FIRE IN CALIFORNIA'S ECOSYSTEMS

FIRE IN CALIFORNIA'S ECOSYSTEMS

NEIL G. SUGIHARA

JAN W. VAN WAGTENDONK

KEVIN E. SHAFFER

JOANN FITES-KAUFMAN

ANDREA E. THODE

UNIVERSITY OF CALIFORNIA PRESS

Berkeley   Los Angeles   London

University of California Press, one of the most distinguished university presses in the United States, enriches lives around the world by advancing scholarship in the humanities, social sciences, and natural sciences. Its activities are supported by the UC Press Foundation and by philanthropic contributions from individuals and institutions. For more information, visit www.ucpress.edu.

University of California Press
Berkeley and Los Angeles, California

University of California Press, Ltd.
London, England

Library of Congress Cataloging-in-Publication Data

Fire in California's ecosystems / [edited by] Neil G. Sugihara . . . [et al.].
   p. cm.
  Includes bibliographical references.
  ISBN-13 948-0-520-24605-8
  ISBN-10 0-520-24605-5 (case : alk. paper)
 1. Fire ecology—California.   2. Fire management—California.
I. Sugihara, Neil. G. QH105.C2F57 2006
  577.2'409794—dc22

                    2006014986

Manufactured in the United States of America
10 09 08 07 06
10 9 8 7 6 5 4 3 2 1

The paper used in this publication meets the minimum requirements of ANSI/NISO Z39.48-1992 (R 1997) (Permanence of Paper). ⊖

Cover photograph: [caption and credit].

To Harold Biswell, who can truly be called the father of fire ecology in California. His patience, persistence, humor, and devotion to managing wildlands and fire in harmony with nature have been an inspiration to all of us.

CONTENTS

LIST OF CONTRIBUTORS

JAMES K. AGEE University of Washington, Seattle

SURAJ AHUJA U.S. Forest Service, Willows, CA

M. KAT ANDERSON University of California, Davis

MICHAEL J. ARBAUGH U.S. Forest Service, Riverside, CA

BERNIE BAHRO U.S. Forest Service, McClellan, CA

MICHAEL G. BARBOUR University of California, Davis

HEATHER BELL U.S. Fish and Wildlife Service, Hadley, MA

JAN L. BEYERS U.S. Forest Service, Riverside, CA

MARK I. BORCHERT U.S. Forest Service, Ojai, CA

ANNE F. BRADLEY The Nature Conservancy, Santa Fe, NM

MATTHEW L. BROOKS U.S. Geologic Survey, Henderson, NV

FRANK W. DAVIS University of California, Santa Barbara

LYNN M. DECKER The Nature Conservancy, Salt Lake City, UT

TOM DUDLEY University of Nevada, Reno, NV

TODD C. ESQUE U.S. Geological Survey, Henderson, NV

JOANN FITES-KAUFMAN U.S. Forest Service, Nevada City, CA

ROBERT E. GRESSWELL U.S. Geologic Survey, Bozeman, MT

KEN HUBBERT Hubbert and Associates, Apple Valley, CA

SUSAN J. HUSARI National Park Service, Oakland, CA

JON E. KEELEY U.S. Geologic Survey, Three Rivers, CA

MARYBETH KEIFER National Park Service, Three Rivers, CA

JEFFREY L. KERSHNER Utah State University, Logan

ROBERT C. KLINGER University of California, Davis

WILLIAM F. LAUDENSLAYER U.S. Forest Service, Fresno, CA

TRAVIS LONGCORE The Urban Wildlands Group, Los Angeles, CA

AMY G. MERRILL University of California, Berkeley

RICHARD F. MILLER Oregon State University, Corvallis

RICHARD A. MINNICH University of California, Riverside

H. THOMAS NICHOLS National Park Service, Boise, ID

LAURIE PERROT U.S. Forest Service, Davis, CA

JOHN M. RANDALL The Nature Conservancy, Davis, CA

GREGG M. RIEGEL U.S. Forest Service, Bend, OR

KEN ROBY U.S. Forest Service, Susanville, CA

KEVIN E. SHAFFER California Department of Fish and Game, Sacramento

JOE SHERLOCK U.S. Forest Service, Vallejo, CA

CARL N. SKINNER U.S. Forest Service, Redding, CA

SYDNEY E. SMITH U.S. Forest Service, Alturas, CA

SCOTT L. STEPHENS University of California, Berkeley

JOHN D. STUART Humboldt State University, Arcata, CA

NEIL G. SUGIHARA U.S. Forest Service, McClellan, CA

ALAN H. TAYLOR The Pennsylvania State University, University Park

ANDREA E. THODE Northern Arizona University, Flagstaff

JAN W. VAN WAGTENDONK U.S. Geologic Survey, El Portal, CA

ROBIN WILLS National Park Service, Oakland, CA

PETER M. WOHLGEMUTH U.S. Forest Service, Riverside, CA

FOREWORD

James K. Agee

Fire was finally recognized as an important ecological factor in the mid-twentieth century in Rexford Daubenmire's *Plants and Environment*. Before then, it had largely been considered an allogenic factor even by ecologists such as Fredric Clements, who had done some of the first work on fire-dependent lodgepole pine in the Rocky Mountains. The volume you have in your hand is the most comprehensive work ever on a state's fire ecology, and demonstrates tremendous progress in understanding the role of fire in California wildlands. Although the destructive fires of southern California in 2003 have captured the headlines at the time of this writing, it is the less dramatic truths in this volume that will have a far more lasting effect on wildland fire in California.

Fire and people have interacted for millennia in California. Native Americans burned the landscapes of the state for a variety of purposes, including protection of their villages (the first wildland-urban interface), resources such as basket-weaving materials, the many food plants that were favored by fire, hunting game animals, and signaling and warfare. Their fires, often starting at low elevations, complemented those started from lightning, more common at high elevations. The long dry seasons typical of the Mediterranean climate ensured a prolonged fire season every year. Although fire did visit almost every landscape in California, it did so with a remarkable variety in frequency, intensity, and effects. California has always been and will continue to be a fire environment unmatched in North America.

Institutionalized fire policy in California began early in the twentieth century when the great fires of Idaho and Montana in 1910 galvanized the fledging Forest Service to promulgate a policy of total fire exclusion. A battle to retain *light burning*, as prescribed fire was called in those days, was fought both in the southern states and in California. Forest industry was leading the charge for light burning, not because of altruistic sentiments about natural forests but because they believed it would help protect the old growth forests until they were ready to be harvested.

Aided by the passage of the Federal Clarke-McNary Act in 1924 that funneled fire protection dollars to the states and by research from the Forest Service, fire exclusion was firmly entrenched in California. Yet some of the same research used to support the fire protection policy, such as that by Bevier Show and Edward Kotok in the Sierra Nevada and Emmanuel Fritz in the coast redwood belt, also showed that fire had played a very significant historical role in forest ecosystem dynamics. The fire exclusion policy remained unchallenged until the 1950s, when it came under attack by a few courageous men, such as Harold Weaver who worked for the Bureau of Indian Affairs and Harold Biswell from the University of California at Berkeley.

Dr. Biswell, more than anyone, actually bent the old fire culture in California. The idea of underburning forests to prevent more destructive wildfires was a revolutionary idea in California in the 1950s and 1960s, although fire then was routinely used in some shrublands. It is important to keep in mind that during those times, Harold was widely criticized for the same ideas, presented in the same way, for which he received so much favorable response later in his career, including his classic integration of science and interpretation, *Prescribed Burning in California Wildland Vegetation Management* (UC Press 1989). Harold was an advocate of fire prevention, but he believed that a balance between fire suppression, prevention, and use was critical. Smokey Bear just couldn't say it all in one sentence anymore. One had to be very courageous in those days, and Harold strode on, focusing on spreading his message and taking the high road in terms of his professional demeanor. The logic of that message attracted many of us, including me, to become interested in fire science as a career.

Where have we come since then, when we at least were providing lip service to the important role of fire in California wildlands? We have made some great strides in some areas, and seem to be mired in the muck elsewhere. The technology needed to conduct prescribed burns continues to improve. We now have computer models that incorporate fire behavior information with geographic information systems to predict fire spread across landscapes. It works well. We have more sophisticated fire effects models to predict the ecological outcome of fire. We can tell what size classes of the various tree species on a site are likely to die in fires with various flame lengths. Our technological fixes are not complete, but in comparison to our knowledge about other ecological disturbance factors, such as wind, insects, or fungi, fire technology is at the head of the pack.

We use this technology only sparingly, and a strong case remains that we could do much more. The phrase "forest health" emerged in the late 1980s to explain why we see so many trees dead and dying across western landscapes, and high-density, multi-layered forests caused by fire exclusion are at the root of the problem. Current forest health situations at Lake Arrowhead are unprecedented, with millions of drought-killed pines helping to fuel current wildfires. Insects and disease epidemics are at historic highs, and intense wildfires are expanding like never before on western landscapes. California, as well as Oregon, New Mexico, and Colorado, have experienced their largest-ever wildfires in recorded history since the turn of the millennium. We continue to despair at the state of our western forests, but the solutions have become mired in political debates. Yet there are some radiant examples of fire use in the state: California state parks are burning in a wide variety of forest and shrub vegetation types; nature organizations such as The Nature Conservancy have been using prescribed fire in prairie restoration and oak woodland maintenance, and are coordinating the pooling of resources of large private landowners to effect landscape burns in the Sacramento Valley; and the National Park Service is continuing to move forward with prescribed fire plans in chaparral and forested portions of national park system lands in the Sierra Nevada and elsewhere. These programs are complex: They require knowledge of plant and animal response to fire, and the effects of varying the frequency of fire, its intensity and extent, the season of burning, and its interaction with other ecosystem processes.

The national forests will see expanded fire programs in the coming years, too. Professor Biswell's idea in the 1950s to use the large federal emergency firefighting fund upfront to do fuel treatment was recently championed by Secretary of the Interior Bruce Babbitt on behalf of all the federal land management agencies. It made perfect sense 40 years ago, but took almost half a century to become part of the fire culture. A portion of the fund became authorized and available in 1998 for prescribed burning on all federal lands. This will have a tremendous impact on project funding, and will result in much more prescribed fire, and reduced threat of wildfire, over millions of acres of the West. The National Fire Plan and the Western Governors' Association are providing consensus polices in the wildland-urban interface. Whether or not the president's Healthy Forests Initiative, recently enacted into law, is embraced as part of the solution depends on whether it is perceived as a real opportunity to increase forest health or simply a way to expedite logging.

The intrusion of residences into wildlands, with its attendant fire problems, was always a major concern of Biswell's, and in his book he warned of impending catastrophic fire in the Berkeley Hills. His warning was based on precedence, in that one of the most devastating urban–wildland interface fires prior to 1991 occurred in the Berkeley Hills in 1923. A fire started in the hilltop area, and blown by hot, dry autumn winds, swept down right to the edge of the University of California campus. Fire marshals were considering dynamiting entire residential blocks to save the rest of the town, when fog blew in from the Golden Gate and helped extinguish the fire. The burned area sprouted back with residences, just as the brush and eucalyptus trees sprouted back, and the residences spread further into the wildlands over the subsequent decades.

The Berkeley Hills are not unique in this regard. They are but one of innumerable communities where residences are invading wildlands, but Harold lived in the Berkeley Hills, so it was of special interest and concern to him. His late 1980s prediction of a major catastrophic fire there came true in 1991. No one was saddened more than Harold Biswell when the fire killed 25 people, destroyed more than 3,000 homes, and cost more than $1.5 billion—and it was preventable. Sadly, these property losses were exceeded in the 2003 southern California fires.

This growing fire problem in what is called the *urban-wildland interface* will continue to plague fire managers. Of all the institutional problems with fire, these are the most complex: most land is privately owned; myriad jurisdictional problems exist for zoning, building codes, fire protection; and attitudes persist that the disaster will strike somewhere else, or will never strike twice.

The volume you hold now will become the secular bible of fire ecology for Californians. But what does the future hold for new knowledge and application? Peruse the list of contributors, and it is clear that agency people are by far the majority of authors. This was also true of the Sierra Nevada Ecosystem Project, which began as a federally funded grant to the University of California, Davis, in the mid-1990s and ended with most of the papers on ecological change completed by late-added agency scientists. Academic trends over the last decade have disfavored small, technically oriented programs (i.e., fire ecology, forest management) in favor of more general and efficient programs (environmental science) that attract larger numbers of students. California's universities, while not disfavoring fire ecologists, will be hiring general ecologists in order to meet their teaching mandates. Those that can attract research funding in fire ecology may be able to carve a niche for themselves, but few universities will be advertising specifically for fire ecologists.

At the same time, the complex nature of resource management argues for more technically trained managers. The agencies have hired many more doctorate-level fire scientists than have the academic systems, and this demand will continue to grow. But there is a major supply and demand problem emerging: Prospects for long-term supply are meager, given the trend in academia to avoid specialist faculty who would guide these students. The typical historical solution to these types of problems has been cooperative programs partly funded by the federal government at selected universities to maintain viable teaching and research capability in a specific discipline. My prediction is that the federal agencies will develop a series of National Fire Science Centers to help meet their own demands in fire science, including fire ecology. A major caveat to this prediction is the general lack of attention to natural resources issues at the federal level. Disasters such as the 2003 fires in southern California spark a few congressional brushfires, but they usually fade as quickly as the headlines. I think Fire Science Center–like programs are likely to be initiated, but may not expand as fully as they perhaps should.

In wildlands, history does repeat itself. Fire environments of yesterday are those of today, and will be those of tomorrow. California and the West are fire environments without parallel in North America. Harold Biswell would say that our mountains will always stand majestically, and dry summers and windy spells will always be part of our western heritage. We can only intervene in the fire behavior triangle by managing the vegetation. Biswell and his contemporaries gave us the tools to manage change through controlled fire, integrating it with naturally occurring fire in wilderness and intelligent, cost-effective fire suppression. It is now time for us to recognize that fire is part of our culture, and we need to make good decisions about the use of fire, not just its control. The solutions will be complex, will vary by place, and will occur in a changing environment. This book tells us what we know now, but we have the ability to learn much more as we manage, and we will need to feed this information back into better decision making. There are many treatments we can apply, in various places with unique land-use histories, and at different scales, in stochastic environments, and perhaps permanently changing climates. Fire ecology will inform this debate, with no better place to start than this book. We hope you enjoy it, learn a lot, and finish with more questions than when you started.

PREFACE

Alterations to fire regimes have resulted in many changes to the biological communities including changes in vegetation composition and structure and vegetation type conversions or ecosystem migrations. This text details many of these changes, explains how fire has changed as an ecosystem process, and provides insights for determining the direction that the changes might take in the future. As with introductory treatments of any of the elements of natural ecosystems, we are prone to generalization, simplification, and standardization of processes and interactions that are inherently complex. In describing fire effects and regimes we are by necessity guilty of continuing that trend toward simplification. However, we hope that by communicating the concepts of the role that fire plays as a dynamic ecological process, we can communicate the importance of fire's role in defining what we know as California ecosystems.

This book is intended for use both as a text for learning and teaching the basics of fire ecology and as a reference book on fire in California ecosystems. It synthesizes and expands upon our knowledge of fire as an ecological process and facilitates a better understanding of the complex and dynamic interactions between fire and the other physical and biological components of California ecosystems. Modern western society has tended to view ecosystems within narrowly defined ranges of time and space. Focused studies of ecosystems from the standpoint of individual species within their habitats, individual stands of trees, populations, plant communities, fire events, or watersheds allow us to know specific mechanics of ecosystems but, by nature, do not help us develop a broad view of large dynamic landscapes. On the other hand, studies of broad spatial or temporal application are usually quite limited in their application to specific exam-

ples. Understanding fire in ecosystems requires us to greatly expand our spatial and temporal context to include both discrete fire events that occur on finite landscapes and complex multi-scale burning patterns and processes that are dynamic on large landscapes. We intend this text to present an integrated view of fire in California ecosystems from as wide a spectrum of temporal and spatial scales as possible.

This text is divided into three parts. Part I is an introduction to the study of fire ecology that is intended for use in teaching the basics of fire ecology. It includes overviews of fire in California, fire as a physical process, fire regimes, and interactions of fire with the biological and physical components of the environment. Part II is a treatment of the history, ecology, and management of fire by bioregions and is intended for use as a reference and for teaching fire ecology within the various bioregions within California. Part III is a treatment of fire management issues and is intended for use as a reference and for teaching fire management from a historical, policy, and issue perspective.

Obviously, a book such as this is not written without the help of many people. First, we would like to thank the many authors of all the chapters; they endured structured outlines, tight deadlines, and an authoritarian group of editors. Heath Norton drew the figures, Daniel Rankin prepared the maps, Scott Dailey formatted the tables, Gail Bakker formatted tables and chapters, and Lester Thode created the fire regime graphs. Without their help, the book would have lacked the consistency and attractiveness that add greatly to its readability. Finally, we would like to thank the Joint Fire Science Program board and Ray Quintanar of the Forest Service's Pacific Southwest Region for providing the funds and time necessary to write the book. Their support was essential.

CHAPTER 1

Fire and California Vegetation

NEIL G. SUGIHARA AND MICHAEL G. BARBOUR

In California, vegetation is the meeting place of fire and ecosystems. The plants are the fuel and fire is the driver of vegetation change. Fire and vegetation are often so interactive that they can scarcely be considered separately from each other.

M. G. BARBOUR, B. PAVLIK, F. DRYSDALE, AND S. LINDSTROM, 1993

During the last decades of the twentieth century and early years of the twenty-first century, fire ecology has emerged as a rapidly expanding area of study. Since the first article on fire ecology appeared in *Scientific American* in 1961 (Cooper 1961), several books have been published on the subject (Kozlowski and Ahlgren 1974, Wright and Bailey 1982, Agee 1993, Whalen 1995, Arno and Allison-Bunnel 2002). However, no book has been published that focuses specifically on the ecological role of fire in California. Wildland fire is a complex, dynamic, and often spectacular force that plays a richly complex role in California's diversity of ecosystems. Human interactions with fire have developed around our need to simultaneously protect ourselves from its harm and use it as a tool. As we get more effective at controlling wildfire, we are gaining an appreciation of the value that fire has to ecosystems and biological diversity. We are also recognizing that exclusion of fire from wildlands is not always the most effective way of protecting ourselves from fire or managing ecosystems. Managing wildland fire has developed into one of the largest ecosystem restoration efforts ever undertaken. Our need to understand fire and the consequences of its occurrence—or exclusion—have become great. This book is the first effort at a comprehensive synthesis of our knowledge of fire in California ecosystems.

Fire as an Ecological Process

Part I of this book is an introduction to the study of fire ecology and provides a basic framework and perspective on fire as an ecological process. Much of California has a mediterranean climate conducive to the occurrence of fire (Pyne et al. 1996), with long dry summers and periods of thunderstorms, low relative humidity, and strong winds. These patterns vary through an extremely wide range of climatic zones and complex topography.

Fire is a physical process as well as an ecological process. The heat it produces, the rate at which it spreads, and the effects it has on other ecosystem components are all part of the physical process. Watersheds, soils, air, plants, and animals are affected in one way or another by fire. Water quality and quantity, erosion, smoke, and plant and animal mortality are some of the more obvious effects. Other ecosystem effects are less obvious, but perhaps even more important. Dead biomass accumulates in mediterranean ecosystems because weather conditions are favorable for growth while decomposition is active for a relatively short part of the year. Fire complements decomposition in these systems by periodically removing debris through combustion. Fire has a differential effect on plant species mortality, allowing those that are best adapted to fire to be perpetuated.

Pyrogenic vegetation has evolved with recurring fire and includes species that tolerate or even require fire in order to complete their life cycles. There is a feedback loop between fire and vegetation. Fire feeds on vegetation as fuel and cannot reoccur without some minimum burnable, continuous biomass; and vegetation cannot maintain its occupation of a site without recurring fire. Fire and vegetation are often so interactive that they can scarcely be considered apart from one another. Indeed, the properties of any fire regime—its seasonality, fire return interval, fire size, spatial complexity, fireline intensity, fire severity, and fire type—require specific responses by the vegetation to persist.

Animal populations and communities have developed in habitats where fire has been the dynamic perturbation. The distribution of animal species on landscapes has been driven by the patterns of fire, controlled by climate, weather, and topography, over space and time. Perpetuation of California's biological diversity certainly requires fire to be present as a vital ecological process.

It is difficult to overstate the importance of fire in California ecosystems. A central theme of this book is that wildfire is a pervasive, natural, environmental factor throughout much of the state, and ignoring its role in ecosystems will seriously limit our ability to understand or manage wildlands in a sustainable, ecologically appropriate manner.

Bioregions and the California Landscape

The diversity of the California landscape is well known; from the mist-shrouded mountains of the north coast to the searing heat of the southeastern deserts, and from the sun-drenched beaches of the south coast to the high Sierra Nevada, the range of climate, geomorphology, and vegetation mirrors this diversity. Similarly, fire's role in each of these bioregions of the state is equally diverse.

If we add up the areas of vegetation types generally regarded as fire maintained, about 54% of California's 39,400,000 ha (985,000,000 ac) requires fire to persist (Barbour and Major 1988). Only desert scrub, alpine tundra, subalpine woodland, and a few other, less widespread, vegetation types are not fire dependent. Even some wetlands—such as tule marsh, riparian forest, and California fan palm *(Washingtonia filifera)* oases—have experienced fires set by both indigenous human populations and lightning strikes (Anderson 2005). Knowledge of how fire operates as an ecological process within the state's various bioregions is part of the foundation for wise management and conservation of California's natural heritage. In Part II of this book, we examine each bioregion in detail to see how that bioregion's physical features influence the interactions among fire, vegetation, and other ecosystem components. But first we take a statewide look at the bioregions and the vegetation within them.

California's Bioregions: Climate and Geography

Bailey (1996) and Bailey et al. (1994) developed an ecosystem classification based on climate, as affected by latitude, continental position, elevation, and landform. Located at the mid-latitudes, California receives a moderate amount of solar radiation, placing it in the temperate thermal zone with both a summer and a winter. California's position on the western edge of the North American continent provides the western portion of the state with a moderate marine climate. Bailey (1996) included this area in the Humid Temperate Domain. East of the crest of the Cascades, the Sierra Nevada, and the Peninsular ranges, where the influence of the ocean is much decreased, lies the Dry Domain.

In California, the Humid Temperate Domain comprises two divisions: the Mediterranean Division and the Mediterranean Regime Mountains Division with alternating wet winters and dry summers (Bailey 1996). In the mountains, the climatic regimes differ from the adjacent lowlands and results in climate zones that change with elevation. Two divisions make up the Dry Domain as well: the Tropical/Subtropical Division occurs in the southeastern desert portion of the state, whereas the Temperate Desert Division includes areas of the Great Basin.

Bailey (1996) further divided these divisions into provinces based on macro features of the vegetation. Ecological subregions of California including provinces, sections, and subsections were described by Miles and Goudey (1997). They divided the Mediterranean Division into the California Coastal Chaparral Forest and Shrub Province, the California Dry Steppe Province, and the California Coastal Steppe, Mixed Forest, and Redwood Forest Province. The Mediterranean Regime Mountains Division comprises the Sierran Steppe–Mixed Forest–Coniferous Province and the California Coastal Range Open Woodland–Shrub–Coniferous Forest–Meadow Province. In the Dry Domain in California, the Tropical/Subtropical Desert Division has only the American Semi-Desert Province. The Temperate Desert Division includes the Intermountain Semi-Desert and Desert Province and the Intermountain Semi-Desert Province.

The next level in Bailey's (1996) classification is the section. A section is defined by landform, the overall shape of the surface. For example, mountain ranges are differentiated as are coastal steppes, deserts, and the Central Valley. We have combined the 19 sections described by Miles and Goudey (1997) that comprise California into nine bioregions based on relatively consistent patterns of vegetation and fire regimes (Map 1.1). In the northeastern portion of the state, tall volcanoes and extensive lava flows characterize the Southern Cascade Range and Northeastern Plateaus bioregions. To the west of the Cascades lies the Klamath Mountains bioregion, a complex group of mountain ranges. Numerous valleys and steep coastal and interior mountains are typical of the North Coast, Central Coast, and South Coast bioregions. The Sacramento and San Joaquin Rivers flow through broad interior valleys with extensive, nearly flat alluvial floors. These valleys constitute the Central Valley bioregion. Immediately east of the valley is the Sierra Nevada bioregion, a high range of north-to-south trending mountains. Finally, the vast southeast corner of California constitutes the Southeastern Desert bioregion. Table 1.1 lists the sections from Miles and Goudey (1997) that are included in each bioregion.

Coastal California is characterized by a long chain of steep, geologically complex mountains known collectively as the Coast Ranges. In general, the climate (and vegetation) progress from mesic to dry on a gradual gradient from north to south and a much more abrupt transition from the coast to the interior. A montane gradient, with cooler and wetter conditions at high elevations, is also present. The Coast Ranges are composed of three bioregions: the North Coast, Central Coast, and South Coast.

The North Coast bioregion supports north coastal scrub and prairie, north coast pine forest, and Sitka spruce *(Picea sitchensis)* forest on the immediate coast. Upland forests and woodlands that are farther away from the marine influence include coast redwood *(Sequoia sempervirens)*, Oregon white oak *(Quercus garryana)*, and mixed evergreen. At the higher elevations, the vegetation is typically mixed conifer lower montane forest and Shasta red fir *(Abies magnifica* var. *shastensis)* upper montane forests.

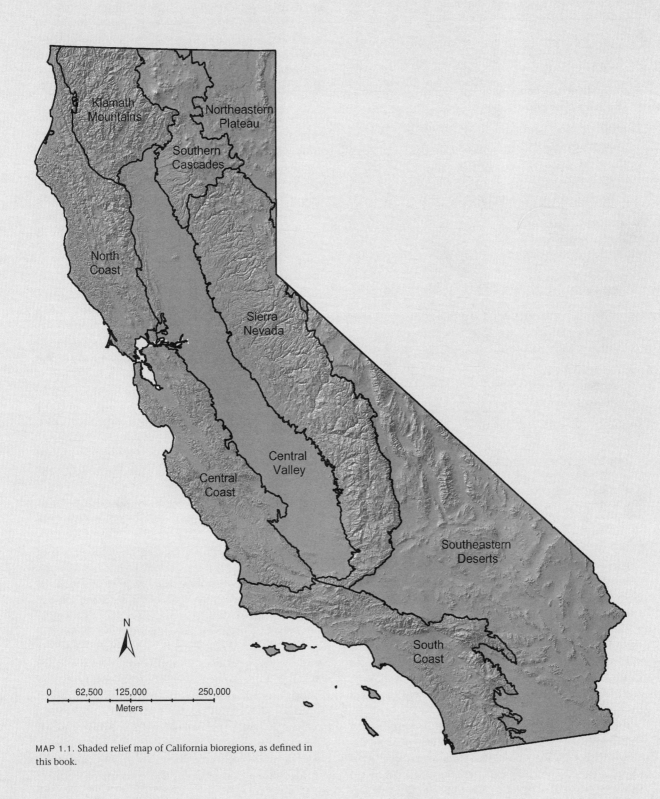

Klamath
Mountains

Northeastern
Plateau

Southern
Cascades

North
Coast

Sierra
Nevada

Central
Valley

Central
Coast

Southeastern
Deserts

South
Coast

N

0   62,500   125,000   250,000
Meters

MAP 1.1. Shaded relief map of California bioregions, as defined in
this book.

TABLE 1.1

Sections from Miles and Goudey (1997) assigned to bioregions used in this book

North Coast Bioregion
    Northern California Coast
    Northern California Coast Ranges

Klamath Mountains Bioregion
    Klamath Mountains

Southern Cascades Bioregion
    Southern Cascades

Northeastern Plateaus Bioregion
    Modoc Plateau
    Northwestern Basin and Range

Sierra Nevada Bioregion
    Sierra Nevada
    Sierra Nevada Foothills

Central Valley Bioregion
    Great Valley Section
    Northern California Interior Coast Ranges

Central Coast Bioregion
    Central California Coast

South Coast Bioregion
    Southern California Coast
    Southern California Mountains and Valleys

Southeastern Deserts Bioregion
    Mojave Desert
    Sonoran Desert
    Colorado Desert
    Mono
    Southeastern Great Basin

The Central Coast bioregion is an area of transition between the bioregions to the north and south. Ridge tops are generally less than 1,200 m (3,800 ft) in elevation, but a few peaks rise up to 1,800 m (5,700 ft). The region supports a mixture of the vegetation types found to the north and south in a more complex mosaic including coastal prairie, north and south coastal scrub, redwood forest (in isolated locations), mixed evergreen forest, chaparral, oak woodland, and some mixed conifer forest in the lower montane belt of the Santa Lucia Range.

The South Coast bioregion contains the east–west-running Transverse Range and the north–south-oriented Peninsular Range. Except for the alpine zone, both ranges have a full complement of montane zones. Elevations extend from sea level to over 3,500 m (11,400 ft). In addition to montane vegetation types, low-elevation vegetation includes interior grassland, south coastal scrub, chaparral, foothill woodland, and mixed evergreen forest. Despite the fact that Coastal California is greatly urbanized, including the San Francisco Bay Area, Los Angeles, San Diego, and their adjacent urban centers, these bioregions do still have large areas of wildland with relatively low human population densities.

The Klamath Mountains bioregion lies between the North Coast bioregion on the west and the Southern Cascade Range bioregion on the east. These mountains are characterized by steep, complex topography dissected by a number of large river valleys. The area is noted for its exceptionally rich flora, which results from several factors. First, the Klamath area is a meeting ground for three regional bioclimates and floras—the Pacific Northwest, California, and the Great Basin—and this increases the number of species present. In addition, the area has served as a refugium for millions of years, hence the presence of many woody species near the edges of their ranges or even restricted to the region. Finally, the diversity of geologic substrates is impressive, ranging from acid granite, to basic marble, metamorphosed shale, and chemically unique ultramafic extrusions (Franklin and Dyrness 1973, Franklin and Halpern 2000). As a consequence, the mosaic of vegetation types does not fall neatly into broadly continuous zones or belts, as it does in the Coast Ranges or the Sierra Nevada (Whittaker 1960, Sawyer and Thornburgh 1988).

The Central Valley bioregion is a wide, flat, low-elevation trough of sediments bounded by the Coast Ranges to the west and Sierra Nevada to the east. The northern part is drained by the Sacramento River; and the southern part, by the San Joaquin and Kern Rivers and their tributaries. The valley floor and adjacent foothills have largely been converted to agriculture or urbanized but were once dominated by a combination of chaparral, foothill woodland, riparian forest, bunchgrass prairie, forb fields, tule marsh, and in the dry southern San Joaquin Valley, saltbush scrub. Recent research has questioned previous assumptions that bunchgrass prairie characterized most of the landscape (Holstein 2001).

The Sierra Nevada and Cascade Ranges form an axis of high mountains east of the Central Valley and Klamath Mountains. The Southern Cascade Range bioregion is the southern end of an extensive chain of volcanoes and volcanic flows extending northward from Oregon and Washington. Mount Shasta and Mount Lassen are the two largest and most well-known Cascade volcanoes in California. The Sierra Nevada bioregion extends south from the Cascade Range 600 km (373 mi) to the Tehachapi Mountains. Vegetation generally occurs in elevation bands with oak woodlands and chaparral in the extensive foothills on the west side of these mountains. The lower montane zone consisting of mixed conifers gives way to an upper montane fir forest and montane chaparral at higher elevations. The highest mountains and ridge tops support subalpine forests and alpine meadows and shrublands.

The western edge of the huge intermountain Great Basin extends into the northeastern corner of California forming the Northeastern Plateaus bioregion. This is a semi-arid region of mountain ranges separated by lower-elevation basins and includes the Modoc Plateau. Major vegetation types include western juniper (*Juniperus occidentalis* var. *occidentalis*) woodland, sagebrush scrub, mixed ponderosa pine (*Pinus ponderosa*), and Jeffrey pine (*Pinus jeffreyi*) forest, upper montane fir forest, and whitebark pine (*Pinus albicaulis*) subalpine woodland.

The southeastern portion of the state is extremely arid. Except for isolated desert mountains, rainfall is <25 cm (10 in). Portions of the Mojave and Sonoran warm deserts, and the southwestern tongue of the Great Basin cold desert comprise the Southeastern Deserts bioregion. Major vegetation types include various desert scrubs (creosote bush [*Larrea tridentata*], blackbrush [*Coleogyne ramosissima*], sagebrush [*Artemisia* spp.]), halophytic scrubs in alkaline sinks (greasewood [*Sarcobatus vermiculatus*], saltbush [*Atriplex* spp.]), desert riparian woodland, pinyon (*Pinus monophylla*) woodland, montane conifer forest dominated by white fir (*Abies concolor*), and, in the Panamint and White Mountains, a subalpine woodland with scattered western bristlecone pine (*Pinus longaeva*) and limber pine (*Pinus flexilis*). Fire is typically limited by the lack of fuel continuity.

California's Floristic Provinces: Evolution of the Vegetation

Floristically, California is divided into three provinces (Hickman 1993). The California Floristic Province corresponds to the Humid Temperate Domain and comprises the portion of California west of the mountainous crest. Both the Great Basin Floristic Province and the Desert Floristic Province are in the area of the Dry Domain. The three provinces are further divided into 10 regions, 24 subregions, and 50 districts. The regions most closely correspond to our bioregions and various combinations of the subregions "or districts" approximate sections. The vegetation in the provinces evolved from different floras. Today, the Arcto-Tertiary Flora dominates in the Northwestern California, Sierra Nevada, Klamath Mountains, and Cascade Ranges regions. Species from the Madro-Tertiary Flora are most common in the Great Central Valley, Central Western California, Modoc Plateau, east of Sierra Nevada, Mojave Desert, and Sonoran Desert regions.

The modern array of bioregions is a product of millions of years of plant evolution, geologic upheavals, and climate change. For the purposes of this chapter, let's begin some 40–60 million years ago, in the Paleocene Epoch, when California was low lying. Large embayments of the sea covered much of what today are the Coast Ranges and the Central Valley. At that time, the highest mountains were only low hills. Judging from plant fossils deposited then, the climate was temperate, with wet summers and mild winters. Forests were composed of a much richer mix of tree types and species than now: an overstory of evergreen conifers, winter-deciduous conifers, evergreen broad-leaf trees, and winter-deciduous hardwoods; and an understory of winter-deciduous shrubs and summer-active perennial herbs. This collection of species has been called the Arcto-Tertiary Geoflora by Axelrod (1976, 1988), which is thought to have

dominated the north-temperate region of the world. Today, no existing forest contains such diversity, but various elements and mixtures exist along the northern California coast, in mountains at middle and upper elevations, and along riparian corridors.

In the Miocene Epoch, about 25 million years ago, the North Coast Range, Diablo Range, and Transverse Range began to form. Water retreated from the Sacramento Valley, but remained in the San Joaquin Valley. From fossils dating to that time, we know that the climate had become warmer and drier, with precipitation more evenly distributed throughout the year. The Arcto-Tertiary Geoflora had begun to fragment and retreat, being slowly replaced by more drought-tolerant plants moving north from what is Mexico today—members of the Madro-Tertiary Geoflora such as chamise (*Adenostoma fasciculatum*), *Ceanothus* spp., pinyons, junipers (*Juniperus* spp.), manzanitas (*Arctostaphylos* spp.), brittlebrush (*Encelia farinosa*), *Agave* spp., and cactus (*Cactaceae*) (Axelrod 1958).

By 5–10 million years ago (Pliocene Epoch), a mediterranean-type semi-arid climate was in place at low elevations. This was a time of spread for grasslands, chaparral, mixed evergreen sclerophyllous forest, and oak woodlands. Elements of the Madro-Tertiary Geoflora became dominant throughout low elevations, whereas Arcto-Tertiary taxa and vegetation retreated to high elevations, riparian areas, or the coastal strip. The Sierra Nevada, Klamath Mountains, and Transverse Ranges were thrust up to ever higher elevations, creating rain shadows to the east that deepened and expanded over time to become today's hot and cold deserts, dominated by drought-tolerant shrubs, succulent cacti, and short-lived ephemeral herbs.

Periods of glacial advances in the last 2 million years (Quaternary Period) forced species and vegetation types to migrate downslope or southward. Because California's mountain chains are largely oriented north-to-south, montane taxa driven south were able to migrate back north during warmer interglacial periods, including the current period. The most recent glacial retreat was completed about 10,000 years ago, but abnormally cold and warm periods continued to alternate after that time. These relatively short-term climate fluctuations undoubtedly affected the location of ecotones between vegetation belts in the mountains and along the coast, and their location may still be slowly rebounding from those times. Tree-ring records for the past several hundred years (Michaelsen et al. 1987) show continuing fluctuations in temperature, precipitation, and interannual variation at the time scale of one-to-several decades; but there does not appear to have been any cumulative, directional change.

Californians and Fire

The third part of this book describes how the succession of dominant cultures that have lived in California viewed fire, used it, tried to suppress it, and finally incorporated it in complex policy issues concerning air quality, watershed resources, rare species, and the reduction of fires that threaten people and property. Relatively speaking, the landscapes of California have changed little in the 3,000 years prior to the arrival of European settlers. Few plant species have become extinct and the belts of vegetation in mountains have remained the same; the height of mountain peaks, the thickness of sediments beneath meadows and grasslands, the amount of snow falling in winter, the degree of summer aridity, the distribution of wetlands, the location of sea level, and the gradients of humidity and aridity from coastal west to interior east have not shifted. The most change has occurred just in the past two centuries, due to exotic and aggressive plants, agriculture, fire exclusion, domesticated livestock, and human populations that are approaching 100 times denser than those of precontact time.

It is not the occurrence of fire in an ecosystem that constitutes an ecological disturbance; rather it is our actions that have led to changes to the existing fire regimes. Fire regimes have probably never been static, but the pace and magnitude of changes to California fire regimes accelerated with the arrival of humans from Asia more than 12,000 years ago and again with the arrival of large numbers of settlers of European origin with the Gold Rush in the mid-1800s. Despite intensive efforts to suppress wildland fires over the past century, fires have continued. We can identify several historic periods of time during which fire regimes were altered, and each time the changes also profoundly altered the ecosystems. Changes to fire regimes are fundamental changes to ecosystems that have occurred while climate, landforms, and species compositions were also changing. It is the result of these processes that give us today's California vegetation.

The Era Prior to Human Settlement

We know that humans have occupied California for at least 11,000 years. Prior to that time, fire regimes were dependent upon the time required for continuous fuel to build up to the point at which it would support a spreading flame ignited by lightning. Fires were also started by much rarer events, such as volcanic eruptions or a spark initiated by rocks falling and striking each other. Only broad generalizations can be drawn from the evidence that has been documented regarding the history of fire in California prior to human settlement. Much of what is known is very general in nature and has been reconstructed from paleoecological evidence. For example, we do know that in the Southern California Coast Ranges, pulses of charcoal deposition in sediments indicate a fire regime dominated by infrequent, large fires (Byrne et al. 1977, Mensing 1998, Mensing et al.1999). Similarly, extensive charcoal deposits in the Sierra Nevada indicate that fire was prevalent at least 5,000 years ago (Smith and Anderson 1992).

The Native American Era

Once humans arrived in California, they changed fire patterns with additional ignitions that were focused on their resource needs (Stewart 2002). Using fire to manipulate vegetation was universal among Native Americans at the time of European contact. Studies show that vegetation changes occurred following the arrival of Native Americans (Keeter 1995) and again with their demise (Mensing 1998). At the time of European contact, California was already inhabited with large populations of indigenous people living and influencing broad landscapes throughout the state (Cook 1972). As detailed in Chapter 17, fire was the most significant, effective, efficient, and widely employed vegetation management tool utilized by California Indian tribes. The pattern of burning was often very specific and focused on particular ecosystem effects. Indigenous burning practices defined and maintained the physiognomy of many vegetation types, encouraging particular suites of understory plants. The area that burned during this time period was extensive: Martin and Sapsis (1992) estimate that between 2.2 and 5.2 million ha (5.6–13 million acres) burned annually from both lighting-caused and human-caused ignitions. However, given the diversity of ecosystems, uneven indigenous occupation patterns, and the complex fire characteristics of the vegetation types, the effect of burning by indigenous people was neither uniform nor equally applied across landscapes. These effects formed a continuum encompassing a range of human modifications from very little or no Native American influence to fully human-created ecosystems. Vale (2002) concludes that the pre-European landscape in the American West was a mosaic of areas that were altered by native peoples and areas that were primarily affected by natural processes.

The Era of European and Asian Settlement

During the early settlement era, several widespread changes in the patterns of wildland fire took place. The changes were largely due to the removal of indigenous people (and their approach to the land) and replacement with newcomers who had a very different land-use philosophy and an array of tools to modify the landscape. In those ecosystems where Indian burning had been a regular practice—foothill woodland, montane meadow, and coastal prairie—the demographic change led to changes in species composition, invasion of non-native plants, and even type conversion of the vegetation. Mining and livestock, initially localized, also had widespread influence. An intensive pulse of sheep grazing during the late 1800s greatly changed fire in much of the western United States. Pyne et al. (1996) state, "More than any 'fire practice' per se, the wholesale introduction of domesticated animals reconfigured the fire regimes of the continent."

Fuel continuity in the herbaceous layer and ignition patterns controlled how and when fires occurred because it was in this layer that fire most commonly spread in many California ecosystems. In open forest and woodland ecosystems with herbaceous understory, the reduction and fragmentation of the herbaceous layer greatly reduced a fire's ability to spread. The result was a reduction in the number of days with conditions under which an area could burn, and a drastic reduction in the frequency of fire. This indirect fire exclusion also allowed vegetation to accumulate biomass, developing different fuel structures, changing species mixes, and shifting the geographic distributions of vegetation types.

The introduction of non-native, invasive plant species during this time had important impacts on fire patterns in many California ecosystems. In the grasslands and oak woodlands of the Central Valley, non-native species extended the late summer and fall fire season. In general, exotics have had a greater impact in mesic, lower elevations than in harsher habitats at high elevations, on unusual geologic substrates, or in arid deserts. Exotics can aggressively colonize following high-severity fires.

The impact of humans on fire frequency at this time can be deduced in several ways. As a general rule we have detailed records of recent fire patterns, but as we move back in time, this record becomes more fragmented and less specific. Current fire records are available through land management and fire fighting agency records and can be supplemented by remote sensing studies to very fine scales of detail. Written records often go back to the early 1900s, but they are very generalized and describe only unusually large and destructive fires in the early part of the century. Historic photographs, land survey records, and newspaper accounts from the 1800s can supplement fire records (Egan and Howell 2001). Tree-ring studies extend these records back several centuries (and in some cases for millennia in ecosystems containing long-lived species), but they cannot always reconstruct the details of fire intensity, severity, complexity, or area burned. Studies of charcoal deposits, phytoliths, and pollen in lake sediments allow fire history studies to be extended 10,000 years or more into the past, but the interpretations are more generalized and lack the resolution needed to provide the detailed information derived from other methods. Our knowledge of fire history and fire-related vegetation change is largely built on information developed from a combination of these methods.

The Fire-Suppression Era

The industrialization of America in the early to mid-1900s brought demands for the extraction of wildland resources. Protection of forests and rangelands from "the scourge of fire" was a central part of this era. A fire-protection philosophy, developed in Europe, was applied to most plant communities in North America (Wright and Bailey 1982). The primary focus of management in the early National Forest Reserves (1905–1910) was protecting the timber supplies and watersheds. Fire was seen as a potential threat to both, and a great deal of effort was committed to the removal of fire in America's forests.

Stephen Pyne (2001) states, "The great fires of 1910 shaped the American fire landscape more than any other fire in any other year throughout the twentieth century." Seventy-eight firefighters were killed and several million acres of national forest land burned. These fires instigated the creation of a national system of wildland fire protection that still dominates fire management.

During World War II, the firefighting effort was intensified in the interest of national defense and was paired with a public education campaign that included Smokey Bear. The public was now well shielded from the history of human–fire relationships and fighting fires had become "The moral equivalent of war" (Pyne 1997). After World War II, firefighting efforts were intensified. Science and technology allowed important strides to be made in understanding wildfire spread and its control. The study of fire at this time concentrated on fire physics, fire behavior, and the relationships between meteorology and fire. Subsequently, the focus broadened into fire's effects on ecosystems and a creation of the field we know today as fire ecology.

The Ecosystem Management Era

A number of factors are driving the continuing change of fire patterns in wildlands. A major factor is the increasing density and spread of humans on the landscape. A second factor is that the technology used for fire suppression continues to become more sophisticated, effective, and efficient. Third, the intentional use of fire as a tool for fuel management, natural resource management, and the protection of communities at the wildland–urban interface is increasing.

Starting in the 1960s and continuing today, the emphasis of fire study has become focused on natural resource values and the influence of fire as an ecosystem process. There has been widespread acceptance of the notion that fire is an important part of many ecosystems and that changes in the patterns of occurrence of fire have had many large-scale ecosystem effects. Fire ecology and fire management have become central issues in land management and there has been a greater recognition of the radiating impact of decisions about how to manage fire. Today, the practice of managing wildland fuels to modify future fire behavior has become an important land management activity. The wildland–urban interface has become the contentious focal point for application of fuel management to difficult situations.

In this book, we provide a great deal of information on the ecological role of fire and how our culture has evolved to recognize and appreciate fire as an ecological process. So are we mounting a massive effort to restore fire to all of our wildlands? No. Why? Because our culture also values other wildland attributes including clean air and water, species and habitats, and living in desirable locations without fire to threaten our health and quality of life.

Wildland fires produce smoke and other combustion byproducts and particulate matter that are potentially harmful to human health and welfare, and reduce visibility. These are natural byproducts of fire but are simply unpleasant to people. Uncontrolled wildfires are clearly responsible for the most widespread, prolonged, and severe periods of air quality degradation. The challenge in managing wildland fire is to understand the tradeoffs of balancing public interest objectives while sustaining ecological integrity. Minimizing the adverse effects of smoke on human health and welfare, while maximizing the effectiveness of using wildland fire, is an integrated and collaborative activity.

We also value clean water, and water quality is impacted by fire. California's watersheds include a diversity of intermittent, ephemeral, and perennial streams of various sizes that are shaped by the dynamics of water and sediment. The balance of water and sediment is continually influenced by fire and other physical and biological perturbations. A pulse of erosion due to removal of vegetation, surface cover, and the structural support that the root systems provide commonly follows wildfire. The scale and intensity of these erosion events is dependent on characteristics of the ecosystem and the pattern and severity of the fires and precipitation. Today, landscapes are highly altered with historic fire regimes greatly modified by human activities. Past and current management practices including water development, mining, road building, urbanization, fire suppression, timber harvest, and recreation influence watersheds. The largest erosion events typically follow very large, uniformly high-severity wildfires in steep erosive landscapes. Fire and its associated pulses of sedimentation, mass wasting, and flooding are natural processes that work within ecosystems and are part of the process that creates and maintains watershed. However, like air quality regulation, the focus of the watershed impact regulatory process is to minimize the impacts of discretionary managed fires. Until watershed managers and aquatic ecologists actively support and prescribe the restoration of fire regimes, fire regimes that benefit watersheds are unlikely.

Although fire is a natural process, the effects of fire are not always what they once were. One of the most significant impacts to California ecosystems is the effect of invasive species from other parts of the world that have been introduced since the earliest European contact. Fire can facilitate the expansion of non-native invasive species, and in other cases fire can be used to select against invasive species. In the grass–fire cycle, invasive grass species become established in an area dominated by woody vegetation. As the invasive grasses increase in abundance, a continuous layer of highly combustible fine fuel develops, resulting in increased rates of fire spread and fire frequency. Shrublands and forests composed of native species are converted to grasslands comprised mainly of non-native species. Invasive species are responsible for altering fire regimes in large areas in southern California chaparral, the Great Basin, the Central Valley, and the Mojave Desert. Using or excluding fire to manage invasive species is an important area of future work.

The Federal Endangered Species Act (1972) and the California Endangered Species Act (1986) were specifically enacted to protect native plants and animals that are threatened or endangered. In California, fire and fuel management

and at-risk species conservation and protection have more often been in conflict than in accord with one another because addressing species and habitat needs takes additional planning, time, and resources, and restricts project implementation. Although there are difficulties, there are also potential opportunities for fire management to aid in the protection of at-risk species. The use of prescribed fire may provide the best opportunity for at-risk species where the absence of fire has degraded habitat or where fire is not likely to be allowed to return naturally. There are numerous examples across California where fire and fuel management activities, prescribed burning, fire suppression, or post-fire rehabilitation and restoration can be integrated while conserving and protecting at-risk species, their habitats, and ecological processes. Many at-risk species, and the ecological systems they depend on, cannot be sustained or recovered without the immediate and longer-term ecological functioning provided by fire.

The story of fire in California ecosystems is an epic adventure played out over millennia in a spectacular setting. This book sets the scenes, introduces the characters and situations, and provides you, the future of fire ecology, with the tools to write the next act.

References

Agee, J. K. 1993. Fire ecology of Pacific Northwest forests. Island Press, Washington, D.C. 493 p.

Anderson, M. K. 2005. Tending the wild: Native American knowledge and the management of California's natural resources. University of California Press, Berkeley, CA. 555 p.

Arno, S. F., and S. Allison-Bunnel. 2002. Flames in our forests. Island Press, Washington, D.C. 227 p.

Axelrod, D. I. 1958. Evolution of Madro-Tertiary geoflora. Botanical Review 24:433–509.

Axelrod, D. I. 1976. History of the coniferous forests, California and Nevada. University of California Publications in Botany 70:1–62.

Axelrod, D. I. 1988. Outline history of California vegetation. P. 139–192 in M. G. Barbour and J. Major (eds.), Terrestrial vegetation of California, expanded edition. California Native Plant Society, Special Publication No. 9, Sacramento.

Bailey, R. G. 1996. Ecosystem geography. Springer, New York. 204 p.

Bailey, R. G., P. E. Avers, T. King, and W. H. McNab (eds.). 1994. Ecoregions and subregions of the United States (map). U.S. Geological Survey, Washington, D.C. Scale 1:750,000; colored.

Barbour, M., B. Pavlik, F. Drysdale, and S. Lindstrom. 1993. California's changing landscapes—Diversity and conservation of California vegetation. California Native Plant Society, Sacramento. 244 p.

Barbour, M. G., and J. Major (eds.). 1988. Terrestrial vegetation of California, expanded edition. California Native Plant Society, Special Publication No. 9, Sacramento.

Byrne, R., J. Michaelsen, and A. Soutar. 1977. Fossil charcoal as a measure of wildfire frequency in Southern California: a preliminary analysis. Proceedings of the symposium on environmental consequences of fire and fuel management in Mediterranean ecosystems. USDA Forest Service Gen. Tech. Rep. WO-3, p. 361–367.

Cook, S.F. 1972. The aboriginal population of Upper California. In R.F. Heizer and M.A. Whipple (eds.), The California Indians. University of California Press, Berkeley.

Cooper, C.F. 1961. The ecology of fire. Scientific American 209:150–160.

Egan, D., and E.A. Howell. 2001. The historical ecology handbook: a restorationist's guide to reference ecosystems. Island Press, Washington, D.C. 457 p.

Franklin, J.F., and C.T. Dyrness. 1973. Natural vegetation of Oregon and Washington. USDA Forest Service, GTR PNW-8, Portland, OR.

Franklin, J.F., and C.B. Halpern. 2000. Pacific Northwest forests. P. 123–159 in M.G. Barbour and W.D. Billings (eds.), North American terrestrial vegetation, second edition. Cambridge University Press, New York.

Hickman, J.C. (ed.). 1993. The Jepson manual—Higher plants of California. University of California Press, Berkeley. 1400 p.

Holstein, G. 2001. Pre-agricultural grassland in central California. Madroño 48:253–264.

Keeter, T.S. 1995. Environmental history and cultural ecology of the North Fork of the Eel River Basin, California. USDA Forest Service, R5-EM-TP-002, Eureka, CA. 116 p.

Kozlowski, T.T., and C.E. Ahlgren (eds.). 1974. Fire and ecosystems. Academic Press, New York. 542 p.

Martin, R.E., and D.B. Sapsis. 1992. Fires as agents of biodiversity: pyrodiversity promotes biodiversity. In R.R. Harris, D.E. Erman, and H.M. Kerner. Proceedings of symposium on biodiversity of Northwestern California. University of California Wildland Resource Center Report No. 29, Berkeley. 316 p.

Mensing, S.A. 1998. 560 years of vegetation change in the region of Santa Barbara, CA. Madrono 45: 1–11.

Mensing, S.A., J. Michaelsen, and R. Byrne. 1999. A 560-year record of Santa Ana fires reconstructed from charcoal deposited in the Santa Barbara Basin, California. Quaternary Research 51: 295–305.

Michaelsen, J., L. Haston, and F.W. Davis. 1987. Four hundred years of California precipitation reconstructed from tree rings. Water Research Bulletin 23:809–818.

Miles, S.R., and C.B. Goudey. 1997. Ecological subregions of California: section and subsection descriptions. USDA Forest Service, R5-EM-TP-005, San Francisco, CA.

Pyne, S.F. 1997. America's fires: management on wildlands and forests. Forest History Society, Durham, NC. 54 p.

Pyne, S.F. 2001. Year of the fires: the story of the great fires of 1910. Viking Penguin, New York. 322 p.

Pyne, S.F., P.L. Andrews, and R.D. Laven. 1996. Introduction to wildland fire. John Wiley and Sons, New York. 769 p.

Sawyer, J.O., and D.A. Thornburgh. 1988. Montane and subalpine vegetation of the Klamath Mountains. P. 699–732 in M.G. Barbour and J. Major (eds.), Terrestrial vegetation of California, expanded edition. California Native Plant Society, Special Publication No. 9, Sacramento.

Smith, S.J., and R.S. Anderson. 1992. Late Wisconsin paleoecologic record from Swamp Lake, Yosemite National Park, California. Quaternary Research 38:91–102.

Stewart, O.C. 2002. Forgotten fires: Native Americans and the transient wilderness, edited and with introductions by Henry T. Lewis and M. Kat Anderson. University of Oklahoma Press, Norman. 364 p.

Vale, T.R. (ed.). 2002. Fire, native peoples, and the natural landscape. Island Press, Washington, D.C. 238 p.

Whalen, R.J. 1995. The ecology of fire. Cambridge University Press, Cambridge, England. 356 p.

Whittaker, R.H. 1960. Vegetation of the Siskiyou Mountains, Oregon and California. Ecological Monographs 30:279–338.

Wright, H.R., and A.W. Bailey. 1982. Fire ecology: United States and Southern Canada. John Wiley and Sons, New York. 501 p.

PART I

INTRODUCTION TO FIRE ECOLOGY

Part I presents and explains the essential aspects of fire ecology. In Chapter 2 we describe how weather and climate influence fires and fire regimes. We then delve into the factors that affect fire as a physical process in Chapter 3, before discussing fire as an ecological process and fully developing a new concept of fire regimes in Chapter 4. Next we discuss the interactions of fire with the soil, water, and air components of the physical environment in Chapter 5. Finally, in Chapters 6 and 7, we cover the effects of fires on biological communities, first looking at interactions with plants and then with animals. This foundation in fire ecology will provide the basis for understanding fire's varying role in the bioregions of California and the issues confronting fire in today's society.

CHAPTER 2

California Climate and Fire Weather

RICHARD A. MINNICH

I've lived in good climate, and it bores the hell out of me.
I like weather rather than climate.

JOHN STEINBECK, 1962

To understand fire as a natural process in California ecosystems, it is necessary to evaluate how climate (average and predictable weather properties over long time scales) contributes to vegetation flammability, and how short-term weather influences the propagation of flame lines (fire weather). The flammability of vegetation can be envisioned as a "tug of war" between the organic energy of plants (carbohydrate) as a heat source, and plant water vital for transport of nutrients and leaf transpiration as a heat sink. Fires occur when fuel energy exceeds the heat capacity of water—that is, the carbohydrate-to-water energy ratio in vegetation is positive (Rothermel 1972).

Climate and weather both affect plant growth and fuel build-up, as well as water/fuel moisture in vegetation and soils, but these two terms reflect different time scales and processes. Climatic parameters, including mean precipitation and temperature, affect annual cycles of soil wetting, water loss by evapotranspiration and runoff, plant growth and phenology, and desiccation of vegetation, as well as natural ignitions from thunderstorms. The predictable properties of California's mediterreanean climate are winter precipitation, summer drought, and mild temperatures in most areas of the state. Climate variability at interannual to decadal time scales is believed to correlate with periodic perturbations in fire regime. The weather, especially relative humidity and wind velocity, affects fuel moisture, heat transfer in flames (fire intensity), and available fuel consumed in pyrolysis. Relative humidity and wind speed influence plant transpiration and water diffusion in dead fuel. Because organic fuels are poor conductors, and radiative heat transfer is inversely related to distance, wind speed (advection) is the dominant mechanism of heat transfer in the propagation of flame lines. Decreasing relative humidity and increasing wind velocity tend to result in higher fire spread rates and intensities, as well as the consumption of ever-coarser fuels.

This review first examines some basic principles of weather. It then discusses California's mediterranean climate from the standpoint of atmospheric circulation. This is followed by short-term weather conditions associated with fire spread, and climate variability and its possible role in fire regimes.

Weather Principles

Atmospheric and oceanic circulation can be understood in terms of radiant solar energy and the behavior of gases. In short, differential heating of the tropics and high latitudes by the sun result in temperature gradients that drive atmospheric motion. Upward air motions can lead to clouds and precipitation; horizontal air motions (winds) are a major factor in atmospheric heat transport and ocean circulation. Ocean circulation in turn influences ocean temperature distribution, whose effects reach back to atmospheric temperature gradients.

Radiant Energy

Solar energy heats the earth's surface unevenly. In the tropics, solar energy intercepts the earth's surface close to right angles with land and ocean surfaces receiving the most radiation during the year of anywhere on Earth. These surfaces and the overlying atmosphere have the highest temperatures on the planet relative to their elevation. At high latitudes, the sun's rays arrive obliquely, with the same amount of solar energy spread out over larger areas of the earth's surface. There, a given unit of land, air, or water receives less solar energy and is colder than in the tropics.

Sunlight is absorbed by the land and water that in turn radiate infrared energy that is absorbed by atmospheric greenhouse gases, especially water vapor and carbon dioxide (the "greenhouse effect"). Thus the air is mostly heated

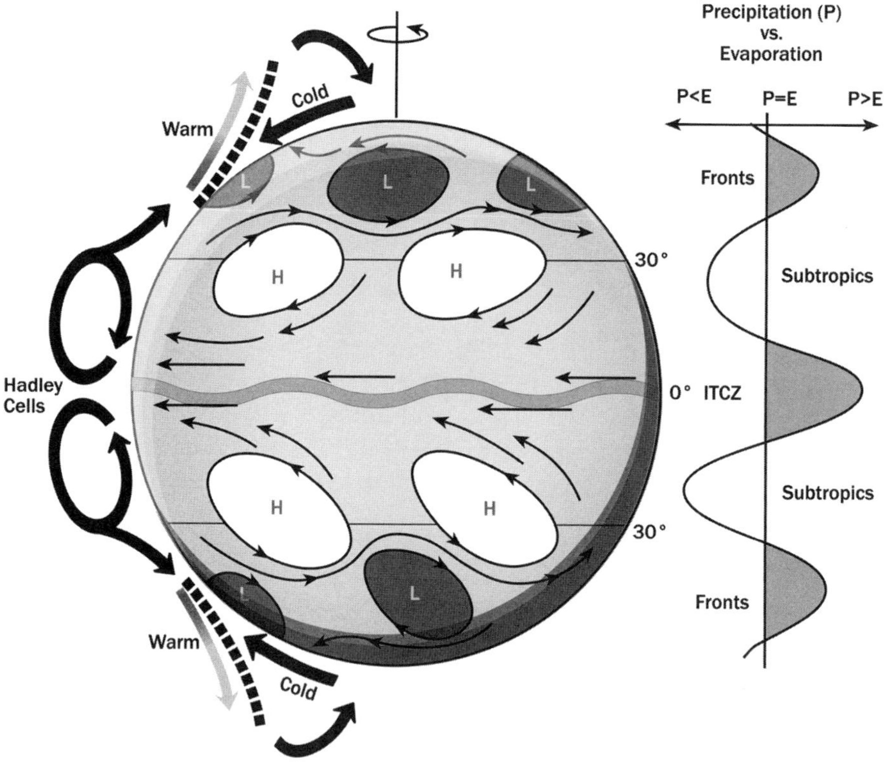

FIGURE 2.1. Global atmospheric circulation. Heated air rises at the intertropical convergence zone (ITCZ) near the equator and sinks in the subtropics as part of the Hadley cell. Additional poleward heat transfer occurs along frontal cyclones at mid- and higher latitudes. Precipitation exceeds evapotranspiration in the tropics and mid-latitudes. Dry sinking air produces more evaporation than precipitation in the subtropics. (Redrawn from Ruddiman 2001.)

through energy exchanges at the earth's surface. In a radiation budget, tropical regions receive more energy than they emit, whereas polar regions radiate more energy than they receive. Over long time scales, the tropics do not become hotter, nor do the polar regions become colder, because of the heat transfer accomplished by atmospheric circulation.

Behavior of Gases

Air motion responds to the *ideal gas law,* which states that increasing the temperature of a gas results in increasing gas pressure at constant volume, and that increasing the temperature increases its volume at constant pressure. These relationships break down with water vapor, which can condense from a gas to a liquid (water) and freeze into a solid (ice). The amount of water vapor that air can hold before condensation increases exponentially with increasing air temperature.

Clouds, Rain, and Air Stability

When air masses move vertically upward (downward), air pressure decreases (increases) with altitude because the proportion of the mass of the atmosphere exerting weight decreases (increases). Air lifting into an environment of lower air pressure results in the expansion and cooling of air parcels, which may eventually lead to condensation, seen as clouds and precipitation (rain, snow, sleet, etc.). In descending air masses, air parcels move into an environment of increasing air pressure. Consequently, the mass is compressed

and heated. Clouds disappear by evaporation to water vapor. Thus, cloudy wet weather is associated with rising air masses, fair weather with descending air masses.

Air masses that resist upward motion are classified as *stable.* Air masses that are easily triggered into upward motion are *unstable.* Dense air, like any fluid, will sink through lighter air and, conversely light air will rise through denser air due to buoyancy. However, air density is related to temperature: Air tends to expand and become lighter with increasing temperature, so that at constant pressure, cold air is denser than warm air. Putting the density and temperature effects together, the capacity for air to rise from the earth's surface depends in part on the temperature profile of the atmosphere *(lapse rate).* If the air layers aloft are relatively cold (dense) and air layers at the surface are relatively warm (light), air masses from the surface will tend to mix high into the atmosphere (unstable air), and convection, cloud formation, and rain are likely. In fact, the condensation and freezing processes (change of state from water vapor to water and water to ice) and precipitation are accelerated by the release of latent heat into the atmosphere. If surface air layers are relatively cold and the air aloft is relatively warm (light), the cold air at the surface, being dense, will remain there at rest (stable air).

Global Atmospheric Circulation

Atmospheric motion is driven by latitudinal temperature gradients that in turn produce horizontal pressure gradients unopposed by gravity. Air moves from high pressure to low

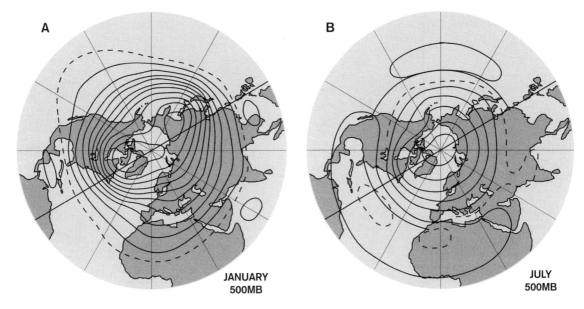

A

B

JANUARY
500MB

JULY
500MB

FIGURE 2.2. Mean 500 mbar contours for: (A) January, and (B) July. Low pressure is centered near the pole, with westerly winds moving around the hemisphere in a direction parallel to contours (geostrophic wind). The entire counter-clockwise flowing system is the circumpolar vortex. The westerlies are strongest in January when the latitudinal temperature gradient is strongest and the jet stream (where contours are closest together) arrives at the Pacific coast in Oregon and Washington. Westerlies are weakest in July when the mean position of the jet stream retreats to western Canada. (Redrawn from Palmén and Newton 1965.)

pressure. However, wind direction is turned to the right in the northern hemisphere and to the left in the southern hemisphere by the rotation of the earth on its axis (the *Coriolis force*). In the northern hemisphere, air moves clockwise around high-pressure areas *(anticyclones)* and counterclockwise around areas of low pressure *(cyclones)*. In the southern hemisphere, moving air is turned to its left: Cyclones rotate clockwise and anticyclones counterclockwise. Surface air always moves out of anticyclones and into cyclones, that is, from high pressure to low pressure.

The northern and southern hemispheres each have a three-cell atmospheric circulation structure (Fig. 2.1). In the Hadley cell of the northern hemisphere, air leaving the equator and moving poleward aloft turns to the right and increases in speed to about 160 km hr^{-1} (100 mi hr^{-1}) as it moves over an increasingly slow rotational spin of the earth. When the air reaches the subtropics, the northward upper air movement is spent; the convection cell is truncated and air descends back to the surface. Air then returns to the equator at the surface as *trade winds*. Seasonal circulations in the Hadley cell, particularly surface trade winds, are very steady. Air masses are warm and moist, and winds are constantly from the northeast in the northern hemisphere and from the southeast in the southern hemisphere. These winds come together at the intertropical convergence zone (ITCZ), a zone of uplift and heavy precipitation near the equator. The Hadley cell is a thermally direct system driven by heating and latent heat released from precipitation along the ITCZ.

Poleward of the Hadley cell is the Ferrel cell. This is a thermally indirect system in which flow is driven by mechanical processes in combination with strong atmospheric tempera-

ture gradients at high latitudes. The Ferrel cell is dissimilar from the Hadley cell of the tropics in that most motion is driven by strong pressure gradients of the polar front jet stream. The jet stream (latitude 30°–60°) is a belt of strong west winds aloft that results from strong air temperature gradients in the upper troposphere (Fig. 2.2).

The jet stream has sinusoidal-shaped waves with "troughs" that extend toward the equator and intervening "ridges" that arc toward the pole. Areas of rising and descending air motion flank the troughs (Fig. 2.3). The east side of a trough (west side of a ridge) is associated with rising air motion and surface low pressure. The subsiding motion on the west side of a trough (east side of a ridge) is associated with subsiding air and surface high pressure. Note that the vertical motion field of the atmosphere causes the areas of surface low pressure and high pressure. The pattern of upper level waves, with the accompanying surface cyclones and anticyclones migrates from west to east, causing changeable weather at mid-latitudes. The waves and associated surface low- and high-pressure systems can be viewed as large interactive "eddies" that transport warm air poleward from the subtropics and cold air equatorward from the poles. The entire global circulation system moves latitudinally with the seasons, toward the equator in winter and toward the pole in summer.

The Ocean Circulation

The oceans have far greater mass than does the atmosphere. Water is also a fluid within which mixing leads to large thermal capacity. As a result, ocean circulation is less rapid than air motion and its temperature changes are more conservative.

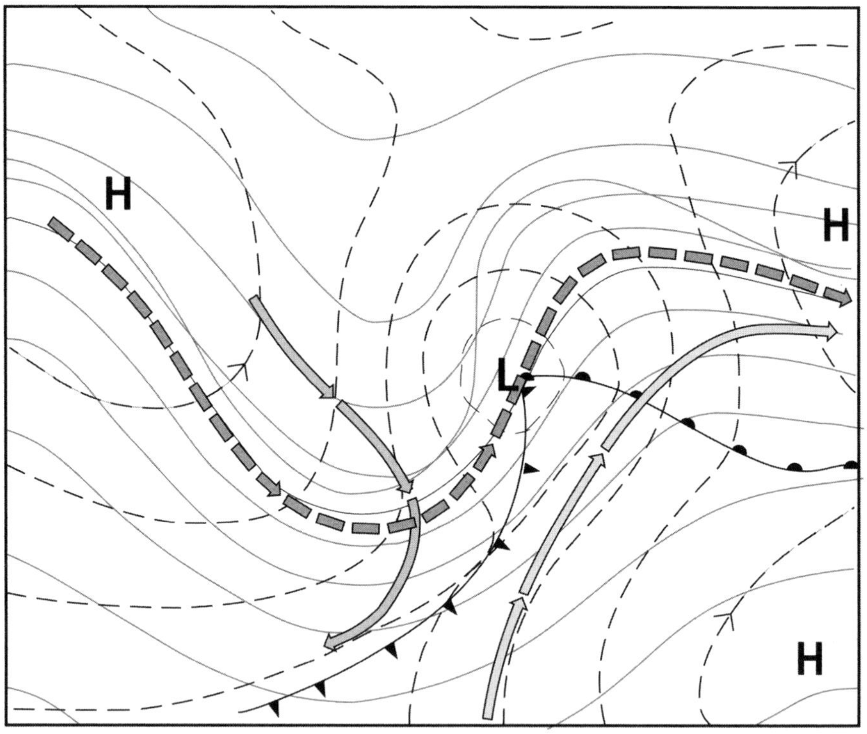

FIGURE 2.3. Schematic of a model cyclone. Pressure pattern (dashed lines) of surface cyclone in middle and anticyclones on right and left shown against wave in the jet stream (solid lines). Frontal boundaries are shown as solid ticked boundaries. Broad arrows show the trajectories of air motion through the system, with sinking air west of the front and rising air east of the front. (Redrawn from Palmén and Newton 1965.)

In summer, the land is warmer than the oceans; in winter, oceans are warmer than the land. Land surfaces, being solid, have low thermal capacity that leads to rapid temperature changes on daily and annual cycles. Land–sea temperature differences affect atmospheric motions like the latitudinal temperature differences.

The oceans have deep currents and surface circulations. Deep ocean circulation is driven by density-driven currents that are very cold, relatively dense waters derived from the melting of ice sheets at the poles. Dense waters sink and move at depth toward the equator. Surface waters are warmer (lighter), being heated by the sun. They float stably on top of deep waters. The two water masses are divided at the *thermocline,* a zone of rapid temperature change at approximately 50–200 m (164–656 ft) below the ocean surface. Surface ocean currents are largely driven by the winds; hence they have nearly the same geographic configuration as surface air flows. Currents move from east to west in the tropics and from west to east in mid and high latitudes. Currents also tend to move poleward off east coasts of continents and equatorward off west coasts of continents. In general, waters off west coasts of continents, including California, are cold due to advection from the poles and upwelling of deeper waters as the surface water is driven offshore by the trade winds. The thermocline is thus brought up closer to the surface. The converse occurs on the east sides of continents.

Climate

California's mediterranean climate of winter rain and dry summers results in inefficient decomposition of organic mat-

ter, fuel build-up, and high fire hazard. The outstanding variety of climate in California is accompanied by remarkable vegetation diversity and associated fire regimes, as well as the weather conditions associated with fire.

The mediterranean climate results from seasonal changes in global circulation, including California's marginal position to the jet stream and the presence of cold, upwelling ocean waters offshore. During winter, large latitudinal temperature gradients support a strong circumpolar vortex with the mean position of jet stream westerlies extending equatorward to the latitude of northern California. Troughs in the jet stream bring low-pressure systems and precipitation. At the surface, low pressure in the Gulf of Alaska brings strong onshore flows of moist westerlies to northern California and the Pacific Northwest, and mild temperatures through the state. Annual rainfall is greatest in the mountains due to orographic lift of air masses, and is lowest in the deserts due to the rain shadow effect of the mountains. During summer, reduced latitudinal temperature gradients weaken the circumpolar vortex, and the mean position of the westerlies and precipitation shifts northward to British Columbia. Surface low pressure in the Gulf of Alaska is replaced by high pressure covering most of the northeast Pacific Ocean. California is dominated by strong onshore flows from the Pacific high to thermal low pressure over the hot desert interior. Air masses are warmer than the ocean, except for a thin layer of cool, moist air, immediately over the ocean surface, called the *coastal marine layer.* The marine layer is also the northeastern boundary of the trade wind layer of the Hadley cell in the North Pacific Ocean. The presence of warm light air overlying the marine layer results in stable air masses, which leads to protracted drought.

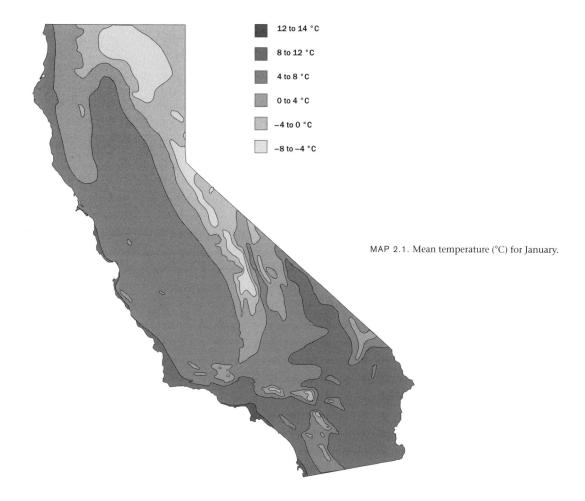

MAP 2.1. Mean temperature (°C) for January.

Temperature

The position of the jet stream is coupled with broadscale latitudinal temperature gradients and lapse rates. Hence, pressure–wind relationships require that latitudinal ambient temperature gradients be gradual over the state. Mean winter temperatures increase southward, and in the mountains reflect atmospheric lapse rates (Map 2.1). Sea level temperatures increase from 9°C (48°F) in coastal northern California to 14°C (57°F) in coastal southern California and 12°C (54°F) in the southeastern deserts. Mean temperatures in the mountains reach freezing at about 1,500 m (4,921 ft) in northern California and 2,200 m (7,218 ft) in southern California. Many low-lying basins contain persistent ground inversions resulting from the combination of radiational cooling and low insolation. In the Central Valley, where ground inversions are maintained by reflective ground fogs, mean January temperatures average 8°C (46°F). From the high northeastern plateaus to Lake Tahoe, ground inversions result in mean temperatures as low as –3°C (27°F) on valley floors.

During summer, the coastal valleys and coastal slopes of the mountains are influenced by the coastal marine layer, a steady-state feature that forms from the cooling and moistening of the tropospheric boundary layer overlying the cold California current. The marine layer is associated with extensive coastal low clouds (stratus) over the ocean and is capped by a strong thermal inversion that divides it from warm, subsiding air masses aloft. Northwesterly gradient winds combined with sea breezes and anabatic valley winds, and mountain slope winds (winds created by local surface heating) transport marine air inland to the coastal ranges usually within 100 km (62 mi) of the coast before the marine layer dissipates from diabatic heating and mixing with warm air aloft (Glendening et al. 1986). Mean July temperatures along the coast reflect local sea surface temperatures, ranging from 14°C–16°C (57°F–61°F) in strong upwelling zones north of Point Conception to 18°C–22°C (64°F–72°F) in the southern California bight (Map 2.2), the embayment between Point Conception and the Mexican border. Temperatures increase to 24°C–28°C (75°F–82°F) in the inland valleys of southern California and along the Central Valley. The deserts beyond the reach of marine air penetration average 26°C–35°C (79°F–95°F) and 38°C (100°F) in Death Valley. Temperatures in mountains reflect ambient lapse rates and isoclinal with latitude, decreasing to 20°C–24°C (68°F–75°F) at 1,500 m (4,921 ft) and 14°C–18°C (57°F–64°F) at 2,500 m (8,202 ft).

Precipitation

Winter precipitation in California results from frontal cyclones and associated troughs of the jet stream that move

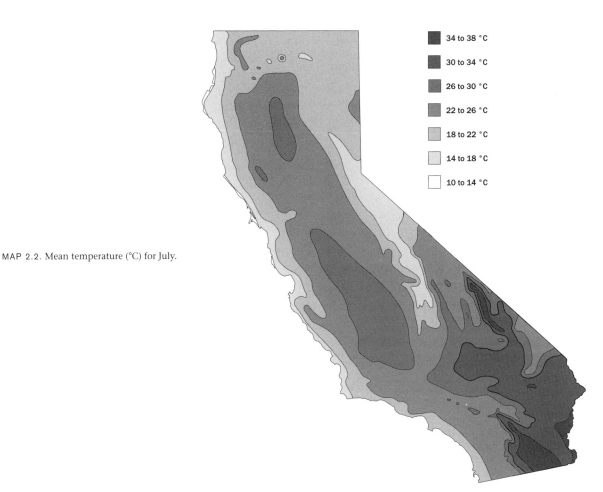

■	34 to 38 °C
■	30 to 34 °C
■	26 to 30 °C
■	22 to 26 °C
■	18 to 22 °C
■	14 to 18 °C
□	10 to 14 °C

MAP 2.2. Mean temperature (°C) for July.

over the area from the North Pacific Ocean. Because the mean position of the jet stream lies in northern California (Fig. 2.2), storms decrease in frequency southward through the state. Most precipitation falls during the prefrontal zone (usually 100–300 km east of the cold front, Fig. 2.3) where upward air motions that may involve deepening of the marine layer cause cold fronts to have the properties of occluded fronts, producing long periods of steady rain in stable air. Winds aloft are predominantly southwesterly because frontal zones precede trough axes, and low-level winds are southerly to southeasterly. Postfrontal precipitation consists of convective showers concentrated over high terrain with veering southwesterly to westerly winds at the surface and aloft. Clouds and precipitation decrease rapidly with the onset of subsidence and advection of dry air following the passage of the trough, with winds aloft turning westerly to northwesterly.

The interaction between prefrontal circulation and terrain results in strong gradients in average annual precipitation throughout California. Because storm air masses are stable, the variation in local precipitation is normally a consequence of physical lifting of air masses over mountain barriers (orographic lift) rather than from thermal convection. Orographic lift is most intense on the south- to southwest-facing escarpments that lie at right angles to storm winds. Amounts

decrease downwind to inland ranges—regardless of altitude—due to depletion of storm air mass moisture and descending airflow in rain shadows.

The average annual precipitation along the northern California coast varies from 50 cm (20 in) at San Francisco to 100 cm (39 in) north of Ft. Bragg, with locally higher amounts where mountains skirt the coastline (Map 2.3). The highest amounts occur in the coastal mountains north of Eureka and near Cape Mendocino where the annual average is > 250 cm (> 98 in). Totals in the North Coast Ranges decrease downwind to 150–200 cm (59–79 in) in the Salmon and Siskiyou Ranges, and decrease southward with the declining general altitude of the mountains to 100 cm (39 in) near Santa Rosa. Rain shadows from the North Coast Ranges produce average annual precipitation of 35–50 cm (14–20 in) in the Sacramento Valley. Orographic lift along the uniformly gentle western slope of the northern Sierra Nevada produces an average annual precipitation of 60 cm (24 in) along the lower foothills to 150–200 cm (59–79 in) at the crest of the range north of Lake Tahoe. To the east of the mountain axis, rain shadows in descending air reduce the average annual precipitation to only 20–60 cm (8–24 in) in the Modoc Plateau, and 60–80 cm (24–31 in) in the Lake Tahoe Basin.

In the South Coast Ranges of central California, the average annual precipitation is 100–150 cm (39–59 in) on the

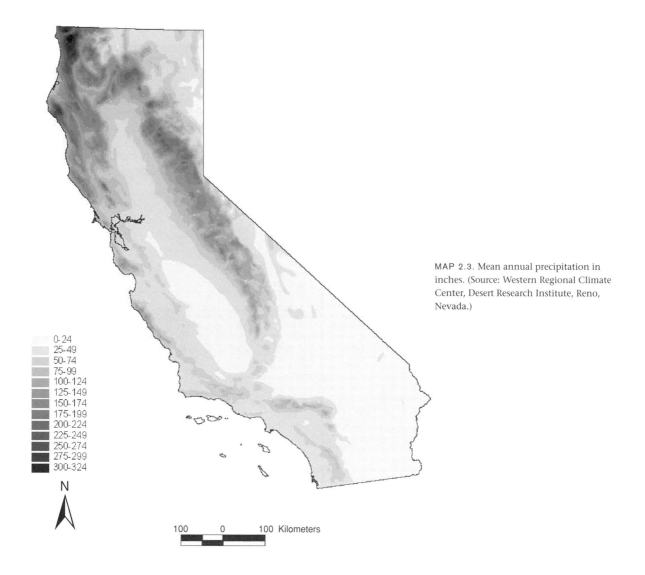

MAP 2.3. Mean annual precipitation in inches. (Source: Western Regional Climate Center, Desert Research Institute, Reno, Nevada.)

0-24
25-49
50-74
75-99
100-124
125-149
150-174
175-199
200-224
225-249
250-274
275-299
300-324

N

100   0   100 Kilometers

steep coastal escarpments of the Santa Cruz and Santa Lucia Mountains but amounts in the rain-shadowed Diablo Ranges to the east seldom exceed 50 cm (20 in). Intervening basins including Salinas Valley receive 30–40 cm (12–16 in). Rain shadows extending from the South Coast Ranges into the San Joaquin Valley produce an average annual precipitation of 30 cm (12 in) near the Sacramento delta, lowering to 15 cm (6 in) near Bakersfield and the Carrizo Plain. Amounts then increase with orographic lift to 35–50 cm (14–20 in) in the Sierra Nevada foothills. The topographic complexity of the southern Sierra Nevada results in large variability in average annual precipitation along the west slope. Steep southwestern exposures have averages of 100–150 cm (39–59 in) from Yosemite to Kaiser Ridge, the Great Western Divide, and the Greenhorn Range. Leeward slopes on the coastal front receive 50–100 cm (20–39 in), including the upper Tuolumne River, Mono Creek Basin, the upper Kings River, and the Kern River plateau northward to Mt. Whitney. The average annual precipitation seldom exceeds 50 cm (20 in) in the southernmost Sierra Nevada and Tehachapi Mountains due to low altitude and leeward position to the western Transverse and South Coast Ranges.

In southern California, precipitation is highest in the Transverse Ranges (average annual precipitation, 80–110 cm [31–43 in]) due to intense orographic lift on their steep southern escarpments. Amounts decrease to 60–80 cm (24–31 in) in the "downwind" San Rafael Mountains, Pine Mountain Ridge, and eastern San Bernardino Mountains. Farther inland, relatively high ranges that include Mt. Pinos, San Emigdio, Tehachapi and Liebre Mountains, and drainages north and east of Big Bear Basin, receive 35–60 cm (14–24 in). The average annual precipitation is only 40–60 cm (16–24 in) on the coastal escarpments of the Peninsular Ranges because slopes parallel storm winds. Amounts reach 80–100 cm (31–39 in) on local southern escarpments of the Santa Ana Mountains, Palomar Mountain, and Cuyamaca Peak. Despite their high altitude, the San Jacinto Mountains receive 40–70 cm (16–28 in) and the Santa Rosa Mountains < 50 cm (< 20 in) due to their leeward position to the Santa Ana and Palomar Mountains. The average annual precipitation in the southern California coastal plain varies from 25–35 cm

(10–14 in) at the shoreline to 40–50 cm (16–20 in) at the base of the mountains.

The average annual precipitation in the southeastern deserts is mostly 10–15 cm (4–6 in), with totals as low as 5 cm (2 in) in Death Valley and the Salton Sea trough. Amounts locally reach 25 cm (10 in) in the Panamint and Inyo Mountains, and the ranges in the northeast Mojave Desert.

Snowfall

In most of California, the replenishment of soil water reflects the timing of rainstorms during the winter, which mostly end by March or April. In high mountain watersheds, an accumulating winter snow pack melt serves to increase available soil moisture in summer because melt is delayed until sun angles become high in April and May, thereby postponing plant desiccation and drying of dead fuels compared with rain-dominated lands below. In effect, the snow pack represents a second layer of water storage on top of moisture in storage in the soil layer.

The ratio of average frozen precipitation (mostly snow hypothetically melted to a liquid depth) ratioed to the average annual precipitation shows a linear relationship with altitude. In southern California, little snowfall occurs below 1,000 m (3,281 ft). The ratios increase to 25% at 1,750 m (5,741 ft), 75% at 2,750 m (9,022 ft), and 100% at 3,000 m (9,843 ft) (Minnich 1986). Average snow lines are about 200–400 m (656–1,312 ft) lower in the Sierra Nevada (Barbour et al. 1991). With an average annual precipitation of 100 cm (39 in), the water equivalent snowfall in southern California reaches 50 cm (20 in) at 2,300 m (7,546 ft) and 75 cm (30 in) at 2,700 m (8,858 ft). With an average annual precipitation of 150 cm (59 in) near Yosemite, the water equivalent snowfall reaches 50 cm (20 in) at 1,900 m (6,234 ft) and 75 cm (30 in) at 2,200 m (7,218 ft). At Mt. Lassen (average annual precipitation, 200 cm [79 in]), 50 cm (20 in) water equivalent amounts are reached by 1,400 m (4,593 ft) and 100 cm (39 in) by 2,000 m (6,562 ft). Interannual snow levels in California tend to increase with increasing total annual precipitation due largely to greater advection of moist subtropical air masses during El Niño events (Minnich 1986). In southern California, average annual snow lines increase from 2,000 m (6,562 ft) with 70% normal precipitation to 2,400 m (7,574 ft) with 140% of normal. The average snow line during the floods of January 1969 was 2,700–3,000 m (8,858–9843 ft). The snowline during the New Year's 1997 flood at Yosemite was > 2,500 m (> 8,202).

The North American Monsoon

From July to early September, the North American monsoon brings occasional afternoon thunderstorms and lightning to California. For 10–20 days per summer, the western margin of the North American monsoon, a deep layer of moist, unstable tropical air, extends northward from Mexico into

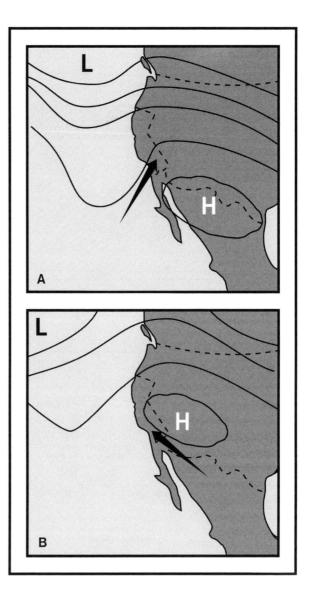

FIGURE 2.4. 500 mbar circulation models in California: (A) dry southwesterly flow over California, and (B) southeasterly North American monsoon types. (Source: Minnich et al. 1993.)

the eastern mountains and deserts of California (Tubbs 1972). The monsoon arrives from the tropical Pacific and Gulf of California around an anticyclone in the midtroposphere centered over the southwestern U.S. desert. The anticyclone is sustained by intense convective heating off the high-elevation land surfaces of the Great Basin, Colorado Plateau, and Mexican Plateau (Hales 1974, Adams and Comrie 1997, Stensrud et al. 1997).

The occurrence of thunderstorms in California and Baja California is related to the position of the anticyclone (Minnich et al. 1993). When the jet stream passes over the Pacific Northwest, the anticyclone is centered over northern Mexico (Figs. 2.4A and 2.5A). Dry southwesterly flow over California results in mostly clear skies, even over the highest mountains. Monsoon moisture is steered northeastward into northwestern Mexico and Arizona. Deep troughs destabilize

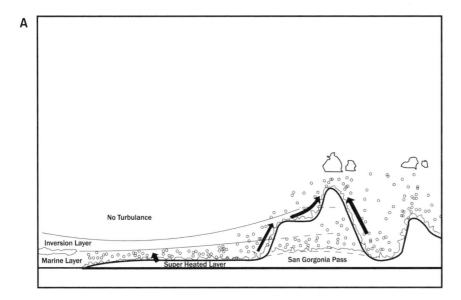

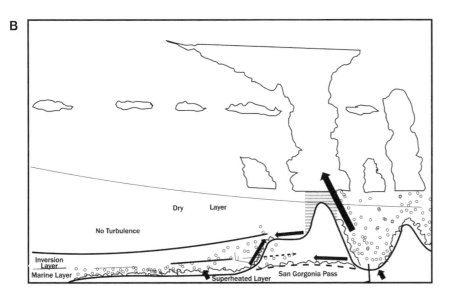

FIGURE 2.5. Conceptual model of afternoon weather conditions for (A) dry southwesterly flow, and (B) southeasterly North American monsoon types. MR = hypothetical mixing ratio profiles of atmospheric moisture. Chaotic lines and bubbles represent superheated air updrafts. Barbs show wind directions and velocities aloft (Redrawn from Minnich et al. 1993)

Pacific Ocean air masses and produce thunderstorms in the mountains of far northern California. When the jet stream is displaced northward into British Columbia, the center of the anticyclone shifts northward over the Colorado Plateau or Great Basin. South to southeasterly winds aloft transport tropical moisture (Figs. 2.4B and 2.5B) into southwestern California and the Sierra Nevada. Moisture arrives at upper levels (3–4 km [1.9–2.5 mi]) as convective debris from afternoon and night thunderstorms and mesoscale convective systems over the Sierra Madre Occidental of northwestern Mexico and Gulf of California. Below 2 km (1.2 mi), low-level moist air masses—derived from convective outflows of thunderstorms over Mexico—surge into the Salton Sea trough, Colorado River Valley, and occasionally as far north as Owens Valley (Hales 1974, Adams and Comrie 1997, Stensrud et al. 1997). Moisture surges also result from the lift of the trade

wind layer overlying the Gulf of California by Mexican Pacific tropical cyclones passing to the south.

Convection tends to be concentrated over high terrain, especially in mountains exposed to low-level Gulf of California air masses, primarily east of a line from the Peninsular Ranges and eastern San Bernardino Mountains to the eastern escarpment of the Sierra Nevada. Average annual summer precipitation (July–September) averages 5–10 cm (2–6 in) in the most favorable areas of convection. Amounts decrease toward the west because of stable air produced by Pacific marine layer intrusions. Infrequent surges of very moist air encourage outbreaks of thunderstorms throughout California, even along the Pacific Coast. Large potential evapotranspiration (PET) rates compared to summer precipitation limits soil wetting to shallow soils (Franco-Vizcaíno et al. 2002), and monsoon rains seldom interrupt the fire season. Mexican

TABLE 2.1
Lightning strikes by bioregion in California, 1985–2000

Bioregion	Lightning Strikes		
	Total	Average	No./yr/l00km^2
North Coast	15,530	971	2.97
Klamath Mountains	46,187	2,887	12.81
Cascade Range	58,560	3,660	18.81
Northeast Plateaus	73,187	4,574	22.49
Sierra Nevada	210,277	13,142	19.59
Central Valley	35,188	2,199	3.89
Central Coast	18,264	1,142	2.96
South Coast	68,365	4,273	10.17
Southeast Deserts	480,673	30,042	27.34
Total	1,006,231	62,889	16.97

SOURCE: van Wagtendonk and Cayan (2007).

Pacific tropical cyclones *(Chubascos)* enter the state about once a decade, mostly in southern California. These storms are steered northward by southerly upper air winds of the first seasonal troughs or cutoff lows west of California, usually in September, and may produce copious precipitation of 5–20 cm (2–8 in) per day (Smith 1986).

Lightning

In 1985, the Bureau of Land Management installed a system of electromagnetic direction finders in the western United States that record radiation emitted by cloud-to-ground lightning strikes, with lightning located by triangulation within 5 km (3.1 mi) resolution. Over short time scales, the detection of lightning reflects the paths of individual thunderstorm cells. However, over time scales of weeks to months and years, the distribution of lightning strikes reflects a combination of regional circulation and differences in air mass instability with terrain primarily during the North American monsoon. Lightning detections are highest from Peninsular Ranges of southern California to the eastern crest of the Sierra Nevada and the desert ranges and basins.

During the period from 1985 through 2000, more than 1,000,000 lightning strikes were detected in California (van Wagtendonk and Cayan 2007), with nearly half of those occurring in the Southeast Desert bioregion (Table 2.1). On a per area basis, the number varied from 2.96 strikes yr^{-1} 100 km^{-2} for the Central Coast bioregion to 27.34 strikes yr^{-1} 100 km^{-2} for the Southeast Deserts.

The spatial distribution of lightning strikes varies within the state. As can be seen in Map 2.4, the Southeastern Deserts, Northeastern Plateaus, and the northern Sierra Nevada have the highest density of lightning strikes.

July and August were the months with the most prevalent lightning in all bioregions except the Central Coast where more lightning was detected during August and September (Table 2.2). The areas with the densest lightning strikes also have the greatest summer precipitation (Minnich et al. 1993). Statewide, the period from noon to 4:00 pm received the greatest number of strikes, whereas the morning hours from 4:00 am to 8:00 am received the least (Table 2.2).

One should not assume that rates of landscape scale burning are proportional to lightning strike densities. The success of ignitions depends on whether they strike flammable targets. Fire record statistics on ignitions are seldom correlated with vegetation successional status of the fuel cycle and configuration of patch mosaic elements. Clearly, lightning strikes in recently burned areas have less chance of establishing a fire than in areas with high fuel loads.

The frequency of ignitions falling upon a patch of vegetation in ecological time scales requires data for three variables: (1) the ignition detection rate (strikes per area per time); (2) the time required for patch elements in a mosaic to reach flammability; and (3) the size frequency distribution of the patch mosaic.

The patch ignition rate (Ip) is estimated by the equation:

$$I_p = (I_{ltg} + I_{anth})\ P\ F,$$

where I_{ltg} is the lightning detection rate (number km^{-2} yr^{-1}), I_{anth} is the anthropogenic ignition rate (number km^{-2} yr^{-1}), P is the patch size (km^2), and F is the vegetation fuel threshold, or the time required for vegetation to become flammable (yr).

Each variable contributing to ignition frequency exhibits a spatial pattern. Lightning (I_{ltg}) occurs periodically in summer, with higher strike densities in the mountains.

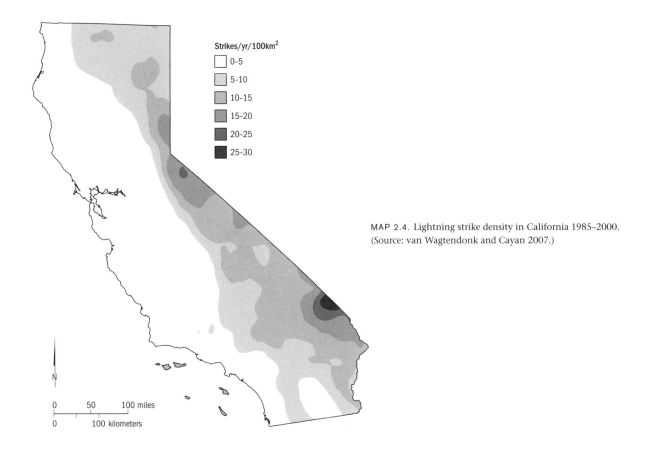

MAP 2.4. Lightning strike density in California 1985–2000. (Source: van Wagtendonk and Cayan 2007.)

TABLE 2.2

Temporal distribution of lightning strikes by 2-month and 4-hour periods in California, 1985–2000

Hour	Number of Strikes						
	Jan–Feb	Mar–Apr	May–Jun	Jul–Aug	Sep–Oct	Nov–Dec	Total
0–4	969	987	10,505	25,864	16,258	1,447	56,030
4–8	1,062	637	7,565	23,064	21,999	1,079	55,406
8–12	1,071	5,023	24,236	71,544	22,661	752	125,287
12–16	3,686	19,872	87,523	256,581	71,545	1,683	440,890
16–20	2,912	8,118	51,976	136,918	47,834	2,581	250,339
20–24	1,242	2,047	14,970	38,517	17,850	3,653	78,279
Total	10,942	36,684	196,775	552,488	198,147	11,195	1,006,231

Anthropogenic ignitions (I_{anth}) concentrate in heavily populated areas or near roads. With respect to the fuel mosaic, large patches (P) have a greater probability of ignitions than small patches because they are larger targets. The fuel threshold (F) depends on productivity and vegetation status in the fire cycle. In a fire mosaic, patch elements sustain abundant lightning discharges in a single fire cycle. For example, at detection rates of 1.0 km^{-2} yr^{-1}, a 1,000 ha patch of chaparral is struck about 5×10^2 times in a 50-year fire interval. The equation holds that the proportion of ignitions that initiate fires is inversely related to the flammability thresholds of ecosystems. Few ignitions establish fires of significant size even without fire control. In Baja California (BCA), < 1% of lightning discharges is required to initiate the number of landscape burns observed there (Minnich and Chou 1997).

A universal property of fire regimes is that most ignitions—regardless of source—fail to grow into large fires because of insufficient fuel. Failure rates increase directly with increasing fuel threshold periods and are also the basis of long-tailed fire size frequency distributions observed in all ecosystems; that is, the distribution comprises a continuum of numerous small burns grading to relatively few large fires accounting for most burn area (Minnich and Chou 1997, Malamud et al. 1998, Minnich et al. 2000a). The addition of anthropogenic ignitions would be expected to contribute to the same frequency distribution as natural ignitions.

Potential Evapotranspiration and Runoff

During summer, the accumulated soil water from winter storms is pumped out by vegetation through transpiration, leading to soil depletion and reduced live fuel moisture in vegetation. *Potential evapotranspiration*—the hypothetical moisture returned to the atmosphere from evaporation of wet surfaces and transpiration from plants with unlimited water availability—is largely a function of temperature. Amounts also vary locally in response to wind speeds and relative humidity. The lowest estimated annual rates of 80–100 cm (31–39 in) occur in areas with the coldest summers, notably the crest of the Sierra Nevada and the immediate Pacific Coast. Rates increase with mean annual temperature to 100–150 cm in the Central Valley and inland valleys of southern California, and 150–250 cm (59–98 in) in the southeastern deserts (Kahrl et al. 1979). Actual evapotranspiration is much less because available water is finite, especially in arid regions. Potential evapotranspiration exceeds precipitation throughout the state in the summer drought, leading to depletion of soil water and plant live fuel moisture. With respect to runoff and stream flow, the average annual precipitation is greater than the actual evapotranspiration by 100 cm (39 in) only in the northwest coast and in the northern Sierra Nevada. Surpluses of 10–20 cm (4–8 in) occur > 1,500 m (> 4,921 ft) in the North Coastal Ranges, Santa Lucia Mountains of the Central Coast, the central Sierra Nevada, and > 2,000 m (> 6,562 ft) in the southern California Coastal Ranges. Runoff is < 10 cm (4 in) over the rest of the state.

Plant Phenology and the Fire Season

The fire season begins in early summer in most parts of California, within two months of the last winter storms. By this time, plant fuel moisture has declined to < 100% dry weight, and most species have completed growth flushes. Patterns of plant phenology depend largely on seasonal temperature and precipitation cycles that vary with altitude. At lower elevations (< 1,000 m [< 3,281 ft]) covered by non-native annual grassland, coastal scrub, and desert scrub, and where mean winter temperatures range from 5°C–10°C (41°F–50°F), the growth flush begins with the first winter rains and peak productivity is in spring. Above 1,000 m (3,281 ft), chaparral, woodlands, and conifer forests dominate the vegetation. Precipitation is

heavier, and shrubs and trees have deeper rooting that utilizes accumulated seasonal soil water. Growth flushes center in late spring after temperatures have warmed. Although evergreen sclerophyllous shrubs possess strong capacity for water regulation (Poole and Miller 1975, 1981), live fuel moisture declines to flammable levels by late spring or early summer.

In high mountain conifer forests, the growth flush occurs after snow melt, usually in early summer (Royce and Barbour 2001a, b). The onset of drought is not significantly delayed compared to forests and woodlands at lower elevations because moisture is rapidly depleted in porous soils, especially in glaciated terrain. Fire hazard begins when moisture in soil litter and shrub biomass is depleted, usually by June or July. Snowmelt and the onset of the fire season may be postponed to August in subalpine forest after wet winters. Summer thundershowers have limited effect on soil moisture. Lysimeter data for the Sierra San Pedro Mártir in Baja California and the San Jacinto Mountains show that summer rain is countered by high summer transpiration rates, with limited wetting of the root zone (Franco-Vizcaíno et al. 2002).

Fire Weather

Fire weather refers to the boundary-layer weather governing the motion of flame fronts over short time scales. The weather influences fire outcomes by altering vegetation fuel moisture and the efficiency of heat transfer in combustion (Albini 1993). Most important are the temporal and spatial distributions of wind and relative humidity by synoptic circulations associated with fire weather. Wind speed directly affects flame-front spread rates and intensities by advection. Relative humidity is defined as:

$$\frac{e_a}{e_s} \times 100 = (in\ percent),$$

where e_a is the actual vapor pressure, and e_s is the saturation vapor pressure.

Relative humidity affects dead fuel moisture by hygroscopic diffusion and plant stress by evapotranspiration. According to the equation, relative humidity is not only a function of absolute water vapor, but is also a function of saturation vapor pressure that increases exponentially with temperature. Relative humidity decreases with increasing temperature without changes in absolute water vapor.

Because California is dominated by dry air masses during the dry season, most of the state experiences weather risk states that can propagate fire virtually every day in this season, except areas dominated by the marine layer along the coast. Indeed, in the nineteenth century before fire control, fires persisted for months in California wildlands (Minnich 1987, 1988). Hence, it is important not to focus on the most extreme weather states inclusively, but also to review fire weather that dominates for the entire season. Prevailing weather conditions have predictable properties that can be used for planned burns. In addition, prehistoric fires that shaped California ecosystems very likely burned during "average" weather.

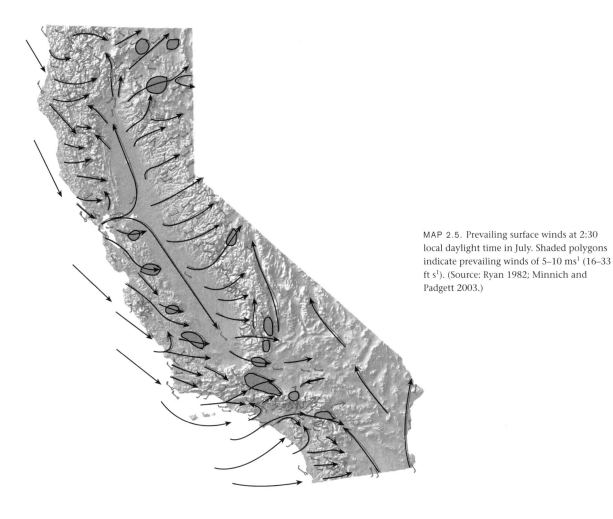

MAP 2.5. Prevailing surface winds at 2:30 local daylight time in July. Shaded polygons indicate prevailing winds of 5–10 ms[1] (16–33 ft s[1]). (Source: Ryan 1982; Minnich and Padgett 2003.)

Because atmospheric circulations are fundamentally different during summer and fall, the following discussion is divided by season. Emphasis is made on weather conditions at mid-day when the diurnal fire hazard is greatest.

Summer

Fire hazard tends to increase when the marine layer is shallow due to lower relative humidity, but day-to-day wind direction and speed that steer fire movement are generally unchanging through the season. Prevailing winds in surface air layers over California are northwesterly in response to the geostrophic balance between a subtropical anticyclone over the east Pacific Ocean and thermal low pressure over the desert. Surface winds reflect the combination of onshore pressure gradients and terrain effects (Map 2.5). The gap in the Coastal Ranges at San Francisco Bay results in divergent low-level wind fields inland, with southerly winds in the Sacramento Valley and northwesterly winds in the San Joaquin Valley. In the southern California bight northwesterly winds offshore turn cyclonically to produce southwesterly to southeasterly winds, termed the "Catalina Eddy." Land heating gradually dissipates the marine layer as it moves onshore, with warm dry air aloft mixing down to the surface.

Intense land heating generates local winds in the form of afternoon sea breezes and anabatic circulations on mountain slopes (DeMarrias et al. 1965, Ryan 1982, Hayes et al. 1984, Zack and Minnich 1991). Local winds predominate because upper wind velocities are < 10 m s^{-1} (< 29 ft s^{-1}) below 700 mbar ($\sim$3,000 m [$\sim$9843 ft]), decoupling low-level winds from the upper flow (Deacon 1969, Ryan 1977).

The "locking" of surface wind fields to local terrain results in more predictable motion of head fires than in autumn when fires spread under a greater diversity of wind directions under broad-scale circulation systems of the jet stream. In anabatic circulations, the warming of slopes causes buoyant surface air layers to move upslope across valley axes, with onshore valley flows moving parallel to valley axes (Stull 1988). Because the marine layer is stably stratified, air flows are also subject to mechanical flow channeling through complex terrain (Böhm 1992), as seen in circulations reported for the Los Angeles Basin and central California (DeMarrias et al. 1965, Fosberg and Schroeder 1966, Schroeder et al. 1967, Schultz and Warner 1982, Hayes et al. 1984, Lu and Turco 1995).

Wind data reveal possible lee slope wakes and convergence zones downwind from higher coastal mountains, such as the Riverside-Perris Plain leeward of the Santa Ana Mountains, the San Fernando Valley leeward of the Santa Monica

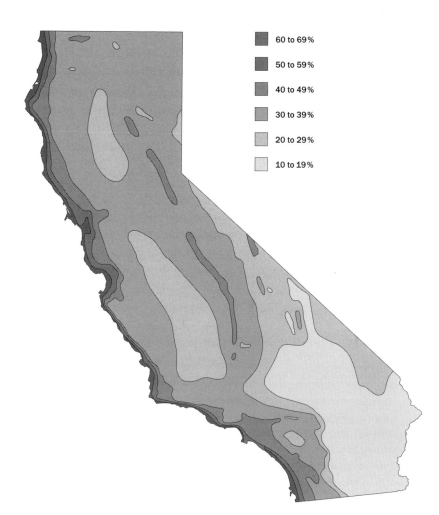

■	60 to 69%
■	50 to 59%
■	40 to 49%
■	30 to 39%
■	20 to 29%
□	10 to 19%

MAP 2.6. Mean relative humidity at 2:30 local daylight time in July. (Source: Ryan 1982; Minnich and Padgett 2003.)

Mountains, and the Salinas Valley leeward of the Santa Lucia Mountains (Map 2.5). Marine air is then transported up mountain slopes by anabatic flows (e.g, Edinger et al. 1972) or escapes to the deserts through gaps in the mountains. In southern California, marine air spills through the Palmdale Gap, Cajon Pass, and San Gorgonio Pass into the Mojave and Sonoran Deserts. In central California, low-level air masses in the San Joaquin Valley push eastward through Walker and Tehachapi Passes to the Mojave Desert (Map 2.5). Strong winds pass through the Trinity Gorge in northern California. Surface winds on mountain slopes are typically at right angles to local contours. Wind speeds are generally in the range of 3–5 m s^{-1} (10–16 ft s^{-1}) and as high as 5–10 m s^{-1} (16–33 ft s^{-1}) on mountain summits and passes (Ryan 1982; Minnich and Padgett 2003). Stably stratified marine air may establish lee waves on the east side of mountain chains, as reported or modeled for southern California (Schroeder et al. 1967, Zack and Minnich 1991, Lu and Turco 1995).

Although the marine layer depth ranges from 300 to 800 m (984–2,625 ft) in summer, spatially uniform relative humidity gradients are encouraged by temperature inversions restricting upward mixing (King et al. 1987). Increasing temperatures of the marine layer as it moves onshore results

in decreasing mid-afternoon relative humidity from 60% along the coast to 20%–30% in the Central Valley and southern California interior valleys (Map 2.6). Adiabatic cooling combined with limited mixing of anabatic flows results in increasing relative humidity with elevation to as high as 40%–50% at 2,000 m (6,562 ft) in the coastal front of the southern California mountains and the Sierra Nevada. The relative humidity in the deserts is normally < 10%–20%, but values occasionally increase to 40% during pulses of tropical moisture of the North American monsoon.

The depth of the marine layer fluctuates with perturbations in the jet stream, deepening with the approach of troughs and shallowing with approaching ridges. When the marine layer is > 1,500 m (> 4,921 ft), cool moist air penetrates as far inland as the coastal slopes of the Sierra Nevada and southern California Coastal Ranges. The highest fire danger occurs during episodes of low humidity associated with a shallow marine layer.

Wind has less influence than relative humidity on fire danger because prevailing onshore flow and anabatic slope winds have small daily fluctuations. The regions that experience the highest winds, such as mountain passes, tend to have high

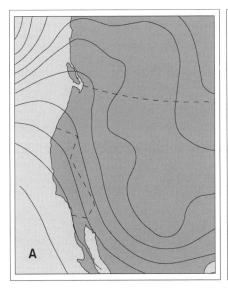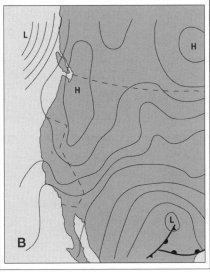

FIGURE 2.6. Weather maps of a strong Santa Ana wind event on November 10, 1970: (A) 500 mbar; (B) surface pressure. At 500 mbar, a trough in New Mexico and a ridge just off the Pacific coast produce a strong north-northwesterly jet stream over California. Strong surface high pressure over the northern Great Basin combined with surface low pressure over Texas and extending west to the California coast cause strong northeasterly winds across southern California. (Redrawn from U. S. Department of Commerce 1970.)

winds almost daily because surface onshore pressure gradients are a steady-state feature. Strong northwesterly winds also occur along the coast and the offshore southern California Channel Islands, but these are associated with a moist marine layer. The coastal plains near Santa Barbara occasionally experience strong, dry northwesterly to northerly winds, called "sundowners," that descend the Santa Ynez Mountains during the evening. Sundowners take place under strong north-to-south pressure gradients between San Francisco and Los Angeles. The term refers to the fact that these winds typically reach the Santa Barbara coastal plain with dissipation of sea breezes, usually at sundown. Leeward mountain slopes and deserts, beyond normal marine layer intrusions, experience the lowest humidity and greatest fire hazard in early summer (late June–early July), when maximum insolation of the summer solstice supports the hottest air masses of the year. The establishment of the North American monsoon, usually by early July, brings slightly cooler tropical maritime air masses to these areas.

Night radiational cooling results in downslope katabatic (air drainage) flows in the mountains and ground inversions in basins. Except in the desert, relative humidity increases to >40% almost everywhere due to decreasing temperatures. Another predictable property of fire weather in summer is that the diurnal shift between daylight upslope wind and night air drainage typically occurs close to sunrise and sunset. At these times, local winds shift as positive net radiation in daylight becomes negative at night.

Autumn

The return of the jet stream in autumn brings greater day-to-day variability in fire weather including episodes of dry offshore winds from the Great Basin. As with summer, fires can persist or spread most days until the onset of the rainy season, normally by October/November in northern California and November/December in southern California (Minnich 1987).

On average, the fire hazard lessens during autumn due to decreasing insolation and temperature. Troughs of the jet stream deepen the marine layer more frequently, with higher relative humidity in the inland valleys and mountains than in summer. Intervening ridges in the jet stream depress the marine layer, resulting in episodes of warm dry days similar to summer. Daylight surface air flows are onshore from the Pacific most days, and sea breezes and anabatic flows still dominate on mountain slopes, although with decreasing importance compared with summer as sun angles and surface heating decrease. The strengthening of the jet stream also produces episodes of dry offshore winds from the Great Basin into the coastal regions normally influenced by the marine layer. Offshore winds are produced by ridging in the jet stream following the passage of cold fronts, strong subsidence over the western United States, and offshore pressure gradients between high pressure over the Great Basin and thermal low pressure along the Pacific coast (Fig. 2.6). Although offshore events are associated with cold air advection, surface temperatures are warm in the interior valleys and along the coast because of adiabatic compression of descending air masses and displacement of the marine layer.

Not all areas are affected by offshore winds because airflows are shunted by the Sierra Nevada. Because of the very high altitude of this range, postfrontal air masses are diverted southward toward southern California, or westward through the Trinity River region and southward through the Sacramento Valley and San Francisco Bay. In southern California, strong offshore winds, called "Santa Anas," develop in mountain passes in the form of low-level jets that frequently exceed 20–30 m s^{-1} (66–98 ft s^{-1}), especially at Cajon Pass, Santa Ana Canyon, San Gorgonio Pass, the Palmdale Gap, and the Peninsular Range at the international boundary (Fosberg et al. 1966). Offshore winds expand throughout coastal southern California if atmospheric subsidence brings jet stream energy toward the surface, or if mountain waves develop leeward of physiographic barriers. Southeasterly offshore winds occasionally surface in the southern San Joaquin Valley and the coastal valleys near Santa Maria. Many areas directly affected by offshore flows experience the highest wind and lowest humidity of the fire season. The Central Valley south of around Stockton is normally protected from offshore flows by the Sierra Nevada. Persistent ground inversions and tule fogs, especially from November to early February, cover the entire valley.

The Fire Weather "Window" in Vegetation

The *fire weather window* at a site is the full range of weather conditions capable of propagating fires, ranging from a moist threshold to the driest weather of the climate. The window varies with changing fuel properties along vegetation gradients, as well as vegetation status in the fire cycle. Cured grassland with low fuel moisture and fine fuels can burn in relatively moist conditions (broad window; RH ≤ 50%) because cured ground canopy is entirely "dead fuel" in summer. Woody shrub and forest assemblages with coarser fuels and higher fuel moisture burn only in a drier "window" than grasslands. Open woody assemblages such as pinyon-juniper and desert scrub with low fuel continuity in open stand arrangements may burn in extreme weather exclusively (narrow window). Hyperarid deserts and mountains above the tree line may be fireproof.

In woody vegetation types, the weather window tends to enlarge with time-since-fire due to cumulative fuel buildup and, in canopy, increasing dead fuel and increasing landscape transpiration demand. All these factors tend to increase the carbohydrate-to-water energy ratio. In principle, if patch flammability increases with time-since-fire, the resulting differential weather window with age class contributes to nonrandom turnover in patch mosaics (patch heterogeniety dependent on fire history; see sidebar 2.1). In a given weather state, fires spreading from patches with high fuel loads may encounter resistance in adjoining patches with less fuel. Fires still overlap across stands from high to low fuel loads due to momentum of the fire. The flame line initially retains high energy release rates until it accommodates to energy levels of the new stand (the fire slows down or eventually dissipates). The magnitude of successive fires at a site fluctuates within the weather window at a modest range of variance because ignitions establish fires at random. The unique weather conditions with each fire cause successive patch mosaic configurations to shift over time (shifting mosaic). Standing mosaics, that is, fixed patch configurations through multiple fire sequences, occur rarely. The burning of young classes should not be interpreted as evidence against age-dependent flammability. Most fire-overlap zones are "slivers" covering small areas due largely to flame-line momentum. Hence, in the analysis of fire-overlap sequences, it is more instructive to examine the age of vegetation of the entire fire, rather than to focus on edge effects.

Post-fire flammability may increase if successions are dominated by herbaceous fuels, leading to a positive feedback in which fires encourage shorter-interval recurrences. This is a significant problem with European invasive grasses in the oats and brome genera (D'Antonio and Vitousek 1992). The enlarged weather window combined with shorter microbial recycling of herbaceous cover reduces the importance of time-dependent fuel accumulation and temporal mosaic element interactions regardless of weather conditions. Not all herbaceous species are fuels. Most California valley wildflowers, forbs that dominate early successions in chaparral and coastal sage scrub, and a few exotics such as red-stemmed filaree disarticulate upon curing and leave little fuel. Forbs also decline in abundance with the development of shrub canopy after a few years.

Climate Cycles

Climatic change is important in fire ecology because variability in temperature and precipitation at scales of years or decades influences regional vegetation productivity, fuel moisture, and fire occurrence. In recent decades, atmospheric scientists have recognized that interannual to interdecadal changes in climate that lead to regional floods and droughts, are linked to coupled ocean-atmosphere feedbacks that are difficult to interpret because deep-ocean dynamics are poorly understood. Most important are changes in ocean currents and sea surface temperatures, as in the El Niño/Southern Oscillation and the Pacific Decadal Oscillation, which influence the amount and distribution of water vapor that is evaporated into the air, condensed into clouds, and rained back to earth.

The El Niño/Southern Oscillation

The El Niño/Southern Oscillation (ENSO) comprises the largest source of interannual variability in the troposphere (Lau and Sheu 1991, Diaz and Markgraf, 1992). Precipitation variability in California is related to the interannual dislocation of the polar front jet stream along the Pacific coast by ENSO. During ENSO events, the dissipation of trade winds and eastward Kelvin wave propagation of warm surface water masses from the western Pacific Ocean results in above-normal sea surface temperatures in the central and eastern equatorial Pacific Ocean. The release of latent heat and divergent outflow from enhanced tropical convection in the central equatorial Pacific Ocean results in the dislocation of the jet stream and anomalous, highly variable rainfall patterns in many areas of the Pacific Basin (Philander 1990, Lau and Sheu 1991).

In La Niña events and ENSO neutral years, the climatic norm, the warmest sea surface temperatures cover the western equatorial Pacific because the eastern equatorial Pacific is influenced by upwelling and advection of cold water of the Humboldt Current. The center of convection lies along the intertropical convergence zone in the western Pacific and causes ridging of the jet stream in the North Pacific, and troughing of the jet stream over the Pacific Northwest and Canada. The jet stream lies mostly poleward of California, with weak onshore advection of moist surface westerlies onto the West Coast of North America, except in northern California and the Pacific Northwest (Fig. 2.6).

At any given site, fires establish over a wide range of weather conditions depending on season, local atmospheric circulation, or the time of day. Although individual fires are each associated with a unique combination of weather and fuel conditions, the cumulative impact of fires scaling over centuries or millennia results in fire occurrence with modal weather states of the local climate over time, if ignitions occur at random.

A model that integrates fire weather and fuel-driven patch dynamics is proposed to explain the discontinuity in fire regime from infrequent large burns and coarse mosaics in California and frequent small burns in Baja California (Minnich and Chou 1997) (Figure 2.1.1). Without fire control in Baja California, numerous fires produce fine-grained mosaics and discrete local-scale fuel heterogeneity linked to stand-replacement fire behavior. Fires consistently establish in old stands and their expansion is constrained in adjoining younger patches with less fuel. Fire suppression in California reduces the number of fires, thereby increasing the size of old-growth patch elements and fires, but fires still spread largely in old stands.

Minnich and Chou (1997) found a shift from dominantly Santa Ana wind-driven fires in southern California to fires carried by onshore anabatic flows in Baja California, Mexico, where fire control does not exist, with a discontinuity in fire weather occurrence along the international boundary (Figure 2.1.1).

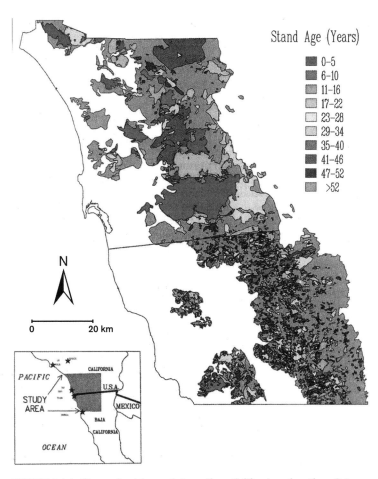

FIGURE 2.1.1. Chaparral patch mosaic in southern California and northern Baja California in 1971.

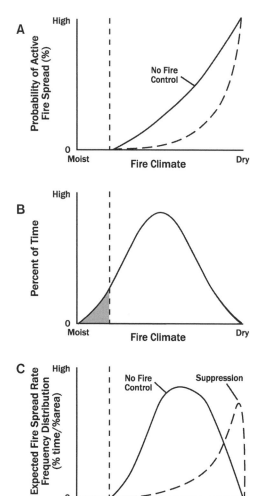

FIGURE 2.1.2. Conceptual model of the expected portion of landscape patch mosaic that burns along a continuum of fire weather risk states of the climate from moist to dry (left to right in all three figures): (A) probability of active fire spread on the landscape; (B) fire climate; and (C) average landscape fire weather and spread rates.

Satellite imagery documents a disparate seasonality of burning—summer in Baja California and fall in southern California (Minnich 1983). The difference in the weather of fires across the international boundary reflects the nonrandomization of large fire occurrence to extreme weather states by suppression.

Fig. 2.1.2 is a conceptual drawing that shows how the probability distribution of fire climate and active fire spread combine to produce an expected fire spread rate probability distribution at a landscape scale. Assuming random ignition rates, (A) describes the probability of active fire spread and fire spread rates, these properties both increasing in value as weather turns drier. The dashed curve in (A) represents the probability of active fire spread and is influenced by initial attack suppression of fire starts. Without fire control, burning is not possible in moist weather but involves an increasing proportion of the mosaic as weather becomes ever drier. With fire control, nearly all ignitions are suppressed except in the driest weather. In (B), the fire climate is described as the proportion of time in weather states in a normal statistical distribution. By definition, there is more time in "normal" weather than in the moist or dry extremes. In (C), (A) and (B) are graphically multiplied together and describe the expected proportion of landscape that burns along the climatic continuum.

With or without fire control there is little burning in moist weather (C) because the fire hazard risk in (A) and the percent of climate in moist weather in (B) are both low. Fire control has little effect because suppressed fire starts would have dissipated at a small size. In normal weather, the expected spread rate frequency distribution in (C) reaches a maximum value without control because modest spread rates (A) are phased with a large portion of time in the fire season (B). In other words, slow burning consumes large landscape area. Fire spread rate distributions in dry weather are low because of the consumption of fuels by slow burning in normal weather; high extreme-weather risk states represent a small proportion of time. With fire control, the nonrandom elimination of fire starts in normal weather reduces burn area in normal weather states. It follows that ignition-stage suppression selectively nonrandomizes the occurrence of large fires to severe-weather risk states compared with those occurring by chance. The expected spread rate frequency distribution is skewed toward extreme weather, resulting in higher-than-average spread rates and flame-front intensities (Figure 2.1.2).

The random establishment of fire starts in "normal" weather is a tenable assumption in presuppression California wildlands because of the abundance of natural ignitions and the long-term persistence of "live" ignitions in coarse fuels (logs, snags) through glowing combustion (see chapter section on lightning detection). The spread of large burns results in numerous other trees storing fire as future ignition sources. It follows that the longer live ignitions persist, the lower the average integrated departure of weather from the long-term mean. Nineteenth-century newspaper reports before fire control indicate that fires alternatively smoldered in large fuels, then formed flame lines intermittently at intervals of a week or longer, and persisted for months until doused by the first autumn rains (Minnich 1987, 1988). Season-long burns still occur in Baja California (Minnich and Chou 1997, Minnich et al. 2000).

The random establishment of mass fires is also made certain by the high failure rate of fire starts in a patch mosaic. The rare fire starts that do establish mass burns have a high probability of coinciding with normal weather by chance. Finally, people set fires in independent actions; that is, there is no "conspiracy" to establish fires in specific weather states. Most such ignitions would also fail except in cured herbaceous vegetation.

Suppression would have no effect on the weather of fires only if the firefighting system had a uniform capacity to influence the spread of flame lines during the course of a fire, regardless of its size or weather risk state. This premise of course is unrealistic because the effectiveness of suppression actions is dependent on the energy output of fire. All fires begin at an infinitely low rate of energy release (the ignition). Energy levels then increase exponentially with increasing length of flame lines at the perimeter. Suppression forces extinguish virtually all ignitions at the ignition stage, but have little effect on escaped large burns because energy release rates exceed the energy of suppression by orders of magnitude; that is, flame lines spread with little interference from suppression actions.

The weather risk state also influences energy levels at the ignition stage, with ignitions in severe weather (and high-energy release states) having the highest probability of expanding past initial attack efforts. Because the continuity of weather operates in time scales of days (in association with synoptic shifts in atmospheric circulation) and because fires in the flaming stage seldom persist more than a few

FIGURE 2.1.3. Patchy chaparral burn in the central Sierra Juárez of Baja California.

days under suppression, the weather characteristics of major fires have a high probability of resembling the weather risk state of escaped fire starts. Weather office personnel are keenly aware of the "persistence" forecast; that is, the next day's weather will most likely resemble the previous day's. In Baja California frequent or long-lived ignition sources produce a pattern in which mass burns establish when weather risk advances past the "moist threshold" of combustion. Fires periodically rise above or descend below the moist threshold, the burning periods often at marginal to the combustion threshold. On the landscape, this is seen in reticulate ("weavy") burning in which separated flame lines merge and separate with fluctuations in terrain, fuels, and weather, even in headfires. Figure 2.1.3 shows a patchy chaparral burn in the central Sierra Juárez of Baja California. Chaparral burns in Baja California burns typically have numerous fire islands of unburned vegetation collectively adding to 10%–30% of the vegetation inside perimeters. Hence, complex patch mosaics can arise from single burns. In California, suppression mass fires begin in extreme risk states due to efficient initial attack extinction of ignitions. Mass fires cease only after the weather risk decreases to the "moist threshold," usually after many days.

It has been argued that differences in transnational fire weather reflect the infrequency of Santa Ana winds in Baja California compared to southern California (Keeley et al. 1999). However, the discontinuity in fire regimes along the international boundary indicates that differences in fire weather are related to divergent fire management practices.

Santa Ana winds arise from hemispheric circulations operating at scales of thousands of kilometers, and the 200-km span of the Peninsular Ranges is too small for large gradients in wind fields to occur. Without distinctive suppression histories, changes in fire weather and patch dynamics should be expressed in a continuum of fire weather, not in the discontinuity presently seen along the international boundary (Minnich and Chou 1997). Climatic gradients, especially temperature and precipitation, change largely in response to elevation and distance from the Pacific Ocean, and run east to west, orthogonal to the international boundary.

In evaluating presuppression fire regimes, fire ecologists and land managers in California should be careful not to judge "average" fire weather conditions from the history mass burns of the twentieth century. Observations of fires in Baja California indicate that fires occurred in a broader range of weather environments than in California, including "normal" weather states when ignitions are efficiently suppressed.

The role of weather risk states shifts with the kind of vegetation. For example, in cured grassland, a shift in the moist threshold for active fire spread (to the far left) in (A) would result in more burning under suppression compared to fire control (Fig. 2.1.1). Initial attack is less efficient in suppressing fire starts here than in woody assemblages because grass fires enlarge rapidly from ignition point. In vegetation characterized by a shift in the combustion threshold to very dry weather (e.g., pinyon–juniper woodland), active fire spread is possible only in extreme weather, with or without fire control.

During warm-phase El Niño events, the center of convection along the intertropical convergence zone lies east of the International Dateline. This results in subnormal 500-mbar heights in the Gulf of Alaska, high pressure aloft in western Canada, and an enhanced southern branch jet stream across California and the southwestern United States (Renwick and Wallace 1996, Hoerling et al. 1997). The recurrence interval of warm-phase El Niño events is variable, but power spectra give a robust period of four years. La Niña events are equally infrequent. However, sea surface temperature fields in "neutral" years resemble La Niña events because the warmest equatorial sea surface temperatures still lie in the western Pacific.

Statistical studies for California show that annual precipitation correlates with ENSO (McGuirk 1982, Ropelewski and Halpert 1987, Schonher and Nicholson 1989, Cayan and Webb 1992, Montiverdi and Null 1997, Minnich et al. 2000b). In moderate and intense La Niña/cold episodes, precipitation departures decrease equatorward along the Pacific coast. Amounts tend to be above normal in northern California, normal from San Francisco to San Luis Obispo, and below normal south of Point Conception. In El Niño events, precipitation departures increase equatorward along the Pacific coast, with maximum values in southern California and northern Baja California. Precipitation amounts during weak El Niños show a similar trend for increasing precipitation departures equatorward, but values are less extreme than those for strong events.

Pacific Decadal Oscillation

The Pacific Decadal Oscillation (PDO) is a rotating sea surface temperature anomaly around the North Pacific gyre. The oscillation affects both precipitation and temperature in the western United States over time scales of decades. Two models have been put forward to explain the oscillation. In one model, the mechanism of the rotating sea surface temperature anomaly appears to be the spin rate of the gyre that occurs in two phases (Latif and Barnett 1994). In the negative or cool phase of the PDO, sea surface temperatures are above normal from Japan to the Gulf of Alaska and below normal from California to New Guinea. The reduced latitudinal temperature gradient over the North Pacific Ocean results in a northward shift of the jet stream and extratropical cyclones, and a weakening of the Aleutian low (drought in California). The cool phase is associated with a "spin up" of the North Pacific gyre (increasing gyre rotation), with enhanced advection of warm sea waters poleward off Japan. The dominance of high pressure over the entire North Pacific increases frictional wind drag (wind stress curl) and the spin rate of the gyre. After about 10–25 years of the spin-up mode, the increased gyre spin rate results in rotational advection of the warm pool to the North American coast and then southwestward to the tropics. The increase in the latitudinal temperature gradient in the North Pacific Ocean (positive-phase PDO) results in the intensification and equatorward displacement of the jet stream and

extratropical cyclones, enlargement of the Aleutian (above-normal precipitation in California), and reduced spin rate of the gyre (the positive or warm phase of the PDO). This mode also persists for one or two decades when the "spin-down" phase is reversed by a phase change back to the negative mode.

In another model, Psonis et al. (2003), arguing from a thermodynamic perspective, suggest that El Niño cyclicity tied to global temperature change produces the decadal oscillations. Given earth-sun geometry, decades of global warming (e.g, 1910–1940, 1977–1999) are primarily expressed in increasing temperature in tropical seas, the enhanced latitudinal temperature gradient in the Pacific generating more frequent El Niños. More frequent Kelvin wave transfer of warm seas to the central Pacific reduces warm water advection off Japan (a conservation of thermal energy), further increasing latitudinal temperature gradients in a positive feedback. Decades of global cooling (1940–1977) result in a reduced frequency of El Niños (greater frequency of La Niñas), and enhanced advection of warm water off Japan.

Minobe (1997) identifies four shifts (two cycles) in the PDO, with each complete cycle interval spanning about 50–70 years. The last two shifts included a negative phase from 1948 to 1976 and a positive phase from 1976 to 1999. The phase transition in the mid-1970s divided a period of protracted drought from 1944 to 1968 and above-normal precipitation since 1977 in California, the latter period having increased ENSO frequency. The two previous shifts were a positive phase in 1925–1947 and a negative phase in 1890–1925. However, precipitation records indicate that these phases were not coincident with prolonged wet or dry spells in California. Over the western United States, both negative-phase shifts were associated with cold winters and springs, and both positive-phase shifts with warm winters and springs.

Analysis of instrumental records (1880–1994) and tree ring data (back to 1700) shows a north-to-south seesaw in precipitation variability in western North America, pivoting at 40° N (Dettinger et al. 1998). Precipitation at California latitudes are positively correlated with the Southern Oscillation Index (SOI), which causes southward displacements of precipitation distribution at interannual and decadal time scales. The overall precipitation amount delivered to the west coast has little variation both in the instrumental record and in tree ring records, consistent with the century scale analysis of tree ring data in the Sierra Nevada by Graumlich (1993).

Climate Variability and Fire History

With respect to climatic change, fire ecologists are most concerned with precipitation variability, especially drought caused by subnormal winter precipitation that may result in deficits in summer live fuel moisture, especially in woody assemblages (annual grasslands provide cured fuel regardless of precipitation). However, it should be recognized that in most wildlands the total annual precipitation alone is an incomplete predictor

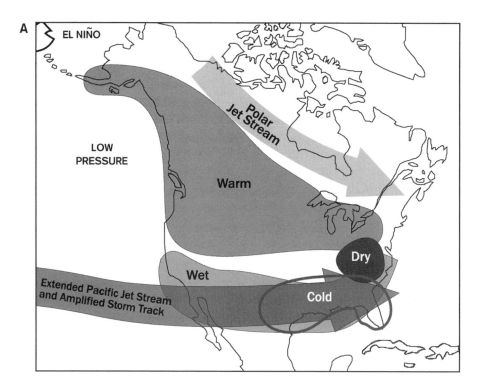

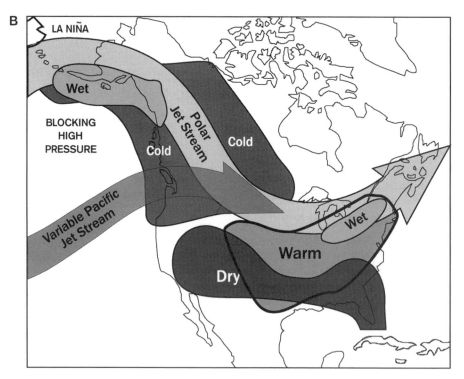

FIGURE 2.7. Map of jet stream in (A) El Niño and (B) la Niña. (After NOAA, Climate Prediction Center: The El Niño Cycle; redrawn from: www.cpc.ncep.noaa.gov/products/analysis_monitoring/ensocycle/enso_cycle.html.)

of drought because mean annual precipitation greatly exceeds soil field capacities (total soil water available to plants in the soil). In mesic mountainous regions, where subnormal annual precipitation may saturate the soils in wet years, only runoff is reduced (Franco-Vizcaíno et al. 2002). Soil water deficits may occur only in the most extreme droughts, as in Lake Tahoe basin in 1989–1992 and in southern California in 1999–2003.

The relationship between climatic variability and the long-term fire history is also dependent on the dynamics and spatial heterogeneity of fuel build-up in ecosystem mosaics. Clearly the effect of drought on fire hazard is expected to be less in a fresh burn than in an old stand that has built up canopy and accumulated fuels over decades or centuries. It is important to recognize that young stands may resist fire in spite of drought; old stands may burn preferentially over young stands due to fuels rather than climatic variability.

At regional scales, the effect of climatic variability on regional burning rates is modulated by patch mosaic status in a negative feedback, especially if landscape fire regimes exist in some form of steady state. As such, patch turnover, stand age frequency distribution, and regional carbohydrate-to-water energy ratios remain relatively constant at broad scales due to a negative feedback between fire hazard and vegetation status. Multi-year drought may reduce the age of patches subject to fire, thereby increasing burning rates. This may be balanced by large fire outbreaks that would lead to overall reduction in the age and fuel hazard of the landscape mosaic. Likewise, moist periods may temporarily postpone burning but lead to regional build-up of fuels. Fire weather is unlikely to influence long-term burning rates as long as the occurrence of large events is random (see sidebar).

It is often tempting to place "cause" of specific fire outbreaks with short-term climatic perturbations such as a single dry-year or a multi-year drought. However, in a heterogeneous patch mosaic, climatic relationships with fire regimes must integrate production and fuel accumulation dynamics of forest and brushlands at time scales commensurate with ecosystems in question. In short, do the fire outbreak and climate perturbation explain the dynamics of the whole landscape? For example, the denudation of an entire patch mosaic, regardless of age, would suggest that the short-term perturbation provides the highest explanatory power (Swetnam and Betancourt 1998). On the other hand, if a fire burned only old-growth vegetation, then the explanation may lie in the integrated dynamics of the mosaic, including the fire history linked to growth patterns and cumulative fuel build-up over long time scales. In this case, the role of climatic shifts should be examined at time scales of vegetation dynamics, for example, centuries for forests that turnover in centuries. In summary, the effect of precipitation variability is modulated by patch structure in which changes in regional fire hazard result in only finite portions of stands achieving flammability thresholds. Statistical tests correlating fire and climatic change should therefore involve running averages of the climatic variability scales to mean fire intervals, not specific climate events (Lovell et al. 2002).

Recent studies have correlated climate variability with fire-scar dendrochronology records in which it is assumed that fire intervals can be directly computed from the fire scars in tree rings of few individual trees or sites. Studies have correlated fire variability with ENSO (e.g., Norman and Taylor 2003) and decadal scales (e.g., Swetnam and Betancourt 1998, Westerling and Swetnam 2003). Millennial scale trends reported for California have been obtained from giant sequoia (Swetnam 1993). Although the scarring frequency documents a site, scaling the scar-year data to regional patterns requires high resolution spatial sampling because fire-size frequency distributions are "long tailed"—a property found in all ecosystems. An alternative hypothesis is that most fires are small, and collectively add to limited spatial extent, the preponderance of landscape burning being accomplished by relatively few large fires (Minnich et al. 2000a). Over time scales of fire cycles, abundant small fires may scar trees as frequently as the few large fires that consume most fuels in western pine forests. Because fire-scar methods cannot directly differentiate mass burns from microburns, regional burning rates in space and time may not covary with scarring rates; that is, the assumption that fire intervals can be directly computed from the fire scar in tree rings is not constrained. It follows that transient fluctuations in the scarring record may also arise from site-specific microburns (lightning fires, anthropogenic starts), rather than from rates of burning at the landscape scale. For example, although the decline of scarring in the Sierra San Pedro Mártir from 1790 to 1830 (Stephens et al. 2003) could reflect climate change, it is also plausible that the decline reflects the demise of Native Americans as a source of campfires. The San Pedro Mártir mission was established in the 1790s. Lengthening fire intervals due to the introduction of mission livestock (Stephens et al. 2003) is not verified by paleobotanical data. Most herbaceous cover, as in most California ranges, grows in riparian or aquatic meadows due to protracted summer drought. Likewise, the extraordinarily short two- to four-year fire intervals in giant sequoia groves of the Sierra Nevada (Swetnam 1993) could be an outcome of cooking fires and patterns of Native American occupation.

In contrast to woody assemblages, the relationship between climatic variability and burn area in herbaceous ecosystems would be expected to correlate over short scales because herbaceous biomass is recycled on annual cycles. Regional fuel patterns and burning rates are independent of fire history. Fire hazard in grasslands tends to increase with total annual precipitation, not drought, due to increased productivity and cured fuel.

References

Adams, D.K., and A.C. Comrie. 1997. The North American monsoon. Bulletin of the American Meterorological Society 78:2197–2213.

Albini, F.A. 1993. Dynamics and modeling of vegetation fires: observations. In J.J. Crutzen and J.G. Goldammer (eds.), Fire in the environment: the ecological, atmospheric, and climatic importance of vegetation fires. Dahlem Workshop Reports, Environmental Sciences Research Report No. 13. Wiley, New York. 400 p.

Barbour, M.G., N.H. Berg, T.G.F. Kittel, and M.E. Kunz. 1991. Snowpack and the distribution of a major vegetation ecotone in the Sierra Nevada of California. Journal of Biogeography 18: 141–149.

Böhm, M. 1992. Air quality and deposition. P. 64–152 in R.K. Olson, D. Binkley, and M. Böhm (eds.), The response of western forests to air pollution. Ecological Studies, Vol. 97. Springer Verlag, New York. 532 p.

Cayan, D.R., and R.H. Webb. 1992. El Niño/southern oscillation and stream flow in the western United States. P. 29–68 in H.F. Diaz and V. Markgraf (eds.), El Niño, historical and paleoclimatic aspects of the southern oscillation. Cambridge University Press, New York.

D'Antonio, C.M., and P.M. Vitousek 1992. Biological invasions by exotic grasses, the grass/fire cycle, and global change. Annual Review of Ecology and Systematics 23:63–87.

Deacon, E.L., 1969. Physical processes near the earth's surface. P. 39–104 in H. Flöhn (ed.), World Survey of Climatology, Vol. 2. Elsevier.

DeMarrias, G.A., G.C. Holzworth, and C.D. Hosler. 1965. Meteorological summaries pertinent to atmospheric transport and dispersion over southern California. U.S. Weather Bureau Paper No. 54. Washington.

Dettinger, M.D., D.R. Cayan, H.F. Diaz, and D.M. Meko. 1998. North-south precipitation variations in western North America on interannual-to-decadal time scales. Journal of Climate 11:3095–3111.

Diaz, H.F. and V. Markgraf. 1992. El Niño: historical and paleoclimatic aspects of the southern oscillation. Cambridge University Press.

Edinger, J.G., M.H. McCutchan, P.R. Miller, B.C. Ryan, M.J. Schroeder, and J.V. Behar. 1972. Penetration and duration of oxidant air pollution in the South Coast Air Basin of California. Air Pollution Control Association Journal 2:882–886.

Fosberg, M.A., C.A. O'Dell, and M.J. Schroeder. 1966. Some characteristics of the three-dimensional structure of Santa Ana winds. USDA Forest Service Research Paper PSW-30. Berkeley, CA.

Fosberg, M.A., and M.J. Schroeder. 1966. Marine air penetration in central California. Journal of Applied Meteorology 5:573–579.

Franco-Vizcaíno, E., M. Escoto-Rodríguez, J. Sosa-Ramírez, and R.A. Minnich. 2002. Water balance at the southern limit of the Californian mixed-conifer forest and implications for extreme-deficit watersheds. Arid Land Research and Management 16:133–147.

Glendening, G.W., B.L. Ulrickson, and J.A. Businger. 1986. Mesoscale variability of boundary layer properties in the Los Angeles Basin. Monthly Weather Review 114:2537–2549.

Graumlich, L.J. 1993. A 1000-year record of temperature and precipitation in the Sierra Nevada. Quaternary Research 39: 249–255.

Hales, J.E., Jr. 1974. Southwestern United States Summer Monsoon Source: Gulf of Mexico or Pacific Ocean? Journal of Applied Meteorology 13:331–342.

Hayes, T.P., J.J.R. Kinney, and N.J.M. Wheeler. 1984. California surface wind climatology. Aerometric Data Division, California Air Resources Board, Sacramento. 73 p.

Hoerling, M.P., A. Kumar, and M. Zhong. 1997. El Niño, La Niña, and the nonlinearity of their teleconnections. Journal of Climate 10:1769–1786.

Kahrl, W.L., W.A. Bowen, S. Brand, M.L. Shelton, D.L. Fuller, and D.A. Ryan. 1979. The California water atlas. California Department of Water Resources.

Keeley, J.E., C.J. Fotheringham, and M. Morais. 1999. Reexamining fire suppression impacts on brushland fire regimes. Science 294:1829–1832.

King, J.A., F.H. Shair, and D.D. Reible. 1987. The influence of atmospheric stability on pollutant transport by slope winds. Atmospheric Environment 21:53–59.

Latif, M., and T.P. Barnett. 1994. Causes of decadal climatic variability over the North Pacific and North America. Science 266:634–637.

Lau, K.M., and P.J. Sheu. 1991. Teleconnections in global rainfall anomalies: seasonal to inter-decadal time scales. In M.H. Glantz, R.W. Katz, and N. Nicholls (eds.), Teleconnections Linking Worldwide Climate Anomalies. Cambridge University Press.

Lovell, C., A. Mandondo, and P. Moriarty. 2002. The question of scale in integration natural resource management. Conservation Ecology 5(2): 25.

Lu, R., and R.P. Turco. 1995. Air pollution transport in a coastal environment: II. Three dimensional simulations over Los Angeles Basin. Atmospheric Environment 29:1499–1518.

Malamud, B.D., G. Morein, and D.L. Turcotte. 1998. Forest fires: an example of self-organized critical behavior. Science 281: 1840–1842.

McGuirk, J.P. 1982. A century of precipitation variability along the Pacific coast of North America and its impact. Climate Change 4:41–56.

Minnich, R.A. 1983. Fire mosaics in southern California and northern Baja California. Science 219:1287–1294.

Minnich, R.A. 1986. Snow levels and amounts in the mountains of southern California. Journal of Hydrology 86:37–58.

Minnich, R.A. 1987. Fire behavior in southern California chaparral before fire control: the Mount Wilson burns at the turn of the century. Annals of the Association of American Geographers 77:599–618.

Minnich, R.A. 1988. The biogeography of fire in the San Bernardino Mountains of California: a historical survey. University of California Publications in Geography 28:1–120.

Minnich, R.A., M.G. Barbour, J.H. Burk., and J. Sosa-Ramírez. 2000a. Californian mixed-conifer forests under unmanaged fire regimes in the Sierra San Pedro Mártir, Baja California, Mexico. Journal of Biogeography 27:105–129.

Minnich, R.A., and Y.H. Chou. 1997. Wildland fire patch dynamics in the chaparral of southern California and northern Baja California. International Journal of Wildland Fire 7:221–248.

Minnich, R.A., E. franco-Vizcaíno, and R.J. Dezzani. 2000. The El Niño/southern oscillation and precipitation variability in Baja California, Mexico. Atmosféra 13:1–20.

Minnich, R.A., E. franco-Vizcaíno, J. Sosa-Ramírez, and Y.H. Chou. 1993. Lightning detection rates and wildland fire in the mountains of northern Baja California, Mexico. Atmosféra 6:235–253.

Minnich, R.A., and P.E. Padgett. 2003. Geology, climate and vegetation of the Sierra Nevada and the mixed-conifer zone: an introduction to the ecosystem. P. 1–31 in A. Bytnerowicz, M.J. Arbaugh, and R. Alonso (eds.), Ozone air pollution in the Sierra Nevada: distribution and effects on forests. Elsevier. 402 p.

Minobe, S. 1997. A 50–70 year climatic oscillation over the North Pacific and North America. Geophysical Research Letters 24:683–686.

Monteverdi, J., and J. Null. 1997. El Niño and California precipitation. Western Technical Attachment No. 97-37. National Weather Service. National Oceanic and Atmospheric Administration.

Norman, S.P., and A.H. Taylor. 2003. Tropical and North Pacific teleconnections influence fire regimes in pine-dominated forests of north-eastern California, USA Journal of Biogeography 30(7): 1081–1092.

Palmén, E., and C.W. Newton. 1965. Atmospheric circulation systems: their structure and physical interpretation. International Geophysics Series Vol. 13. Academic Press. 603 p.

Philander, S.G. 1990. El Niño, La Niña, and the southern oscillation. Academic Press, New York.

Poole, D.K, and P.C. Miller. 1975. Water relations of selected species of chaparral and coastal sage species. Ecology 56:1118–1128.

Poole, D.K., and P.C. Miller. 1981. The distribution of plant water stress and vegetation characteristics in southern California chaparral. American Midland Naturalist 105:32–43.

Renwick, J., and J.M. Wallace. 1996. Relationships between North Pacific wintertime blocking, El Niño and the PNA pattern. Monthly Weather Review 124:2071–2076.

Ropelewski, C.F., and M.S. Halpert. 1987. Global and regional scale precipitation patterns associated with the El Niño/southern oscillation. Monthly Weather Review 115: 1606–1626.

Rothermel, R.C. 1972. A mathematical model for fire spread predictions in wildland fuels. USDA Forest Service Research Paper INT-115. 40 p.

Royce, E.B., and M.G. Barbour. 2001a. Mediterranean climate effects I. Conifer water use across a Sierra Nevada ecotone. American Journal of Botany 88:911–918.

Royce, E.B., and M.G. Barbour. 2001b. Mediterranean climate effects II. Conifer growth phenology across a Sierra Nevada ecotone. American Journal of Botany 88:919–932.

Ruddiman, W.F. 2001. Earth's climate: past and future. W.H. Freeman. 465 p.

Ryan, B.C. 1977. A mathematical model for diagnosis and prediction of surface winds in mountainous terrain. Journal of Applied Meteorology 16:571–584.

Ryan, B.C. 1982. Estimating fire potential in California: atlas and guide for fire management planning. USDA For. Serv. Pac. Southwest For. and Range Exp. Sta., Riverside, CA.

Schonher, T., and S.E. Nicholson. 1989. The relationship between California rainfall and ENSO events. Journal of Climate 2: 1258–1269.

Schroeder, M.J., M.A. Fosberg, O.P. Cramer, and C.A. O'Dell. 1967. Marine air invasion of the Pacific coast: a problem analysis. Bulletin of the American Meteorological Society 48:802–808.

Schultz, P., and T.T. Warner. 1982. Characteristics of summertime circulations and pollutant ventilation in the Los Angeles Basin. Journal of Applied Meteorology 21:672–682.

Smith, W. 1986. The effects of eastern North Pacific tropical cyclones on the southwestern United States.U.S. National Oceanic and Atmospheric Administration Technical Memorandum NWS WR-197. 220 p.

Steinbeck, J. 1962. Travels with Charley: in search of America. Viking Press, New York.

Stensrud, D.J., R.L. Gall, and M.K. Nordquist. 1997. Surges over the Gulf of California during the Mexican monsoon. Monthly Weather Review 125:417–437.

Stephens, S.L., C.N. Skinner, and S.J. Gill. 2003. A dendrochronology based fire history of Jeffrey pine-mixed conifer forest in the Sierra San Pedro Martir, Mexico. Canadian Journal of Forest Research 33:1090–1101.

Stull, R.B. 1988. An introduction to boundary layer meteorology. Kluwer Academic Publishers, Dordrecht. 666 p.

Swetnam, T.W. 1993. Fire history and climatic change in giant Sequoia groves. Science 262:885–890.

Swetnam, T.W., and J.L. Betancourt. 1998. Mesoscale disturbance and ecological response to decadal climatic variability in the American Southwest. Journal of Climate 11:3128–3147.

Tubbs, A.M. 1972. Summer thunderstorms over southern California. Monthly Weather Review 100:799–807.

U.S. Department of Commerce. National Oceanic and Atmospheric Administration. Daily Weather Map. November 10, 1970. Environmental Data Service. Government Printing Office. Washington, D.C.

van Wagtendonk, J.W., and D. Cayan. 2007. Temporal and spatial distribution of lightning strikes in California in relationship to large-scale weather patterns. Fire Ecology. (in press)

Westerling, A., and T.W. Swetnam. 2003. Interannual to decadal drought and wildfire in the western United States. Bulletin of the American Meteorological Society 84:595–604.

Zack, J.A., and Minnich, R.A., 1991. Integration of geographic information systems with a diagnostic wind field model for fire management. Forest Science 37:560–573.

CHAPTER 3

Fire as a Physical Process

JAN W. VAN WAGTENDONK

Where there's smoke, there's fire.

ANONYMOUS

In many California ecosystems, the process of decomposition is too slow to completely oxidize accumulated organic material, and another process, such as fire, steps in to perform that role. The mediterranean climate in California, with its hot, dry summers and cool, wet winters, is not conducive to decomposition. When it is warm enough for decomposer organisms to be active, it's too dry. Conversely, when it's wet enough, it's too cold. As a result, decomposition is unable to keep up with the deposited material, and organic debris begins to accumulate. This debris becomes fuel available for the inevitable fire that will occur. All that is needed is a sufficient amount of fuel, an ignition source, and weather conditions conducive to burning. In this chapter we will look at fire as a physical process including combustion, fuel characteristics, fuel models, fire weather, ignition sources, mechanisms for fire spread, and fire effects.

Combustion

Combustion is one of many types of oxidation processes. These processes combine materials that contain hydrocarbons with oxygen and produce carbon dioxide, water, and energy. Oxidation is the reverse of photosynthesis, where energy is used in combination with carbon dioxide and water to produce organic material. The rate of oxidation can vary from the slow hardening of a coat of linseed oil in a paint film to the instantaneous explosion of a petrochemical. Combustion is a chain reaction that occurs rapidly at high temperatures.

Combustion Chemistry

Byram (1959) presents the chemical equation for combustion using a formula for wood that approximates its carbon, hydrogen, and oxygen contents. Although moisture content affects the amount of fuel available for combustion, water does not take part in the combustion reaction. Nitrogen, which is also a constituent of organic material, has little effect on combustion. If moisture and nitrogen are not included, the combustion equation is:

$$4C_6H_9O_4 + 25O_2 \rightarrow 18H_2O + 24CO_2 + 5{,}264{,}729 \text{ kJ}.$$

The energy produced by this reaction is called the *heat* of combustion. The 5,264,729 kJ (4,990,000 Btu) for the 4 moles of fuel is equivalent to 20 MJ kg^{-1} (8,600 Btu lb^{-1}) of fuel. See sidebar 3.1 for further discussion on different units and their derivation. The heat is produced from the fuel once it is ignited. For combustion to occur, fuel, oxygen, and heat must be present. These three factors form the *fire triangle* and fire control measures are based on breaking the link among them (Fig. 3.1). For example, a fire can be extinguished by removing the fuel, reducing the amount of oxygen, or by lowering the temperature of the fuel. In most wildland fires, combustion is incomplete and not all fuel is consumed.

The amount of heat produced by a fire is less than would occur under conditions of complete combustion. Some heat is lost through radiation, but the primary loss comes from the vaporization of moisture. Four separate steps are involved in this process: (1) heat is required to raise the temperature of the water in the fuel to boiling, (2) bound water must be released from the fuel, (3) the water must be vaporized, and (4) the water vapor must be heated to flame temperature. Only the heat necessary to release the bound water and to vaporize the water can be considered true losses (Byram 1959). The result of subtracting these two values from the heat content is called the *low heat content* or *heat yield*. If there is too much moisture in the fuel, combustion is unable to occur. The threshold level of moisture is called the *moisture of extinction*.

We are all familiar with calories—the nutritional content of food and the curse of all dieters. There are several other energy units that are less familiar but equally important. *British thermal units* (Btu) are used to measure the output of furnaces and air conditioners, and *kilowatt hours* (kW h) keep track of our electricity use. There are many types of energy, but all energy can be measured using the same unit, the *joule* (J). It was named after the British physicists James Prescott Joule and is the amount work done to produce the power of one watt (w) for one second (s), such as lifting 102 g (e.g., a small apple) through one meter under the earth's gravity. The joule is the preferred metric unit for energy, and the *megajoule* (MJ) is the unit used by fire scientists to measure the amount of heat energy in fuels.

The nutritional calorie is actually 1,000 calories (cal) and is called a *kilocalorie* (kcal). A calorie (cal) is the amount of heat necessary to raise the temperature of one gram of water one degree Celsius from 15°C–16°C and is equal to 4.184 J. Similarly, the Btu is the amount of heat necessary to raise one pound of water one degree Fahrenheit from 60°F to 61°F. It is equivalent to 1,054 J.

The kilowatt hour (kW h) corresponds to one kilowatt (kW) of power being used over a period of one hour and is equal to 3.6×10^6 J. Although the kW h is not used to describe fire behavior, the kilowatt (kW) is part of one measure of fire intensity. Fireline intensity, which is described as the amount of energy received per second along one meter of the fire front, is measured in units of kW m^{-1}.

Regardless of what units are used, the basic concept remains the same. Energy is stored in fuel and is released during combustion. The rate of that release is governed by many factors discussed in the remainder of this chapter.

FIGURE 3.1. The fire triangle illustrates the requirements for combustion; heat must be applied to fuel in the presence of oxygen for combustion to occur.

Heat Transfer

The heat resulting from combustion is transferred by three primary mechanisms: conduction, convection, and radiation. *Conduction* occurs when heat moves from molecule to molecule and is the only mechanism that can transfer heat through an opaque solid. Conduction is the reason you are likely to drop a frying pan that has been on the fire when you grab it by its handle. Heat moves by conduction through branches and into the center of logs. Fuel temperature is thus increased and water is driven out of the solid fuels. Conduction also occurs when flames come into direct contact with unburned fuels.

Convection is the movement of heat in a gas or a liquid. You can feel heat moving by convection when you put your hand above a campfire. As heat rises from a flaming front, convection transfers heat to the canopy of trees and preheats fuels in front of the flames. This can lead to torching of individual trees and to crown fires. Heat transfer by convection is enhanced by wind and steep slopes and is instrumental in

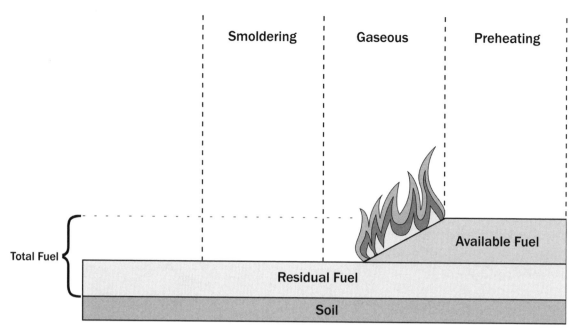

FIGURE 3.2. The three phases of combustion. Available fuel is the amount of fuel actually consumed. Combustion continues during the smoldering phase after passing of the flaming front.

lofting firebrands that produce new fires, called *spot fires,* ahead of the flaming front.

Heat transfer by *radiation* occurs in a straight line through transparent solids, liquids, and gases. Radiation preheats fuels and can cause spontaneous ignitions. This heat is felt while standing in front of a fire and is inversely proportional to the square of the distance away from the source. If you move half the distance toward a campfire, you will receive four times as much heat through radiation. This is why flames that are bent over by wind or are closer to adjacent fuels due to the slope are more effective in preheating and drying those fuels.

Combustion Phases

In wildland fuels, combustion occurs in three phases: preheating, gaseous, and smoldering (Fig. 3.2). During the *preheating* phase, fuels ahead of the fire are heated, water is driven out of the fuel, and gases are partially distilled (Byram 1959). The *gaseous* phase starts with ignition as gases continue to be distilled and active burning begins. During this phase oxidation is initiated and an active flaming front develops. The flames come from the burning distilled gases; both water and carbon dioxide are given off as invisible combustion products. Incomplete combustion results in condensation of some of the gases, and water vapor as small droplets of liquid or solid are suspended over the fire and produce smoke. During the *smoldering* phase, charcoal and other unburned material remaining after the flaming phase continue to burn leaving a small amount of residual ash (Byram 1959). During this phase the fuel burns as a solid and oxidation occurs on the surface of the charcoal. One of the products of incomplete combustion during the soldering phase is carbon monoxide.

Fuel

Fuel is the source of heat that sustains the combustion process. Fuels are characterized by physical and chemical properties that affect combustion and fire behavior.

Fuel Characteristics

Under constant weather and topographic conditions, the characteristics of the fuels determine the rate of combustion. For example, a fire burning in dry-grass fuels on a 20% slope with an 8 km h^{-1} (5 mi h^{-1}) wind would have a higher rate of spread and be more intense than would a fire burning an equivalent weight of woody debris under identical conditions. Similarly, a tall brush field would burn more intensely than would an equivalent amount of fuel arranged into a fuel complex with larger particles and less depth. Fine, porous fuels heat more quickly and burn more readily than coarse, compact fuels. The moisture contained in grass, wood, or shrub fuels also affects combustion—the drier the fuel, the more rapid the combustion.

SURFACE AREA TO VOLUME RATIO

Fuel coarseness, or fineness, is a function of fuel particle size. Imagine trying to start a log on fire in your wood stove with a single match. The log would not ignite because you would not be able to raise its temperature to ignition temperature. Instead you would split the log into many individual pieces of kindling. Although the volume of wood has not changed, the surface area of all the kindling is much greater than the surface area of the log (Box 3.1). The smaller the size of a fuel

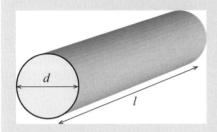

particle, the larger the ratio between its surface and the vol-
ume. The surface area to volume ratio is measured in units of
$m^2 \, m^{-3}$ ($ft^2 \, ft^{-3}$) or, for simplicity, m^{-1} (ft^{-1}). For long, cylin-
drical fuel particles such as conifer needles, twigs, branches,
and grasses, the area of the ends can be ignored, and the ratio
is determined by dividing the diameter into the number 4
(Burgan and Rothermel 1984). Leaves from broad-leaved
plants also have high surface area to volume ratios that can
be approximated by dividing the leaf thickness into the number 2. For example, an oak leaf with a thickness of 0.0005 m
(0.0016 ft) would have a surface area to volume ratio of
4,000 m^{-1} (1,220 ft^{-1}). This ratio is an extremely important
fuel characteristic because as more surface area is available for
combustion, heating of the entire particle is quicker, and
moisture is driven off more easily.

FUEL MOISTURE TIMELAG CLASS

The proportion of a fuel particle that contains moisture is
a primary determinant of fire behavior. The interaction of
a fuel particle with the ambient moisture regime is dependent on its size or its depth in the organic layer called duff.
The size classes that are traditionally used to categorize
fuels correspond to fuel moisture timelag classes (Deeming
et al. 1977). *Timelag* is the amount of time necessary for a
fuel component to reach 63% of its equilibrium moisture
content at a given temperature and relative humidity (Lancaster 1970). Table 3.1 shows the various timelag classes
and the corresponding woody size classes and duff depth
classes.

One-hour timelag fuels consist of dead herbaceous plants
and small branchwood as well as the uppermost litter on
the forest floor. These fuels react to hourly changes in relative humidity. Day-to-day changes in moisture are
reflected in the 10-hour fuels. The 100-hour fuels capture
moisture trends spanning from several days to weeks,
whereas 1,000-hour fuels reflect seasonal changes in moisture. The firewood analogy applies here as well. Your large
logs would take several months to dry if left out in the rain
for the winter, yet kindling, if brought inside, would dry in
a few hours.

PACKING RATIO

Fuelbed compactness is another fuel characteristic that affects
fire behavior. Again, imagine compressing all the kindling
you just split into a tight bundle and trying to light the bundle; the kindling would probably not ignite. Remembering
all the campfires you have lit, you would instead arrange the
kindling into a small log cabin or teepee. The volume of
wood has not changed, but the amount of air in the fuel bed
has increased (Box 3.2). Fuelbed compactness, called the
packing ratio, is measured by dividing the bulk density of the
fuelbed, including fuel and air, by the fuel particle density
(Burgan and Rothermel 1984). A solid block of wood has a
packing ratio of one. If the packing ratio is too high, not
enough oxygen can reach the fuel and combustion cannot
occur. Conversely, if the packing ratio is too low, the fire has
trouble spreading from particle to particle as the distance
between particles increases and radiation decreases. The compactness at which maximum energy release occurs is called
the *optimum* packing ratio. The closer the *actual* packing ratio
is to the *optimum*, the more intense the fire will be. This concept is similar to adjusting the carburetor or fuel injectors on
your car to reach the optimum mixture of fuel and air. If the
mixture is too rich or too lean, the engine will not burn fuel
efficiently.

FUEL LOAD

The amount of fuel that is potentially available for combustion has a differential effect on fire spread and intensity. As
a heat source, the more fuel available, the greater the amount

TABLE 3.1
Moisture timelag classes and corresponding woody fuel size and duff fuel depth classes

Timelag Class	Time Period	Woody Fuel Size Class		Duff Fuel Depth Class	
		(cm.)	(in.)	(cm.)	(in.)
1-hour	Hourly	0.00–0.64	0.00–0.25	0.00–0.64	0.00–0.25
10-hour	Daily	0.25–2.54	0.25–1.00	0.64–1.91	0.25–0.75
100-hour	Weekly	2.54–7.62	1.00–3.00	1.91–l0.16	0.75–4.00
1,000-hour	Seasonally	7.62–22.86	3.00–9.00	10.16+	4.00+

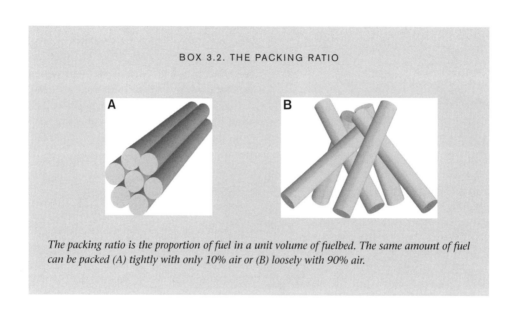

BOX 3.2. THE PACKING RATIO

The packing ratio is the proportion of fuel in a unit volume of fuelbed. The same amount of fuel can be packed (A) tightly with only 10% air or (B) loosely with 90% air.

of energy released. Rate of spread may actually decrease as fuel load increases, however, because the extra fuel also becomes a greater heat sink, and more heat is required to raise it to ignition temperature. Much of the response depends on the size class of the fuel, its packing ratio, and whether or not it is dead or live fuel. Procedures for inventorying downed woody fuels are found in Brown (1974) and Brown et al. (1982).

HEAT CONTENT

The low heat content of the fuel provides the energy to drive combustion. Rate of spread varies directly with heat content; doubling the heat content results in a two-fold increase in rate of spread. Heat content is measured in MJ kg^{-1} (Btu lb^{-1}).

Fuel Models

Fuel types that have similar characteristics are grouped into stylized "fuel models" that include the variables important for combustion. Fuel models for predicting surface fire spread were developed by Rothermel (1972) and adapted for predicting fire behavior by Albini (1976) and for assessing fire danger by Deeming et al. (1977). Anderson (1982) provided aids for determining fuel models for estimating fire behavior and showed how the models in the two systems were similar. The Albini (1976) and Deeming et al. (1977) models contained the necessary fuel information for calculating reaction intensity and rate of spread. However, the two systems use different algorithms for determining characteristic values to be representative of the entire fuel array. The fire behavior system uses the surface area to volume ratio for weighting, whereas the danger rating system uses fuel load. Rothermel's (1972) surface fire spread model was not designed to predict crown fire spread, account for the large fuels that burn after the fire front goes by, or predict fire effects such as duff consumption and smoke production.

Acknowledging these limitations of existing fuel models, Sandberg et al. (2001) proposed a new system of fire characteristic classes that would provide all the information necessary for predicting fire behavior, fire danger, and fire effects. Fuel characteristic classes are defined for a vegetation type and contain data for fuels in up to six strata representing potentially independent combustion environments. For example, a ponderosa pine *(Pinus ponderosa)* type might have fuels in the tree canopy, shrub, woody fuel, and ground fuel strata. A stratum can contain one or more fuelbed categories that contribute available biomass and flammable surfaces to the stratum. Continuing with the ponderosa pine example, there might be overstory and understory categories in the tree stratum, and sound wood, rotten wood, and snags in the woody fuel stratum. The physiognomy of each fuelbed category determines a set of morphological, chemical, and structural features that define a fuelbed component (Sandberg et al. 2001). Fuelbed components combust differently and have a unique influence on fire behavior and effects. Examples of fuelbed components include the different size classes of sound woody fuels and the foliage and twigs of shrubs. Each component is defined by a set of quantitative variables that specify physical, chemical, and structural characteristics of the fuelbeds.

TREE CANOPY FUELS

The tree canopy stratum contains understory and overstory fuel that lead to and sustain crown fires. Continuity in the vertical distribution of these fuels provides the avenue for fire to spread into the upper canopy. Quantitative variables for canopies include mean live crown base height, mean canopy height, canopy bulk density, and percent cover. Low live crown bases and the presence of understory trees contribute to *ladder fuels* that allow a fire to reach into the upper crowns. The bulk density of the crowns, measured in kg m^{-3} (lb ft^{-3}), directly affects crown fire spread. Percent cover relates to the spatial homogeneity of the canopy stratum and affects subcanopy wind speeds and fuel shading.

SHRUB FUELS

The shrub stratum is described by height to live crown base, mean shrub height, the live to dead ratio, and percent cover. The heat content, moisture of extinction, surface area to volume ratio, and load by size class of the live leaves and twigs and the dead twigs and branches are additional variables that need to be quantified. Of all of these variables, the mean shrub height and total fuel load are the most important determinants of fire behavior. Chaparral fires in southern California become very intense because of their heavy loads and near-optimum compactness.

LOW VEGETATION FUELS

Low vegetation fuels include grasses, sedges, and forbs. These fuels are classified by their surface area to volume ratio and whether they are annuals or perennials. Mean height, load, percent cover, and maximum percent that can be live are the quantitative variables that describe grasses and sedges. Mean height and load affect the packing ratio, and percent live affects the ratio between live and dead herbage and, consequently, their moisture content.

Sound logs, rotten logs, snags, and stumps are included in the woody fuel stratum. Sound woody fuel is divided into components that correspond to the moisture timelag classes with the addition of a greater than 22.86 cm (9 in) component. For each of these components, a load, surface area to volume ratio, fuelbed depth, heat content, and moisture of extinction need to be specified. Sound wood particles less than 7.62 cm (3 in) in diameter contribute to spread of the flaming fire front, roughly in proportion to their corresponding surface area to volume ratios. Although the larger fuels are ignited by the flaming front, they do not contribute to surface fire spread. Instead, they burn or smolder for hours or days and their heat and emissions are instrumental in producing fire effects such as tree mortality and smoke. The rotten wood category includes wood in the advanced rot stage that usually does not burn with the passing of the flaming front but smolders afterwards, contributing to smoke and other emissions. Snags are standing dead trees that, once ignited, produce firebrands. These burning embers can be lofted into the air and carried down wind, starting spot fires. Snags are classified by class, diameter, and height.

LITTER FUELS

Litter fuels include moss, lichen, needles, or leaves, and all can contribute to the spread of the fire front. Physiognomic variables for litter fuels include moss type, litter type, and litter arrangement. Percent cover and mean depth are used to infer the biomass of these fuels.

GROUND FUELS

The ground fuel stratum is divided into upper duff, lower duff, basal accumulation, and animal middens fuelbed categories. The upper duff is defined as the weathered or fermentation layer, whereas the lower duff component consists of the humus or decomposed layer. Both duff components contribute to emissions and smoke and are measured by their depth, load, and percent of rotten wood. The accumulation of fuel occurs in middens or around the bases of large trees and can become very deep and smolder for days, generating enough heat that can kill the tree through cambium mortality and loss of fine root hairs.

Fire Weather

Simply having enough fuel on the ground is not sufficient to produce a fire; an ignition source must be present to start a fire, and weather conditions must be such that the fire will continue to spread once ignited. As we learned in the previous chapter, weather is the state of the atmosphere surrounding the earth and the atmosphere's changing nature (Schroeder and Buck 1970). Fire weather is concerned with weather variations within the first 8–16 km (5–10 mi) above the earth's surface that influence wildland fire behavior. Fire weather includes air temperature, atmospheric moisture, atmospheric stability, and clouds and precipitation.

Air Temperature

Ambient air temperature affects fuel temperature, which is one of the key factors determining when fires start and how they spread (Schroeder and Buck 1970). The amount of heat necessary to evaporate the fuel moisture and raise the temperature of the fuel to the ignition point is directly related to the initial fuel temperature and the temperature of the air. As the air temperatures rise, less heat is required. As discussed in the section on fuel moisture timelag classes, these processes can take only seconds for fine fuels and minutes to hours for large fuels. Fire effects such as scorch height are also affected by air temperature. Air temperature indirectly affects fire behavior through its influence on other factors such as winds, atmospheric moisture, and atmospheric stability.

Atmospheric Moisture

Moisture in the air is one of the key elements of fire weather (Schroeder and Buck 1970). Atmospheric moisture directly affects fuel moisture and is indirectly related to other fire weather factors such as thunderstorms and lightning. The maximum amount of moisture that can be held in air is directly related to the air temperature and the atmospheric pressure. At a given pressure, as temperature rises, more water vapor can be held. The actual amount of water vapor in the air is called the *absolute humidity*. The ratio between the actual amount and the maximum amount at any particular temperature and pressure is called the *relative humidity*. There is a continuous exchange of water vapor between the air and dead fuels. Fuel gives off moisture when the relative humidity is low. The exchange continues until the equilibrium moisture content is reached. Fuels absorb water vapor when the relative humidity is higher than the fuel moisture content and give off moisture when the relative humidity is lower. The rate of exchange is related to the difference between the air and fuel moisture contents and the surface area to volume ratio of the fuels. Extremely low relative humidity can also affect live fuel moisture content as plants transpire increasingly more water vapor as temperature increases.

Atmospheric Stability

Fire behavior is greatly affected by atmospheric motion and the properties affected by that motion (Schroeder and Buck 1970). Surface winds are the most obvious result of differences in atmospheric pressure as air moves from areas of high pressure to areas of low pressure. Vertical motions within the atmosphere can have dramatic effects on fire behavior. Heat from the fire generates vertical motion near the surface and creates a convective column that is affected directly by the stability of the air (Schroeder and Buck 1970). Unstable air

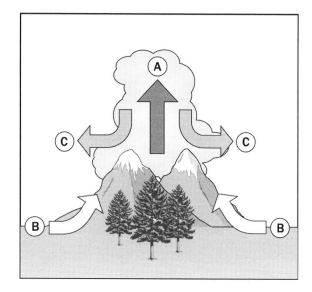

FIGURE 3.3. Under conditions of atmospheric instability, heat from the fire rises to form an updraft (A), causing an indraft of air near the surface (B). As the column collapses, strong downdraft winds can blow the fire in several directions (C).

allows the convection column to grow, causing an indraft into the fire at the surface and eventually leading to a downdraft as the column collapses (Fig. 3.3). These winds can cause erratic and severe fire behavior. Ironically, unstable air provides the best conditions for dispersing smoke into the atmosphere. Subsidence of air from high-pressure areas to low-pressure areas brings with it strong hot and dry winds caused by air moving across a steep pressure gradient. The Santa Ana in southern California and the Mono in the Sierra Nevada are well-known examples of gradient winds that have an extreme effect on fire behavior.

Wind Speed and Direction

Of all the weather or weather-related factors affecting fire behavior, winds are the least predictable and the most variable. Winds affect fire behavior by carrying away moisture in the air, thereby drying the fuels, and by increasing the oxygen supply and accelerating combustion. This is the reason we blow on a campfire in order to get it going—more oxygen, faster combustion. Gradient and frontal winds are associated with pressure differences and movements of large air masses. The passage of a dry cold front can cause strong, gusty winds and dry, unstable air. Local heating and cooling and the shape of the topography affect convective winds near the earth's surface. For example, up-canyon winds in the morning and down-canyon winds in the evening are the result of differential heating and cooling of terrain surfaces. Fire spread is enhanced by transferring heat by convection and by bending the flames closer to the fuel. Embers from torching trees and burning snags are carried by the wind, starting spot fires ahead of the main fire and increasing its lineal and areal rate of growth.

Clouds and Precipitation

Clouds and precipitation affect fire behavior primarily through their effects on fuel moisture. Shade from clouds lowers the air temperature and raises the relative humidity. As a result, fuel temperature decreases and fuel moisture content increases. Thunderstorm clouds, however, can portend unstable atmosphere, erratic winds, and severe fire behavior. The amount of precipitation and its seasonal distribution determine the beginning, ending, and severity of the fire season (Schroeder and Buck 1970). Precipitation has the direct effect of raising fuel moisture.

Ignition

Now that we have an abundant array of fuel available for burning and fire weather conducive to fire spread, all we need is an ignition. Lightning and humans are the primary ignition sources, although volcanoes ignite fires when their infrequent eruptions occur. Not all ignitions result in a fire, however, because several conditions must be met before an ignition can become a fire and spread.

Ignition Sources

Lightning develops in thunderstorms that form as a result of frontal activity or air mass movements (Schroeder and Buck 1970). Thunderstorms associated with fronts occur when warm, moist air is forced over a wedge of cold air. Lightning is usually more prevalent with cold-front thunderstorms. Orographic lifting of air masses is also a common cause of thunderstorms and lightning as air moves over mountain ranges. As a thunderstorm develops, positive charges accumulate in the top of the cloud and negative charges in the lower portion. Lightning occurs in thunderstorms when the electrical energy potential builds up to the point that it exceeds the resistance of the atmosphere to a flow of electrons between areas of opposite charge (Schroeder and Buck 1970). Cloud-to-ground lightning accounts for about one third of all strikes, and these strikes are primarily negative (Fuquay 1982). Ignitions occur when the lightning strike has a long continuing current, as do approximately 80% of positive strikes and 10% of negative strikes. Lightning is pervasive in the state of California but is most prevalent in the mountains and the southeastern deserts. The temporal and spatial distribution of lightning strikes is discussed in Chapter 2.

Native Americans have been cited as an ignition source for fires throughout California (Anderson 1996). Their fires were set for many reasons including nurturing plants used for food such as California black oaks (Quercus kelloggii), enhancing the quality of plants shoots used in basketry, clearing vegetation around village sites, and driving game for easier hunting. Anderson (1996) states that some ecosystems can be labeled anthropogenic because they were probably dependent on human activities for their perpetuation. Examples of this practice are patches of deer grass in chaparral, montane meadows, desert fan-palm oases, coastal prairies, and oak woodlands. Although fires set by Native Americans certainly burned areas occupied or used by them, the areal extent of those fires remains uncertain. In the chapter *Use of Fire by Native Americans* (Chapter 17), Anderson states that their use spanned a gradient from intensive use to no use at all. Vale (1998) suggests that non-human processes determined the landscape characteristics of over 60% of Yosemite. In these areas there were scattered Native American camps and few, if any, fires. For the remaining 40%, Vale (1998) states that there were more frequent fires that were possibly made more numerous by ignitions by Native Americans, and that around village sites, fires were likely to be more frequent as a result of their fires. In all likelihood, ignitions by Native Americans were an addition to lightning ignitions rather than a substitute for them, and the landscape was a mosaic of both natural and cultural characteristics.

Ignition Probability

Not all ignitions result in a fire. Ignition by a lightning strike or a firebrand occurs in four stages (Deeming et al. 1977). First, contact with a receptive fuel must be made. Once contact is made, the moisture in the fuel must be driven off. The temperature of the fuel must then be raised to the point of pyrolysis. And finally, the gasses must be heated to ignition temperature. The probability that a firebrand will start a fire is a function of the fine dead fuel moisture (1-hour timelag fuel moisture) content; fuel temperature; surface area to volume ratio and packing ratio; and characteristics of the firebrand such as temperature, rate of heat release, length of time it will burn, and whether it is flaming or glowing (Deeming et al. 1977). In the fire behavior prediction system, ignition probability is calculated using fine dead fuel moisture, air temperature, and percent shading (Rothermel 1983). In addition to those three, the ignition component in the National Fire Danger Rating System includes the spread component in order to determine the probability of detecting an ignition that requires suppression action (Deeming et al. 1977).

Using simulated lightning discharges, Latham and Schlieter (1989) found that ignition probabilities for duff of short-needled conifers such as lodgepole pine (Pinus contorta ssp. murrayana) depend almost entirely on duff depth. Ignition of litter and duff from long-needled conifers including ponderosa pine and western white pine (Pinus monticola) was affected primarily by the moisture content. Ignition was also dependent on the duration of the arc, indicating that a lightning strike's length of time could have an effect on starting a fire.

Arnold (1964) found that only 25% of the lightning's long-continuing discharges actually started fires. In Yosemite National Park, the 7,250 lightning strikes that occurred from 1985 through 1990 produced 361 fires, an ignition rate of only 5% (van Wagtendonk 1994). Many discharges might have resulted in fires that did not grow large enough to be detected and went out before they could be located. Other discharges

TABLE 3.2
Fire types, fuel strata, and categories in which they burn

Fire Type	Fuel Bed Stratum	Fuel Category
Ground	Ground fuel	Duff, peat, basal accumulation, animal middens
Surface	Litter fuel	Litter, lichens, moss
	Woody fuel	Sound wood, rotten wood, piles and jackpots, stumps
	Shrub	Shrubs, needle drape
	Low vegetation	Grasses and sedges, forbs
Passive Crown	Litter fuel	Litter, lichens, moss
	Woody fuel	Sound wood, rotten wood, piles and jackpots, stumps
	Shrub	Shrubs, needle drape
	Low vegetation	Grasses and sedges, forbs
	Tree canopy	Canopy, snags, ladders
Active Crown	Litter fuel	Litter, lichens, moss
	Woody fuel	Sound wood, rotten wood, piles and jackpots, stumps
	Shrub	Shrubs, needle drape
	Low vegetation	Grasses and sedges, forbs
	Tree canopy	Canopy, snags, ladders
Independent Crown	Tree canopy	Canopy, snags, ladders

might have struck rock, snow, or other noncombustible substances. Deeming et al. (1977) combined ignition probability with rate of spread to an index for the chance that an ignition will result in a detectable fire.

Fire Behavior

Finally, we have the necessary ingredients for a fire: sufficient fuel, conducive weather, and an ignition. We now look at how these factors, combined with topography, cause a fire to spread. Fires can spread through ground fuels, surface fuels, crown fuels, or combinations of all three. Spot fires ignited by lofted firebrands can also spread fires. Each method has unique physical mechanisms necessary to sustain fire spread. The fuel stratum that is burned and the method of spread define fire types (Table 3.2). Ground fires burn the duff or other organic matter such as peat and usually burn with slow-moving smoldering fires, often after the surface fire as passed. Surface fires burn the litter, woody fuels (up to 7.62 cm [3 in]), and low vegetation such as shrubs, with and active flaming front. *Passive* crown fires burn surface fuels and single trees or groups of trees, *active* crown fires burn in the canopies in conjunction with a surface fire, and *independent* crown fires spread through the canopies without a surface fire.

Flaming Front

The flaming front is the area of the fire at its leading edge and is defined by its forward rate of spread, residence time, and flaming zone depth. These characteristics are used to calculate additional characteristics including reaction intensity, fireline intensity, flame length, and heat per unit of area. Equations for calculating these characteristics are included in Box 3.3. *Rate of spread* is the speed at which the flaming front moves forward and is measured in units of distance per unit of time. Rate of spread is affected by many fuel, weather, and topographic variables. The time the flaming front takes to pass over a point is called the *residence time*. The *flaming zone depth* is defined as the distance from the front to the back of the active flaming front and is calculated by multiplying the rate of spread by the residence time. Anderson (1969) found that the residence time was related to the size of the particles that were being burned.

The rate of energy release is characterized by the reaction intensity and the fireline intensity. *Reaction intensity* is the rate of energy release per unit of flaming zone area. The reaction intensity is the source of heat that keeps the chain reaction of combustion in motion and is a contributor to fire effects.

Fireline intensity is the rate of energy release per unit length of fire front and is likened to the amount of heat you would be exposed to per second while standing immediately in front of a fire. It is equivalent to the product of the available energy (in terms of heat per unit of area) and the forward rate of spread and can also be determined from reaction intensity and flaming zone depth (Box 3.3). Fireline intensity is related to flame length, the average distance from the base of the

BOX 3.3. EQUATIONS FOR THE FLAMING FRONT CHARACTERISTICS

Characteristic	Metric		English	
Fireline Intensity(FLI)				
FLI = (Heat/Area) × Rate of Spread)/60	FLI	Kw m^{-1}	Btu ft^{-1} s^{-1}	
	H/A	kJ m^{-2}	Btu ft^{-2}	
	ROS	m min^{-1}	ft min^{-1}	
FLI = (Reaction Intensity × Flaming Zone Depth)/60	FLI	Kw m^{-1}	Btu ft^{-1} s^{-1}	
	RI	kJ m^{-2} min^{-1}	Btu ft^{-2} min^{-1}	
	FZD	m	ft	
FLI = (Reaction Intensity × Rate of Spread × Residence Time)	FLI	Kw m^{-1}	Btu ft-1 s^{-1}	
	RI	kJ m^{-2} min^{-1}	Btu ft^{-2} min^{-1}	
	ROS	m min^{-1}	ft min^{-1}	
	RT	min	min	
FLI = 258 × (Flame Length)$^{2.17}$	FLI	Kw m^{-1}		
	FL	m		
FLI = 5.67 × (Flame Length)$^{2.17}$	FLI		Btu ft^{-1} s^{-1}	
	FL		ft	
FLame Length (FL)				
FLame Length (FL)				
FL = 0.237 × (Fireline Intensity)$^{0.46}$	FL	m		
	FLI	Kw m^{-1}		
FL = 0.237 × (Fireline Intensity)$^{0.46}$	FL		ft	
	FLI		Btu ft^{-1} s^{-1}	
Heat per Unit Area (H/A)				
H/A = (60 × Fireline Intensity)/Rate of Spread	H/A	Kw m^{-2}	Btu ft^{-2}	
	FLI	Kw m^{-1}	Btu ft^{-1} s^{-1}	
	ROS	m min^{-1}	ft min^{-1}	

ROS = Rate of Spread; RI = Reaction Intensity, FZD = Flaming Zone Depth, RT = Residence Time

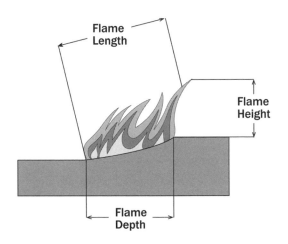

FIGURE 3.4. Flame dimensions for a wind-driven fire. Flame length is related to the fireline intensity and is measured from the base of the flame to its tip.

flame to its highest point. Figure 3.4 shows flame dimensions with flame length as the hypotenuse and flame height the vertical distance to the highest point.

Byram (1959) provided the approximate relationship between fireline intensity and flame length (Box 3.3). His equations can be reversed to obtain simple expressions for fireline intensity in terms of flame length. Byram (1959) cautioned that the equations for fireline intensity based on flame length are better approximations for low-intensity fires rather than for high-intensity fires. Although not without its difficulties, flame length is the only measurement that can be taken easily in the field that is related to fireline intensity (Rothermel and Deeming 1980).

Available fuel energy is the energy that is actually released by the flaming front, while *total* fuel energy is the maximum energy that *could* be released if all the fuel burns. Energy release is measured in heat per unit of area and can be

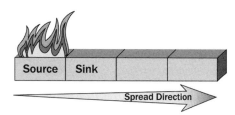

FIGURE 3.5. Rate of spread is the ratio between the heat source and the heat sink. As more heat is generated by the source, the more quickly the heat sink ignites.

calculated from the fireline intensity and the rate of spread (Box 3.3). Heat per unit area is the primary contributor to fire effects since it is independent of time.

Surface Fire Spread

The first attempt to describe fire spread using a mathematical model was by Fons (1946). He theorized that because sufficient heat is needed at the fire front to ignite adjacent fuels, fire spread is a series of successive ignitions controlled by ignition time and the distance between fuel particles. Conceptually, this is analogous to viewing a fuelbed as an array of units of volume of fuel, each unit being ignited in turn as its adjacent unit produces enough heat to cause ignition. The unit being ignited is the *heat sink,* whereas the unit currently burning is the *heat source* (Fig 3.5).

Frandsen (1971) developed the first theoretical model of this process by applying the conservation of energy principle to a unit volume of fuel ahead of a fire front. The unit of fuel that is currently burning serves as the heat source for the unit ahead which acts as a heat sink. Sufficient heat must be generated by the source to ignite the adjacent unit. The rate of spread is determined by the rate at which adjacent fuel units are ignited.

The equation for Frandsen's (1971) quasi—steady-state rate of spread in uniform fuels is shown in (Box 3.4). The numerator is the heat source and contains two terms, one for the horizontal propagating heat flux (I_{xig}) and another for the gradient of the vertical intensity flux ($[\delta Z_c/\delta Z]z_c$). The horizontal flux is a measure of the heat received by the adjacent fuel unit through internal convection and conduction and through radiation from the vertical flame. The gradient flux measures the additional heat received through flame contact, convection, and radiation as the slope or wind brings the flame closer to the adjacent unit. The denominator is the heat sink and contains two terms, one for the effective bulk density of the adjacent fuel, which is the proportion of that fuel that actually ignites (ρ_{be}), and one for the heat necessary to bring it to ignition (Q_{ig}). The proportion that ignites is a function of fuel particle size: the smaller the particle, the greater the proportion that burns. For example, once a large log starts burning, only the outer portion has been raised to ignition temperature. The result of the interaction of the numerator and the denominator in the equation is that fire spreads faster as more heat is produced but spreads slower as

it becomes necessary to ignite greater quantities and sizes of fuel.

Because some of the terms in Frandsen's (1971) equation contained unknown heat transfer mechanisms, Rothermel (1972) devised experimental and analytical methods to determine these terms using fuel, weather, and topographic variables. His model of surface fire spread has been the most commonly used model in the United States since the mid-1970s. The first predictions using Rothermel's (1972) methods were made with the nomograms contained in Albini (1976). Procedures for field use of handheld calculator versions of the model were developed by Burgan (1979) and Sussott and Burgan (1986). Rothermel (1983) formalized the procedures for training fire behavior analysts to use the spread model for use on wildland fires. The model was subsequently computerized by Andrews (1986) in the BEHAVE fire prediction and fuel modeling system. The advent of laptop computers made it possible to combine the fire spread model with other fire behavior models into the FARSITE model, which performs simulations of areal fire spread (Finney 1998). Attempts are under way in Australia to refine the surface spread model, but results are not yet complete.

Box 3.5 shows the surface fire spread equation and defines each of its terms. In the numerator, the propagating fluxes were divided into terms that accounted for the total heat release, the proportion of the heat reaching the adjacent fuel unit, and wind and slope effects. Using the campfire analogy, the total heat release is all of the heat produced by the fire, whereas the heat reaching you sitting at the fire's side would be the proportion reaching the adjacent fuel. Imagine how much hotter you would become if you were able to sit while hovering just above the fire. In the denominator, empirical relationships were used to define bulk density, the effective heating number, and the heat of pre-ignition. The final formulation provided an approximate solution to the equation (Burgan and Rothermel 1984). Each of the terms in the surface combustion, their weight must be removed from the calculation of reaction velocity. A mineral content value of 5.55 % is used for all standard fuel models.

The low heat content (h) provides the heat necessary to sustain combustion. There is some variation in heat content for fuels of different species. Conifers tend to have higher values than do hardwoods because of the presence of resins and higher lignin content. Sclerophyllous shrubs contain oils and waxes in their leaves that increase their heat content. Albini (1976) uses a standard value of 18.61 MJ kg^{-1} (8,000 Btu lb^{-1}).

The moisture damping coefficient (0_M) and mineral damping coefficient (0_s) account for the effects that moisture and minerals have in reducing the potential reaction velocity (Rothermel 1972). The moisture damping coefficient is derived from the fuel moisture content and the fuel moisture content of extinction, which is the moisture level at which combustion can no longer be sustained. The mineral damping coefficient is a function of the silica free ash content, termed the *effective* mineral content. A value of 1.00% is used for the standard fuel models (Albini 1976).

The proportion of heat reaching adjacent fuel is calculated under the assumption that the fire is burning without any wind and on flat terrain (Burgan and Rothermel 1984). The propagating flux ratio (ξ) is a dimensionless fraction that accounts for the fact that not all of the reaction intensity reaches adjacent fuels. For example, in the no-wind, no-slope situation pictured in Figure 3.6, most of the heat energy moves upward by convection, whereas only a smaller proportion is directed at the adjacent fuel by radiation and convection. The minimum value for the flux ratio is zero when no heat reaches adjacent fuels, and the maximum value is 1 when all the heat reaches adjacent fuels. These extreme values are seldom reached, and a more practical range would be from 0.01 to 0.20 because most of the heat is convected upward.

fire spread equation will be examined individually to gain insight into the complex effects of fuels, weather, and topography on surface fire spread. First we cover the terms in the numerator and then the terms in the denominator.

Reaction intensity (I_R) is made up of several factors explained below that relate to the rate of energy release (Box 3.6). Reaction velocity ($\ni'$) is a ratio that expresses how efficiently the fuel is consumed compared to the burnout time of the characteristic particle size (Burgan and Rothermel 1984). This ratio is a function of the actual and optimum packing ratios and the surface area to volume ratio. The actual packing ratio is found by dividing the fuelbed bulk density by the oven-dry fuel particle density. Albini (1976) specifies a standard value of 51.25 kg m^{-3} (32 lb ft^{-3}) for fuel particle density. The optimum packing ratio is a function of the surface area to volume ratio. Fine fuels, such as grass and long-needled pine litter, have near-optimum packing ratios and large surface area to volume ratios. These fuels burn thoroughly in a short period of time and have the highest reaction velocity.

The net fuel loading (w_n) is equal to the oven-dry fuel loading multiplied by 1 minus the fuel particle total mineral content (Albini 1976). Because minerals do not contribute to

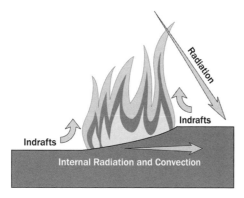

FIGURE 3.6. Under no-wind, no-slope conditions, heat is transferred by radiation from the flame and by internal radiation and convection. Indrafts move air up into the flame.

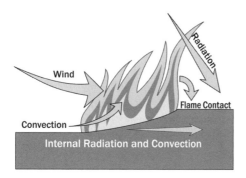

FIGURE 3.7. Under no-slope conditions, wind bends the flame closer to the adjacent fuel resulting in increased radiation, convective heat, and flame contact.

The surface area to volume ratio andthe the packing ratio are the determinants of the propagating flux ratio. As these two ratios increase, the flux ratio increases, with fine fuels having the most pronounced effect.

Both the wind coefficient (Φ_w) and the slope coefficient (Φ_s) have the effect of increasing the proportion of heat reaching the adjacent fuel. They act as multipliers of the reaction intensity. In the no-slope case, the wind coefficient increases rapidly with increases in wind speed in loosely packed fine fuels (Burgan and Rothermel 1984). Direct contact and increased convection and radiation heat transfer occur as the flame tips toward the unburned fuel (Fig. 3.7). Although the smoke might have caused you to move away from the campfire first, if you had remained, you would have felt the added heat from the closer flames. The wind coefficient is affected by surface area to volume ratio, packing ratio, and wind speed. Finer fuels have more surface area exposed to the increased radiation than do coarse fuels. Increasing the surface area to volume ratio increases the wind coefficient, and this effect becomes greater at higher wind speeds as the distance between the flame and the fuel decreases (Burgan and Rothermel 1984). The wind effect is less pronounced as the packing ratio moves beyond the optimum, and fuel particles begin to obstruct the convective flow. There

FIGURE 3.8. Under no-wind conditions with a slope, the convection component is not as pronounced as it would be with wind. Radiation and flame contact are still important factors for increasing spread.

is a maximum wind speed beyond which the wind coefficient does not increase (Burgan and Rothermel 1984). At that point, the power of the wind forces exceeds the convective forces. This occurs when the wind speed in km h^{-1} is twice the reaction intensity in kJ min^{-1} m^{-2} (or the wind speed in mi h^{-1} is 1/100 of the reaction intensity in Btu ft^{-2} min^{-1}). For typical annual grass fires with sparse fuels, wind speeds in excess of 19 km h^{-1} (12 mi h^{-1}) will not increase the rate of spread. In tall grasses, rate of spread will not increase after wind speeds reach 68 km h^{-1} (42 mi h^{-1}).

Under no-wind conditions, the slope coefficient increases as the slope becomes steeper. The effect is similar, but less pronounced, than that of wind. Although flames are brought closer to the unburned fuels, without wind to bring heated air in contact with the fuel, there is only a slight increase in convection (Fig. 3.8). If you are standing above a fire on a slope, you will feel much hotter than if you were standing below. The packing ratio and the tangent of the slope are used to calculate the slope coefficient. The packing ratio has a slight influence on the sensitivity of the coefficient to increases in slope steepness (Burgan and Rothermel 1984). This effect is small in comparison to the other effects due to changes in the packing ratio. The wind and slope coefficients do not interact, but their combination can have a dramatic effect on fire behavior.

Now we take a look at the terms in the denominator of the Rothermel (1972) spread equation that constitute the heat sink. The denominator represents the amount of heat necessary to bring the fuel up to ignition temperature. The first term is *fuelbed bulk density* (ρ_b), the total amount of fuel that is potentially available. It is defined as the oven-dry weight of the fuel per unit of fuelbed volume and is calculated by dividing the oven-dry fuelbed load by the fuelbed depth. Because bulk density is in the denominator of the spread equation, an increase in density will tend to cause a decrease in spread rate (Burgan and Rothermel 1984). This can happen by either increasing the fuel load or by decreasing the fuelbed depth. However, an increase in load also causes the reaction intensity to increase. In addition, an increase in bulk density can cause the propagating flux and the wind and slope coefficients to go up or down depending on the relative packing ratio.

Not all of the fuel that is available will burn with the passing of the flaming front. Often only the outer portion of a large log or other fuel particle is heated to ignition temperature. The effective heating number (ε) defines the proportion of the fuel that will burn as the flaming front passes and is dependent on fuel particle size as measured by the surface area to volume ratio. Small particles will heat completely through and ignite, whereas decreasing proportions of larger particles will ignite as size increases. Not only do the thinner particles heat all the way through, but also their increased surface area allows heating by radiation to occur rapidly. Multiplying the fuelbed bulk density by the effective heating number yields the amount of fuel that must be heated to ignition temperature (Burgan and Rothermel 1984).

How much heat is required? The heat of pre-ignition quantifies the amount of heat necessary to raise the temperature of a 1-kg (2.2-lb) piece of moist fuel from the ambient temperature to the ignition point. First the moisture must be driven off and then the fuel must be heated. Most of these temperature values are fairly constant and can be calculated in advance (Burgan and Rothermel 1984). Moisture content does vary and is used to calculate the heat required for ignition. As fuel moisture content increases, there is a steady increase in the heat of pre-ignition. The units are in kJ kg^{-1} (Btu lb^{-1}). The product of the fuelbed bulk density, effective heating number, and the heat of pre-ignition is the heat per unit of area in kJ m^{-2} (Btu ft^{-2}) necessary to ignite the adjacent fuel cell.

Crown Fire Spread

A crown fire occurs when the fire moves from the surface fuels into the canopies of trees. Although shrub canopies can be considered crowns, the models developed for predicting crown fire behavior are specific to trees. Van Wagner (1977) defined three stages of crown fire. The first stage of crowning is a *passive* crown fire, which begins with the torching of trees from a surface fire. If the fire spreads through the crowns in conjunction with the surface fire, it is called an *active* crown fire. A crown fire spreading through the crowns far ahead of or in the absence of the surface fire is an *independent* crown fire.

In a passive crown fire, single trees or groups of trees torch out and there might be some movement of fire into adjacent tree crowns (Fig. 3.9). Torching can occur at low wind speeds with relatively low crown bulk densities if the crown bases are low enough to be ignited by the surface fire. Although a passive crown fire does not spread from crown to crown, embers from torching trees can start fires ahead of the fire front. Transition to passive crowning

FIGURE 3.9. Passive crown fires can occur under conditions of low crown base heights, even with relatively low wind speeds and low crown bulk densities.

begins when the fireline intensity of the surface fire exceeds that necessary for igniting the crowns. This point is dependent on the height to the base of the live crowns and the foliar moisture content (Alexander 1988). Ladder fuels are considered in the calculation of the crown base height. Under conditions of low foliar moisture content, the crowns will ignite when the surface fire intensity is great enough to bring the crowns to ignition temperature either through direct contact with flames or through convective heat. Once ignited, the fire in the crowns will spread some, but, as long as the actual rate of spread of the crown fire is less than the threshold for active crown spread, the fire will remain passive. Actual spread rate can be calculated from surface fire spread rate, the proportion of the trees that are involved in the crowning phase, and the maximum crown fire spread rate (Rothermel 1991).

An active crown fire can occur when winds increase to the point that flames from torching trees are driven into the crowns of adjacent trees (Rothermel 1991). The heat generated by the surface fire burning underneath the canopy sustains the fire through the crowns (Fig. 3.10). The fire becomes a solid wall of flame from the surface to the crown and spreads with the surface fire (Scott 1999). Lower crown base heights, higher wind speeds, and higher crown bulk densities than those necessary for passive crowning are required for active crowning. The threshold for transition from passive to active crowning is dependent on the crown bulk density and a constant related to the critical mass flow through the canopy necessary for a continuous flame (Alexander 1988). Active crowning continues as long as the surface fire intensity exceeds the critical intensity for initiation of crown fire, and the actual spread rate, as calculated from the Rothermel (1972) equation, is greater than the critical crown fire spread rate. The critical spread rate for active crowning decreases rapidly as crown bulk density increases from 0.01 to 0.05 kg

FIGURE 3.10. Higher wind speeds and crown bulk densities with low crown base heights lead to active crown fires.

FIGURE 3.11. Very high wind speeds and crown bulk densities can lead to independent crown fires that race ahead of the surface fire.

m^{-3} (0.01–0.03 lb ft^{-3}). Consequently, the actual spread rate necessary to initiate crown fire spread becomes less (Scott 1999). As tree canopies become closer and denser, fire is able to spread more easily from tree to tree. After crown bulk densities reach 0.15 kg m^{-3} (0.09 lb ft^{-3}), there is little additional effect on the critical spread rate. Once an active crown fire is initiated, its intensity is calculated using the combined loading of the available surface fuels and crown fuels and the crown rate of spread (Finney 1998). The crown fuel loading is derived from the crown fraction burned, the mean canopy height, the crown base height, and the crown bulk density. The crown fraction burned is dependent on the critical surface spread associated with the critical intensity for initiating a crown fire (Van Wagner 1993).

Independent crown fires burn in aerial fuels substantially ahead of the surface fire and are rare, short-lived phenomena (Fig. 3.11). It is unlikely that these stand-replacing fires occurred over extensive areas during the past several centuries as evidenced by the lack of large areas of even-aged vegetation. Although Swetnam (1993) reported the occurrence of widespread fires from several locations in the Sierra Nevada in 1297, the fires were not severe enough to erase the fire scar record of their occurrence and were not likely to have been independent crown fires. Steep topography, very high wind speeds, and bulk densities greater than 0.05 kg m^{-3} (0.03 lb ft^{-3}) lend themselves to the extreme behavior of these wind-driven fires. Independent crown fires occur when the surface fire intensity exceeds the critical intensity, the actual rate of spread is greater than the critical rate of spread, and the actual energy flux is less than the critical energy flux for independent crown fires in the advancing direction. Finney (1998) did not model independent crown fires because of their ephemeral nature.

Independent crown fires can also occur under low wind and unstable air conditions. Rothermel (1991) describes fires under those conditions as *plume-dominated* fires. Byram (1959) introduced the concept of energy flow rates in the wind field and in the convection column above a line of fire to explain the behavior of plume-dominated fires. The power of the wind is the rate of flow of kinetic energy through a vertical plane of unit area at a specified height in a neutrally stable atmosphere (Nelson 1993). The wind energy is a function of the air density, the wind speed, the forward rate of spread of the fire, and the acceleration due to gravity. The power of the fire is the rate at which thermal energy is converted to kinetic energy at the same specified height in the convection column. It is calculated from the fireline intensity, the specific heat of air, and the air temperature at the elevation of the fire. When the power of the fire is greater than the power of the wind for a considerable height above the fire, extreme fire behavior can occur (Byram 1959). Both Byram (1959) and Rothermel (1991) give equations for the wind and fire power functions, and Nelson (1993) has generalized the equations for use with any applicable system of units.

Spotting

Trees that are ignited during any of the crown fire stages and snags ignited by any fire are sources of firebrands that could ignite spot fires. The spread of a fire is increased dramatically by ignition of numerous spot fires ahead of the flaming front. Albini (1979) developed a model for calculating spot fire distance from a torching tree and enhanced his original model to accommodate embers generated from wind-driven fires (Albini 1983). The model calculates the height to which an ember is lofted, the time it remains burning, and the distance it travels. Characteristics of the torching tree and embers, the intervening area, and the receiving fuelbed all determine the distance and probability of ignition of a new spot fire (Fig. 3.12). Large embers are not lofted as high nor do they travel as far as small embers. Therefore, they are often still burning by the time they can land and start spot fires. Small embers usually burn out before they can land.

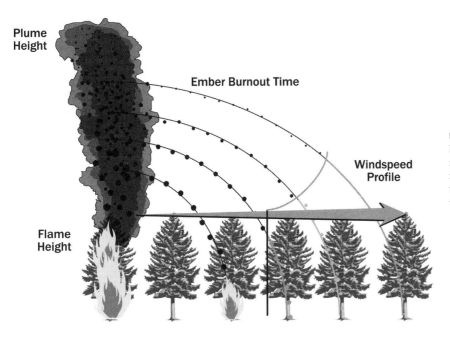

Plume Height

Ember Burnout Time

Windspeed Profile

Flame Height

FIGURE 3.12. Large embers are not lofted as high as small ones but they remain lit long enough to ignite new spot fires. Small embers are lofted great distances but often are extinguished before they land. (Redrawn from Finney 1998.)

Tree species, height, and diameter, and number of torching trees in a group affect the flame height and time of steady burning. Ember characteristics include size, shape, density, and starting height in the tree. While the embers are in flight, the wind speed and direction, and the evenness and vegetative cover of the intervening terrain influence the distance traveled. If the ember lands on a receptive fuelbed, the fine fuel moisture and temperature determine whether a spot fire is ignited. Chase (1981, 1984) adapted the spot fire distance model for use in a programmable pocket calculator and it has been incorporated in BEHAVE (Andrews 1986) and FARSITE (Finney 1998).

Fire Effects

Once a fire is ignited, it starts to affect other components of the ecosystem. Plants, animals, soil, water, and air all interact in one way or another with fire. This section introduces the physical parameters of fire behavior that affect fire severity, spotting, tree scorch height, plant mortality, biomass consumption, and microclimate. The ecological ramifications of these effects are discussed in subsequent chapters.

Fire Severity

Fire severity is the magnitude of the effect that the fire has on the environment, and is commonly applied to a number of ecosystem components. We include in this definition fire effects that occur while the fire is burning over an area as well as those effects that occur in the post-fire environment. This differs from the definition used by burn area emergency rehabilitation (BAER) teams who use *fire* severity for the immediate fire environment and *burn* severity for post-fire environment (Jain 2004).

Different patterns of fire line intensity, fire duration, and the amount of dead and live fuel affect the level of fire severity. For example, a high-intensity fire of short duration could result in the same level of severity as a low-intensity fire of long duration. Furthermore, the same fire behavior can result in different severity effects to soils and understory and overstory vegetation. A high-intensity fire that moves quickly through the crowns may kill all of the trees but have relatively little effect on the soil, whereas a low-intensity fire might leave trees untouched but smolder for days and result in severe soil heating. Precise measures of severity will vary from one ecosystem to the next, depending upon the degree of change to biotic and physical ecosystem components.

Tree Crown Scorch Height

Scorch occurs when the internal temperature of the leaves or needles of a plant are raised to lethal levels. Both the temperature and its duration are important (Davis 1959). Exposure to temperatures of about 49°C (120°F) for an hour can begin to kill tissues, whereas temperatures of approximately 54°C (130°F) can kill within minutes, and temperatures over 64°C (147°F) are considered instantaneously lethal. Van Wagner (1973) related crown scorch height to the ambient air temperature, fireline intensity, and wind speed. Under conditions of warm air, less intensity is necessary to raise the tissue temperature to the lethal level (Fig. 3.13). For a given fireline intensity, scorch height is reduced sharply as wind speed increases. Winds cool the hot plume as entrained ambient air moves through the canopy (Albini 1976). Scorch height calculations are included in BEHAVE (Andrews and Chase 1989) and in FARSITE (Finney 1998).

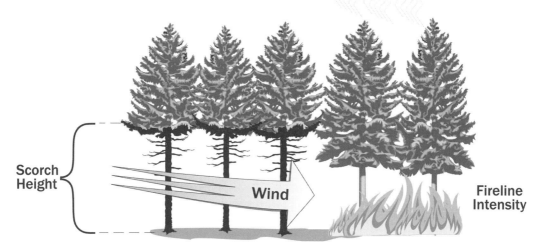

FIGURE 3.13. Scorch height is affected by fireline intensity, wind speed, and air temperature.

Plant Mortality

Mortality can occur when plants are either entirely consumed or certain tissues are raised to lethal temperatures for a sufficient duration. However, some species are able to sprout after complete canopy removal or scorch. For other species, if too much cambium or canopy is killed, the plant cannot survive. Ryan et al. (1988) studied long-term fire-caused mortality of mature Douglas-fir *(Pseudotsuga menziesii)* and found that the amount of cambium killed was the best predictor of tree mortality and that the percent of the crown scorch was a better predictor than was crown scorch height. Ryan et al. (1988) did not have flame length data available, but van Wagtendonk (1983) found that flame length was the best predictor of understory mortality of Sierra Nevada conifers. Peterson and Ryan (1986) used bark thickness, crown scorch height, and Rothermel's (1972) equation to predict cambial damage and mortality for northern Rocky Mountain species. Ryan and Reinhardt (1988) developed a model for predicting percent mortality based on percent volume crown scorch and bark thickness. Bark thickness was derived from species and diameter, while percent crown scorch was calculated from the scorch height, tree height, and crown ratio. Fire-induced mortality calculations based on their work is included in the FIRE 2 module of BEHAVE (Andrews and Chase 1989). Stephens and Finney (2002) found that mortality of Sierra Nevada mixed conifers was related to percent canopy scorched and local ground fuel consumption.

Biomass Consumption

The amount of biomass consumed by the flaming front can be calculated from the heat per unit of area released by the fire. Fire effects are often more related to the heat given off

after passage of the flaming front, however. Van Wagner (1972) provided equations for estimating the amount of the combined litter and fermentation layers that would burn based on the average moisture content of those layers. Similar results for litter and duff layers in the Sierra Nevada were found by Kauffman and Martin (1989). They found that consumption of the litter and fermentation layers was inversely related to the moisture content of the lower duff layer. Albini et al. (1995) modeled burnout of large woody fuels including the influence of smoldering duff. The rate at which these fuels burn is a balance between the rate of heat transfer to the fuel and the amount of heat required to raise the fuel to a hypothetical pyrolysis temperature. CONSUME, a computer program developed by Ottmar et al. (1993), predicts the amount of fuel consumption on logged units based on weather data, the amount and fuel moisture of fuels, and a number of other factors.

Microclimate

The effect of fire on microclimate can be determined by comparing canopy densities before and after a fire. These secondary effects are manifested through changes in the vegetation. For example, a fire that thins a stand of trees will increase wind speed and temperature at the ground surface and decrease relative humidity and fuel moisture (Fig. 3.14). A more open canopy allows more sunlight to reach the surface fuels and offers less resistance to winds above the canopy. These changes will, in turn, affect the behavior of subsequent fires. The rationale for adjusting wind speed 6.5 m (20 ft) above the canopy to midflame wind speeds is given in Albini and Baughman (1979), and adjustment factors for various fuel models are given by Rothermel (1983). Rothermel et al. (1986) explain the procedures for modeling the moisture

FIGURE 3.14. Solar radiation, temperature, and wind speeds are increased, and relative humidity is decreased after a fire has opened up a stand of trees.

content of fine dead fuels based on particle size, weather conditions, and exposure to sun and wind.

Summary

In this chapter we have covered fire as a physical process. A fire cannot occur unless there is sufficient fuel available to support combustion, weather conditions are conducive for burning, and an ignition source is present. Combustion is an oxidation process that combines hydrocarbons in the form of vegetative fuels with oxygen to produce carbon dioxide, water, and energy. This basic ecosystem process occurs in three phases: a preheating phase, a gaseous flaming phase, and a smoldering phase. Heat from combustion is transferred through conduction, convection, and radiation. Fuel characteristics determine the amount of fuel energy available and its rate of release. Fireline intensity is the rate of energy release per unit of length of fire front, and the reaction intensity is the rate of release per unit of area. Important fuel characteristics include the size of the fuels, their ability to absorb and release moisture, their compactness, and their total weight. Fuels are categorized into models that include all the various characteristics that affect fire behavior and fire effects. Strata that are included in these models are tree canopy fuels, shrub fuels, low-vegetation fuels, woody fuels, litter fuels, and ground fuels.

Fire weather is a critical determinant of fire behavior. Elements of primary importance are relative humidity, which affects fine-fuel moisture, and wind speed, which affects the rate of energy release and rate of spread. Strong wind or atmospheric instability can lead to severe fire behavior including crowning and spotting. Ignition sources include lightning, volcanoes, and humans. Air temperature and the fine-fuel moisture content determine whether an ignition results in a fire.

Once ignited, the fire begins to spread on the surface as the heat generated from a cell of fuel reaches the temperature necessary to ignite the adjacent cell. The heat source is generated by the heat content present in the fuel and is affected by the surface area to volume ratio, packing ratio, moisture content, and mineral content. Surface fire spread is accelerated by wind and steep topography. The heat sink is composed of the bulk density of the fuel of the adjacent cell, its surface area to volume ratio, and its moisture content. Crown fire spread occurs when the heat from the surface fire crosses the threshold necessary to ignite crowns. Factors affecting that threshold include the height to the live crown base, the foliar moisture content, and the crown bulk density. Torching trees can loft embers that ignite spot fires downwind from the main fire.

Fires affect vegetation by consuming complete plants or raising the temperature of live tissues to lethal levels. Consumption of fine fuels is related to the reaction intensity, whereas consumption of large fuels is influenced primarily by moisture content. Microclimate is affected indirectly through the effects of fire on vegetation.

Fire plays a dynamic role in natural ecosystems. As a physical process, it reacts to and influences other ecosystem components. The current physical and biological environments of California ensure that fire will continue to be present and that humans must learn to adapt to fire as part of that environment. In the following chapter, we will see how the physical process of fire is integrated within ecosystems as an ecological process.

References

Albini, F. A. 1976. Estimating wildfire behavior and effects. USDA For. Serv. Gen. Tech. Rep. INT-30. 74 p.

Albini, F. A. 1979. Spot fire distance from burning trees: a predictive model. USDA For. Serv. Gen. Tech. Rep. INT-56. 73 p.

Albini, F. A. 1983. Potential spotting distance from wind-driven surface fires. USDA Gen. Tech. Rep. INT-309. 27 p.

Albini, F. A., and R. G. Baughman. 1979. Estimating windspeeds for predicting fire behavior. USDA For. Serv. Res. Pap. INT-221. 12 p.

Albini, F. A., J. K. Brown, E. D. Reinhardt, and R. D. Ottmar. 1995. Calibration of a large fuel burnout model. International Journal of Wildland Fire 5(3):173–192.

Alexander, M. E. 1988. Help with making crown fire hazard assessments. P. 147–156 in W. C. Fischer, and S. F. Arno (comps.), Protecting people and homes from wildfire in the interior West. USDA For. Serv. Gen. Tech. Rep. INT-251. 156 p.

Anderson, H. E. 1969. Heat transfer and fire spread. USDA For. Serv. Res. Pap. INT-69. 20 p.

Anderson, H. E. 1982. Aids for determining fuel models for estimating fire behavior. USDA For. Serv. Gen. Tech. Rep. INT-122. 22 p.

Anderson, M. K. 1996. Tending the wilderness. Restoration Management. Notes 14(2):154–166.

Andrews, P. L. 1986. BEHAVE: fire behavior prediction and fuel modeling system—BURN subsystem. USDA For. Serv. Gen. Tech. Rep. INT-194. 130 p.

Andrews, P. L., and C. H. Chase. 1989. BEHAVE: fire behavior prediction and fuel modeling system—BURN subsystem, Part 2. USDA For. Serv. Gen. Tech. Rep. INT-260. 93 p.

Arnold, R. K. 1964. Project skyfire lightning research. Proceedings of the Annual Tall Timbers Fire Ecology Conference 3:121–130.

Brown, J. K. 1974. Handbook for inventorying downed woody material. USDA For. Serv. Gen. Tech. Rep. INT-16. 24 p.

Brown, J. K., R. D. Oberhue, and C. M. Johnston. 1982. Handbook for inventorying surface fuels and biomass in the interior West. USDA For. Serv. Gen. Tech. Rep. INT-129. 48 p.

Burgan, R. E. 1979. Fire danger/fire behavior computations with the Texas Instruments TI-59 calculator: user's manual. USDA For. Serv. Gen. Tech. Rep. INT-61. 25 p.

Burgan, R. E., and R. C. Rothermel. 1984. BEHAVE: fire behavior prediction and fuel modeling system—FUEL subsystem. USDA For. Serv. Gen. Tech. Rep. INT-167. 126 p.

Byram, G. M. 1959. Combustion of forest fuels. P. 61–89 in K. P. Davis, Forest fire control and use. McGraw-Hill, New York. 584 p.

Chase, C. H. 1981. Spot fire distance equations for pocket calculators. USDA For. Serv. Res. Note INT-310. 21 p.

Chase, C. H. 1984. Spot fire distance from wind-driven fires—extensions of equations for pocket calculators. USDA For. Serv. Res. Note INT-346. 21 p.

Davis, K. P. 1959. Forest fire control and use. McGraw-Hill, New York. 584 p.

Deeming, J. E., R. E. Burgan, and J. D. Cohn. 1977. The National Fire Danger Rating System—1978. USDA For. Serv. Gen. Tech. Rep. INT-39. 63 p.

Finney, M. A. 1998. FARSITE: fire area simulator-model development and evaluation. USDA For. Serv. Res. Rep. RMRS-RP-4. 47 p.

Fons, W. 1946. Analysis of fire spread in light forest fuels. Journal of Agriculture Research 7(3):93–121.

Frandsen, W. H. 1971. Fire spread through porous fuels from the conservation of energy. Combustion and Flame 16:9–16.

Fuquay, D. M. 1982. Cloud-to-ground lightning in summer thunderstorms. Journal of Geophysical Research 87:7131–7140.

Jain, T. B. 2004. Tongue-tied. Wildfire Magazine, July–August, 2004.

Kauffman, J. B., and R. E. Martin. 1989. Fire behavior, fuel consumption, and forest floor changes following prescribed understory fires in Sierra Nevada mixed-conifer forests. Canadian Journal of Forest Research 19:455–462.

Lancaster, J. W. 1970. Timelag useful in fire danger rating. Fire Control Notes 31(3):6–8.

Latham, D. J., and J. A. Schlieter. 1989. Ignition probabilities of wildland fuels based on simulated lightning discharges. USDA For. Serv. Res. Pap. INT-411. 16 p.

Nelson, R. M. 1993. Byram's energy criterion for wildland fires: units and equations. USDA For. Serv. Res. Note INT-415. 5 p.

Ottmar, R. D., M. F. Burns, J. N. Hall, and A. D. Hanson. 1993. CONSUME users guide. USDA For. Serv. Gen. Tech. Rep. PNW-GTR-304. 17 p.

Peterson, D. L., and K. C. Ryan. 1986. Modeling postfire conifer mortality for long-range planning. Environmental Management 10(6):797–808.

Rothermel, R. C. 1972. A mathematical model for fire spread predictions in wildland fuels. USDA For. Serv. Res. Pap. INT-115. 40 p.

Rothermel, R. C. 1983. How to predict the spread and intensity of forest fires. USDA For. Serv. Gen. Tech. Rep. INT-143. 161 p.

Rothermel, R. C. 1991. Predicting behavior and size of crown fires in the northern Rocky Mountains. USDA For. Serv. Res. Pap. INT-438. 46 p.

Rothermel, R. C., and J. E. Deeming. 1980. Measuring and interpreting fire behavior for correlation with fire effects. USDA For. Serv. Gen Tech. Rep. INT-93. 4 p.

Rothermel, R. C., R. A. Wilson, G. A. Morris, and S. S. Sackett. 1986. Modeling moisture content of fine dead wildland fuels input to the BEHAVE fire prediction system. USDA For. Serv. Res. Pap. INT-359. 61 p.

Ryan, K. C., D. L. Peterson, and E. D. Reinhardt. 1988. Modeling long-term fire-caused mortality of Douglas-fir. Forest Science 34:190–199.

Ryan, K. C., and E. D. Reinhardt. 1988. Predicting post-fire mortality of seven western conifers. Canadian Journal of Forest Research. 18:1291– 1297.

Sandberg, D. V., R. D. Ottmar, and G. H. Cushon. 2001. Characterizing fuels in the 21st century. International Journal of Wildland Fire. 10 (3 and 4): 381–387.

Schroeder, M. J., and C. C. Buck. 1970. Fire weather . . . a guide for application of meteorological information to forest fire control operations. USDA For. Serv. Agric. Handbook 360. 229 p.

Scott, J. H. 1999. NEXUS: a spread sheet based crown fire hazard assessment system. Fire Management Notes 59(2): 20–24.

Stephens, S. L., and M A. Finney. 2002. Prescribed fire mortality of Sierra Nevada mixed conifer tree species: effects of crown damage and forest floor consumption. Forest Ecology and Management 162:261–271.

Sussott, R. A., and R. E. Burgan. 1986. Fire behavior computations with the Hewlett-Packard HP-71B calculator. USDA For. Serv. Gen. Tech. Rep. INT-202. 80 p.

Swetnam, T. W. 1993. Fire history and climate change in giant sequoia groves. Science 292(5):885–889.

Vale, T. R. 1998. The myth of the humanized landscape: an example from Yosemite National Park. Nat. Areas J. 18:231–236.

Van Wagner, C. E. 1972. Duff consumption by fire in eastern pine stands. Canadian Journal of Forest Research 2(34):34–39.

Van Wagner, C. E. 1973. Height of crown scorch in forest fires. Canadian Journal of Forest Research 3(3):373–378.

Van Wagner, C. E. 1977. Conditions for the start and spread of crownfire. Canadian Journal of Forest Research 7(1):23–34.

Van Wagner, C. E. 1993. Prediction of crown fire behavior in two stands of jack pine. Canadian Journal of Forest Research 18:818–820.

van Wagtendonk, J. W. 1983. Prescribed fire effects on forest understory mortality. Proc. 7th Conf. Fire and Forest Meteorology. 7:136–138.

van Wagtendonk, J. W. 1994. Spatial patterns of lightning strikes and fires in Yosemite National Park. Proc. 12th Conf. Fire and Forest Meteorology 12:223–231.

CHAPTER 4

Fire as an Ecological Process

NEIL G. SUGIHARA, JAN W. VAN WAGTENDONK, AND JOANN
FITES-KAUFMAN

> Removing fire from . . . ecosystems would be among the greatest
> upsets in the environmental system that man could impose—
> possibly among the most severe stresses since the evolution of
> the fire-dependent biota evolved. I cannot predict the outcome,
> but a fundamental reordering of the relationships between all
> plants and animals and their environments would occur. Many
> species could be lost through extinction.
>
> M.L. HEINSELMAN, 1981

Fire is an integral part of California ecosystems; for without fire, few of the state's native ecosystems, habitats, or even species, would persist as we know them today. Fire's dynamic nature and great complexity are amplified by the state's diverse topography, climate, and vegetation. For millennia, California ecosystems have developed in tandem with fire. Long-term alterations of fire patterns have occurred with climatic changes and with interactions with humans. In the past two centuries, the pace of human-induced alteration has accelerated, resulting in a number of changes in species and ecosystems. Many of these species and ecosystem changes occurred previously, some are currently occurring, and others are yet to manifest themselves. To understand the importance of the changing ecological role of fire, it is necessary to understand fire as an ecosystem process.

Fire can be viewed within two distinct time frames: individual fires and repeated patterns of fire occurrence. When an individual fire is seen as a discrete event, its physical characteristics are important to understanding how fire functions as an ecosystem process. Individual fires range from simple to extremely complex in their behavior, size, pattern of burning, and ecosystem effects. Individual fires in a limited area affect fuel dynamics, the physical attributes of the ecosystem, and the biological systems at the individual, species, population, and community levels. These direct influences are discussed in detail in subsequent chapters in Part I of this text.

Landscapes have repeated patterns of fire occurrence, fire magnitude, and fire type that vary over space and time. When fire is considered over centuries or millennia and on large landscapes, this repeated pattern of fire occurrence and its properties affect ecosystem function. Compounding the influences of individual fires, existing patterns greatly influence the dynamics of species composition, vegetation structure, and subsequent fire patterns. While recognizing that the patterns of fire occurrence over large expanses of space and long periods of time are extremely complex, they can be distilled into useful summaries known as *fire regimes*.

Fire is an integral part of ecosystems, and there is a continuous feedback of fire, fuels, and vegetation within the ecosystem. Fire interacts with, and is affected by, species composition, vegetation structure, fuel moisture, air temperature, biomass, and many other ecosystem components and processes over several scales of time and space. These ecosystem components are so interdependent that changes to one, including fire, often result in significant changes to others. This dynamic view of ecosystems is the key to understanding fire as an ecosystem process.

In this chapter we explore fire as a dynamic ecosystem process by first examining fire in the context of general ecological theory, then discussing the concept of fire regimes, and finally by developing and applying a new framework for classifying fire regimes that better allows us to understand the patterns of fire as processes within ecosystems. This fire regime framework will be used in the bioregional chapters that follow in Part II.

Fire in the Context of Ecological Theory

As ecological theory has evolved, so has the manner in which fire along with climate, insects, fungi, and weather are considered in that theory. We first look at succession theory and then proceed through ecosystem, disturbance, and hierarchical theory. Finally we present our view of fire as an ecological process.

Succession Theory

Classical succession is an ecological concept that was developed and championed by Clements (1916) in the early 1900s. Since it was first published, his framework for viewing plant communities as complex entities that develop over time has

FIGURE 4.1. Clements viewed succession as a stepwise, predictable, directional process. As time passes, bare ground eventually becomes covered with a mature climax vegetation.

Bare Ground → Grassland → Shrub → Young Forest → Mature Forest → Climax

TIME ▶

served as a basis from which successional ecology theory has developed. Clements (1936) defined *succession* as a predictable, directional, and stepwise progression of plant assemblages that culminates in a self-perpetuating *climax* community controlled by climate. For example, bare ground might first be colonized by grasses, followed by shrubs, and then by a young forest, and finally be covered by a mature forest (Fig. 4.1). According to Clements, the climatic climax is stable, complex, self-perpetuating, and considered to be the adult version of the "complex organism" or plant community.

Clements (1916) considered bare areas created by lightning fires as one of the natural sources for the initiation of succession. He expressed the view that lightning fires were numerous, and often very destructive, in regions with frequent dry thunderstorms. In fact, the early twentieth century witnessed some of the most destructive wildland fires known in this country. Clements considered areas where such fires maintained vegetation that differed from the climatic climax to be *subclimax*, because they were continually reset to seral plant assemblages by recurrent fire before they reached climax conditions. He cited chaparral in California and lodgepole pine *(Pinus contorta* ssp. *murrayana)* in Colorado as examples of fire subclimaxes (Clements 1916). Fire was viewed as a retrogressive process that sets back the directional, stepwise progression of succession toward the stable climactic climax. Clements (1936) refined his ideas about the nature and structure of the climax and developed a complex terminology for classifying units of vegetation. Fire subclimaxes were still part of this complex system, and he added California's Monterey pine *(Pinus radiata)*, Bishop pine *(Pinus muricata)*, and knobcone pine *(Pinus attenuata)* as examples. He used the term *disclimax* for communities that had been degraded by human activities such as logging, grazing, and burning, but seemed to not apply the term to natural fires (Clements 1936).

Gleason (1917) reacted to Clements' theory by proposing the individualistic concept of the plant association. He argued that succession was not inherently directional, but was the result of random immigration of species into a variable environment. As the environment changes, the assemblage of associated species changes based on individual attributes of each species. As an example, he cited the gradual replacement of grasslands by California oak *(Quercus spp.)* forests as one ascends the foothills and precipitation increases (Fig 4.2). Similarly, Gleason (1917) argued that entirely different plant associations might occupy physiographically and climatically identical environments. For instance, the alpine areas of the Sierra Nevada have essentially the same environment as in the Andes, but their floras are entirely different. Although Gleason (1926) felt that the environment had a strong influence on plant community development, he referred to fire as an unnatural disturbance that limited the duration of the original vegetation.

Daubenmire (1947) was one of the first ecologists to recognize fire as an ecological factor rather than as an allogenic factor. With regard to succession, however, he followed the same terminology as Clements (1916) but considered fire to be one of five different climaxes. *Primary* climaxes included climatic, edaphic, and topographic climaxes, whereas fire and zootic climaxes were termed *secondary* climaxes (Daubenmire 1968). Specific examples included the forests of the Sierra Nevada where episodic fires replaced fire-sensitive species with fire-tolerant pines. Daubenmire (1968) felt that the fire climax could appropriately be called a disclimax because its maintenance depended on continued disturbance.

Whittaker (1953) examined both the organismic (Clements 1916) and individualistic (Gleason 1926) concepts of the climax community and proposed an alternative approach that views the climax as a pattern of vegetation resulting from environmental variables. He postulated that: (1) the climax is a steady state of community productivity, structure, and population, with a dynamic balance determined in relationship to its site; (2) the balance among plant populations shifts with changes in the environment; and (3) the climax composition is determined by all factors of the mature ecosystem. A major

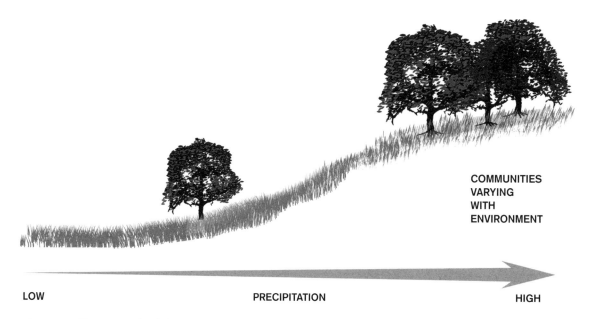

COMMUNITIES
VARYING
WITH
ENVIRONMENT

LOW   PRECIPITATION   HIGH

FIGURE 4.2. Gleason considered plant communities to be distributed according to environmental gradients, such as grasses being gradually replaced by oaks as precipitation increases with elevation.

contribution that Whittaker (1967) made to ecological theory was his use of gradient analysis to delineate how plant assemblages change in space and time. Whittaker (1953) considered periodic fire to be one of the environmental factors to which some climaxes are adapted. In the absence of fire, the climax plant populations might develop into something entirely different, but that development might never occur. A key point he makes is that burning may cause population fluctuations that make it difficult to distinguish between fire as an environmental factor and fire as a disturbance introduced from outside the ecosystem. For example, in climates between forests and deserts, fire could shift the balance among woodlands, shrublands, and grasslands (Whittaker 1971).

Ecosystem Theory

Tansley (1935) refuted the organism concept of a plant community put forward by Clements (1916) and proposed that succession in a community is a trajectory of a dynamic system with many possible equilibria. That is, depending on the environment, a plant community could develop in one of many different directions and reach a point of equilibrium regardless of which trajectory was followed. He also introduced the term *ecosystem* to describe the entire system to include not only the biotic components but also the abiotic factors that make up the environment. In the ecosystem, these components and factors are in a dynamic equilibrium. Succession leads to a relatively stable phase termed the *climatic climax*. He recognized other climaxes determined by factors such as soil, grazing, and fire. Tansley (1935) considered vegetation that was subjected to constantly recurring fire to be a fire climax, but thought that catastrophic fire was destructive and external to the system.

Odum (1959) defined ecology as the study of structure and function of ecosystems and emphasized that the ecosystem

approach had universal applicability. He related the ecosystem concepts of nutrient and energy flow to evolutionary ecological growth and adaptation (Odum 1969). Fire was seen as an important ecological factor in many terrestrial ecosystems, as both a limiting and as a regulatory factor (Odum 1963). He cited examples of fire consuming accumulated undecayed plant material and applying selective pressure favoring the survival and growth of some species at the expense of others.

A systems approach was advocated by Schultz (1968), applying the concepts of energy dissipation to ecosystem function. He described ecosystems as open systems with material being both imported and exported. Rather than reaching an equilibrium, an open system attains a steady state with minimum loss of energy. Fire is considered a negative feedback mechanism that prevents the complete destruction of natural ecosystems by returning some of the energy to the system (Schultz 1968).

Disturbance Theory

Traditional theories of natural disturbance considered that disturbance must be a major catastrophic event and that it must originate in the physical environment (Agee 1993). Much discussion has centered on these points and various definitions and thresholds have been applied to distinguish disturbances from processes. Watt (1947) introduced the concept that plant communities were composed of patches in various stages of development that were dynamic in time and space. The patches were initiated by some form of disturbance, be it the death of a single tree or larger factors such as storms, drought, epidemics, or fires. Other than mentioning size differences, he did not distinguish among factors that were internal or external to an ecosystem. Similarly, White (1979) urged that the concept of disturbance not be limited to large catastrophic events that originate from within the physical environment but also include external factors. White and Pickett (1985) define disturbance as "any relatively discrete event in time that disrupts ecosystem, community, or population structure and changes resources, substrate availability, or the physical environment." They included disasters and catastrophes as subsets of disturbance. Fire was specified as a source of natural disturbance. Agee (1993) proposed that disturbance comprises a gradient that ranges from minor to major; he did not differentiate between internal and external sources. He did distinguish between fires of natural origin and fires set by Native Americans or European Americans, calling the former *natural disturbances*.

Walker and Willig (1999) follow the terminology of White and Pickett (1985) and treat fire as a natural disturbance. They go on to state that disturbances that originate inside the system of interest are considered to be endogenous. Fire is driven by an interplay of *exogenous* factors from outside of the system such as climate and topography and *endogenous* factors such as soil and biota. In this sense, Walker and Willig (1999) consider fire to be an inherent ecological process. They characterize disturbances by their frequency, size, and magnitude. These characteristics are used for grouping disturbances into disturbance regimes.

Turner and Dale (1998) state that large, infrequent disturbances are difficult to define because they occur accoss a continuum of time and space. One definition they propose is that disturbances should have statistical distributions of extent, intensity, or duration greater than two standard deviations (SDs) of the mean for the period and area of interest. Romme et al. (1998) distinguish large, infrequent disturbances from small, frequent ones by a response threshold—when the force of the disturbance exceeds the capacity of internal mechanisms to resist disturbance or where new means of recovery become involved. For example, an area that burns with a very high-severity fire as a result of unnaturally heavy accumulations of fuels would be qualitatively different from an area that burns with frequent, low-severity fires. However, not all high-severity fires cross the response threshold. Romme et al. (1998) cite the example of jack pine *(Pinus banksiana)*, an ecological equivalent of lodgepole pine, that re-establishes itself after stand-replacing fires, regardless of size, through the dispersal of seed throughout the area from serotinous cones. These criteria (Turner and Dale 1998, Romme et al. 1998) form a basis for separating endogenous fires from those arising from outside the environment of the ecosystem.

Hierarchical Theory

O'Neill et al. (1986) proposed a hierarchical concept of the ecosystem to reconcile the species-community and process-function schools of thought. The authors define the ecosystem as being composed of plants, animals, incorporated abiotic components, and the environment. In their view, the ecosystem is a dual organization determined by structural constraints on organisms and functional constraints on

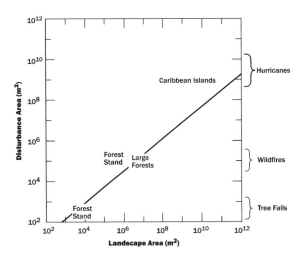

FIGURE 4.3. Relative size of disturbance area and landscape units. Landscapes above the diagonal line are in disequilibrium because they are smaller than the characteristic perturbations. (Redrawn from Shugart and West 1981.)

processes. These dual hierarchies have both temporal and spatial components.

Disturbances are termed *perturbations* and are associated with a particular temporal and spatial scale. O'Neill et al. (1986) describe fire as a perturbation that ensures landscape diversity and preserves seed sources for recovery from any major disturbance. They state that viewing ecosystems on the arbitrary scale of the forest stand results in seeing fire as a catastrophic disturbance. If, however, fire is viewed at the scale appropriate to the frequency of occurrence, it can be seen as an essential ecosystem process that retains the spatial diversity of the landscape and permits reaching a dynamic equilibrium after disturbance. O'Neill et al. (1986) consider a perturbation to be *incorporated* if the ecosystem structure exerts control over some aspect of the abiotic environment that is uncontrolled at a lower level of organization.

Systems that are large relative to their perturbations maintain a relatively constant structure (O'Neill et al. 1986). For example, ponderosa pine *(Pinus ponderosa)* forests are usually larger than the fires that burn within them; therefore the perturbation is incorporated in the sense that the fires do not threaten the survival of the ecosystem but are in fact necessary to perpetuate the spatial diversity of the landscape. This concept is illustrated in Figure 4.3 (Shugart and West 1981). Above the diagonal line are disequilibrium systems that are the same size or smaller than their characteristic perturbations. Wildland fires would be considered a perturbation in forest stands but would be an incorporated process in large forests.

Pickett et al. (1989) linked the hierarchical organization of ecosystem components with the concept of disturbance. They state that any persistent ecological object such as a tree will have a minimal structure that permits its persistence, and that disturbance is a change in that structure caused by a factor external to the level of interest. Disturbance, then, is identified with specific ecological levels, or hierarchies, of the organization (Pickett et al. 1989). In this view, periodic fire perpetuates a variety of structures that allow the ecosystem to persist.

Our View of Fire

Each of the aforementioned views is based on careful observation and carry something of the truth. In developing our view of fire, we synthesize and build on previous theory. We consider fire to be an incorporated ecological process rather than a disturbance. In its natural role, fire is not a disturbance that impacts ecosystems; rather it is an ecological process that is as much a part of the environment as precipitation, wind, flooding, soil development, erosion, predation, herbivory, carbon and nutrient cycling, and energy flow. Fire resets vegetation trajectories, sets up and maintains a dynamic mosaic of different vegetation structures and compositions, and reduces fuel accumulations. Humans have often disrupted these processes, and the result can be that fire behavior and effects are outside of their range of natural variation. At that point, fire is considered an exogenous disturbance factor.

Fire Regimes

It is relatively simple to understand the influence of a single fire on specific ecosystem properties, but the importance of fire as an ecosystem process becomes greatly amplified by the complex pattern of fire effects over long time periods, multiple fire events, and numerous ecosystem properties. To synthesize these patterns of fire occurrence, ecologists use the concept of *fire regimes*. Fire regimes are a convenient and useful way to classify, describe, and categorize the pattern of fire occurrence for scientific and management purposes. Like any classification, a fire regime classification necessarily simplifies complex patterns. Although fire regimes are typically assigned to ecosystems defined by either land areas or vegetation types, or to some combination of area and vegetation, they often vary greatly within a vegetation type and over time on the same piece of land.

Previous Fire Regime Descriptions

Fire regime classification systems have been based on a very small number of attributes that could be described and used to explain basic patterns of ecosystem change. The classifications offer a variety of information ranging from simple, single-attribute descriptions (e.g., mean fire return interval) to a few attributes, but usually have not provided descriptions of the patterns of fire over time and space, and by magnitude. Recent fire history studies have focused on the importance of multi-scaled spatial and temporal variation of fire. As our knowledge of ecosystems and complex processes such as fire grows, our need for more sophisticated descriptive tools such as fire regime classifications expands. It is important to recognize that any classification system is an oversimplification of some portion of nature for the convenience of humans, and there is no single "complete" or "right" way to describe fire regimes. The appropriate system to use for classification of fire regimes depends on the character of the ecosystems, the fire regimes, and the intended use of that system.

Kilgore (1981) observed that fire is known to be important in so many ecosystems that it is becoming less meaningful to merely refer to ecosystems as fire dependent or fire independent. Instead, he suggests that it is more appropriate to speak of ecosystems with varying fire regimes that are made up of such factors as fire frequency and intensity (Sando 1978, Heinselman 1981), season (Gill 1975), pattern (Keeley 1977), and depth of burn (Methven 1978).

Heinselman (1981) defined a fire regime as a summary of the fire history that characterizes an ecosystem. He distinguished seven fire regimes based on: (1) fire type and intensity (crown fires or severe surface fires vs. light surface fires), (2) size (area) of typical ecologically significant fires, and (3) frequency or return intervals typical for specific land units. Although these fire regime types described the patterns that he observed in the midwestern United States, this system has served as the basis for fire regime classification throughout the western United States. The classification was not intended to imply mutually exclusive or exhaustive categories; rather it was intended to provide a tool for discussing general fire-occurrence patterns. Heinselman (1981) states, "The purpose here is not to set up a precise classification but to make it possible to discuss important differences in the way fire influences ecosystems." His fire regimes are defined in Box 4.1.

Heinselman (1981) described multiple fire regimes that occur when there are several types of fires in a single ecosystem, and each type can be described with its own fire regime. This occurs under the following three conditions: (1) the ecosystem can have more than one type of fire, (2) the types of fires occur under different sets of conditions, and (3) the conditions allow the different types of fires to occur at different frequencies. Multiple fire regimes occur most commonly in vegetation types that have multiple fuel layers that can carry a fire. Heinselman (1981) described red pine (*Pinus resinosa*) forests in the lake states to have both a frequent light surface fire regime carried in the herbaceous layer and a regime of much-less-frequent higher-intensity fire carried in the forests canopy. Many California ecosystems including some Douglas-fir (*Pseudotsuga menziesii* var. *menziesii*), red fir (*Abies magnifica* var. *magnifica*), and mixed conifer forest burn with both surface and crown fires that occur at different frequencies and under different weather conditions and can be termed *multiple fire regimes* (Heinselman 1981).

After applying the Heinselman (1981) fire regimes, designed for northern forests, to the forests and scrublands of the western United States, Kilgore (1981) made a number of observations. There are complex relationships between fire and other attributes of the ecosystem on the variable topography of the western states. Fire acts with different frequencies and intensities, varying with the vegetation, topography, and climate that determine the coincidence of ignitions and burning conditions. Vegetation composition and structure depend on climate, fire frequency, and fire intensity, whereas fire frequency and intensity in turn depend on vegetation structure, topography, and climate. Kilgore (1981) concluded that because of almost annual coincidence of ignitions with suitable burning conditions, western forests, such as some of those found in the Sierra Nevada, have frequent fires of low intensity. Although ignitions are as frequent in many Rocky Mountain forests, they do not coincide as often with dry fuel conditions. These Rocky Mountain forests tend to have less frequent, high-intensity crown fires.

Hardy et al. (2001) modified Hienselman's (1981) six original regimes by replacing types of fire with levels of fire severity. They grouped regimes into three levels of frequency and three levels of severity (Box 4.2). These groups are currently being used to determine natural fire regime condition classes across the landscape (Hann and Bunnell 2001). Departures from natural fire regime conditions form the basis for fire- and fuel-management programs.

Vegetation types can be combined into fire regime groups based on the response of dominant plant species to fire, potential frequency of fire, and similarity in post-fire succession. Davis et al. (1980) defined fire regime groups in Montana, as did Bradley et al. (1992) for eastern Idaho and western Wyoming. Agee (1993) considers fire regime groups to be a useful way to catalog fire and ecological information when a management system is based on similar vegetation units, such as habitat types; but the simplicity of the system begins to bog down when one considers the literally hundreds of fire groups, or vegetation communities, across the western United States. Agee (1993) considers fire regime groups to be best applied on a local basis as in the Pacific Northwest.

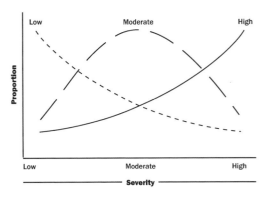

FIGURE 4.4. Variation in fire severity within a general fire regime type (redrawn from Agee 1993). Within a single fire regime type, there could be a combination of low-, moderate-, and high-severity fires.

Agee (1993) also describes another system of fire regime classification based on the severity of fire effects on dominant tree species for forests of the Pacific Northwest. To display the variability in fire that occurs within or between fires on a site, he used a set of distribution curves for illustrating fire severity patterns. The low, moderate, and high fire severity types are presented as distributions composed of different proportions of severity levels (Fig. 4.4). This allows for a range of severity variability within a regime type. The following section greatly expands on Agee's (1993) treatment of conceptual distributions to include seven fire regime attributes.

A New Framework for Defining Fire Regimes

Fire regimes distill useful information about continuous variation of fire occurrence patterns into simple categories that help us describe predominant patterns in fire and its effects on ecosystems. As land management objectives evolve, there is a need to re-evaluate what constitutes useful information. Societal objectives for land management have shifted in the past few decades, emphasizing ecosystem and biological values over consumptive uses. The amount and detail of information needed to manage fire to meet these new objectives are greater than ever before. Heinselman (1981) used various combinations of fire severity, frequency, and type to define fire regimes. Although this system could be refined to meet new management information needs, we have chosen to develop a new framework that includes and expands on his fire regime attributes.

This new framework describes fire regimes using three groups of seven attributes of fire patterns (Box 4.3). Although there are many other attributes that could be used, these seven include those that are most commonly considered to be important to ecosystem function.

Attributes are grouped into temporal, spatial, and magnitude variables. Temporal attributes include *seasonality* and *fire return interval*. Spatial attributes include *fire size* and *spatial complexity* of the fires. Magnitude attributes include *fireline intensity*, *fire severity*, and *fire type*.

Fire regimes are depicted using a set of conceptual distribution curves similar to those presented by Agee (1993) for fire severity. For each attribute, there might be several curves with different shapes representing the variability in the distribution of that attribute within different ecosystem types. A fire regime for a particular ecosystem type includes distributions for all seven attributes representing the pattern of variability within that ecosystem.

Figure 4.5 is an example of fire regime distribution curves for fire return interval. The x-axis of each distribution curve represents the range of values for fire return intervals in three different ecosystem types. The y-axis always represents the proportion of the burned area with different return interval distributions. The sum of the area underneath each curve is equal to unity and accounts for all of the area that actually burns with that regime type. The three distribution types that are illustrated are short, medium, and long, with each representing a range of short to long, but in different proportions.

The conceptual distribution curves allow us to illustrate the features of a fire regime that will affect a specific ecosystem function. For example, if a closed-cone conifer is the only species that distinguishes an ecosystem from the surrounding chaparral ecosystem, the persistence of that closed-cone conifer is key to the persistence of the ecosystem. In this case, the distribution of fire return intervals in the two ecosystems may be largely the same, differing only in the presence or absence of the low-frequency events at the extremes of the range of variability (distribution tails) (Fig. 4.6). If the fire return interval extends outside of the range of time (either

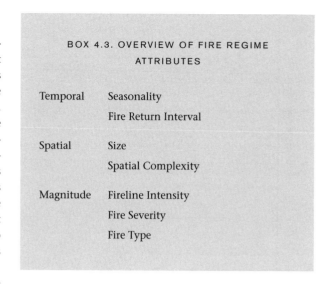

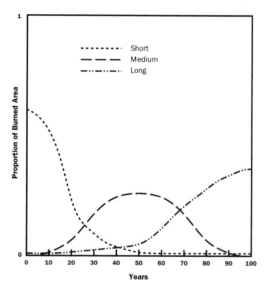

FIGURE 4.5. Example fire regime distribution curve for fire return interval. For short-return interval regimes, the majority of the burned area has intervals of only a few years. Medium-return interval regimes range from a few years to several but, the majority of the burned area has intervals in the middle range. Similarly, long fire-return interval regimes have predominantly long intervals.

shorter or longer) when the closed-cone conifer can produce seed, then there is a predicted conversion to the chaparral ecosystem type. For this example, the fire-return interval distributions for the two ecosystems have the same general shape, differing only in the absence of the tails of the distribution curve in the conifer type. The tails of the distribution are outside of the range of variability for length of fire-return interval within which the conifers can be sustained.

Information for defining and refining the distributions can be obtained using a number of data sources including tree rings with fire scars, charcoal deposits in sediment cores, fire records, and stand-age distributions. These methods require intensive studies and, when used alone, will typically yield

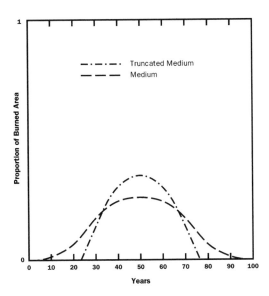

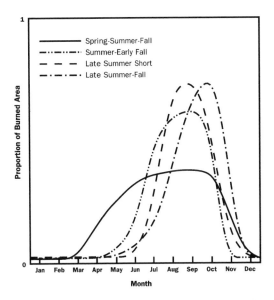

FIGURE 4.6. Example of fire regime distribution curves for fire-return interval for a closed-cone conifer ecosystem and a surrounding chaparral ecosystem. The curves are the same except for the absence of tails for the closed-cone conifer.

FIGURE 4.7. Fire regime distributions for seasonality. Four different distributions are displayed for fire seasons ranging from spring to fall.

only parts of the overall fire regime. Additional information can be obtained through a number of sources that are not currently used in development of fire regime descriptions. The following information should be useful in developing conceptual fire regime attribute distributions for specific ecosystems: (1) geographic location and topography; (2) plant species life history characteristics and fire adaptations; (3) spatial and temporal patterns of fuel quantity, structure, and flammability; and (4) climate and weather patterns.

Although there may be no case where we have all of the data needed to know the actual distributions of all of the fire regime attributes for any one ecosystem, we can conceptually describe the distributions of these attributes for most ecosystems. These descriptions are based on characteristics of the physical environment and knowledge of the fire relationships of the plant species composing the vegetation types, as well as other vegetation types that interface with it on the landscape. There are different combinations of fire regime attributes that are biologically important and influence stand structure and density, species composition, and distribution and stability of vegetation types with changing fire regimes. Defining the general patterns of fire regimes for ecosystems allows us to gain insight into fire's role in ecosystems. We now examine each group of fire regimes attributes and display their conceptual distribution curves.

Temporal Fire Regime Attributes

The temporal attributes of fire regimes are described in two ways: seasonality and fire return interval. *Seasonality* is a description of *when* fires occur during the year; *fire return interval* describes *how often* fires occur over several years. The patterns that are described here for ecosystems are not static on

landscapes and can migrate or change in response to changing climate, fuel, continuity, ignition, or species composition. When temporal fire patterns change, there is commonly a change in vegetation type or the distribution of vegetation types.

SEASONALITY

Although California in general can be described as having warm, dry summers and cool, moist winters, season alone does not determine when ecosystems are likely to burn. Other factors, including elevation, coastal influences, topography, characteristics of the vegetation, ignition sources, and seasonal weather patterns, also influence the fire season. Season of burning is especially important biologically because many California ecosystems include species that are only adapted to burning during a fairly limited part of the year. Figure 4.7 illustrates the four conceptual seasonality patterns that occur in California ecosystems with proportion of the burned area on the y-axis and the annual calendar on the x-axis.

Spring–Summer–Fall Fire Season The longest fire season type that occurs in California has fire burning well distributed from May to November. It occurs in ecosystems with early spring warming and drying and in which fire is primarily carried in rapidly curing herbaceous layer fuels. The spring–summer–fall fire season type occurs in low elevations and deserts that cure early in the spring and persists until wetting rains occur in the late fall. This fire season type is characteristic of many low-elevation grasslands and oak woodlands, and the Mojave, Colorado, and Sonoran deserts.

Summer–Fall Fire Season This is the characteristic fire season type for many of the lower- and middle-elevation, montane conifer forests of California such as mixed conifer and ponderosa pine forests. Fires are primarily carried in herbaceous, duff, and needle layers. Most of the area burns from July to October.

Late Summer, Short Fire Season This is the shortest fire season type that occurs in California. It is characteristic of alpine and subalpine ecosystems where there is a very short period late in the summer when the vegetation is dry enough to burn. The climate excludes fire for the remainder of the year. Although lightning is abundant, fuels are mostly sparse and discontinuous, resulting in few fires.

Late Summer–Fall Fire Season This is the characteristic fire season type for central and south coastal California chaparral. Fire occurrence and size are greatly influenced by Santa Ana and north winds that most commonly occur in the late summer and early fall. This is the end of the dry season and live fuel moisture levels are lowest at this time of year. Most of the area that burns does so from September to early November.

FIRE-RETURN INTERVAL

Fire-return interval is the length of time between fires on a particular area of land. Fire rotation (Heinselman 1973) and fire cycle (Van Wagner 1978) are related concepts that display the average time required for fire to burn over an area equivalent to the total area of an ecosystem. Fire-return interval distributions illustrate the range and pattern of values that are characteristic of an ecosystem and are critical in determining the mixture of species that will persist as the vegetation of a given area. A species cannot survive if fire is too frequent, too early, or too infrequent to allow that species to complete its life cycle (Hendrickson 1991). For example, survival of a nonsprouting species in a given area may be threatened by fires that occur before there has been time for a seed pool to accumulate or after the plant's longevity has been exceeded and the store of seed is lost (Bond and vanWilgen 1996). The significance of fire-return interval in determining the species composition or vegetation structure through time is illustrated when fire burns often enough to prevent Oregon white oak *(Quercus garryana)* woodlands from changing to a Douglas-fir forest, which can tolerate a wider range of return intervals (Sugihara and Reed 1987). Figure 4.8 illustrates six conceptual fire-return interval patterns occurring in California ecosystems with proportion of the burned area on the y-axis and the fire-return interval on the x-axis.

Truncated Short Fire-Return Interval All of the area that burns does so with short fire-return intervals. Long intervals allow the establishment and growth of species that will convert these ecosystems to another type. Many oak woodlands, montane meadows, grasslands, and other Native American–maintained ecosystems are typical of this fire-return interval pattern.

Short Fire-Return Interval Most of the area burns at short fire-return intervals, but there is a wide range including a

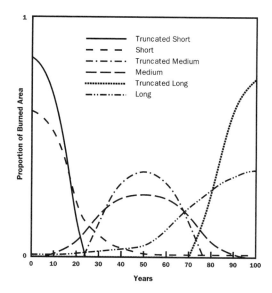

FIGURE 4.8. Fire regime distributions for fire return interval. Six different distribution curves describe the variety of possible return interval regimes.

small proportion of longer intervals. Ponderosa pine forests typify this pattern with the short intervals maintaining the open nature of the stand and ponderosa pine as the dominant species. The occasional low-probability long intervals promote the establishment of a mixture of canopy species but do not prevent ponderosa pine from maintaining dominance as long as short intervals are typical.

Truncated Medium Fire-Return Interval The area that burns does so within a range of fire-return intervals that has both upper and lower limits that are defined by the life histories of characteristic species. Intervals outside of that range result in conversion to another ecosystem. This is a variation of the previous pattern with upper and lower boundaries on the length of fire-return intervals. Many of the closed-cone pine and cypresses *(Cupressus* spp.) are examples of ecosystems in which fires must occur within a specific range of intervals for the characteristic species to regenerate. If fires are too close or too far apart in time, the conifers cannot persist.

Medium Fire-Return Interval Most of the area burns at medium-return intervals, but occasional strong deviation will not usually facilitate conversion to another ecosystem type. This set of fire-return interval distributions includes a variety of means, ranges, and shapes. Although the distribution on Figure 4.8 shows a symmetrical shape, this is not always the case. The presence of a relatively wide range of intervals within the regime is characteristic. This pattern includes many chaparral types, live oak forests, and upper-montane forest types including red fir and white fir *(Abies concolor)* forests.

Truncated Long Fire-Return Interval In all of the burned area, intervals are long (typically greater than 70 years), and fires burning over the same area within a few years or even decades do not occur without conversion to another ecosystem type.

This return interval pattern is characteristic of ecosystems with discontinuous fuels or very short burning seasons such as most very arid deserts, sand dunes, and alpine and subalpine ecosystems. Plant species are generally not adapted to fire. Mountain hemlock *(Tsuga mertensiana)*, whitebark pine *(Pinus albicaulis)*, foxtail pine *(Pinus balfouriana* ssp. *balfouriana)*, bristlecone pine *(Pinus longaeva)*, Sitka spruce *(Picea sitchensis)*, and alpine meadows have this return interval pattern.

Long Fire-Return Interval In most of the burned area, fire-return intervals are long. Fires burning over the same area at shorter intervals can occur within this ecosystem type but account for only a small proportion of the overall burned area. This pattern is characteristic of ecosystems that are geographically isolated, do not normally have a fuel layer that will typically carry a fire, have discontinuous fuels or very short burning seasons, or lack ignition sources. Ecosystems in which this pattern is typical include some desert scrubs that only develop herbaceous layers in wet years, low-density Jeffrey pine *(Pinus jeffreyi)*, or lodgepole pine on glaciated bedrock that will not support continuous vegetative cover, and singleleaf pinyon pine *(Pinus monophylla)* and beach pine *(Pinus contorta* spp. *contorta)* forests.

Spatial Fire Regime Attributes

The spatial attributes of fire regimes are described in two ways: fire size and spatial complexity. *Fire size* is the characteristic distribution of area within the fire perimeter. *Spatial complexity* describes pattern of area burned at different levels of fire severity. Although we have little direct evidence of pre–fire-suppression-era spatial patterns for most of California's vegetation types, much information can be inferred from the structure of the vegetation and typical burning patterns and conditions.

FIRE SIZE

Fire size is displayed as the distribution of burned area in fires of various sizes. The size of an individual fire is the area inside the perimeter of the fire. This is not the same as the total amount of area burned by the fire because it also includes unburned islands and the entire mosaic of burned and unburned areas. The size a fire attains is determined by fuel continuity, site productivity, topography, weather, and fuel conditions at the time of the fire. Figure 4.9 illustrates four different fire size patterns that occur in California ecosystems, with proportion of the burned area on the y-axis and fire size on the x-axis. Care should be taken to interpret each curve separately. Small fires do not necessarily burn more area than large fires; the range of fire sizes is less for small fire regimes than for medium or large regimes, and therefore the proportion is larger.

Small Fire Size Most of the area that burns does so in fires smaller than 10 ha (25 ac) with larger fires accounting for much less of the total area burned. Open Jeffrey pine woodlands on glaciated surfaces with discontinuous fuels are examples.

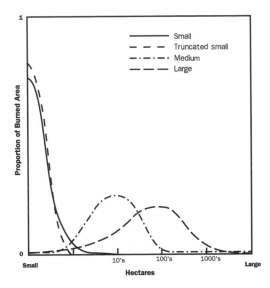

FIGURE 4.9. Fire regime distributions for size. Small, truncated small, medium, and large fire size regimes are displayed.

Truncated Small Fire Size All of the burned area is in small fires, usually less than 1 ha (2.5 ac). This is characteristic of areas with very discontinuous fuels such as whitebark pine, foxtail pine, bristlecone pine, and alpine meadow ecosystems.

Medium Fire Size Most of the area that burns does so in medium-sized fires that range from 10 to 1,000 ha (25 to 2,500 ac). Smaller and larger fires do occur but account for a small proportion of the total area burned in these ecosystems. This fire size pattern is characteristic of ecosystems that occur with patchy fuel conditions and have limited stand size, limited burning periods, or limited fuel continuity. Many red fir and white fir forests are examples of this fire size pattern.

Large Fire Size Most of the area that burns is in large fires that are greater than 1,000 ha (2,500 ac) in size with smaller fires accounting for a lower proportion. This pattern is characteristic of ecosystems occurring over extensive areas with fires typically spreading in continuous fuel layers. Many of California's grassland, chaparral, and oak woodland ecosystems fit into this category.

SPATIAL COMPLEXITY

Spatial complexity, or patchiness, is the spatial variability in fire severity within the fire perimeter. Figure 4.10 illustrates four distribution curves for spatial complexity patterns that occur in California ecosystems, with the proportion of the burned area on the y-axis and spatial complexity ranging from low to high on the x-axis.

Low Spatial Complexity Most of the area within the perimeter of the fire is homogeneous with few unburned islands and a relatively narrow range of severity producing a course-grained vegetation mosaic. Oak woodlands, grasslands, and chamise *(Adenostoma fasiculatum)* chaparral are often examples of this spatial type.

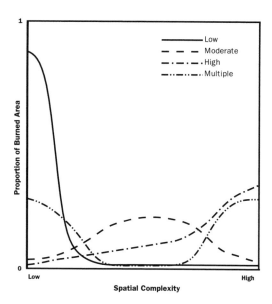

FIGURE 4.10. Fire regime distributions for spatial complexity. Burned areas can have low to high spatial complexity as well as a mixture of multiple complexities.

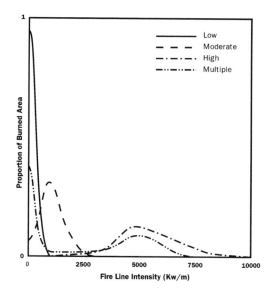

FIGURE 4.11. Fire regime distributions for fireline intensity. Fire regimes include low-, moderate-, high-, and multiple-intensity distribution curves.

Moderate Spatial Complexity   Most of the area within the burn perimeter has an intermediate level of complexity. Burned and unburned areas and severity levels produce a mosaic of fine- and coarse-grained vegetation pattern. Douglas-fir and ponderosa pine are examples.

High Spatial Complexity   Most of the area burns in a highly complex pattern of burned and unburned areas and severity levels producing a fine-grained vegetation mosaic. Mixed conifer and giant sequoia (*Sequoiadendron giganteum*) forests are examples.

Multiple Spatial Complexity   Most of the area burns in fires that are of two distinct types: one has a complex burn pattern of burned and unburned areas and severity levels producing a fine-grained vegetation mosaic; the other has a mostly uniform pattern of burned area and severity levels and produces a coarse-grained vegetation mosaic. This is characteristic of ecosystems in which two distinct fire types occur with flaming fronts in two different fuel layers. Red fir and white fir forests are examples in which complex surface fires and homogenous crown fires result in two very different spatial complexity patterns.

Magnitude Fire Regime Attributes

Fire magnitude is separated into three separate attributes: fireline intensity, fire severity, and fire type. *Fireline intensity* is a description of the fire in terms of energy release pattern. *Fire severity* is a description of fire effects on the biological and physical components of the ecosystem. *Fire type* is a description of different types of flaming fronts. Although fire severity is related to fire intensity and fire type, their relationship is very complex depending on which elements of severity are assessed

and how they are directly and indirectly influenced by fire intensity and type. Similarly, fire severity is interrelated with fire seasonality and fire-return interval through fire intensity.

FIRELINE INTENSITY

Fireline intensity is a measure of energy release per unit length of fire line. Intensity is described in detail in Chapter 3 and summarized here as it applies to fire regimes. Figure 4.11 illustrates four different fire intensity distribution patterns that occur in California ecosystems with proportion of the burned area on the y-axis and level of intensity on the x-axis.

Low Fireline Intensity   Most of the area that burns does so in fires that are low intensity with flame lengths less than 1.2 m (4 ft) and fireline intensities less than 346 kW m^{-1} (100 Btu ft^{-1} s^{-1}). A smaller proportion of the area burns at moderate to high-intensity levels. Persons using hand tools can generally attack the fire at the head or flanks. Fire remains on the surface and occasionally consumes understory vegetation. Annual grasslands and blue oak (*Quercus douglasii*) woodlands are examples of ecosystems that typically burn with this intensity pattern.

Moderate Fireline Intensity   Most of the area burned does so in fires of moderate intensity with flame lengths from 1.2 to 2.4 m (4 to 8 ft) and fireline intensities between 346 and 1,730 kW m^{-1} (100 and 500 Btu ft^{-1} s^{-1}). Fire is too intense for direct attack at the head by persons using hand tools. Fire usually remains on the surface, although there could be complete consumption of understory vegetation. Mixed conifer and giant sequoia forests are examples of ecosystems that typically burn with this intensity pattern.

High Fireline Intensity   Most of the area that burns has fires that are of high to very high intensities greater than 1,730 kW m^{-1} (500 Btu ft^{-1} s^{-1}) with flame lengths over 2.4 m (8 ft). A smaller proportion of the area burns at low to moderate intensity levels. Some crowning, spotting, and major runs are probable. These intensities usually result in complete consumption and mortality of vegetation, and consumption of entire individual plants occurs. Lodgepole pine and many chaparral ecosystems often burn with this intensity pattern.

Multiple Fireline Intensity   Most of the burned area has fires that are mostly of two types: low-intensity surface fires and high-intensity crown fires. A smaller proportion of the area burns at moderate or very high intensity levels. Red fir, white fir, and some Douglas-fir and mixed conifer forests are examples of ecosystems that commonly burn with this intensity pattern.

SEVERITY

Fire severity is the magnitude of the effect that fire has on the environment, and is applied to a variety of ecosystem components, including vegetation, soil, geomorphology, watersheds, wildlife habitat, and human life and property. Separate, and often very different, distributions are appropriate when severity is displayed for multiple ecosystem characteristics. Fire severity is not always a direct result of fireline intensity, but results from a combination of fireline intensity, residence time, and moisture conditions at the time of burning. This treatment of severity emphasizes the effect that fire has on the plant communities, especially the species that characterize the ecosystem. Figure 4.12 illustrates five severity patterns that occur in California ecosystems with proportion of the burned area on the y-axis and severity on the x-axis.

Low Fire Severity   Most of the area burns in low-severity fires that produce only slight or no modification to vegetation structure; most of the mature individual plants survive. A small proportion of the area burns at higher severity levels. Interior Douglas-fir forests in the Klamath Mountains, ponderosa pine, and blue oak woodlands are often examples of this fire severity pattern.

Moderate Fire Severity   Most of the area burns in fires that are moderately stand modifying, with most individual mature plants surviving. A small proportion of the area burns at lower and higher severity levels. Mixed conifer and giant sequoia are typical examples of this severity pattern.

High Fire Severity   Fire kills the aboveground parts of most individual plants over most of the burned area. Most mature individual plants survive below ground and resprout. A small proportion of the area burns at lower and higher severity levels. Chamise and many sprouting chaparral types are often examples of this fire severity pattern.

Very High Fire Severity   Fires are mostly stand replacing over much of the burned area. All or nearly all of the individual mature plants are killed. A smaller proportion of the area burns at lower severity levels. Lodgepole pine, mountain hemlock, knobcone pine, Monterey pine, and many cypress and nonsprouting chaparral types frequently display this fire severity pattern.

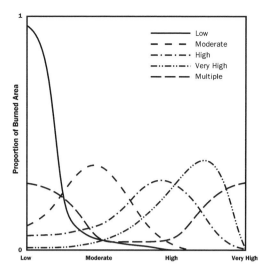

FIGURE 4.12. Fire regime distributions for severity. Five different distribution curves describe the variation in severity for different fire regimes.

Multiple Fire Severity   The area burned is mostly divided between two distinct fire types: low severity and high to very high severity. A smaller proportion of the area burns at moderate severity levels. Red fir and white fir forests are often examples of this fire severity pattern.

FIRE TYPE

Fire type is a description of the flaming front patterns that are characteristic of an ecosystem. The types are defined in Chapter 3 and include surface, passive crown, active crown, and independent crown fires. Although fire type is a categorical variable, it can be expressed as a continuous variable by using fireline intensity to scale the fire types. Ground fires, although a significant contributor to fire effects, are not part of the flaming front. There are four fire regime types that represent different combinations of the fire types. These are the surface-passive crown fire regime, the passive–active crown fire regime, the active-independent crown fire regime, and the multiple-fire-type regime. Figure 4.13 illustrates the four different patterns for fire type regimes that occur in California ecosystems. The proportion of the burned area is on the y-axis, and the x-axis depicts increasing values for fireline intensity with points along the axis for fire type.

Surface-Passive Crown Fire   Most of the area that is burned does so with a surface fire. Although as much as 30% of the area may experience torching of individual trees or groups of trees, the flaming front is primarily a surface fire. Organic layers are burned by ground fires, and small amounts of active crowning can burn stands of trees. Grasslands, blue oak woodlands, ponderosa pine, and low-elevation desert shrublands are typical examples of this fire-type distribution.

Passive–Active Crown Fire   Most of the burned area has fire that is a combination of surface fire supported by passive and active crown fire. Active crown fire is dependent on and

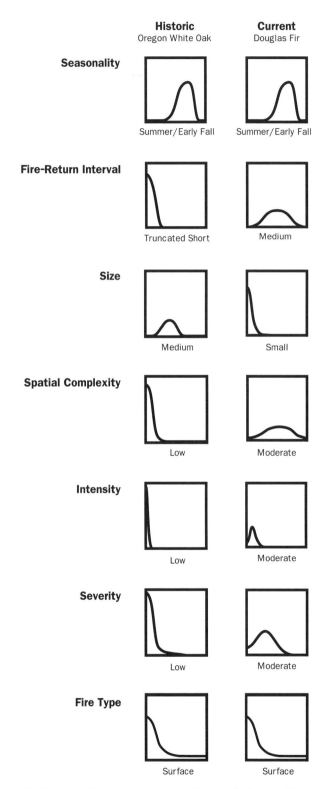

FIGURE 4.1.1. Fire regime attribute distributions for Oregon white oak/Douglas-fir forest ecosystems.

This chapter has defined fire regimes and outlined a method for describing them as a set of conceptual distributions. This example applies the description method to a California ecosystem to better illustrate this approach. We demonstrate how the persistence of this ecosystem is dependent on specific fire regime attributes.

Since the mid-1800s, there has been a general change in the fire regime patterns and a concomitant change in forest composition from Oregon white oak woodland to Douglas-fir forest. Figure 4.1.1 displays two sets of distributions that define the historic fire regime and the current fire regime that has replaced the historic one in the past 200 years. The narrative description explains the dynamics of the change and some of the options for future management. This example is intended to display the use of the fire regime distributions but not to fully describe all of the possible complexities. In-depth descriptions of the issues are developed in the chapters on bioregions.

Fire Regime Attributes

Seasonality Summer–Early Fall. The seasonality of fire has remained relatively unchanged from the historic to current period.

Fire-Return Interval Oregon white oak woodlands within the coast redwood *(Sequoia sempervirens)* forest were maintained by annual or nearly annual burning (truncated short fire-return interval) by the Native Americans. Douglas-fir was a constituent of the redwood forest. The interval has changed to a medium-return interval with fires occurring much less frequently.

Size   Historically, fires were typically 10–100 ha (25–250 ac) due to the size and pattern of the vegetation on the landscape. Currently, the fires are mostly smaller than 10 ha (25 ac) due to the effectiveness of fire suppression.

Spatial Complexity   Historically, the complexity of any particular fire was low due to the uniform herbaceous fuels in which the fires spread. As Douglas-fir becomes established and changes the fuel conditions, the spatial complexity increases to moderate.

Intensity   Historically, fire was limited to low to moderate intensity due to the short fire-return intervals and the lack of opportunity for heavy fuel accumulations. With fire exclusion, the longer intervals allow more fine fuels and heavier woody fuels to accumulate. Moderate- to high-intensity fires now occur.

Severity   Historically, fire severity was low, with plant species adapted to frequent fires and frequent surface fires having little effect on the Oregon white oak overstory. Douglas-fir is sensitive to low- to moderate-severity fire when it is young but is very resistant to damage from moderate-severity fire as a large tree. After long fire-free intervals, high-severity fires can eliminate Douglas-fir from the stand.

Fire Type   Historically, surface fires with only occasional torching occurred. Currently, surface fire is still the most common, with more torching and some potential for active crown fires under extreme fire weather conditions.

Fire Regime Changes

Since the late 1800s, there have been changes in the fire regime largely due to elimination of the annual or nearly annual burning by Native Americans. Encroachment of Douglas-fir from the adjacent forest and invasion of non-native annual grass species have greatly influenced the ecosystem. The season during which the grasses are dry enough to burn has probably started earlier in the summer because of the change in species composition to more non-native annual grasses that cure earlier in the season. Fire-suppression efforts have reduced the opportunity for fires to burn these woodlands. Spatial complexity, intensity, and severity of the fires have all increased. Originally, surface fires were the most common fire type. Now there is mixture of surface fires and crown fires.

Plant Community Response

The changes in fire regime have resulted in conversion from Oregon white oak woodland to Douglas-fir forest. This represents a significant change in biodiversity of the area, because it represents a reduction in plant community diversity. The Oregon white oak woodlands are replaced by expansion of the adjacent Douglas-fir forests.—NGS

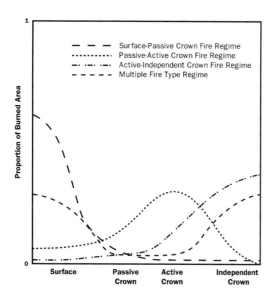

FIGURE 4.13. Fire regime distributions for type. Fire type regimes include surface fires, crown fires, and multiple type fires.

synchronous with a surface fire and is the most common type of sustained crown fire. This fire regime type occurs in north coastal pine forests, Sitka spruce, knobcone pine, coastal sage *(Salvia* spp.) scrub, and desert riparian woodlands and oases.

Active-Independent Crown Fire   In California forests, independent crown fires are very rare but do occur occasionally in combination with active crown fires. When they do occur, the crown fire burns independently of the surface fire and advances over a given area ahead of the surface fire. Examples are lodgepole pine in northeastern California and some closed-cone conifer ecosystems. Areas supporting hardwood or conifer forests with dense canopies in very steep complex topography can also fit into this fire type distribution. In chaparral ecosystems, independent crown fires are the norm, although some active crowning might occur. Examples of vegetation types with a greater preponderance for independent crowning include knobcone pine embedded in chaparral, similarly situated Sargent cypress *(Cupressus sargentii)*, and south coast and Sierra Nevada chaparral.

Multiple Fire Type   Both surface fire and crown fire are characteristic of these ecosystems with multiple fire types. Each fire type occurs in a complex spatial mosaic within the same fire under different fuel, topographic, and weather conditions. In the Sierra Nevada, red fir, lodgepole pine, and tanoak *(Lithocarpus densiflorus)*–mixed evergreen are examples of ecosystems in which this fire type pattern is characteristic. Additional types include Coulter *(Pinus coulteri)*, Bishop pine, and Monterey pine.

Combining Attributes to Develop a Comprehensive Fire Regime

Comprehensive fire regimes are developed for vegetation types by combining the appropriate attribute distribution curves for each attribute. Similar combinations could be grouped into fire regime types such as those described by Hardy et al. (2001). Sidebar 4.1 describes how all seven attributes are combined to depict the fire regime for Oregon white oak woodlands and how those attributes might change as the woodlands convert to a Douglas-fir forest as a result of fire exclusion.

Summary

Fire is an important ecological process that occurs regularly and has predictable spatial, temporal, and magnitude patterns. That is not to say, however, that we can always predict when and where a fire will occur. In the fire-prone ecosystems of California, fire is inevitable and general patterns are predictable, but the extremes are not. Species adapt to fire by having characteristics that make them competitive in the presence of recurring fire. Because fire patterns interact with biotic communities and depend on them to provide fuel, the dynamics of ecosystems are intimately tied to fire regimes. Changing fire regimes inherently affect biological change. Changes to any of the fire regime attributes are large-scale alterations to ecosystem function, producing shifts in the composition and distribution of species and ecosystems.

Fire regimes have always been dynamic at multiple scales. In addition to the scale represented by the distribution curves, fire regimes also operate at larger scales on much larger landscapes over centuries and millenia. Ecosystems and their associated fire regimes have migrated across landscapes with climate changes, human occupation, and geologic and biologic changes. Ecosystems adjust to changes in fire regime by changing composition and structure and by migrating up- and downslope, and north and south.

Although humans have altered fire regimes throughout California for thousands of years, the pace of fire regime change has accelerated over the past 200 years. Recent and current management strategies have imposed directional changes on the pattern of fires in many California ecosystems. For example, fire exclusion from some forests that historically had frequent fires has lengthened fire-return intervals, allowing greater fuel accumulations. Until 2000, the trend had been to less total area burned, with the reduction mostly in area burned by fires of low to moderate intensity and severity. Today the trend is toward more area burned by a larger number of high-severity fires. Because current technology has enabled increased human intervention in eliminating the low- to moderate-severity fires, the historic fire regime distributions have now shifted toward a greater proportion of high-severity, large, stand-replacing fires (McKenzie et al. 2004). Although it is unlikely that we will ever universally restore California's ecosystems to any historic condition, it is apparent that we cannot totally eliminate fire.

In recent decades, ecologists and land managers have become very concerned with mitigating the effects of our changes to historic fire regimes. Scientists and land managers have devoted considerable effort to improving our understanding of historic fire regimes and our changes to them. We know that fire's role in ecosystems and fire regime dynamics serve as mechanisms for driving habitat change for many species. An understanding of fire regimes is critical in assessing current conditions and developing strategies for achieving land management objectives. It is also vital in assessing the threat that wildfire poses to people on the urban–wildland interface.

The system used here for describing fire regimes allows description of the attributes involved, comparison of how they differ from those in other ecosystems, and how they change over time. Additionally, fire regime descriptions allow us to view in a structured manner how changing attributes influence fire's role as an ecological process. Knowledge of fire regime–ecosystem interactions allows us to understand mechanisms for ecosystem change due to changing fire regimes. This knowledge further allows prediction of the direction of ecological change that will occur with future planned and unplanned changes to fire regimes.

Today we have the opportunity to manage dynamic ecosystems and maintain many of their important processes and attributes. Society is redefining its land management objectives and strategies, and managing fire regimes has emerged as a major element of managing ecosystems. We must also decide where it is appropriate to manage altered fire regimes and ecosystems to meet society's desires and demands. The fire regime system described in this chapter is designed to aid in meeting these challenges by giving us a tool for assessing fire regime–ecosystem dynamics and to help us to understand the mechanisms of fire-related ecosystem change.

References

Agee, J.K. 1993. Fire ecology of Pacific Northwest forests. Island Press, Washington, D.C. 493 p.

Bond, W.J., and B.P. van Wilgen. 1996. Fire and plants. Chapman and Hall, London. 263 p.

Bradley, A.F., W.C. Fischer, and N.V. Noste. 1992. Fire ecology of the forest habitat types of eastern Idaho and western Wyoming. USDA For. Serv. Gen. Tech. Rept. INT-290. 98 p.

Clements, F.E. 1916. Plant succession. Carnegie Inst. Washington Pub. 242. 512 p.

Clements, F.E. 1936. Nature and structure of the climax. Journal of Ecology 22:39–68.

Daubenmire, R. 1947. Plants and environment. Wiley, New York. 424 p.

Daubenmire, R. 1968. Plant communities. Harper and Row, New York. 300 p.

Davis, K.M., B.D. Clayton, and W.C. Fischer. 1980. Fire ecology of Lolo National Forest habitat types. USDA For. Serv. Gen. Tech. Rep. INT-79.

Gill, A.M. 1975. Fire and the Australian flora: a review. Australian Forestry 38:4–25.

Gleason, H.A. 1917. The structure and development of the plant association. Bulletin Torrey Botanical Club 43:463–481.

Gleason, H.A. 1926. The individualistic concept of the plant association. Bulletin of the Torrey Botanical Club 53:7–26.

Hann, W.J., and D.L. Bunnell. 2001. Fire and land management planning and implementation across multiple scales. International Journal of Wildland Fire 10(3 and 4):389–403.

Hardy, C.C., K.M. Schmidt, J.P. Menakis, and R.N. Sampson. 2001. Spatial data for national fire planning and management. International Journal of Wildland Fire 10(3 and 4):353–372.

Heinselman, M.L. 1973. Fire in the virgin forests of the Boundary Waters Canoe Area, Minnesota. Quaternary Research 3:329–382.

Heinselman, M.L. 1981. Fire intensity and frequency as factors in the distribution and structure of northern ecosystems. P. 7–57 in H.A. Mooney, T.M. Bonnicksen, N.L. Christensen, J.E. Lotan, and W.A. Reiners (eds.), Fire regimes and ecosystem properties, proceedings of the conference. USDA For. Serv. Gen. Tech. Rep. WO-26. 593 p.

Hendrickson, W.H. 1991. Perspective on fire and ecosystems in the United States. P. 29–33 in Proc. Symp. Fire and Environ. USDA For. Serv. Gen. Tech. Rep. SE-69. 429 p.

Keeley, J.E. 1977. Fire dependent reproductive strategies in *Arctostaphylos* and *Ceanothus*. P. 371–376 in H.A. Mooney and C.E. Conrad (eds.), Proceedings of the symposium on the environmental consequences of fire and fuel management in Mediterranean ecosystems. USDA For. Serv. Gen. Tech. Rep. WO-3. 498 p.

Kilgore, B.M. 1981. Fire in ecosystem distribution and structure: western forests and scrublands. P. 58–89 in H.A. Mooney, T.M. Bonnicksen, N.L. Christensen, J.E. Lotan, and W.A. Reiners (eds.), Fire regimes and ecosystem properties, proceedings of the conference. USDA For. Serv. Gen. Tech. Rep. WO-26. 593 p.

McKenzie, D., Z. Gedalof, D.L. Peterson, and P. Mote. 2004. Climatic change, wildfire, and conservation. Conservation Biology 14(4):890–902.

Methven, I.R. 1978. Fire research at the Petawawa Forest Experiment Station: the integration of fire behavior and forest ecology for management purposes. In Fire ecology in resource management workshop proceedings. P. 23–27 in D.E. Dube (ed.), Inf. Rep. NOR-X-210. North For. Res. Cent., Can. For. Serv., Edmonton, Alberta.

Odum, E.P. 1959. Fundamentals of ecology, 2nd ed. Saunders, Philadelphia. 451 p.

Odum, E.P. 1963. Ecology. Holt, Reinhart, and Winston, New York. 152 p.

Odum, E.P. 1969. The strategy of ecosystem development. Science 154:262–270.

O'Neill, R.V., D.L. DeAngelis, J.B. Waide, and T.F.H. Allen. 1986. A hierarchical concept of ecosystems. Princeton University Press, Princeton, New Jersey. 253 p.

Pickett, S.T.A., J. Kolasa, J.J. Armesto, and S.L. Collins. 1989. The ecological concept of disturbance and its expression at various hierarchical levels. Oikos 54(2):129–136.

Romme, W.H., E.H. Everham, L.E. Frelich, M.A. Moritz, and R.E. Sparks. 1998. Are large, infrequent disturbances qualitatively different from small, frequent disturbances? Ecosystems 1(6): 524–534.

Sando, R.W. 1978. Natural fire regimes and fire management—foundations and direction. Western Wildlands 4(4):34–42.

Schultz, A.M. 1968. The ecosystem as a conceptual tool in the management of natural resources. P. 139–161 in S.V. Ciriacy-Wantrup and J.J. Parsons (eds.), Natural resources: quality and quantity. University of California Press, Berkeley. 217 p.

Shugart, H.H., and D.C. West. 1981. Long-term dynamics of forest ecosystems. American Scientist 69:647–652.

Sugihara, N.G., and L.R. Reed. 1987. Vegetation ecology of the Bald Hills oak woodlands of Redwood National Park. Redwood National Park Research and Development Technical Report 21. 78 p.

Tansley, A.G. 1935. The use and abuse of vegetational concepts and terms. Ecology 16:196–218.

Turner, M.G., and V.H. Dale. 1998. Comparing large, infrequent disturbances: what have we learned? Ecosystems 1(6): 493–496.

Van Wagner, C.E. 1978. Age class distribution and the forest fire cycle. Canadian Journal of Forestry Research 8:220–227.

Walker, L.R., and M.R. Willig. 1999. An introduction to terrestrial disturbances. P. 1–6 in L.R. Walker (ed.), Ecosystems of disturbed ground. Elsevier, Amsterdam. 868 p.

Watt, A.S. 1947. Pattern and process in the plant community. J. Ecol. 39:599–619.

White, P.S. 1979. Pattern, process, and natural disturbance in vegetation. Botanical Review 45:229–299.

White, P.S., and S.T.A. Pickett. 1985. Natural disturbance and patch dynamics: an introduction. P. 3–13 in S.T.A. Pickett and P.S. White (eds.), The ecology of natural disturbance and patch dynamics. Academic Press, New York. 472 p.

Whittaker, R.H. 1953. A consideration of climax theory: the climax as a population and pattern. Ecological Monographs 23:41–78.

Whittaker, R.H. 1967. Gradient analysis of vegetation. Biological Review 42:207–264.

Whittaker, R.H. 1971. Communities and ecosystems. McMillan, New York. 162 p.

CHAPTER 5

Fire and Physical Environment Interactions

Soil, Water, and Air

PETER M. WOHLGEMUTH, KEN HUBBERT,
AND MICHAEL J. ARBAUGH

Therefore, as fire is to air, so is air to water, water to Earth. And again, as the earth is to the water, so is water to air, and air to fire.

HENRY CORNELIUS AGRIPPA, 2000

Interactions of fire with soil, water, and air play an important role in the ecology of forests, brushfields, and grasslands throughout California. Soil is a primary factor in site productivity, and the effects of burning can both enhance and degrade soil quality. Water is especially sensitive to upland environmental changes and is an excellent indicator of ecosystem condition. Fire affects water quantity and water quality both for aquatic and riparian ecosystems and for downstream human consumption. Fire impacts air quality by degrading aesthetic vistas and potentially redistributing airborne pollutants. It can combine with urban-generated air pollution to affect both forests and human health and well-being at areas distant from the fire. By understanding the effects of fire on soil, water, and air resources, we are in a better position to manage the consequences of burning, whether for wildfire mitigation or for developing a program of prescribed burning.

Soils develop in response to geology, topography, climate, vegetation, and time. Formed over the years by the weathering of rock and the incorporation of organic material, soil is a dynamic medium that is very sensitive to ecosystem change. Soils provide the natural base for the growth of terrestrial ecosystems and the platform on which fire interactions on the landscape are played.

Hydrology is the cyclic movement of water through the landscape. Precipitation falls to the earth as rain or snow and runs off in surface streams or percolates as groundwater. Some of this water is held in the soil column and is taken up by the local vegetation. Water is returned to the atmosphere by evaporation from land and water bodies and by transpiration from the plant communities. Fire generally changes the water balance at a site by enhancing runoff at the expense of percolation.

Smoke emissions may affect forest biota, human health, and visibility. The disposition of smoke is an important aspect of fire management due to the effect of particulates on human health and the visibility even far removed from the fire's location. Deposition of smoke in the ecosystem may have direct effects on plant function and affect the nutritional status in combination with urban-generated air pollution.

Fire Interactions with Soils

Effects of fire on the soil's physical and chemical properties differ with fire temperature, intensity, duration, and frequency and season of occurrence. The aspect of the slope also affects both chemical and physical soil properties (Box 5.1). Fire can change soil properties such as soil texture, bulk density and porosity, infiltration and permeability, color and mineralogy, water and organic matter content, acidity, exchangeable cations, and rates of mineralization of nitrogen (N) and phosphorus (P). Indirect effects of fire to soils include erosion due to changes in soil hydrological properties; leaching of elements; and changes in litterfall, nutrient uptake, and plant growth rate (Raison et al. 1990).

Soil Physical Properties

SOIL TEMPERATURE

The intensity and duration of soil heating depends on the kind and spatial distribution of live and dead fuels, topography and micro-relief, weather (relative humidity, wind, and temperature), and soil texture and moisture content. Factors of wildland fuels that influence soil heating include fuel types (grasses, shrubs, timber litter, slash, and litter and duff), fuel characteristics (fuel moisture), size and shape (light, heavy), fuel loading (quantity), and horizontal continuity and vertical arrangement of fuels (uniform, patchy). Less heat is produced in the soil during a fast-moving fire on an uphill run than during a slow-moving backing fire (DeBano 1981). Fast-propagating, high-energy surface fires produce relatively low soil temperatures compared to low-intensity, slow-spreading or smoldering fires that have a much longer residence time (10–15 hr) (Wells et al. 1979).

Most of the heat from a fire is directed upward. Of the total energy released during burning of chaparral fuels, only about 8% is transmitted into the underlying soil (DeBano 1974). Recorded soil temperatures for wildfires range from 250°C (482°F) in grass fuels to 700°C (1,292°F) in shrublands and under slash piles (DeBano and Rice 1971, Wells et al. 1979). In Sierra Nevada lower-montane forests, typical soil surface temperatures were ~210°C (~410°F) (DeBano et al. 1998). A soil temperature of 66°C (151° F) is conservatively considered to be instantaneously lethal for giant sequoia (*Sequoiadendron giganteum*) and sugar pine (*Pinus lambertiana*) roots (Haase and Sackett 1998). Rapid heating of the humus layer to 100°C (212°F) is lethal to most organisms and can result in altered microbial community structures (Pieti-kainen et al. 2000). Figure 5.1 shows the effects of soil heating on physical, chemical, and biological soil processes.

Heat transfer into soil depends not only on the surface temperature and duration of exposure but also on soil water content, soil texture, and the soil pore distribution. Thermal conductivity of soil depends on the arrangement and contact of soil particles, and the proportion of water and air in the pore spaces (Jury et al. 1991). Dry soils are good insulators of heat, with surface temperatures rapidly attenuating with depth into the soil column (DeBano et al. 1979). A chaparral fire with surface soil temperatures of 700°C (1,292°F) produced temperatures of less than 200°C (424°F) at a depth of 2.5 cm (1 in), and a grass fire with surface soil temperatures of 250°C (482°F) generated temperatures of less than 100°C (212°F) at a depth of 1.3 cm (0.5 in) (Wells et al. 1979) (see Fig. 5.2).

Moist soils have a greater heat capacity than dry soils and therefore require more energy to induce a comparable temperature rise. Temperature of a wet soil will not exceed 100°C (212°F) until the water evaporates or moves deeper into the soil (DeBano et al. 1979). Likewise, water needs to be evaporated in moist litter and duff layers before combustion of organic matter can begin (Oswald et al. 1999). At volumetric water content of 0.20 in both sand and clay, the thermal conductivity of sand is approximately double that of clay (Jury et al. 1991); thus, depth of soil heating is greater in the sand as compared to the clay. Contiguous macropores can

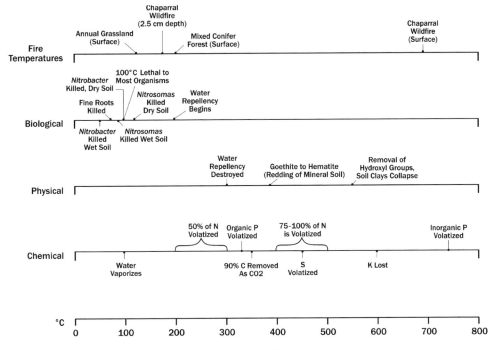

FIGURE 5.1. Wildland fire temperatures and the effects of soil heating on biological, physical, and chemical soil processes.

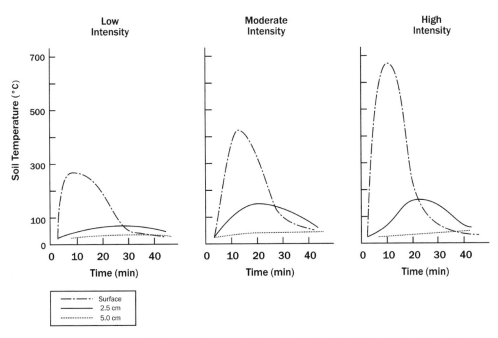

FIGURE 5.2. Soil temperatures for low-, moderate-, and high-intensity fires. Note the insulation effect with increasing soil depth. (Adapted from DeBano 1981.)

TABLE 5.1
Effects of heating by experimental fires on particle size distribution and aggregate stability at 0 to 2.5 cm depth of mineral soil

Heating Temp.°C	Sand %	Silt %	Clay %	Aggregate
25	34	34	32	42
89	36	33	31	41
184	42	33	25	50
307	45	33	22	50
395	47	33	20	51
558	52	30	17	61

NOTE: Adapted from Giovaninni and Lucchesi (1997).

channel heat from a fire to deeper soil horizons, and in turn, burning roots can heat soil at depths well below the soil surface.

LITTER AND DUFF COVER

Post-fire spatial variability of litter and duff cover strongly reflects the pre-fire moisture content. In a study conducted by Sweeney and Biswell (1961), the greatest amounts of litter and duff remaining after prescribed burning were in the low areas where litter and duff were the deepest and wettest. In another study, the thinnest post-burn duff depths were located near the top of draws where the heat from the fire had funneled up (Robichaud and Miller 1999). Fire can also induce its own micro-weather conditions, making it hard to predict where the consumption of duff and litter will be the greatest.

SOIL TEXTURE AND STRUCTURE

Soil texture refers to the relative proportions of sand (0.05–2 mm [0.002–0.08 in] in diameter), silt (0.002–0.05 mm [0.0008–0.002 in] in diameter), and clay (<0.002 mm [0.0008 in] in diameter) particles in the soil. Soil structure is the arrangement of soil particles into aggregates exhibiting distinctive patterns (e.g., columnar, prismatic, blocky, platy).

The textures of severely burned soils usually become coarser (from decreased clay content) as a result of the melting and fusion of clay minerals. Heating the soil above 150°C (302°F) will produce the aggregation of finer clay particles into greater silt and sand particles (Giovaninni and Lucchesi 1997) (Table 5.1). Alternatively, fire can make some soil textures finer by consuming the organic matrix that binds primary mineral grains into aggregates (Ulery and Graham 1993), thereby increasing porosity and permeability (Ahlgren and Ahlgren 1960). Decomposing kaolinized sand grains can decrease in particle size, resulting in finer textures (Ulery and Graham 1993), thereby increasing the soil erodibility (Durgin 1985).

Soil aggregation and structure are promoted by organic matter, organometallic cementing agents, and microbial organisms. Fungal mycelia can surround the soil particles and intertwine among them to form aggregates with a high degree of stability. Aggregation can reduce erosion by making the soil particles more resistant to soil detachment. Fire consumes the organic matter and fungi that promote soil aggregation.

BULK DENSITY, POROSITY, AND PORE SIZE DISTRIBUTION

Bulk density is the mass of dry soil per unit bulk volume (g cm^{-3} [lb ft^{-3}]). *Porosity* is an index of the relative pore volume of the soil. *Pore size distribution* is the arrangement of macropores, mesopores, and micropores in the soil profile.

Fire's consumption of organic glues and fungal mycelium reduces soil aggregation, thus increasing soil bulk density and reducing infiltration (Welling et al. 1984). Fire can also kill burrowing insects and soil microorganisms, indirectly reducing the production of macropores, thereby increasing bulk density (Ahlgren and Ahlgren 1960). However, consumption of organic particles within the surface horizon can leave void spaces in the surface soil (Wells et al. 1979), suggesting a decrease in bulk density and an increase in porosity. Coarse-textured soils with low carbon content generally show a lack of post-fire change in bulk density. Pore size distribution can be changed as a result of surface sealing or plugging of macropores by smaller particles moving downward into the underlying aggregate soil, effectively reducing infiltration and soil permeability (Welling et al. 1984). In addition, the thermal contact between soil particles is enhanced when bulk density increases (Jury et al. 1991). Therefore, an increase in bulk density can result in deeper heat pulse into the soil profile.

SOIL COLOR

Post-fire color of the mineral soil is influenced by the type and amount of organic matter and iron oxides present before the burn (Ketterings and Bigham 2000). Low-intensity burns with surface temperatures of 100°C–250°C (212°F–482°F) are characterized by black ash and scorched liter and duff. Moderate burning, where surface temperatures reach 300°C–400°C (572°F–752°F), consumes most of the litter, depositing gray and black ash. In areas not covered with ash, the soil is not altered in color. High-intensity burning produces surface soil temperatures in excess of 500°C (932°F) and results in white ash remaining after the complete combustion of fuel and reddening of the mineral soil surface (Wells et al. 1979). Soil color becomes darker when mixed with black ash, lowering the *albedo* (percent of incoming solar radiation that is reflected at the soil surface); therefore less incoming radiation is reflected. The charred or blackened surfaces absorb more heat than an unburned litter layer, resulting in higher soil temperatures during the day and greater diurnal temperature ranges and extremes (Neal et al. 1965).

Soil water repellency or *hydrophobicity* is a physical property of soil that limits water infiltration, as well as a chemical property in it that consists of organic compounds (DeBano et al. 1998). In a hydrophobic soil, water will not readily penetrate and infiltrate into the soil, but will "ball up" and remain on the surface (DeBano 1981). Surface attraction or repellency for water originates from the attractive forces between water and solid surfaces. If the attraction is greater between water and soil particles than between individual water molecules, the water will spread out and be absorbed. However, when the attraction between water molecules is greater than that between the water and soil surface, the water will be repelled by the soil particle rather than infiltrate (Letey 1969, DeBano 1981).

Hydrophobic substances are naturally occurring and are derived from organic compounds of most living or decomposing plant species or microorganisms in grasslands, shrublands, and forests. Chaparral, pine, and fir species are most commonly associated with water repellency, especially those containing a considerable amount of resins, waxes, or aromatic oils (DeBano 1981). Fungal growth can also produce water repellency and is important in areas where soil fungal net biomass may equal or even exceed aboveground biomass production (Fogel and Hunt 1979).

Coarser particles are more susceptible to developing water repellency because of their smaller surface area per unit volume compared with soils of finer texture. For example, surface area for a medium-size sand particle is $0.0077 \text{ m}^2 \text{ g}^{-1}$ (DeBano 1981), whereas clay can have a surface area as large as $800 \text{ m}^2 \text{ g}^{-1}$ (Jury et al. 1991). Therefore, it would take less of the hydrophobic substance to coat the larger-sized sand particles than the finer clay particles. Thus, subsurface layers of repellency are usually thicker in coarse-grained soils than in fine-textured soils.

The thickness, depth, intensity, persistence, and spatial distribution of soil water repellency depends on the temperature and duration of the fire, depth of the litter and duff layer, species composition of the litter, soil moisture, and soil texture (DeBano 1981). Heat from the fire vaporizes the organic matter and drives it down into the soil profile, where it re-condenses along thermal gradients on individual soil particles, thereby thickening the band of repellency (DeBano 1981). Consequently, there is a lower frequency of occurrence of post-fire repellency in the surface layers of soil. Water repellency is generally intensified at temperatures of 175°C–200°C (347°F–424°F), but can be eliminated above 270°C–300°C (518°F–572°F) (Savage 1974). Under unburned conditions, continuous layers of the non-wettable substances are generally not formed because rodent, worm, insect, and root activity continuously disrupts the soil-column structure, and forms conduits for water to enter. Little is known of the breakdown and re-establishment of water repellency in soils (Doerr et. al. 2000). Soil moisture will break down repellent compounds (Dekker et al. 1998), but after long dry periods, there can be a re-establishment of soil water repellency (Shakesby et al. 2000) (Fig. 5.3).

Post-fire soil water repellency may increase water availability for some resprouting chaparral shrubs by channeling water deep into the soil profile following preferential flow pathways, while at the same time reducing evaporation due to partial dryness of the surface soil layer. Live roots, old root channels, and cracks can serve as penetrating points for preferential flow of water through these layers providing water to the deeper-rooted chaparral species (Scott 1993). In the post-fire environment, chaparral shrubs are not affected directly by the water-repellent layer, because their root systems remain intact, both above and below the repellent layer.

Soil Chemical Properties

Chemical soil properties are important because they govern nutrient relations. The direct effects of fire on soil chemistry include oxidation of litter and organic horizons, increased mineral mobility caused by ashing, heat-induced changes in soil microflora, and nutrient volatilization, especially nitrogen (N). Indirect fire effects on nutrients include changes in soil moisture and temperature caused by decreased shading and precipitation interception by vegetation and litter, changes in rates of organic matter decomposition and other microbial processes, and selective mortality of soil biota caused by heat. Other indirect effects include changes in N_2 fixation rates, mycorrhizal relationships, and hydrologic export of nutrients by way of mobilization and water movement through the ecosystem (Overby and Perry 1996).

Combustion releases nutrients stored in live and dead plant biomass and makes them readily available to the soil (McNabb and Cromack 1990). Nutrients are rapidly incorporated into new foliar growth, especially evident in resprouting species, promoting establishment of the post-fire plant community. However, the majority of fire-generated nutrient flush is transported offsite by the actions of wind, runoff, leaching, and volatilization (Wells et al. 1979).

ORGANIC MATTER

Surface organic matter (litter and duff) is important to the health and productivity of shrublands and forested areas because of its nutrient and water content; its influence on physical, chemical, and biological characteristics; and its ability to be a medium for fine roots and mycorrhizae. The forest floor consists of the *litter layer* (L or Oi), defined as the intact recognizable plant material; the *fermentation layer* (F or Oe), defined as partially decomposed but recognizable litter; and the *humus layer* (H or Oa), defined as well-humified, extensively decayed organic matter. The L layer is comparable to litter fuels described in Chapter 3, whereas the F and H layers combined are often referred to as the *duff layer* and correspond to ground fuels.

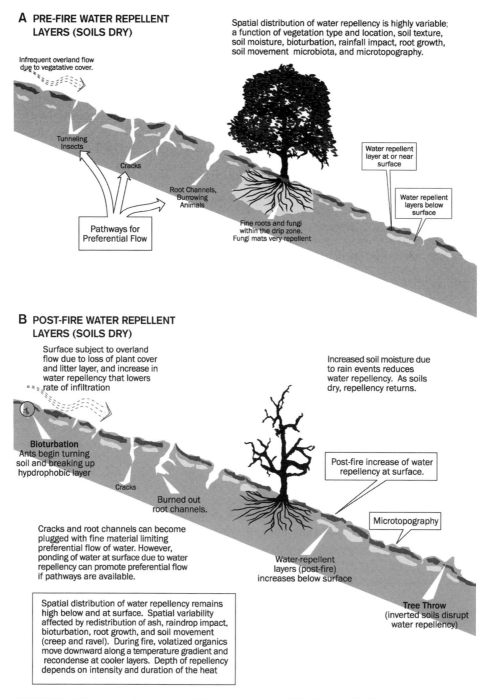

A PRE-FIRE WATER REPELLENT LAYERS (SOILS DRY)

Spatial distribution of water repellency is highly variable; a function of vegetation type and location, soil texture, soil moisture, bioturbation, rainfall impact, root growth, soil movement microbiota, and microtopography.

Infrequent overland flow due to vegetative cover.

Tunneling Insects

Cracks

Root Channels, Burrowing Animals

Pathways for Preferential Flow

Fine roots and fungi within the drip zone. Fungi mats very repellent

Water repellent layer at or near surface

Water repellent layers below surface

B POST-FIRE WATER REPELLENT LAYERS (SOILS DRY)

Surface subject to overland flow due to loss of plant cover and litter layer, and increase in water repellency that lowers rate of infiltration

Increased soil moisture due to rain events reduces water repellency. As soils dry, repellency returns.

Bioturbation
Ants begin turning soil and breaking up hypdrophobic layer

Cracks

Burned out root channels.

Cracks and root channels can become plugged with fine material limiting preferential flow of water. However, ponding of water at surface due to water repellency can promote preferential flow if pathways are available.

Post-fire increase of water repellency at surface.

Microtopography

Water-repellent layers (post-fire) increases below surface

Tree Throw
(inverted soils disrupt water repellency)

Spatial distribution of water repellency remains high below and at surface. Spatial variability affected by redistribution of ash, raindrop impact, bioturbation, root growth, and soil movement (creep and ravel). During fire, volatized organics move downward along a temperature gradient and recondense at cooler layers. Depth of repellency depends on intensity and duration of the heat

FIGURE 5.3. Soil water repellency and hydrologic consequences (A) before and (B) after a fire.

Fire decreases soil organic matter resulting in lower cation exchange capacity, lower soil moisture content, and loss of soil aggregation. Percentage loss of carbon is dependent on fire temperature and intensity, the degree to which organic matter is incorporated into the mineral soil, and the nature and structure of pre-existing vegetation. At 220°C (428°F), Fernandez et al. (1997) reported that 37% of carbon was lost, and at 350°C (662°F), 90% of carbon was lost. The rapid loss of carbon as carbon dioxide (CO_2) during fire lowers the C/N ratio. With carbon in short supply, bacteria and fungi (their

mass being high in N) die and decompose, releasing the N to the soil solution (Donahue et al. 1983).

NITROGEN (N) CYCLING

Nitrogen is the nutrient most likely to limit plant growth in the wildland soils. Long periods of fire exclusion result in wildlands with N-limiting conditions (Kimmins 1996). Soil N is taken up and held in the organic form resulting in high C/N ratios (e.g., greater than 30:1); thus only a small portion of total N is available for plant uptake. Combustion of organic matter by fire lowers the C/N ratio releasing a flush of available N to the soil, but heating by fire also volatizes N. Where fuel load has increased the risk of catastrophic fires, fire during the dry season can result in total biomass consumption and decreases of N in excess of 1,120 kg ha^{-1} (1,000 lb ac^{-1}). Box 5.2 is a simplified example of fire's effect on the N cycle.

During pyrolysis, organic nitrogen (mainly amino acids in plant material and litter) is converted to volatile, gaseous forms including NH_3 (ammonia), molecular N, and various oxides of nitrogen. DeBell and Ralston (1970) found that 62% of the nitrogen content of pine needles and litter was lost during combustion, mostly as molecular nitrogen. The loss of nitrogen is partially compensated by the increased availability of the nitrogen that remains after the fire. Soluble forms of nitrogen, ammonium (NH_4^+-N), and nitrate (NO_3^--N) were higher in burned soil than in unburned soil in California chaparral (Christensen 1973). Higher amounts of NO_3^--N after fire as reported by Christensen and Muller (1975) suggest that increases in NO_3^--N after fire are due to mineralization and nitrification.

Exchangeable NH_4^+-N can increase during fire (Prieto-Fernandez et al. 1998). In a ponderosa pine forest, NH_4^+-N concentrations remained higher than did the unburned control for a year, with initial post-fire concentrations of NH_4^+-N for wildfire of 19.5 μg g^{-1} as compared to the unburned control of 1.9 μg g^{-1} (Choromanska and DeLuca 2001). Exchangeable NH_4^+-N may originate from the thermal decomposition at 200°C (392°F) of organic matter amino acids (DeBano 1988). Studies also indicate that inorganic and labile N (readily available) concentrations can remain reduced for an indefinite period of time, depending on burning intensity, soil water content, climate, and other ecological drivers that govern post-fire recovery (Neary et al. 1999).

Nitrogen fixation is the conversion of molecular N (N_2) to ammonia (NH_3) and, in rapid order, to organic combinations or to forms readily usable in biological processes (Donahue et al.1983). Symbiotic N fixation is accomplished by microorganisms (commonly rhizobia or actinomycetes) associated with roots of the host plant that supplies the energy for fixing N. Free-living, nonsymbiotic bacteria perform N fixation by utilizing energy supplied by the breakdown of organic matter (DeBano et al. 1998). Post-fire conditions favor nitrogen fixation by free-living microorganisms. In the Sierra Nevada Mountains of California, mountain whitehorn *(Ceanothus cordulatus)* with nitrogen-fixing symbionts in root nodules, and broadleaf lupine *(Lupinus latifolius)*, an herbaceous perennial legume, are both colonizers of recently burned soils and can be expected to add significantly to total soil nitrogen (St. John and Rundel, 1976).

PHOSPHORUS (P) AND SULFUR (S) CYCLING

The majority of phosphorus is lost during volatilization of the litter and biomass. Fire temperatures above 300°C (572°F) increase the volatilization losses of organic P (Giovaninni and Lucchesi 1997). Water-soluble, available P increased after burning (Giovaninni and Lucchesi 1997) (Table 5.2). Volatized P from the litter and surface organic matter can be translocated down the soil profile along a decreasing temperature gradient, subsequently condensing on the intervening soil particles (Overby and Perry 1996). As soil organic P is thermally mineralized, available P increases with the rising heating temperature (Giovaninni and Lucchesi 1997).

During fire, sulfur is volatized at higher temperatures than N, but in much smaller quantities. The reduction of S relative to N is between 5% and 9% of the nitrogen content of the fuels. Sulfur reduction showed a highly significant correlation with fuel weight loss, and an increase of 30%–70% as the temperature of combustion increased (Tiedemann and Anderson 1980). Sulfur cannot be fixed by biological processes, and is primarily added to sites through precipitation and volcanic eruptions.

CATION EXCHANGE CAPACITY AND INDIVIDUAL CATIONS

Cation exchange capacity (CEC) is the sum of the exchangeable cations found on organic and inorganic soil colloids. Total CEC can be decreased by burning, and may remain low for at least one year, because organic matter, which provides a large reactive surface area, is consumed (St. John and Rundel 1976). Even though CEC is reduced, the plant-available nutrient status of the soil is increased in response to the fire-induced release of organically bound nutrients such as potassium (K), calcium (Ca), and magnesium (Mg) now found in the ash. In the majority of wildland soils, these major cations are not normally deficient, and all have high temperature thresholds. Burning increased exchangeable K and Mg, and dramatically increased exchangeable Ca, as a result of virtually all of the Ca from the litter being deposited on the mineral soil (St. John and Rundel 1976). At Lake Tahoe, Stephens et al. (2004) found that prescribed fires released calcium and raised soil pH, and may have resulted in the incorporation of phosphorus into insoluble forms.

Copper (Cu), aluminum (Al), molybdenum (Mo), and manganese (Mn) showed increases following fire, whereas iron (Fe), strontium (Sr), barium (Ba), and zinc (Zn) showed medium to large reductions (Hough 1981). Increases of Mn in the surface horizons were attributed to the deposition of ash from the burnt vegetation, whereas increases of Mn in subsurface horizons were due to its transportation in the form of organic complexes through soil macropores (Gonzalez-Parra et al. 1996).

pH AND ASHBED EFFECT

Burning affects the chemical properties of soils by converting organic matter, including the residues in the litter layer, to ash. Precipitation washes and leaches the ash into the soil, affecting the pH and the concentration of solutes (Wells et al. 1979). The basic cations in the ash can raise the pH of the

BOX 5.2. FIRE AND THE NITROGEN CYCLE

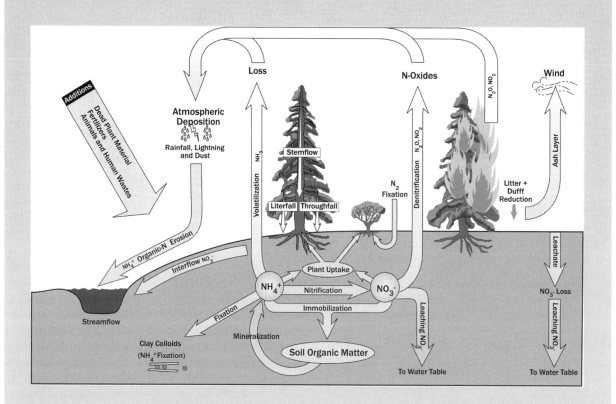

Accelerated losses

Volatilization   Heating during fire. Between 400°C and 500°C, 75% to 100% of N is lost; between 300°C and 400°C, 50% to 75% is lost; from 200°C to 300°C, up to 50% of N is lost; and below 200°C only small amounts of N are lost (DeBano et al., 1979).

Ash   Combustion of living and dead plant material. Litter is removed by wind and contains small amounts of N, but has increased amounts of cations that were present in the fuels before burning.

Leaching   The transport of NO_3^-, which is less easily attached to soil particles, downward through the profile to below the root zone. Post-fire, more NO_3^- is available to be leached because of absence of uptake by vegetation.

Surface erosion   Removal of NH_4^+ attached to clay particles.

Nitrification

Oxidation of ammonium (NH_4^+) to nitrite (NO_2^-), and then to nitrate (NO_3^-). *Nitrosomonas* bacteria can be killed in dry soil at 140°C and in wet soil at 75°C. *Nitrobacter* are more sensitive and are killed at 100°C in dry and 50°C in wet soil (Dunn and DeBano, 1977).

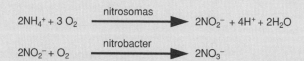

$$2NH_4^+ + 3\,O_2 \xrightarrow{\text{nitrosomas}} 2NO_2^- + 4H^+ + 2H_2O$$

$$2NO_2^- + O_2 \xrightarrow{\text{nitrobacter}} 2NO_3^-$$

(Continued)

(Continued)

Mineralization and immobilization

Mineralization   Conversion of organic N to the ammonium form, through decomposition. This process is accelerated by fire.

Immobilization NH_4^+ is taken up and assimilated again as plants and microbes grow and synthesize new organic N compounds. R = Organic compounds.

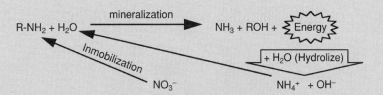

Biological N_2 fixation

Conversion of atmospheric N_2 to organic combinations (post-fire *Lotus* and *Lupinus* spp., *Ceanothus* spp., alder, lichens, bacteria in downed logs).

TABLE 5.2

The effect of experimental fires on some chemical properties of the 0 to 2.5 cm depth of soil

Heating Temp. °C	CEC meq/100g	OM %	N-NH4+ mg/kg	P-Org. mg/kg	P-Avail. mg/kg
25	44	26	40	208	39
89	40	25	34	204	40
184	36	21	60	184	50
210	36	20	33	160	50
312	36	15	50	70	88
395	29	13	52	60	92
457	27	12	52	40	95
558	23	12	54	30	103

NOTE: Adapted from Giovaninni and Lucchesi (1997).

surface soil as much as three units (to pH 10.5), thus fundamentally altering many chemical weathering reactions (Ulery and Graham 1993). Soil pH increased after burning in a giant sequoia grove (St. John and Rundel 1976); however, no change in post-fire pH was reported for a prescribed burn in chaparral (Overby and Perry 1996).

The ash is highly soluble and most compounds are removed from the soil in the first post-fire wet season (Tiedemann et al. 1979). Calcite, which is less soluble, can still be present in the soil 3 years after burning, resulting in surface soils of moderate alkaline pH (Ulery and Graham 1993).

Winds associated with very intense wildfires may remove most of the ash from a site.

Fire Interactions with Water

Fire alters the water balance on burned sites, which promotes changes in the hydrology of the hillslopes, the stream channels, and whole watersheds. These hydrologic changes in turn affect the erosion and sedimentation response of burned landscapes at all spatial scales.

Hillslope Hydrology

The disposition of water on hillslopes reflects a balance between the inputs and outputs of the hydrologic cycle (Fig. 5.4). Hillslope hydrology changes after a fire, in part because of altered soil conditions of structure and water repellency. These hydrologic changes have serious implications for hillslope erosion and the delivery of sediment and water to the stream channels.

INTERCEPTION, SNOW ACCUMULATION, AND SNOWMELT

Some of the precipitation falling on a watershed never reaches the ground. *Interception* is that portion of rain (or snow) that is retained in the plant canopy until it evaporates. Interception in unburned vegetation may be as high as 11% (Rowe and Colman 1951). Interception reduces raindrop impact, soil water storage, and transpiration. By removing the vegetation, fire reduces interception, thereby potentially increasing water on the hillsides (Baker 1990).

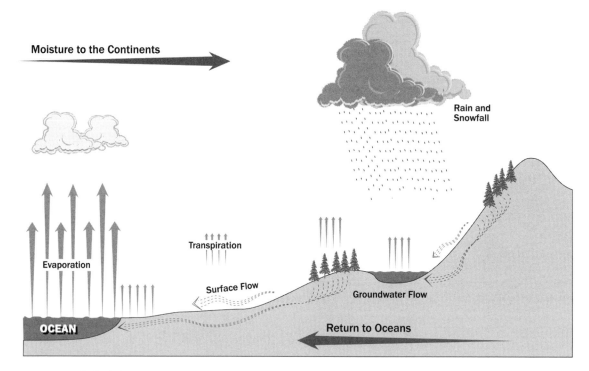

FIGURE 5.4. The hydrologic cycle. Water moves from oceans to continents and back again.

The rates of snowfall accumulation and snowmelt are not uniform across the landscape. Apart from obvious differences in elevation and aspect, snow accumulation is generally inversely proportional to vegetation cover. Thus, snow depths would be enhanced on severely burned sites where the vegetation has been removed. However, accumulation would be less in large bare areas that were subject to snow removal by wind scour (Tiedemann et al. 1979).

Vegetation has a moderating influence on local weather conditions. With the removal of vegetation, burned areas are susceptible to extremes of surface temperatures, affecting soil freezing and snowmelt rates (Baker 1990). Scorched ground in burn areas may increase the long-wave solar re-radiation into the snowpack (Tiedemann et al. 1979), thereby enhancing snowmelt.

INFILTRATION

Fire affects infiltration by altering ground cover and soil properties. Often the changes in infiltration mirror the changes in soil texture and porosity explained previously. Infiltration is reduced if soil aggregate bonds are destroyed, promoting surface sealing by the newly liberated fine soil grains subject to unimpeded raindrop impacts (Ahlgren and Ahlgren 1960, Wells et al. 1979, Baker 1990). However, where fire enhances soil aggregation and permeability, infiltration will be increased (Scott and Burgy 1956).

Other factors also influence post-fire infiltration. The litter layer can act like a sponge during rainfall, and if it is consumed by fire, infiltration will be reduced (Wells et al. 1979). Water-repellent soils will initially sharply reduce infiltration on burned sites, although the water-repellent substances are slightly water soluble and will eventually wet up and infiltrate normally (DeBano 1981). The temperature extremes on burn sites can also promote more soil freezing, which will reduce infiltration (Tiedemann et al. 1979).

EVAPOTRANSPIRATION

Generally, site evaporation increases but transpiration is sharply curtailed after a fire. The greater daytime temperature extremes experienced in burned areas promote greater evaporation. Post-fire evaporation is also enhanced by the loss of plant canopy shading and protection (Ahlgren and Ahlgren 1960). Conversely, water-repellent substances can reduce evaporation by disrupting the forces of capillary rise (DeBano 1981).

Obviously, post-fire transpiration is negligible if the vegetation is completely consumed. Partially burning a watershed unit should reduce transpiration in proportion to the percentage of totally burned area (Rowe and Colman 1951). Lightly and moderately burned sites will have transpiration reduced to the degree that foliage is consumed and roots are killed. Even with initial vegetation recovery, site transpiration rates will be reduced, as biomass is limited and the herbaceous fire-followers lack great rooting depths to significantly de-water the soil mantle (Sampson 1944).

SOIL MOISTURE

Soil moisture content on any site results from a balance between infiltration and evapotranspiration. Soil moisture in burned areas reflects any consequent changes in vegetation or soil properties. Reduced infiltration, whether by surface sealing (Ahlgren and Ahlgren 1960) or by water repellency (DeBano 1981), can lower soil moisture levels. However, soil moisture can also increase after a fire, as interception and transpiration are negligible (Rowe and Colman 1951). On some post-fire sites, both conditions can occur simultaneously. Soil moisture in the upper mantle is lower due to greater evaporation and transpiration by herbs and forbs, whereas soil moisture in the lower mantle is higher, as it is beyond the depth of herbaceous root systems (Sampson 1944).

OVERLAND FLOW

Hillslope surface runoff, or *overland flow*, occurs when precipitation intensity exceeds the rate of infiltration. On unburned areas with a complete canopy and/or litter cover, overland flow is a rare event, produced only during the most intense rains. In post-fire environments where infiltration and water storage capacities are severely reduced by altered canopy and soil properties, however, overland flow can be substantial (Tiedemann et al. 1979, DeBano 1981). Rice (1974) estimated that surface runoff could be as much as 40% of the rainfall on a freshly burned chaparral site in southern California. In their review of fire in forested ecosystems, Ahlgren and Ahlgren (1960) reported that burned watersheds in the Sierra Nevada increased overland flow by 31–463 times the unburned rate.

A special type of surface runoff is the flow from springs. Spring flow has been observed to increase after fire in the Sierra Nevada foothills (Biswell and Schultz 1957). In this case, increased flow has less to do with the relative rates of precipitation and infiltration than with reduced transpiration from vegetation uphill of the spring.

Hillslope Erosion

The fire-induced changes in soil conditions and hillslope hydrology discussed previously can produce dramatic increases in post-fire hillslope erosion. Fire renders the landscape more sensitive to erosional forces, and large storms can result in substantial quantities of rock and soil being stripped off the hillslopes and delivered to the stream channels.

SURFACE EROSION

Surface erosion generally increases following a fire, but the amount of accelerated erosion depends on the complex combination of site conditions, fire characteristics, and rainfall patterns. Burning increases surface erosion by removing the protective barriers of vegetation and litter, thereby increasing the erosional effectiveness of rainsplash, wind scour, and overland flow. Fire also alters soil properties (structure, porosity, and water repellency) that enhance hillslope erosional processes (Wells et al. 1979, DeBano 1981).

Accelerated surface erosion can actually start while the fire is still burning. As organic barriers on the ground surface are consumed, trapped soil and rock material that have accumulated behind them are liberated and move downhill under the influence of gravity. This pulse of dry ravel (Rice 1974) is more pronounced in steep terrain, and may continue for days or weeks after the fire until a new geomorphic equilibrium is reached.

A second flush of surface erosion begins with the first post-fire rains, when gravity is augmented by hydrologic processes. Overland flow, often promoted by a water-repellent layer and reduced soil water storage, is an especially effective erosional process. Well-developed networks of micro-channels or *rills* are a distinctive feature on burned hillslopes (Wells 1981).

Post-fire surface erosion levels can increase by several orders of magnitude over pre-burn rates. Fire increased both wet and dry hillslope erosion by a total of 17 times over pre-burn levels in southern California chaparral (Krammes 1960). Ahlgren and Ahlgren (1960) reported that post-fire surface erosion in the Sierra Nevada was 2–239 times greater than pre-burn rates. With vegetation regrowth and the depletion of easily mobilized surface material, hillslope erosion attenuates with time since fire and returns to pre-burn rates within 2–3 years (Heede et al. 1988, Wohlgemuth et al. 1998).

MASS EROSION

Contrary to popular notions, fire is not an important factor in directly generating mass erosion on hillslopes. Mudflows, earthflows, and nonseismic landslides are almost exclusively produced by excess soil moisture during the rainy season. However, as noted previously, infiltration is often reduced in the post-fire environment, resulting in more overland flow and less percolation to subsurface slip zones. Burning can indirectly foster mass movement, but this is associated with the loss of root strength in fire-killed trees and may not occur for nearly a decade after the burn (Ziemer and Swanston 1977). Debris flows are important post-fire mass erosion events, but they are confined almost exclusively to stream channels and are covered in the following section.

Channel Hydrology

Fires can directly impact stream channels by killing the instream vegetation and changing riparian habitats. However, the most direct consequence of burning on streams is the extra sediment and water delivered from the hillslopes. The attendant changes in water quantity, water quality, and erosion and sedimentation can drastically alter the character of channel systems.

WATER QUANTITY

In the post-fire environment there is a change in watershed hydrology. Increased hillslope overland flow—from the reduction in vegetation cover and transpiration, and the

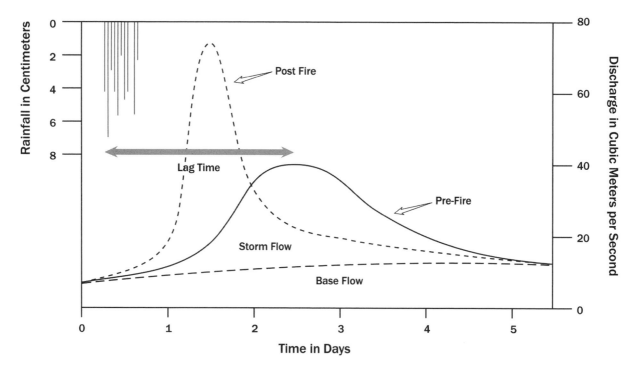

FIGURE 5.5. Streamflow hydrograph (discharge plotted against time) following a rainstorm showing lag time and peak flow changes with fire events.

production of water repellent soils—generates more stream-flow. Fire increases the contributing area of hillslope delivery to the channels, and the rill networks quickly convey water off the slopes into the streams (Wells 1981). Thus, in post-fire environments, a larger number of storms produce flow than before the burn, with greater total water yield, and with intermittent flows often becoming perennial (Tiedemann et al. 1979).

Peak flows are the greatest instantaneous discharge rates experienced in stream channels for individual flood events, whereas *storm flows* are the total amounts of water produced by a rainstorm or a related series of storms (Fig. 5.5). Burning has been shown to increase peak flows in California forests and chaparral (Anderson, 1949), in Arizona chaparral (Rich 1962), and in Australian scrub forests (Brown 1972). Using comparable storms both before and after a high-severity fire in southern California chaparral, Krammes and Rice (1963) were able to document that post-fire peak flows were 200–800 times greater than unburned levels. Tiedemann et al. (1979) reported that extreme increases in post-fire peak flows could be up to 10,000 times those in unburned watersheds. Increases in peak flow are generally inversely proportional to watershed area. Thus, the largest increases occur in the smallest catchments. Light and moderate severity burns can produce peak flows that are 5–100 times greater than from unburned conditions (Tiedemann et al. 1979).

Storm flows also increase after burning. In one of two adjacent watersheds with extensive pre-fire streamflow records in southern California chaparral, fire increased storm flow by 3–5 times compared to its unburned companion (Colman

1953, Sinclair and Hamilton 1955). Brown (1972) and Tiedemann et al. (1979) reported similar post-fire storm flow responses. Storm flows remain elevated for 3 years following a fire and may persist for 5–10 years (Baker 1990).

Base flows are the background streamflow levels over which the rainy season storm flows are superimposed (Fig. 5.5). Base flows are typically evaluated at the end of the dry season. Burned watersheds have been shown to increase base flows compared with pre-fire conditions (Pase and Ingebo 1965) or similar unburned catchments (Tiedemann et al. 1979). Base flow increases have been specifically attributed to the reduced transpiration of fire-killed riparian vegetation (Colman 1953), but increased base flow would also be expected to result from the consumption of all vegetation across the burned area.

Flow timing refers to the shape of the streamflow runoff curve (or *hydrograph*). Fires can alter hydrograph shape by producing multiple storm peaks and reducing the lag time from rainfall initiation to peak flow (see Fig. 5.5). Brown (1972) reported secondary flow peaks in a burned watershed that he attributed directly to the fire. Lag time to peak flows are shorter in burned catchments because water is shed rapidly off the hillslopes and more quickly delivered to the streams. Reduced lag times can also be the result of earlier snowmelts (Tiedemann et al. 1979).

WATER QUALITY

Not only is the amount and timing of streamflow affected by fire, so is the character of the water itself. Changes in turbidity, temperature, and stream chemistry may alter water quality, sometimes to the detriment of aquatic ecosystems and downstream water supplies.

Turbidity is a measure of the suspended solids in streamflow. Stream discharge from unburned watersheds is normally clear, barring any ground-disturbing activity. On the other hand, streamflow from burned catchments is typically laden with ash and fine soil grains, giving the water a sooty or muddy appearance. Increased turbidity is the most dramatic post-fire water quality response. However, turbidity is difficult to characterize, being highly transient and extremely variable. The source of the stream sediment load is primarily soil stripped off the hillslopes and also includes material scoured from the channel bed and banks (Tiedemann et al. 1979, Baker 1990).

Stream temperatures are elevated in the post-fire environment with the loss of protective shade. Temperature increases depend on the topography (governing exposure), distance from the water source, and size of the burned area. Elevated temperatures are partially offset by increased streamflow (Tiedemann et al. 1979).

Changes in post-fire water chemistry can be tremendous. Nutrients and soluble compounds in the ash are flushed off the hillslopes during the first post-fire storms and are incorporated into the streamflow. Much of the nutrient load is attached to sediment particles, and is exported with the suspended sediments (Tiedemann et al. 1979). However, fires significantly increase solute concentrations in the stream water. Concentrations of these solutes remain elevated long after sediment transport has returned to pre-burn levels (Williams and Melack 1997). Stephens et al. (2004) reported that stream water calcium concentrations increased in burned watersheds in the Tahoe basin, whereas soluble reactive phosphorus concentrations did not change. Monitoring indicated that the water quality effects in this latter study lasted for approximately 3 months.

Channel Erosion and Sedimentation

Stream channels are very dynamic systems that erode, transport, and deposit sediment in a quasi-continuous fashion, eventually routing hillslope-derived rock and soil to the watershed outlet. Fire greatly accelerates the activity rate of this process, and can alter riparian structure and geomorphology. Channel stability is often a function of the material making up the bed and banks. Alluvial channels, composed of sand-sized grains, are very mobile and respond quickly to changes in flow regime or sediment load. Conversely, bedrock channels are very stable and are only modified by the highest magnitude flows (Leopold et al. 1964). Channels composed of cobbles or boulders show few morphologic changes in the absence of fire (Doehring 1968).

With the changes in soils, hillslope hydrology, and surface erosion following a fire, the initial channel response is to fill with colluvial sediments from adjacent side slopes (Heede et al. 1988, Florsheim et al. 1991). This sediment is delivered to the channels first by dry ravel and second by overland flow with the onset of the rainy season.

The generally observed pattern of channel fill and subsequent downcutting is well documented (Doehring 1968, Heede et al. 1988, Florsheim et al. 1991). Initial post-fire storms laden with hillslope sediment cause channel filling, while later storms tend to scour the channels, as hillslope sediment supply becomes depleted. However, in alluvial channels and on steeper channel gradients, initial scour can be followed by subsequent filling (Doehring 1968). Post-fire channel sedimentation will preferentially fill stream pools, smoothing both the longitudinal and transverse profiles (Keller et al. 1997).

Channel scour can also occur by post-fire debris flows. *Debris flows,* a form of mass erosion, are slurries of water and sediment that have incredible erosive power. Some debris flows originate on hillslopes as transformed ground-saturated landslides. But, as noted previously, these are not post-fire features. Instead, post-fire debris flows form and propagate exclusively in the stream channels, as stored sediment is mobilized by the influx of water derived from hillslope overland flow (Wells 1987). Despite their impressive ability to alter channel morphology, debris flows are relatively rare events. Post-fire channel flushing is more likely to occur by normal stream transport processes than by high-magnitude debris flows (Keller et al. 1997).

Post-fire channel sedimentation, subsequently scoured, will eventually migrate downstream out of the burned area. These post-fire sediments are periodically flushed by flood flows and temporarily held in storage sites until they reach the outlet of larger watersheds (Heede et al. 1988). This transported sediment can alter riparian habitats and can reduce channel capacity, thereby increasing downstream flood risk (Keller et al. 1997).

Watershed Hydrology and Erosion

The effects of fire on water at a landscape level can be ascertained in studies of whole watersheds. Catchments integrate the local vagaries of fire response into general trends in water yield and sediment yield.

WATER YIELD

The unanimous consensus of published research is that fire increases catchment water yield, as might be expected in light of the foregoing discussions of hillslope hydrology and streamflow quantity. Whether comparing the response of adjacent burned and unburned watersheds (Hamilton et al. 1954, Glendening et al. 1961, Brown 1972) or the response of similar storms in watersheds before and after a fire (Krammes and Rice 1963), burning enhances water yield. Unless this difference can be accounted for by the concomitant reduction in transpiration, this would suggest that there is an overall reduction in soil moisture across the watershed. Elevated levels of water yield can persist for years after a fire (Rowe et al. 1954, Baker 1990).

Not surprisingly, because of accelerated hillslope erosion and enhanced channel transport, fire appears to universally increase watershed sediment yield (Anderson 1949; Hamilton et al. 1954, Glendening et al. 1961, Brown 1972). The source of the sediment comes from both hillslope material and mobilized stream channel deposits. The timing of post-fire sediment yield can vary as a function of watershed size. Smaller catchments respond very quickly, but because of temporary storage, there may be a considerable lag time before sediment arrives at the outlet of larger watersheds (Heede et al. 1988).

Documented rates of post-fire sediment yield vary considerably, depending on topography, soil characteristics, vegetation type, fire severity, and precipitation patterns. In forested environments, post-fire sediment yields can exceed unburned levels by as much as 50 times (Anderson 1949). Post-fire sediment yields in Arizona chaparral can be 100 times greater than those from unburned watersheds (Pase and Ingebo 1965). Burned watersheds in southern California chaparral produce an average of 35 times more sediment than unburned watersheds (Rowe et al. 1954), but can experience 1,000 times more sediment yield than comparably sized unburned catchments (Kraebel 1934). Post-fire sediment yields can remain elevated for 8–10 years after burning (Rowe et al. 1954).

Fire Interactions with Air

Fire affects air quality by introducing smoke and the residues of combustion into the atmosphere. These byproducts of burning can be transported to areas distant from the fire and may have profound effects on plant communities.

Air Quality

Smoke is produced as fires burn live and dead vegetation. Wildland fires result in complex combustion of many types of biomass, and smoke composition varies with topography, weather, and fuel density. Emissions from prescribed fires and wildfires contain a number of air pollutants, including particulate matter, carbon monoxide, nitrogen oxides, volatile organic compounds, and certain toxic pollutants (DeBano et al. 1998). The quantity and type of emissions produced depend on the amounts and types of vegetation burned, its moisture content, and the temperature and altitude of combustion (USEPA 1998).

As biomass is consumed, thermal energy is released. This energy creates buoyancy that lifts smoke particles and other pollutants above the fire. In hot fires (Fig. 5.6) buoyancy can result in a fast-rising central convective column with counterrotating vortices, which entraps the surrounding air. This active column may also produce turbulent downdrafts that ignite new fires distant from the original fire. If fire intensity is lower, then the central column may not form, or it may collapse as fire intensity diminishes. The result is smaller convective cells that do not carry smoke as high into the atmosphere. Low-intensity smoldering fires produce little buoyancy, often resulting in smoke that fills local valleys and basins at night (Sandberg et al. 2002).

Once aloft, smoke plumes are subject to complex chemical reactions. These reactions depend on dilution rates, photolysis rates, position, altitude, and temperature. Dilution occurs when dense smoke mixes with the surrounding "clean" air. Chemical reactions within smoke plumes decrease as smoke gets diluted with this air. For instance, increasing dilution by a factor of 2 will decrease the reaction rate by a factor of 4. Photolysis reactions are chemical reactions that occur due to the presence of sunlight in which molecules are split into their constituent atoms. These reactions occur largely at the top of plumes, especially when thermal inversion layers of air limit plume height. As plumes are diluted with surrounding air, sunlight penetrates deeper into the plume and photolysis reaction rates increase.

Concentration also influences particulate formation. Particles can form from gases as a result of nucleation of gases (molecules of gas combining together) or condensation (entrapment of gases in water droplets). These processes commonly occur as the plume temperature cools, thus plume height, temperature, and concentration may act in combination to control the total particulate and trace gas composition and concentration.

Downwind air also mixes with the plume, which in California typically includes urban-generated air pollution. Urban air pollution sources are predominantly the result of gasoline and diesel combustion. Inorganic compounds including nitrogenous compounds are injected into the atmosphere along with light hydrocarbons and particles. O_3 is formed by photolytic reaction during transport of air masses eastward.

Several biomass combustion and secondary products are classified as *criteria* pollutants (pollutants with established air quality standards) under the Clean Air Act, including O_3, CO, NO_x, and particulate matter. Under the current regulatory framework, prescribed fire is generally considered an *anthropogenic*, as opposed to *natural*, source of air pollutants by state and regional air quality agencies. However, an effort is underway to re-classify prescribed fires that are used to maintain functional and fire-resilient ecosystems as natural fire emission sources. California air-quality districts do not yet generally recognize this classification, and thus consider most prescribed-fire emissions to be subject to control strategies designed to help meet state and federal air quality standards.

Transport

In California, prevailing ground-level winds are northwesterly because of the geotropic balance between a subtropical anticyclone over the east Pacific Ocean and thermal low pressure over the desert during the summer. In gaps along the Coastal Ranges, the onshore winds create air streams flowing

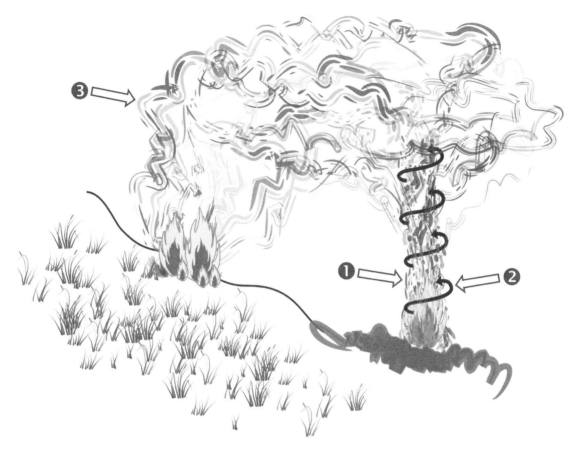

FIGURE 5.6. Illustration of smoke plume dynamics for a hot fire. A central convective column (1) occurs due to heated air becoming more buoyant than the surrounding air. As this air rises it may become a counter-rotating vortex (2) that develops strong ground winds as air is pulled up from the ground into the plume. The rapidly developing smoke plume can also form down drafts (3) that ignite new fires at distant points from the original fire.

into the inland valleys. Warm boundary-layer air masses overlying these valleys in summer are stratified by weak thermal inversions at 1,000–1,300 m (3,281–4,265 ft). Daylight land heating generates local anabatic winds from the southwest and west along the western slopes, which transport air masses into the interior mountain ranges.

The onshore winds and boundary-layer air masses contribute to complex plume transport characteristics in California. Advection (lateral diffusion) is often easterly for low-elevation fires, but can quickly change with prevailing wind patterns. The inversion layer of air also often limits upward diffusion of the plume and reduces dissipation of the smoke plume in the upper atmosphere. Smoke from higher-elevation fires, such as in the Sierra Nevada, is less affected by thermal inversions but may burn at lower intensities for longer duration. Dispersion is also less predictable in mountainous areas as inversion air masses that normally constrain upward diffusion weaken due to complex high-elevation topography. When this occurs, plumes penetrate higher-elevation air mass layers and may be transported hundreds or thousands of miles before the plume dissipates.

Emissions inventories for all sources, including fire, are compiled on an annual basis by the California Air Resources Board (CARB). Fire emissions for state inventories are developed by multiplying the area burned by timber/brush emission factor and fuel loading. Results are reported as the amount of pollutant produced per year for the entire state, by individual air basins, and by county. Particulate matter (PM) in smoke emissions is the constituent of greatest concern due to its impacts on visibility (Billington et al. 2000) and human health. Particulate emissions are projected to increase for most air basins in the Sierra Nevada and southern California through 2010 (CARB 2001). The majority of particulates produced by biomass burning are less then ten microns in diameter, small enough to enter the human respiratory system (Billington et al. 2000). Slow-burning fires generate much greater amounts of fine particles (<2.5 microns), whereas high-intensity fires (such as wildfires) release higher proportions of coarse particles (Cahill et al. 1996).

Ozone (O_3) formation may also result from chemical reactions during smoke transport (Sandberg et al. 2002). O_3 forms by photolysis of nitrogen oxides in the presence of nonmethane hydrocarbons such as volatile organic compounds. It primarily forms in smoke plumes many kilometers from the actual fire. Concentrations of ozone as great as

80–90 ppb above background have been measured in smoke plumes.

Although fire emissions can be modeled, it is not possible at this time to accurately measure emissions on site. To estimate smoke from wildland burning, land cover and fuel condition data must be combined with meteorological information (Fox et al. 2000). Simply expressed, smoke emissions are calculated by multiplying the area burned by the fuel loading and an emissions factor, which is the amount of pollutant produced per unit of fuel consumed. Emissions factors and fuel-loading estimates may represent general categories such as grass or brush, or be specific to an individual vegetation type (e.g., coastal sage scrub). As may be inferred, more reliable emissions information is produced by site- and vegetation-specific emission factors and fuel-loading parameters.

Smoke Effects on Ecosystems

Chemicals generated by smoke affect vegetation in a variety of ways. Smoke may reduce photosynthetic efficiency at low levels, and cause acute toxicity and tissue necrosis at high levels. For instance, nitric acid vapor is a strong oxidant that can cause cuticular degradation of leaf waxes in ponderosa pine *(Pinus ponderosa)* and California black oak *(Quercus kelloggii)*, perhaps predisposing plants to insect or pathogen attacks or the effects of other air pollutants (Bytnerowicz et al. 2001).

Smoke may also *protect* vegetation from fungal infection. After plant surfaces were exposed to smoke, germination and growth of several fungi, including annosus root rot *(Heterobasidion annosum)*, were reduced in laboratory studies (Parmeter and Uhrenholdt 1976). This suggests that smoke may impact microbial communities that exist in forest and shrub ecosystems.

Smoke has also been shown to induce germination of many annual species in chaparral ecosystems. Smoke and charred wood induced germination in annual and some perennial species present in chaparral ecosystems (Keeley and Fotheringham 1998). Some responses have been linked to exposure to NO_x, which induces germination in several annual species (Keeley 2000), but others appear to be caused by chemicals present both in smoke and in charred wood. In addition, some species have a long-term storage requirement before they will germinate in response to smoke exposure.

Other effects of smoke may be due to NO_3^-, NH_4^+, and O_3 created as secondary compounds during the transport process. O_3 is the most toxic of these compounds for plants. As previously discussed, O_3 is produced both from smoke and from urban-generated air pollution sources. O_3 is taken into the plant through the stomates, and due to its strong oxidizing capacity it reduces photosynthesis rates, decreases foliar chlorophyll, and accelerates foliar senescence. Field and fumigation chamber studies of conifer species have indicated that ponderosa pine, Jeffrey pine *(Pinus jeffreyi)*, white fir *(Abies concolor)*, Coulter pine *(Pinus coulteri)*, incense-cedar *(Calocedrus decurrens)*, big cone Douglas-fir *(Pseudotsuga macrocarpa)*, and sugar pine are susceptible to O_3 in California (Miller et al. 1983).

Negative impacts of atmospheric N deposition may also be occurring in California's ecosystems. Although small increases of N deposited from smoke act to stimulate growth and regeneration in clean environments, they may have the opposite effect in areas where high deposition of N from urban-generated air pollution has occurred. High levels of N in soils can accelerate community structure changes, and high N deposition has been shown to increase nitrate export through the soil and water systems. Subsequent exposure of high N deposition areas to O_3 has been associated with physiological changes in ponderosa pine, and can lead to replacement of some pine species with nitrophilous-, shade, and O_3-tolerant tree species (Takemoto et al. 2000). Issues related to smoke impacts are discussed further in Chapter 21.

Summary

Fire interactions with soil, water, and air resources range from minute changes in soil structure, to alterations in stream water quantity and quality, to potential degradation of air quality across broad regions. However, these are not isolated effects, as fire interactions in one part of the landscape can influence outcomes in other areas.

Heat from a fire can alter soil structure, chemistry, and soil biota, which may radically modify hillslope hydrology, especially infiltration and overland flow. Increased post-fire dry ravel and surface runoff greatly accelerate hillslope surface erosion. The delivery of soil and water from the hillslopes can overwhelm the stream channels by increasing the water quantity, changing the water quality, and modifying the patterns of erosion and sedimentation. The net result is an increase in both water yield and sediment yield from upland watersheds that will last for many years. Similarly, smoke from wildland fires can affect the health and well-being of human and biological communities, both adjacent to and at some distance from the burning.

Much is known about the interactions of fire with soil, water, and air; yet many knowledge gaps remain. Although we believe we conceptually understand these fire interactions, attempts at predictive modeling and risk analysis are woefully inadequate. Only by better understanding the effects of fire on soil, water, and air resources are we in a better position to manage the consequences of burning.

References

Agrippa, H.C. 2000. Three books of the occult philosophy or of magic. P. 1-678 in D. Tyson (ed.), Three books of the occult philosophy written by Henry Cornelius Agrippa of Nettlesheim. Llewellyn Press, St. Paul.

Ahlgren, I. F., and C. E. Ahlgren. 1960. Ecological effects of forest fires. Botanical Review 26:483–533.

Anderson, H. W. 1949. Does burning increase surface runoff? Journal of Forestry 47:54–57.

Baker, M.B., Jr. 1990. Hydrologic and water quality effects on fire. P. 31–42 in J.S. Krammes (technical coordinator), Proceedings of the symposium on the effects of fire management on southwestern natural resources, November 15–17, Tucson, Arizona, USDA Forest Service, Rocky Mountain Research Station, General Technical Report RM-191.

Billington, J., L. Ommering, C. Haden, E. Linse, R. Ramalingam, and K. Black. 2000. Proposed amendments of California's agricultural burning guidelines. Staff Report. CALEPA, Air Resources Board, Planning and Technical Support Division, Sacramento, CA.

Biswell, H.H., and A.M. Schultz. 1957. Spring flow affected by brush. California Agriculture 11:3–4, 10.

Brown, J.A.H. 1972. Hydrologic effects of a bushfire in a catchment in southeastern New South Wales. Journal of Hydrology 15:77–96.

Bytnerowicz, A., P.E. Padgett, S.D. Parry, M.D. Fenn, and M.J. Arbaugh. 2001. Concentrations, deposition, and effects of nitrogenous pollutants in selected California ecosystems. In Optimizing nitrogen management in food and energy production and environmental protection, Proceedings of the 2nd international nitrogen conference on science and policy. In The Scientific World, Vol. 1. http://www.thescientificworld.com.

Cahill, T.A., T. Carroll, D. Campbell, and T.E. Gill. 1996. Sierra Nevada ecosystem project, final report to Congress, Vol. II, Chapter 48, p. 1227–1262.

California Air Resources Board (CARB). 2001. Emissions projections 2000–2010. Technical Support Division, Sacramento, CA.

Choromanska, U., and T.H. DeLuca. 2001. Prescribed fire alters the impact of wildfire on soil biochemical properties in a ponderosa pine forest. Soil Science Society of America Journal 65:232–238.

Christensen, N.L. 1973. Fire and the nitrogen cycle in California chaparral. Science 181:66–68.

Christensen, N.L., and C.H. Muller. 1975. Effects of fire on factors controlling plant growth in Adenostoma chaparral. Ecological Monographs 45:29–55.

Colman, E.A. 1953. Fire and water in southern California's mountains. USDA Forest Service, California Forest and Range Experiment Station, Miscellaneous Paper 3. 7 p.

DeBano, L.F. 1974. Chaparral soils. P. 19–16 in M. Rosenthal (ed.), Proceedings of a symposium on living with the chaparral, March 30–31, 1973, Riverside, CA. Sierra Club, San Francisco.

DeBano, L.F. 1981. Water repellent soils: a state-of-the-art. USDA Forest Service, Pacific Southwest Forest and Range Experiment Station, General Technical Report PSW-46. 21 p.

DeBano, L.F. 1988. Effects of fire on the soil resource in Arizona chaparral. P. 65–77 in J.S. Krammes (tech. coord.), Effects of fire management of southwestern natural resources. Gen. Tech. Rep. RM-191. Fort Collins, CO: USDA Forest Service, Rocky Mountain Forest and Range Experiment Station.

DeBano, L.F., D.G. Neary, and P.E. Ffolliott. 1998. Fire's effects on ecosystems. John Wiley and Sons, New York.

DeBano, L.F., and R.M. Rice. 1971. Fire in vegetation management—its effect on soil. P. 327–346 in Interdisciplinary aspects of watershed management. Symposium proceedings, Bozeman, MT.

DeBano, L.F., R.M. Rice, and C.E. Conrad. 1979. Soil heating in chaparral fires: effects on soil properties, plant nutrients, erosion, and runoff. USDA Forest Service, Pacific Southwest Forest and Range Experiment Station, Research Paper PSW-145.

DeBell, D.S., and C.W. Ralston. 1970. Release of nitrogen by burning light forest fuels. Soil Science Society of America Proceedings 34:936–938.

Dekker, L.W., C.J. Ritsema, K. Oostindie, and O.H. Boersma. 1998. Effect of drying temperature on the severity of soil water repellency. Soil Science 163:780–796.

Doehring, D.O. 1968. The effect of fire on geomorphic processes in the San Gabriel Mountains, California. University of Wyoming, Contributions to Geology 7(1):43–65.

Doerr, S.H., R.A. Shakesby, and R.P.D. Walsh. 2000. Soil water repellency: its causes, characteristics and hydro-geomorphological significance. Earth-Science Reviews 51:33–65.

Donahue, R.L., R.W. Miller, and J.C. Shickluna. 1983. Soils: an introduction to soils and plant growth. Prentice Hall, Englewood Cliffs, NJ.

Durgin, P.B. 1985. Burning changes the erodibility of forest soils. Journal of Soil and Water Conservation 40:299–301.

Fernandez, I., A. Cabaneiro, and T. Carballas. 1997. Organic matter changes immediately after a wildfire in an Atlantic forest soil and comparison with laboratory soil heating. Soil Biology and Biochememistry 29:1–11.

Florsheim, J.L., E.A. Keller, and D.W. Best. 1991. Fluvial sediment transport in response to moderate storm flows following chaparral wildfire, Ventura County, southern California. Geological Society of America Bulletin 103:504–511.

Fogel, R., and G. Hunt. 1979. Fungal and arboreal biomass in a western Oregon Douglas fir ecosystem: distribution patterns and turnover. Canadian Journal of Forestry Research 9:245–25.

Fox, D.G., A.R. Riebau, K.A. Eis, T.H. Vonder Haar, and W. Malm. 2000. Technically Advanced Smoke Estimation Tools: report to the National Park Service and the Joint Fire Science Program under Agreement Number CA 1268-2-9004 TA CSU-187, 99 p.

Giovaninni, G., and S. Lucchesi. 1997. Modifications induced in soil physico-chemical parameters by experimental fires at different intensities. Soil Science 162:479–486.

Glendening, G.E., C.P. Pase, and P. Ingebo. 1961. Preliminary hydrologic effects of wildfire in chaparral. P. 12–15 in Proceedings of the Arizona watershed symposium, September, 1961.

Gonzalez-Parra, J., V. Cala Rivera, and I.T. Glesias Lopez. 1996. Forms of Mn in soils affected by a forest fire. Science for the Total Environment 181:231–236.

Haase, S.M., and S.S. Sackett. 1998. Effects of prescribed fire in giant sequoia-mixed conifer stands in Sequoia and Kings Canyon National Parks. P. 236–234 in T.L. Pruden and L.A. Brennan (eds.), Fire in ecosystem management: shifting the paradigm from suppression to prescription. Tall Timbers ecology conference proceedings, no. 20. Tall Timbers Research Station, Tallhassee, FL.

Hamilton, E.L., J.S. Horton, P.B. Rowe, and L.F. Reimann. 1954. Fire-flood sequences on the San Dimas Experimental Forest. USDA Forest Service, California Forest and Range Experiment Station, Technical Paper No. 6. 29 p.

Heede, B.H., M.D. Harvey, and J.R. Laird. 1988. Sediment delivery linkages in a chaparral watershed following a wildfire. Environmental Management 12:349–358.

Hough, W.A. 1981. Impact of prescribed fire on understory and forest floor nutrients. USDA Forest Service, Southeastern Forest Experiment Station, Research Note SE-303.

Jury, W.A., W.R. Gardner, and W.H. Gardner. 1991. Soil physics. John Wiley and Sons, New York.

Keeley, J.E. 2000. Chaparral. P. 203–24 in M.G. Barbour and W.D. Billings (eds.), North American terrestrial vegetation, second edition. Cambridge University Press, Cambridge, U.K.

Keeley, J.E., and C.J. Fotheringham. 1998. Mechanism of smoke-induced seed germination in Californian chaparral. Journal of Ecology 86:27–36.

Keller, E.A., D.W. Valentine, and D.R. Gibbs. 1997. Hydrological response of small watersheds following the southern California Painted Cave Fire of June 1990. Hydrological Processes 11: 401–414.

Ketterings, Q.M., and J.M. Bigham. 2000. Soil color as an indicator of slash-and-burn severity and soil fertility in Sumatra, Indonesia. Soil Science Society of America Journal 64: 1826–1833.

Kimmins, J.P. 1996. Importance of soil and role of ecosystem disturbance for sustained productivity of cool temperate and boreal forests. Soil Science Society of America Journal 56: 1643–1654.

Kraebel, C.J. 1934. The La Crescenta flood. American Forests 40:251–254, 286–287.

Krammes, J.S. 1960. Erosion from mountain side slopes after fire in southern California. USDA Forest Service, Pacific Southwest Forest and Range Experiment Station, Research Note 171. 8 p.

Krammes, J.S., and R.M. Rice. 1963. Effect of fire on the San Dimas experimental forest. P. 31–34 in Proceedings of Arizona's 7th annual watershed symposium, September 18, 1963.

Leopold, L.B., M.G. Wolman, and J.P. Miller. 1964. Fluvial processes in geomorphology. W.H. Freeman and Company, San Francisco: 522 p.

Letey, J. 1969. Measurement of contact angle, water drop penetration time, and critical surface tension. P. 43–47 in Proceedings of the symposium on water-repellent soils, University of California, May 1968.

McNabb, D.H., and K. Cromack, Jr. 1990. Effects of prescribed fire on nutrients and soil productivity. P. 125–141 in J.D. Walstad, S.R. Radosevich, and D.V. Sandberg (eds.), Natural and prescribed fire in Pacific Northwest forests. Oregon State University Press, Corvallis, OR.

Miller, P.R., G.J. Longbotham, and C.R. Longbotham. 1983. Sensitivity of selected western conifers to ozone. Plant Disease 67: 1113–1115.

Neal, J.L., E. Wright, and W.B. Bolen. 1965. Burning Douglas fir slash: physical, chemical and microbial effects in the soil. Forestry Research Laboratory, Research Paper 1. Oregon State University, Corvallis, OR. 32 p.

Neary, D.G., C.C. Klopatek, L.F. DeBano, and P.F. Ffolliott. 1999. Fire effects on belowground sustainability: a review and synthesis. Forest Ecology and Management 122:51–71.

Oswald, B.P., D. Davenport, and L.F. Neunschwander. 1999. Effects of slash pile burning on the physical and chemical soil properties of Vassar soils. Journal of Sustainable Forestry 8:75–86.

Overby, S.T., and H.M. Perry. 1996. Direct effects of prescribed fire on available nitrogen and phosphorus in an Arizona chaparral watershed. Arid Soil Resources and Rehabilitation 10:347–357.

Parmeter, J.R., Jr., and B. Uhrenholdt. 1976. Effects of smoke on pathogens and other fungi. 1976. In Tall Timbers fire ecology conference and fire and land management symposium, Missoula, MT, No. 14, Tall Timbers Research Station, Tallahassee, FL.

Pase, C.P., and P.A. Ingebo. 1965. Burned chaparral to grass: early effects on water and sediment yields from two granitic soil watersheds in Arizona. P. 8–11 in Proceedings of the Arizona watershed symposium, September 22, 1965, Tempe, AZ.

Pietikainen, J., R. Hiukka, and H. Fritze. 2000. Does short-term heating of forest humus change its properties as a substrate for microbes? Soil Biology and Biochemistry 32:277–288.

Prieto-Fernandez, A., M.J. Acea, and T. Carballas. 1998. Soil microbial and extractable C and N after wildfire. Biology and Fertility of Soils 27:132–142.

Raison, R.J., H. Keith, and P.K. Khanna. 1990. Effects of fire on the nutrient supplying capacity of forest soils. P. 39–44 in W.J. Dyck and C.A. Mees (eds.), Impact of intensive harvesting on forest site productivity. FRI Bulletin No. 159, Rotorua, New Zealand.

Rice, R.M. 1974. The hydrology of chaparral watersheds, P. 277–334 in M. Rosenthal (ed.), Proceedings of a symposium on living with the chaparral, March 30–31, 1973, Riverside, CA, Sierra Club, San Francisco.

Rich, L.R. 1962. Erosion and sediment movement following a wildfire in a ponderosa pine forest of central Arizona. USDA Forest Service, Rocky Mountain Forest and Range Experiment Station, Research Note 76. 12 p.

Robichaud, P.R., and S.M. Miller. 1999. Spatial interpolation and simulation of post-burn duff thickness after prescribed fire. International Journal of Wildland Fire 9:137–143.

Rowe, P.B., and E.A. Colman. 1951. Disposition of rainfall in two mountain areas of California. USDA Technical Bulletin No. 1048, 84 p.

Rowe, P.B., C.M. Countryman, and H.C. Storey. 1954. Hydrologic analysis used to determine effects of fire on peak discharge and erosion rates in southern California watersheds. USDA Forest Service, California Forest and Range Experiment Station. 49 p.

Sampson, A.W. 1944. Effect of chaparral burning on soil erosion and soil moisture relationships. Ecology 25:171–191.

Sandberg, D.V., R.D. Ottmar, J.L. Peterson, and J. Core. 2002. Wildland fire on ecosystems: effects of fire on air. USDA Forest Service, Rocky Mountain Research Station, General Technical Report RMRS-GTR-42-vol.5. 79 p.

Savage, S.M. 1974. Mechanism of fire-induced water repellency in soil. Soil Science Society of America Proceedings. 38:652–657.

Scott, D.F. 1993. The hydrological effects of fire in South African mountain catchments. Journal of Hydrology 150:409–432.

Scott, V.H. and R.H. Burgy. 1956. Effects of heat and brush burning on the physical properties of certain upland soils that influence infiltration: Soil Science 82:63–70.

Shakesby, R.A., S.H. Doerr, and R.P.D. Walsh. 2000. The erosional impact of soil hydrophobicity: current problems and future research directions. Journal of Hydrology. 231–232:178–191.

Sinclair, J.D., and E.L. Hamilton. 1955. Streamflow reactions of a fire-damaged watershed. In proceedings of the hydraulic division, American Society of Civil Engineers. 18 p.

St. John, T.V., and P.W. Rundel. 1976. The role of fire as a mineralizing agent in a Sierran coniferous forest. Oecologia 25:35–45.

Stephens, S.L., T. Meixner, M. Poth, B. McGurk, and D. Payne. 2004. Prescribed fire, soils, and stream water chemistry in a watershed in the Lake Tahoe Basin, California. Int. J. Wildland Fire 13:27–35.

Sweeney, J.R., and H.H. Biswell. 1961. Quantitative studies of the removal of litter and duff by fire under controlled conditions. Ecology 42:572–575.

Takemoto, B. R., A. Bytnerowicz, and M. A. Fenn, M. A. 2000. Current and future effects of ozone and atmospheric nitrogen deposition on California's mixed conifer forests. Forest Ecology and Management 144:159–173.

Tiedemann, A. R., and T. D. Anderson. 1980. Combustion losses of sulfur from native plant materials and forest litter. Fire and Forest Meteorology Conference Proceedings 6:220–227.

Tiedemann, A. R., C. E. Conrad, J. H. Dieterich, J. W. Hornbeck, W. F. Megahan, L. A. Viereck, and D. D. Wade. 1979. Effects of fire on water, a state-of-knowledge-review. USDA Forest Service, General Technical Report WO-10. 28 p.

Ulery, A., L. and R. C. Graham. 1993. Forest fire effects on soil color and texture. Soil Science Society of America Journal 57:135–140.

USEPA. 1998. Interim Air Quality Policy on Wildland and Prescribed Fires. http://www.epa.gov/ttn/oarpg/t1/memoranda/firefnl.pdf.

Welling, R., M. Singer, and P. Dunn. 1984. Effects of fire on shrubland soils. P. 42–50 in J.J. DeVries (ed.), Proceedings of the chaparral ecosystems research conference, University of California, Davis, Water Resources Center, Report No. 62.

Wells, C. G., R. E. Campbell, L. F. DeBano, C. E. Lewis, R. L. Fredricksen, E. C. Franklin, R. C. Froelich, and P. H. Dunn. 1979. Effects of fire on soil: a state of knowledge review. USDA Forest Service, General Technical Report WO-7.

Wells, W. G., II. 1981. Some effects of brushfires on erosion processes in coastal southern California. P. 305–342 in Proceedings of a symposium on erosion and sediment transport in Pacific Rim steeplands, January 25–31, 1981, Christchurch, New Zealand, International Association of Hydrological Sciences Publication No. 132.

Wells, W. G., II. 1987. The effects of fire on the generation of debris flows in southern California. Geological Society of America, Reviews in Engineering Geology 7:105–114.

Williams, M. R., and J. M. Melack. 1997. Effects of prescribed burning and drought on the solute chemistry of mixed-conifer forest streams of the Sierra Nevada. Biogeochemistry 39:225–253.

Wohlgemuth, P. M., J. L. Beyers, C. D. Wakeman, and S. G. Conard. 1998. Effects of fire and grass seeding on soil erosion in southern California chaparral. P. 41–51 in S. Gray (chair), Proceedings of the 19th forest vegetation management conference, January 20–22, 1998, Redding, CA.

Ziemer, R. R., and D. N. Swanston. 1977. Root strength changes after logging in southeastern Alaska. USDA Forest Service, Pacific Northwest Forest and Range Experiment Station, Research Note PNW-306. 10 p.

Fire and Plant Interactions

JOANN FITES-KAUFMAN, ANNE F. BRADLEY,
AND AMY G. MERRILL

Pyrodiversity creates biodiversity . . .

BOB MARTIN AND DAVID SAPSIS, 1992

Charcoal records show that fire has been present in California for millions of years (Weide 1968, Keeley and Rundel 2003), creating a long history of fire interacting with plants. In an ecological context, fire is neither "good" nor "bad" for biota—it is an integral part of the ecological process in most plant communities of California (see Part II). Many plants in California have characteristics that enable them to survive—and even thrive—in response to fire and in particular fire regimes.

Fire's effects on plants result from the interaction between fire's chemical and physical properties and characteristics of the individual plant or microorganism. Since each fire behaves differently, and each species has a unique combination of physiological and physical traits, there is a wide array of resulting fire effects on the plants or microorganisms (Box 6.1). These effects are also influenced by post-fire weather conditions, heterogeneity of adjacent unburned land, and surviving or immigrating biota.

The heat, smoke, and charcoal that fires produce (Chapter 3) affect plants and their living tissues in different ways. In biological terms, fire consumes biomass, causes mortality, affects hormone production in growing tissues, alters the physical and chemical characteristics of the soil, and modifies interactions between species. Fire effects on plants and microorganisms include physical effects of fire on living tissue, individuals, populations, communities, and ecosystems.

Many fire ecology studies have investigated the effects of a single fire on a specific species, area, or study site. These studies can address only a tiny fraction of the relationships between fires and plant communities. Species adapt and evolve in context of the entire ecosystem. Fire, as an ecosystem process, has effects at the landscape scale and over many generations and fire events—the fire regime (see Chapter 4). Species are not adapted to fire per se, but to a fire regime. Species persist because the traits they possess are tolerant of a specific fire regime. To best understand the relationship between fire and plants, it is important to understand the relationship between species communities and fire regimes (Box 6.2).

Variation in fire regimes and in the species that make up plant communities generates a myriad of effects within those plant communities. In this chapter we describe fire interactions with plants and microorganisms including effects on individual tissues, species, populations, communities, and ecosystems. More detail on species and plant community responses are described for different parts of California in the bioregional chapters in Part II.

Direct Effects on Individuals

Fire affects individual plants directly by impacting the plant itself and indirectly by changing the plant's environment. Direct effects on individuals are a function of fire characteristics—namely, fire behavior—and the individual's morphological and physiological characteristics. *Morphology* refers to plant structure and includes plant size, the location of regenerating tissues such as buds, and different plant tissues and organs. Plant *physiology* refers to the production, interaction, and regulation of chemicals within living plant tissue that govern plant growth, development, and senescence. Individual plants or species respond to fire by resisting or persisting. Plants *resist* fire by having structures that protect them from heat damage, such as thick bark protecting sensitive growing cambium tissue in the stem. Plants *persist* with fire by regenerating after topkill, by sprouting, or with seeds that survive fire—such as those buried in the soil. In this section, we first focus on plant structures that resist fire and second on persistence of vascular plants. Then we discuss nonvascular plants (mosses and lichens) and microbes (bacteria and fungi).

Resistance

Heat is a primary output of fire that affects plants, and there are numerous morphological traits that plants have developed to resist heat. Heat kills plant cells by causing structural damage and breakdown of cellular metabolism and chemical bonds. The degree of heat damage sustained by a plant depends on the number and type of cells injured or killed. Both the absolute amount of heat and the length of time plant tissue is exposed to heat are important in determining the amount of damage to individual plants. Subjecting plants to high temperatures can result in tissue death in a few seconds. On the other hand, even moderate temperatures can kill plant tissues when they continue for minutes or hours. Many California plants have morphological structures that permit them to resist heat. These structures and life history responses to fire are summarized in Table 6.1, and some are described below. Further detail on the responses for many California plant species to fire are catalogued at the Fire Effects Information System (www.fs.fed.us/database/feis/).

Individual plants survive fire either by having insulating tissues (e.g., bark) above ground or by growing tissues underground where they are protected by the insulating soil. A plant's lifeform, size, and structure determine how it is affected by fire. The basic lifeforms of vascular plants include perennial trees and shrubs, and perennial and annual grasses and herbs. Plants that live several or more years are perennial, and those that only live one year are annuals (Box 6.3). Plants of each lifeform can differ in their responses to fire in several ways. When the crowns of annual plants are killed by fire, they generally cannot grow new shoots because they lack buds and energy reserves Annuals may have died and gone to seed by the time they burn. In order to persist after fire, they rely on seed present on the site or on colonization by plants from seeds from adjacent unburned areas. Buds capable of sprouting and the position of these buds in relation to both heat and the protection of insulating tissue or soil cover are of critical importance to the survival of perennial plants. Depending on exposure of the plant to lethal heat, perennials often grow new roots, stems, and leaves following fire.

We now look at how different plant structures contribute to a plant's response to fire. These structures include crowns, foliage, and leaves; buds, stems, and trunks; roots; and basal meristems.

BUDS

Buds are masses of plant tissue from which new shoots or stems and leaves form (Box 6.3, Fig. 6.1). Plants exposed to fire can lose a lot of their foliage from heat damage to leaf tissue. Because most plants depend on leaves for energy production, survival of damaged plants depends on the rapid regeneration of foliage burned by a fire. Buds occur on many perennial species and at different locations on the plant body. Buds below the mineral soil surface are most likely to survive fires, because they are insulated from heat (Fig. 6.2). Conversely, buds at or near the soil surface are most sensitive to heat-kill, because they are located where active fuel consumption and heat flux occur. Aerial buds, located in the plant crown, vary in their response to fire depending on how far they are above the heat source. Thus, buds in mature tree crowns are less likely to be affected by heat from surface fires compared to buds on low-growing shrubs. Buds also vary in their degree of protection depending on the amount and type of insulating tissues surrounding them.

CROWNS, FOLIAGE, AND LEAVES

Plant foliage (e.g., the leaves and needles) plays a crucial role in plant growth by producing all of a plant's energy through photosynthesis. Crown structure and moisture content are primary determinants of fire effects on plant foliage. The likelihood of crown survival depends on its shape, size, and height, and the degree of protection afforded its buds. Foliage

TABLE 6.1
Plant structures and associated definitions, factors associated with fire response and examples

Vegetative Structures	Definition	Potential Factors Associated with Fire Response	Examples
Foliage	Leaves and needles	Phenology, moisture level, leaf thickness, shape, area	Chamise (*Adenostoma fasciculatum*)
Crowns	Sum of all leaves or needles of a plant	Crown height and bulk density	Ponderosa pine (*Pinus ponderosa*)
Bark	Layer of dead, protective cells around outside of stem, phloem	Bark thickness and density, volatile substances	Ponderosa pine giant sequoia (*Sequoiadendron giganteum*)
Roots	Underground structures that absorb water and nutrients, and anchor plant	Amount and duration of heat, depth below surface, concentration and distribution of system	Mountain misery (*Chamaebatia foliolosa*)
Sprouting structures			
Epicormic buds	Buds in stem capable of sprouting	Fire intensity, fire duration	Big-cone Douglas-fir (*Pseudotsuga macrocarpa*), many hardwoods
Basal burls, buds at stems	Woody tissue from which roots and stems originate, often covered with buds	Fire intensity, fire duration	Manzanita (*Artostaphylos* spp.), ceanothus (*Ceanothus* spp.), bigleaf maple (*Acer macrophyllum*)
Caudexes, corms, bulbs	Stem base that stores energy may also produce new leaves/stems	Depth and degree of heat from fire	Mule's ears (*Wyethia* spp.), lily (*Lilium* spp.), iris (*Iris* spp.)
Stolons	Above-ground lateral stems form new plants	Depth of litter layer, depth and degree of heat	Strawberry, (*Fragaria* spp.) snowberry (*Symphoricarpus* spp.)
Rhizomes	Below-ground lateral stems form new plants	Depth of heat from fire, soil moisture	Spirea (*Spiraea* spp.), Oregon grape (*Berberis* spp.), mountain misery
Sprouting roots	Roots that have primordial buds capable of sprouting	Magnitude and duration, soil moisture	Aspen (*Populus* spp.)
Sexual reproduction			
Fire-stimulated flowering	Plants that flower or flower more with fire	Sensitive to fire intensity: temperature over threshold kills flowering tissue	Mariposa lily (*Calochortus* spp.)
Serotinous cones	Cones storing seeds: cones only open with high heat	Temperature of fire, longevity of seeds in relation to fire return interval	Knobcone pine (*Pinus attenuata*), Bishop pine (*Pinus muricata*), cypresses (*Cupressus* spp.)
Seed Banks	Supply of viable seeds buried in soil	Depth and degree of soil heating, soil moisture	Bigpod ceanothus (*Ceanothus megacarpus* var. *megacarpus*)

BOX 6.3. LIFE HISTORY AND REPRODUCTION OF PLANTS

Annual	Plants live one year
Perennial	Plants live more than one year
Meristems	Masses of embryonic cells that can form stems, roots, or leaves
Buds	Protected meristems found on most plants except grasses
Sprouts	After death or injury to part of a plant, growth from protected buds and energy reserves underground or in the stem

BRANCH WITH BUDS

BUDS LEAFED OUT

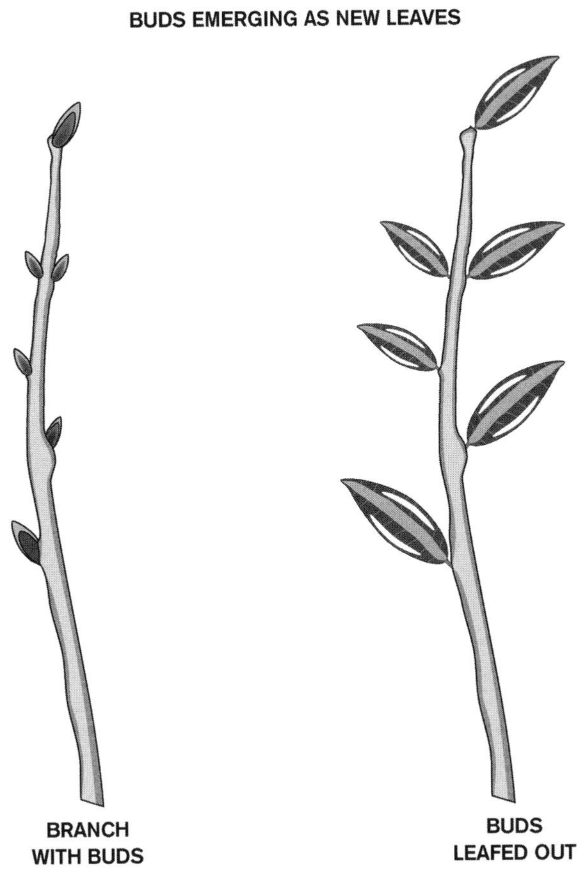

FIGURE 6.1. Buds before and after sprouting. Fire can damage buds in either stage.

closer to the flames and heat is more likely to experience tissue death. Plants with crowns that extend from or near the soil surface to the top of the plant usually have greater tissue mortality because branches and foliage near the ground forms a "ladder" of vertical fuels providing a conduit for combustion and heat from the base to the top of the crown. For example, western junipers *(Juniperus occidentalis* ssp. *occidentalis)* prevalent in the Northeastern Plateaus bioregion (see Chapter 11) have crowns that descend to the ground and fire often results in complete crown combustion. Foliar loss or damage can also increase with crown density and the proportion of dead branches and leaves in the crown because of increased heat released (Schwilk 2003). This dead material, termed *decadence,* is characteristic of some shrubs such as the chamise, a prevalent species in chaparral in the South Coast and Central Coast bioregions (Schwilk 2003).

Species differences influence the amount of foliar tissue death from fire that individual plants can survive. For sprouting species, the entire crown may be consumed and the plant can still regenerate the crown from protected buds and energy reserves underground or in the stem. Examples include black oak *(Quercus kelloggii)* or bigcone Douglas-fir. Details about the variation in sprouting response are covered in the section on persistence. For nonsprouting species, such as most conifer trees, the ability to recover from foliar damage depends on the resistance of the aerial buds to heat damage and proportion of crown retained. Aerial buds in white fir *(Abies concolor)* and Douglas-fir *(Pseudotsuga menziesii)* are small and relatively unprotected by bracts or foliage. Conversely, ponderosa pine and Jeffrey pine *(Pinus jeffreyi)* buds are larger, have greater tissue protection in the form of bracts, and have some protection from the long needles that extend beyond the terminal buds. Consequently, ponderosa and Jeffrey pine are able to survive even when most of the foliage is damaged because many of the

buds are still alive. White fir and Douglas-fir typically sustain both foliage and bud damage, allowing no means to regenerate foliage.

If foliar moisture levels are low, the heat required for foliar damage is reduced. Foliar moisture content varies seasonally, and plants tend to have the lowest moisture content during the summer and early fall, when most fires occur (Dell and Philpot 1965). Low foliar moisture can also occur during winter at higher elevations when water availability is low due to cold or frozen soil water. Foliar moisture is usually highest in the spring, and actively growing tissues are more susceptible to heat damage at this time. Fires are likely to cause greater crown damage when foliage is actively growing, regardless of foliar moisture levels. Foliar moisture reaches its lowest level in perennial plants when several years of drought have depleted soil moisture, thereby reducing the ability of plants to replenish their water.

STEMS AND TRUNKS

Plant stems and trunks provide growth, structural support for foliage, and nutrient and water transport between the roots and crowns. Cambium is the layer of tissue that develops into vascular tissues called *xylem* and *phloem* cells (Fig. 6.3). Xylem forms on the inside of the cambium and transports water from roots to crowns. Phloem forms on the outside and

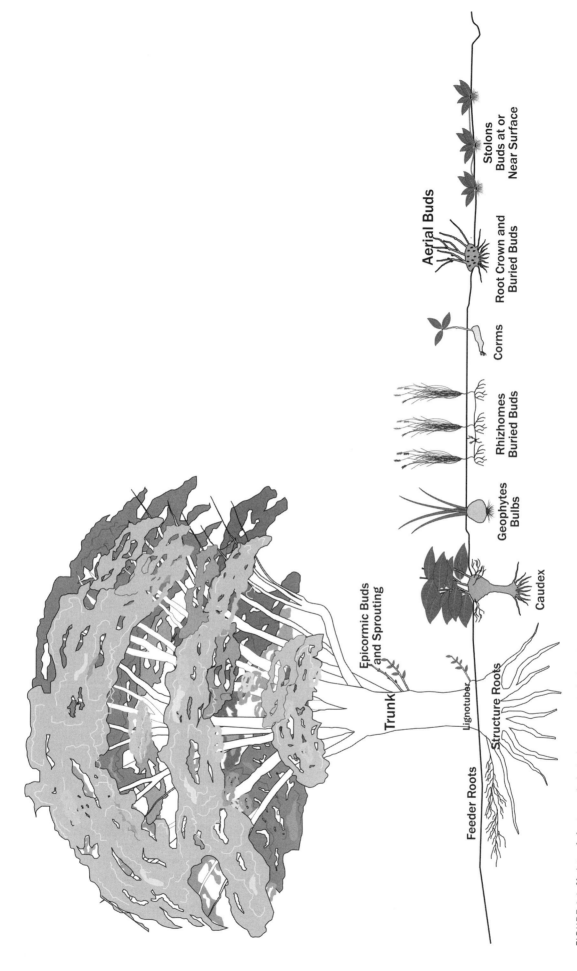

FIGURE 6.2. Variety of plant morphological structures, including those that sprout. The location of the buds relative to the heat source determines the response to fire.

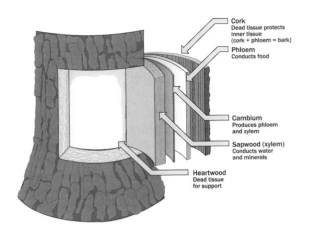

Cork
Dead tissue protects
inner tissue
(cork + phloem = bark)

Phloem
Conducts food

Cambium
Produces phloem
and xylem

Sapwood (xylem)
Conducts water
and minerals

Heartwood
Dead tissue
for support

FIGURE 6.3. Cross-section of tree trunk showing protective bark and underlying fire-sensitive tissues. The xylem grows inward of the cambium and forming wood, while the phloem grows outward forming bark.

transports carbohydrates produced in the foliage down to the roots. Phloem cells die over time, forming layers of bark. Cambium tissue is responsible for stem diameter growth. Injury or death to the cambium can have a great, even lethal, impact on a plant. The cambium of most trees, shrubs, and many herbs is located on the outside of the stem. Resistance of these plant stems to fire is dependent in large part on how well bark insulates the cambium from heat. In monocots—including grasses (Poaceae), lilies (Liliaceae), and palm trees (Arecaceae)—the cambium and xylem and phloem tissues are distributed throughout the stem and not just the outside.

Cambial death is a function of both temperature and duration of heat during a fire and can occur both by exposure to very high heat or by extended exposure to low heat. Accumulation of downed woody fuel or duff at the bases of plants, which burns primarily as smoldering combustion, is a common cause of cambial kill (Ryan and Reinhardt 1980, Sackett and Haase 1992). *Girdling* occurs when the cambium around the entire circumference of the plant stem is killed. Ultimately, girdling will kill the plant by constricting or eliminating water and nutrient transport.

Bark provides insulation from heat for cambium and buds in the stem. The insulating effectiveness of bark depends on its thickness, chemical composition, and flammability. In general, stems with thicker bark provide greater insulation and resistance to heat (Gill 1981). Trees can have thick bark, and conifers usually have thicker bark than do hardwoods. Shrubs and perennial herbs tend to have thin bark. As trees grow old, bark thickness increases; consequently the likelihood of survival increases with greater age and size (Fig. 6.4) (Peterson and Ryan 1986). Other bark characteristics such as the chemical composition, anatomy, and structure (e.g., flakiness) can influence the rate of heat diffusion or flammability of the stem (Spalt and Reifsnyder 1962). Bark flammability has been little studied in the United States but has been documented as a key factor in effects of fire on Eucalyptus (*Eucalyptus* spp.) trees in Australia (Gill 1981). In California, the flaky bark of ponderosa

pine is often observed as being more flammable than other co-occurring species such as black oak (Plumb 1979).

Plants such as palms and lilies cannot be girdled by fire. They have many independent bundles of vascular tissue distributed throughout the stem. Oases of California fan palms (*Washingtonia filifera*) were burned repeatedly by Native Americans to clear the oases for human habitation and to enhance palm fruit production (Vogl 1968). Each successive fire burned some of the palm vascular bundles causing a reduction in trunk diameter and crown size, potentially reducing transpiration to the dry desert air, but not necessarily causing mortality.

ROOTS AND UNDERGROUND TISSUES AND ORGANS

Root systems primarily function to absorb water and nutrients from the soil and provide structural stability. *Feeder* roots are primarily involved in absorbing water and nutrients, and are closer to the soil surface. *Structural* roots anchor the plant to the ground and are generally larger and deeper. Death of feeder roots may cause stress to plants even if root mortality does not lead to immediate plant death after fire (Wade 1993). Some plants also have underground stems, called *rhizomes*, which can be important for sprouting species (Fig. 6.2).

The effects of fire on roots and rhizomes are a function of how much heat the tissues are exposed to and their physiological state. The amount of heat that penetrates into the soil is a function of soil type, soil moisture, and surface fuel loading (as described in Chapter 5). Wet soils conduct heat more readily to plant tissues than dry soils up to a point, and temperatures will remain at 100°C (212°F) until the water evaporates. In very wet soils, all of the heat may go into heating water at the surface and not get conducted down into the soil profile. On the other hand, fuel consumption, and thus heat output, can be greater when both fuels and soils are dry. Root depth and physiological activity determine how sensitive they are to heat from fire. Deep roots are more protected by soil and less exposed to heat.

Feeder roots are most susceptible to heat-kill during the season of active growth (often in early spring) and are more tolerant when dormant. For example, ponderosa pine mortality was higher after spring (30%) than after fall (20%) burning in central Oregon, corresponding to differences in root mortality (Swezy and Agee 1991). Although the exact mechanism has not been determined, it is likely that the young growing tissues were more sensitive to fire or that the trees' water and nutrient requirements are greater during periods of active growth. In contrast, Kummerow and Lantz (1983) reported that fine roots of red shank, a chaparral species that grows in southern California, increased following fire. They attributed this increase to enhanced nutrient availability and higher soil moisture.

Root tissue mortality is a function of both the temperature and duration of heat. As with stems, smoldering combustion rather than the passing of the flaming front often

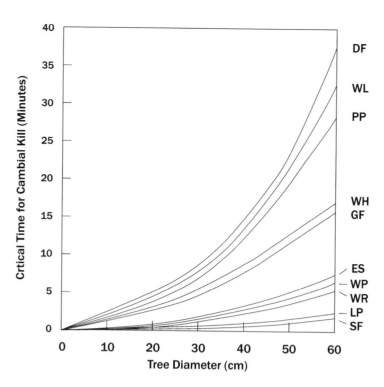

FIGURE 6.4. Variation in time to kill cambium by species and diameter. DF = Douglas fir, WL = western larch *(Larix occidentalis)*, PP = ponderosa pine, WH = western hemlock *(Tsuga heterophylla)*, GF = grand fir *(Abies grandis)*, ES = Engleman spruce *(Picea engelmannii)*, WP = western white pine *(Pinus monticola)*, WR = western redcedar *(Thuja plicata)*, LP = lodgepole pine *(Pinus contorta* ssp. *contorta)*, SF = subalpine fir *(Abies lasiocarpa)*. (Redrawn from Peterson and Ryan 1986.)

causes the greatest root mortality because of the longer duration of the fire (Miller 2000). This is particularly evident where litter has accumulated at the base of plants and where feeder roots are growing into the duff or litter. Heat for long periods of time, even at relatively low temperatures can be as lethal as a short duration of high temperatures. Smoldering combustion also increases the likelihood of heat penetration into the soil as the lower organic layers are consumed.

GRASSES AND GRASS-LIKE PLANTS

Instead of buds and cambium, grasses and like grass-like plants such as sedges *(Carex* spp.*)* and rushes *(Juncus* spp.*)* have growing tissues called *meristems* that allow them to survive repeated burning. Unlike the terminal buds on trees, shrubs, and herbs, meristems are located at the base of the leaves rather than at the tip. Thus, the plants can continue to grow after repeated grazing or mowing. The location of meristems relative to the soil surface and level of decadence, or dead foliage, influences both how much heat they receive and the level of tissue damage or mortality. Just as with tree or shrub crowns, decadent material generates more heat in close proximity to the foliage and meristems, increasing tissue damage and mortality.

Lifeforms of grasses that are important to fire responses include annuals, perennial bunchgrasses, and perennial stoloniferous or rhizomatous grasses (Miller 2000). Annual grasses only live one year and are typically killed outright by fire or, if already cured, are completely consumed. Their seeds may survive, depending on how heat resistant they are or how well-insulated the seeds are in the soil. Perennial grass survival depends on how well their meristems or buds are

protected from heat and the amount of decadent material. Stoloniferous grasses are more susceptible to fire damage because the stolons are exposed above the soil surface (Fig. 6.2). The effect of fire on rhizomatous and bunch grasses depends on the depth of the buried buds or meristems (Miller 2000). For example, Idaho fescue *(Festuca idahoensis)* is relatively fire sensitive, because its meristematic tissue is near the soil surface. In contrast, squirreltail is more fire tolerant, because its meristematic tissue is more than an inch below the soil surface. However, even with deeper meristematic tissues, accumulations of adjacent fuel or high levels of decadent material may result in meristematic tissue death.

Individual Plant Vigor

The condition of a plant affects its ability to survive a fire. Plants already stressed by disease, drought, or herbivory are more likely to die under the additional stress of fire. Moreover, weakened or suppressed plants develop fire-resistant characteristics, such as thick bark, more slowly than do healthier plants of similar age (Wade 1993). Plants with compromised health are also less likely to generate vigorous sprouts, since underground energy stores are lower than those of more healthy individuals.

Colonization and Persistence

As discussed previously, resistance to heat is one means of surviving fire. Another means of individual plant or species survival is by persistence through sprouting or seeds. Sprouting is the growth of new tissues (e.g., stems, leaves) from buds. Many plants respond to top-kill by fire through sprouting, improving their chances of crown regrowth and survival. Plants can persist on site with seeds that are buried in the ground (seed bank) or enclosed in serotinous cones. Some plants also respond to fire through colonization—seed dispersal from adjacent unburned sites.

SPROUTING

Sprouting is a physiological response that is stimulated by damage to the top or crown of plants (Miller 2000). Damage can come from heat as well as from wind, flooding, and animals. Factors controlling the sprouting response include species, age, size, phenology, bud location, and bud structure. The temperature and duration of heat relative to the location of buds affects the amount of plant top-kill, bud damage, and the sprouting response.

Bud-bearing structures (Fig. 6.2) vary in size, number of buds, and location of buds relative to heat from fire, all of which contribute to plant response to fire. A number of different plant structures may contain buds with the potential to resprout after fire including aerial stems, rhizomes, bulbs, corms, lignotubers, and roots (Fig. 6.2). Many sprouting structures also store energy (e.g., starch) needed by emerging sprouts. For example, *geophytes*, or plants with bulbs, such as death camas (*Zigadensus* spp.) (Tyler and Borchert 2002) often sprout following fire utilizing the starch contained in their bulbs.

Fire intensity and duration, together with the location of buds relative to flames, influence the potential sprouting response to fire. Sprouting tissues, like other plant tissues, can be killed by either a short exposure of high-intensity fire or a long duration of low-intensity fire. The greatest sprouting response often comes with moderate-intensity fires, where some buds are killed and some are stimulated to sprout (Miller 2000). Long-duration fires, even of low intensity, will often result in the poorest sprouting response because of the greater heat penetration through the soil and exposure of sprouting structures.

Sprouting structures that are protected by soil or heat-resistant tissues (e.g., thick bark) are most likely to survive and respond positively to fires of varied intensity and duration. Sprouting from stolons or root crowns is most easily reduced by fire, especially surface fires, because these structures occur above or near the soil surface. Bulbs, rhizomes, or roots are less likely damaged by fire, because they occur below the soil surface, insulated by soil.

Sprouting response of a particular species and between species with similar sprouting structures can vary. Vesk and Westoby (2004) suggested that sprouting response was better characterized as a continuum, with a probability of 0 to 1, rather than as a dichotomy (i.e., does sprout or does not sprout). For example, Vesk et al. (2004) reported a 79% probability of sprouting for "strong" sprouters after fire in contrast with a 6% probability for "weak" sprouters. The strong sprouters tended to have deeper buds. Overall, a dichotomous approach to sprouting works best where intense fires remove more of the above-ground biomass, such as in chaparral in the South Coast or Sierra Nevada bioregions (Chapters 12 and 15). A dichotomy is less clear in systems with surface fire regimes, where there is greater variation or patchiness in intensity and some above-ground plant parts survive (Vesk and Westoby 2004). There can be within-species variation in the sprouting response as well, such as is displayed by bitterbrush in the Northeastern Plateaus bioregion (see Chapter 11). This variable response may be partly genetic variation and may also be due to a greater variation in sprouting response observed with the more variable fire patterns in areas dominated by surface fire regimes.

Plant size or age, phenology, and time since the last fire can influence sprouting response to fire by affecting levels of starch storage. There is often an increased sprouting response with larger or older plants because of the development of greater numbers of buds and/or greater accumulation of stored carbohydrates and nutrients (James 1984), particularly in species with variable sprouting (Vesk et al. 2004). The direct importance of stored carbohydrates to sprouting has been documented by reduced levels of carbohydrates in several species following fire-induced sprouting (Bond and Midgley 2001, Tyler and Borchert 2002). It can take two or more years to recover stored starch levels.

Phenology refers to the timing of plant life cycle events, including growth, reproduction, dormancy, and death. These phases affect a plant's energy reserves and hormonal patterns that govern sprouting (James 1984). Levels of carbohydrates in roots or lignotubers are usually highest before the onset of growth. Reserves then decline, reaching their minimum shortly after growth begins. Reserves are lowest during the energy-intensive stages of flowering and seed production (Fig. 6.5). Generally, plants are less able to sprout during times of active growth when carbohydrate reserves are lowest. If burning occurs when plants are dormant, their sprouting response may be delayed until the following growing season. Two other plant conditions that can influence sprouting during the growing season or later in the growing cycle are hormones and water status (James 1984). Hormones that suppress sprouting have been found to be greater during the summer when temperatures are highest. Sprouting response may be greater when plants have more available water. Plants stressed by drought or pollution have lower vigor and may have a reduced ability to sprout following fire.

Although riparian plants are thought to be particularly vulnerable to fire, they are often vigorous sprouters. Riparian areas are typically wetter and less flammable than other portions of the landscape, but they do burn. Many riparian plants have strong sprouting responses that permit them to survive not only flooding but also to survive and even flourish with fire (Szalay and Resh 1997). In fact, some riparian species are the first to resprout following fires, often within the same week. The favorable moisture for plant growth found in riparian areas contributes to this rapid response. Observations after wildfires indicate that some widely distributed riparian shrubs, such as varied willows (*Salix* spp.) and mountain alder (*Alnus incana* ssp. *Tenuifolia*), and trees such as cottonwood (*Populus* spp.), resprout vigorously after

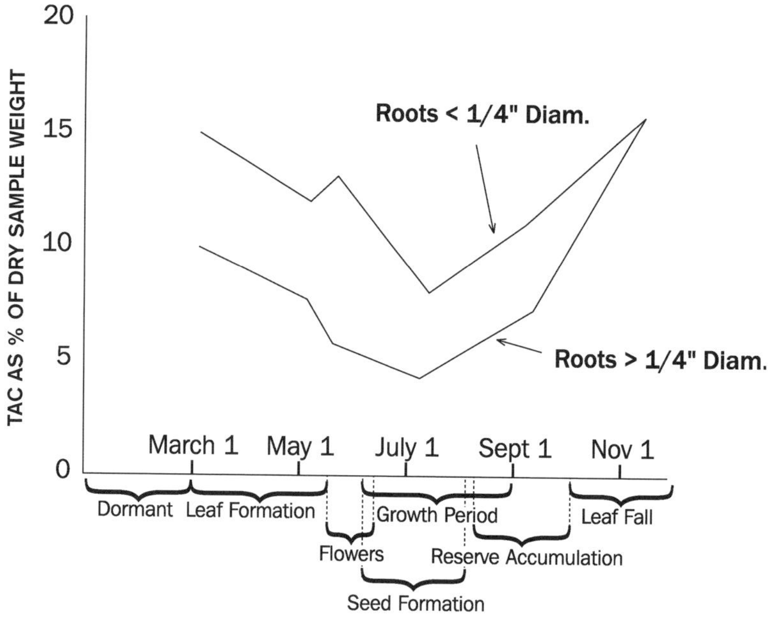

FIGURE 6.5. Seasonal changes in carbohydrate levels in bitterbrush *(Purshia tridentata)*. Levels reach the lowest point after flowering, during the growth period, and during seed formation. (Redrawn from McConnell and Garrison 1966)

fires. Native American burning in California for basketry materials included numerous riparian species such as willow, bigleaf maple, and hazelnut *(Corylus cornuta)* (see Chapter 17).

SEEDS

After fire, seeds are essential to the perpetuation of many plant species, particularly those that do not sprout or do not have heat-resistant characteristics. Seed and post-fire seed germination responses to fire include (1) survival through soil seed banks, (2) germination or release of seed stimulated by the fire, (3) fire-enhanced seedling establishment and survival, and (4) dispersal from outside the burned area. The first two aspects of seed and post-fire seed germination response are discussed in this section, and the latter two in the following section on dispersal and colonization.

The soil seed bank is the accumulation of seeds on a site and includes both long-lived, persistent seed as well as transient seeds that are viable for only a few weeks or months. The effect of fire on the seed bank depends on what types of seeds are present (long-lived or transient), how much heat penetrates the soil in relation to the distribution of seeds in the soil profile, the heat tolerance of the seeds, and the mechanisms that initiate germination. Plant species that quickly exploit recently burned sites are often able to do so because they have large quantities of soil-stored, long-lived seed. For example, snowbrush seeds may germinate after being dormant for an estimated 200–300 years (Noste and Bushey 1987) and can readily dominate sites after fires. Large seed densities may accumulate, sometimes as high as 2,000–21,000 seeds per square meter (Zammit and Zedler 1988). Species that have transient seeds that are not viable for long periods (i.e., several years or less) do not accumulate large seed banks and often depend on other means to survive fire—especially frequent fire—such as sprouting. Examples of species with

transient seeds include toyon *(Heteromeles arbutifolia)* and California coffeeberry *(Rhamnus californica)* found in California chaparral in several bioregions including the South Coast, Central Coast, North Coast, and Sierra Nevada.

Soil provides seeds and seed banks with insulation from heat similar to roots and rhizomes or other underground sprouting tissues. Seeds closer to the surface are exposed to more heat, which either causes seed mortality or stimulates germination in some species. Many of these hard-seeded species have seed coats that are ruptured following heat from fire or a few from chemicals derived from charcoal. The genus *Ceanothus* has numerous species with heat-stimulated germination that occur across all bioregions in California including desert ceanothus in the South Coast bioregion, mountain whitethorn *(Ceanothus cordulatus)* in the Sierra Nevada, Southern Cascades, Klamath Mountain, and Northeastern Plateaus bioregions; and blue blossom in the North Coast bioregion. Some chaparral seeds require dry heat to germinate but are killed by low temperature if they have imbibed water (Parker 1986). Species with water-imbibing seeds are more likely to sustain high seed mortality if fire occurs when soils are moist. Plant species also vary in the degree of heat-induced germination. For example, in coastal sage in the South Coast bioregion, seeds of purple sage *(Salvia leucophylla)*, black sage *(Salvia mellifera)*, coast buckwheat *(Eriogonum cinereum)*, and California buckwheat are "polymorphic" (see Chapter 15). Some of the seeds are heat stimulated, but not all are.

Chaparral in California, particularly in the South Coast and Central Coast bioregions, have many annual species as well as shrubs with germination closely tied to fire (Keeley and Keeley 1987, Zammit and Zedler 1988, Borchert and Odion 1995). The most common mechanism for fire-induced germination is heat. Seeds of some annuals in chaparral in the South Coast bioregion are stimulated not by heat, but by chemicals in smoke and charred wood. For example, the annual whispering bells *(Emmenanthe penduliflora)* germinates when exposed to the nitrogen dioxide (NO_2) in smoke (Keeley and Fotheringham 1997). Concentrations of NO_2 sufficient to initiate germination are generated both by the fire and by the elevated nitrification in many post-burn soils. NO_2 is also a common air pollutant. Deposition of NO_2 in southern California chaparral exceeds those levels identified as necessary to elicit germination in the lab. These recent findings raise questions about air pollution effects on some fire-adapted species (Malakoff 1997).

In addition to seeds surviving fire in the soil seed bank, other species, in particular some California conifers persist with fire through serotinous cones. Unlike cones on most conifers that release seeds when they are mature and open, serotinous cones remain sealed or shut under normal weather conditions. However, when temperatures are high enough to melt the resin that bonds the cone scales, usually between 45°C and 50°C (113°F and 122°F), serotinous cones open and release seeds (Lotan 1976). These relatively low fire temperatures allow the seed to remain viable. Lodgepole pine cones are capable of withstanding brief exposure to temperatures as high as 900°C (1,652°F) for 30 seconds in crown fires and still produce viable seeds. In California, serotinous species include knobcone pine, lodgepole pine, Bishop pine, Monterey pine *(Pinus radiata)*, Coulter pine *(Pinus coulteri)*, giant sequoia, and many cypresses (e.g., Tecate *[Cupressus forbesii]* and Cuyamaca *[Cupressus arizonica* spp. *stephensonii]*). Closed cones can remain on the tree for a decade or more until a fire opens the cone and releases the stored seeds during the post-fire period. Lodgepole pine and Coulter pine produce both serotinous and non-serotinous cones. The degree of serotiny in Coulter pine varied across California amongst plant communities (Borchert 1985). Serotiny was greater in plant communities with fire regimes characterized by uniform, high-intensity crown fires, such as chaparral, and lower in communities where variable surface fires are more common, such as blue oak *(Quercus douglasii)* woodlands.

SEED DISPERSAL, COLONIZATION, AND ESTABLISHMENT

For some species, establishment of seedlings on burned sites is important to their persistence with fire. Turner et al. (1998) characterized species as residual or colonizers. *Residual* species are those that survive fire as individual plants, through the seed bank, or by sprouting. *Colonizers* are those that do not survive the fire or may not have been present at the site before the fire but travel to burned areas after a fire and become established.

The ability of plants to colonize a burned area where they were previously absent or where all of the adults were killed depends on how far seeds disperse or travel. Seeds with attached wings, such as big-leaf maple or white fir, can travel short distances through the air. Other plants such as cottonwood, thistle, or willow, have small, light seeds and feathery or fluffy tissues that can travel long distances, particularly with the wind. Animals carry seeds on their fur that have burs or hooks, such as some grasses or fiddlenecks. Animals also eat fruits, ingest the seeds and disperse them through their scat while traveling through a burned area. Other animals, particularly rodents, gather and bury nuts, acorns, or seeds. This has been shown to be an important dispersal and recolonization mechanism for Coulter pine (Borchert 1985).

A number of species have enhanced seedling survival in conditions created by fire. For example, seeds of many conifers are better able to become established and survive when they germinate on bare mineral soil exposed by fire (see giant sequoia example in Chapter 12). It is essential for roots to penetrate into the soil in order for the seedlings to survive. When seeds land on bare mineral soil, the new roots can rapidly reach the soil (Stark 1965). In contrast, when they land on accumulations of duff or litter, it may be difficult for the root of a newly germinated seed to penetrate through the duff or litter layer into the soil. The duff and litter layer often do not provide the water or nutrients required by the seedlings.

Predicting Species Responses to Fire

Although the response to fire of individual plant structures (e.g., stem resistance to heat) or characteristics (e.g., sprouting) determines whether an individual plant dies, the entire suite of characteristics of an individual species governs their response to fire and particularly fire regimes (Keeley 1998). Various conceptual models of the response of individual plant species to fire have been developed for the purpose of characterizing and predicting fire effects of individual plant species or entire plant communities (e.g., Nobble and Slayter 1980, Rowe 1983, and Bond and van Wilgen 1996). Pausas et al. (2004) based their model on the "premise that predicting vegetation change can be accomplished with the use of plant functional types . . . the combination of life-history traits and species into a set of functional groups that best represent the range of strategies present."

Much of the focus of plant fire response classifications have been on shrub systems with crown fire regimes, such as chaparral of southern California, fynbos of South Africa, and the garrigue and maquis in Mediterranean areas of Europe. In these crown fire systems, emphasis has been on adaptive syndromes, or suites of characteristics, and the tradeoffs such as sprouting compared to seed-dependent regeneration species (see Chapter 15). There has been less attention to the variation in adaptive syndromes across varied fire regimes, such as is found throughout the varied bioregions of California. However, when comparing the species and plant community responses to varied fire regimes across California, there are some general patterns in the types and proportion of species with different adaptive syndromes that vary by overall fire type regime such as crown fire, surface fire, or multiple fire regimes. In this section, we have modified one of the more recent plant response classifications developed by Bond and van Wilgen (1996) for crown fire systems to incorporate a broader range of plant responses to other fire regimes (Table 6.2).

TABLE 6.2
Modified Bond and van Wilgen (1996) model of plant fire response classification for California flora (with examples)

| | | Reproductive Strategy | |
| | | Non-Sprouters | |
Fire-Stimulated	Sprouters	NOT KILLED BY FIRE	KILLED BY FIRE
Fire-dependent	Flowering only or almost entirely after fire (mariposa lily, Death camas)	Fire-stimulated flowering, germination, seed release (Golden-eyes)	Seed release from heat (knobcone and Bishop pines, bigpod ceanothus)
Fire-enhanced	Species increase after fire, but establishment occurs in fire-free interval too (black oak, aspen)	Seed release and seedling establishment enhanced (ponderosa pine)	Seed germination enhanced (tobacco brush, mountain white thorn)
Not fire-stimulated Fire-neutral	Sprouting recruitment same following fire as in fire-free interval; continuous sprouters (scrub oak, bigleaf maple, cottonwood, sedges)	Seed germination same following fire as in fire-free interval; seed producers survive fire (Douglas-fir, sugar pine)	Long-distance seed dispersal (fireweed, thistle)
Fire-inhibited	Sprouting recruitment less following fire than in fire-free interval	Seed germination less following fire than in fire-free interval (mature firs)	Mature and seedling individuals killed by fire; post-fire recruitment low (Sitka spruce, Santa Lucia fir, fir seedlings)

Fire responses are divided into two broad categories based on whether the plant is or is not stimulated by fire. Fire-stimulated responses are those that increase with fire, such as seed germination or sprouting. Fire-stimulated plants are further divided into fire-dependent and fire-enhanced categories, while plants not stimulated by fire are either fire-neutral or fire-inhibited. Fire-dependent responses occur *only* with fire, such as seed germination requiring heat, smoke, or chemicals from charcoal. Fire-enhanced responses (e.g., sprouting) are those that are increased by fire but that also occur from other types of damage to the plant.

Reproductive strategies are based on whether a plant is a sprouter or a nonsprouter. Nonsprouters are further divided into plants that tend to be killed or not killed by fire. Nonsprouters that often survive fire tend to have fire-resistant traits such as thick bark. Plants that tend to be killed by fire and do not sprout tend to be more abundant where fire is less frequent or more patchy. Specific strategies are listed in Table 6.2 based on recruitment in relation to fire events, including seed germination and establishment, or vegetative reproduction (sprouting).

Some general patterns emerge among the fire response characteristics of species in different bioregions throughout California. These patterns are associated with different floras

and fire regimes. In general, there is a high proportion of species with fire-stimulated and fire-dependent germination (e.g., desert ceanothus) and species with strong fire response sprouting (e.g., chamise) in plant communities and bioregions with shrub crown fire regimes, such as chaparral in the Central Coast and South Coast bioregions (see Chapters 14 and 15). In communities that have a predominately surface-type fire regime, such as most montane ponderosa pine and mixed conifer forests in the Sierra Nevada, Southern Cascades, and Northeastern Plateaus bioregions, there tends to be a mixture of species with varied responses to fire. Examples include nonsprouters that are fire resistant (e.g., ponderosa pine) with reproduction often enhanced by fire, sprouters that sprout strongly or moderately following fire but are not dependent on fire (e.g., black oak, bitterbrush [*Purshia* spp.]), and species with germination (e.g., deer brush [*Ceanothus intergerrimus*], mountain whitethorn) or flowering (e.g., mariposa lilies) enhanced by fire. In bioregions with more variable or higher fire severity and intensity, and longer-return interval fire regime patterns, such as in the Southeastern Desert ands North Coast bioregions, common species are those that do not resist fire well or that lack fire-stimulated germination or sprouting. However, throughout most of California's bioregions, many species are enhanced by fire or are able to take advantage of post-fire conditions for recruitment. Some species are dependent on these conditions.

Effects on Microorganisms and Nonvascular Plants

There are other important groups of organisms including moss, fungi, lichen, algae, bacteria, and protozoa that comprise important components of biotic communities and are affected by fire. In this section, we refer to these organisms as either as *microorganisms* or *nonvascular plants*. They live primarily in or on the soil; in the duff; or on plants, rocks, downed wood, or other substrates above ground. They perform critical ecosystem functions related to nutrient cycling and decomposition. Of particular importance is their role in breaking down fuels into different forms, eventually converting them into soil. In this section, we introduce the ways that fire affects microorganisms and nonvascular plants. Discussion on ecosystem processes mediated by microorganisms, such as nutrient cycling, can be found in Chapter 5.

Characteristics, Life History, and Distribution of Microorganisms

Bacteria, fungi, and protozoa live primarily in the soil and in decomposing organic material including standing and down dead trees, the duff layer, and the upper meter (3 ft) of soil. Microbes are particularly active in the upper 10 cm (4 in) of soil and in the *rhizosphere,* the area of soil directly surrounding active roots. Algae can grow on exposed areas of the soil or rock surface. Lichens (a symbiotic combination of algae and fungi) can be found on tree boles, hanging from tree branches, and on rocks. They are capable of photosynthesis and have the ability to absorb nutrients from the substrate. Mosses are small, nonvascular plants. Most reproduce via *spores*—small seed-like structures that are able to travel great distances via water, animals, or the wind. Although the spores of most nonvascular plants are fire resistant, the plants are not. They either avoid fire or rely on insulation from soil to survive, and unlike many vascular plants, they lack the ability to sprout.

Fire Effects on Microorganisms

Although desiccation can kill microorganisms, fire affects nonvascular plants and microorganisms primarily through heat. While some bacteria are able to survive temperatures as high as 210°C (410°F), many fungi are readily destroyed at temperatures just above 94°C (201°F) (Neary et al. 1999). The foliage of lichen and mosses are more sensitive to heat, although the resistance of the spores of some species may vary. Their habitat varies from in the soil to the tops of trees, and as a result, their exposure to heat varies with their location and fire behavior. In addition to direct effects, fire indirectly affects processes (e.g., nutrient cycling) that are mediated by the interaction of fire on biota, including changes in the pH of the soil, availability of nitrogen, and decomposition of fuels (see Chapter 5).

The interaction of fire and nonvascular plants and microorganisms can be categorized into three key types based on their habitat. Microorganisms that reside in the soil tend to survive fire depending on the amount and duration of heat in the soil. Specialized mychorrhizael fungi, which depend on vascular plant hosts for nutrition, are affected by fire to the same degree as their host plants. Microorganisms and nonvascular plants that occur in litter or on downed wood are particularly vulnerable to fire. The impact of fire on these organisms depends upon variation in the intensity and the patchiness of fire. The effect of fire on microorganisms and nonvascular plants living on the boles, branches, or leaves of plants depends upon their proximity to flames and the proportion of them affected. Surface fires have little effect on arboreal microorganisms or nonvascular plants, but crown fires can have a major effect.

Fire affects microbial decomposition and nutrient cycling by combusting organic material, accelerating decomposition, and converting much of the organic C and N to gaseous forms. Periodic surface fires apparently played an important role in maintaining low litter and woody debris loads on forest floors of many California ecosystems during pre-settlement times (see Chapters 9, 10, and 12). Increased stand density and fuel build up due to fire exclusion has led to stagnation or slowing of nutrient cycling in many forests (Covington and Sackett 1984, Monleon and Cromack 1996). By temporarily removing vegetation and blackening the soil, fire increases soil insolation and heat absorption, resulting in warmer surface soil temperatures on first-year post-burn sites (Ahlgren 1974). An increase in soil temperature increases microbial metabolism exponentially, so that decomposition and nutrient cycling in post-burn soils occur at higher rates than in soils of unburned sites (Paul and Clark 1989).

Because fire burns the duff layer more completely than the surface organic soil, fungal populations are usually more affected by fire than are bacterial populations. Vazquez et al. (1993) reported that the bacterial population was 25 times larger in soil one month after burning than in unburned soil. Conversely, fire resulted in an overall reduction of the soil fungal population one month following the fire: soil fungi numbers were approximately 5% of those found in unburned soil (Vasquez et al. 1993). Fungal populations can remain suppressed from one to ten years after a severe fire (Klopatek et al. 1994). A shift from a microbial community dominated by fungi to one dominated by bacteria can affect plant species composition by favoring nonmycorrhizal-dependent species or plant species dependent on mycorrhizal fungi that survive or quickly recolonize the site. Many non-native invasive plant species are not mycorrhizal dependent, and a shift in microbial community following severe fires may enhance their colonization and expansion (Perry et al. 1992). The shift can also limit decomposition and N mineralization, since fungi play a key role in breaking down more recalcitrant organic material.

Plant Population–Fire Interactions

A *population* is defined as a group of individuals of a species that are potentially interbreeding and together form a gene pool. The key to population persistence is survival and reproduction. An important aspect of populations is the spatial distribution of a species, including both the size of the area occupied and the distribution within that area. Metapopulations are useful in characterizing the pattern of changes and significance of those changes to overall population trends in space and time. *Metapopulations* are subpopulations within a portion of the entire extent of a species. General patterns of plant population and fire regime interactions vary by the fire regime, in particular crown fire and surface-fire-type regimes. The suite of plant characteristics, including morphology and life history traits (adaptive syndromes), tends to vary among fire-type regimes. The combination of species with different adaptive syndromes and different patterns of surface and crown fire regimes results in different interactions between populations and fire. In this section, we discuss fire effects on populations of species with different adaptive syndromes by the seven fire regime attributes (as described in Chapter 4).

Plant Populations and Fire Regime Characteristics

The response of populations to fire regimes is based on the entire fire regime, not on a single attribute. In the bioregional chapters, examples of responses of species to entire fire regimes are discussed. Here we describe general patterns of responses of populations of species with different adaptive syndromes to individual fire regime attributes.

FIRELINE INTENSITY, FIRE SEVERITY, AND FIRE TYPE

The magnitude of a fire affects the size and extent of populations through direct mortality and indirect effects on survival, reproduction, and recruitment. Fire type and intensity interact with species characteristics to produce different fire severities. Fire intensity affects plant populations in various ways, depending on patterns of survival, reproduction, and recruitment in response to fire. Depending on the species response and fire characteristics, fires of any given intensity can increase the total population by stimulating recruitment of more individuals than what originally existed, reducing the population by killing mature individuals and seedlings, destroying the seed bank, or not significantly stimulating regeneration. Crown fires result in high mortality above ground and species with populations that persist tend to do so with sprouting, regenerating from the seed bank, or colonizing. Surface fires, dominated by low to moderate intensities, produce lower mortality and more varied individual responses within a population. Some individuals may be

killed or have above-ground mortality, whereas others may be unaffected or only partially consumed.

Populations of most fire-resistant plant species fluctuate little with low- to moderate-intensity fires, but are significantly affected by very high-intensity fires. For example, mature individuals of ponderosa pine and Douglas-fir are only slightly affected by low- to moderate-intensity fires—their fire-resistant characteristics lead to low mortality—but are greatly affected by high-intensity fires, which result in high mortality. For some plants, the younger cohorts of a population may be more susceptible than the older individuals. Ponderosa pine seedlings are more vulnerable to fire than are older trees—they are more likely to die from moderate- or even low-intensity fire. This means that low-intensity fires may affect the overall tree population of a species for centuries, even if only younger trees are affected. Conversely, lack of fire may result in large changes in population structure and species composition. Ponderosa pine can reach greater densities in the absence of fire, leading to greater mortality from tree competition. Conversely, fires of any intensity may reduce mature plant survival and population levels in species that lack fire-resistant characteristics. Brewer spruce *(Picea breweriana)* in the Klamath Mountains bioregion has thin bark, and fire of any intensity causes high mortality.

Fireline intensity affects population recruitment from sprouts or the seed bank. Low-intensity fire enhances seedling establishment of some species, including pines *(Pinus* spp.) (Vale 1979), provided mineral soil is exposed. However, the response of a population to fire intensity is not always straightforward. In one low-intensity fire, high regeneration from root sprouts occurred in snowbrush but did not induce seed germination of the heat-dependent seeds (Noste 1985). After a more intense burn, root sprouting was very low, but seed germination was high. Thus, intensity did not affect the population occurrence but did affect the age structure.

FIRE SIZE

The size of fire relative to the distribution of a plant population determines the effects that fire might have on the population. A small (e.g., 0.1%) or large (e.g., 90%) fraction of a plant population can be affected by a fire, depending on the species distribution in relation to fire size. Interactions between fire size and population distribution are most likely to influence a population at the landscape scale, and there are broad-scale implications for plant populations.

Rarely does a single fire extend across the entire range of a species. Generalizing patterns of plant distributions allows for understanding basic fire extent–population interactions. Plant population distributions occur in three general patterns: endemic, patchy, and continuous. A population with an *endemic* distribution is one in which the distribution of the plant is limited geographically to a small area (Cox and Moore 2000). Examples include Brewer spruce in the Klamath Mountains bioregion and Santa Lucia fir in the Central Coast bioregion. A *patchy* distribution pattern refers to

TABLE 6.3
Potential population effects of an individual fire event on varying population distribution and
types of fire response by plants

Plant Distribution	Fire Response Type			
	Fire-dependent	Fire-enhanced	Fire-neutral	Fire-inhibited
Endemic	Maintains or increases distribution and abundance unless season results in mortality	Same as fire-dependent unless severity and season of fire result in high mortality and low establishment	May greatly restrict population if effects are severe	Decrease in distribution and abundance; degree of decrease increases with severity of fire
Patchy	Maintains or increases distribution and abundance across fraction of population affected	Same as fire-dependent unless severity and season of fire result in high mortality and low establishment	May negatively affect portion of distribution where fire occurs if effects are severe; recolonization may be limited due to patchy distribution	Decrease in portion of distribution where fire occurs; recolonization may be limited due to patchy distribution
Continuous	Maintains or increases distribution across fraction of population affected	Same as fire-dependent unless severity and season of fire result in high mortality and low establishment	May affect portion of distribution where fire occurs; but recolonization opportunities not limited	Decrease in portion of distribution where fire occurs; but recolonization opportunities not limited

a geographic extent that is widespread, but within that broad area individual occurrences are patchy. Examples include Pacific dogwood or trailplant found in the North Coast, Southern Cascades, Klamath Mountains, and Sierra Nevada bioregions. A *continuous* distribution pattern refers to a geographic extent that is widespread with consistent and uniform individual occurrences. Ponderosa pine exhibits a continuous distribution.

Population distributions usually refer to the distribution of plants. However, the distribution of viable seeds in the seed bank is as important and does not necessarily overlap with the living, above-ground population. Determining the potential distribution of plants that have long-lived seeds accumulated in the soil can be difficult (Parker 1986).

The relative importance of plant population varies with the distribution pattern of the species (Table 6.3). For example, a single fire can have a large effect on an endemic population, since a single fire could encompass most or all of the population. Conversely, a single fire is unlikely to have a large effect on a wide-ranging species, because the fire would only affect a relatively small portion of the overall population. The exception would be if the fire event fragmented the population by creating a barrier to dispersal and colonization.

The interaction between a fire and a species population also depends on whether the species is fire-dependent, fire-

enhanced, fire-neutral, or fire-inhibited. For fire-dependent species, a single fire will often have a positive effect on abundance and distribution within the extent of the fire. For example, the rare geophyte, club-haired mariposa lily, was thought to be very limited in distribution in the central Sierra Nevada until a major wildfire occurred. The Cleveland fire in Eldorado County stimulated flowering of the plant, and the known distribution and abundance increased significantly. For fire-dependent species, the greater the overlap between fire and the population, the greater the positive effect on the overall population. Fire-enhanced species respond similar to fire-dependent species but may be more influenced by the severity of the fire, how it changes the physical environment for the plant, and how it affects the plant's competitive ability relative to other species. The effect of fire on populations of fire-intolerant species is typically negative. As with fire-dependent species, the degree of negative effect on the population is in proportion to the population burned by the fire.

SPATIAL COMPLEXITY

The effects of spatial patterns of fire on populations are influenced by the spatial pattern of the species (whether it is widespread or restricted, or continuously or patchy in

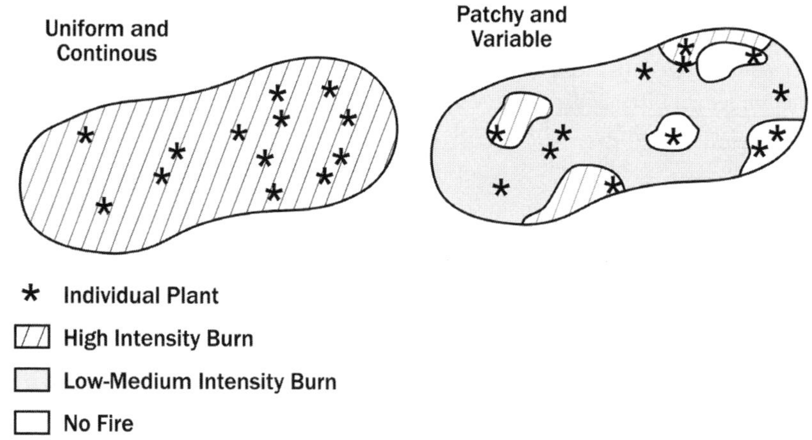

FIGURE 6.6. Interaction of fire spatial complexity and effects to plant populations. A fire of uniform intensity will have uniform effects, whereas a fire with variable intensities will have variable effects.

Uniform and Continous

Patchy and Variable

*   Individual Plant

High Intensity Burn

Low-Medium Intensity Burn

No Fire

distribution), the dispersal characteristics of the species, and fire magnitude. Spatial patterns of intensity and severity range from variable and complex to continuous and uniform (Chapter 4). The spatial pattern of fire intensity influences the effect of fire on the portion of a plant population within a fire (Fig. 6.6). At one extreme, a fire with uniform intensity will have uniform effects, either positive or negative, on the survival, age-class distribution, abundance, and distribution of individuals in a population. At the other extreme, a complex fire, with variable intensity, will have varied effects on a plant population within the area burned. Crown fires tend to be more uniform, whereas surface fires more complex, particularly at fine spatial scales. Multiple fire types are also complex, but on a more coarse, often patchy scale.

As long as the characteristics of a fire are within the distributions of the suitable fire regime, fire-dependent and fire-enhanced species will have a greater positive population response to a uniform fire than one that is variable. This is because more of the individuals will be burned or otherwise positively affected. For fire-inhibited or fire-intolerant species, uniform fires may result in large decreases in local abundance, including local extirpation, compared to the effects of a more discontinuous fire. Fires with greater spatial complexity would result in a higher probability of at least some individuals of each fire response type surviving.

Several studies from southern California chaparral illustrate interactions between fire pattern and plant population distribution. In chamise chaparral communities, variation in the amount and distribution of dead branches on the ground can cause variation in surface heating, which in turn can affect the distribution of surviving seeds and sprouting tissues. High surface heating in dense shrub clumps can reduce regeneration of most species in those clumps (Odion and Davis 2000). Small-scale patterns of germinable seeds and seedlings can result (Borchert and Odion 1995). Patchiness of plant populations in post-fire chaparral has also been attributed to uneven pre-fire seed distributions, such as those of annuals that are concentrated in old canopy gaps (Davis et al. 1989).

For many fire-dependent species, distribution patterns remain relatively stable through repeated burns. This is due to

at least two mechanisms (Odion and Davis 2000). First, seeds of many fire-dependent species have thick, heavy coats, and therefore do not disperse widely. Second, persistent-sprouting species retain roughly constant spatial distributions since they regenerate "in place." As a result, many fire-dependent populations retain fairly fixed spatial distributions.

Plant dispersal and recolonization strongly affect plant species distribution (Hanski 1995). A fire's spatial pattern can affect plant dispersal and recolonization, thereby affecting the plant population as a whole. For example, large burned areas are more likely to be recolonized by species with continuous distributions because the seeds are usually proximate to the burned areas. A complex fire could overlap with a patchy species distribution, however, significantly reducing that species' ability to survive and recolonize after the fire. Similarly, a fire that results in mortality and extirpation of a subpopulation or significant proportion of the entire population can create a gap in the distribution of a species that extends beyond typical dispersal distances between populations; consequently, the likelihood of recolonization is reduced (Hamrick and Nason 1996).

The distance seed can travel is affected by differences in speed, mode (e.g., air, water, animal), and timing. Species that have high dispersal distances, such as fireweed, will be more able to recolonize large burned areas than those that have low dispersal distances.

FIRE-RETURN INTERVAL

The consequences of fire-return intervals on plant populations depend on the length of the fire interval relative to the age at which plants reach reproductive maturity and on the ability of plants to survive between fires. The effects of fire-return interval are most pronounced with fire-dependent species. Both the length of time between fires and the regularity of these intervals influences the effect on populations.

Zedler (1995) described three effects of fire intervals on fire-dependent or fire-enhanced plants. *Senescence risk* occurs when time intervals between fires exceed survival time, thereby reducing reproductive abilities of populations during the fire-free period. Similarly, when a species depends on fire for reproduction, a population can become extirpated when its longevity is less than the fire interval. *Recruitment risk* occurs in species that rely upon recruitment by seed when the fire return interval is shorter than the time required for individuals to mature and set seed. *Immaturity risk* occurs when the fire return interval is shorter than the time required for individuals to grow to a fire-resistant stage.

Some plants are able to minimize senescence risk by producing seeds that remain viable for long periods of time. For example, the longevity of desert ceanothus is less than the average intervals between fires (Zedler 1995), and the perpetuation of the species is dependent on seed bank accumulations. Some ceanothus seeds maintain viability for hundreds of years (Noste 1985), so the populations may be able to overcome senescence risk through reliance on seed banks. Similarly, geophytes, such as species of onion (*Allium* spp.), brodiaea (*Brodiaea* spp.), and death camas, can persist in a dormant state for decades with little growth or flowering (Keeley 1991). Long-lived species, such as giant sequoia, can overcome senescence risk by individuals surviving extended fire-free periods. Reproduction and recruitment of giant sequoia are heavily dependent on fire; the cones are serotinous, and seeds require mineral soil for optimum establishment and survival (Rundel 1969). However, because individuals live for thousands of years, the fire-return interval can vary widely, and the population will still be able to successfully reproduce and recruit new cohorts to perpetuate the population.

Variability in intervals between fires can also influence populations. Although the focus in fire regime literature is often on the *average* fire-return interval, the *distribution* of intervals as discussed in Chapter 4 may be more important in understanding plant–fire interactions. Regular, short, fire-return intervals tend to favor abundant populations of fire-resistant or fire-tolerant species. For example, populations of annual plants or sprouters may be little affected by recurrent frequent fire because they are able to reproduce or survive following fire and maintain abundant population levels. In contrast, populations of species that are not fire resistant or fire tolerant may persist with fire-return intervals that are on average frequent but that include occasional long intervals between fires. For example, white fir achieves fire tolerance at maturity but is vulnerable to fire before then. Because it is long-lived and persists for centuries, populations of white fir can exist in an area when there are longer intervals between fires at least occasionally. Population abundance would be lower than with longer fire-return intervals on average, but irregular intervals provide for population persistence.

The season of fire influences plant populations in two ways. First, plants in a population at a sensitive stage of development are more susceptible to injury and mortality and are disproportionately affected by fire. Second, fire may reduce new seed production and recruitment for that year.

These individual effects can influence population size and age distribution, which influence population growth and reproductive viability. These fire effects can be short term, such as destruction of that year's progeny recruitment or the elimination or reduction of particular age-classes, or long term, such as depressed reproductive capacity or change in the population's competitive advantage in the community.

Fires that burn during the flowering or seed development stages result in greater mortality and population reduction than fires that burn during other times of the year because seeds may not be produced that season. Even if the population reproduction is not directly affected, energy reserves may be reduced or utilized for responding to the effects of the fire. As a result, population recovery can be slow and seed production for the year reduced. The degree of effect that fire has on a population is also a function of life cycle or lifeform. Annual species, dependent on annual seed production and recruitment, are more likely affected by variation in the seasonality of fire regime than are perennial species.

Populations depending on seed banks for reproduction or persistence also can be affected by the timing of a fire. Seasonal fluctuations in soil moisture influences heat transfer through the soil and seed mortality (Parker 1986). The seed bank for a species may be heavily affected when fire occurs while soils are wet enough to conduct heat deeply but not wet enough to absorb the heat. This is particularly important for populations of species that have seeds that imbibe water and are easily stem-killed.

Populations of sprouting species can be enhanced by early-growing-season fire even though there may be high above-ground mortality. During this time, above ground, newly formed foliage is sensitive to heat; but individuals have high below-ground energy reserves to produce a vigorous sprouting response.

Plant Community–Fire Interactions

The ecological community is the most visible biological unit that interacts with fire (Bond and van Wilgen 1996). In this section, we focus on the community characteristics and landscape distribution of community types that change with fire. California is host to an amazing array of plant communities and associated fire regimes. Plant community–fire interactions are often specific to each type of community and fire regime. Many characteristic, unique, and dominant plant community–fire interactions are presented in more comprehensive discussions in Part II of this book.

Communities and Their Components

Plant communities are comprised of all the species that occur together and interact on a particular site. Three major aspects of plant communities include species composition, community structure, and interactions among plants and between plants and their environment. Plant *composition* refers to the

Vegetative Growth
Flowering
Fruit Maturity

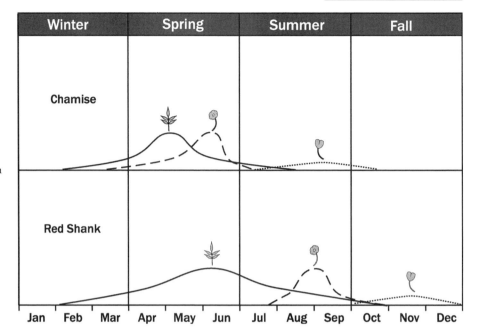

| Winter | Spring | Summer | Fall |

Chamise

Red Shank

Jan Feb Mar Apr May Jun Jul Aug Sep Oct Nov Dec

FIGURE 6.7. Different phenologic patterns for two co-occurring southern California chaparral species in a typical year. An early spring fire is likely to cause more damage to chamise than to red shank because the chamise would be flowering at that time. (Redrawn from Hanes 1965.)

number and proportion of different species in a given community. The size, arrangement, density, and plant lifeform, or *physiognomy* (e.g., shrub, tree, grass, herb, moss), make up the plant community *structure*.

Researchers have observed that not only does fire affect vegetation, but also vegetation affects fire (Agee 1996, Chang 1996). These reciprocal effects are most evident at the community level and through landscape patterns of vegetation. The influence of vegetation structure and community composition on fire is illustrated in Chapter 3 by detailing the effect of vegetation on fuel type, loading, and arrangement and consequently on fire behavior. Fire, along with other factors, such as fluctuations in climate, can greatly influence plant community dynamics. In addition, animals can influence plant communities by themselves or in concert with fire. The influence of animals on plant communities is discussed in Chapter 6. Here we discuss the relationship of plant composition and fire, fire and community structure, and indirect environment and climate effects on fire and community interactions.

Fire and Species Composition

The overall response of plant communities to fire is a result of the relative difference in the fire response of the individual species present. Variation in species responses to the fire regime attributes of season, fire return interval, and fireline intensity determine the effects of fire on the community.

SEASONALITY

Each plant species within a community will respond differently to seasonal patterns of fire based on that species' phenology. For example, chamise and red shank (*Adenostome sparsifolium*) are two common shrub species that often co-occur in southern California plant communities but have different phenological patterns (Fig. 6.7). Fires that occur in the early spring are likely to result in greater mortality of chamise than of red shank because the chamise flowers earlier and is in a phenological state that is more sensitive to fire. As a result, the season in which the fire occurs can change the plant species composition of a community.

Species composition can also affect the season when fires burn most readily. In areas of the Great Basin and the southeastern deserts where composition has shifted to annual grasses, fires tend to occur earlier in the year and earlier relative to the life cycles of other species. Annuals typically die early in the year and, if present in sufficient densities, provide a readily available fuel source. A clear example is a community that has become dominated by cheatgrass (*Bromus tectorum*) (see Chapters 11, 16, and 22 for details). Cheatgrass dies back by early to mid summer, creating a carpet of very flammable, available fuel. Ignitions spread easily during this time of year, and the fire season shifts toward early rather than late summer. This creates a positive feedback mechanism with the earlier fire season favoring cheatgrass because cheatgrass has already produced seed. In contrast, re-establishment of perennials that generally flower and produce seeds later in the year is diminished.

Both the length and regularity of the fire intervals are important in determining community composition. Longer fire intervals allow establishment and persistence of species that are fire inhibited, or fire neutral. Shorter fire intervals prevent fire-inhibited species from establishing and favor fire-enhanced and fire-dependent species. For example, ponderosa pine, a fire-enhanced species, often dominates communities where fire intervals are short. When occasional long fire intervals occur or when longer fire intervals occur on average, fire-inhibited young individuals such as Douglas-fir or white fir co-dominate communities with ponderosa pine or dominate communities at the expense of ponderosa pine.

Similarly, post-fire conditions can favor species through fire-induced changes in the physical environment, such as availability of light or limitation of nutrients. For example, post-fire succession in chaparral includes an immediate pulse of annual and perennial herbs along with sprouting shrubs (Keeley 1981). Grasses and herbs are often able to out-compete young shrubs and saplings for water, nutrients, and light. In grassland systems, there is often a similar pattern of plant community responses to fire that retards or halts encroachment of woodland species.

Species composition of a community can also influence fire return intervals (Mutch 1970). Communities dominated by ponderosa pine, with high annual production of flammable litter, are more likely to burn frequently because of the presence of that accumulation of available fuel. Similarly, communities dominated by species with naturally high concentrations of volatile oils, such as chamise (Montgomery and Cheo 1969, Rothermel 1976) or bearclover (McDonald et al. 2004), may have higher fire frequencies because of the greater flammability of the community.

FIRELINE INTENSITY

High-intensity fires can often lead to plant communities with lower diversity and increased dominance of a few species. High-intensity fires favor species that have some mechanism for resistance to fire-related mortality or have their establishment and recruitment favored by fire through sprouting, fire-stimulated seed banks, or widespread seed dispersal. These reproductive strategies enable rapid growth following fire and can allow one or several species to rapidly dominate a site where high-intensity fire has killed most other species. Chamise chaparral is a good example of this type of post-fire domination by a single species.

If the fire is very intense, the burned forest or shrubland may be converted to herbs or grasses, at least temporarily, until shrubs and trees recolonize the area. The time needed for shrubs and trees to become re-established depends on burn intensity, topography, the species of herbaceous or graminoid plants immediately taking over the site, and the presence of surviving seed on-site, or the presence of adjacent vegetation supplying seed. Often, only a few years are needed for some shrub communities to become re-established, such as those dominated by chamise, some manzanitas, or ceanothus shrub species. Tree-dominated communities take much longer to repopulate sites, but the transition can begin within 10–20 years if trees quickly become established and out-compete shrubs.

Community response to low-intensity fires can differ from that of high-intensity fires. More species with low fire resistance or low regeneration response to fire can survive low-intensity fires. However, due to increased species survival, competition among all species can be very high in post-burn, low-intensity fire communities. In these situations, fire-dependent or fire-enhanced species may have a competitive advantage.

Fire and Community Structure

Shifts in forest or shrubland structure can occur after fires. Canopy closure can be reduced, and vertical or horizontal continuity can be altered, thereby influencing subsequent fire behavior. Fires affect the density and vertical structure of forests by reducing overall biomass, including dead and live fuel (Kilgore and Sando 1975). In general, stands are differentially thinned, leaving some areas intact and other areas with many fewer live plants immediately following fire. The result is a mosaic of unburned areas resembling the pre-fire condition, and burned areas with more open surface and canopy. Formation of such a burn mosaic increases the variety of habitats and the extent of *ecotones,* or the edge effect, within an area.

Recurrent fire generally results in reduced densities of small trees (Kilgore and Sando 1975, Lathrop and Martin 1982, Keifer 1998) and a shift in tree diameter distribution toward larger trees (Gordon 1967). More frequent fire also reduces recruitment because younger, more vulnerable individuals are killed by fire. As a result, each cohort of individuals is less abundant, reducing not only the number of younger individuals, but also the recruitment pool for older individuals over the long run. With more frequent fires, it is also more likely that a plant community will either be composed of small (young) individuals or have an open midstory. In forests, frequent fires can lead to higher crown bases and thus have fewer ladder fuels. Long fire intervals allow the densest vegetation to develop.

Not only do fires affect plant community structure, but also the resulting structure can also influence subsequent fire behavior and effects. Forest communities with high representation of young or understory trees have more ladder fuels, which can increase fire intensity and severity. Similarly, crown fires can occur in coniferous forests when the trees are densely packed, have low-moisture contents, and high accumulations of litter (van Wagtendonk 1996).

Plant traits present in many fire-prone ecosystems have been interpreted as adaptations to fire. At the outset it is important to distinguish *adaptations* from *exaptations* (Gould and Vrba 1982). The former refers to traits that perform a particular function and have been selected for that function; the latter refers to traits that serve a particular function but that originated through selection for some other function. Distinguishing between the two is shaded by anthropogenic perspective—in many cases it is doubtful one can clearly distinguish between the two—and thus the term *apparent adaptation* may be appropriate.

The nature of fire adaptations is closely aligned with fire regime such that traits present in crown fire chaparral are far more similar to traits in other crown fire ecosystems such as boreal jack pine forests and South African fynbos than to adjacent ponderosa forests with a surface fire regime. In chaparral, crown sprouting and post-fire seed germination have been interpreted as fire adaptations. Sprouting in response to fire is almost certainly an exaptation as sprouting is nearly ubiquitous in dicotyledonous plants and likely has risen multiple times in response to many different processes (Keeley 1981). Relatively unique, however, are the large basal burls or lignotubers present in the chaparral species, *Adenostoma fasciculatum* and *Xylococcus bicolor;* and species of *Arctostaphylos, Ceanothus,* and *Garrya.* Although many woody species will produce ground-level tubers in response to various disturbances such as cutting, this coppicing effect is different because burls in chaparral species are normal ontogenetic structures that appear early in development.

Many chaparral species have fire-dependent reproduction with seed dormancy triggered by fire; this is likely a mix of adaptations and exaptations. Most species that recruit after fire can be classified as having heat-stimulated seeds or smoke- or charred wood–stimulated seeds (Keeley and Fotheringham 2000). High temperatures produced by solar heating of bare soil are sufficient to break dormancy in the former species, thus making this trait of selective value as a means of cueing germination to openings created by many types of disturbance. Smoke-stimulated germination would appear to be a clear adaptation to fire but the chemical cue in some species is nitrogen oxides that could be produced under other conditions. Another crown fire trait that is an apparent adaptation to fire is serotiny (Schwilk and Ackerly 2001), which is present in a few pines associated with chaparral, as well as lodgepole pine and jack pine, and widespread in mediterranean shrublands in South Africa and Western Australia (Lamont et al. 1991).

Surface fire regimes have selected for a very different suite of fire adaptations and generally these traits are not tied directly to reproduction. The dominant trees in most of our conifer forests and savanna woodlands have thick bark that is an apparent adaptation to fire. It has been argued that thick bark could have arisen in response to other environmental factors such as high and low ambient temperatures. However, the genus *Pinus* illustrates the overriding importance of fire in the determination of bark thickness. Also, all species from fire-prone habitats have very thick bark, whereas the desertic pinyon pines and the tree-line white pines have the thinnest bark (Keeley and Zedler 1998). The importance of fire regime characteristics is illustrated by the extraordinarily thick bark in savanna oaks compared with the rather thin bark in scrub oaks adapted to crown fire regimes (Zedler 1995). Typically in pines and oaks adapted to surface fire regimes, thick bark is also coupled with self-pruning of dead branches, traits that enhance survivorship of mature trees. This is critical since recruitment is often in post-fire environments and is dependent on the survival of parent seed trees.

One of the more controversial ideas related to fire adaptations is the hypothesis of species evolving characteristics that enhance flammability (Mutch 1970). Some have written this idea off as "group selectionist," which is considered unlikely in the context of inclusive fitness theory that forms the basis of modern evolutionary theory. Bond and Midgely (2001) resurrected this idea and provided sufficient reasons to consider it a possibility that flammability arose through effects on individual fitness. For example, in chaparral, some species such as chamise and species of manzanita and ceanothus fail to self-prune dead branches. It has been shown that this greatly affects fire intensity over what would occur if those branches were dropped and remained as surface fuels (Schwilk 2002). The selective advantage is that by contributing to higher-intensity fires, these species that are dependent on fire for reproduction may gain an advantage by creating greater openings for post-fire seedling recruitment.—*Jon E. Keeley*

Removal of some of the trees through partial harvesting should decrease fire severity and mortality. However, this is not always the case. In a retrospective study after a wildfire, Weatherspoon and Skinner (1995) found that uncut forest stands had lower mortality than those with partial harvest. They attributed at least part of the higher-severity fires found in harvested stands to increased flame height, winds, and accumulations of fuel from harvesting residues (see Fig. 3.14).

Community structure in relation to its landscape position can also have important effects on fire. For example, Coulter pine patches surrounded by chaparral burned at higher severity than did similar stands surrounded by grassland (Vale 1979). The Coulter pines were short in stature and formed an open canopy. The heavy fuel load in the adjacent chaparral created a high-intensity fire that was able to sweep into the Coulter pine stand and burn trunks high into the canopy. In contrast, fuel loads in the grasslands were not as high, so only a low-intensity surface fire moved underneath the adjacent pine stand.

Indirect Environment and Climate Effects on Community–Fire Interactions

In addition to direct, physical effects of fires on plant communities, fires also change the physical and chemical environment of the communities. These changes, in turn, influence weather in the short term and climate in the long term. As a result, fire, plant communities, and fire–plant community interactions are all affected in some manner.

SHORT-TERM ENVIRONMENT–FIRE–PLANT COMMUNITY INTERACTIONS

Fires alter availability of nutrients, water, light, soil surface substrate and chemistry, and microclimate of plant communities (see Chapter 5). These changes can differentially affect sprouting, growth, colonization, and establishment of varied species in a community.

Vegetation mortality can increase the light, water, and nutrients available to surviving or establishing plants by decreasing competition between plants for these resources. Also, increased solar radiation and loss of litter cover can increase soil temperature fluctuations. Warmer soil and increased light levels after a fire have been found to enhance the sprouting response. In annual grass communities, late-spring fires have been shown to induce prolific flowering and seed production, apparently due to the positive effects of greater light and nutrient availability on photosynthesis rates.

The litter layer is often completely consumed by surface fires, leaving bare mineral soil. Many plants have greater establishment and seedling survival on mineral soil than on litter. After fire, species that sprout, have fire-stimulated seeds in the soil, colonize from external seed sources, or have enhanced germination on mineral soil often have a competitive advantage.

Weather preceding and following fire can influence plant community response to fire. If conditions preceding fire have been dry, the plants may be drought-stressed and less able to respond to increased stress imposed by fire. After a fire, weather can play an important role in determining sprouting levels, germination levels, and seedling survival. Moisture following fire provides plants with the conditions necessary for successful seedling survival and successful sprouting. Moderate to intense rains after a fire can also increase erosion of topsoil and ash-derived nutrients, particularly in steep chaparral lands. Loss of topsoil and nutrients can affect short-term plant survival, growth, and species interactions.

LONG-TERM CLIMATE CHANGES

Climate is never static. Changes in climate can shift fire–plant community interactions by affecting plant community characteristics and distributions. Fire weather and fuel availability are also affected through indirect, reciprocal effects that alterations in vegetation and fire regime have on each other.

Climate change influences plant communities directly by changing the conditions favorable for individual plant species to migrate to different parts of the landscape, which, over long time periods, results in development of new plant communities. Over shorter time scales, climate changes can also affect stand-age structure through effects on germination and establishment. Climate change can affect species composition by altering competitive species advantages under changing climate conditions. Climate also affects community structure and fire patterns through changes in fuel loads by increased stress-induced mortality and altered litter decomposition rates. These shifts in plant community composition and structure affect flammability, fire–season interactions, and community response to periodic fires. Changes in climate that directly affect fire frequency and intensity include changes in duration and frequency of drought, precipitation and temperature, lightning ignitions, and winds.

Evidence of climatically driven shifts in fire regimes has been inferred from correlations between fluctuations in charcoal levels and shifts in climate inferred from pollen over centuries and millennia (Anderson and Smith 1997). These findings indicate that fire frequencies and intensities varied over long time periods. Over the scale of thousands of years, Swetnam (1993) found variation in both fire intervals and synchronicity between cohorts of giant sequoias based on fire scars and apparent changes in climate, deduced through tree-ring analyses. Millar and Woolfenden (1999) took a more detailed look at interactions between climate, fire regimes, and plant communities on the east side of the southern Sierra Nevada. These communities include long-lived species such as red fir *(Pinus albicaulis)*, whitebark pine *(Abies magnifica)*, and lodgepole pine, all of which can live for well over 400 years. The authors found that fire-return intervals, recorded as fire scars on trees, varied substantially on the scale of centuries. Some centuries, including the most recent, had little evidence of fire. Other centuries had more regular and frequent fires, and others had longer, more irregular intervals. The plant community compositions and age structures varied with changes in fire-return intervals, with shifts in dominance of lodgepole pine or red fir in various cohorts, depending on the century. These studies illustrate that plant community–fire interactions may vary over time, even at the relatively short temporal scale of centuries.

Fire and Communities' Geographic or Landscape Patterns

Plant communities also respond to fire by changes in the geographic distribution of the community. Communities expand or contract, are converted to different type, and change their community landscape patterns.

Repeated low-intensity fire or occasional high-intensity fire can result in contraction or expansion of adjacent plant communities in relation to each other. For example, some grassland communities in various bioregions of California are maintained or expand with recurrent fire. Without recurrent fire, trees from adjacent forests or woodlands become established in grasslands and eventually shade out the grass. This results in an expansion of the forest or woodland communities into the grassland. In contrast, with recurrent fire in the grasslands, the less fire-resistant tree seedlings are unable to survive repeated fire and fail to establish or survive. Examples discussed in the bioregional chapters in Part II of this text include: (1) the grass prairies and Oregon white oak *(Quercus garryana)* or Douglas-fir forests in the North Coast bioregion, (2) lodgepole pine and meadows in the Northeastern Plateaus and Sierra Nevada bioregions, and (3) coast live oak *(Quercus agrifolia)* in the Central Coast bioregion. Often the expansions or retractions are influenced not only by fire but also by fluctuations in climate and/or soil moisture conditions.

Even more dramatic changes in plant communities can occur related in part to fires that are less ephemeral and are more dynamic, long lasting, and extensive. These type conversions are particularly associated with either severe fires or with presence of invasive, non-native species (see Chapter 22 for more detail).

Boundaries of ecosystems, such as those between the east slopes of the Sierra Nevada and the Great Basin, or those between the foothills of the Sierra Nevada and the Central Valley, are characterized by differences in precipitation and temperature that result in changes in the suite of plant communities present. As precipitation increases, forests or woodlands replace grasslands or open shrublands. The climate at the boundaries may represent the limit of what tree species can tolerate and survive. Precipitation might be insufficient for survival or surface temperatures might be too high. Sometimes, the tree seedlings at the boundaries of ecosystems are dependent on the protection of shade from overstory trees to establish and survive. With high-intensity fire that kills the protective overstory, conversion of the plant community to shrubland, chaparral, or grassland may occur. This change or conversion to an entirely new community may persist for decades or centuries because of the relatively harsh conditions for the tree species, making establishment and survival limited.

Type conversions also occur following intense fire when non-native species invade and dominate an area after fire. Examples include conversions to non-native annual grasslands from sage scrub in the South Coast bioregion, desert scrub in the Southeastern Deserts bioregion, and sagebrush steppe in the Northeast Plateaus bioregion.

Summary and Conclusions

Fire directly affects plants through heat, smoke, or charrate, and indirectly affects plants through fire-induced changes in nutrient and light availability and germination conditions. Plants respond to these direct and indirect effects in myriad ways. Many species have physical characteristics, such as thick bark, that enable them to survive fires. Fires, depending on fire intensity, distribution, and season, also enhance reproduction in some species. Other species are negatively affected by fire and proliferate during long fire-free periods. Fire seasonality, return interval, size, spatial complexity, intensity, severity, and type all affect plant survival and reproduction and plant community structure and composition. Plant community structure and composition have feedback effects on fire frequency, intensity, extent, and season. As we learn more about fire interactions among plant, animal, and microbial communities, we will be able to understand how fire functions as an ecological process and how we might best manage fire in California ecosystems.

References

Agee, J. K. 1996. The influence of forest structure on fire behavior. Proceedings: Forest vegetation management conference, Redding, CA.

Ahlgren, I. F. 1974. The effect of fire on soil organisms. In T. T. Kozlowski and C. E. Ahlgren (eds.), Fire and ecosystems. Academic Press, New York.

Anderson, R. S., and S. J. Smith. 1997. The sedimentary record of fire in montane meadows, Sierra Nevada, California, USA: a preliminary assessment. P. 313–327 in J. S. Clark, H. Cachier, J. G. Goldammer, and B. J. Stocks (eds.), Sediment records of biomass burning and global change. NATO ASI Series 51.

Bond, W. J., and B. W. van Wilgen. 1996. Fire and plants. Chapman and Hall, New York (Population and Community Biology Series, vol. 14). 263 p.

Bond, W. J., and J. J. Midgley. 2001. Ecology of sprouting in woody plants: the persistence niche. Trends in Ecology and Evolution 16:45–51.

Borchert, M. I. 1985. Serotiny and cone-habitat variation in populations of *Pinus coulteri* (Pinaceae) in the southern coast ranges of California. Madroño 32(1):29–48.

Borchert, M. I., and D. C. Odion. 1995. Fire intensity and vegetation recovery in chaparral: a review. P. 91–100 in J. E. Keeley and T. Scott (eds.), Brushfires in California: ecology and resource managements. International Association of Wildland Fire, Fairfield, WA.

Chang, C. 1996. Ecosystem responses to fire and variations in fire regimes. In Sierra Nevada ecosystem project: final report to congress. University of California, Centers for Water and Wildland Resources, vol. II, Chapter 39.

Covington, W. W., and S. S. Sackett. 1984. The effect of prescribed fire in Southwestern ponderosa pine on organic matter and nutrients in woody debris and forest floor. Forest Science 30:183–192.

Cox, C. B., and P. D. Moore. 2000. Biogeography: an ecological and evolutionary approach, 6th edition. Blackwell Science, Oxford. 298 p.

Davis, F. W., M. I. Borchert, and D. C. Odion. 1989. Establishment of microscale vegetation pattern in maritime chaparral after fire. Vegetatio. 84:53–67.

Dell, J. D., and C. W. Philpot. 1965. Variations in the moisture content of several fuel size components of live and dead chamise. USDA, Forest Serv. Res. Note PSW-83.

Gill, A. M. 1981. Fire adaptive traits of vascular plants. P. 208–230 in H. A. Mooney, T. M. Bonnicksen, N. L. Christensen, J. E. Lotan, and W. A. Reiners (eds.), Proceedings of the conference, fire regimes and ecosystem properties. USDA Forest Serv., Gen. Tech. Rep. WO-26.

Gordon, D. T. 1967. Prescribed burning in the interior ponderosa pine type of northeastern California. USDA, Forest Serv. Res Pap. PSW-45.

Gould, S. J., and E. S. Vrba. 1982. Exaptation—a missing term in the science of form. Paleobiology 8:4–15.

Hamrick, J. L., and J. D. Nason. 1996. Consequences of dispersal in plants. P. 203–236 in O. E. Rhodes, R. K. Chesser, and M. H. Smith (eds.), Population dynamics in ecological space and time. University of Chicago Press, Chicago.

Hanes, T. D. 1965. Ecological studies on two closely related chaparral shrubs in southern California. Ecol. Monogr. 35(2): 213–235.

Hanski, I. 1995. Effect of landscape pattern on competitive interactions. In L. Hansson, L. Fahrig, and G. Merriam (eds.), Mosaic landscapes and ecological processes. Chapman and Hall, New York. 356 p.

James, S. 1984. Lignotubers and burls: their structure, function and ecological significance in Mediterranean ecosystems. Botanical Review 50:225–266.

Keeley, J. E. 1981. Reproductive cycles and fire regimes. P. 231–277 in H. A. Mooney, T. M. Bonnicksen, N. L. Christensen, J. E. Lotan, and W. A. Reiners (eds.), Proceedings of the conference, fire regimes and ecosystem properties. Washington, DC, USDA, Forest Service, General Technical Report WO-26.

Keeley, J. E. 1991. Seed germination and life history syndromes in the California chaparral. The Botanical Review 57:81–116.

Keeley, J. E. 1998. Coupling demography, physiology and evolution in chaparral shrubs. P. 257–264 in P. W. Rundel, G. Montenegro, and F. M. Jaksic (eds.), Landscape disturbance and biodiversity in Mediterranean-type ecosystems. Springer, New York.

Keeley, J. E., and C. J. Fotheringham. 1997. Trace gas emissions and smoke-induced seed germination. Science 276:1248–1250.

Keeley, J. E., and S. C. Keeley. 1987. Role of fire in the germination of chaparral herbs and suffrutescents. Madroño 34: 240–249.

Keeley, J. E., and P. W. Rundel. 2003. Evolution of CAM and C4 carbon-concentrating mechanisms. Int. J. Plant Sci. 164(suppl. 3): S55–S77.

Keeley, J. E., and P. H. Zedler. 1998. Evolution of life histories in *Pinus*. P. 219–250 in D. M. Richardson (ed.), Ecology and biogeography of *Pinus*. Cambridge University Press, Cambridge UK.

Keifer, M. B. 1998. Fuel load and tree density changes following prescribed fire in the giant sequoia-mixed conifer forest: the first 14 years of fire effects monitoring. In L. A. Brennan and T. L. Pruden (eds.), Fire in ecosystem management: shifting the paradigm from suppression to prescription. Proceedings of the Tall Timbers Fire Ecology Conference 20:306–309.

Kilgore, B. M., and R. W. Sando. 1975. Crown-fire potential in a sequoia forest after prescribed burning. Forest Science 21:83–87.

Klopatek, C. C., C. Friese, M. F. Allen, and J. M. Klopatek. 1994. Comparisons of field and laboratory studies on the effects of fire on VA mycorrhizal fungi. P. 762–776 in Proceedings of the 12th conference on fire and forest meteorology, October 26–28, 1993. Jekyll Island, GA. SAF Publ. 94-02. Society of American Foresters, Bethesda, MD.

Kummerow, J., and R. K. Lantz. 1983. Effect of fire on fine root density in red shank (*Adenostoma sparsifolium Torr.*) chaparral. Plant and Soil 70:236–347.

Lamont, B. B., D. C. L. Maitre, R. M. Cowling, and N. J. Enright. 1991. Canopy seed storage in woody plants. Botanical Review 57:277–317.

Lathrop, E. W., and B .D. Martin. 1982. Response of understory vegetation to prescribed burning in yellow pine forests on Cuyamaca Rancho state park, California. Aliso. 10:329–343.

Lotan, J. E. 1976. Cone serotiny—fire relationships in lodgepole pine. P. 267–278 in Proceedings, 14th Tall Timmbers fire ecology conference. Tall Timbers Research Station, Tallahassee, FL.

Malakoff, D. A. 1997. Nitrogen oxide pollution may spark seeds' growth. Science 276:1199.

Martin, R. E., and D. B. Sapsis. 1992. Fires as agents of biodiversity: pyrodiversity promotes biodiversity. P. 150–157 in H. M. Kerner (ed.). Proceedings of the symposium on biodiversity of Northwestern California, Oct. 28–30, 1991, Santa Rosa, CA. Wildland Resources Center Report 29, Berkeley, CA.

McConnell, B. R., and G. A. Garrison 1966. Seasonal variations of available carbohydrates in bitterbush. J. Wildl. Manage. 30(1): 168–172.

McDonald, P. M., G. O. Fiddler, and D. A. Potter. 2004. Ecology and manipulation of bearclover (*Chamaebatia foliolosa*) in northern and central California: the status of our knowledge. USDA For. Serv. Gen. Tech. Rep. PSW-GTR-190. 26 p

Millar, C. I., and W. Wolfenden. 1999. The role of climate change in interpreting historical variability. Ecological Applications 9:1207–1216.

Miller, M. 2000. Fire autecology. P. 9–34 in J. K. Brown and J. K. Smith (eds.), Wildland fire in ecosystems. USDA Forest Service, Rocky Mountain Research Station, GTR-42, vol. 2. 257 pages.

Montgomery, K. R., and P. C. Cheo. 1969. Moisture and salt effects on fire retardance in plants. American Journal of Botany 56(9):1028–1032.

Monleon, V. J., and K. J. Cromack. 1996. Long-term effects of prescribed underburning on litter decomposition and nutrient release in ponderosa pine stands in central Oregon. For. Ecol. Manage. 81:143–152.

Mutch, R. W. 1970. Wildland fires and ecosystems: a hypothesis. Ecology 51:1046–1051.

Neary, D. G., C. C. Klopatek, L. F. DeBano, and P .F. Ffolliott. 1999. Fire effects on belowground sustainability: a review and synthesis. Forest Ecology and Management 122:51–71.

Nobble, I. R., and R. O. Slayter. 1980. The use of vital attributes to predict successional changes in plant communities subject to recurrent disturbances. Vegetatio. 43:5–21.

Noste, N. V. 1985. Influence of fire severity on response of evergreen ceanothus. P. 91–96 in J. E. Lotan and J. K. Brown (eds.), Fire's effects on wildlife habitat, symposium proceedings, Missoula, MT. USDA Forest Service, Intermountain Res. Station, Gen. Tech. Rep. INT-18, Ogden, UT.

Noste, N. V., and C . L. Bushey. 1987. Fire response of shrubs of dry forest habitat types in Montana and Idaho. USDA Forest Service, Intermountain Forest and Range Experiment Station, Gen. Tech. Rep. INT-239, Ogden, UT. 22 pp.

Odion, D. C., and F. W. Davis. 2000. Fire, soil heating, and the formation of vegetation patterns in chaparral. Ecological Monographs 70:149–169.

Parker, V. T. 1989. Maximizing vegetation response on management burns by identifying fire regimes. P. 87–91 in N. H. Berg (ed.), Proceedings of the symposium on fire and watershed management. USDA Forest Service, Pacific Southwest Forest and Range Experiment Station, General Technical Report PSW-109.

Parker, V. T. 1986. Evaluation of the effect of off-season prescribed burning on chaparral in the Marin municipal water district watershed. Marin Municipal Water District.

Paul, E. A., and F. E. Clark. 1989. Soil microbiologyand biochemistry. Academic Press, New York.

Pausas, J. G., R. A. Bradstock, D. A. Keith, and J. E. Keeley. 2004. Plant functional trait analysis in relation to crown-fire ecosystems. Ecology 85:1085–1100.

Perry, D.A., T. Bell, and M. P. Amaranthus. 1992. Mycorrhizal fungi in mixed-species forests and other tales of positive feedback,redundancy and stability. P. 151–179 in M.G.R. Cannell, D. C. Malcolm, and P. A. Robertson (eds.), The ecology of mixed species stands of trees. Blackwell, Oxford.

Peterson, D. L., and K .C. Ryan. 1986. Modeling postfire conifer mortality for long-range planning. Environ. Manage. 10(6): 797–808.

Plumb, T. R. 1979. Responses of oaks to fire. P. 202–215 in T. R. Plumb (tech. coord.), Ecology, maagement, and utilization of California oaks. USDA Forest Serv. Gen. Tech. Rep. PSW-44. 368 p.

Rothermel, R. C. 1976. Forest fires and the chemistry of forest fuels. P. 245–259 in F. Shafizadeh, K. V. Sarkanen, and D. A. Tillman (eds.), Thermal uses and properties of carbohydrates and lignins. Academic Press, New York.

Rowe, J. S. 1983. Concepts of fire effects on plant individuals and species. P. 135–154 in R. W. Wein and D. A. MacLean (eds.), The role of fire in northern circumpolar ecosystems. Scope 18. Wiley, New York.

Rundel, P. W. 1969. The distribution and ecology of the giant Sequoia ecosystem in the Sierra Nevada, California. Ph.D. Thesis, Duke Univ. 204 p.

Ryan, K. C., and E. D. Reinhardt. 1980. Predicting postfire mortality of seven western conifers. Canadian Journal of Forest Research 18:1291–1297.

Sackett, S. S., and S. M. Haase. 1992. Measuring soil and tree temperatures during prescribed fires with thermocouple probes. USDA Forest Serv. Gen. Tech. Rep. PSW-131. 15 p.

Schwilk, D. W. 2003. Flammability is a niche construction trait: canopy architecture affects fire intensity. Am. Nat. 162(6): 725–733.

Schwilk, D.W., and P.D. Ackerly 2001. Flammability and serotiny as strategies: correlated evolution in pines. Oikus 94:326– 336.

Spalt, K. W., and W. E. Reifsnyder. 1962. Bark characteristics and fire resistance: a literature survey. USDA Forest Serv. Occasional Paper S-193.

Stark, N. 1965. Natural regeneration of Sierra Nevada mixed conifers after logging. J. Forestry 63:456–457.

Swetnam, T. W. 1993. Fire history and climate change in giant sequoia groves. Science 262:885–889.

Swezy, D. M., and J. K. Agee 1991. Prescribed fire effects on fine root and tree mortality in old growth ponderosa pine. Canadian Journal of Forest Research 21:626–634.

Szalay, F. A., and V. H. Resh. 1997. Responses of wetland invertebrates and plants important in waterfowl diets to burning and mowing of emergent vegetation. Wetlands 17(1):149–156.

Turner, M. G., W. L. Baker, C. J. Peterson, and R. K. Peet. 1998. Factors influencing succession: lessons from large, infrequent natural disturbances. Ecosystems 1:511–523.

Tyler, C., and M. Borchert. 2002. Reproduction and growth of the chaparral geophyte, *Zigadenus fremontii* (Liliaceae), in relation to fire. Plant Ecology 165:11–20.

Vale, T. R. 1979. *Pinus coulteri* and wildfire on Mount Diablo, California. Madroño 26:135–140.

van Wagtendonk, J. W. 1996. Use of a deterministic fire growth model to test fuel treatments. In Sierra Nevada ecosystem project: final report to Congress, vol. II, Chapter 43. University of California, Davis, Wildland Resources Center Rep. 37. 1528 p.

Vazquez, F. J., M. J. Acea, and T. Carballas. 1993. Soil microbial populations afterwildfire. FEMS Microbiology Ecology 13: 93–104.

Vesk, P. A., and M. Westoby. 2004. Sprouting ability across diverse disturbances and vegetation types worldwide. J. Ecol. 92(2): 310–320.

Vesk, P. A., D. I. Warton, and M. Westoby. 2004. Sprouting by semi-arid plants: testing a dichotomy and predictive traits. Oikos 107:72–89.

Vogl, R. J. 1968. Fire adaptations of some southern California plants. P. 79–109 in E. V. Komarek, Sr. (conf. chair), Proceedings on Tall Timbers fire ecology conference: California. Lake County, CA. Tall Timbers Research Station 7, Tallahassee, FL.

Wade, D. D. 1993. Thinning young loblolly pine stands with fire. International Journal of Wildland Fire 3:169–178.

Weatherspoon, C. P., and C. N. Skinner. 1995. An assessment of factors associated with damage to tree crowns from the 1987 wildfires in northern California. Forest Science 41: 430–451.

Weide, D. L. 1968. The geography of fire in the Santa Monica Mountains. Master's thesis, California State University, Los Angeles.

Zammit, C. A., and P. H. Zedler. 1988. The influence of dominant shrubs, fire, and time since fire on soil seed banks in mixed chaparral. Vegetatio. 75:175–187.

Zedler, P. H. 1995. Are some plants born to burn? Trends in Ecology and Evolution 10:303–395.

CHAPTER 7

Fire and Animal Interactions

KEVIN E. SHAFFER AND WILLIAM F. LAUDENSLAYER, JR.

> Big game creatures do not eat mature trees—they feed on
> sun-drenched browse, new grass, and lush regrowth, all
> of which rely on fire to rewind their biotic clocks.
>
> STEPHEN PYNE, 1995

The previous chapter addressed the effects of fire on individual plants, plant populations, and plant communities. As with plants, fire affects animals at the individual, population, and community levels. Effects on animals include direct mortality, changes in animal physiology and behavior, shifts or displacements in animal populations and communities, and immediate and longer-term alterations to habitat structure, composition, and function. In this chapter we explore how fire affects: (1) animals that inhabit different habitats; (2) terrestrial and aquatic animal populations and communities; and (3) animal habitat structure, composition, and function.

The study of animal–fire interactions has historically been focused in two areas: (1) effects on a single or a few species and (2) the response of animals, as individual organisms, to actual fire events. Some research and syntheses focus on the broader relationship between fire and animal communities, usually addressing the longer-term effects to animals from fire-induced changes to habitat (Lyon et al. 1978, Smith 2000). Research in California, as in many other regions of North America, has generally focused on mammals and birds. The ecological relationship between fire and animal communities is poorly understood, and there is little known about fire effects on most animal species existing in California.

Emphasis has been placed on understanding the effects of fire on animal habitat, including cover and shelter, the physical dimensions of an area, dominant plant species, food and forage, and other attributes important to a species, including various seasonal, life history, and reproductive needs. Fire affects the presence and condition of various habitat elements and temporal and spatial characteristics of habitat critical to animal populations, including patch size, juxtaposition, and connectivity (Cooperrider et al. 2000).

Fire Regime Attributes and Effects on Animals

Each of the components of fire regime is significant to animals. The interaction between animals and fire, including the implications of altered regimes or fire management practices, may be best understood when viewing individual fire regime attributes and their particular effects on animals. The temporal, spatial, and magnitude attributes of a fire all influence animals and their habitat.

Temporal Attributes of Fire

The seasonality, frequency, and regularity of fire represent the cycling of fire through an ecosystem and are the foundation of the ecological relationship of fire and animal interactions. Of all of the fire regime attributes, seasonality of fire may have the greatest potential for affecting individual animals and animal populations. Most animal species have specific temporal behaviors and resource needs associated with nesting, mating, raising young, foraging, and periods of inactivity. In many regions of California, late summer to autumn represents the period when fire is most frequent, although fire can and does occur in other seasons of the year. For most animals, the fire season occurs after breeding and rearing of young is completed. Thus, under normal, natural conditions, timing of animal reproduction and rearing ties well ecologically with fire. Fires burning in other seasons may have significant implications for plant species and communities, and thus, considerable short- and long-term implications for animals. The question is: how significant are these effects and how long do they last? These ideas are addressed further in the section on direct and indirect effects to populations and communities.

Like seasonality, a given bioregion has a number of characteristic fire-return intervals that occur within its ecological zones. Changes in return intervals can have long-term effects on vegetation communities, animal habitat, and animal communities. A reduction in the interval between fires can affect plant populations and can even contribute to plant community-type conversion (Zedler et al. 1983, Haidinger and Keeley 1993). In other regions of North America, shorter fire-return intervals have been shown to result in the loss of birds due to emigration and changes in behavior (Smith 2000). Increased fire frequency can disrupt behavior essential to reproducing, rearing young, defending territory, and acquiring resources. Too-frequent fire could have the additive effect of removing enough individuals from a population to affect reproduction or survival or to cause animals to emigrate or cease to immigrate. On the other hand, too infrequent fire could eventually render an animal's habitat unsuitable due to changes in composition and structure.

Spatial Attributes of Fire

The spatial complexity and size of a fire affect animals in several ways. The most obvious may be that differential burning in an area results in a varied, more complex vegetation mosaic comprised of different plant communities and resources in different conditions. The significance to animals varies with size of fire and scale of patches within the mosaic. For animals such as salamanders, relevant patches are of square meters within centimeters above the ground, but for larger animals such as bears and large ungulates, they are of square kilometers and meters above the ground. Spatial complexity can be caused by variation within one fire or by the pattern of multiple fires at various times in a landscape.

The size of a fire or consecutive fires has ramifications for animals by creating broad areas of similar vegetation structure and condition or altering too much or too little habitat. A fire's complexity and size can alter the connectivity from one area to another, the size of habitat patch, and the pattern of animal habitat on the landscape.

Intensity and Severity Attributes of Fire

Fire intensity is a measure of the heat released by the fire that is responsible for most direct mortality and injury. Temperatures above 100°C (212°F) can be considered lethal for most living organisms (DeBano et al. 1998), whereas much lower temperatures (40°C–60°C [104°F–140°F]) are lethal for animals. Longer residence times can increase lethality, and shorter residence times may reduce lethality, at least at lower temperatures at the edge of the lethal threshold.

Fire intensity determines whether animals are injured or killed by a fire, whereas severity provides an indication of the degree of habitat alteration. Alterations to the plant and soil communities can affect the shelter, nesting, and forage components of animal habitat. The extent and depth of heating in soil and woody debris is an important factor to many animal species. Soil and woody material can reduce the lethal effects of heat on animals through their insulating properties.

Fire severity also affects animals through changes in their habitat. Animals associated with more open habitats, dominated by herbaceous plant species and a younger age-class of shrubs or trees, generally benefit from fire severe enough to remove vegetation, eliminate older plants, and maintain those open conditions. Animals associated with more homogenous habitats benefit from fires of more uniform severity and low spatial complexity. Low-severity fire allows existing species to remain or quickly recolonize, whereas moderate- to high-severity fires allow new species to establish themselves into the resulting, altered landscape. Animals associated with plant community ecotones benefit from fires of varying severity that leave a relatively diverse patchwork of unburned and burned areas and a range of habitat conditions.

Crown fires (see Chapter 3) reduce or eliminate crowns of trees and shrubs, stressing or killing them. The response of animals to these changes can be varied. Crown reduction can substantially reduce habitat for invertebrates and nesting vertebrates by reducing nesting sites and material, forage, cover, and escape routes from predators. Conversely, the removal of vegetation structure associated with crown fires creates or enhances habitat for species preferring more open canopy or exposed surfaces.

Direct Effects of Fire on Individuals

Although fire does kill animals, even the immediate, direct effects to animals and animal populations are complex and difficult to quantify. Direct mortality counts or estimates likely do not completely reveal either the immediate or the long-term effects on animal populations. Animals can move in from adjacent areas or be displaced, reproductive rates may decline or increase, and fewer inter- or intra-specific competitors may benefit those individuals that survive fire. A properly functioning, fire regime–animal community interrelationship, complete with some degree of mortality and habitat change for those resident species, should be the focus for understanding animal–fire interactions. The ensuing discussion relates to "properly functioning" fire regime–animal community relationships and what new information is needed on the subject. The most complete source of information concerning the fire and effects to animal species occurring in California and elsewhere in North America is the Fire Effects Information System (USDA Forest Service 1999).

Direct Mortality of Animals from Fire

Although much attention and interest have been given to how animals respond to actual fire events, little is known or documented. Mortality rates are difficult to quantify,

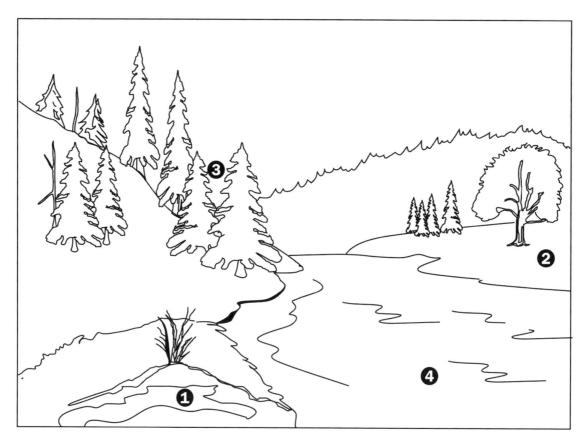

FIGURE 7.1. Animal habitat zones: (1) Subterranean, (2) Ground-dwelling, (3) Arboreal, and (4) Aquatic.

FIGURE 7.2. Subterranean fauna habitat zone.

because scavengers often consume the majority of carcasses within 24 hours of a fire (M. Brooks, pers. comm., 2004). And, without knowledge of pre- and post-fire population densities, mortality rates alone are of little use. Knowledge concerning animal response to fire events is often based on inferences from observations of animal behavior before and after fires, and what is believed to be happening where and when observations cannot be conducted (e.g., in burrows, under tree or brush canopy). Escaping the fire's heat is the most common way for animals to escape direct mortality.

Animals can either flee or take shelter from fire, and any behavior can be explained as a variation of these two strategies. Slower-moving animals, by necessity, have to take shelter from fire. Such might be the case with small mammals, reptiles, and amphibians. More mobile animals (e.g., deer, birds) will depart burning areas. If escape is not possible, their size or particular habitat use, such as ground or tree nesting, can become a liability in relation to fire.

To understand animal behavioral response to fire, one must consider the habitats and vertical zones occupied by the species in question. Where and how an animal moves about, forages, finds shelter, and nests is dependent on an animal's morphology, physiology, and behavioral abilities as well as the characteristics of the habitat at the time of a fire. These factors govern animal response to fire. We discuss animal reaction to fire by generalizing the landscape into four vertical zones: subterranean, ground level, arboreal, and aquatic (Fig. 7.1).

SUBTERRANEAN FAUNA

Subterranean fauna include species that live in or under the ground and species that either spend a considerable amount of time underground or the underground habitat serves an essential function (Fig. 7.2). Subterranean animals propel themselves through the earth, create burrows, or utilize burrows made by other species (Box 7.1).

Subterranean species will typically respond to fire by taking shelter underground. The insulating properties of soil or below-ground shelters generally protect animals under most fire conditions. For species that find protection underground or by some other means, direct mortality due to fire is often avoided (Harestad 1985, Yensen et al. 1992, Koehler and Hornocker 1997) (Box 7.2). Though some of these species can be fast moving (e.g., rabbits), most are relatively slow or immobile. For some species (e.g., earthworms), there is no option for escaping the effects of fire other than sheltering with the thermal protection of the soil. Conversely, mobile species such as rabbits can leave the immediate area, returning once the fire has passed. Heated soil and smoke can also cause mortality in underground fauna. As discussed in Chapter 5, as depth increases, the insulating properties of soil reduce the heat penetration beneath the surface. However, the insulating effects of soils are altered depending on the residence time of the fire coupled with soil texture and soil moisture. Longer residence time will drive the heat deeper into the soil. Both smoke and fire's consumption of oxygen and production of carbon monoxide also threaten underground-dwelling animals. In addition to providing multiple escape routes, multiple entrances may have value for burrowing mammals during a fire by allowing for a continual supply of breathable air thereby avoiding asphyxiation (Bendell 1974, Sullivan 1996).

GROUND-DWELLING FAUNA

Animals living above soil and on the ground constitute the ground-dwelling fauna (Fig. 7.3). For these animals, the ground surface is where the majority of activities occur (e.g., nesting, rearing of young, foraging). The surface faunal community has the widest variation in size, ranging from small snails and beetles to large mammals, and has a wide

FIGURE 7.3. Ground-dwelling fauna habitat zone.

> ## BOX 7.3. GROUND-DWELLING ANIMAL COMMUNITY: RELATIVE MOBILITY AND RESPONSE TO FIRE
>
> | | |
> |---|---|
> | *Limited mobility and likely cannot flee fire, taking shelter or seeking refuge* | Snails, slugs, arachnids, centipedes, millipedes, beetles and other insects, tortoises, toads |
> | *Moderate mobility, and fleeing versus taking shelter likely a function of rate of approaching fire front* | Amphibians (e.g., western toad, *Bufo boreas*), many salamanders, reptiles (e.g., rattlesnakes, lizards), some ground-nesting birds (e.g., quail, turkeys), many rodent species (e.g., mice, voles, chipmunks, woodrats) |
> | *Highly mobile and likely fleeing fire* | Flying insects (e.g., grasshoppers, some ground-nesting birds (e.g., meadowlark, wild turkeys mid- to large-sized mammals (e.g., many carnivores, ungulates) |

range of mobility. Some animals move extremely slowly, and if also small, cannot move sufficient distances quickly enough to escape fire. Other animals, both small and large, are much more mobile. Size and mobility contribute to how animals can respond to fire (Box 7.3).

Many surface fauna try to escape fire by sequestering themselves inside or under surface features, such as the litter layer, downed and decaying woody matter, ground nests, dens, talus, and rocky outcrops. Animal morphological characteristics and mobility determine what form of shelter they seek.

Smaller, slower species, such as woodrats (*Neotoma* spp.), take shelter by retreating to dens or cavities in rocks or talus piles (Howard et al. 1959, Wright and Bailey, 1982), whereas toads hide underneath logs or under wet litter in depressions (Komarek 1969). Some animals den in dense vegetation (e.g., riparian brush rabbit) or create their dens from dead vegetation and sticks (e.g., woodrats). These materials are highly flammable, and direct mortality of species seeking shelter from fire in such places has been recorded (Williams et al. 1992) or postulated to be likely during a fire (Basey 1990). Many surface inhabitants utilize or nest in downed wood, which is differentially affected by fire (see following). In Arizona and Utah, research has revealed that many surface species (e.g., snakes, lizards, rodents, lagomorphs, ground birds) appeared in burned areas shortly after fire, suggesting they avoided the fire in some way (Esque et al. 1995).

Larger animals, such as black bears *(Ursus americanus)*, mule deer *(Odocoileus hemionus)*, and pronghorn *(Antilocapra americana)*, often evade a fire, and are rarely killed during fires (National Park Service 1966). For other species for which escape may be the primary response, such as bighorn sheep and American pine martens *(Martes americana)*, data regarding direct effects to and responses of these species to fire are lacking (Tesky 1993, Koehler and Hornocker 1997). However, even species that may be thought of as being relatively slow movers, such as toads, have been observed moving ahead of oncoming fires (Sullivan 1994).

ARBOREAL FAUNA

Animals living in vegetation above the ground, whether in main stems, branches, or crowns, constitute arboreal fauna (Fig. 7.4). Some of these species spend their time primarily above the ground, nesting and foraging in the canopy of shrubs and trees (e.g., tree squirrels *[Sciurus* and *Tamiasiurus]*, porcupine *[Erethizon dorsatum]*, tree frogs *[Hyla* spp.*]*), but also traverse the ground. Others are able to either glide or fly, perhaps leaving branches or the canopy to forage but otherwise remaining above the ground (e.g., many insects, arboreal nesting birds, northern flying squirrel *[Glaucomys sabrinus]*, bats).

Like animals occupying other zones, some arboreal animals seem to respond to fire by taking shelter, whereas others take flight. Again, there is little direct evidence to confirm how a species responds to fire. Animals that construct or occupy existing nest cavities within trunks may find suitable shelter from fire. However, unlike the protection provided by a soil layer for benthic fauna, the protection from plant matter may be more tenuous for arboreal animals. Heat convection is greater and the material providing the protection itself is flammable. Thus, moderate to severe fires may pose a threat to animals sheltering within standing trees, especially if the trees are already dead.

Observations of birds suggest that they are not frightened by fire (Lyon et al. 1978), perhaps because of their ability to easily and quickly avoid fire and its effects. Instead, many flying insects and birds respond quickly to fires by taking advantage of injured plants, whereas other bird species immigrate to feed on species attracted to the burned area. Bark beetles (e.g., *Dendroctonus* spp., *Scolytus* spp.) and other beetles (e.g., long-horned beetle *[Cerambydidae]* and flat-headed boring beetle *[Buprestidae]*) that forage on the cambial tissues quickly arrive to lay their eggs under the bark of stressed trees, and the resulting larvae on the cambium, contributing to tree mortality. In turn, predaceous insects and insectivorous birds, such as woodpeckers and nuthatches, quickly take advantage of new, prolific food supplies, whereas raptors congregate in burned areas to prey on rodents.

AQUATIC FAUNA

Animals that live entirely in water (e.g., fishes, some mollusks and insects), have an aquatic life stage (e.g., amphibians, some insects), or primarily occupy or use aquatic, wetland, or riparian ecosystems for nesting and shelter, reproduction, or foraging (e.g., many amphibians and reptiles, river otter, beaver, many waterfowl and wading birds) constitute aquatic fauna (Fig. 7.5).

Aquatic species are likely buffered from the effects of most fires. Research conducted in eastern and southern North America suggests that reptiles and amphibians inhabiting such environments suffer little to no mortality during fire, and there is no evidence that populations are affected (Ford et al. 1999, Russell et al. 1999). Many bird species occupy marsh, wetland, riparian, and other aquatic habitats. They are also highly mobile and likely to avoid the direct effects of fire by escaping.

Little is known about direct effects to species or life stages occurring in water environments, whether fully aquatic or amphibious. Animals living along a body of water likely retreat to the water, as they would when faced with other threats. Thus, non-flying vertebrates (e.g., amphibians and reptiles, many ducks, and mammals able to swim) occupying the shores of a pond or lake or the banks of a stream or river take refuge in the water. Increased water temperature and decreased oxygen due to fire are potential direct threats to aquatic life. Many more indirect effects to the aquatic environment, as with its terrestrial counterpart, influence aquatic animals, populations, and communities. Fires of higher magnitude or greater extent likely would have more effect on aquatic systems than smaller fires or those of lesser magnitude; both of these regime attributes could impact water temperature and oxygen concentration and affect terrestrial features influencing the aquatic environment. Similarly, temporal characteristics of fire indirectly affect the aquatic environment by affecting terrestrial elements, such as soil and vegetation, which then change aquatic environments. As Chapter 3 described, the amount of heat necessary to change liquid water to gas is considerable, and water provides good insulation for animals. Certainly, the volume of the water mass inhabited by aquatic animals would determine the level of protection afforded them. Lakes, large ponds, rivers, and perennial streams provide considerable protection from fire. Interestingly, California has a unique

FIGURE 7.4. Arboreal fauna habitat zone.

aquatic ecosystem; vernal pools, which are both ephemeral and relatively shallow. This would seem to be one aquatic environment that potentially could be affected by fire. But as with other ecosystems in California, vernal pools, and the native fauna, appear to be in synchrony with the fire regimes where they occur (see Chapter 13 on the Central Valley).

Direct Effects of Fire on Populations and Communities

The same factors that are important to individual animals are important to populations and communities. Fires over large

spatial and temporal scales influence the availability, condition, and spatial distribution of key habitat features such as migration corridors and refugia. In fact, unburned areas adjacent to burned areas function as biological refugia for animals during and immediately after fire and during the period of recovery from the fire. In addition to direct mortality, fire directly influences intra- and inter-specific behavior including population residency and displacement, migration, colonization, foraging and predation, and reproduction.

Only in situations where populations are in dangerously poor condition, such as low abundance, restricted age-class distribution, or already-established decline, or where the fire

FIGURE 7.5. Aquatic fauna habitat zone.

regime is drastically altered, does a single fire or series of fires pose a real threat to an animal species or community (e.g., desert tortoise; see sidebar in Chapter 16). Alteration of fire regimes and vegetation communities, along with the fragmentation of animal populations, create situations in which fire can significantly affect a particular aquatic or terrestrial species population or community.

Although there is little research regarding the effects of fire at the population and community levels (Smith 2000), for the west and all of North America, fire effects to bird communities are known best. Within California, there have been studies on fire effects on southern California rodent populations and communities, the Stephen's kangaroo rat *(Dipodomys stephensi)*, California gnatcatcher *(Polioptila californica)*, and mule deer. The most comprehensive summary of fire–animal population and community interactions is by Smith (2000).

Residence and Displacement

Animal populations disrupted by fire are often dispersed from nests, shelters, and foraging areas. Resident species may be displaced only during the actual fire, but others are displaced for varying periods. In contrast, some species may exploit the burned area, even to point of colonization and establishment as long as post-fire habitat conditions are suitable. Each fire regime attribute has the potential to influence the residency or displacement of animal populations and, by extension, the entire animal community (Table 7.1). The season of the fire

would dictate if, and what, behaviors of animals might be altered, and if changes in fire frequency occurred, animal populations and entire communities might be altered. The fire's size and complexity would determine how much of the range of a population was affected and how each species' essential habitat was distributed. Likewise, the magnitude of the fire determines whether habitat elements remain and how they might be distributed across the area, dictating whether and where a species can continue to reside.

Studies of rodent communities in southern California illustrate how fire affects populations of different species and how these populations, and the resulting community, continue to adjust as the burned area continues to change following fire (Price et al. 1995, Wirtz 1995). In grasslands and coastal sage scrub, rodent communities with different vegetation structure and forage requirements differentially occupy and respond to burned and unburned areas. The mixture and juxtaposition of patches of unburned and burned areas affect species composition and distribution of the rodent species, and this effect is evident for up to ten years. Fires created a wide variety of habitats, opening up some areas—an essential condition for rodents such as kangaroo rats *(Dipodomys* spp.)—and providing for a wider array of plants species, used as both shelter and forage by animals. In unburned areas, rodent diversity was lower, and some species abundances declined due to lack and gradual loss of habitat.

Table 7.2 displays a comparison between rodent species showing survival and response following fire in coastal sage

TABLE 7.1
Potential change in animal residence and displacement with changes in fire regime attributes

Temporal	
Seasonality	Changes in the seasonality of fire can cause shifts in which species are disturbed or displaced. Critical activities, such as reproduction and nesting, can be irrevocably disturbed for the season. Slow-moving young or newborn nestlings can be killed by unusually early fire.
Frequency	Increased frequency could cause displacement or behavioral change frequently enough that species do not continue to reside in that area. Decreased or increased frequency each over time could alter habitat structure and other resources so that the area is no longer inhabitable for some species but is perhaps suitable for other species.
Spatial	
Size	Large fires affect more habitat and could displace animals for a season or until enough area becomes suitable again for residency.
Complexity	Heterogeneity can determine whether a suitable habitat persists and the quantity and distribution of that habitat. Thus, the presence, number, and distribution of resident species could change with the degree of a fire's heterogeneity. Species benefiting from a more uniform environment would benefit more from a more homogeneous fire.
Magnitude	
Severity	Severity can either create or destroy the habitat attributes required by resident species. Too severe fire could pose a greater threat for direct mortality, potentially impacting the future reproductive success of populations. And, it could destroy habitat structure and function, displacing species for variable periods after fire. On the other hand, fire not severe enough could as easily displace a species due to inadequate habitat conditions in the future that would have been initiated by an adequately severe fire.
Type	Surface fires might not displace species occupying habitat above the ground any longer than the time it takes for smoke to dissipate. Crown fires greatly alter habitat in all three dimensions, displacing species for as long as it takes to regain the habitat structure. However, crown fires kill more trees, allowing species that require dead trees and openings.

scrub and southern chaparral. Species were first detected at different periods following fire, from less than four months for Pacific kangaroo rats *(Dipodomys agilis)* in coastal sage scrub to up to 11 months for dusky-footed woodrats *(Neotoma fuscipes).* Peak abundance ranged from as early as immediately after fire (e.g., deer mouse *[Peromyscus maniculatus]* in both plant communities) to several years following fire (e.g., cactus mouse *[Perumyscus eremicus]* in coastal sage scrub). The presence and period of occupation of each rodent species was related to the habitat condition over time after fire. At first, the area had the most contrasting mosaic of unburned and burned patches—open space and sparse vegetation in burned patches, with abundant and accessible seed from the surviving and flourishing plant species. Over time, the open areas regained vegetation structure and density, closing in the open areas and changing available forage as plant community composition changed.

Fire's Influence on Animal Migration

Migration is an obligatory, annual activity for many animal species. It involves unique behavior and considerable energy expenditure, contributes to the crucial genetic exchange between populations, and affects animal community health and composition. Each attribute of fire regime can affect migration. Fires occurring during active migration times can cause migration routes to be interrupted. The size, complexity, and magnitude of the fire could alter the path of subsequent migrations because of the juxtaposition of altered habitat gaps with past migration routes, adequacy of maintenance of migration corridors, and behavioral response of other species (e.g., predators) to changes in migration corridors (Table 7.3).

Ungulate response provides some understanding of fire's importance to animal migration. Migration is one of many animal population life history activities studied following the 1988 Yellowstone fires that consumed both forest and range vegetation. The more open post-fire forests were found to allow pronghorn different routes to summer foraging areas (Scott and Geisser 1996). For migration to successfully occur through a particular area, the essential food and cover needed by the species in question must be present. Fire can affect such characteristics, either positively or negatively, thus changing the quality, or perhaps use, of burned corridors. Native Californians were aware of the vegetation changes that fire caused and used fire to create or manipulate animal habitat to both benefit preferred wildlife and create easier hunting opportunities (see Chapter 17).

TABLE 7.2
Survival, time of appearance, and post-fire abundance of rodent species following fire in coast sage scrub and southern chaparral communities of southern California

	Survive Fire?	Time to Appear at Burned Sites	Post-Fire Peak Abundance	Study
Coastal Sage Scrub				
Pacific kangaroo rat *Dipodomys agilis*	Unknown	4 months or less	2–4 years	Price et al. 1995
San Diego pocket mouse *Chaetodipus fallax*	Unknown	4 months or less	3–7 years	Price et al. 1995
Deer mouse *Peromuscus maniculatus*	Yes	6–9 months	Post-fire	Wirtz 1995
Cactus mouse *Peromyscus eremicus*	Unknown	Unknown	3–7 years	Price et al. 1995
Southern Chaparral				
California pocket mouse *Perognathus californicus*	Yes	6–7 months	Unknown	Wirtz 1995
Brush mouse *Peromyscus boylli*	Yes	6–9 months	Unknown	Wirtz 1995
Parasitic mouse *Peromyscus californicus*	Yes	6–9 months	Unknown	Wirtz 1995
Deer mouse *Peromyscus maniculatus*	Yes	6–9 months	Post-fire	Wirtz 1995
Pacific kangaroo rat *Dipodomys agilis*	Unknown	8–9 months	Unknown	Wirtz 1995
Dusky-footed wood rat *Neotoma fuscipes*	No	8–11 months	Unknown	Wirtz 1995

TABLE 7.3
Potential change in animal migration with changes in fire regime attributes

Temporal
Seasonality   Fires burning during migration season could alter the path migrant species take.
Frequency   Change in frequency causes changes in habitat that could, depending on the species, either increase or decrease its use during the migration period.

Spatial
Size   The size of a fire might (1) dictate whether migration routes are kept sufficiently open or (2) create gaps too wide for animals to cross or hide from predators.
Complexity   Independent of size, complexity probably has little effect on migration. But increased spatial complexity could mean more variability in migration routes, benefiting more species. Decreased complexity in combination with large fires can significantly shift migration routes.

Magnitude
Severity   High severity could establish or maintain migration routes necessary for larger species while destroying the cover or finer scale of routes important to smaller species. Low-severity fires might not be sufficient to maintain the habitat structure needed by migrating animals.
Type   Crown fires could cause the most change in habitat structure that may be better or worse for different migrating species. Crown fires could remove the arboreal structure used by migrating birds.

TABLE 7.4
Potential change in animal reproduction with changes in fire regime attributes

Temporal

Seasonality   In-season fire could allow resident animals to maintain reproductive and rearing behaviors and activi-ties exploit normally. Out-of-season could impact those same behaviors or activities or kill slower-moving offspring or offspring confined to nests.

Frequency   Repeated disturbance of reproduction or longer-term alterations in an area's habitat could have suc-cessive influence on reproductive success. This could result in a decline in a population. If the affected animal species are of greater significance (e.g., keystone, integral in food web) to the ecosystem, the entire community can be affected.

Spatial

Size   Larger fires have the potential of affecting a larger portion of reproductively active members or off-spring of a population, more mating pairs' territories, greater foraging or hunting range of females with offspring.

Complexity   Independent of other fire regime attributes, complexity probably has little effect on reproduction. For rearing, if offspring or parents searching for food require a diverse environment or specific habitat to remain after or be created by fire, a more complex fire likely benefits these young. Offspring or forag-ing/hunting parents of species that benefit from more homogeneous areas would benefit from a less complex fire.

Magnitude

Severity   Independent of other fire regime attributes, severity probably has no unique effects on reproduction. Fire of any magnitude that has disturbed reproductive or rearing activities would have the same net effect. And, heat from a low to moderate fire could pose the same threat to mortality of young as high intensity. However, severity would come into play with forage for lactating mammals and species that collect food for their young.

Type   As with other animal activities, fire type has differential effects on animals living in different zones. Ground fires would be a threat to ground-nesting species but not to species high in the canopy or main stem of plants.

Fire's Influence on Animal Reproduction

For a population to remain viable, a sufficient number of individuals must survive and reproduce in the course of short- and long-term changes that fire brings to their envi-ronment. Fire affects mating and rearing activity, can kill young, and can affect the amount of food available for new-born, juvenile, and adult animals alike. Environmental con-ditions can both benefit and negatively affect populations. For example, abundant forage after high rainfall that allows for greater reproductive success in a population may also fuel fires in subsequent years just as immature individuals are rearing on the landscape (see sidebar in Chapter 16). If enough animals in a population are affected, the dynamics and health of that population will change.

Animals subjected to fire may leave the burned area tem-porarily or be displaced for longer periods. Animal popula-tions might benefit from newly made-available food, reduced predators, or reduced competition. Any of these changes following a fire could contribute to more adults surviving to produce and raise offspring or simply more off-spring surviving. But fire could have equally negative impacts on the reproductive success of animal populations. Adults, or more likely their slowly moving or immobile

young, could be killed by fire. And essential forage or prey could be affected, decreasing fecundity or survival of young. As with other characteristics of animals, the attrib-utes of fire regime affect reproduction in different ways (Table 7.4).

Seasonality of fire and fire return interval can have a dra-matic effect on reproductive viability. Many times, different groups within a population are differentially affected. Entire age-classes (e.g., newborn) or life stages (i.e., eggs) can be affected once (i.e., an out-of-season fire) or repeat-edly (i.e., more frequent fires than the return interval would indicate over a period of time), affecting not only the num-ber of individuals within a population but also an entire or substantial proportion of a brood year. For example, nesting of ground- and tree-nesting birds, fawning of ungulates, and emergence from or initiation of aestivation (e.g., rep-tiles, amphibians, mammals) are closely linked to season, bioregion, latitude, and elevation. In prairie and grassland systems in the Midwestern states, research has shown that fires out of synchrony with historic patterns of seasonality can be lethal to young animals confined to nests or dens or unable to escape from fire. The occurrence of a fire can affect an entire animal population within the bounds of the fire for at least one breeding cycle (Erwin and Stasiak 1979,

Finch et al. 1997, Smith 2000). Invertebrate populations are equally susceptible. Longcore (2003) studied the relationship of fire and butterflies in southern California chaparral and found that some life stages (i.e., eggs, larvae, pupae) are quite vulnerable to fire, and that even adults may suffer direct mortality due to low flight speed and high site fidelity. Thus, fire may affect the age structure of these butterfly populations. However, increased post-fire plant production, changes in plant community composition, and increased structural complexity resulted in overall beneficial conditions for butterflies. Huntzinger (2003) found that butterfly diversity increased two to three times in open areas created by fire in forest communities and doubled in riparian communities.

Change in vegetation structure, biomass, and nutritional content contribute to the reproductive success of each animal population inhabiting or using a burned area. Because fire severity and fire type alter vegetation differently, some populations' young of the year will benefit, whereas others will not. Bird and mammal adults searching for food will have differing success both in nesting and in gaining food for their young depending on the changes to vegetation brought on by the severity and size of the fire. Both surface fires and crown fires may provide access to more food for animals such as rodents and woodpeckers. Maturation of young may be enhanced because fires can increase the amount and nutritional value of forage and access to that forage. Fires also can create nesting platforms for bird species such as the spotted owl (Strix occidentalis).

Reproduction and survival of animal species with extended breeding and foraging seasons, such as chipmunks and bark beetles, may be significantly affected by a long fire season. Fire affects availability of food necessary for over-wintering or migrating birds and mammals putting on fat and energy stores. Fire, coupled with one or more years of low primary production, could reduce health and reproduction in many animals, including many insect and bird species, ungulate mammals, and food cachers such as rodents and several species of birds.

Fire's Influence on Animal Foraging and Predation

Fire's alteration of the vegetation community affects reproductive success of animals by influencing the amount and nutritional value of available food. Fire can result in alterations to available animal prey and plant food, including forage, fruits, and seed. Following fire, trophic structure of the pre-fire animal community can be altered, and the changed landscape may attract different species that feed on new food sources, including plant species that germinate or sprout only after fire, regrowth of previously occurring plants, and newly available seed. New herbivores attract predators, some new and some not, to the burned area. The result is an altered food web, including some animals from the pre-fire community, as well as new species stimulated by the fire itself. Over decades, the response of the vegetation

community to subsequent fires continues to affect the animal population–food web relationships.

An interesting relationship of fire to animal feeding behavior is the effect smoke has on various animals. Smoke affects animals by attracting or repelling different species. The net effect is an immediate, usually short-lived, change in animal community composition and structure. Smoke has both beneficial and detrimental effects on animals. Obviously, asphyxiation due to smoke is a threat to individual terrestrial animals. As with humans trapped in structures, smoke may pose a greater threat to life than heat. Many species escape the threat of smoke by fleeing fires, while others find shelter beneath materials such as logs and rocks.

There is evidence that fire and smoke attract some insects (Hart 1998) and inhibit activities of some beetle species. Some birds are attracted to the fire front, preying on other animals fleeing the fire and scavenging freshly killed animals. However, it is unclear if the smoke, fire, or other physical or chemical attributes of fire attract them. In addition, some bird species increase in abundance while the fires are active and for days and weeks following fire. In California, this has been documented for ravens (Wirtz 1979), screech-owls (Elliott 1985), woodpeckers (Moriarty et al. 1985), raptors and scavengers (Dodd 1988), golden eagles (Aquila chrysaetus), and peregrine falcons (Falco peregrinus) (Lehman and Allendorf 1989). Of particular interest is the community change related to woodpeckers. Stand-replacing fires kill large numbers of trees, leaving many others dying or susceptible to insects or diseases that can eventually kill them. Many species of insects are attracted to the dead and dying trees, followed by predaceous insects and insectivorous birds. In these environments, some species of woodpeckers are known to be the primary or exclusive occupant, or to dramatically increase following fire where dead and dying trees are abundant.

Some mammals are also known to be attracted to active or recently active fires. Deer are attracted to newly available forage and in turn attract mountain lions (Puma concolor) (Quinn 1990). French and French (1996) documented bears, raptors, and scavenging birds foraging along actively burning fire fronts of the 1988 Yellowstone fires. Grizzly and black bears, in particular, did not seem to be inhibited by either smoke or fire while foraging on ungulate carcasses resulting from fire mortality. Fire also can affect the type and quantity of food and forage available to animals but this topic is more properly discussed below under the indirect effects of fire.

Indirect Effects of Fire on Terrestrial Animals

Indirect fire effects are among the most important to animals, since both the animals' biotic and abiotic environments may be affected for a considerable period. Influences include alterations to (1) plant community composition and structure, (2) soil and litter, and (3) aquatic habitat and ecosystems. These habitat changes determine the short-term conditions for survival of individuals residing in the area before the fire, newly arriving individuals, and the long-term consequences for entire animal populations and communities.

Fire alters both the structure and the composition of vegetation, temporarily or permanently reduces or eliminates some food types while increasing others, and opens up areas previously closed by vegetation. If essential physical features or food items are lost, animal species dependent on them will leave the area until those features or food items return, if they do. This is also the case for cover needed for shelter, protection, or migration, and even thermal requirements of animals (Esque et al. 1995; Rinne 1996; Brooks and Esque 2002). On the other hand, changes to habitat benefit other animal species. For example, species requiring more openings, downed or dying vegetation, or types of food enhanced by fire may establish themselves in post-fire environments until the resources that attracted them are exhausted or are lost to vegetation growth following fire.

Habitat Structure

Perhaps one of the most significant roles of fire, with regard to animal populations and communities, is the alteration of vegetation and the subsequent shift in available habitat and habitat quality. These alterations are temporal, and some changes, such as the elimination of forbs and grasses, may be relatively short-lived (e.g., one to ten years). However, other changes, such as the re-establishment of snags, downed wood, or re-establishment of mature shrubs and trees, can take decades. Fire alters individual plants, the density of vegetation, the age-class distribution of plant species, the three-dimensional structure of habitat, and the composition of plant species. Each of these changes can potentially influence animal occupation and use of a burned area for various periods of time, from months, to years, to decades.

WOODY PLANTS

Woody plants constituting the canopy structure may be altered in several ways that affect animals. Fires can kill mature trees creating new snags, burn down snags creating new downed logs, and consume old logs creating ash beds for new tree seedlings. Some microhabitat elements are also created or facilitated by fire or by scorching such as fire scars, cat faces, and hollowing of trees.

Fire can repeatedly scar individual mature trees, eventually resulting in "cat faces," or deeply burned sections of the bole. Cat faces permit the invasion of insects and fungi into the exposed cambium, sapwood, and heartwood of trees, accelerating tree decline but providing food sources for invertebrates and vertebrates such as wood boring insects, insectivorous birds, and flying squirrels. Scorching can either kill trees or induce physiological stress, permitting invasion by insects and fungi. As with scarring, scorching provides habitat for insects and other invertebrates, and abundant food (e.g., bark beetles *Dendroctonus* spp. and *Scolytus* spp.) for vertebrates such as woodpeckers and nuthatches. The decay sequence

lasts from years in moist, mild climates to decades, or even centuries, for large wood in very cold, dry subalpine environments and supports an everlasting but changing array of organisms associated with decay.

Fire can facilitate the development of hollow trees by either entering through existing fire scars and cat faces or facilitating decay in heart and sapwood. Hollow trees provide shelter, nests, and food for many species of animals, including woodpeckers, bats, rodents, mustelids, and black bears.

PLANT DENSITY AND SIZE

Fires alter the configuration and degree of canopy closure and juxtaposition and density of plants in shrub, woodland, and forest communities. These changes affect the condition of habitat in the canopy as well as of that of the forest or woodland floor. Opening up of mature vegetation improves the habitat for some animals (e.g., chipmunk, *Tamias* spp., ground squirrels, *Spermophilus* and *Ammospermophilus* spp.). For other animal species, fires that open up the canopy degrade or remove essential habitat, such as creating excessively large openings, destroying nesting sites, or eliminating snags. Species such as northern flying squirrels and chipmunk (e.g., Townsend's, *Tamias townsendii*), or species associated with denser forest habitats, would be expected to be reduced by either greater canopy opening or reduced tree density. Similarly, the desert tortoise, which requires shrub cover to escape intense desert sun, typically displays population declines in areas where shrub cover is lost due to fire (Brooks and Esque 2002; see sidebar in Chapter 16, this volume).

Decreasing plant density can also improve primary productivity by decreasing competition and increasing growth rate, which benefits animal species associated with larger diameter and/or taller shrubs and trees. Large trees, in particular, appear to be of great value to animals in woodlands and forests. Their dimension and volume provide habitat for animals that cannot be provided by smaller trees. Large animals, such as nesting birds of prey, bears, and porcupines may find it impossible to use small trees because of dimensional constraints alone. Smaller animals, such as passerine birds or rodents, may prefer larger trees to avoid predators. If large trees are missing, these animals have to find alternatives or are forced to move to areas where habitat conditions are appropriate. Large trees also provide a greater abundance of cambium for invertebrate food and habitat than do smaller trees. It is possible that some of the larger boring insects can find sufficient habitat only in larger trees. Small trees do perform some important animal habitat functions. Some insects prefer habitat in smaller, dying trees or in the branches of larger trees. The larger density of smaller trees provides a constant background of habitat for invertebrates and fungi that serve as food for predators.

Like trees, changes in shrub size and density have important consequences for animals. Fire often consumes a very large proportion of the plant biomass in shrubland communities. The effects on animals vary and are related to the effects on individual plant species, the entire plant community, and to the ecological needs of the animals. Often, shrub canopy reduction benefits animals that (1) forage in more open habitat or on newly available food (i.e., kangaroo rats), or (2) are more mobile in the more open habitat (e.g., mule deer). For example, opening up shrub communities initially benefits animals consuming seeds (Wirtz et al. 1988). However, other animals require a more mature shrub community or one with greater canopy cover. Beyers and Wirtz (1997) found that the California gnatcatcher inhabited coastal sage scrub with 50% cover or more, with plants typically taller than one meter. When fire burned occupied scrub communities, gnatcatchers typically did not recolonize the area for four to five years.

SOIL AND LITTER

Fires generally consume much of the litter, duff, and small dead wood, and may also consume a large proportion of the organic matter in the upper soil layers. Consumption of litter fuels generally releases a flush of nutrients to plants, encouraging growth. While reducing litter, fire also initiates deposition of a new pulse of organic matter, which will initiate the new litter and duff layers.

Deposition of new organic material has two immediate wildlife-related results. First, deposition provides the only available habitat for species whose habitat was, at least partially, consumed. Second, the deposition and/or sprouting of various species' seeds (e.g., cone- and acorn-bearing trees) provide substantial readily available food for rodents, especially sciurids, ants, and seed-eating birds.

SNAGS AND DOWNED WOOD

Dead and dying woody plants, snags, and downed wood and logs (coarse woody debris) provide important habitat for hundreds of vertebrate (CDFG 1999) and invertebrate species in shrub, woodland, and forest ecosystems. Fire, alone and in combination with other agents such as rusts, fungi, and insects, facilitates the production of new snags, downed wood, and coarse woody debris and other deadwood. Fire regime attributes of severity, extent, and spatial complexity cause differences in creation and distribution of snags and coarse woody debris and consumption of dead wood existing before fire. Often single trees and large shrubs are killed, but large patches of shrubs and trees, and even entire stands, may be killed depending on the size, intensity, and severity of the fire. During the deadwood cycling process, a wide range of animals utilizes the wood in various ways, including food, shelter, and nesting (Box 7.4).

Fire also consumes existing snags and coarse woody debris. Since these habitat elements are essential to animals, uniform loss over large extensive geographic areas could threaten the continued occurrence or recolonization of animals after a fire. Consumption may not be complete, and instead of reducing all of these woody materials to ash, fire often reduces portions of the snags and logs to ash, converting other portions to charcoal and leaving other portions intact (Sidebar 7.1).

Habitat Distribution

In addition to changing the structural nature of habitat, fire also alters the spatial relationship of distinct patches of habitat—the number and size of the patches, the juxtaposition of the suitable habitat for any given animal species, and the connectivity between these habitat patches. The spatial distribution of burned and unburned patches of animal habitat, or *mosaic*, dictates animal community composition and carrying capacity for each population in an area (Sidebar 7.2). Unburned areas can function as refugia for resident animals during fires, sites for immediate occupation or recolonization

Dead wood in forests, expressed as standing dead trees *(snags)* and logs, is an important habitat component for many animals ranging from insects to vertebrates. For some species, such as many beetles of the Families Scolytidae, Cerambycidae, and Buprestidae, dying and dead trees are essential to their existence. Fire has often been portrayed as a villain to wildlife because of its propensity to consume snags and logs. While this view is somewhat correct, it is incomplete; the role of fire relative to snags and logs is much more complex than simply consuming dead material that has value to wildlife. One of the recurring themes in this chapter and the entire book is the patchy mosaic of different habitat compositions and structures and the resetting of habitat development trajectories following fire or other ecological processes. Fire has an essential role in the cycling of dead wood in forest, woodland, and shrub communities.

Not all of the dead wood is necessarily consumed by fire; patches within the perimeter of the burn often contain areas that are not burned at all or are so lightly burned that many of the snags, and to a lesser extent logs, continue to persist (Horton and Mannan 1988, Laudenslayer 2002). The scale of these patches of unburned or lightly burned habitat can vary considerably from a few square meters to hectares—and the reason for the fire's lack of consumption include those presented elsewhere in this book such as change in fuel density, topography, and weather conditions. It is not clear what causes fire to consume only a portion of the wood within a fire's perimeter. The amount of bark remaining, deposition of duff and litter around the dead wood, and certainly moisture content of the dead wood and the continuity of fuels between the dead wood and other portions of the fire all probably contribute to the consumption or lack of consumption of dead wood.

The response of snags and logs to fire is not that they are either consumed or not consumed—partial consumption is a common result of fires in dead wood (Horton and Mannan 1988, Laudenslayer 2002). However, partial consumption can change the characteristics of the dead material substantially, and the surface area of the dead wood affected by partial consumption varies considerably. Partial consumption of dead wood varies from light scorching, where a thin layer of the surface bark or wood is consumed, producing a veneer of carbonized wood, to deep charring, where the bark or wood is converted to charcoal to a depth up to several centimeters. The surface areas of pieces of dead wood can vary considerably in the proportion unburned, scorched, and charred, with some trees exhibiting only a small degree of scorching, to others where the entire tree was heavily charred or scorched. These changes in the external characteristics of dead wood are substantial and probably change the internal environment of the dead wood altering habitat for animals. However, little is known about wildlife responses to scorching and charring at this time.

Fire can remove dead wood or change its character but it also is one of the initiators of new dead wood. Fire-induced mortality, whether causing immediate death or stressing trees to permit the action of secondary mortality factors (e.g., insects and disease) to eventually kill trees, is a common result of fire. Fire-induced mortality can be instantaneous, as when the crowns are consumed or largely scorched, or it can be delayed for a number of years after the cambium or rootlets are subjected to lethal heat (Ryan and Reinhardt 1988, Reinhardt and Ryan 1989, Ryan 1990, Swezy and Agee 1991, Sackett and Haase 1996). The potential for mortality is related to topography, amount of fuels associated with the tree bole, area where fine rootlets are near the soil surface, as well as weather conditions. The mixture of trees immediately killed by fire and those that die months and years later provide a time sequence of dead material that likely have differing characteristics due to the potential differences in insect and fungal invaders through time.

Indeed, the deterioration and fall rates of snags created by fire compared to snags created by some other agent of mortality (e.g., bark beetles) appear to differ (Keene 1955, Kimmey 1955, Harrington 1996, Laudenslayer 2002), with fire-killed trees deteriorating and falling more quickly than other dead trees. These differences probably do have a profound effect on the microorganisms and invertebrates associated with decaying dead material and most likely also have an effect on vertebrates but little is currently known about these responses.

It is clear that fire has a profound effect on snags and logs in forested situations. It removes some, can change the characteristics of those remaining, and creates new snags and logs. This renewing of the snag and log resource, coupled with the potential variation in snag and log characteristics, may well be an essential element in maintaining a diverse and functional forest, including the array of animals existing therein.—*WFL*

TABLE 7.5
Potential change in animal colonization and exploitation with changes in fire regime attributes

Temporal		
	Seasonality	In-season fire would allow resident animals to exploit resources (e.g., food, nesting sites) normally and while out-of-season could either impact those same resources or fail to affect them in a manner necessary for a segment of the resident animal community.
	Frequency	Changes in frequency alter both habitat structure and composition, which in turn could lead to new species being able to exploit an area. Long-term shifts might mean colonization and establishment of invading animal species; shorter-term shifts might mean relatively shorter periods of exploitation.
Spatial		
	Size	Larger fires have the potential to reduce or increase habitat quality for different species across larger areas.
	Complexity	Independent of size, complexity probably has little effect on colonization. But increased spatial complexity could mean more variability in habitat quality affecting more species positively or negatively. Decreased complexity in combination with large fires could significantly change the capability of the habitat to support some species.
Magnitude		
	Severity	High severity could establish or maintain habitat necessary for larger species while removing the cover or finer scale of habitat patches important to smaller species. Low-severity fires might not be sufficient to maintain the habitat structure needed by some species.
	Type	Crown fires would cause the most obvious change in habitat structure, benefiting some resident species while negatively affecting others. Crown fires could remove the arboreal structure used by birds and insects and other arboreal animals.

following the fire, temporary shelter, or provide forage for migrating and early succession species (Esque et al. 1995). Burned areas can function for foraging or hunting of resident or immigrant species or newly available habitat for some resident or immigrant species. Different fire regimes alter habitat differently, influencing if and how burned areas will be colonized or exploited by animals (Table 7.5)

The mosaics created by fire elicit different responses from different species. Small habitat patches are necessary for animals that require either small openings or denser vegetation

One of the most vexing problems in managing wildlife forest habitat is providing continuous habitat for all species so that relatively isolated populations can remain in genetic contact through time. Recently, great concern has been raised about the lack of continuous habitat for some species. This concern is based on understandings about the isolation of populations restricted to islands of habitat separated from other populations or suitable habitat by different, effective filters, such as a water body or unsuitable habitat. The common solution for these problems in terrestrial systems has been to propose development and maintenance of corridors, bands of suitable habitat connecting larger areas supporting populations of the species of interest or suitable habitat. However, these concerns and proposed solutions have generally been raised for species associated with relatively stable forests characterized by large numbers of old, large-diameter trees and high canopy closure. To date, little concern has been raised about contiguity of habitat for species associated with forest openings dominated by shrubs or herbaceous plants and especially for short-lived species associated with openings that are ephemeral. Consideration of habitat contiguity for such species necessarily requires not only spatial but also temporal aspects of these relatively short-lived habitats.

Historically, fire created and maintained a dynamically shifting mosaic of different sizes and types of habitat patches for many animal species. Fire at the extremes of the range of fire regime—from low-severity surface fires at relatively small spatial and temporal scales (ha and years) to high-severity stand-replacement fires at a variety of spatial and temporal scales from small to relatively large scales (perhaps up to square kilometers and centuries)—contributed to these dynamic habitat mosaics.

Suitable patches for any species must be sufficiently large and sufficiently adjacent in space and time for the species to find and exploit. Historically, habitats dominated by large-diameter trees were relatively contiguous and were maintained through frequent, light, surface fires. However, there were a relatively few fires that shifted habitat structure to large-scale openings dominated by herbaceous vegetation, shrubs, and small trees. More ephemeral habitats were contiguous temporally with frequent, relatively low-severity fires helping to maintain such habitats and newer patches of such habitats created through more intensive stand-replacing fires (and subsequently maintained by lower-intensity fires).

Perhaps of greater importance than the spatial and temporal continuity of suitable habitat is the character of the *gaps* between patches of contiguous habitat. Species that require habitats needing a great deal of time to develop, are long-lived, have great reproductive capability, or have great capability to move should be better able to tolerate larger gaps (spatial and temporal). Species associated with ephemeral habitats and that have relatively short lives, limited reproductive capability, and limited capability of movement would be expected to tolerate much smaller habitat gaps.

What constitutes a gap is also dependent on the species' biology. Gaps can represent an absolute barrier to movement if the gap habitat offers no forage or cover, or, when the gap has habitat capability but is excessively wide for animals to cross, does not allow for some movement. Generally, gaps in terrestrial systems operate as filters for most species, reducing but not eliminating movement between suitable patches.

A variety of plants are known to respond positively to fires; other plants are known to respond to the openings left in forests or shrublands following fires. Many animals are associated with such plants; some are dependent on the plants themselves, and thus also require moving openings to maintain genetic contact with others of their species.—*WFL, KES* patches to be scattered in an otherwise homogeneous landscape. Some rodents need open areas to forage or to move within their range, whereas other rodent species and birds need cover for shelter and nesting. For example, the California gnatcatcher occupies and nests in coastal sage communities with shrub cover of 50% or more (Beyers and Wirtz 1997). Similarly, for many voles (e.g., *Microtus* spp.), shorter grasses or more open situations following fire make it difficult to conceal their movements from potential predators. When fires open up this plant community, some bird and rodent species cease to occupy the habitat.

The interface between severely burned areas and the adjacent unburned or very lightly burned areas forms a complex mosaic of edges and openings. The shapes of these mosaics depend on a complex mix of variables affecting fire behavior, including the presence and types of fuels, topography, and weather during the burn. Openings at the edges of most closed forests are utilized by browsing and predatory animals, which take advantage of newly available forage and exposed prey, respectively. Larger openings dominated by herbaceous plants provide habitat for species including pocket gophers, voles, and ground-foraging birds. The edges of larger openings can also provide forage for deer. However, research into ungulate presence and use of seasonal habitats over entire population ranges suggests that pronghorn (Scott and Geisser 1996) and elk (Norland et al. 1996) do not measurably alter their occupation following fires. Norland et al. (1996) concluded that fire effects on ungulates are still not understood.

The relationships among fire regime, habitat alteration, and species and community response can be quite complicated. Fire's modification of individual plants, canopy, and habitat has a cumulative effect. Spatial and temporal variation among fires creates a complex, varied environment for animals.

In California, the interaction of fire and the northern goshawk *(Accipiter gentilis)* illustrates the complex relationship of fire regime and animal habitat (Graham et al. 1997, Russell et al. 1999). Northern goshawks occupy forests with various fire regimes, ranging from surface fires in Ponderosa pine communities to stand-replacing fires of coastal Douglas-fir and western larch forests in the Pacific Northwest. Smaller openings within the forests are preferred by many prey species of the northern goshawk, both birds and mammals. The goshawks themselves hunt at the edges of larger openings. Additionally, openings of adequate size adjacent to suitable nest sites are needed for adequate clearance for flight to and from nests, and for detection of predators. The northern goshawk requires a spectrum of opening sizes in order to prey, breed, and successfully rear young. An inadequate diversity of opening sizes likely would reduce population viability for the northern goshawk.

Plant Community Composition

Fire has even larger-scale, indirect effects on animals by altering plant community composition and condition. These longer-term, larger-scale changes affect available suitable habitat for animal populations and communities. As the plant community develops after fire, animal populations respond accordingly and changes in animal community composition and structure occur.

FOOD AVAILABILITY

Fire alters the type, quantity, and nutritional value of plant matter, including foliage, fruit, and nuts. At a broader level, the species composition and age–class distribution of plant species in the vegetation community dictates the composition and structure of the animal community. In California, fire in chaparral ecosystems may benefit mule deer and upland bird species (Biswell 1957, 1969; Kie 1984) by increasing forage and forage value as well as opening up areas for access to foliage.

The type and quantity of food and forage available to animals during years immediately following fire depends on both the fire type and the plant community condition. As mentioned previously, food for granivorous and insectivorous animals may be greatly increased after a fire. This effect may remain for two to five years following a fire in a grass or shrub community, and many more years in forests, depending on the ever-changing patterns and types of plant communities. Newly available or newly depleted food may mean an introduction or displacement of animal species (Price et al. 1995, Van Dyke et al. 1996).

For grasslands, fire has been shown to increase forage productivity and quality (Norland et al. 1996, Tracy and McNaughton 1996, Van Dyke et al. 1996); however, mixed results in various studies indicate that this is not always the case. Fire has been shown to reduce nutritional value of elk winter forage in Yellowstone National Park (DelGiudice and Singer 1996) and to have no effect (positive or negative) on mule deer in pine-oak scrub of Trinity County (Kie 1984). Biswell (1957, 1969) suggested that fire in various types of California chaparral communities increased both deer utilization and deer fecundity.

PLANT COMMUNITY SHIFTS

Plant communities can be altered by changes in species composition and structure, or more likely, by a combination of both. If the fire regime is altered by the occurrence of one uncharacteristic fire, an uncharacteristic sequence of fires, or fire exclusion, plant communities can change on a given site; forests can be converted to another forest type, shrublands, or herbaceous vegetation; and shrublands may be converted to herbaceous vegetation. The time needed for shrubs and trees to become re-established depends on variables such as the severity of the burn, topography, reproductive strategies of the species making up the plant community, the species of plants colonizing the site, the seed bank, and adjacent vegetation that can supply seed.

Changing from a forest or shrub community to a herbaceous-dominated community will immediately shift the fauna from those associated with trees and shrubs to those relying on herbaceous plants, if suitable animals are nearby and the size of the opening is sufficient. This shift in species composition will, on establishment of shrubs and trees, begin to revert to the fauna present before the fire. Often only a few years are needed for some rapidly developing shrub communities like those dominated by chamise and *Ceanothus* species, to become re-established. Tree-dominated communities take much longer to re-establish themselves, but the transition can begin immediately; within 10 to 20 years, tree heights exceed those of the shrubs, and the shade provided by the trees begins to cause the loss of the shrubs. In grassland systems, the pattern of plant community response often retards or halts encroachment of woody shrubs and trees, at least for a time. Grasses and forbs often out-compete young shrubs and saplings for nutrients, light, and especially water. Many animal species, including solitary bees, rodents, and birds, are dependent on native grasses for food, and frequent fires in these areas maintain suitable habitat.

Shifts in forest or shrubland structure also occur after fire. Stands are differentially thinned by fire, leaving some areas intact and other areas with many fewer plants alive, immediately following fire. Additionally, canopy closure and canopy layering is reduced. The result is a mosaic of unburned areas, resembling the pre-fire condition, and areas of more open surface and canopy. This creates a greater variety of both habitats and ecotones, or *edge effect,* which many animals exploit.

Changes in plant species composition can have a profound effect on the composition of the fauna associated with the site. Invertebrates are often closely tied to specific species or genera of plants and can be lost until required plant species, consumed by fire, recolonize the burned area. Animals that are resource generalists (e.g., squirrels, chipmunks, jackrabbits [*Lepus* spp.], and jays) tend to be more tolerant of changes in vegetation composition because they do not require specific plant species for food, shelter, or nesting.

Indirect Effects of Fire on Aquatic Animals

Aquatic and amphibian communities and habitat can be indirectly affected by fire in several ways. Among these effects are changes to water flow, increased sedimentation, changes in supply and distribution of woody debris, and changes in composition and structure of riparian vegetation. In California, one of the most important questions about fire is its relationship to native aquatic species and communities. Knowledge learned from other western states, and likely to be applicable to California, indicates that: (1) fire has an important ecological function for aquatic ecosystems and the adjacent mesic vegetation communities, and (2) fire is a threat to aquatic systems only when either natural fire regime has been compromised or native populations are highly fragmented, disjunct, or depressed (Sidebar 7.3).

Delivery of Large Woody Debris, Sediment, and Water

Indirect fire effects to river and lake systems primarily involve shorter-term increase in water discharge and longer-term increases in sediment, nutrients, and large woody debris influx to the aquatic habitat. The annual, seasonal, and spatial distribution of each influences aquatic habitat and its quality. The materials delivered to aquatic systems can have beneficial or detrimental effects on aquatic animals and their habitat. Animals that inhabit riverine environments can benefit from increased water flow as long as pulse or sustained flow is not so strong as to degrade aquatic habitat or displace species downstream.

Large woody debris delivered from uplands is an essential aquatic habitat element for many species, such as salamanders, fishes, and benthic invertebrates, by creating pools and backwaters, increasing stream structural complexity, and stabilizing lake and stream banks and substrate. Large moderate- to high-severity fires cause mortality in woody plants, resulting in significant quantities of woody debris being transported into water bodies over many years. In-stream wood forms log jams, and these log jams form barriers to some aquatic species moving up- or downstream. Generally, log jams rarely form barriers that last long or prove to be complete blockage to upstream or downstream migration. In addition, the water held behind the log jams is habitat for other species. Fire plays a crucial role in the ecological cycling of large woody debris, both creating new sources of debris and decreasing the stability of existing debris (Young and Bozek 1996).

Large, severe fires also can result in extreme erosion conditions, producing large quantities of sediment moving into water bodies. Sediment and organic material deposition can impact the benthic environment by filling in gravel substrate essential for spawning fishes, and the benthic habitat for macroinvertebrates, covering benthic plants or habitat or creating a shallower environment. Animals inhabiting lacustrine systems may be especially susceptible, because the filling in of ponds and lakes alters the benthic environment, creates a shallower water body, and affects aquatic plants. Suspended sediment can also detrimentally affect aquatic animals by damaging gills and increasing respiratory stress and by temporarily decreasing photosynthesis by reducing light penetration. Decreased light reduces aquatic plants and algae, affecting herbivorous and predatory aquatic species.

The alterations to aquatic habitat resulting from fire, and the runoff from post-fire, successive storms, can cause mortality of aquatic animals and impact animal community density and diversity. However, animal communities appear to be resilient, if not adapted, to the interrelated cycles of fire, water, and transport of upslope sediment.

In montane Sierra Nevada conifer forests, natural fire regime and storm runoff result in a pulse disturbance regime. Post-fire erosion and runoff produce episodic delivery of both woody debris and sediment to headwater and mid-elevation stream channels and maintain delivery and transport of both aquatic habitat elements. A pulse event *(perturbation)* allows an ecosystem to remain within its normal bounds and return to prior conditions (Bender et al. 1984, Yount and Niemi 1990). During the period between fires, woody debris delivery to headwater channels decreases,

Direct and indirect effects of fire can substantially alter the physical characteristics of aquatic systems (Swanson et al. 1990), and in some cases these changes may lead to fish mortality (Novak and White 1990; Bozek and Young 1994; Rieman et al.1997). These consequences are generally linked to changes in watershed hydrology after a large proportion of a drainage is burned and little vegetation or woody debris remains on the landscape. Effects on population dynamics of salmonid fishes are usually temporary, however; and persistence is rarely affected (Gresswell 1999). Exceptions generally occur in areas where relict populations of indigenous salmonids have been isolated in small headwater streams. For example, Rinne (1996) reported that intense fire, followed by strong precipitation events and associated flooding, resulted in local extirpation of two populations of brook trout *(Salvelinus fontinalis)* and one population of rainbow trout *(Oncorhynchus mykiss)* in central Arizona, and one of the few remaining populations of endangered Gila trout *(O. gilae)* in New Mexico.

Fortunately, such conditions are uncommon, and recolonization by fishes in areas where mortalities have occurred is generally rapid if access is adequate. For example, Rieman et al. (1997) reported that despite trout mortalities following fires that burned through the Boise River basin in 1992 and 1994, fish were present in defaunated reaches within one year, and approached densities in unaffected reaches in one to three years. Novak and White (1990) attributed rapid increases in rainbow trout density and biomass in the year following a post-fire flood event to movement of spring-spawning adfluvial rainbow trout. In contrast, beaver dams and low discharge in the same stream apparently limited access to fall-spawning adfluvial brown trout *(Salmo trutta),* and this species did not demonstrate rapid post-disturbance increases (Novak and White 1990). Ultimately, recolonization is influenced by proximity and relative location of refugia and the occurrence of complex life history patterns and overlapping generations (Warren and Liss 1980; Rieman et al. 1997).

In most streams, effects of fire on fish populations appear to be less severe (Gresswell 1999). Response to fire events in individual watersheds generally occurs at spatial scales of hundreds to thousands of meters, and effects can be observed over time periods of tens to hundreds of years. In second- or third-order streams, effects would be most noticeable in stream segments, geomorphic reaches, individual habitat units, and microhabitats (Frissell et al. 1986). Given that salmonids have evolved in North America since the late Miocene (approximately 6 · million years; Stearley and Smith 1993), there is little doubt that they have developed strategies to survive perturbations that occur at the spatial extent (1–1 million ha) and frequency of wildland fires (10–100 years). It is apparent that fire is a natural process that has been occurring for millennia; and in watersheds with adequate connectivity and sufficient species pool, there is no evidence that fire-related effects limit persistence of fish species. On the contrary, there is a growing body of evidence suggesting that episodic fire plays an important role in the creation and maintenance of salmonid habitat at multiple spatial scales (Reeves et al. 1995; Rieman et al. 2003).

The influence of fire on lakes is less distinct. Post-fire research on lakes has generally focused on water quality and plankton, and detectable responses are uncommon (Gresswell 1999, Lamontagne et al. 2000, Patoine et al. 2000). Mortality of fish, either directly associated with loss of watershed vegetation or indirectly resulting from post-fire allocthonous inputs, has not been documented. Although it may be reasonable to expect that fish populations would be especially sensitive to changes in top-down and bottom-up trophic interactions related to nutrient dynamics following fire, to date there is no strong evidence of a growth-response in fish (St-Onge and Magnan 2000, Gresswell 2004). Even in small ponds (< 2 ha) there is little evidence of change in water quality, or abundance or diversity of aquatic biota (plankton and amphibians), during the initial year following fire (Gresswell unpublished data).

In recent years there has been a growing concern that persistence of dwindling salmonid assemblages may be threatened by putative increases in the probability of large stand-replacing wildfires that are associated with the accumulation of fuels and climate change (Rieman and Clayton 1997, Gresswell 1999). On the other hand, management activities that are focused on reducing the probability of uncharacteristic fire events are not independent of fire, and interaction of the two may cause more substantial change in aquatic systems than either would alone. In reality, it may be more prudent to focus on the root causes of habitat loss and population decline, rather than the proximal factors that may influence the loss of remaining individuals. A broad-based management strategy that focuses on protecting remaining populations and habitat from further anthropogenic degradation and restoring degraded habitat and connectivity among habitats may provide greater long-term protection than expending limited resources in attempts to prevent stochastic events that may be beyond the control of human technology.—*Robert E. Gresswell*

decreasing pool size and frequency and in-stream large woody debris amounts. In mid-elevations, alluvial channel sedimentation is cyclical due to accumulation and subsequent flushing of sediment. The contemporary regime has shifted to increased interval, extent, and severity of fires (Parenti 2002). The change in fire regime, in part owing to efficient exclusion of low- and mid-severity fires, has resulted in a shift from a pulse event regime to a press disturbance regime. A press disturbance regime pushes an ecosystem to a different domain (i.e., outside the normal, historic bounds; Bender et al. 1984, Yount and Niemi 1990, Parenti 2002). Consequently, the frequency and quality of headwater pools decreases, and mid-elevation stream alluvial channels experience degradation and increased cross-sectional area. Such a shift in the fire regime could have profound effects on riparian and riverine ecosystems. Minshall and Brock (1991) speculated that such fire regimes pose the greatest long-term significance to streams and aquatic habitat.

Thermal Regime

Heat influx from fire to aquatic ecosystems has not been documented and is likely not typically significant due to water's thermal and insulating properties. The potentially significant effect fire can have on the aquatic temperature regime results from fires severe enough to remove the vegetation that shades streams and lakes. Elevated water temperature has several effects, including reduced available dissolved oxygen, increased metabolism, and increased susceptibility of fishes to pathogens. For coho salmon (*Oncorhynchus kisutch*) in British Columbia, Holtby (1988) demonstrated that increased water temperature contributed to early emergence of fry, early and less favorable smolt migration, and lowered abundance and diversity of prey species. In California, elevated water temperatures following decreased riparian cover have been documented for salmonid streams, but neither fish mortality nor reduced population viability has been observed (Cafferata 1990).

Riparian Communities

Fire is a common ecological process in riparian communities, as it is in other natural communities, but usually burns under different fire regimes than in upland areas (DeBano et al. 1998, Dwire and Kauffman 2003; also see Chapter 20, this volume). Little is known regarding the fire regimes of riparian areas in California. Recent investigations of fire in riparian systems at low and mid elevations of the Southern Cascades and Klamath Mountain bioregions demonstrates that fire return intervals in riparian areas are twice those of areas upslope, and that riparian habitats in higher elevations of a given watershed may, in fact, experience greater fire intensities than surrounding vegetative communities (see Chapter 8, this volume). The nature of water channels themselves, as well as the fact that many of these water courses are intermittent, creates wind funnels that sustain a fire. This same research is showing that fire occasionally is intense enough to remove the majority of riparian vegetation.

In most instances, fire removes much of the dead wood, litter, and duff deposits, as well as trees from riparian areas. Effects on animals would result from the interrelationship of fire severity, vegetation conditions, and soil moisture, and whether standing or moving water was present. However, despite these potential effects on animals residing in riparian areas, it is generally believed that animals that inhabit riparian areas are rarely affected by fire (Smith 2000).

Streams and riparian systems are some of the most altered systems in California. Placer mining as well as other stream-channeling activities and reduction of beaver populations contributed to significantly changing the stream and riparian environments, especially in wider-bottom and low-gradient areas. Historically, these areas were broader laterally, consisting of multiple braided channels. The microclimate was moister, with more extensive riparian vegetation. Though characteristics such as fire return interval likely would not have been different, fires probably would have moved through valley bottoms and low-gradient areas differently and affected the animal populations differently (Decker, pers. comm., 2005).

Fire and Ecosystem Interactions

The relationship of fire to animals, especially populations and communities, is of great importance in California. The more significant relationship, however, is the role of fire within an ecosystem. In this context, fire is one of several critical ecological processes (e.g., energy, water, nutrients, geomorphic reaches, weather, and climate) that interact with the entire biotic community. Interactions among vegetation, wildlife, soil microbes, and fire can play an important part in determining how the entire system responds to single burns or changes in the fire regime. In this section, we discuss the kinds of interactions that can occur and possible ramifications at the broader ecological levels. It is at these broader levels that there are important management implications as well as questions for which further research is needed.

Ecosystem Feedbacks from Animal and Fungi Activity

Biotic interactions among plants, herbivores, insects, fungi, or other soil biota all influence plant community responses. Changing from a forest or shrubland to herbaceous vegetation will immediately shift the fauna from those associated with trees and shrubs to those relying on herbaceous plants, if a suitable reservoir of those animals is within a reasonable distance to immigrate. Herbivores, ranging from insects to ungulates, can browse newly sprouted shoots following a fire, depleting the plant's energy reserves and reducing its ability to become established. Selective herbivory can favor regeneration of some plant species while suppressing regeneration of others, thereby influencing the post-fire succession trajectory.

Insect or fungus attack of already-weakened species can also influence plant species composition. A cause of plant mortality associated with fire can come from attack by insects attracted to the burned area or insects that were already present before the burn. The level of the insect population at the time of the fire, as well as whether the trees were already physiologically stressed from drought at the time of the fire, all interact to cause additional stress and secondary mortality. Secondary mortality can also favor re-establishment of some plant species while suppressing establishment of others, thereby affecting the overall composition and succession pathway of the ecosystem.

Animals and other biota can also have reciprocal effects on an area's fire regime. Grazing and pathogens can greatly alter vegetation structure and composition. Fire can also increase the dominance of non-native plants (see Chapter 22). Such changes in vegetation structure affect litter and woody debris inputs, litter chemistry and decomposition rates, and therefore fuel loading. These changes directly affect fire conditions. For example, increased grazing in the African Serengeti decreased overall fuel levels and reduced fire frequency and intensity over several decades (Norton-Griffiths 1979). In North America, intensive grazing has also contributed to the reduction of grasses and forbs (that become fine fuels after drying), which can reduce fire frequency but has also led toward increases in dense stands of advanced tree reproduction (Rummell 1951, Biswell 1972, Wright 1974, Savage 1991) that can alter fire behavior and severity.

Ecosystem Relationships between Animals and Other Environmental Processes

Fire does not simply affect a single animal species or animals alone. Across California, the interrelationship of effects to one or more animal species, plant species, and ecological cycles, such as water or chemical cycles, can be seen. Plant species dominance and distribution, which affects animal population occurrence, density, and distribution, is altered by fire. Those same animal species have different population demographics after the fire, and new animal species may either temporarily thrive or colonize the area. In chaparral and grassland ecosystems of the Central Valley and South Coast bioregions, rodent and insect herbivores may take advantage of new growth or abundant seed, even aiding in transporting seed to or within the burned area. Predators may take advantage of less cover, birds or mammals of altered nesting structure in the vegetation. Loss of vegetation affects available water, affecting the resident and colonizing animals alike, and products of the fire affect nutrient cycling, influencing plant response as well as detritus-consuming animals. All of this, in turn, affects the very vertebrates inhabiting or using a burned area.

In forest-dominated systems of the Sierra Nevada, fire's effects on forest structure and density also alter the distribution, density, and viability of many prominent vertebrates, including California spotted owl, northern goshawk, northern flying squirrel, pine marten, and fisher. Fire affects vegetation, fungi, and animal prey species, which in turn affect one another and other animal populations both individually and synergistically. Often, researchers attempt to investigate the relationship of fire with one species, the vegetation forest composition and structure it needs, and possibly some animal species that make up the prey base, when the species in question is carnivorous. But fire influences carnivores, herbivores, omnivores, and scavengers simultaneously. Research at Black Mountain Experimental Forest has revealed some of the ecological relationships among forest trees, insects, and insectivorous birds during and after fire, but little is known about the interactions or relationships of the broader faunal communities. As fire regimes continue to be altered in the Sierra Nevada and other forest-dominated bioregions such as the Southern Cascades Range and Klamath Mountains, little is known about the ecological relationships of fire, animal communities, the forests, and other ecosystem processes such as water and nutrient cycling, or how changes in fire regimes may affect the health of animals. Research in oak woodland communities of the Central Coast bioregion has investigated the response of oak species and communities to fire and the response of several populations of small vertebrates, including mammals, birds, and reptiles, to both fire and the changed oak community (Vreeland and Tietje 2002).

In spite of such endeavors, there is a lack of understanding of the interrelationships of fire, vegetation, and other ecological processes with animal communities. Such understanding requires both time, as measured in successive fires and animal population generations interacting, and interdisciplinary research, focused on crucial information about those same fires' effects on hydrology, vegetation, and nutrient cycling.

Summary and Conclusions

To remain viable, animal species must adapt to the conditions of the regions they inhabit. Fire has been historically and still is an essential ecological process in California's bioregions, and is a dominant force for many plant communities. Therefore, many animal populations and communities in California have adapted and persist in a fire-prone environment. Though individuals obviously perish in fires and, in some cases, populations may be reduced or absent for a time, animal community health and interrelationships are tied to fire fulfilling its ecological functions. Fire maintains habitat complexity and ecotones; recycles and makes available nutrients, water, and other ecological elements; and changes the trophic relationships among the various animal species in a given community or area.

Little has been documented about fire–animal interactions in California. This shortcoming needs to be rectified as fire has become (1) an important social issue (see Part III), and (2) an essential tool in managing and conserving the state's remaining wildlands, and by extension, the animal communities that inhabit these lands.

Information is lacking most for invertebrates, herpetofauna, and aquatic communities. Fire interactions with these specific groups of animals need to be better understood before solid conclusions can be developed about the effects of fire on these organisms. Research and knowledge regarding California invertebrates is sparse. Internationally, much attention has been given to some invertebrate groups, including snails,

earthworms, and grasshoppers, but in California, the most attention has been given to butterflies. As stated earlier, most fire information on North American herpetofauna has not been collected in California or the West, and the researchers who have conducted the research have warned against applying their work and results too widely. Last, investigation into the relationship of fire and native fishes has occurred in the western United States, but not in California.

As Biswell (1989) noted, fire has been a crucial process in many California forests, woodlands, and grasslands for thousands of years. As a process, fire affects a myriad of animals both directly and indirectly through effects on their habitats. Recent alterations in fire regimes have resulted in changes in California landscapes. In some cases, fires have become more intense, directly affecting larger numbers of animals more severely in a single event than most fires likely did historically. Fire regime changes also have indirectly affected California's wildlife through the alteration of habitat composition and structure; habitat quality for some of these species has improved but for others it has declined. It is not clear whether these current conditions will be sustained through time. Although we know that contemporary fire regimes differ from historical regimes in many bioregions in California, the effects of these changes to animal species and communities are not yet understood, and the changes in populations or communities likely would take generations of animals to be detectable. This change in fire regimes has resulted in changes in vegetation composition and structure that have altered the habitats for many animals that reside in these areas. For some, the changes have improved the quality of their habitat whereas for others, the changes have reduced the quality of their habitat. Yet, in many of these habitats, fire will eventually return regardless of attempts to suppress it. The question is: what kind of fire will it be?

Investigating the Broader Relationships of Fire, Animals, and Ecosystems

Some research in California has gone beyond fire's effects on animals or animals' responses to fire. As mentioned earlier, the relationship of insects, birds, fire, and vegetation structure has been studied at Klamath National Forest and at Black Mountain Experimental Forest in northeast California. Further south in the Sierra Nevada, studies (e.g., Kings Canyon and Yosemite National Parks) have attempted to understand fire's effects on several species of the biotic community. In oak woodlands of the Central Coast bioregion, researchers have studied the relationship of oak species, small vertebrates, and fire. In the South Coast, research has focused on the mammal and bird species of coastal sage scrub, while in the Southeast Desert bioregion, investigators have tried to understand the relationship of fire, vegetation, precipitation, and ground-dwelling animals.

Such efforts need to continue. Additional studies need to commence in bioregions or plant communities where investigations are lacking. Years of investigation are needed to understand the relationships of fire regime and fire cycles, animal populations, vegetation changes, climate, hydrology, and nutrient cycling. It will be these types of investigations—studies that focus on broader ecological processes and multiple animal populations—that will give the best insight into the ecological effects of fire on animals in California and provide the best options to conserving both the ecosystems and the animal populations.

References

Basey, G. E. 1990. Distribution, ecology, and population status of the riparian brush rabbit *(Sylvilagus bachmani riparus)*. Master's Thesis, California State University, Stanislaus. 76 p.

Bendell, J. F. 1974. Effects of fire on birds and mammals. P. 73–138 in T. T. Kozlowski and C. E. Ahlgren (eds.), Fire and ecosystems. Academic Press, New York.

Bender, E. A., T. J. Case, and M. E. Gilpin. 1984. Perturbation experiments in community ecology: theory and practice. Ecology 65:1–13.

Beyers, J. L., and W. O. Wirtz, II. 1997. Vegetative characteristics of coastal sage scrub sties used by California gnatcatchers: implications for management in a fire-prone ecosystem. P. 81–90 in J. A. Greenlee (ed.), Proceedings: first conference on fire effects on rare and endangered species and habitats, Coeur d'Arlene, Idaho, November 1995. International Association for Wildland Fire, November 13–16, 1995. Hot Springs, SD.

Biswell, H. H. 1957. The use of fire in California chaparral for game habitat improvement. P. 151–155 in 57th Annual Meeting of the Society of American Foresters, November 10–13, 1957. Syracuse, NY.

Biswell, H. H. 1969. Prescribed burning for wildlife in California brushlands. P. 438–446 in Transactions of the 34th North American wildlife and natural resources conference, March 2–5, 1969. Wildlife Management Institute.

Biswell, H. H. 1972. Fire ecology in ponderosa pine-grassland. Proceedings, Annual Tall Timbers Fire Ecology Conference 12:69–96.

Biswell, H. H. 1989. Prescribed burning in California wildlands vegetation management. University of California Press, Berkeley. 255 p.

Bozek, M. A., and M. K. Young. 1994. Fish mortality resulting from delayed effects of fire in the Greater Yellowstone ecosystem. Great Basin Naturalist 54:91–95.

Brooks, M. L., and T. C. Esque. 2002. Alien plants and fire in desert tortoise *(Gopherus agassizii)* habitat of the Mojave and Colorado deserts. Chelonian Cons. Biol. 4(2):330–340.

Cafferata, P. 1990. Temperature regimes of small streams along the Mendocino coast. Jackson Demonstration State Forest Newsletter, No. 39:4–7.

California Department of Fish and Game. 1999. California Department of Fish and Game. California Wildlife Habitat Relationships Program, Sacramento, CA.

Cooperrider, A., R. F. Noss, H. H. Welsh, Jr., C. Carroll, W. Zielinski, D. Olson, S. K. Nelson, and B. G. Marcot. 2000. Terrestrial fauna of redwood forests. In R. F. Noss (ed.), The redwood forest: history, ecology, and conservation of the coast redwoods. Save the Redwood League. Island Press, Washington, D.C.

DeBano, L. F., D. G. Neary, and P. F. Ffolliott. 1998. Fire's effects on ecosystems. Wiley, New York.

DelGiudice, G. D., and F. J. Singer 1996. Physiological responses of Yellowstone elk to winter nutritional restriction before and after the 1988 fires: a preliminary examination. P. 133–135 in J. A. Greenlee (ed.), Proceedings: the ecological implications of fire in Greater Yellowstone, the second biennial conference on the greater Yellowstone ecosystem. September 12–21, 1993. Yellowstone National Park. International Association for Wildland Fire.

Dodd, N. L. 1988. Fire management and southwestern raptors. P. 341–347 in R. L. Glinski et al. (eds.), Proceedings of the southwest raptor symposium and workshop. May 21–24, 1986, Tuscon, AZ. NWF Scientific and Technology Series No. 11. National Wildlife Federation.

Dwire, K. A., and J. B. Kauffman. 2003. Fire and riparian ecosystems in landscapes of the western USA. Forest Ecology and Management 178(1–2):61–74.

Elliott, B. 1985. Changes in distribution of owl species subsequent to habitat alteration by fire. Western Birds 16(1): 25–28.

Erwin, W. J., and R. H. Stasiak. 1979. Vertebrate mortality during the burning of reestablished prairie in Nebraska. American Midland Naturalist 10(1):247–249.

Esque, T. C., T. Hughes, L. A. DeFalco, B. E. Hatfield, and R. B. Duncan. 1995. Effects of wildfire on desert tortoises and their habitats. P. 153–154 in A. Fletcher-Jones (ed.), 19th proceedings of the desert council, Tucson, AZ.

Finch, D. M, J. L. Ganey, W. Young, R. T. Kimball, and R. Sallasbanks. 1997. Effects and interactions of fire, logging, and grazing. P. 103–136 in W. M. Block and D. M. Finch (tech. eds.), Songbird ecology in southwestern ponderosa pine forests: a literature review. Gen. Tech. Rep. RM-GTR-292. Fort Collins, CO. USDA Forest Service, Rocky Mountain Forest and Range Experiment Station.

Ford, W. M., M. A. Menzel, D. W. McGill, J. Laerm, and T. S. McCay. 1999. Effects of a community restoration fire on small mammals and herpetofauna in the southern Appalachians. Forest Ecology and Management 114:233–243.

French, M. G., and S. P. French. 1996. Large mammal mortality in the 1988 Yellowstone fires. P. 113–116 in J. M. Greenlee (ed.), Proceedings: the ecological implications of fire in greater Yellowstone, the second biennial conference on the greater yellowstone ecosystem. September 12–21, 1993. Yellowstone National Park. International Association for Wildland Fire.

Frissell, C. A., W. J. Liss, C. E. Warren, and M. D. Hurley. 1986. A hierarchical framework for stream habitat classification: viewing streams in a watershed context. Environmental Management 10:199–214.

Graham, R. T., T. B. Jain, R. T. Reynolds, and D. A. Boyce. 1997. The role of fire in sustaining northern goshawk habitat in Rocky Mountain forests. P. 69–76 in J. A. Greenlee (ed.), Proceedings: first conference on fire effects on rare and endangered species and habitats, Coeur d'Arlene, Idaho, November 1995. International Association for Wildland Fire.

Gresswell, R. E. 1999. Fire and aquatic ecosystems in forested biomes of North America. Transactions of the American Fisheries Society Volume 128:193–221.

Gresswell, R. E. 2004. Effects of wildfire on growth of cutthroat trout in Yellowstone Lake. P. 143–164 in L. Wallace (ed.), After the fires: the ecology of change in Yellowstone National Park. Yale University Press.

Haidinger, T. L., and J. E. Keeley. 1993. Role of high fire frequency in destruction of mixed chaparral. Madroño 40(3):141–147.

Harestad, A.S. 1985. *Scaphiopus intermontanus* (Great Basin spadefoot toad) mortality. Herp. Review 16(1): 24.

Harrington, M.G. 1996. Fall rates of prescribed fire-killed ponderosa pine. Res. Paper INT-RP-489. Ogden, UT. Intermountain Research Station, USDA Forest Service. 7 p.

Hart, S. 1998. Beetle mania: an attraction to fire. BioScience 48(1): 3–5.

Holtby, L.B. 1988. Effects of logging on stream temperatures in Carnation Creek, British Columbia, and associated impacts on the coho salmon. Can. J. Fish Aquat. Sci. 45:502–515.

Horton, S.P., and R.W. Mannan. 1988. Effects of prescribed fire on snags and cavity-nesting birds in southeastern Arizona pine forests. Wildlife Society Bulletin 16:37–44.

Howard, W.E., R.L. Fenner, and H.E. Childs, Jr. 1959. Wildlife survival in brush burns. J. Range Manage. 12:230–234.

Huntzinger, P.M. 2003. Effects of fire management practices on butterfly diversity in the forested western United States. Biol. Cons. 113:1–12.

Keen, F.P. 1955. The rate of natural falling of beetle-killed ponderosa pine snags. Journal of Forestry 53(10): 720–725.

Kie, J.G. 1984. Deer habitat use after prescribed burning in northern California. Research Note PSW-369, Pacific Southwest Forest and Range Experiment Station, USDA Forest Service. 4 p

Kimmey, J.W. 1955. Rate of deterioration of fire-killed timber in California. Circular No. 962. U.S. Department of Agriculture, Washington, D.C. 22 p.

Koehler, G.M., and M.G. Hornocker. 1977. Fire effects on marten habitat in the Selway-Bitterroot Wilderness. Journal of Wildlife Management 41(2): 500–505.

Komarek, E.V. 1969. Fire and animal behavior. P. 161–207 in Proceedings of the 9th conference on fire ecology. April 10–11, 1969. Tallahassee, FL. Tall Timbers Station, Tallahassee, FL.

Lamontagne, S., R. Carignan, P. D'Arcy, Y.T. Prairie, and D. Pare. 2000. Element export in runoff from eastern Canadian Boreal Shield drainage basins following forest harvesting and fires. Canadian Journal of Fisheries and Aquatic Sciences 57: 118–128.

Laudenslayer, W.F., Jr. 2002. Effects of prescribed fire on live trees and snags in eastside pine forests in California. P. 256–262 in N.G. Sugihara, M.E. Morales, and T.J. Morales (eds.), Proceedings of the symposium, fire in California ecosystems, integrating ecology, prevention, and management. Assoc. Fire Ecology. Misc. Pub 1. November 17–20, 1997. San Diego, CA.

Lehman, R.N., and J.W. Allendorf. 1989. The effects of fire, fire exclusion, and fire management on raptor habitats in the western United States. In B.A. Giron Pendleton (ed.), Western Raptor Management Symposium and Workshop. 1987. Boise, Idaho. National Wildlife Federation.

Longcore, T. 2003. Ecological effects of fuel modification on arthropods and other wildlife in an urbanizing wildland. P. 111–117 in K.E.M. Galley, R.C. Klinger, and N.G. Sugihara (eds.), Proceedings of fire conference 2000: the first national congress on fire ecology, prevention, and management, November 27–December 1, 2000, San Diego, CA. Tall Timbers Research Station, Miscellaneous Publication No. 13.

Lyon, J.L., H.S. Crawford, E. Czuhai, R.L. Fredricksen, R.F. Harlow, L.J. Metz, and H.A. Pearson. 1978. Effects of fire on fauna: a state-of-the-knowledge review. USDA Forest Service, GTR-WO-6. 22 p.

Minshall, G.W., and J.T. Brock. 1991. Observed and anticipated effects of forest fire on Yellowstone stream ecosystems. In R.B. Keiter and M.S. Boyce (eds.), The greater Yellowstone ecosystem: redefining America's wilderness heritage, New Haven, CT, Yale University Press.

Moriarty, D.J., R.E Farris, D.K. Noda, and P.A. Stanton. 1985. Effects of fire on a coastal sage scrub bird community. Southwestern Naturalist 30(3): 452–453.

National Park Service. 1966. Conservation plan: Wind Cave National Park, Custer County Conservation District. Department of the Interior, National Park Service, Wind Cave National Park, SD. 46 p.

Norland, J.E., F.J. Singer, and L. Mack. 1996. Effects of the Yellowstone fires of 1988 on elk habitat. P. 223–232 in J.A. Greenlee (ed.), Proceeding: the ecological implications of fire in Greater Yellowstone, the second biennial conference on the greater Yellowstone ecosystem. September 12–21, 1993. Yellowstone National Park. International Association for Wildland Fire.

Norton-Griffiths, M. 1979. The influence of grazing, browsing, and fire on vegetation dynamics in the Serengeti, Tanzania, Kenya. P. 310–352 in A.R.E. Sinclair and M. Norton-Griffiths (eds.), Serengeti: dynamics of an ecosystem. University of Chicago Press, Chicago, IL.

Novak, M.A., and R.G. White. 1990. Impact of fire and flood on the trout population of Beaver Creek, Upper Missouri Basin, Montana. P. 120–127 in F. Richardson and R.H. Hamre (eds.), Wild Trout IV: Proceedings of the symposium. September 18–19, 1985. Yellowstone National Park. U.S. Government Printing Office, Washington, DC.

Quinn, R.D. 1990. Habitat preferences and distribution of mammals. In California chaparral. USDA Forest Service, Research Paper PSW-RP-202. Berkeley, CA.

Parenti, M.J. 2002. Altered fire regimes and changes in stream channel morphology in the Sierra Nevada. P. 273–278 in N.G. Sugihara, M.E. Morales, and T.J. Morales (eds.), Proceedings of the symposium: fire in California ecosystems, integrating ecology, prevention, and management. Assoc. Fire Ecology, Misc. Pub 1. November 17–20, 1997. San Diego, CA.

Patoine, A., B. Pinel-Alloul, E.E. Prepas, and R. Carignan. 2000. Do logging and forest fires influence zooplankton biomass in Canadian Boreal Shield lakes? Canadian Journal of Fisheries and Aquatic Sciences 57:155–164.

Price, M.V., N.M. Waser, K.E. Taylor, and K.L. Pluff. 1995. Fire as a management tool for Stephens' kangaroo rat and other small mammal species. P. 51–61 in J.E. Keeley and T. Scott, Brushfires in California wildlands: ecological and resource management. May 6–7, 1994. Irvine, CA. International Association of Wildland Fire.

Pyne, S.J. 1995. World fire: the culture of fire on earth. University of Washington Press, Seattle, WA.

Reeves, G.H., L.E. Benda, K.M. Burnett, P.A. Bisson, and J.R. Sedell. 1995. A disturbance-based ecosystem approach to maintaining and restoring freshwater habitats of evolutionarily significant units of anadromous salmonids in the Pacific Northwest. American Fisheries Society Symposium 17:334–349.

Reinhardt, E.D., and K.C. Ryan. 1989. Estimating tree mortality resulting from prescribed fire. P. 41–44 in D.M. Baumgartner, D.W. Breuer, B.A. Zamora, L.F. Neuenschwander, and R.H. Wakimoto (eds.), Prescribed fire in the Intermountain Region forest site and range improvement. Washington State University, Pullman, WA.

Rieman, B.E., and J.L. Clayton. 1997. Fire and fish: issues of forest health and conservation of native fishes. Fisheries (Bethesda) 22(11):6–15.

Rieman, B.E., D. Lee, D. Burns, R. Gresswell, M. Young, R. Stowell, J. Rinne, and P. Howell. 2003. Status of native fishes in the western United States and issues of fire and fuels management. Forest Ecology and Management 178(1–2):197–211.

Rieman, B.E., D. Lee, G. Chandler, and D. Myers. 1997. Does wildfire threaten extinction for salmonids? Responses of redband trout and bull trout following recent large fires in the Boise National Forest. P. 47–57 in J. Greenlee (ed.), Proceedings of the symposium on fire effects on rare and endangered species and habitats. Coeur d'Arlene, Idaho, November 13–16, 1995. International Association of Wildland Fire, Hot Springs, SD.

Rinne, J.N. 1996. Short-term effects of wildfire on fishes and aquatic macroinvertebrates in the southwestern United States. North American Journal of Fisheries Management 16:653–658.

Rummell, R.S. 1951. Some effects of livestock grazing on ponderosa pine forest and range in central Washington. Ecology 32:594–607.

Russell, K.R., D.H. van Lear, and D.C. Guynn, Jr. 1999. Prescribed fire effects on herpetofauna: review and management implications. Wildlife Society Bulletin 27(2):374–384.

Ryan, K.C. 1990. Predicting prescribed fire effects on trees in the interior west. P. 148–162 in M.E. Alexander and B.F. Bisgrove (tech. coords.), The art and science of fire management: Proceedings of the first interior west fire council annual meeting and workshop, Kananaskis Village, Alberta, October 24–27, 1988. Information Report NOR-X-309, Edmonton, Alberta, Forestry Canada, Northwest Region, Northern Forestry Centre.

Ryan, K.C., and E.D. Reinhardt. 1988. Predicting postfire mortality of seven western conifers. Canadian Journal of Forest Research 18:1291–1297.

Sackett, S.S., and S.M. Haase. 1996. Fuel loadings in southwestern ecosystems of the United States. P. 187–192 in P.F. Ffolliott, L.F. DeBano, M.B. Baker, Jr., G.J. Gottfried, G. Solis-Garza, C.B. Edminster, D.G. Neary, L.S. Allen, and R.H. Hamre (tech. coords.), Effects of fire on Madrean Province ecosystems: a symposium proceedings. Gen. Tech. Rep. RM-GTR-289, Fort Collins, CO, Rocky Mountain Forest and Range Experiment Station, USDA Forest Service.

Savage, M. 1991. Structural dynamics of a southwestern pine forest under chronic human influence. Annals of the Association of American Geographers 81(2):271–289.

Scott, M.D., and H. Geisser. 1996. Pronghorn migration and habitat use following the 1988 Yellowstone fires. P. 123–132 in J.A. Greenlee (ed.), Proceeding: the ecological implications of fire in Greater Yellowstone, the second biennial conference on the greater Yellowstone ecosystem. September 12–21, 1993. Yellowstone National Park. International Association for Wildland Fire.

Smith, J.K., ed. 2000. Wildland fire in ecosystems: effects of fire on fauna. Gen. Tech. Rep. RMRS-GTR-42-vol. 1. Ogden, UT, USDA Forest Service, Rocky Mountain Research Station.

St-Onge, I., and P. Magnan. 2000. Impact of logging and natural fires on fish communities of Laurentian Shield lakes. Canadian Journal of Fisheries and Aquatic Sciences 57:165–174.

Stearley, R.F., and G.R. Smith. 1993. Phylogeny of the Pacific trouts and salmons (Oncorhynchus) and genera of the family Salmonidae. Transactions of the American Fisheries Society 122:1–33.

Sullivan, J. 1994. Bufo boreas. In W.C. Fisher (comp.), The fire effects information system [data base], Missoula, MT. USDA, USFS, Intermountain Research Station.

Sullivan, J. 1996. Taxidea taxus. In W.C. Fisher (comp.), The fire effects information system [data base], Missoula, MT. USDA, USFS, Intermountain Research Station.

Swanson, F.J., J.F. Franklin, and J.R. Sedell. 1990. Landscape patterns, disturbance, and management in the Pacific Northwest, USA. P. 191–213 in I.S. Zonneveld and R.T.T. Forman (eds.), Changing landscapes: an ecological perspective. Springer-Verlag, New York.

Swezy, D.M., and J.K. Agee. 1991. Prescribed-fire effects on fine-root and tree mortality in old-growth ponderosa pine. Canadian Journal of Forest Research 21:626–634.

Tesky, J.L. 1993. Ovis canadensis. In W.C. Fisher (comp.), The fire effects information system [data base], Missoula, MT. USDA, USFS, Intermountain Research Station.

Tracy, B.F., and S.J. McNaughton. 1996. Comparative ecosystem properties in summer and winter ungulate ranges following the 1988 fires in Yellowstone National Park. P. 181–191 in J.A. Greenlee (ed.), Proceeding: the ecological implications of fire in Greater Yellowstone, the second biennial conference on the greater Yellowstone ecosystem. September 12–21, 1993. Yellowstone National Park. International Association for Wildland Fire.

USDA Forest Service. 1999. Fire Effects Information Service. USDA Forest Service, Rocky Mountain Research Laboratory, Fire Science Laboratory, Missoula, MT. www.fs.fed.us/database/feis.

Van Dyke, F., M.J. Deboer, and G.M. Van Beek. 1996. Winter range plant production and elk use following prescribed burning. P. 193–200 in J.A. Greenlee (ed.), Proceeding: the ecological implications of fire in Greater Yellowstone, the second biennial conference on the greater Yellowstone ecosystem. September 12–21, 1993. Yellowstone National Park. International Association for Wildland Fire.

Vreeland, J.K., and W.D. Tietje. 2002. Numerical response of small vertebrates to prescribed fire in a California oak woodland. P. 269–279 in Proceedings of the fifth symposium on oak woodland: oaks in California's changing landscape, San Diego, CA, October 22–25, 2001. USDA Forest Service, Gen. Tech. Rep. PSW-GTR-184.

Warren, C.E., and W.J. Liss. 1980. Adaptation to aquatic environments. P. 15–40 in R.T. Lackey and L. Nielsen (eds.), Fisheries management. Blackwell Scientific Publications, Oxford.

Williams, D.F., J. Verner, H.F. Sakai, and J.R. Waters. 1992. General biology of major prey species of the California spotted owl. P. 207–221 in Forest Service Gen.Tech.Rep. PSW-GTR-133.

Wirtz, II, W.O. 1979. Effects of fire on birds in chaparral. Cal-Neva Wildlife Transactions 1979:114–124.

Wirtz II, W.O. 1995. Responses of rodent populations to wildfire and prescribed fire in southern California chaparral. P. 63–67 in J.E. Keeley and T. Scott. Brushfires in California wildlands: ecological and resource management. May 6–7, 1994. Irvine, California. International Association of Wildland Fire.

Wirtz, W., D. Hoekman, J. Muhm, and S. Souze. 1988. Postfire rodent succession following prescribed fire in southern California chaparral. In R. Szaro, K. Severson, and D. Patton (eds.), Management of amphibians, reptiles, and mammals in North America. USDA Forest Service General Technical Report, GTR-RM-166.

Wright, H.A. 1974. Range burning. Journal of Range Management 27:5–11.

Wright, H.A., and A.W. Bailey. 1982. Fire ecology: United States and southern Canada. Wiley and Sons, New York.

Yensen, E., D.L. Quinney, K. Johnson, K. Timmerman, and K. Steenhof. 1992. Fire, vegetation changes, and population fluctuations of Townsend's ground squirrels. The American Midland Naturalist 128:299–312.

Young, M.K., and M.A. Bozek. 1996. Post-fire effects on coarse woody debris and adult trout in northwestern Wyoming streams. In J. Greenlee (ed.), Proceeding: the ecological implications of fire in greater Yellowstone, the second biennial conference on the greater Yellowstone ecosystem. September 12–21, 1993. Yellowstone National Park. International Association of Wildland Fire.

Yount, J.D., and G.J. Niemi. 1990. Recovery of lotic communities and ecosystems from disturbance: a narrative review of case studies. Environmental Management 14:547–570.

Zedler, P.H., C.R. Gautier, and G.S. McMaster. 1983. Vegetation changes in response to extreme events: the effects of short interval fire in California chaparral and coastal scrub. Ecology 64:809–818.

PART II

THE HISTORY AND ECOLOGY OF FIRE IN CALIFORNIA'S BIOREGIONS

Part II of this book describes nine bioregions and their fire regimes, beginning in the humid northwest and ending in the arid southeast. We start in Chapter 8 with the North Coast bioregion in northwestern portion of the state where numerous valleys and steep coastal and interior mountains create moisture gradients in response to numerous winter storms. In Chapter 9, we describe the Klamath Mountains bioregion, a complex group of mountain ranges and a diverse flora. Tall volcanoes and extensive lava flows characterize the Southern Cascades (Chapter 10) and Northeastern Plateaus (Chapter 11) bioregions. Immediately south of the Cascades is the Sierra Nevada bioregion (Chapter 12), extending nearly half the length of the state. The Sacramento and San Joaquin rivers flow through broad interior valleys with extensive, nearly flat alluvial floors that constitute the Central Valley bioregion (Chapter 13). Coastal valleys and mountains and interior mountains are also typical of the Central Coast bioregion (Chapter 14). Southern California with its coastal valleys and the prominent Transverse and Peninsular Ranges are included in Chapter 15 on the South Coast bioregion. Finally, in Chapter 16, we discuss the vast southeast corner of California that constitutes the Southeastern Deserts bioregion. Each bioregion is divided in ecological zones, which are defined by the interaction of biotic communities and soil, hydrology, climate, elevation, topography, and aspect. Within ecological zones can be found vegetation alliances, defined by existing dominant or codominant plant species. Part II chapters describe ecological zones and discuss fire regimes in different alliances.

CHAPTER 8

North Coast Bioregion

JOHN D. STUART AND SCOTT L. STEPHENS

> In the early days of forestry we were altogether too dogmatic
> about fire and never inquired into the influence of fire on
> shaping the kind of forests we inherited.
>
> EMANUEL FRITZ, 1951

Description of Bioregion

Physical Geography

The North Coast California bioregion is classified as being within the California Coastal Steppe, Mixed Forest, and Redwood Forest Province of the Mediterranean Division of the Humid Temperate Domain (Bailey 1995). Specifically, it is composed of the Northern California Coast and the Northern California Coast Ranges Sections (Map 8.1) (Miles and Goudey 1997). The bioregion ranges from southwestern Oregon to north of the Golden Gate in Marin County. Its eastern boundary is adjacent to the Klamath Mountains in the north and the Northern California Interior Coast Ranges in the central and southern portions. The North Coast section stretches from San Francisco Bay to the Oregon border. Other notable landmarks include Humboldt Bay, Cape Mendocino, Clear Lake, and Point Reyes. The North Coast Ranges are bounded by the North Coast section, the Interior Ranges, and the Klamath Mountains.

Sedimentary rocks from the Franciscan Formation dominate in the bioregion. Sandstone, shale, and mudstone are most common with lesser amounts of chert, limestone, and ultramafic rocks. Basalt, andesite, rhyolite, and obsidian can be found in the volcanic fields of Sonoma, Napa, and Lake Counties, whereas granitic rocks similar to those found in the Sierra Nevada are located west of the San Andreas Fault near Point Reyes and Bodega Bay (Harden 1997). Soils in the northwestern California ecological units have been classified as Alfisols, Entisols, Inceptisols, Mollisols, Spodosols, Ultisols, and Vertisols (Miles and Goudey 1997).

The bioregion is topographically diverse. Elevations range from sea level to around 1,000 m (3,280 ft) in the Northern California Coast Section and from around 100 to 2,470 m (328 to 8,100 ft) in the Northern California Coast Ranges (Miles and Goudey 1997). Slope gradients vary from flat in valley bottoms to moderate to steep on mountain slopes. Gradients of over 50% are common in the mountains. Mountain ranges are generally parallel to each other and are oriented in a northwesterly direction. Mountains and ridges are typically long and separate parallel river valleys and steep, narrow canyons. Prominent mountain ranges include the Kings Range, South Fork Mountain, Yolla Bolly Mountains, and the Mayacamas Mountains. The North Coast is home to the Smith, Klamath, Mad, Van Duzen, Mattole, Eel, Noyo, Navarro, Gualala, Russian, and Napa Rivers, as well as Redwood Creek.

Climatic Patterns

Three predominant climatic gradients help determine the vegetation patterns in northwestern California: (1) a west–east gradient extending from a moist, cool coastal summer climate to a drier, warmer interior summer climate; (2) a north–south gradient of decreasing winter precipitation and increasing summer temperatures; and (3) a montane elevational gradient of decreasing temperature and increasing precipitation. These gradients, although important individually, interact in a complex fashion, especially away from the coast.

The bioregion enjoys a mediterranean climate with cool, wet winters and cool to warm, dry summers. Over 90% of the annual precipitation falls between October and April (Elford and McDonough 1964). Annual precipitation varies from 500 to 3,000 mm (20 to 118 in.) (Miles and Goudey 1997). The Pacific Ocean greatly moderates temperature, resulting in sharp west to east temperature gradients. The mean maximum monthly temperature at Fort Ross, for example, varies from 13.8°C in January to 20.2°C in September, a difference of only 6.4°C. In contrast, the mean maximum monthly temperature at Angwin, near the Napa Valley, varies from 11.2°C in January to 30.5°C in July, a difference of 19.3°C

TABLE 8.1

Number of days of temperature and relative humidity observations in Prairie Creek Redwoods State Park (coastal redwood forest) and Humboldt Redwoods State Park (interior redwood forest)

	Coastal Flat	Coastal Slope	Interior Flat	Interior Slope
No. days maximum temperature >21°C	4	23	106	208
No. days maximum temperature >27°C	0	0	16	78
No. days relative humidity <50%	0	27	46	172
No. days relative humidity <35%	0	0	2	37

NOTE: Data were collected between July 1986 and November 1987. (After Pillers 1989.)

(Western Region Climate Center 2001). Most coastal forests, and especially coast redwood *(Sequoia sempervirens)* forests, experience summer fog. Fog can be an important source of water for trees, boosting soil moisture and reducing plant moisture stress (Azevedo and Morgan 1974, Dawson 1998). Summer relative humidity and temperature are strongly influenced by proximity to the Pacific Ocean and the presence of summer fog. Pillers (1989) found that coastal redwood forests in Humboldt County had many fewer days with temperatures above 21°C and relative humidity lower than 50% than comparable interior sites (Table 8.1).

Although lightning does occur during the fire season, it is much less prevalent than on the higher ridges and mountains to the east (Elford and McDonough 1964, Keeley 1981, Automated lightning detection system 1999). Notwithstanding lightning's potential to ignite fires in northwestern California, Native American ignitions likely accounted for most fires (Fritz 1931, Agee 1993, Lewis 1993).

Synoptic weather systems in northwestern California influence critical fire danger (Hull et al. 1966). Gripp (1976), in a study of critical fire weather in northwestern California, found that 37.5% of fires larger than 120 ha (300 ac) were associated with the Pacific High (Postfrontal) Type. The Great Basin High Type accounted for 29.7% of the fires, the Subtropical High Aloft Pattern was linked with 21.9%, and other miscellaneous types were associated with 10.9%. The Pacific High (Postfrontal) and the Great Basin High Types produce warm, dry east winds *(foehn winds)* that displace the marine air mass off the coast (Hull et al. 1966). The Subtropical High Aloft Pattern produces abnormally high temperatures and low humidity (Hull et al. 1966). The most hazardous weather pattern is the Pacific High (Postfrontal) Type, having produced an average of 1.4 fires larger than 120 ha (300 ac)

every ten days it occurs. The Great Basin High Type was associated with 0.5 fires/10 days and the Subtropical High Aloft Pattern had 0.3 large fires/10 days (Gripp 1976).

Between 1955 and 1974 there were 64 fires larger than 120 ha (300 ac) in Humboldt and Del Norte Counties. Twelve of these fires occurred in cool, moist coastal areas, and 52 fires were located in warm, dry interior regions. All of the large fires in coastal areas and 86% of those in interior regions were associated with the Pacific High (Postfrontal) Type, the Great Basin High Type, or the Subtropical High Aloft Pattern (Gripp 1976).

Ecological Zones

In general, low-elevation conifer forests dominate along the coast and in the northern part of the bioregion. Woodlands and montane forests increasingly dominate to the south and east. Interspersed among these vegetation types and along the coast can be found grasslands and shrublands. Montane scrubs are found at higher elevations in the Northern California Coast Ranges, whereas chaparrals are more common on volcanic soils in the southeastern part of the bioregion. These plant communities can be described as occurring in six broad ecological zones.

The north coastal scrub and prairie zone (Fig. 8.1) is found in the fog belt along the California coast in a discontinuous band below 1,000 m elevation from Santa Cruz north to the Oregon border (Heady et al. 1988). Its distribution along the north coast varies from locally extensive to sporadic to absent. North Coastal Scrub is found immediately inland of the coastal strand in a narrow strip extending from southern Oregon to the Bay Area. The vegetation is characteristically compact having been sculpted by strong salt-laden ocean winds. North Coastal Scrub was described by Munz (1959) and is variously dominated by species such as coyotebrush *(Baccharis pilularis)*, yellow bush lupine *(Lupinus arboreus)*, salal, and evergreen huckleberry *(Vaccinium ovatum)*. Scrubs dominated by salal *(Gaultheria shallon)*, evergreen huckleberry, ferns, and blackberry are more common in the northern part of the bioregion and are more likely to form two-layered communities. One-layered communities are more common to the south (Heady et al. 1988). Coastal Prairie is dominated by an assortment of grass and herbaceous species and may have the greatest plant diversity of any North American grassland type (Stromberg et al. 2001).

The north coastal pine forest zone (Fig. 8.2) is made up of isolated stands along the north coast. Principal species include beach pine *(Pinus contorta* ssp. *contorta)*, Bishop pine *(Pinus muricata)*, Bolander pine *(Pinus contorta* ssp. *bolanderi)*, and pygmy cypress *(Cupressus goveniana* ssp. *pigmaea)*.

The Sitka spruce *(Picea sitchensis)* forest zone (Fig. 8.3) is generally found inland of the north coastal scrub and prairie zone in a narrow strip approximately 1 to 2 km (0.6 to 1.2 mi) wide (Zinke 1988) extending south from the Oregon border and terminating near Fort Bragg. Along rivers and in the Wildcat Hills south of Ferndale, Sitka spruce forests can extend inland as far as 25 km (15.5 mi) (Zinke 1988).

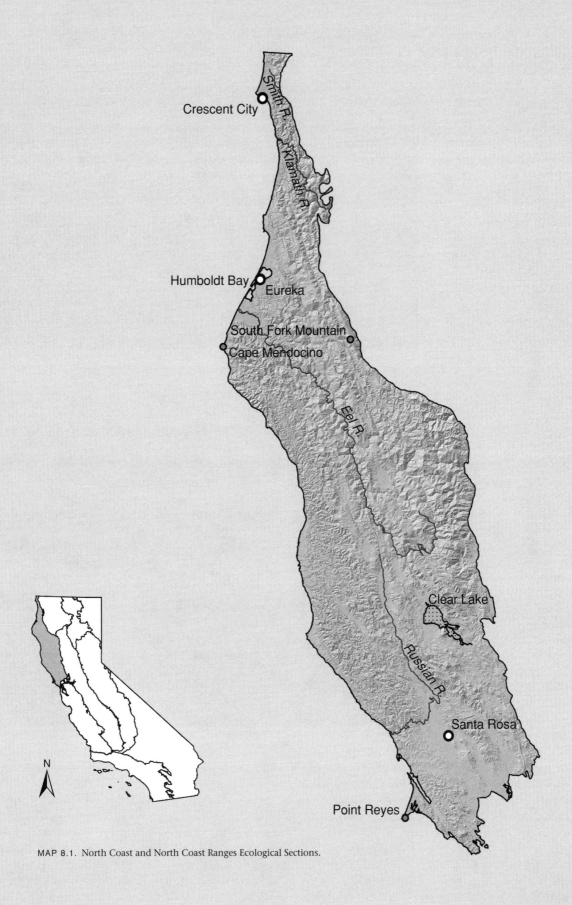

Crescent City

Smith R.

Klamath R.

Humboldt Bay
Eureka

South Fork Mountain
Cape Mendocino

Eel R.

Clear Lake

Russian R.

Santa Rosa

Point Reyes

N

MAP 8.1. North Coast and North Coast Ranges Ecological Sections.

FIGURE 8.1. North coastal scrub and prairie zone. Coastal prairie at Sea Ranch, Sonoma County. (Photograph by Rand Evett.)

FIGURE 8.2. North coastal pine forest zone. Bishop pine forest regeneration following fire. (Photograph by Scott Stephens.)

The redwood forest zone (Fig. 8.4) is inland of the Sitka spruce forest zone. Redwood is intolerant of salt spray and strong, desiccating winds (Olson et al. 1990). On the north, east, and south, the redwood zone is mostly limited by inadequate soil moisture and excessive evapotranspiration (Mahony and Stuart 2001). Redwood forests occur in an irregular narrow strip, ranging in width from 8 to 56 km (5 to 35 mi) (Olson et al. 1990). Stands in Napa County are 68 km (42 mi) from the coast (Griffin and Critchfield 1972). The

tallest and largest trees are confined to moist, wind-protected canyons and lower slopes.

Increased evapotranspiration inland limits the coastal conifers allowing for complex mixtures of Douglas-fir *(Pseudotsuga menziesii)* and a variety of evergreen and deciduous broadleaved trees defining the Douglas-fir–tanoak *(Lithocarpus densiflorus)* forest zone (Fig. 8.5). Notable among the tree species present are tanoak, Pacific madrone *(Arbutus menziesii)*, Oregon white oak *(Quercus garryana)*, and California black oak *(Quercus*

FIGURE 8.3. Sitka spruce forest zone. Young Sitka spruce forest at Patrick's Point State Park. (Photograph by John Stuart.)

FIGURE 8.4. Redwood forest zone. Old-growth redwood forest in Redwood National Park. (Photograph by John Stuart.)

FIGURE 8.5. Douglas-fir–tanoak forest zone. Young Douglas-fir–tanoak forest in Humboldt County. (Photograph by John Stuart.)

*kelloggii) (Zinke 1988, Stuart and Sawyer 2001). Douglas-fir and tanoak forests dominate inland lower montane forests. Montane forests characteristically have Douglas-fir mixed with ponderosa pine *(Pinus ponderosa),* and then at higher elevations Douglas-fir is intermixed with white fir *(Abies concolor).*

The Oregon white oak woodland zone (Fig. 8.6) occurs sporadically throughout the North Coast and North Coast Ranges. In the redwood forest zone and the Douglas-fir–tanoak forest zone, Oregon white oak woodlands often occur in patches of a few to hundreds of hectares in size, usually near south- and west-facing ridges. In the warmer, drier parts of the North Coast and North Coast Ranges, Oregon white oak can form open savannas or be interspersed with other broadleaved trees or conifers.

A few of the higher mountains support red fir *(Abies magnifica)* forests and on the highest peaks, foxtail pine *(Pinus balfouriana* spp. *balfouriana)* and Jeffrey pine *(Pinus jeffreyi)* woodlands can be found. These are discussed in the Klamath Mountains chapter (Chapter 9). Blue oak *(Quercus douglasii)* woodlands, chaparrals, and grasslands are found in the interior lowlands on the eastern border of the region (Stuart and Sawyer 2001) and are discussed in the Central Valley chapter (Chapter 13).

Overview of Historic Fire Occurrence

Prehistoric Period

Holocene fire history reconstructions from lake sediments in western Oregon (Long et al. 1998, Long and Whitlock 1999) and the Klamath Mountains (Mohr et al. 2000) indicate relatively frequent fire during the warm, dry early to mid Holocene and less frequent fire as climate became cooler and wetter.

Pollen analyses reveal increased levels of fire-adapted vegetation concomitant with thicker charcoal deposits and a warm, dry climate (Long and Whitlock 1999). Similar patterns, presumably, apply to California's North Coast and North Coast Ranges.

The North Coast Ranges have experienced three major climatic periods since the end of the Pleistocene: a cool, somewhat continental climate from the early Holocene to about 8,500 years B.P.; a warmer period with presumably drier summers from 8,500 to about 3,000 years B.P.; and a cool, moist climate since about 3,000 years B.P. (Keter 1995). Native Americans are known to have lived in the region since around 8,200 to 8,600 years B.P., and by the middle of the Holocene, humans lived throughout the North Coast region (Sawyer et al. 2000). The pollen record demonstrates that vegetation differed during the three periods. Open pine forests with sparse shrubs and herbs dominated during the early Holocene in parts of the North Coast Ranges. As the climate warmed and dried, pine pollen counts remained high and oak counts increased while Douglas-fir pollen decreased. The cool, moist climate in the late Holocene enabled Douglas-fir, tanoak, and true fir pollen counts to increase and oak counts to decrease (Keter 1995). Fire was presumably more frequent during the warm, dry period and less frequent during the cool, moist period.

Fire history studies from the last 1,000 years reveal a variable pattern of fire frequencies throughout northwestern California. The most frequently burned landscapes were ignited on a nearly annual basis by Native Americans (Lewis 1993, Keter 1995) and were generally near villages, or were in vegetation cultured for food and basketry materials such as in grasslands and oak woodlands. Vegetation adjacent to Native American use areas experienced more frequent fire than would be found in the same vegetation type farther away (Vale 2002, Whitlock and Knox 2002). In general, the

FIGURE 8.6. Oregon white oak woodland zone. Oregon white oak woodland in Humboldt County. (Photograph by John Stuart.)

most frequent fire occurred in grasslands and oak woodlands, with decreasing fire frequencies in chaparral, mixed evergreen, and montane mixed conifer. The least frequent fire occurred in moist, coastal conifer forests.

Native American ignitions presumably accounted for the most fire starts in the coastal region, as lightning is infrequent during the summer months (Automated lightning detection system 1999, Stephens and Libby 2006). Lightning fires are more numerous at higher elevations in the North Coast Ranges than the in coastal regions, but not as numerous as in the Klamath, Shasta, or Trinity National Forests (Show and Kotok 1923, Keeley 1981). Van Wagtendonk and Cayan (2007) found that lightning strike density increased with distance from the Pacific Ocean (Fig. 8.7) and increasing

elevation for the period between 1985 and 2000. The number of lightning strikes per year per 100 km² (39 mi²) in northwestern California during this period ranged from 0.9 to 9.3 (median = 1.7, mean = 3.0, SD = 2.5).

Historic Period

The prevention of Native-American–ignited fires, the introduction of cattle and sheep by ranchers, and logging altered fire regimes during the historic period. New fire regimes were created as Euro-American settlement moved north from the Bay Area in the early nineteenth century to the northern counties in the mid to late nineteenth century. Coastal areas were usually settled earlier than inland areas.

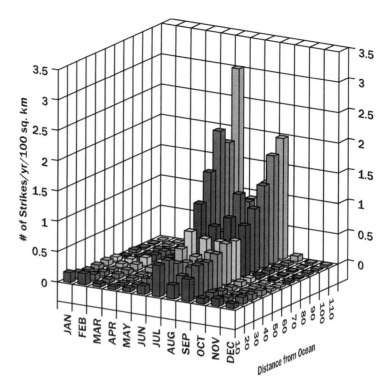

FIGURE 8.7. Average annual lightning strike density as a function of distance from the Pacific Ocean in the North Coast bioregion, 1985–2000. (Data from van Wagtendonk and Cayan 2007.)

Indian burning was interrupted in the early 1800s near the Bay Area, in the 1830s to 1840s near Clear Lake, and the mid 1860s in northern Mendocino and Humboldt Counties (Keter 2002). Traditional burning practices were curtailed as Indian populations were decimated by disease and warfare and as survivors were relocated to reservations (Keter 1995).

Early settler fires either originated from escaped campfires or were deliberately set to improve forage for livestock (Barrett 1935, Gilligan 1966). Ranchers primarily grazed cattle during the early to mid nineteenth century with sheep grazing increasing in the mid to late nineteenth century. Sheepherders were notorious as indiscriminate users of fire. Barrett (1935) wrote, "[T]he largest percentage of the most destructive fires in the mountains of California were caused by sheepmen during the thirty years preceding the establishment of the National Forests." Fire use by ranchers was not as skillfully employed as by Indians. Rather than burning for a single reason, Indians burned for multiple purposes at different times of the year and with variable intensities and severities (Lewis 1993).

Loggers during the mid to late nineteenth century regularly burned recently cut lands to remove bark and facilitate log extraction by draft animals. The potential for fire to escape and burn into unlogged forests was high. Fortunately, most of the early logging was done in cool, moist coastal forests where fire hazards were generally low (O'Dell 1996). By the late nineteenth century and through the 1920s, mechanical yarding systems and railroads enabled logging of whole watersheds in coastal and interior drainages. Following logging, many timberland owners attempted to convert forestland to grassland by repeatedly burning the logging slash and sowing grass seed (O'Dell 1996). Fire frequency, intensity, and severity were high throughout this period.

Large fires were frequent in northwestern California during the historic period. For example, Gripp (1976) conducted an extensive review of northwestern California newspapers and various other documents and found that large fires in Humboldt and Del Norte Counties from about 1880 to 1945 were common with an average interval between severe fire seasons of 3 years.

Fire suppression began on National Forest Land in northwestern California in 1905 (Keter 1995, Stephens and Ruth 2005). Fire suppression on private and state land, in the latter part of the nineteenth century through the early twentieth century, was largely the responsibility of the counties and various landowner associations. During the 1920s, fire wardens used their power of conscription to recruit firefighters and by the early 1930s, the California Division of Forestry assumed the role of fire suppression (Clar 1969). Effective fire suppression on private, state, and federal land, however, did not begin until after 1945 when the State Forest Practice Act curtailed logging activities, more effective firefighting equipment became available, and returning soldiers from World War II helped to suppress fires.

Current Period

Fire records dating back to around 1915 exist for the bioregion, although reasonably complete records for large fires are only available since 1945, and complete records in digital format for fires of all sizes are available for only the past couple of decades. The records for fires larger than approximately 120 ha (300 ac) (CDF-FRAP 2001) reveal that two to three times as many fires occurred in the 1950s as in subsequent decades. In addition, there were consistently more fires in the

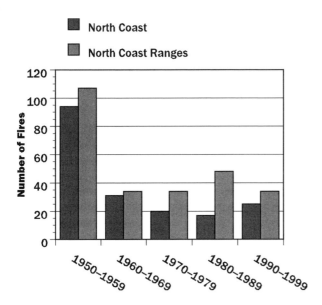

North Coast

North Coast Ranges

FIGURE 8.8. Number of fires larger than 120 ha (300 ac) by decade in the North Coast and North Coast Ranges Ecological Sections.

North Coast Ranges Section than in the North Coast Section (Fig. 8.8). The vast majority of fire records did not identify fire cause, although the large number of fires in the 1950s coincided with a period of increased logging. Fewer large fires in ensuing decades can be attributed to more effective fire prevention and suppression.

The North Coast has experienced a consistent decrease in cumulative hectares burned since the 1950s, and the North Coast Ranges similarly experienced progressively fewer hectares burned from 1950 through the 1970s; but in the past two decades cumulative fire size has dramatically increased, possibly due to fuel load and structural changes associated with fire suppression (Fig. 8.9) (Talbert 1996, Stuart and Salazar 2000).

The *natural fire rotation,* a measure of fire frequency defined as "the length of time necessary for an area equal in size to the study area to burn" (Agee 1993), in northwestern California has lengthened appreciably since fire prevention and suppression were initiated. Overall, the North Coast had a natural fire rotation from 1950 through 1999 of 485 years, and the North Coast Ranges had a value of 261 years. When analyzed by latitude, the North Coast had longer natural fire rotations in the central and southern parts of the ecological section, while the North Coast Ranges had a longer natural fire rotation in the north (Fig. 8.10).

Major Ecological Zones

North Coastal Scrub and Prairie Zone

North coastal scrub extends from Monterey County into Oregon in a narrow strip generally ranging in width from tens to hundreds of meters. Belsher (1999) found that scrubs north of Sonoma County were variously dominated by coyotebrush, yellow bush lupine, salal, evergreen huckleberry,

and various blackberry species. Salal in combination with blackberry species and a rich mix of other shrubs, subshrubs, and herbaceous species often forms thickets and brambles. Yellow bush lupine stands, in contrast, can be monotypic (Heady et al. 1988). A transition zone between north coastal scrub and coastal sage scrub lies in Marin and San Mateo Counties. Tolerance to salt spray is the dominant ecological factor in these communities.

Prior to European settlement, the North Coastal Prairie was probably dominated by native perennial grasses, including California oatgrass *(Danthonia californica),* purple needlegrass *(Nassella pulchra),* Idaho fescue *(Festuca idahoensis),* and tufted hairgrass *(Deschampsia cespitosa)* (Heady et al. 1988). Highly susceptible to invasion, coastal prairie now includes many mediterranean annual species as well as non-native perennial grasses, notably velvetgrass *(Holcus lanatus)* and sweet vernalgrass *(Anthoxanthum odoratum)* (Hektner and Foin 1977).

FIRE ECOLOGY

Salal, evergreen huckleberry, coyotebrush, thimbleberry *(Rubus parviflorus),* salmonberry *(Rubus spectabilis),* and California blackberry *(Rubus ursinus)* are all fire-neutral, facultative sprouters (Table 8.2). Although regeneration is not fire dependent, these species have the capability to aggressively recolonize burned landscapes through sprouting, seeding, or germination from buried seed.

Because the pre-European settlement prairie community composition is speculative, and the present communities have been significantly altered by invasion, fire responses must be examined for each species individually. The only published study of coastal prairie native bunchgrass fire responses showed no significant changes in foliar cover or frequency for California oatgrass, purple needlegrass, and foothill needlegrass *(Nassella lepida)* after burning (Hatch et al. 1999). Tufted hairgrass in other plant communities is resistant to all but the highest intensity fires and recovers to pre-burn levels in a few years (Walsh 1995). Idaho fescue is resistant to low-intensity burning but can be killed at higher intensities (Zouhar 2000). A small unpublished study at The Sea Ranch in Sonoma County showed temporary decreases in the cover of velvetgrass and sweet vernalgrass following prescribed burns with little effect on tufted hairgrass (Evett 2002).

FIRE REGIME–PLANT COMMUNITY INTERACTIONS

Fire is relatively uncommon in North Coastal Scrub because of its proximity to the cool, humid climate of the Pacific Ocean. Native Americans would most likely have ignited any fires that did burn and fire spread would have been probably dependent on warm, dry east winds. Pre-European fire intervals are unknown, but may have varied from a few years near Native American habitations to hundreds of years. North Coastal Scrub is capable of self-perpetuating with or without fire.

The role of fire in maintaining coastal prairie prior to European settlement is poorly documented but is likely to have included widespread burning (Blackburn and Anderson

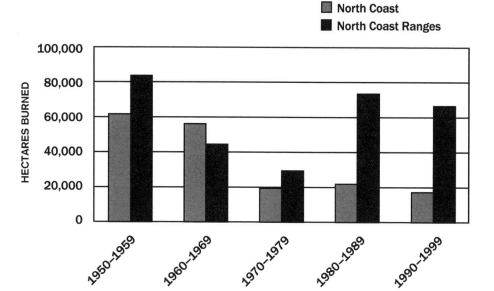

FIGURE 8.9. Number of hectares burned for fires larger than 120 ha (300 ac) by decade in the North Coast and North Coast Ranges Ecological Sections.

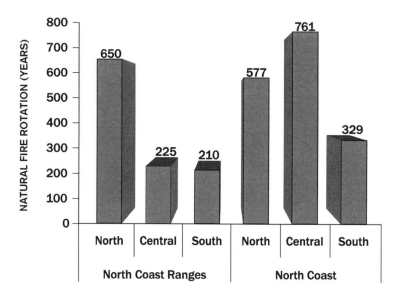

FIGURE 8.10. Natural fire rotation based on fires larger than 120 ha (300 ac) between 1950 and 1999 by latitude in the North Coast Ranges and the North Coast Ecological Sections. For the North Coast Ranges, North = Humboldt, Trinity, and Tehama Counties; Central = Glenn and Mendocino Counties; and South = Lake, Colusa, Sonoma, and Napa Counties. For the North Coast, North = Del Norte and Humboldt Counties; Central = Mendocino and Lake Counties; and South = Sonoma, Napa, Solano, and Marin Counties.

1993). A few accounts by early European travelers in coastal California mention fires and comment on lush grasslands on coastal terraces. Because lightning frequency is very low in north coastal California, fires were probably deliberately set by Native Americans to maintain grasslands with their rich sources of grain, bulbs, and tubers. Soil and phytolith evidence suggests that many coastal prairie sites have been grassland for thousands of years (Bicknell et al. 1992). In the absence of burning or grazing, many of these sites with high grass phytolith content in the soil have been invaded by

shrubs and trees, suggesting that regular aboriginal burning was required to maintain the coastal prairie (Bicknell et al. 1993, Evett 2000). Following displacement of the native population, many ranchers practiced deliberate burning to maintain the prairie and promote understory forage in forested areas (Bicknell et al. 1993). For the past 150 years, continuous livestock grazing has replaced frequent burning as the most important change agent throughout the coastal prairie. During this time, non-native mediterranean annuals have largely replaced native perennial grasses. Whether this

TABLE 8.2

Fire response types for important species in the North Coast bioregion

| | | *Type of Fire Response* | | |
	Sprouting	Seeding	Individual	*Species*
Tree	None	Neutral	Killed	Beach pine, Sitka spruce, western hemlock, western redcedar
	None	Neutral	Survive	Grand fir, Port Orford-cedar
	None	Stimulated (establishment)	Survive	Douglas-fir
	None	Stimulated (release)	Killed	Bishop pine, Bolander pine, pygmy cypress
	Stimulated	Neutral	Survive/ Top-killed	Bigleaf maple, California bay, canyon live oak, golden chinquapin, tanoak
	Stimulated	Stimulated (establishment)	Survive/ Top-killed	Redwood, California black oak, Oregon white oak, Pacific madrone
Shrub	Stimulated	Neutral	Survive/ Top-killed	Evergreen huckleberry, salal
	Stimulated	Stimulated (establishment)	Survive/ Top-killed	Evergreen blackberry, coyotebrush, salmonberry, thimbleberry
Grass	Stimulated	Stimulated (establishment)	Survive/ Top-killed	California oatgrass, Idaho fescue, purple needle-grass, tufted hairgrass

replacement would have been as extensive under continued frequent burning is unknown.

There is little data on mean fire return intervals in coastal prairie. Greenlee and Langenheim (1990) estimated pre-European settlement fire return intervals near Monterey Bay were 1–2 years; post-European settlement intervals, confounded by the simultaneous introduction of livestock grazing, were 20–30 years. Aboriginal fires were probably small and of low intensity due to the discontinuous nature of the coastal prairie and lack of fuel accumulation under a high-frequency regime. Seasonality of aboriginal fires is unknown; fires were probably more likely in the summer or early fall dry season (Table 8.3).

The removal of fire and livestock grazing from the coastal prairie has profound effects on the plant community composition. Sites at The Sea Ranch in northern Sonoma County, where livestock grazing was removed in the late 1960s and fires have been excluded, show a shift from mixed annual and perennial grasses to overwhelming dominance of non-native perennial grasses, a decline in biodiversity indices, and dangerously increased fuel loads (Foin and Hektner 1986, Evett 2002).

Small-scale attempts to reintroduce fire to coastal prairie sites to reduce non-native species and restore native species dominance have met with mixed success. Burning at The Sea Ranch sites reduced cover of the non-native grasses, velvetgrass and sweet vernalgrass, but increased cover of another non-native grass, hairy wallaby grass (*Rytedosperma pilosum*) (Evett 2002). Biological diversity increased because of increased cover of non-native forbs and annual grasses. Native grass species were mostly unaffected by burning; this was also true in a study in coastal San Mateo County (Hatch et al. 1999).

North Coastal Pine Forests Zone

Bishop, beach, and Bolander pine forests are sporadically arranged along coastal bluffs and marine terraces from the Oregon border to the Bay Area. Bishop pine occurs in disjunct populations in coastal California from Humboldt County to Santa

TABLE 8.3
Fire regime classification for the north coastal scrub and prairie zone

Temporal	
Seasonality	Summer–fall
Fire-return interval	Long
Spatial	
Size	Small
Complexity	Low
Magnitude	
Intensity	Multiple
Severity	High
Fire type	Passive-active crown

NOTE: Fire regime terms used in this table are defined in Chapter 4.

TABLE 8.4
Fire regime classification for the north coastal pine forest zone

Temporal	
Seasonality	Summer–fall
Fire-return interval	Truncated medium
Spatial	
Size	Medium
Complexity	Low
Magnitude	
Intensity	High
Severity	Very high
Fire type	Passive-active crown

NOTE: Fire regime terms used in this table are defined in Chapter 4.

Barbara County. It is also found on Santa Cruz and Santa Rosa Islands as well as in Baja California, Mexico (Metcalf 1921, Critchfield and Little 1966, Little 1979). Beach pine is much more widely distributed than Bolander pine and is found along the Pacific Coast from Yakutat Bay, Alaska, to Mendocino County (Little 1971, Critchfield 1980, Bivin 1986, Oliphant 1992). Bolander pine is endemic to the pygmy forests of western Mendocino County and is associated with pygmy cypress.

FIRE ECOLOGY

Bishop pine is a fire-dependent, obligate seeder (Table 8.2). Regeneration is dependent on a crown-stored seed bank. Cones can remain closed for years and only open after fire or on hot, low-humidity days (Van Dersal 1938). Fire is a critical process in the establishment and maintenance of Bishop pine ecosystems (Vogl et al. 1977). Older trees have thick bark that enables them to survive multiple surface fires (McCune 1988). Many Bishop pine stands, however, are very dense and stand-replacing crown fires are common. Cone serotiny is somewhat variable, with northern populations less serotinous than southern populations (Zedler 1986). Morphological differences in cones have been observed, but this does not result in a significant difference in cone-opening temperatures (Ostoja and Klinger 1999). Mycorrhizal colonization of Bishop pine is rapid after stand-replacement fires, and the source of the inoculum is probably heat-resistant propagules in the soil (Barr et al. 1999).

Beach pine is a fire-neutral, obligate seeder, whereas Bolander pine and pygmy cypress are fire-dependent, obligate seeders (Table 8.2). Beach pines are non-serotinous; Bolander pines and pygmy cypresses are variably so (Lotan and Critchfield 1990). Beach pine, Bolander pine, and pygmy cypress all have persistent cones and begin to produce cones within 10 years (Krugman and Jenkinson 1974). Bolander pine and pygmy cypress cones will open after fire or by desiccation (Johnson 1974, Vogl et al. 1977). Detached cones commonly open, but this rarely results in seedling establishment because of the need for bare mineral seedbeds and high amounts of sunlight.

FIRE REGIME– PLANT COMMUNITY INTERACTIONS

Bishop pine is adapted to stand-replacement high-severity fires (Table 8.4). Pre-historically, the majority of these fires probably occurred in the late summer and fall when fuel moisture contents were low. High-severity fires were probably mostly associated with warm, dry east winds. The spatial scale of fires is difficult to estimate. No fire history data exists to estimate the spatial extent of the fires, but in areas where the trees were in isolated groves surrounded by shrublands the fires were probably of moderate or large size (hundreds of ha or larger). Some high-frequency, low-intensity surface fires were ignited by Native Americans and ranchers in Bishop pine forests (B. Baxter, personal communication). Lightning-ignited fires are unusual (Keeley 1981), so anthropogenic ignitions were probably the main source of fires. The majority of Bishop pine forests have not burned in the last 40 to 70 years because of fire suppression. The lack of fire could threaten the long-term existence of Bishop pine because it relies on high-severity crown fires that prepare seed beds, enable the release of large quantities of seed, and remove the canopy thereby increasing the light reaching the forest floor. Conversely, fire at high frequency could extirpate Bishop pine because there would be insufficient time for the trees to produce viable seed between successive fires. Introduction of non-native grasses into recently burned areas would increase the risk of extirpation because the grasses could produce a highly continuous fuel bed in 1 to 2 years.

Little is known about the role of fire in Bolander pine and pygmy cypress forests. Wind, rather than fire, appears to be the primary significant source of change in beach pine stands (Green 1999).

Sitka Spruce Forest Zone

Sitka spruce forests are variously dominated by Sitka spruce, western hemlock *(Tsuga heterophylla)*, Douglas-fir, western redcedar *(Thuja plicata)*, Port Orford-cedar *(Chamaecyparis law-soniana)*, grand fir *(Abies grandis)*, or red alder *(Alnus rubra)*.

FIRE ECOLOGY

In general, Douglas-fir and red alder regenerate well following fire, timber harvest, floods, or windthrow, whereas Sitka spruce, western hemlock, grand fir, western redcedar, and Port Orford-cedar regenerate well in either undisturbed or disturbed forests. Douglas-fir is a fire-enhanced obligate seeder, and red alder is a fire-neutral facultative sprouter (Table 8.2). Both species require full sunlight and mineral soil to regenerate. Young red alder trees sprout vigorously, but older trees rarely sprout (Harrington 1990). Sitka spruce, western hemlock, grand fir, western redcedar, and Port Orford-cedar are all fire-inhibited obligate seeders and regenerate well on organic seedbeds in shade or partial shade (Foiles et al. 1990, Harrington 1990, Harris 1990, Hermann and Lavender 1990, Packee 1990, Zobel 1990). Sitka spruce, western hemlock, western redcedar, and Port Orford-cedar are capable of reproducing by layering (Harris 1990, Packee 1990, Zobel 1990), although Port Orford-cedar layers only occasionally.

With the exception of Douglas-fir and larger Port Orford-cedar (Zobel et al. 1985), other potential canopy dominants and co-dominants in these forests are not fire resistant. Western hemlock, Sitka spruce, western redcedar, and red alder are shallow rooted and have thin bark (Uchytil 1989, Packee 1990, Griffith 1992). Furthermore, western hemlock has flammable foliage and a low branching habit (Tesky 1992). Grand fir is fire sensitive when small, but can develop bark thick enough to resist light surface fires (Howard and Aleksoff 2000).

FIRE REGIME–PLANT COMMUNITY INTERACTION

Fires were generally uncommon in Sitka spruce forests. Lightning ignitions were scarce and Native Americans either ignited the few fires that did burn significant areas or fires spread from inland areas and were most likely accompanied by warm, east winds. Fuel moisture is almost always too wet to support fire in these coastal forests with the exception of late summer and early fall after summer fog has run its course. Even then, temperature and humidity are usually not conducive to burning so close to the Pacific Ocean. With the exception of Native American ignitions in prairies or near villages, fire intervals were long to very long. When fires did burn, however, they were surface fires or with warm, dry east winds they developed into passive/active crown fires. Fires were small to moderate in size, with moderate spatial complexity and intensity, and had multiple severity levels (Table 8.5).

Fire history in Sitka spruce forests is not well documented. Inferences can be made from fire histories from the cool, moist redwood forests in Del Norte County and from similar forest types along the coast of Oregon and Washington. Veirs (1982) found that redwood forests in coastal Del Norte County had fire intervals between 250 and 500 years. Impara (1997) found similar patterns in Sitka spruce forests in the central Oregon Coast Range with pre-settlement (1478–1845)

TABLE 8.5

Fire regime classification for the Sitka spruce forest zone

Temporal	
Seasonality	Summer–fall
Fire-return interval	Truncated long
Spatial	
Size	Small–Medium
Complexity	Moderate
Magnitude	
Intensity	Moderate
Severity	Multiple
Fire type	Passive-active crown

NOTE: Fire regime terms used in this table are defined in Chapter 4.

fire intervals averaging around 300 years. Agee (1993) reported fire intervals of around 200 years for the southern Oregon coast, 400 years for the northern Oregon coast, and 1,146 years in Sitka spruce forests of western Washington (Fahnestock and Agee 1983). Wind is the more frequent cause of change in these coastal forests (Agee 1993, Green 1999).

Red alder is known as an early seral species that aggressively colonizes moist, mineral soils in full sunlight. Early growth is rapid and it usually dominates competitors for the first 25 years or so until it is overtopped by other conifers (Uchytil 1989). If Douglas-fir is present, it may eventually overtop red alder and potentially dominate in the overstory for centuries. If Douglas-fir is not present, then Sitka spruce, western hemlock, grand fir, or Port Orford-cedar (Hayes 1958) may develop into canopy dominants. Port Orford-cedar and western hemlock can regenerate in the shade of a canopy (Franklin and Dyrness 1973), whereas Sitka spruce and grand fir, though not as shade tolerant as Port Orford-cedar or western hemlock, can self-perpetuate following windthrow or pockets of overstory mortality (Franklin and Dyrness 1973).

There has been little change in fire regime from pre-European time to the current time period. The 60 to 70 years of effective fire suppression is much shorter than the pre-European fire intervals. Even though many coastal stands were logged and presented different stand structures than old growth, a benign climatic regime, rapid plant recolonization, rapid plant growth, and rapid fuel decomposition have allowed many stands to approximate fire environments seen in old growth stands. Effective fire suppression should continue to minimize the probability of wildfire in these forests into the future.

Redwood Forest Zone

FIRE ECOLOGY

Redwood is a fire-enhanced facultative sprouter (Table 8.2). Seedling establishment is problematic in the absence of fire, windthrow, or flooding because of low seed viability (Olson et al. 1990) and unsuitable seedbeds. It is rare to find redwood seedlings that have become established on their own litter because of the combination of damping-off fungi (Davidson 1971) and low light intensities commonly found beneath redwood canopies (Jacobs 1987). However, exposure of mineral soil following fire, windthrow, or flooding often results in successful redwood seedling establishment. Redwood is also capable of establishing from seed on duff (Olson et al. 1990), logs (Bingham 1984), debris (Olson et al. 1990), and litter from other species (Jacobs 1987). Seedling establishment is better under high light intensities (Jacobs 1987), and juvenile growth is best in full sunlight (Olson et al. 1990).

Sprouting in redwood can occur from lignotubers at the root crown, induced lignotubers on layered branches, trunk burls, and from adventitious buds on tree trunks (Del Tredici 1998). Sufficiently intense surface fires can stimulate basal lignotubers to sprout, whereas crown fires often result in redwood "fire columns" (Jepson 1910, Fritz 1931) whose denuded trunks sprout new leaves and eventually develop new branches. The development of redwood lignotubers and axillary meristems are a normal part of seedling development (Del Tredici 1998) and may represent an evolutionary response to fire, windthrow, or flooding.

Redwood bark serves as either a resister or enabler of fire damage to the cambium layer depending on its thickness and the water content of its loosely packed, sponge-like fibers. Bark, 15 to 30 cm (6 to 12 in.) thick (Fritz 1931), protects the cambium from heat damage, especially when moist. Thin-barked trees, however, are susceptible to fire damage and are readily top-killed (Fritz 1931, Finney and Martin 1989, 1993) as are large trees that have had their once-thick bark reduced by recurring fires. Dead cambium acts as an infection court for sapwood and heartwood rots. Surface fires burn into the rotten sapwood or heartwood hollowing out tree bases (goosepens). Subsequent fires in goosepens continue to expand the cavity with the result that many trees are consumed standing (Fritz 1931). Fire scars have been recorded to be as tall as 70 m (Sawyer et al. 2000). Such tall scars were initiated by dry bark burning in long strips. The burned strips are enlarged by ensuing fires and can further develop into scars up to a meter wide.

Redwood stands are among the most productive in the world (Fritz 1945, Fujimori 1977) and consequently produce impressive fuel loads. Rapid litter decomposition helps to keep the litter loads relatively low. Pillers and Stuart (1993) found that the time to decompose 95% of the weight of oven-dried litter ranged from approximately 7 to 11 years on four sites in Humboldt County.

Litterfall is episodic and varies by site and by species. In general, most litter falls in a few weeks to a few months. Redwood litter is particularly flammable after it falls. Its leaves have had several weeks to air dry on the tree and, because leaves do not abscise individually but as sprays of leaves, the resultant fuel bed is made up of loosely compacted fuel enabling the litter to quickly respond to moisture changes

TABLE 8.6
Fire regime classification for the redwood forest zone

Temporal	
Seasonality	Summer–fall
Fire-return interval	Short–long
Spatial	
Size	Small–medium
Complexity	Moderate
Magnitude	
Intensity	Moderate
Severity	Low
Fire type	Surface

NOTE: Fire regime terms used in this table are defined in Chapter 4.

and to increased oxygen supply during combustion (Pyne et al. 1996).

Accretion rates for larger fuels such as branches and logs are episodic and may not be dependent on significant wind events. Although fuels less than 25 cm (10 in.) in diameter accrete every year, large branches and trees may take centuries to fall. In addition to wind, snow and wildfire can cause stem breakage or mortality that eventually augments the large forest floor dead fuels.

Decomposition of Douglas-fir, western hemlock, and Sitka spruce logs in redwood forests can take hundreds of years (Harmon et al. 1986). Redwood's renowned decay resistance (Agee 1993) suggests even slower decomposition rates.

Understory plants can either inhibit or intensify fire behavior. Coastal redwood forests in Del Norte County, for example, include many plants (Mahony 1999) with moisture high enough to retard fire spread. Inland redwood forests, in contrast, have a higher proportion of sclerophyllous understory trees and shrubs that can exacerbate fire behavior. Stuart (1986) found that during prescribed burns in Humboldt County, flame lengths on redwood litter and duff were 10 to 90 cm (4 to 35 in.) long, yet beneath evergreen huckleberry the flames were 300 to 500 cm (9 to 16 ft) long.

FIRE REGIME–PLANT COMMUNITY INTERACTIONS

Redwood forests typically burned in the summer and early fall with variable fire intervals. The wettest sites had long fire intervals and drier sites had short fire intervals. Many fires ignited by Native Americans in vegetation adjacent to redwood forests were likely extinguished as they spread into cool, moist fuels usually associated with forest floors in old-growth redwood stands. Occasionally, though, fires larger than 10 ha (25 ac), and some larger than 1,000 ha (2,400 ac), would occur, especially during droughts and under the influence of warm, dry east winds.

Redwood forests generally experienced moderate-intensity surface fires that consumed irregular patches of surface fuel and understory vegetation (Table 8.6). Occasional passive

TABLE 8.7
Fire intervals in redwood forests

	Fire Interval (years)	Composite Area (ha)	Source
Del Norte and northern Humboldt Counties	50–500	1	(Veirs 1982)
East of Prairie Creek Redwoods State Park	8	0.25–3	(Brown and Swetnam 1994)
Humboldt Redwoods State Park	11–44	7	(Stuart 1987)
Southern Humboldt County	25	12	(Fritz 1931)
Jackson State Forest	6–20	4–20	(Brown and Baxter 2003)
Salt Point State Park	6–9	~200	(Finney and Martin 1989)
Annadel State Park	6–23	14 trees[a]	(Finney and Martin 1992)
Near Muir Woods National Monument	22–27	75	(Jacobs et al. 1985)
Western Marin County	8–13	5–10; 10 trees in 1 stand	(Finney 1990) (Brown et al. 1999)
Jasper Ridge Preserve, Santa Clara County	9–16	1–3	(Stephens and Fry 2005)
Big Basin Redwoods State Park	~50	Variable, dependent on estimated fire area	(Greenlee 1983)

[a]Point data.

crown fires occurred, especially along the southern and eastern edges of the range. On average, fire severities were lowest in the coolest, wettest regions and highest in the warmer, drier areas.

Redwood forests have a complex fire history. In general, pre-suppression fire intervals correspond to the three predominant climatic gradients described earlier where the longest fire intervals are found in moist, cool coastal sites in the north, and the shortest fire intervals are found in the drier, warmer interior and southern sites. Fire intervals from 125 to 500 years have been reported for coastal forests in Del Norte County where redwood grows in association with Sitka spruce, western hemlock, and western redcedar (Veirs 1982, Mahony and Stuart 2001). Drier, warmer redwood forests in eastern Del Norte County with higher proportions of Douglas-fir, tanoak, and Pacific madrone have pre-suppression fire intervals of approximately 50 years (Veirs 1982). Fire intervals to the south generally range between 6 and 44 years (Table 8.7). Some redwood stands had fire intervals of 1 or 2 years due to regular burning by Native Americans of prairies surrounded by redwood forest, near villages, and along travel corridors (Fritz 1931, Gilligan 1966, Lewis 1993). Other redwood stands had intervals in excess of 50 years because of their remoteness from Native American ignitions (Fritz 1931, Lewis 1993), fire-inhospitable microclimates, or fuel anomalies.

Few studies have attempted to estimate fire size in redwood forests. Stuart (1987) estimated fire sizes in old-growth redwood stands in Humboldt Redwoods State Park to be approximately 786 ha (1,940 ac) for the pre-settlement period, 1,097 ha (2,710 ac) for the settlement period, and 918 ha (2,270 ac) for the post-settlement period. California Department of Forestry fire records for Humboldt Redwoods State Park and nearby areas for the period 1940 through 1993 indicate that 30 fires larger than 120 ha (300 ac) burned, averaging 505 ha (1,250 ac) and ranging in size from 100 to 1,787 ha (250 to 4,400 ac) (Stuart and Fox 1993). Most of these fires were not located in old-growth redwood forests. Several fires were ignited in other vegetation types and burned into the redwood forest but were not sustained. One fire, however, that began on logged land outside of the park, did burn approximately 300 ha (740 ac) of old-growth redwood forest. Settlers during this period adopted the burning practices of the Sinkyone Indians and regularly burned the prairies in the upper basin to increase the production of livestock feed. Most fires burned into the old-growth Douglas-fir, "burning the vegetation and debris of the forest floor without destruction of the forest stands" (Gilligan 1966).

Succession and the climax status of redwood forests have been discussed since the early 1900s. Some authors contend that redwood is a seral species that, in the absence of fire, windthrow, or flooding, would eventually be succeeded by more understory-tolerant species as individual redwoods die (Cooper 1965, Osburn and Lowell 1972). Most ecologists, however, have argued that redwood is self-perpetuating and should be considered climax or as a fire sub-climax (Fisher et al. 1903, Weaver and Clements 1929, Fritz 1938, Whittaker 1960, Roy 1966, Becking 1967, Stone and Vasey 1968, Daubenmire and Daubenmire 1975, Veirs 1982, Olson et al. 1990, Agee 1993). It is difficult to imagine a scenario where redwood is unable to maintain itself in forests. Redwood's survival is ensured because of its great height, longevity, and resistance to fire by thick-barked individuals, ability to sprout, and capacity to establish seedlings on disturbed seedbeds.

Whether redwood is dependent on fire is an open question and should be answered on a case-by-case basis with each redwood community assigned a place on a fire-dependency continuum. A Redwood-Western Hemlock/Salmonberry association (Mahony and Stuart 2001) in coastal Del Norte County, for example, is fire tolerant but not fire dependent (Veirs 1982). Low to moderate surface fires kill fire-susceptible species such as western hemlock, western redcedar, and Sitka spruce. These moisture-loving understory-tolerant species quickly regenerate, grow, and have the capacity to develop into important ecosystem structural elements. A Redwood-Tanoak/Round Fruited Carex-Douglas Iris association (Borchert et al. 1988) near the droughty southern limits of the range, in contrast, could be thought of as fire dependent (Veirs 1982). In these areas, redwoods primarily regenerate from sprouts following recurring fires (Noss 2000). Reproduction from seed is difficult because of the inability of these relatively dry sites to meet redwood's soil moisture requirements (Olson et al. 1990, Noss 2000). The vast majority of redwood's range is found on sites intermediate to those described above with individual stands occupying intermediate positions on the fire-dependency continuum. Although the redwood species may not be dependent on fire to perpetuate in these forests, its ecosystem structures and functions may well be. Fire in redwood forests can determine size and spacing of dominant and co-dominant trees, snags, dead limbs, and logs. These features could provide critical habitat for a variety of wildlife species. Additionally, fire can increase the availability and cycling of soil nutrients, influence the establishment and perpetuation of understory species, and create natural edges (Hanson 2002).

Fire regime changes are evident in the drier portions of redwood's range, but not necessarily so in the wet north. Post-World War II (1950–2003) natural fire rotations for the northern, central, and southern redwood zones for fires larger than 134 ha were 1,083, 717, and 551 years, respectively (Oneal et al. 2004). The current fire interval in the north is probably not beyond the natural range of variability. However, the current fire intervals in the central and southern redwoods zones greatly exceed the 6- to 44-year pre-suppression intervals (Table 8.7).

It is possible, however, that a fire regime change in the north will eventually become evident because of modifications in fuel loading and structure following logging and land clearing. Only about 10% of the range of redwood is currently old-growth forest (Fox 1988). The other 90% of redwood's range is composed of young growth—some of which is more than 100 years old and dominated by large redwoods with fuel complexes not dissimilar to old growth, but much of the young growth is composed of small-diameter, dense complexes of conifers intermixed with broadleaved trees and shrubs. Other fuel complex alterations include the presence of large, persistent redwood stumps and logging slash, as well as greater shrub and herbaceous plant cover. In general, available fuel and horizontal and vertical fuel continuity have increased. Eventually, fire size, intensity, and severity

may increase, whereas fire complexity may change to multiple and the fire type may become passive-active crown fire. The above speculation assumes that the current successes the redwood forest has benefited from in fire management and suppression will not be sustained. It is likely, however, that aggressive fire suppression on land that is largely the responsibility of the state of California will continue and that less-frequent, small fires may remain the norm in the redwood forests for the foreseeable future.

Douglas-Fir–Tanoak Forest Zone

Douglas-fir–tanoak forests are widely distributed in the bioregion in areas inland from the redwood belt. Both tanoak and Douglas-fir are major components of northern mixed evergreen forests and Douglas-fir–hardwood forests (Sawyer et al. 1988). Douglas-fir dominates the overstory, while tanoak dominates a lower, secondary canopy. Other important tree associates may be Pacific madrone, golden chinquapin *(Chrysolepis chrysophylla)*, bigleaf maple *(Acer macrophyllum)*, California bay *(Umbellularia californica)*, canyon live oak *(Quercus chrysolepis)*, ponderosa pine, sugar pine *(Pinus lambertiana)*, incense-cedar *(Calocedrus decurrens)*, California black oak, and Oregon white oak.

FIRE ECOLOGY

Douglas-fir regeneration is often episodic in part due to irregular seed crops (Strothmann and Roy 1984). Douglas-fir establishment is enhanced if a good seed crop follows a low to moderate surface fire. If, however, there was a poor seed crop, other species would become established and inhibit Douglas-fir seedlings in ensuing years. Seedlings are most likely to become established on moist mineral soil, whereas relatively few seedlings are found on thick organic seedbeds (Hermann and Lavender 1990). Douglas-fir is considered moderately shade tolerant in northwestern California (Sawyer et al. 1988) and relatively shade intolerant in western Oregon and Washington (Hermann and Lavender 1990). Young seedlings are better able to tolerate shade than older seedlings, although Douglas-fir seedlings growing on dry sites need more shade. In northwestern California, optimum seedling survival occurs with about 50% shade, but optimum seedling growth occurs with 75% full sunlight (Sawyer et al. 1988).

Mature Douglas-fir has thick corky bark and is fire resistant. Other fire adaptations include great height with branches on tall trees over 30 m (100 ft) above the ground, rapid growth, longevity (up to 700 to 1,000 years old), and the ability to form adventitious roots (Hermann and Lavender 1990).

Douglas-fir and tanoak litter decomposes to 5% of original dry weight in 7 and 9 years, respectively (Pillers 1989). Because of this, fuel beds are typically thin. Douglas-fir leaves are short and fall individually, resulting in compact litter. Dry tanoak litter, however, is deeper and more porous.

Tanoak, Pacific madrone, chinquapin, canyon live oak, bigleaf maple, and California bay are all fire-neutral facultative sprouters (Table 8.2). Tanoak generally dominates its associated broadleaved trees and reproduces from seed under most light conditions, but fares best in full sunlight (Sawyer et al. 1988). Although tanoak is very tolerant of shade, regeneration from seed in dense shade is limited. Tanoak can be easily top-killed by fire but vigorously sprouts from dormant buds located on burls or lignotubers (Plumb and McDonald 1981). Stored carbohydrates and an extensive root system aid in a rapid and aggressive post-fire recovery (McDonald and Tappeiner 1987). Resistance to low-intensity surface fires increases with size because of increased bark thickness (Roy 1957, Plumb and McDonald 1981). Dried tanoak leaves are very flammable in comparison to other mixed evergreen forest species. Dried tanoak leaves in a dead crown can enable long flames and torching fire behavior. Many older tanoak trees may initially survive low-intensity fires, but bole wounds facilitate the entry of insects and disease that may eventually kill the tree (Roy 1957). Wind and infrequent heavy snow loads in tanoak canopies can cause branch and stem breakage resulting in heavy, hazardous surface fuels (Tappeiner et al. 1990). Tanoak mortality from sudden oak disease may produce hazardous wildfire conditions, and areas with high infection rates may find increases in fire intensity, severity, and the potential for crown fires (McPherson et al. 2000).

FIRE REGIME–PLANT COMMUNITY INTERACTIONS

Pre-European settlement fires were relatively frequent in Douglas-fir–tanoak forests due to their warmer, drier, inland locations and increased lightning activity at higher elevations (Keeley 1981). In the North Fork of the Eel River, for example, an average of about 25 lightning strikes occur per year (Keter 1995). Native American ignitions were the primary ignition source in the North Coast Ranges, though, as they regularly burned to culture tanoak, true oaks, and basketry materials (Keter 1995). As with other regional forest types, fires are most likely to occur during the months of July through September (Keeley 1981, Lewis 1993) (Table 8.8).

There is scant literature describing pre-European settlement fire size, intensity, and severity. Ethnographic data on indigenous populations and fire history data suggest that fire sizes, intensities, and severities were highly variable. In areas subject to frequent Native American burning, fire intensities and severities were low (Lewis 1993, Adams and Sawyer). Other areas experienced fire intensities and severities that varied spatially and temporally across the landscape resulting in a complex mosaic of mostly multi-aged stands of varying sizes (Rice 1985, Lewis 1993, Wills and Stuart 1994). Fires in interior sites spread more extensively than those closer to redwood forests. Surface fires were common and were intermixed with areas that supported passive/active crown fires (Table 8.8).

TABLE 8.8

Fire regime classification for the Douglas-fir–tanoak forest zone

Temporal	
Seasonality	Summer–fall
Fire-return interval	Short
Spatial	
Size	Medium
Complexity	Moderate
Magnitude	
Intensity	Multiple
Severity	Low–moderate
Fire type	Surface

NOTE: Fire regime terms used in this table are defined in Chapter 4.

The few fire history studies of Douglas-fir–tanoak forests indicate that average pre-suppression fire intervals varied from 10 to 16 years (Rice 1985, Wills and Stuart 1994, Adams and Sawyer n.d.). Pre-suppression fire sizes were undoubtedly variable. Rice (1985) reported fires in the hundreds of hectares.

In addition to environmental factors such as soil type, aspect, and so forth, successional trajectories depend on fire severity, seed availability, and sprout density. The climax forest is characterized by an overstory of Douglas-fir with tanoak dominating the lower, secondary canopy. Surface fires appear to be the norm in all-aged and all-sized old-growth Douglas-fir–tanoak forests in the Six Rivers National Forest (Adams and Sawyer). Fire suppression has increased the density of shade-tolerant tanoak in many Douglas-fir–tanoak forests (Tappeiner et al. 1990, Talbert 1996, Hunter 1997, Hunter et al. 1999). Douglas-fir, though, is able to maintain its dominance because of its large size and longevity. Sawyer and others (1988) described several successional pathways for Douglas-fir–tanoak forests. Following a severe, extensive stand-replacing fire, seed-producing Douglas-firs are killed leaving the sprouting tanoak or other sprouting hardwoods to dominate during early succession. Salvage logging and broadcast burning can enhance sprouting hardwood dominance, while not-salvage logging will ensure that shrubs in combination with sprouting hardwoods will dominate during early succession (Stuart et al. 1993). Eventually, Douglas-fir will reinvade as growing space is created by maturing, self-thinning hardwoods. A moderate- to low-severity surface fire, in contrast, would not kill potential seed-producing overstory Douglas-fir, but would kill Douglas-fir seedlings and saplings (Rice 1985). Douglas-fir seedling establishment would then occur in the partial shade beneath the surviving mixed canopies of Douglas-fir and tanoak (or other hardwoods). Douglas-fir will continue to dominate the overstory and tanoak will continue to perpetuate in the understory and secondary canopy. A third scenario in more open mixed stands would allow both Douglas-fir and tanoak to persevere.

There isn't enough evidence to deduce whether the current fire regime in old-growth Douglas-fir–tanoak forests has changed since European contact. Fire regimes in young stands, though, have been modified. The most significant change in old growth is the greater density of understory shrubs and trees creating greater vertical fuel continuity, increasing the probability that a surface fire could burn into the crown. Many Douglas-fir–tanoak forests, however, have been logged or have experienced stand-altering wildfire. The current regime in these forests can be characterized as having longer fire return intervals due to effective and aggressive fire suppression, greater intensity because of increased fuel loadings from slash and from increased densities of understory shrubs and trees, and greater severity because of the accumulated ladder fuels and increased loading of large, dead surface fuels. Fine fuels decompose too rapidly to have increased beyond that of pre-European conditions. Seasonality of fire occurrence complexity is probably unchanged. The current fire regime probably accounts for a higher proportion of forest area burned in passive crown fires. Because pre-European fire size is not known with any certainty, we can't speculate whether there have been any changes.

Oregon White Oak Woodland Zone

Oregon white oak is distributed from southwestern British Columbia through western Washington and Oregon into California in the North Coast Ranges and Sierra Nevada (Little 1971). Oregon white oak woodlands often occur in the margin between conifer forest and prairies in the North Coast Ranges. Oregon white oak can also be found in open savannas, closed-canopy stands, mixed stands with conifers, or with other broadleaved trees (Burns and Honkala 1990).

FIRE ECOLOGY

Oregon white oak and California black oak are fire-enhanced, facultative sprouters (Table 8.2). Oregon white oak is frequently top-killed by fire but vigorously sprouts from the bole, root crown, and roots (Griffin 1980, McDonald et al. 1983, Sugihara et al. 1987). Sprouting has been reported to decrease with age (Sugihara and Reed 1987). As in most oak species, sprouts grow more rapidly than seedlings because of stored carbohydrates and an extensive root system. Seedling establishment is enhanced by the removal of the litter layer (Arno and Hammerly 1977).

FIRE REGIME–PLANT COMMUNITY INTERACTIONS

Pre-historically, Oregon white oak woodlands experienced frequent, low-intensity surface fires, many of which were ignited by Native Americans. Mean fire return intervals varied from 7 to 13 years in Oregon white oak woodlands in Humboldt County (Reed and Sugihara 1987). Fires probably spread in cured herbaceous fuels. There is no information on fire sizes in this vegetation type, but they probably were diverse. Fires ignited by Native Americans under moister

TABLE 8.9

Fire regime classification for the Oregon white oak woodland zone

Temporal	
Seasonality	Summer–fall
Fire-return interval	Truncated short
Spatial	
Size	Medium
Complexity	Low
Magnitude	
Intensity	Low
Severity	Low
Fire type	Surface

NOTE: Fire regime terms used in this table are defined in Chapter 4.

conditions probably would not have spread far into adjoining conifer forests (Gilligan 1966), whereas those ignited in the summer and fall could have been extensive because of continuous dry herbaceous fuels. Frequent surface fires produced open savannas in the Bald Hills in Humboldt County (Sugihara et al. 1987) (Table 8.9).

Fire suppression has dramatically affected this plant community. Frequent surface fires once inhibited seedling establishment and reduced the density of Douglas-fir and other competing conifers (Barnhardt et al. 1996). In the absence of fire, conifers can over-top, suppress, and eventually produce enough shade to kill Oregon white oak. Management-ignited prescribed fires have been ineffective in reducing the density of competing conifers when they are over 3 m (10 ft) in height (Sugihara and Reed 1987). Hand removal of small Douglas-fir has been used in some areas and larger trees can be girdled to increase the dominance of the oak (Hastings et al. 1997). To maintain oak dominance, a minimum fire frequency of 3 to 5 years has been recommended (Sugihara and Reed 1987).

Management Issues

The management challenges in the ecosystems of the North Coast bioregion are diverse. In general, fire once occurred frequently in grasslands and oak woodlands, with decreasing fire frequencies in chaparral, mixed evergreen, and montane-mixed conifer. Some redwood forests also experienced very frequent fires, particularly the populations that are on relatively xeric sites. Fire was less frequent in moist, coastal conifer forests.

Native American ignitions presumably accounted for the most fire starts in this area, as lightning is infrequent during the summer months. Indian burning was interrupted in the mid 1860s largely because of the impacts of introduced diseases. Managers in this region must answer an important question: Should restoration and management objectives include the influence of past Native American ignitions? Because Native Americans were an integral component of this region for thousands of years it is logical that current plans should include their influences.

Removal of fire from coastal grasslands and Oregon white oak woodlands has dramatically changed these ecosystems. In the absence of fire, conifers can over-top, suppress, and eventually produce enough shade to kill Oregon white oak. Frequent surface fires also produced open savannas in the Bald Hills in Humboldt County. The use of fall-ignited prescribed fires should be used to enhance and maintain these ecosystems.

The majority of Bishop pine forests have not burned in the last 40 to 70 years because of fire suppression. The lack of fire could threaten the long-term existence of Bishop pine because it relies on high- and mixed-severity fires to prepare seed beds, enable the release of large quantities of seed, and remove the canopy thereby increasing the light reaching the forest floor. Conversely, fire at high frequency could extirpate this species because there would be insufficient time for the trees to produce viable seed between successive fires.

Redwood forests once experienced fire at different intervals depending on their geographic location. The wettest sites had long fire intervals, and drier sites had short fire intervals. Redwood sites that are in relatively dry areas should use fall-ignited prescribed fires to reintroduce fire as an ecosystem process. Some prescribed fire is presently occurring in parks in this area but this should be expanded. Although the redwood species may not be dependent on fire to perpetuate in these forests, its ecosystem structures and functions may well be.

Pre-European settlement fires were relatively frequent in Douglas-fir–tanoak forests due to their warmer, drier, inland locations and increased lightning activity at higher elevations. Fire suppression has reduced fire frequency, particularly in young-growth forests. The most significant change in old growth is the greater density of understory shrubs and trees that has increased vertical fuel continuity. This increase in vertical fuel continuity has increased the probability of high-severity crown fires. Past forest harvesting operations may have had the most influence on forest structure in this forest zone.

Fire has been an integral part of coastal prairie ecology and fire exclusion has led to undesirable consequences. Livestock grazing can mitigate some of these consequences (Hayes 2002), but effective management should include prescribed burning. The sparse published data on burning of coastal prairie in California combined with anecdotal evidence and evidence from outside the region suggest regular burning on a 3- to 5-year rotation will slow the invasion of some non-native species without reducing cover of existing native species. If the seed bank contains viable seeds of displaced native species, burning may stimulate increased cover of these species. To achieve satisfactory restoration on most sites, extensive reseeding of desirable native species is required, followed by a regular prescribed burning and/or grazing program (Evett 2002).

Scientific information on the influences of fire on the ecosystems of the North Coast bioregion should be expanded through adaptive management and experimentation. This area includes significant amounts of federal and state land along with the state's largest amount of industrial forests. Site-specific questions on fire's role in North Coast ecosystems need to be addressed on the full spectrum of private and public lands. Most fire-related research has been on public land and relatively little has been done on the extensive private lands found in this bioregion. More general ecologiclandscape questions such as species viability will have to be answered on a regional basis.

References

Adams, S., and J. O. Sawyer. n.d. Past fire incidence in mixed evergreen forests of northwest California. Unpublished draft. Humboldt State University, Arcata, CA.

Agee, J. K. 1993. Fire ecology of Pacific Northwest forests. Island Press, Covelo, CA.

Arno, S. F., and R. P. Hammerly. 1977. Northwest trees. The Mountaineers, Seattle, WA.

Automated lightning detection system. 1999. Program for climate, ecosystem, and fire application. In Desert Research Institute and USDI Bureau of Land Management, Reno, Nevada. Available: www.dri.edu/Programs/CEFA/Cefa_Products/cefaprod_index.htm.

Azevedo, J., and D. L. Morgan. 1974. Fog precipitation in coastal California forests. Ecology 55:1135–1141.

Bailey, R. G. 1995. Description of the ecoregions of the United States, 2nd ed. U. S. Department of Agriculture, Forest Service, Washington, D.C.

Barnhardt, S. J., J. R. McBride, and P. Warner. 1996. Invasion of northern oak woodlands by *Pseudotsuga menziesii* (Mirb.) Franco in the Sonoma Mountains of California. Madroño 43:28–45.

Barr, J., T. R. Horton, A. M. Kretzer, and T. D. Bruns. 1999. Mycorrhizal colonization of *Pinus muricata* from resistant propagules after a stand replacing wildfire. New Phytol. 143:409–418.

Barrett, L. A. 1935. A record of forest and field fires in California from the days of the early explorers to the creation of the forest reserves. Report to the Regional Forester, October 14, 1935. U.S. Department of Agriculture, Forest Service, California Region, San Francisco, CA.

Becking, R. W. 1967. The ecology of the coastal redwood forest of northern California and the impact of the 1964 floods upon redwood vegetation. National Science Foundation grant GB-3468, Arcata, CA.

Belsher, J. B. 1999. Coastal shrublands of Humboldt and Del Norte Counties, California. Master's thesis. Humboldt State University, Arcata, CA.

Bicknell, S. H., A. T. Austin, D. J. Bigg, and R. P. Godar. 1992. Late prehistoric vegetation patterns at six sites in coastal California. Bulletin of the Ecological Society of America 73:112.

Bicknell, S. H., R. P. Godar, D. J. Bigg, and A. T. Austin. 1993. Salt Point State Park prehistoric vegetation. Final report, interagency agreement no. 88-11-013. California Department of Parks and Recreation, Arcata, CA.

Bingham, B. B. 1984. Decaying logs as a substrate for conifer regeneration in an upland old-growth redwood forest. MS. Humboldt State University, Arcata, CA.

Bivin, M. M. 1986. A fifth subspecies of lodgepole pine in northwest California and southwest Oregon. MA. Humboldt State University, Arcata, CA.

Blackburn, T. C., and K. Anderson (eds.). 1993. Before the wilderness: environmental management by Native Californians. Ballena Press, Menlo Park, CA.

Borchert, M., D. Segotta, and M. D. Purser. 1988. Coast redwood ecological types of southern Monterey County, California. Gen. Tech. Rep. PSW-107. U.S. Department of Agriculture, Forest Service, Pacific Southwest Forest and Range Experiment Station, Berkeley, CA.

Brown, P. M., and W. T. Baxter. 2003. Fire history in coast redwood forests of Jackson Demonstration State Forest, Mendocino coast, California. Northwest Science 77:147–158.

Brown, P. M., M. W. Kaye, and D. Buckley. 1999. Fire history in Douglas-fir and coast redwood forests at Point Reyes National Seashore, California. Northwest Science 73:205–216.

Brown, P. M., and T. W. Swetnam. 1994. A cross-dated fire history from coast redwood near Redwood National Park, California. Canadian Journal of Forest Research 24:21–31.

Burns, R. M., and B. H. Honkala. 1990. Silvics of North America. Vol. 2. Hardwoods. Agriculture Handbook 654. U.S. Department of Agriculture, Forest Service, Washington, DC.

CDF-FRAP. 2001. Fire Perimeters. In CA Dept. of Forestry and Fire Protection, USDA Forest Service.

Clar, C. R. 1969. Evolution of California's wildland fire protection system. California State Board of Forestry, Sacramento.

Cooper, D. W. 1965. The coast redwood and its ecology. University of California, Agricultural Extension Service, Berkeley.

Critchfield, W. B. 1980. Genetics of lodgepole pine. Research Paper WO-37. U.S. Department of Agriculture, Forest Service, Washington, DC.

Critchfield, W. B., and E. L. Little. 1966. Geographic distribution of the pines of the world. P. 97 in Misc. Publ. 991. U.S. Department of Agriculture, Forest Service, Washington, DC.

Daubenmire, R., and J. Daubenmire. 1975. The community status of the coastal redwood *Sequoia sempervirens*. Report Redwood National Park.

Davidson, J. G. N. 1971. Pathological problems in redwood regeneration from seed. Ph.D. University of California, Berkeley.

Dawson, T. E. 1998. Fog in the California redwood forest: ecosystem inputs and use by plants. Oecologia 117:476–485.

Del Tredici, P. 1998. Lignotubers in Sequoia sempervirens: development and ecological significance. Madroño 45:255–260.

Elford, R. C., and M. R. McDonough. 1964. The climate of Humboldt and Del Norte Counties. Agricultural Extension Service, University of California, Eureka.

Evett, R. R. 2000. Research on the pre-European settlement vegetation of the Sea Ranch coastal terraces. Final report, unpublished. Sea Ranch Association.

Evett, R. R. 2002. Sea Ranch grassland vegetation inventory and monitoring program associated with the prescribed burn program. Final report, unpublished. Sea Ranch.

Fahnestock, G. R., and J. K. Agee. 1983. Biomass consumption and smoke production by prehistoric fires in western Washington. Journal of Forestry 81:653–657.

Finney, M. A. 1990. Fire history from the redwood forests of Bolinas Ridge and Kent Lake Basin in the Marin Municipal Water District. In Vegetation and fire management baseline studies: The Marin Municipal Water District and the Marin County Open Space District (Northridge Lands), unpublished report. Leonard Charles and Associates and Wildland Resource Management, Marin County, California.

Finney, M. A., and R. E. Martin. 1989. Fire history in a *Sequoia sempervirens* forest at Salt Point State Park, California. Canadian Journal of Forest Research 19:1451–1457.

Finney, M. A., and R. E. Martin. 1992. Short-fire intervals recorded by redwoods at Annadel State Park. Madroño 39:251–262.

Finney, M. A., and R. E. Martin. 1993. Modeling effects of prescribed fire on young-growth coast redwood trees. Canadian Journal of Forest Research 23:1125–1135.

Fisher, R. T., H. von Schrenk, and A. D. Hopkins. 1903. The redwood. A study of the redwood. U.S. Department of Agriculture, Bur. For. Bull. No. 38.

Foiles, M. W., R. T. Graham, and D. F. Olson. 1990. *Abies grandis* (Dougl. ex D. Don) Lindl. Grand fir. P. 52–59 in R. M. Burns and B. H. Honkala (eds.), Silvics of North America. Volume 1, Conifers. Agriculture Handbook 654. U.S. Department of Agriculture, Forest Service, Washington, DC.

Foin, T. C., and M. M. Hektner. 1986. Secondary succession and the fate of native species in a California coastal prairie community. Madroño 33:189–206.

Fox, L. 1988. A classification, map, and volume estimate for coast redwood forest in California. The Forest and Rangeland Resources Assessment Program, California Department of Forestry and Fire Protection, Sacramento.

Franklin, J. F., and C. T. Dyrness. 1973. Natural vegetation of Oregon and Washington. U.S. Department of Agriculture, Forest Service, Pacific Northwest Forest and Range Experiment Station, General Technical Report, PNW-8, Portland, OR.

Fritz, E. 1931. The role of fire in the redwood region. Journal of Forestry 29:939–950.

Fritz, E. 1938. Growth of redwood trees left after selective logging. Timberman 39:14–16, 53–55.

Fritz, E. 1945. Twenty years' growth on a redwood sample plot. Journal of Forestry 43:30–36.

Fujimori, T. 1977. Stem biomass and structure of a mature *Sequoia sempervirens* stand on the Pacific Coast on northern California. J. Jpn. For. Soc. 59:435–441.

Gilligan, J. P. 1966. Land use history of the Bull Creek Basin. P. 42–57 in Proceedings of the symposium, Management for park preservation: a case study at Bull Creek, Humboldt Redwoods State Park, California. School of Forestry, University of California, Berkeley.

Green, S. 1999. Structure and dynamics of a coastal dune forest at Humboldt Bay, California. MA. Humboldt State University, Arcata, CA.

Greenlee, J. M. 1983. Vegetation, fire history and fire potential of Big Basin Redwoods State Park, California. Ph.D. University of California, Santa Cruz.

Greenlee, J. M., and J. H. Langenheim. 1990. Historic fire regimes and their relation to vegetation patterns in the Monterey Bay Area of California. American Midland Naturalist 124:239–253.

Griffin, J. R. 1980. Sprouting in fire damaged valley oaks, Chews Ridge, California. P. 219–219 in T. R. Plumb (ed.), Proceedings of the symposium on the ecology, management, and utilization of California oaks; June 26–28, 1979; General Technical Report PSW-44. U.S. Department of Agriculture, Forest Service, Pacific Southwest Forest and Range Experiment Station, Claremont, CA.

Griffin, J. R., and W. B. Critchfield. 1972. The distribution of forest trees in California. Research Paper, PSW-82 U.S. Department of Agriculture, Forest Service, Pacific Southwest Forest and Range Experiment Station, Berkeley.

Griffith, R. S. 1992. *Picea sitchensis*. U.S. Department of Agriculture, Forest Service, Rocky Mountain Research Station, Fire Sciences Laboratory. Fire Effects Information System, http://www.fs.fed.us/database/feis/.

Gripp, R. A. 1976. An appraisal of critical fire weather in northwestern California. MS. Humboldt State University, Arcata, CA.

Hanson, J. 2002. Vegetation responses to fire created edge environments and subsequent salvage logging in Douglas-fir/hardwood forests, Klamath Mountains, California. MS. Humboldt State University, Arcata, CA.

Harden, D. R. 1997. The Coast Ranges: mountains of complexity. P. 252–288 in California geology. Prentice Hall, Inc., Upper Saddle River, NJ.

Harmon, M. E., J. F. Franklin, F. J. Swanson, P. Sollins, S. V. Gregory, J. D. Lattin, N. H. Anderson, S. P. Cline, N. G. Aumen, J. R. Sedell, G. N. Lienkaemper, K. Cromack, and K. W. Cummins. 1986. Ecology of coarse woody debris in temperate ecosystems. P. 133–302 in Advances in Ecological Research. Academic Press, Inc., Orlando, FL.

Harrington, C. A. 1990. *Alnus rubra* Bong. Red alder. P. 116–123 in R. M. Burns and B. H. Honkala (ed.), Silvics of North America. Volume 2, Hardwoods. Agriculture Handbook 654. U.S. Department of Agriculture, Forest Service, Washington, DC.

Harris, A. S. 1990. *Picea sitchensis* (Bong.) Carr. Sitka spruce. P. 260–267 in R. M. Burns and B. H. Honkala (eds),. Silvics of North America. Volume 1, Conifers. Agriculture Handbook 654. U.S. Department of Agriculture, Forest Service, Washington, DC.

Hastings, M. S., S. J. Barnhardt, and J. R. McBride. 1997. Restoration management of northern oak woodlands. U.S. Department of Agriculture, Forest Service General Technical Report PSW-160, Albany, CA.

Hatch, D. A., J. W. Bartolome, J. S. Fehmi, and D. S. Hillyard. 1999. Effects of burning and grazing on a coastal California grassland. Restoration Ecology 7:376–381.

Hayes, G. L. 1958. Silvical characteristics of Port Orford-cedar. Silvical Series No. 7. U.S. Department of Agriculture, Forest Service, Pacific Northwest Forest and Range Experiment Station, Portland, OR.

Heady, H. F., T. C. Foin, M. M. Hektner, M. G. Barbour, D. W. Taylor, and W. J. Barry. 1988. Coastal prairie and northern coastal scrub. P. 733–760 in M. G. Barbour and J. Major (eds.), Terrestrial vegetation of California, new expanded edition. California Native Plant Society, Sacramento.

Hektner, M. M., and T. C. Foin. 1977. Vegetation analysis of a northern California prairie: Sea Ranch, Sonoma County, California. Madroño 24:83–103.

Hermann, R. K., and D. P. Lavender. 1990. *Pseudotsuga menziesii* (Mirb.) Franco Douglas-fir. P. 527–540 in R. M. Burns and B. H. Honkala (eds.), Silvics of North America. Volume 1, Conifers. Agriculture Handbook 654. U.S. Department of Agriculture, Forest Service, Washington, DC.

Howard, J. L., and K. C. Aleksoff. 2000. *Abies grandis*. U.S. Department of Agriculture, Forest Service, Rocky Mountain Research Station, Fire Sciences Laboratory (2001, October). Fire Effects Information System, http://www.fs.fed.us/database/feis/.

Hull, M. K., C. A. O'Dell, and M. J. Schroeder. 1966. Critical fire weather patterns—their frequency and levels of fire danger. U. S. Department of Agriculture, Forest Service, Pacific Southwest Forest and Range Experiment Station, Berkeley, CA.

Hunter, J. C. 1997. Fourteen years mortality in two old-growth *Pseudotsuga-Lithocarpus* forests in northern California. Journal of the Torrey Botanical Society 124:273–279.

Hunter, J. C., V. T. Parker, and M. G. Barbour. 1999. Understory light and gap dynamics in an old-growth forested watershed in coastal California. Madroño 46:1–6.

Impara, P. C. 1997. Spatial and temporal patterns of fire in the forests of the central Oregon Coast Range. Ph.D. Oregon State University, Corvallis.

Jacobs, D. F. 1987. The ecology of redwood (*Sequoia sempervirens* [D. Don] Endl.) seedling establishment. Ph.D. University of California, Berkeley.

Jacobs, D. F., D. W. Cole, and J. R. McBride. 1985. Fire history and perpetuation of natural coast redwood ecosystems. Journal of Forestry 83:494–497.

Jepson, W. L. 1910. The silva of California. The University Press, Berkeley, CA.

Johnson, L. C. 1974. *Cupressus* L. Cypress. P. 363–369 in C. S. Schopmeyer (ed.), Seeds of woody plants in the United States. Agriculture Handbook 450. U.S. Department of Agriculture, Forest Service, Washington, DC.

Keeley, J. E. 1981. Distribution of lightning and man caused wildfires in California. P. 431–437 in C. E. Conrad and W. C. Oechel (eds.), Proceedings of the symposium on Dynamics and management of Mediterranean-type ecosystems. General Technical Report GTR-PSW-58. U.S. Department of Agriculture, Forest Service, Pacific Southwest Forest and Range Experiment Station, Berkeley, CA.

Keter, T. S. 1995. Environmental history and cultural ecology of the North Fork of the Eel River Basin, California. U.S. Department of Agriculture Forest Service, Pacific Southwest Region, R5-EM-TP-002, Eureka, CA.

Keter, T. S. 2002. Telephone conversation with author, May 8. Arcata, CA.

Krugman, S. L., and J. L. Jenkinson. 1974. Pinaceae—pine family. P. 598–637 in C. S. Schopmeyer (ed.), Seeds of woody plants in the United States. Agriculture Handbook 450. U.S. Department of Agriculture, Forest Service, Washington, DC.

Lewis, H. T. 1993. Patterns of Indian burning in California: ecology and ethnohistory. P. 55–116 in T. C. Blackburn and K. Anderson (eds.), Before the wilderness: environmental management by Native Californians. Ballena Press, Menlo Park, CA.

Little, E. L. 1971. Atlas of United States trees: Volume I. Conifers and important hardwoods. U.S. Department of Agriculture, Forest Service Miscellaneous Publication No. 1146, Washington, DC.

Little, E. L. 1979. Checklist of United States trees (native and naturalized). Agriculture Handbook 541. USDA Forest Service, Washington, DC.

Long, C. J., and C. Whitlock. 1999. A 4600-year-long fire and vegetation record from Sitka spruce forests of the Oregon Coast Range. P. 440 in Conference Geological Society of America, 1999 annual meeting, Denver, CO, Oct. 25–28, 1999. Geological Society of America.

Long, C. J., C. Whitlock, P. J. Bartlein, and S. H. Millspaugh. 1998. A 9000-year fire history from the Oregon Coast Range, based on a high-resolution charcoal study. Canadian Journal of Forest Research 28:774–787.

Lotan, J. E., and W. B. Critchfield. 1990. *Pinus contorta* Dougl. ex Loud. lodgepole pine. P. 302–315 in R. M. Burns and B. H.

Honkala (eds.), Silvics of North America. Volume I. Conifers. Agriculture Handbook 654. U.S. Department of Agriculture, Forest Service, Washington, DC.

Mahony, T.M. 1999. Old-growth forest associations in the northern range of redwood. MS. Humboldt State University, Arcata, CA.

Mahony, T.M., and J.D. Stuart. 2001. Old-growth forest associations in the northern range of coastal redwood. Madroño 47:53–60.

McCune, B. 1988. Ecological diversity in North American pines. American Journal of Botany 75:353–368.

McDonald, P.M., D. Minore, and T. Atzet. 1983. Southwestern Oregon–Northern California hardwoods. P. 29–32 in R.M. Burns (ed.), Silvicultural systems for the major forest types of the United States. Agriculture Handbook 445. U.S. Department of Agriculture, Forest Service, Washington, DC.

McDonald, P.M., and J.C. Tappeiner. 1987. Silviculture, ecology, and management of tanoak in northern California. P. 64–70 in T.R. Plumb and N.H. Pillsbury (eds.), Proceedings of the symposium on multiple-use management of California's hardwood resources. U.S. Department of Agriculture, Forest Service, Pacific Southwest Forest and Range Experiment Station, San Luis Obispo, CA.

McPherson, B.A., D.L. Wood, A.J. Storer, P. Svihra, D.M. Rizzo, N.M. Kelly, and R.B. Standiford. 2000. Oak mortality syndrome: sudden death of oaks and tanoaks. Tree Notes 26:1–6.

Metcalf, W. 1921. Notes on the bishop pine (*Pinus muricata*). Journal of Forestry 19:886–902.

Miles, S.R., and C.B. Goudey. 1997. Ecological subregions of California: section and subsection descriptions. U.S. Department of Agriculture, Forest Service, Pacific Southwest Region, San Francisco, CA.

Mohr, J.A., C. Whitlock, and C.N. Skinner. 2000. Postglacial vegetation and fire history, eastern Klamath Mountains, California, USA. The Holocene 10:587–601.

Munz, P.A., and D.D. Keck. 1959. A California flora. University of California Press, Berkeley and Los Angeles.

Noss, R.F. 2000. The redwood forest: history, ecology, and conservation of the coast redwoods. Island Press, Washington, DC.

O'Dell, T.E. 1996. Silviculture in the Redwood Region: an historical perspective. P. 15–17 in J. LeBlanc (ed.), Proceedings of the Conference on coast redwood forest ecology and management. University of California Cooperative Extension, Humboldt State University, Arcata, CA.

Oliphant, J.M. 1992. Geographic variation of lodgepole pine in Northern California. MA. Humboldt State University, Arcata, CA.

Oneal, C.B., L. Fox, J.D. Stuart, and S.J. Steinberg. 2004. Modern fire history of the coast redwood forest. In Mixed severity fire regimes: ecology and management. Association for Fire Ecology, Spokane, WA.

Olson, D.F., D.F. Roy, and G.A. Walters. 1990. *Sequoia sempervirens* (D. Don) Endl., redwood. P. 541–551 in R.M. Burns and B.H. Honkala (eds.), Silvics of North America, Volume 1, Conifers. U.S. Government Printing Office, Washington, DC.

Osburn, V.R., and P. Lowell. 1972. A review of redwood harvesting. State of California, The Resources Agency, Department of Conservation, Division of Forestry, Sacramento, CA.

Ostoja, S.M., and R.C. Klinger. 1999. The relationship of bishop pine cone morphology to serotiny on Santa Cruz Island, California. In D.R. Brown, K.L. Mitchell, and H.W.

Chaney (eds.), Proceedings of the 5th Channel Islands Symposium. Santa Barbara Museum of Natural History.

Packee, E.C. 1990. *Tsuga heterophylla* (Raf.) Sarg., western hemlock. P. 613–622 in R.M. Burns and B.H. Honkala (eds.), Silvics of North America. Volume I. Conifers. U.S. Department of Agriculture, Forest Service, Washington, DC.

Pillers, M.D. 1989. Fine fuel dynamics of old-growth redwood forests. MS. Humboldt State University, Arcata, CA.

Pillers, M.D., and J.D. Stuart. 1993. Leaf-litter accretion and decomposition in interior and coastal old-growth redwood stands. Canadian Journal of Forest Research 23:552–557.

Plumb, T.R., and P.M. McDonald. 1981. Oak management in California. General Technical Report PSW-54. U.S. Department of Agriculture, Forest Service, Pacific Southwest Forest and Range Experiment Station, Berkeley, CA.

Pyne, S.J., P.L. Andrews, and R.D. Laven. 1996. Introduction to wildland fire, second ed. John Wiley and Sons, Inc., New York.

Reed, L.J., and N.G. Sugihara. 1987. Northern oak woodlands— ecosystem in jeopardy or is it already too late? In T.R. Plumb and N.H. Pillsbury (eds.), Symposium on multiple-use management of California's hardwood resources. U.S. Department of Agriculture, Forest Service, Pacific Southwest Forest and Range Experiment Station, San Luis Obispo, CA.

Rice, C.L. 1985. Fire history and ecology of the North Coast Range Preserve. P. 367–372 in J.E. Lotan, B.M. Kilgore, W.C. Fischer, and R.W. Mutch (eds.), Wilderness Fire Symposium. U.S. Department of Agriculture, Forest Service, Intermountain Forest and Range Experiment Station, Missoula, MT.

Roy, D.F. 1957. Silvical characteristics of tanoak. Technical Paper 22. U.S. Department of Agriculture, Forest Service, California [Pacific Southwest] Forest and Range Experiment Station, Berkeley, CA.

Roy, D.F. 1966. Silvical characteristics of redwood (*Sequoia sempervirens* [D. Don] Endl.). U.S. Department of Agriculture Forest Service Pacific Southwest Forest and Range Experiment Station Research Paper PSW-28.

Sawyer, J.O., J. Gray, G.J. West, D.A. Thornburgh, R.F. Noss, J.H. Engbeck Jr., B.G. Marcot, and R. Raymond. 2000. History of redwood and redwood forests. P. 7–38 in R.F. Noss (ed.), The redwood forest: history, ecology, and conservation of the coast redwoods. Island Press, Washington, DC.

Sawyer, J.O., D.A. Thornburgh, and J.R. Griffin. 1988. Mixed evergreen forest. P. 359–381 in M.G. Barbour and J. Major (eds.), Terrestrial vegetation of California, new expanded edition. California Native Plant Society, Sacramento, CA.

Show, S.B., and E.I. Kotok. 1923. Forest fires in California 1911–1920: an analytical study. U.S. Department of Agriculture, Department Circular 243, Washington, DC.

Stephens, S.L., and D.L. Fry. 2005. Fire history in coast redwood stands in the northeastern Santa Cruz Mountains, California. Fire Ecology 1:2–19.

Stephens, S.L., and W.J. Libby. 2006. Anthropogenic fire and bark thickness in coastal and island pine populations from Alta and Baja California. Journal of Biogeography 33:648–652.

Stephens, S.L. and L.W. Ruth. 2005. Federal forest fire policy in the United States. Ecological Applications, 15(2):532–542.

Stone, E.C., and R. Vasey. 1968. Preservation of coast redwood on alluvial flats. Science 159:157–161.

Stromberg, M.R., P. Kephart, and V. Yadon. 2001. Composition, invisibility, and diversity in coastal California grasslands. Madroño 48:236–252.

Strothmann, R. O., and D. F. Roy. 1984. Regeneration of Douglas-fir in the Klamath Mountains Region, California, and Oregon. General Technical Report PSW-81. U.S. Department of Agriculture, Forest Service, Pacific Southwest Forest and Range Experiment Station, Berkeley, CA.

Stuart, J. D. 1986. Redwood fire ecology. Final report California Department of Parks and Recreation, Weott, CA.

Stuart, J. D. 1987. Fire history of an old-growth forest of *Sequoia sempervirens* (Taxodiaceae) in Humboldt Redwoods State Park, California. Madroño 34:128–141.

Stuart, J. D., and L. Fox. 1993. Humboldt Redwoods State Park unit prescribed fire management plan. California Department of Parks and Recreation, Arcata, CA.

Stuart, J. D., M. C. Grifantini, and L. Fox. 1993. Early successional pathways following wildfire and subsequent silvicultural treatment in Douglas-fir/hardwood forests, NW California. Forest Science 39:561–572.

Stuart, J. D., and L. A. Salazar. 2000. Fire history of white fir forests in the coastal mountains of northwestern California. Northwest Science 74:280–285.

Stuart, J. D., and J. O. Sawyer. 2001. Trees and shrubs of California. University of California Press, Berkeley.

Sugihara, N. G., and L. J. Reed. 1987. Prescribed fire for restoration and maintenance on Bald Hills oak woodlands. In T. R. Plumb and N. H. Pillsbury (eds.), Symposium on multiple-use management of California's hardwood resources. U.S. Department of Agriculture, Forest Service, Pacific Southwest Forest and Range Experiment Station, San Luis Obispo, CA.

Sugihara, N. G., L. J. Reed, and J. M. Lenihan. 1987. Vegetation of the Bald Hills oak woodlands, Redwood National Park. Madroño 34:193–208.

Talbert, B. J. 1996. Management and analysis of 30-year continuous forest inventory data on the Six Rivers National Forest. MS. Humboldt State University, Arcata, CA.

Tappeiner, J. C., P. M. McDonald, and D. F. Roy. 1990. *Lithocarpus densiflorus* (Hook. & Arn.) Rehd. Tanoak. In R. M. Burns and B. H. Honkala (eds.), Silvics of North America: Volume 2, Hardwoods, Agriculture Handbook 654. U.S. Department of Agriculture, Forest Service, Washington, DC.

Tesky, J. L. 1992. *Tsuga heterophylla*. In U.S. Department of Agriculture, Forest Service, Rocky Mountain Research Station, Fire Sciences Laboratory. Fire Effects Information System, http://www.fs.fed.us/database/feis.

Uchytil, R. J. 1989. *Alnus rubra*. In U.S. Department of Agriculture, Forest Service, Rocky Mountain Research Station, Fire Sciences Laboratory (2001, October). Fire Effects Information System, http://www.fs.fed.us/database/feis.

Vale, T. R. 2002. The pre-European landscape of the United States: pristine or humanized? P. 1–39 in T. R. Vale (ed.), Fire, native peoples, and the natural landscape. Island Press, Washington, D.C.

Van Dersal, W. R. 1938. Native woody plants of the United States, their erosion control and wildlife values. U.S. Department of Agriculture, Washington, DC.

van Wagtendonk, J. W., and D. R. Cayan. 2007. Temporal and spatial distribution of lightning strikes in California in relationship to large-scale weather patterns. Fire Ecology (in press).

Veirs, S. D. 1982. Coast redwood forest: stand dynamics, successional status, and the role of fire. P. 119–141 in J. E. Means (ed.), Proceedings of the symposium, Forest succession and stand development research in the northwest. Forest Research Laboratory, Oregon State University, Corvallis.

Vogl, R. J., W. P. Armstrong, K. L. White, and K. L. Cole. 1977. The closed-cone pines and cypress. P. 295–358 in M. G. Barbour and J. Major (eds.), Terrestrial vegetation of California. John Wiley and Sons, New York.

Walsh, R. A. 1995. Deschampsia cespitosa. U.S. Department of Agriculture, Forest Service, Rocky Mountain Research Station, Fire-Sciences Laborator. Fire Effects Information System, http://www.fs.fed.us/database/feis.

Weaver, J. E., and F. C. Clements. 1929. Plant ecology. McGraw-Hill Book Company, Inc., New York.

Western Region Climate Center. 2001. Western U.S. climate historical summaries: Crescent City and Angwin Pacific Union College. Desert Research Institute, http://www.wrcc.dri.edu/Summary/Climsmnca.html.

Whitlock, C., and M. A. Knox. 2002. Prehistoric burning in the Pacific Northwest: human versus climatic influences. P. 195–231 in T. R. Vale (ed.), Fire, native peoples, and the natural landscape. Island Press, Washington, DC.

Whittaker, R. H. 1960. Vegetation of the Siskiyou Mountains, Oregon and California. Ecological Monographs 30:279–338.

Wills, R. D., and J. D. Stuart. 1994. Fire history and stand development of a Douglas-fir/hardwood forest in northern California. Northwest Science 68:205–212.

Zedler, P. H. 1986. Closed-cone conifers of the chaparral. Fremontia 14:14–17.

Zinke, P. J. 1988. The redwood forest and associated north coast forests. P. 679–698 in M. G. Barbour and J. Major (eds.), Terrestrial vegetation of California: new exp. ed. Wiley-Interscience, 1977. Reprint, Sacramento: California Native Plant Society, New York.

Zobel, D. B. 1990. *Chamaecyparis lawsoniana* (A. Murr.) Parl. Port Orford-cedar. P. 88–96 in R. M. Burns and B. H. Honkala (eds.), Silvics of North America. Volume 1, Conifers. Agriculture Handbook 654. U.S. Department of Agriculture, Forest Service, Washington, DC.

Zobel, D. B., L. F. Roth, and G. M. Hawk. 1985. Ecology, pathology, and management of Port Orford-cedar (*Chamaecyparis lawsoniana*). U.S. Department of Agriculture, Forest Service, Pacific Northwest Forest and Range Experiment Station, Portland, OR.

Zouhar, K. L. 2000. Festuca idahoensis. U.S. Department of Agriculture, Forest Service, Rocky Mountain Research Station, Fire-Sciences Laboratory, Fire Effects Information System, http://www.fs.fed.us/database/feis.

CHAPTER 9

Klamath Mountains Bioregion

CARL N. SKINNER, ALAN H. TAYLOR, AND JAMES K. AGEE

Fires ... have been ground fires, and easily controlled. A trail will
sometimes stop them.

R. B. WILSON, 1904

Description of Bioregion

The Klamath Mountains bioregion makes up a major portion of northwestern California continuing into southwestern Oregon to near Roseburg. In California, the bioregion lies primarily between the Northern California Coast
bioregion on the west and the southern Cascade Range to
the east. The southern boundary is made up of the Northern California Coast Ranges and Northern California Interior Coast Ranges (Miles and Goudey 1997). The very steep
and complex terrain of the Klamath Mountains covers
approximately 22,500 km² (8,690 mi²), or 6% of California.
The bioregion includes the Klamath and Trinity River systems, the headwaters of the Sacramento River, the most
extensive exposure of ultramafic rocks in North America
(Kruckeberg 1984), and the most diverse conifer forests in
North America (Cheng 2004) (Map 9.1).

Physical Geography

The Klamath Mountains have been deeply dissected by the
Klamath, McCloud, Sacramento, and Trinity Rivers with no
consistent directional trends. Only two sizable alluvial valleys, Scott Valley and Hayfork Valley, occur here (Oakeshott
1971, McKee 1972). Elevations in the Klamath Mountains
range from 30 m (100 ft) to 2,755 m (9,038 ft). From north
to south, several prominent ranges or ridge systems comprise
the Klamath Mountains with Mt. Eddy being the highest
peak (Oakeshott 1971, McKee 1972). The crests of these ridge
systems are usually between 1,500 m (4,900 ft) and 2,200 m
(7,200 ft) (Irwin 1966).

The complexity of the geology and terrain has a strong
influence on the structure, composition, and productivity of
vegetation in the Klamath Mountains (Whittaker 1960). The
topography and vegetation influence fire regimes. Spatial
variation in soil productivity combined with steep gradients
of elevation and changes in slope aspect across landscapes
control the connectivity, structure, and rates of fuel accumulation.

Climatic Patterns

The climate of the Klamath Mountains is mediterranean,
characterized by wet, cool winters and dry, warm summers.
However, the local expression of this climate regime is
remarkably variable due to a strong west to east moisture and
temperature gradient caused by proximity to the Pacific
Ocean and steep elevation gradients that influence temperature and the spatial pattern of precipitation via orographic
effects. The contemporary climatic phase appears to have
become established about 3,500–4,000 years ago (West 1985,
1988, 1989, 1990; Mohr et al. 2000).

Table 9.1 shows normal January and July maxima and
minima temperatures for Willow Creek (west), Sawyers Bar
(central), Dunsmuir (east), and other selected stations from
west to east. These data demonstrate the warm temperatures
that exist during the long, annual summer drought. These
temperature records in the Klamath Mountains are only from
valleys or canyon bottoms because no regularly reporting stations are located above 1,000 m (3,280 ft).

Although most precipitation falls between October and
April, there is considerable local and regional geographic
variation in the amount of annual precipitation. Generally,
less precipitation falls in valleys and canyons than in the surrounding uplands with strong gradients over short horizontal distances. Precipitation declines with distance from the
coast in both the northern and southern Klamaths. The driest areas occur along the eastern edge of the range adjacent
to the Shasta and Sacramento Valleys. However, there is no
west to east precipitation gradient in the eastern Klamaths in
the watersheds of the Sacramento, McCloud, and Pit
Rivers. The high precipitation of the eastern-most Klamaths

MAP 9.1. Map of the Klamath Mountains. The Klamath bioregion includes the Trinity River watershed, western portion of the Klamath River watershed, and the headwaters of the Sacramento River.

TABLE 9.1

Average annual, January, and July precipitation and normal daily January and July maxima and
minima temperatures for representative stations (elevations noted) in the Klamath Mountains

	Average Precipitation cm (in)	Normal Daily Maximum Temperature °C (°F)	Normal Daily Minimum Temperature °C (°F)
Willow Creek (141 m)			
Annual	143.5 (56.5)		
January	24.3 (9.6)	11.1 (52)	1.5 (35)
July	0.4 (0.2)	34.7 (95)	11.5 (53)
Sawyers Bar (659 m)			
Annual	117.6 (46.3)		
January	21.6 (8.5)	9.1 (48)	−2.9 (27)
July	2.3 (0.9)	32.8 (91)	10.9 (52)
Fort Jones (830 m)			
Annual	57.6 (22.3)		
January	10.8 (4.3)	6.6 (44)	−5.1 (23)
July	0.9 (0.4)	32.9(91)	8.6(48)
Weaverville (610 m)			
Annual	101.2 (39.8)		
January	18.8 (7.4)	8.3 (47)	−2.8 (27)
July	0.5 (0.2)	34.2 (94)	9.6 (49)
Whiskeytown (367 m)			
Annual	160.4 (63.1)		
January	30.0 (11.8)	12.0 (54)	2.1 (36)
July	0.7 (0.3)	35.3 (96)	17.4 (63)
Dunsmuir (703 m)			
Annual	163.6 (64.4)		
January	29.7 (11.7)	9.9 (50)	−0.9 (30)
July	0.7 (0.3)	31.8 (89)	12.1 (54)

is probably caused by orographic uplift of moist air masses.
The eastern Klamaths are the first major range encountered
by southwesterly flowing winds moving northeast across the
Sacramento Valley. At higher elevations, most precipitation
falls as snow. The average annual early April snowpack depth
and water content for high-elevation sites in the Klamath
Mountains are shown in Table 9.2.

WEATHER SYSTEMS

Critical fire weather in the Klamath Mountains is generated
by conditions of both the California and Pacific Northwest
weather types described by Hull et al. (1966). Overall, critical
fire weather is associated with any weather condition that creates sustained periods of high-velocity winds with low humidity. In the Klamath Mountains, critical fire weather conditions
are created by three different weather patterns described by

Hull et al. (1966): (1) Pacific High–Post-Frontal (Post-Frontal),
(2) Pacific High–Pre-Frontal (Pre-Frontal), and (3) Subtropical
High Aloft (Subtropical High).

Post-Frontal conditions occur when high pressure following the passage of a cold front causes strong winds from the
north and northeast. Temperatures rise and humidity
declines with these winds. Examples of fires fanned by Post-
Frontal conditions occurred in 1999 when the Megram, east
of Hoopa, burned more than 57,000 ha (141,000 ac) and the
Jones fire, northeast of Redding near Lake Shasta, consumed
more than 900 structures while burning more than 10,000 ha
(25,000 ac).

Pre-Frontal conditions occur when strong, southwesterly
or westerly winds are generated by the dry, southern tail of a
rapidly moving cold front. Strong winds are the key here
because temperatures usually drop and relative humidity
rises as the front passes. These strong winds are able to spread

TABLE 9.2

Average April 1 snowpack data for representative courses ordered from
north to south (CCSS 2002)

	Elevation m (ft)	Snow Depth cm (in)	Water Content cm (in)
Etna Mountain	1,798 (5,900)	190.2 (74.9)	76.2 (30.0)
Sweetwater	1,783 (5,850)	94.2 (37.1)	34.5 (13.6)
Parks Creek	2,042 (6,700)	231.9 (91.3)	92.5 (36.4)
Deadfall Lakes	2,195 (7,200)	174.5 (68.7)	72.6 (28.6)
North Fork Sacramento R	2,103 (6,900)	153.9 (60.6)	59.9 (23.6)
Gray Rock Lakes	1,890 (6,200)	246.6 (53.8)	57.2 (22.5)
Middle Boulder 3	1,890 (6,200)	136.7 (97.1)	103.4 (40.7)
Wolford Cabin	1,875 (6,150)	218.7 (86.1)	91.4 (36.0)
Mumbo Basin	1,737 (5,700)	145.0 (57.1)	59.9 (23.6)
Whalan	1,646 (5,400)	124.5 (49.0)	53.1 (20.9)
Highland Lakes	1,829 (6,000)	172.5 (67.9)	74.9 (29.5)
Slate Creek	1,737 (5,700)	163.6 (64.4)	73.9 (29.1)
Red Rock Mountain	2,042 (6,700)	259.8 (102.3)	111.8 (44.0)
Bear Basin	1,981 (6,500)	197.6 (77.8)	84.8 (33.4)

fires rapidly through heavy fuels such as happened in 2001 when the Oregon fire west of Weaverville burned more than 650 ha (1,600 ac) and 13 homes.

Subtropical High conditions occur when the region is under the influence of descending air from high pressure that causes temperatures to rise and humidity to drop. In the Klamath Mountains, these conditions lead to fires controlled mostly by local topography. Subtropical High conditions also promote the development of strong temperature inversions that inhibit smoke from venting out of the canyons and valley bottoms. The combination of smoke and lack of vertical mixing created by strong inversions, especially following initiation of widespread lightning-caused fires, reduces fire intensity. Under Subtropical High conditions, fires create mainly low- to moderate-severity effects. An example of recent major fire episodes burning under these conditions includes the Hayfork fires in 1987 where 70% of the burned area sustained low- to moderate-severity fire effects (Weatherspoon and Skinner 1995). Fires burning above the inversion layer and immediately after dissipation of the inversion often burn at much higher intensity (Weatherspoon and Skinner 1995).

LIGHTNING

Lightning is common in the Klamath Mountains with 12.8 strikes (range 6.4–26.4)/yr/100 km^2 (33.7 strikes [range 16.8–69.4]/yr/100 mi^2). Lightning-caused fires have accounted for most area burned in recent decades (e.g., 1977, 1987, 1999, and 2002). Lightning may ignite hundreds of fires in a 24-hour period. As a result of the large number of simultaneous fires combined with poor access for fire-suppression forces, steep topography, and extensive strong canyon inversions (see above), widespread lightning events have contributed to

situations where fires burn for weeks to months and cover very large areas. For example, widespread lightning during the last week of August in 1987 ignited fires that ultimately burned more than 155,000 ha (380,000 ac). These fires burned until rain and snow extinguished them in November (Biswell 1989). The Biscuit fire, also caused by lightning and burned in both California and Oregon in 2002, burned more than 186,000 ha (450,000 ac).

Lightning occurrence increases with distance from the coast and with increasing elevation (van Wagtendonk and Cayan 2007). It is interesting to note that the two years with the least number of lightning strikes recorded—1987 and 1999—were the same two years with the greatest amount of area burned by lightning-caused fires during the period of lightning strike data (Fig. 9.1).

Though it seems counterintuitive, the number of lightning-caused fires in a region is not necessarily related to the number of lightning strikes. Storms that produce lightning-caused fires are associated with higher instability and higher dew point depression (drier air) than storms that produce the most lightning strikes (Rorig and Ferguson 1999, 2002). Additionally, in both 1987 and 1999, a single storm episode was responsible for nearly all of the area burned by lightning-caused fires.

Ecological Zones

The Klamath Mountains are an area of exceptional floristic diversity and complexity in vegetative patterns (Whittaker 1960, Stebbins and Major 1965). The diverse patterns of climate, topography, and parent materials in the Klamath Mountains create heterogeneous vegetation patterns more complex than that found in the Sierra Nevada or the Cascade

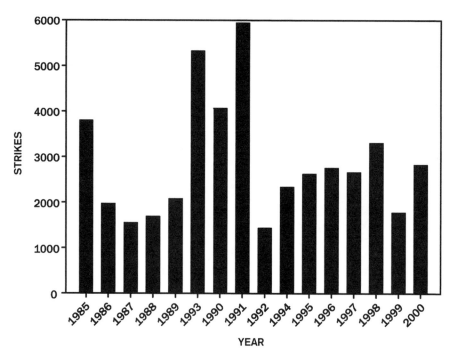

FIGURE 9.1. Variation in number of lightning strikes by year.

Range (Sawyer and Thornburgh 1977). The Klamath Mountains are thought to be of central importance in the long-term evolution and development of western forest vegetation because of this diversity and the mixing of floras from the Cascade/Sierra Nevada axis and the Oregon/California coastal mountains that intersect in the Klamath Mountains (Whittaker 1961, Smith and Sawyer 1988). Vegetation and species diversity generally increases with distance from the coast and species diversity is highest in woodlands with a highly developed herb strata (Whittaker 1960). Conifer forests and woodlands are found in all elevational zones throughout the bioregion.

The rugged, complex topography and resulting intermixing of vegetation in the Klamath Mountains defies a simple classification of ecological zones by elevation. Nevertheless, this chapter discusses three general zones: (1) a diverse lower montane zone of mixed conifer and hardwood forests, woodlands, and shrublands; (2) a mid-upper montane zone where white fir *(Abies concolor)* is abundant and hardwoods are less important; and (3) a subalpine zone where white fir, Douglas-fir *(Pseudotsuga menziesii* var. *menziesii)*, sugar pine *(Pinus lambertiana)*, and ponderosa pine *(Pinus ponderosa)* drop out and are replaced by upper montane and subalpine species such as Shasta red fir *(Abies magnifica* var. *shastensis)*, mountain hemlock *(Tsuga mertensiana)*, western white pine *(Pinus monticola)*, Jeffrey pine *(Pinus jeffreyi)*, whitebark pine *(Pinus albicaulis)*, lodgepole pine *(Pinus contorta* spp. *murrayana)*, foxtail pine *(Pinus balfouriana)*, and curl-leaf mountain-mahogany *(Cercocarpus ledifolius)*.

LOWER MONTANE

The lower- and mid-montane zone is characterized by a very complex and diverse intermixing of vegetation assemblages (Fig. 9.2). This heterogeneity is caused by rugged complex terrain, diverse lithology, and a diversity of fire regimes.

Grasslands are most extensive in the two alluvial valleys (e.g., Scott and Hayfork). Shrublands are found throughout the Klamath Mountains. At lower elevations, shrublands are found on warm or rocky, dry sites and on ultramafic and limestone-derived soils. Species that commonly dominate lower-montane shrublands are whiteleaf *(Arctostaphylos viscida)* and greenleaf manzanitas *(Arctostaphylos patula)*, Brewer oak *(Quercus garryana* var. *breweri)*, and deer brush *(Ceanothus intergerrimus)*. Shrublands also occupy extensive areas around historic mining districts, such as those near Lake Shasta and Whiskeytown Reservoirs where the combination of heavy cutting to support mining and air pollution from smelters drastically reduced site quality and increased soil erosion. The northern-most stands of chamise *(Adenostoma fasciculatum)* are found in the Whiskeytown area. Douglas-fir–dominated and mixed evergreen forests are found throughout this zone.

MID TO UPPER MONTANE

In the western Klamath Mountains are areas on upper slopes and ridgetops locally known as prairies supporting a dense sward of perennial grasses. Grasslands also occur on shallow ultramafic soils and on cemented glacial till, whereas wet montane meadows are scattered throughout the upper-montane and subalpine areas. Shrublands occur at higher elevations on poor sites and where severe fires have removed tree cover. Important shrubs here are tobacco brush *(Ceanothus velutinus* var. *velutinus)*, shrub tan oak *(Lithocarpus densiflorus* var. *echinoides)*, golden *(Chrysolepis chrysophylla)* and bush chinquapin *(Chrysolepis sempervirens)*, huckleberry oak *(Quercus vaccinifolia)*, and greenleaf manzanita.

Woodlands dominated or co-dominated by any combination of blue oak *(Quercus douglasii)*, Oregon white oak *(Quercus garryana)*, California black oak *(Quercus kelloggii)*, gray pine

FIGURE 9.2. Lower montane zone. This photo shows the diversity typical of the lower montane zone in the Klamath Mountains. This scene is from the McCloud River Canyon. Left side of photo shows Douglas-fir stands, California black oak stands and Brewer oak intermixed on soils derived from weathered metasediments. Right side of photo shows gray pine woodland, buck brush, and Brewer oak on soils derived from limestone. (Photo by Carl N. Skinner.)

FIGURE 9.3. Mid montane zone. Douglas-fir usually dominates conifer forests in this zone. Jud Creek looking north toward Hayfork Bally. (Photo by Carl Skinner, USDA Forest Service.)

(Pinus sabiniana), or ponderosa pine are found on sites similar to grasslands. Woodlands are also found on steep, dry, south- and west-facing slopes such as those along the Trinity River west of Junction City. Dry woodlands of ponderosa pine, western juniper *(Juniperus occidentalis* ssp. *occidentalis)*, Douglas-fir, Oregon white oak, and incense-cedar *(Calocedrus decurrens)* dominate sites around the Scott and Shasta Valleys. Woodlands are also common on harsh sites in the upper-montane zones where they may be dominated by western white pine, Jeffrey pine, incense-cedar, Shasta red fir, or curl-leaf mountain-mahogany.

The conifer component of montane forests can be quite diverse and up to 17 conifer species have been identified in some watersheds in the north central Klamath Mountains (Keeler-Wolf 1990). However, stands usually have Douglas-fir in combination with any of five other conifer species: sugar pine, ponderosa pine, incense-cedar, Jeffrey pine, and white fir (Fig. 9.3). Areas of ultramafic soils are an exception, however, and instead support stands usually dominated by Jeffrey pine or gray pine. Douglas-fir is the dominant conifer in the western portion of the range. Ponderosa pine becomes an important associate on drier sites and may co-dominate or even dominate sites in the eastern part of the range. White fir is of significant importance throughout except on ultramafics where Jeffrey pine becomes more important. With increasing elevation, white fir generally gives way to Shasta red fir and then mountain hemlock. Western white pine is commonly an important species throughout the upper montane areas.

The hardwood component of Klamath montane forests is equally diverse and distinguishes them from montane forests in the Sierra Nevada and Cascade Range. Hardwoods commonly present in the subcanopy include golden chinquapin, bigleaf maple *(Acer macrophyllum)*, Pacific madrone *(Arbutus menziesii)*, tanoak *(Lithocarpus densiflorus)*, California black oak, and canyon live oak *(Quercus chrysolepis)*. Tanoak and golden chinquapin, dominant hardwoods in the west, are replaced by California black oak in the central and eastern Klamath Mountains.

SUBALPINE

Subalpine woodlands and forests dominate the highest elevations in the Klamath Mountains (Fig. 9.4). There is no upper limit to this zone as trees are able to grow to the tops of the highest peaks (Sawyer and Thornburgh 1977). The alpine character of the higher elevations of the Klamath Mountains is primarily due to shallow soils (Sharp 1960) or soils derived from strongly ultramafic parent materials and not due to low temperatures that prevent forest growth (Sawyer and Thornburgh 1977). Forests in the subalpine zone are generally open, patchy woodlands of widely spaced trees with a discontinuous understory of shrubs and herbs. Extensive bare areas are common (Sawyer and Thornburgh 1977). However, dense stands are found on deeper soils.

Stands on mesic sites are dominated by mountain hemlock, whereas xeric sites are usually occupied by Shasta red fir (Sawyer and Thornburgh 1977, Keeler-Wolf 1990). Woodlands are also common on harsh sites in the upper-montane and subalpine zones where any mixture of western white pine, Jeffrey pine, whitebark pine, foxtail pine, mountain hemlock, or curl-leaf mountain-mahogany may occur.

Overview of Historic Fire Occurrence

Prehistoric Period

Vegetation assemblages have varied considerably over the Holocene, and there have been long periods (thousands of yrs) with assemblages unlike any found today. Contemporary vegetation assemblages coalesced approximately 3,000 to 4,000 years ago when the climate cooled and became moister compared to the previous several millennia (West 1985, 1988, 1989, 1990; Mohr et al. 2000). Because the dominant tree species have potential life spans of 500 to 1,000+ years (Brown 1996, 2002), the current forest assemblages have existed for only a few life spans of the dominant tree species.

Fire regimes have varied over millennia primarily due to variations in climate. The record of fire in the Klamath Mountains covers the post-glacial Holocene and extends back to about 13,000 to 15,000 years B.P. and is preserved as variation in fossil charcoal abundance in lake sediments (West 1985, 1988, 1989, 1990; Mohr et al. 2000; Daniels 2001; Whitlock et al. 2001; Briles 2003). The frequency of fire

episodes over this period track variation in precipitation and temperature (Whitlock et al. 2003). Fire episodes were more frequent during warm, dry periods such as the early Holocene and the Medieval Warm Period than in cool, wet periods (Whitlock 2001). Fire regimes characteristic of the pre-settlement period (i.e., 1600 A.D.–1850 A.D.) have been in place for approximately the last 1,000 years (Mohr et al. 2000). The fossil charcoal record indicates that the frequency of fire episodes per century, and millennia, has not been stable over the Holocene. Charcoal influx appears to be more closely related to trends in regional burning reflective of the amount of available biomass rather than to local fire frequency (Whitlock et al. 2004). Importantly, the paleoecological evidence suggests there is only a loose coupling between fire regimes and any particular vegetation assemblage (Whitlock et al. 2003).

Native people of the Klamath Mountains used fire in many ways: (1) to promote production of plants for food (e.g., acorns, berries, roots) and fiber (e.g., basket materials); (2) for ceremonial purposes; and (3) to improve hunting conditions (Lewis 1990, 1993; Pullen 1995). Though native ignitions appear to have been widespread, we do not know the extent of their influence on fire regimes and vegetation at broad scales.

Several fire history studies describe fire regimes in parts of the Klamath Mountains over the last few centuries (Agee 1991; Wills and Stuart 1994; Taylor and Skinner 1997, 1998, 2003; Stuart and Salazar 2000; Skinner 2003a, 2003b; Fry and Stephens 2006). These studies indicate there are two periods with distinctly different fire regimes: (1) the Native American period, which usually includes both the pre-historic and European settlement period, and (2) the fire suppression period. Though there is variation among sites as to when fire suppression became effective, the temporal patterns of fire occurrence in the pre–fire suppression period indicate that most stands experienced at least several fires each century. This suggests a general fire regime of frequent, low- to moderate-intensity fires.

Historic Period

Europeans began to explore the Klamath Mountains by the 1820s (Sullivan 1992, Pullen 1995). Following the 1848 discovery of gold along the Trinity River (Jackson 1964, Hoopes 1971), people of European, Asian, and other non-native cultures began to enter the Klamath Mountains in large numbers and permanently settle the area. Settlers are reported to have set fires to make travel easier, to clear ground for prospecting, to drive game, and to encourage forage production for sheep and cattle (Whittaker 1960). Though settlement is thought to have increased fire frequency and perhaps fire intensity, no increases in fire occurrence during the settlement period are evident in fire scar studies (Agee 1991; Wills and Stuart 1994; Taylor and Skinner 1998, 2003; Stuart and Salazar 2000). It may be that fires caused by settlers, either intentional or accidental, replaced fires ignited by Native Americans as the latter

FIGURE 9.4. A subalpine landscape looking southwest from Mount Eddy toward the Trinity Alps. Most of the trees in the foreground and middle ground are foxtail pines. (Photo by Carl N. Skinner.)

Thompson Ridge

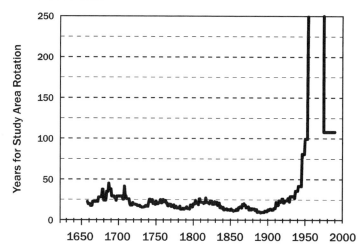

FIGURE 9.5. Charts showing the dramatic increase in fire rotations for two large study areas: Thompson Ridge near Happy Camp (Taylor and Skinner 1998), and Rusch/Jud creek watersheds near Hayfork (Taylor and Skinner 2003).

Judd & Rusch Creeks

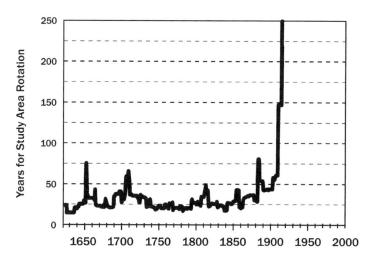

populations declined. In any case, many areas in the Klamath Mountains experienced a pre-settlement fire regime until fire suppression became effective sometime after establishment of the Forest Reserve system in 1905 (Shrader 1965). Fire suppression had become effective in more-accessible areas by the 1920s (Agee 1991; Stuart and Salazar 2000; Skinner 2003a, 2003b; Taylor and Skinner 2003; Fry and Stephens 2006), whereas fire suppression did not become effective in more remote areas until after 1945 (Wills and Stuart 1994, Taylor and Skinner 1998, Stuart and Salazar 2000).

Current Period

Fire occurrence declined dramatically with the onset of fire suppression. This is illustrated by the steep rise in fire rota-

tion for two large study areas: (1) near Happy Camp (Taylor and Skinner 1998) and (2) near Hayfork (Taylor and Skinner 2003) (Fig. 9.5).

Over the 400 years prior to effective fire suppression, there are no comparable fire-free periods when large landscapes experienced decades without fires simultaneously across the bioregion (Agee 1991; Wills and Stuart 1994; Taylor and Skinner 1998, 2003; Stuart and Salazar 2000; Skinner 2003a, 2003b).

Along with these changes in the fire regimes are changes in landscape vegetation patterns. Before fire suppression, fires of higher spatial complexity created openings of variable size within a matrix of forest that was generally more open than today (Taylor and Skinner 1998). This heterogeneous pattern has been replaced by a more homogenous pattern of smaller openings in a matrix of denser forests (Skinner 1995a). Thus, spatial complexity has been reduced. The ecological consequences of these changes are likely to be regional in scope, but they are not yet well understood. When modern fires burn under relatively stable atmospheric conditions conducive to thermal inversions in the narrow canyons, patterns of severity appear to be similar to historical patterns (Weatherspoon and Skinner 1995, Taylor and Skinner 1998). However, when inversions break and/or strong winds accompanied by low humidity occur, large areas of severe burn are possible such as those of the Megram fire in 1999 (Jimerson and Jones 2003) and the Biscuit fire in 2002 (USDA Forest Service 2003). The extent of the recent high-severity burns appears to be different than historic burning patterns. More area is burning at high intensity, and this is related, in part, to higher quantities and more homogeneous fuels caused by accumulation during the fire-suppression period.

Major Ecological Zones

Fire Regimes

The steep and complex topography of the Klamath Mountains provides for conditions that make it difficult to separate fire regimes by ecological zones. The most widespread fire regime in the Klamath Mountains is found from the lower montane through the mid-montane into the upper montane and it crosses ecological zones. Indeed, the patterns we present run the elevational gradient from the lowest canyon bottoms to nearly 2,000 m (6,250 ft). Generally, the steep, continuous slopes that run from low to higher elevations interact with changes in slope aspect and the dominating influence of the summer drought, to create conditions for frequent, mostly low- and moderate-intensity fires in most ecological zones in the Klamath Mountains. Given the importance of topographical controls on fire regimes in the Klamath Mountains we discuss the fire regimes more generally rather than assign them to specific ecological zones as in other bioregions.

TOPOGRAPHY

The long-term record of fires from intensive studies of fire scars, tree age-classes, and species composition demonstrates that topography strongly influenced Klamath Mountain fire regimes. The spatial pattern of fire occurrence appears to be related to differences in timing of fires from place to place and topographically related differences in fire severity rather than to fire frequency. With the exception of riparian zones (Skinner 2002a, 2003b), only small differences in median fire-return intervals have been found within watersheds of several thousand hectares despite considerable variability in elevation, slope aspect, and tree species composition; and they vary from landscape to landscape following no consistent pattern (Taylor and Skinner 1998, 2003).

Areas of similar timing of fires were found to be of several hundred hectares and were bounded by topographic features (e.g., ridgetops, aspect changes, riparian zones, lithologic units) that affect fuel structure, fuel moisture, and fire spread (Taylor and Skinner 2003). It is likely that the size of areas of similar fire occurrence probably varied from landscape to landscape depending on topographic complexity. Although areas separated by topographic boundaries often had similar fire return interval distributions, they often experienced fires in different years than in adjacent areas. The topographic boundaries between fire occurrence areas were not simple barriers to fire spread, but acted more like filters. In many years these features contained fires, but in other years, especially those that were very dry, fires would spread across boundaries (Taylor and Skinner 2003) (Fig. 9.6).

RIPARIAN ZONES

Few fire history data are available from riparian zones, but available data suggest that fire-return intervals, and possibly fire behavior, are more variable within riparian zones than in adjacent uplands (Skinner 2002a, 2003b). Median fire-return intervals were generally twice as long on riparian sites than on neighboring uplands. However, large differences in the range of fire return intervals were not found between riparian zones and adjacent upland sites (Skinner 2002a, 2003b). It should be noted that these data are from riparian sites adjacent to perennial streams and are probably not representative of riparian areas associated with ephemeral and intermittent streams. Riparian areas associated with ephemeral and intermittent streams dry out over the warm summers and probably have a fire regime similar to the surrounding uplands (Skinner 2002a, 2003b).

Thus, riparian areas along perennial watercourses served as effective barriers to spread of many low-intensity and some moderate-intensity fires and strongly influenced patterns of fire occurrence beyond their immediate vicinity. Consequently, by affecting fire spread, riparian areas are a key topographic feature that also contributes to the structure and dynamics of upland forest landscapes (Skinner 2002a, 2003b; Taylor and Skinner 2003).

FIRE SEVERITY

Patterns of fire severity, an important determinant of stand and landscape structural diversity, have been associated with topographic position in both the pre-fire suppression and contemporary periods (Weatherspoon and Skinner 1995, Taylor and Skinner 1998, Jimerson and Jones 2003). A typical pattern of fire severity is illustrated in Figure 9.7 (Taylor and Skinner 1998). Generally, the upper third of slopes and the ridgetops, especially on south- and west-facing aspects, experience the highest proportion of high-severity burn. In the landscape, this is seen as larger patches of shrubs, young even-aged conifer stands, and stands of knobcone pine (*Pinus attenuata*). The lower third of slopes and north- and east-facing aspects

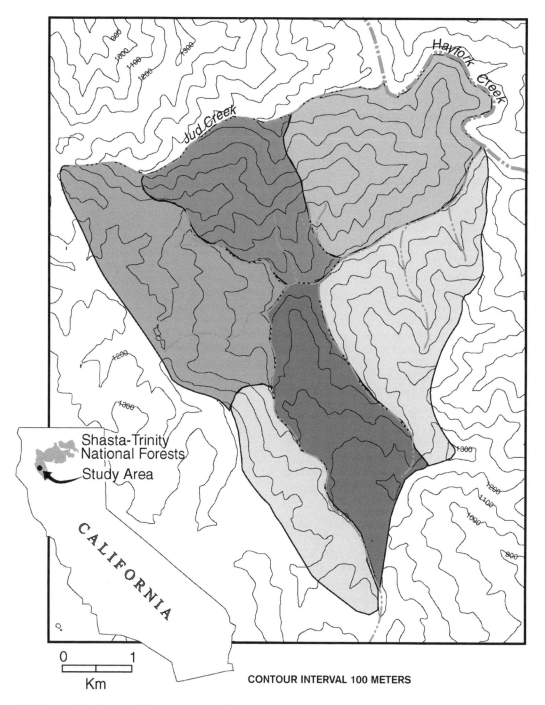

FIGURE 9.6. Map of areas with similar timing of fire occurrence in the Rusch/Jud creek watersheds near Hayfork. This figure illustrates how topographic features limited the spread of fires in most years. Even though fire frequency did not vary significantly from area to area, the year of fire occurrence was often different from one area to its neighbors. (Adapted from Taylor and Skinner 2003.)

experience mainly low-severity fires. Thus, more extensive stands of multi-aged conifers with higher densities of old trees are found in these lower slope positions. Middle slope positions are intermediate between lower and upper slopes in severity pattern. Middle and upper slope positions, especially on south- and west-facing aspects, are more likely to experience higher

fire intensities than other slope positions due to differentials in factors that affect fire behavior. The effect of greater drying and heating of fuels on these slopes contributes to greater fire intensity and makes it more likely that these slope positions experience higher-intensity burns (Rothermel 1983). The common occurrence of strong thermal inversions in the steep, narrow

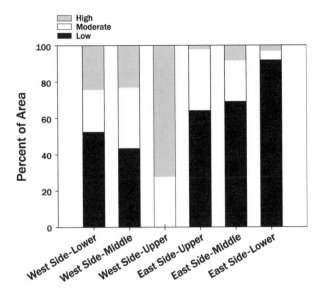

FIGURE 9.7. Chart depicting the distribution of cumulative fire severity patterns on Thompson Ridge near Happy Camp (Taylor and Skinner 1998).

canyons of the Klamath Mountains amplifies differentials in temperature, humidity, and fuel moisture between the canyon bottoms and the ridgetops (Schroeder and Buck 1970). Diurnal patterns of local sun exposure and wind flow combine with slope steepness to affect fire behavior (Schroeder and Buck 1970, Rothermel 1983). Thus, upper slopes would have a greater tendency to support higher-intensity fires running uphill through them in contrast to the tendency for lower slopes to support lower-intensity backing fires. The exposure to wind and solar insulation combines with position on steep slopes to create conditions where upper slopes experience higher-intensity fires more often than do lower slopes. The cumulative effects of the interaction of these factors on landscape patterns are depicted in Figure 9.8 (Sidebar 9.1).

Lower Montane

Tables 9.3 and 9.4 summarizes the fire regime information of common alliances in the lower montane ecological zone of the Klamath Mountains.

FIRE RESPONSES OF IMPORTANT SPECIES

More fire ecology information is available for alliances that include Douglas-fir as an important species than for any other alliances in the Klamath Mountains. Douglas-fir, once mature, is very resistant to low- to moderate-intensity surface fires due to a variety of characteristics. Douglas-fir has very thick bark, a deep rooting habit, high crowns (Agee 1993), short needles, heals fire wounds rapidly, and does not slough bark. In fact, Douglas-fir is the most fire-resistant tree species in the Klamath Mountains. Its common conifer associates, ponderosa, Jeffrey, and sugar pine, are also fire resistant and have thick bark, root deeply, and have high, open crowns. The pines, however, have longer needles and slough bark that forms a less compact litter bed so surface fires are more intense at the base of pine

trees. It is not unusual for these three pine species to exhibit open fire wounds (cat faces). In contrast, Douglas-fir rarely maintains open fire wounds. Wounds generally heal rapidly and are bark covered after only a few years. Moreover, Douglas-fir has shorter needles than the pines and does not slough bark so litter beds beneath the trees are compact, which reduces fire intensity at the base of the tree. Thus, Douglas-fir has advantages in this bioregion following occasional extended periods (20–30 years) without fire when Douglas-fir is less likely to incur basal bole damage than the pines.

Canyon live oak, generally considered sensitive to fire, is common in the lower montane zone of the Klamath Mountains. They may be easily top-killed by fire due to a dense canopy and thin bark that makes them highly susceptible to crown scorch and cambium damage. As with most oaks, if the top is killed, canyon live oak sprouts vigorously from the root crown (Tirmenstein 1989).

California black oaks, common throughout lower and mid-montane forests in the Klamath Mountains, have thin bark and are fire sensitive compared with conifer associates (e.g., Douglas-fir, ponderosa pine, sugar pine, white fir) that invade oak stands during long fire-free periods. However, oak litter beds decompose rapidly and usually have low accumulations of fuel so fires that burn in oak litter have a low intensity and rarely damage mature stems. Moreover, California black oak crowns are open and do not usually support crown fires. With regular burning, the understory fuels are light, generally composed of grasses, forbs, scattered shrubs, and oak litter. Additionally, if black oaks are top-killed they sprout vigorously from the root crown and are able to maintain their presence on a site.

Stands with a major component of buck brush (Ceanothus cuneatus var. cuneatus) are found scattered throughout the lower- to mid-montane zones in the Klamath Mountains on xeric sites with shallow soils on limestone, ultramafic, or granitic bedrock. Often associated with buck brush are the shrubs birch-leaf mountain-mahogany (Cercocarpus betuloides var. betuloides), holly-leaf redberry (Rhamnus ilicifolia), California buckeye (Aesculus californica), and the trees California bay (Umbellularia californica) and California black oak. It is interesting that buck brush does not sprout but establishes from seed following fires, whereas its associates are all strong sprouters (Table 9.5).

Dense stands of shrubs dominated by Brewer oak are common and often support a diverse association of woody species. Brewer oak–dominated stands are found well into the mid-montane areas. Common associates are deer brush, poison oak (Toxicodendron diversilobum), snowdrop bush (Styrax officinalis), foothill ash (Fraxinus dipetala), birch-leaf mountain-mahogany, wild mock orange (Philadelphus lewisii), redbud (Cercis occidentalis), and California buckeye. All of these species sprout vigorously following fires (Skinner 1995b) (Table 9.5).

FIRE REGIME–PLANT COMMUNITY INTERACTIONS

The fire regimes of forests dominated by Douglas-fir are discussed at length in the section describing the common fire regimes of the Klamath Mountains. As these fire regimes are

FIGURE 9.8. This photo of Figure-head Mountain in the Thompson Creek watershed illustrates how patch size varies with topographic position as a response to variation in fire intensity. The largest patches with mostly young trees are on the upper thirds of the slopes as a response to higher-intensity fires above the inversion. Intermediate patches are in the middle-third slope position. The lower-third slope position has a fine-grain pattern of dense large, old trees indicating fires burned primarily as low-intensity surface fires in these locations (Taylor and Skinner 1998). This photo was taken in 1992—five years after the entire landscape shown had burned in the 1987 fires. (Photo by Carl Skinner, USDA Forest Service.)

TABLE 9.3
Fire regime characteristics—for lower-montane forest and woodlands

Vegetation type	Douglas-fir–dominated	Canyon live oak	California black oak	Oregon oak
Temporal				
Seasonality	Summer–fall	Summer–fall	Summer–fall	Summer–fall
Fire-return interval	Short	Short–Medium	Short	Short
Spatial				
Size	Medium–large	Medium	Medium	Medium–Large
Complexity	Moderate–high	Moderate–high	Low–moderate	Low–moderate
Magnitude				
Intensity	Low–moderate	Low–moderate	Low	Low
Severity	Low–moderate	Low–moderate	Low–moderate	Low–moderate
Fire type	Surface	Surface	Surface	Surface

NOTE: Fire regime terms used in this table are defined in Chapter 4.

not specific to this zone, we do not elaborate on them here. Here we concentrate on alliances more common in this zone than in others.

In the lower- to mid-montane zone, canyon live oaks commonly achieve tree stature and dominate steep, xeric slopes in landscapes that experienced frequent, low- to moderate-intensity fires. Canyon live oaks on these sites sometimes have open cat faces with fire scars evident. However, the fire record is generally undatable due to decay around the wound. Fire scar records collected from ponderosa pines, sugar pines, and Douglas-firs scattered in five canyon live oak stands near Hayfork had median fire-return intervals of 6 to 22 years (Taylor and Skinner 2003). This fire scar record

covered the period from the mid 1700s to the last recorded fire in 1926.

Sites where canyon live oak makes up a major portion of the canopy are often rocky, unproductive (Lanspa n.d.), and have sparse, discontinuous surface fuels that do not carry fire well except under more extreme conditions (Skinner and Chang 1996). Slopes with canyon live oak are often so steep that surface fuels collect mainly in draws, small benches, and on the upslope side of trees. Fires on these slopes would likely follow the draws and burn in a discontinuous manner. The fire record comes from trees located near the head of ephemeral draws on the upper third of slopes. The presence of fire scars in the canyon live oaks

TABLE 9.4

Fire regime characteristics—Lower-montane shrublands

Vegetation type	Buck brush	Brewer oak	Whiteleaf manzanita
Temporal			
Seasonality	Summer–fall	Summer–fall	Summer–fall
Fire-return interval	Medium–long	Short–medium	Medium–long
Spatial			
Size	Medium	Small–large	Medium–large
Complexity	Moderate	Moderate–high	Low–high
Magnitude			
Intensity	High	Low–high	Low–high
Severity	High	Moderate–high	Moderate–high
Fire type	Passive-active crown	Surface–passive crown	Surface to active-independent crown

NOTE: Fire regime terms used in this table are defined in Chapter 4.

TABLE 9.5

Fire response types for important species in the lower-montane zone of the Klamath Bioregion

	Type of Fire Response			
	Sprouting	Seeding	Individual	*Species*
Conifer	None	Stimulated (establishment)	Resistant/killed	Douglas-fir, ponderosa pine
	None	Stimulated (seed release)	Resistant/killed	Gray pine
	None	Fire stimulated (seed release)	Killed	Knobcone pine
Hardwood	Fire stimulated	Stimulated (establishment)	Top-killed/survive	California black oak
	Fire stimulated	None known	Top-killed/survive	Brewer oak, tan oak, foothill ash, Oregon ash, Fremont cottonwood, white alder
Shrub	None	Stimulated (germination)	Killed	Whiteleaf manzanita
	Fire stimulated	Stimulated (germination)	Top-killed/survive	Chamise, deer brush, greenleaf manzanita, mahala mat
	Fire stimulated	None	Top-killed/survive	California buckeye, Lemmon's ceanothus, shrub tan oak, birch-leaf mountain-mahogany, wild mock orange, snowdrop bush, poison oak

TABLE 9.6
Fire regime characteristics—Upland forests in mid- to upper-montane zones

Vegetation type	Jeffrey pine	White fir	Shasta red fir	Knobcone pine
Temporal				
Seasonality	Summer–fall	Summer–fall	Late summer–early fall	Late summer–early fall
Fire-return interval	Short	Short–medium	Short–medium	Truncated medium
Spatial				
Size	Small–large	Small–large	Medium	
Complexity	Moderate	Moderate–high	Moderate–high	Low–moderate
Magnitude				
Intensity	Low–moderate	Low–moderate	Low–moderate	Multiple
Severity	Multiple	Multiple	Multiple	Moderate–high
Fire type	Surface	Surface to crown	Surface to crown	Crown

NOTE: Fire regime terms used in this table are defined in Chapter 4.

suggests they were scarred by very light fires that burned in fuel that had collected on the uphill side of the stem.

Stands dominated by California black oak are common throughout lower- and mid-montane areas especially in the central and eastern Klamath Mountains. The highly nutritious acorns of California black oaks were an important food source for the native people of the bioregion. To perpetuate this food source, the native people promoted and maintained California black oak stands by regular burning (Lewis 1993). Since the onset of fire suppression, conifers have invaded many of these stands and they are poised to overtop and replace the oaks on many sites.

California black oak usually suffers the greatest damage when moderate-intensity fires burn in stands that have a significant component of conifers. Greater fuel accumulates under conifers because conifer litter decomposes more slowly than California black oak litter. Moreover, oaks in mixed stands often have lower vigor due to competition from the conifers, and lower-vigor trees are more susceptible to fire damage, especially with the altered fuelbeds. In these mixed stands, conifers often survive fires because they have thicker bark, whereas many oaks may be top-killed. If much of the conifer canopy remains, the oaks then sprout in the shade of the conifers and are often not able to reach the main canopy as they do in an open environment or under other oaks.

Black oak (as well as tan oak and Pacific madrone) seedlings can survive for many years in the shaded understory of conifers. During this time, they are able to develop a large root system with a long taproot with limited top growth. Top growth on the seedlings may die back to the root crown and re-sprout several times waiting to quickly put on height growth following formation of a canopy gap. In this way, California black oaks are able to survive for long periods as isolated trees in relatively dense conifer stands. Additionally, when a high-intensity fire kills much of the conifer overstory, existing oak seedlings are poised to quickly grow and reclaim

dominance of the site (McDonald and Tappeiner 2002). Subsequent frequent fires will maintain the oak dominance. An example of this process can be seen near Volmers along Interstate 5 where a severe fire in 1986 killed several hundred hectares of mixed Douglas-fir, ponderosa pine, and sugar pine. The burned area is now dominated by fast-growing California black oak on mesic sites, and knobcone pine on xeric sites.

Extensive stands of California black oaks survived the approximately 12,000 ha (29,600 ac) High Complex near Lake Shasta reservoir in 1999. Even though this fire burned in August and early September, the driest time of the year, the light fuel beds under oak stands supported mostly low-intensity surface fire.

Mid- to Upper Montane

Forests in this zone are differentiated from lower-elevation forests by the increased importance of white fir throughout and Shasta red fir in higher portions and the decreased importance of hardwoods, especially tan oak, giant chinquapin, and California black oak. Specified in this way, the lower extent of the zone varies from approximately 600 m (2,000 ft) in the west to about 1,300 m (4,250 ft) in the eastern portion of the range (Sawyer and Thornburgh 1977). Table 9.6 summarizes the fire regime information for vegetation common in the mid- to upper-montane ecological zone of the Klamath Mountains.

FIRE RESPONSES OF IMPORTANT SPECIES

White fir has thin bark when young, but its bark is not shed and thickens with age, making it more fire tolerant when mature. Shasta red fir is similar but appears to be more sensitive than white fir at all ages.

Port Orford-cedar (*Chamaecyparis lawsoniana*), commonly associated with mesic conditions on soils derived from ultramafic material, is found in two disjunct areas in the

TABLE 9.7
Fire regime characteristics—riparian forests, wetlands, and upland shrub types in the mid- to upper-montane zone

Vegetation type	Port orford-cedar	California pitcher plant	Ceanothus shrub fields	Greenleaf manzanita
Temporal				
Seasonality	Late summer–fall	Late summer–fall	Summer–fall	Summer–fall
Fire-return interval	Short–medium	Short–medium	Medium–long	Medium–long
Spatial				
Size	Small–medium	Small	Small–large	Small–large
Complexity	Moderate–high	Moderate–high	Low–high	Low–high
Magnitude				
Intensity	Low–high	Low–moderate	Moderate–high	Moderate–high
Severity	Low–high	Low–high	Moderate–high	Moderate–high
Fire type	Surface to crown	Surface	Crown	Crown

Klamath Mountains. The largest stands of Port Orford cedar occur in the western Klamath Mountains, especially in the Siskiyous. Inland, Port Orford cedar stands are primarily found in riparian settings in the Trinity Pluton ultramafic formation (Jimerson et al. 1999), mostly in the Trinity and Sacramento River watersheds. Port Orford cedar stands often include trees more than 300 years old with open, charred wounds (cat faces) indicating they commonly survived low- to moderate-intensity surface fires (Table 9.7).

Knobcone pine, a serotinous cone pine with relatively thin bark, is common in the Klamath Mountains in areas that burn intensely.

Stands dominated by Jeffrey pine are found primarily on soils derived from ultramafic rock and they occur in the lower-montane through the subalpine zones (Sawyer and Thornburgh 1977). Incense-cedar is a common associate with huckleberry oak and California coffeeberry as common understory shrubs. Jeffrey pine is similar to ponderosa pine in that it develops thick bark relatively early in life rendering it resistant to most low- and moderate-intensity fires. Incense-cedar becomes very resistant to low- and moderate-intensity fires as it approaches maturity due to thick, insulating bark and high crowns. Incense-cedar has also been found to withstand high levels of crown scorch (Stephens and Finney 2002).

Important shrub-dominated alliances of the upper-montane Klamath Mountains are greenleaf manzanita, deer brush, tobacco brush, and huckleberry oak. All of the dominant shrubs in these alliances sprout vigorously following fire. Moreover, manzanitas and most *Ceanothus* spp, also establish after fire from long-lived seeds stored in soil seed banks (Tabel 9.8).

FIRE REGIME–PLANT COMMUNITY INTERACTIONS

Most information on fire regimes and fire effects in white fir forests comes from areas on the edges of the Klamath Moun-

tains. On the western edge, Stuart and Salazar (2000) found median fire-return intervals of 40 years in the white fir alliances, and shorter 26- and 15-year median intervals where white fir was found in the Douglas-fir and incense cedar associations. Atzet and Martin (1992) reported a 25-year fire-return interval for white fir, and Agee (1991) found a range from 43 to 64 years from dry to moist white fir forest in the Siskiyous. Thornburgh (1995) reported a 29-year fire-return interval for the centrally located Marble Mountains.

Before the fire suppression era, the severity of most fires was not high, due to the fire tolerance of mature white fir and generally low to moderate fire intensities. Generally, more fires are dated from fire scars than from fire-initiated cohorts of regeneration (Taylor and Skinner 1998, Stuart and Salazar 2000), allowing inference that most fires were underburns. The natural forest structure is patchy, and this structure was maintained by fire. Areas that burn with high severity usually are young stands of pure white fir, open stands of white fir with a shrub understory, or montane chaparral that may contain a few white firs (Thornburgh 1995), and these high-severity patches create coarse scale heterogeneity.

Our understanding of the frequency and extent of high-severity fire and its role in stand and landscape dynamics in the white fir zone is limited. Fire likely interacted with wind to influence dead fuel accumulations. In the Klamaths and in the Cascades to the east, white fir stand structure is often all-aged and sites often have pit and mound topography created by windthrow, suggesting that wind is an important disturbance that creates gaps (Agee 1991, Taylor and Halpern 1991, Taylor and Skinner 2003). Moreover, at these higher elevations, winter snowfall is common, and when followed by high winds, can cause substantial snapping of treetops, as in 1996 in the central Klamath Mountains. Wind-generated stem snap and windthrow were responsible for the high fuel accumulations that generated the higher-severity burn patterns in the 1999

TABLE 9.8
Fire response types for important species in the mid- to upper-montane zone of the Klamath bioregion

| | Type of Fire Response | | | |
	Sprouting	Seeding	Individual	*Species*
Conifer	None	Fire stimulated (seed release)	Killed	Knobcone pine
	None	Fire stimulated (establishment)	Resistant/killed	Douglas-fir, ponderosa pine, Jeffrey pine
	None	None	Resistant/killed	Incense cedar, Port Orford-cedar, sugar pine, western white pine, red fir, white fir, western juniper
	None	None	Killed	Brewer's spruce, lodgepole pine
Hardwood	Fire stimulated	None	Top-killed/survive	Bigleaf maple, tanoak, canyon live oak, Pacific dogwood, white alder, Oregon ash, water birch
	Fire stimulated	None	Resistant/top-killed/survive	California black oak, blue oak, Pacific madrone, golden chinquapin
	Fire stimulated	Stimulated (establishment)	Resistant/top-killed/survive	Oregon white oak
	None	None	Killed	Curl-leaf mountain-mahogany
Shrub	Fire stimulated	Stimulated (germination)	Top-killed/survive	Tobacco brush, greenleaf manzanita, mahala mat
	Fire stimulated	None	Top-killed/survive	Bush chinquapin, shrub tanoak, huckleberry oak, California buckeye, wild mock orange, vine maple, mountain maple

Megram fire (Jimerson and Jones 2003). The degree to which higher stand densities and surface fuel accumulations due to fire exclusion stimulated this synergistic effect is not clear.

Forest density in white fir forests has tended to increase with fire suppression, with the shade-tolerant white fir generally showing the largest increases (Stuart and Salazar 2000). Fire-tolerant species such as ponderosa pine, sugar pine, and California black oak are declining and this will most likely continue as long as fire exclusion is effective.

Though Shasta red fir is common throughout the Klamath Mountains in upper montane and subalpine environments (Sawyer and Thornburgh 1977), Shasta red fir has been studied most extensively in the Cascades and more detail will be presented in that chapter (Chapter 10).

In the Klamath Mountains, fire history has been documented in one Shasta red fir stand near Mumbo Lakes. Important associates were western white pine, white fir, Jeffrey pine, and mountain hemlock (Skinner 2003a). Six fire-scarred samples were collected from a 2-ha (5-ac) site within this stand. The fire record extended from 1576 to 1901. The composite median fire-return interval for all samples was 10 years and the median fire-return interval for individual trees ranged from 9 to 30 years. However, there was considerable variation in fire-return intervals with a minimum interval of 2 years from 1698 to 1700 and a maximum of 118 years from 1752 to 1870. No fires were detected after 1901. The fire-free period since 1901 is exceeded only by the 118-year interval.

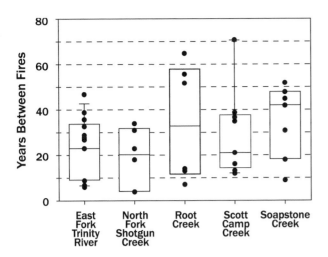

FIGURE 9.9. Port Orford-cedar stand fire intervals. Chart shows distribution of fire-return intervals in inland stands of Port Orford-cedar. (Source: Skinner 2003a).

Though Port Orford-cedar is resistant to low- and moderate-intensity fires, there has been extensive mortality to Port Orford-cedars in stands where high-intensity fires have burned in recent years. For example, in the 1994 Bear fire, mortality was so high in the No Man's Creek drainage (a proposed Research Natural Area) that there was concern that Port Orford-cedar would disappear due to lack of seed source (Creasy and Williams 1994). Since Port Orford-cedar stands are located on mesic, riparian sites and their wood is highly resistant to decay, it is likely these stands are able to produce heavy fuel loadings, especially following longer periods without fire as in the more recent fire suppression era. When these areas finally do burn in the inevitable dry years, high-intensity burns should be expected with accompanying mortality of the Port Orford-cedars.

The previous discussion on the influence of riparian areas on Klamath Mountain fire regimes was based on information from inland sites in the Trinity and Sacramento River watersheds dominated by Port Orford-cedar. These fire-scar data for the inland Port Orford-cedar stands indicate that fires burned with median fire-return intervals of 16 to 42 years (Fig. 9.9). In each case, the median fire-return interval in the Port Orford-cedar stands was at least twice that of forests in the surrounding uplands (Skinner 2003b). Though there was considerable variation in length of fire intervals, the length of time since the last fire (the fire-suppression period) exceeds the longest interval previously recorded in each of the sampled stands.

Knobcone pine in the Klamath Mountains exhibits a unique bimodal geographical distribution related to areas at higher and lower elevations that experience high-intensity fires. As in other bioregions, knobcone pine is found at low elevations intermixed with chaparral as around Lake Shasta and Whiskeytown Lake reservoirs. However, in the Klamath Mountains, knobcone pine is also found in the upper montane zone on upper slopes and ridgetop positions, especially on south- and west-facing slopes. As discussed previously,

these are locations that experience more extreme fire weather conditions (e.g., low humidity, high temperature, high winds) than the surrounding landscape.

Jeffrey pine forests are generally thought to have fire regimes similar to ponderosa pine forests—frequent, low- to moderate-intensity fires. However, Jeffrey pine sites often have more variation in fire-return intervals than sites that support ponderosa pine (Skinner and Chang 1996, Taylor 2000, Stephens 2001, Stephens et al. 2003). This variation is probably due to the combination of nutrient-poor soils and shorter growing seasons, especially at higher elevations, which increases variability in fuel production compared with typical ponderosa pine sites.

Fire-scar data from ultramafic sites with Jeffrey pine in the Klamath Mountains are available from 7 sites in the vicinity of Mt. Eddy (Skinner 2003a) and 10 sites near Hayfork (Taylor and Skinner 2003). The median fire-return interval for the Jeffrey pine sites near Mt. Eddy ranged from 8 to 30 years and 8 to 15 years for those near Hayfork. For the sites near Mt. Eddy, the current fire-free periods of 57 to 129 years exceed the 95th percentile pre-fire suppression fire-free interval for 5 of 7 sampled stands. At Hayfork, the current fire-free periods of 68 to 125 years exceed the longest pre-fire suppression intervals recorded on all 10 sites.

Considerable differences in the flammability of shrub stands have been noted. Shrub stands dominated by manzanita, particularly greenleaf and whiteleaf manzanita, burn more readily than stands dominated by ceanothus (either deer brush or tobacco brush) or stands with a significant component of shrub canyon live oak, tan oak, or chinquapin (Weatherspoon and Skinner 1995). Stands dominated by huckleberry oak appear to be similar to those dominated by California-lilac or other oaks (Table 9.8).

The occurrence of montane shrub stands may be associated with either poor edaphic conditions unsuitable for tree growth or high-intensity, stand-replacing fires. Once established, because of the nature of shrub fuels, fires that burn in these communities are more likely to be high-intensity, stand-replacing events.

Thus, where shrub communities established following stand-replacing forest fires, recurring fire plays a key role in the maintenance of these communities by preventing shrub replacement by trees (Wilken 1967, Nagel and Taylor 2005). More information on fire regimes of shrub-dominated alliances can be found in Chapter 10.

The only known herbaceous alliance with fire ecology information in the Klamath Mountains is for the California pitcher plant *(Darlingtonia californica)*. Pitcher plant seeps are common in open habitats saturated with running water, usually on serpentine substrate (Sawyer and Keeler-Wolf 1995). The continuous presence of flowing water through these herbaceous communities would seem to limit opportunities for fires and little is known of their fire ecology (Crane 1990). However, Port Orford-cedar, incense-cedar, western white pine, or Jeffrey pine trees with cat faces, are commonly scattered in and adjacent to the seeps.

FIGURE 9.10. A pitcher plant seep in September following an early hard frost in the Scott Camp Creek watershed near Castle Lake. (Photo by Carl N. Skinner.)

A prescribed burn in September 1997 in the Cedar Log Flat Research Natural Area on the Siskiyou National Forest was found to spread easily through dead herbaceous material in sedge and pitcher plant seeps under the following conditions: humidity 27%, temperature 20°C–25°C (68°F–77°F), 10-hour fuel moisture 12%, and 100-hour fuel moisture 20% to 26% (Borgias et al. 2001). These are conditions easily achieved, or exceeded, in the summer where pitcher plant is found. Though a decline in pitcher plant cover was detected three years post-fire, unburned controls experienced a similar decline suggesting little effect from the burn (Borgias et al. 2001).

Fire histories from fire-scarred trees in pitcher plant seeps have been documented in the North Fork of Shotgun Creek (NFSC) and Soapstone Creek (SC). Median fire return intervals for these sites were18 years and 42 years, respectively (sites 2 and 5 in Fig. 9.9) (Skinner 2003b), whereas individual tree fire-return intervals ranged from 24 to 73 years at NFSC, and 40 to 140 years at SC. Differences in the length of fire-return intervals in these seeps are probably related to conditions in the surrounding forests. NFSC is located in the upper third of a steep, southeast-facing slope and is surrounded by mixed stands of Jeffrey pine, white fir, incense-cedar, sugar pine, and Douglas-fir. Consequently, it would be expected to have relatively short fire return intervals. On the other hand, SC is near the bottom of a U-shaped canyon on a gentle slope surrounded by mixed stands of Shasta red fir, white fir, western white pine, Jeffrey pine, sugar pine, and Douglas-fir. Thus, SC would be expected to have relatively long fire return intervals. Port Orford-cedar is the most common tree on both sites, however.

Fires burning in these environments probably occur very late in the season when water is low, in very dry years, or possibly after an early frost has killed much of the herbaceous material above ground as in Figure 9.10.

Subalpine

FIRE RESPONSES OF IMPORTANT SPECIES

Most tree species in the subalpine zone, including mountain hemlock, Shasta red fir, whitebark pine, western white pine, foxtail pine, lodgepole pine, and curl-leaf mountain-mahogany have thinner bark than species found at lower elevations and are easily damaged or killed by moderate-intensity fire or the consumption of heavy surface fuels at the base of the tree. Tables 9.9 and 9.10 summarize the fire regime information for vegetation discussed in the subalpine ecological zone of the Klamath Mountains.

FIRE REGIME–PLANT COMMUNITY INTERACTIONS

Landscapes of this zone are a heterogeneous mosaic of stands, rock outcrops, talus, morainal lakes, and riparian areas, so fuels are discontinuous. Moreover, deep snowpacks persist into late June or July in most years, so the fire season is very short. Fuel beds from the short-needled species are compact and promote slow-spreading, mostly smoldering surface fires. Fuel build-up tends to be slow because of the short growing season. Higher-intensity fires that do burn in

TABLE 9.9

Fire response types for important species in the subalpine zone of the Klamath Bioregion

	Type of Fire Response			
	Sprouting	Seeding	Individual	*Species*
Conifer	None	None	Resistant/killed	Red fir, mountain hemlock, Jeffrey pine, foxtail pine, western white pine, whitebark pine
	None	None	Killed	lodgepole pine
Hardwood	None	None	Killed	Curl-leaf mountain-mahogany

TABLE 9.10

Fire regime characteristics—Subalpine

Temporal	
Seasonality	Late summer–fall
Fire-return interval	Short–long
Spatial	
Size	Small–medium
Complexity	Moderate–high
Magnitude	
Intensity	Low
Severity	Multiple
Fire type	Surface

subalpine forests primarily occur in areas of locally heavy fuel accumulations during periods of extreme fire weather.

The only fire history data for the subalpine zone in the Klamath Mountains are from stands on China Mountain (Mohr et al. 2000, Skinner 2003a). Species present in these stands are mountain hemlock, Shasta red fir, whitebark pine, western white pine, foxtail pine, and lodgepole pine.

Fire-scar samples were collected from 14 trees on three 1-ha (2.5-ac) sites in the Crater Creek watershed. Over the period spanned by the fire-scar record (1404–1941), the median fire return intervals for these sites were 11.5, 12, and 13 yrs. However, 44 of 51 fires were detected on only single trees. This suggests that fires in this subalpine basin were mainly low intensity and small. Ranges of individual-tree median fire-return intervals were 9 to 276 years with a grand median of 24.5 years. No fires were detected after 1941.

Management Issues

Managers face several fire-related challenges in the Klamath Mountains but most are similar to those faced by managers in other parts of California and the western United States (e.g., smoke management, heavy fuel accumulations). How-ever, two issues—wildlife habitat and wildland-urban interface—stand out in this bioregion.

Wildlife Habitat

Management objectives often include the desire to maintain forest ecosystems within their historic range of variability (HRV; see, e.g., Swanson et al. 1994, Manley et al. 1995) using ecological processes (FEMAT 1993, USDA-USDI 1994) as a means to sustain a mix of desirable wildlife habitats. Recent studies suggest that vegetation patterns and conditions generated by pre–fire-suppression fire regimes (Taylor and Skinner 1998, 2003) may be advantageous for wildlife species of concern such as the northern spotted owl *(Strix occidentalis caurina)* (Franklin et al. 2000) and several species of butterflies (Huntzinger 2003). Fire suppression has been ubiquitously applied throughout the bioregion. Consequently, there is a need to better understand the role of frequent low- and moderate-intensity fires on development of the forest landscape mosaic from stand to watershed scales (Agee 1998, 2003). This understanding will help managers better assess risks associated with different management alternatives (Attiwill 1994, Mutch and Cook 1996, Arno et al. 1997, Cissel et al. 1999, Arno and Allison-Bunnell 2002, Agee 2003).

More-recent management activities, such as logging and replacement of multi-aged old-growth forests with even-aged forest plantations and continued fire suppression have reduced forest heterogeneity, increased the proportion of even-aged forests, and altered habitat conditions for forest-dwelling species compared to conditions in the pre–fire-suppression landscape (USDAs-USDI 1994). Large wildfires with large proportions of stand-replacing or near-stand-replacing fire have burned in the Klamath Mountains in the last three decades (1977, 1987, 1995, 1996, and 2002). These fires have reduced the extent, in some places dramatically, of multi-aged, old-growth stands. Areas burned by these fires are now occupied by plantations, even-aged hardwood stands, or brushfields and, in some watersheds (e.g., north and south forks of the Salmon River, Chetco River), these vegetation types are now the landscape matrix. Moreover, some areas that burned

Prior to fire suppression, parts of the forested landscape in the Klamath Mountains were occupied by stands of trees with similar ages, but there is little evidence that they covered large areas (i.e., hundreds–thousands ha) (Atzet and Martin 1992, Agee 1993, Taylor and Skinner 1998, 2003). We believe the origin of even-aged stands is not just the result of punctuated establishment following stand-replacing fire. Certainly, high-severity, stand-replacing fire is the process responsible for the location and extent of some even-aged stands (e.g., Agee 1993; Taylor and Skinner 1998) but two other pathways of even-aged stand development are also possible.

Frequent low- to moderate-severity fires often kill conifer seedlings and occasionally kill dominant trees leading to the development of large forest openings over long periods (i.e., decades to centuries) especially in upper-slope topographic positions. The interruption of these frequent fires with a longer fire-free period, combined with a good seed crop, perhaps associated with cooler and moister conditions, could then trigger establishment of even-aged stands. This pathway appears to be responsible for some of the even-aged stands of white fir or Douglas-fir we observed in forests on Thompson Ridge near Happy Camp (Taylor and Skinner 1998).

Another pathway to even-aged stand development we have observed is associated with fire suppression. In some forest types, punctuated regeneration of fire-sensitive species occurred over wide areas following suppression of fire. For example, young even-aged forests of Douglas-fir now occupy large areas in parts of the Klamath Mountains where frequent fire had originally maintained dominance by black oak. The result of this process has increased the proportion of landscapes occupied by even-aged conifer forests at low to middle elevation.

intensely in 1977 (e.g., Hog fire) burned intensely again in 1987 (e.g., Yellow fire). The 1987 fires also burned large areas of multi-aged, old-growth forest at high intensity. Thus, young even-aged forests that will have high fuel loads as plantations are thinned, and old-growth stands with high fuel loads due to fire suppression, may amplify conditions for even-aged landscape development. Positive feedbacks between management (i.e., fire suppression, plantations), stand conditions in the new even-aged vegetation matrix, and intense fire have the potential to maintain or even expand an even-aged forest matrix that is unusual with respect to the pre-historical period.

Wildland-Urban Interface

With an average of less than 1.2 people/km^2 (3 people/mi^2), the Klamath Mountains have a low human population compared with California as a whole (USCB 2002). Yet, a large proportion of the bioregion is classified as mixed interface (CDF 2002b) because of the dispersed nature of dwellings in small, scattered communities in flammable, wildland vegetation. As a result, several hundred homes have been lost to wildfires that originated in the bioregion in just the last three decades (CDF 2002a). Examples of major suppression efforts in wildland-urban interfaces in the bioregion include fires near Hayfork and Happy Camp (1987), Redding and Lakehead (1999), Weaverville (2001), and Jones Valley (Bear fire) and French Gulch (2004). The Jones fire (1999) alone burned more than 900 structures (CDF 2002a), including nearly 200 homes in and around Redding. The fire problem at the wildland-urban interface will continue to grow as more people move into low-density housing at the edges of communities throughout the bioregion.

Future Directions

There is a critical need to better understand the synergistic relationships between low-, moderate-, and high-intensity fire and pre–fire-suppression vegetation patterns. There is a particular need for quantitative estimates of the proportion of landscapes in different stand types (i.e., old-growth, young even-aged, hardwood) and how they were patterned on the landscape to provide a stronger foundation for applying concepts of historical range of variability to forest management in the Klamath Mountains. There is great potential for fire and landscape ecologists to work with wildlife ecologists to examine wildlife responses to landscape dynamics across a range of spatial and temporal scales.

Hardwoods, especially oaks, provide important habitat elements for many species of wildlife. As a result, managers may use prescribed fire to inhibit conifer encroachment into oak stands as well as to improve acorn crops (Skinner 1995b). Oak woodlands have also been associated with rich vegetation diversity. Yet, their ecology is little studied in these montane forest environments. We need to better understand the ramifications of the potential loss of large areas of hardwoods to conifers for associated vegetative diversity and wildlife habitat.

The temporal and spatial dynamics of large, dead woody material in areas where pre–suppression fire regimes are characterized by frequent, low- to mixed-severity fires is not known but it is probably very different than those identified by current standards and guidelines used by both federal and state agencies. Quantities of large woody material for standards and guidelines were developed from contemporary old-growth forests that had experienced many decades of fire suppression. These quantities of woody material were probably unusually high compared to typical pre–fire-suppression values. Consequently, a management emphasis on meeting or exceeding standards and guidelines for dead woody material has and will increase fire hazard over time and threatens the very habitat the standards and guidelines were designed to improve (Skinner 2002b).

Summary

Primarily due to the annual summer drought and ample winter precipitation, fires were historically frequent and generally of low to moderate and mixed severity in most vegetation assemblages, especially those that cover large portions of the Klamath Mountains. Fire exclusion and other management activities have led to considerable changes in Klamath Mountain ecosystems over the last century. Of all management activities that have contributed to altering ecosystems in the Klamath Mountains, fire suppression has been the most pervasive since it alone has been ubiquitously applied. Though there is much current discussion of the need for restoring fire as an ecological process, or at least creating stand structures that would help reduce the general intensity of fires to more historical levels, there are many competing social/political concerns and objectives (e.g., fine filter approaches to managing wildlife habitat and air quality) that make doing anything problematic (Agee 2003). Regardless of how these controversies are resolved, the ecosystems of the Klamath Mountains will continue to change in response to climate and social/political choices for the use of forest resources and their associated fire-management alternatives.

References

Agee, J. K. 1991. Fire history along an elevational gradient in the Siskiyou Mountains, Oregon. Northwest Science 65:188–199.

Agee, J. K. 1993. Fire ecology of Pacific Northwest forests. Island Press, Washington, D.C.

Agee, J. K. 2003. Burning issues in fire: will we let the coarse-filter operate? Tall Timbers Research Station, Miscellaneous Publication No. 13:7–13.

Arno, S. F., and S. Allison-Bunnell. 2002. Flames in our forest: disaster or renewal? Island Press, Washington, DC.

Arno, S. F., H. Y. Smith, and M. A. Krebs. 1997. Old growth ponderosa pine and western larch stand structures: influences of pre-1900 fires and fire exclusion. USDA Forest Service, Intermountain Research Station, Ogden, UT, Research Paper INT-RP-495.

Attiwill, P. M. 1994. The disturbance of forest ecosystems: the ecological basis for conservative management. Forest Ecology and Management 63:247–300.

Atzet, T., and R. Martin. 1992. Natural disturbance regimes in the Klamath Province. In R. R. Harris, D. C. Erman, and H. M. Kerner (eds.), Symposium on biodiversity of northwestern California. Berkeley, CA: University of California, Wildland Resources Center Report No. 29.

Biswell, H. H. 1989. Prescribed burning in California wildlands vegetation management. University of California Press, Berkeley, CA.

Borgias, D., R. Huddleston, and N. Rudd. 2001. Third year post-fire vegetation response in serpentine savanna and fen communities, Cedar Log Flat Research Natural Area, Siskiyou National Forest. Unpublished report for challenge cost-share agreement 00-11061100-010 from The Nature Conservancy to the Siskiyou National Forest. On file at the Siskiyou National Forest, Grants Pass, OR.

Briles, C. E. 2003. Vegetation and fire history near Bolan Lake in the northern Siskiyou Mountains of Oregon. M.S. Thesis. University of Oregon, Eugene.

Brown, P. M. 1996. OLDLIST: a database of maximum tree ages. P. 727–731 in J. S. Dean, D. M. Meko, and T. W. Swetnam (eds.), Tree rings, environment, and humanity. The University of Arizona, Tucson, Radiocarbon 1996.

Brown, P. M. 2002. OLDLIST: a database of ancient trees and their ages. Rocky Mountain Tree-ring Research, Inc. Available online: http://www.rmtrr.org/oldlist.htm.

CCSS. 2002. Historical course data. California Resources Agency, Department of Water Resources, Division of Flood Management, California Cooperative Snow Surveys. Data online at: http://cdec.water.ca.gov/snow/.

CDF. 2002a. Historical Statistics. In Fire and Emergency Response. California Department of Forestry and Fire Protection, Sacramento, Available online at http:/www.fire.ca.gov/FireEmergencyResponse/HistoricalStatistics/HistoricalStatistics.asp.

CDF. 2002b. Information and data center. In Fire and Resource Assessment Program. California Department of Forestry and Fire Protection, Sacramento, Available online at http://frap.cdf.ca.gov/infocenter.html.

Cheng, S. T. E. 2004. Forest Service Research Natural Areas in California. General Technical Report PSW-GTR-188. Pacific Southwest Research Station, Forest Service, U.S. Department of Agriculture, Albany, CA.

Cissel, J.H., F.J. Swanson, and P.J. Weisberg. 1999. Landscape management using historical fire regimes: Blue River, Oregon. Ecological Applications 9:1217–1231.

Crane, M.F. 1990. Darlingtonia califomica. In: Fire Effects information System, [Online]. U.S. Department of Agriculture, Forest Service, Rocky Mountain Research Station, Fire Sciences Laboratory (Producer). Available: http://www.fs.fed.us/database/feis/ [2005 July 7].

Creasy, M., and B. Williams. 1994. Bear fire botanical resources report. In Dillon Complex burn area rehabilitation report, USDA Forest Service, Klamath National Forest, Yreka, CA.

Daniels, M.L. 2001. Fire and vegetation history since the late Pleistocene from the Trinity Mountains of California. M.S. Thesis. Northern Arizona University, Flagstaff, AZ.

FEMAT. 1993. Forest ecosystem management: an ecological, economic, and social assessment., Portland, OR, Report of Forest Ecosystem Management Assessment Team.

Franklin, A.B., D.R. Anderson, R.J. Gutierrez, and K.P. Burnham. 2000. Climate, habitat quality, and fitness in northern spotted owl populations in northwestern California. Ecological Monographs 70:539–590.

Fry, D.L., and S.L. Stephens. 2006. Influence of humans and climate on the fire history of a ponderosa pine-mixed conifer forest in the southeastern Klamath Mountains, California. Forest Ecology and Management 223:428–438.

Hoopes, C.L. 1971. Lure of Humboldt Bay region. Kendall/Hunt Publishing, Dubuque, IW.

Hull, M.K., C.A. O'Dell, and M.J. Schroeder. 1966. Critical fire weather patterns: their frequency and levels of fire danger. USDA Forest Service, Pacific Southwest Research Station, Berkeley, CA.

Huntzinger, M. 2003. Effects of fire management practices on butterfly diversity in the forested western United States. Biological Conservation 113:1–12.

Irwin, W.P. 1966. Geology of the Klamath Mountains province. P. 19–28 in E.H. Bailey (ed.), Geology of northern California. California Division of Mines and Geology, Sacramento, CA, Bulletin 190.

Irwin, W.P. 1981. Tectonic accretion of the Klamath Mountains. P. 29–49 in W.G. Ernst (ed.), The geotectonic development of California. Prentice-Hall, Englewood Cliffs, NJ.

Irwin, W.P., and J.L. Wooden. 1999. Plutons and accretionary episodes of the Klamath Mountains, California and Oregon. US Geological Survey Open-file Report 99-374.

Jackson, J. 1964. Tales from the mountaineer. The Rotary Club of Weaverville, Weaverville, CA.

Jimerson, T.M., S.L. Daniel, E.A. McGee, and G. DeNitto. 1999. A field guide to Port Orford cedar plant associations in northwest California and Supplement. USDA Forest Service, Pacific Southwest Region, Washington, DC, R5-ECOL-TP-002.

Jimerson, T.M., and D.W. Jones. 2003. Megram: blowdown, wildfire, and the effects of fuel treatment. Tall Timbers Research Station, Miscellaneous Report No. 13:55–59.

Keeler-Wolf, T. (ed.). 1990. Ecological surveys of Forest Service Research Natural Areas in California. USDA Forest Service, Pacific Southwest Research Station, Berkeley, CA, General Technical Report PSW-125.

Kruckeberg, A.R. 1984. California serpentines: flora, vegetation, geology, soils, and management problems. Berkeley: University of California.

Lanspa, K.E. n.d. Soil survey of Shasta-Trinity Forest area, California. USDA Forest Service, Pacific Southwest Region, n.a., National Cooperative Soil Survey.

Lantis, D.W., R. Steiner, and A.E. Karinen. 1989. California: the Pacific connection. Creekside Press, Chico, CA.

Lewis, H.T. 1990. Reconstructing patterns of Indian burning in southwestern Oregon. P. 80–84 in N. Hannon and R.K. Olmo (eds.), Living with the land: the Indians of southwest Oregon. Southern Oregon Historical Society, Ashland, OR, Proceedings of the 1989 symposium on the Prehistory of Southwest Oregon.

Lewis, H.T. 1993. Patterns of Indian burning in California: ecology and ethnohistory. P. 55–116 in T.C. Blackburn and K. Anderson (eds),. Before the wilderness: environmental management by native Californians. Ballena Press, Menlo Park, CA.

Manley, P.N., G.E. Brogan, C. Cook, M.E. Flores, D.G. Fullmer, S. Husari, T.M. Jimerson, L.M. Lux, M.E. McCain, J.A. Rose, G. Schmitt, J.C. Schuyler, and M.J. Skinner. 1995. Sustaining ecosystems: a conceptual framework, R5-EM-TP-001. San Fransisco, CA: USDA Forest Service, Pacific Southwest Region.

McDonald, P.M., and I.I. Tappeiner John C. 2002. California's hardwood resource: seeds, seedlings, and sprouts of three important forest-zone species. USDA Forest Service, Pacific Southwest Research Station, Albany, CA, General Technical Report PSW-GTR-185.

McKee, B. 1972. Cascadia: the geologic evolution of the Pacific Northwest. McGraw Hill, New York.

Miles, S.R., and C.B. Goudey (eds.). 1997. Ecological subregions of California: section and subsection descriptions. USDA Forest Service, Pacific Southwest Region, San Francisco, CA, R5-3M-TP-005.

Mohr, J.A., C. Whitlock, and C.N. Skinner. 2000. Postglacial vegetation and fire history, eastern Klamath Mountains, California, USA. The Holocene 10:587–601.

Mutch, R.W., and W.A. Cook. 1996. Restoring fire to ecosystems: methods vary with land management goals. P. 9–11 in C.C. Hardy and S.F. Arno (eds.), The use of fire in forest restoration. Ogden, UT: USDA Forest Service, Intermountain Research Station. General Technical Report INT-GTR-341.

Nagel, N., and A.H. Taylor. 2005. Fire and persistence of montane chaparral in mixed conifer forest landscapes in the northern Sierra Nevada, Lake Tahoe Basin, California, USA. Journal of the Torrey Botanical Society 132:442–454.

Oakeshott, G.B. 1971. California's changing landscapes: a guide to the geology of the state. McGraw-Hill, San Francisco.

Pullen, R. 1995. Overview of the environment of native inhabitants of southwestern Oregon, late prehistoric era. Pullen Consulting, Bandon, OR, Report for the USDA Forest Service, Grants Pass, OR.

Rorig, M.L., and S.A. Ferguson. 1999. Characteristics of lightning and wildland fire ignition in the Pacific Northwest. Journal of Applied Meteorology 38:1565–1575.

Rorig, M.L., and S.A. Ferguson. 2002. The 2000 fire season: lightning-caused fires. Journal of Applied Meteorology 41: 786–791.

Rothermel, R.C. 1983. How to predict the spread and intensity of forest and range fires. USDA Forest Service, Intermountain Research Station, Ogden, UT, General Technical Report INT-143.

Sawyer, J.O., and T. Keeler-Wolf. 1995. A manual of California vegetation. California Native Plant Society, Sacramento, CA.

Sawyer, J.O., and D.A. Thornburgh. 1977. Montane and subalpine vegetation of the Klamath Mountains. P. 699–732 in M. G. Barbour and J. Major (eds.), Terrestrial Vegetation of California. John Wiley & Sons, New York.

Schroeder, M.J., and C.C. Buck. 1970. Fire weather—a guide for application of meteorological information to forest fire control operations. US Department of Agriculture, Washington, DC, Agricultural Handbook 360.

Sharp, R.P. 1960. Pleistocene glaciation in the Trinity Alps of northern California. American Journal of Science 258:305–340.

Shrader, G. 1965. Trinity Forest. Yearbook of the Trinity County Historical Society. P. 37–40.

Skinner, C.N. 1978. An experiment in classifying fire environments in Sawpit Gulch, Shasta County, California. M.A. Thesis. California State University, Chico.

Skinner, C.N. 1995a. Change in spatial characteristics of forest openings in the Klamath Mountains of northwestern California, USA. Landscape Ecology 10:219–228.

Skinner, C.N. 1995b. Using prescribed fire to improve wildlife habitat near Shasta Lake. Unpublished file report, USDA Forest Service, Shasta-Trinity National Forest, Shasta Lake R.D., Redding, CA.

Skinner, C.N. 2002a. Fire history in riparian reserves of the Klamath Mountains. Association for Fire Ecology Miscellaneous Publication 1:164–169.

Skinner, C.N. 2002b. Influence of fire on dead woody material in forests of California and southwestern Oregon. P. 445–454 in W. F. Laudenslayer Jr., P. J. Shea, B. E. Valentine, C. P. Weatherspoon, and T. E. Lisle (eds.), Proceedings of the symposium on the ecology and management of dead wood in western forests. November 2–4, 1999; Reno, NV. USDA Forest Service, Pacific Southwest Research Station, Albany, CA, General Technical Report PSW-GTR-181.

Skinner, C.N. 2003a. Fire regimes of upper montane and subalpine glacial basins in the Klamath Mountains of northern California. Tall Timbers Research Station Miscellaneous Publication 13:145–151.

Skinner, C.N. 2003b. A tree-ring based fire history of riparian reserves in the Klamath Mountains. In California riparian systems: processes and floodplains management, ecology, and restoration. 2001 Riparian Habitat and Floodplains Conference Proceedings, March 12–15, 2001, Sacramento, CA, edited by P. M. Farber. Sacramento: Riparian Habitat Joint Venture.

Skinner, C.N., and C. Chang. 1996. Fire regimes, past and present. P. 1041–1069 in Sierra Nevada Ecosystem Project: Final report to Congress. Volume II: Assessments and scientific basis for management options. Centers for Water and Wildland Resources, University of California, Davis, Water Resources Center Report No. 37.

Smith, J.P., Jr., and J.O. Sawyer, Jr. 1988. Endemic vascular plants of northwestern California and southwestern Oregon. Madrono 35:54–69.

Stebbins, G.L., and J. Major. 1965. Endemism and speciation in the California flora. Ecological Monographs 35:1–35.

Stephens, S.L. 2001. Fire history differences in adjacent Jeffrey pine and upper montane forests in the Sierra Nevada. The International Journal of Wildland Fire 10:161–167.

Stephens, S.L., and M.A. Finney. 2002. Prescribed fire mortality of Sierra Nevada mixed conifer tree species: effects of crown damage and forest floor combustion. Forest Ecology and Management 162(2):261–271.

Stephens, S.L., C.N. Skinner, and S.J. Gill. 2003. A dendrochonology based fire history of Jeffrey pine-mixed conifer forests in the Sierra San Pedro Martir, Mexico. Canadian Journal of Forest Research 33:1090–1101.

Stuart, J.D., and L.A. Salazar. 2000. Fire history of white fir forests in the coastal mountains of northwestern California. Northwest Science 74:280–285.

Sullivan, M.S. 1992. The travels of Jededia Smith. University of Nebraska Press, Lincoln.

Swanson, F.J., J.A. Jones, D.O. Wallin, and J.H. Cissel. 1994. Natural variability—implications for ecosystem management. P. 80–94. In M. E. Jensen and P.S. Bourgeron (eds), Eastside forest ecosystem health assessment, Vol. II: Ecosystem management: principles and applications. USDA Forest Service, Pacific Northwest Research Station, Portland, OR.

Taylor, A.H. 2000. Fire regimes and forest changes along a montane forest gradient, Lassen Volcanic National Park, southern Cascade Mountains, USA. Journal of Biogeography 27:87–104.

Taylor, A.H., and C.N. Skinner. 1997. Fire regimes and management of old growth Douglas fir forests in the Klamath Mountains of northwestern California. P. 203–208 in J. Greenlee (ed.), Proceedings—Fire Effects on Threatened and Endangered Species and Habitats Conference, Nov. 13–16, 1995. Coeur d'Alene, Idaho. International Association of Wildland Fire, Fairfield, WA.

Taylor, A.H., and C.N. Skinner. 1998. Fire history and landscape dynamics in a late-successional reserve in the Klamath Mountains, California, USA. Forest Ecology and Management 111: 285–301.

Taylor, A.H., and C.N. Skinner. 2003. Spatial patterns and controls on historical fire regimes and forest structure in the Klamath Mountains. Ecological Applications 13:704–719.

Tirmenstein, D. 1989. *Quercus chrysolepis*. In The fire effects information system [Online]. USDA Forest Service, Rocky Mountain Research Station, Fire Sciences Laboratory, Missoula, MT. Accessed July 15, 1995. http://www.fs.fed.us/database/feis/plants/tree/quechr/index.html.

Thornburgh, D.A. 1995. The natural role of fire in the Marble Mountain Wilderness. P. 273–274 in J. K. Brown, R. W. Mutch, C. W. Spoon, and R. H. Wakimoto (eds.), Proceedings: Symposium on fire in wilderness and park management. USDA Forest Service, Intermountain Research Station, Ogden, UT, General Technical Report INT-GTR-320.

USCB. 2002. Census 2000 data for the state of California. In United States Census 2000. US Census Bureau, Washington, D.C. Available online at: http://www.census.gov/census2000/states/ca.html.

USDA Forest Service. 2003. Biscuit post-fire assessment—Rogue River and Siskiyou National Forests: Josephine and Curry Counties. Siskiyou National Forest. Grants Pass, OR.

USDA-USDI. 1994. Record of decision for amendments to Forest Service and Bureau of Land Management planning documents within the range of the northern spotted owl; standard and guidelines for management of habitat for late-successional and old-growth forest related species within the range of the northern spotted owl. USDA Forest Service and USDI Bureau of Land Management, Portland, OR.

van Wagtendonk, J.W., and D. Cayan. 2007. Temporal and spatial distribution of lightning strikes in California in relationship to large-scale weather patterns. Fire Ecology (in press).

Waring, R.H. 1969. Forest plants of the eastern Siskiyous: their environmental and vegetational distribution. Northwest Science 43:1–17.

Weatherspoon, C. P., and C. N. Skinner. 1995. An assessment of factors associated with damage to tree crowns from the 1987 wildfires in northern California. Forest. Science 41:430–451.

West, G.J. 1985. Holocene vegetation and climatic changes in California's North Coast Ranges. P. 8–29 in J.F. Hayes and W.R. Hildebrandt (eds.), Archaeological investigations on Pilot Ridge: Results from the 1984 field season. Center for Anthropological Studies Center, Sonoma State University, and Center for Anthropological Research, San Jose State University. Unpublished report on file at the Six Rivers National Forest., Eureka, CA.

West, G.J. 1988. Holocene vegetation and climatic history of the Trinity River region: the pollen record. P. 13–28 in E. Sundahl (ed.), Cox Bar (CA-TRI-1008): a borax lake pattern site on the Trinity River, Trinity County, California. Unpublished report on file at the Shasta College Archaeology Lab, Redding, CA.

West, G.J. 1989. Late Pleistocene/Holocene vegetation and climate. P. 36–55 in M. E. Basgall and W. R. Hildebrandt (eds.), Prehistory of the Sacramento River canyon, Shasta County, California. Center for Archaeological Research at Davis, Publication Number 9. University of California, Davis, CA.

West, G.J. 1990. Holocene fossil pollen records of Douglas fir in northwestern California: reconstruction of past climate. P. 119–122 in J.L. Betancourt and A.M. MacKay (eds.), Proceedings of the Sixth Annual Pacific Climate (PACLIM) Workshop. California Department of Water Resources, Sacramento, CA, Interagency Ecological Studies Program Technical Report 23.

Whitlock, C. 2001. Variations in Holocene fire frequency: a view from the western United States. Biology and Environment 101B(1–2): 65–77.

Whitlock, C., and R. S. Anderson. 2003. Fire history reconstructions based on sediment records from lakes and wetlands. P. 3–31 in T.T. Veblen, W.L. Baker, G. Montenegro, and T.W. Swetnam (eds.), Fire and climatic change in temperate ecosystems of the western Americas. Springer-Verlag, New York.

Whitlock, C., J. Mohr, T. Minckley, and J. Marlon. 2001. Holocene vegetation and fire history from Cedar Lake, northern California. Final report for Cooperative Agreement USFS PSW-99-0010CA. Department of Geography, University of Oregon, Eugene, OR.

Whitlock, C., C.N. Skinner, T. Minckley, and J.A. Mohr. 2004. Comparison of charcoal and tree-ring records of recent fires in the eastern Klamath Mountains. Canadian Journal of Forest Research 34:2110–2121.

Whitlock, C., S.L. Shafer, and J. Marlon. 2003. The role of climate and vegetation change in shaping past and future fire regimes in the northwestern US and the implications for ecosystem management. Forest Ecology and Management 178:5–21.

Whittaker, R.H. 1960. Vegetation of the Siskiyou Mountains, Oregon and California. Ecological Monographs 30:279–338.

Whittaker, R.H. 1961. Vegetation history of the Pacific Coast States and the "central" significance of the Klamath region. Madrono 16:5–23.

Wilken, G.C. 1967. History and fire record of a timberland brush field in the Sierra Nevada of California. Ecology 48:302–304.

Wills, R.D., and J.D. Stuart. 1994. Fire history and stand development of a Douglas-fir/hardwood forest in northern California. Northwest Science 68:205–212.

Wilson, R.B. 1904. Township descriptions of the lands examined for the proposed Trinity Forest Reserve, California. U.S. Department of Agriculture, Bureau of Forestry, Washington, DC.

CHAPTER 10

Southern Cascades Bioregion

CARL N. SKINNER AND ALAN H. TAYLOR

> In ... the southern portions of ... the Cascades ... where the forests are largely or mainly of yellow pine in open growth, with very little litter or underbrush, destructive fires have been few and small, although throughout these regions there are few trees which are not marked by fire, without, however, doing them any serious damage.
>
> HENRY GANNETT, 1902

Description of the Bioregion

Physical Geography

The Cascade Range extends from British Columbia, Canada, south to northern California where it meets the Sierra Nevada. The Southern Cascades bioregion in California is bounded on the west by the Sacramento Valley and the Klamath Mountains, and on the east by the Modoc Plateau and Great Basin. The bioregion encompasses the Southern Cascades section of Miles and Goudey (1997) and covers approximately 4% (16,740 km² [6,460 mi²]) of the area of California. Mt. Shasta and Mt. Lassen are located in this bioregion.

The Cascades are geologically young and characterized by prominent volcanic peaks (some recently active) that stand above an extensive mainly basaltic plateau. In parts of the central and southern Cascades, volcanics overlie granitic and metamorphic rocks similar to those of the Klamath Mountains and Sierra Nevada (Oakeshott 1971). Soils are derived from volcanic material and are classified as Alfisols, Entisols, Inceptisols, Mollisols, Ultisols, and Vertisols (Miles and Goudey 1997).

Overall, topography in the southern Cascades is gentler than that in the Klamath Mountains or the Sierra Nevada. Elevations range from about 60 m (196 ft) in the southwestern foothills adjacent to the Sacramento Valley to 4,317 m (14,162 ft) at the summit of Mt. Shasta. Other notable topographic features include Mt. Lassen, the Medicine Lake Highlands, Butte Valley, Hat Creek Valley, Burney Falls, Shasta Valley, and the Pit River canyon. Both the Klamath and the Pit rivers originate east of the Cascade crest and breach the range as they flow westward toward the Pacific Ocean (Map 10.1).

Climatic Patterns

The climate in the southern Cascades is mediterranean with wet, cool winters and dry, warm summers. The expression of this climate regime within the southern Cascades is mediated by location along three predominant climatic gradients: (1) a west-to-east gradient in annual precipitation and winter temperature where wetter and warmer conditions prevail on the west side of the range south of Mt. Shasta, (2) a north-to-south gradient where annual precipitation is lower on the west side of the range north of Mt. Shasta due to a rain shadow effect from the Klamath Mountains, and (3) decreasing temperatures and increasing annual precipitation with increasing elevation (Table 10.1).

The driest areas are Butte and Shasta Valleys to the north of Mt. Shasta. Most precipitation falls as snow at higher elevations. The average early April snowpack depth and water content for selected sites in the Cascade Range are shown in Table 10.2.

The west-to-east gradient in precipitation and temperature help to create very different environments at similar elevations on the west side of the crest compared to the east side of the crest, albeit not as dramatically as in the Sierra Nevada. Nevertheless, distinctly different vegetation develops in response to the different climatic regimes. Therefore, the term *westside* is used to refer to environments typical of the west side of the crest and *eastside* for those typical of the east side of the range.

WEATHER SYSTEMS

The southern Cascades are susceptible to the critical fire weather conditions of high winds and low humidity that are caused by weather patterns characteristic of both California and the Pacific Northwest (Hull et al. 1966). Three types of fire weather conditions that occur during the dry period of the year (fire season) are important in the southern Cascades: (1) Pacific High–Post-Frontal (Post-Frontal), (2) Pacific High–Pre-Frontal (Pre-Frontal), and (3) Subtropical High Aloft (Subtropical High).

The Post-Frontal type occurs when high pressure follows the passage of a cold front and causes strong foehn winds

TABLE 10.1

Normal annual, January, and July precipitation and normal maxima and minima January and July temperatures for representative stations (elevation noted) of the southern Cascade Range (WRCC 2002)

	Average Precipitation cm (in)	Normal Daily Maximum Temperature °C (°F)	Normal Daily Minimum Temperature °C (°F)
Paradise (533 m), West Side			
Annual	139.7 (55.0)		
January	28.2 (11.1)	12.1 (53.7)	3.1 (37.5)
July	0.3 (0.1)	33.1 (91.6)	17.6 (63.6)
Mt. Shasta City (1,204 m), West Side			
Annual	99.1 (39.0)		
January	18.8 (7.4)	5.9 (42.6)	−3.5 (25.7)
July	0.8 (0.3)	29.2 (84.6)	10.1 (50.2)
Mineral (1,486 m), West Side			
Annual	141.0 (55.5)		
January	25.7 (10.1)	4.9 (40.8)	−5.8 (21.5)
July	1.0 (0.2)	27.1 (80.7)	5.9 (42.7)
Burney (956 m), East Side			
Annual	70.6 (27.8)		
January	12.4 (4.9)	6.4 (43.5)	−7.7 (18.1)
July	0.5 (0.2)	30.8 (87.4)	6.2 (43.2)
Mt. Hebron (1,295 m), East Side			
Annual	30.0 (11.8)		
January	3.3 (1.3)	3.9 (39.1)	−9.2 (15.5)
July	1.0 (0.4)	28.3 (83.0)	5.9 (42.6)
Chester (1,379 m), East Side			
Annual	86.1 (33.9)		
January	16.5 (6.5)	5.5 (41.9)	−6.9 (19.6)
July	0.8 (0.3)	29.4 (85.0)	6.7 (44.0)

TABLE 10.2

Average April 1 snowpack data for representative snow courses in the southern Cascade Range ordered from north to south (CCSS 2002)

	Elevation m (ft)	West/East Side	Snow Depth cm (in)	Water Content cm (in)
Medicine Lake	2,042 (6,700)	East	202.7 (79.8)	81.3 (32.0)
Dead Horse Canyon	1,372 (4,500)	East	65.3 (25.7)	29.0 (11.4)
Burney Springs	1,433 (4,700)	East	12.7 (5.0)	5.1 (2.0)
Blacks Mountain	2,042 (6,700)	East	56.9 (22.4)	20.3 (8.0)
Chester Flat	1,402 (4,600)	East	40.6 (16.0)	16.5 (6.5)
Mount Shasta	2,408 (7,900)	West	307.3 (121.0)	106.2 (41.8)
Stouts Meadow	1,646 (5,400)	West	206.5 (81.3)	95.8 (37.7)
Snow Mountain	1,859 (6,100)	West	161.8 (63.7)	81.8 (32.2)
Thousand Lakes	1,981 (6,500)	West	206.2 (81.2)	86.4 (34.0)
Lower Lassen Peak	2,515 (8,250)	West	454.2 (178.8)	202.7 (79.8)
Mill Creek Flat	1,798 (5,900)	West	234.7 (92.4)	98.0 (38.6)

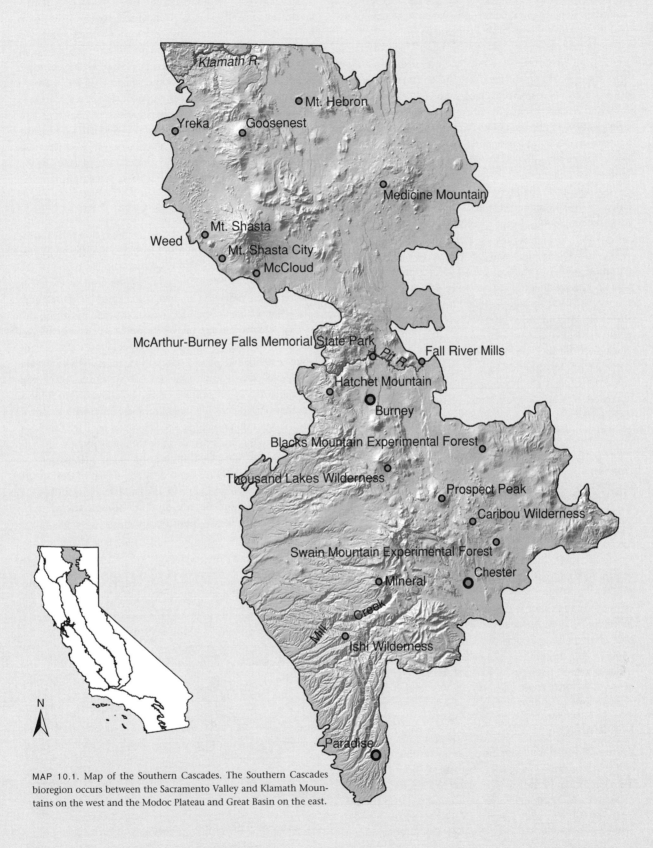

MAP 10.1. Map of the Southern Cascades. The Southern Cascades bioregion occurs between the Sacramento Valley and Klamath Mountains on the west and the Modoc Plateau and Great Basin on the east.

from the north and northeast. The Cone fire in September 2002 that burned 812 ha (2006 ac), mostly in the Blacks Mountain Experimental Forest, is an example of a major fire that burned under Post-Frontal conditions.

The Pre-Frontal type occurs when the southern dry tail of a cold front crosses the area and generates strong southwest or west winds. The strong winds are the key fire weather component in this type because it is common for temperatures to drop and relative humidity to rise. The Lost fire in the Hat Creek Valley that burned more than 9,700 ha (24,000 ac) in September 1987 and the Fountain fire of August 1992 that burned more than 26,000 ha (64,250 ac) on Hatchet Mountain are examples of fires driven by Pre-Frontal conditions.

The Subtropical High type occurs when stagnant high pressure produces high temperatures and low relative humidity for extended periods. In the Cascades, Subtropical High conditions lead to fires controlled mainly by local fuel conditions, diurnal wind flow, and topography. In areas with steep elevation gradients, shifting diurnal winds cause fires to continually change direction. An example was seen in the Bolam fire that burned approximately 390 ha (960 ac) on the north slopes of Mt. Shasta in August 1970. Afternoon upslope winds tended to push this fire toward Military Pass. However, glaciers sitting high on the mountain provided a source of cooling for pulses of downslope winds that occasionally overcame the general afternoon upslope flow. This led to what appeared to be erratic fire behavior as the fire "front" shifted direction in relation to the shifting dominance of the general afternoon upslope winds and the pulses of downslope winds.

LIGHTNING

The Cascade Range averages 18.8 lightning strikes (range 5.5–33.8)/100 km²/yr (49.5 strikes [range 14.5–89.1]/100 mi²/yr), which are a common source of ignition. Although lightning is common throughout the range, the density of strikes increases from south to north (van Wagtendonk and Cayan 2007). Occasionally, incursions of subtropical moisture that moves north from the eastern Pacific and the Gulf of California produce widespread thunderstorms that result in numerous fires. Hundreds of lightning fires can be ignited over short periods during these events. The occurrence of widespread, simultaneous, lightning ignitions has contributed to fires that burn for weeks and cover very large areas as in 1977, 1987, 1990, and 1999.

Ecological Zones

South of the latitude of Mt. Shasta, vegetation composition and species dominance in the lower and mid-montane zones is similar to that in the northern Sierra Nevada, but the upper montane and subalpine zones are more similar to the Klamath Mountains and northern Cascades (Parker 1991). When compared to the Sierra Nevada, vegetation composition in the Cascades is more strongly controlled by local topography and substrate and less so by elevation (Parker

1995), likely due to less dramatic elevation differences and youthful geology with young soils. Open woodlands, shrublands, and areas of sparse vegetation occur over wide areas on harsh sites. These conditions are common where young lava flows or other young volcanic materials with shallow, poor soils inhibit vegetative growth regardless of ecological zone. North of Mt. Shasta, in the rain shadow of the Klamath Mountains, the vegetation of the west side of the Cascades resembles vegetation more characteristic of the drier east side of the Cascades. Lower elevations on both sides of the Cascades are dominated by grasslands, shrublands, and woodlands. However, there is considerable variability in the composition and physiognomy of these vegetation types.

SOUTHWESTERN FOOTHILLS

The southwestern foothills of the Cascades, along the northeastern edge of the Sacramento Valley, is a low-elevation, dissected volcanic plateau with vegetation similar to that in the Sierra Nevada foothills (Fig. 10.1). Common alliances in this portion of the bioregion are blue oak (*Quercus douglasii*), gray pine (*Pinus sabiniana*), interior live oak (*Quercus wislizenii*), valley oak (*Quercus lobata*), buck brush (*Ceanothus cuneatus* var. *cuneatus*), annual grassland, and vernal pools (Miles and Goudey 1997). Two other important alliances in this zone are ponderosa pine (*Pinus ponderosa*) and California black oak (*Quercus kelloggii*). This ecological zone corresponds to subsection M261Fa (Tuscan Flows) of Miles and Goudey (1997). Three major creeks (Mill, Antelope, and Deer) flow from the Cascades westward to the Sacramento Valley through this area.

The southwestern foothills area has a complex pattern of vegetation primarily influenced by the depth of the underlying soil (Biswell and Gilman 1961). Blue oak woodland is the most common alliance, and it varies from forest to savanna in terms of tree density (Appendix 3).

NORTHWESTERN FOOTHILLS

The northwestern foothills zone is north of Mt. Shasta and generally corresponds to subsections M261Db and M261Dc of Miles and Goudey (1997). This zone includes the Shasta Valley and adjacent foothills. As this area lies in the rain shadow of the Klamath Mountains and is above 790 m (2,600 ft) in elevation, it is more of an eastside type (Fig. 10.2). Common alliances include big sagebrush (*Artemisia tridentata* vars.), western juniper (*Juniperus occidentalis* ssp. *occidentalis*) woodlands, meadows (mostly sedges [*Carex* spp.]), buck brush, California black oak, and ponderosa pine (Miles and Goudey 1997). Extensive areas are dominated by introduced grasses, especially cheat grass (*Bromus tectorum*). See Chapter 11 on the Northeastern Plateau for more on vegetation alliances common to this zone.

LOW ELEVATION EASTSIDE

Lower elevations of the east side of the Cascades occur primarily along the Pit River corridor and the lower reaches

FIGURE 10.1. Southwestern Foothills occur on a dissected volcanic plateau. The thin, rocky soils often support blue oak and gray pine as shown here in Bidwell Park, Chico. (Photo by Carl N. Skinner.)

FIGURE 10.2. Northwestern Foothills. Shrublands on north slopes of Mt. Shasta looking northwest into the Shasta Valley. Shrubs in photo are mostly greenleaf manzanita, tobacco brush, and bitterbrush. (Photo by Carl N. Skinner.)

of Hat Creek. This zone corresponds roughly to the lower portions of Miles and Goudey's (1997) subsection M261Dj (Hat Creek Rim). The low elevation of the Pit River gorge may have allowed it to serve as a corridor for plant species characteristic of westside habitats to migrate into eastside environments. For example, between Burney and Fall River, gray pine, California black oak, Oregon white oak *(Quercus garryana)*, and buck brush, usually associated with westside environments, co-occur with western juniper and bitterbrush *(Purshia tridentate)* (Fig. 10.3). See Chapter 11 on the Northeastern Plateau for more on vegetation alliances common to this zone.

The Pit River corridor near Burney Falls also has disjunct stands of mountain misery *(Chamaebatia foliolosa)* that grow

in association with ponderosa pine, California black oak, Douglas-fir *(Pseudotsuga menziesii* var. *menziesii)*, Oregon white oak, and other conifers. For more information on mountain misery, which commonly occurs throughout the montane zone in the Sierra Nevada south of the Feather River canyon, see Chapter 12.

MID-MONTANE WESTSIDE/EASTSIDE

Conifer forests dominate the mid-montane zone on both sides of the range and they are intermixed with woodlands and shrublands. Few natural meadows or grasslands occur on the west side of the range. Species composition varies from

FIGURE 10.3. Lower Montane East-side. Gray pine mixed with western juniper on rim of Pit River Canyon near Fall River Mills depicting the mixing of vegetation usually found on the west side of the range with that more characteristic of the east side of the Cascades. (Photo by Carl Skinner, USDA Forest Service.)

FIGURE 10.4. Mid-Montane West-side. Mixed stand of Douglas-fir, pon-derosa pine, sugar pine, incense-cedar, California black oak, white fir, and mountain dogwood in the Flatwoods near Big Bend. Stand was mechani-cally thinned for fire hazard reduction ten years prior to the photograph. (Photo by Derrick B. Skinner.)

west to east over the crest but less so than in the Sierra Nevada because the crest is lower in elevation and mountain passes are relatively low (Griffin 1967). Nevertheless, the mid-montane zone of the southern Cascades is quite differ-ent on the east compared to the west side of the crest because of the rain shadow effect and differences in tem-perature. Consequently, our discussion is split between west-side and eastside alliances. The mid-montane westside cor-responds to subsections M261Dg and M261Di of Miles and Goudey (1997). The mid-montane eastside corresponds to subsections M261Da and M261Dj of Miles and Goudey (1997).

Mixed-species conifer forests dominate the mid-montane zone on the west side of the Cascade Range (Fig. 10.4). Any of six conifer species (ponderosa pine, Douglas-fir, incense-cedar [*Calocedrus decurrens*], sugar pine [*Pinus lambertiana*], Jeffrey pine [*Pinus jeffreyi*], and white fir [*Abies concolor*]) may co-occur and share dominance (Barbour 1988, Parker 1995, Beaty and Taylor 2001). A subcanopy of the deciduous hardwoods California black oak, bigleaf maple (*Acer macrophyllum*), and mountain dogwood (*Cornus nutallii*) and the evergreen canyon live oak (*Quercus chrysolepis*) may occur beneath the conifer canopy. Stand composition is influenced by elevation, slope aspect, soil moisture conditions, and substrate (Griffin 1967).

FIGURE 10.5. Upper Montane. Shrub fields intermixed with patches of conifers on Snow Mountain (named for the large patch of snow in the center of the photo that lasts through the summer except in very dry years). Dominant shrubs are tobacco brush, greenleaf manzanita, bitter cherry, and bush chinquapin. (Photo by Carl N. Skinner.)

Mixed white fir–red fir *(Abies magnifica* var. *shastensis)* forests occur above the elevation of the mixed conifer zone in the Cascades (Parker 1995). The forest cover is often interrupted by stands of montane chaparral. The most common shrubs of the Cascade Range montane chaparral are greenleaf manzanita *(Arctostaphylos patula), Ceanothus* spp., and shrub oaks. Montane chaparral appears to occupy sites that are unable to support trees due to shallow soils; exposed slopes where cold, high winds and ice damage are common; or sites that have experienced severe fire (Wilken 1967; Weatherspoon 1988; Bolsinger 1989; Beaty and Taylor 2001).

Extensive areas east of the Cascade crest are dominated by ponderosa pine, Jeffrey pine, or a combination of both. Other conifers, such as white fir and incense cedar, may be locally important but do not usually attain dominance, especially on the drier sites (Rundel et al. 1977). Western juniper and curl-leaf mountain-mahogany *(Cercocarpus ledifolius)* may be associates on drier and rockier sites. Widely scattered, small stands of quaking aspen occur throughout this zone east of the Cascade crest around seeps, on meadow edges, and on young exposed basalt.

UPPER MONTANE

Upper-montane-zone conifer forests and shrublands have similar species composition on both sides of the crest. However, species dominance varies widely and is influenced by total annual precipitation, topography, and substrate. The more common conifers in this zone are Jeffrey pine, ponderosa pine, white fir, red fir, lodgepole pine *(Pinus contorta* ssp. *murrayana)*, and western white pine *(Pinus monticola)*. Common shrubs include bush chinquapin *(Chrysolepsis sempervirens)*, greenleaf manzanita, pinemat manzanita *(Arctostaphylos nevadensis)*, mountain whitethorn *(Ceanothus cordulatus)*, tobacco brush *(Ceanothus velutinus* var. *velutinus)* (commonly called snowbrush in this bioregion), huck-leberry oak *(Quercus vaccinifolia)*, Parry's rabbitbrush *(Chrysothamnus parryi)*, rubber rabbitbrush *(Chrysothamnus nauseosus)*, and big sagebrush. As in the mid-montane zone, forest cover can be interrupted by stands of montane shrubs on harsh sites or where there has been a history of severe fires (Fig. 10.5). The drier portions of this zone are found on the eastern edge of the bioregion and correspond to subsections M261Dd and M261Dh of Miles and Goudey (1997). See Chapter 11 for more on herbaceous and shrub vegetation alliances common to the eastern part of this zone.

Large, seasonally wet, montane meadows are characteristic of the upper-montane zone east of the crest. The remainder of the zone corresponds to the portions of subsections M261Df, M261Di, and M261Dm of Miles and Goudey (1997) that are at elevations lower than the subalpine zone.

SUBALPINE

Subalpine and alpine vegetation is generally limited to the highest peaks in the southern Cascades such as Mt. Shasta, Mt. Lassen, and Crater Peak. Common alliances are mountain hemlock *(Tsuga mertensiana)*, whitebark pine *(Pinus albicaulis)*, and red fir. These areas are the higher elevations of subsections M261Df, M261Di, and M261Dm of Miles and Goudey (1997) (Fig. 10.6).

Overview of Historic Fire Occurrence

There are generally two periods with distinctly different fire regimes in the Cascades. First was a Native American period, before 1905, when fires were generally frequent. This period includes both the pre-historic and the European-settlement periods. The Native American period was followed by the fire-suppression period ensuing with the establishment of the national forest reserves in 1905 when fire occurrence decreases dramatically (Skinner and Chang 1996; Taylor

FIGURE 10.6. Subalpine woodland of mountain hemlock near Reading Peak in Lassen Volcanic National Park. (Photo by Carl N. Skinner.)

1990, 1993, 2000; Beaty and Taylor 2001; Bekker and Taylor 2001; Norman 2002; Norman and Taylor 2002, 2005).

Prehistoric Period

As discussed in Chapter 17, native people of the southern Cascade Range used fire to promote production of food and basketry materials, to help gather grasshoppers and other insects, to improve hunting conditions, and for ceremonial purposes (Lewis 1990, 1993). Though the use of fire by native people appears to have been widespread, the extent of its influence on vegetation at broad scales is unknown.

The mediterranean climate, the commonality of lightning ignitions, and the widespread use of fire by native people in the Cascades promoted frequent surface fires of mostly low to moderate intensity with frequency decreasing with elevation. Pronounced local variations in fire frequency also occur due to interruptions in fuel connectivity caused by volcanics (e.g., lava flows, scoria depositions, debris flows; Taylor 2000).

Historic Period

Parts of the bioregion began to experience a decrease in fire occurrence as early as the late nineteenth century (Norman and Taylor 2005). The decrease was pronounced near meadows and coincided well with a documented period of heavy sheep grazing (Taylor 1990b, Norman and Taylor 2005). Most areas did not experience a fire frequency decline until the beginnings of organized fire suppression. The earliest accounts of wildland fire suppression are from 1887 for fires burning along the railroad lines near what is now the city of Mt. Shasta (Morford 1984). The first recorded organized fire protection in wildland areas was by the Central Pacific Railroad in 1898, which supported mounted patrols to suppress fires in the McCloud flats east of Mt. Shasta (Morford 1984).

Current Period

The total area burned by fires was greatly reduced in the twentieth century compared with pre-historic levels, due to highly effective fire suppression in the relatively gentle terrain. The gentle terrain also allowed early logging of the large fire-resistant trees which, combined with the effects of fire suppression, has left forests heavily stocked with young trees. Forests in parks and wilderness areas that were not logged have also developed high densities of young trees due to fire suppression (Dolph et al. 1995, Taylor 2000). Thus, where surface fires were frequent and extensive (e.g., foothill through mid-montane) and mostly low to moderate intensity, fires are now either kept small or they escape initial fire suppression efforts and become large, mostly high-intensity fires. Examples of these large, severe fires include the Pondosa (1977; 6,000 ha [about 15,000 ac]), Lost (1987; 9,700 ha [24,000 ac]), Campbell (1990; more than 48,500 ha [120,000 ac]), Fountain (1992; about 26,000 ha [64,250 ac]), and Gunn (1999, more than 24,000 ha [59,000 ac]). All of these fires except the Fountain fire were started by lightning.

Further indication that the reduction in fire occurrence that has occurred during last century is largely due to fire suppression is that the nature of climate variation over the last approximately 150 years has been such that one would have expected fire occurrence to have increased rather than decline (Swetnam 1993, Stine 1996, Chang 1999). The climate has generally warmed since the mid-1800s and precipitation, although variable, was relatively high in the late 1800s and early 1900s and declined at the time when fire-suppression policies were initially implemented (Graumlich 1987, Hughes and Brown 1992, Earle 1993, Stine 1996). The longer fire season associated with a warming climate (Flannigan and Van Wagner 1991, Chang 1999, Swetnam and Baisan 2003) and the accumulation of burnable fuel biomass as a result of increased precipitation (Chang 1999, Swetnam and Baisan 2003) would likely have contributed to more frequent, widespread fires. Yet, just the opposite has taken place.

The southwestern Cascade foothills were assessed for biotic integrity (Moyle and Randall 1996) and fire risk (McKelvey and Busse 1996) by the Sierra Nevada Ecosystem Project (SNEP). This area has a high fire risk based on area burned through the twentieth century compared with other areas included in the SNEP assessment (McKelvey and Busse 1996). The southwestern foothills portion of the Cascades has the greatest proportion of area burned over the period 1910–1993 of all major watersheds included in the SNEP assessment area (SNEP 2003). However, Moyle and Randall (1996) found the biological integrity of the three major tributaries (Mill, Antelope, and Deer Creeks) to be unusually high compared to the rest of the SNEP assessment area with much of the native fish and amphibian faunas intact "... and the biotic communities ... still largely governed by natural processes" despite the frequent occurrence of large fires in the twentieth century. Thus, the relatively frequent, large twentieth-century fires did not have a detrimental effect on aquatic communities at least in this part of the Cascades. Notably, two more large fires have burned in the watershed since the SNEP assessment—the Barkley occurred in 1994 and burned more than 10,000 ha (24,700 ac), whereas in 1999 the Gunn fire burned more than 24,000 ha (60,000 ac).

Major Ecological Zones

Fire Patterns

To adequately convey the importance of widespread fire regime characteristics, we must break with the protocol of the other bioregional chapters and discuss the fire regimes more generally, without assigning them necessarily to a specific ecological zone. To assign them to a specific ecological zone could potentially convey a misleading impression to the reader that these characteristics are specific to a particular ecological zone.

SEASONALITY

The position of fire scars identified in tree-ring fire-scar studies demonstrates that most fire scars occur in latewood or at the ring boundary (Fig. 10.7). This indicates that fires burned mostly in mid-summer through fall, which is typical of forests under the influence of long, dry summers characteristic of mediterranean climates (Skinner 2002). Both dead and live fuels reach their lowest moisture levels at that time and ignite and burn easily. However, there is temporal and spatial variation in the seasonal timing of fires suggesting a complex set of interactions among slope aspect, elevation, climate variation, and the seasonal occurrence of fire (Taylor 2000, Beaty and Taylor 2001, Bekker and Taylor 2001, Norman 2002, Norman and Taylor 2002, Norman and Taylor 2003). Fires occurred earlier in the season on drier pine-dominated sites (i.e., south- and west-facing aspects) at lower elevation compared to more mesic sites (i.e., north- and east-facing aspects) and high-elevation sites (Taylor 2000; Bekker and Taylor

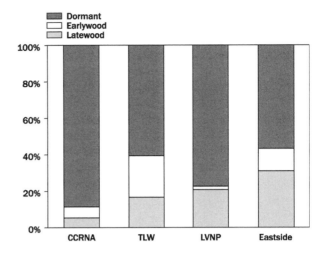

FIGURE 10.7. Distribution of intra-ring locations for fire scars from fire history studies in the Cascade Range of California. Study areas were Cub Creek Research Natural Area (CCRNA; Beaty and Taylor 2001), Thousand Lakes Wilderness Area (TLW; Bekker and Taylor 2001), Lassen Volcanic National Park (LVNP; Taylor 2000), and Eastside pine and mixed conifer sites (Eastside; Norman and Taylor 2003).

2001). Seasonality has also varied over time. In pine-dominated forests east of the Cascade crest, fire scars were more common in earlywood during a cool, wet period between 1790 and 1820 than in decades before or after (Norman and Taylor 2003). Fires that burned in years with normal or above normal precipitation burned mainly in the late summer and fall.

TOPOGRAPHY

As in the Klamath Mountains, dendroecological records of historical fire regimes that include the pre–fire-suppression period demonstrate that variability in fire-return intervals and fire severity are strongly influenced by topography, especially slope aspect, elevation, and slope position. Statistically significant differences in fire-return intervals have been identified within the same forest type on different slope aspects, and fire-return interval lengths increase with elevation between the montane and upper-montane zone (Taylor 2000, Beaty and Taylor 2001, Bekker and Taylor 2001). Fire-return interval lengths have also been found to vary with slope position. Upper slopes had shorter median fire return intervals than middle and lower slopes (Norman and Taylor 2002). Fire-return intervals also vary with other terrain characteristics. Forests interspersed with lava flows, scoria fields, or other features with little or no vegetation cover that impede fire spread have longer fire return intervals than areas with continuous forest cover (Taylor 2000). Riparian zones affected landscape patterns of fire occurrence by acting as barriers to the spread of some fires as in the Klamath Mountains (Beaty and Taylor 2001, Norman and Taylor 2002) (Sidebar 10.1).

FIRE SEVERITY

Patterns of fire severity during the pre–fire-suppression period were associated with topographic position, at least in deeply incised terrain. In the Cub Creek Research Natural Area, Beaty

Fire-return intervals in most fire-scar studies from the Cascade Range have been estimated primarily from fire scars removed in wedges from trees with exposed wounds *(cat faces)* (Taylor and Halpern 1991, Taylor 2000, Beaty and Taylor 2001, Bekker and Taylor 2001, Taylor and Solem 2001). In only a few cases were stumps available to see full cross-sections of the trees (Taylor 1993, Norman and Taylor 2002, Norman 2002). Relying only on trees with open wounds may bias estimates of fire-return intervals. Wounds induced by low-intensity surface fires often heal over completely, especially on true firs *(Abies* spp.*)* and Douglas-fir, leaving no external evidence of past fires (Taylor 1993, Stuart and Salazar 2000, Taylor and Skinner 2003). Cross-sections of stumps often yield abundant evidence of past fires, although the trees have no external evidence of having been scarred by fire (Fig. 10.1.1).

For example, Taylor and Skinner (2003) found that 86% of Douglas-fir trees (stumps) with internal fire records had no external evidence of being damaged by fire. Importantly, true firs and Douglas-fir trees with open wounds often exhibit extensive rot when compared to trees with healed wounds. This may further reduce the ability to detect a full fire scar record using only trees with open wounds.

For example, Taylor and Halpern (1991) relied primarily on fire scars from cat faces of live trees in two mixed red fir–white fir stands and supplemented this sample with a few cross-sections from cut stumps next to the stands. Later, full cross-sections were sampled from cut stumps by Taylor (1993) on two 3-ha (7.5-ac) plots adjacent to the stands originally sampled by Taylor and Halpern (1991). The two new plots were located within an area that had been logged as a shelter wood, leaving abundant exposed stump surfaces to detect otherwise hidden fire scars. Mean fire-return intervals using full cross-sections from the two new plots ranged from 18.6 to 26.3 years, whereas those using the original cat-face samples were longer at 41 to 42 years. The values obtained from the new cross-sections are similar to mean

FIGURE 10.1.1. Photo of Douglas-fir stump with hidden fire scars (indicated by arrows). These scars would not be evident without seeing the full cross-section of the stump. (Photo by Carl N. Skinner, USDA Forest Service.)

fire-return intervals identified by Skinner (2003) also using full cross-sections in a red fir stand in the Klamath Mountains.

Due to variation in climate and differences in fuel beds, there are likely real differences in fire-return interval between slope aspects and along elevation gradients. However, as species composition changes from pine-dominated (with many well-preserved fire scars in open wounds) to true fir– or Douglas-fir–dominated stands (where rapid healing hides most scars and open wounds have a tendency to rot), differences detected using only cat-faced trees may be exaggerated compared to estimates from full stem cross-sections.

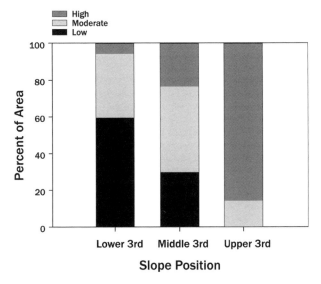

FIGURE 10.8. Topographic distribution of severity patterns in the Cub Creek Research Natural Area (Beaty and Taylor 2001).

and Taylor (2001) found that the upper thirds of slopes and ridgetops, especially on south- and west-facing aspects, experienced the highest proportion of high-severity burns. Lower thirds of slopes and north- and east-facing aspects experienced the smallest proportion of high-severity burns and the highest proportion of low-severity burns. Middle slope positions were intermediate (Fig. 10.8). This pattern is strongly pronounced in the Klamath Mountains and is discussed in detail in Chapter 9.

Southwestern Foothills

FIRE RESPONSES OF IMPORTANT SPECIES

Blue oak woodland is the most common alliance in this sub-region and it varies from forest to savanna in terms of tree density (Sawyer and Keeler-Wolf [in review]). Most dominant shrubs and hardwood trees in the foothills sprout following fire (Table 10.3). These include scrub oak (*Quercus berberidifolia*), interior live oak, birch-leaf mountain-mahogany (*Cercocarpus betuloides* var. *betuloides*), yerba santa (*Eriodictyon californicum*), bearbrush (*Garrya fremontii*) (commonly called Fremont silk tassel in this bioregion), flannel-bush (*Fremontodendron californicum*), and California bay (*Umbellularia californica*). A different regeneration strategy, germination after fire from a soil seedbank, is characteristic of three dominant shrubs: buck brush, whiteleaf manzanita (*Arctostaphylos viscida*), and common manzanita (*Arctostaphylos manzanita*) (Biswell and Gilman 1961). California nutmeg (*Torreya californica*), a sprouting conifer, is commonly found in the steep canyons, especially on north-facing slopes (Griffin and Critchfield 1972).

Additional important species in this zone are gray pine, ponderosa pine, California black oak, and California juniper (*Juniperus californica*). Each of these species survives surface fires of low to moderate intensity. Among these species, ponderosa pine is most fire resistant; California black oak, least fire resistant. Moreover, both gray pine and California black oak have characteristics that promote regeneration after more severe fire. When top-killed, California black oak sprouts vigorously from the root crown and gray pine is semi-serotinous. Gray pine's heavy cones protect the seeds from heat and cones open slowly over several years. California junipers have dense crowns that inhibit herbaceous understory growth so fires mostly scorch the edges of individual crowns. However, California juniper is not resistant to fire and is killed by moderate-intensity surface fires.

FIRE REGIME–PLANT COMMUNITY INTERACTIONS

Chapter 12 discusses fire regimes of the Sierra Nevada foothills which are likely to be similar to those of this ecological zone (Table 10.4) (see Sidebar 10.2).

TABLE 10.3
Fire response types for important species in the southwestern foothills zone of the South Cascades bioregion

	Type of Fire Response			
Lifeform	Sprouting	Seeding	Individual	*Species*
Conifer	None	Stimulated (seed dispersal)	Resistant/killed	Gray pine
	Fire stimulated	None	Resistant/top-killed/survive	California nutmeg
	None	None	Resistant/killed	Ponderosa pine
Hardwood	Fire stimulated	None	Resistant/top-killed/survive	California black oak, blue oak
	Fire stimulated	None	Top-killed/survive	Interior live oak, valley oak, California bay, bigleaf maple, Pacific dogwood, foothill ash, Fremont cottonwood
Shrub	None	Stimulated (germination)	Killed	Buck brush
	Fire stimulated	None	Top-killed/survive	California buckeye, Lemmon's ceanothus, flannel bush, birch-leaf mountain-mahogany, toyon, yerba santa, poison oak

TABLE 10.4
Fire regime characteristics for southwestern foothills ecological zone

Vegetation type	Southwestern foothills–woodlands	Southwestern foothills–conifers	Southwestern foothills–shrubs
Temporal			
Seasonality	Summer–fall	Summer–fall	Summer–fall
Fire-return interval	Short	Short	Medium
Spatial			
Size	Medium–large	Medium–large	Medium–large
Complexity	Moderate	Moderate	Multiple
Magnitude			
Intensity	Low–moderate	Low–moderate	Multiple
Severity	Low–moderate	Low–moderate	Moderate–high
Fire type	Surface	Surface	Crown

NOTE: Fire regime terms used in this table are defined in Chapter 4.

In the transition from the southwestern foothills to mid-montane forest are topographic features that support open stands of ponderosa pine and California black oak. These forests are best developed on broad, flat ridgetops. Examples are the Graham and the Beaver Creek Pinery in the Deer Creek watershed (Fig. 10.2.1). Though it survived the 1990 Campbell fire largely intact, the Graham Pinery suffered significant pine mortality in the Barkley fire of 1994. The Beaver Creek Pinery (BCP), which is approximately 250 ha (615 ac), was also burned by both fires with only patchy tree mortality.

FIGURE 10.2.1. Lower-Montane Westside. The Beaver Creek Pinery sits on this flat ridgetop in the Ishi Wilderness Area. (Photo by Carl Skinner, USDA Forest Service.)

FIGURE 10.2.2. Typical stand structure in the Beaver Creek Pinery. Note the two people standing in front of a large ponderosa pine at lower, right of center. (Photo by Carl Skinner, USDA Forest Service.)

FIGURE 10.2.3. Stand treated with mechanical thinning (whole tree harvest) followed by prescribed fire at the Blacks Mountain Experimental Forest. (Photo by Carl Skinner, USDA Forest Service.)

FIGURE 10.2.4. Stand treated with only mechanical thinning (whole tree harvest) at the Blacks Mountain Experimental Forest. (Photo by Carl Skinner, USDA Forest Service.)

Fire scars indicate the BCP burned frequently in the twentieth century. Thus, it is thought that the BCP may broadly represent stand conditions that were similar to pre–fire suppression westside ponderosa pine forests (Taylor 2002) (Fig. 10.2.2). The fire scar record (n = 36 cross-dated samples) from the BCP indicates that it burned five times during the twentieth century. However, there was a 66-year period without fire scars between 1924 and 1990. The pre–fire-suppression composite mean fire-return interval for fires that scarred 50% or more of the samples was 6 years, indicating that fires that burned throughout the BCP were frequent prior to fire suppression. There has been a four-fold increase in the mean fire-return interval to 24.5 years since the onset of the fire-suppression period. Most fire scars occurred in latewood and late-earlywood indicating that they burned during the growing season (Taylor 2002). Frequent fires seem to have promoted a fine-grained patchy stand structure with tree clumps of 100 m^2 (1,076 ft^2) to 1,500 m^2 (16,146 ft^2; Taylor 2002), similar to that described for other ponderosa pine forests that experienced frequent pre-settlement fires (e.g., Cooper 1961, Morrow 1986, White 1985).

Interestingly, diameter distributions for unlogged stands on the east side of the Cascade Range dominated by ponderosa and Jeffrey pine in the Blacks Mountain Experimental Forest (BMEF) in 1938 were similar to current diameter distributions of ponderosa pine forests in the BCP (Oliver 2001). Stands of this type at BMEF have been treated with a combination of thinning followed by prescribed fire and thinning without prescribed fire (Oliver 2000). Stands treated with both thinning and prescribed fire have developed diameter distributions very similar to those of 1938 at BMEF and found currently in the BCP (Fig. 10.2.3). However, where thinning alone was used, diameter distributions remained quite different because small-diameter trees were not subsequently thinned by prescribed fire (Oliver 2001) (Fig. 10.2.4).

TABLE 10.5

Fire regime characteristics for mid-montane westside and eastside ecological zones

Vegetation type	Mid-montane conifers—west side	Mid-montane shrubs—west side	Mid-montane conifers—east side	Knobcone pine	Mid-montane shrubs—east side
Temporal					
Seasonality	Summer–fall	Summer–fall	Summer–fall	Summer–fall	Summer–fall
Fire-return interval	Short	Medium–long	Short	Truncated Medium	Medium–long
Spatial					
Size	Small–medium	Medium–large	Small–large	Medium	Small–large
Complexity	Moderate	Low–moderate	Moderate	Low–moderate	Low–high
Magnitude					
Intensity	Low–moderate	Moderate–high	Low–moderate	Multiple	Low–high
Severity	Multiple	Moderate–high	Multiple	Moderate–high	Moderate–high
Fire type	Surface	Passive	Surface	Passive	Crown

NOTE: Fire regime terms used in this table are defined in Chapter 4.

TABLE 10.6
Fire response types for important species in the mid-montane westside zone of the South Cascades bioregion

Lifeform	Sprouting	Seeding	Individual	Species
		Type of Fire Response		
Conifer	None	Fire stimulated (establishment)	Resistant/killed	Ponderosa pine, Douglas-fir, Jeffrey pine
	None	None	Resistant/killed	Incense-cedar, sugar pine, white fir, western juniper
	None	Fire stimulated (seed dispersal)	Killed	Knobcone pine, Modoc cypress
	None	None	Killed	Pacific yew
Hardwood	Fire stimulated	None	Resistant/top-killed/ survive	California black oak
	Fire stimulated	None	Top-killed/survive	Bigleaf maple, canyon live oak, white alder, Oregon ash, quaking aspen
Shrub	Fire stimulated	Stimulated (germination)	Top-killed/killed	Greenleaf manzanita
	None	Stimulated (establishment)	Killed	Curl-leaf mountain-mahogany
	Fire stimulated	Stimulated	Top-killed/survive	Deerbrush, tobacco brush, mahala mat
	None	Stimulated (germination)	Killed	Buck brush
	Fire stimulated	None	Top-killed/survive	Birch-leaf mountain-mahogany, Lemmon's ceanothus, shrub tanoak, vine maple, mountain maple, bush chinquapin

Northwestern Foothills

Chapter 11 discusses fire regimes of the Northeastern Plateau which are likely similar to those of this area since many species and alliances are common to both areas.

Mid-Montane Westside

Most information available on fire ecology and fire history in the mid-montane zone is for woody plants in conifer-dominated landscapes (Table 10.5).

FIRE RESPONSES OF IMPORTANT SPECIES

All of the more common conifer species (ponderosa pine, Douglas-fir, incense cedar, sugar pine, Jeffrey pine, and white fir) survive frequent surface fires of low to moderate intensity

when mature (Table 10.6). The primary difference is how early in life they become resistant to these fires. All of the common deciduous hardwoods, California black oak, big-leaf maple, and mountain dogwood, and the evergreen canyon live oak are able to survive low-intensity surface fires, and they sprout vigorously when top-killed by fire. Stand composition is influenced by elevation, slope aspect, soil moisture conditions, and substrate (Griffin 1967). With few exceptions, the more common shrubs such as greenleaf manzanita, *Ceanothus* species, and shrub oaks sprout vigorously after being top-killed. One exception is whiteleaf manzanita, which is easily top-killed by even low-intensity fires and relies on soil seed banks to germinate following fires. Manzanitas and *Ceanothus* spp. generally germinate from seed following fires. One exception is Lemmon's ceanothus which relies entirely on sprouting after being top-killed.

Fire regimes in mixed-species mid-montane forests have been documented in the Cub Creek Research Natural Area (CCRNA) in the Deer Creek drainage and vary with forest species composition and environment (i.e., slope aspect, slope position, elevation), which co-vary on the western slope of the Cascades (Beaty and Taylor 2001). Median composite and point fire-return intervals on pine-dominated south-facing slopes (9 years, 19 years) were shorter than those on fir-dominated north-facing slopes (34 years, 54 years); other slope aspects had intermediate values. Variation in fire-rotation lengths paralleled that for fire return intervals, and they were longest on north-facing slopes (42.5 years) and shortest on south-facing slopes (17.4 years). Fire extent in the 1,590-ha (3,900-ac) study area also varied by year and by slope aspect. The average extent of a burn was 106 ha (range, 7–379 ha). Most fires burned only one or two slopes but five burned across three or more slopes. Average fire sizes were largest on north-facing (80 ha, range 37–120 ha) and south-facing (75 ha, range 21–105 ha) slopes and smaller on other slope aspects. Most of these burns (90%) occurred after trees had stopped growth for the year (dormant) (see Sidebar 10.2). Topographic variation in fire severity in the Cub Creek watershed, which is deeply incised, was particularly pronounced as interpreted from the spatial distribution of forest structural types throughout the watershed (Fig. 10.8). Multi-aged and multi-sized forests were concentrated on lower slopes and valley bottoms whereas more even-aged and even-sized stands that develop after high-severity burns mainly occupied upper slopes and ridgetops. Similar landscape structural patterns have been described in the steep, complex terrain of the Klamath Mountains (Taylor and Skinner 1998). This suggests that topography may be an important control on fire severity and forest structure at landscape scales. Upper- and mid-slope positions often experience higher fire intensities due to pre-heating of fuels, higher effective wind speeds, and lower canopy cover (Rothermel 1983, Weatherspoon and Skinner 1995, Taylor and Skinner 1998; Chapter 3 this volume).

Fire frequency in CCRNA also varied by time period. Mean composite fire-return intervals were similar in the Native American (6.6 years) and settlement (7.7 years) periods but longer (30.7 years) in the fire suppression period. Only two fires burned in the study area after 1905. The dramatic increase in fire rotation length from 28 to 407 years after 1905 underscores the decline in the role of fire in these ecosystems that begins coincident with the implementation of fire suppression. There was no evidence in CCRNA, or in other mid-montane forests on the west slope of the Cascades (Norman and Taylor 2002), of a fire frequency decline during the settlement period like that reported for mid-montane forests in the southern Sierra Nevada (Caprio and Swetnam 1995). Thus, there appears to be considerable regional variation in when fire frequency changed in California montane forests, and this may be reflected in the type and magnitude of vegetation changes that are associated with altered fire regimes.

The mixed-species conifer forests on the west side of the Cascades have changed since the onset of the fire-suppression period (Beaty 1998, Norman and Taylor 2002). Forest density has increased, and there has been a shift in species composition toward increasing density of fire-sensitive white fir. Moreover, many areas that were montane chaparral early in the twentieth century have been invaded by trees, especially white fir, and are now closed forests. Thus, it is likely that fire suppression was an important factor in vegetation changes that have reduced the structural diversity of both forest stands and forested landscapes in the mid-montane zone.

Mid-Montane Eastside

FIRE RESPONSES OF IMPORTANT SPECIES

Most of the more-common conifer species (Jeffrey pine, ponderosa pine, incense cedar, and white fir) survive frequent surface fires of low to moderate intensity when mature (Table 10.7). As on the west side of the range, the primary difference is how early in life they become resistant to these fires. Western juniper is more easily killed by fires that the other conifers would survive and it invades open sites from refugia during longer fire-free periods. Three conifers in this zone— knobcone pine *(Pinus attenuate)*, MacNab cypress *(Cupressus macnabiana)*, and Modoc cypress *(Cupressus bakeri)*—have serotinous cones. These species rely on occasional severe crown fires to induce regeneration.

The more common hardwoods of this zone are Oregon white oak, curl-leaf mountain-mahogany, quaking aspen *(Populus tremuloides)*, and California black oak. Oregon white oak is resistant to low- to moderate-intensity surface fires and is able to sprout vigorously if top-killed by fire. Curl-leaf mountain-mahogany is killed by even low-intensity surface fires. It reinvades burned sites from rocky outcrops and other fire refugia during periods of reduced fire activity. The fire ecology of quaking aspen has not been well studied in this zone. However, quaking aspen is fire sensitive but sprouts vigorously after it has been top-killed by fire.

Mahala mat *(Ceanothus prostrates)* is a common understory shrub in the mid- to upper montane forests of the range on both sides of the crest. It germinates from stored seed banks following fires.

FIRE REGIME–PLANT COMMUNITY INTERACTIONS

Of the three species of serotinous cone conifers, Modoc cypress and MacNab cypress occur in small, widely scattered groves on rocky, shallow soils (Griffin and Critchfield 1972).

The most widespread of the serotinous-cone species is knobcone pine. Knobcone pine has not been well studied in the Cascade Range. More information on the fire ecology of knobcone pine can be found in Chapters 9 and 12. Although primarily a westside species through most of its range, knobcone pine is found on both sides of the Cascades. The most extensive stands occur on the south- and east-facing slopes of Mt. Shasta. On the

TABLE 10.7
Fire response types for important species in the low elevation eastside zone of the South Cascades bioregion

| Lifeform | Type of Fire Response | | | Species |
	Sprouting	Seeding	Individual	
Conifer	None	Stimulated (seed dispersal)	Resistant/killed	Gray pine
	None	None	Resistant/killed	Ponderosa pine, western juniper
Hardwood	Fire stimulated	None	Top-killed/killed	California black oak
	Fire stimulated	Stimulated (establishment)	Survive/top-killed	Oregon white oak
Shrub	None	Stimulated (germination)	Killed	Buck brush
	Fire stimulated when young	None	Top-killed/sometimes survive when young	Bitterbrush
	Fire stimulated	Stimulated (germination)	Top-killed/survive	Mahala mat
	Fire stimulated	None	Top-killed/survive	Mountain misery

east side of the Cascades, knobcone pine extends to the lava beds north of Fall River Valley and into the Northeast Plateau along the base of the Big Valley Mountains. The widespread distribution of this serotinous cone species suggests that severe fires were an important component of mid-montane fire regimes at least in some locations. Knobcone pines are short lived and usually begin dying after 50 or more years without fire (Vogl et al. 1977). Thus, after decades of fire suppression and the associated low fire occurrence, many stands are experiencing widespread mortality (e.g., Imper 1991). Severe crown fires are advantageous to mature, standing trees because these fires move quickly through the stands and melt heavy resin coating the cones. This promotes seed dispersal onto mineral soil soon after the passage of the fire. Conversely, as time since fire increases and stands die, the dead, fallen trees accumulate as dry fuel leaving the seedlings and cones susceptible to intense fires that consume cones and kill seeds and seedlings. Consequently, contemporary stands may lose the ability to regenerate and this species may experience a range contraction in the Cascades.

The low-growth habit of mahala mat situates green, relatively moist leaves on and near soil and litter surfaces. This low-growing shrub often does not burn well except under extreme burning conditions. Unburned patches of the shrub on the forest floor provide refuge for small, fire-susceptible seedlings and saplings of conifers and other shrubs (e.g., white fir, bitterbrush, curl-leaf mountain-mahogany) that establish in them. By giving protection to young woody plants, mahala mat may have played an important role in

long-term stand dynamics and vegetative diversity of Cascadian forests.

The historical fire regimes of yellow pine-dominated alliances (Jeffrey pine and ponderosa pine), especially in the area transitioning from mid-montane to upper-montane environments in the southern portion of the bioregion, have been described by Taylor (2000) and Norman (2002). Fires were frequent in yellow pine forests until late in the nineteenth century or the onset of the fire-suppression period (Table 10.5).

Norman (2002) identified pre–fire suppression fire regimes and stand structure across an approximately 800-km^2 landscape between Eagle Lake and Butte Creek. Both open pine forest sites (OPF) and closed pine forest sites (CPF) were studied. Median fire-return intervals composited for 1- to 3-ha sites were 12 years (range 6–17) for OPF sites and 14.4 years (range 7–22) for CPF sites. Notably, widespread fires, detected on multiple sites across the large study area, had a median return interval of 20.5 years (range 7–49). These results are similar to mixed pine forests in the nearby Blacks Mountain Experimental Forest.

These conifer forests have changed, often considerably, coincident with the period of fire suppression (Norman 2002). Forest density has increased, and there has been a shift in species composition toward increasing density of pines and more fire-sensitive white fir. Moreover, many areas that were montane meadows early in the twentieth century have been invaded by trees, especially Jeffrey and lodgepole pine, and are becoming forests (Norman and Taylor 2005). Thus, fire suppression, interacting with climatic variation and more

TABLE 10.8
Fire-response types for important species in the upper-montane zone of the South Cascades bioregion

	Type of Fire Response			
Lifeform	Sprouting	Seeding	Individual	Species
Conifer	None	None	Resistant/killed	Jeffrey pine, ponderosa pine, white fir, red fir, western white pine
	None	None	Killed	Lodgepole pine
Hardwood	Fire stimulated	None	Top-killed/survive	Quaking aspen, willows, black cottonwood
Shrub	Fire stimulated	Stimulated (seed production)	Top-killed/survive	Bush chinquapin, mountain whitethorn,
	Fire stimulated	Stimulated (germination)	Top-killed/survive	Greenleaf manzanita, tobacco brush
	None	Stimulated	Killed	Pinemat manzanita
	Fire stimulated	None	Top-killed/survive	Huckleberry oak, rubber rabbitbrush
	None	None	Killed	Big sagebrush

locally with other land uses such as grazing and logging, has contributed to vegetation changes that have reduced the structural diversity of both forest stands and forested landscapes.

Small stands of quaking aspen are scattered throughout the montane and upper-montane zone east of the Cascade crest. Though quaking aspen is not well studied in the Cascades, years of observation suggest several important relationships between quaking aspen and fire. In quaking aspen stands with few conifers, the high fuel moisture of the herbaceous understory and generally low fuel loads reduce fire intensity as fire enters stands. This occurs even under more severe burning conditions. Severe passive crown fires in adjacent conifer stands have been observed to change to low-intensity surface fires when they enter quaking aspen stands. However, if the quaking aspen stand has been heavily invaded by conifers, the fires continue to burn severely. Conifers are capable of replacing quaking aspen, and fires were probably a key process that maintained quaking aspen stands before the fire suppression period. Since the onset of fire suppression, many quaking aspen stands have been invaded and overtopped by conifers. Where heavy conifer invasion has gone on long enough to have significantly reduced the vigor of quaking aspen clones, the clones may have difficulty sprouting following severe fires. In some areas, quaking aspen has already been replaced by conifers and contemporary quaking aspen stands probably cover less area than before the fire suppression period.

Young basalt flows with little or no soil cover large areas such as in the Hat Creek Valley. These low-productivity sites limit fuel accumulations, and fires are unable to burn well except under severe weather conditions. These sites also seem to serve as fire refugia for many fire-sensitive species, including curl-leaf mountain-mahogany, western juniper, bitterbrush, and quaking aspen.

Many yellow pine-dominated forests and woodlands today have a relatively continuous understory of bitterbrush, such as seen in stands surrounding Butte Valley and other areas. Bitterbrush in the Cascades is fire sensitive and easily killed by even low-intensity fires. It does not sprout well unless young and vigorous. Where it is mature and robust it is highly flammable, burns with high intensity, and fires usually kill the plants outright. Given these traits, it is unlikely the contemporary widespread continuity of bitterbrush, especially the mature robust shrubs, was typical of these environments under pre-historic fire regimes. Fires were too frequent. It is likely bitterbrush took advantage of refugia provided by basalt flows and mahala mat to maintain itself in this generally fire-prone ecosystem.

Upper Montane

FIRE RESPONSES OF IMPORTANT SPECIES

Fire ecology information is available for montane shrubs and four common tree-dominated alliances in the southern Cascade Range: white fire, red fir, lodgepole pine, and Jeffrey pine (Table 10.8). Of the more common conifer species found in the upper montane of the Cascades, Jeffrey pine is most fire resistant, followed by white fir, red fir, western white pine, and lodgepole pine, respectively (Agee 1993).

TABLE 10.9
Fire regime characteristics for upper-montane ecological zone

Vegetation type	Yellow pine-dominated	True fir-dominated	Lodgepole pine	Upper-montane shrubs
Temporal				
Seasonality	Summer–fall	Late summer–fall	Late summer–fall	Late summer–fall
Fire-return intervals	Short	Short–long	Medium–long	Medium–long
Spatial				
Size	Small–large	Small–medium	Small–medium	Medium
Complexity	Moderate–high	Moderate–high	Low–high	Low–high
Magnitude				
Intensity	Low–moderate	Low–high	Low–high	Moderate–high
Severity	Low–moderate	Low–high	Moderate–high	Moderate–high
Fire type	Surface	Surface	Surface	Crown

NOTE: Fire regime terms used in this table are defined in Chapter 4.

Shrub species dominance varies with substrate, soils, and other conditions. However, nearly all dominant, woody species in upper-montane shrub fields sprout following fires, including bush chinquapin, huckleberry oak, and bitter cherry *(Prunus emarginata)*. Important species that both sprout and germinate from seed from long-lived soil seed banks include tobacco brush, greenleaf manzanita, mountain whitethorn, deer brush, and pinemat manzanita.

FIRE REGIME–PLANT COMMUNITY INTERACTIONS

The influence of commercial thinning and prescribed burning on the germination and establishment of tobacco brush and manzanita (greenleaf and pinemat) have been studied in young-mature, even-aged white fir and red fir stands that had regenerated in a shrub field near Jenny Springs on the Lassen National Forest just outside of the Swain Mountain Experimental Forest (Weatherspoon 1985, 1988). Though no live shrubs and few shrub skeletons were present in plots before treatments were applied, more than 15 million tobacco brush seeds/ha (6 million/ac) were found in the top 10 cm (4 in) of soil. Mechanical treatments included: (1) unthinned controls, (2) moderate thinning, and (3) heavy thinning. Prescribed burning treatments were: (1) unburned controls in each level of thinning; (2) under burn half of the plots in spring before thinning; and (3) under burn all plots except controls after thinning, half in spring and half in fall (Weatherspoon 1985).

After treatments, the density of tobacco brush and manzanita seedlings was higher on burned than on unburned, and on thinned than on unthinned plots and varied with the amount of fuel consumed (Weatherspoon 1985). Apparently, most seedlings died that germinated in shaded, unthinned plots. Fuel consumption was generally greater in fall burns compared to spring burns. Seedling density was lowest in unburned areas, somewhat greater in shallow burns (litter consumed), highest in areas of moderate depth of burn (fermentation layer consumed), and lower again in deeply burned areas (humus layer consumed). Seed stores were not reduced by shallow burns, but 94% of the seeds were killed to 10 cm (3.9 in) soil depth, and 100% were killed to 4 cm (1.6 in) depth where humus was consumed (Weatherspoon 1988). Overall, seedling density varied with fuel consumption, suggesting that highly consumptive pre-thinning burns may be effective at reducing stored seed reserves (Weatherspoon 1985).

The Jenny Springs study suggests that recurring, consumptive fires under dry, late summer conditions probably served to reduce seed stores of montane shrub species more rapidly than would otherwise have occurred. Thus, stands of trees that have been in place for longer periods (centuries) and experienced many fires would be expected to have less seed stored in the soil than young stands that have recently emerged from a shrub field or stands that experienced fewer fires. A high-intensity fire occurring as the stand was emerging from a shrub field when seed stores are high, or in an older stand that had experienced relatively few fires may kill many seeds—but the more open environment may increase survivorship of the seedlings. Conversely, older stands that had been burned many times over the years by low- to moderate-intensity fires would likely have considerably fewer seeds stored in the seed bank. A high-intensity fire may not induce as great a flush of seedlings due to the long-term depletion of the seed bank. Where shrubs such as huckleberry oak and bush chinquapin that do not develop seed banks were extirpated from a site by conifer competition, they would have to re-invade similarly to conifers following a high-intensity, stand-replacing fire.

Truffle abundance was also evaluated 10 years after thinning and 9 years after burning in the Jenny Springs study area (Waters et al. 1994). Interestingly, no difference in the frequency or biomass of truffles was found between thinning treatments with or without the use of prescribed fire (Waters et al. 1994). However, the composition of the truffle species assemblage differed between the thinned and unthinned environments.

There are few data on the fire history of montane shrub fields because the severe nature of brushfield fires consumes most evidence needed to reconstruct fire histories (Skinner and Chang 1996). However, fire scar data collected by Nagel and Taylor (2005) in the central Sierra Nevada from trees along the edges and scattered within stands of montane chaparral had a median point fire-return interval of 28 years (range 6–77) (Table 10.9). In contrast, surrounding forests had a median point fire return interval of 14 years. This suggests that fire-return intervals in montane chaparral may be longer and more variable than in surrounding conifer forests. Fuel structure, conditions needed for burning, and rates of fuel recovery in montane chaparral are different than in adjacent conifer forests and are probably responsible for the longer and more variable fire-return intervals. The absence of fire, primarily due to fire suppression, has also led to widespread conversion of montane shrublands to forest in the northern Sierra Nevada and southern Cascades (Bock and Bock 1977, Conard and Radosevich 1982, Beaty and Taylor 2001, Bekker and Taylor 2001, Nagel and Taylor 2005).

White fir-dominated stands in the Cascades are common in the transition area from mid-montane to upper-montane environments, especially on mesic sites. Stands are usually mixed with either Jeffrey pine or red fir at lower and higher elevations, respectively. Fire regimes generally vary between those characteristic of these other two species depending on which is more important. Figure 10.9 shows how conditions have changed in stands where white fir is a major component during the twentieth century in Lassen Volcanic National Park.

Stands where red fir is dominant or co-dominant are common, especially on mesic sites, in the upper-montane zone of the southern Cascades (Laacke 1990, Parker 1991). Where the upper-montane transitions to subalpine environments, red fir is found most frequently on xeric sites (Taylor 1990). Common red fir associates include white fir, western white pine, Jeffrey pine, lodgepole pine, and mountain hemlock (Laacke 1990).

Pinemat manzanita is a common, prostrate understory shrub in upper montane forests and woodlands. Its low growth habit situates green, relatively moist leaves on and near soil and litter surfaces. Thus, pinemat manzanita burns well only under extreme burning conditions, and burns are usually patchy. Unburned islands of pinemat manzanita serve as fire refugia for small, fire-susceptible conifer seedlings and saplings. Consequently, by giving protection to the small conifers, pinemat manzanita may play an important role in long-term stand dynamics of upper-montane forests, similar to that described for mahala mat in mid- and upper-montane forests.

Fire occurrence in red fir forests has diminished considerably since the onset of the fire suppression period in the early twentieth century (Taylor 1993, McKelvey et al. 1996, Taylor 2000). Along with the ever-increasing time between fires, there has been an increase in forest density, similar to forest changes that are occurring in lower- and mid-montane forests (Taylor 2000). Figure 10.10 is representative of the ongoing changes in stand conditions that are representative of upper-elevation red fir forests in the southern Cascades since the early 1920s.

Fire regimes in red fir–dominated landscapes are characterized by mixed-severity burns (Agee 1993) that occur mainly in the late summer or fall after trees have stopped growth for the year (Taylor 2000). Mean fire-return intervals for points (individual trees) in forests dominated by red fir range from 25–110 years with the median being 70 years (Taylor and Halpern 1991, Taylor 1993, Taylor 2000). This is similar to a mean value (i.e., 65 years) reported for high-elevation red fir–western white pine forests in the southern Sierra Nevada (Pitcher 1987). However, most studies in red fir forests have used fire scars extracted from open wounds and did not have access to stumps. Open wounds on trees in these environments tend to rot. Access to stumps would allow the discovery of hidden scars in trees that successfully healed following the wound. Without access to stumps, frequency of fire occurrence may be underestimated (Sidebar 10.1).

Stands dominated by lodgepole pine in the Cascades are more similar to those of central Oregon (e.g., Stuart et al. 1989; Parker 1991, 1995; Agee 1993) than they are to lodgepole pine stands in the Sierra Nevada (e.g., Parker 1986; Potter 1998). In the Cascades, lodgepole pine dominates topographic settings conducive to cold-air ponding, high water tables, or sites with infertile, coarse volcanic material (Parker 1991, 1995; Agee 1994; Bekker and Taylor 2001; Taylor and Solem 2001). Red fir and white fir are often important associates, especially on more upland sites (Parker 1991, 1995), where the firs may eventually replace lodgepole pine after long periods without fire (Bekker and Taylor 2001, Taylor and Solem 2001).

Lodgepole pines are considered fire sensitive because they have thin bark and are easily damaged or killed by moderate-intensity surface fires (Agee 1993, Cope 1993). In the southern Cascades, average point fire-return intervals were 63 years (range 59–67 years) in the Caribou Wilderness (Taylor and Solem 2001) and 47 years (range 38–54 years) in the Thousand Lakes Wilderness (Bekker and Taylor 2001). These are more comparable to upper-montane, red fir forests than montane forests dominated by yellow pines. Fire-return intervals in the southern Cascades are shorter than those reported for lodgepole pine in central Oregon (Agee 1993). However, lodgepole stands north and east of Mt. Shasta may be more similar to those of central Oregon because they too are most extensive on pumice and andesite flats.

A mixed-severity fire regime consisting of small, low-severity fires and larger fires with significant portions of stand-replacing, high-severity effects appears to have been common in lodgepole pine forests (Fig. 10.11). These recurring mixed-severity fires, interacting with beetles and wind

FIGURE 10.9. Paired photos showing representative changes in structure of white fir/Jeffrey pine forests in Lassen Volcanic National Park. Photo A taken in 1925. Photo B taken at same location in 1993. (Photo A by A. E. Weislander; photo B by Alan Taylor, from Taylor 2000, used with permission of Blackwell Publishing.)

events, created variable multi-aged forests at both plot and landscape scales (Bekker and Taylor 2001, Taylor and Solem 2001). Average extent of pre–fire-suppression fires in lodgepole pine forests were 150 ha (370 acres) in the Caribou Wilderness (Taylor and Solem 2001) and 405 ha (1,000 acres) in the Thousand Lakes Wilderness (Bekker and Taylor 2001).

Fire rotations in lodgepole pine forests vary by time period. During the Native American period, fire rotations in the Caribou Wilderness were 76 years and lengthened to 177 years

during the settlement period (1850–1910) (Taylor and Solem 2001). During the settlement period, fire rotation for lodgepole pine forests in the Thousand Lakes Wilderness was shorter at 46 years (Bekker and Taylor 2001). The fire rotation period has lengthened considerably in both study areas since the onset of fire suppression. In the Caribou Wilderness, the fire rotation has increased to 577 years (Taylor and Solem 2001) and no fires were detected in fire scars in lodgepole pine forests in the Thousand Lakes Wilderness since the beginning of fire suppression (Bekker and Taylor 2001).

FIGURE 10.10. (A) October 1925, on the west side of Prospect Peak. The scene shows a red fir–western white pine stand with few seedlings and saplings on the forest floor. There are also patches of tobacco brush and bush chinquapin in the understory but little herbaceous cover. Fire scars on a nearby sample tree indicate the stand last burned in 1883. (B) July 1993. Trees in the stand have increased in height and diameter and new seedlings and saplings have established in the understory since 1925. The tree in the foreground (left) of the 1925 scene died and fell; seedlings and saplings have established in this opening. Ground fuels (needles, twigs, branches, boles) have also increased on the forest floor. (Photo A by A. E. Weislander; photo B by Alan Taylor, from Taylor 2000, used with permission of Blackwell Publishing.)

Stand density in eastside yellow pine forests has increased during the twentieth century (Dolph et al. 1995), and the onset of the increase corresponds with the beginning of the fire suppression period (Taylor 2000, Norman 2002). Repeat photography of eastside pine forests in Lassen Volcanic National Park that have never been logged (Weislander 1935)

illustrates changes in forest conditions between the 1920s and 1993. As discussed previously, these changes are unlikely to be due to climate change. They are due mainly to the dramatic reduction of area burned as a result of fire suppression and are typical of changes observed in eastside pine forests throughout the park (Fig. 10.12).

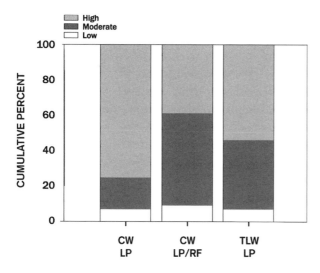

FIGURE 10.11. Distribution of fire severity classes in lodgepole pine of the Caribou Wilderness Area (CW; Taylor and Solem 2001) and the Thousand Lakes Wilderness Area (TLW; Bekker and Taylor 2001).

Jeffrey-pine-dominated forests occupy the lower elevations on south-, east-, and west-facing slopes in eastside environments. In eastern Lassen Volcanic National Park (LVNP), median point fire-return interval (individual tree scale) (n = 36) for this type of forest was 16 years and ranged from 13 years on east-facing slopes to 32 years and 31 years on south- and west-facing slopes, respectively. Longer fire-return intervals on slopes that dry earlier each year (i.e., south, west), and hence are more fire prone, were unexpected. Lava flows and scoria fields, however, were present on the south- and west-facing slopes and apparently reduced import of fire from adjacent areas lengthening fire-return intervals (Taylor 2000). This effect underscores the importance of local topographic conditions as a control on fire regimes. The fire scar record for lower-elevation mixed-pine forests had a grand median fire return interval of 14 years (Norman 2002), similar to pine forests in eastern LVNP, but the range of median values on LVNP was wider (Taylor 2000).

Changes in stand density and species composition in the twentieth century have been documented in unlogged stands in the Blacks Mountain Experimental Forest (BMEF; Dolph et al. 1995). The density of small-diameter trees (<38 cm [15 in]) in BMEF stands increased fourfold or more between 1938 and 1991, whereas the density of large-diameter trees (>70 cm [27.5 in]) declined by 3.5 per hectare (1.4/ac) (Dolph et al. 1995). It has been hypothesized that the loss of larger trees has been at least partly due to increased competition from the smaller trees that have established since the onset of fire suppression. Increased competition for moisture and nutrients may have created stressful conditions for the larger trees making them more susceptible to fatal insect attack, especially during dry periods. Intense competition between small- and intermediate-size trees also reduces growth of intermediate-sized trees and their recruitment into larger size-classes as existing larger trees die (Dolph et al. 1995, Minnich et al. 1995).

Subalpine

Lightning is frequent in the subalpine zone of the Cascade Range (van Wagtendonk and Cayan 2007). Yet, there is little evidence that fire plays a significant role in this zone. Trees in this zone are generally very sensitive to even low-intensity fires. Though lightning is frequent, the few fires that ignite rarely spread beyond individuals or small groups of trees. This is the result of climatic conditions and sparse fuels that are not conducive to fire spread. Historic fire regimes were likely similar to that described for the adjacent Sierra Nevada bioregion (see Chapter 12).

Management Issues

Managers in the Cascade Range face several fire-related challenges (e.g., smoke management, fuel accumulations, increasing stand density, wildland-urban interface) but none are unique. However, three issues—wildlife habitat, wildland-urban interface, and changing stand structures—stand out in this bioregion.

Wildlife Habitat

There is a need to better understand the role frequent low- and moderate-intensity fires once had on wildlife habitat through their influence on the development of the forest mosaics at watershed and landscape scales. Especially important is an improved understanding of the influence of fire on development of old forest ecosystems and patterns of large, dead woody material in the relatively gentle terrain of the Cascade Range. The topography of the Cascades, which is more conducive to extensive fires (Norman and Taylor 2003) than that of the Klamath Mountains (Taylor and Skinner 2003), suggests that relationships with these habitat factors may be different than those described for the Klamath Mountains or other bioregions. Describing these patterns would have important implications for management of such species as spotted owls *(Strix occidentalis occidentalis)* (Weatherspoon et al. 1992), fur-bearers, and northern goshawks *(Accipiter gentilis)*. An improved understanding will help managers to better assess risks associated with different management alternatives that inadequately consider fire as a process in fire-prone ecosystems (e.g., Attiwill 1994, Mutch and Cook 1996, Arno et al. 1997, Cissel et al. 1999, Arno and Allison-Bunnell, 2002).

Wildland-Urban Interface

A large proportion of the bioregion is classified as mixed interface (CDF 2002b) because dwellings are widely dispersed in small, scattered communities that are embedded in wildland vegetation. This pattern has resulted in the loss of hundreds of homes to wildfires in just the last three decades (CDF 2002a). The Fountain fire alone burned more than 300 homes in 1992 (CDF 2002a). The wildland-urban interface fire problem will continue to grow as development inexorably expands throughout the bioregion.

FIGURE 10.12. (A) October 1925, on the south side of Prospect Peak. The scene shows a mixed Jeffrey pine–white fir stands with few seedlings, saplings, or small-diameter stems in the forest understory. A small patch of tobacco brush is present in the foreground (right) but there is little herbaceous cover. Note the charred bark on the large-diameter stems. Fire scars on a nearby sample tree indicate the stand last burned in 1892. (B) June 1993. A dense stand of mostly white fir now dominates the forest understory and ground fuels (needles, twigs, branches) have accumulated on the forest floor. Stand density in this scene is now 820 trees (more than 4.0 cm dbh) ha^{-1}. This site was revisited in 1994. All large-diameter Jeffrey pines in the stand had died due to bark beetles. (Photo A by A. E. Weislander; photo B by Alan Taylor in 1994, from Taylor 2000, used with permission of Blackwell Publishing.)

Changing Stand Structures

Nearly a century of minimal fire occurrence due mostly to fire exclusion in forests that once experienced frequent fires has greatly altered compositional and structural diversity in forest stands and forested landscapes. The reduction in frequency and extent of fire has resulted in an increase in stand density, a shift from fire-tolerant to fire-intolerant species, and has reduced structural heterogeneity in both forest stands and forested landscapes in many parts of the western United States (Agee 1993, Arno and Allison-Bunnell 2002). Forests in the Cascade Range of California have also experienced these changes (Dolph et al. 1995, Taylor 2000), and these changes appear to be contributing to the increase in area burned by severe wildfires in this region, especially in lower- and mid-elevation forests (McKelvey et al. 1996, Weatherspoon and Skinner 1996, Stephens 1998). A similar shift to more severe fires may also begin to occur in less fire-prone, higher-elevation forests as stand density and time since last fire increase with continuing fire suppression (Taylor 2000).

Future Directions

Ecological Effects of Fuels Treatments and Altering Stand Structures

The changing stand and fuel conditions in fire-prone, lower-elevation forests have led many to conclude that widespread treatment of forest fuels is necessary to restore ecological integrity and to reduce the high risk of destructive, uncharacteristically severe fires (e.g., Hardy and Arno 1996, Terhune 2002). Treatments that are being discussed for widespread application include selective tree removal, mechanical manipulations of fuels, and prescribed fire, but the effectiveness of these treatments and their ecological effects are poorly known (Weatherspoon and Skinner 2002). Resource managers need much better information about the ecological consequences of creating different stand structures with mechanical thinning or fire as they develop plans to reduce fire hazard (Zack et al.1999, Oliver 2000, Weatherspoon and Skinner 2002).

To address this need, three large, stand-manipulation studies have been initiated in the Cascade Range of California by the U.S. Forest Service, Pacific Southwest Research Station's Redding Silviculture Laboratory. The three large studies are: (1) the Blacks Mountain Ecological Research Project (BMERP; Oliver 2000), (2) the Little Horse Peak Research Project (GAMA [Goosenest Adaptive Management Area]; Zack et al. 1999; Ritchie 2005), and (3) the Southern Cascades Fire/Fire Surrogates Site which is part of the National Fire and Fire Surrogates Study (FFS; McIver et al. 2001). These studies are interdisciplinary, complimentary, and are designed to assess both the short- and long-term ecological effects of altering stand structures by using mechanical thinning, prescribed fire, or both. With the completion of the FFS treatments in November 2002, all initial treatments for each study are in place.

Fire-Climate Interactions

The southern Cascade Range sits in an intermediate position along a latitudinal gradient in regional to hemispheric-scale climate variation and fire regimes in this area may be especially sensitive to changes in the strength of these climatic teleconnections (e.g., El Niño Southern Oscillation [ENSO], Pacific/North American pattern [PNA], Pacific Decadal Oscillation [PDO]). For example, wet conditions in northern Mexico and southern California and dry conditions in Washington are associated with a warm ENSO, whereas an opposite wet (north)-dry (south) pattern is typical of a cold ENSO. However, in the intermediate geographic position occupied by the southern Cascade Range, both wet (e.g., 1997) or dry (e.g., 1977) years can be associated with a similar ENSO signal. Focused work on fire–climate interactions in this transitional area is needed to better understand variation in fire–climate relationships. Moreover, this understanding can be used to develop tools for predicting the nature of upcoming fire seasons. Prediction of problematic fire seasons months to years in advance will enhance allocation of resources to suppression and fire readiness, in the case of severe seasons, and to fuels treatment using prescribed fire in favorable seasons. Early results indicate that extensive fires in eastside pine forests were associated with droughts influenced by associations of the PDO and ENSO in distinctive phases (Norman and Taylor 2003).

Summary

Annual summer drought, ample winter precipitation, and abundant lightning combined to make fire frequent and generally low or moderate in severity in most of the southern Cascade Range during the Native American period. Fire exclusion, grazing, and logging have dramatically changed fire regimes and forest structure in Cascade ecosystems over the last century. Of all management activities, it is likely that fire suppression has been the most pervasive because it alone has been ubiquitously applied. There is considerable discussion about the need to reduce fire hazard by manipulating fuels and stand structure either mechanically or with the use of prescribed fire. However, accomplishing fire hazard reduction is often problematic due to competing social/political objectives for Cascade forests (e.g., wood production, preservation for wildlife, maintenance of air quality). Regardless of how these controversies are resolved, the ecosystems of the Cascade Range will continue to change in response to historic and contemporary management activities in expected and unexpected ways.

References

Agee, J.K. 1993. Fire ecology of Pacific Northwest forests. Island Press, Washington, D.C.

Agee, J.K. 1994. Fire and weather disturbances in terrestrial ecosystems of the eastern Cascades. USDA Forest Service, Pacific Northwest Research Station, Portland, OR, General Technical Report PNW-GTR-320.

Agee, J.K. 1996. The influence of forest structure on fire behavior. P. 52–68 in S.L. Cooper (comp.), Proceedings 17th annual forest vegetation management conference. Forest Vegetation Management Conference, January 16–18, 1996, Redding, CA. University of California, Shasta County Cooperative Extension, Redding.

Agee, J.K. 1997a. Fire management for the 21st century. P. 191–202 in K. Kohm and J.F. Franklin (eds.), Creating a forestry for the 21st century: the science of ecosystem management. Island Press, Washington, DC.

Agee, J.K. 1997b. The severe weather wildfire—too hot to handle? Northwest Science 17:153–156.

Agee, J.K. 1998. The landscape ecology of western forest fire regimes. Northwest Science 72:24–34.

Agee, J.K. 1999. A coarse-filter strategy. Forum for Applied Research and Public Policy 14:15–19.

Agee, J.K. 2003. Burning issues in fire: will we let the coarse-filter operate? P. 7–13 in K.E.M. Galley, R.C. Klinger, and N.G. Sugihara (eds.), Proceedings of fire conference 2000. Tall Timbers Research Station Misc. Pub 13. 226 p.

Agee, J.K., B. Bahro, M.A. Finney, P.N. Omi, D.B. Sapsis, C.N. Skinner, J.W. van Wagtendonk, and C.P. Weatherspoon. 2000. The use of shaded fuelbreaks in landscape fire management. Forest Ecology and Management 127:55–66.

Arno, S.F., and S. Allison-Bunnell. 2002. Flames in our forest: disaster or renewal? Island Press, Washington, DC.

Arno, S.F., H.Y. Smith, and M.A. Krebs. 1997. Old growth ponderosa pine and western larch stand structures: influences of pre-1900 fires and fire exclusion. USDA Forest Service, Intermountain Research Station, Ogden, UT, Research Paper INT-RP-495.

Attiwill, P.M. 1994. The disturbance of forest ecosystems: the ecological basis for conservative management. Forest Ecology and Management 63:247–300.

Barbour, M.G. 1988. Californian upland forests and woodlands. P. 131–164. In M.G. Barbour and W.D. Billings (eds), North American terrestrial vegetation. Cambridge University Press, New York.

Beaty, R.M. 1998. Spatial and temporal variation in fire regimes and forest dynamics along a montane forest gradient in the southern Cascades, California. M.S. Thesis. Pennsylvania State University.

Beaty, R.M., and A.H. Taylor. 2001. Spatial and temporal variation of fire regimes in a mixed conifer forest landscape, southern Cascades, California, USA. Journal of Biogeography 28:955–966.

Bekker, M.F. 1996. Fire history of the Thousand Lakes Wilderness, Lassen National Forest, California, USA. M.S. Thesis. Pennsylvania State University, State College.

Bekker, M.F., and A.H. Taylor. 2001. Gradient analysis of fire regimes in montane forests of the southern Cascade Range, Thousand Lakes Wilderness, California, USA. Plant Ecology 155:15–28.

Biswell, H.H., and J.H. Gilman. 1961. Brush management in relation to fire and other environmental factors on the Tehama deer winter range. California Fish and Wildlife 47: 357–389.

Bock, C.E., and J.H. Bock. 1977. Patterns of post-fire succession on the Donner Ridge Burn, Sierra Nevada. P. 464–469 in H.A. Mooney and C.E. Conrad (tech. coords.), Proceedings of the symposium on the environmental consequences of fire and fuel management in mediterranean ecosystems. USDA Forest Service, Washington, D.C., General Technical Report WO-3.

Bolsinger, C.L. 1989. Shrubs of California's chaparral, timberland, and woodland: area ownership, and stand characteristics. USDA Forest Service, Pacific Northwest Research Station, Portland, OR, Resource Bulletin PNW-RB-160.

Caprio, A.C., and T.W. Swetnam. 1995. Historic fire regimes along an elevational gradient on the west slope of the Sierra Nevada, California. P. 173–179 in J.K. Brown, R.W. Mutch, C.W. Spoon, R.H. Wakimoto (tech. coords.), Proceedings: Symposium on fire in wilderness and park management. USDA Forest Service, Intermountain Research Station, Ogden, UT, General Technical Report INT-GTR-320.

CCSS. 2002. Historical course data. California Resources Agency, Department of Water Resources, Division of Flood Management, California Cooperative Snow Surveys. Data online at: http://cdec.water.ca.gov/snow/.

CDF 2002b. Information and data center in Fire and Resource Assessment Program. California Department of Forestry and Fire Protection, Sacramento, Available online at http://frap.cdf.ca.gov/infocenter.html.

Chang, C. 1999. Understanding fire regimes. Ph.D. Dissertation. Duke University, Durham, NC. 184.

Cissel, J.H., F.J. Swanson, and P.J. Weisberg. 1999. Landscape management using historical fire regimes: Blue River, Oregon. Ecological Applications 9:1217–1231.

Conard, S.G., and S.R. Radosevich. 1982. Post-fire succession in white fir (Abies concolor) vegetation of the northern Sierra Nevada. Madrono 29:42–56.

Cooper, C.F. 1961. Pattern in ponderosa pine forests. Ecology 42:493–499.

Cope, A.B. 1993. Pinus contorta var. murrayana. In W.C. Fischer and (compiler) (eds.), The fire effects information system [Data base]. USDA Forest Service, Intermountain Research Station, Intermountain Fire Sciences Laboratory, Missoula, MT. Magnetic tape reels; 9 track; 1600 bpi, ASCII with Common LISP present.

Dolph, K.L., S.R. Mori, and W.W. Oliver. 1995. Long-term response of old-growth stands to varying levels of partial cutting in the eastside pine type. Western Journal of Applied Forestry 10:101–108.

Earle, C.J. 1993. Asynchronous droughts in California streamflow as reconstructed from tree rings. Quaternary Research 39: 290–299.

Eyre, F.H. 1980. Forest cover types of the United States. Society of American Foresters, Washington, DC.

Farris, K.L., E.O. Garton, P.J. Heglund, S. Zack, and P.J. Shea. 2002. Woodpecker foraging and the successional decay of ponderosa pine. P. 237–246 in J. Laudenslayer, F. William, P.J. Shea, B.E. Valentine, C.P. Weatherspoon, and T.E. Lisle (eds.), Proceedings of the symposium on the ecology and management of dead wood in western forests. USDA Forest Service, Pacific Southwest Research Station, Albany, CA, General Technical Report PSW-GTR-181.

Flannigan, M.D., and C.E. Van Wagner. 1991. Climate change and wildfire in Canada. Canadian Journal of Forest Research 21:66–72.

Gannett, H. 1902. The forests of Oregon. Professional Paper No. 4, Series H, Forestry, 1. U.S. Geological Survey, Washington, DC.

Griffin, J.R. 1967. Soil moisture and vegetation patterns in northern California forests. USDA Forest Service, Pacific Southwest Research Station, Berkeley, CA, Research Paper PSW-46.

Griffin, J.R., and W.B. Critchfield. 1976. The distribution of forest trees in California, with supplement. USDA Forest Service,

Pacific Southwest Research Station, Berkeley, CA, Research Paper PSW-82.

Graumlich, L. J. 1987. Precipitation variation in the Pacific Northwest (1675–1975) as reconstructed from tree rings. Annals of the Association of American Geographers 77:19–29.

Hughes, M. K., and P. M. Brown. 1992. Drought frequency in central California since 101 B.C. recorded in giant sequoia tree rings. Climate Dynamics 6:161–167.

Hull, M. K., C. A. O'Dell, and M. J. Schroeder. 1996. Critical fire weather patterns: their frequency and levels of fire danger. USDA Forest Service, Pacific Southwest Research Station, Berkeley, CA.

Imper, D. K. 1991. Ecological survey of the proposed Mayfield Research Natural Area, SAF Type 248 (Knobcone Pine), Lassen National Forest. Unpublished report PO #40-9AD6-0409 on file U.S. Forest Service, Pacific Southwest Research Station, Albany, CA.

Laacke, R. J. 1990. *Abies magnifica* A. Murr. California red fir. P. 71–79 in R. M. Burns, B. H. Honkala (tech. coords.), Silvics of North America, 1, Conifers. USDA Forest Service, Washington, DC.

Leathers, D. J., B. Yarnal, and M. A. Palecki. 1991. The Pacific/North American teleconnection pattern and the United States climate. Part I: regional temperature and precipitation association. Journal of Climate 5:517–527.

Lewis, H. T. 1990. Reconstructing patterns of Indian burning in southwestern Oregon. P. 80–84 in N. Hannon, R. K. Olmo (eds.), Living with the land: the Indians of southwest Oregon. Southern Oregon Historical Society, Ashland, OR.

Lewis, H. T. 1993. Patterns of Indian burning in California ecology and ethnohistory. P. 55–116 in T. C. Blackburn and K. Anderson (eds.), Before the wilderness: environmental management by native Californians. Ballena Press, Menlo Park, CA.

McIver, J., C. P. Weatherspoon, and C. Edminster. 2001. Alternative ponderosa pine restoration treatments in the western United States. P. 104–109 in R. K. Vance, C. B. Edminster, W. W. Covington, and J. A. Blake (eds.), Ponderosa pine ecosystems restoration and conservation: steps towards stewardship—conference proceedings. USDA Forest Service, Rocky Mountain Research Station, Ogden, UT, Proceedings RMRS-P-22.

McKelvey, K. S., and K. K. Busse. 1996. Twentieth-century fire patterns on Forest Service lands. P. 1119–1138 in Sierra Nevada Ecosystem Project: final report to Congress. Volume II: Assessments and scientific basis for management options. Centers for Water and Wildland Resources, University of California, Davis, Water Resources Center Report No. 37.

McKelvey, K. S., C. N. Skinner, C. Chang, D. C. Erman, S. J. Husari, D. J. Parsons, J. W. van Wagtendonk, and C. P. Weatherspoon. 1996. An overview of fire in the Sierra Nevada. P. 1033–1040 in Sierra Nevada Ecosystem Project: final report to Congress. Volume II: Assessments and scientific basis for management options. Centers for Water and Wildland Resources, University of California, Davis, Water Resources Center Report No. 37.

Miles, S. R., and C. B. Goudey (eds.). 1997. Ecological subregions of California: section and subsection descriptions. USDA Forest Service, Pacific Soutwest Region, San Francisco, CA, R5-3M-TP-005.

Minnich, R. A., M. G. Barbour, J. H. Burk, and R. F. Fernau. 1995. Sixty years of change in California conifer forests of the San Bernardino Mountains. Conservation Biology 9:902–914.

Morford, L. 1984. 100 years of wildland fires in Siskiyou County. [Publisher not available] Siskiyou County Library Reference No. R 634.9618 M, Yreka, CA.

Morrow, R. J. 1986. Age structure and spatial pattern of old-growth ponderosa pine in Pringle Falls Experimental Forest, central Oregon. M. S. Oregon State University, Corvallis.

Moyle, P. B., and P. J. Randall. 1996. Biotic integrity of watersheds. P. 975–985 in Sierra Nevada Ecosystem Project: final report to Congress. Volume II: Assessments and scientific basis for management options. Centers for Water and Wildland Resources, University of California, Davis, Wildland Resources Center Report No. 37.

Mutch, R. W., and W. A. Cook. 1996. Restoring fire to ecosystems: methods vary with land management goals. P. 9–11. In C. C. Hardy and S. F. Arno (eds), The use of fire in forest restoration, Ogden, UT: USDA Forest Service, Intermountain Research Station. General Technical Report INT-GTR-341.

Nagel, T. A., and A. H. Taylor. 2005. Fire and persistence of montane chaparral in mixed conifer forest landscapes in the northern Sierra Nevada, Lake Tahoe Basin, California, USA. Journal of the Torrey Botanical Society 132:442–457.

Norman, S. P. 2002. Legacies of anthropogenic and climate change in fire prone pine and mixed conifer forests of northeastern California. Ph.D. Dissertation. Pennsylvania State University, State College.

Norman, S., and A. H. Taylor. 2002. Variation in fire-return intervals across a mixed-conifer forest landscape. P. 170–179 in N. Sugihara, M. Morales, and T. Morales (eds.), Symposium on fire in California ecosystems: integrating ecology, prevention, and management. Nov. 1997, San Diego, CA, Associate for Fire Ecology, [NA], Miscellaneous Publication No. 1.

Norman, S. P., and A. H. Taylor. 2003. Tropical and north Pacific teleconnections influence fire regimes in pine-dominated forests of north-eastern California, USA. Journal of Biogeography 30:1081–1092.

Norman, S. P., and A. H. Taylor. 2005. Pine forest expansion along a forest-meadow ecotone in northeastern California, USA. Forest Ecology and Management 215:51–68.

Oakeshott, G. B. 1971. California's changing landscapes: a guide to the geology of the state. McGraw-Hill Book Co., San Francisco.

Oliver, W. W. 2000. Ecological research at the Blacks Mountain Experimental Forest in northeastern California. USDA Forest Service, Pacific Southwest Research Station, Albany, CA, General Technical Report PSW-GTR-179.

Oliver, W. W. 2001. Can we create and sustain late successional attributes in interior ponderosa pine stands? Large-scale ecological research studies in northeastern California. P. 99–103 in R. K. Vance, C. B. Edminster, W. W. Covington, and J. A. Blake (eds.), Proceedings—Ponderosa pine ecosystems restoration and conservation: steps toward stewardship, April 25–27, 2000, Flagstaff, AZ. USDA Forest Service, Rocky Mountain Research Station, Ogden, UT, Proceedings RMRS-P-22.

Parker, A. J. 1986. Persistence of lodgepole pine forests in the central Sierra Nevada. Ecology 67:1560–1567.

Parker, A. J. 1991. Forest/environment relationships in Lassen Volcanic National Park, California, USA. Journal of Biogeography 18:543–552.

Parker, A. J. 1995. Comparative gradient structure and forest cover types in Lassen Volcanic and Yosemite National Parks, California. Bulletin of the Torrey Botanical Club 122:58–68.

Pitcher, D. C. 1987. Fire history and age structure in red fir forests of Sequoia National Park, California. Canadian Journal of Forest Research 17:582–587.

Ritchie, M. W. 2005 Ecological research at the Goosenest Adaptive Management Area in northeastern California. USDA Forest Service, Pacific Southwest Research Station, Albany, CA, General Technical Report PSW-GTR-192.

Rothermel, R. C. 1983. How to predict the spread and intensity of forest and range fires. USDA Forest Service, Intermountain Research Station, Ogden, UT, General Technical Report INT–143.

Rundel, P. W., D. J. Parsons, and D. T. Gordon. 1977. Montane and subalpine vegetation of the Sierra Nevada and Cascade ranges. P. 559–599 in M. G. Barbour and J. Major (eds.), Terrestrial vegetation of California. Wiley, New York.

Show, S. B., and E. I. Kotok. 1925. Fire and the forest: California pine region. U.S. Department of Agriculture, Washington, DC., Department Circular 358.

Show, S. B., and E. I. Kotok. 1929. Cover type and fire control in the National Forests of northern California. U.S. Department of Agriculture, Washington, DC, Department Bulletin No. 1495.

Skinner, C. N. 2002. Influence of fire on dead woody material in forests of California and southwestern Oregon. P. 445–454 in W. F. Laudenslayer, Jr., P. J. Shea, B. E. Valentine, C. P. Weatherspoon, and T. E. Lisle (eds.), Proceedings of the symposium on the ecology and management of dead wood in western forests. November 2–4, 1999, Reno, NV. USDA Forest Service, Pacific Southwest Research Station, Albany, CA, General Technical Report PSW-GTR-181.

Skinner, C. N. 2003. Fire regimes of upper montane and subalpine lake basins in the Klamath Mountains of northern California. Tall Timbers Research Station, Miscellaneous Report No. 13:145–151.

Skinner, C. N., and C. Chang. 1996. Fire regimes, past and present. P. 1041–1069 in Sierra Nevada Ecosystem Project: final report to Congress. Volume II: Assessments and scientific basis for management options. Centers for Water and Wildland Resources, University of California, Davis, Water Resources Center Report No. 37.

SNEP. 2003. Analysis results from SNEP GIS database summarized by county or hydrologic basin. Sierra Nevada Ecosystem Project. Data accessed online May, 28, 2003 at: http://www.biogeog.ucsb.edu/projects/snner/snepgis/select.html.

Stine, S. 1996. Climate, 1650–1850. P. 25–30 in Sierra Nevada Ecosystem Project: final report to Congress. Volume II: Assessments and scientific basis for management options. Centers for Water and Wildland Resources, University of California, Davis.

Stephens, S. L. Evaluation of the effects of silvicultural and fuels treatments on potential fire behavior in Sierra Nevada mixed-conifer forests. Forest Ecology and Management 105:21–35.

Stuart, J. D., J. K. Agee, and R. I. Gara. 1989. Lodgepole pine regeneration in an old, self-perpetuating forest in south central Oregon. Canadian Journal of Forest Research 19:1096–1104.

Stuart, J. D., and L. A. Salazar. 2000. Fire history of white fir forests in the coastal mountains of northwestern California. Northwest Science 74:280–285.

Swetnam, T. W. 1993. Fire history and climate change in giant sequoia groves. Science 262:885–889.

Swetnam, T. W., and C. H. Baisan. 2003. Tree-ring reconstructions of fire and climate history in the Sierra Nevada and southwestern United States. P. 158–195 in T. T. Veblen, W. L. Baker, G. Montenegro, and T. W. Swetnam (eds.), Fire and climatic change in temperate ecosystems of the western Americas. Springer, New York.

Swezy, D. M., and J. K. Agee. 1991. Prescribed fire effects on fine root and tree mortality in old growth ponderosa pine. Canadian Journal of Forest Research 21:626–634.

Taylor, A. H. 1990a. Habitat segregation and regeneration patterns of red fir and mountain hemlock in ecotonal forests, Lassen Volcanic National Park, California. Physical Geography 11: 36–48.

Taylor, A. H. 1990b. Tree invasion in meadows of Lassen Volcanic National Park. Professional Geographer 53:457–470.

Taylor, A. H. 1993. Fire history and structure of red fir (Abies magnifica) forests, Swain Mountain Experimental Forest, Cascade Range, northeastern California. Canadian Journal of Forest Research 23:1672–1678.

Taylor, A. H. 1995. Forest expansion and climate change in the mountain hemlock (Tsuga mertensiana) zone, Lassen Volcanic National Park, California, U.S.A. Arctic and Alpine Research 207–216.

Taylor, A. H. 2000. Fire regimes and forest changes along a montane forest gradient, Lassen Volcanic National Park, southern Cascade Mountains, USA. Journal of Biogeography 27: 87–104.

Taylor, A. H. 2002. Fire history and stand dynamics in ponderosa pine forests in the Ishi Wilderness, Lassen National Forest, California. Unpublished final report for cost share agreement between The Pennsylvania State University and the Lassen National Forest. On file at Lassen National Forest Supervisor's Office, Susanville, CA.

Taylor, A. H., and C. B. Halpern. 1991. The structure and dynamics of Abies magnifica forests in the southern Cascade Range, USA. Journal of Vegetation Science 2:189–200.

Taylor, A. H., and C. N. Skinner, 1998. Fire history and landscape dynamics in a late-successional reserve in the Klamath Mountains, California, USA. Forest Ecology and Management 111: 285–301.

Taylor, A. H., and C. N. Skinner. 2003. Spatial patterns and controls on historical fire regimes and forest structure in the Klamath Mountains. Ecological Applications 13:704–719.

Taylor, A. H., and M. N. Solem. 2001. Fire regimes and stand dynamics in an upper montane forest landscape in the southern Cascades, Caribou Wilderness, California. Journal of the Torrey Botanical Club 128:350–361.

Thomas, T. L., and J. K. Agee. 1986. Prescribed fire effects on mixed conifer forest structure at Crater Lake, Oregon. Canadian Journal of Forest Research 16:1082–1087.

Turhune, G. 2002. The QLG defensible fuelbreak strategy. Association for Fire Ecology Miscellaneous Publication 1:253–255.

Veblen, T. T., T. Kitzberger, and J. Donnegan. 2000. Climatic and human influences on fire regimes in ponderosa pine forests in the Colorado Front Range. Ecological Applications 10:1178–1195.

Vogl, R. J. W. P. Armstrong, K. L. White, and K. L. Cole. 1977. The closed-cone pines and cypresses. P. 295–358 in M. G. Barbour and J. Major (eds.), Terrestrial vegetation of California. Wiley, New York.

van Wagtendonk, J. W., and D. Cayan. 2007. Temporal and spatial distribution of lightning strikes in California in relationship to large-scale weather patterns. Fire Ecology (in press).

Waters, J.R., K.S. McKelvey, C.J. Zabel, and W.W.Oliver. 1994. The effects of thinning and broadcast burning on sporocarp production of hypogeous fungi. Canadian Journal of Forest Research 24:1516–1522.

Weatherspoon, C.P. 1983. Residue management in the eastside pine type. P. 114–121 in T. F. Robson and R.B. Standiford (eds.), Management of the eastside pine type in northeastern California: proceedings of a symposium. Northern California Society of American Foresters, Arcata, CA.

Weatherspoon, C.P. 1985. Preharvest burning for shrub control in a white fir stand: preliminary observations. P. 71–88 in S.L. Cooper (comp.), Proceedings—6th annual forest vegetation management conference, November 1–2, 1984, Redding, California. University of California, Shasta County Cooperative Extension, Redding.

Weatherspoon, C.P. 1988. Preharvest prescribed burning for vegetation management: effects on *Ceanothus velutinus* seeds in duff and soil. P. 125–141 in S. L. Cooper (comp.), Proceedings—9th annual forest vegetation management conference; November 3–5, 1987, Redding, California. University of California, Shasta County Cooperative Extension, Redding.

Weatherspoon, C.P. 1996. Fire-silviculture relationships in Sierra forests. P. 1167–1176 in Sierra Nevada Ecosystem Project: final report to Congress. Volume II: Assessments and scientific basis for management options. Centers for Water and Wildland Resources, University of California, Davis, Water Resources Center Report No. 37.

Weatherspoon, C.P., and C.N. Skinner. 1995. An assessment of factors associated with damage to tree crowns from the 1987 wildfires in northern California. Forest Science 41:430–451.

Weatherspoon, C.P., and C.N. Skinner. 1996. Landscape-level strategies for forest fuel management. P. 1471–1492 in Sierra Nevada Ecosystem Project: final report to Congress. Volume II: Assessments and scientific basis for management options. Centers for Water and Wildland Resources, University of California, Davis, Water Resources Center Report No. 37.

Weatherspoon, C.P., and C.N. Skinner. 2002. An ecological comparison of fire and fire surrogates for reducing wildfire hazard and improving forest health. Association for Fire Ecology Miscellaneous Publication 1:239–245.

Weatherspoon, C.P., G.A. Almond, and C.N. Skinner. 1989. Tree-centered spot firing—a technique for prescribed burning beneath standing trees. Western Journal of Applied Forestry 4:29–31.

Weatherspoon, C.P., S.J. Husari, and J.W. van Wagtendonk. 1992. Fire and fuels management in relation to owl habitat in forests of the Sierra Nevada and Southern California. P. 247–260 in J. Verner, K.S. McKelvey, B.R. Noon, R.J. Gutierrez, G.I. Gould Jr., and T.W. Beck (tech. coords.), The California spotted owl: a technical assessment of its current status. USDA Forest Service, Pacific Southwest Research Station, Albany, CA, General Technical Report PSW-133.

Weislander, A.E. 1935. First steps of the forest surveys in California. Journal of Forestry 3:877–884.

White, A.S. 1985. Presettlement regeneration patterns in a southwestern ponderosa pine stand. Ecology 66:589–594.

Wilken, G.C. 1967. History and fire record of a timberland brush field in the Sierra Nevada of California. Ecology 48:302–304.

WRCC. 2002. Historical climate data. Western Regional Climate Center, Desert Research Institute, Reno, NV. Data available online at: http://www.wrcc.sage.dri.edu.

Zack, S., W.F. Laudenslayer, Jr., T.L. George, C. Skinner, and W. Oliver. 1999. A prospectus on restoring late-successional forest structure to eastside pine ecosystems through large-scale, interdisciplinary research. P. 343–355 in J.E. Cook and B. P. Oswald (comps.), First Biennial North American Forest Ecology Workshop. Society of American Foresters, (na), Forest Ecology Working Group.

Northeastern Plateaus Bioregion

GREGG M. RIEGEL, RICHARD F. MILLER, CARL N. SKINNER,
AND SYDNEY E. SMITH

> The only means for taking deer wholesale was by kupi't (firing)
> and was practiced in late summer, about the middle of August.
> When deer were sighted on a hill, a group of hunters hastened
> there, some on either side of the mountain. They started fires,
> working them around until the band was completely encircled.
> This accomplished the fires were brought closer, constricting the
> circle until the animals were bunched on the crest on a hill
> where they could be shot conveniently. Deer firing was ordinar-
> ily executed without undue noise, but if a bear were accidentally
> caught in the fire, a great hue and cry was set up to warn others
> and to inform them which direction the animal was headed.
>
> *Fire use by Northern Paiute Indians, as told to* ISABEL T. KELLY, 1932

Description of the Bioregion

Northeastern California landscape is a mixture of vast arid basins and uplands, and forested mountain ranges interspersed with both fresh water and alkaline wetlands. The entire bioregion is significantly influenced by the rain shadow effect of the Cascade Range to the west. Three ecological unit subsections are treated in this chapter: (1) Modoc Plateau Section (M261G), (2) northwestern Basin and Range Section (342B), and (3) extreme northern portion of the Mono Section (341Dk). The Cascade Range defines the western edge of the Modoc Plateau, and the Sierra Nevada defines the western boundary for the southern portion of the northwestern Basin and Range and Mono Sections. There is no one overriding feature that cleanly depicts this bioregion to the north and east as the political borders of the states of Oregon and Nevada, respectively, define the boundaries (Map 11.1).

Physical Geography

The Northeastern Plateaus bioregion extends east of the southern Cascade Range and south along the east slopes of the Sierra Nevada. This region represents California's portion of the Great Basin. The climate is dry, cold, and continental. Volcanism dominates the geology, topography, and geomorphic processes of the area. The most conspicuous feature of the region is the Modoc Plateau, a high, flat terrain characterized by basalt plains and volcanic shields (MacDonald and Gay 1966). The topography is extremely abrupt and

elevations, ranging from 1,204 m (3,950 ft) to 3,016 m (9,892 ft), can change quickly. The Pit River, with headwaters in the Warner Mountains and, until 1877, Goose Lake, traverses the Modoc Plateau from east to west where it enters the Cascade Range and flows into the Sacramento River (Pease 1965). The Modoc Plateau is also scattered with seasonal ponds and pluvial lakebeds. Several rivers, including the Susan, which drains into the Honey Lake basin, and the Carson and Walker in the northern Mono section, flow from west to east and transect the steppe.

Several vegetation zones occur in the Northeastern Plateaus bioregion. The general sequence, from the lowest elevations to the highest, are: sagebrush steppe (includes Wyoming big sagebrush and western juniper series zones), lower montane (ponderosa pine series zone), mid-montane (lower-elevation white fir series zone), upper montane (upper-elevation white fir series), and subalpine (whitebark pine series zone). The bioregion as defined in this publication is too dry and cold to support red fir (*Abies magnifica*) and mountain hemlock (*Tsuga mertensiana*), and only a few Douglas-fir (*Pseudotsuga menziesii*) or sugar pines (*Pinus lambertiana*) are found on the extreme western edge of this bioregion. Several species reach the extent of their ranges in this area, as detailed below (Smith and Davidson 2003).

The volcanism that shaped the area is fairly recent, dating from the Pliocene to Pleistocene eras, and includes volcanic ash deposits, lava flows, talus jumbles, obsidian deposits, and lava rims. Soils that have weathered in place, particularly at the lowest elevations of the region, are often poorly developed, shallow, and rocky. Clays weathered from basalt are a typical soil texture component in many locations. River deposits include Mollisols and Aridisols, and lakebed deposits include silt, sandstones, and diatomite (Young et al. 1988). At higher elevations in the bioregion, most residual soils are Mollisols, often weathered from basalt parent materials. Soils transported to lower-lying areas via alluvial processes are often Vertisols. Soil temperature regimes are mesic, frigid, and cryic, and soil moisture regimes are mostly xeric and aridic.

Climatic Patterns

Climate data in northeastern California is somewhat inaccurate because of historically few and somewhat widely spaced long-term climate stations confounding the difficulty in interpolating the marked rain shadow effects from topographic features. The PRISM climate model (Daly et al. 1994) uses extrapolations from weather station data points, and if the data are sparse then errors result in the extrapolations. In arid climates such as northeastern California, slight differences in precipitation and temperature show up in vegetation expression more readily than in wetter climates, and current climate models sometimes fail to predict this. We expect this will change in the next couple of decades as there are now more and spatially denser automated stations that should result in better predictive climate, vegetation, and fire models. In the meantime, structured observations of vegetation on zonal sites (sites reflecting the regional climate more than local topography or soils) are the best way to infer the climate of this bioregion.

FIRE CLIMATE VARIABLES

The bioregion is buffered from Pacific storms by being in the rain shadow of the Cascade Range and Sierra Nevada. Most of the precipitation occurs between October and May; with most occurring between November and April as snow. The summer months from May to October are mostly rainless with the exception of summer thunderstorms. Summer thunderstorms can be locally significant and are the source of lightning ignitions. The range of annual precipitation in the Northeastern Plateaus bioregion is from 17.8 to 121.9 cm (7–48 in) (Daly et al. 1994). The overall bioregional average is 43.2 cm (17 in). However, local orographic enhancement boosts precipitation from 91.4 to 121.9 cm (36–48 in) in the northern Warner Mountains. Temperatures range from January minimums of $-11°C$ to $-2°C$ ($12°F–28°F$) to July maximums of $21°C$ to $32°C$ ($69°F–89°F$). The majority of fires occur from June to September, and certain fire weather conditions can affect fire ignitions and fire behavior during those months.

WEATHER SYSTEMS

There are four basic fire weather patterns that can significantly affect fire behavior and natural ignitions in northeastern California during the May-to-October fire season.

These are: (1) the Pre-Frontal Winds, (2) Lightning with Low Precipitation, (3) Moist Monsoon, and (4) Strong Subsidence/Low Relative Humidity patterns. The pre-frontal and subsidence patterns mostly affect fire behavior and spread, whereas the lightning with low precipitation and moist monsoon patterns are important for their fire ignition potential.

Pre-Frontal Winds   Pre-frontal wind events are frequent in springtime and again in late summer and fall. They are of most consequence in the latter period, when both live and dead fuel moistures are low. The pre-frontal weather pattern occurs in advance of spring or fall cold fronts, or upper low-pressure troughs. Tight pressure gradients aloft produce moderate to strong south to west winds, which can surface strongly on the lee side of the Cascade Range and Sierra Nevada. As the downward-moving air masses lose elevation, they gain temperature and lose humidity due to adiabatic compression. These phenomena are combined with moderate to strong wind speeds of 24 to 56 km h^{-1} (15–35 mi h^{-1}), with gusts as high as 80 km h^{-1} (50 mi h^{-1}). This pattern usually occurs between 5 and 10 times a year, with one or two significant events during the fall season of most years. These conditions can lead to rapid fire spread and extreme fire behavior.

Lightning with Low Precipitation   This weather pattern typically affects northeastern California to varying degrees, once or twice per fire season, although it can occur as many as four or five times in a single year. Though not a term generally recognized by meteorologists, local fire and resource mangers use "dry lightning" to describe this pattern because it includes episodes of thunderstorms that are more likely to cause fires than others. The pattern is most common in July and August, but can occur from June through mid-September. It sets up when the dominant high pressure aloft becomes oriented from roughly northern Nevada down through Arizona. When the main high-pressure center is in northern Nevada, it draws mid-level moisture northwestward, tracking along the western flank of the high-pressure mass toward northern California. Often, this moisture transport roughly parallels the Sierra Nevada, with the greatest moisture from near the crest eastward. When relatively cool disturbances aloft are caught up in this larger-scale flow pattern they can act as "triggers," destabilizing the mid and upper layers enough to generate high-based thunderstorms. Because the resulting cells have high bases, much of the precipitation associated with them evaporates before reaching the ground. The events usually result in many fire ignitions over a relatively short time, a situation that can be rapidly compounded by the gusty erratic downdraft winds associated with the thunderstorms (Rorig and Ferguson 1999, 2002).

Moist Monsoon   The moist monsoon pattern is the "true" southwestern monsoon, and it is rare in the Northeastern Plateaus and the rest of northern California. The pattern is characterized by unstable air masses, high humidity, and fairly widespread wet thunderstorm activity. Although it is a

MAP 11.1. Northeastern Plateaus bioregion map. Note the inclusion of
Carson Valley and the Pine Nut Mountains in the northern Mono sections of the Great Basin, southeast of Lake Tahoe.

common summer feature from Arizona/New Mexico northward into the Great Basin and southern Rocky Mountains, northeastern California usually lies just beyond its western fringes. About once in 10 to 15 years the pattern is displaced far enough westward to affect northeastern California. When it does so, sites can receive a total of 5 to 12.5 cm (2–5 in) of precipitation from thunderstorms over a span of 4 to 6 weeks. This occurred during the unusually wet July and August of 2003. Many wildfires can be ignited during this weather pattern. However, due to the accompanying precipitation they do not spread much, and therefore do not become a significant problem if standard levels of local firefighting resources are available.

Strong Subsidence/Low Relative Humidity A fourth pattern, strong subsidence/low relative humidity (RH) can, with enough duration, cause a significant increase in Northeastern Plateau fire potentials, even without much wind. The pattern occurs when a strong mid- and/or upper-level high-pressure area is centered to the west of northeastern California for a period of at least several days. High pressure over the area leads to diverging air at the surface. The surface divergence induces large-scale slow sinking of the mid/upper air mass over northeastern California. This phenomenon is called *subsidence* and it leads to adiabatic compression that warms and dries the lower atmosphere. Perhaps its most important effect is the hindrance of normal nighttime RH recovery. Non-subsidence pattern recovery occurs on lower slopes and in drainage bottoms. The RH recovery ranges from 35% to 45%, and may reach 55%. In a subsidence situation, which is most common in August or September and only pertains to mid-slopes and above, the daytime minimum RH usually drops to 4% to 12%, but nighttime recovery is very low, reaching only the 15% to 30% range. Dead fuel moistures drop; live fuels become more stressed; and fires ignite, spread, and spot more easily. Fire seasons characterized by large fires and/or extreme fire behavior are often preceded by one to several years of drought.

LIGHTNING

Lightning strikes are most common from June through August and peak in July; though they may occur from May through September (van Wagtendonk and Cayan 2007). Ignition probability is highest in late July through September as fuel moistures are typically at their lowest. Total number of lighting strikes from 1985 to 2000 was 73,187 covering 2,034,103 km^2 with 22.49 yr^{-1} 100 km^{-2}. The top three lightning-impacted areas by total number of strikes (in parentheses) and number year^{-1} 100 km^{-2} within this bioregion are: (1) Devil's Garden (8,475) 19.76; (2) Fredonyer Peak (6,876) 24.91; (3) Tule Mt. to McDonald Peak (6,697) 25.06; and (4) Shaffer and Skedaddle Mountains to Eagleville (6,395) 21.08. Lightning occurrence is not linearly related to an increase in elevation in this bioregion. The distance lightning can travel in this area ranges from 180 km (112 mi), which is the longest at the lower end range of all bioregions, to 340 km (211 mi), which is second to the Southeast Desert bioregion.

Ecological Zones

The quantity of available moisture from precipitation or soil is the primary determinant of vegetation and fire regimes in the Northeastern Plateaus bioregion. Major zones include: sagebrush steppe, lower montane, mid-montane, upper montane, and subalpine zones.

The most widespread zone is the sagebrush steppe, which occurs across the driest areas in the bioregion, typically on the extensive flatter, lower-elevation areas. This zone is predominately shrub steppe, shrub desert, juniper woodlands and pinyon-Sierra juniper woodlands in the northern Mono section (Vasek and Thorne 1988, Young et al. 1988). The sagebrush steppe extends from California across the Intermountain Region into Wyoming, occupying a total of 44.4 million ha (110 million ac) (West 1983). It is generally characterized by an overstory dominated by short to tall forms of sagebrush with an understory of forbs and grasses.

Three coniferous forest-dominated zones occur with increasing elevation and precipitation associated with mountains or topographic relief. The lower montane zone is dominated by ponderosa pine *(Pinus ponderosa)* and mixed ponderosa pine/Jeffrey pine *(Pinus jeffreyi)* woodlands and forests. The mid-montane zone contains mixed forests of ponderosa pine, Jeffrey pine, and various amounts of white fir *(Abies concolor)*. The upper-montane zone is defined as the area where the climate supports the higher-elevation white fir forests in pure stands and in mixes with western white *(Pinus monticola)*, ponderosa, Jeffrey, and Washoe *(Pinus washoensis)* pines. The subalpine zone occurs in limited locations in the highest elevations of the Warner Mountains, dominated by whitebark pine *(Pinus albicaulis)* woodlands with some white fir, lodgepole pine *(Pinus contorta* ssp. *murryana)*, and western white pine.

Overview of Historic Fire Occurrence

Prehistoric Period

The Northeastern Plateaus bioregion appears to have been a dry region for more than a million years since the building of the Cascade Range began to block moisture from Pacific winter storms. Over this period the assemblages of vegetation across the bioregion appear to have remained relatively stable, though oscillating from grasslands to sagebrush and juniper to pine woodlands and forests depending on the trends in effective moisture as the climate changed between glacial and interglacial periods (Adam et al. 1989). During the Wisconsin glacial interval (the last major glaciation), several periods of extreme cold created conditions where Grass Lake, at only 1,537 m (5,043 ft) in the Cascade Range to the north of Mt. Shasta, appears to have been above treeline. The last of these cold periods appears to have occurred between 18.9 and 17.6 ka (thousands of years before present) (Hakala and Adam 2004). This coincides with glacial advances in several areas of the south Warner Mountains where the more extensive evidence of glacial activity is from the Pine Creek and

Owl Creek drainages. What is now Paterson Lake was then covered with glacial ice (Osborn and Bevis 2001).

We are aware of only two paleoecological studies looking at the association of climate, fire, and vegetation in this bioregion: one by Wigand et al. (1995) in the Eagle Lake area on the southwestern edge of the bioregion, and one by Minckley (2003) at Patterson and Lily Lakes in the Warner Mountains.

In the southeastern portion of the bioregion around Eagle Lake, it appears that most of the early and mid-Holocene (11.5–4 ka) was characterized by warm and very dry conditions. Vegetation appears to have oscillated between grasslands and shrublands during this period. Fire frequency appears to have been variable at this time with little charcoal produced. Juniper woodlands had their greatest expansion during the cool, moist period of 4 to 2 ka. This was accompanied by changes in the fire regime that indicated the greater available biomass would promote occasional extensive fires that would be followed by short-term expansion of grasslands that would then give way again to juniper woodlands. Eventually, a general increase in effective moisture over the last millennium appears to have increased vegetative productivity and promoted more frequent fires. As a result, the juniper woodlands gave way to the eastside yellow pine–dominated forests and woodlands that are characteristic of the area today (Wigand et al. 1995).

The Warner Mountains show warming and drying trends from 11.5 to 9 ka with sagebrush expansion similar to the rest of the Great Basin. However, fir expansion begins between 9 and 8 ka indicating greater effective moisture in contrast to other Great Basin locales. This also coincides with increased fire activity, as evidenced by charcoal influx to lakes in the Warner Mountains. Fir and pine continue to increase and modern forest conditions appear to assemble between 4.5 and 3 ka. Two other periods of high fire activity took place between 4 and 3 ka and from 2 to 1 ka. Interestingly, the mixed conifer vegetation at Lily Lake in the north Warners has been unusually stable in spite of the oscillations in fire activity. Here, variation in fire activity appears to have been independent of trends in vegetation. However, variation in fire activity, as indicated in charcoal influx, has been similar to variation in fire activity across the region (Minckley 2003). Recent work suggests that background levels of charcoal from lake sediments are an indicator of extralocal or regional fire activity (Whitlock et al. 2004). It may be that Lily Lake is capturing a more regional picture of fire activity and that local fires were of low intensity or patchy enough for locally produced charcoal to not overwhelm the regional picture (Minckley 2003).

Historic Period

In 1880, there were reported 16,000 beef cattle, 23,000 resident sheep, and 6,000 horses in Modoc County. By 1909, the reported numbers had increased to 44,000 beef cattle, 76,500 resident sheep, and 15,000 horses (Pease 1965, cited in Laudenslayer et al. 1989). In addition, transient sheep from neighboring areas of California, Oregon, and Nevada came

TABLE 11.1

Number and area of fires recorded on the Modoc National Forest, 1910–2005

	Total Number of Fires	Fires ≥2000 Acres	Total Acres Burned
1910–1919	64	2	212,652
1920–1929	65	6	57,847
1930–1939	73	7	74,847
1940–1949	78	7	91,733
1950–1959	49	12	162,487
1960–1969	34	2	13,087
1970–1979	65	10	282,736
1980–1989	47	6	37,058
1990–1999	123	10	109,381
2005	39	4	56,431

NOTE: These values include human-caused and lightning ignitions (data on file, Modoc N.F., Alturas, CA).

through parts of the bioregion in the spring, summer, and fall. The intensive, largely unmanaged livestock grazing affected fire regimes by reducing fine fuels, reducing some plant life forms such as the perennial native bunchgrasses and palatable shrubs (e.g., antelope bitterbrush [*Purshia tridentata*]), and facilitating other life forms such as annual grasses and unpalatable trees and shrubs (e.g., sagebrushes and western juniper [*Juniperus occidentalis* var. *occidentalis*]) (Laudenslayer et al. 1989).

Ponderosa and Jeffrey pine stand structures were generally more open at the time of Euro-American settlement. Many early accounts of settlers, soldiers, surveyors, and others mention stands composed of large, widely scattered trees (Laudenslayer et al. 1988). Fire was almost certainly one of the main factors that affected the forest structures observed in those early accounts. Historic period disturbances of logging, grazing, mining, agriculture, rail networks, highways, and so forth began in the region in the 1860s, and were in full swing by the 1920s. This area, however, was always more sparsely populated than the main California Gold Rush regions to the south and west.

Timber harvesting was always an important activity in the forested areas of this bioregion. The main species harvested were ponderosa and Jeffrey pine. Most of the early timber harvest was used locally. By the mid 1930s, the local timber industry became economically dependent on sales of timber outside the eastside pine region, much of which is included in the northeastern California bioregion. Fire suppression was actively pursued and promoted as a means of protecting the economic resource provided by the region's forests, and was probably effective in the flatter areas of the bioregion (Laudenslayer et al. 1989).

The number of fires and area burned from 1910 to 1999 in the Modoc National Forest is depicted in Table 11.1. Though only two fires were recorded to have burned greater than 800 ha (2,000 ac) from 1910 to 1919, the area burned was the second largest in the 90-year record. Many small fires were started by trains, escaped warming fires, and fires set to clear land for agriculture. As railroad and highway traffic increased, so did the number of ignitions along travel corridors in this bioregion. The highest number of hectares burned between 1970 and 1979 were after several above-average years of precipitation in the early 1970s followed by drought in the latter part of the decade. During the time period between 1990 and 1999, 123 fires were recorded, the highest recorded for this area of the Northeastern Plateaus bioregion.

The Sugar Hill fire, probably the most famous large and destructive fire in early Modoc County history, was ignited by sparks from a train on the Southern Pacific Railroad on the west side of the North Warner Mountains on July 22, 1929 (Brown and Brown 1991). The fire started around one in the afternoon when relative humidity was zero with high temperatures and near-gale winds. The fire quickly spread to the east, and at the peak of the fire storm, "the fire swept a half mile across Lassen Creek Canyon in an immense sheet of flame from tree tops on one side to those on the other, without igniting the ranch buildings and haystacks in the canyon bottom" (Brown and Brown 1991). It was finally controlled by 600 men after burning 2,400 ha (6,000 ac) of forest in two days. Though Crane Creek sawmill was heroically saved, many of the mill workers' homes were destroyed in the blaze. Thought to be totally extinguished, the fire erupted from smoldering roots and burned an additional 200 ha (500 ac) on August 5 before being controlled by 300 firefighters. There was no loss of life, but the loss of timber that was to be cut and milled was significant.

NATIVE AMERICANS

Information on the use of fire by Native Americans in this bioregion, either prehistoric or during initial contact with settlers is rare. Deer firing *(kupi't)* was an effective tool used by the Northern Paiute to move and corral frightened mule deer *(Odocoileus hemionus)* into a waiting party of hunters (see full quotation at the beginning of this chapter, Kelly 1932). Pease (1965) questioned the local legend that Native Americans used fire to keep the forest understory clear of shrubs to increase game and facilitate hunting. Fire use by Native Americans, Pease (1965) argued, would have reduced understory forest vegetation from repeated burning. In the lower-montane sites, Native American fire use coupled with lightning ignitions would have favored herbaceous species over fire-sensitive shrubs such as antelope bitterbrush, which is a key browse plant of mule deer and a major food source of the Native Americans (see Sidebar 11.1). However in the mid-montane zone, repeated fire promotes fire-adapted shrub species (e.g., ceanothus and manzanita), which make wildlife and human travel difficult and are not preferred browse species of mule deer.

Current Period

Since the turn of the century, fire regimes have changed among many of the semi-arid plant associations in northeastern California. These changes are largely attributed to the reduction of fine fuels through livestock grazing, fire suppression, the introduction of highly flammable, exotic annual herbs, and climate change. Since the late 1870s, some plant associations within ecological zones burn more frequently and others less frequently than prior to this period. Where fires were historically more frequent and have currently become less frequent, fire severity has increased.

Major Ecological Zones

Sagebrush Steppe

The predominant sagebrush species are (1) big sagebrush *(Artemisia tridentata)*, which include subspecies Wyoming *(Artemisia tridentata* ssp. *wyomingensis)*, basin big *(Artemisia tridentata* ssp. *tridentata)*, and mountain *(Artemisia tridentata* ssp.*vaseyana)*; and (2) low *(Artemisia arbuscula)*; and to a lesser extent black sagebrush *(Artemisia nova)* (Rosentreter 2005) (Fig. 11.1). Series associated with the sagebrush steppe are western juniper woodlands, quaking aspen *(Populus tremuloides)*, riparian, and associations dominated by antelope bitterbrush and curl-leaf mountain-mahogany *(Cercocarpus ledifolius)*. Presettlement juniper communities were primarily shrub savannas, which usually occupy shallow rocky soils. Most present day juniper woodlands in northeastern California have become established since the late 1800s and have replaced sagebrush steppe communities where precipitation is sufficient to support western juniper. Generally this occurs in areas that receive a minimum of 30 cm (12 in) of precipitation. In addition, introduced plant species such as cheat grass *(Bromus tectorum)*, medusahead *(Taeniatherum caput-medusae)*, tumble mustard *(Sisymbrium altissimum)*, and the native western tansy mustard *(Descurainia pinnata)* have successfully invaded and replaced shrub steppe communities throughout this region resulting in a shift to annual grasslands.

The pluvial valley bottoms, primarily found in the Surprise Valley and Honey Lake areas, are occupied by the greasewood and shadscale series. Greasewood *(Sarcobatus vermiculatus)* is also found in the lowlands around Alturas and in the Klamath Basin around Tule Lake and Klamath Marsh (Young et al. 1988). These environments have soils that are too saline or precipitation that is too low for most species of sagebrush to be a dominant component. Predominant shrub species are fourwing saltbush *(Atriplex canescens)*, greasewood, hop-sage *(Grayia spinosa)*, and winterfat *(Krascheninnikovia lanata)*. Tables 11.2 and 11.3 describe the fire regimes of important species of the shrub steppe.

FIRE RESPONSES OF IMPORTANT SPECIES

One of the largest changes in community composition following fire is the immediate reduction of the shrub layer. Shrubs, associated with sagebrush steppe plant communities across the bioregion are composed of fire-tolerant and fire-intolerant species (Tables 11.4 and 11.5). The composition of

Antelope bitterbrush *(Purshia tridentata)* is the dominant understory species in pine forests throughout the Northeastern Plateaus bioregion. How it responds to fire is of concern to land managers because of its high value as a wildlife browse species (Guenther et al. 1993). Antelope bitterbrush provides 73% to 84% of mule deer's diet from June to July in the pumice zone of south-central Oregon (Gay 1998) and is a major portion of their winter diet where both species occur (Salwasser 1979, Gay 1998). It is also important as small-mammal food source (Vander Wall 1994) and habitat (Smith and Maguire 2004), as well as neotropical bird nesting habitat (Dobkin and Sauder 2004), and contributor to soil productivity via symbiotic nitrogen fixation (Busse 2000a, 2000b).

Antelope bitterbrush grows from the sagebrush steppe to the mid-montane zone in the 30 cm to 89 cm (12 in to 35 in) precipitation range, respectively. It is adapted to forested environments where fire burned with low intensity, (function of energy content of the fuel, the mass of the fuel consumed, and the rate of the fire spread [Agee 1993]), low severity (effect of fire on plants [Agee 1993]), and frequent fire-return intervals (4 to 24 years) (Arno 1976, Wright and Bailey 1982, McArthur et al. 1983, Bork 1985, Agee 1993, see also West 1968, Sherman and Chilcote 1972, Martin 1983, Vander Wall 1994). Historically very frequent fires (<10 years) probably limited the ability of bitterbrush to occupy a site and favored fire resilient herbaceous species, especially graminoids (Riegel unpublished data). Because of lower precipitation in the sagebrush steppe, plant distribution is more dispersed with greater distances between shrubs and herbaceous species and seed production is limited (Young and Clements 2002. Riegel unpublished data). The heterogeneity of vegetation structure and biomass production prior to fire suppression and livestock grazing allowed for some plants to survive a mixed fire regime with low to moderate fire intensities and longer fire-return intervals (>30 years). This allowed for the potential to develop 50- to 98-year-old plants (Adams 1975, Clements and Young 2001, Riegel unpublished data). The largest antelope bitterbrush specimen in California reported to date was from Janesville, at the edge of Sierra Nevada and Northeastern Plateaus bioregions Nord (1965). It was 128 years old, 3.7 m (12 ft) tall, and 6.1m (20 ft) across.

Livestock grazing from 1880 through the early 1920s promoted an increase in antelope bitterbrush cover by: (1) selectively reducing competition between the historic graminoid-dominated understory, allowing antelope bitterbrush to expand and occupy a greater percentage of the understory, and (2) reducing the major source of fine fuels—graminoids—needed for carrying fire through the understory to the detriment of bitterbrush (Weaver 1943, Adams 1975, Peek et al. 1978, Shinn 1980). These factors, coupled with above-average precipitation during this time period (Antevs 1938, Graumlich 1987, Miller et al. 1994), allowed antelope bitterbrush and ponderosa pine to become established in higher densities than during the presettlement fire regime (Agee 1933).

The ability of antelope bitterbrush to persist in fire-prone environments is a function of sprouting (Blaisdell 1950, Blaisdell and Muggler 1956, Martin and Johnson 1979, Clark et al. 1982, Martin 1982, 1983, Martin and Driver 1983, Hurley and Ratcliff 1986, Cook et al. 1994) and rodent seed caching (West 1968, Sherman and Chilcote, Martin 1983, Vander Wall 1994). The literature on antelope bitterbrush's response to fire is often confusing. Fire is commonly reported to be very destructive to antelope bitterbrush (Hormay 1943, Billings 1952, Wagstaff 1980). Some plants have been observed to sprout after burning under favorable conditions (Nord 1959, 1965), while some populations have exhibited abilities to sprout reasonably well following burning (Blaisdell 1950, Blaisdell and Muggler 1956, Martin and Johnson 1979, Clark et al. 1982, Hurley and Ratcliff 1986, Cook et al. 1994). Antelope bitterbrush growing in pumice soils of central Oregon and northeastern California has been reported to sprout infrequently following fire (Driscoll 1963, Nord 1965, Sherman and Chilcote 1972, Martin 1982, 1983, Martin and Driver 1983).

However, Busse et al. (2000) found 25% of a bitterbrush population that sprouted was still alive by year five. There are a variety of factors and their interactions that may contribute to antelope bitterbrush's ability to sprout: genetics, plant age, phenology, soil moisture, soil texture, fuel moisture, fuel loads, fire intensity, and fire severity. Given the genetic potential to produce sprouts from the basal crown (Alderfer 1977, Winward and Alderfer-Finley 1983, Agee 1993, Jabbes 2000), plants older than 5 years and younger than 20 to 40 years typically produce the most sprouts (Martin and Driver 1983, Simon 1990). Early-season spring burns have the highest potential for successful sprouting when: (1) soil moisture is high enough to reduce heat flux to the basal crown and roots and allow for sufficient regrowth, (2) moisture content of small fuel (woody material <0.6cm [1/4"in] in diameter, generally drying out in 1 hour, with a comparatively high surface area-to-volume ratio) is low enough for rapid fire (low residence time), (3) and moisture content of heavy fuels (large diameter wood such as large limbs, logs, and snags) is relatively high so that these fuels do not burn. These abiotic factors interact with plant phenology; burning early versus late in the growing season may yield higher sprouting success as the plants have a greater amount of time to resprout and resume photosynthesis if the basal crown was not killed and the plant has sufficient carbohydrate reserves to facilitate resprouting (Agee 1993). The percentage of successful sprouting appears to be inversely related to fire severity as measured by Blaisdell (1950, 1953), Nord (1959), and Driscoll (1963). Thus, dry fuels produce the highest heat yields, but high soil moisture reduces the heat flux to the crown and root tissues, mitigating the effect of intensity.

Establishment and recruitment of antelope bitterbrush occurs primarily by seed from rodent caching (West 1968, Sherman and Chilcote 1972, Martin 1983, Vander Wall 1994). Successful caches are made in the interspaces between shrubs where litter is sparse. Though a sprouting plant may produce flowers and seed the first year following fire, it takes typically 9 to 15 years to reach pre-burn production (Pechanec et al. 1954, Wright 1972, in Noste and Bushey 1987). Fire-return intervals shorter than 20 years yield the highest sprouting potential of antelope bitterbrush (Simon 1990) but result in lower density and cover, while fire-return intervals greater than 20 to 40 years allow for a sufficient population of seed bearing shrubs but only a small percentage may retain the ability to sprout (Simon 1990, Gay 1998).

Mule deer populations have been declining in this bioregion for several decades (Salwasser 1979, Clements and Young 1997) There are many causal factors that contribute to mule deer habitat loss: (1) increased frequencies of wildfires in sagebrush steppe that comprise winter ranges, (2) suppression of fire in the lower- and mid-montane zone that are key transition and summer ranges have facilitated western juniper expansion (Clements and Young 1997), and increased Jeffrey and ponderosa pine stand density and canopy development limiting light levels for regeneration (Peek et al. 2001), and (3) in the lower elevation sites, the introduction of highly competitive exotic annual grasses that reduce antelope bitterbrush regeneration success and also facilitate frequent fires that are extremely flammable when dry (Clements and Young 1997). In south central Oregon mule deer preferred canopy closures ≤40% in their core home ranges (Gay 1998). Thinning forest stand density to <40% canopy cover will provide antelope bitterbrush with the higher light levels that are optimal for establishment and growth (Gillespie and Loik 2004). The paradox for land managers is how to maintain acceptable fuel loads, which includes pine needle drape on antelope bitterbrush (*pine needle drape* acts as accelerant that increases flame heights 2 to 5 fold), while growing bitterbrush for habitat and dietary needs of mule deer. See Young and Clements (2002) for a thorough and practical approach to understanding the biology and management of antelope bitterbrush.

FIGURE 11.1. Sagebrush steppe zone. This mountain big sagebrush site had recently burned. Rabbitbrush has resprouted and bitterbrush appears to be growing in the background. (Photo by Rick Miller.)

TABLE 11.2

Fire regime characteristics for sagebrush types in shrub steppe ecological zones in northeastern California

Vegetation type				
	Low sage	Basin big sage	Wyoming sage	Mountain big sage
Temporal				
Seasonality	Summer–early fall	Summer–early fall	Summer–early fall	Summer–early fall
Fire-return interval	Truncated medium	Truncated medium	Truncated medium	Truncated medium
Spatial				
Size	Medium	Small	Large	Large
Complexity	High	High	Multiple	Multiple
Magnitude				
Intensity	Moderate	Moderate	Moderate	Moderate
Severity	Very high	Very high	Very high	High
Fire type	Surface	Multiple	Multiple	Multiple

fire-tolerant and fire-intolerant shrubs prior to the burn influences shrub composition during the early years following fire.

Sagebrush   Species of sagebrush found in the northeast bioregion are easily killed by fire with the exception of silver sagebrush *(Artemisia cana)* and snowfield sagebrush *(Artemisia speciformis)*, both of which resprout (Winward 1985) (Table 11.4). Reestablishment of the big sagebrush subspecies and the two forms of low sagebrush *(Artemisia arbuscula)* is entirely dependent on unburned seed. The potential for large inputs of sagebrush seed following a fire is limited and dependent on the amount of unburned edge and the amount and distribution of unburned sagebrush shrubs in the burn. Sagebrush seed is mainly distributed by wind, with no evidence of seed caching by animals. Seed movement from adjacent unburned areas has been reported to be slow, taking many years to move into the interior of the burn (Mueggler 1956, Johnson and Payne 1968, Ziegenhagen 2003, EOARC data*). The majority of sagebrush seed (more than 90%) is disseminated within

*EOARC is the Eastern Oregon Agricultural Research Center, jointly operated by Oregon State University and USDA Agricultural Research Service, Burns, OR.

TABLE 11.3
Fire regime characteristics for non-sagebrush types in shrub steppe ecological zones in the Northeastern Plateaus bioregion

Vegetation type					
	Bitterbrush	Mountain mahogany	Juniper	Quaking aspen	Cheat grass
Temporal					
Seasonality	Summer–early fall	Summer–early fall	Late summer–early fall	Late summer	Summer–early fall
Fire-return interval	Truncated medium	Truncated medium	Truncated long	Medium	Short
Spatial					
Size	Medium	Small	Small–large	Small	Large
Complexity	Multiple	Multiple	Multiple	Low	Low
Magnitude					
Intensity	Moderate	High	High	Multiple	Low
Severity	Multiple	Very high	Very high	High	Low
Fire type	Multiple	Multiple	Multiple	Surface	Surface

TABLE 11.4

Relative response of common shrubs in the sagebrush biome and salt deserts to fire

Tolerant	Moderately Tolerant	Intolerant
Yellow rabbitbrush (s)	Rubber rabbitbrush (s)	Low sagebrush
Wax currant (s)		Big sagebrush
Desert gooseberry (s)		Fourwing saltbrush
Wood rose (s)		Curl-leaf mountain-mahogany
Greasewood (s)		Hop-sage
Mountain snowberry (s)		Antelope bitterbrush (ws)
Horsebrush (s)		

NOTE: s = sprouter, ws = weak sprouter. Derived from Blaisdell 1953, Wright et al. 1979.

9 m (30 ft) of the parent plant and nearly 100% within 30 m (98 ft) (Harniss and McDonough 1974, Johnson and Payne 1968). This suggests the rate of recovery is highly dependent on soil seed pools immediately following the fire, particularly on large fires with few unburned islands and unburned plants in the burn perimeter.

Sagebrush seed matures and disperses in the autumn and winter (Young and Evans 1989, Meyer and Monsen 1991). The majority of wild and prescribed fires occur during the summer and early fall, prior to maturity of the current year's seed crop. So soil seed pool reserves are determined by the previous year(s) seed crop(s).

Although seed crop production is highly variable from year to year, seed production is usually not a limiting factor for big sagebrush establishment (Harniss and McDonough 1974). Goodwin (1956) reported that sagebrush produced 350,000 seeds m^{-2} of canopy annually. In the first year after

fire, sagebrush seedling density can be high (Blaisdell 1953, Mueggler 1956). However, with little seed input, seed pool reserves will decline through germination, loss of viability, and predation within the first two years following fire. Hassan and West (1986) reported Wyoming big sagebrush seed densities following a summer fire were 0.7 viable seeds m^{-2} compared to 3.7 viable seeds m^{-2} on an adjacent unburned site. In the second fall after the fire, viable seed densities declined to 0.3 m^{-2}.

In northwestern Nevada, a 4,000-ha (9,900-ac) wildfire occurred in 1994 prior to seed maturation and left few surviving sagebrush plants. In 1993, an extremely wet year, large seed crops were produced. During the first two growing seasons following the fire, rapid establishment of mountain big sagebrush and antelope bitterbrush occurred (Ziegenhagen 2003) (Fig. 11.2). During this period, 0.3 and 0.9 shrubs m^{-2} were successfully established. In mountain big sagebrush

TABLE 11.5
Relative response of common perennial forbs in the sagebrush biome to fire

None to Slight	Moderate to Severe
Yarrow (*Achillea millefolium*)	Pussy-toes (*Antennaria* spp.)
Agoseris (*Agoseris* spp.)	Sandwort (*Arenaria* spp.)
Onion (*Allium* spp.)	Matted buckwheat (*Eriogonum caespitosum*)
Aster (*Aster* spp.)	Parsnipflower buckwheat (*Eriogonum heracleoides*)
Milkvetch (*Astragalus* spp.)	Douglas' buckwheat (*Eriogonum douglasii*)
Woollypod milkvetch (*Astragalus purshii*)	Slender buckwheat (*Eriogonum microthecum*)
Balsam-root (*Balsamorhiza* spp.)	Sulfur flower (*Eriogonum umbellatum*)
Indian paintbrush (*Castilleja* spp.)	Spiny phlox (*Phlox hoodii*)
Hawksbeard (*Crepis* spp.)	
Fleabane daisy (*Erigeron* spp.)	
Geranium (*Geranium* spp.)	
Avens (*Geum macrophyllum*)	
Prickly lettuce (*Lactuca serriola*)	
Lomatium (*Lomatium* spp.)	
Lupine (*Lupinus* spp.)	
Bluebells (*Mertensia* spp.)	
Slender phlox (*Phlox gracilis*)	
Penstemon (*Penstemon* spp.)	
Longleaf phlox (*Phlox stansburyi*)	
Cinquefoil (*Potentilla* spp.)	
Lambstongue ragwort (*Senecio integerrimus*)	
Goldenrod (*Solidago* spp.)	
Dandelion (*Taraxacum* spp.)	
Goat's beard (*Tragopogon* spp.)	
Largehead clover (*Trifolium macrocephalum*)	
Foothill death camas (*Zigadenus paniculatus*)	

NOTE: Derived from Blaisdell 1953, Pechanec et al. 1954, Lyon and Stickney 1976, Klebenow and Beall 1977, Wright et al. 1979, Volland and Dell 1981, Bradley et al. 1992.

associations, shrub densities in fully established stands ranged between 0.8 and 1.2 shrubs m^{-2} (Ziegenhagen 2003, EOARC data). The decline in seedling establishment in 1997 and 1998, both wetter-than-average years, was attributed to depleted seed pools due to germination of seed, loss of seed viability, granivory, and limited input from newly established plants. In several other fires, seedling establishment began to increase 8 to 10 years after the fire as earlier established plants matured and began producing adequate seed.

Rate of big sagebrush recovery following fire is highly variable but tends to be slower in the more arid plant associations (Bunting 1984a). Within 15 to 25 years following the fire, mountain big sagebrush canopy cover can be 15% to 25% (Bunting et al. 1987, Ziegenhagen 2003). Rate of recovery is highly dependent on soil seed pools and moisture availability in growing seasons immediately following the fire.

Antelope Bitterbrush Antelope bitterbrush is a weak sprouter in the Northeastern Plateaus bioregion, and its response to fire is highly variable (Tables 11.4 and 11.5).

Blaisdell and Mueggler (1956) reported survival from resprouting in eastern Idaho was 49% in a light burn, 43% in a moderate burn, and 19% in a hot burn. They also reported greater survival of resprouting in plants less than 15 years old. Driscoll (1963) concluded survival of antelope bitterbrush resprouts was related more to soil surface texture than fire intensity in central Oregon. In California, 5% to 25% of the antelope bitterbrush successfully resprouted in 5 of 13 fires (Nord 1965). Survival from resprouting was also greater in spring burns than fall burns (Clark et al. 1982).

In northwestern Nevada, less than 1% of the antelope bitterbrush survived by resprouting (Ziegenhagen 2003). The majority of shrub establishment occurred from soil seed reserves. However, unlike sagebrush, an important vector of antelope bitterbrush seed dispersal is small mammal seed caches. When antelope bitterbrush successfully resprouts following fire, the species can recover to nearly fully stocked stands within 9 to 10 years after fire (Wright et al. 1979). However, on sagebrush-associated sites evaluated

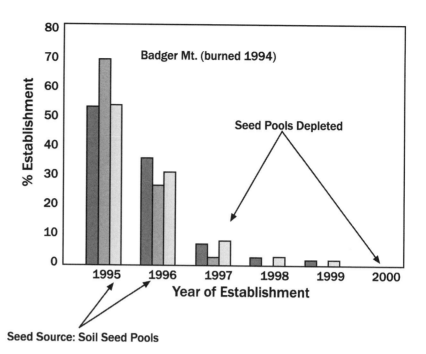

FIGURE 11.2. Mountain big sagebrush seedlings became established from soil seed pools only in the first two years post-fire. The seed pool decline was precipitous in the first year and by the third year the pools were exhausted, emphasizing the short-lived seeds of sagebrush. Beyond the second year, recruitment largely occurs from new seed that is wind dispersed on the site (Ziegenhagen 2003).

several years after fire in northern California, southeastern Oregon, and northwestern Nevada, reestablishment was primarily from seed and occurred at the same rate as sagebrush on the same sites. On a heavily browsed deer winter range in south central Oregon, antelope bitterbrush did not recover to preburn levels 40 years after the fire (EOARC data). Antelope bitterbrush seedlings also compete poorly with cheat grass, which can severely limit reestablishment (Holmgren 1956).

Rabbitbrush and Horsebrush Rubber and yellow rabbitbrush and horsebrush are capable of sprouting and more rapidly recovering immediately following fire than big sagebrush (Tables 11.4 and 11.5). However, rubber rabbitbrush is more sensitive to fire than yellow rabbitbrush (Wright et al. 1979). In some areas, establishment is from both seeds and shoots (Young and Evans 1978). In eastern Idaho and northeastern California, establishment was primarily from crown and root shoots with little from seed (Bunting et al. 1987, EOARC data). Although percent composition is usually higher for these sprouting species during the early years following fire, percent cover of these sprouters often does not exceed preburn levels on good condition sites (Bunting et al. 1987, EOARC data). The abundance of these sprouting species also usually declines over time as sagebrush abundance increases and the intervals between disturbance increase (Young and Evans 1978, Whisenant 1990). However, density and cover of these species can exceed preburn levels, especially on degraded sites (Chadwick and Dalke 1965, Young and Evans 1978). Abundance of horsebrush (*Tetradymia* spp.) remained higher than preburn levels 30 years after the fire (Harniss and Murray 1973). Heavy grazing following fire can also increase the abundance of

rabbitbrush and horsebrush as these taxa are not palatable to livestock.

Curl-Leaf Mountain-Mahogany Curl-leaf mountain-mahogany, a weak sprouter, is highly susceptible to fire (Wright et al. 1979) (Tables 11.4 and 11.5). Presettlement-aged plants are usually found on rocky ridges, which are fire protected (Dealy 1975, Gruell et al. 1984, Davis and Brotherson 1991). Postsettlement stands are commonly found in communities where presettlement fire return intervals were less than 20 years, but have significantly increased since the late 1800s (Dealy 1975, Gruell et al. 1984, Miller and Rose 1999). Age analysis indicates a large increase of curl-leaf mountainmahogany since the late 1800s.

Reestablishment following fire is largely dependent on seedling establishment (Wright et al. 1979); thus a nearby seed source is important. Curl-leaf mountain-mahogany has regenerated in several large burns in northeastern California (Tule Mountain 1959 and Three Peaks 1957) where mature plants, often located on rocky micro sites, survived the fire. However, little recruitment has occurred in a large curl-leaf mountain-mahogany stand following the 1973 Ninemile fire where few plants survived as a result of high fire severity.

Herbs and Grasses Ground cover of native herbaceous vegetation can quickly recover and exceed preburn levels in some plant associations and decrease or equal preburn levels in others (Blaisdell 1953). Rate of recovery and composition following a fire is largely determined by moisture regime, ecological site plant composition prior to the burn, soil seed reserves, fire tolerance of species on the site, fire intensity, weather conditions, and management following the fire. In general, ground cover of native grasses and forbs growing in the more mesic sagebrush communities—characterized by mountain big sagebrush, Columbia needlegrass (*Achnatherum lemmonii*), Idaho fescue (*Festuca idahoensis*), and bluebunch wheatgrass (*Pseudoroegnaria spicata*)—recovers rapidly and often exceeds preburn levels within 1 to 3 years after fire. However, in more arid plant associations and plant associations with fire-sensitive grasses and forbs, recovery is slower and cover will often not exceed preburn levels for many years. If density of native species is less than 2 plants m^{-2} (Bates et al. 2000), and cheat grass is abundant in the understory, burning will likely convert the site to introduced annual grassland.

In general, broad-leaf grasses such as squirreltail (*Elymus elymoides*), bluebunch wheatgrass, and Columbia needlegrass are relatively resistant to fire, recovering quickly and often producing greater amounts of biomass following a fire (Blaisdell 1953, Wright 1971, Bunting et al. 1987, EOARC data). In contrast, fine-leaf grasses such as Idaho fescue and Thurber needlegrass (*Achnatherum thurberianum*) are more sensitive to fire, suffering greater crown mortality and slower recovery rates than broad-leaf grasses (Blaisdell 1953, Wright 1971). Fine-leaf grasses usually accumulate more dead material in the crown, which causes the plant to burn more slowly, transferring more heat to the growing points (Wright 1971).

Conrad and Poulton (1966) reported grazed Idaho fescue and bluebunch wheatgrass plants were less damaged than ungrazed plants. In a Wyoming big sagebrush plant association in south central Oregon, bluebunch wheatgrass was severely damaged in an ungrazed exclosure where considerable dead leaf material had accumulated in the crowns (EOARC data). Outside of the exclosure on the grazed portion of the study area, bluebunch wheatgrass biomass and ground cover was near preburn levels in the first year following fire.

Although the majority of literature reports Idaho fescue is fire sensitive and declines in the first year following fire (Blaisdell 1953, Conrad and Poulton 1966, Countryman and Cornelius 1957), this species usually recovers, and biomass and cover can exceed preburn levels within 3 to 5 years after the fire (EOARC data). In Lassen County, Idaho fescue crown area decreased by one third in the first year following fire but was 35% greater than preburn levels in the third growing season.

Forb species, which resprout below ground from a caudex, corm, bulb, rhizome, or rootstock, usually exhibit rapid recovery following fire. The majority of these forbs are dormant at the time of the fire and their growing points are protected from heat. However, forbs that are *suffrutescent* or mat forming, such as sandwort (*Arenaria*) and wild buckwheat (*Eriogonum*) species, have their growing points above ground and can be severely damaged by fire, resulting in crown area reduction or mortality. Perennial forb production usually increases two- to threefold following fire in the more mesic sagebrush plant associations (Blaisdell 1953, EOARC data). However, perennial forb response is usually less in the drier plant associations (Blaisdell 1953, Bunting et al. 1987, Fischer et al. 1996, EOARC data).

In relatively good condition sites, the largest increases in vegetation during the first several years following fire are often the native annuals, if sufficient moisture is available. Most species have completed their life cycle by early summer, prior to most fire events. During the first growing season following fire, annuals are able to take advantage of increased nutrient availability and decreased competition from perennials. In several fires in northeastern California and northwestern Nevada, native annuals increase three- to fivefold in the first and second year following fire (EOARC data). However, annual response typically lasts only two to five growing seasons following a fire event. Their response can also be greatly limited by dry conditions in the spring. In heavily disturbed or warmer sites (e.g., Wyoming big sagebrush series), the native annual response is replaced by exotic annuals and biennials, which dominate the site.

FIRE REGIME–PLANT COMMUNITY INTERACTIONS

Proxy information must be used to develop fire regimes for much of the sagebrush steppe zone since little direct information is available. The lack of large presettlement wood or trees that repeatedly scar, such as ponderosa pine, across most of the sagebrush biome, limits our ability to date presettlement fires and determine mean fire return intervals. Presettlement fire-return intervals for some of the wetter mountain big sagebrush associations adjacent to forested communities have been described (Houston 1973, Miller and Rose 1999, Heyerdahl et al. 2006). But descriptions of fire regimes for the majority of plant associations in the sagebrush steppe are lacking. Here we use available literature and ecological–fire–climate relationships to describe presettlement fire regimes for shrub steppe, desert shrub, and woodland associations. This includes: (1) fire scars and charred wood, (2) fine fuel load potentials, and (3) juniper age structure to describe presettlement fire regimes in several mountain big sagebrush plant associations. Tables 11.2 and 11.3 show the fire regimes for the shrub steppe plant communities.

Juniper trees less than 50 years old are easily killed by fire (Burkhardt and Tisdale 1969, 1976; Bunting 1984b; Miller and Rose 1999). Taking into consideration the variability of fire-return intervals, mean fire-return intervals were probably less than 50 years to inhibit woodland encroachment. As fire-return intervals increase in length (more than 50 years) the potential for some trees to survive fire increases. In mountain big sagebrush it is not uncommon to see scattered presettlement trees on less-productive south slopes. However, on the opposing north aspect, evidence of presettlement trees is typically absent unless present on fuel-limited micro sites. In these arid land plant communities, the potential for shorter fire-return intervals decreases along an increasing moisture gradient resulting in more abundant fuels and greater fuel continuity.

Frost (1998) estimated a very general presettlement fire-return interval of 13 to 25 years for the sagebrush region in the Intermountain West. However, this was based on fire-return intervals reported for the more mesic mountain big sagebrush communities in Yellowstone, Wyoming (Houston 1973). Brown (2000) estimated the presettlement fire-return interval for this same region as varying between 35 and 100 years, which probably better characterizes the more arid sagebrush associations that occupy a larger portion of this zone. The combined range of both authors, 13 to 100 years, probably best captures the range of complexity of fire-return intervals that occurred across much of the sagebrush steppe, with return intervals getting increasingly longer going from the mesic to arid big sagebrush communities. In the fuel-limited low sagebrush and black sagebrush communities, fire-return intervals were more commonly greater than 150 years (Young and Evans 1981, Miller and Rose 1999).

Pre- and postsettlement fire regimes among and within desert shrub, salt desert shrub, shrub steppe, and juniper woodlands of northeastern California are spatially and temporally complex. Presettlement fire regimes varied from low-intensity fires occurring at intervals of less than 20 years in some mountain big sagebrush associations (that were more likely grasslands or shrub grassland mosaics) to events rarely occurring in desert salt shrub associations. Even with the mountain big sagebrush series presettlement fire-return intervals on the Lava Beds National Monument range from less than 20 years to greater than 200 years among different plant associations (Miller et al. 2003). Since the late 1800s, fire regimes have significantly changed among many of the plant associations in northeastern California. The reduction of fine fuels through grazing, introduction of exotic weeds, fire suppression, and the removal of anthropogenic burning have significantly altered fire interval, intensity, severity, and season (Burkhardt and Tisdale 1969, 1976; Whisenant 1990; Miller and Rose 1999, Miller and Tausch 2001).

Amount and continuity of fuels are often limiting among many plant associations in the sagebrush biome (Bunting et al. 1987) and associated plant communities. Fire models that describe rate of spread and behavior are usually inadequate for most of these plant associations due to the patchiness of fuels and presence of bare ground (Brown 1982). Minimum levels of fuels required to carry fire in sagebrush steppe communities are 20% shrub cover, 200 to 300 lb ac^{-1} of herbaceous fuel, 8 to15 mph winds, 15% to 20% RH, and 21°C (70°F) to 27°C (80°F) temperatures (Britton et al. 1981). Brown (1982) reported shrub canopies began influencing fire spread at 30% to 40% cover. For fire to carry through woodland under relatively dry conditions, Klebenow and Bruner (1976) reported a minimum of 40% to 60% pinyon, juniper, and shrub cover were required. Wright et al. (1979) concluded that 600 to 700 lbs of fine fuel were necessary to carry a fire through pinyon-juniper woodland. However, wildfires that burn under severe weather conditions are capable of burning across plant communities having very limited fuels.

Areas in this zone with short fire-return regimes were probably grass grasslands or sagebrush-grassland mosaics. As MFRI (median fire-return interval) increase, the physiognomy shifts from grassland to shrub steppe. Sparse stands of western juniper occupied sites with MFRI greater than 50 years. Since the late 1800s, fire events have generally decreased across the mountain big sagebrush series, especially those where presettlement MFRI were less than 100 years. In north-

ern California, the result has been an increase in shrub cover and density and decline in the herb layer, and often a shift from shrub steppe communities to western juniper woodlands (see Sidebar 11.2).

More than 90% of the presettlement fires dated in this region occurred between mid-summer and early fall (Miller and Rose 1999, EOARC data). The likely ignition source was lightning, which usually occurs in dry thunderstorms during July and August. During a two-week period in August of 2001, more than 100,000 strikes occurred in Lassen and Modoc Counties in California and adjacent Lake and Harney Counties in Oregon (BLM, personal communication) resulting in numerous fire starts. Although there is evidence of Native Americans burning in this region, there is no consensus as to magnitude of human-caused fire starts compared with those caused by lightning.

The northwesternmost populations of pinyon pine are found on the edge of the Northeastern Plateaus bioregion and the eastern slopes of the Sierra Nevada; Long Valley Creek in the foothills of the Diamond Mountains, which drains into the Honey Lake 40 km (25 mi) to the east, and is 30 km (19 mi) north of the Loyalton population in Sierra County (David Charlet and Robin Tausch, personal communication). Both stands consist of only a few scattered trees and have been spared by several wildfires that have burned in the vicinity since 1989. Much more expansive stands of pinyon pine occur in the northern Mono section of the bioregion. Their fire ecology is discussed in Chapter 16.

Lower-Montane Zone

The lower-montane zone is wetter and cooler than the sagebrush steppe, and generally occurs in this bioregion where precipitation levels range from approximately 40 cm (16 in) to about 64 cm (25 in) (Figs. 11.3 and 11.4). Vegetation within the lower-montane zone is characterized by ponderosa and Jeffrey pine forests growing on sites with moderately deep to deep well-drained soils. The lower-montane zone in this bioregion occurs on the lower slopes of the Warner and Big Valley Mountains, at the base of the Diamond Mountains, and in large patches on the flat, expansive Devil's Garden area. Slopes are generally less than 30%. At the north end of the bioregion, ponderosa pine is the sole native yellow pine, although Jeffrey pine can be found in older tree plantations such as Sugar Hill (reforested after the 1929 fire) in the north Warner Mountains. South of a latitude line corresponding with Alturas, California, Jeffrey pine mixes with ponderosa pine. Common tree and shrub species are ponderosa pine, Jeffrey pine, western juniper, incense-cedar (Calocedrus decurrens), California black oak (Quercus kelloggii), antelope bitterbrush, mountain big sagebrush, low sagebrush, greenleaf manzanita (Arctostaphylos patula), curl-leaf mountain-mahogany, Utah service-berry (Amelanchier utahensis), and western choke-cherry (Prunus virginiana) (Smith and Davidson 2003).

This zone was heavily affected in the twentieth century by logging, grazing, fire exclusion, and possibly climate change.

The northwestern portion of the pinyon and juniper region is represented by western juniper *(Juniperus occidentalis)*. This subspecies occupies more than 3.64 million hectares (9 million acres) in northeast California, eastern Oregon, northwest Nevada, southwest Idaho, and a few outlying stands in southeast Washington (Miller et al. 2005). In California, woodlands (more than 10% tree canopy cover) occupy 520,000 ha (1,284,948 ac), and juniper shrub savannas (less than 10% tree canopy cover) occupy 323,000 ha (798,150 ac) (Bolsinger 1989). It is typically the only conifer occupying the site except where juniper woodlands integrate with ponderosa pine. Precipitation typically averages from 30 to 40 cm (12 to 16 in) across the majority of these woodlands. In its southern limit, south of Susanville, western juniper integrates with the subspecies Sierra juniper *(Juniperus occidentalis* spp. *australis)*, which occurs along the upper-elevation slopes of the Sierra Nevada Mountains.

During the Pleistocene period, the northern range of western juniper was in the Lahontan Lake basin (Thompson et al. 1986, Tausch 1999). In California, it grew in Kings Canyon during maximum glaciation (Thompson 1990). At the end of the Pleistocene (10,000 years B.P.), western juniper began migrating north, reaching northeast California and southeast Oregon during the mid-Holocene period, between 7,000 and 4,000 years B.P. (Bedwell 1973, Mehringer and Wigand 1987). At Lava Beds National Monument in northern California, western juniper seeds and twiglets were found in an ancient wood rat midden dated 5,400 years old (Mehringer and Wigand 1987). From the mid-Holocene to Euro-American settlement, the abundance of western juniper populations have increased and decreased with climate and fire throughout their current range (Mehringer and Wigand 1987, 1990; Wigand 1987). However, expansion of western juniper woodlands during the past 130 years appears to be unprecedented when compared with any other time period in the last 10,000 years (Miller and Wigand 1994).

Prior to settlement, which began around the late 1860s, juniper was primarily confined to rocky surfaces or ridges and pumice sands with sparse vegetation (West 1984, Miller and Rose 1995, Waichler et al. 2001, Johnson and Miller in press). In northeastern California, the most extensive stands of old juniper are found on shallow, heavy clay soils supporting low sagebrush and Sandberg bluegrass *(Poa secunda* ssp. *secunda)*. These stands are typically open with less than 10% canopy cover. On fuel-limited sites, such as rocky outcrops, western juniper can attain ages exceeding 1,000 years (Waichler et al. 2001). In Devil's Garden, located north of Alturas, the majority of old-growth trees growing in association with low sagebrush and Sandberg bluegrass ranged between 200 and 500 years of age (EOARC data 1940) with some exceeding 700 years (Fig. 11.2.1). The widely scattered old trees (canopy cover less than 5%) would suggest the occurrence of infrequent stand-replacing fires.

Western juniper is capable of growing in a broad range of soils. Since the late 1800s, western juniper has rapidly expanded into deeper, more productive soils (Burkhardt and Tisdale 1969, 1976; Adams 1975; Miller and Rose 1995, 1999; Gruell 1999). In northeast California, western juniper has encroached into the mountain big sagebrush and quaking aspen alliances and riparian series. Expansion has been attributed to a decline in fire occurrence, the introduction of livestock, and wetter-than-average conditions between 1870 and 1915. In northeast California and southeast Oregon, western juniper expansion coincides with the reduced occurrence of fire in the late 1800s following the introduction of livestock (Miller and Rose 1999, EOARC data). The lack of old wood or trees on the more productive plant associations suggests fire was frequent enough to limit juniper encroachment into these communities. In nearly a dozen mountain big sagebrush/Idaho fescue sites and adjacent ponderosa pine alliances located in southeast Oregon and northeast California, mean fire-return intervals between 1700 and 1870 varied between 10 and 20 years for small fires and 32 years for large fires (Miller and Rose 1999, EOARC data). Since the

FIGURE 11.2.1. Sagebrush steppe zone. Old-growth western juniper growing in low sagebrush and Sandberg bluegrass in the Devil's Garden, Modoc County. Low site productivity on heavy clay soils yields widely spaced shrubs and herbaceous species making fire ignition and spread difficult. Though the Devil's Garden has the highest number of lightning strikes within the bioregion, fire-return intervals are very long, which has allowed western juniper trees to live up to 500 years in this area. (Photo by Rick Miller.)

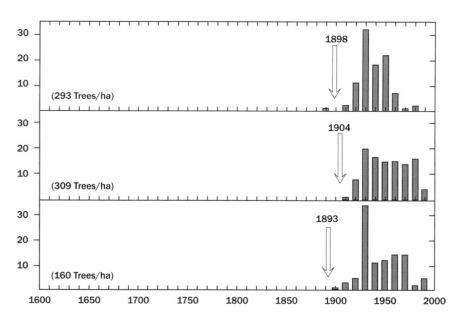

FIGURE 11.2.2. Establishment dates of western juniper trees on three different sites in the Lava Beds National Monument. Prior to settlement these communities were open ponderosa pine/Idaho fescue with scattered mountain big sagebrush and bitterbrush. Presettlement fire-return intervals were 8 to 10 years; last fire is reported in the graph (from Miller et al. 2003).

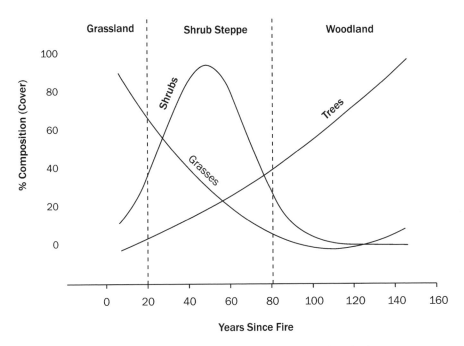

FIGURE 11.2.3. Model of the rate of post-fire succession from grassland to shrub steppe to western juniper woodland. Shrubs and trees co-dominate during the period shown in gray. Percentage composition is derived from measured cover of existing herb, shrub (excluding mountain-mahogany), and overstory (western juniper and mountain-mahogany) at Lava Beds National Monument. Moist sites are those plant associations that contain Idaho fescue while arid sites are those that contain western needlegrass (from Miller et al. 2003).

decline in fire, western juniper is invading these sites. On the Lava Beds National Monument, fire-return intervals were between 8 and 10 years during 1750 and 1904 in open ponderosa pine/Idaho fescue communities (Miller et al. 2003). Following the cessation of fire on these sites, mountain big sagebrush increased followed by the rapid establishment of western juniper and the decline of sagebrush (Figs. 11.2.2 and 11.2.3). Although presettlement fire events were likely less frequent in more arid mountain big sagebrush associations, fire-return intervals would probably have to have been less than 50 years to limit western juniper encroachment into shrubland communities (Burkhardt and Tisdale 1976, Bunting 1984a, 1984b, Miller and Rose 1999). As the length of fire-return intervals increases with more limited fuels on increasingly drier sagebrush communities, scattered trees can establish and occupy the site. A relatively dry western juniper, mountain big sagebrush, and Thurber needlegrass plant association in the Lava Beds National Monument supported infrequent moderate- to high-severity fires. Two fire events recorded on this site, one in the early 1700s and a second in 1856, resulted in scattered patches of old western juniper trees and an abundance of charred wood and stumps (Miller et al. 2003).

The majority of western juniper woodlands in Oregon and California are still in transition from shrub steppe to juniper woodland. Although western juniper has increased tenfold in the past 130 years, it currently occupies far less land than it is capable of under current climatic conditions (Miller et al. 2000). During the early stages of encroachment, juniper initially adds structural diversity to shrub steppe communities, which often increases wildlife abundance and diversity (Reinkensmeyer 2000, Miller 2001). However, structural diversity declines as woodlands become fully developed and structural complexity, productivity, and diversity of understory vegetation declines (Miller et al. 2000). In Modoc County north

FIGURE 11.2.4. Sagebrush steppe zone. Many of the lower-elevation and drier aspen stands have succumbed to juniper succession. This process has occurred due to: (1) reduction of competition from herbaceous plants primarily by livestock grazing, (2) browsing of aspen regeneration by livestock and native ungulates, (3) soil compaction primarily by livestock, (4) fire exclusion, and (5) the complex interactions of factors 1 through 4. (Photo by Rick Miller.)

of Alturas, western juniper overstory increased and live shrubs decreased in permanent transects measured from 1957 to 1998 (Schaefer et al. 2003). Sagebrush, an important ladder fuel during the early stages of woodland development decreases as juniper dominance on the site increases. The production of fine fuels can also decrease with the decline of sagebrush, essentially fire-proofing the site.

Western juniper began invading quaking aspen communities in the 1890s, with peak establishment occurring between 1900 and 1940 (Fig. 11.2.4). In nearly 100 quaking aspen stands studied across north eastern California, southeastern Oregon, and northwestern Nevada below 2,100 m (6,890 ft), western juniper was present in over 90% of the stands (Wall et al. 2001). They reported 12% of the quaking aspen stands were completely replaced by western juniper; juniper was the dominant tree species in 23% of the stands and was common to codominant in 42%. No juniper tree more than 140 years of age was measured across these stands, nor was large juniper wood found. Prior to 1900, disturbance intervals within relatively large quaking aspen groves occurred between 10 to 16 years, with total stand replacement occurring about 60 to 100 years (Romme et al. 1996, Wall et al. 2001). In southeastern Oregon, juniper trees have been rapidly encroaching into riparian areas (EOARC data). The lack of old wood or presettlement trees in both of these series suggests mature western juniper was probably absent prior to Euro-American settlement.

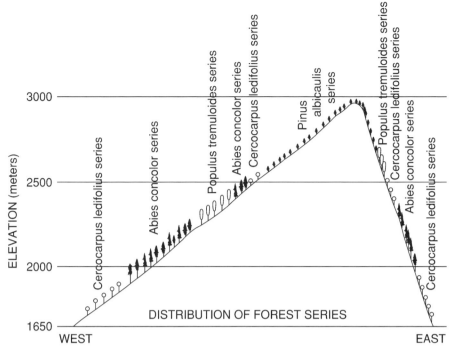

FIGURE 11.3. Distribution of climatic potential vegetation types and elevation relationships in the South Warner Mountains (Riegel et al. 1990). Fire suppression has allowed for white fir expansion into (1) Jeffrey and ponderosa pine sites in the lower-montane zone that typically occur from 1,670 to 2,043 m (5,479 to 6,703 ft), and (2) Washoe pine sites from 1,890 to 2,195 m (6,201 to 7,201 ft) in the mid-montane to upper-montane zones. The upper-montane zone spans from 1,829 to 2,390 m (6,001 to 7,841 ft) where white fir is both the historic dominant under a natural fire regime as well as the climatic potential with occasional stands of western white pine.

FIGURE 11.4. Lower-montane zone. Landscape view of ponderosa and Jeffrey pines, California black oak, western juniper, and antelope bitterbrush dispersed between large expanses of low and mountain big sagebrush on the Big Valley Ranger District, Modoc National Forest. (Photo by Sydney Smith.)

In general, stands are much denser than in the late nineteenth century, and trees are much smaller, larger ones having been removed mostly by logging. Fuel loadings are likely quite high compared to pre-twentieth century levels because of dense trees, dead trees, and accumulations of logging slash (Smith and others, personal observations).

FIRE RESPONSES OF IMPORTANT SPECIES

Before the twentieth century, frequent surface fires of low to moderate intensity removed needle and branch litter and created exposed surface mineral soil where yellow pines, both ponderosa and Jeffrey, and incense cedar seeds can germinate and grow (Table 11.6). Winged seeds of these species are wind dispersed in the late summer through fall. Depending on the time at which fire returns to a site these seeds may be eaten or cached by animals, consumed by fire, or fall on mineral surface soil.

Jeffrey pine occurs on the coldest sites, higher elevations, steeper slopes, and shallower soils relative to ponderosa pine (Smith 1994). Thus, Jeffrey pine sites are generally lower in productivity compared with ponderosa pine sites (Jenkinson 1990). Antelope bitterbrush is the most widespread understory dominant associated with Jeffrey pine forests.

TABLE 11.6
Fire response types for important species in the lower montane zone

| Lifeform | Type of Fire Response | | | Species |
	Sprouting	Seeding	Individual	
Conifer	None	None	Resistant/killed	Ponderosa pine, Jeffrey pine, incense cedar, western juniper
Hardwood	Fire stimulated	None	Resistant/killed	California black oak
Shrub	Fire stimulated	Fire stimulated	Top-killed	Mahala mat, greenleaf manzanita, western choke-cherry
	Fire stimulated	None	Top-killed	Utah service-berry, bitter cherry, Modoc plum
	+/−Fire stimulated	None	Killed	Antelope bitterbrush
	None	None	None	Mountain big sagebrush
Forb	Fire stimulated	None	Top-killed	Woolly mule's ears, arrowleaf balsam-root, lambs tongue ragwort, lupine, Nevada wild pea, lomatium, peony, Indian paintbrush
Graminoids	+/− Tillering	None	Top-killed	Idaho fescue
	Tillering	None	Top-killed	Squirreltail, Ross' sedge, Canby bluegrass
	None	None	Killed	Cheat grass

Utah service-berry may be slightly injured by fire, depending on moisture conditions and flame lengths but is generally considered to be fire tolerant (Crane 1982, Bradley et al. 1992). However, mortality does occur if a thick litter layer is present at the time of the fire. Utah service-berry sprouts from adventitious buds at the root crown and it is also a prolific seed producer with persistent animal-dispersed berries.

Fire often kills aboveground choke-cherry stems and foliage, but it quickly resprouts from root crowns and rhizomes (Volland and Dell 1981, Young 1983). Fire-induced sprouts can be produced within the growing year following a spring burn, or if a fall burn, by the next spring. It can double its stem density within one growing season prior to being burned. Large, animal-dispersed seeds aid in post-fire regeneration. Scarification of the seed coat by the heat from fire improves germination.

The primary response of herbaceous plants to a prescribed fire on the Fremont National Forest, in south-central Oregon, was a slight increase in diversity and a change in the relative dominance of graminoid species, Ross' sedge (Carex rossii), and Idaho fescue (Busse et. al. 2000). Squirreltail and Ross' sedge both increased in biomass and cover, whereas fescue cover declined. Fire stimulates squirreltail root and shoot biomass of surviving plants and increases seedling recruitment (Young and Miller 1985, Vose and White 1991). Ross' sedge has shal-

low rhizomes and is capable of responding rapidly to disturbance. In comparison, fescue, a tufted bunchgrass, varies from moderate to severe susceptibility to fire, depending on the amount of detritus in the basal tufts that cause fire to linger and kill the perennating buds (Wright 1971, Johnson 1998) (see further discussion in the sagebrush steppe zone above). The most common species typically found after burning are tailcup lupine (Lupinus caudatus), Nevada pea (Lathyrus lanszwertii), nineleaf biscuitroot (Lomatium triternatum), sticky cinquefoil (Potentilla glandulosa), Brown's peony (Paeonia brownii), and fireweed (Epilobium angustifolium).

FIRE REGIME–PLANT COMMUNITY INTERACTIONS

Though no fire history studies have been conducted in the Jeffrey pines forests in northeastern California, Smith (1994) speculates that return intervals were short, probably ranging from 5 to 20 years (Table 11.7). In the ponderosa pine/antelope bitterbrush-tobacco brush/needlegrass plant association on Pringle Butte in Central Oregon (Deschutes National Forest), between 1362 and 1900, the MFRI ranged from 7 to 20 years where mean annual precipitation was 61 cm (24 in) (Bork 1985). However, Jeffrey pine, which reaches its eastern geographic range limit in Modoc County (Little 1971, Griffin

TABLE 11.7
Fire regime characteristics for the lower montane zone in the Northeastern Plateaus bioregion

Vegetation type	Jeffrey pine	Ponderosa pine	Jeffrey-ponderosa pine
Temporal			
Seasonality	Summer–early fall	Summer–early fall	Summer–early fall
Fire-return interval	Short–medium	Short	Short–medium
Spatial			
Size	Medium	Medium	Medium
Complexity	Medium–high	Low–medium	Low–high
Magnitude			
Intensity	Low	Low	Low–moderate
Severity	Low	Low	Low–moderate
Fire type	Surface	Surface	Surface

and Critchfield 1972), is absent from these Central Oregon sites. Thus the fire-return intervals may be shorter than would be expected for Jeffrey pine. The harsher conditions usually associated with Jeffrey pine sites, as noted above, usually leads to slower fuel accumulation, typically resulting in longer fire return intervals than found on sites dominated by ponderosa pine (Skinner and Chang 1996, Taylor 2000, Stephens 2001, Skinner 2003, Stephens et al. 2003) (see also Chapters 9 and 10, this volume).

Within the lower montane zone, fire-return intervals were probably longer at the drier and/or lower-elevation sagebrush steppe zone ecotone than in the mid and upper elevations, regardless of dominance Jeffrey pine or ponderosa pine. Bork (1985) reported an MFRI of 16 to 38 years, from 1460 to 1970, in a ponderosa pine/antelope bitterbrush-mountain big sagebrush/Idaho fescue plant association on pumice soils, where mean annual precipitation is 24 cm (9 in). Fire history was reconstructed from scattered ponderosa pine growing within mountain big and low sagebrush communities in the upper Chewaucan River basin near Paisley, Oregon, where precipitation was approximately 40 cm (16 in). MFRI ranged from 3 to 38 years between the years 1601 and 1897 (Miller and Rose 1999). Fire return intervals from a relatively small sample size were reported along an elevation and vegetation gradient in the Buck Creek watershed on the west side of the North Warner Mountains (Goheen 1998). For the period between 1650 and 1879, return intervals were four times longer (MFRI ranged from 2 to 56 years) on a lower-elevation (1,567 m [5,140 ft]) juniper and ponderosa pine site than in the middle-elevation (1,735 to 1,905 m [5,690 to 6,250 ft]) ponderosa pine sites (MFRI ranged from 1 to 11 years). Vegetation spatial pattern is more heterogeneous on these lower-elevation sites as limited soil moisture regulates plant density and biomass production. Both limited fuel quantities and lack of continuity result in longer intervals between fires. Additionally, slopes are not as steep on the lower-elevation sites and would be less likely to produce fires intense enough to scar trees as on steeper slopes.

Busse et al. (2000) demonstrated that low-intensity prescribed fire following a prolonged period of wildfire exclusion produced a significant, yet slight reduction in tree growth in thinned ponderosa pine stands. Basal area growth reduction was proportional to the level of crown scorch and "O" horizon reduction during burning. No evidence was found to suggest that prescribed fire will have a long-term impact on stand productivity. Specifically, soil resources, including nutrient content and exposed mineral soil, were unaffected by fire.

Woolly mule's ears (Wyethia mollis) is a common and abundant understory species of Jeffrey, ponderosa, and Washoe pine forests east of the Cascade Range from south-central Oregon and northeastern California through the eastern Sierra Nevada of California and Nevada (Hopkins 1979, Riegel 1982, Smith 1994, Sawyer and Keeler-Wolf 1995), as an associate species in the montane and subalpine sagebrush steppe throughout this range (Cronquist 1994). An herbaceous, disturbance-adapted long-lived perennial (more than 50 years) with a deep taproot and fleshy resinous foliage, woolly mule's ears was most likely an early successional plant with low frequency and cover prior to Euro-American arrival (Young and Evans 1979, Williams 1995). Woolly mule's ears is also one of the first plants to initiate growth in the spring and typically completes its flower and fruit set by early August. Under current fire regimes, its early season phenology and taproot provide a competitive advantage to exploit soil resources for expansion and dominance (Rundel et al. 1988, Agee 1993, Barbour and Minnich 2000). Heavy livestock grazing of palatable plants from 1860 to the 1930s, primarily by sheep, also resulted in increased woolly mule's ears abundance (Coville 1898, Kennedy and Doten 1901, Leiberg 1902, USDA Forest Service 1937, Olmstead 1957). Woolly mule's ears continues to dominate sites in Lassen National Park that have been excluded from livestock grazing for more than 80 years (Oswald et al. 1995). Woolly mule's ears-dominated sites may suppress succession to mid-seral

FIGURE 11.5. Mid-montane zone. The mid-montane zone provides habitat for many woody species. In the foreground, ponderosa pine is regenerating at the edge of a mountain big sagebrush and woolly mule's ears site. Sagebrush is edaphically controlled by higher soil clay content, which limits plant-available water. Quaking aspen occurs, as both small clones comprised of several trees growing within conifer stands or as larger clones that are topographically controlled where the water table is closer to the surface. Historically, discontinuous fuel types and varying biomass productivity contributed to complex burn patterns and fire intensity. With fire exclusion, many smaller quaking aspen clones are being lost to conifer succession. In the background, mid-montane through subalpine zones are visible in the South Warner Wilderness Area. (Photo by Gregg Riegel.)

conifer regeneration for up to 100 years (Kennedy and Doten 1901, Evanko 1951, Parker and Yoder-Williams 1989) and can persist in the understory of mid- and late-seral Jeffrey pine overstories as an infrequent, low cover (less than 5 %) associate (Smith 1994).

Water-extractable allelochemicals from woolly mule's ears have been suggested as an additional factor in suppressing Jeffrey pine regeneration (Heisey and Delwiche 1983, Yoder-Williams and Parker 1987, Parker and Yoder-Williams 1989, Williams 1995). In a field bioassay, Yoder-Williams and Parker (1987) found woolly mule's ears litter leachates inhibited germination and reduced radicle elongation of pine seedlings. However, results of a greenhouse study did not support the field bioassays discussed above and concluded that allelochemicals or soil nutrients do not limit regeneration of Jeffrey pine (Riegel et al. 2002).

Hardwood species are relatively rare in northeastern California due to extreme cold minimum temperatures and aridity. Current populations of California black oak and Oregon ash *(Fraxinus latifolia)* are at their furthest northeast distribution (Little 1971, Griffin and Critchfield 1972) and are considered relict remnants from a time when the regional climate experienced warmer minimum temperatures, higher precipitation, and lower evapotranspiration (Major 1988). Oregon oak achieves its most interior distribution here with the exception of those found along the Columbia River (Little 1971,

Griffin and Critchfield 1972). These disjunct populations are primarily found on shallow clay-textured soils within fractured basalt flows (e.g., Egg Lake and Ash Creek) and secondarily, in the Pit River Canyon. Fire-return intervals were likely less frequent because ignition must be initiated on site due to the discontinuity of vegetation in basalt flows and shallow soils matrix.

The largest population of Modoc cypress *(Cupressus bakeri)* occurs on the northwestern edge of the bioregion on the corners of Modoc, Shasta, and Siskiyou counties (Stone 1965, Griffin and Critchfield 1972). This 2,833-ha (7,000-ac) population is found on recent basalt flows near Timbered Crater at elevations from 1,067 to 1,219 m (3,500 to 4,000 ft). Fire is the only effective process that opens the serotinous cones and creates conditions for successful regeneration required for reproduction (Vogl et al. 1988). Most cones remain closed until the resinous seal between the ovuliferous scales is heated by fire, allowing seeds to shed for up to several months. Stands with limited fuel continuity probably lived longer than those growing within ponderosa pine with more frequent fire return intervals. Heat generation from low fire intensity may not be hot enough for resins to come to a boil and melt. Cones will also open when the resinous seals dry, though not as wide as with fire, following mechanical detachment such as disturbance caused during logging operations. Knobcone pine *(Pinus attenuata)*,

TABLE 11.8
Fire response types for important species in the mid-montane zone

Lifeform	Type of Fire Response			Species
	Sprouting	Seeding	Individual	
Conifer	None	None	Resistant, killed	Ponderosa pine, Jeffrey pine, white fir, incense cedar
Shrub	Fire stimulated	Fire stimulated	Top-killed	Mahala mat, greenleaf manzanita, tobacco brush
	Fire stimulated	None	Top-killed	Bitter cherry, western choke-cherry, Modoc plum, mountain snowberry, creeping barberry
	None	None	None	Mountain big sagebrush
Forb	Fire stimulated	None	Top-killed	Heartleaf arnica, tuber starwort, hawkweeds, lupines, Nevada wild pea, Sierra pea, sweet cicely
Graminoids	Tillering	None	Top-killed	Squirreltail, Ross' sedge, Wheeler's bluegrass, Canby bluegrass, needlegrasses, orcutt brome

another closed-cone fire-adapted species is discussed in Chapters 9, 10, and 14.

Mid-Montane Zone

The mid-montane zone in this bioregion is defined as the area where the climate supports the lower-elevation white fir forests (Figs. 11.3 and 11.5). The mid-montane zone occurs in the Big Valley Mountains, the northern part of the Devil's Garden, and in the Warner Mountains. This zone is colder and wetter and usually at higher elevations than the lower montane zone. Average annual precipitation in this zone ranges from about 64 cm (25 in) to 82 cm (32 in) and elevations range from about 1,430 to 1,980 m (4,700 to 6,500 ft) in the Big Valley Mountains and about 1,615 m (5,300 ft) to as high as 2,225 m (7,300 ft) in the Warner Mountains (Smith and Davidson 2003). White fir occurs mixed with ponderosa pine, Jeffrey pine, incense cedar, and as more-or-less pure stands. Common tree and shrub species in addition to those already mentioned include western juniper, quaking aspen, California black oak, antelope bitterbrush, mountain big sagebrush, low sagebrush, bitter cherry (*Prunus emarginata*), western choke cherry, Modoc plum (*Prunus subcordata*), Utah service-berry, roundleaf snowberry (*Symphoricarpos rotundifolius*), greenleaf manzanita, and tobacco brush (*Ceanothus velutinus* var. *velutinus*) (Smith and Davidson 2003).

This zone presents unusual fuels management challenges because of: (1) changes in stand species composition and structure in the twentieth century, and (2) susceptibility of trees to mortality from drought, disease, and insects. Because of preferential logging of ponderosa pine, fire exclusion, and climate variation, white fir has generally increased, whereas the pines have decreased. These changes have dramatically altered the fire regime in this zone. Stand physiognomy has generally changed from less dense or relatively open stands of large trees to much denser stands of small trees. Extensive tree mortality from insects and diseases has accompanied periodic droughts. Thus, the potential for high-intensity fires increases as these mortality episodes lead to increased fuel accumulations from standing and fallen dead trees (Smith and others, personal observations).

FIRE RESPONSES OF IMPORTANT SPECIES

Jeffrey pine, ponderosa pine, incense cedar, and white fir all develop thick bark as they age which allows for their survival in characteristic frequent and low-intensity fire (Table 11.8). Jeffrey and ponderosa pine are more resistant to fire when young compared with white fir or incense cedar (van Wagtendonk 1983, Agee 1993). White fir sapling and pole-sized trees are very susceptible to fire-caused mortality due to (1) numerous resin blisters on the bark that increase potential for flammability, (2) flat, lateral branches that often extend to the ground especially in trees that are in canopy gaps and isolated "wolf trees", and (3) comparatively shallow roots that increase susceptibility to lethal temperatures when surface fires slowly burn through high fuel loads in deep and compact litter (Agee 1993, Miller 2000).

Fire profoundly affects individual species responses which in turn greatly influence successional dynamics in the mid-montane zone. Surface fires burn litter, temporarily leaving an ashy mineral soil surface that ponderosa and Jeffrey pines seeds require for successful germination, whereas incense cedar tolerates a variety of surface substrates (Powers and Oliver 1990). White fir is the only tree species in this bioregion that can germinate on top of litter, which typifies sites with longer fire-return intervals.

Following fire, greenleaf manzanita and tobacco brush prolifically spout, whereas long-lived seed bank reserves are released from dormancy ensuring the establishment or perpetuation of seral montane shrubfields. Mountain snowberry response to fire is quite variable. Most plants survive fire and typically resprout from basal buds at the root crown. However, mountain snowberry is considered a weak sprouter, especially after severe fire (Young 1983) (Table 11.5). Low-severity fire can kill branches as well as all the above-crown portions of a plant, making it difficult to predict individual plant survival. Even following severe fires, mountain snowberry root crowns usually survive (Pechanec et al. 1954, Kuntz 1982). Sprouting can occur the first year but may be initially limited, eventually reaching preburn levels within 15 years (Pechanec et al. 1954, Kuntz 1982).

FIRE REGIME–PLANT COMMUNITY INTERACTIONS

Historic fire regimes are similar to those described for the east montane zone of the Sierra Nevada and the mid-montane eastside zone of the Southern Cascade Range. Fire-return intervals were short, and intensity and severity were low (Table 11.9). Intensive logging of ponderosa pine, coupled with fire suppression and exclusion, has shifted species composition from pine-dominated and co-dominated stands to overstories where white fir is the dominant species. Fire helped to regulate stand density and suppressed the continual recruitment of white fir. The exclusion of fire has helped promote the shift to white fir dominance. White fir seedlings, which establish best in partial shade, can survive under the canopy of montane shrubs and dense forests, but once established, grow best in full sunlight (Laacke 1990). Shade-tolerance ranking for tree regeneration (seedlings and saplings) from most to least tolerant is white fir, incense cedar, and ponderosa pine and Jeffrey pine (Minore 1979). White fir is also a prolific tree, producing up to 1.5 million seeds ha^{-1} (6,000,000 ac^{-1}) generally every 2 to 5 years, beginning at age 40 and continuing beyond 300 years (Laacke 1990).

When precipitation is greater than or equal to the annual mean for a site, white fir can be very successful with rapid growth and continual reproduction and recruitment. However, in the 64-cm (25-in) precipitation zone in northeastern California, due to recurring droughts, white fir tends to become stressed, especially where the denser stands have developed, and eventually succumbs to insects and diseases—often *before* a fire occurs. White fir's stomatal regulation, water

TABLE 11.9

Fire regime characteristics for the mid-montane zone in the Northeastern Plateaus bioregion

Vegetation type	White fir and incense-cedar
Temporal	
Seasonality	Summer-early fall
Fire-return interval	Medium
Spatial	
Size	Medium
Complexity	Medium
Magnitude	
Intensity	Multiple
Severity	Multiple
Fire type	Multiple

use efficiency (WUE), and ability to control transpiration per unit of fixed carbon is far less than that of ponderosa pine (Hinckley et al. 1982). If white fir is under moisture stress (−2.0 or greater MPa) for several summers, they are more susceptible to successful fir engraver attacks than are trees under less stress (Ferrel 1978). Recurring drought is the common denominator that regulates a site's ability to produce more leaf area and stand density. Cochran (1998) advises that if prolonged droughts are forecast, removal of white fir on drier sites is recommended. Fire would have regulated white fir regeneration under a function of historic fire regime on these sites.

Despite extended drought in the southeastern Warner Mountains, Vale (1975) found that white fire invaded the mountain big sagebrush ecotone between 1915 and 1944. He concluded that heavy livestock grazing of competing vegetation was the main factor and that successful fire suppression, which did not occur until after the trees had been established, was secondary. Eventually these trees on the ecotone will be eliminated by (1) drought, (2) stress, (3) insect interactions, or (4) fire.

Outbreaks of Modoc budworm defoliating white firs occurred during the years 1959 to 1962 and 1973 to 1975 in the Warner Mountains and nearby ranges of northeastern California (Ferrel 1980). These outbreaks were associated with periods of three years or more when precipitation averaged at least 25% below the historic mean annual precipitation. A Douglas-fir Tussock Moth infestation occurred from 1959 to 1962 on 182 ha (450 ac), and from 1964 to 1965 another infestation defoliated white fir populations in second-growth pine stands in the Warner Mountains between 1,700 and 1,900 m (5,600 and 6,200 ft). Wickman (1978) interpreted from the existing number and size of stumps that the pre-logged forest had been a ponderosa and Washoe pine stand with large trees, 91 to 102 cm dbh (36 to 40 in), before being logged around the early 1900s. Though the area had been

FIGURE 11.6. Upper-montane zone. Landscape perspective of the Owl Creek watershed on the east side of the Warner Mountains showing the patchy, discontinuous nature of forest in this zone. Photo was taken during an August thunderstorm. (Photo by Carl Skinner.)

logged a second time for white fir overstory trees in 1954, Wickman noted that no fires had burned in the area for at least 50 years and more likely 75 years. The effect of logging the pine and suppressing and excluding fire has been to allow white fir to become the dominant tree species in all structural and age classes. The consequence of this change is that the current forest is more susceptible to high-intensity fire because of large amounts of live and dead fuels. The ensuing high-intensity fires have produced large landscape-level stand-replacing events such as the Scarface fire (1977), the Crank fire (1987), and the Blue fire (2001).

After a forest is removed by fire or logging, the developing shrub and herbaceous understory often suppresses conifer regeneration as a result of competition for soil moisture (Conard and Radosevich 1981, 1982; McDonald 1983b; Lanini and Radosevich 1986; Shainsky and Radosevich 1986; Parker and Yoder-Williams 1989). Though there are many pathways succession can take following disturbance in mid-montane pine forests, a generalized summary includes: (1) early seral–woolly mule's ears dominance (discussed above in the lower-montane zone) with associated herbaceous species and some conifer regeneration; (2) mid-seral–greenleaf manzanita, tobacco brush, mahala mat (Ceanothus prostratus), and antelope bitterbrush shrub dominance with pole-sized conifers; and (3) late seral–conifer dominance with some shade-tolerant herbs and shrubs.

The shrub species associated with the mid-seral stage compete with establishing conifers for light, water, and nutrients (Conard and Radosevich 1981, 1982; McDonald 1983a, 1983b; Roy 1983; Radosevich 1984; Shainsky and Radosevich 1986). A shrub canopy also provides a shaded microenvironment, however, that reduces evaporative demand and improves the water balance of trees, which may be less physiologically stressful than competition for soil resources on hot, dry sites (Conard and Radosevich 1982, Lanini and Radose-

vich 1986). Soil moisture availability on shrub-dominated sites can be significantly greater than on woolly mule's ears–dominated sites during the latter part of the growing season (Williams 1995).

Shrub dominance in the mid-seral phase should increase the soil nutrient capital with time-between-fire-and-logging disturbance intervals that temporarily reduce the cover of nitrogen-fixing shrubs, tobacco brush, mahala mat, and antelope bitterbrush (Conard et al. 1985; D. W. Johnson 1995; Busse et al. 1996; Busse 2000a, 2000b). Nitrogen fixation occurs from actinorhizal symbionts associated with tobacco brush, mahala mat (Delwiche et al. 1965; Conard et al. 1985; Busse 2000a, 2000b), and antelope bitterbrush (Webster et al. 1967; Busse 2000a, 2000b). Annual nitrogen fixation in forests east of the Sierra Nevada and Cascade Range crest varies from 5 to 15 kg ha^{-1} (5 to 15 lb ac^{-1}) for tobacco brush and 1 kg ha^{-1} (1 lb ac^{-1}) for mahala mat and antelope bitterbrush (Busse 2000a, 2000b). Busse et al. (1996) found increased soil carbon, nitrogen, and microbial biomass in the upper horizon of a ponderosa pine forest due to long-term retention of shrubs from longer fire return intervals due to fire exclusion. D. W. Johnson (1995) also found improved soil nitrogen status at pine sites with a dominance of tobacco brush. With successful fire exclusion for nearly 50 years, nitrogen-fixing shrubs that would have been periodically consumed in historic fire regimes increased radial-increment growth in naturally regenerated ponderosa pine stands in Central Oregon (Cochran and Hopkins 1991). Succession in these forests may be more influenced by competition for soil moisture and changes in microclimate.

Upper Montane Zone

The upper montane zone in this bioregion is defined as the area where the climate supports the higher-elevation white fir forests (Figs. 11.3, 11.6, and 11.7). The upper-montane

FIGURE 11.7. Upper-montane zone. Photo shows the pattern of exposed slopes dominated by shrubs and herbaceous plants with trees confined mostly to more protected sites such as the draw in the foreground and the patch of trees in the upper center on the lee side of the crest. (Photo taken by Carl Skinner near High Grade Spring north of Mt. Vida.)

zone occurs at elevations of about 1,830 to 2,225 m (6,000 to 7,300 ft) in the Big Valley Mountains, and at elevations between about 1,800 and 2,430 m (5,900 to 8,000 ft) in the Warner Mountains (Smith and Davidson 2003). This zone is cold and wet compared to the mid-montane zone. Average annual precipitation in this zone exceeds 81.5 cm (32 in). The vegetation of the zone is quite patchy responding to soil moisture, edaphic variation, and winter wind patterns. The patches are of several general types: (1) conifer-dominated, (2) shrub-dominated, (3) herbaceous-dominated, and (4) rocky, relatively barren areas primarily along exposed ridges. White fir occurs in pure stands and in mixes with western white pine, lodgepole pine, quaking aspen, occasional yellow pines (ponderosa, Jeffrey, or Washoe pines), and whitebark pine at the upper elevations of this zone (Riegel et al. 1990, Smith 1994). Western juniper at these higher elevations can still be found on exposed sites with shallow soils. Common shrubs include mountain big sagebrush, snowfield sagebrush, low sagebrush, creeping snowberry *(Symphoricarpos mollis)*, sticky currant *(Ribes viscosissimum)*, bitter cherry, tobacco brush, curl-leaf mountain-mahogany, and pinemat manzanita *(Arctostaphylos nevadensis)* (Riegel et al. 1990, Smith and Davidson 2003). We are aware of no published fire research conducted in this zone. Most of the following discussion is based on the authors' observations and discussions with local fire and resource managers.

Although this zone has been affected by twentieth-century logging, grazing, and climate change, the fire regime, as indicated by conifer and shrub species composition, has likely been affected the least of the montane zones in this bioregion. One major change, however, is the decrease in the extent and occurrence of quaking aspen. For comparison, relative changes from historic to current fire regime ranked from least changed zone to the most changed zone are upper montane, lower montane, and mid-montane.

FIRE RESPONSES OF IMPORTANT SPECIES

Scouler's willow *(Salix scouleriana)* is fire sensitive, and crown mortality can be 0% to 100% depending on fire intensity (Owens 1982) (Table 11.10). Severe fires may result in 100% aboveground mortality (Lyon and Stichney 1976). Following low- to moderate-intensity fire, Scouler's willow will quickly resprout. High-intensity fire that kills live foliage but does not kill the vascular cambium will cause vigorous epicormic sprouting from the root crown (Weixelman et al. 1998). Sprouting typically occurs within days following a fire and it is not uncommon for a plant to reach and exceed preburn frequency and cover in 5 years or less. Scouler's willow also produces wind-borne seeds that can travel for considerable distances off site.

Bitter cherry response to fire is variable. It can be killed if burned while actively growing or if fire intensity is high (Young 1983). Resprouting occurs from the root crown. It also establishes from large buried seed or seed dispersed from off site by animals, primarily birds.

Creeping snowberry is usually top-killed by fire; however, vegetative regrowth does occur from rhizomes (Volland and Dell 1981). Fire will kill rhizomes if surface litter layers are thick and/or organic matter constitutes a significant portion of the upper soil horizon (Neuenschwander n.d., cited in FEIS).

Sticky currant is considered only moderately resistant to fire (Volland and Dell 1981). Low- to moderate-intensity fire can stimulate rapid resprouting from basal stems. Seeds are relatively heavy and animal dispersed. Heat scarification increases germination rates.

Pinemat manzanita is killed by fire but re-establishes from seed during the first post-fire growing season. Kruckeberg

TABLE 11.10
Fire-response types for important species in the upper-montane zone

Lifeform	Type of Fire Response			Species
	Sprouting	Seeding	Individual	
Conifer	None	None	Resistant/killed	White fir, Washoe, ponderosa, Jeffrey, and western white pine, lodgepole pine
Hardwood	Fire stimulated	None	Top-killed	Quaking aspen
Shrub	Fire stimulated	Fire stimulated	Top-killed	Tobacco brush, bush chinquapin
	Fire stimulated	None	Top-killed	Bitter cherry, creeping snowberry, mountain snowberry, Scouler's willow, sticky currant, snowfield sagebrush
	None	Fire stimulated	Top-killed	Pinemat manzanita
	None	None	Killed	Mountain big sagebrush
Forb	Fire stimulated	None	Top-killed	Heartleaf arnica, tuber starwort, hawkweeds, lupines, slender penstemon, whiteveined wintergreen, sweet cicely
Graminoids	Tillering	None	Top-killed	Squirreltail, Ross' sedge, Wheeler bluegrass, needlegrasses, orcutt brome, Brainerd's sedge

(1977) speculated that it may be an obligate seeder, requiring fire and/or leachate from smoke or charred wood to break seed dormancy.

FIRE REGIME–PLANT COMMUNITY INTERACTIONS

Fuel-accumulation rates—not ignitions—are probably the limiting factor for fire occurrence in this zone of frequently occurring summer thunderstorms. The generally dry climate coupled with cold winters contributes to slow fuel accumulation. Although episodes of widespread lightning are common in summer, ignitions are not likely a limiting factor for fire occurrence. The predominance of short-needle conifers and the winter snow compact the fuel bed. Thus, fires started by the frequently occurring thunderstorms are often slow-spreading, patchy, low-intensity surface fires becoming more intense only where concentrations of fuels from dead trees or small thickets, usually of white fir regeneration, have developed. Accumulations of dead fuels are generally caused by (1) the stem-exclusion phase of white fir regeneration patches, (2) beetle-killed patches, or (3) deaths of individual large trees.

Some areas in this zone that were once dominated by very large yellow pines have converted to lodgepole pine and white fir (Vale 1977). Examples of this are found: (1) on the north-facing slopes near Lily Lake where large stumps of both yellow pines and incense-cedar are found in what are now dense thickets of mostly lodgepole pine, and (2) along the west side of the main crest of the Warner Mountains in the vicinity of the headwaters of the south fork of Davis Creek where large stumps of yellow pines are found in lodgepole pine/white fir stands. In both of these cases no yellow pine regeneration is evident. It is likely the original fire regimes for these specific sites have changed dramatically with this change in species. The South Warner Wilderness Area provides an outstanding example of succession from yellow pines to white fir without logging but with fire exclusion (Riegel et al. 1990).

There are three yellow or three needle pines (subgenus *Diploxylon of Pinus*)—ponderosa, Jeffrey, and Washoe—that occur in the upper montane zone in the South Warner Mountains (Haller 1961, Critchfield and Allenbaugh 1969, Griffin and Critchfield 1972, Riegel et al. 1990, Smith 1994). Washoe pine, which grows at elevations from 1,890 to 2,195 m (6,199 to 7,200 ft) has attracted considerable interest to the Warner Mountains from taxonomists and geneticists (Haller 1961, Smith 1967, 1971, 2000, Critchfield 1984, Conkle and Critchfield 1988, Niebling and Conkle 1990, Lauria 1997, Mitton et al. 1997, Rehfeldt 1999, Patten and Brunsfeld 2002). Land managers have been concerned that Washoe pine would respond differently than ponderosa or Jeffrey pines to silviculture treatments (letter from W. B. Critchfield, PSW Research Geneticist, to Dick Lund, Forest Supervisor, 20 July 1972, on file Modoc N.F.). Our observations concur with Critchfield

TABLE 11.11
Fire history data derived from crossdated fire scars at six sites of less than 10 ha each in the Horse
Creek watershed of the Warner Mountains

Site	Number of Trees	Number of Scars	Median FRI	Mean FRI	Minimum FRI	Maximum FRI
Horse A	8	21	7.5	13.3	1	51
Horse B	9	17	3.5	8.4	1	43
Horse C	10	12	37.0	33.0	8	55
Horse D	6	6	40.0	35.3	1	65
Horse F	14	20	5.5	7.1	1	20
Horse H	14	19	15.5	20.6	4	56

NOTE: FRI = fire return interval.

(1984) that the ecological response of Washoe pine to various land management activities such as logging and prescribed fire differs from ponderosa and Jeffrey pines. Washoe pine has distinctive adaptive characteristics that favor its survival in more severe climate and environments at higher elevations and slow growth rates (Rehfeldt 1999). Recent genetic research of Rehfeldt (1999) supports the distinction of Washoe pine as a robust and resilient taxon in the Warner Mountains. The ancestral lineage of Washoe pine continues to be of interest (Critchfield 1984, Lauria 1997, Rehfeldt 1999, Patten and Brunsfeldt 2002), which further emphasizes the need for land mangers to work with researchers to develop an adaptive fire management program to ensure survival of this unique species. The primary threats to Washoe pine are: (1) the potential destruction by stand-replacing fires where white fir succession has altered the fire regime, and (2) loss of habitat due to climate change (Brunsfeld 1999).

The only cross-dated fire scar record in the Warner Mountains is from this zone (Table 11.11). These data are from stands dominated by white fir with lodgepole pine and western white pine as associates. The fire scar record was developed from stumps of mostly white fir, lodgepole pine, and white pine. The record of fires extends from 1746 to 1957. Median fire-return intervals ranged from 3.5 to 40 years. Intra-ring position of fires scars was 90.6% ring boundary, 7.8% latewood, 1.6% in middle-earlywood (S. Smith unpublished data). This indicates that seasonality was mostly late summer to early fall and was similar to other upper-montane forests in northern California (Taylor 2000, Skinner 2003) (see Chapters 9 and 10).

In this zone, western juniper often occupies exposed, almost barren ridgelines. These are areas where fire rarely spreads due to very limited fuels. The barren nature of these ridgelines often limits the spread of fires from one watershed to the next. Many of the larger trees in these locations appear to be quite old, although no formal aging has been done.

Curl-leaf mountain-mahogany is often found on sites exposed to both the winter winds that remove snow and more intense summer insolation. Curl-leaf mountain-mahogany plants appear to initiate in small areas protected from wind and sun by rock outcrops. These sites are often surrounded by open, sparse stands of low shrubs and herbaceous plants. They can then survive for long periods as these areas appear to not carry fire well (e.g., the Blue fire in August 2001). Larger curl-leaf mountain-mahogany plants in one location of this type north of Fandango Pass have been aged at more than 400 years (unpublished data on file, Forest Service Pacific Southwest Research Station, Redding).

With the exception of the more-extensive stands to the east of Dismal Swamp, quaking aspen is generally found in small clones associated with increased soil moisture and surrounded by one of the other types of patches described above. The trees in larger quaking aspen clones affected by the Blue fire often survived even though the surrounding conifer stands sustained considerable mortality. The fire burning intensely in adjacent conifer stands appears to have dropped to the ground when entering the larger quaking aspen groves and burned through as a low-intensity surface fire. This change in fire behavior was likely due to higher moisture in the live and dead fuels, higher humidity, and the open nature of the crowns. None of the clones with this effect had significant encroachment of conifer regeneration.

Conifer stands in this zone likely have similar responses to fire as found in other bioregions, and the reader should reference Chapters 9, 10, and 12. The character of lodgepole pine stands varies from more open stands of larger trees and scattered individuals in the south Warner Mountains to more extensive and denser stands north of Highway 299, such as around Dismal Swamp, continuing through the Warner Mountains into Oregon. It is likely the fire regimes will vary with the nature of the stands, being more like the Cascade Range in the north (Chapter 10) and the Sierra Nevada in the south (Chapter 12).

Subalpine Zone

The subalpine zone is limited in this bioregion to the Warner Mountains with the majority of the zone found in the South

FIGURE 11.8. Subalpine zone. Photo looking south from Warren Peak toward Eagle Peak along the main crest of the Warner Mountains. All of the forests (foreground, middle ground, and background) shown in this photo are nearly 100% whitebark pine. The patches of whitebark pine are interspersed with patches of shrubs and herbaceous plants dominated mostly by snowfield sagebrush. Photo was taken during an August thunderstorm. (Photo by Carl Skinner.)

TABLE 11.12
Fire response types for important species in the subalpine zone

| Lifeform | Type of Fire Response | | | Species |
	Sprouting	Seeding	Individual	
Conifer	None	None	Resistant/killed	Whitebark pine
Shrub	Fire stimulated	None	Top-killed	Mountain snowberry, snowfield sagebrush
	+/−Fire stimulated	Fire stimulated	Top-killed	Gooseberry currant
Forb	Fire stimulated	None	Top-killed	Slender penstemon, prickly sandwort, Davidson's penstemon, phlox
Graminoids	Tillering	None	Top-killed	Western needlegrass, Wheeler's bluegrass, Ross' sedge

Warner Wilderness Area at elevations starting at about 2,253 m (7,390 ft) (Riegel et al. 1990). Whitebark pine forms nearly pure stands in this zone (Figs. 11.3 and 11.8). White fir can be either rare or common at the lower ecotonal edge; however, lodgepole pine, western white pine, and quaking aspen are relatively rare (Vale 1977, Riegel et al. 1990, Figura 1997). Common shrubs include snowfield sagebrush, Utah snowberry (*Symphoricarpos oreophilus* var. *utahensis*), mountain gooseberry *(Ribes montigenum)*, and rabbitbush *(Ericameria bloomeri)*. Common herbaceous species include western needlegrass (*Achnatherum occidentale*), pussypaws (*Calyptridium umbellatum*), Wheeler's bluegrass (*Poa wheelerii*), slender penstemon (*Penstemon gracilentus*), prickly sandwort (*Arenaria aculeata*), Davidson's penstemon, and spreading phlox.

FIRE RESPONSES OF IMPORTANT SPECIES

Whitebark pine is the only subalpine tree species in northeastern California. Chapter 12 contains a discussion of the fire response of whitebark pine. Snowfield sagebrush can resprout from root crowns or lower stem bases after being top-killed by fire (Winward 1985) (Table 11.12).

FIRE REGIME–PLANT COMMUNITY INTERACTIONS

The fire regimes are similar to that described for the subalpine zone of the Sierra Nevada and Cascade Range, with infrequent and small, low-intensity fires due to the lack and discontinuity of fuels. The largest and most contiguous stands are found in South Warner Wilderness Area from Mill

Creek to the southern slopes of Eagle Peak where relatively high-elevation ridges occur on a gentle west slope. Heavy sheep grazing in the late nineteenth century greatly reduced primarily perennial grasses and forbs in the subalpine sagebrush allowing for downslope expansion (Figura 1997). These lower-elevation stands, below approximately 2,470 m (8,102 ft), are characterized as relatively young (most trees established between 1915 and 1965) with a few older trees (200 to 300 years), yielding low stem density and basal area. Figura (1997) noted the lack of standing snags, large fallen logs, burnt coniferous wood, and downed wood in the lower-elevation stands, supporting his downslope migration hypothesis. High-elevation forests are old (400 to 800 years), self-perpetuating stands. Fire-scarred trees were found in the upper-elevation stands, though all trees cored by Figura (1997) were rotten, precluding dating historic fires. Lightning strikes are very common at these elevations yet fuel continuity and cool, moist conditions limit the ability of fire to spread beyond one to several multi-stemmed trees. We are unaware of evidence that suggests large fires have burned sizeable whitebark pine stands in the Warner Mountains. Small, old wind- and snow-shaped krummholz whitebark pine grow to the summit of Eagle Peak (3,016 m [9,892 ft]), which is the highest peak in the bioregion (Riegel et al. 1990). There is no alpine zone (land above treeline) in this bioregion (Riegel et al. 1990).

Non-Zonal Vegetation

Riparian areas, including wetlands, meadows, and riparian forests, are dispersed throughout the bioregion in all ecological zones due to both topographic and edaphic controls of surface and subsurface water. To our knowledge no fire ecology research has been done in these hydric vegetation types in this bioregion. Fire regimes in riparian areas probably differ from those in adjacent uplands but are interconnected through shared disturbance events. We speculate that presettlement fire return intervals were longer and were typically more spatially complex than adjacent uplands. When these sites did burn, fire intensity was moderate to high with mixed severity due to microtopograhic and surface–water table interactions. Livestock removal of fine fuels in the form of forage has altered these fire regimes since postsettlement.

One of the most obvious changes has been tree invasion—mostly lodgepole pine—into meadows. The reasons for invasion are complex, but the combination of reduced competition from herbaceous species and fine fuel removal due to livestock grazing coupled with fire exclusion has reduced the number and size of meadows in this bioregion. Because lodgepole pine is an evergreen conifer, it continues to transpire as long as the soil within the rooting zone is not frozen (Running 1980, Running and Reid 1980, Sparks et al. 2001). This increased, nearly year-long transpiring leaf area significantly reduces water to the meadow and is a net water loss to a watershed.

Common riparian hardwood trees and shrubs, comprised mostly of black cottonwood (*Populus balsamifera* ssp. *trichocarpa*), willows, silver sagebrush, interior rose (*Rosa woodsii* var. *ultramontana*), and scattered populations of mountain (*Alnus incana* ssp. *tenuifolia*) and white alder (*Alnus rhombifolia*), and dwarf (*Betula nana*) and water birch (*Betula occidentalis*), can sprout from stumps, stems, and root crowns following low- and, sometimes, moderate-intensity fires (Dwire and Kauffman 2003).

Quaking aspen, considered a facultative or facultative upland wetland species occurs in different settings in the Northeastern Plateaus bioregion, depending on the zone and location. In the sagebrush steppe zone, quaking aspen trees are somewhat rare; if they do occur, they are confined to sites such as streams, springs, and talus rock "reservoirs" that have perennial moisture. In the lower- and mid-montane zones, quaking aspen stands are more common and are similarly associated with sites containing perennial water. The most extensive occurrences of quaking aspen in the Northeastern Plateaus bioregion are in the upper-montane zone, mainly in the Warner Mountains. In this zone, quaking aspen stands are found on sites with added moisture from streams, meadows, and springs, as well as sites with added moisture from snowdrifts. In the subalpine zone, quaking aspen occurrence declines with increasing elevation. In areas where snow accumulations can persist well into the growing season (typically June through July), nivial or snow-morphed stands occur (Riegel et al. 1990), which are very important to many wildlife species in this zone.

Quaking aspen are clonal. The clones can be extremely long lived, hundreds to perhaps thousands of years, although the aboveground stems *(ramets)* usually only live for 125 years or so. Continuous successful regeneration from root suckers is necessary for clone survival over time. Quaking aspen has very low shade tolerance. Healthy clones with a range of size and age classes are stimulated and regenerated by stand-replacing fire.

Quaking aspen stands in this bioregion occur in two broad "themes": "Meadow" quaking aspen and "Upland" quaking aspen. Meadow quaking aspen that grow on wetter sites on stream sides and meadow edges are often not susceptible to conifer succession. If the aboveground stems senesce and are not replaced by younger stems, the clones will often thin out or disappear and the sites will be occupied by forb communities, such as corn lily (*Veratrum californicum*) in the upper-montane zone, or even mountain big sagebrush if the sites are also dewatered. Upland quaking aspen grow in drier sites and are susceptible to conifer succession in the absence of fire or other disturbances that remove or kill the conifers. Quaking aspen in both environments have decreased in the last 150 years. Meadow quaking aspen have been more affected by livestock grazing than by changes in fire regimes in the twentieth century. Upland quaking aspen stands have been profoundly affected by changed fire regimes, and have largely become dominated by conifers. These stands appear to occupy but a small fraction of their former extent, judging from scattered

Sage grouse *(Centrocercus urophasianus)* are a sagebrush-obligate and depend on the fire-sensitive plant for both food and cover. During late summer and fall, sagebrush leaves make up the majority of their diet and constitute 100% of their diet during the winter (Crawford et al. 2004). During the early spring and throughout summer (depending on availability), forbs are an important part of their diet. Prior to the twentieth century, sage grouse were able to adapt to an ecosystem where fire was an important ecosystem process. However, fire regimes have drastically changed across much of the sagebrush biome since Euro-American settlement, resulting in large losses of habitat. Ironically, fire-return intervals have significantly lengthened in the mountain big sagebrush series and greatly shortened in the Wyoming big sagebrush series (Wright and Bailey 1982, Miller and Rose 1999, Miller and Tausch 2001). In northeast California, exotic annuals have replaced large areas of warmer, drier sagebrush communities, which are potentially important winter habitat. On cooler, more mesic sagebrush communities, western juniper woodlands are rapidly increasing, resulting in the decline of sagebrush and forbs. Both scenarios of altered fire regimes resulting in conifer and exotic weed encroachment have caused a significant loss in sage grouse habitat (Miller and Eddleman 2000, Crawford et al. 2004). A primary question related to sage grouse is "How do we manage fire"?

There is considerable debate on the pros and cons of using fire to enhance sage grouse habitat. The decision to use or suppress fire for the enhancement of sage grouse habitat must be made on a site-by-site basis. Five factors that determine the negative or positive outcomes of fire on sage grouse habitat are: (1) site potential, (2) site condition, (3) functional plant group(s) (4) what is limiting in the habitat, (5) pattern and size of the burn, and (6) plant community composition on a landscape basis. Because sage grouse have extensive home ranges, habitat limitations must be considered at large scales.

Fire can be a useful tool to enhance the availability of native perennial forbs and grasses among many of the mountain big sagebrush plant associations. This is primarily in communities where sagebrush cover exceeds 30%, good populations of native herbs are present, and exotic species are limited. Perennial forb abundance can increase two- to threefold following fire (Pyle and Crawford 1996, EOARC data). Fire also enhances nutrient quality of forbs, especially protein content (McDowell 2000), and lengthens the growing season. The affects of fire on beetles and ants (important chick food) are mixed. Pyle and Crawford (1996) reported that fire did not affect beetle populations, whereas Fischer et al. (1996) reported decreases in beetle populations following fire. Fire also has a negative impact on thatch ants (J. McIver, USFS PNW Research Station, La Grande, OR, personal communication). Burning in good condition mountain big sagebrush affected species composition but not abundance of caterpillars (EOARC data), an important food for sage grouse chicks (Mike Gregg, USDI Fish and Wildlife Service, personal communication). In Nevada, sage grouse have been reported to be attracted to burn areas during the summer (Klebenow and Beall 1977, Martin 1990). Small burns with adjacent stands of sagebrush have also been used as leks. Possibly the most important justification for the use of fire for the restoration or maintenance of sage grouse habitat is that of limiting the development of juniper woodlands across many of these shrub steppe communities.

The use of fire in arid sagebrush plant associations for improving sage grouse habitat is probably very limited. Burning in good condition Wyoming big sagebrush communities or low sagebrush/Sandberg bluegrass associations usually does not increase desirable forbs used as sage grouse food (Fischer et al. 1996, EOARC file). In addition, Fischer et al. (1996) reported a decrease in beetle populations, an important chick food (Pyle and Crawford 1996). Many Wyoming big sagebrush sites also have depleted understories and have a low resistance to invasion of exotic plant species. With little to gain and the potential to increase populations of exotic weeds, the use of fire as a tool to enhance sage grouse habitat in these drier sagebrush communities is limited and very risky.

living and dead remnants throughout the mid- and upper montane zones. Quaking aspen clones respond vigorously to stand-replacing fire by producing thousands of suckers per hectare. Often the extent of a degraded clone with a few surviving stems per hectare is not apparent until a stand-replacing fire event releases the clone and multitudes of quaking aspen suckers appear where before there was nothing but white fir or some other conifer.

Management Issues

Altered fire regimes have likely caused large-scale changes in plant composition and structure across many plant communities. These changes affect important ecological processes, including the water, nutrient, and energy cycles, in addition to wildlife habitat and forage production.

The reintroduction of fire has been proposed to restore some of these arid-land communities. However, there is considerable debate over the use of fire as a tool to restore these habitats. Much of the debate is due to a lack of research on fire ecology from this bioregion. Concerns related to the use of fire, including the rapid expansion of exotic weedy species further loss of habitat for sagebrush obligates, watershed, and liability, are fueled primarily by a lack of local information. However, the lengthening periods without fire in some plant communities in the quaking aspen and mountain big sagebrush series will likely lead to their loss.

Besides altered fire regimes, the primary issues in the Northeastern Plateaus bioregion include grazing effects, wildlife needs, and impacts of invasive plant species, especially cheat grass (see Chapter 22). However, due to the lack of investigation and interest, this region is one of the most poorly understood with regard to fire ecology. In the future, more attention and investigation need to be given to the fire ecology of the various brush and woodland communities that occur in this region.

Grazing

Both the presence and level of grazing have issues for many areas in the Northeastern Plateaus bioregion and have affected a wide variety of species, including Idaho fescue, bluebunch wheatgrass, Wyoming big sagebrush, antelope bitterbrush, rabbitbrush, white fir, and whitebark pine. In some instances, grazing maintains conditions suitable for native vegetation by keeping areas more open and preventing excessive accumulation of dead material. On the other hand, direct impacts to plants occur from foraging and trampling, and indirect impacts occur when both native and invasive plant species are promoted by livestock grazing, reducing competition for resources, primarily soil moisture.

Because grazing affects the vegetation composition and condition, the regime of fire is influenced by grazing regimes (Miller et al. 1994). Thus, subsequent fire regimes that affect native vegetation communities are affected by how grazing has been conducted. Prescribed burning is used

to improve range conditions and such burning can have dramatic effects on sagebrush and grass species, as well as on junipers. Grazing timing and regimes, as well as prescribed burning conducted for range value, need to integrate the unique fire ecology of the various northeast plateau plant communities to minimize both impacts to native vegetation and alterations to future fire regimes.

Wildlife

Many key plant species in the shrub and woodland communities of the northeast plateaus are greatly affected by fire. These species, such as antelope bitterbrush, rabbitbrush, and junipers, are also significant habitat and food for wildlife species. Mule deer, pronghorn (*Antilocapra americana*), hares and rabbits, and sage grouse and other ground-nesting birds are dependent on the cover, shelter, and food that the scattered native grass, brush, and woodland vegetation provide.

Greatly altered fire regimes and the spread of exotic plant species have affected this bioregion's wildlife. As in other areas of the state, the use of prescribed fire has become a topic of interest among land managers and agencies responsible for the conservation of wildlife. One example of this debate is the sage grouse, a species that in recent years has shown a decline in numbers sufficient to raise concerns about its health and viability. Whether prescribed fire has a conservation role for the sage grouse or any other wildlife species is still unknown (see Sidebar 11.3).

Summary

This bioregion has a rich history of fire throughout the vast arid basins, uplands, and forested mountain ranges interspersed with fresh and alkaline wetlands. Both lightning and Native American burning patterns abruptly changed when fuel continuity was disrupted, and non-native invasive species were introduced, with the arrival of large numbers of domestic livestock in the last two decades of the 1800s. Fire suppression and agriculture have further altered historic fire regimes. Changes to fire regimes have caused changes in plant community composition and structure, and wildlife habitat in many plant communities. Although fire once limited woody plants, juniper now takes advantage of longer fire return intervals; its expanding range into the sagebrush steppe has also affected fire regimes. Fire has also become less frequent throughout the montane zones with the mid-montane more changed than the lower montane, and upper montane the least changed of the three. Fire continues to be an important ecological process throughout the Northeastern Plateaus bioregion but its role has greatly changed.

References

Adam, D. P., A. M. Sarna-Wojcicki, H. J. Rieck, J. P. Bradbury, W. E. Dean, and R. M. Forester. 1989. Tulelake California: the last 3 million years. Palaeogeography, Palaeoclimatology, Palaeoecology 72:89–103.

Adams, A. W. "Bud." 1975. A brief history of juniper and shrub populations in southern Oregon. Oregon State Wildlife Commission, Wildlife Research Report No. 6, Corvallis, OR.

Agee, J. K. 1993. Fire ecology of Pacific Northwest forests. Island Press, Washington, D.C.

Alderfer, J. M. 1977. A taxonomic study of bitterbrush [*Purshia tridentata* (Pursh). DC.] in Oregon. M.S. Thesis. Oregon State University, Corvallis

Antevs, E. 1938. Rainfall and tree growth in the Great Basin. Carnegie Institution of Washington, Publication 469, American Geographers Society, Special. Publication 21. New York, N.Y.

Arno, S. F. 1976. The historical role of fire on the Bitterroot National Forest. USDA Forest Service, Intermountain Forest and Range Experiment Station, General Technical Report, INT-187, Ogden, UT.

Barbour, M. G., and R. A. Minnich. 2000. California upland forests and woodlands. P. 161–202 in M. G. Barbour and W. D. Billings (eds.), North America terrestrial vegetation, 2nd. ed. Cambridge University Press, New York.

Bates, J., R. F. Miller, and T. S. Svejcar. 2000. Understory dynamics in cut and uncut western jumper woodlands. Journal of Range Management 53:119–126.

Bedwell, S. F. 1973. Fort Rock Basin prehistory and environment. University of Oregon Books, Eugene, OR.

Billings, W. D. 1952. The environmental complex in relation to plant growth and distribution. Quarterly Review of Biology 27:251–265.

Blaisdell, J. P. 1950. Effects of controlled burning on bitterbrush on the Upper Snake River Plains. USDA Forest Service, Intermountain Forest and Range Experiment Station, INT Research Paper 20, Ogden, UT.

Blaisdell, J. P. 1953. Ecological effects of planned burning of sagebrush-grass range on the upper Snake River Plains. U.S. Department of Agriculture, Technical Bulletin No. 1075.

Blaisdell, J. P., and W. F. Mueggler. 1956. Sprouting of bitterbrush (*Purshia tridentata*) following burning or top removal. Ecology 37:365–370.

Bolsinger, C. L. 1989. California's western juniper and pinyon-juniper woodlands: area, stand characteristics, wood volume, and fenceposts. USDA Forest Service Pacific Northwest Research Station, Bulletin PNW-RB-166, Berkeley, CA.

Bork, J. L. 1985. Fire history in three vegetation types on the east side of the Oregon Cascades. Ph.D. Thesis, Oregon State University, Corvallis, OR.

Bradley, A. F., N. V. Noste, and W. C. Fischer. 1992. Fire ecology of forests and woodlands in Utah. USDA Forest Service Research, Intermountain Research Station, General Technical Report INT-287, Ogden, UT.

Britton, C. M., R. G. Clark, and F. A. Sneva. 1981. Will your sagebrush range burn? Rangelands 3:207–208.

Brown, J. K. 1982. Fuel and fire behavior predication in big sagebrush. USDA Forest Service Research, Intermountain Forest and Range Experiment Station, Research Paper INT-290, Ogden UT.

Brown, J. K. 2000. Introduction and fire regimes. P. 1–7 in J. K. Brown and J. K. Smith (eds.), Wildland fire in ecosystems: effects of fire on flora. USDA Forest Service, Rocky Mountain Research Station, General Technical Report RMRS-GTR-42-Volume 2, Fort Collins, CO.

Brown, V. A., and W. S. Brown. 1991. The Sugar Hill fire and reforestation, and lookout tower. Journal of the Modoc County Historical Society (Warner Mountains Issue) 13:173–183.

Bunting, S. C. 1984a. Fire in sagebrush grass ecosystems: successional changes. In K. Sanders and J. Durham (eds.), Rangeland fire effects. USDI Bureau of Land Management Idaho State Office, Boise.

Bunting, S. 1984b. Prescribed burning of live standing western juniper and post-burning succession. P. 69–73 in T. E. Bedell (comp.), Oregon State University Extension Service Proceedings, Western juniper short course. October 15–16, Bend, OR.

Bunting, S. C., B. M. Kilgore, and C. L. Busbey. 1987. Guidelines for prescribed burning sagebrush-grass rangelands in the northern Great Basin. USDA Forest Service General Technical Report INT-231.

Burkhardt, J. W., and E. W. Tisdale. 1969. Nature and successional status of western juniper vegetation in Idaho. Journal of Range Management 22:264–270.

Burkhardt, J. W., and E. W. Tisdale. 1976. Causes of juniper invasion in southwestern Idaho. Ecology 76:472–484.

Busse, M. D. 2000a. Ecological significance of nitrogen fixation by actinorhizal shrubs in interior forests of California and Oregon. P. 23–41 in R. F. Powers, D. L. Hauxwell, and G. M. Nakamura (tech. coords.), Proceedings of the California Forest Soils Council conference on forest soil biology and forest management. USDA Forest Service General Technical Report GTR-PSW-178, Albany, CA.

Busse, M. D. 2000b. Suitability and use of the ^{15}N-istope dilution method to estimate nitrogen fixation by actinorhizal shrubs. Forest Ecology and Management 136:85–95.

Busse, M. D., P. H. Cochran, and J. W. Barrett. 1996. Changes in ponderosa pine site productivity following removal of understory vegetation. Soil Science Society of America Journal 60:1614–1621.

Busse, M. D., S. A. Simon, and G. M. Riegel. 2000. Tree-growth and understory responses to low-severity prescribed burning in thinned *Pinus ponderosa* forests of Central Oregon. Forest Science 46:258–268.

Chadwick, H. W., and P. D. Dalke. 1965. Plant succession on dune sands in Fremont County, Idaho. Ecology 46:765–780.

Clark, R. G., C. M. Britton, and R. A. Sneva. 1982. Mortality of bitterbrush after burning and clipping in eastern Oregon. Journal of Range Management 35:711–714.

Clements C. D., and J. A. Young. 1997. A viewpoint: Rangeland health and mule deer habitat. Journal of Range Management 50:129–138.

Clements, C. D., and J. A. Young. 2001. Antelope bitterbrush seed production and stand age. Journal of Range Management 54:269–273.

Cochran, P. H. 1998. Examples of mortality and reduced annual increments of white fir induced by drought, insects, and diseases at different stand densities. USDA Forest Service, Pacific Northwest Research Station, Research Note PNW-RN-525, Portland, OR.

Cochran, P. H., and W. E. Hopkins. 1991. Does fire exclusion increase productivity of ponderosa pine? P. 224–228 in A. E. Harvey and L. F. Neuenschwander (comps.), Proceedings: management and productivity of western montane forest soils. USDA Forest Service Research, Intermountain Research Station, General Technical Report GTR-INT-280, Ogden, UT.

Conard, S. G., and S. R. Radosevich. 1981. Photosynthesis, xylem pressure potential, and leaf conductance of three montane chaparral species in California. Forest Science 27:627–639.

Conard, S. G., and S. R. Radosevich. 1982. Growth responses of white fir to decreased shading and root competition by montane chaparral shrubs. Forest Science 28:309–320.

Conard, S. G., A. E. Jaramillo, K. Cromack, Jr., and S. Rose. 1985. The role of *Ceanothus* in western forest ecosystems. USDA Forest Service, Pacific Northwest Forest and Range Experiment Station, General Technical Report PNW-182, Portland, OR.

Conkle, M. T., and W. B. Critchfield. 1988. Genetic variation and hybridization of Ponderosa Pine. P. 27–43 in D. M. Baumgartner and J. E. Lotan. Ponderosa pine: the species and its management, symposium proceedings, Washington State University, Pullman.

Conrad, C. E., and C. E. Poulton. 1966. Effect of a wildfire on Idaho fescue and bluebunch wheatgrass. Journal of Range Management 19:148–141.

Cook, J. G., T. J. Hershey, and L. L. Irwin. 1994. Vegetative response to burning on Wyoming, mountain-shrub big game ranges. Journal of Range. Management 47:296–302.

Countryman, C. M., and D. R. Cornelius. 1957. Some effects of fire on perennial range type. Journal of Range Management 10:39–41.

Coville, F. 1898. Forest growth and sheep grazing in the Cascade Mountains of Oregon. U.S. Department of Agriculture, Division of Forestry Bulletin 15, Washington, DC.

Crane, M. F. 1982. Fire ecology of Rocky Mountain Region forest habitat types. Final Report Contract No. 43-83X9-1-884. Missoula, MT: USDA Forest Service, Region 1. 272 p. On file with: USDA Forest Service, Intermountain Research Station, Fire Sciences Laboratory, Missoula, MT.

Crawford, J. C., R. A. Olson, N. E. West, J. C. Mosley, M. A. Schroeder, T. D. Whitson, R. F. Miller, M. A. Gregg, and C. S. Boyd. 2004. Ecology and management of sage-grouse and sage-grouse habitat. Journal of Range Management 57:2–19.

Critchfield, W. B. 1984. Crossability and relationships of Washoe pine. Madroño 31:144–170.

Critchfield, W. B., and G. L. Allenbaugh. 1969. The distribution of the Pinaceae in and near northern Nevada. Madroño 19:12–26.

Cronquist, A. 1994. Asterales. P. 17 in A. Cronquist, A. H. Holmgren, N. H. Holmgren, J. L. Reveal, and P. K. Holmgren. Intermountain Flora: Vascular Plants of the Intermountain West, U.S.A, Volume 5, New York Botanical Gardens, Bronx, NY.

Daly, C., R. P. Neilson, and D. L. Phillips. 1994. A statistical-topographic model for mapping climatological precipitation over mountainous terrain. Journal of Applied Meteorology 33:140–158.

Davis, J. N., and J. D. Brotherson. 1991. Ecological characteristics of curl-leaf mountain-mahogany (*Cercocarpus ledifolius* Nutt.) communities in Utah and implications for management. Great Basin Naturalist 51:153–166.

Dealy, J. E. 1975. Ecology of curl-leaf mountain-mahogany *(Cercocarpus ledifolius)* in eastern Oregon and adjacent area. Ph.D. Thesis, Oregon State University, Corvallis.

Delwiche, C. C., P. J. Zinke, and C. M. Johnson. 1965. Nitrogen fixation by *Ceanothus*. Plant Physiology 40:1045–1047.

Dobkin, D. S., and J. D. Sauder. 2004. Shrubsteppe landscapes in jeopardy. Distributions, abundances, and thee uncertain future of birds and small mammals in the Intermountain West. High Desert Ecological Research Institute, Bend, OR.

Driscoll, R. S. 1963. Sprouting bitterbrush in central Oregon. Ecology 44:820–821.

Dwire, K. A., and J. B. Kauffman. 2003. Fire and riparian ecosystems in landscapes of the western USA. Forest Ecology and Management 178:61–74.

Evanko, A. B. 1951. Response of *Wyethia* to 2,4-D. USDA Forest Service North. Rocky Mt. Forest Range Experiment Station Research Note No. 98, Fort Collins, CO.

Ferrel, G. T. 1978. Moisture stress threshold of susceptibility to fir engraver beetles in pole-sized white firs. Forest Science 24:85–92.

Ferrel, G. T. 1980. Growth of white firs defoliated by Modoc budworm in northeastern California. USDA Forest Service, Pacific Southwest Forest and Range Experiment Station, Research Paper PSW-154, Berkeley, CA.

Figura, P. J. 1997. Structure and dynamics of whitebark pine forests in the South Warner Wilderness Area. M. S. Thesis, Humboldt State University, Arcata, CA.

Fischer, R. A., K. P. Reese, and J. W. Connelly. 1996. An investigation on fire effects within xeric sage grouse brood habitat. Journal of Range Management 49:194–198.

Frost, C. C. 1998. Presettlement fire frequency regimes of the United States: A first approximation. P. 70–81 in T. L. Pruden and L. A. Brennan (eds.), Fire in ecosystem management: shifting the paradigm from suppression to prescription. Tall Timbers Fire Ecology Conference Proceedings, No. 20 Tall Timbers Research Station, Tallahassee, FL.

Gay, D. 1998. A test of the southcentral Oregon mule deer habitat suitability index. M. S. Thesis, University of Idaho, Moscow.

Gillespie, I. G., and M. E. Loik. 2004. Pulse events in Great Basin Desert shrublands: Responses of *Artemisia tridentata* and *Purshia tridentata* seedlings to summer rainfall pulses. Journal of Arid Environments 59:41–57.

Goheen, A. 1998. Buck Creek Drainage fire analysis: the ecological consequences of aggressive fire suppression. Technical Fire Management 11, Washington Institute, Colorado State University, Fort Collins.

Goodwin, D. L. 1956. Autecological studies of *Artemisia tridentata* Nutt. Ph.D. Dissertation, State College of Washington, Pullman.

Graumlich, L. J. 1987. Precipitation variation in the Pacific Northwest (1675–1975) as reconstructed from tree rings. Annals of the Association of American Geographers. 77:19–29.

Griffin, J. R., and W. B. Critchfield. 1972. The distribution of forest trees in California. Research Paper, PSW-82, USDA Forest Service, Pacific Southwest Forest and Range Experiment Station, Berkeley, CA.

Gruell, G. E., S. Bunting, and L. Neuenschwander. 1984. Influence of fire on curl-leaf mountain-mahogany in the Intermountain West. P. 58–72 in J. K. Brown and J. Lotan (eds.), Proceedings: fire's effects on wildlife habitat. USDA Forest Service Research, Intermountain Research Station, General Technical Report GTR-INT-186, Ogden, UT.

Gruell, G. E., 1999. Historical and modern roles of fire in pinyon-juniper. P. 24–28 in S. B. Monsen and R. Stevens (comps.), Proceedings: ecology and management of pinyon-juniper communities within the interior West, Sept. 15–18, 1997, Provo, UT. USDA Forest Service, Rocky Mountain Research Station Proceedings RMRS-P-9, Fort Collins.

Guenther, G. E., C. L. Wambolt, and M. R. Frisina. 1993. Characteristics of bitterbrush habitats that influence canopy cover and mule deer browsing. Journal of Environmental Management 36:175–181.

Hakala, K.J., and D.P. Adam. 2004. Late Pleistocene vegetation and climate in the southern Cascade Range and the Modoc Plateau region. Journal of Paleolimnology 31:189–215.

Haller, J.R. 1961. Some recent observations on ponderosa, Jeffrey and Washoe pines in northeastern California. Madroño 16: 126–132.

Harniss, R.O., and W.T. McDonough. 1974. Yearly variation in germination in the subspecies of big sagebrush. Journal of Range Management 29:167–168.

Harniss, R.O., and R.B. Murray. 1973. 30 years of vegetal change following burning of sagebrush-grass range. Journal of Range Management 29:322–325.

Hassan, M.A., and N.E. West. 1986. Dynamics of soil seed pools in burned and unburned sagebrush semi-deserts. Ecology 67:269–272.

Heisey, R.M., and C.C. Delwiche. 1983. A survey of California plants for water-extractable and volatile inhibitors. Botanical Gazette 144:382–390.

Heyerdahl, E.K., R.F. Miller, and R.A. Parsons. (2006). History of fire and Douglas-fir establishment in a savanna and sagebrush-grassland mosaic, southwestern Montana, USA. Forest Ecology and Management 230:107–118.

Hinckley, T.M., R.O. Teskey, R.H. Waring, and Y. Morikawa. 1982. The water relations of true firs. P. 85–94 in C.D. Oliver and R.M. Kenady (eds.), Proceedings of the biology and management of true fir in the Pacific Northwest symposium. University of Washington, College of Forest Resources, Contribution, No. 45, Seattle, WA.

Holmgren, R.C. 1956. Competition between annuals and young bitterbrush (Purshia tridentata) in Idaho. Ecology 37:370–377.

Hopkins, W.E. 1979. Plant associations of the Fremont National Forest. U.S. Department of Agriculture Forest Service, Pacific Northwest Region, R6-ECOL-79-004, Portland, OR.

Hormay, A.L. 1943. Bitterbrush in California. USDA Forest Service, Pacific Southwest Forest and Range Experiment Station, Research Note 34, Berkeley, CA.

Houston, D.B. 1973. Wildfires in northern Yellowstone National Park. Ecology 54:1109–1117.

Hurley, J., and T. Ratcliff. 1986. Resprouting success in antelope bitterbrush following a prescribed burn. Unpublished report on file, USDA Forest Service, Plumas National Forest, Quincy, CA.

Jabbes, M. 2000. Hybridization and its evolutionary consequences in Purshia Purshia and Cowania. Ph.D. dissertation. University of Idaho, Moscow.

Jenkinson, J.L. 1990. Pinus jeffreyi Grev. & Balf. Jeffrey Pine. P. 359–369 in R.M. Burns and B.H. Honkala (tech. coords.), Silvics of North America: Volume I. Conifers. USDA Forest Service, Agricultural Handbook 654. Washington, DC.

Johnson, C.G., Jr. 1998. Vegetation responses after wildfire in national forests of northeastern Oregon. USDA Forest Service, Pacific Northwest Region, R6-NR-ECOL-TP-06-98.

Johnson, D.D., and R.F. Miller. (in press). Structure and development of expanding western juniper as influenced by two topographic variables. Forest Ecology and Management. (in press).

Johnson, D.W. 1995. Soil properties beneath Ceanothus and pine stands in the eastern Sierra Nevada. Soil Science Society of America Journal 59:918–924.

Johnson, J.R., and G.F. Payne. 1968. Sagebrush reinvasion as affected by some environmental influences. Journal of Range Management 21:209–213.

Kennedy, P.B., and S.B. Doten. 1901. A preliminary report on the summer ranges of western Nevada sheep. Nevada State University, Agricultural Experiment Station, Bulletin, No. 51, Reno.

Kelly, I.T. 1932. Ethnography of the Surprise Valley Paiute. University of California, Publications in American Archaeology and Ethnology 31:67–209.

Klebenow, D.A., and R.C. Beall. 1977. Fire impacts on birds and mammals on Great Basin rangelands. In Proceedings, Joint Intermountain Rocky Mountain Fire Research Council, Casper, WY.

Klebenow, D.A., and A. Bruner 1976. Determining factors necessary for prescribed burning. P. 69–47 in Use of prescribed burning in western woodland and range ecosystems. Utah State University, Logan, UT.

Kruckeberg, A.R. 1977. Manzanita (Arctostaphylos) hybrids in the Pacific Northwest: effects of human and natural disturbance. Systematic Botany 2: 233–250.

Kuntz, D.E. 1982. Plant response following spring burning in an Artemisia tridentata subsp. vaseyana/Festuca idahoensis habitat type, M.S. Thesis, University of Idaho, Moscow.

Laacke, R.J. 1990. Abies concolor (Gord. & Glend.) Lindl. ex Hildebr. White fir. P. 36–46 in R.M. Burns and B.H. Honkala (tech. coords.), Silvics of North America: Volume I. Conifers. USDA Forest Service, Agricultural Handbook 654. Washington, DC.

Lanini, W.T., and S.R. Radosevich. 1986. Response of three conifer species to site preparation and shrub control. Forest Science 32:61–77.

Laudenslayer, W.F., Jr., H.H. Darr, and S. Smith. 1989. Historical effects of forest management practices on eastside pine communities in northeastern California. P. 26–34 in A. Tecle, W.W. Covington, R.H. Hamre (tech. coords.), Multiresource management of ponderosa pine forests: Proceedings of the symposium, November 14–16, 1989, Flagstaff, AZ. USDA Forest Service, Rocky Mountain Forest and Range Experiment Station, General Technical Report, GTR-RM-185, Fort Collins, CO.

Lauria, F. 1997. The taxonomic status of Pinus washoensis H.Mason & Stockw. (Pinaceae). Annalen des Naturhistorischen Museums in Wien 99:655–671.

Leiberg, J.B. 1902. Forest conditions in the northern Sierra Nevada, California. U.S.Geological Survey Professional Paper No. 8, U.S. Government Printing Office, Washington DC.

Little, E.L., Jr. 1971. Conifers and important hardwoods. Vol. 1. Atlas of the United States trees. USDA Forest Service, Miscellaneous Publication No. 1146, Washington, DC.

Lyon, L.J., and P.F. Stickney. 1976. Early vegetal succession following large northern Rocky mountain wildfires. In Proceedings Montana Tall Timbers Fire Ecology Conference and Fire and Land Management Symposium. No. 14:355–375. Tall Timbers Research Station, Tallahassee, FL.

MacDonald, G.A., and T.E. Gay, Jr. 1966. Geology of the southern Cascade Range, Modoc Plateau, and Great Basin areas in northeastern California. In Mineral resources of California. California Division of Mines and Geology Bulletin 191:43–48.

Major, J. 1988. California climate in relation to vegetation. P. 11–74 in M.G. Barbour and J. Major (eds.), Terrestrial vegetation of California. California Native Plant Society Special Publication Number 9, new expanded edition.

Martin, R.C. 1990. Sage grouse responses to wildfire in spring and summer habitats. M.S. Thesis. University of Idaho, Moscow.

Martin, R.E. 1982. Fire history and its role in succession. P. 92–99. In Means, J.E. (ed.), Forest succession and stand development in the Northwest, Forest Research Lab, Oregon State University, Corvallis.

Martin, R. E. 1983. Antelope bitterbrush seeding establishment following prescribed fire in the pumice zone of the southern Cascade Mountains. P. 92–99. In A. R. Tiedemann, and K. L. Johnson (comps.), Proceedings-research and management of bitterbrush and cliffrose in western North America, USDA Forest Service, Intermountain Forest and Range Experiment Station, General Technical Report, INT-152, Ogden, UT.

Martin, R. E., and C. H. Driver. 1983. Factors affecting antelope bitterbrush reestablishment following fire. P. 266–279. In A.R. Tiedemann, and K.L. Johnson (eds.), Proceedings-research and management of bitterbrush and cliffrose in western North America, USDA Forest Service, Intermountain Forest and Range Experiment Station, General Technical Report INT-GTR-152, Ogden, UT.

Martin, R. E., and A. H. Johnson. 1979. Fire management of Lava Beds National Monument. P. 1209–1217 in R. E. Linn (ed.), Proceedings of the First Conference of Science and Research in the National Parks. USDI National Parks Service Transactions Proceedings Series No. 5.

McArthur, E. D., H. C. Stutz, and S. C. Sanderson. 1983. Taxonomy, distribution, and cytogenetics of *Purshia, Cowania,* and *Fallugia* (Rosoideae, Rosaceae). P. 4–24. In A.R. Tiedemann, and K.L. Johnson (eds.), Proceedings-research and management of bitterbrush and cliffrose in western North America, USDA Forest Service, Intermountain Forest and Range Experiment Station, General Technical Report INT-GTR-152, Ogden, UT.

McDonald, P. M. 1983a. Climate, history, and vegetation of the eastside pine type in California. P. 1–16 in T. F. Robson and R. B. Standiford (eds.), Management of the eastside pine type northeastern California: proceedings of a symposium. Northern California Society of American Foresters, S.A.F. 83-06, Arcata, CA.

McDonald, P. M. 1983b. Weeds in conifer plantations of northeastern California . . . management implications. P. 70–78 in T. F. Robson and R. B. Standiford (eds.), Management of the eastside pine type northeastern California: proceedings of a symposium. Northern California Society of American Foresters, S.A.F. 83-06, Arcata, CA.

McDowell, M.K.D. 2000. The effects of burning in mountain big sagebrush on key sage grouse habitat characteristics in southeastern Oregon. M.S. Thesis, Oregon State University, Corvallis.

Mehringer, P.J., Jr., and P. E. Wigand. 1987. Western juniper in the Holocene. P. 13–16 in R. L. Everett (ed.), Proceedings: Pinyon Juniper Conference. USDA Forest Service Research, Intermountain Research Station, General Technical Report GTR-INT-215.

Mehringer, P. J., and P. E. Wigand. 1990. Comparison of late Holocene environments from woodrat middens and pollen. P. 294–325 in J. L. Betancourt, T. R. Van Devender, and P. S. Martin (eds.), Packrat middens: the last 40,000 years of biotic change. University of Arizona Press, Tucson.

Meyer, S. E., and S. B. Monsen. 1991. Habitat-correlated variation in mountain big sagebrush (*Artemisia tridentata* ssp. *vaseyana*) seed germination patterns. Ecology 72:739–732.

Miller, M. 2000. Fire autecology. In J. K. Brown and J. K. Smith (eds.), Wildland fire in ecosystems: effects of fire on flora. General Technical Report RMRS-GTR-42-vol-2, USDA Forest Service, Rocky Mountain Research Station, Ogden, UT.

Miller, R. F. 2001. Managing western juniper of wildlife. Woodland Fish and Wildlife. Pub. No. MISC0286.

Miller, R. F., J. D. Bates, T. J. Svejcar, F. B. Pierson, and L. E. Eddleman. 2005. Biology, ecology, and management of western juniper (*Juniperus occidentalis*). Oregon State University Agricultural Experiment Station Technical Bulletin 152.

Miller, R. F., P. Doescher, and T. Purrington. 1991. Dry-wet cycles and sagebrush in the Great Basin. The Grazier 30:5–10, Oregon State University, Department of Rangeland Resources, Corvallis.

Miller, R. F., and L. E. Eddleman. 2000. Spatial and temporal changes of sage grouse habitat in the sagebrush biome. Oregon State University Agricultural Experiment Station, Technical Bulletin 151, Corvallis.

Miller, R. F., E. K. Heyerdahl, and K. Hopkins. 2003. Fire regimes, pre- and post-settlement vegetation, and the modern expansion of western juniper at Lava Beds National Monument, California. Final Report to the USDI Lava Beds National Monument.

Miller, R. F., and J. A. Rose. 1995. Historic expansion of *Juniperus occidentalis* (western juniper) in southeastern Oregon. Great Basin Naturalist 55:37–45.

Miller, R. F., and J. A. Rose. 1999. Fire history and western juniper encroachment in sagebrush steppe. Journal of Range Management 52:520–559.

Miller, R. F., T. Svejcar, and J. A. Rose. 2000. Western juniper succession in shrub steppe: impacts on community composition and structure. Journal of Range Management 53:574–585.

Miller, R. F., T. Svejcar, and N. E. West. 1994. Implications of livestock grazing in the intermountain sagebrush region: plant composition. P. 101–146 in M. Vavra, W. A. Laycock, and R. D. Pieper (eds.), Ecological implications of livestock herbivory in the West. Western Society for Range Management. Denver, CO.

Miller, R. F., and R. J. Tausch. 2001. The role of fire in pinyon and juniper woodlands: a descriptive analysis. Tall Timbers Research Station. Miscellaneous Publication 11:15–30, Tallahassee, FL.

Miller, R. F., and P. Wigand. 1994. Holocene changes in semiarid pinyon-juniper woodlands: response to climate, fire and human activities in the U.S. Great Basin. BioScience 44:465–474.

Minckley, T. A. 2003. Holocene environmental history of the northwestern Great Basin and the analysis of modern pollen analogues in western North America. Ph.D. Dissertation, University of Oregon, Eugene.

Minore, D. 1979. Comparative autecological characteristics of northwestern tree species—a literature review. USDA Forest Service, General Technical Report PNW-87, Pacific Northwest Forest and Range Experiment Station, Portland, OR.

Mitton, J. B., R. G. Latta, and G. E. Rehfeldt. 1997. The pattern of inbreeding in Washoe pine and survival of inbred progeny under optimal environmental conditions. Silvae Genetica 46:215–219.

Mueggler, W. F. 1956. Is sagebrush seed residual in the soil of burns or is it wind borne? USDA Forest Service INT-RN-35.

Niebling, C. R., and M. T. Conkle. 1990. Diversity of Washoe pine and comparisons with allozymes of ponderosa pine races. Canadian Journal of Forest Research 20: 298–308.

Nord, E. C. 1959. Bitterbrush Ecology—Some recent findings. USDA Forest Service, Pacific Southwest Forest and Range Experiment Station, PSW Res. Note 148, Berkeley, CA.

Nord, E. C. 1965. Autecology of bitterbrush in California. Ecological Monographs 35:307–334.

Noste, N. V., and C. L. Bushey. 1987. Fire response of shrubs of dry forest habitat types in Montana and Idaho. USDA Forest Service, Intermountain Forest and Range Experiment Station, General Technical Report INT-GTR-239, Ogden, UT.

Olmstead, P. 1957. The Nevada-California-Oregon border triangle: a case study in sectional history. M.A. Thesis, University of Nevada, Reno.

Osborn, G., and K. Bevis. 2001. Glaciation in the Great Basin of the western United States. Quaternary Science Reviews 20:1377–1410.

Oswald, V. H., D. W. Showers, and M. A. Showers. 1995. A flora of Lassen National Park, California. California Native Plant Society, Sacramento, CA.

Owens, T. E. 1982. Postburn regrowth of shrubs related to canopy mortality. Northwest Science 56:34–40.

Parker, V. T., and M. P. Yoder-Williams. 1989. Reduction of survival and growth of young *Pinus jeffreyi* by an herbaceous perennial, *Wyethia mollis*. American Midland Naturalist 121:105–111.

Patten, A. M., and S. J. Brunsfeld. 2002. Evidence of a novel lineage within the *Ponderosae*. Madroño 49:189–192.

Pease, R. W. 1965. Modoc County: a geographic time continuum on the California volcanic tableland. University of California Publications in Geography Vol. 17. University of California Press, Berkeley.

Pechanec, J. F., G. Steward, and J. P. Blaisdell. 1954. Sagebrush burning—good and bad. U.S. Department of Agriculture, Farmer's Bulletin 1948.

Peek, J. M., F. D. Johnson, and N. N. Pence. 1978. Successional trends in a ponderosa pine/bitterbrush community related to grazing by livestock, wildlife, and to fire. Journal of Range Management 31:49–53.

Peek J. M., J. J. Korol, D. Gay, and T. Hershey. 2001. Overstory-understory biomass changes over a 35-year period in south-central Oregon Forest Ecology and Management 150:267–277.

Powers, R. F., and W. W. Oliver. 1990. *Libocedrus decurrens* Torr. Incense-cedar. P. 173–180 in R. M. Burns and B. H. Honkala (tech. coords.), Silvics of North America: Volume I. Conifers. USDA Forest Service, Agricultural Handbook 654. Washington, DC.

Pyle, W. H., and J. A. Crawford. 1996. Availability of foods of sage-grouse chicks following prescribed fire in sagebrush-bitterbrush. Journal of Range Management 49:320–324.

Radosevich, S. R. 1984. Interference between greenleaf manzanita (*Arctostaphylos patula*) and ponderosa pine (*Pinus ponderosa*). P. 259–270 in M. L. Dureya and G. N. Brown (eds.), Seedling physiology and reforestation success. Martinus Nijhoff/Dr. W. Junk Publishers, Dordrecht, The Netherlands.

Rehfeldt, G. E. 1999. Systematics and genetic structure of Washoe pine: applications in conservation genetics. Silvae Genetica 48:167–173.

Reinkensmeyer, D. P. 2000. Habitat associations of bird communities in shrub-steppe and western juniper woodlands. M.S. Thesis, Oregon State University, Corvallis.

Riegel, G. M. 1982. Forest habitat types of the South Warner Mountains, Modoc County, northeastern California. M.S. Thesis, Humboldt State University, Arcata, CA.

Riegel, G. M., T. J. Svejcar, and M. D. Busse. 2002. Does the presence of *Wyethia mollis* limit growth of affect growth of *Pinus jeffreyi* seedlings? Western North American Naturalist 62: 141–150.

Riegel, G. M., D. A. Thornburgh, and J. O Sawyer. 1990. Forest habitat types of the South Warner Mountains, Modoc County, California. Madroño 37:88–112.

Romme, W. H., M. L. Floyd-Hanna, D. Hanna, and E. J. Bartlett. 1996. Landscape analysis for the South Central Highlands Section, southwestern Colorado and northwestern New Mexico, Chapter 5: Aspen forests. Unpublished draft; final report of the San Juan National Forest, Durango, CO.

Rosentreter, R. 2005. Sagebrush Identification, Ecology, and Palatability Relative to Sage-Grouse. P. 3–16 in N.L. Shaw, M. Pellant, and S.B. Monsen (comps.), Sagegrouse habitat restoration symposium proceedings; 2001 June 4–7; Boise, ID, USDA Forest Service, Rocky Mountain Research Station, Proceedings RMRS-P-38, Fort Collins, CO.

Rorig, M. L., and S. A. Ferguson. 1999. Characteristics of lightning and wildland fire ignition in the Pacific Northwest. Journal of Applied Meteorology 38:1565–1575.

Rorig, M. L., and S. A. Ferguson. 2002. The 2000 fire season: lightning-caused fires. Journal of Applied Meteorology 41: 786–791.

Roy, D. F. 1983. Natural regeneration. P. 87–102 in T. F. Robson and R. B. Standiford (eds.), Management of the eastside pine type in northeastern California, proceedings of a symposium. Northern California Society of American Foresters, S.A.F. 83-06, Arcata, CA.

Rundel, P. W., D. J. Parsons, and D. T. Gordon. 1988. Montane and subalpine vegetation of the Sierra Nevada and the Cascade Ranges. P. 559–599 in M. G. Barbour and J. Major (eds.), Terrestrial vegetation of California. California Native Plant Society Special Publication Number 9, new expanded edition.

Running, S. W. 1980. Environmental and physiological control of water flux through *Pinus contorta*. Canadian Journal of Forest Research 10: 82–91.

Running, S. W., and C. P. Reid. 1980. Soil temperature influences on root resistance of *Pinus contorta*. Plant Physiology 65:635–640.

Salwasser, H. 1979. The ecology and management of the Devil's Garden interstate deer herd and its range. University of California, Berkeley, Ph.D. dissertation.

Sawyer, J. O., and T. Keeler-Wolf. 1995. A manual of California vegetation. California Native Plant Society, Sacramento, CA.

Schaefer, R. J., D. J. Thayer, and T. S. Burton. 2003. Forty-one years of vegetation change on permanent transects in northeastern California: implications for wildlife. California Fish and Game 89:55–71.

Shainsky, L. J., and S. R. Radosevich. 1986. Growth and water relations of *Pinus ponderosa* seedlings in competitive regimes with *Arctostaphylos patula* seedlings. Journal of Applied Ecology 23:957–966.

Sherman R. L., and W. W. Chilcote. 1972. Spatial and chronological patterns of *Purshia tridentata* as influenced by *Pinus Ponderosa*. Ecology 53:294–298.

Shinn, D. A. 1980. Historical perspectives on range burning in the Inland Pacific Northwest. Journal of Range Management 33:415–422.

Simon, S. A. 1990. Fire effects from prescribed underburning in central Oregon ponderosa pine plant communities: first and second growing season after burning. Unpublished report on file, USDA Forest Service, Fremont National Forest, Lakeview, Oregon.

Skinner, C. N. 2003. Fire regimes of upper montane and subalpine glacial basins in the Klamath Mountains of northern California. Tall Timbers Research Station Miscellaneous Publication 13:145–151, Tallahassee, FL.

Skinner, C. N., and C. Chang. 1996. Fire regimes, past and present. P. 1041–1069 in Sierra Nevada Ecosystem Project: final report to Congress. Volume II: Assessments and scientific basis for management options. Centers for Water and Wildland Resources, University of California, Davis, Water Resources Center Report No. 37.

Smith, R. H. 1967. Variations in the monoterpene composition of the wood resin of Jeffrey, Washoe, Coulter, and lodgepole pines. Forest Science 13:246–252.

Smith, R. H. 1971. Xylem monoterpenes of *Pinus ponderosa, P. washonesis,* and *P. Jeffreyi* in the the Warner Mountains of California. Madroño 21:26–32.

Smith, R. H. 2000. Xylem monoterpenes of pines: distribution, variation, genetics, function. USDA Forest Service, Pacific Southwest Research Station, General Technical Report PSW-GTR-177, Albany, CA.

Smith, S. 1994. Ecological guide to eastside pine plant associations, northeastern California: Modoc, Lassen, Klamath, Shasta-Trinity, Plumas, and Tahoe National Forests. USDA Forest Service, Pacific Southwest Region R5-ECOL-TP-004, San Francisco, CA.

Smith, S., and B. Davidson. 2003. User's manual: Terrestrial Ecological Unit Inventory (TEUI), land type associations, Modoc National Forest. USDA Forest Service, Pacific Southwest Region, R5-TP-015, Version 1.0.

Smith, T. G., and Maguire. 2004. Small-mammal relationships with down wood and antelope bitterbrush in ponderosa pine forests of Central Oregon. Forest Science 50:711–728.

Sparks, J. P., G. S. Campbell, and R. A. Black. 2001. Water content, hydraulic conductivity, and ice formation in winter stems of *Pinus contorta:* a TDR case study. Oecolgia 27:469–475.

Stephens, S. L. 2001. Fire history differences in adjacent Jeffrey pine and upper montane forests in the Sierra Nevada. International Journal of Wildland Fire 10:161–167.

Stephens, S. L., C. N. Skinner, and S. J. Gill. 2003. A dendrochonology based fire history of Jeffrey pine-mixed conifer forests in the Sierra San Pedro Martir, Mexico. Canadian Journal of Forest Research 33:1090–1101.

Stone, C. G. 1965. Modoc cypress, *Cupressus bakeri,* does occur in Modoc County. Aliso 6:77–87.

Tausch, R. J. 1999. Historic woodland development. P. 12–19. In R. Stevens, R. J. Tausch, R. Miller, and S. Goodrich (eds.), Ecology and management of pinyon and juniper communities with the interior west. USDA Forest Service, Rocky Mountain Research Station Proceedings RMRS-P-9, Fort Collins, CO.

Taylor, A. H. 2000. Fire regimes and forest changes along a montane forest gradient, Lassen Volcanic National Park, southern Cascade Mountains, USA. Journal of Biogeography 27:87–104.

Thompson, R. S. 1990. Late quaternary vegetation and climate in the Great Basin. P. 200–239 in J. L. Betancourt, T. VanDevender, and P. S. Martin (eds.), Packrat middens: the last 40,000 years of biotic change. University of Arizona Press, Tucson.

Thompson, R. S., L. Benson, and E. M. Hattori. 1986. A revised chronology for the last Pleistocene Lake cycle in the central Lahontan Basin. Quaternary Research 25:1–10.

USDA Forest Service. 1937. Range Plant Handbook. U.S. Government Printing Office, Washington, DC.

Vale, T. R. 1975. Invasion of big sagebrush *(Artemisia tridentata)* by white fir *(Abies concolor)* on the southeastern slopes of the Warner Mountains, California. Great Basin Naturalist 35:319–324.

Vale, T. R. 1977. Forest changes in the Warner Mountains, California. Annals of the Association of American Geographers 67:28–45.

van Wagtendonk, J. K. 1983. Prescribed fire effects on understory mortality. Fire and Forest Meteorology Conference 7:136–138.

van Wagtendonk, J. W., and D. Cayan. 2007. Temporal and spatial distribution of lightning strikes in California in relationship to large-scale weather patterns. Fire Ecology (in press).

Vander Wall, S. B. 1994. Seed fate pathways of antelope bitterbrush: dispersed by seed-caching yellow pine chipmunks. Ecology 75:1911–1926.

Vasek, F. C., and R. F. Thorne. 1988. Transmontane coniferous vegetation. P. 797–832 in M. G. Barbour and J. Major (eds.), Terrestrial vegetation of California. California Native Plant Society Special Publication Number 9, new expanded edition.

Vogl, R. J., W. P. Armstrong, D. L White, and K. L. Cole. 1988. The closed-cone pines and cypress. P. 295–358 in M. G. Barbour and J. Major (eds.), Terrestrial vegetation of California. California Native Plant Society Special Publication Number 9, new expanded edition.

Volland, L. A., and J. D. Dell. 1981. Fire effects on Pacific Northwest forest and range vegetation. USDA Forest Service, Pacific Northwest Region. Range Management and Aviation and Fire Management, R6 Rm 067 1981, Portland OR.

Vose, J. M., and A. S. White. 1991. Biomass response mechanisms of understory species the first year after prescribed burning in an Arizona ponderosa-pine community. Forest Ecology and Management 40:175–187.

Wagstaff, F. J. 1980. Impact of the 1975 Wallsburg Fire on antelope bitterbrush (*Purshia tridentata*). The Great Basin Naturalist 40:299–302.

Waichler, W. S., R. F. Miller, and P. S. Doescher. 2001. Community characteristics of old-growth western juniper woodlands. Journal of Range Management 54:518–527.

Wall, T. G., R. F. Miller, and T. Svejcar. 2001. Juniper encroachment into aspen in the Northwest Great Basin. Journal of Range Management 54:691–698.

Weaver, H. 1943. Fire as an ecological and silvicultural factor in the ponderosa pine region of the pacific slope. Journal of Forestry 41:7–14.

Webster, S. R., C. T. Youngberg, and A. G. Wollum. 1967. Fixation of nitrogen by bitterbrush (*Purshia tridentata* [Pursh] D.C.). Nature 216:392–393.

Weixelman, D. A., T. R. Bowyer, and V. Van Ballenberghe. 1998. Diet selection by Alaskan moose during winter: effects of fire and forest succession. In W. B. Ballard and A.R.J. Rodgers (eds.), Proceedings, 33rd North American moose conference and workshop; 4th international moose symposium, May 17–23, 1997, Fairbanks, AK. Alces 34:213–238.

West, N. E. 1968. Rodent-influenced establishment of ponderosa pine and bitterbrush seedlings in central Oregon. Ecology 49:1009–1011.

West, N. E. 1983. Western intermountain sagebrush steppe. P. 351–374 in N. E. West (ed.), Ecosystems of the world: temperate deserts and semi-deserts. Elsevier Scientific Publishing Company, New York.

West, N. E. 1984. Successional patterns and productivity potentials of pinyon-juniper ecosystems. P. 1301–1332 in Developing strategies for rangeland management: a report prepared by the committee on developing strategies for rangeland management. Westview Press, Boulder, CO.

Whisenant, S. G. 1990. Changing fire frequencies on Idaho's Snake River plains: ecological and management implications. P. 4–10 in Proceedings: symposium on cheatgrass invasion, shrub die-off, and other aspects of shrub biology and management. USDA Forest Service General, Technical Report GTR-INT-276, Ogden, UT.

Whitlock, C., C. N. Skinner, P. J. Bartlein, T. Minckley, and J. A. Mohr. 2004. Comparison of charcoal and tree-ring records of recent fires in the eastern Klamath Mountains. Canadian Journal of Forest Research 34:2110–2121.

Wickman, B. E. 1978. A case study of a Douglas-fir tussock moth outbreak and stand conditions 10 years later. USDA Forest Service, Research Paper, PNW-244, Pacific Northwest Forest and Range Experiment Station, Portland, OR.

Wigand, P. E. 1987. Diamond Pond, Harney County, Oregon: vegetation history and water table in the eastern Oregon desert. Great Basin Naturalist 47:427–458.

Wigand, P. E., M. L. Hemphill, S. Sharpe, and S. Patra [Manna]. 1995. Eagle Lake Basin, northern California, paleoecological study: semi-arid woodland and montane forest dynamics during the late quaternary in the northern Great Basin and adjacent Sierras. University and Community College System of Nevada, Reno.

Williams, M. P. 1995. Inhibition of conifer regeneration by an herbaceous perennial, *Wyethia mollis,* in the eastern Sierra Nevada, California. Ph.D. Dissertation, University of Washington, Seattle.

Winward, A. H. 1985. Fire in the sagebrush-grass ecosystem—the ecological setting. P. 2–6 in K. Sanders and J. Durham (eds.), Rangeland fire effects: a symposium. USDI Bureau of Land Management, Idaho State Office, Boise.

Winward, A. H., and J. Alderfer-Finely. 1983. Taxonomic variations of bitterbrush (*Purshia tridentata*) in Oregon. P. 25–30. in A. R. Tiedemann, and K. L. Johnson (eds), Proceedings-research and management of bitterbrush and cliffrose in western North America, USDA Forest Service, Intermountain Forest and Range Experiment Station, General Technical Report INT-GTR-152, Ogden, UT.

Wright, H. A. 1971. Why squirreltail is more tolerant to burning than needle and thread. Journal of Range Management 24:277–284.

Wright, H.A. 1972. Shrub response to fire. P. 204–217. In Wildland shrubs- their biology and utilization, An International Symposium, Utah State University Logan, USDA Forest Service Intermountain Forest and Range Experiment Station, General Technical Report INT-1, Ogden, UT.

Wright, H. A., and A. W. Bailey. 1982. Fire ecology: United States and southern Canada. Wiley, New York.

Wright, H. A., and J. O. Klemmedson. 1965. Effects of fire on bunchgrasses of the sagebrush-grass region in southern Idaho. Ecology 46:680–688.

Wright, H. A., L. F. Neuenschwander, and C. M. Britton. 1979. The role and use of fire in sagebrush-grass and pinyon-juniper plant communities: a state of the art review. USDA Forest Service General Technical Report GTR-INT-58, Ogden, UT.

Yoder-Williams, M. P., and V. T. Parker. 1987. Allelopathic interference in the seedbed of *Pinus jeffreyi* in the Sierra Nevada, California. Canadian Journal of Forest Research 17:991–994.

Young, J. A., and C. D. Clements. 2002. Purshia: The Wild and Bitter Roses. University of Nevada Press, Reno.

Young, J. A., and R. A. Evans. 1978. Population dynamics after wildfires in sagebrush grasslands. Journal of Range Management 31:283–289.

Young, J. A., and R. A. Evans. 1979. Arrowleaf balsamroot and mules ears seed germination. Journal of Range Management 32:71–74.

Young, J. A., and R. A. Evans. 1981. Demography and fire history of a western juniper stand. Journal of Range Management 34:501–505.

Young, J. A., and R. A. Evans. 1989. Dispersal and germination of big sagebrush (*Artemisia tridentata*) seeds. Weed Science 37:201–206.

Young, J. A., R. A. Evans, and J. Major. 1988. Sagebrush steppe. P. 763–796 in M. G. Barbour and J. Major (eds.), Terrestrial vegetation of California. California Native Plant Society Special Publication Number 9, new expanded edition.

Young, R. P. 1983. Fire as a vegetation management tool in rangelands of the intermountain region. P. 18–31 in S. B. Monsen and N. Shaw (comps.), Managing intermountain rangelands—improvement of range and wildlife habitats: proceedings, September 15–17, 1981, Twin Falls, ID; June 22–24, 1982, Elko, NV. USDA Forest Service, Intermountain Forest and Range Experiment Station, General Technical Report.GTR-INT-157. Ogden, UT.

Young, R. P., and R. F. Miller. 1985. Response of *Sitanion hystrix* (Nutt.) J.G. to prescribed burning. American Midland Naturalist 113:182–187.

Ziegenhagen, L. 2003. Shrub reestablishment following fire in the mountain big sagebrush (*Artemisia tridentata* Natt. ssp. *vaseyana* [Rydb.] Beetle) alliance. Oregon State University, M. S. Thesis, Corvallis.

CHAPTER 12

Sierra Nevada Bioregion

JAN W. VAN WAGTENDONK AND JO ANN FITES-KAUFMAN

> In the main forest belt of California, fires seldom or never sweep
> from tree to tree in broad all-enveloping sheets . ... Here the fires
> creep from tree to tree, nibbling their way on the needle-strewn
> ground, attacking the giant trees at the base, killing the young,
> and consuming the fertilizing humus and leaves.
>
> JOHN MUIR, 1895

The Sierra Nevada is one of the most striking features of the state of California, extending from the southern Cascade Mountains in the north to the Tehachapi Mountains and Mojave Desert 700 km (435 mi) to the south (Map 12.1). The Central Valley forms the western boundary of the Sierra Nevada bioregion, and the Great Basin is on the east. The bioregion includes the central mountains and foothills as described by the Sierra Nevada Section and the Sierra Nevada Foothills Section of Miles and Goudey (1997). The area of the bioregion is 69,560 km² (26,442 mi²), approximately 17% of the state of California. Significant features along the length of the range include Lake Tahoe, Yosemite Valley, and Mount Whitney.

Description of the Bioregion

The natural environment of the Sierra Nevada is a function of the physical factors of geomorphology, geology, and regional climate interacting with the available biota. These factors are inextricably linked to the abiotic and biotic ecosystem components including local climate, hydrology, soils, plants, and animals. The distribution and abundance of the ecological zones of the Sierra Nevada are directly influenced by these interactions. The ecological role of fire in the bioregion varies with changes in the natural environment.

Physical Geography

The Sierra Nevada is a massive block mountain range that tilts slightly to the south of west and has a steep eastern escarpment that culminates in the highest peaks. This block of the Earth's crust broke free along a bounding fault line and has been uplifted and tilted (Huber 1987). Elevations range from 150 m (492 ft) on the American River near Sacramento to 4,418 m (14,495 ft) at Mount Whitney.

The relatively moderate western slope of the Sierra Nevada is incised with a series of steep river canyons from the Feather River in the north to the Kern River in the south. As the mountain block was uplifted, the rivers cut deeper and deeper into underlying rock (Huber 1987). The foothills are gently rolling with both broad and narrow valleys. At the mid elevations, landforms include canyons and broad ridges that run primarily from east-northeast to west-southwest. Rugged mountainous terrain dominates the landscape at the higher elevations.

The oldest rocks of the Sierra Nevada were metamorphosed from sediments deposited on the sea floor that collided with the continent during the early Paleozoic Era (Huber 1987). These rocks grade into early Mesozoic Era metasediments and metavolcanics west of the crest of the Sierra Nevada. Granites began to form 225 million years ago, and pulses of liquid rocks continued for more than 125 million years, forming the granite core of the range (Schweickert 1981). During the first half of the Tertiary Period, mountains were uplifted and erosion stripped the metamorphic rocks from the granite and exposed large expanses of the core throughout the range. Meandering streams became deeply incised as gradients became steeper. By the Eocene Epoch, about 55 million years ago, this high "proto-Sierra Nevada" had been eroded into an Appalachian-like chain of low mountains. Violent volcanic eruptions during the second half of the Tertiary Period blanketed much of the subdued landscape of the northern Sierra Nevada and portions of the higher central Sierra Nevada with ash that dammed streams, filled narrow valleys, and covered passes (Hill 1975). Today, volcanic rocks occur primarily in the northern and central Sierra Nevada, although small outcrops can be seen throughout the range. The sharp relief and high altitude of the modern Sierra Nevada are the products of recent uplift associated with extension of the Great Basin. This uplift began 2 to 3 million years ago and continues today.

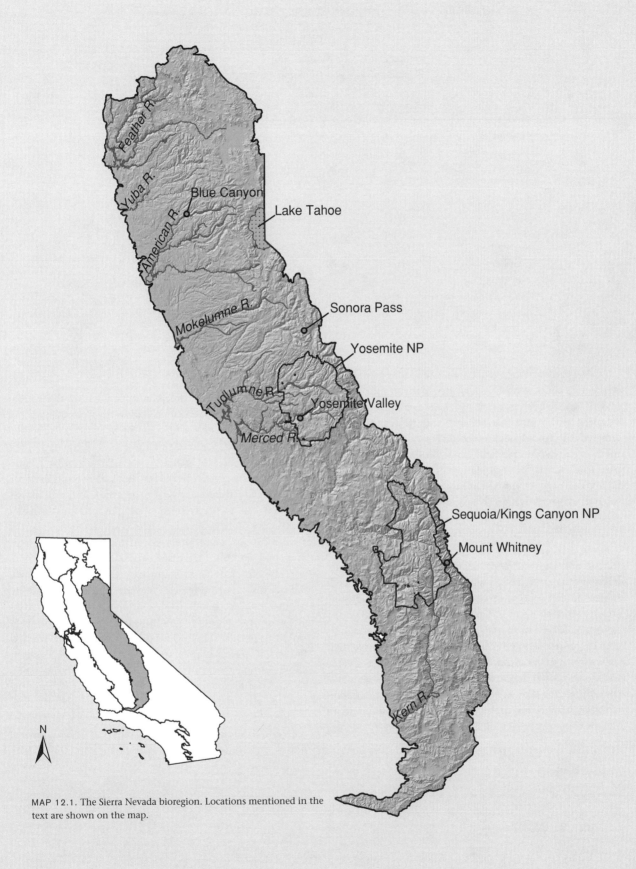

Feather R.

Yuba R.

Blue Canyon

American R.

Lake Tahoe

Sonora Pass

Mokelumne R.

Yosemite NP

Tuolumne R.

Yosemite Valley

Merced R.

Sequoia/Kings Canyon NP

Mount Whitney

Kern R.

N

MAP 12.1. The Sierra Nevada bioregion. Locations mentioned in the
text are shown on the map.

TABLE 12.1
Normal maxima, normal minima, record high, and record low temperatures at Blue
Canyon, elevation 1,609 m (5,391 ft), northern Sierra Nevada

	Normal Daily Maximum (°C)	Normal Daily Minimum (°C)	Record High (°C)	Record Low (°C)
January	6.4	−0.8	21.7	−15.0
February	6.3	−0.7	22.8	−14.4
March	7.9	0.4	22.2	−12.8
April	11.7	3.3	25.6	−8.3
May	15.7	6.7	30.0	−6.1
June	19.6	10.6	33.3	−2.2
July	25.0	15.0	32.8	4.4
August	24.8	13.8	33.3	1.7
September	22.2	12.2	33.9	−1.7
October	16.8	7.4	29.4	−5.6
November	12.1	3.1	25.6	−0.6
December	8.6	0.6	23.9	−2.8

During the Pleistocene Epoch, snow and ice covered most of the high country, and glaciers filled many of the river valleys (Hill 1975). Several glaciations are recognized to have occurred in the Sierra Nevada, but only two can be reconstructed with confidence (Huber 1987). The Tahoe glaciation reached its maximum extent about 60,000 to 75,000 years ago, whereas the Tioga glaciation peaked about 15,000 to 20,000 years ago. These glaciers further deepened valleys and scoured ridges, leaving the exposed granite landscape so prevalent today. Modern glaciers are scattered on high peaks between Yosemite and Sequoia National Parks.

Seven soil orders occur in the Sierra Nevada. *Alfisols* are formed under forest cover with the bulk of the annual production of organic matter delivered above ground. *Andisols* most commonly occur on steep slopes formed by volcanic activity. *Aridisols* occur in semi-arid areas where local conditions impose aridity. *Entisols* and *Inceptisols* are found where climate or bedrock limits soil development. Most *Mollisols* have formed under meadow or grassland vegetation. Deeply weathered *Ultisols* develop in moist, cold areas under acidic conditions. The different soil orders occur in combination with wet, frigid or frozen soil temperature regimes and dry to aquatic soil moisture regimes.

Climatic Patterns

The pattern of weather in the Sierra Nevada is influenced by its topography and geographic position relative to the Central Valley, the Coast Ranges, and the Pacific Ocean. Winters are dominated by low pressure in the northern Pacific Ocean while summer weather is influenced by high pressure in the same area.

FIRE CLIMATE VARIABLES

The primary sources of precipitation are winter storms that move from the north Pacific and cross the Coast Ranges and Central Valley before reaching the Sierra Nevada. The coastal mountains catch some of the moisture, but the gap in the mountains near San Francisco Bay allows storms to pass through producing the heaviest precipitation to occur in the Sierra Nevada in areas to the east and north. As the air masses move up the gentle western slope, precipitation increases and, at the higher elevations, falls as snow. Once across the crest, most of the moisture has been driven from the air mass and precipitation decreases sharply. Precipitation also decreases from north to south with nearly twice as much falling in the northern Sierra Nevada as does in the south. Mean annual precipitation ranges from a low of 25 cm (10 in) at the western edge of the foothills to more than 200 cm (79 in) north of Lake Tahoe. More than half of the total precipitation falls in January, February, and March, much of it as snow. Summer precipitation is associated with afternoon thunderstorms and subtropical storms moving up from the Gulf of California.

Sierra Nevada temperatures are generally warm in the summer and cool in the winter. Table 12.1 shows normal monthly maxima and minima and highest and lowest temperatures recorded for the Blue Canyon weather station at 1,609 m (5,391 ft) in the northern Sierra Nevada. Temperatures decrease as latitude and elevation increase, with a temperature lapse rate of approximately 6.5°C with each 1,000 m of elevation (3.3°F in 1,000 ft). At Blue Canyon, normal 10:00 am relative humidity is highest in January at 60% and lowest in July at 30%. Extremely low relative humidity is common in the summer. Wind speeds are variable, averaging

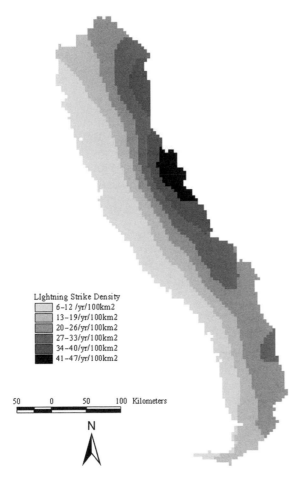

Lightning Strike Density
- 6–12 /yr/100km2
- 13–19/yr/100km2
- 20–26/yr/100km2
- 27–33/yr/100km2
- 34–40/yr/100km2
- 41–47/yr/100km2

50 0 50 100 Kilometers

N

MAP 12.2. Spatial distribution of lightning strikes in the Sierra Nevada bioregion, 1985–2000. The density increases from west to east and reaches a maximum just east of the crest north of Sonora Pass.

up to 11 km hr^{-1} (7 mi hr^{-1}) but have been recorded as high as 113 km hr^{-1} (70 mi hr^{-1}) out of the north at Blue Canyon during October.

Lightning is pervasive in the Sierra Nevada, occurring in every month and on every square kilometer with over 210,000 strikes occurring from 1985 through 2000 (van Wagtendonk and Cayan 2007). However, there are spatial and temporal patterns. Map 12.2 shows the spatial distribution of the average annual number of lightning strikes for the 16-year period. The highest concentration of lightning strikes occurs 15 km (9.3 mi) northeast of Sonora Pass. In the Sierra Nevada, there is a strong correlation between the number of lightning strikes and elevation, with strikes increasing with elevation (Fig. 12.1) (van Wagtendonk 1991a). Summer afternoon heating of slopes causes uplift in the mountains and results in the development of thunderstorms. Ridge tops receive more strikes than valley bottoms, but there is no significant relationship between strikes and either slope steepness or aspect. The temporal distribution of lightning strikes is shown in Table 12.2. The greatest number of strikes occurs in the afternoon in July and August.

WEATHER SYSTEMS

Fires are associated with critical fire weather patterns that occur with regularity during the summer (Hull et al. 1966). For California, there are four types of patterns: (1) the Pacific High–Post-Frontal, (2) the Great Basin High, (3) the Subtropical High Aloft, and (4) the Meridional Ridge with Southwest Flow Aloft. The Pacific High–Post-Frontal type is a surface type where air from the Pacific moves in behind a cold front and causes north to northwest winds in northern and central California (Hull et al. 1966). A foehn effect is produced by steep pressure gradients behind the front causing strong winds to blow down slope. The Great Basin High type often follows the Pacific High–Post-Frontal type with air stagnating over the Great Basin. Combined with a surface thermal trough off the California coast, the Great Basin High creates strong pressure gradients and easterly or northeasterly winds across the Sierra Nevada (Hull et al. 1966). Although this type is often present during winter months when fires are not expected to occur, the Great Basin High can produce extreme fire weather during the summer.

During the Subtropical High Aloft type, the belt of westerly winds is displaced northward and a stagnant air pattern effectively blocks advection of moist air from the Gulf of Mexico. High temperatures and low relative humidities are associated with this type. The Meridional Ridge with Southwest Flow pattern requires a ridge to the east and a trough to the west, allowing marine air penetration in coastal and inland areas. Above the marine layer in the Sierra Nevada, temperatures are higher and relative humidities are lower as short wave troughs and dry frontal systems pass over the area (Hull et al. 1966). Table 12.3 shows the percentage of days each month that would be expected to have each critical fire weather pattern based on records from the Blue Canyon station. During June, July, and August, the maximum temperatures associated with each of these types range from 27°C to 33°C (81°F–91°F) and the relative humidity from 8% to 21%.

Ecological Zones

The vegetation of the Sierra Nevada is as variable as its topography and climate. In response to actual evapotranspiration and the available water budget, the vegetation forms six broad ecological zones that roughly correspond with elevation (Stephenson 1998). These zones include: (1) the foothill shrubland and woodland zone, (2) the lower-montane forest zone, (3) the upper-montane forest zone, (4) the subalpine forest zone, (5) the alpine meadow and shrubland zone, and (6) the eastside forest and woodland zone. These zones are arranged in elevation belts from the Central Valley up to the Sierra Nevada crest and back down to the Great Basin (Fig. 12.2). The ecological zones increase in elevation from the north to southern Sierra Nevada.

FOOTHILL SHRUBLAND AND WOODLAND

The foothill shrubland and woodland zone covers 15,777 km^2 (5,993 mi^2) from the lowest foothills at 142 m (466 ft) to occasional stands at 1,500 m (5,000 ft), reaching a maximum

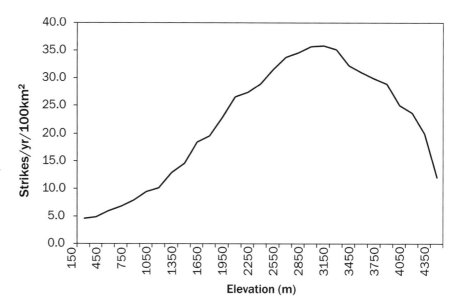

FIGURE 12.1. Lightning strikes by elevation in the Sierra Nevada bioregion, 1985–2000. The density of strikes is greatest at 3,000 m and decreases as elevation increases above that point.

TABLE 12.2
Temporal distribution of lightning strikes by 2-month and 4-hour periods for the Sierra Nevada, 1985–2000

| Hour | Number of Strikes | | | | | | |
	Jan–Feb	Mar–Apr	May–Jun	Jul–Aug	Sep–Oct	Nov–Dec	Total
0–4	88	159	1,661	3,645	1,505	156	7,214
4–8	61	111	858	6,402	1,919	39	9,390
8–12	105	610	7,946	21,902	4,204	85	34,852
12–16	665	3,688	28,124	64,692	17,430	377	114,976
16–20	482	1810	10,025	15,344	6,685	762	35,110
20–24	162	434	3,344	2271	1723	801	8,735
Total	1,565	6,812	51,958	114,256	33,466	2,220	210,277

extent between 150 m and 300 m (1,000–1,500 ft). The primary vegetation types in this zone are foothill pine–interior live oak *(Pinus sabiniana-Quercus wislizenii)* woodlands, mixed hardwood woodlands, and chaparral shrublands. Blue oak *(Quercus douglasii)* woodlands occur at the lower end of the zone and are treated in Chapter 13 (Central Valley Bioregion).

LOWER-MONTANE FOREST

The lower montane forest is the most prevalent zone in California and in the Sierra Nevada bioregion, occupying 21,892 km² (8,316 mi²) primarily on the west side of the range just above the foothill zone. Ninety-five percent of the stands occur below 2,400 m (8,000 ft), and the greatest occupied area is between 1,500 and 1,650 m (5,000–5,500 ft). Major vegetation types include California black oak *(Quercus kelloggii)*, ponderosa pine *(Pinus ponderosa)*, white fir *(Abies concolor)*

mixed conifer, Douglas-fir *(Pseudotsuga menziesii var. menziesii)* mixed conifer, and mixed evergreen forests. Interspersed within the forests are chaparral stands, riparian forests, and meadows and seeps.

UPPER MONTANE FOREST

This ecological zone covers 11,383 km² (4,324 mi²) and extends from as low as 750 m (2,500 ft) to 3,450 m (11,500 ft). The upper-montane forest is most widely spread between 1,950 and 2,100 m (6,500–7,000 ft) where it covers 1,800 km² (695 mi²). Forests within this zone include extensive stands of California red fir *(Abies magnifica var. magnifica)* along with occasional stands of western white pine *(Pinus monticola)*. Woodlands with Jeffrey pine *(Pinus jeffreyi)* and Sierra juniper *(Juniperus occidentalis* ssp. *australis)* occupy exposed ridges, whereas meadows and quaking aspen *(Populus tremuloides)* stands occur in moist areas.

TABLE 12.3
Percent of days each month with critical fire weather types for Blue Canyon, 1951–1960

	Percentage of Days Per Month									
Weather Type	Mar	Apr	May	Jun	Jul	Aug	Sep	Oct	Nov	Dec–Feb
Pacific High, Post-frontal	6.8	8.0	5.2	7.0	3.2	4.5	5.7	7.4	5.3	4.9
Great Basin High (Pacific)	16.1	12.0	11.3	11.0	7.4	6.1	12.3	18.7	15.7	16.1
Subtropical High Aloft	0.0	0.0	0.0	10.3	32.3	24.8	16.3	1.6	0.0	0.0
Meridional Ridge SW Flow Aloft	3.9	6.3	11.6	17.0	16.5	27.4	17.3	9.0	7.7	1.9

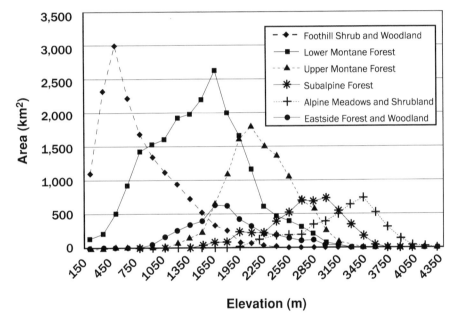

FIGURE 12.2. Area of ecological zones by 500-m elevation bands. The elevational distribution of ecological zones is evident as area cover by each zone increases and then decreases as elevation increases.

SUBALPINE FOREST

The subalpine forest zone ranges from 1,650 m (5,500 ft) to 3,450 m (11,500 ft) and reaches its maximum extent between 3,000 m to 3,450 m (9,500–10,000 ft). The subalpine zone encompasses 5,047 km² (1,917 mi²) and consists of lodgepole pine *(Pinus contorta* ssp. *murrayana)*, mountain hemlock *(Tsuga mertensiana)* forests and limber pine *(Pinus flexilis)*, foxtail pine *(Pinus balfouriana* ssp. *balfouriana)*, and whitebark pine *(Pinus albicaulis)* woodlands, with numerous large meadow complexes.

ALPINE MEADOW AND SHRUBLAND

Sitting astride the crest of the Sierra Nevada is the 4,423-km² (1680-mi²) alpine meadow and shrubland ecological zone. The

zone extends from 2,000 m (7,000 ft) to 4,350 m (14,500 ft), with the largest area between 3,300 m and 3,450 m (11,000–11,500 ft). Willow *(Salix spp.)* shrublands and alpine fell fields containing grasses, sedges, and herbs are the dominant vegetation types.

EASTSIDE FOREST AND WOODLAND

On the eastern side of the Sierra Nevada, forest and woodlands cover a total of 3,907 km² (1,484 mi²). The woodlands are comprised of single-leaf pinyon pine *(Pinus monophylla)*, while the forests consist of Jeffrey pine, white fir, and mixed white fir and pine. The zone ranges in elevation from 1,050 m to 2,850 m (3,500–9,500 ft) and is most prevalent between 1500 m and 1,650 m (5,000–5,500 ft).

Overview of Historic Fire Occurrence

Fire has been an ecological force in the Sierra Nevada since the retreat of the Tioga glacier more than 10,000 years ago. Flammable fuels, abundant ignition sources, and hot, dry summers combine to produce conditions conducive to an active fire role. Whereas this role has varied over the millennia as climate has changed, fire continues to shape vegetation and other ecosystem components. Fire's role is also influenced by the elevation gradient of the Sierra Nevada, which affects fuels, ignition sources, and climate.

Prehistoric Period

The earliest evidence of the presence of fire in the Sierra Nevada can be seen in lake sediments more than 16,000 years old in Yosemite National Park (Smith and Anderson 1992). Charcoal does not appear in meadow sediments until about 10,000 B.P. (Anderson and Smith 1997). Six separate peaks in charcoal deposits were recorded between 8,700 and 800 years B.P. in seven meadows from Yosemite south to Sequoia National Park. Such increases in charcoal abundance above the background level indicate large individual fires or fire periods. With the exception of the peak between 8,700 and 9,500 years B.P., charcoal was less prevalent in the early Holocene Epoch than in the late Holocene, suggesting that the climate was drier during the earlier period (Anderson and Smith 1997).

Pollen and macrofossils in the sediments indicate that the forests were more open during the early Holocene, possibly producing less fuel and less extensive fires. Anderson and Smith (1997) hypothesized that, during the late Holocene, climatic changes and possible increases in winter storms or El Niño-like conditions led to denser forests with greater fuel loads and more intense fires. Pollen data from sediment cores taken from subalpine lakes confirmed the meadow data showing open, dry vegetation consisting of pines and chaparral during the early Holocene and closed, wet forests of firs and hemlocks during the late Holocene (Anderson 1990).

Fire scars are another source of information for documenting the historical role of fire. Wagener (1961b) reexamined fire scar records from mixed conifer stands on the western slope of the Sierra Nevada between the Feather River on the north and the San Joaquin River on the south. Included in his analysis were five stands originally investigated by Boyce (1920) and two additional stands north and south of Yosemite. Based on all seven of those stands, fire-return intervals ranged from seven to nine years. In a study area 50 km (31 mi) west of Lake Tahoe, Stephens et al. (2004) recorded fires between 1649 and 1921 with median fire intervals between 5 and 15 years. For the mountains just to the southeast of Lake Tahoe, Taylor (2004) reported a mean pre-settlement fire return interval of 10.4 years. Further south in Kings Canyon National Park, Kilgore and Taylor (1979) found that fires scarred trees every 7 years on west-facing slopes and every 16 years on east-facing slopes.

Fire scar records from five giant sequoia (*Sequoiadendron giganteum*) groves located from Yosemite to south of Sequoia National Park confirm the presence of fire in the Sierra Nevada for the past 3,000 years with the earliest recorded fire occurring in 1125 B.C. (Swetnam 1993). Based on independent climate reconstructions, years with low precipitation amounts were likely to have fires occur synchronously across the region. The scars showed that extensive fires burned every 3.4 to 7.7 years during the cool period between A.D. 500 and A.D. 800 and every 2.2 years to 3.7 years during the warm period from A.D. 1000 to A.D.1300. After 1300, fire-return intervals increased, except for short periods, during the 1600s for one grove and during the 1700s for two other groves (Swetnam 1993). Fire-free intervals ranged from 15 to 30 years during the long-interval period and were always less than 13 years during the short-interval years.

Although lightning would have been present for millennia prior to charcoal appearing in late sediments 16,000 years ago, ignitions by Native Americans probably did not occur until 9,000 years ago (Hull and Moratto 1999). Their use of fire was extensive and had specific cultural purposes (Anderson 1999). It is currently not possible to determine whether charcoal deposits or fire scars were caused by lightning fires or by fires ignited by Native Americans. However, Anderson and Carpenter (1991) attributed a decline in pine pollen and an increase in oak pollen coupled with an increase in charcoal in sediments in Yosemite Valley to expanding populations of aboriginal inhabitants 650 years ago. Similarly, Anderson and Smith (1997) could not rule out burning by aboriginals as the cause of the change in fire regimes beginning 4,500 years ago. It is reasonable to assume that the contribution of ignitions by Native Americans was significant but varied over the spectrum of inhabited landscapes (Vale 2002).

Historic Period

The arrival of European Americans in the Sierra Nevada affected fire regimes in several ways. Native Americans were often driven from their homeland, and diseases brought from Europe decimated their populations. As a result, use of fire by Native Americans was greatly reduced. Settlers further exacerbated the situation by introducing cattle and sheep to the Sierra Nevada, setting fires in attempts to improve the range, and excluding fires from other areas to protect timber and watershed values. Extensive fires occurred as a result of slash burning associated with logging activities and prospectors who burned large areas to enhance the discovery of mineral outcrops (Lieberg 1902).

Evidence of the changed fire regimes is found in charcoal deposits and fire scars. The meadow sediments examined by Anderson and Smith (1997) showed a drop in charcoal particles during the most recent century, which they attributed to fire suppression. Giant sequoias also showed a reduction in fire scars after 1850, assumed by Swetnam (1993) to be the result of sheep grazing, elimination of fires set by Native Americans, and fire suppression. Similar decreases in fire scars were noted by Wagener (1961b) throughout the Sierra Nevada and by Kilgore and Taylor (1979) in the southern part of the range.

Of all the activities affecting fire regimes, the exclusion of fire by organized government suppression forces has had the greatest effect. Beginning in the late 1890s, the U.S. Army attempted to extinguish all fires within the national parks in the Sierra Nevada (van Wagtendonk 1991b). When the Forest Service was established in 1905, it developed both a theoretical basis for systematic fire protection and considerable expertise to execute that theory on national forests (Show and Kotok 1923). This expertise was expanded to the fledgling National Park Service when it was established in 1916. Fire control remained the dominant management practice throughout the Sierra Nevada until the late 1960s. Fire exclusion resulted in an increase in accumulated surface debris and density of shrubs and understory trees. Although the number of fires and the total area burned decreased between 1908 and 1968, the proportion of the yearly area burned by the largest fire each year increased (McKelvey and Busse 1996). Suppression forces were able to extinguish most fires while they were small but during extreme weather conditions they were unable to control the large ones.

Current Period

Based on early work by Biswell (1959) and Hartesvelt (1962), the National Park Service changed its fire policy in 1968 to allow the use of prescribed fires deliberately set by managers and to allow fires of natural origin to burn under prescribed conditions (van Wagtendonk 1991b). The Forest Service followed suit in 1974, changing from a policy of fire control to one of fire management (DeBruin 1974). As a result, fire was reintroduced to the Sierra Nevada landscape through programs of prescribed burning and wildland fire use (Kilgore and Briggs 1972, van Wagtendonk 1986). Giant sequoias recorded the new program with fire scars from two prescribed burns in 1969 and 1971 and a wildfire in 1988 (Caprio and Swetman 1995).

For much of the Sierra Nevada, however, routine fire suppression is still the rule. Fire regimes are altered with a shift from frequent, low-intensity fires to less frequent, large fires (McKelvey and Busse 1996). Fuel accumulations, brush, small trees, and dense forests produce very different conditions for the inevitable fire that occurs, whether from lightning or from human sources. Some headway is being made in wilderness areas and areas where prescribed fire can be applied safely and effectively.

Major Ecological Zones

The six ecological zones of the Sierra Nevada are comprised of different vegetation types and species. Each species has different adaptations to fire and varies in its dependency on fire. Similarly, the fire regimes and plant community interactions of the zones vary.

Foothill Shrubland and Woodland

The foothill shrubland and woodland zone is the first ecological zone above the Central Valley bioregion. It is bounded below by the valley grasslands and blue oak woodlands and above by the montane, conifer-dominated zone. The terrain is moderately steep with deep incised canyons. Sedimentary, metavolcanic, and granitic rocks form the substrate and soils are thin and well drained. The climate is subhumid with hot, dry summers and cool, moist winters. Lightning is relatively infrequent, averaging only 8.25 strikes yr^{-1} 100 km^{-2} (75.9 strikes yr^{-1} 100 mi^{-2}).

The vegetation is a mix of large areas of chaparral, live oak woodland with scattered or patchy foothill or ponderosa pines (Fig. 12.3). These species form dense continuous stands of vegetation and fuels. Chamise (Adenostoma faciculatum), manzanita (Arctostaphylos spp.), and California-lilac (Ceanothus spp.) dominate the chaparral. Interior live oaks or canyon live oaks (Quercus chrysolepis) are extensive on steep slopes of large canyons. Tall deciduous shrubs or forests dominate riparian areas with dense vertical layering and a cooler microclimate.

FIRE RESPONSES OF IMPORTANT SPECIES

Many foothill species of the Sierra Nevada have fire responses and characteristics that are similar to those of the interior South Coast zone described in Chapter 15. Some species are dominant, such as chamise in extensive chaparral areas and stands of interior live oak. Chaparral includes many sprouting species but few that require heat for seed germination. The two live oaks are vigorous sprouters. The most prevalent conifers, such as ponderosa pine, are fire resistant or have serotinous cones, such as gray pine and knobcone pine. There has been less research in Sierra Nevada chaparral than in southern California and the proportion of species with fire-dependent characteristics is unknown. Establishment, survival, and abundance of many species are enhanced by fire. The fire responses for knobcone pine (Pinus attenuata), ponderosa pine, and chamise are covered in more detail in the North Coast (Chapter 8), Northeastern Plateaus (Chapter 11), and South Coast (Chapter 15) chapters, respectively. Table 12.4 lists the fire responses of the important species in the foothill zone.

Numerous chaparral shrubs sprout following fire. These include chamise, flannelbush (Fremontodendron californicum), poison oak (Toxicodendron diversilobum), coyote brush (Baccharis pilularis), birch-leaf mountain-mahogany (Cercocarpus betuloides var. betuloides), redshank (Adenostoma sparsifolium), yerba santa (Eriodictyon californicum), California coffeeberry (Rhamnus californica), and Christmas berry (Heteromeles arbutifolia) (Biswell 1974). Non-sprouting shrubs can be dominant as well, with seeds that are heat resistant and have fire-enhanced germination—such as whiteleaf manzanita (Arctostphylos viscida), Mariposa manzanita (Arctostaphylos viscida spp. mariposa), chaparral whitethorn (Ceanothus leucodermis), and buck brush (Ceanothus cuneatus var. cuneatus). Exposure to heat can more than double germination rates. Laurel sumac (Malosma laurina)

FIGURE 12.3. Foothill shrub and woodland. Foothill pine and interior live oak are dominant overstory species in this stand with non-native grasses and species of manzanita and California-lilac in the understory. Fire is common and keeps the understory relatively clear.

seed germination increased from 17% to more than 50% with exposure to 100°C (212°F) (Wright 1931). Many chaparral species produce seed at an early age that can remain viable in the soil for decades or more. Buck brush produces seeds from age 5 to 7 years. Growing in dominantly single-species patches, buck brush resists burning until decadent or foliar moistures are extremely low. Several crops of seed are often produced before fire returns, enhancing post-fire dominance.

Sierra Nevada chaparral can be more productive than its southern California counterparts, with four times the biomass accumulation over 37 years (Rundel and Parsons 1979). As stands age, the proportion of dead biomass increases. By the time chamise stands reach 16 years of age, the combination of dead branches and live resinous foliage make them extremely flammable.

Numerous geophytes, or bulb-bearing plants, that show an increased flowering and growth response following fire are scattered in chaparral. Common examples are soap plant *(Chlorogalum pomeridianum)*, death camas *(Zigadenus* spp.*)*, and mariposa lilies *(Calochortus* spp.*)*. Annual plants respond to fire by prolific seeding.

Interior and canyon live oaks sprout both from root and canopy crowns following fire and their seedlings develop burls early. Canyon live oak bark resists low-intensity fires (Paysen and Narog 1993), whereas the relatively thin bark of interior live oak results in top-kill with all but lowest-intensity fires (Plumb 1980). Both species can also sprout new branches from epicormic buds on the stem.

Foothill pines persist after high-intensity fires in surrounding chaparral by developing cones and seeds at an early age, producing plentiful seeds (Fowells 1979), and by having cones that are opened by heat (Sudworth 1908) and

seedlings that survive well on mineral soil. Pitch running down the bole is common and increases crown torching (Lawrence 1966). The tolerance of foothill pine for rocky, thin soils and drought conditions also enables it to avoid burning because fuels are scattered and fire infrequent. Because foothill pine seeds are large and wingless, dispersal of seeds is dependent on seed caching by rodents and birds.

Native Americans maintained small patches of native grasslands such as deergrass *(Muhlenbergia rigens)*, which is a large, coarse-leaved perennial bunchgrass (Anderson 1996). It responds to periodic burning with vigorous growth. Fires, particularly if set in the fall, favored native species, including fire-stimulated flowers of bulb-species like brodiaea *(Brodiaea* spp.*)* (York 1997). Fire exclusion has led to invasion of these patches by annual, non-native grasses such as cheat grass *(Bromus tectorum)*.

FIRE REGIME–PLANT COMMUNITY INTERACTIONS

Fire regimes in the foothill zone vary with topography and vegetation. In the lower portions with more gentle topography, the oak grassland savannah areas burned frequently and with low to moderate intensity as described in the Central Valley chapter (Chapter 11). Fire season would have begun in early summer extending to fall. Steeper areas dominated by chaparral and scattered trees or pockets of conifers burned less frequently and with higher-intensity crown fires, resulting in highly severe effects to vegetation (Table 12.5). These are among the driest areas in the bioregion, with less than 62.5 cm (25 in) average annual precipitation being characteristic. Fire season is long and begins in early summer. Given the high numbers of species with fire-enhanced responses, the vegetation overall is resilient to high-severity fires. Where severe fires

TABLE 12.4
Fire response types for important species in the foothill shrub and woodland ecological zone

| Lifeform | Type of Fire Response | | | Species |
	Sprouting	Seeding	Individual	
Conifer	None	None	Resistant, killed	Ponderosa pine
	None	Fire stimulated (seed release)	Resistant, killed	Foothill pine, knobcone pine
Hardwood	Fire stimulated	None	Top-killed or branch killed	Blue oak, interior live oak, canyon live oak
Shrub	Fire stimulated	None or unknown	Top-killed	Poison oak, flannelbush, coyote bush, birch-leaf mountain-mahogany, redshank, yerba santa, California coffeeberry, Christmas berry
	Fire stimulated	Fire stimulated	Top-killed	Chamise, redbud
	None	Fire stimulated	Killed	Whiteleaf manzanita, chaparral whitethorn, buck brush
	None	None	Killed	
Forb	Fire stimulated	None	Top-killed	Soap plant, death camas, mariposa lilies
	None	None		
Grass	Fire stimulated	None	Top-killed	Deergrass
	None	None	Killed	Cheat grass

have occurred at the upper end of the foothill shrubland zone, the boundary between the shrublands and the lower-montane forest has shifted. Reestablishment of the conifers in those areas could take decades to centuries, and frequent recurring fires may perpetuate the shrub species.

Little direct information exists on the patterns of historic vegetation shaped by fire. Biswell (1974) described three different kinds of California chaparral, of which two occur in the Sierra Nevada foothills. One is on shallow soils and steep slopes with chamise, California-lilac, manzanita, and scrub oaks; and the second is on deeper productive soils, often developed from grasslands when fires become less frequent. Other species occur such as flannelbush and coyote brush. This type of chaparral has increased with fire suppression and development in the foothills.

Recurrent fire and dominance by sprouters tend to perpetuate large patches of single-species dominated chaparral or oak forest. Chamise dominates large areas, particularly on dry, shallow soil sites with both post-fire sprouting and heat-enhanced germination. But not all chamise plants resprout, and these openings allow California-lilac to germinate and persist in mixed chamise patches. Similarly, live oak often dominates large areas and sprouts vigorously with rapid growth following fire (Biswell 1974).

Frequent fire in the grasslands of the foothills, in part from burning by Native Americans, reduced encroachment by chaparral. With fire suppression and elimination burning by Native Americans, chaparral has increased in extent. Chaparral has also increased on sites where it previously co-occurred with ponderosa pine. Ponderosa pine remains in the foothills in limited patches on more mesic north-facing slopes. It has a reduced distribution due to preferential logging during European settlement. Natural re-establishment of ponderosa pine in the foothills is limited by the reduction in fires, which provided canopy openings and mineral soil for successful survival. In some locations, the boundary for conifer communities is rising in elevation due, in part, to current patterns of fire. In the foothills to the west of Yosemite National Park, recurrent, large, high-intensity fires have resulted in establishment of vast shrub fields and annual grasslands. Ponderosa pine is at its lower limit in the foothills as moisture becomes less available, especially in large open areas. Establishment of ponderosa pine is difficult since seed sources are somewhat distant.

Foothill pine stands respond to the fire regimes of the surrounding chaparral and live oak stands, surviving those of low severity and succumbing to moderate- to high-severity fires. Partial serotiny allows reestablishment after stand-replacing fires. Woody and duff fuel loads are among the lowest of

TABLE 12.5
Fire regime attributes for vegetation types of the foothill shrub and
woodland ecological zone

Vegetation type	Chaparral	Oak woodlands/ grasslands	Conifer forest patches
Temporal			
Seasonality	Summer–fall	Summer–fall	Summer–fall
Fire-return interval	Medium	Short	Medium
Spatial			
Size	Large	Large	Small
Complexity	Low	Low	Low
Magnitude			
Intensity	High	Low	High
Severity	High	Low	High
Fire type	Crown	Surface	Crown

NOTE: Fire regime terms used in this table are defined in Chapter 4.

any Sierra Nevada conifer and do not contribute significantly to fire spread and intensity (van Wagtendonk et al. 1998). Although relatively uncommon, patches of knobcone pine exist in the Sierra Nevada foothills surrounded by chaparral. Locations are typically steep on large canyon walls. These patches are dependent on high-intensity fire because of their serotinous cones. Current practices of fire exclusion may reduce the persistence of some knobcone pine patches.

Lower-Montane Forest

The lower-montane forest ecological zone is the first continuous zone of conifers as one ascends the Sierra Nevada. The foothills are below with the upper montane forest above. The relatively gentle western slope consists of ridges and river canyons. Metavolcanic, metasedimentary, and granitic rocks form the majority of the geologic substrates and soils are relatively deep and well drained. Summers are hot and dry, and winters are cold and wet. Lightning is moderately frequent, averaging 15.6 strikes yr^{-1} 100 km^{-2} (40.3 strikes yr^{-1} 100 mi^{-2}).

Vegetation and fire within the lower-montane zone vary with elevation, landscape position, and latitude. At the lowest elevations, California black oak and ponderosa pine dominate large areas, particularly in the southern Sierra Nevada. Intermixed with the oak-pine forests are various-sized patches of chaparral and canyon live oak—extensions of foothill types. Manzanita and California-lilac species dominate chaparral, whereas canyon live oak is extensive on steep slopes of large canyons. With increasing elevation, the proportion of white fir or Douglas-fir increases on mesic slopes they can dominate. Incense-cedar (Calocedrus decurrens) and sugar pine (Pinus lambertiana) are found throughout. Figure 12.4 shows

a stand of ponderosa pines, incense-cedars, and sugar pines with an understory of mountain misery (Chamaebatia foliolosa). Giant sequoia–mixed conifer forests are concentrated in several river basins in the central and southern Sierra Nevada, occupying sites where soils are wet. At the highest elevation, at the boundary with upper montane forests, white fir often becomes dominant on all aspects except where soils are shallow or very rocky. Here, pine or shrub communities often dominate.

Throughout the zone, riparian plant communities characterized by deciduous trees, shrubs, large herbs, and grasses occur with varied proportions of intermixed conifers. White alder (Alnus rhombifolia), gray alder (Alnus incana), or black cottonwood (Populus balsamifera ssp. trichocarpa) dominate larger streams or wetter sites. Bigleaf maple (Acer macrophyllum) and mountain dogwood (Cornus nuttallii) occur along smaller or intermittent streams. Small patches of quaking aspen occur in the higher-elevation white-fir–dominated forests but are more prevalent in the upper-montane zone. Meadows and seeps tend to be small and scattered.

Partly due to increasing precipitation, Douglas-fir becomes important from the Mokelumne River basin to the north. Mixed-evergreen forests comprised of tanoak (Lithocarpus densiflorus), Pacific madrone (Arbutus menziesii), and other montane hardwoods and conifers occupy large areas in the western Yuba and Feather River basins further north where precipitation exceeds 152 cm (60 in) annually.

FIRE RESPONSES OF IMPORTANT SPECIES

The majority of lower-montane species have characteristics resulting in resistance to fire and often have favorable responses to fire. Sprouting hardwood trees, shrubs, vines,

FIGURE 12.4. Lower-montane forest. This open stand of ponderosa pine, incense-cedar, and sugar pine with mountain misery in the understory burned in 1978 and in 1996.

herbs, and grasses are common and mostly fire enhanced; conifers have at least some fire-resistant characteristics.

Giant sequoia, ponderosa pine, sugar pine, Douglas-fir, and white fir have thick bark when mature (Table 12.6). The trees vary in their level of resistance to low- and moderate-intensity fires. Ponderosa pine has a thicker bark as a seedling and is more resistant to fire than the other lower-montane conifers. As ponderosa pine grows older, its high crowns and large, protected buds provide additional fire resistance. Rapid growth of giant sequoia seedlings produces early fire resistance. Douglas-fir, white fir, and incense-cedar have thick bark when mature, but are killed by fire when young because of thin bark, low, flammable crowns, and small, unprotected buds. Sugar pine is intermediate in fire resistance with thick bark and high crowns but potentially more susceptible to cambial or root damage from heat (Haase and Sackett 1998).

All conifers show improved establishment with mineral soil. Giant sequoias have serotinous cones that are exposed by heat or by small mammals and show increased seedling density with higher-intensity fire (Kilgore and Biswell 1971). Giant sequoia is the only Sierra Nevada conifer that sprouts, but this response is apparently limited to younger trees (Weatherspoon 1986). See sidebar on giant sequoias for more information about responses of this species to fire. Pacific yew *(Taxus brevifolia)* and California nutmeg *(Torreya californica)* are uncommon, relict conifers that have thin bark. They have survived in the fire-prone landscape by their restricted habitats in wet, mostly riparian areas and can apparently survive low-intensity fire as evidenced by observed fire scars and sprouting (Fites-Kaufman 1997).

The montane hardwoods, including tanoak, Pacific madrone, California black oak, canyon live oak, California bay *(Umbellularia californica)*, mountain dogwood, bigleaf maple, white alder, and black cottonwood, all sprout from basal burls or root crowns following fire. Sprouting can be vigorous with up to 100 sprouts produced on individual California black oak stumps (McDonald 1981). Sprouting can also can change with tree size. Tanoak sprouts are smaller when originating from smaller trees (Tappenier et al. 1984). Epicormic sprouting from the stem following low-intensity fire was observed in California black oak, tan oak, and mountain dogwood (Kauffman and Martin 1990). California black oak is the only species that develops bark sufficiently thick to resist low- to moderate-intensity fire in larger trees (>16 cm [6.3 in] dbh) (Plumb 1980). Riparian hardwoods all sprout following fire. Native Americans

TABLE 12.6
Fire response types for important species in the lower montane ecological zone

Lifeform	Type of Fire Response			Species
	Sprouting	Seeding	Individual	
Conifer	None	None	Resistant, killed	Ponderosa pine, Douglas-fir, white fir, sugar pine, incense-cedar
	None	Fire stimulated (seed release)	Resistant, killed except sprouts when young	Giant sequoia
	None	None	Low resistance, killed	Pacific yew
Hardwood	Fire stimulated	None	Top-killed	Black oak, tan oak, canyon live oak, big-leaf maple, Pacific madrone, white alder
Shrub	Fire stimulated	None	Top-killed	Mountain misery, greenleaf manzanita, poison oak, hazelnut, willow
	Fire stimulated	Fire Stimulated	Top-killed	Deer brush, Scotch broom
	None	Fire stimulated	Killed	Whiteleaf manzanita
Forb	Fire stimulated	None	Top-killed	Penstemon, many lilies, iris, Pacific starflower, trail plant, sanicle, mountain lady's slipper
Grass	None	None		
	Fire stimulated	None	Top-killed	Red fescue, melic, sedges
	None	None	Killed	Cheat grass

burned riparian areas to enhance shoot production of bigleaf maple and hazelnut (Coylus cornuta) shrubs (Anderson 1999).

Many shrubs have fire-enhanced regeneration with both sprouting and heat-stimulated seeds (Kauffman and Martin 1990) (Table 12.6). Sprouters include mountain misery, deer brush (Ceanothus intergerrimus), greenleaf manzanita (Arctostaphylos patula), bush chinquapin (Chrysolepis sempervirens), mountain whitethorn (Ceanothus cordulatus), and riparian shrubs hazelnut, thimbleberry (Rubus parviflorus), and gray alder. The burning season can affect sprouting response. Bush chinquapin, Sierra gooseberry (Ribes roezlii), deer brush, greenleaf manzanita, and thimbleberry all showed greater sprouting following early spring burns than fall or late spring burns (Kauffman and Martin 1990). But mountain whitethorn showed the greatest post-fire sprouting after higher-intensity fall burns. Sprouting occurs from burls, root crowns, and rhizomes.

Shrubs sprouting from deeply buried rhizomes, such as mountain misery, can readily dominate sites with frequent and intense fire. Mountain misery occupies extensive areas, 4 to 40 ha (10–100 ac), through extensive networks of rhizomes

protected from heat more than 20 cm (8 in) below the soil surface. With highly flammable foliage containing volatile oils and with highly dissected leaves, mountain misery promotes burning. Rundel et al. (1981) found that regrowth was stimulated by spring and fall burns but that summer burns inhibited resprouting for at least two years. Further enhancing its competitive advantage, mountain misery is able to fix nitrogen from nodules that develop after burning (Heisey et al.1980).

Some shrubs, particularly California-lilac, have heat-stimulated seed germination. Heat-stimulated seed of deer brush can produce extensive seedling patches, as dense as 15,800 seedlings ha^{-1} (6,500 seedlings ac^{-1}) after burning (Kilgore and Biswell 1971). Mountain whitethorn also produces many seeds that can persist in the soil for decades or centuries. The dual fire-enhanced sprouting and seed germination responses of the native deer brush and non-native Scotch broom (Cytisus scoparius) make them particularly successful in rapidly colonizing burned sites. Scotch broom is an aggressive, non-native shrub that has animal-dispersed and fire-stimulated seed, vigorous sprouting, and rapid early

One is in no danger of being hemmed in by sequoia fires, because they never run fast, the speeding winds flowing only across the treetops, leaving the deeps below calm, like the bottom of the sea. Furthermore, there is no generally distributed fire food in sequoia forests on which fires can move rapidly. Fire can only creep on the dead leaves and burrs, because they are solidly packed.

—JOHN MUIR, 1878

Probably better than any other species, giant sequoia exemplifies a truly fire-adapted species. Not only does it have thick bark that protects it from periodic surface fires, but also its cones are opened by heat and its regeneration is dependent on exposed mineral soil, such as occurs after a moderately severe fire. Biswell (1961) was one of the first scientists to explore the relationships between giant sequoias and fire. He reported fire scar dates in the Mariposa Grove in Yosemite National Park from as early as A.D. 450 with periods between fire scars averaging 18 years. He also looked at the number of lightning fires in 93-km^{-2} (36-mi^{-2}) areas surrounding sequoia groves and found that during the years from 1950 through 1959, 36 fires had been suppressed in the Mariposa Grove and 39 in the Tuolumne Grove. These data along with observations of dense thickets of white firs and incense-cedars and large increases in forest floor debris led him to conclude the groves should be managed with fire as part of the environment.

Hartesveldt (1962) conducted the first detailed scientific study of giant sequoias and fire in the Mariposa Grove and concluded that the greatest threat to the survival of the big trees was catastrophic fire burning through accumulated surface and understory fuels as a result of decades of fire exclusion. His recommendation was to reintroduce fire to the giant sequoia ecosystem through the use of prescribed burning (Hartesveldt 1964).

Subsequently, Hartesveldt and Harvey (1967) and Harvey et al. (1980) studied factors associated with giant sequoia reproduction in the Redwood Mountain Grove of Kings Canyon National Park. Using experimental fires and mechanical manipulations, they measured seedling survival and growth and investigated the role of vertebrate animals and arthropods in giant sequoia reproduction. Seedlings established on the hottest areas burned survived at a higher rate than those on other soils. Fire did not greatly affect vertebrate populations, and only one species had a significant effect on sequoia reproduction. The Douglas squirrel feeds on the scales of two- to five-year-old giant sequoia cones and cuts and caches thousands of cones each year. This greatly aids the distribution of cones and, subsequently, seedlings because the squirrels could not relocate most cached cones. Although more than 150 arthropods were found to be associated with giant sequoias, only two significantly affected regeneration. The gelechiid moth (*Gelechia* spp.) feeds on one-year-old cones, while the small long-horned beetle mines the main axis of cones older than five years, which causes them to dry and drop their seeds.

Based on these findings, the national Park Service began a program of prescribed burning and research in giant sequoia groves in Yosemite, Sequoia, and Kings Canyon National Parks (Kilgore 1972). Detailed information on fires and minerals (St. John and Rundel 1976), fuel accumulation (Parsons 1978), and fire history (Kilgore and Taylor 1979) added to the knowledge about the role of fire in these forests.

Burning in sequoia groves was not without controversy, however. Charred bark from a prescribed burn in Sequoia National Park prompted an investigation and a report on the burning programs in the groves (Cotton and McBride 1987). As a result, additional research was conducted to refine the scientific basis for the programs (Parsons 1994). Fire history studies extended the fire scar record back to 1125 B.C., with an average interval between fires from 2 to 30 years (Swetnam 1993). Pollen and charcoal in sediments cores taken in the groves indicated that giant sequoias became more prevalent about 5,000 years ago and that fires occurred throughout the record (Anderson 1994, Anderson and Smith 1997).

Studies on the effects of fire on fungi and insect relationships with giant sequoias led Piirto (1994) to conclude that fire does influence the types and population levels of numerous organisms but that their interactions are not well understood. Other studies looked at the role of fire severity in establishing and maintaining giant sequoia groves. Of particular interest was the finding that patchy, intense fires existed in presettlement times and that these fires were important determinants of grove structure and composition (Stephenson et al. 1991). Leading to these intense fires in giant sequoia groves are the heaviest woody fuel loads found for any Sierra Nevada conifer species (van Wagtendonk et al. 1998).

All the research to date indicates that fires have always played an important role in giant sequoia ecology and that the survival of the species depends on the continued presence of fire. Management programs must recognize this fact and must be designed to include fire in as natural a role as practicable. Restoration targets must include process goals as well as structural goals based on sound science (Stephenson 1999). Only through such a program can we ensure the survival of this magnificent fire species.

growth and seed production. It is taller than mountain misery and can out-compete deer brush and even mountain misery at times.

Deer brush is one of the most ubiquitous shrubs throughout the lower montane zone. Germination with wet seed can be greater than from dry heat (Kauffman and Martin 1990). This could explain its greater prevalence, especially after fires on moister portions of the landscape, such as north and east aspects or lower slopes. It gains height rapidly but can be limited by deer browsing (Kilgore and Biswell 1971). It persists under shaded canopies, but in a decadent, highly flammable state.

Little formal research has been conducted on fire response of herbs and grasses in the Sierra Nevada. But observations of morphology and fire responses indicate many understory species are enhanced by fire. Numerous perennial plants with sprouting structures including rhizomes, corymbs, or stolons exist and have been observed sprouting following fire. These include Pacific starflower (*Trientalis latifolia*), trail plant (*Adenocaulon bicolor*), western blue flag (*Iris missouriensis*), Bolander's bedstraw (*Galium bolanderi*), bear-grass (*Xerophyllum tenax*), sanicles (*Sanicula* spp.), many-stemmed sedge (*Carex multicaulis*), Ross' sedge (*Carex rossii*), needlegrasses (*Achnantherum* spp.), oniongrass (*Melica bulbosa*), and red fescue (*Festuca rubra*). On the other hand, some species like the Mountain lady's slipper (*Cypripedium montanum*) are killed outright by fire. Other plants exhibit sprouting or enhanced flowering following fire. Mariposa lilies and penstemons (*Penstemon* spp.) are two examples.

FIRE REGIME–PLANT COMMUNITY INTERACTIONS

Fire regime attributes for major vegetation types of the lower montane ecological zone are shown in Table 12.7. Fire was generally frequent in the lower-montane zone, ranging from 2 to 20 years on average at the stand or landscape scale (Wagener 1961b, Skinner and Chang 1996). There was noticeable variation in fire pattern with latitude and elevation related to shifts in fire season and in precipitation. Drier areas with longer fire seasons experienced the most frequent and regular fires. These areas are most prevalent in the southern and central Sierra Nevada and throughout the range on south aspects, ridges, and lower elevations. These areas tend to be dominated or co-dominated by ponderosa pine and California black oak. Throughout the zone, relatively cooler and wetter sites have had frequent but less regular fire and are more likely to have a presence or dominance of Douglas-fir and white fir. Fire patterns and vegetation interactions also varied at fine-spatial scales for all portions of this zone.

The interrelationships between vegetation and fire regimes make it difficult to distinguish which pattern drives the other. Fire-return interval estimates for this zone vary by the size of area examined. Average fire-return intervals reported for larger sample areas (more than 50 ha [122 ac]) generally fall under 10 years and are often as short as 4 years (Caprio and Swetnam 1995). Fire-return intervals for smaller areas (fewer than several ha) are more variable, ranging from 5 to more than 30 years (Kilgore and Taylor 1979, Fites-Kaufman 1997).

TABLE 12.7
Fire regime attributes for major vegetation types of the lower montane ecological zone

Vegetation type	Ponderosa pine/ black oak	Douglas-fir/ white fir	Tanoak-mixed evergreen
Temporal			
Seasonality	Summer–fall	Summer–fall	Summer-fall
Fire-return interval	Short (regular)	Short (variable)	Medium (variable)
Spatial			
Size	Large	Large	Medium
Complexity	Low	Multiple	Multiple
Magnitude			
Intensity	Low	Low–moderate	Multiple
Severity	Low–moderate	Low–moderate	Multiple
Fire type	Surface	Surface–multiple	Multiple

NOTE: Fire regime terms used in this table are defined in Chapter 4.

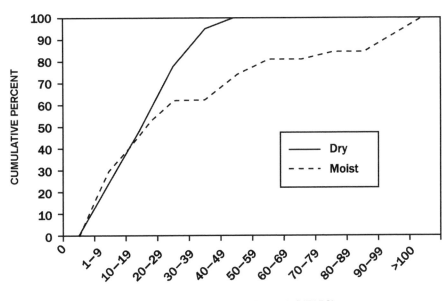

FIGURE 12.5. Distribution of fire-return intervals from small sample areas (1–3 ha, 2.5–7.5 ac) showing variation between moist and dry sites. Return intervals for dry sites peak at 50 years, whereas moist sites can have intervals of more than 100 years. (Adapted from Fites Kaufman 1996.)

North–south gradients in climate and vegetation parallel changes in fire patterns. Fire seasons are longer and precipitation lower in the southern portions of the westside lower montane zone. In ponderosa pine–California black oak forests of the southern Sierra Nevada, fire-return intervals increased with increasing elevation (Caprio and Swetnam 1995). In the northern Sierra Nevada, mean fire-return intervals were shorter (5–15 years) on drier, south- and west-facing upper slopes than on mesic, north- and east-facing lower slopes (15–25 years) (Fites-Kaufman 1997). More important than the average fire-return intervals, the distribution of fire-return intervals can vary substantially among locations in the landscape (Fig. 12.5), with associated differences in forest composition. The distribution of return intervals for xeric sites is more skewed toward small return intervals than for mesic sites. The more frequent, regular fire pattern is more often associated with ponderosa pine-dominated sites. Ponderosa pine develops resistance to fire at a young age and can best tolerate frequent, regular fire. The less regular fire pattern is more often associated with the presence of Douglas-fir or white fir. These latter species require more time for young trees to develop fire resistance. Spatial complexity of vegetation within forest stands has been linked to fire (Bonnickson and Stone 1982, Fites-Kaufman 1997, Knight 1997).

Diverse and variable species in both the tree and shrub layers resulted in variable fuel and fire patterns. For example, ponderosa pine fuels are more loosely packed than those of white fir, allowing the pine fuels to burn more readily (van Wagtendonk et al. 1998). High levels of contrasting fire environments, such as varying slope, aspect, elevation, and weather, as well as topographically controlled diurnal changes in fire behavior, overlap with variable fuel patterns to create fine-scale patterns of variation in forest density, height, tree sizes, and understory vegetation. With fire suppression, density and uniformity in structure and composition have increased. Across many sites in the mid-elevations of the central and southern Sierra Nevada, white fir and incense cedar have increased, shifting composition away from ponderosa pine and creating more uniformly dense forests (Vankat and Major 1978, Parsons and deBenedetti 1979, Minnich et al.1995, Bouldin 2000). Douglas-fir responds similarly in the northern Sierra Nevada (Fites-Kaufman 1997). At lower elevations, bordering the foothills, these shade-tolerant species are scarce or absent but ponderosa pine has increased in density (Parsons and deBenedetti 1979, Fites-Kaufman 1997). Similarly, at higher elevations, white fir dominates but with increased uniformity and density attributed to lack of fire (Parsons and deBenedetti 1979).

Historically, open or more variable forest structure occurred as a result of more frequent fire (Gruell 2001). Not only did fire favor different species with different return interval patterns, but also it affected forest structure by thinning the young trees, leaving a patchier or more open forest, and selectively retaining larger, fire-resistant trees (Bonnickson and Stone 1982, van Wagtendonk 1985). Exactly what the landscape was like overall and what proportion was low density are unknown. Early observers emphasized open, park-like pine-dominated forests (Muir 1895, Jepson 1921) but also noted dense patches (Sudworth 1900, Leiburg 1902). Gruell (2001) chronicled the ecological changes since 1849 through a series of repeat photographs. Portions of the landscape that exhibited more variable fires included north and east aspects and higher elevations. These areas had greater portions of the landscape with moderate to high cover forests, evidenced by the historic prevalence of shade-tolerant white fir and Douglas-fir (Fites-Kaufman 1997).

Questions remain concerning the intensity and severity of presettlement fires. All sites in the lower-montane zone experienced fire frequently enough to reduce fuel accumulations and vegetation density, and, as a result, these fires were primarily of low to moderate intensity and severity. Long-term evidence in giant sequoia suggests that high-severity fires occurred in small patches (Stephenson et al. 1991). Large patches of California black oak or chaparral persist, evidently the result of large, severe fires. Some patches may have originated or expanded during the last century of suppression (Vankat and Major 1978), but others were apparently from earlier fires (Leiburg 1902).

There is a lack of historical information on the size or distribution of high-severity fires in the lower-montane zone. It is likely that they occurred infrequently and were related to drought cycles, which would create larger areas of highly flammable vegetation. It is also possible that locations in the northern Sierra Nevada with high average annual rainfall (more than 203 cm [80 in] mean annual precipitation) and continuous fuels (conifer and tan oak) would have a higher proportion of high-severity fires (Fites-Kaufman 1997). Moister conditions and higher foliar water content reduce fire in many years but allow more fuels to accumulate. These locations also overlap with steep terrain. When the canyons are aligned with prevailing southwest winds, the likelihood of larger, severe fire increases.

Currently, most of the area burned does so with fires of high intensity and severity. The Sierra Nevada contains some of the most productive fire-prone areas in the western United States (Franklin and Agee 2003). The increased stand densities and reduced decomposition rates result in accumulated fuels (Kilgore 1973, Vankat and Major 1978, Agee et al. 2000). This increases the tendency for high-intensity and high-severity fire through both increased fuels and increased susceptibility of dense smaller vegetation. It is unknown if current fires are larger but the extent of high-severity fire has certainly increased (Skinner and Chang 1996).

Most fires occur between mid-summer and early fall. The fire season is longer in the southern portion of the Sierra Nevada because of drier conditions. Some fires have always occurred in the spring and early summer and occasionally in the winter. Historic fire patterns in lower-elevation and drier landscapes maintained open pine and California black oak woodlands with resprouting shrubs and perennial grasses and herbs. Suppression of fire in combination with harvest patterns has resulted in an increase in the density of these forests (Parsons and deBenedetti 1979) but not always in changes of pine dominance (Parsons and deBenedetti 1979, Fites-Kaufman 1997). At higher elevations, trees with greater shade tolerance and less fire-resistant seedlings such as white fir, Douglas-fir, and incense-cedar, have become established and form dense understories (Parsons and deBenedetti 1979, van Wagtendonk 1985, Vale 1987,). Lower light levels and possibly lack of fire have resulted in sparse shrub and herb presence. On more mesic north or east slopes at mid-elevations, white fir and Douglas-fir were historically present but have also increased in density (Fites-Kaufman 1997). High-elevation white fir–mixed conifer forests have often retained similar composition but increased in density (Parsons and deBennedetti 1979).

Historically, Sierra Nevada lower-montane forests were more heterogeneous with clumps or patches of shrubs present in varying amounts. Fire promoted a greater distribution of younger, more vigorous sprouting shrubs. Deer brush is able to persist in the forest through changes in density until fire or some other activity opens the overstory and heats the soil, stimulating germination or sprouting. Current low levels of fire have resulted in increasingly tall and decadent deer brush, slowly being shaded out under dense forest cover. Thick patches of mountain misery decrease ponderosa pine regeneration, precluding dense stands of pines from

FIGURE 12.6. Upper-montane forest. This stand is characterized by large red fir, western white pine, and Jeffrey pine in the overstory with an understory of prostrate and erect manzanita and California-lilac species. Fire is infrequent but can burn extensive areas.

developing. This has resulted in the maintenance of relatively open pine stands over mountain misery, even with fire suppression. Fire restoration in these settings has been achieved in only two applications in Yosemite National Park.

Upper-Montane Forest

The upper-montane forest is located just above the lower-montane forest and occurs on both sides of the crest of the Sierra Nevada. The forest ranges in elevation with latitude. On the west side of the crest, elevations are generally lower than on the east side, with the differences greater in the south than in the north (Potter 1998). The terrain is relatively moderate on the west side but drops precipitously on the east. The geology underlying this zone is primarily volcanic in the north and granitic in the south. Soils are weakly developed and are typically medium to coarse textured and often lack a clay zone (Potter 1998).

The climate of the upper-montane forest is moderate with warm summers and cold winters. Total annual precipitation, although less than that which occurs in the lower montane forest, is still relatively high with 65% to 90% falling as snow (Major 1988). Barbour et al. (1991) propose that the ecotone between the lower and upper-montane zones is determined by the winter-long snowpack. The upper-montane forest zone receives as many lightning strikes as might be expected by chance (van Wagtendonk 1991a). The average number of lightning strikes that occurred in the zone between 1985 and 2000 was 29.3 strikes yr^{-1} 100 km^{-2} (75.9 strikes yr^{-1} 100 mi^{-2}) (van Wagtendonk and Cayan 2007).

The vegetation of the upper-montane forest is characterized by the presence of California red fir (Potter 1998). Figure 12.6 shows a stand of California red fir and western white pine with a sparse understory of montane chaparral. Other alliances include western white pine, quaking aspen, western juniper, Jeffrey pine, and tufted hairgrass (Deschampsia cespitosa ssp. holciformus). Interspersed in the forests are wet meadows and stands of montane chaparral.

FIRE RESPONSES OF IMPORTANT SPECIES

Many upper-montane species have fire-resistant characteristics and respond favorably to fire (Table 12.8). Shrubs and hardwood trees typically sprout, whereas herbs and grasses either reseed or regrow quickly after fire. Conifers are protected from the heat from fire by thick bark layers.

The conifers in the upper-montane ecological zone vary in their resistance to fire. California red fir has thin bark when it is young, making it susceptible to fire. As California red fir matures, its bark becomes thicker and it is able to survive most fires (Kilgore 1971). Similarly, mature Jeffrey pines have thick bark, and a slightly thicker bark when young that allows them to survive low-intensity fires. Western white pine and western juniper are more susceptible to fire at a young age than California red fir or Jeffrey pine. The percentage of crown scorch that a species can sustain is also variable. Like ponderosa pine, up to 50% of the buds of a Jeffrey pine can be killed and it can still survive (Wagener 1961a). The other upper-montane conifers can sustain only 30% to 40% scorch (Kilgore 1971).

Quaking aspen is the primary hardwood species in the upper montane forest and occurs in small stands where moisture is available. It is a vigorous and a profuse sprouter after fire (DeByle 1985). It becomes increasingly resistant to fire as

TABLE 12.8
Fire-response types for important species in the upper-montane forest ecological zone

| Lifeform | Type of Fire Response | | | Species |
	Sprouting	Seeding	Individual	
Conifer	None	None	Resistant, killed	Red fir, Jeffrey pine, western white pine, western juniper
Hardwood	Fire stimulated	None	Resistant, top-killed	Quaking aspen
Shrub	Fire stimulated	Abundant seed production	Top-killed	Bush chinquapin, mountain whitethorn, huckleberry oak
	None	Fire stimulated	Killed	Whiteleaf manzanita, pinemat manzanita
Forb	Fire stimulated	None	Top-killed	Woolly mule's ears
	None	None	Top-killed	Corn lily
Grass	Fire stimulated	Off-site	Top-killed	Tufted hairgrass
	Tillers	Off-site	Top-killed	Western needlegrass

its diameter increases beyond 15 cm (6 in) (Brown and DeByle 1987).

Bush chinquapin, mountain whitehorn, and huckleberry oak (*Quercus vaccinifolia*) form extensive stands in the open and underneath conifers. They are all sprouters and are top-killed by fire (Biswell 1974, Conard et al.1985). Mountain whitethorn is also a relatively prolific seeder after fire. Pine-mat manzanita (*Arctostaphylos nevadensis*) and greenleaf manzanita are usually found in the understory. Although these non-sprouting manzanitas are killed by intense heat, they are able to reestablish by seed the first year after fire. Both species may be obligate seeders, requiring fire and/or charred wood leachate to break seed dormancy (Kruckeberg 1977).

Woolly mule's ears (*Wyethia mollis*) apparently resprouts after fire but the sprouting might not be fire dependent (Mueggler and Blaisdell 1951). The density of mule's ears has been noted to increase after fire (Young and Evans 1978). Corn lily (*Veratrum californicum*) grows in wet meadows and is not usually affected by fire. Based on its ability to resprout each year after being top-killed by frost, it is reasonable to assume that corn lily would sprout the year after being burned.

Western needlegrass (*Achnantherum occidentalis*) occurs in the understory of the conifer forests and is a tussock-forming grass that seeds into burns from off-site (Brown and Smith 2000). The above-ground biomass is consumed, and intense fires can kill the rootstock. Tufted hairgrass is one of many grass and sedge species common in wet meadows. Although it burns infrequently, tufted hairgrass generally survives all but the most intense fires and sprouts from the root crown, as do most sedges.

FIRE REGIME–PLANT COMMUNITY INTERACTIONS

Although the upper-montane forest receives a proportionally higher number of lightning strikes on a per area basis than the lower montane forest, fewer fires result (van Wagtendonk 1994). Lightning is often accompanied with rain, and the compact fuel beds are not easily ignited. Those fires that do occur are usually of low intensity and spread slowly through the landscape except under extreme weather conditions. Natural fuel breaks such as rock outcrops and moist meadows prevent extensive fires from occurring (Kilgore 1971).

California red fir fuel beds are among some of the heaviest and most compact found for conifers in the Sierra Nevada. Although duff weight was just above average, woody fuel weight was surpassed only by giant sequoia (van Wagtendonk et al. 1998). The bulk density of California red fir duff fuels was above average, and the fuel bed bulk density, including woody and litter fuels, was only exceeded by limber pine. Such dense fuels ignite and carry fire only under extremely dry and windy conditions.

Fire regimes tend to be more variable in frequency and severity than those in the lower montane forest (Table 12.9) (Skinner and Chang 1996). Median fire-return interval estimates from fire scars range from 12 to 69 years (Skinner and Chang 1996). Based on lightning fires that were allowed to burn under prescribed conditions in Yosemite National Park, van Wagtendonk (1995) calculated the fire rotation in California red fir to be 163 years. Occasional crown fires occur in California red fir stands, but normally fires spread slowly because of compact surface fuels and the prevalence of natural terrain breaks.

TABLE 12.9

Fire regime attributes for major vegetation types of the upper montane forest ecological zone

Vegetation type	Red fir	Jeffrey pine, western white pine, mountain juniper	Tufted hairgrass
Temporal			
Seasonality	Late summer–fall	Summer–fall	Late summer–fall
Fire-return interval	Medium	Medium	Long
Spatial			
Size	Medium	Truncated small	Small
Complexity	Multiple	Low	Low
Magnitude			
Intensity	Multiple	Low	Low
Severity	Multiple	Low	Low
Fire type	Multiple	Surface	Surface

NOTE: Fire regime terms used in this table are defined in Chapter 4.

At the higher elevations in the upper-montane zone, fire has an important role in the successional relationship between California red fir and lodgepole pine (Kilgore 1971). Fire creates canopy openings by killing mature lodgepole pine and some mature California red fir. Where lodgepole pine occurs under a California red fir canopy, it is eventually succeeded by California red fir. Pitcher (1987) concluded that fire was necessary for creating openings where young California red fir trees could get established. In areas where crown fires have burned through California red fir forests, montane chaparral species such as mountain whitethorn and bush chinquapin become established. Within a few years, however, California red fir and Jeffrey pine begin to overtop the chaparral.

Fires in Jeffrey pine, western juniper, and western white pine stands are usually moderate in intensity, burning through litter and duff or, if present, through huckleberry oak or greenleaf manzanita. Older trees survive these fires, although occasionally an intense fire may produce enough heat to kill an individual tree (Wagener 1961a). Fuel bed bulk density and woody fuels weights are comparable for the three species, but Jeffrey pine has three times as much litter and twice as much duff (van Wagtendonk et al. 1998). As a result, surface fires tend to be more intense in Jeffrey pine stands. Jeffrey pine will be replaced by huckleberry oak and greenleaf manzanita if fires of high severity occur frequently, or by California red fir if the period between fires is sufficiently long (Bock and Bock 1977). Western juniper is slow to return to burned areas and, like Jeffrey pine and western white pine, will seed in from adjacent stands.

Although quaking aspen stands in the Sierra Nevada usually burn only if a fire from adjacent vegetation occurs at a time when the stands are flammable, the decline of quaking aspen stands has been attributed to the absence of natural fire regimes (Lorentzen 2004). Quaking aspen stands burn in late summer when the herbaceous plants underneath the quaking aspens have dried sufficiently to carry fire. Because quaking aspen is a vigorous sprouter, it is able to recolonize burns immediately at the expense of non-sprouting conifers. Similarly, meadows consisting primarily of tufted hairgrass burn if fires in adjacent forests occur during the late summer. Occasional fires reduce encroachment into the meadows by conifers (deBennedetti and Parsons 1979).

Subalpine Forest

The subalpine forest lies between the upper-montane forest and the alpine meadows and shrublands. Extensive stands of subalpine forest occur on the west side of the Sierra Nevada and a thin band exists on the east side of the range. Like the upper-montane zone below, the terrain is moderate on the west side and steep on the east. Volcanic rocks are prevalent in the north and granitic rocks occur throughout the zone. Soils are poorly developed.

The climate of the subalpine forest is moderate with cool summers and extremely cold winters. Other than occasional thundershowers, precipitation falls as snow. The snow-free period is short, from mid June to late October. Lightning is pervasive in the subalpine forest with many more lightning strikes than might be expected by chance (van Wagtendonk 1991a). Between 1985 and 2000, the average number of strikes was 33.6 strikes yr^{-1} 100 k^{-2} (87.1 strikes yr^{-1} 100 mi^{-2}) (van Wagtendonk and Cayan 2007).

The vegetation of the subalpine forest is dominated by lodgepole pine (Fig. 12.7). As tree line is approached, lodgepole pine is replaced by mountain hemlock and whitebark pine. On the east side of the Sierra Nevada, limber pine

FIGURE 12.7. Subalpine forest. Lodgepole pine forms extensive stands in this zone. Fire is infrequent but when it occurs it burns from log to log or creeps through the sparse understory vegetation and litter.

occurs with whitebark pine, and in Sequoia National Park, foxtail pine is found at tree line. Extensive meadows of short-hair sedge *(Carex filifolia* var. *erostrata)* and Brewer's reedgrass *(Calamagrostis breweri)* are mixed within the forest.

FIRE RESPONSES OF IMPORTANT SPECIES

Subalpine trees are easily killed by fire at a young age but increase their resistance as they grow older (Table 12.10). Clements (1916) was one of the first ecologists to consider lodgepole pine to be a fire type. Its thin bark, flammable foliage, and serotinous cones all fit into the classical definition of a fire-adapted species. The cones of the Sierra Nevada subspecies, however, are not fully serotinous, open at maturity, and are dispersed over a two-year period (Lotan 1975). Parker (1986) concluded that fire was not necessary for the perpetuation of lodgepole pine, but fire-induced openings sup-

plemented those created by tree-falls. When surface fires occur in lodgepole pine forests, individual trees are killed (deBennedetti and Parsons 1984). Occasional crown fires can consume entire stands, which are quickly recolonized by released seed.

The combination of thin bark, flammable foliage, low-hanging branches, and growth in dense groups make mountain hemlocks susceptible to fire (Fischer and Bradley 1987). As the trees mature, the bark thickens giving them some protection. Whitebark pine survives fires because large refugia trees are scattered in areas of patchy fuels (Keane and Arno 2001). Clark's nutcrackers *(Nucifraga columbiana)* facilitate post-fire seedling establishment (Tomback 1986). Bark thickness is moderate and mature trees usually survive low- and sometimes moderate-intensity surface fires, whereas smaller trees do not. Limber pines also have moderately thin bark, and young trees often do not survive surface fires

TABLE 12.10
Fire response types for important species in the subalpine forest ecological zone

	Type of Fire Response			
Lifeform	Sprouting	Seeding	Individual	*Species*
Conifer	None	Fire stimulated	Killed	Lodgepole pine
	None	None	Resistant, killed	Mountain hemlock
	None	None	Resistant, killed	Whitebark pine, limber pine, foxtail pine
Grass	Fire stimulated	None	Top-killed	Brewer's reedgrass

TABLE 12.11

Fire regime attributes for vegetation types of the subalpine forest ecological zone

Vegetation type	Lodgepole pine	Mountain hemlock	Whitebark pine, limber pine, foxtail pine
Temporal			
Seasonality	Late summer–fall	Late summer–fall	Late summer–fall
Fire-return interval	Long	Long	Truncated long
Spatial			
Size	Small	Small	Small
Complexity	Low	Low	Low
Magnitude			
Intensity	Multiple	Low	Low
Severity	Multiple	Low	Low
Fire type	Multiple	Surface	Surface

NOTE: Fire regime terms used in this table are defined in Chapter 4.

(Keeley and Zedler 1998). Terminal buds are protected from the heat associated with crown scorch by the tight clusters of needles around them. Foxtail pine occurs where fuels to carry fires are practically nonexistent (Parsons 1981). The charred remains of trees struck by lightning are evidence that periodic fires do occur, although they seldom spread over large areas.

FIRE REGIME–PLANT COMMUNITY INTERACTIONS

Although lightning strikes are plentiful in the subalpine forest zone, ignitions are infrequent. Between 1930 and 1993, lightning caused only 341 fires in the zone in Yosemite National Park, (van Wagtendonk 1994). Those fires burned only 2,448 ha (5,953 ac), primarily in the lodgepole forest. During the period between 1972 and 1993 when lightning fires were allowed to burn under prescribed conditions, only six fires in lodgepole pine grew larger than 123 ha (300 ac).

Lodgepole pine fuel beds are relatively shallow and compact (van Wagtendonk et al. 1998). Often herbaceous plants occur in the understory, precluding fire spread except under extremely dry conditions. When fires do occur, encroaching California red firs and mountain hemlocks are replaced by the more prolific–seeding lodgepole pines. In areas where lodgepole pines have invaded meadows, fires will kill back the trees (deBennedetti and Parsons 1984). Stand-replacing fires are rare, but when they do occur, lodgepole pines become reestablished from the released seeds.

Keeley (1981) estimated the fire-return interval in lodgepole pine to be several hundred years. Data from fires that have burned in the wildland fire-use zone in Yosemite suggest a fire rotation of 579 years (van Wagtendonk 1995). Caprio (2002), however, found that prior to 1860, widespread fires were recorded in 1751, 1815, and 1846 in lodgepole pine stands in Sequoia National Park. In any case, fires are relatively rare and usually light to moderately severe. (Table 12.11)

Little information exists for the role of fire in mountain hemlock forests in the Sierra Nevada. In Montana, however, fires in the cool, wet mountain hemlock forests generally occur as infrequent, severe stand-replacing crown fires (Fischer and Bradley 1987). Fire-return intervals are estimated to be between 400 and 800 years (Habeck 1985). During the 28-year period prior to 1972, no fires burned in hemlock forests in the wildland fire-use zone of Yosemite National Park (van Wagtendonk et al. 2002). Litter and duff fuels of mountain hemlocks were some of the deepest, heaviest, and most compact of any Sierra Nevada conifer, indicating long periods between fires (van Wagtendonk et al. 1998). Mountain hemlock is replaced by lodgepole pine in areas where both are present before a fire. Seeding from adjacent areas is possible but can take several years to be successful.

Fire seldom burns in the pine stands that occur at tree line. There have been only 25 lightning fires in whitebark pine during the past 70 years in Yosemite (van Wagtendonk 1994). Only four of these fires grew larger than 0.1 ha (0.25 ac), and they burned a total of 4 ha (9 ac). Based on the area burned in the type, van Wagtendonk (1995) calculated a fire rotation of more than 23,000 years. Although no records exist showing fires in limber pine stands in the Sierra Nevada, it is reasonable to assume equally long fire-return intervals for that species as well. Scattered pockets of fuel beneath both whitebark pine and limber pine attest to the long period between fires. Limber pine recorded the heaviest litter and duff load of any Sierra Nevada conifer (van Wagtendonk et al. 1998). On the other hand, foxtail pine had hardly any fuel beneath it. Keifer (1991) found only occasional evidence of past fires in foxtail stands. She noted sporadic recruitment in those stands that did not appear to be related to fire and suggested that the thick bark on the mature trees protected them from low-intensity fires.

Little is known about fire in subalpine meadows. These meadows are sometimes ignited when adjacent forests are burning. Brewer's reedgrass can become re-established after fire from seeds and rhizomes. Meadow edges are maintained by fire as invading lodgepole pines are killed (deBenndetti and Parsons 1984, Vale 1987).

Alpine Meadow and Shrubland

The alpine meadow and shrubland zone consists of fell fields and willows along riparian areas. The short growing season produces little biomass and fuels are sparse. Lighting strikes occur regularly in the alpine zone but result in few fires (van Wagtendonk and Cayan 2007). The 16-year average number of strikes in the Sierra Nevada is 32.2 yr^{-1} 100 k^{-2} (83.5 strikes yr^{-1} 100 mi^{-2}). Weather, coincident with lightning, is usually not conducive to fire ignition or spread. Fires are so infrequent that they probably did not play a role in the evolutionary development of the plants that occur in the alpine zone. The 70-year record of lightning fires in Yosemite includes only eight fires, burning a total of 12 ha (28 ac), primarily in a single fire (van Wagtendonk 1994).

Eastside Forest and Woodland

The width of the eastside montane zone of the Sierra Nevada varies from north to south. In the north, the width of the zone is more than 12.5 km (20 mi), but to the south it quickly becomes less than 1 km (0.6 mi) due to the high elevation of the crest, increased importance of the rain shadow effect, and the sharp gradient from upper montane to Great Basin vegetation. In the northern Sierra Nevada, the eastside montane zone increases in width, as the crest of the Sierra Nevada becomes lower and less distinct. The area to the north and east of Lake Tahoe basin comprises large expanses of eastside forest and woodland vegetation. Some of the species, such as Jeffrey pine, are at the eastern edge of their distribution. Others, such as pinyon pine and sagebrush, are at their western edge of distribution (Fig. 12.8). Small climatic shifts may have resulted in dramatic shifts in vegetation, fire, and plant community–fire interactions. Lightning is common in the eastside zone with 28.9 strikes yr^{-1} 100 k^{-2} (74.8 strikes yr^{-1} 100 mi^{-2}) for the period between 1985 and 2000 (van Wagtendonk and Cayan 2007). Proportionally more lightning strikes occur in the northern part of the zone than in any other zone in the Sierra Nevada.

The vegetation of the eastside of the Sierra Nevada is often transitional between upper montane and lower-elevation Great Basin species. A variable, but often coarse-scale mosaic of open woodlands or forests and shrublands or grasslands, is characteristic. This is similar to the east side of the Cascades or northeastern California. The most prevalent tree-dominated types include Jeffrey pine or mixed Jeffrey and ponderosa pine woodlands, mixed white fir and pine forests, white fir, and quaking aspen groves. In some locations, particularly in the central and southern portions, pinyon pine occurs. Typically, westside species (i.e., Douglas-fir and black oak) occur in small amounts in the northern Sierra Nevada. The shrublands can be extensive and variable, ranging from typical Great Basin species of sagebrush (*Atemisia* spp.) and bitterbrush (*Purshia* spp.) to chaparral comprised of tobacco brush (*Ceanothus velutinus* var. *velutinus*), greenleaf manzanita, bearbrush (*Garrya fremontia*), and bush chinquapin. Curl-leaf mountain-mahogany (*Cercocarpus ledifolia*) occurs in patches on rocky and particularly dry sites. Riparian and wetland areas occur throughout, and, although this is the most xeric portion of the Sierra Nevada, meadows can be extensive. Quaking aspen, black cottonwood, and various willow species dominate the overstory of riparian communities of larger streams. Lodgepole pine is also common in riparian areas or localized areas with cold air drainage.

Because of the Sierra Nevada bioregion's similarities with the Northeastern Plateaus (Chapter 11) and Southern Cascades (Chapter 10) bioregions, the focus of this chapter is on the Jeffrey pine woodlands, mixed Jeffrey pine–white fir forests, and montane chaparral. Additional information on communities dominated by Great Basin or desert species

FIGURE 12.8. Eastside forest and woodland. This stand of Jeffrey pine and red fir was recently burned and shows evidence of manzanita mortality.

such as juniper, pine, and sagebrush or bitterbrush, can be found in the Northeastern Plateaus chapter (Chapter 11) and Southeastern Deserts chapter (Chapter 16).

FIRE RESPONSES OF IMPORTANT SPECIES

Some of the dominant species in this zone are also prevalent in the upper montane or adjacent lower montane zones and are only described as they co-occur in this zone. Species in this zone tend to be a mixture of those with fire-resistant or fire-enhanced characteristics and those that are fire inhibited (Table 12.12). Jeffrey pine has thick, fire-resistant bark; large, well-protected buds; and self-pruning that often results in high crowns. Pinyon pine is not very fire resistant, with crowns low to the ground; relatively thin bark; and a ten-

dency to have pitchy bark, branches, and foliage, making it flammable. In this zone, pinyon pine often occupies rocky sites with sparse vegetation and fuels that decrease the likelihood of frequent fire. Seeds of both ponderosa pine and lodgepole pine show a high tolerance to heat, showing germination over 50% after 5-minute exposures to heat as high as 930°C (200°F) (Wright 1931).

Shrub species vary from those that have enhanced sprouting or seed germination following fire to those that have little fire resistance. Greenleaf manzanita, bearbrush, bush chinquapin, and tobacco brush all sprout from basal burls following fire. Where branches are pressed against the soil from snow, layering results in sprouting; however, these sprouts can be more susceptible to fire mortality. Tobacco brush also has enhanced germination from fire.

TABLE 12.12
Fire response types for important species in the eastside forest and woodland ecological zone

| Lifeform | Type of Fire Response | | | Species |
	Sprouting	Seeding	Individual	
Conifer	None	None	Resistant, killed	Jeffrey pine, ponderosa pine
	None	None	Low resistance, killed	Pinyon pine
Hardwood	Fire stimulated	None	Top-killed	Quaking aspen, black cottonwood, willow
Shrub	Fire stimulated	None	Top-killed	Bush chinquapin, greenleaf manzanita, huckleberry oak, snowberry, willow, bitterbrush[a]
	Fire stimulated	Fire stimulated	Top-killed	Tobacco brush
	None	None	Killed	Sagebrush, bitterbrush[a]
Herb	Fire stimulated	None	Top-killed	Woolly mule's ears
	None	None		
Grass	Fire stimulated	None	Top-killed	Sedges
			Killed	Cheat grass

[a] Bitterbrush has a variable sprouting response to fire.

TABLE 12.13
Fire regime attributes for vegetation types of the eastside forest and woodland ecological zone

Vegetation type	Jeffrey pine, ponderosa pine	White fir and mixed conifer	Chaparral
Temporal			
Seasonality	Summer–fall	Summer–fall	Summer–fall
Fire-return interval	Short	Medium	Medium
Spatial			
Size	Small–Medium	Medium	Medium
Complexity	Multiple	Multiple	Low
Magnitude			
Intensity	Low	Multiple	High
Severity	Low	Multiple	High
Fire type	Surface	Multiple	Crown

NOTE: Fire regime terms used in this table are defined in Chapter 4.

FIRE REGIME–PLANT COMMUNITY INTERACTIONS

Only a few fire history studies have been conducted in the eastern montane zone. In an area east of the crest near Yosemite, Stephens (2001) found median fire-return intervals of 9 years for Jeffrey pine and 24 years for adjacent upper-montane forest consisting of California red fir, lodgepole pine, and western white pine. Taylor's (2004) work southeast of Lake Tahoe showed a mean fire return interval of 11.4 years for presettlement mixed Jeffrey pine and white fir stands. As recent, severe fires have burned on the lower slopes of the eastside forests, the boundary between forests and sagebrush has retreated up slope.

Fire regimes vary with both vegetation type and landscape location (Table 12.13). The most-frequent fires and lowest-intensity fires occurred in the lower elevation, open pine-dominated areas of this zone, with responses similar to that described in the Northeastern Plateaus (Chapter 11). On less productive or more southern portions, Jeffrey pine woodlands likely had a fire regime similar to those described for upper montane Jeffrey pine woodlands, with a range of intervals from 5 to 47 years (Taylor 2004). White fir forests occurred in a mosaic with chaparral on the more mesic sites on north slopes and at higher elevations. The fire regimes included a greater variety of severities, due, in part, to less-consistent fire intervals and patterns. The fire season was primarily from summer through fall, with longer seasons at lowest elevations in open pine forests.

The fire regime for the white fir–chaparral type apparently included some high-severity fires in the past (Russell et al. 1998), although the importance of settlement activities on contributing to these types of fires is unclear. The structure of white fir forests leads to higher crown-fire potential (Conard and Radosevich 1982). Branch retention, high stand densities, and low and uniform crowns are all common. Regeneration of white fir is continuous (Bock et al.1978, Conard and Radosevich 1982) until a fire occurs. Subsequently, portions of the forest are converted to chaparral dominated by sprouting greenleaf manzanita and both sprouting and heat-stimulated germination of tobacco brush (Conard and Radosevich 1982). The duration of this fire-generated chaparral can last for more than 50 years (Russell et al. 1998). The relative amounts of pine and white fir regeneration are affected by fire. Pine regeneration can increase from 25% in forests with no fire to greater than 93% in forests with fire (Bock and Bock 1969). Fire can also serve as a control over regeneration by limiting the density of white fire recruitment (Bock et al. 1976), but white fir can also regenerate well under the shade of chaparral (Conard and Radosevich 1982).

Management Issues

Private property owners, land managers, and the public in the Sierra Nevada face many issues as a result of changed fire regimes and population growth. Primary among the issues is the accumulation of fuels both on the ground and in tree canopies. Dealing with these fuels has become more complicated by increased urbanization, at-risk species, and air quality considerations.

Urbanization

The population of the Sierra Nevada more than doubled between 1970 and 1990 (Duane 1996). Much of this growth has occurred in the foothills of the Sierra Nevada. In particular, the central Sierra Nevada contains one of the largest areas of intermixed urban and wildlands in California. This creates changes in fire patterns and restricts restoration or fuels reduction. The relatively higher productivity chaparral of the Sierra Nevada foothills means that growth rates are higher and maintenance of fuel-reduction areas more frequent and costly. There

are two contrasting fire management conditions in the montane and eastern portions of the Sierra Nevada: one where communities are adjacent to and mixed with wildlands; the second where vast areas are undeveloped, often bordering higher-elevation wilderness. The former creates conditions in which intensive and frequent fuel-reduction treatments around communities are important because of the frequent occurrence of fire in this area. The latter is well suited for wildland fire use, a program that restores naturally occurring fires through less intensive and expensive means. The situation in the intermix areas has serious ramifications for fire management. Property owners demand that fire suppression forces protect their homes first, thus diverting them from protecting resources.

FIRE AND FUELS MANAGEMENT

Each new catastrophic fire increases the clamor to do something about fuels. Homeowners expect fire and land management agencies to act, yet are often unwilling to accept some of the responsibility themselves. The most immediate problem exists around developments and other areas of high societal values. Mechanical removal of understory trees followed by prescribed burning is the most likely treatment to succeed in these areas. Where houses have encroached into shrublands, removal of shrubs up to 30 m (100 ft) may be necessary. Less compelling are treatments in remote areas where there is less development and access is difficult. Prescribed burning and the use of naturally occurring fires are more appropriate in areas beyond the urban-wildland interface.

The call to thin forests to prevent catastrophic fires has confused the issue. As we have learned in Chapter 3, only in rare occasions can a fire move independently through the crowns of trees without a surface fire to feed it. Thinning forests to prevent crown fires without treating surface fuels is ecologically inappropriate and economically unjustifiable. A combination of treatments including understory thinning and prescribed fire will probably be most productive.

Species at Risk

Several species at risk occur in the Sierra Nevada, and many of these, including the Pacific fisher (*Martes pennanti pacifica*), American marten (*Martes americana*), and California spotted owl (*Strix occidentalis occidentalis*), evolved in fire-dependent or fire-maintained habitats. Concurrent changes in fire regimes and vegetation in the lower-elevation portions of the Sierra Nevada foothill and lower montane zones have resulted in region-wide changes in vegetation and wildlife habitats, including the stability of those habitats. Low-severity fire regimes made low-contrast changes to previous regional patterns of vegetation and habitat. Today, moderate- to high-severity fires produce high-contrast changes. These changes have implications for wildlife habitat that varies with vegetation. Habitat with denser forests was more distributed and less widespread. Currently, however, denser forests dominate but are punctuated with large, non-forest openings created by severe fires.

The question becomes how to restore natural fire regimes without adversely affecting at-risk species and their habitats. To do nothing only makes the situation worse, predisposing the species and habitats to destruction by catastrophic fire. These species evolved with fire and the answer must include fire. Care must be taken, however, to ensure that fragmented populations are not adversely affected by fire treatment activities.

Air Quality

One of the biggest impediments to conducting prescribed burns or using wildland fires to achieve resource benefits in the Sierra Nevada is restrictions on air quality. Smoke is a byproduct of burning, whether it comes from a prescribed fire, a wildland fire burning under prescribed conditions, or a wildfire. Catastrophic wildland fires produce extreme concentrations of smoke that exceed public health standards (see Chapter 21 for additional information). Society is faced with deciding to accept periodic episodes of low concentrations of smoke from managed fires or heavy doses from wildfires. Either reduced emission restrictions for wildland management activities or exemptions for federal agencies from the local air pollution control district regulations will be necessary if fire is to be allowed to play its natural role in the Sierra Nevada.

Research Needs

Skinner and Chang (1996) developed a comprehensive list of research needs during the Sierra Nevada Ecosystem Project. They identified six research topics, which we have grouped into three general areas: (1) spatial and temporal dynamics of fire, (2) presettlement forest conditions, and (3) effects of fire on ecosystem processes.

Spatial and Temporal Dynamics of Fire

Although much has already been learned about the dynamics of fire and Sierra Nevada ecosystems, several specific topics still need to be addressed. Fire history data are sparse through much of the Sierra Nevada. Isolated studies are the rule, although comprehensive data sets exist for the national parks and the area around Lake Tahoe. Complete fire histories would elucidate the spatial and temporal aspects of landscape-level fire interactions. Related studies on the spatial and temporal interactions of climate, vegetation, and fire are needed.

There is also a need for more information about the effects of frequent low- to moderate-severity fires on vegetation patterns. Most information available today is on low-severity prescribed fire or high-severity wildfires. Naturally occurring low- to moderate-intensity fires were probably the norm, and their ecological role is not well understood. Similarly, little is known about the interaction of fire with some of the other dynamic ecosystem processes, such as insect and fungi population fluctuations. These processes combine to affect fire behavior and subsequent fire effects and vegetation responses.

Presettlement Forest Conditions

Researchers have been uncertain about the vegetation conditions of the Sierra Nevada in presettlement times. Understanding those conditions and the factors that led to them gives insights into possible management targets and methods to reach those targets. Comparative photos have proven useful, but detailed re-measurement of historic vegetation surveys holds the greatest promise. Several of these surveys were conducted in the late 1800s and early 1900s in many parts of the Sierra Nevada and should prove productive if they can be relocated. Information derived from resurveys would give the best estimate of what have been called "old forest" or "late successional" conditions because the original surveys included the effects of naturally occurring ecological processes such as fire.

Effects of Fire on Ecosystem Properties

Although it will never be possible to know all of the effects of fire, investigators should continue to determine those effects of greatest importance to society and to ecosystem function. These include the effects of fire on coarse woody debris including logs and snags. The role fire plays in the dynamics of these structural habitat components is not well understood.

Smoke is another ecosystem process that warrants additional study. Some preliminary investigations have looked at the interactions of smoke with fungi and bacteria in forested ecosystems. Attempts need to be made to determine the presettlement air quality conditions for comparison to those now experienced with wildland fire use, suppressed wildland fires, and prescribed fires.

Summary

John Muir named the Sierra Nevada the Range of Light; an even better name might have been the Range of Fire. Fires have been a part of the Sierra Nevada for millennia and will continue to be so in the future. This chapter has looked at the factors that have contributed to make fire an important process in the ecological zones of the range and how fire has interacted with vegetation in each zone. The success of our management of the Sierra Nevada is contingent on our ability and willingness to keep fire an integral part of these ecosystems. To not do so is to doom ourselves to failure; fire is inevitable and we must try to manage only in harmony with fire.

References

Agee, J. K., B. Bahro, M. A. Finney, P. N. Omi, D. B. Sapsis, C. N. Skinner, J. W. van Wagtendonk, and C. P. Weatherspoon. 2000. The use of fuel breaks in landscape fire management. Forest Ecology and Management 127:55–66.

Anderson, M. K. 1996. The ethnobotany of deergrass, *Muhlenbergia rigens* (Poaceae): its uses and fire management by California Indian tribes. Econ. Bot. 50:409–422.

Anderson, M.K. 1999. The fire, pruning, and coppice management of temperate ecosystems for basketry material by California Indian tribes. Human Ecology 27:79–113.

Anderson, R.S. 1990. Holocene forest development and paleoclimates within central Sierra Nevada, California. J. Ecology 78:470–489.

Anderson, R.S. 1994. Paleohistory of a giant sequoia grove: the record from Log Meadow, Sequoia National Park. P. 49–55 in P.S. Aune (tech. coord.), Proceedings of symposium on giant sequoias: their place in ecosystem and society. USDA For. Serv. Gen. Tech. Rep. PSW-151. 170 p.

Anderson, R.S., and S.L. Carpenter. 1991. Vegetation changes in Yosemite Valley, Yosemite National Park, California, during the protohistoric period. Madrono 38:1–13.

Anderson, R.S., and S.J. Smith. 1997. The sedimentary record of fire in montane meadows, Sierra Nevada, California, USA: a preliminary assessment. P. 313–327 in J.S. Clark, H. Cachier, J. G. Goldammer, and B.J. Stocks (eds.), Sediment records of biomass burning and global change. NATO ASI Series 51.

Barbour, M.G., N.H. Berg, T.G.F. Kittel, and M. E. Kunz. 1991. Snowpack and the distribution of a major vegetation ecotone in the Sierra Nevada of California. Journal of Biogeography 18:141–149.

Biswell, H.H. 1959. Man and fire in ponderosa pine in the Sierra Nevada of California. Sierra Club. Bul. 44:44–53.

Biswell, H.H. 1961. The big trees and fire. National Parks Magazine 35:11–14.

Biswell, H.H. 1972. Fire ecology in ponderosa pine-grassland. Proceedings Tall Timbers Fire Ecology Conference 12:69–96.

Biswell, H.H. 1974. Effects of fire on chaparral. P. 321–364 in T.T. Kozlowski and C.E. Ahlgren (eds.), Fire and ecosystems. Academic Press, New York. 542 p.

Bock, C.E., and J.H. Bock. 1977. Patterns of post-fire succession on the Donner Ridge burn, Sierra Nevada. P. 464–469 in H.A. Mooney and C.E. Conrad (tech. coords.), Proceedings symposium, environmental consequences of fire and fuel management in mediterranean ecosystems. USDA, For. Serv. Gen. Tech. Rep. WO-3. 498 p.

Bock, J.H., and C.E. Bock. 1969. Natural reforestation in the northern Sierra Nevada-Donner Ridge burn. Proceedings Tall Timbers Fire Ecology Conference 9:119–126.

Bock, J.H., C.E. Bock, and V.M. Hawthorne. 1976. Further studies of natural reforestation in the Donner Ridge burn. Proceedings of the Annual Tall Timbers Fire Ecology Conference 14:195–200.

Bock, J.H., M. Raphael, and C.E. Bock. 1978. A comparison of planting and natural succession after a forest fire in the northern Sierra Nevada. Journal of Applied Ecology 15:597–602.

Bonnickson, T.M., and E.P. Stone. 1982. Reconstruction of a presettlement giant sequoia–mixed conifer forest community using the aggregation approach. Ecology: 63:1134–1168.

Bouldin, J.R. 2000. Twentieth century changes in forests of the Sierra Nevada, California. Unpub. PhD diss. University of California, Davis. 219 p.

Boyce, J.S. 1920. The dry rot of incense cedar. USDA Bul. 871. 58 p.

Brown, J.K., and N.V. DeByle. 1987. Fire damage, mortality, and suckering in aspen. Canadian Journal of Forest Research 17: 1100–1109.

Brown, J. K., and J.K. Smith. 2000. Wildland fire in ecosystems: effects of fire on flora. USDA For. Serv. Gen. Tech. Rep. RMRS-GTR-42-vol. 2. 257 p.

Caprio, A.C. 2002. Fire history of lodgepole pine on Chagoopa Plateau, Sequoia and Kings Canyon National Parks. P. 38 in Abstracts 2002 fire conference, managing fire and fuels in the remaining wildlands and open spaces of the southwestern United States. Association for Fire Ecology. 98 p.

Caprio, A.C., and T.W. Swetnam. 1995. Historic fire regimes along an elevational gradient on the western slope of the Sierra Nevada, California. P. 173–179 in J.K. Brown, R.W. Mutch, C. W. Spoon, and R. H. Wakimoto (tech. coords.), Proceedings symposium on fire in wilderness and park management. USDA Forest Service Gen. Tech. Rep. INT-GTR 320.

Christensen, N., L. Cotton, T. Harvey, R. Martin, J. McBride, P. Rundel, and R. Wakimoto. 1987. Review of fire management programs for sequoia–mixed conifer forests of Yosemite, Sequoia, and Kings Canyon national parks. Unpub. Report, National Park Service, Western Region, San Francisco.

Clements, F.E. 1916. Plant succession. Carnegie Inst. Washington Pub. 242. 512 p.

Conard, S.G., A.E. Jaramillo, K. Cromack, and S. Rose. 1985. The role of the genus *Ceanothus* in western forest ecosystems. USDA For. Serv. Gen. Tech. Rep. PNW-182. 72 p.

Conard, S.G., and S.R. Radosevich. 1982. Post-fire succession in white fir (*Abies concolor*) vegetation of the northern Sierra Nevada. Madrono 29:42–56.

deBennedetti, S.H., and D.J. Parsons. 1979. Natural fire in subalpine meadows: a case description from the Sierra Nevada. Journal of Forestry 77:477–479.

deBennedetti, S.H., and D.J. Parsons. 1984. Post-fire succession in a Sierran subalpine meadow. American Midland Naturalist 111:118–125.

DeBruin. H. W. 1974. From fire control to fire management: a major policy change in the Forest Service. Proceedings of the Tall Timbers Fire Ecology Conference 14:11–17.

DeByle, N.V. 1985. The role of fire in aspen ecology. In J. E. Lotan, B. M. Kilgore, W.C. Fischer, and R.W. Mutch (tech. coords), Proceedings—Symposium and workshop on wilderness fire. USDA For. Serv. Gen. Tech. Rep. INT-182. 326 p.

Duane, T.P. 1996. Human settlement, 1850–2040. In Sierra Nevada Ecosystem Project: Final report to Congress, Volume II, Chapter 11. University of California, Davis, Wildland Resources Center Rep. 37. 1528 p.

Fischer, W.C., and A.F. Bradley. 1987. Fire ecology of western Montana forest habitat types. USDA For. Serv.Gen. Tech. Rep. INT-223. 95 p.

Fites-Kaufman, J. 1997. Historic landscape pattern and process: fire, vegetation, and environment interactions in the northern Sierra Nevada. Unpub. PhD Dissertation, University of Washington. 175 p.

Fowells, 1979. Silvics of forest trees of the United States. USDA Agric. Handbook 271. 761 p.

Franklin, J.F., and J.K. Agee. 2003. Foraging a science-based national forest fire policy. Issues in Science and Tech. Fall 2003.

Gruell, G.E. 2001. Fire in Sierra Nevada forests: a photographic interpretation of ecological change since 1849. Mountain Press, Missoula, MT. 238 p.

Haase, S.M., and S.S. Sackett. 1998. Effects of prescribed fire in giant sequoia–mixed conifer stands in Sequoia and Kings Canyon National Parks. Proceedings Tall Timbers Fire Ecology Conference 20:236–243.

Habeck, J.R. 1985. Impact of fire suppression on forest succession and fuel accumulations in long-fire-interval wilderness habitat types. P. 110–118 in J. E. Lotan, B. M. Kilgore, W. C. Fischer, and R. W. Mutch (tech. coords.), Proceedings symposium and workshop on wilderness fire. USDA Forest. Serv. Gen. Tech. Rep. INT-182. 434 p.

Hartesveldt, R. J. 1962. Effects of human impact on *Sequoia gigantean* and its environment in the Mariposa Grove, Yosemite National Park, California. Unpub. PhD diss. University of Michigan, Ann Arbor. 310 p.

Hartesveldt, R. J. 1964. Fire ecology of the giant sequoias: controlled fire may be one solution to survival of the species. National History Magazine 73:12–19.

Hartesveldt, R. J., and H. T. Harvey. 1967. The fire ecology of sequoia regeneration. Proceedings of the Annual Tall Timbers Fire Ecology Conference 7:65–77.

Harvey, H. T., H. S. Shellhammer, and R. E. Stecker. 1980. Giant sequoia ecology. National Park Service Sci. Monog. 12. 182 p.

Heisey, R. M., C. C. Delwiche, R. A. Virginia, A. F. Wrona, and B. A. Bryan. 1980. A new nitrogen-fixing non-legume: *Chamaebatia foliolosa (Rosaceae)*. Amer. J. Botany 67(3):429–431.

Hill, M. 1975. Geology of the Sierra Nevada. University of California Press, Berkeley. 232 p.

Huber, N. K. 1987. The geologic story of Yosemite National Park. U. S. Geol. Surv. Bul. 1595. 64 p.

Hull, K. L., and M. J. Moratto. 1999. Archeological synthesis and research design, Yosemite National Park, California. Yosemite Research Center Publications in Anthropology No. 21. Yosemite National Park.

Hull, M. K., C. A. O'Dell, and M. K. Schroeder. 1966. Critical fire weather patterns—their frequency and levels of fire danger. USDA For. Serv. Pacific Southwest Forest and Range Expt. Sta., Berkeley. 40 p.

Jepson, W. L. 1921. The fire type of forest of the Sierra Nevada. The Intercollegiate Forestry Club Annual 1:7–10.

Kauffman, J. B., and R. E. Martin. 1990. Sprouting shrub response to different seasons and fuel consumption levels of prescribed fire in Sierra Nevada mixed conifer ecosystems. Forest Science 36:748–764.

Keane, R. E., and S. F. Arno. 2001. Restoration concepts and techniques. P. 367–400 in D. Tomback, S. F. Arno, and R. E. Keane (eds.), Whitebark pine communities: ecology and restoration. Island Press, Washington, DC. 328 p.

Keeley, J. E. 1981. Reproductive cycles and fire regimes. P. 231–277 in H. A. Mooney, T. M. Bonnicksen, N. L. Christensen, J. E. Lotan, and W. A. Reiners (tech. coords.), Proceedings—conference on fire regimes and ecosystem properties. USDA For. Serv. Gen. Tech. Rep. WO-26. 594 p.

Keeley, J. E., and P. H. Zedler. 1998. Evolution of life histories in *Pinus*. P. 219–250 in D. M. Richardson (ed.), Ecology and biogeography of *Pinus*. Cambridge University Press, Boston. 527 p.

Keifer, M. B. 1991. Age structure and fire disturbance in southern Sierra Nevada subalpine forests. Unpub. MS Thesis, University of Arizona. 111 p.

Kilgore, B. M. 1971. The role of fire in managing red fir forests. Transactions North American wildlife and natural resources conference 36:405–416.

Kilgore, B. M. 1972. Fire's role in a sequoia forest. Naturalist 23:26–37.

Kilgore, B. M. 1973. The ecological role of fire in Sierran conifer forests: its application to national park management. Quartnary Research 3:496–513.

Kilgore, B. M., and H. H. Biswell. 1971. Seedling germination after prescribed fire. California Agriculture 25:163–169.

Kilgore, B. M., and G. M. Briggs. 1972. Restoring fire to high elevation forests in California. Journal of Forestry 70:266–271.

Kilgore, B. M., and D. Taylor. 1979. Fire history of a sequoia mixed-conifer forest. Ecology 60:129–142.

Knight, R. 1997. A spatial analysis of a Sierra Nevada old-growth mixed-conifer forest. Masters Thesis, University of Washington. 84 p.

Kruckeberg, A. R. 1977. Manzanita (*Arctostaphylos*) hybrids in the Pacific Northwest: effects of human and natural disturbance. Systematic Botany 2:233–250.

Lawrence, G. E. 1966. Ecology of vertebrate animals in relation to chaparral fire in the Sierra Nevada foothills. Ecol. 47:278–291.

Leiburg, J. B. 1902. Forest conditions in the northern Sierra Nevada, California. USGS Prof. Pap. 8. U.S. Government Printing Office, Washington, DC. 194 p.

Lorentzen, E. 2004. Aspen delineation project. Bureau of Land Manage., California State Office, Resource Note 72. 2 p.

Lotan, J. E. 1975. Cone serotiny—fire relationships in lodgepole pine. Proceedings Tall Timbers Fire Ecology Conference 14:267–278.

Major, J. 1988. California climate in relation to elevation. P. 11–74 in M. C. Barbour and J. Major. Terrestrial vegetation of California. Wiley-Interscience, New York. 1002 p.

McDonald, P. M. 1981. Adapatations of woody shrubs. P. 21–29 in S. D. Hobbs and O. T. Helgerson (eds.), Reforestation of skeletal soils: proceedings of a workshop. Oregon State University, Forest Research Laboratory.

McKelvey, K. S., and K. L. Busse. 1996. Twentieth century fire patterns on Forest Service lands. In Sierra Nevada Ecosystem Project: Final report to Congress, Volume II, Chapter 41. University California, Davis, Wildland Resources Center Rep. 37. 1528 p.

Minnich, R. A., M. G. Barbour, J. H. Burk, and R. F. Fernau. 1995. Sixty years of change in California conifer forests of the San Bernadino Mountains. Conservation Biology 9:902–914.

Miles, S. R., and C. B. Goudy (comps.). 1997. Ecological subregions of California. USDA For. Serv. RM-EM-TP-005. 216 p.

Muir, J. 1895. Thoughts upon national parks. P. 350–354 in L. M. Wolfe (ed.), 1979. John of the mountains: the unpublished journals of John Muir. University of Wisconsin Press, Madison. 459 p.

Mueggler, W. F., and J. P. Blaisdell. 1951. Replacing wyethia with desirable forage species. Journal of Range Management 4: 143–150.

Parker, Albert J. 1986. Persistence of lodgepole pine forests in the central Sierra Nevada. Ecology 67:1560–1567.

Parsons, D. J. 1978. Fire and fuel accumulation in a giant sequoia forest. Journal of Forestry 76:104–105.

Parsons, D. J. 1981. The role of fire management in maintaining natural ecosystems. 1981 P. 469–488 in H. A. Mooney, T. M. Bonnicksen, N. L. Christensen, J. E. Lotan, and W. A. Reiners (tech. coords.), Proceedings conference fire regimes and ecosystem properties. USDA For. Serv. Gen. Tech. Rep. WO-26. 594.

Parsons, D. J. 1994. Objects or ecosystems: giant sequoia management in national parks. P. 109–115 in P. S. Aune (tech. coord.), Proceedings—symposium on giant sequoias: their place in ecosystem and society. USDA For. Serv. Gen. Tech. Rep. PSW-151. 170 p.

Parsons, D.J., and S.H. deBennedetti. 1979. Impact of fire suppression on a mixed-conifer forest. Forest Ecology and Management 2:21–33.

Payson, T.E., and M.G. Narog. 1993. Tree mortality 6 years after burning a thinned *Quercus chrysolepis* stand. Canadian Journal of Forest Research 23:2236–2241.

Piirto, D.D. 1994. Giant sequoia insect dsease, and ecosystem interactions. P. 82–89 in P.S. Aune (tech. coord.), Proceedings—symposium on giant sequoias: their place in ecosystem and society. USDA For. Serv. Gen. Tech. Rep. PSW-151. 170 p.

Pitcher, D.C. 1987. Fire history and age structure of red fir forests of Sequoia National Park, California. Canadian Journal of Forest Research 17:582–587.

Plumb, T.R. 1980. Response of oaks to fire. P. 202–215 in T.R. Plumb (tech. coord.), Proceedings of symposium on ecological management and utilization of California Oaks. USDA Forest Service, PSW-GTR-44: 202–215. 368 p.

Potter, D.A. 1998. Forested communities of the upper montane in the central and southern Sierra Nevada. USDA For. Serv. Gen. Tech. Rep. PSW-169. 319 p.

Rundel, P.W., G.A. Baker, and D.J. Parsons. 1981. Productivity and nutritional response of *Chamaebatia foliolosa (Rosaceae)* to seasonal burning. P. 191–196 in N.S. Margaris and H.A. Mooney (eds.), Components of productivity of mediterranean-climate regions. Dr. W. Junk, The Hague, Netherlands. 279 p.

Rundel, P.W., and D.J. Parsons. 1979. Structural changes in chamise *(Adenostoma fasciculatum)* along a fire-induced age gradient. J. Range Manage. 32:462–466.

Russell, W.H., J. McBride, and R. Rowntree. 1998. Revegetation after four stand-replacing fires in the Lake Tahoe Basin. Madrono 45:40–46.

St. John, T.V., and P.W. Rundel. 1976. The role of fire as a mineralizing agent in a Sierran coniferous forest. Oecologia 25:35–45.

Schweickert, R.A. 1981. Tectonic evolution of the Sierra Nevada range. P. 87–131 in W.G. Ernst (ed.), The geotectonic development of California, Rubey Vol 1. Prentice-Hall, Englewood Cliffs, NJ. 706 p.

Show, S.B., and E.I. Kotok. 1923. Forest fires in California. USDS Cir 243. 80 p.

Skinner, C.N., and C. Chang. 1996. Fire regimes, past and present. In: Sierra Nevada Ecosystem Project: Final report to Congress, Volume II, Chapter 38. University of California, Davis, Wildland Resources Center Rep. 37. 1528 p.

Smith, S.J., and R.S. Anderson. 1992. Late Wisconsin paleoecologic record from Swamp Lake, Yosemite National Park, California. Quaternary Research 38:91–102.

Stephens, S.L. 2001. Fire history of adjacent Jeffrey pine and upper Montane forests in the eastern Sierra Nevada. International Journal of Wildland Fire 10:161–167.

Stephens, S.L., F.A. Finney, and H. Schantz, H. 2004. Bulk density and fuel loads of ponderosa pine and white fir forest floors: impacts of leaf morphology. Northwest Science 78:93–100.

Stephenson, N.L.1994. Long-term dynamics of giant sequoia populations: implications for managing a pioneer species. P. 56–63 in P.S. Aune (tech. coord.), Proceedings symposium on giant sequoias: their place in ecosystem and society. USDA For. Serv. Gen. Tech. Rep. PSW-151. 170 p.

Stephenson, N.L. 1998. Actual evapotranspiration and deficit: biologically meaningful correlates of vegetation distribution across spatial scales. Journal of Biogeography 25: 855–870.

Stephenson, N.L. 1999. Reference conditions for giant sequoia forest restoration: structure, process and precision. Ecol. Appl. 9:1253–1265.

Stephenson, N.L., D.J. Parsons, and T.W. Swetnam. 1991. Restoring natural fire to the sequoia–mixed conifer forest: should intense fire play a role? Proceedings Tall Timbers Fire Ecology Conference 17:321–337.

Sudworth, G.B. 1900. Stanislaus and Lake Tahoe Forest Reserves, California, and adjacent territory. In annual reports of the Department of Interior, 21st annual report of the U.S. Geological Survey, part 5, 505–561.

Sudworth, G.B. 1908. Forest trees of the Pacific Slope. USDA Government Printing Office, Washington, DC. 441 p.

Swetnam, T.W. 1993. Fire history and climate change in giant sequoia groves. Science 262:885–889.

Tappeiner, J.C., T.B. Harrington, and J.D. Walstad.1984. Predicting recovery of tanoak *(Lithocarpus densiflorus)* and pacific madrone *(Arbutus menziesii)* after cutting or burning. Weed Science 32:413–417.

Taylor, A.H. 2004. Identifying forest reference conditions on early cut-over lands, Lake Tahoe basin, USA. Ecological Applications 14(6): 1903–1920.

Tomback, D.F. 1986. Post-fire regeneration of krummholz whitebark pine: a consequence of nutcracker seed caching. Madrono 33:100–110.

Vale, T.R. 1987. Vegetation change and park purposes in the high elevations of Yosemite National Park. Annals of the Assoc. American Geographer 77:1–18.

Vale, T.R. 2002. Fire, native peoples, and the natural landscape. Island Press, Washington, DC. 238 p.

Vankat, J.L. 1985. General patterns of lightning ignitions in Sequoia National Park, California. P. 408–411 in J.E. Lotan, B.M. Kilgore, W.C. Fischer, and R.W. Mutch (tech. coords.), Proceedings—symposium and workshop on wilderness fire. USDA For. Serv. Gen. Tech. Rep. INT-182. 434 p.

Vankat, J.L., and J. Major. 1987. Vegetation changes in Sequoia National Park. Journal of Biogeography 5:377–402.

van Wagtendonk, J.W. 1985. Fire suppression effects on fuels and succession in short-fire-return interval wilderness ecosystems. P. 119–126 in J.E. Lotan, B.M. Kilgore, W.C. Fischer, and R.W. Mutch (tech. coords.), Proceedings—symposium and workshop on wilderness fire. USDA Forest. Serv. Gen. Tech. Rep. INT-182. 434 p.

van Wagtendonk, J.W. 1986. The role of fire in the Yosemite Wilderness. P. 2–9 in Proceedings national wilderness research conference: currentresearch USDA For. Serv. Gen. Tech. Rep. INT-212. 553 p.

van Wagtendonk, J.W. 1991a. Spatial analysis of lightning strikes in Yosemite National Park. Proceedings 11th conference on fire and forest meteorology 11:605–611.

van Wagtendonk, J.W. 1991b. The evolution of National Park Service fire policy. Fire Management Notes 52:10–15.

van Wagtendonk, J.W. 1994. Spatial patterns of lightning strikes and fires in Yosemite National Park. Proceedings 12th conference on fire and forest meteorology 12:223–231.

van Wagtendonk, J.W. 1995. Large fires in wilderness areas. P. 113–116 in J.K. Brown, R.W. Mutch, C.W. Spoon, and R.H.

Wakimoto (tech. coords.), Proceedings—symposium on fire in wilderness and park management. USDA Forest Service Gen. Tech. Rep. INT-GTR 320. 283 p.

van Wagtendonk, J. W., J. M. Benedict, and W. M. Sydoriak. 1998. Fuel bed characteristics of Sierra Nevada conifers. Western Journal of Applied Forestry 13:73–84.

van Wagtendonk, J. W., and D. Cayan. 2007. Temporal and spatial distribution of lightning strikes in California in relationship to large-scale weather patterns. Fire Ecology (in Press).

van Wagtendonk, J. W., K. A. van Wagtendonk, J. B. Meyer, and K. J. Paintner. 2002. The use of geographic information for fire management planning in Yosemite National Park. The George Wright Forum 19(1): 19–39.

Wagener, W. W. 1961a. Guidelines for estimating the survival of fire-damaged trees in California. Misc. Paper 60. Berkeley, CA: USDA, For. Serv. Pacific Southwest Forest and Range Exp. Sta. Misc. Pap. 60. 11 p.

Wagener, W. W. 1961b. Past fire incidence in Sierra Nevada forests. Journal of Forestry 59:739–748.

Weatherspoon, C. P. 1986. Silvics of giant sequoia. P. 4–10 in C. P. Weatherspooon, Y. R. Iwamoto, and D. Piirto (tech. coords.), Proceedings of the workshop on management of giant sequoia, Reedly, California. USDA Forest Service, PSW Research Station PSW-GTR-9. 170 p.

Wright, E. 1931. The effect of high temperatures on seed germination. Journal of Forestry 29:679–687.

York, D. 1997. A fire ecology study of a Sierra Nevada foothill basaltic mesa grassland. Madrono 44:374–383.

Young, J. A., R. A. Evans. 1978. Population dynamics after wildfires in sagebrush grasslands. Journal of Range Management 31:283–289.

CHAPTER 13

Central Valley Bioregion

ROBIN WILLS

> When I first saw this central garden, the most extensive and
> regular of all the bee-pastures of the state, it seemed all
> one sheet of plant gold, hazy and vanishing in the distance,
> distinct as a new map along the foothills at my feet.
>
> JOHN MUIR, 1894

Description of Bioregion

The Central Valley creates one of the most important defining physical features of the California landscape. Lying between the Sierra Nevada and the Coast Ranges, this massive valley is nearly 800 km (500 mi) long and up to 120 km (75 mi) across (Map 13.1). More than 15% of the state's total area is included within its boundaries. Although still one of the most spectacular elements of California's geography, this bioregion is among the state's most highly impacted. A long history of significant alteration has resulted in a landscape with little resemblance to its presettlement past. The valley once supported a diverse array of prairies, oak (*Quercus* spp.) savannas, semi-arid grasslands, freshwater marshes, and riparian woodlands. From its earliest periods of human occupation until today, the Central Valley has supported large and diverse populations of people, plants, and animals. These assemblages thrived in the context of complex vegetation patterns and dynamic ecological processes.

Physical Geography

The Central Valley is most appropriately described as two valleys lying end to end. Each is drained by a major river, which also provides the valleys with their respective names. The Sacramento Valley lies north of San Francisco Bay and is drained by the Sacramento River. South of the Bay lies the San Joaquin Valley and its associated San Joaquin River. These two rivers find their confluence at the Sacramento–San Joaquin Delta. The bay-delta formed a massive 1900-km^2 (1180 m^2) wetland that, today, is one of California's most important agricultural centers. Complex irrigation projects, moving water throughout the valley, have converted the arid Southern San Joaquin into one of the world's most productive agricultural sites.

The analogy comparing California's Central Valley to a bath tub is supported by the elevation gradient found along the valley floor. Much of the Central Valley occurs at an elevation approximating sea level. At both its northern and southern ends, elevations rise to near 120 m (400 ft). At the valley's center, east of San Francisco bay, elevations below sea level are recorded. Consequently, river systems in this portion of the Valley are still tidally influenced.

A description of this bioregion's precise boundary can be complex. Ecotones between valley and foothill vegetation types occur in an irregular pattern. Elevation indicators are also confusing. Vegetation types are associated with a series of terraces, which vary on the eastern and western sides of the Valley. Additionally, a number of low-lying valleys in the Coast Ranges and Sierra Nevada foothills are dominated by biological communities that are typically associated with the Central Valley. One useful boundary description defines the Great Central Valley where alluvial soils grade into bedrock features and the landscape becomes dominated by foothill woodland (Schoenherr 1992).

The character of the valley has been changed most significantly through alteration in the pattern, frequency, and magnitude of flood events. As a result of intensive land use, fundamental changes have occurred in the valley's hydrology. Flooding was possibly the most important natural process affecting the valley's vegetation. Today, flood control structures dominate nearly every river draining the Sierra Nevada. Structures control the extent, magnitude, and intensity of flood events and in most cases have confined flow to a narrow portion of the original flood plain. The volume of water available to valley ecosystems has also been greatly reduced. Three massive lakes formally occurred in the southern San Joaquin. Tule, Buena Vista, and Kern lakes have all been eliminated from the valley landscape. The shores of these lakes once supported expansive fresh water marsh systems, providing critical habitat to an impressive array of resident and migratory species. These lake shores also concentrated a large portion of the valley's early human occupants.

Geologists have often described the Great Central Valley as a large trough of mud. Indeed the basin has been a repository of sediments during the last 145 million years of geologic activity. Deep sedimentary soils characterize this landscape, with a seemly endless input of alluvial material from the surrounding mountains. Sand and gravel deposits more than 9,000 m (30,000 ft) deep currently cover parent material, angling westward from the slopes of the Sierra Nevada. Following that alignment the deepest sediment layers occur near the eastern edge of the coast range. Here too, a thrust fault zone parallels the western edge of the valley. The underlying basement rocks are a continuation of the landform that makes up the Sierra Nevada. The long, slow processes that resulted in the valley's formation have left much of the underlying rock materials relatively unbroken.

Climatic Patterns

Climate in the Central Valley varies significantly in a north to south gradient. Temperature and rainfall patterns promote herbaceous vegetation types throughout the valley landscape, with moderately wet winters and hot dry summers (Table 13.1). Precipitation is generally limited to winter months, although summer rainfall can occur in the northern Sacramento Valley. The north Sacramento Valley receives a moderate amount of annual precipitation, while the San Joaquin Valley can experience rainfall levels similar to desert climates.

Relative humidity can vary tremendously across the Sacramento and San Joaquin Valleys. During the warm season, humidity is characteristically low. Under the influence of the north winds, humidity readings may drop to below 10%. Surrounding the bay-delta, a strong inflow of marine air during the summer creates a transition zone between the high humidity of the coast and the low readings of the valley. Winter values are usually moderate to high across the Central Valley.

The location of the Central Valley and its influence on weather systems can have significant effects on the surrounding bioregions (Map 13.2). Cold air draining from the surrounding mountains collects in the deep basin of the Central Valley. As temperatures drop at higher elevations, downslope flows pour cold air into the valley, filling it to the crest of the coast range. This dense pool of cold air can be impenetrable to wind and persist for days. The resulting temperature inversion produces dense, ground-hugging fog, known locally as *tule fog* during the winter. During summer and early fall months, inversion layers often burn off quickly and photochemical smog can become a significant problem.

FIRE CLIMATE VARIABLES

The tightly arranged topography of the Central Valley strongly influences important fire climate variables. The Coast Range and Sierra Nevada provide a fairly consistent boundary of high mountains surrounding the valley. This limits the chance for offshore air flow and the development of foehn style winds (Mitchell 1969). Prevailing summer winds are southwestern and tend to increase in speed during daylight hours. Synoptic-scale winds do occur and become more common in fall months (Schroeder and Buck 1970). These winds, resulting from the combination of a Great Basin high-pressure cell and Pacific Coast low-pressure trough, come from the north and may be of considerable strength.

The persistent pattern of Central Valley temperature inversions has implications for behavior on free-burning wildfires. Thermal belts may occur above the dense layer of cold air pooled in the valley bottom. Fire burning out of the valley or slowly backing downslope may encounter these bands of drier fuels, higher temperatures, and lower relative humidity. A resulting increase in fire spread, during early and mid morning hours, may significantly contribute to fire size.

Lightning occurs at an extremely low density in the valley with only 3.9 strikes yr^{-1} 100 km^{-2} (35.8 strikes yr^{-1} 100 mi^{-2}). Thunderstorms may occur in California at any time of the year, and over the Central Valley there appears to be no definite season. When they do occur these storms are generally light with few positive downstrikes. Although it is true that lightning strikes on the valley floor may have contributed little to presettlement fire regimes, numerous fires from the surrounding mountains may have eventually spread downslope into these lower-elevation plant communities. Storms generating lightning in surrounding bioregions are generally limited to late-summer months.

WEATHER SYSTEMS

Central Valley storms develop as areas of low pressure in the north Pacific. Prevailing northwesterly winds track these storm cells down the California coast. The position of the Pacific high will determine how far south the storms will travel. Spinning counterclockwise, these systems continue to pull moisture from the ocean while dumping rainfall on the land. A gradient of increasing land temperatures and air pressure results in significantly more rainfall occurring in northern than in southern California. As summer approaches and strong high-pressure systems develop over southern California, storms are deflected toward the Pacific Northwest.

Ecological Zones

The Central Valley exhibits distinct and neatly arranged ecological zones. Variations in topography, soils, water availability, and climate define the pattern of plant occurrence. With the large number of mountain-draining river systems entering the valley from both the Sierra Nevada and the Coast Range, the vegetation is often partitioned into discrete blocks. Still, a clear pattern of vegetation types can be described for the San Joaquin and portions of the

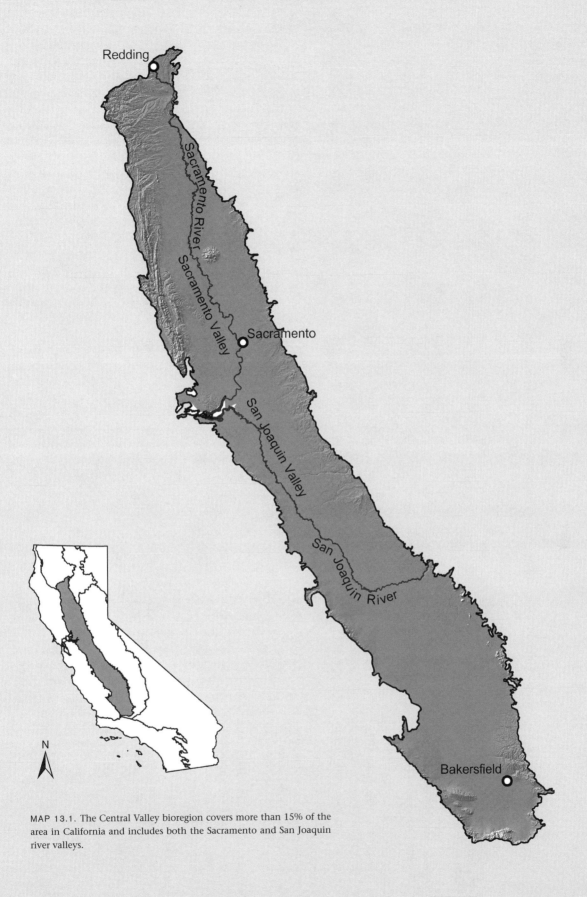

MAP 13.1. The Central Valley bioregion covers more than 15% of the area in California and includes both the Sacramento and San Joaquin river valleys.

TABLE 13.1

Average minimum and maximum temperature and average total precipitation for representative weather stations in the Central Valley

	Jan	Feb	Mar	Apr	May	Jun	Jul	Aug	Sep	Oct	Nov	Dec	Annual
Redding, 1/11/1931 to 4/30/1979													
Average Max. Temperature (°F)	54.9	59.7	65.2	72.5	81.7	90.2	98.4	96.4	90.7	78.7	64.6	55.7	75.7
Average Min. Temperature (°F)	37.4	40.5	43.3	47.9	54.9	62.3	68.1	65.9	61.3	53.2	44.4	38.8	51.5
Average Total Precipitation (in.)	7.96	5.89	5.00	2.99	1.48	0.97	0.16	0.31	0.78	2.19	4.69	6.95	39.37
Chico, 1/08/1906 to 3/31/2003													
Average Max. Temperature (°F)	53.9	60.2	65.6	72.8	81.2	89.7	96.4	94.8	89.5	78.6	64.9	54.9	75.2
Average Min. Temperature (°F)	35.6	38.6	40.9	44.6	50.5	56.4	60.3	58.0	54.2	47.1	40.1	35.9	46.8
Average Total Precipitation (in.)	5.32	4.45	3.50	1.86	0.97	0.47	0.02	0.09	0.48	1.36	2.95	4.41	25.87
Sacramento, 1/01/1941 to 3/31/2003													
Average Max. Temperature (°F)	53.2	59.8	64.5	71.6	80.0	87.2	92.7	91.5	87.6	77.9	63.6	53.6	73.6
Average Min. Temperature (°F)	37.8	41.0	43.0	45.9	50.6	55.2	58.0	57.7	55.8	50.2	42.7	38.1	48.0
Average Total Precipitation (in.)	3.68	3.08	2.38	1.11	0.48	0.16	0.03	0.06	0.29	0.88	2.14	2.90	17.18
Hanford, 12/1/1927 to 3/31/2003													
Average Max. Temperature (°F)	54.5	61.6	67.6	75.4	83.8	91.1	97.4	95.7	90.1	80.5	66.3	55.2	76.6
Average Min. Temperature (°F)	35.5	38.7	42.3	46.6	52.6	58.2	62.4	60.5	55.7	47.8	38.7	34.9	47.8
Average Total Precipitation (in.)	1.54	1.53	1.45	0.72	0.23	0.08	0.01	0.01	0.14	0.36	0.83	1.24	8.14
Bakersfield, 10/1/1937 to 3/31/2003													
Average Max. Temperature (°F)	57.4	63.6	68.8	75.9	84.2	92.2	98.6	96.7	90.9	80.7	67.4	57.7	77.8
Average Min. Temperature (°F)	38.4	42.1	45.3	49.8	56.5	63.1	68.9	67.5	62.8	53.9	44.0	38.3	52.5
Average Total Precipitation (in.)	1.06	1.17	1.15	0.65	0.21	0.08	0.01	0.04	0.11	0.29	0.63	0.78	6.19

MAP 13.2. The relationship of the Central Valley to surrounding bioregions has strongly affected weather and possibly the pattern of fire occurrence.

Sacramento Valley (Fig. 13.1). Although vegetation has certainly changed in response to human disturbance and annual variations in precipitation, it seems reasonable to assume that no major shifts in plant formations have occurred in the Central Valley during the last 6,000 years (Webb 1988).

An analysis of prehistory data indicates a valley dominated by vegetation significantly different from that seen by early Europeans. Several researchers have suggested that the area surrounding Tule Lake was Great Basin–like during the last Pleistocene and early Holocene (Adams 1985, Davis 1990). Still, the associated faunal record for the same period is dominated by large grazing herbivores like bison, horses, mammoths, and ground sloths. The presence of these species has been interpreted as evidence for large grasslands dominating this portion of the valley (Fenenga 1991). Fenenga

(1994) has suggested some portion of both these models may hold true. The Tulare Lake Basin was likely a mosaic of plant communities, with shrublands containing a significant cover of perennial grasses.

The pattern of vegetation does differ between the two valleys. Throughout its history, the Sacramento Valley has maintained some connection to coastal influences via the San Francisco bay-delta. The smaller spatial scale, higher latitude, and moderating marine influence have resulted in more plant communities dominated by woody species. Grassland remnants also support the hypothesis that perennial grasses may have been more prevalent in this portion of the Central Valley.

With its large expanse and strong continental influence the San Joaquin represents a more xeric landscape. Grasslands in this portion of the valley were likely dominated by annual vegetation and exhibited less structural diversity.

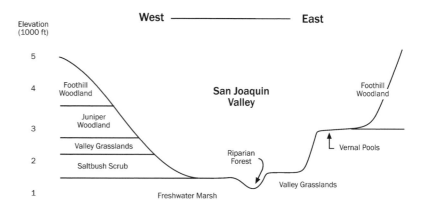

West —————————— East

Elevation
(1000 ft)

5

4 Foothill   San Joaquin   Foothill
   Woodland   Valley   Woodland

   Juniper
3 Woodland

   Valley Grasslands   Vernal Pools

2 Saltbush Scrub   Riparian
                                          Forest
                                                          Valley Grasslands
1   Freshwater Marsh

FIGURE 13.1. Vegetation in the Central Valley is neatly organized along elevation and directional gradients.

Saltbrush *(Atriplex* spp.*)* scrub communities were once common in the southern San Joaquin. Juniper *(Juniperus* spp.*)* woodlands were also a significant component of the western valley foothills.

Although tremendous amounts of diversity can be described within these generalized vegetation communities, four primary ecological zones dominated the presettlement Central Valley. Freshwater marsh, valley grasslands, foothill woodlands, and riparian forests were arranged in a mosaic most strongly influenced by moisture and elevation gradients. An array of grassland and vernal pool assemblages was thought to be the most abundant valley vegetation, covering more than 9 million ha (22 million ac). Freshwater marshes, fed by a combination of winter precipitation and spring runoff may have occupied nearly 1.6 million ha (4 million ac). Long linear riparian woodlands patterned the length of the valley, covering more than 400,000 ha (1 million ac) in the early 1800s. In all cases, these once-expansive vegetation types now exist in less than 10% of their former range.

This strong patterning of distinctly different vegetation types created a diverse landscape unlike any other on the continent. Vast in scale and rich in species, this portion of California has also been a strong attraction for humans. The combination of intense human occupation, large quantities of fine fuels, and extensive fire compartments has set the stage for a highly pyretic landscape.

Overview of Historic Fire Occurrence

Prehistoric Period

Unlike most other bioregions in California, little is known of the presettlement pattern of fire within the Central Valley landscape. With the absence of long-lived trees, a record of fire occurrence for the several hundred years prior to European contact was never recorded. Other methods, like sediment core analysis for documenting the abundance of fire in a given landscape, are complicated by the significant input of sediments from the surrounding mountains.

Fire is an ecological process commonly associated with grass-dominated ecosystems throughout the world (Noss 1994, Pyne 1995, Whelan 1995). The combined presence of

abundant ignition sources and receptive fuels results in a high likelihood of frequent fire events. The extent of these events, in time and space, is currently difficult to determine. Still, some evidence suggests a rich history of fire occurrence throughout the Great Central Valley.

The high density of Native Americans occupying the Central Valley lends support to the idea that frequent burning of grasslands and savannah vegetation occurred (Map 13.3). Although there are numerous records of burning by aboriginals, there is minimal agreement on the effect of these fires on vegetation (Wickstrom 1987, Anderson and Moratto 1996, Keeley 2002). The influence Native Americans had on local fire regimes was affected by the background pattern of lightning occurrence. The exceptionally low density of lightning strikes in the Central Valley may have increased the relative impact of burning by Native Americans on vegetation. The importance of Native American fire would have increased in topographically complex areas or where natural ignitions were infrequent (Frost 1998). Burning in the valley was certainly complicated by the continuous nature of fine fuels. Native Americans may have shifted the seasonality of fire, taking advantage of valley wetlands to control fire spread. There is also evidence that Native Americans made use of abundant foot trails as control lines (Siefkin, pers. comm.). Much evidence has supported the idea that Native American burning patterns relate strongly to the location of settlements and food production areas (Clark et al 1996). In many cases, burning was used as a tool to protect assets from the threat of future wildfire (Williams 1998). Closer examination of the valley's occupation, rainfall patterns, and vegetation may reveal much about past fire occurrence.

Population densities may help to describe a pattern of presettlement fire. Estimates place California's largest populations in the Central Valley. It is likely that these tribes represent the highest density of human occupation west of the Mississippi River (Wallace and Riddell 1988, 1991, 1993). Cook (1974) estimated that before Hispanic contact, populations reached 76,100 and 83,800 for the Sacramento and San Joaquin valleys, respectively. This intense occupation of nonagricultural hunter-gathers clearly affected vegetation at both fine and coarse scales. There is some evidence to support native Californians burning more often in the fall than in the spring in

The term *vernal pool* represents a diverse array of seasonal wetlands scattered throughout the entire pre-settlement Central Valley. Though vernal pool communities are present in a few southern California and Coast Range locations, the largest number and densest assemblage of pools occurs in the Central Valley (Fig. 13.1.1). Vernal pools may be considered one of California's most negatively affected natural habitats with up to 95% of pre-settlement pools being lost to agriculture and development (Holland 1978).

Grasslands of the Central Valley are currently characterized by a large group of non-native annual plants. Still, scattered throughout the sea of introduced plants are relatively intact islands of native plant diversity. Holland and Jain (1988) found that vernal pools typically remain dominated by native plants. The unique pattern of winter inundation and extremely dry summers has resulted in tremendous floristic diversity and a rich invertebrate fauna (Zedler 1987, Eng et al.1990). Pools combine patchy spatial elements with a discontinuous temporal life history. These extremes of vernal pool existence have helped to generate high levels of endemism among its associated plants and animals.

The Central Valley is dominated by three types of pools: valley pools, pools on volcanic substrate, and terrace pools (Schoenherr 1992). Valley pools are possibly the most heavily impacted of these wetland systems. Occurring in alkaline soil types, the floras of these pools include salt-tolerant plants like saltgrass *(Distichlis spicata)* and Ahart's dwarf rush *(Juncus leiospermus* var. *ahartii)*. The plant series Northern claypan vernal pools seems to best describe the plant assemblage associated with these areas (Sawyer and Keeler-Wolf 1995). Although pools of this type do occur in the Sacramento Valley, they are much more widespread in the southern San Joaquin.

Outside the Central Valley, pools forming on volcanic soils are common. Basalt caps and heavy clay soils create an ideal location for small depressions to retain winter rainwater. These pools seem to have the greatest elevation range as well as highly variable soils (Sawyer and Keeler-Wolf 1995). The diversity of this group of pools may justify additional series. Excellent examples of basalt flow pools can be found on the Vina Plains of Tehama County.

FIGURE 13.1.1. Vernal pools pocket the landscape in some areas of the Central Valley. This plant community is one of the most threatened in California, having been heavily impacted by agricultural and residential development.

Terrace pools are commonly found on old soils, deposited on ancient flood terraces. These soil types, including the Redding, Corning, and San Joaquin series, contain high levels of iron silica and readily form hardpans. The topography associated with these pools is the classic hogwallows and mima mounds that ring much of the northern valley. These pools are best described as Northern hardpan vernal pools and may represent the highest level of diversity amongst these vegetation types (Sawyer and Keeler-Wolf 1995). One of the better remaining examples of this vegetation complex occurs at Jepson Prairie Preserve in Solano County.

Little published research has been completed regarding fire in vernal pool ecosystems. As these communities are generally embedded within a matrix of grassland vegetation, we may assume that similar fire regimes have shaped these plant assemblages. Although it may be reasonable to expect similar rates of fire occurrence between grasslands and vernal pools, other components of their fire regimes may differ greatly. Certainly, measures of intensity and severity vary significantly from upland communities. Due to very low fuel loads, discontinuous arrangements, as well as the possible presence of water, it has been my experience that vernal pools rarely sustain fire spread (Fig. 13.1.2). Fire may still have played an important part in developmental history of this flora, affecting significantly its striking ecotone and adjacent vegetation.

Vernal pools have been described as one of the most pristine of California vegetation types (Holland and Griggs 1976). Still, many pools have experienced heavy infestations of medusahead. The presence of this annual grass may change significantly the pattern of fire events in vernal pool communities.

Both livestock grazing and burning are recognized as important tools for vernal pool management (Menke 1992, Barry 1995). A number of important plant and animal species have declined sharply in the absence of disturbance. Several authors have reported declines of rare plants following cattle removal (Davis and Sherman 1992, Muir and Mosely 1994). It has been reported that pools excluded from grazing have seen local extinction of some populations of fairy shrimp *(Branchinecta* spp.*)* (Bratton, 1990, Bratton and Fryer 1990). These negative effects on pool invertebrates and plants are presumed to be a result of increased residual mulch.

FIGURE 13.1.2 Low fuel volumes and phenology that differs from surrounding plant communities can minimize fire spread in vernal pools.

Some active burning of vernal pools has been implemented on selected sites. Pollak and Kan (1996) found early spring burns to be an effective management tool for both vernal pools and grassland communities at the Jepson Prairie Preserve. This study demonstrated a significant reduction in medusahead cover and residual dry matter, as well as a robust response from native grasses and early season forbs. Native species dominance was significantly increased, particularly in mound and intermound communities adjacent to the pools.

an effort to promote food plants and limit the impact on deer browse (Lewis 1973). Reference to the common use of tarweed (*Holocarpha virgata* and *Hemizonia congesta*) seeds as a food source (Barret and Gifford 1933) supports floristic evidence that these species were dominant in the presettlement grasslands of the southern San Joaquin (Holstein 2001).

No evidence currently exists documenting a pattern of repeated fire events in the presettlement Central Valley. What is obvious is a set of conditions creating a high *probability* of fire events. Weather conditions supporting fire spread, abundant dry fuels, and sources of ignition all align for some communities during some years. Open grasslands and savannas around the world are likely to experience a high occurrence of fire events (Bond and van Wilgen 1996). The exact description of past fire regimes within the plant communities of the Central Valley will never be known. Still, most ecologists would agree that a history of fire occurrence helped shape the pattern and structure of plant communities in the valley. The flat plains, large open fire compartments, available fuel, and high densities of Native Americans indicate a potential fire frequency of one to three years for the Central Valley (Frost 1998).

Historic Period

Writings from early visitors to the Central Valley provide evidence of fire use by California Native Americans (Roquefeuil 1823, Gordon 1977, Litke 1992). Spanish expeditions describe a well-populated valley with closely spaced, small villages and occasional large settlements. Father Munoz mentions burning by Indians during his visit of 1806 (Cook 1960). Jepson (1923) interpreted the density of oak stems to be a direct result of annual fire treatments by Native Americans. Later expeditions and small military raids to the interior of California occurred between the years 1820 and 1840 (Cook 1962). Brief reports and letters from this period document frequent use of fire, by both Native Americans and explorers, to facilitate warfare and capture of individuals.

The history of fire in the Central Valley is further complicated by the very early influence of non-native plant species and land use. Several early accounts document the presence of non-natives in the Central Valley prior to the introduction of extensive cattle or sheep grazing (Cook 1960). Redstem filaree (*Erodium cicutarium*), mustard (*Brassica* spp.), and wild oats (*Avena* spp.) were well established in the San Joaquin by the early part of the nineteenth century (Torrey 1859). The presence of these non-natives may have changed both the frequency and timing of fire events. Invasion by annual grasses, in particular, have substantially changed fuels characteristics of valley plant communities. These thatch-forming grasses have likely lengthened the season of burning, increased probabilities of ignitions, and created a more continuous fuel bed than that of presettlement grassland vegetation.

By the 1840s, ranching began to have a significant influence on plant communities in the Central Valley (Webster 1981). Horses were known to exist in the valley as early as 1807, with large numbers being documented after 1830 (Bryant 1848, Fremont, 1848, Cook 1960). Although the impact of overgrazing may not have occurred prior to the droughts of 1860s, the presence of large numbers of livestock likely influenced elements of early fire regimes. During the mid-1800s, the alignment of low-rainfall years and intensive grazing pressure likely reduced fire occurrence. No direct evidence documents the use of fire by early settlers for rangeland improvement or the clearing of agricultural lands. Still, it is likely that fire was used for these purposes through the early part of the twentieth century.

Current Period

Unlike other bioregions, the Central Valley has seen less-significant effects from changes in fuels or climate. Human ignitions result in frequent fires, but fragmentation and land conversion limits fire size in the contemporary valley landscape. Few fires extend beyond initial suppression activity

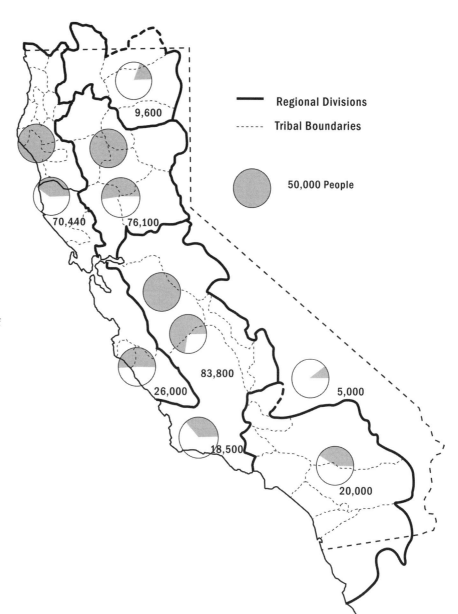

MAP 13.3. The Central Valley supported some of the highest known densities of Native Americans west of the Mississippi River. (Adapted from Baumhoff 1978.)

boundaries due to the fuel types and their restricted spatial arrangement. The vast majority of fires are contained at less than 4 ha (10 ac), and the largest was just over 6,000 ha (15,000 ac). This pattern of fire events has changed little over the last 50 years.

The use of prescribed fire was a common agricultural practice throughout the 1970s. More than 40,000 ha (100,000 ac) of agricultural wastes were burned annually, with the majority of treatment being targeted at rice stubble and orchard waste. Deteriorating air quality and stricter regulation has nearly eliminated agricultural burning in the Central Valley. The reduced number of permissible burn days and permitting difficulties has forced farmers to seek alternative methods to preparing agricultural fields. The prescriptive burning of wildlands, while never frequent, has also been limited by revisions to the state's air quality regulations.

Major Ecological Zones

Foothill Woodland

The Great Central Valley is characteristically framed by a rim of foothill oak woodlands defining the transition from modern valley grasslands to hillslope vegetation types (Fig. 13.2). Though widely used, the term "foothill" may be deceiving, as this community also grows on the floor of the valley and in some locations may occur at relatively high elevations. Still, this collection of vegetation types is very strongly associated with the hill terrain ascending from the central valley. Foothill woodlands cover several million hectares and nearly encircle the Central Valley. Though these vegetation types are characterized by the presence of either blue oak (*Quercus douglasii*) or gray pine (*Pinus sabiniana*), soil depth, aspect, and

FIGURE 13.2. Foothill woodlands support a diverse and structurally complex assemblage of plants. Both California black oak *(Quercus kelloggii)* and blue oak dominate the overstory of this mid-elevation foothill site.

elevation strongly influence the composition and structure of the tree-dominated communities. Where soils are deep and well-developed, valley oak *(Quercus lobata)* woodlands are not uncommon. In addition to the development of hillslope oak woodlands, ribbons of riparian forest often partition this ecological zone. Although this vegetation formation includes a number of different assemblages, blue oak is clearly the dominant tree and a critical focus for describing fire regimes.

An open savannah structure is most common in the low foothills rimming the valley. Blue oak savannahs appear to be strongly correlated with exposed south-facing slopes and shallow soils. These communities generally have few additional tree and shrub species present. An occasional California buckeye *(Aesculus californica)* or interior live oak *(Quercus wislizenii)* may appear in the canopy. Shrubs in the understory are sparse, with buck brush *(Ceanothus cuneatus* var. *cuneatus)* and whiteleaf manzanita *(Arctostaphylos viscida)* being the most common.

Overstory trees are scattered in a sea of grasses and forbs that have been dramatically altered by a non-native plant invasion. In some locations, as much as 95% of the herbaceous layer biomass is made up of non-native species (Gerlach et al. 1998). Though their percentage of plant biomass may be small, native herbaceous species are abundant in these communities and contribute significantly to species diversity. The presence of mediterranean annual grasses has significantly increased moisture stress on oak seedlings and may negatively impact recruitment (Adams et al.1992, Gordon and Rice 1993). Prominent amongst non-native forbs is yellow star-thistle *(Centaurea solstitialis)*. Introduced during the mid 1800s, it remained limited in its distribution until the 1940s. Changes in agricultural practices saw the expansion of yellow star-thistle from the valley floor to the bordering foothills. Since the 1960s this plant has expanded its range at an explosive rate. The result

is a significant change in species composition of both grassland and woodland ecosystems and a possible altering of fire regimes.

Though the percentage of plant biomass may be small, native herbaceous species are abundant in these communities and contribute significantly to species diversity. Within the range of blue oak woodlands, the assemblage of herbaceous species varies considerably. A number of researchers have documented the difference in species composition under oaks compared with open grassland (Marañon and Bartolome 1994, Rice and Nagy 2000). This may be particularly true following fire events (Marty 2002). Borchert et al. (1991) found the compositional pattern of selected herbs to be strongly correlated with crown cover, slope, solar insolation, and elevation. Soil and moisture gradients have also been noted as important factors influencing the arrangement of herbaceous plants in the blue oak understory. Native perennial grasses, purple needlegrass *(Nassela pulchra)*, California melic *(Melica californica)*, squirreltail *(Elymus elymoides)*, and blue wildrye *(Elymus glaucus)* may be common. A rich collection of forbs may be found among blue oaks. Parry's larkspur *(Delphinium parryi)*, dotseed plantain *(Plantago erecta)*, Johnny-jump-up *(Viola pendunculata)*, and popcornflower *(Plagiobothrys nothofulvus)* all add to a diverse display of spring wildflowers.

Further upslope from the valley floor, blue oaks are likely to occur in a more continuous overstory. Higher stem densities and the addition of other tree species create a woodland stand structure. Additional rainfall or cooler north aspects result in a denser and more structurally complex community. Additional tree species commonly include gray pine in the north and central portions of the valley. California juniper *(Juniperus californica)* may also be present throughout the southern valley foothills, though frequency of occurrence is higher on the east side.

TABLE 13.2
Fire response of selected foothill woodland plant species

Lifeform	Type of Fire Response			Species
	Sprouting	Seeding	Individual	
Hardwood	Fire stimulated	Fire neutral	Top-killed or branch killed	Blue oak, valley oak, coast live oak
Conifer	None	Fire stimulated	Killed	Gray pine
Shrub	Fire stimulated	Fire neutral	Top-killed	Mountain-mahogany
Herb	Fire stimulated	Fire stimulated	Top-killed	Blue larkspur
Grass	Fire stimulated	Fire neutral	Top-killed	Oniongrass

Both the density and diversity of shrub species increase significantly in blue oak woodlands. Many shrubs not found in lower-elevation savannahs may now be found spilling downslope from adjacent chaparral communities. Birch-leaf mountain-mahogany *(Cercocarpus betuloides* var. *betuloides)*, California coffeeberry *(Rhamnus californica)*, redbud *(Cercis occidentalis)*, and poison oak *(Toxicodendron diversilobum)* can occur in relatively dense patches scattered throughout the understory. The composition of herbaceous species may closely resemble that occurring in savannahs, though their arrangement may be much more discontinuous.

The arrangement of vegetation communities differs on the east and west sides of the valley. In the Sierra Nevada foothills, blue oak savannahs can become established as low as 150 m (500 ft) in elevation. This band of blue-oak–dominated vegetation is often sandwiched between vernal pool grassland in the valley and mixed chaparral types above 1,500 m (5,000 ft). On the east side of the valley, blue oaks tend to occur at higher elevations, following juniper woodlands and mixed shrublands above 1,000 m (3,500 ft).

On deep soils, valley oak may form extensive, monotypic stands of large trees, with very little understory. Williamson (1853) noted extensive oak stands in the southern San Joaquin: "The whole of this delta is covered with a luxuriant growth of oak. The soil is rich, producing spontaneously many kinds of grasses. The contrast between this beautifully-green spot and the arid plains on each side is very striking." Though valley oak is most often the dominant species, coast live oak *(Quercus agrifolia)* or interior live oak stems may be present. These stands are most common on recent alluvial terraces of large valleys, but can also appear on hillslope terrain (Griffin 1977). Valley oak woodlands are characteristically heterogeneous with varied structure (Conard et al. 1977). Smaller trees tend to occur at higher densities in a matrix of more open savannah-like structures.

FIRE ECOLOGY OF IMPORTANT SPECIES

A number of studies have shown no positive effect of fire on blue oak seedling establishment or survival (Allen-Diaz and Bartolome 1992, Swiecki and Bernhardt 2002). A number of other research efforts have indicated that fire may not be a limiting factor in seedling recruitment, as most seedlings are vigorously respouting (Table 13.2) (Lathrop and Osborne 1992, Haggerty 1994). It has also been suggested that alteration of presettlement fire regimes has contributed to weak seedling recruitment (Pavlik et al. 1991). Mature trees seem to persist, following fire events, and may experience an increase in crown vigor (Mooney 1977, Fry 2002). Indeed, factors other than fire may be more likely to limit seedlings from recruiting into the sapling stage of development. Predicting post-fire response of blue oak is difficult, as phenological variation, unique to individual fire events, may explain the majority of variation.

Information reported in the literature has often characterized oak seedlings as ephemeral and short lived (Biswell 1956, White 1966). Contrary to previous assumptions, Allen-Diaz and Bartolome (1992) found mortality of blue oak seedlings was not well correlated with age or size, and that both fire and sheep grazing appeared to have no effect on the seedling recruitment. Their study supports the idea that blue oaks may not require fire, but have developed a strategy to survive in the presence of frequent disruptive events. Seedlings are always present in the understory, providing advance regeneration for that time when the canopy is removed and release occurs.

Mature oaks suffer very little mortality following low- or moderate-intensity fire events. However, higher-intensity events can result in severe damage and significant mortality of mature trees (Plumb 1980). Significant variability can be seen in post-fire response of various oak species. Survival

TABLE 13.3
Fire regime components in foothill woodlands of the
Central Valley

Temporal
    Seasonality — Summer–fall
    Fire-return interval — Short

Spatial
    Size — Small–medium
    Complexity — High

Magnitude
    Intensity — Low to moderate
    Severity — Low to moderate
    Fire type — Surface

NOTE: Fire regime terms used in this table are defined in Chapter 4.

Temporal	
Seasonality	Summer–fall
Fire-return interval	Short
Spatial	
Size	Small–medium
Complexity	High
Magnitude	
Intensity	Low to moderate
Severity	Low to moderate
Fire type	Surface

may be strongly correlated with sprouting ability and bark thickness (Plumb and Gomez 1983). Rundel (1980) identified suites of traits in many California oak species that allow survival in areas where fires are frequent.

FIRE REGIME–PLANT COMMUNITY INTERACTIONS

Unlike some other portions of the California landscape, little evidence of past fire patterns exists for contemporary foothill woodlands. Although some long-lived tree species are present in these communities, none readily retain fire scar records. Additional evidence of past fire patterns based on the contemporary arrangement of vegetation is confounded by the strong influence of edaphic factors. Also, because of the dramatic changes in fuel type, load, and arrangement, recent fire events may differ dramatically from those of the past.

Although patterns of past fire occurrence may be difficult to describe, efforts have been made to predict changes in future fire events. Urban and suburban development trends are having a pronounced effect on oak woodland vegetation, particular in the northwestern Sierra Nevada foothills. As the density of development has increased, substantially lower rates of burning have occurred (Spero 2002).

Some studies have indicated that repeated fire events played an important role in maintaining the structure of blue oak woodlands (McClarn and Bartolome 1989, Mensing 1992). Though information remains limited, several studies have used scar data to reconstruct past patterns of fire and its relationship to age-class distribution (McClaran and Bartolome 1989, Mensing 1992, Haggerty 1994). Though information remains limited, pre-settlement fire regimes likely supported frequent, low-severity events (Table 13.3). The correlation of fire events and oak regeneration may result from increased growth rates of sprouts as well as reduced competition from herbaceous vegetation (McClaren and Bartolome 1989, Mensing 1990). These same fire effects have resulted in noted improvement of structural elements in blue oak savan-

nahs. Haggerty (1994) found savannah-like characteristics to be, at least temporarily, enhanced within a wildfire perimeter outside Sequoia and Kings Canyon National Parks. Although some small-diameter trees were top-killed, little change occurred in relative dominance or basal area of oaks.

Swiecki and Bernhardt (2002) described blue oak seedling growth and survivorship following a 1996 wildfire in the northern San Joaquin. Although on a similar site Tietje et al. (2001) found small blue oak mortality to be very low, with seedlings sprouting vigorously following fire events, their observations indicate that fire damage has hindered the advancement of small saplings into the overstory. They suggest a 1.5- to 2-m height or about a 4- to 5.5-cm diameter are critical thresholds for complete top-kill. Additional data from these same authors, collected at Pinnacles National Monument, indicate some potential negative impacts from frequent fire events. Plots with fire-free intervals of less than five years were least likely to contain sapling-sized trees (Swiecki and Bernhardt 1998).

Although actual mortality of blue oaks may be infrequent following fire events, there does not seem to be a demonstrated stimulatory effect on regrowth or regeneration (Bartolome et al.2002). Most studies seem to indicate that blue oak grows fastest when protected from both grazing pressure and burning. This is not a clear indication that fire is incompatible with successful oak recruitment, but that the timing and frequency of fire events are critical (Bartolome et al. 2002, Swiecki and Bernhardt 2002).

Even with concerns about fire impacts, the model for blue oak regeneration supports a role for re-occurring fire in foothill woodlands (Swiecki and Bernhardt 1998, Allen-Diaz and Bartolome 1992). It is conceivable that fire was a significant agent of change, occasionally killing overstory trees and promoting the transition of seedlings to the sapling type. Still, blue oak recruitment may not be limited by fire patterns (White 1966), and the effects of browsing may have a more significant effect on recruitment (Vankat and Major 1978). The possibility that stand-replacing fire events, initiating the single-age cohorts dominating many stands, seems unlikely as fuels necessary to support this type of fire spread rarely occur within these sites.

Valley Grasslands

Much discussion has occurred regarding the original composition of valley grasslands (Fig. 13.3). Many ecologists have contributed to the perception that Central Valley plant communities are dominated by native perennial grasses (Clements 1934, Clements and Shelford 1939, Beetle 1947, Munz and Keck 1949, Clark 1956, Benson 1957, Burcham 1957, Hull and Muller 1977, Heady 1977, Kuchler 1977). Clements and Shelford (1939) described the needlegrass community as a diverse assemblage of perennial grasses including blue wildrye, pine bluegrass (*Poa secunda*), and deergrass (*Muhlenbergia rigens*). The arrangement of grassland communities in the Central Valley was likely organized by soil types,

FIGURE 13.3. Valley grasslands represent a rich collection of grasses and forbs that vary tremendously depending on specific site factors and land-use history. Meadow barley *(Hordeum brachyantherum)* and seep monkeyflower *(Mumulus guttatus)* are dominant on this mesic grassland site.

levels of available soil moisture and annual precipitation. In wet soils of the central San Joaquin Valley, extensive stands of creeping wildrye *(Leymus triticoides)* were thought to dominate (Barry 2003). Similar sites in the southern San Joaquin, with more alkaline soils, likely supported alkali sacaton *(Sporobolus airoides)*-dominated grasslands or, on drier flats, saltgrass. Barry (2003) has promoted the idea of a gradient on dry valley sites from needlegrass prairie communities to xeric bunchgrass steppe assemblages.

Although questions remain concerning the composition of early Central Valley grasslands, what is well documented is that by the mid-1800s much of the valley was clearly dominated by non-natives (Thurber 1880). Some researchers believe the cover of perennial grasses decreased dramatically with the onset of intensive grazing by cattle and sheep (Barry 1972, Heady et al. 1991, Barbour et al. 1993, Noss 1994). It was also assumed that periods of intensive drought during the 1860s and extensive plowing for early dry-land farming facilitated the decline of perennial grasses. This alignment of factors resulted in conditions that promoted introduced European annuals over the native grassland flora (Jackson 1985, Barbour et al. 1993, Knapp and Rice 1994).

Still, some research efforts have demonstrated a beneficial response of bunchgrasses to grazing (Noy-Meier et al. 1989, Menke 1992). Some combination of factors, including the reduction of thatch and its effect on the germination and establishment of perennial grasses, may explain the response (Fowler 1986, Noy-Meier et al. 1989, Langstroth 1991, Dyer et al. 1996). Although not dependent, many of the valley's bunchgrasses appear well adapted to persisting in the presence of repeated burning or grazing.

A number of researchers have questioned the dominance of bunchgrasses in the valley grasslands (Cooper 1922, Biswell 1956, Twisselmann 1967, Wester 1981, Schiffman 1994, Hamilton 1997, Holstein 2001). Certainly, native perennial bunchgrasses were present in the pre-settlement Central Valley. Still the pattern and organization of these species may differ significantly from common perceptions. Utilizing a combination of survey data and historical accounts, Holstein (2001) has argued that topography and precipitation affected community composition and pattern, with much of the dry southern San Joaquin being dominated by annual species. Documentation from early explorers supports this idea (Williamson 1853).

Still other investigators have suggested a Central Valley dominated by shrublands (Cooper 1922, Bauer 1930, Wells 1964, Naveh 1967, Keeley 1989). The ultimate loss of shrubs and type conversion to annual vegetation may have resulted from repeated burning and grazing (Huenneke 1989, Keeley and Fotheringham 2001, Keeley 2002). The use of frequent fire by California tribes is well documented, suggesting type conversion may have begun well before the influence of European settlers (Timbrook et al.1982, Anderson and Moratto 1996).

The stability of current annual vegetation in the Central Valley is somewhat unique compared with other mediterranean grasslands (Blumler 1984, Jackson 1985). Very little invasion of perennials seems to occur within existing grassland sites (Bartolome and Gemmill 1981) This resistance of annual grasslands may support the hypothesis that the vegetation on the valley floor was composed primarily of annual vegetation (Piemeisel and Lawson 1937, Hoover 1970, Schiffman 1994). The composition of these herbaceous communities likely varied across the valley landscape. Frenkel (1970) proposed a vegetation type, comprised largely of annual grasses, dominating lower-elevation sites. Other evidence, including a number of historical accounts, seems to indicate a plant community dominated by annual forbs (Muir 1894, Roundtree 1936).

Journals from colonial expeditions to the Central Valley provide some insights on pre-settlement vegetation patterns.

TABLE 13.4
Fire response of selected valley grassland plant species

| | Type of Fire Response | | | |
Lifeform	Sprouting	Seeding	Individual	Species
Herb	Fire stimulated	Fire neutral	Top-killed	Brodiaea, navarretia
Grass	Fire stimulated	Fire neutral	Top-killed	Purple needlegrass, creeping wildrye, alkaline sacaton
	None	Fire stimulated	Killed	One-sided bluegrass

FIGURE 13.4. Purple needlegrass sprouts vigorously three days following a spring prescribed fire.

Father Zalvidea, in July of 1806, described large areas of the southern San Joaquin as characterized by sparse vegetation with no grass (Cook 1960). The only well-developed vegetation identified during this expedition are all associated with riparian systems. Included in these journals are descriptions of large tule stands on the shores of Lake Buena Vista and impressive cottonwood *(Populus* spp.*)* forest associated with the San Joaquin River. The latter contained an understory of "good pasture." Given the location, this may be a reference to creeping wildrye. Father Munoz also traveled throughout the southern Central Valley during 1806 (Cook 1960). His chosen route appears to have included foothill portions of the west valley. His descriptions of vegetation appear similar to other explorers. He notes a "great scarcity of grass" as well as areas of alkaline soils. His descriptions of riparian vegetation identify large willow *(Salix* spp.*)* thickets with some good pasture. Both journals note a lack of firewood in this portion of the valley.

Evidence does seem to indicate the importance of perennials on more mesic sites in the north valley (Bartolome and Gemmill 1981, Gerlach et al. 1998). Still, much of the San Joaquin seems more likely to have been occupied by wetland vegetation or ephemeral annual vegetation on drier sites (Webster 1981, Hamilton 1997, Meyer and Schiffman 1999). Much of the southern valley may have been devoid of vegetation for portions of the year when fire occurrence was likely. On extremely dry or alkaline sites, xerophytic shrubs seem more likely to have occured than bunchgrass prairies (Twisselmann 1967, Menke 1989).

Questions regarding the exact makeup of grassland communities prior to the nineteenth century will remain unanswered. What does seem clear is that perennial-dominated stands did occur in some valley locations, with increasing importance in the Sacramento Valley, Coast Range, and Sierra Nevada foothills. The dominance of perennials on other valley locations appears to be driven primarily by variations in soil and available moisture. The central and southern portions of the valley were more likely to support annual vegetation on upland sites. Evidence would seem to indicate that forbs were more common than grasses. Additionally, in the southern San Joaquin, many sites presumed to have been grasslands perhaps were occupied by a desert scrub plant assemblage.

FIRE ECOLOGY OF IMPORTANT SPECIES

Given the history of ecological thought in Central Valley grasslands, it may not be surprising that much of the fire effects literature has focused on perennial grasses. Physiology supporting fire response is common among all guilds of valley grassland species (Table 13.4). Many native bunchgrasses are known to respond favorably to fires, with vigorous resprouting and flower production after fire (Keeley 1981, Axelrod 1985, Young and Miller, 1985, Glenn-Lewis et al. 1990, Fehmi and Bartolome 2003). In particular, the vigorous response of purple needlegrass to fire events has been documented in a number of studies (Bartolome 1979, Ahmed 1983, Menke 1989, Dyer et al. 1996, Wills 2001). Purple needlegrass commonly will begin to sprout just days after late spring fire events (Fig. 13.4). Bartolome (1981) noted the success of seedling establishment following fire or grazing. Menke (1982) observed an overall benefit to periodic burning of purple needlegrass–dominated communities and recommended treatment every three to four years. It has been suggested that the persistence of purple needlegrass on Central Valley sites is a result of strong adaptation to frequent fire and heavy grazing (Sampson 1944, Jones and Love 1945, Bartolome and Gemmill 1981, Ahmed 1983).

If water is limited, fire may reduce the productivity of perennial grasses during the first post-fire growing season (Blaisdell 1953, Daubenmire 1968, Wright 1974, Robberecht and Defosse 1995). Rates of regrowth for Idaho fescue (*Festuca idahoensis*) following fire were shown to increase with no significant mortality recorded for a variety of fire severities (Defosse and Robberecht 1996).

Much attention has been given to fire effects on nonnative species currently occupying much of the valley's former grassland habitat. Although certain non-native species have responded positively to burn treatments, some effective fire prescriptions have been developed. Yellow star-thistle, a particularly problematic weed was significantly less abundant in burned versus unburned plots of several studies. DiTomaso et al. (1999) found that several years of repeated burning were necessary to sufficiently control yellow star-thistle. The effect of fire on this and other species is covered in greater detail in Chapter 22.

Annual forbs represent a critical component of valley grassland communities, but often receive little focus during restoration planning and implementation. It is true that little is known of the specific tolerance individual species may have to burning. Still, some research in California grasslands has shown that certain native species increase in the post-fire

TABLE 13.5

Fire regime components in grasslands of the Central Valley

Temporal	
Seasonality	Summer–fall
Fire-return interval	Short
Spatial	
Size	Medium–large
Complexity	Low
Magnitude	
Intensity	Low
Severity	Moderate–high
Fire type	Surface

environment (Parsons and Stohlgren 1989, Meyer and Schiffman 1999). On a grassland site at Beale Air Force Base, Marty (2002) found variable linanthus (*Linanthus parviflorus*) absent from all plots prior to treatment. Following burning and grazing, variable linanthus was found only in plots that had experienced fire.

Parsons and Stohlgren (1989) documented increases in the biomass of several native forbs following fire events implemented during a variety of seasons. Following three consecutive fall prescribed fires, Indian paintbrush (*Orthocarpus attenuatus*) experienced a significant increase in biomass. Following the same number of spring burns, smallhead clover (*Trifolium microcephalum*) also increased among treated plots. Chilean bird's-foot trefoil (*Lotus subpinnatus*) increased in biomass following both fall and spring burns.

On another foothill site, York (1997) found eight native annuals and a perennial to respond positively to a single fire event (1997). Dwarf brodiaea (*Brodiaea terrestris*), common stickyseed (*Blennosperma nanum*), California goldfields (*Lasthenia californica*), marigold navarretia (*Navarretia tagetina*), and butter-and-eggs (*Triphysaria eriantha*) all seemed to demonstrate some adaptation to growing season fire events. Pygmyweed (*Crassula connata*) and water chickweed (*Montia fontana*) seemed to respond well to the removal of thatch.

In contrast to much of what had previously appeared in the literature, Marty (2002) found burn treatments to negatively affect stands of purple needlegrass. Across a variety of grazing treatments, bunchgrass mortality was 10% higher in burned versus unburned plots. Burning treatments did elicit a positive seedling response, with densities 100% higher in burned versus unburned plots two years after the burn. Still, during the period of this research, seedling densities did not attain pre-burn levels.

FIRE REGIME–PLANT COMMUNITY INTERACTIONS

Although accurate estimates of pre-settlement fire-return intervals do not exist for the Central Valley, investigations

FIGURE 13.5. Rich galley forest once followed river corridors throughout the Central Valley. Levees follow most major rivers in the valley today, limiting both flooding and riparian forest development.

from other grassland systems may help to interpret fire regimes (Table 13.5). Greenlee and Langeheim (1990) estimated fire frequency in grasslands of the Monterey Bay area to be between 1 and 15 years prior to 1880. The timing of fire events is less clear, though it is likely that some Native American burning took place as soon as fuels were receptive. Biswell (1989) stated fires were set by Native Americans as soon as patches of vegetation dried sufficiently to sustain fire spread. Summer and fall fires continued following both natural (lightning strikes) and anthropogenic causes (Vogl 1974, Biswell 1989).

D'Antonio et al. (2002) analyzed existing data on the effects of fire and grazing on contemporary California grasslands and concluded there has been much variation in community response. They found that precipitation has generally been more important than the type of burn treatment in influencing the pattern of perennial grasses and forbs. Native forbs benefited most from burning, but this same response was commonly seen in non-native forbs. They also found little long-term effect on the abundance of native grasses demonstrated in the literature. With the exception of purple needlegrass and California oatgrass (*Danthonia californica*),

TABLE 13.6
Fire response of selected riparian woodland plant species

| Lifeform | Type of Fire Response | | | Species |
	Sprouting	Seeding	Individual	
Hardwood	Fire stimulated	Fire stimulated	Survive or top-killed	Arroyo willow, (Salix lasiolepis), western sycamore (Platanus racemosa)
	Fire neutral	Fire inhibited	Survive or top-killed	Black cottonwood (Populus balsamifera ssp. trichocarpa)
Shrub	Fire stimulated	Fire stimulated	Top-killed	Coyote brush (Baccharis pilularis) Mexican elderberry (Sambucus mexicana)
	Fire stimulated	Fire neutral	Top-killed	Mule fat (Baccharis salicifolia)
Grass	Fire stimulated	Fire neutral	Top-killed	Deergrass (Muhlenbergia rigens)

there was a lack of data on native perennial grass species. Although prescribed fire treatments may temporarily increase the cover of natives and suppress some non-native annual grasses, the specific approach to successful fire application is not well defined and may have significant spatial and temporal variability.

Investigating the impacts of grazing and burning on spatial patterns of purple needlegrass, Fehmi and Bartolome (2003) recommend repeated burning and grazing exclusion as the most effective management regime for mixed coastal grasslands. These recent results support earlier work (Hatch et al. 1991) in coastal grasslands systems. On sites where perennial grasses occupy significant cover, varied burning regimes appear to be effective conservation strategies (Wills 2000). Still, caution should be exercised when applying these results to Central Valley systems, as both historic and contemporary conditions appear to differ significantly.

Questions addressing the effect of timing on grassland diversity have drawn little attention. Meyer and Schiffman (1999) compared the effects of different seasons of burning and mulch reduction on annual grassland plant communities at the Carrizo Plain Natural Area. Their results document a significant increase in native species cover and diversity following late spring and fall burns, whereas winter burning showed minimal effect on native cover or diversity. Other studies have also documented changes in diversity patterns following fire events. York (1997) demonstrated a significant change in grassland species composition and diversity following a single fire event. Marty (2002) noted increases in species richness across all functional groups. Similar groups

of native forbs increased in biomass and cover following spring fire events in southern California grasslands (Wills 2000, Klinger and Messner 2001).

Numerous authors have noted that fire can reduce competition from annual grasses (Hervey 1949, Zavon 1982, Ahmed 1983, Keeley 1990, George et al. 1992). Hopkinson et al. (1999) noted timing and intensity as significant variables affecting the response of non-native annual grasses.

Riparian Forest

Riparian forests in California reached their highest level of development in the Central Valley (Fig. 13.5). The Sacramento, the San Joaquin, and their tributaries all supported extensive gallery forests. Growing on raised terraces slightly above the stream channel, these forests varied in their size, structure, and composition. An impressive collection of winter-deciduous trees crowded the dense canopy of this community. Western sycamore, box elder (Acer negundo var. californicum), Fremont cottonwood (Populus fremontii), Goodding's black willow (Salix gooddingii), and valley oak all occurred in complex multi-story stands.

Estimates suggest about 400,000 ha (1 million ac) of riparian forest occupied the valley in the mid nineteenth century. Although riparian forest certainly occurred in the southern San Joaquin, historical accounts seem to indicate a larger portion of the Sacramento Valley being occupied by this vegetation type (von Kotzebue 1830). An additional traveler, William Dane Phelps, traveled up the Sacramento in 1841 and noted tall trees along the high banks (Busch

TABLE 13.7
Fire regime components in riparian woodlands of the Central Valley

Temporal	
Seasonality	Summer–fall
Fire-return interval	Long
Spatial	
Size	Small–medium
Complexity	High
Magnitude	
Intensity	Low–high
Severity	Low–high
Fire type	Surface–crown

NOTE: Fire regime terms in this table are defined in Chapter 4.

1983). Williamson (1853), in a survey of the southern San Joaquin to identify potential railroad routes to the Pacific, stated that his views of the valley were obscured by large riparian forests. Very little of California's riparian forest is left today, and less still has maintained a semblance of pre-settlement structure.

FIRE ECOLOGY OF IMPORTANT SPECIES

It seems clear that plants of the Central Valley riparian forest are not dependent on fire to successfully regenerate. Still, fire has influenced the structure and composition of riparian vegetation (Bendix 1994, Ellis 2001). Although the dominant tree and shrub species may not be specifically adapted to fire events, most species are physiologically capable of surviving a variety of events (Table 13.6) (Ellis 2001).

In more coastal riparian vegetation, Davis et al. (1989) found sprouting to be the dominant means of recovery for tree species. Sycamore showed rapid rates of recovery, while other less-vigorous sprouters, like alder *(Alnus spp.)*, were very slow to respond. Although easily killed by moderate- or high-severity fire, cottonwood has also demonstrated the ability to persist following fire events (Ellis 1999). Studies on other southwestern riparian forest document variable responses and inefficient recovery of native trees (Busch and Smith 1993). Cottonwood was eliminated from burn sites on the lower Colorado River, whereas on these same sites willow did persist (Busch 1995). Size may contribute significantly to sprouting ability, with smaller-diameter trees responding more vigorously than larger ones (Blaisdell and Mueggler 1956).

Severity appears to significantly affect response of both trees and shrubs. Even moderate-severity fire events may result in complete overstory mortality and limited response of sprouting trees (Busch 1995, Ellis 2001). The number of fires may also significantly affect community structure and composition (Busch 1995). Compressed fire-return intervals may facilitate the invasion of weedy species.

FIRE REGIME–PLANT COMMUNITY INTERACTIONS

Very little documentation of fire effects on riparian communities has been developed for California's Central Valley. More research has been initiated in riparian systems of the Southwest. Several investigators have suggested fire to be a novel event in riparian plant communities (Dobyns 1981, Bahre 1985, Kirby et al. 1988, Busch 1995). However, it is possible to predict fire regime components for riparian woodlands (Table 13.7). Evidence does seem to support the claims that in riparian woodland vegetation, fires are increasing in both frequency and severity (Busch 1995, Busch and Smith 1995, Stuever et al. 1997). The presence of more flammable, non-native vegetation may be driving shifts in fire regimes (Ohmart and Anderson 1982, Busch and Smith 1993). More fundamental changes in salinity level, available nutrients, and plant-water relations may be transitioning gallery forests to a riparian scrubland (Busch and Smith 1993). The lack of flooding in these systems may also contribute to excessive fuel accumulation and more severe fire events (Ellis 2001).

Assuming a repeated pattern of fire in upland vegetation types, riparian forests of the Central Valley must also have experienced periodic fire occurrence (Table 13.7). During some seasons, conditions could have made riparian systems effective barriers to fire spread. These systems may have been significant boundaries to fire events, hence defining an important component of valley fire regimes. The widespread distribution of riparian forests partitioned the valley into discrete blocks of upland vegetation. It is not unreasonable to assume Native Americans made use of these barriers to control fire spread and ultimately fire size.

It is also fair to assume that during periods of prolonged drought, riparian forests did burn readily, increasing fire size and altering vegetation patterns. Contemporary examples of valley riparian forest often exhibit high fuel loads in a continuous vertical and horizontal arrangement. Fire events on these sites can be of extremely high severity, with all overstory trees being killed (Stuever 1997). Fire behavior in some recent events has been strongly influenced by non-native species, most notably giant reed *(Arundo donax)* and salt cedar *(Tamarix spp.)*. The past pattern of fire within these vegetation types will remain unknown, though contemporary evidence would indicate an important role for riparian forest in the fire regimes of the Central Valley.

Freshwater Marsh

Our contemporary image of the Central Valley has been so strongly affected by changes wrought by land use that it has become difficult to imagine its pre-settlement splendor. Possibly the single most striking feature of the pre-contact landscape was the scale and scope of its massive freshwater wetlands (Fig. 13.6). This element of the valley has been changed so fundamentally it may be impossible to fully define its former extent. European explorers noted a valley hydrology quite different from today with large expanses of water and marshes (Williamson 1853, M'Collum and Morgan 1960, Cronise

FIGURE 13.6. Freshwater marshes once covered significant portions of the valley, creating unique plant communities and important wildlife habitat.

TABLE 13.8

Fire response of selected freshwater marsh plant species

Lifeform	Type of Fire Response			Species
	Sprouting	Seeding	Individual	
Grass	Fire stimulated	Fire stimulated	Top-killed	Cord grass
	Fire inhibited	Fire inhibited	Top-killed	Saltgrass
	Fire neutral	Fire neutral	Top-killed	Bulrush
	Fire stimulated	Fire neutral	Top-killed	Cattail

1868). Missing from the contemporary landscape are the interconnected Tulare, Buena Vista, and Kern Lakes that formed the largest wetland in California. These large, former lakes of the Central Valley combined with an intricate network of sloughs and marshes wherever water settled in low portions of the landscape. This incredible wetland system was estimated to contain more than 3,400 km (2,100 mi) of shoreline prior to active dewatering (Schoenherr 1992).

In all cases, marsh vegetation is arranged in distinct units based on water depth and ecological requirements. It appears that near-shore portions of the valley's wetlands were dominated by various reedlike plants. A variety of cattail species, California bulrush (*Scirpus californicus*), and slenderbeak sedge (*Carex athrostachya*) may all have been abundant in these locations (Keeler-Wolf 1996). Following the gradient to higher, better-drained soils, willows are also an important component of freshwater marsh habitats. Goodding's black willow, red willow (*Salix laevigata*), and shining willow (*Salix*

TABLE 13.9

Fire regime components in freshwater marshes of the Central Valley

Temporal	
Seasonality	Summer–fall
Fire-return interval	Short
Spatial	
Size	Small–medium
Complexity	High
Magnitude	
Intensity	High
Severity	High
Fire type	Surface

NOTE: Fire regime terms in this table are defined in Chapter 4.

FIGURE 13.7. Wetlands and small tributaries partitioned significant parts of the Central Valley landscape and may have formed effective barriers to fire spread.

lucida ssp. *lasiandra)* were likely common. Although the tree form of these species may have been present, more individuals likely branched close to the ground resembling large shrubs. On drier, more alkaline sites, mule fat may have replaced willows.

FIRE ECOLOGY OF IMPORTANT SPECIES

Several studies have demonstrated significant change following fire events in wetland ecosystems (Johnson and Knapp 1993, Gabrey et al. 1999, Clark and Wilson 2001). Following prescribed fire events, Johnson and Knapp (1993) noted pronounced increases in soil pH, organic matter, and available nutrients in rush *(Juncus* spp.) and cord grass *(Spartina* spp.) marsh vegetation. Changes occurring in soils may contribute to significantly greater biomass production, inflorescence density, and plant height in annually burned prairie cordgrass *(Spartina pectinata)* wetlands (Johnson and Knapp 1993). Smith and Kadlec (1985) noted no difference in production of broad-leafed cattail *(Typha latifolia)*, bulrush *(Scirpus lacustris)*, and cosmopolitan bulrush *(S. maritimus)* on burned sites versus controls. Increased protein in post-fire vegetation may have resulted in preferential grazing by wetland vertebrates (Smith and Kadlec 1985). Specific response of Central Valley marsh vegetation is still in need of further investigation, though some adaptations to fire seem clear (Table 13.8).

FIRE REGIME–PLANT COMMUNITY INTERACTIONS

No spatially explicit records of fire patterns exist for pre-settlement marsh habitats of the Central Valley. Still, historical descriptions place native Californians and active burning in locations of abundant freshwater marsh habitat. Much research in other locations has documented a history of naturally occurring fires in wetland habitats (Viosa 1931, Loveless 1959, Cohen 1974, Wade et al.1980, Wilbur and Chris-

tensen 1983, Izlar 1984). Based on these studies, fire regime components in freshwater marshes of the Central Valley can be postulated (Table 13.9).

The effect these long, linear, mesic environments had on fire spread is unknown. Certainly, during portions of the year, the combinations of riparian forest and freshwater marsh provided an effective barrier to fire spread. This extremely wet environment split the valley in half and may have partitioned much of the east side (Fig. 13.7). During years of above-average rainfall these features likely held abundant water all summer.

Freshwater marsh vegetation may have also contributed significantly to enlarging fire events. Particularly in the San Joaquin, much of the uplands may have produced low volumes of discontinuous fuels. Marsh habitats are known to be extremely productive (Bakker 1972) and would have contributed tremendous amounts of fuel to the valley's fire environment. Although species like cattails may not be available for burning during significant portions of the year, these fuels do burn readily with great intensity, under a particular alignment of factors. The linear arrangement of these vegetation types may have contributed to extensive north-south fire spread, during periods of low rainfall and dry conditions.

Management Issues

The Central Valley is arguably the most highly altered bioregion in California. Its long history of occupation and intensive use has resulted in a contemporary landscape largely devoid of natural vegetation. This conversion has been occurring over long periods of time. Land use stretches deep into the valley's past, though it is modern agriculture that remains the single most significant agent of change. With few exceptions, the conservation landscape here has been defined long ago. Lands fall into clear patterns of protected or intensively used areas. There are very few areas in which remnant, unprotected plant communities still exist.

Given the condition of the valley's open space, restoration is the obvious priority for management action. Restoring Central Valley plant communities has been a high priority for conservation in this portion of the state. Yet, with so few intact remnants left, reference conditions have been difficult to define. Much work is still needed to identify vegetation targets at multiple scales.

Agreement on restoration goals is only helpful when supported by adequate research, technologies, and resources. The hard work of many has improved our ability to establish particular elements of valley plant communities. Still, a number of important guilds of species remain unavailable and untested in restoration settings. The process of restoration, particularly in grasslands and riparian forest, is further complicated by the presence of invasive non-native species, the control of which is absolutely critical to management success.

Recent efforts have demonstrated how commonly used management practices affect grassland composition and how various environmental factors interact with these practices. Late spring (June–July) burning has become an often-used tool for increasing native species richness and cover in grasslands or preparing sites for more active restoration. Prescriptive grazing has been used to similar effect. On sites of various conditions, moderate levels of grazing do not seem to have an overwhelming negative or positive effect on species composition.

Fire management in the valley's future makes sense only in this context of restoring native plant communities. Elevated fuel loads and the resulting threat to social infrastructure is clearly not an issue in this bioregion. The alterations to historic patterns of fire also appear less important here than in other bioregions of the state. The parallel changes that have occurred in plant community composition and structure make burning alone ineffective. Targeted fire use, aimed at invasive, non-native species control, site preparation, and specific species response seems the clear future for fire management activities of the valley.

Even these modest goals for prescribed fire may see limited success. Throughout much of the twentieth century, agricultural burning was a common practice in the Central Valley. The fall burning of rice (Oryza sativa) straw stubble, in particular, resulted in notoriously poor air quality. Nonattainment in many of the valley's air sheds has reduced acceptable burn windows to a small number of days each year. Burn permitting is competitive, with both agricultural and wildland units attempting to implement during the same periods. The unlikely resolution to the air quality issue will continue to minimize fire applications.

References

Adams, D.P. 1985. Quaternary pollen records from California. P. 125–140 in V.M. Bryant, Jr. and R.C. Holloway (eds.), Pollen records of late-quaternary North American sediments. American Association of Stratigraphic Palynologists Foundation.

Adams, T.E., P.B. Sands, W.H. Weitkamp, and N.K. McDonald 1992. Oak seedlings establishment on California rangelands. Journal of Range Management 45(1):93–98.

Ahmed, E.O. 1983. Fire ecology of Stipa pulchra in California annual grassland. Ph.D Dissertation, University of California, Davis.

Allen-Diaz, B.H., and J.W. Bartolome. 1992. Survival of Quercus douglasii seedlings under the influence of fire and grazing. Madrono 39(1):47–53.

Allen-Diaz, B.H., and B.A. Holzman. 1991. Blue oak communities in California. Madrono 38:80–95.

Anderson, M.K., and M.J. Moratto. 1996. P. 187–206 in Native American land-use practices and ecological impacts. In Sierra Nevada Ecosystem Project: Final Report to Congress: Status of the Sierra Nevada, Vol. 2 (eds.), SNEP team. Centers for Water and Wildland Resources, University of California, Davis.

Axelrod, D.I. 1985. Rise of the grassland biome, central North America. Botanical Review 62:116–1183.

Bahre, C.J. 1985. Wildfire in southeastern Arizona between 1859 and 1890. Desert Plants 7:190–194.

Bakker, E. 1972. An island called California. University of California Press, Berkeley.

Barbour, M., B. Pavlik, F. Drysdale, and S. Lindstrom. 1993. California's changing landscape. California Native Plant Society, Sacramento.

Barret, S.A., and E.W. Gifford 1933. Miwok material culture. Bulletin of the Milwaukee Public Museum 2(4):117–376.

Barry, S. 1995. Vernal pools on California annual grasslands. Rangelands 17:173–175.

Barry, W.J. 1972. California prairie ecosystems (Vol. 1): The Central Valley prairie. State of California, Resources Agency, Dept. of Parks and Recreation, Sacramento.

Barry, W.J. 2003. California primeval grasslands and management in the State Park System. Grasslands 13(3):5–8.

Bartolome, J.W. 1979. Germination and seedling establishment in California annual grassland. Journal of Ecology 67:273–281.

Bartolome, J.W., and B. Gemmill. 1981. The ecological status of Stipa pulchra (Poaceae) in California. Madrono 28:172–184.

Bartolome, J.W., M.P McClaran, B.H. Allen-Diaz, J. Dunne, L.D. Ford, R.B. Standiford, Neil K. McDougald, and L. C. Forero 2002. Effects of fire and browsing on regeneration of blue oak. In Proceedings of the fifth symposium on oak woodlands: oaks in California's changing landscape. USDA Forest Service Gen. Tech. Rpt. PSW-GTR-184.

Bauer, H.L. 1930. Vegetation of the Tehachapi Mountains, California. Ecology 11:263–280.

Baumhoff, M.A. 1978. Historical demography. P. 91–98 in R.F. Heizer (ed.), Environmental background. In Handbook of North American Indians, Vol. 8, California. Smithsonian Institute, Washington DC.

Beetle, A.A. 1947. Distribution of the native grasses of California. Hilgardia 17:309–357.

Bendix, J. 1994. Among-site variation in riparian vegetation in the Southern California Transverse Ranges. American Midland Naturalist 132:136–151.

Benson, L. 1957. Plant classification. D.C. Heath, Boston.

Biswell, H.H. 1956. Ecology of California grasslands. Journal of Range Management 9:19–24.

Biswell, H.H. 1989. Prescribed burning in California wildlands vegetation management. University of California Press, Berkeley.

Blaisdell, J.P. 1953. Ecological effects of planned burning of sagebrush-grass range on the upper Snake River plains. USDA Tech. Bull. 1075.

Blaisdell, J.P., and W.F. Mueggler. 1956. Sprouting of bitterbush (*Purshia tridentate*) following burning or top removal. Ecology 37:365–370.

Blumler, M.A. 1984. Climate and the annual habitat. M.A. thesis. University of California, Berkeley.

Bond, W.J., and B.W. van Wilgen 1996. Fire and plants. Chapman and Hall, London. 258 p.

Borchert, M., F.W. Davis, and B. Allen-Diaz. 1991. Environmental relationships of herbs in blue oak (*Quercus douglasii*) woodlands of central coastal California. Madrono 38(4).

Bratton, J.H. 1990. Seasonal pools: an overlooked invertebrate habitat. British Wildlife 2:22–29.

Bratton, J.H., and G. Fryer 1990. The distribution and ecology of *Chirocephalus diaphanous* Prevost (Branchiopoda: Anostraca) in Britain. Journal of Natural History 24:955–964.

Bryant, E. 1848. What I saw in California. Appleton, New York.

Burcham, L.T. 1957. California rangeland. Calif. Dept. Nat. Resources, Div. Forestry, Sacramento.

Busch, B.D. (ed.). 1983. Alta California 1840–1842: the journal and observations of William Dane Phelps. Arthur H. Clark Co., Glendale, CA.

Busch, D.E. 1995. Effects of fire on southwestern riparian plant community structure. Southwestern Naturalist 40:259–267.

Busch, D.E., and S.D. Smith. 1993. Effects of fire on water and salinity relations of riparian woody taxa. Oecologia 94:186–194.

Busch, D.E., and S.D. Smith. 1995. Mechanisms associated with decline of woody species in riparian ecosystems of the southwestern U.S. Ecological Monographs 65:347–370.

Clark, A.K. 1956. The impact of exotic invasion on the remaining New World mid-altitude grasslands. P. 737–762 in W.L. Thomas (ed.), Man's role in changing the face of the earth. University of Chicago Press, Chicago.

Clark, J.S., T. Hussey, and P.D. Royall. 1996. Presettlement analogs for Quaternary fire regimes in eastern Northern America. Journal of Paleolimnology 16:79–96.

Clements, F.E. 1934. The relict method in dynamic ecology. J. Ecol. 22:39–68.

Clements, F.E., and V.E. Shelford. 1939. Bioecology. Wiley, London.

Cohen, A.D. 1974. Evidence of fires in the ancient everglades and coastal swamps of southern Florida. P. 213–218 in P.J. Gleason (ed.), Environments of south Florida past and present. Miami Geological Society Memoir 2, Miami, FL.

Conard, S.G., R.L. MacDonald, and R.F. Holland. 1977. Riparian vegetation and flora of the Sacramento Valley. In Riparian forest in California: their ecology and conservation. University of California, Institute of Ecology Publication No. 15.

Conise, T.F. 1868. The natural wealth of California. H.H. Bancroft & Co., San Francisco.

Cook, S.F. 1960. Colonial expeditions to the interior of California: Central Valley, 1800–1820. University of California Antrrhropological Records 16(6):239–292.

Cook, S.F. 1962. Colonial expeditions to the interior of California: Central Valley, 1820–1840. University of California Antrrhropological Records 20(5):151–214.

Cook, S.F. 1974. The Esselen: territory, villages, and populations. Quarterly of the Monterey County Archaeological Society 3(2):1–12.

Cooper, W.S. 1922. The broad-sclerophyll vegetation of California. Carnegie Inst. Wash. Pub. 319. 124 p.

Daubenmire, R. 1968. Ecology of fire in grasslands. P. 209–267 in J.B. Cragg (ed.), Advances in ecological research. Academic Press, New York/London.

D'Antonio, C.D., S. Bainbridge, C. Kennedy, J. Bartolome, and S. Reynolds 2002. Ecology and restoration of California grasslands with special emphasis on the influence of fire and grazing on native grassland species. Report to the David and Lucille Packard Foundation. University of California, Berkeley.

Davis, F.W, E.A. Keller, A. Parikh, and J. Florsheim. 1989. Recovery of the chaparral riparian zone after fire. In Proceedings of the California riparian systems conference: protection, management and restoration for the 1990s. Gen. Tech. Rep. PSW-110.

Davis, L.H., and R.J. Sherman. 1992. Ecological study of rare *Chorizanthe valida* (Polygonaceae) at Point Reyes National Seashore, California. Madrono 39:271–280.

Davis, O.K. 1990. Preliminary report of the pollen analysis of Tulare Lake. Newsletter of the Tulare Lake Archaeological Research Group 3(8):2–4.

Defosse, G.E., and R. Robberecht. 1996. Effects of competition on the post-fire recovery of 2 bunchgrass species. Journal of Range Management 49(2):137–142.

Dobyns, H.F. 1981. From fire to flood: historic human destruction of Sonoran Desert riverine oases. Ballena Press, Socorro, NM. 222 p.

Driver, H.E., and W.C. Massey. 1957. Comparative studies of North American Indians. Transactions of the American Philosophical Society 47(2):165–456.

Dyer, A., H. Fossum, and J. Menke 1996. Emergence and survival of *Nassella pulchra* in a California grassland. Madrono 43:316–366.

Ellis, L.M. 1999. Floods and fire along the Rio Grande: the role of disturbance in the riparian forest. Doctoral Dissertation, University of New Mexico, Albuquerque.

Ellis, L.M. 2001. Short-term response of woody plants to fire in a Rio Grande riparian forest, Central New Mexico, USA. Biological Conservation 97:159–170.

Eng, L.L., D. Belk, and C.H. Ericksen. 1990. California Anostraca: distribution, habitat, and status. Journal of Crustacean Biology 10:247–277.

Fehmi, J.S., and J.W. Bartolome. 2003. Impacts of livestock and burning on the spatial patterns of grass *Nassella pulchra* (Poaceae). Madrono 50(1):8–14.

Fenenga, G.L. 1991. A preliminary analysis of faunal remains from early sites in the Tulare Lake Basin. P. 11–22 in W.J. Wallace and F.A. Riddell (eds.), Contributions to Tulare Lake archaeology I: background to a study of Tulare Lake's archaeological past. Tulare Lake Archaeological Research Group, Redondo Beach, CA.

Fenenga, G.L. 1994. Alternative interpretations of Late Pleistocene paleoecology in the Tulare Lake Basin, San Joaquin Valley, California. Kern County Archaeological Society Journal 5:105–117.

Fowler, N.L. 1986. Microsite requirements for germination and establishment of three grass species. American Midland Naturalist 115:131–145.

Fremont, J.C. 1848. Geographical memoir upon upper California. 30th Congress, 1st Session, Senate Misc. Doc. 148.

Frenkel, R.E. 1970. Ruderal vegetation along some California roadsides. University of California Press, Berkeley.

Frost, C.C. 1998. Presettlement fire frequency regimes of the United States: a first approximation. P. 70–81 in T. L. Pruden and L. A. Brennan (eds.), Fire in ecosystem management: shifting the paradigm from suppression to prescription. Tall Timbers Fire Ecology Conference Proceedings, No. 20 Tall Timbers Research Station, Tallahassee, FL.

Fry, D.L. 2002. Effects of a prescribed fire on oak woodland stand structure. In Proceedings of the fifth symposium on oak woodlands: oaks in California's changing landscape. USDA Forest Service Gen. Tech. Rpt. PSW-GTR-184.

George, M.R., J.R. Brown, and W.J. Clawson. 1992. Application of nonequilibrium ecology to management of mediterranean grasslands. Journal of Range Management 45:436–440.

Gerlach, J., A. Dyer, and K. Rice. 1998. Grassland and foothill woodland ecosystems of the Central Valley. Fremontia 26:4.

Glenn-Lewis, D.C., L.A. Johnson, T.W. Jurik, A. Akey. M. Loeschke, and T. Rosburg. 1990. Fire in central North American grasslands: vegetative reproduction, seed germination, and seedling establishment. P. 28–45 in S.L. Collins and L.L. Wallace (eds.), Fire in North American tallgrass prairies. University of Oklahoma Press, Norman.

Gordon, B.I. 1977. Monterey Bay Area: natural history and cultural imprints. Boxwood, Pacific Grove, CA.

Gordon, D.R., and K.J. Rice 1993. Competitive effects of grassland annuals on soil water and blue oak (Quercus douglasii) seedlings. Ecology 74(1):68–82.

Greenlee, J.M., and J.H. Langeheim. 1990. Historic fire regimes and their relation to vegetation patterns in the Monterey Bay Area of California. American Midland Naturalist 124:239–253.

Griffin J.R. 1977. Oak woodland. P. 383–415 in M.G. Barbour and J. Major (eds.), Terrestrial vegetation of California. Wiley, New York.

Haggerty, P.K. 1994. Damage and recovery in southern Sierra Nevada foothill oak woodland after a severe ground fire. Madrono 41(3): 185–198.

Hamilton, J.G. 1997. Changing perceptions of pre-European grasslands in California. Madrono 44:311–333.

Hatch, D.A., J.W. Bartolome, and D.S. Hillyard. 1991. Testing a management strategy for restoration of California's native grasslands. P. 343–349 in Proceedings of the Yosemite centennial symposium. Yosemite Association, El Portal, CA.

Heady, H.F. 1977. Valley grassland. P. 491–514 in M. G. Barbour and J. Major (eds.), Terrestrial vegetation of California. Wiley, New York.

Heady, H.F., J.W. Bartolome, M.D. Pitt, G.D. Savelle, and M.C. Stroud. 1991. California Prairie. P. 313–335 in R. T. Coupland (ed.), Natural grasslands. Series: Ecosystems of the world. Vol. 8A. Introduction and Western Hemisphere. Elsevier, New York.

Hervey, D.F. 1949. Reaction of a California annual-plant community to fire. Journal of Range Management 2:116–121.

Holland, R., and S. Jain. 1988. Vernal pools. P. 515–533 in M.G. Barbour and J. Major (eds.), Terrestrial vegetation of California. Wiley, New York.

Holland, R.F. 1978. The geographic and edaphic distribution of vernal pools in the Great Central Valley, California. California Native Plant Society special publication.

Holland, R.F., and F.T. Griggs. 1976. A unique habitat—California's vernal pools. Fremontia 4(3):3–6.

Holstein, G. 2001. Pre-agricultural grassland in central California. Madrono 48(4):253–264.

Hoover, R.F. 1970. The vascular plants of San Luis Obispo County, California. University of California Press, Berkeley.

Hopkinson, P.J., S. Fehmi, and J.W. Bartolome. 1999. Summer burns reduce cover but not spread of barbed Goatgrass in California grassland. Ecological Restoration 17:168–169.

Huenneke, L.F. 1989. Distribution and regional patterns of California grasslands. P. 1–12 in L.F. Huenneke and A. Mooney (eds.), Grassland structure and function: California annual grassland. Kluwer Academic, Dordrecht, Netherlands.

Hull, J.C., and C.H. Muller. 1975. The potential for dominance by Stipa pulchra in a California grassland. The American Midland Naturalist 97:47–175.

Izlar, R.L. 1984. Some comments on fire and climate in the Okefenokee swamp-marsh complex. P. 70–85 in A.D. Cohen, D.J. Casagrande, M.J. Andrejko, and G.R. Best (eds.), The Okefenokee Swamp: its natural history, geology and geochemistry. Wetlands Surveys, Los Alamos, NM.

Jackson, L.E. 1985. Ecological origins of California's mediterranean grasses. Journal of Biogeography 12:349–361.

Jepson, W.L. 1923. The trees of California, 2nd. ed. Sather Gate, Berkeley, CA.

Jepson, W.L. 1910. The silva of California. University of California Mem., Vol. 2. 480 p.

Jones, B.J., and R.M. Love. 1945. Improving California ranges. University of California Agricultural Experiment Station Circular 129:1–48.

Keeley, J.E. 1981. Reproductive cycles and fire regimes. P. 231–277 in H.A. Mooney, T.M. Bonnicksen, N.L. Christensen, J.E. Lotan, and W.A. Reiners (eds.), Proceedings of the conference fire regimes and ecosystems properties. USDA Forest Service, General Technical Report WO-26.

Keeley, J.E. 1989. The California valley grassland. P. 2–23 in A. A. Schoenherr (ed.), Endangered plant communities of southern California. California State University, Fullerton. Southern California Botanists. Special Publication No. 3.

Keeley, J.E. 2002. Native American impacts on fire regimes of the California coast ranges. Journal of Biogeography 29:303–320.

Keeley, J.E., and C.J. Fotheringham. 2001. The historic fire regime in southern California shrublands. Conservation Biology 15:1536–1548.

Kirby, R.E., Lewis, S.J., and Sexton, T.N. 1988. Fire in North American wetland ecosystems and fire-wildfire relations: an annotated bibliography. Biol Rep 88(1), U.S. Fish and Wildl. Serv., Washington, DC, 146 p.

Klinger, R.C., and I. Messer. 2001. The interaction of prescribed burning and site characteristics on the diversity and composition of a grassland community on Santa Cruz Island, California. P. 66–80 in K.E.M. Galley and T. P. Wilson (eds.), Proceedings of the invasive species workshop: the role of fire in the control and spread of invasive species. Fire Conference 2000: The First National Congress on Fire Ecology, Prevention, and Management. Tall Timbers Research Station, Tallahassee, FL.

Knapp, E.E., and K.J. Rice. 1994. Starting from seed: genetic issues in using native grasses for restoration. Restoration and Management Notes 12:40–45.

Knoop, W.T., and B.H. Walker. 1976. The interactions of woody and herbaceous vegetation in a southern African savanna. Journal of Ecology 73:235–253.

Komarek, E. V. 1964. The natural history of lightning. Tall Timbers Fire Ecology Conference Proceedings 8:169–197.

Kotzebue, O. von. 1830. A new voyage round the world in the years 1823–1826. De Capo Press, New York.

Kuchler, A. W. 1977. The map of the natural vegetation of California. P. 909–938 in M. G. Barbour and J. Major (eds.), Terrestrial vegetation of California. Wiley-Interscience, New York.

Langstroth, R. 1991. Fire and grazing ecology of *Stipa pulchra* grassland: a field study at Jepson Prairie, California. M.S. Thesis, University of California, Davis.

Lathrop, E. W., and C. D. Osborne. 1991. Influence of fire on oak seedlings and saplings in southern oak woodland on the Santa Rosa Plateau Preserve, Riverside, CA. P. 366–370 in Proceedings of the symposium on oak woodlands and hardwood rangeland management. USDA Forest Service, Pacific Southwest Forest and Range Experimental Station , Berkeley, CA. General Technical Report PSW-126.

Lewis, H. T. 1973. Patterns of Indian burning in california: ecology and ethnohistory. Ballena Press Anthropological Papers 1:1–101.

Litke, F. P. 1992. Diary written during the round the world voyage of the sloop Kamchatka. P. 135–163 in L. A. Shur (S. Watrous, trans.), To the shores of the new world. Nauka, Moscow, 1975.

Loveless, C. M. 1959. A study of vegetation in the Florida Everglades. Ecology 40:1–9.

Mack, R. N. 1989. Temperate grasslands vulnerable to plant invasions: characteristics and consequences. P. 155–179 in J. A. Drake, H. A. Mooney, F. di Castri, R. H. Groves, F. J. Kruger, M. Rejmanek, and M. Williamson (eds.), Biological invasions: a global perspective. John Wiley & Sons, Chichester, NY.

Maranon, T., and J. W. Bartolome. 1994. Coast live oak (*Quercus agrifolia)* effects on grassland biomass and diversity. Madrono 41:39–52.

Marty, J. T. 2002. Managing and restoring California annual grassland species: an experimental field study. Ph.D. Dissertation. University of California, Davis.

McClaran, M. P. and J. W. Bartolome, 1987. Factors associated with oak regeneration in California. P. 86–91 in T. R. Plumb and N. H. Pillsbury (tech. coords.), Proceedings of the symposium on multiple-use management of California's hardwood resources. USDA Forest Service General Technical Report PSW-100.

McClaran, M. P. and J. W. Bartolome 1989. Fire-related recruitment in stagnant *Quercus douglasii* populations. Can. J. Forest Res. 19:580–585.

Menke, J. W. 1989. Management limits on productivity. P. 173–199 in L. F. Heunneke and H. Mooney (eds.), Grassland structure and function: California annual grassland. Kluwer Academic Publishers, Dordrecht, Netherlands.

Menke, J. W. 1992. Grazing and fire management for native perennial grass restoration in California grasslands. Fremontia 20(2):22–25.

Mensing, S. A. 1990. Blue oak regeneration in the Tehachapi Mountains. Fremontia 18:38–41. Meyer, M. D., and P. M. Schiffman. 1999. Fire season and mulch reduction in California annual grassland: a comparison of restoration strategies. Madrono 46:25-37.

Mensing, S. A. 1992. The impact of European settlement on blue oak (*Quercus douglasii*) regeneration and recruitment in the Tehachapi Mountains, California. Madrono 39(1):36–46.

Mitchell, V. L. 1969. The regionalization of climate in montane areas. Ph.D. dissertation. Univerisity of Wisconsin, Madison.

Mooney, H. A. (ed.) 1977. Convergent evolution in Chile and California mediterranean climate ecosystems. Dowden, Hutchinson and Ross, Inc., Stroudsberg, PA.

Morgan, D. L. 1960. California as I saw it. Incidents of travel by land and water by William M'Collum. The Talisman Press, Los Gatos, CA.

Muir, J. 1894. The mountains of California. Century, New York.

Muir, P. S., and R. K. Morseley. 1994. Response of *Primula alcalina,* a threatened species of alkaline seeps, to site and grazing. Natural Areas Journal 14:269–279.

Munz, P. A., and D. D. Keck. 1949. California plant communities. Aliso 2:87–105.

Naveh, Z. 1967. Mediterranean ecosystems and vegetation types in California and Israel. Ecology 48:445–459.

Noss, R. 1994. Managing rangelands. P. 220–262 in Saving nature's legacy. Island Press, Washington, DC.

Noy-Meier, I., M. Gutman, and Y. Kaplan. 1989. Responses of mediterranean grassland plants to grazing and protection. Journal of Ecology 77:290–310.

Ohmart, R. D., and Anderson, B. W. 1982. North American desert riparian ecosystems. P. 433–479 in G. L. Bender (ed.), Reference handbook on the deserts of North America. Greenwood Press, Westport, CN.

Parsons, D. J., and T. J. Stohlgren 1989. Effects of varying fire regimes on annual grasslands in the southern Sierra Nevada of California. Madrono 36(3):154–168.

Pavlik, B. M., P. C. Muick, S. Johnson, and M. Popper. 1991. Oaks of California. Cachuma Press, Los Olivos, CA.

Piemeisel, R. L., and F. R. Lawson. 1937. Types of vegetation in the San Joaquin Valley of California and their relation to the beet leafhopper. United States Department of Agriculture, Washington, DC.

Plumb, T. R. 1980. Response of oaks to fire. P. 205–215 in Proceedings of the symposium on ecology, management and utilization of California oaks, June 26–28, 1979. USDA Forest Service, Pacific Southwest USDA Forest Service 44.

Plumb, T. R., and A. P. Gomez. 1983. Five southern California oaks: identification and post fire management. USDA Forest Service, Pacific Southwest Forest and Range Experimental Station, Berkeley, CA. General Technical Report PSW-71.

Pollak, O., and T. Kan. 1996. The use of prescribed fire to control invasive exotic weeds at Jepson Prairie Preserve. P. 241–249 in C. W. Witham et al. (eds.), Ecology, conservation and management of vernal pool ecosystems—Proceedings from a 1996 conference. California Native Plant Society, Sacramento, CA, 1998.

Pyne, S. J. 1995. World fire. Henry Holt and Company, New York.

Rice, K. J., and E. S. Nagy. 2000. Oak canopy effects on the distribution patterns of two annual grasses: the role of competition and soil nutrients. American Journal of Botany 87:1699–1706.

Roquefeuil, M. C. 1823. A voyage round the world between the years 1816–1819. Phillips, London.

Rundel, P. R. 1980. Adaptations of mediterranean-climate oaks to environmental stress. P. 43–54 in Proceedings of the symposium on the ecology, management and utilization of California oaks. USDA Forest Service, Pacific Southwest Forest and Range Experimental Station, Berkeley, CA. General Technical Report PSW-44.

Sampson, A. W. 1944. Plant succession on burned chaparral lands in northern California. California Agricultural Experiment Station Bulletin 685:1–144.

Sawyer, J., and T. Keeler-Wolf. 1995. A manual of California vegetation. California Native Plant Society, Sacramento.

Schiffman, P.M. 1994. Promotion of exotic weed establishment by endangered giant kangaroo rats (*Dipodomys ingens*) in a California grassland. Biodiveristy and Conservation 3:524–537.

Schoenherr, A.A., 1992. A natural history of California. University of California Press, Berkeley.

Schroeder, M.J., and C.C. Buck. 1970. Fire weather: a guide for application of meteorological information to forest fire control operations. Washington, D.C. USDA Forest Service, Agricultural Handbook 360.

Spero J.G. 2002. Development and fire trends in oak woodlands of the Northwestern Sierra Nevada foothills. In Proceedings of the fifth symposium on oak woodlands: oaks in California's changing landscape. USDA Forest Service Gen. Tech. Rpt. PSW-GTR-184.

Stohlgren, T.J. 1993. Evaluating human effects on vegetation: an example from the Sierran foothills. P. 110–131 in S. D. Veirs, T. J. Stohlgren, and C. Schonewald-Cox (eds.), Proceedings of the fourth conference on research in California's National Parks. Transactions and Proceedings Series 9. National Park Service, Washington, DC.

Stuever, M.C. 1997. Fire induced mortality of Rio Grande Cottonwood. Master's Thesis. University of New Mexico, Albuquerque.

Swiecki, T.J., and E.A. Bernhardt. 1998. Understanding blue oak regeneration. Fremontia 26:1.

Swiecki, T.J., and E.A. Bernhardt. 2002. Effects of fire on blue oak saplings. In Proceedings of the fifth symposium on oak woodlands: oaks in California's changing landscape. USDA Forest Service Gen. Tech. Rpt. PSW-GTR-184.

Swiecki, T.J., E.A. Bernhardt, and R.A. Arnold. 1990. Impacts of diseases and arthropods on California's rangeland oaks. Report to Forest and Rangeland Resources Assessment Program, CDF, Sacramento, CA.

Thurber, G. 1880. Gramineae. P. 253–328 in S. Watson (ed.), Geological survey of California: botany of California, Vol. II. John Wilson and Son, University Press, Cambridge, MA.

Tietje, W.D., J.K. Vreeland, and W.H. Weitkamp. 2001. Live oak saplings survive prescribed fire and sprout. Calif. Agric. 55(2): 18–22.

Timbrook, J., J.R. Johnson, and D.D. Earle. 1982. Vegetation burning by the Chumash. Journal of California and Great Basin Anthropology 4:163–186.

Torrey, J. 1859. Botany of the boundary. In Report on the United States and Mexican boundary survey, Vol. 2, Pt. 1, 24th Congress, 1st Session, Exec. Doc., 135.

Twisselmann, E.C. 1956. A flora of the Temblor Range and the neighboring part of the San Joaquin Valley. The Wasmann J. Biol. 14:161.

Twisselmann, E.C. 1967. A flora of Kern County. University of San Francisco Press, San Francisco.

Vankat, J.L., and J. Major. 1978. Vegetation changes in Sequoia National Park, California. J. Biogeog. 5:377–402.

Viosa, P., Jr. 1931. Spontaneous combustion in the marshes of southern Lousiana. Ecology 12:439–442.

Vogl, R. 1974. Effect of fire on grasslands. P. 139–194 in T. T. Kozlowski and C. E. Ahlgren (eds.), Fire and ecosystems. Academic Press, New York.

Vreeland, J.K., and W.D. Tietje. 2002. Numerical response of small vertebrates to prescribed fire in a California oak woodland. In Proceedings of the fifth symposium on oak woodlands: oaks in California's changing landscape. USDA Forest Service Gen. Tech. Rpt. PSW-GTR-184.

Wade, D., J. Ewel, and R. Hosfstetter. 1980. Fire in south Florida ecosystems. USDA Forest Service General Technical Report SE-17. Southeastern Forest Experiment Station, Asheville, NC.

Wallace, W.J., and F.A. Riddell 1988. Archaeological background of Tulare Lake, California. P. 87–101 in J. A. Willig, C. M. Aikers, and J. L. Fargan (eds.), Early occupations in far western North America: the Clovis-Archaic interface. Nevada State Museum Anthropological Papers No. 21.

Wallace, W.J., and F.A. Riddell 1991. Contributions to Tulare Lake archaeology I: Background to a study of Tulare Lake's archaeological past. Tulare Lake Archaeological Research Group, Redondo Beach.

Wallace, W.J., and F.A. Riddell 1993. Contributions to Tulare Lake archaeology II: Finding the evidence: the quest for Tulare Lake's archaeological past. Tulare Lake Archaeological Research Group, Redondo Beach.

Webster, L. 1981. Composition of native grasslands in the San Joaquin Valley, California. Madrono 28:231–241.

Wells, P.V. 1964. Antibiosis as a factor in vegetation patterns. Science 144:889.

Whelan, R.J. 1995. The ecology of fire. Cambridge University Press, Cambridge, England.

White, K.L. 1966. Structure and composition of foothill woodland in central coastal California. Ecology 47(2):229–237.

Wickstrom, C.K.R. 1987. Issues concerning Native American use of fire: a literature review. Yosemite National Park, CA, Yosemite Research Center, Publ. Anthropol. 6.

Wilbur, R.B., and N.L. Christensen. 1983. Effects of fire on nutrient availability in a North Carolina Coastal Plain pocosin. American Midland Naturalist 110:54–61.

Williams, G.W. 1998. References on the American Indian use of fire in ecosystems. Manuscript and bibliography. USDA Forest Service, Pacific Northwest Region, Portland, OR.

Williamson, R.S. 1853. Reports of exploration and surveys to ascertain the most practical and economical route for the railroad from the Mississippi River to the Pacific Ocean. Vol. 5. Beverley Tucker, Washington, DC.

Wills, R. 1999. Effective fire planning of California grasslands. In J. E. Keeley (ed.), Second interface between ecology and land development in California. USGS Open-File Report 00-62.

Wills, R. 2001. Effects of varying fire regimes in a California native grasslands. Ecological Restoration 19:92–109.

York, D. 1997. A fire ecology study of the Sierra Nevada foothill basaltic mesa grassland. Madrono 44(4):374–383.

Young, J.A., and R.F. Miller. 1985. Response of *Sitanion histrix* (Nutt.) J. G. to prescribed burning. American Midland Naturalist 113:182–187.

Zavon, J.A. 1982. Grazing and fire effect on annual grassland composition and sheep diet selectivity. Master's Thesis. University of California, Davis. 41 p.

Zedler, P.H. 1987. The ecology of southern California vernal pools: a community profile. Biological Report 85(7.11). National Wetlands Research Center, U.S. Fish and Wildlife Service.

CHAPTER 14

Central Coast Bioregion

FRANK W. DAVIS AND MARK I. BORCHERT

Branches broken by this storm in one night added more fuel
than had accumulated in more than thirty years of fire control.
Thus, the stage was set for the fury that erupted when lightning
set four fires in the Ventana Wilderness.

JIM GRIFFIN *on the Marble Cone fire of 1977*

Description of Bioregion

The Central Coast bioregion includes the Central California
Coast and Central California Coast Ranges Sections (Map
14.1) (Miles and Goudey 1997) in the California Coastal
Chaparral Forest and Shrub Province of the Mediterranean
Division of the Humid Temperate Domain (Bailey 1995). The
bioregion extends from Napa County south to northern
Santa Barbara County, altogether covering 38,830 km^2
(14,992 mi^2). The eastern boundary of the bioregion adjoins
the western edge of the San Joaquin Valley. Familiar coastal
landmarks include San Francisco Bay, Monterey Bay, Big Sur,
and Morro Bay. Notable interior landmarks include Mt. Diablo, San Benito Mountain, and the Carrizo Plain.

Physical Geography

The topography of the region consists of rugged, northwest-
to-southeast trending ranges, notably the Santa Cruz Mountains, Santa Lucia Ranges, San Rafael Mountains, Diablo
Range, Gabilan Range, and Temblor Range. Expansive intervening valleys include the Santa Clara, Salinas, and Santa
Maria River valleys. Elevations range from sea level to over
1,800 m (5,906 ft). Half of the area in the Central California
Coast Section is below 160 m elevation (525 ft), versus 488 m
(1,600 ft) in the Central California Coast Ranges.

Geology exerts a strong control on landforms, soils, and vegetation of the region (Wells 1962, Griffin 1975). The lithology
of the region is dominated by folded and faulted Cenozoic
marine and nonmarine sediments, with the exception of the
northern Santa Lucia Range and northern Gabilan Range,
which are composed of Mesozoic granitic and Triassic metamorphic rocks. Marine sediments are predominantly interbed-
ded sandstones and shales.

In the Central California Coast Section, rugged terrain,
complex geology, local topo-climatic variability and disturbance history result in complex local vegetation mosaics
(Wells 1962). In general, upland natural vegetation changes
from coastal prairies and coastal sage scrub below 300 m
(984 ft) through chaparral-dominated slopes to roughly
1,200 m (3,937 ft), to montane hardwood and mixed hardwood forests at the higher elevations. Conifer forests are
prevalent at elevations above 1,500 m (4,921 ft). Interior valleys and annual grasslands, oak woodlands, and chaparral-
dominated foothills lie to the east of the coastal ridges.
Annual grasslands, semi-desert chaparral, and oak woodlands
dominate the driest interior portion of this section.

Azonal grasslands, shrublands, and woodlands are associated with scattered serpentinite outcrops of the Mesozoic
Franciscan Complex, a mélange of metamorphosed sedimentary and volcanic rocks. These outcrops are especially
widespread in the South Coastal Santa Lucia Range. In the
Diablo Range, San Benito Mountain is the upper portion of
a highly altered ultrabasic plug with large patches of highly
mineralized serpentine (Griffin 1975). Stabilized Pleistocene
sand dunes support distinctive maritime chaparral vegetation
in the Santa Maria and Salinas River valleys, east of Pismo
and Morro Bays and at other stretches near the coast as far
north as Sonoma County (Van Dyke and Holl 2001).

Climatic Patterns

The regional climate is strongly mediterranean with cool wet
winters and warm dry summers. More than 80% of seasonal
rain falls between November and March, primarily due to
occluded fronts and occasional cold fronts from the west-
northwest (Null 1995). Precipitation decreases from north to
south, but topography exerts an equally strong influence on climate with the highest rainfall in the coastal mountains and
lowest rainfall in rain shadows along the eastern edge of the
region (Map 14.2). To illustrate these patterns, at the northern
end of the region, long-term mean annual precipitation

decreases from 1,250 mm (49.2 in) in Big Basin Redwoods State Park to 767 mm (30.2 in) in Santa Cruz to 427 mm (16.8 in) at Pinnacles National Monument. At the southern end of the region, mean annual rainfall ranges from 575 mm (22.7 in) at San Luis Obispo to 140 mm (5.5 in) at interior station Cuyama. In general, the highest rainfall is associated with El Niño years and lower rainfall with La Niña years (Cayan et al. 1999).

Seasonal temperatures also vary considerably with latitude, elevation, and distance from the coast (Map 14.3) (Thornton et al. 1997). At coastal stations, mean monthly temperatures at sea level range from 10°C–13°C (50°F–55°F) in the winter months to 16°C–18°C (60.8°F–64.4°F) in the summer, with highest temperatures in August through October. The coastal ranges prevent a strong marine influence from reaching more than a few kilometers inland from the coast except via large river valleys, and inland temperature regimes are considerably more continental. For example, mean daily maximum temperatures at coastal Morro Bay for the period 1959–2001 ranged from 16.7°C (62°F) in January to 20.8°C (69.4°F) in October. In contrast, 30 kilometers inland at Paso Robles mean daily maximum temperatures range from 15.2°C (59.4°F) in January to 34.5°C (94.1°F) in July.

WEATHER SYSTEMS

During the fire season, Santa Ana conditions (see Keeley, this volume) are most likely to occur during the fall (Sommers 1978). At the southern end of the region, Santa Ana conditions and local foehn winds increase the risk of large wildfires (Davis and Michaelsen 1995, Moritz et al. 2004). Further north, the relative location of the high-pressure center over Utah and Nevada, as well as the northwest-southeast axis of the Central Coast Ranges, limits the development of strong Santa Ana conditions, but foehn winds can still be locally important.

Summer convective storms and accompanying lightning activity are uncommon in the Central Coast due to a strong atmospheric inversion and cool coastal marine layer. In fact, except for the Northern California Coast, the Central Coast has the lowest incidence of lightning strikes of any region in the state. Lightning network data since 1985 indicate an average of only 2.99 strikes per 100 km^2 per year in the Central Coast bioregion compared to 27.26 strikes/100 km^2/yr for the Sonoran Desert bioregion of California or 19.60 strikes/km^2/yr for the Sierra Nevada bioregion (Jan van Wagtendonk, personal communication; see also Keeley 1982, Keeley 2002a, Keeley and Fotheringham 2003). Lightning-ignited wildfires are accordingly rare but in the right weather and fuel moisture conditions they can become quite large, as exemplified by the 72,500 ha (179,150 ac) Marble Cone fire of 1977 in the northern Santa Lucia Mountains.

Live fuel moisture of chaparral in the region peaks in April and declines steadily to minimum levels in September and October (Fig. 14.1). This general pattern is observed at stations throughout the bioregion, but there is high local variation as well as marked inter-annual variability in fuel moisture associated with late winter and spring precipitation (Davis and

Michaelsen 1995). Between 1976 and 1999, the lowest minimum summer fuel moisture levels (48%–55% across stations) occurred during the multi-year drought from 1984 to 1988. Highest minimum summer fuel moisture levels (60%–78%) followed strong El Niño years (1982–1983, 1997–1998).

Long-term rainfall history data from station records and tree rings indicate two to seven-year wet-dry cycles in coastal California between San Francisco and San Diego for at least the past 400–600 years (Michaelsen et al. 1987; Haston and Michaelsen 1994, 1997). There is no clear relationship between annual precipitation and the El Niño Southern Oscillation (ENSO) over the long-term record. The Central Coast often shows the opposite pattern to southern California south of Point Conception, so that wet years in the south often coincide with dry years in the north, and vice-versa (Haston and Michaelsen 1997).

There is evidence of 20- to 50-year fluctuations in Central Coast rainfall and even longer-term precipitation patterns including a generally wetter climate during the sixteenth and seventeenth centuries followed by a relatively drier climate during the eighteenth and nineteenth centuries (Haston and Michaelsen 1994). Furthermore, the magnitude of climate variability has fluctuated considerably over 50- to 150-year periods and there is evidence that variability has been increasing during the past 30 to 40 years (Haston et al. 1988, Haston and Michaelsen 1997). Such variation in rainfall could have affected the incidence and extent of wildfires in the Central Coast during different eras. Analyzing climate and fire data from 1913 to 2001, Keeley (2003) found a weak but significant positive relationship between the Palmer Drought Severity Index (PDSI) for the current year and fire occurrence in the Central Coast (correlation r = 0.23, p < 0.05) and a modest relationship between previous-year index and fire occurrence (r = 0.45, p < 0.01). However, there was only a weak positive relationship between the index and total area burned (Keeley 2003). The weak relationship between PDSI and fire in this region is in contrast to stronger relationships observed in other regions of the western U.S. (Westerling et al. 2003) and probably indicates the stronger control exerted by autumn foehn wind events than by fine fuels or fuel moisture levels on wildfire risk in the region (Keeley 2004, discussed below).

Human Geography

Since the early Holocene, native peoples have occupied the Central Coast bioregion at relatively high population densities, especially along the immediate coastal plains, foothills, and valleys, where densities may have averaged one to three persons per km^2 (Beals and Hester 1974, cited in Keeley 2002). Spanish settlement began in earnest in the last quarter of the eighteenth century with the construction of missions and the low but steady influx of new settlers during the Mexican era from 1836 to 1850. The population climbed gradually through the early twentieth century and rapid growth did not commence until the 1940s, especially in Bay-area counties (Fig. 14.2).

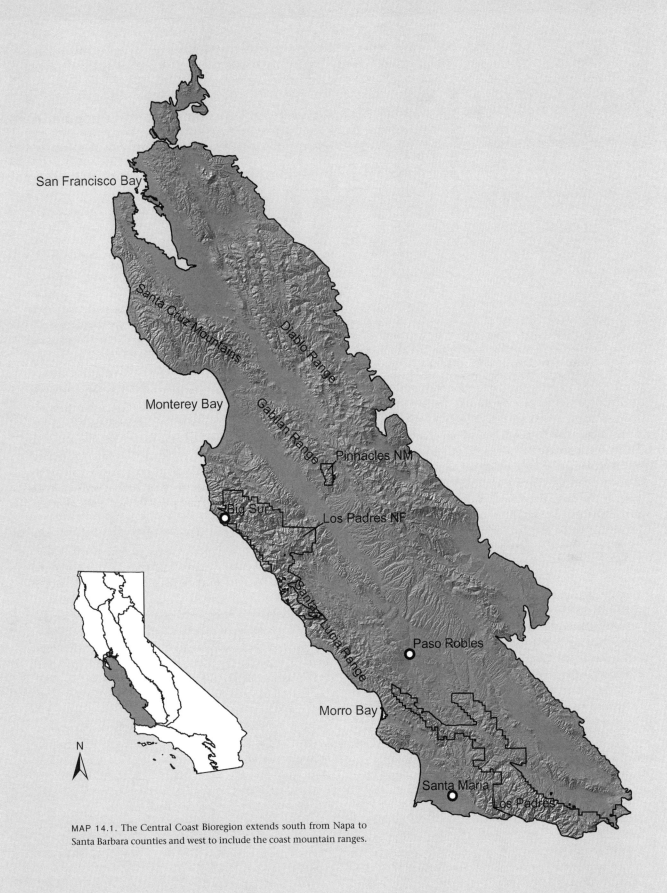

MAP 14.1. The Central Coast Bioregion extends south from Napa to
Santa Barbara counties and west to include the coast mountain ranges.

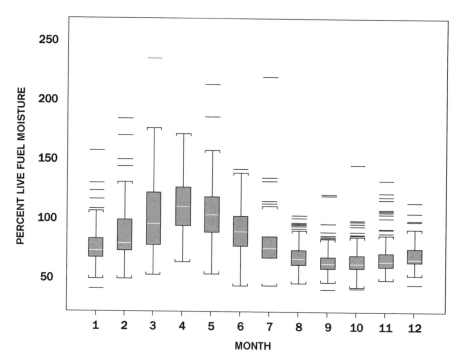

FIGURE 14.1. Boxplots of monthly percentage of live fuel moisture data for chamise sampled from seven locations, Monterey to Santa Barbara County, in Los Padres National Forest. (Data from 1976–1999, courtesy of Los Padres National Forest.)

Most of the population increase has occurred near the coast, whereas the interior of the region remains rural. Today the region is still sparsely settled with the exception of the Bay area and smaller urban centers such as Santa Cruz, Monterey, Salinas, Paso Robles, San Luis Obispo, and Santa Maria. Eighty-seven percent of the region has a housing density of less than one house per 8 ha (20 ac). With the exception of the large wilderness areas, a dense network of public and private roads accesses these rural lands. For example, excluding major state and interstate highways, a 50-m (164-ft) buffer on either side of the mapped roads (U.S. 2000 TIGER data) of Santa Cruz County encompasses roughly 25% of the county. In Monterey and San Luis Obispo Counties the same buffers enclose 15% and 13%, respectively. In general, road-buffer areas range from more than 80% in densely developed areas to less than 20% in rural, sparsely roaded areas of California.

Seventy-eight percent of the region is privately owned. Los Padres National Forest is the largest public landowner with 983,300 ha (2,429,720 ac) in the region, including large wilderness areas in the northern and southern Santa Lucia Ranges. Other large tracts of public land include Fort Hunter-Liggett, comprising 66,800 ha (165,066 ac), which adjoins Los Padres National Forest in southern Monterey County; Fort Ord (11,237 ha [27,767 ac]) on Monterey Bay; and Pinnacles National Monument (5,396 ha [13,333 ac]) in San Benito County.

Ecological Subregions

Miles and Goudey (1997) divided the California Coast Ranges and Central California Coast Ranges Sections into 23 ecological subsections based on geology, geomorphic processes, soil groups, subregional climates, and potential natural plant communities (Table 14.1, Map 14.4). To help discriminate systematic geographic variation in environmental conditions and

associated fire regimes in the Central Coast bioregion, we subjected the subsection data in Table 14.1 (excluding subsection area) to principal components analysis (PCA) using the correlation matrix of the 12 variables. We included modern fire history (Table 14.1, variable 11) in the analysis because, although the modern fire history differs considerably from the historic regimes, the modern pattern of fire occurrence is still highly correlated with environmental factors such as vegetation, climate, land use, and topography and this pattern is most pertinent to current management considerations.

Subsection scores for the first two PCA axes, which account for 33% of the total variance, revealed four geographically and environmentally distinctive clusters (Fig. 14.3 and Map 14.5). We refer to these subregions as: (1) developed plains, valleys, and terraces, (2) the Santa Cruz Mountains, (3) the Santa Lucia Ranges, and (4) the Interior Coast Ranges. The factor loadings in PCA axes 1 and 2 (shown as arrows in Fig. 14.3) can be used to interpret the scores for each subsection. For example, the cluster of subsections with low scores in PCA axis 2 (Subregion 1, as described below) are those with high urban or cropland areas and a small percentage of the region in native vegetation types like blue oak woodland.

The first subregion (developed plains, valleys, and terraces) consists of flat areas dominated by urban and agricultural land use and low fire frequency. There are three disjunct areas including the Santa Maria Valley; the Watsonville Plain/Salinas Valley; and the San Francisco Bay peninsula, bay flats, and East Bay Terraces. Overall, 20% of the Central Coast region has been converted to urban or agricultural uses (California Department of Forestry and Fire Protection Multi-source landcover data, 2002, v.2, http://frap.cdf.ca.gov/data/frapgisdata/select.asp).

Of the remaining subregions, the Santa Cruz Mountains Subregion is distinctive in combining high rainfall, high

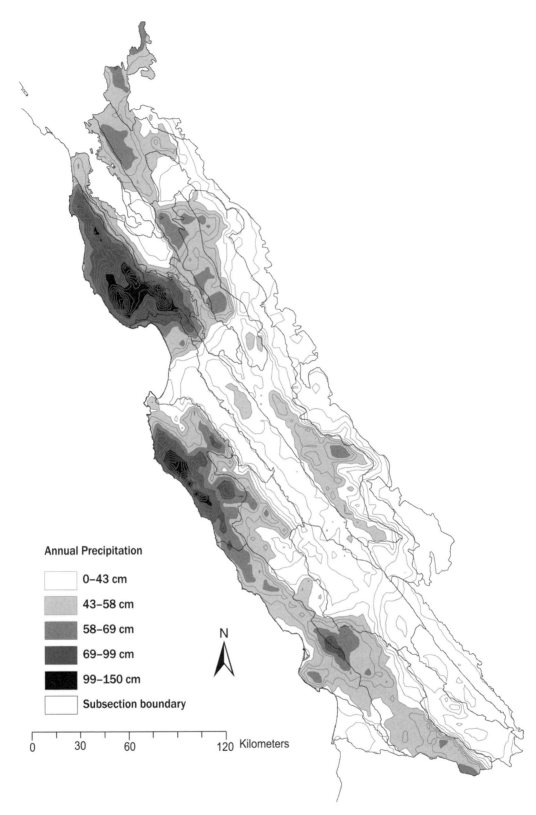

Annual Precipitation

- 0–43 cm
- 43–58 cm
- 58–69 cm
- 69–99 cm
- 99–150 cm
- Subsection boundary

N

0   30   60   120   Kilometers

MAP 14.2. Isohyets of mean annual precipitation interpolated from weather station data for the years 1961–1990. (See Daly et al. [1994] for a description of the interpolation method.)

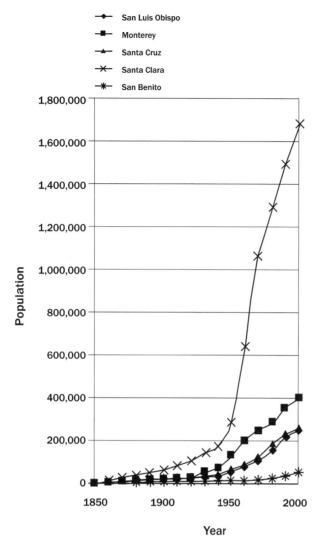

FIGURE 14.2. Population trends for selected counties of the Central Coast bioregion. (From California Department of Finance Demographic Research Unit, "Historical Census Populations of California State, Counties, Cities, Places, and Towns, 1850–2000," http://www.dof.ca.gov/ HTML/DEMOGRAP/Histtext.htm.)

relief, low fire occurrence, and extensive areas of Douglas-fir and coast redwood forests.

The Southern Coastal, North Coastal, and Interior Santa Lucia Ranges form a distinctive subregion characterized by extreme ruggedness, moderate rainfall and continentality, extensive shrublands, montane hardwood forests and mixed hardwood-conifer forests, and a high occurrence of wildfire.

The Interior Coast Ranges are characterized by moderate relief, low rainfall, high summer temperatures, extensive grasslands, and intermediate wildfire frequency. Two ecological subsections—the East Bay Hills–Mount Diablo and the Leeward Hills—are intermediate in character between the Santa Cruz Mountains and the Interior Coast Ranges (Fig. 14.3). However, rather than create a separate subregion, we combined them with the interior subsections.

These four subregions provide a useful construct for comparing and contrasting fire regimes in different areas and plant communities of the Central Coast bioregion. Given the long history of cultivation in developed plains, valleys, and terraces, it is not possible to reconstruct the fire regimes of urban and agricultural valleys except in the broadest sense. We provide separate treatments of the fire history, modern fire regimes, and plant communities in the remaining three ecological subregions: the Santa Cruz Mountains, the Santa Lucia Ranges, and the Interior Coast Ranges. We describe the fire ecology and plant community–fire regime interactions of selected community species and community types associated with the Santa Lucia Ranges. We do not provide such descriptions for the other subregions because the relevant species and community types are covered in other chapters and/or because of the lack of scientific research to support such an analysis.

Santa Cruz Mountains Subregion

Major ecological zones include: (1) coastal prairie and coastal sage scrub, (2) coast redwood–Douglas-fir and coast redwood–mixed evergreen forests, and (3) chaparral and oak woodland. Roughly 12% of the Santa Cruz Mountains subregion has been converted to urban and agricultural uses.

The coastal prairie and coastal scrub zone is most extensive below 300 m (975 ft) elevation between Point Año Nuevo and Pillar Point. Characteristic species include coyotebrush (*Baccharis pilularis*), seaside woolly sunflower (*Eriophyllum staechadifolium*), hairy brackenfern (*Pteridium aquilinum* var. *pubescens*), tufted hairgrass (*Deschampsia cespitosa* ssp. *Holciformis*), and California oatgrass (*Danthonia californica*).

Coast redwood–Douglas-fir and coast redwood–mixed evergreen forests cover many slopes of the Santa Cruz Mountains above 300 m (975 ft) and are the most widespread vegetation types in this subregion. Coast redwood is more common on the western slopes and in more mesic sites. Mixed evergreen forests of tan oak (*Lithocarpus densiflorus*), coast live oak (*Quercus agrifolia*), Pacific madrone (*Arbutus menziesii*), and California bay (*Umbellularia californica*) often occur on drier sites in topomosaics with coast redwood–Douglas-fir forests, and become more widespread in the more interior portions of the Santa Cruz Mountains.

Patches of chaparral and oak woodland are scattered throughout the subregion on xeric sites but also form an extensive zone below 600 m (1950 ft) along the eastern interior edge of the Santa Cruz Mountains. Characteristic species include chamise (*Adenostoma fasciculatum*), buck brush (*Ceanothus cuneatus* var. *cuneatus*), coast live oak, and valley oak (*Quercus lobata*).

Overview of Historic Fire Occurrence

PREHISTORIC PERIOD

Surprisingly little fire history research has been conducted in the Santa Cruz Mountains. As a result, we rely heavily on the

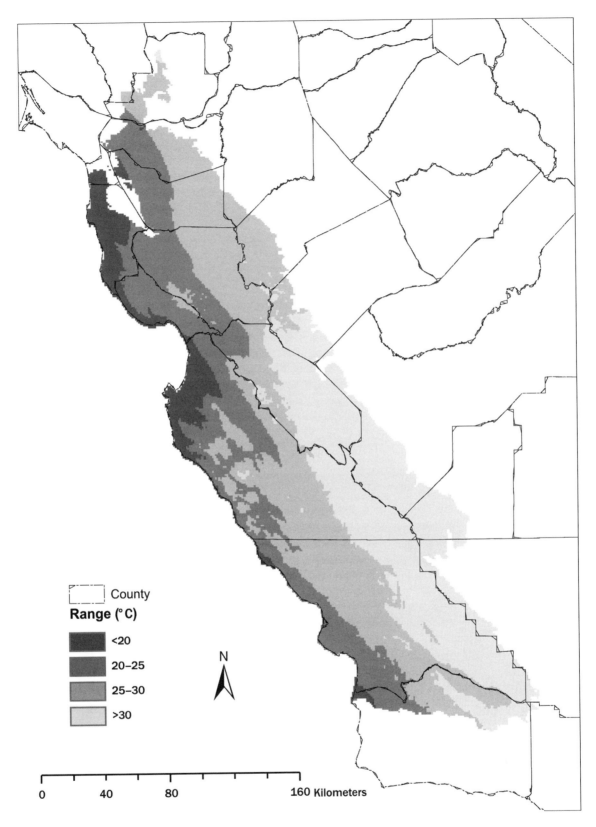

MAP 14.3. Mean annual temperature range in degrees centigrade (From DAYMET US Data Center, http://www.daymet.org/; see Thornton et al. (1997) for details of the method.)

TABLE 14.1

Ecological characteristics of the 23 subsections of the central coast bioregion

Zone / Subsection (Code)	Area (sq. km)	Annual ppt (1)	Ann. Temp. Range (2)	August Max Temp. (3)	Chaparral (4)	Crop (5)	Grassland (6)	Blue oak woodland (7)	Redwood–Douglas Fir (8)	Montane Hardwood–Mixed Hardwood Conifer(9)	Urban (10)	% Burned (11)	Relief (12)
Developed Valleys and Coastal Areas													
1. East Bay Terraces and Alluvium (261Ad)	505	27.08	27.54	26.74	0.00	1.38	1.49	0.02	0.00	0.00	94.51	0.18	2.48
2. San Francisco Peninsula (261Ai)	195	26.67	16.91	23.03	3.92	0.23	1.34	0.03	0.00	0.00	91.92	3.78	7.73
3. Bay Flats (261Ab)	272	19.52	21.90	26.91	0.00	1.10	1.30	0.00	0.00	0.00	80.63	0.00	0.79
4. Santa Clara Valley (261Ae)	1180	19.79	23.43	27.66	0.05	27.10	13.67	0.00	0.00	0.00	57.70	0.69	3.08
5. Watsonville Plain–Salinas Valley (261Ah)	1622	20.64	20.87	25.39	3.24	55.92	10.54	0.78	1.14	0.00	15.88	0.79	5.15
6. Santa Maria Valley (261Al)	620	21.41	20.98	25.65	7.08	45.91	10.83	4.14	0.00	0.33	19.16	6.31	3.72
Santa Cruz Mountains													
7. Santa Cruz Mountains (261Af)	1995	38.42	20.25	23.50	21.07	3.02	7.16	0.44	36.04	0.65	8.88	2.60	24.72
Santa Lucia Ranges													
8. North Coastal Santa Lucia Range (261Aj)	2522	37.41	22.61	23.63	42.98	0.19	9.98	0.12	2.38	10.83	2.77	51.59	34.50
9. Interior Santa Lucia Range (M262Ae)	4974	23.92	27.50	28.62	44.15	4.57	19.26	2.14	0.00	1.54	0.91	40.79	20.62
10. South Coastal Santa Lucia Range (261Ak)	2257	30.23	23.49	26.22	22.77	4.69	31.45	2.11	0.17	6.67	4.29	27.87	21.11
Interior Coast Ranges													
11. Suisun Hills and Valley (261Aa)	889	23.68	26.63	30.52	0.15	7.32	47.86	0.64	0.00	1.01	33.97	6.84	10.28
12. East Bay Hills–Mount Diablo (26lAc)	1190	21.56	23.87	28.04	11.82	0.15	24.76	0.12	0.38	1.37	35.08	4.25	19.36
13. Eastern Hills (M262Ad)	3567	15.45	31.74	33.09	3.83	1.00	83.07	2.97	0.00	0.00	2.23	16.58	16.43
14. Fremont- Livermore Hills and Valleys (M262Aa)	985	18.12	26.14	29.22	1.11	5.58	51.59	2.14	0.00	0.85	21.27	2.52	16.55
15. Leeward Hills (261Ag)	653	28.55	23.61	26.18	16.44	2.99	14.77	0.17	1.99	0.30	25.12	10.41	23.44
16. Diablo Range (M262Ac)	4739	19.58	32.51	31.91	19.74	0.77	33.42	25.98	0.00	0.55	0.35	14.16	24.48
17. Western Diablo Range (M262Ab)	1352	19.33	28.66	29.15	8.95	0.78	32.72	10.98	0.00	3.90	0.34	7.98	29.11
18. Gabilan Range (M262Af)	2424	20.15	29.10	30.05	20.49	1.34	49.01	0.55	0.00	0.51	0.19	14.77	17.29
19. Kettleman Hills and Valleys (M262Ag)	1055	11.09	31.83	34.40	0.00	38.04	52.88	0.06	0.00	0.00	6.22	3.46	4.02
20. Paso Robles Hills and Valleys (M262Ah)	2574	21.75	29.82	31.13	2.81	7.01	73.65	0.75	0.00	0.07	2.55	7.51	8.36
21. Temblor Range (M262Ak)	939	15.03	32.31	32.52	2.19	0.08	72.97	0.04	0.00	0.00	0.28	3.72	17.81
22. Carrizo Plain (M262Ai)	857	13.96	31.27	31.87	0.11	0.01	88.27	0.04	0.00	0.00	0.01	4.26	4.35
23. Caliente Range–Cuyama Valley (M262Aj)	1462	15.72	30.39	30.79	21.82	7.37	44.78	0.82	0.00	0.38	1.22	13.62	13.37

NOTE: Subsections are grouped into four zones for the purpose of describing the fire ecology of the region. Subsection names and codes are based on Miles and Goudy (1997). Climate statistics are based on 1 km climate grids (Thornton and Running 1997). Percentages of the subsection in different land use and land cover types are based on 100-m resolution multi-source land cover data (California Wildlife Habitat Relationship system) obtained from the California Department of Forestry and Fire Protection (CDF&FP).

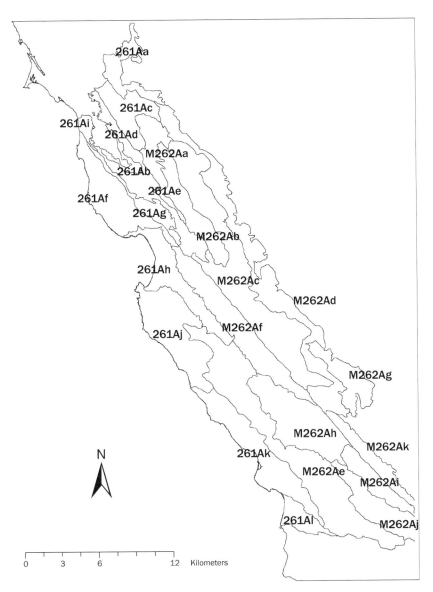

MAP 14.4. Ecological subsections of the study region as defined by Miles and Goudey (1997). See Table 14.1 for subsection names and descriptions.

study by Greenlee and Langenheim (1990) and on the reconstruction of fire history in Douglas-fir *(Pseudotsuga menziesii)* and coast redwood *(Sequoia sempervirens)* forests to the north at Point Reyes National Seashore by Brown et al. (1999).

Based on a simple model of lightning ignitions and fire spread, Greenlee and Langenheim (1990) concluded that, in the absence of aboriginal burning, coast redwood forests of the Santa Cruz Mountains would experience a mean fire interval of around 135 years while mixed evergreen forests might burn every 30 to 135 years. Being warmer and drier, oak woodland and chaparral environments were predicted to have shorter mean fire intervals of 10 to 30 years, while the interval between fires in coastal prairie and coastal sage scrub varied from 1 to 15 years. Given the documented low incidence of lightning in the region, these return intervals are probably too short for the coastal communities.

It is now widely accepted that Native Americans used fire to manage vegetation in central coastal California. Native Americans occupied the entire coast at densities averaging one

to three persons per km[2] (Keeley 2002b). The Ohlone (Castanoans) inhabited an area from San Francisco to Point Sur and regularly burned coastal vegetation to stimulate the seed production of preferred species (Lewis 1973, Gordon 1979). Greenlee and Langenheim (1990) argued that aboriginal burning increased fire frequency and reduced the mean fire interval in coast redwood forests from 135 years to 17–82 years. In contrast to these findings, fire histories from coast redwood–Douglas-fir forests at Point Reyes and the Santa Cruz Mountains suggest a higher pre-Columbian mean fire interval of 8 to 12 years (Brown et al. 1999, Stephens and Fry 2005).

HISTORIC PERIOD

The arrival of the Spanish in the late 1700s brought lasting changes in land use and fire regimes over much of the bioregion. In the Santa Cruz Mountains, prohibitions on burning, population decline, and cattle grazing during the Mission era of the late eighteenth and early nineteenth centuries reduced

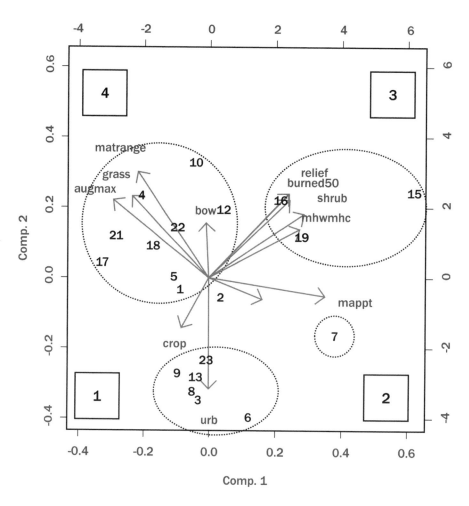

FIGURE 14.3. Scatterplot of PCA scores for 23 ecological subsections (see Table 14.1 for number codes). Loadings of original variables are portrayed as arrows. Variables include topographic relief (relief), mean annual precipitation (mappt), mean annual temperature range (matrange), august maximum temperature (augmax), percentage cropland (crop), percentage urban (urb), percentage grassland (grass), percentage shrubland (shrub), percentage blue oak woodland (bow), percentage montane hardwood/montane hardwood conifer (mhwmhc), and percentage of the subsection that burned at least once since 1950 (burned50). Fire subregions are enclosed in ellipses and numbered (boxes) to correspond with Map 14.5.

fire use by the Castanoans. Using a combination of modeling, newspaper accounts, and fire scars, Greenlee and Langenheim (1990) concluded that over the course of the nineteenth century and early twentieth century, fire frequency decreased in coastal vegetation types like coastal prairie and coastal sage scrub to a mean fire interval of 20 to 30 years and decreased in oak woodlands from a pre-Columbian mean fire interval of 1 to 2 years to 50 to 75 years. At the same time, they concluded that fire frequency increased in chaparral and coast redwood forests to 7 to 29 years and 20 to 50 years, respectively, probably due to fires that escaped from burning of logging slash as well as deliberate burning to convert chaparral to pasture and farmland. Logged areas of the Santa Cruz Mountains likely burned at least once and perhaps as many as three times during the late nineteenth and early twentieth century. Fire scar data from coast redwood forests to the north also show a late nineteenth century increase in fire frequency, but suggest a much shorter mean fire interval of 4 to 12 years (Brown et al. 1999, Stephens and Fry 2005) compared with the 20 to 50 years of Greenlee and Langenheim (1990).

CURRENT PERIOD

Since 1930, fire suppression has successfully controlled most wildfires in the Santa Cruz Mountains. Between 1929 and

1979, 3,765 recorded fires burned only 21,500 ha (53,105 ac), and 92% of the fires burned less than 4 ha (10 ac) (Greenlee and Langenheim 1990). One of the largest recorded fires burned 6,400 ha (15,808 ac) over a seven-day period in 1948 (Stephens et al. 2004). Fire suppression has reduced fire frequency in all major vegetation types, but most dramatically in coastal prairie, where fire now rarely, if ever, occurs. Their estimated mean fire intervals for chaparral/coastal sage scrub, oak woodland, and mixed evergreen forest are on the order of 150 to 250 years. Mean fire interval in a Monterey pine (*Pinus radiata*) forest varied from 40 to 60 years. Recent burning has been most prevalent in coast redwood forests, but even in that type the mean fire interval is estimated to be 100 to 150 years. Brown et al. (1999) report a similar pattern from Point Reyes National, where surface fires in coast redwood and Douglas-fir forests essentially ceased after 1945.

Major Ecological Zones

Coastal Prairie and Coastal Sage Scrub Unfortunately, the fire ecology and plant community–fire regime interactions of coastal prairie and Diablan coastal sage scrub have received little formal study. There is little doubt that fire frequency is much lower today than in prehistoric and historic

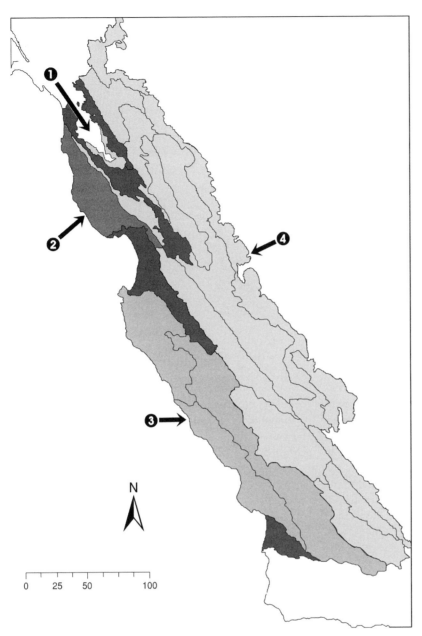

MAP 14.5. Aggregation of ecological subsections into ecological zones based on climate, topography, land use, vegetation, and post-1950 fire history. Subsection boundaries are drawn.

N

0   25   50   100

eras. Like other grassland and coastal scrub ecosystems, these communities are grazed and are also heavily invaded by exotic weeds. Hatch et al. (1999) examined the response of native grasses to fall burning and grazing in coastal prairie at Pomponio State Beach in the northwestern subregion and did not observe a significant effect of a single burn on California oatgrass or needlegrasses. Native species increased slightly under moderate grazing compared to ungrazed controls. The authors note that these responses are different from those obtained from grasslands at inland sites and suggest that fire and grazing exclusion have limited value for restoring coastal prairie.

Coast Redwood–Douglas-fir and Mixed Evergreen Forest Zone Stuart and Stephens (this volume) describe the fire ecology and interactions between fire regime and community

dynamics for coast redwood forest in northwest California. They note that the degree of fire dependence in this community type should be viewed as a continuum and that more southern and drier occurrence of the type may be more fire prone and fire dependent.

They also review the fire ecology and regime characteristics of Douglas-fir–tanoak forests, which bear a close resemblance to the mixed evergreen forests of the Santa Cruz Mountains. Douglas-fir is less prevalent in the mixed evergreen forests of the Santa Cruz Mountains, and we would expect these forests to be somewhat drier and more fire prone during the summer months than those to the north. As noted above, fire suppression has greatly reduced fire occurrence in both coast redwood–Douglas-fir and mixed evergreen forests compared with prehistoric and historic eras.

FIGURE 14.4. Grassland, chaparral, and coastal scrub mosaic in the foothill and lower montane zones of the southern Santa Lucia Ranges sub-region. View is looking northwest from Cuesta Grade toward Morro Bay, San Luis Obispo County. (Photo by Christopher Cogan.)

Chaparral and Oak Woodland Zone Keeley (this volume) discusses the fire ecology of chaparral vegetation and Wills (this volume) discusses the fire ecology of foothill oak woodland and grassland. As noted previously, no large wildfires have occurred in this zone since at least 1950, and Greenlee and Langenheim (1990) estimate that the mean fire interval here is now greater than 150 years. This contrasts sharply with chaparral communities in the other subregions of the Central Coast bioregion and in the South Coast California bioregion, where large wildfires still occur despite intense suppression efforts. This may reflect the patchier distribution of chaparral vegetation in the eastern Santa Cruz Mountains, the somewhat wetter and cooler prevailing climate, or the greater accessibility of the area to suppression forces.

Santa Lucia Ranges Subregion

Viewed along a coast-to-interior transect, major ecological zones of this subregion include: (1) coastal plain and foothills, which support coastal prairie, annual grassland, coastal sage scrub, maritime chaparral, coast live oak forests, and closed cone pine forests; (2) a lower montane zone dominated by topo-mosaics of chaparral, coastal sage scrub, and coast live oak woodlands and forests, but also supporting azonal serpentine grasslands and cypress woodlands; and (3) an upper montane zone supporting mixed evergreen forests, Coulter pine forests, and mixed conifer forests. Inland valleys and the interior edge of this subregion, which are dominated by oak woodland, coastal sage scrub, and annual grasslands, comprise a fourth ecological zone that we refer to as the interior foothill zone. Additionally, roughly 5% of the Santa Lucia Ranges subregion has been converted to urban and agricultural uses (Fig. 14.4).

In the coastal plain and foothills zone, widespread alliances include California annual grasslands, coyote brush, California sagebrush (*Artemesia californica*), blue blossom *(Ceanothus thyrsiflorus)*, and yet-to-be-described alliances of the Diablan, Franciscan, and Lucian coastal sage scrub associations. Coast live oak occurs in many coastal and foothill settings and plant communities including closed forests (typically greater than 60% crown cover), open woodlands and savannas (10%–60% crown closure with an herbaceous understory), coastal sage scrub and chaparral (Griffin 1988, Allen et al. 1991, Sawyer and Keeler-Wolf 1995, Peinado et al. 1997). Localized vegetation types of special interest include closed-cone pine forests and maritime chaparral. The former includes Bishop pine *(Pinus muricata)* forests, knobcone pine *(Pinus attenuata)* forests, and Monterey pine forests along the Monterey and Big Sur Coast. Maritime chaparral combines chamise, coast live oak, and highly localized California-lilac and manzanita species.

Vegetation of the lower montane zone includes a diverse variety of localized types but generally presents a mosaic of coastal scrub, chaparral, and oak woodland. Widespread scrub types include black sage (*Salvia mellifera*), purple sage *(Salvia leucophylla)*, and California buckwheat (*Eriogonum fasciculatum*). Widespread chaparral types include chamise, buck brush, and scrub oak alliances. Coast live oak is the most widespread woodland series. Sargent cypress (*Cupressus sargentii*) forests are one of the many distinctive mid-elevation community types associated with ultramafic-derived soils.

In the upper montane zone, mixed evergreen forests (oak, Pacific madrone, tan oak, California bay, big-leaf maple [*Acer macrophyllum*]) are widespread in the northern Santa Lucia Range. Hardwood-conifer forests (ponderosa pine [*Pinus ponderosa*], Coulter pine [*Pinus coulteri*], sugar pine [*Pinus lambertiana*], canyon live oak [*Quercus chrysolepis*], tan oak) are widespread in the North Coastal Santa Lucia Ranges at the highest elevations (Griffin 1975, 1979). Common single-species alliances include canyon live oak, California bay, tan oak, and Coulter pine.

Santa Lucia fir forests are patchily distributed at mid to high elevations, mainly in the watersheds of the Big Sur, Little Sur, and Upper Carmel Rivers in Monterey County. High elevation coastal forests include ponderosa pine and sugar pine alliances. In the southern Santa Lucia Mountains, mixed evergreen forests, conifer-hardwood forests, and montane conifer forests become highly localized in their distributions. Here Coulter pine/montane chaparral is the most abundant conifer type, especially in the La Panza Range (Borchert et al. 2004).

The interior foothill zone includes extensive blue oak and valley oak woodland, annual grassland, chamise chaparral, and California buckwheat scrub.

Overview of Historic Fire Occurrence

PREHISTORIC AND HISTORIC PERIODS

Analysis of charcoal particles in varved sediments from the Santa Barbara Basin from A.D. 1425 to 1985 furnishes the most detailed, long-term fire history for the southern Santa Lucia Ranges and western Transverse Ranges to the south (Byrne et al. 1977, Mensing et al. 1999). Using a significant correlation between the large charcoal (more than 3,750 μm^2) accumulation rate and total burned area on the coastal Santa Barbara Ranger District of Los Padres National Forest, Mensing et al. (1999) recorded 23 fires burning more than 20,000 ha (49,400 ac) in a 560-year record. The average interval between fires was 24 years (SD $\pm$ 18.4, n = 22) with a range of 5 to 75 years. Remarkably, the mean interval between large fires changed little during four very different periods: the Native American (prior to 1792), Spanish-Mexican (1792–1848), Anglo (1849–1929) and Recent (1930–present). Mensing et al. (1999) also compared a time series analyses of tree-ring data from bigcone Douglas-fir (*Pseudotsuga macrocarpa*) (Haston and Michaelsen 1994) with the varve record and found large fires to be most common in the early years of multi-year drought periods at the end of wet periods that perhaps resulted in higher fuel loads.

The fire history depicted in the varve sediments likely only applies to the southern Santa Lucia Mountains from Santa Barbara north to San Luis Obispo, or possibly to Morro Bay. Still, large fires periodically have burned along the coast of the northern Santa Lucia Mountains, as evidenced by the Marble Cone fire (72,500 ha [179,075 ac]) in 1977 and Kirk Complex (35,100 ha [86,697 ac]) in 1999, both caused by lightning. Even before fire suppression began around 1910, a 20,000-ha (49,400-ac) human-caused fire burned in 1903 and a 60,000-ha (148,200-ac) fire occurred in 1906 (Henson and Usner 1993). In the late 1800s, reports of huge fires were common in newspapers and government reports (Griffin 1978a).

Although fires larger than 20,000 ha (49,400 ac) probably have a long history in this region, prehistoric mudflows in the Big Sur River (Jackson 1977) suggest that the average interval between large fires may have been longer than the interval gleaned from varve cores in the Santa Barbara region. The two most recent mudflow events both coincided with large fires in watersheds of the Big Sur River drainage. Assuming such mudflows have followed all large fires, then the mean interval between fires over the period 1370 A.D. to 1972 A.D. can be estimated as 75 years (SD $\pm$ 19.7, n = 8). However, fire recurrence estimates from varve sediments and mudflows are not directly comparable because the varve sediments represent a much larger area than watersheds of the Big Sur River.

The extent of burning by Native Americans is unknown but was probably sufficient to alter pre-Columbian fire regimes and vegetation patterns over a significant part of the bioregion. The Esselen Indians occupied a comparatively small area from Point Sur to Big Creek and inland to the Salinas River. South and east of the Esselens, the Salinians reached San Carpoforo Creek. Unfortunately, we know little about fire use by either group (Henson and Usner 1993).

Further south, burning likely occurred not only in coastal prairie and oak woodlands, but also in chaparral and coastal sage scrub (Keeley 2002). South of the Salinians, the Chumash territory stretched from the Santa Maria River to the Santa Clara River and east to the upper Cuyama Valley (Keeley 2002b). Using diaries and journals of early explorers and clerics, Timbrook et al. (1982) documented that the Chumash, like the Ohlone to the north, regularly employed burning to encourage the growth of bulbs, green shoots, and seeds of herbs like chia (*Salvia columbariae*) and Brewer's redmaids (*Calandrinia breweri*). Frequent burning could have converted many areas of coastal sage scrub and chaparral to grasslands, although there were certainly large areas that, due to their ruggedness and remoteness, were little affected by Native American burning (Keeley 2002). With the advent of the Mission Era, fire frequency likely was reduced in coastal plain and foothill environments.

CURRENT PERIOD

Although separated by less than 75 km, the northern Santa Lucia Ranges and Santa Cruz Mountains provide a dramatic contrast in modern fire histories. Fire is much more widespread in the Santa Lucia Ranges, where roughly one quarter of the region has burned at least once since 1950 (Table 14.1). Furthermore, fires that have occurred in recent times in the Santa Lucia Ranges are much larger than are those in the Santa Cruz Mountains. The largest modern fires in the Santa Cruz Mountains, including an 8,000-ha (19,760-ac) burn in 1948, the 1,320-ha (3,260-ac) Lincoln Hill fire in 1962, and the 5,314-ha (13,125-ac) Lexington fire of 1985 (which mainly burned east of the Santa Cruz Mountains in the Leeward Hills), are an order of magnitude smaller than the largest fires in the northern Santa Lucia Ranges.

Relatively detailed records of twentieth century fires on Los Padres National Forest have been analyzed by Davis and Michaelsen (1995), Mensing et al. (1999), and Moritz (1997, 2003). A large fraction of area burned in the Santa Lucia Ranges since 1900 can be attributed to a few very large fires. Most of these large fires have been human-ignited (except the aforementioned Marble Cone and Kirk Complex fires) and many of the large fires at the southern end of the region have

TABLE 14.2
Fire response types for important species in the coastal woodlands and forests of the lower montane zone in the coastal plain and foothills subregion

Lifeform	Type of Fire Response			Species
	Sprouting	Seeding	Individual	
Conifer	None	Fire stimulated release of seeds from serotinous or partially open cones; serotiny varies considerably species to species	Killed	Knobcone pine, Sargent cypress, Coulter pine, Bishop pine, Monterey pine
	None	None	Killed; survives in fire-proof locations	Santa Lucia fir
Hardwood	Fire stimulated	None	Top-killed/survive; coast live oak crown sprouts from epicormic buds	Coast live oak, interior live oak, Pacific madrone, tan oak, big-leaf maple, California bay

spread under severe weather conditions of high temperature and winds (Davis and Michaelsen 1995; Moritz 1997, 2003).

Based on analyses of Los Padres fire history data, Moritz (1997, 2003) concluded that fire hazard in the Santa Lucia Ranges is not significantly related to fuel age but is controlled instead by extreme weather events. A combination of rugged terrain and poor access into remote wilderness areas has limited the ability of firefighting agencies to control fire spread in these weather conditions, and, despite an improved suppression effort, there does not seem to be a temporal trend in large fire frequency in this region (Moritz 1997). However, the introduction of fixed-wing aircraft and helicopters after 1950 has proved effective in reducing fire spread under more moderate conditions. For example, since 1950, fires between 500 and 5,000 ha (1235–12,350 ac) are less frequent than they were from 1911 to 1950 (Moritz 1997).

Los Padres National Forest fire history data have also been used to compare fire sizes in the southern ("Main") Division and the Monterey Division in the southern and northern Santa Lucia Ranges, respectively. The Main Division (which extends out of the Central Coast bioregion into the northern Southwestern bioregion) displays a higher frequency of large fires (more than 4,000 ha [9,880 ac]) than does the Monterey Division. For example, 80% of the fires in the Monterey Division are smaller than 900 ha (2,223 ac), whereas for the Main Division, 80% are less than 5,300 ha (13,091 ac) (Moritz 1997).

Major Ecological Zones

The complex vegetation mosaics of the Santa Lucia Ranges do not lend themselves to a simple zonal vegetation classifi-

cation scheme. Instead we focus on those species and community types that are characteristic of this subregion and whose fire ecology has been formally investigated. Unfortunately, most widespread chaparral and coastal sage scrub community types have received practically no study in this region, so we refer the reader to the chapter by Keeley (this volume) for a discussion of these types. Similarly, we are unable to report on the fire ecology of the mixed evergreen forests of the upper montane zone. For a treatment of annual grassland and blue oak woodland of the inland foothill zone, we refer the reader to the chapters by Wills (this volume).

Here we review the ecology of several species and community types that, with the exception of coast live oak, are characteristic of the region but are relatively localized. In the coastal plain and foothills zone we highlight Bishop pine, Monterey pine, maritime chaparral, and coastal live oak forests and woodlands. Of the many species and community types characteristic of the lower montane zone, we discuss knobcone pine and Sargent cypress. Coulter pine is the only species and community type discussed that is characteristic of the upper montane zone.

Bishop Pine

FIRE ECOLOGY

Bishop pine forms distinct northern (northern Bishop pine) and southern (southern Bishop pine) varieties that diverge from one another at Monterey (Millar 1983). Fire research on Bishop pine has focused entirely on the northern borealis variety. Bishop pine is nonsprouting and moderately serotinous (Keeley and Zedler 1998) (Table 14.2).

Sugnet (1981) examined the age structure of six Bishop pine stands along the Inverness Ridge in Point Reyes National Seashore. Three stands were even-aged, showing a single pulse of seedling recruitment that he traced to earlier fires. Indeed, post-fire seedling establishment of Bishop pine can be prolific (Ornduff and Norris 1997). After a 1996 fire on Inverness Ridge, B. Holzman (personal communication) recorded an average of 26 Bishop pine seedlings/m² (2.4 seedlings/ft²), some of which had reached heights of 1.2 m (3.9 ft) by the following year. Even-aged stands, however, did not always result from high-intensity fires.

Sugnet (1981) also observed near-complete mortality in a stand that was subject to a low-intensity backing fire. Even though Bishop pine has thick bark and is resistant to most surface fires, the high mortality was due to basal girdling by prolonged, smoldering combustion in the deep (up to 25 cm [10 in]) litter layer that develops in stands older than 40 years. Thus, while even-aged stands result primarily from high-intensity fires, lethal ground fires also can induce an even-aged structure. Two stands Sugnet (1981) examined were multi-aged but the youngest cohorts were not associated with past fires, indicating that seedling establishment had taken place beneath an older cohort of trees. Bishop pine does not require fire to free seeds from the cones. Cones also open on hot days and seeds released in this way may establish in the understory.

FIRE REGIME–PLANT COMMUNITY INTERACTIONS

Keeley and Zedler (1998) proposed a comprehensive framework for understanding the evolution of the major life history strategies of species in the genus Pinus. Schwilk and Ackerly (2001) have elaborated further on the strategy that has selected for flammable, serotinous species. They postulated that in a regime of frequent, high-intensity fires of large patch size, pines would evolve a suite of "fire-embracing" traits; that is, traits that increase or promote flammability. These traits include serotiny, thin bark, short height at maturity (because of slow growth on low-productivity sites), a lack of self-pruning, more flammable foliage, a relatively early age of cone production, and limited seed dispersal.

Several lines of evidence suggest that within-species variation in Bishop pine may reflect selection for a number of fire-embracing traits along north-to-south and maritime-to-interior gradients of varying fire regimes. Common-garden studies of Bishop pine, for example, have shown that southern Bishop pine populations have genetically slow growth (Millar 1986)—a trait that increases the likelihood that fire will carry from the understory into the tree canopy (Keeley and Zedler 1998).

Serotiny, another fire-embracing characteristic, increases from the northern Bishop pine populations to the southern Bishop pine populations (Duffield 1951). Compared to the southern Bishop pine populations, the northern Bishop pine populations burn relatively infrequently and average fire size tends to be much smaller (Greenlee and Langenheim

1990; also this chapter). Even within the northern Bishop pine variety, Millar described an uncharacteristically high degree of serotiny in five Bishop pine populations growing inland of coastal Inverness populations. In growth form and degree of serotiny, inland populations more closely resembled those of the southern Bishop pine variety. Compared to coastal forests, inland stands had multiple whorls of serotinous cones that remained closed for longer periods of time. Furthermore, stands were growing in or near flammable chaparral and therefore were more likely to burn in crown fires. Millar (1986) speculated that the increased serotiny of the inland populations may be a consequence of the relatively frequent stand-replacing fires in the warmer, drier interior. It would be interesting to know if other traits in Bishop pine such as bark thickness, self-pruning, foliage flammability, age of cone production, and seed dispersal also vary systematically with the north–to-south change in fire regime.

Monterey Pine

FIRE ECOLOGY

Of the three members of the closed-cone pines, Monterey pine is the most restricted in its distribution and also is the least variable genetically (Millar et al. 1988). Like Bishop pine, Monterey pine is a moderately serotinous nonsprouter. Also like Bishop pine, seed release is highest following fires but some cones also open every year, providing continuous seed input for inter-fire regeneration (Table 14.2).

FIRE REGIME–PLANT COMMUNITY INTERACTIONS

There are no long-term fire ecology studies of Monterey pine within its native distribution. In 1994, White (1999) revisited 38 pine stands on the Monterey Peninsula that he had first sampled from 1965 to 1966. He excluded 19 of the original samples for various reasons: partial or complete logging, urban conversion, etc. Two stands burned completely in a 1987 fire. The 19 stands he resampled were highly heterogeneous in structure. Some appeared to be even-aged—the result of high-intensity fires in the past. Others had a wide array of diameter classes indicating that, as in Bishop pine, a small percentage of seedlings in unburned stands become saplings and pole-sized trees. Thus, while seedling establishment is clearly most abundant following fire (more than 100,000 seedlings/ha [247,000 seedlings/ac]), long unburned pine stands do not convert to coast live oak forests, the most frequent understory tree, but continue to be dominated by Monterey pine (Fig. 14.5).

Stephens et al. (2004) investigated the fire history and postfire recruitment of Monterey pine north of Santa Cruz. An analysis of fire scar data revealed average mean fire return intervals of 11.2 to 20.1 years (Table 14.3). Mixed-severity fires dominated the fire regime in this area resulting in multi-aged forests with high spatial heterogeneity. Indeed, 51% of

TABLE 14.3

Fire regime characteristics for coastal shrub and woodland forests

Vegetation type			
	Bishop and monterey pine	Coast live oak	Maritime chaparral
Temporal			
Seasonality	Late summer–fall	Spring/summer–fall	Spring/summer–fall
Fire-return interval	Medium–long	Short–medium	Truncated medium
Spatial			
Size	Medium–large	Small–large	Medium–large
Complexity	Low–moderate	Low–moderate	Low
Magnitude			
Intensity	Multiple	Multiple	High
Severity	Moderate–high	Multiple	Moderate–high
Fire type	Multiple	Surface	Crown

FIGURE 14.5. Monterey pine forest understory near Cambria dominated by blackberry and poison oak. This site has not burned for many decades.

the trees in openings regenerated within 5 years of the most recent fire. In general, however, the evidence suggests that Monterey pine forests do not require periodic fire to persist on the landscape and perhaps urbanization poses the greatest threat to this species.

Coast Live Oak Forest and Woodland

FIRE ECOLOGY

Coast live oak is one of the most fire-resistant oaks in California (Lathrop and Osborne 1991). Coast live oak seedlings and saplings can survive relatively low-intensity surface fires (Snow 1980), although seedling mortality is undoubtedly

higher during high-intensity surface fires and crown fires (Table 14.2). Adult trees exhibit a number of fire adaptations, including dense outer bark, a thick inner bark with high insulating capacity, and an ability to resprout from the base and crown following severe wildfires (Plumb 1980). Adult survival rates exceeding 95% have been documented following severe wildfire, and canopy volume may return to pre-fire levels within 5 to 10 years (Plumb 1980, Dagit 2002). Mortality rates are higher for late-season fires and for oaks growing among chaparral shrubs where fire severity is more extreme (Wells 1962, Plumb and Gomez 1983, Davis et al. 1988a).

FIRE REGIME–PLANT COMMUNITY INTERACTIONS

Pollen records from the Santa Barbara Channel and Zaca Lake in northern Santa Barbara County indicate that coast live oak populations were relatively stable for many centuries prior to European settlement but have increased in the last quarter of the nineteenth century (Mensing 1998).

Coast live oak is widespread in grasslands and oak savannas of the region but appears to be declining in these settings due to tree removal and low recruitment of tree-sized individuals due to drought and herbivory by rodents, deer, cattle, and insects (Plumb and Hannah 1991, Callaway and Davis 1998, Parikh and Gale 1998, Dunning et al. 2003). Because of grazing and fire suppression, fires are now infrequent in this vegetation type (Table 14.3). Unfortunately, the effects of frequent fires in this vegetation, such as may have occurred prehistorically, have not been studied.

Callaway and Davis (1993) documented a shifting mosaic of four vegetation types in Gaviota State Park and on neighboring ranchlands between 1947 and 1989 (Fig. 14.6). Unburned annual grasslands were invaded by coastal sage

FIGURE 14.6. Patches of Coast live oak forest in a matrix of annual grassland on northern footslopes of the Purisima Hills, Los Alamos Valley, Santa Barbara County.

scrub, and unburned coastal sage scrub was invaded by coast live oak leading to the formation of oak woodlands. Coast live oak rarely replaced grassland directly but could invade coastal sage scrub by using the shrubs as seedling nurse plants. However, oak cover declined in oak woodlands with a grass understory, suggesting a long-term return to grasslands, presumably because oak seedlings do poorly in the understory of oak woodlands, except in the most mesic settings. In burned areas, fire slowed the transition of coastal sage scrub to oak woodlands because acorns and seedlings succumbed in fires. Grazing also slowed the transition rate to oak woodlands because it delayed the transition from grassland to coastal sage scrub. In addition to grazing and fire, transition rates also were dependent on soil types.

Coast live oak is shade tolerant (Callaway 1992) and recruits into both chaparral and coastal sage scrub on many substrates as well as into more mesic settings such as north-facing slopes and areas bordering riparian areas of central coastal California (Wells 1962, Callaway and Davis 1993, Callaway and Davis 1998, Parikh and Gale 1998). Nevertheless, high-intensity fires in shrublands probably kill most seedlings and saplings, thereby reversing any increase in oak cover that takes place during fire-free periods (Wells 1962, Callaway and Davis 1993, Van Dyke and Holl 2001). It would appear that on many sites the presence of oak woodland versus chaparral or coastal sage scrub depends on whether sufficient time has elapsed between fires for oaks to establish and grow large enough to endure high-intensity fires (Table 14.3).

In coast live oak forests, the litter layer is often deep, and perennials such as poison oak *(Toxicdendron diversilobum)*, Christmas berry *(Heteromeles arbutifolia)*, and hairy bracken-fern form a discontinuous herb and shrub understory (Campbell 1980, Allen et al. 1991). For much of the year, fuel moisture of the shrubs and litter is high and conditions are not conducive to surface fire ignition and spread.

Little is known about the role of fire in coast live oak forest. Presumably it is less frequent than in adjacent shrubland and grassland community types, but when fire does occur, it is usually a high-severity, passive crown fire that burns all the foliage from the canopy. For example, in 1985 the Wheeler fire in Ventura County top-killed large areas of riparian forests composed of coast live oak, western sycamore *(Platanus racemosa)*, and white alder *(Alnus rhombifolia)*. Within the first year after fire, only 50% of the overstory oaks had resprouted at four monitored sites with the probability of sprouting positively correlated with diameter at breast height (Parikh 1989). Of the surviving oaks at one site, 29% subsequently were toppled by high winds (Davis et al. 1988b).

Maritime Chaparral

Maritime chaparral is associated with sandy substrates in level or rolling terrain within 10–20 km (6–12 mi) of the coast. These areas are under a strong maritime climate characterized by frequent summer fog and low annual temperature range. Stands of northern and central maritime chaparral communities are scattered along the coast from northern Santa Barbara County to Sonoma County. Maritime chaparral supports many rare and endemic plants and thus has received a fair amount of scientific study, especially in recent decades as the type has been heavily reduced and fragmented by coastal residential development and military operations (Lambrinos 2000, Van Dyke and Holl 2001).

FIRE ECOLOGY

Maritime chaparral is usually dominated by chamise in combination with several locally endemic species of California-lilac and manzanita. In the Central Coastal biore-

TABLE 14.4
Fire response types for important species in the maritime chaparral found in the
Santa Cruz and Santa Lucia ranges subregions

| Lifeform | Type of Fire Response | | | Species |
	Sprouting	Seeding	Individual	
Hardwood	Fire stimulated	None	Top-killed /survive	Coast live oak
Shrub	None	Fire stimulated germination of soil-stored seed	Killed	Blue-blossom ceanothus, Purissima manzanita, Hooker's manzanita, Pajaro manzanita, Morro manzanita
	Fire stimulated	Fire stimulated	Top-killed/killed	Shagbark manzanita

gion, characteristic shrub species include obligate-seeding species such as Santa Barbara ceanothus *(Ceanothus impressus)*, sand buck brush *(Ceanothus cuneatus* var. *fasciculatus)*, La Purisima manzanita *(Arctostaphylos purissima)*, Hooker's manzanita *(Arctostaphylos hookeri* ssp. *hookeri)*, sandmat manzanita *(Arctostaphylos pumila)*, Pajaro manzanita *(Arctostaphylos pajaroensis)*, Morro manzanita *(Arctostaphylos morroensis)*, and the resprouting sand mesa manzanita *(Arctostaphylos rudis)* (Griffin 1978, Davis et al. 1988a). Multi-trunked coast live oaks also may attain high cover, especially on deeper soils and at greater distances from the coast. Subshrub and herb layer diversity can be high, especially for the first five years following fire. In general, maritime chaparral communities exhibit higher plant species diversity than other chaparral community types (Davis et al. 1988a).

Many rare and endemic species of obligate-seeding California-lilac and manzanita in maritime chaparral are fire dependent (Table 14.4). Odion and Tyler (2002) observed high levels of fire-induced mortality in the soil seed bank of the endangered Morro manzanita and concluded that the species may require considerably longer than 40 years between burns in order to establish an adequate seed bank to replace adults killed during the fire.

FIRE REGIME–PLANT COMMUNITY INTERACTIONS

Lightning is rare along the coast and it is probably safe to assume that the fire regime of maritime chaparral has been anthropogenic for many millennia, especially given the prehistoric densities of native Americans in coastal areas supporting maritime chaparral (e.g., lower Santa Ynez River Valley, Pismo Bay, Morro Bay, and Monterey Bay [Keeley 2002b]). Greenlee and Langenheim (1990) estimated prehistoric fire return intervals near Monterey Bay to be on the order of 10 to 100 years (Table 14.3). Today, human-caused ignitions are frequent in maritime chaparral but wildfires are quickly suppressed or extinguished at roads and fuel

breaks. As a result, fires now rarely exceed 100 ha (247 ac) (Davis et al. 1988a, Van Dyke and Holl 2001, Odion and Tyler 2002). In maritime chaparral to the east of Vandenberg Air Fore Base near Lompoc, Davis et al. (1989) documented only 27 fires larger than 1 ha between 1938 and 1986 that occurred in 10% to 15% of the maritime chaparral area under investigation.

As in other chaparral communities, many maritime chaparral species are dependent on or promoted by fire (Table 14.2; see Keeley, this volume). Regeneration after fire includes sprouting and recruitment from buried seeds (Fig. 14.7). Exogenous seed sources usually do not play an important role in succession (Davis et al. 1989, Odion and Davis 2000). Chronosequence studies suggest that succession after fire is largely a function of floristic composition prior to burning, differential seedling survivorship and differential adult longevity of species. Vegetation in the first several years after fire is a diverse combination of annuals and short-lived perennials recruited from the seed bank and resprouting geophytes and woody plants (Davis 1988a). Unlike other chaparral communities, the flush of post-fire annuals appears to be mainly related to removal of the shrub canopy rather than fire-induced germination of refractory seed (Tyler 1996). Herb layer biomass and diversity drop rapidly with closure of the shrub canopy 5 to 10 years after burning. After 20 to 40 years, the shorter-lived shrubs, notably the obligate-seeding California-lilac species, senesce and the community is increasingly dominated by long-lived chamise, manzanitas, and coast live oak.

Shrub dieback during the fire-free period can leave conspicuous gaps in the chaparral canopy where some herbaceous species can grow and augment the soil seed bank. These gaps experience less extreme soil heating and associated seed mortality during the next fire, and thus become microsites of higher seedling recruitment for both herbaceous and woody species (Davis et al. 1989, Odion and Davis 2000). Mortality of buried seeds during fire can reduce the

FIGURE 14.7. Maritime chaparral (being sampled by Dennis Odion and Diana Hickson) on Burton Mesa, northern Santa Barbara, two years after burning. Peak rush-rose is a conspicuous member of the diverse post-fire community.

density of viable seed of some species by an order of magnitude or more, so local variations in fuel loading and fire behavior have important consequences for post-fire vegetation composition and pattern (Odion and Davis 2000, Odion and Tyler 2002).

Maritime chaparral is more extensively invaded by exotic plant species than most other chaparral types, perhaps because it is more densely roaded and closer to human developments, and thus more prone to human disturbance and sources of exotic propagules. One alien succulent species, fig-marigold, can be widespread in maritime chaparral and establishes most successfully after fire (D'Antonio et al. 1993). Other invasive exotics include pampas grass (*Cortaderia jubata*), perennial veldt grass (*Erharta calcina*), and French broom (*Genista monspessulana*) (Griffin 1978b, Davis et al. 1988b, Zedler and Scheid 1988, Lambrinos 2000, Odion and Tyler 2002).

Several observers of maritime chaparral argue that, in the absence of fire, the chaparral would eventually be replaced by coastal oak or pine forests (Cooper 1922, McBride and Stone 1976, Griffin 1978b). Davis et al. (1989) reported a significant positive correlation between oak canopy cover and time since burning but noted that the increase in oaks varied widely depending on distance from the coast, soil characteristics, and fire severity. In the coastal sand hills of northern Monterey County, Van Dyke and Holl (2001) found that in the long absence of fire, remnants of Prunedale maritime chaparral had undergone significant changes in species composition and stand structure. Fire-dependent shrubs like sand-scrub ceanothus (*Ceanothus dentatus*), blue blossom, and goldenbush (*Ericmeria ericoides*) present in stands sampled from 1975 to 1976 (Griffin 1978b) were absent in a resurvey in 2000. By 2000, Pajaro manzanita and coast live oak had increased in cover from 86% to 99% and dominated the overstory. Van Dyke and Holl (2001) posited that in the con-

tinued absence of fire, coast live oak would gradually replace the long-lived obligate-seeder Pajaro manzanita, eventually converting maritime chaparral to coast live oak woodland.

Knobcone Pine

FIRE ECOLOGY

Knobcone pine is a medium-sized, relatively short-lived conifer that frequently grows in dense stands. Because trees self-prune poorly, they are easily killed in chaparral crown fires and depend on fire for regeneration (Table 14.2).

Despite its widespread distribution in California, there are remarkably few post-fire studies of knobcone pine. Keeley et al. (1999) studied the regeneration of this species in the central Santa Lucia Mountains after a fire in 1994. Populations of serotinous species are particularly vulnerable to extinction if they reburn before a cone bank develops that is sufficient in size to replace the population after the next fire—what Zedler (1995) terms "immaturity risk" (as discussed in Chapter 6). They examined the regeneration of knobcone stands that reburned after a fire just eight years earlier. Seedling recruitment following the 1985 fire was abundant, and because knobcone pine produces cones at an early age (two years), a partial aerial seed bank had developed by the second fire. Seedling recruitment after the second fire was low (1–2 seedlings/m²) and patchily distributed compared to recruitment after the 1985 fire. Nevertheless, local extinction appeared to be averted by the presence of a relatively low number of new cones.

The impact of two fires just eight years apart likely would have been very different for Coulter pine, another serotinous species growing in the same area. Because Coulter pine does not produce cones until about ten years of age, few, if any, seedlings would have appeared after the second fire.

TABLE 14.5
Fire regime characteristics of lower montane zone and upland forests

Vegetation type			
	Knobcone pine	Sargent cypress	Coulter pine
Temporal			
Seasonality	Spring/summer–fall	Spring/summer–fall	Summer–fall
Fire-return interval	Medium–long	Medium truncated–long	Short–medium
Spatial			
Size	Large	Large	Medium–large
Complexity	Low	Low–moderate	Low–moderate
Magnitude			
Intensity	High	High	Multiple
Severity	High	Moderate–high	Multiple
Fire type	Crown	Crown	Multiple

FIRE REGIME–PLANT COMMUNITY INTERACTIONS

Knobcone pine, like Coulter pine and Sargent cypress, often grows in close association with highly flammable vegetation like chaparral. As a result, knobcone pine stands regularly burn in stand-replacing fires at frequencies matching the surrounding vegetation (Table 14.5).

Sargent Cypress

Within the region, Sargent cypress forms an archipelago of small stands that extend from the northern Santa Lucia Range to the southern part of the bioregion above San Luis Obispo. It is almost entirely confined to serpentine outcrops where other rare plant taxa are associated with it (Hardham 1962). Three of these island-like forests are formally designated botanical areas on Los Padres National Forest.

FIRE ECOLOGY

Among the four cypress species in the region, Sargent cypress is the only species that has been studied after fire (Table 14.2). Sargent cypress is a fire-dependent, obligate-seeding species that releases prodigious numbers of small, wingless seeds after crown fires.

FIRE REGIME–PLANT COMMUNITY INTERACTIONS

After a wildfire swept the Cuesta Ridge Botanical Area in 1994, Ne'eman et al. (1999) reconstructed pre-fire stand characteristics (adult density, cone and seed densities, age, etc.) using the skeletal remains of trees in even-aged stands that ranged from 20 to 95 years. The number of cones per tree increased rapidly after 80 years as tree densities thinned from $0.8/m^2$ in young-aged stands to $0.4/m^2$ in the oldest ones.

Seedling densities ranged from $6.3/m^2$ to $81.7/m^2$ but seedling density was negatively correlated with tree density.

The highest seedling densities occurred in stands younger than 60 years rather than in the oldest stands with the highest number of cones per tree. They attributed low seedling densities in the oldest stands to either reduced seed viability with age or to higher-intensity fires in older stands (Table 14.5). Indeed, for some cypress species, seed viability decreases rapidly with age (De Magistris et al. 2001). They concluded that fires burning at intervals as short as 20 years posed little risk (i.e., immaturity risk) to the regeneration of the species at this site, presumably because 20-year-old stands had an adequate cone bank. Nevertheless, the fire that burned these Sargent cypress forests also reburned the knobcone pine forests described above (Keeley et al. 1999) just a few kilometers away. Had the Sargent cypress stands burned after eight years, as some of the knobcone pine forests did, much of the cypress forest may have been lost.

Coulter Pine

Coulter pine is the most widely distributed closed-cone species in the Central Coastal bioregion. Its range is more or less linear and extends from northern Diablo Range in Contra Costa County along the coastal Santa Lucia Range to Figueroa Mountain. Inland populations are rare and more scattered and trail down the Diablo Range (Ledig 2000).

FIRE ECOLOGY

In the southern Coast Ranges, Coulter pine exhibits considerable cone-habit variation that appears to be directly related to fire regime (Borchert 1985). Over much of its range, Coulter pine grows as an overstory tree in a matrix of dense montane chaparral (Borchert et al. 2004). In this setting, crown fires are inevitable because fire carries easily from the shrub layer into the crowns of the pines that self-prune poorly (Table 14.2). Typically, large tracts of pines

FIGURE 14.8. Aerial view of annual grassland and oak forest topo-mosaics of the Interior Coast Ranges, northeast of Salinas in San Benito County.

succumb. Nevertheless, in some topographic positions (drainages and ridgetops), small stands survive (Borchert 1985, Borchert et al. 2003) where fire intensity is diminished. Despite its relatively thick bark, moderate-intensity fires easily kill Coulter pine (Borchert et al. 2002). Stand-killing fires, however, are not just confined to chaparral. Stands with an understory of dense Sargent cypress or canyon live oak in steep topography often suffer complete mortality.

In an environment of repeated stand-replacing fires, Coulter pine tends to be highly serotinous. Heat from both the burning chaparral and the porous canopy of long needles breaks the resinous seal of the cones and seeds fall *en masse* into the ash bed. Although winged, the heavy seeds do not disperse far from the tree except perhaps in strong winds (Borchert et al. 2003, Johnson et al. 2003). Once on the ground, rodents and birds quickly harvest seeds and bury them in caches of 1 to 15 seeds per cache. In fact, most seedlings emerge from unrecovered caches. Seedlings are drought tolerant and seedling mortality is relatively low, especially when compared to early seedling mortality of other serotinous pines (Borchert et al. 2003).

At about age 10, saplings begin to produce cones but because the cones are heavy, they require the support of the tree bole and only appear on the ends of branches after the limbs are sufficiently stout. As the tree grows, cones accumulate creating an aerial seed bank. Some cones open or are predated by western gray squirrels *(Sciurus griseus)* or white-headed woodpeckers *(Picoides albolarvatus)* (Koch et al. 1970), but seeds that remain encased in the closed cones receive a high degree of protection as evidenced by a seed viability of 95% in 25-year-old cones (Borchert 1985).

FIRE REGIME–PLANT COMMUNITY INTERACTIONS

Coulter pine is not confined to chaparral in its distribution. On the Central Coast, it frequently associates with coast live oak (Campbell 1980, Borchert et al. 2002), and occasionally with valley oak or other hardwoods in both woodlands and forests. In these forests, Coulter pine is not serotinous, or is only moderately so. Where sites are productive and trees grow large, the continuous shrub understory is absent or poorly developed. Thus, surface fires are more common than crown fires and adult Coulter pine mortality is low (Table 14.5). Seedlings establish after fires from cones of the current year or they establish and grow to a fire-tolerant size in the interval between fires (Borchert 1985).

Interior Coast Ranges Subregion

Ecological zonation has been obscured by extensive type conversion of shrublands to grassland, but it is still possible to discriminate two general ecological zones: a lower-elevation grassland zone and a higher-elevation blue oak woodland-chaparral zone. Ten percent of the subregion has been converted to urban and cropland uses.

The interior valleys and foothills are dominated by alliances such as California annual grassland and California buckwheat (Fig. 14.8). Remnant valley oak woodlands are present in larger stream valleys on deeper loamy soils across the region.

Mid to high elevations support blue oak woodlands, chamise chaparral, and other chaparral alliances such as buck brush and Eastwood's manzanita *(Arctostaphylos glandulosa)*, blue oak *(Quercus douglasii)*, and blue oak–gray pine. The latter two alliances are especially widespread in the Diablo Range. The only montane forests in the inland region are the unusually open stands of Jeffrey pine *(Pinus jeffreyi)*, incense-cedar (*Calocedrus decurrens*), and Coulter pine that occupy the serpentine areas of San Benito Mountain.

Overview of Historic Fire Occurrence

PREHISTORIC AND HISTORIC PERIODS

There is little doubt that Native Americans augmented vegetation burning in the Interior Ranges just as they did along the coast. Greenlee and Moldenke (1982) assert that the Castanoans were burning grasslands and oak woodlands annually or semi-annually. Chaparral and foothill pine woodland were likely thinned or reduced in extent by the high frequency of deliberate or inadvertent fires in the region (Keeley 2002b).

Aboriginal burning declined with the advent of the Mission Period in the last quarter of the eighteenth century (Greenlee and Langenheim 1990). By the time Mexico ceded California to the United States in 1850, regular burning of oak woodlands by Native Americans had ceased but chaparral burning probably expanded both to increase rangeland area and to facilitate travel. Fires still occurred but they were more likely to be accidental or lightning-caused rather than deliberate. For example, newspaper accounts during the period 1855 to 1920 recorded roughly 60 wildfires in San Benito County; around the same number were reported in Monterey County (Greenlee and Moldenke 1982). Nearly all of these fires occurred between July and October.

CURRENT PERIOD

Maps of fires that have burned since 1950 have been compiled by the Forest Service and California Department of Forestry and Fire Protection (CDF&FP) (Map 14.6, http://frap.cdf.ca.gov/projects/fire_data/fire_perimeters/index.asp). Only fires larger than 120 ha (300 ac) are mapped on private lands. We also obtained fire history records from Pinnacles National Monument, which provide a more complete and accurate history of fires from the interior Diablo and Gabilan Ranges. In comparing the two datasets we found the CDF&FP data to be incomplete for lands outside of the National Forests. Nevertheless, the CDF&FP data provide a good general picture of fire frequency and size across the region. Based on these records, at least 40% of the region has burned at least once since 1950, with fires concentrated in shrublands and mixed evergreen forests of the northern Santa Lucia Ranges.

Although uncommon, lightning fires occur with greater frequency in the Interior Ranges than in the Santa Lucia Ranges or Santa Cruz Mountains. Between 1930 and 1979, fire history data record 142 lightning-caused fires out of a total of 3,086 fires (4.6%) in the Gabilan and Diablo Ranges (Greenlee and Moldenke 1982). Eighty-six percent of these lightning fires occurred in grasslands or oak woodlands and, with one exception, all lightning fires started between May and October. Nearly half of the fires burned in September.

Humans started 95% of all recorded fires from 1930 to 1979 (Greenlee and Moldenke 1982). Some of this is due to the widespread use of controlled burning for rangeland improvement in the region. Sixteen percent of the fires recorded during this period were characterized as deliberate "brush burning," and over the period 1951 to 1978, 22,814 ha (56,350 ac) were deliberately burned in San Benito and western Fresno Counties alone. Although grass and blue oak woodland cover over 50% of the Gabilan and Diablo Ranges, and despite the relatively high frequency of lightning ignitions in those vegetation types, roughly 55% of the area that burned between 1930 and 1979 was classified as "brush," and less than 30% as grassland or woodland (Greenlee and Moldenke 1980).

At least 15% of the Interior Ranges burned at least once between 1950 and 1998 in fires larger than 120 ha (296 ac) (Map 14.6), compared to 40% of the Santa Lucia Ranges and 3% of the Santa Cruz Mountains. Large fires in the Interior Ranges are most common in southern San Benito County (Hepsedam Peak and San Benito Mountain) and in the Gabilan Ranges north and east of Pinnacles National Monument. Based on fire scar data and maps of fire perimeters, Greenlee and Moldenke (1982) concluded that fire suppression efforts have reduced fire frequency in the region from every 10 to 30 years prior to 1930 to a current recurrence interval of 25 to 35 years, depending on vegetation, topography, and exposure.

In a more recent analysis, Keeley (2004) analyzed CDF&FP fire history data for three counties east of San Francisco Bay (Santa Clara, Alameda, and Contra Costa Counties) and reported a sharp rise in the number of fires after 1950 and then a leveling off after 1990 in the East Bay region. Fire frequency was highly correlated with regional population growth until recent years. Area burned showed little directional change over the same period, although moderate to large fires have become less frequent and small fires more frequent over the period of record. Based on these trends in twentieth-century burning patterns, Keeley (2004) concludes that fire suppression cannot account for the widely observed colonization of grasslands by shrubs and trees and that cessation of grazing is a more likely explanation.

Major Ecological Zones

The fire ecology and fire regimes in widespread and characteristic vegetation types in this zone such as blue oak woodland, annual grassland, and chaparral are covered in other chapters in this volume (see chapters by Wills and Keeley). Systematic comparisons of the fire ecology of these types in the Interior Coast Ranges versus other parts of their distributions are not possible at this time.

Subregional Differences in Modern Fire Regime

Although existing fire history data are too incomplete and too inconsistent to allow detailed quantitative comparisons of the Santa Cruz, Santa Lucia, and Interior Ranges, they do suggest several striking interregional differences in modern

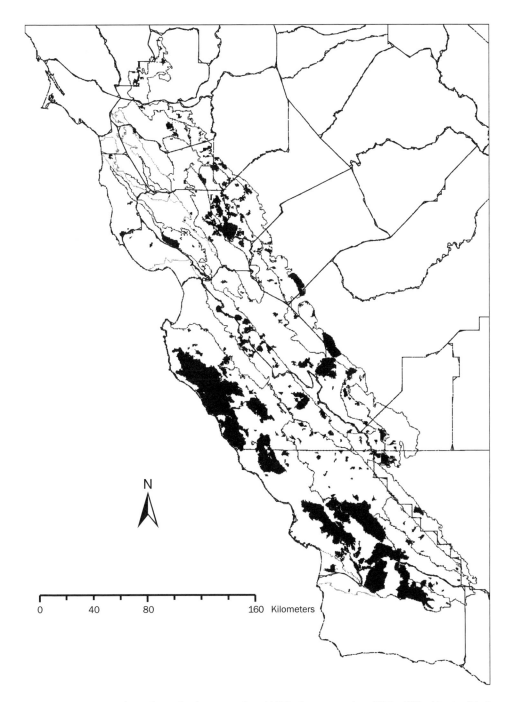

MAP 14.6. Locations of areas burned at least once since 1950 in fires greater than 120 ha (300 ac) in size (black areas), superimposed on the fire regions displayed in Map 14.5. Fire perimeter data were provided by the California Department of Forestry and Fire Protection.

fire regimes that appear related to vegetation, climate, and ease of suppression.

Fire suppression has dramatically altered the fire regime of the Santa Cruz Mountains. Although the terrain is fairly rugged, the mountains are densely roaded and much more accessible to suppression forces than are the Santa Lucia Ranges. Furthermore, many fires in this area begin as understory burns in coast redwood–Douglas-fir forests. Under the more moderate fire weather conditions and higher fuel mois-

tures typical of this area, fires are more readily contained than shrubland fires to the south. This situation may be changing as the forests accumulate more understory ladder fuels (Greenlee 1983).

In contrast to the Santa Cruz Mountains, the Santa Lucia Ranges are characterized by large wildfires occurring mainly in rugged terrain dominated by crown fire–prone shrublands and mixed evergreen forests. Fires are somewhat larger in the chaparral-dominated southern Santa Lucia Ranges of Santa

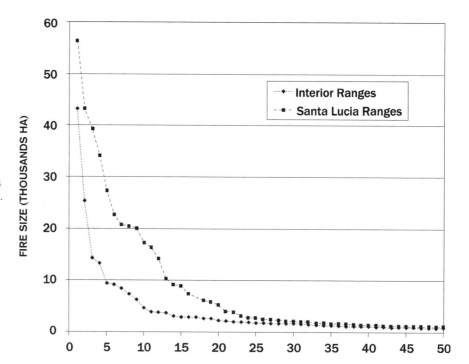

FIGURE 14.9. Rank order of fires vs. burn patch size for the 50 largest fires recorded in the Interior Ranges versus the Santa Lucia Ranges (Regions 3 vs. 4 in Map 14.5) for the period 1950–1997. Mapped fire boundaries for fires larger than 120 ha (300 ac) were analyzed.

Barbara and San Luis Obispo Counties than in the northern Santa Lucia Ranges of Monterey County. Areas experiencing large wildfires occur mainly within Los Padres National Forest where a sparse road network limits access for fire suppression. In the south coastal and interior Santa Lucia Ranges, large fires are promoted by winter and spring drought, heat waves during the fire season, and high winds associated with Santa Ana conditions. However, high winds are not a prerequisite for large wildfires, as evidenced by numerous large burns in the northern Santa Lucia Ranges. It appears that a combination of ample fuel, low summer fuel moisture, high temperatures and low humidity, and steep terrain more than meet the requirements for infrequent, large wildfires. Although modern fire suppression has greatly reduced wildfires near the coast and in the foothills, it appears to have had much less effect on the frequency of large wildfires in the montane zone.

The modern fire regime of the Interior Ranges is more similar to that of the Santa Lucia Ranges than the Santa Cruz Mountains but there are some notable differences: In the Interior Ranges lightning fires are more frequent, more fires are set deliberately for range improvement, and fires do not attain the size of the largest fires in the Santa Lucia Ranges. Although the CFD&FP fire perimeter maps show more fires larger than 120 ha (296 ac) in the Interior Ranges than in the Santa Lucia Ranges for the period 1950 to 1998 (293 vs.189 ha [724 vs. 467 ac]), very large fires are much more likely in the Santa Lucia Ranges and the total area burned is also much greater (Fig. 14.9).

Management Issues

Sound vegetation management using fire depends fundamentally on a good understanding of the fire ecology of the species or plant communities in question. Thus, it is somewhat surprising that the Central California Coast, which has one of the richest arrays of plant communities in the state, has so few fire ecology studies, especially considering the major vegetation types that cover much of the bioregion. For example, four associations of coastal sage scrub are represented and although Venturan, Lucian, Diablan, and Franciscan cover more than 2,500 km^2 (925 m^2) of the region (Davis et al. 1998) we know of only one fire ecology study in Franciscan coastal sage scrub by Ford (1991). Similarly, chaparral makes up 20% (7,765 km^2, 2,998 m^2) of the region but there are only two postburn studies of prescribed fires in nonmaritime chaparral, one in Pinnacles National Monument (Florence 1985) and the other in the Mount Hamilton Range (Dunne et al. 1991). By comparison, the number of fire ecology studies of chaparral in the South Coast bioregion number more than 100. Finally, this region is one of the major repositories of mixed evergreen forests (1,625 km^2) in the state but, except for limited post–Marble Cone fire observations by Griffin (1978c), there are no formal fire ecology studies in this highly variable type.

In sharp contrast to many of the common alliances in the bioregion, rare alliances have received considerably more research attention. This is perhaps not surprising since a number of these types, such as maritime chaparral and Monterey pine forests, are at risk from urbanization and other land conversions (Cylinder 1997, Hillyard 1997, Lambrinos 2000). Other rare types like the narrow endemic Santa Lucia fir (*Abies bracteata*) (Talley 1974) and sugar pine forests in the northern Santa Lucia Mountains are better protected on national forest lands and yet these alliances have not been immune from management activities, like post-fire grass seeding for erosion control, that have threaten their persistence on the landscape (Griffin 1982).

In this chapter we have highlighted some similarities but also some major differences in fire regimes among the geographic subregions and major vegetation types of the Central California Coast bioregion. This heterogeneity and the pressing need for more ecological research notwithstanding, we would be remiss if we did not reiterate four important management issues that face fire and natural resource managers in the Central Coast bioregion, notably: climate change, fire and exotic species, management of fire-dependent species, and fire management at the wildland-urban interface.

Climate Change

Analyses of historical climate data as well as models of predicted future climates under elevated carbon dioxide make it abundantly clear that the recent past that has formed the basis for the design of fire policy and management may not serve as the guide to the future fire regimes and their management in the region. Fire incidence and total area burned depend on the frequency of extreme weather events, longer-term variation in rainfall and drought severity, and associated changes in vegetation productivity and composition (Davis and Michaelsen 1995). The region is warming (Cayan et al. 2001) and the magnitude of interannual variability in climate appears to be increasing (although there is less certainty about the latter) (Haston and Michaelsen 1997). Depending on trends in winter and spring precipitation, we speculate that climate change could well increase the likelihood of wildfires in some vegetation types, notably the coast redwood–Douglas-fir forests of the Santa Cruz Mountains and the mixed evergreen forests of the northern Santa Lucia Ranges.

Fire and Non-Native Species

Coastal and foothill vegetation types of the region are now extensively invaded by non-native plant species and this trend is likely to continue, especially given rapid human population increase and development in some parts of the region. Deliberate use of fire to convert shrublands and closed woodlands to grasslands has promoted invasion of non-native plants into many areas (Keeley 2001). In the past, the spread of some exotics into shrublands was undoubtedly promoted by post-fire seeding, but this practice appears to have become far less prevalent in recent years. Now there is increasing interest by managers in using fire to control non-native plant species, despite the mixed success of efforts to date and the need for better understanding of the fire ecology of target species and communities, especially in response to repeated burning (D'Antonio 1993, Keeley 2001, Alexander and D'Antonio 2003).

Recent widespread mortality of tanoak, black oak *(Quercus kelloggii)*, and coast live oak at the northern end of the bioregion has been linked to the exotic pathogen *Phytophthora ramorum* or Sudden Oak Death Syndrome (SODS) (Rizzo

et al. 2002). The disease now extends over at least 300 km (186 mi) of the Central Coast bioregion. In heavily infested areas of Marin County, mortality of tanoak and coast live oak has been as high as 18% to 50% and 15% to 20%, respectively (Kelly and Meentemeyer 2002, Spencer and O'Hara 2003). The effects of increased dead fuel loading, canopy opening, and associated changes in understory composition and fuel moisture on fire regime and post-fire succession could be profound. Studies are underway to better understand fire behavior in SODS-affected areas. However, we would re-emphasize the need for systematic research on the fire ecology of both mixed evergreen forests and coast live oak forests in both SODS-free and SODS-affected areas to better understand the management implications of this pathogen in the region.

Management of Fire-Dependent Species

As noted in the sections on maritime chaparral and closed-cone conifers, there are many rare and endemic species in the region whose distribution and abundance is closely tied to fire regime. Fire management for many of these species has become increasingly difficult due to their close proximity to residential areas. In some areas, managers have resorted to mechanically clearing fuel breaks, setting prescribed burns in relatively cool and damp spring or early winter conditions, or shortening the time between burns to prevent excessive fuel build-up. Such management can have unintended negative impacts on native species and communities. Mechanical clearing can promote non-native species and native vegetation may be slow to recover (Stylinski and Allen 1999). Burning outside the normal fire season and high-frequency burning favors some species, like sprouters, but can operate strongly against obligate-seeding species, and the benefits for public health and safety are often unclear (Keeley 2002a).

Wildland-Urban Interface

In 1991, the deadly Tunnel fire killed 25 people and destroyed 3,810 dwellings in the Oakland Hills. A combination of drought-dry vegetation, high temperatures, low humidity, steep topography, and Santa Ana-strength winds that forced the fire down slope created a firestorm that defied control for several days (Ewell 1995). Although many of the cities in the bioregion are located in agricultural areas (e.g., the developed plains, valleys and terraces ecological zone) and are immune from wildland fires, others, like San Luis Obispo (which has been threatened twice in the last 25 years by chaparral fires), are vulnerable to fires burning from wildland areas. The historically unprecedented Tunnel fire provides a vivid worst-case example of fire management problems that other areas in the bioregion will face as California's population continues to grow exponentially and the populace pushes into and up against flammable wildlands.

References

Alexander, J.M., and C.M. D'Antonio. 2003. Seed bank dynamics of French broom in coastal California grasslands: Effects of stand age and prescribed burning on control and restoration. Restoration Ecology 11(2):185–197.

Allen, B.H., B.A. Holzman, and R.R. Evett. 1991. A classification system for California hardwood rangelands. Hilgardia 59(2): 1–45.

Axelrod, D.I. 1958. The Pliocene Verdi flora of western Nevada. University of California Publications in Geological Sciences. University of California Publications in Geological Sciences 34:91–160.

Axelrod, D.I. 1967. Geologic history of the California insular flora. P. 276–316 in Proceedings of the symposium on biology of the California islands. Santa Barbara Botanic Garden, Santa Barbara, CA.

Axelrod, D.I. 1980. History of the closed-cone pines, Alta and Baja California. University of California Publications in Geological Sciences 120:1–143.

Axelrod, D.I., and J. Cota. 1993. A further contribution to closed-cone pine (Oocarpae) history. American Journal of Botany 80:743–751.

Bailey, R.G. 1995. Description of the ecoregions of the United States. Washington, D.C., USDA Forest Service.

Bendix, J. 2002. Pre-European fire in California chaparral. P. 269–293 in T.R. Vale (ed.), Fire, native peoples, and the natural landscape. Island Press, Covelo, CA.

Borchert, M. 1985. Serotiny and cone-habit variation in populations of *Pinus coulteri* (Pinaceae) in the southern Coast Ranges of California. Madroño 32:29–48.

Borchert, M., A. Lopez, C. Bauer, and T. Knowd. 2004. Field guide to coastal sage scrub and chaparral alliances of Los Padres National Forest. R5-TP-019. USDA Forest Service, Vallejo, CA.

Borchert, M., M. Johnson, D. Schreiner, and S.B. Vander Wall. 2003. Early postfire seed dispersal, seedling establishment and seedling mortality of *Pinus coulteri* (D. Don) in central coastal California, USA. Plant Ecology 168:207–220.

Borchert, M., D. Schreiner, T. Knowd, and T. Plumb. 2002. Predicting postfire survival in Coulter pine *(Pinus coulteri)* and gray pine *(Pinus sabiniana)* after wildfire in central California. Western Journal of Applied Forestry 17(3):134–138.

Brown, P.M., M.W. Kaye, and D. Buckley. 1999. Fire history in Douglas-fir and coast redwood forests at Point Reyes National Seashore, California. Northwest Science 73(3): 205–216.

Byrne, R., J. Michaelsen, and A. Soutar. 1977. Fossil charcoal as a measure of wildfire frequency in Southern California: a preliminary analysis. P. 361–367 in H.A. Mooney and C.E. Conrad (tech. coords.), Proceedings of the symposium on the environmental consequences of fire and fuel management in mediterranean ecosystems. General Technical Report WO-3, USDA Forest Service, Washington, D.C.

Callaway, R.M. 1992. Morphological and physiological responses of 3 California oak species to shade. International Journal of Plant Sciences 153(3):434–441.

Callaway, R.M., and F.W. Davis. 1993. Vegetation dynamics, fire, and the physical-environment in coastal Central California. Ecology 74(5):1567–1578.

Callaway, R.M., and F.W. Davis. 1998. Recruitment of *Quercus agrifolia* in central California: the importance of shrub-dominated patches. Journal of Vegetation Science 9(5): 647–656.

Campbell, B. 1980. Some mixed hardwood forest communities of the coastal ranges of southern California. Phytocoenologia 8(3/4):297–320.

Cayan, D.R., S.A. Kammerdiener, M.D. Dettinger, J.M. Caprio, and D.H. Peterson. 2001. Changes in the onset of spring in the western United States. Bulletin of the American Meteorological Society 82(3):399–415.

Cayan D.R., K.T. Redmond, and L.G. Riddle. 1999. ENSO and hydrologic extremes in the western United States. Journal of Climate 12:2881–2893.

Cooper, W.S. 1922. The broad-sclerophyll vegetation of California. Carnegie Institute of Washington, Washington, DC.

Cylinder, P. 1997. Monterey pine forest conservation strategy. Fremontia 25(2):21–26.

Dagit, R. 2002. Post-fire monitoring of coast live oaks *(Quercus agrifolia)* burned in the 1993 Old Topanga fire. P. 243–249 in R.B. Standiford, D. McCreary, and K.L. Purcell, Proceedings of the 5th symposium on oak woodlands: oaks in California's changing landscape, October 22–25, 2001, San Diego, CA. USDA Forest Service, Pacific Southwest Research Station. Gen. Tech. Rep. PSW-GTR-184.

Daly, C., R.P. Neilson, and D.L. Phillips. 1994. A statistical-topographic model for mapping climatological precipitation over mountainous terrain. Journal of Applied Meteorology 33: 140–158.

D'Antonio, C.M. 1993. Mechanisms controlling invasion of coastal plant communities by the alien succulent *Carpobrotus edulis*. Ecology 74(1):83–95.

D'Antonio, C.M., D.C. Odion, and C.M. Tyler. 1993. Invasion of maritime chaparral by the introduced succulent *Carpobrotus edulis*. Oecologia 95(1):14–21.

Davis, F.W., M.I. Borchert, and D. Odion. 1989. Establishment of microscale vegetation pattern in maritime chaparral after fire. Vegetation 84(1):53–67.

Davis, F.W., D. Hickson, and D.C. Odion. 1988a. Composition of maritime chaparral related to fire history and soil, Burton Mesa, California. Madroño 35:169–195.

Davis, F.W., E.A. Keller, A. Parikh, and J. Florsheim. 1988b. Recovery of the chaparral riparian zone after wildfire. California Riparian Systems Conference, Davis, California, USFS, Pacific Southwest Research Station.

Davis, F.W., and J. Michaelsen 1995. Sensitivity of fire regime in chaparral ecosystems to climate change. P. 435–456 in J.M. Moreno and W.C. Oechel, Global change and mediterranean-type ecosystems.. Springer, New York.

Davis, F.W., D.M. Stoms, A.D. Hollander, K.A. Thomas, P.A. Stine, Odion D., M.I. Borchert, J.H. Thorne, M.V. Gray, R.E. Walker, K. Warner, and J. Graae. 1998. The California Gap Analysis Project—Final Report. University of California, Santa Barbara, CA. [http://www.biogeog.ucsb.edu/projects/gap/gap_rep.html]

De Magistris, A.A., P.N. Hashimoto, S.L. Masoni, and A. Chiesa. 2001. Germination of serotinous cone seeds in *Cupressus* ssp. Israel Journal of Plant Science 49:253–258.

Duffield, J.W. 1951. Interrelationships of the California closed-cone pines with special reference to *Pinus muricata* D. Don. Ph.D. Dissertation. University of California, Berkeley.

Dunne, J., A. Dennis, J.W. Bartolome, and R.H. Barrett. 1991. Chaparral response to a prescribed fire in Mount Hamilton, Santa Clara County, California. Madroño 38(1):21–29.

Dunning, C.E., R.A. Redak, and T.D. Paine. 2003. Preference and performance of a generalist insect herbivore on *Quercus agrifolia* and *Quercus engelmannii* seedlings from a southern California oak woodland. Forest Ecology and Management 174:593–603.

Ewell, P.L. 1995. The Oakland-Berkeley Hills fire of 1991. P. 7–10 in D.R. Weise and R.E. Martin (eds.), The Biswell symposium: fire issues and solutions in urban interface and wildland ecosystems. USDA Forest Service, Pacific Southwest Research Station. General Technical Report PSW-GTR-158.

Florence, M.A. 1985. Successional trends in plant species composition following fall, winter and spring prescribed burns of chamise chaparral in the central Coast Range of California. M.A. Thesis, California State University, Sacramento, CA.

Ford, L.D. 1991. Post-fire dynamics of northern coastal scrub, Monterey County, California. Ph.D. Thesis, University of California, Berkeley.

Gordon, B.L. 1979. Monterey Bay area: natural history and cultural imprints. Boxwood Press, Pacific Grove, CA.

Greenlee, J.M. 1983. Vegetation, fire history, and fire potential of Big Basin Redwoods State Park, California. Ph.D. Thesis, University of California, Santa Cruz.

Greenlee, J.M., and J.H. Langenheim. 1990. Historic fire regimes and their relation to vegetation patterns in the Monterey Bay Area of California. American Midland Naturalist 124(2): 239–253.

Greenlee, J.M., and A. Moldenke. 1982. History of woodland fires in the Gabilan Mountains region of central coastal California. Paicines, California, National Park Service Pinnacles National Monument.

Griffin, J.R. 1975. Plants of the highest Santa Lucia and Diablo Range Peaks, California. USDA Forest Service Research Paper PSW-110. 50 p.

Griffin, J.R. 1978a. Vegetation damage, Marble-cone fire, Los Padres National Forest, Junipero Sierra Peak, Report 1—*Pinus lambertiana* regeneration. Unpublished report. 20 p.

Griffin, J.R. 1978b. Maritime chaparral and endemic shrubs of the Monterey Bay region, California. Madroño 25(2): 65–81.

Griffin, J.R. 1978c. The Marble-Cone fire ten months later. Fremontia 6(2):8–14.

Griffin, J.R. 1979. Vegetation damage, Marble-Cone fire, Los Padres National Forest. Pine Ridge, Report 1—*Pinus ponderosa* regeneration. Unpublished report. 15 p.

Griffin, J.R. 1982. Pine seedlings, native ground cover, and *Lolium multiflorum* on the Marble-Cone burn, Santa Lucia Range, California. Madroño 29:177–188.

Griffin, J.R. 1988. Oak woodland terrestrial. P. 383–416 in M.G. Barbour and J. Major (eds.), Vegetation of California. John Wiley, New York.

Hardham, C.B. 1962. The Santa Lucia *Cupressus sargentii* groves and their associated northern hydrophilous and endemic species. Madroño 16(6):173–204.

Haston, L., F.W. Davis, and J. Michaelsen. 1988. Climate response functions for bigcone spruce: a mediterranean climate conifer. Physical Geography 9(1):81–97.

Haston, L., and J. Michaelsen. 1994. Long-term central coastal California precipitation variability and relationships to El-Nino-Southern Oscillation. Journal of Climate 7(9):1373–1387.

Haston, L., and J. Michaelsen. 1997. Spatial and temporal variability of southern California precipitation over the last 400 years and relationships to atmospheric circulation patterns. Journal of Climate 10(8):1836–1852.

Hatch, D.A., J.W. Bartolome, J.S. Fehmi, and D.S. Hillyard. 1999. Effects of burning and grazing on a coastal California grassland. Restoration Ecology 7:376–381.

Henson, P., and D.J. Usner. 1993. The natural history of Big Sur. University of California Press, Berkeley, CA.

Hillyard, D. 1997. Challenges in conserving Monterey pine forest. Fremontia 25(2):16–20.

Holland, R.F. (1986). Preliminary descriptions of the terrestrial natural communities of California. Sacramento, California, The Resources Agency, Department of Fish and Game, Natural Heritage Division.

Jackson, L.E., Jr. 1977. Dating and recurrence frequency of prehistoric mudflows near Big Sur, Monterey County, California. Journal of Research U.S. Geological Survey 5(1):17–32.

Johnson, D.L. 1977. The late Quaternary climate of coastal California: evidence for an Ice Age refugium. Quaternary Research 8:154–179.

Johnson, J., S.B. Vander Wall, and M. Borchert. 2003. A comparative analysis of seed and cone characteristics and seed-dispersal strategies of three pines in the subsection Sabinianae. Plant Ecology 168:69–84.

Keeley, J.E. 1982. Distribution of lightning and man-caused fires in California. P. 431–437 in C.E. Conrad and W.C. Oechel (eds.), Proceedings of the symposium on dynamics and management of mediterranean-type ecosystems. USDA Forest Service, Pacific Southwest Forest and Range Experiment Station.

Keeley, J.E. 2001. Fire and invasive species in mediterranean-climate ecosystems of California. Invasive species workshop: the role of fire in the control and spread of invasive species, Tallahassee, FL, Tall Timbers Research Station.

Keeley, J.E. 2002a. Fire management of California shrubland landscapes. Environmental Management 29(3):395–408.

Keeley, J.E. 2002b. Native American impacts on fire regimes of the California coastal ranges. Journal of Biogeography 29(3): 303–320.

Keeley, J.E. 2003. Impact of antecedent climate on fire regimes in coastal California. International Journal of Wildland Fire 13:173–182.

Keeley, J.E., and C.J. Fotheringham. 2003. Impact of past, present and future fire regimes on western North American shrublands. P. 218–262 in T.T. Veblen, W.L. Baker, G. Montenegro, and T.W. Swetnam (eds.), Fire and climatic change in temperate ecosystems of the Western Americas. Springer, New York.

Keeley, J.E., G. Ne'eman, and C.J. Fotheringham. 1999. Immaturity risk in a fire-dependent pine. Journal of Mediterranean Ecology 1:41–48.

Keeley, J.E., and P.H. Zedler. 1998. Evolution of life histories in *Pinus*. P. 219–249 in D.M. Richardson (ed.), Ecology and biogeography of *Pinus*. Cambridge University Press, Cambridge, UK.

Kelly, M., and R.K. Meentemeyer. 2002. Landscape dynamics of the spread of sudden oak death, Photogrammetric Engineering and Remote Sensing 68 (10):1001–1009.

Koch, R. R., A. E. Courchesne, and C. Collins. 1970. Sexual differences in foraging behavior in white-headed woodpeckers. Bulletin of the Southern California Academy of Science 69:60–64.

Lambrinos, J. G. 2000. The impact of the invasive alien grass *Cortaderia jubata* (Lemoine) Stapf on an endangered mediterranean-type shrubland in California. Diversity and Distributions 6:217–231.

Lathrop, E. W., and C. D. Osborne. 1991. Influence of fire on oak seedlings and saplings in southern oak woodland on the Santa Rosa Plateau Preserve, Riverside County, California. P. 366–370 in Proceedings of the symposium on oak woodlands and hardwood rangeland management, Davis, CA, USFS, Pacific Southwest Research Station. Gen. Tech. Rep. PSW-126.

Ledig, F. T. 2000. Founder effects and the genetic structure of Coulter pine. The Journal of Heredity 91(4):307–315.

Lewis, H. T. 1973. Patterns of Indian burning in California: ecology and ethnohistory. Ballena Press Anthropological Papers No. 1, Socorro.

McBride, J. R., and E. C. Stone. 1976. Plant succession on sand dunes of Monterey Peninsula, California. American Midland Naturalist 96(1):118–132.

Mensing, S. A. 1998. 560 years of vegetation change in the region of Santa Barbara, California. Madroño 45(1):1–11.

Mensing, S. A., J. Michaelsen, and R. Byrne. 1999. A 560-year record of Santa Ana fires reconstructed from charcoal deposited in the Santa Barbara Basin, California. Quaternary Research 51(3):295–305.

Michaelsen, J., L. Haston, and F. W. Davis. 1987. 400 years of Central California precipitation variability reconstructed from tree rings. Water Resources Bulletin 23(5):809–817.

Miles, S. R., and C. B. Goudey. 1997. Ecological subregions of California: section and subsection descriptions. San Francisco, CA. USDA Forest Service, Pacific Southwest Region.

Millar, C. I. 1983. A steep cline in *Pinus muricata*. Evolution 37:311–319.

Millar, C. I. 1986. Bishop pine *(Pinus muricata)* of inland Marin County, California. Madroño 33(2):123–129.

Millar, C. I., S. H. Strauss, M. T. Conkle, and R. D. Westfall. 1988. Allozyme differentiation and biosystematics of the Californian closed-cone pines (*Pinus* subsect. Oocarpae). Systematic Botany 13:351–370.

Moritz, M. A. 1997. Analyzing extreme disturbance events: fire in Los Padres National Forest. Ecological Applications 7(4): 1252–1262.

Moritz, M. A. 2003. Spatiotemporal analysis of controls on shrubland fire regimes: age dependency and fire hazard. Ecology 84:351–361.

Moritz M. A., J. E. Keeley, E. A. Johnson, and A. A. Schaffner. 2004. Testing a basic assumption of shrubland fire management: how important is fuel age? Frontiers in Ecology and the Environment 2:67–72.

Ne'eman, G., C. J. Fotheringham, and J. E. Keeley. 1999. Patch to landscape patterns in post fire recruitment of a serotinous conifer. Plant Ecology 145:235–242.

Null, J. 1995. Climate of San Francisco, NOAA Technical Memorandum NWS WR-126 (3rd Revision).

Odion, D. C., and F. W. Davis. 2000. Fire, soil heating, and the formation of vegetation patterns in chaparral. Ecological Monographs 70(1):149–169.

Odion, D. C., and C. M. Tyler. 2002. Are long fire-free periods necessary to maintain the endangered, fire-recruiting shrub, *Arctostaphylos morroensis* (Ericaceae)? Conservation Ecology 6(2):4.

Ornduff, R., and V. Norris. 1997. Rebirth of a Bishop pine forest: first year after the Mount Vision fire. Fremontia 25 (3):22–28.

Parikh, A. 1989. Factors affecting the distribution of riparian tree species in southern California chaparral watersheds. Ph.D. Thesis, Geography. Department of University of California at Santa Barbara: 123.

Parikh, A., and N. Gale. 1998. Coast live oak revegetation on the central coast of California. Madroño 45(4):301–309.

Peinado, M., J. L. Aguirre, and J. Delgadillo. 1997. Phytosociological, bioclimatic and biogeographical classification of woody climax communities of western North America. Journal of Vegetation Science 8:505–528.

Plumb, T. R. 1980. Response of oaks to fire. P. 202–215 in T. R. Plumb (tech. coord.), Proceedings of the symposium on the ecology, management, and utilization of California oaks, Claremont, CA, June, 1979, USDA Forest Service Pacific Southwest Forest and Range Experiment Station.

Plumb, T. R., and A. P. Gomez. 1983. Five southern California oaks: identification and postfire management. Berkeley, California, USDA Forest Service, Pacific Southwest Forest and Range Experiment Station General Technical Report PSW-71. 56 pp.

Plumb, T. R., and B. Hannah. 1991. Artificial regeneration of blue and coast live oaks in the Central Coast. Proceedings of the symposium on oak woodlands and hardwood rangeland management, Davis, CA, USFS Pacific Southwest Research Station.

Rizzo, D. M., M. Garbelotto, J. M. Davidson, G. W. Slaughter, and S. T. Koike. 2002. *Phytophthora ramorum* as the cause of extensive mortality of *Quercus* spp. and *Lithocarpus densiflorus* in California. Plant Disease 86(3):205–214.

Sawyer, J. O., and T. Keeler-Wolf. 1995. A manual of California vegetation. Sacramento, California Native Plant Society.

Schwilk, D. W., and D. D. Ackerly. 2001. Flammability and serotiny as strategies: correlated evolution in pines. Oikos 94:326–336.

Snow, G. E. 1980. The fire resistance of Engelmann and coast live oak seedlings. P. 62–66 in T. R. Plumb (tech. coord.), Proceedings of the symposium on the ecology, management, and utilization of California oaks, Claremont, CA, June, 1979, USDA Forest Service Pacific Southwest Forest and Range Experiment Station.

Sommers, W. T. 1978. LFM forecast variables related to Santa-Ana wind occurrences. Monthly Weather Review 106(9): 1307–1316.

Spencer, M., and K. O'Hara. 2002. The spatial pattern of SOD symptoms in coastal redwood tanoak forests. Presentation Abstract, Sudden Oak Death Science Symposium, December 16–18, 2002, Monterey, California. http://danr.ucop.edu/ihrmp/sodsymp/paper/paper29.html .

Stephens, S. L., D. D. Pirto, and D. F. Caramagno. 2004. Fire regimes and resultant forest structure in native Año Nuevo Monterey pine *(Pinus radiata)* forest, California. American Midland Naturalist 152:25–36.

Stephens, S. L. and D. L. Fry. 2005. Fire history in coast redwood stands in the northeastern Santa Cruz Mountains, California. Fire Ecology 1(1):1–19.

Stylinski, C. D., and E. B. Allen. 1999. Lack of native species recovery following severe exotic disturbance in southern Californian shrublands. Journal of Applied Ecology 36(4): 544–554.

Sugnet, P.W. 1981. Fire history and post-fire stand dynamics of Inverness Bishop pine populations. M.S. Thesis, University of California, Berkeley.

Talley, S.N. 1974. The ecology of Santa Lucia fir (*Abies bracteata*), a narrow endemic of California. Ph.D. Thesis, Duke University.

Thornton, P.E., S.W. Running, and M.A. White. 1997. Generating surfaces of daily meteorology variables over large regions of complex terrain. Journal of Hydrology 190:214–251.

Timbrook, J., J.R. Johnson, and D.D. Earle. 1982. Vegetation burning by the Chumash. Journal of California and Great Basin Anthropology 4(2):163–186.

Tyler, C.M. 1996. Relative importance of factors contributing to postfire seedling establishment in maritime chaparral. Ecology 77(7):2182–2195.

Van Dyke, E., and K.D. Holl. 2001. Maritime chaparral community transition in the absence of fire. Madroño 48(4):221–229.

Wells, P.V. 1962. Vegetation in relation to geological substratum and fire in San Luis Obispo Quadrangle, California. Ecological Monographs 32(1):79–103.

Westerling, A.L., A. Gershunov, T.J. Brown, D.R. Cayan, and M.D. Dettinger. 2003. Climate and wildfire in the western United States. Bulletin of the American Meteorological Society 84:595–604.

White, K.L. 1999. Revisiting native *Pinus radiata* forests after twenty-nine years. Madroño 46:80–87.

Zedler, P.H. 1995. Fire frequency in southern California shrublands: biological effects and management options. P. 101–112 in J.E. Keeley and T. Scott (eds.), Brushfires in California wildlands: ecology and resource management. International Association of Wildland Fire, Fairfield, WA.

CHAPTER 15

South Coast Bioregion

JON E. KEELEY

There is fire on the mountain and lightning in the air ...
"Fire on the Mountain," MARSHALL TUCKER BAND, 1975

Description of Bioregion

Physical Geography

The South Coast bioregion includes the Southern California Coast and the Mountains and Valleys sections as defined by Miles and Goudey (1997). The region is bordered on the north by the Transverse Ranges, on the south by the U.S. border with Mexico, on the east by the Peninsular Ranges, and on the west by the Pacific Ocean (Map. 15.1). The Transverse and northern Peninsular ranges bound the Los Angeles Basin, an extensive floodplain comprising millions of years of alluvial outwash deposited by the Los Angeles, San Gabriel, and Santa Ana rivers. Minor mountain ranges occur within the basin, including the Palos Verde Peninsula on the west, Puente Hills on the east, and San Joaquin Hills on the south. The Orange and San Diego coastlines comprise a series of Pleistocene marine terraces and an uplifted peneplain now incised by east-west-running rivers including the Santa Margarita, San Luis Rey, and San Diego rivers. Other rivers traversing the San Diego coastal plain and emptying into San Diego Bay are the Sweetwater and Otay rivers (Schoenherr 1992).

The Transverse Ranges are one of the few east-west ranges in western North America and are composed of five mountain systems separated by broad alluvial valleys. These include, from west to east, the Santa Ynez, Santa Monica, Castaic or Liebre, San Gabriel, and San Bernardino mountains, with maximum elevations of 1,430, 949, 1,765, 3,074, and 3,508 m, respectively (Norris and Webb 1976). The Channel Islands are geologically part of this formation.

On the western end, the Transverse Ranges fork into a northern extension, the Santa Ynez Mountains and a southern extension, the Santa Monica Mountains (Map 15.1). Both extend nearly to the ocean leaving a very narrow coastal plain and both are relatively low-elevation mountains largely lacking significant coniferous forests. The Santa Ynez geology

is dominated by marine sediments predating the Tertiary and bears much resemblance to the Coast Ranges to the north (Norris and Webb 1976). The Santa Monica Mountains comprise a mixture of Miocene volcanic extrusions and more recent marine terrace deposits. The San Gabriel Mountains are a largely granite fault block, bounded on all sides by faults and with outlying extensions including the Verdugo Mountains to the west and Liebre or Castaic Mountains to the northwest. These mountains have experienced considerable uplift in recent geological time, contributing to the rather steep and highly dissected front that faces the Los Angeles Basin. The eastern-most San Bernardino Mountains are also a rapidly growing granitic fault block, but unlike the San Gabriel Mountains, they have conifer-dominated mid-elevation plateaus between 1,700 and 2,300 m, which includes Arrowhead and Big Bear lakes. Several features in this range represent the most southerly extension of Pleistocene glaciation in California (Sharp et al. 1959), indicative of lower summer temperatures in the region during the last glacial maximum (Owen et al. 2003).

The Peninsular Ranges are a north-south trending series of fault blocks, the bulk of which lie south of the U.S. border (Hinds 1952). In our region they include the San Jacinto Mountains in the north, with a maximum elevation of 3,300 m, and to the southeast the drier Santa Rosa mountains with several peaks over 1,800 m. To the west is another series of lower-elevation ranges separated by broad valleys and include the Santa Ana, Agua Tibia, and Laguna Mountains, mostly below 1,800 m. Unusual and potentially stressful substrates for vegetation include serpentine and breccias in the Santa Ana Mountains and gabbros in the Laguna Mountains and lower foothills to the west, including peaks such as Pinos, Guatay, Mother Grundy, Lawson, Lyons, Tecate, Otay, and Mt. Miguel, all below 1,500 m (Alexander 1993). These gabbro soils are, like serpentine, derived from mafic igneous rocks, and weather

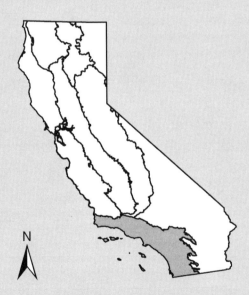

MAP 15.1. The South Coast bioregion extends south from the east-west trending Transverse Ranges to Mexico and from the coast east to the north-south trending Peninsular Ranges.

into reddish iron- and magnesium-rich soils that have lower primary productivity but support a rich diversity of endemic plants (Schoenherr 1992).

This southwestern region includes the highest peaks outside of the Sierra Nevada; however, over 50% of the region is below 500 m (Davis et al. 1995). The extraordinary range of elevations represented in this region translates into a high diversity of vegetation types and fire regimes. The high ranges separated by broad valleys dissected by riparian corridors all play important roles in determining the extent of fire spread. The widespread distribution of substrates such as gabbro has possibly reduced fire frequency by limiting the rate of biomass productivity. The unusually rich diversity of mineral and gem deposits, many of which have been mined since the middle of the nineteenth century (Schoenherr 1992), have likely been responsible for early anthropogenic impacts on wildfire activity in remote mountainous regions (Leiberg 1900a).

Despite comprising only 8% of the land area of the state, this region contains 56% of the total human population (Davis et al. 1995). This pattern of development has placed immense pressure on natural resources and has created a fire management problem of extraordinary proportions.

Climatic Patterns

This is a region of mediterranean climate, consisting of cool, wet winters and hot, dry summers. Average rainfall varies spatially from 200 to 1,200 mm annually, two thirds of which falls November to April in storms of several days' duration, and dry spells of a month or more may occur during the wet season (Major 1977). The distribution of winter rainfall is strongly controlled by the orographic effect, and precipitation increases with elevation. Above 2,100 m a significant portion of winter precipitation comes as snow. Significant summer precipitation is rare near the coast but occasional Mexican monsoons from the Gulf of California affect the interior mountains (Douglas et al. 1993).

Mean winter temperatures near the coast are greater than 10°C and decrease toward the interior and with elevation. Coastal sites may occasionally experience subzero temperatures with lethal effects on some native species (Collett 1992). In the interior foothills and valleys, summer temperatures often exceed 40°C, but are more moderate at higher elevations and toward the coasts. Late spring and early summer marine air delays the onset of the fire season in the coastal mountains (Coffin 1959).

Lightning accompanies both winter and summer storms, and the proportion varies markedly between the coastal and the interior ranges (Fig. 15.1). In the interior ranges, lightning strikes peak in August, a pattern typical in other interior parts of California and the Southwest (van Wagtendonk and Cayan 2003); however, in the coastal ranges, lightning strikes peak later in the autumn (Fig. 15.1B). The coastal ranges also differ in that 35% of all strikes occur in winter and spring, whereas in the interior these two seasons represent less than 12% (Fig. 15.1A, B). Due to high fuel moisture, these winter and spring lightning strikes play essentially no role as ignition sources for wildfires (Conroy 1928), thus a substantially greater proportion of lightning strikes will be ineffective at igniting fires in these coastal ranges.

Regionally, lightning strike density is substantially greater in the interior mountain ranges, which receive several times more strikes than at comparable elevations in the coastal ranges (Fig. 15.2; Wilcoxin's signed rank test, $P < 0.001$, n = 10). Broad comparisons of lightning strike density reveal roughly 25 to 40 lightning strikes per 100 km^2 per year for interior ranges, and this is 5 to 10 times higher than for coastal valleys (Fig. 15.2). Based on the density of fires ignited by lightning in these two regions (Keeley 1982) it appears that only 3% to 5% of all lightning strikes ignite a fire. In the interior ranges, lightning-ignited fires are predictable most years, whereas in the coastal ranges, they are sporadic. For example, in the Santa Monica Mountains, lightning-ignited fires occurred rarely in fire records between 1919 and 1980 (Radtke et al. 1982). Since 1981, there have been lightning-ignited fires on two dates, one in 1982 and one in 1998 (Santa Monica Mountains National Recreation Area fire records, supplied by Marti Witter, NPS, 2003). Thus, in the coastal ranges, lightning is a potential source of fire ignition but a relatively uncommon source. In the interior ranges, they are annual events, with the vast majority of lightning-ignited fires in forests and fewer than 20% in shrublands (Keeley 1982).

A factor of local importance in southern California is the Santa Ana wind. This foehn wind results from a high-pressure cell in the Great Basin, coupled with a low-pressure trough off the coast of southern California, which drives dry air toward the coast. These foehn winds may exceed 100 km hr^{-1} and bring high temperatures and low humidity. Santa Ana winds create the worst fire weather conditions in the country because several days or weeks of these winds occur every autumn, at the time natural fuels are at their driest (Schroeder et al. 1964). Under Santa Ana wind conditions, fire spread is rapid, sometimes covering 30,000 ha in a single day through fuels of any age class (Phillips 1971).

The overwhelming importance of Santa Ana winds is illustrated by the relationship between burning patterns and climate. Throughout the western U.S., there is a strong relationship between antecedent drought and fire activity (Westerling et al. 2002). However, in southern California during the twentieth century, there is a surprisingly weak relationship between antecedent drought and subsequent fire activity (Keeley 2004a). The important role of Santa Ana winds is also shown by the relationship between the Palmer Drought Severity Index and large fires. Those large fires occurring during the autumn months and most likely driven by Santa Ana winds occur regardless of whether or not there is a drought. The primary impact of antecedent drought appears to be one of extending the fire season, since large fires before and after the autumn Santa Ana season occur consistently during drought years.

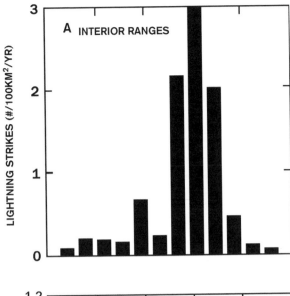

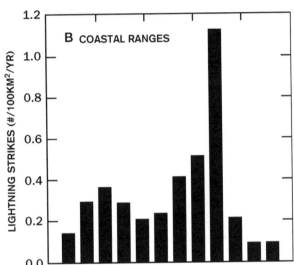

FIGURE 15.1. Monthly distribution of lightning strike density in the interior (A) and coastal (B) zones of southern California as defined by Miles and Goudey 1997 (data from van Wagtendonk and Cayan 2003) and Santa Ana wind days (C) for Los Angeles County (data from Weide 1968), based on (1) 3-mb decrease in mean sea level pressure from Santa Monica to Palmdale, (2) ≥10°C decrease in temperature from Santa Monica to Palmdale, (3) northerly wind speeds of 16 km per hour in the San Fernando Valley and 50 km per hour in the Riverside-San Bernardino area, and (4) relative humidity ≤30%.

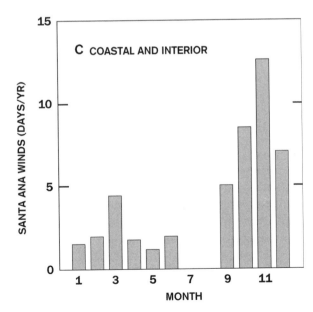

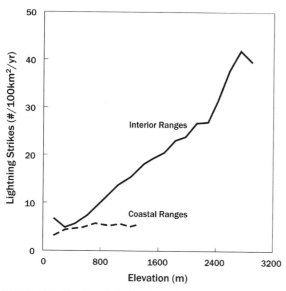

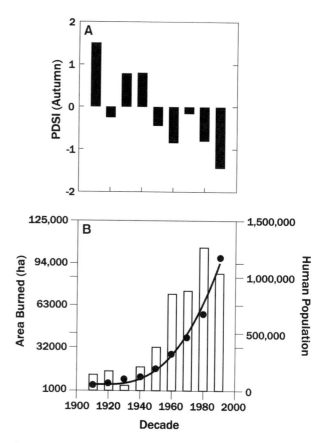

FIGURE 15.2. Elevational distribution of lightning-strike density for the interior and coastal ranges of the South Coast bioregion. Due to limited area in the highest elevations these were combined into the last elevational category plotted. (Data from van Wagtendonk and Cayan 2007.)

Although the weather conditions that produce lightning do not overlap with conditions that generate foehn winds, the seasons do overlap and Santa Ana winds may occur within days or weeks of a lightning-ignited fire (Fig. 15.1C). Although the vast majority of contemporary burning in the region is due to human-ignited fires during Santa Ana wind conditions, it is hypothesized that under natural conditions, occasionally lightning-ignited fires persisted into the autumn foehn wind season and these Santa Ana wind-driven fires accounted for the majority of area burned (Keeley and Fotheringham 2001a).

One of the difficulties in sorting out the role of climate in driving fire regimes is that human ignitions play a major role in this region and complicate the interpretation. For example, in focusing on just the decadal average Palmer Drought Severity Index for Riverside County, it is apparent that it matches closely the area burned during the twentieth century (Fig. 15.3). However, human population growth parallels these changes in area burned, and increased ignitions are likely a major contributor to the late-twentieth-century increase in burning in that county.

Ecological Zones

The South Coast bioregion is a complex mosaic of grassland, shrubland, forest, and woodland (Fig. 15.4) that forms a relatively fine-grained landscape relative to most wildfires, which usually burn large enough areas to encompass a diversity of vegetation types and associations. Thus, fire regimes vary on a rather course scale, and within a vegetation type there is limited association of fire regimes with specific plant associations. In this respect, there are two broad ecological zones: the coastal valleys and foothill zone and the montane

FIGURE 15.3. Decadal variation in Palmer Drought Severity Index (A), area burned (open bars), and human population (closed circles) for Riverside County (B). (Data from Keeley et al. 1999.)

zone. Within each of these zones, fire response is best examined at the scale of broadly defined vegetation types.

In the coastal and foothill zone, the distribution pattern of grasslands, sage scrub, chaparral, and woodlands is driven largely by a combination of soil moisture and disturbance. At the arid end of the gradient, herbaceous and semi-woody subshrub associations predominate, with woodlands and chaparral at the moister end of the gradient. However, there is an important interaction between soil moisture and disturbance, such that under xeric conditions, far less disturbance is required to displace the dominant woody association with herbaceous vegetation (Keeley 2002a).

Southern California grasslands include small, highly fragmented patches of native grassland and more widespread, anthropogenically created non–native-dominated annual grasslands. The native grasslands are dominated by perennial bunchgrasses, purple needlegrass (*Nassella pulchra*), pine bluegrass (*Poa secunda*), and Junegrass (*Koeleria macrantha*), and are distributed on fine-grained soils in localized patches within a mosaic of shrublands and woodlands (Huenneke 1989, Keeley 1993). Native grasslands also include a rich diversity of annual forbs but very few native annual grasses. Significant native grasslands still persist in valleys and shallow slopes on clay soils, which, due to the water-holding capacity of these fine-grained soils, are stressful substrates for competing shrubs.

FIGURE 15.4. Landscape mosaic of southern oak woodland, grassland, sage scrub, arid chaparral on south-facing exposures (slopes on right side of photo), and mesic chaparral on north-facing slopes. (Photo by J. Keeley, location near Black Mountain north of Ramona, San Diego County.)

Most of the grasslands in the region lack any native grasses and are dominated by non-native annual grasses and forbs. They bear little resemblance, in both ecology and distribution, to native grasslands. Most annual grasslands were derived from fire-induced type conversion of shrublands and subsequent invasion by non-native grasses and forbs. They exhibit no strong relationship with soil type or precipitation regime and are the result of anthropogenic disturbance (Cooper 1922, Wells 1962, Keeley 1990b, 1993, 2002a). Although these generalizations are broadly applicable across the region, on a more limited scale there are some annual grasslands that do appear to be derived from native grassland as a result of intensive livestock grazing (Oberbauer 1978) or soil tillage (Kellogg and Kellogg 1990, Stromberg and Griffin 1996).

Semi-deciduous sage scrub dominates lower elevations along the coast and in interior valleys, and in these two subregions, sage scrub forms very different species assemblages (Davis et al. 1994). Thus, it is not surprising that there are significant differences in fire response between coastal and interior sage scrub associations. This appears to be driven partly by floristic differences (Kirkpatrick and Hutchinson 1977) and partly by the impact of the more arid conditions in interior valleys. As treated here, the interior sage scrub is equivalent to the Riversidian Division and the coastal sage scrub is included within the Venturan and Diegan divisions (Axelrod 1978).

At lower elevations, the taller stature evergreen chaparral replaces sage scrub on north-facing exposures or on deeper soils (Fig. 15.5), and with increasing elevation completely displaces it throughout much of the foothills and lower montane. Chaparral comprises a rich array of different floristic associations (Sawyer and Keeler-Wolf 1995), some of which, such as chamise and black sage *(Salvia melliflora)*, have such broad distributions that they include more than a single fire

regime. Although fire response between dominants of different associations varies, different associations are often subject to similar fire regimes because of the fine-grain distribution of associations due to small-scale topographic variation. For example, monotypic stands of the facultative seeder chamise *(Adenostoma fasciculatum)* on south-facing slopes are often juxtaposed with diverse north-facing slopes of obligate resprouters such as scrub oak *(Quercus berberidifolia)*, California coffeeberry *(Rhamnus californica),* and chaparral cherry *(Prunus ilicifolia)*, sometimes separated by ridge tops dominated by the obligate seeder hoaryleaf ceanothus *(Ceanothus crassifolius)*. Most fires burn broad portions of the landscape; thus these three associations typically burn in the same high-intensity fire. Although fire severity may vary in these different associations, the impact of fires on community resilience may be as much a function of pre- and post-fire climate as it is floristic differences.

Within chaparral-dominated landscapes, there are isolated patches of serotinous cypress species, Tecate cypress *(Cupressus forbesii)* or Cuyamaca cypress *(Cupressus arizonica)* (Hickman 1993). They typically occur above 1,200 m in widely disjunct populations, perhaps as relicts of a once-wider distribution. They range from 330 to 1,700 m, primarily on north-facing slopes, and all populations appear to date back to the last fire (Armstrong 1966, Zedler 1977). These small-stature cypress form even-aged monotypic stands from less than 1 ha to more than 100 ha in size, typically embedded within a sea of chaparral, and usually on fine clay soils derived from gabbro or other ultramafic substrates (McMillan 1956, Zedler 1995a).

Several pines are closely associated with chaparral shrublands. In the eastern Transverse and northern Peninsular ranges are pockets of knobcone pine *(Pinus attenuata)* (Minnich 1980a, Pequegnat 1951, Vogl 1973), a species more common further north in the coastal ranges. Coulter pine *(Pinus coulteri)* is widely distributed above 1,200 m throughout

FIGURE 15.5. Mosaic of sage scrub surrounding patch of larger-stature chaparral in the Santa Ana Mountains, Orange County, at approximately 700 m. (Photo by J. Keeley.)

the Transverse and Peninsular ranges, occurring in both chaparral and mixed conifer forests (Griffin and Critchfield 1972). A closely related species is Torrey pine *(Pinus torreyana)*, a rare endemic restricted to a few coastal populations in San Diego County, with one disjunct population on Santa Rosa Island.

Bigcone Douglas-fir *(Pseudotsuga macrocarpa)* occurs in low- to high-density populations between 400 and 1,800 m, although small populations at lower and higher elevations do occur (Gause 1966). Approximately two thirds of this forest type (19,000 ha) are distributed in the San Gabriel Mountains

(Stephenson and Calcarone 1999). They are most abundant on north-facing slopes, particularly on interior sites (Bolton 1966, Minnich 1978). This tree was heavily exploited for timber during the early settlement period because it was the lowest elevation conifer in the region (Minnich 1988). This, plus increased fire frequency accompanying settlement in the Los Angeles Basin, are considered factors accounting for the upward movement of its elevational boundary (Gause 1966). Today, it is commonly restricted to rather steep ravines in association with canyon live oak *(Quercus chrysolepis)* amidst a sea of chaparral and oak woodland (McDonald and Litterell 1976).

Riparian woodlands and shrublands today occupy a relatively small percentage of the region, as it is estimated that 90% of them have been lost (Faber et al. 1989). Historically, the greatest extent of riparian habitat was the Los Angeles coastal plain, much of which was a vast seasonal wetland (Gumprecht 1999). Riparian woodlands have the potential for affecting landscape patterns of fire spread. The dominant woody taxa willow (Salix), alder (Alnus), cottonwood (Populus), elderberry (Sambucus), maple (Acer), mule fat (Baccharis), ash (Fraxinus), arrow weed (Pluchea), poison oak (Toxicodendron), and sycamore (Platanus) are almost all important components of riparian communities throughout the Northern Hemisphere. Nearly all are winter deciduous (Rundel 1998), and in foothill and coastal environments this contrasts with a landscape otherwise dominated by either summer deciduous or evergreen life forms.

Woodlands dominate undisturbed valleys and north-facing slopes, most commonly including the evergreen coast live oak (Quercus agrifolia), sometimes in association with the much rarer evergreen Engelmann oak (Quercus engelmannii). Typically these woodlands are relatively open and in many instances are best considered oak savannas. Today, the understory consists mostly of non-native grasses and forbs, and these are the primary fuels that carry fire. Prior to human entry into California, the oak understory is thought to have comprised coastal sage scrub subshrubs (Wells 1962), and examples of this association are still readily observed today along Highway 101, north of Gaviota Pass in Santa Barbara County. This plant community has long been in direct competition with human development; thus extensive portions of woodlands have been lost. Interior live oak (Quercus wislizenii) is another evergreen oak that often forms closed-canopy forests on mesic sites, often mixing with broadleaf chaparral shrubs. Valley oak woodlands occur in several valleys of the northwestern Transverse Ranges. These represent a southern extension of such woodlands and are covered in more detail in the Central Coastal section by Borchert and Davis, Chapter 14.

One largely endemic association is the California black walnut (Juglans californica)-dominated woodland, widely distributed in the foothills of the Los Angeles Basin (Quinn 1990). This winter-deciduous tree often forms associations with arborescent forms of evergreen chaparral shrubs such as Christmas berry (Heteromeles arbutifolia), chaparral cherry (Prunus ilicifolia), and holly-leaf redberry (Rhamnus ilicifolia) (Keeley 1990a).

In the lower montane zone, winter-deciduous California black oak (Quercus kelloggii) woodlands often dominate between the lower-elevation evergreen sclerophyllous chaparral and the higher-elevation evergreen conifers. This winter-deciduous woodland is more widespread in the other interior ranges of the region.

Montane forest types considered here all exhibit substantial ecological overlap with Sierra Nevada forests. They include yellow pine, mixed conifer, and lodgepole pine forests. Two yellow pines, ponderosa (Pinus ponderosa) and Jeffrey (Pinus jeffreyi), segregate out according to specific climatic parameters, with the latter being predominant on drier and/or colder sites (Thorne 1977, Stephenson 1990). At their lower margins they are associated with Coulter pine (Pinus coulteri) and at higher elevations with white fir (Abies concolor). On more mesic slopes, white fir and incense-cedar (Calocedrus decurrens) dominate with a smaller percentage of sugar pine and Jeffrey pine. Lodgepole pine (Pinus contorta var. murrayana) forests have limited distribution in the highest elevations of the eastern Transverse and northern interior Peninsular ranges. Unlike the lodgepole populations of the northern Rocky Mountains, these southern California pines are not fire-dependent serotinous species, and in this respect are most similar to the Sierra Nevada lodgepole pine forests.

Overview of Historic Fire Occurrence

Prehistoric Period

Chaparral genera, including manzanita (Arctostaphylos), California-lilac (Ceanothus), mountain-mahogany (Cercocarpus), flannelbush (Fremontodendron), Christmas berry (Heteromeles arbutifolia), cherry (Prunus), oak (Quercus), coffeeberry or redberry (Rhamnus), and sumac or sugarbush (Rhus), were present in the south coast region since at least mid to late Miocene—5 to 15 million years ago (Axelrod 1939). Even then, fire was part of this environment, as middle Miocene deposits in the Santa Moncia Mountains contain charcoal and partially burned chaparral fragments (Weide 1968). Chaparral shrub species as well as big-cone Douglas-fir forests were present in southern California since at least middle Pliocene (Axelrod 1950b) and were present much further east into what is today desert habitat (Axelrod 1950c). Throughout the Pliocene and Pleistocene epochs, the region was dominated by closed-cone cypress and pines and included Monterey cypress (Cupressus macrocarpus), Bishop pine (Pinus muricata), and Monterey pine (Pinus radiata), species that today are displaced 560 km northward (Axelrod 1938, Axelrod and Govean 1996, Ledig 1999, 2000). The closed-cone character indicates fire has been a predictable feature of this landscape for at least a couple million years, and this is supported by fossil charcoal records (Johnson 1977). The fact that these species typically burn in stand-replacing crown fires, and are moderately long-lived obligate seeders sensitive to short fire-return intervals (Keeley and Zedler 1998), and growth rates were lower than those today due to 40% less CO_2 during much of the Pleistocene (Ward et al. 2005), suggests the hypothesis that fires were infrequent, on the order of once or twice a century.

Approximately 90% of the past 1.6 million years were cooler conditions, and contemporary plant associations in the region developed only during the last 8,000 years, which comprises the Holocene Epoch. Prior to the Holocene, we know certain dominants currently in southern California were displaced hundreds of kilometers southward and toward lower elevations. For example, the Vizcaino Desert region of central Baja California at 27°N latitude had chamise chaparral only 10,200 years B.P. (Rhode 2002). At comparable elevations (780 m), the present southern boundary of chamise chaparral is more than 500 km north of this Pleistocene population. Further north in Baja California at 30°, Wells (2000) reported a diverse chaparral assembly at 550 to 600 m elevation between 10,000 and 17,000 years B.P., which is more than 400 m lower than that at present. In southern California, late Pleistocene floras were distributed 800 to 900 m lower (Axelrod 1950a, Anderson et al. 2002), likely due to the higher precipitation during glacial episodes (Robert 2004).

There is a relatively scant fossil record for coastal sage scrub species; for this reason, Axelrod (1978) proposed that this is a largely Holocene plant community in southern California. However, arid environments, such as those where sage scrub predominates, seldom preserve much of a fossil record. Illustrative of this is the fact that the nearly ubiquitous chaparral shrub chamise is absent from the fossil record, save some relatively recent packrat midden sites.

The present distribution of vegetation types is a product of Holocene drying and coincides with the first entry of humans into the region. The concomitant emergence of contemporary climate, vegetation distribution, and humans presents a challenge to accurately discerning natural and anthropogenic fire regimes. However, although humans were present more than 10,000 years B.P., a widespread presence significant enough to have an impact on the local ecology is undoubtedly much younger, perhaps only the last few thousand years or less (Jones 1992). Throughout the first half of the Holocene, lightning was likely the dominant or only ignition source in most parts of the region. It has been hypothesized that the coastal region burned when the occasional August or September lightning-ignited fire persisted until picked up and carried by the autumn foehn winds (Keeley and Fotheringham 2003). At the other extreme would have been montane coniferous forests subjected to frequent lightning ignitions, which would have burned on much shorter intervals, controlled largely by the rate of fuel accumulation (Minnich 1988).

By the middle Holocene, a great diversity of Indian groups had settled in the region, and fire was one management practice they all held in common. Numerous uses for burning have been reported, but the one that likely had the greatest impact was burning shrublands for type conversion to herb-dominated associations (Timbrook et al. 1984, Keeley 2002a). The clearest statement of this management practice is a 1792 report by Spanish explorer Jose Longinos Martinez who wrote, "in all of New California from Fronteras northward the gentiles have the custom of burning the brush" (Simpson 1938). It has been said that Native American presence was widespread and touched every part of this region (Anderson et al. 1998). This view would be supported by the fact that the archeological record in San Diego County alone has over 11,000 Indian sites documented, and they are distributed within all 32 USGS 7.5-min quadrangles (Christenson 1990). Two thirds of the settlements were in the coastal valleys and foothills in what currently is chaparral or sage scrub vegetation.

The sudden emergence of charcoal deposits and replacement of woody elements by herbaceous taxa around 5,000 yr B.P. in coastal southern California (Davis 1992) is perhaps a reflection of Native American burning for type conversion. Burning is also a likely contributing factor to the demise of closed-coned cypress along the San Diego coast 1,800 yr B.P. (Anderson and Byrd 1998), because it is not tied to climatic patterns that might account for the extirpation of this species in the area. Cessation of Indian burning following settlement is thought to have been a major contributor to an apparent nineteenth century lowering of the elevational distribution of oak woodlands (Byrne et at. 1991).

Historic Period

Much of our historical information is from written records that often contain misinformation and exhibit various biases. Early reports on fire cause are suspect when it comes to evaluating lightning ignitions. For example, Sargent (1884) reported for 1881 that 340,000 acres burned in California forests, but none were attributed to lightning, whereas hunters, campers, and Indians were thought to be the primary sources of ignition. This report is highly suspect because today we know lightning accounts for a significant portion of all wildfires in the state. Undoubtedly, this source of ignition was not suspected because weather conditions during lightning storms are not conducive to rapid fire spread, and when distant lightning-ignited fires did become noticeable it was often days or weeks later when weather conditions had changed.

The first Spanish settlement in California was the Mission San Diego de Alcala, founded in 1769. In addition to initiating a relentless wave of settlers over the subsequent centuries, these first Europeans most dramatically changed the landscape with the introduction of a wide selection of grasses and forbs (Mack 1989). These non-natives spread rapidly, perhaps facilitated by the highly disturbed landscape resulting from a long history of frequent Indian burning (Keeley 2001, 2004c) and further promoted by the Mexican vaqueros habit of expanding grazing lands by burning off the brush (Kinney 1887).

American occupation and subsequent statehood brought increased competition for grazing land (Kinney 1900, Plummer 1911). In rural San Diego County, a typical late nineteenth-century land-use pattern involved homesteads of 65 ha centered in small grassy potreros or dry meadows that were generally too small to provide a sound economic basis for subsistence (Lee and Bonnicksen 1978). Chaparral dominated the slopes surrounding these potreros (e.g., Fig. 15.4), and stockmen routinely burned the shrublands to supplement meadow grazing with additional forage and to allow easier movement from one canyon to another.

In remote areas, sheep herders routinely used fire to enhance mountain-grazing lands, and miners used fire to open the brush and facilitate exploration. Post-settlement increases in sedimentation have been interpreted to be at least partially the result of this increased fire frequency (Cole and Wahl 2000). Surveys done in the three southern California forest reserves in the late nineteenth century provide some of the best quantitative data on pre–fire-suppression burning patterns. For the chaparral zone, which comprised 50% (San Bernardino) to 90% (San Gabriel) of the new reserve landscapes, USGS biologist J. B. Leiberg presented estimates of burning in annual reports filed in the late 1890s. Based on the area of chaparral in each reserve, and his estimate of how much chaparral had burned in the previous four to nine years, I calculate that he observed rates of burning, expressed as percentage of chaparral landscape burned per decade, of 2.8%, 3.3%, and 5.4% for the San Jacinto (Leiberg 1899a, 1900c), San Bernardino (Leiberg 1899b, 1900b), and San Gabriel (Leiberg 1899c, 1900a) Reserves, respectively. Even this limited extent of burning cannot be entirely ascribed to natural sources. For example, Leiberg (1899c) stated, "It is also noteworthy that the worst-burnt areas in the three reserves examined are to be found in the San Gabriel Reserve in the region of the most extensive mining operations." Although Leiberg's estimates likely did not capture all of the burning on these landscapes, they do indicate that natural fire rotation intervals in the lower-elevation chaparral zone were on the scale of once or twice a century or less, and certainly not on the scale of every few decades as was apparently the case in higher-elevation conifer forests.

These historical records suggest a pre-suppression model of burning in chaparral landscapes of many modest-sized summer lightning-ignited fires that burned a relatively small portion of the landscape, punctuated one to two times a century by massive autumn Santa Ana wind–driven fires (Keeley and Fotheringham 2001a). This model is supported by the historical record of infrequent large Santa Ana fires over the past 500 years (Mensing et al. 1999). It is also supported by life history characteristics of many dominant woody species that are resilient to long fire-free intervals and sensitive to short intervals on the scale of once a decade (Keeley 1986, Zedler 1995a).

Although remote regions were experiencing limited burning, rapidly developing rural areas reported some rather massive wildfires. In 1878, one of the largest fires in Los Angeles County history burned 24,000 ha, and in 1899, well over a quarter million hectares burned in a single fire centered in Orange County (Barrett 1935, Lee and Bonnicksen 1978). In San Diego County, it was reported in 1885 that "At least one third of the land covered with brush, grass and oak timber in the southern part of this county has been burnt off by settlers within the past eighteen months, doing a great deal of damage, not only as regards pasturage, timber, and bees, but also decreasing the reservoirs of water, which the absence of brush will effect...," and in 1889, a huge 37,000-ha fire burned coastal shrublands in the county (Barrett 1935).

It has been proposed that a view of the natural southern California fire regime can be gained by examination of burning patterns south of the U.S. border, where it is presumed humans have had less impact on the natural fire regime. These studies are discussed in the sidebar on fire regimes in southern California and northern Baja California (sidebar 15.1).

Current Period

The nineteenth-century pattern of large fires has continued through the twentieth century, and Moritz (1997) demonstrated that the probabilities for large fires in the central coastal region have not changed due to fire suppression. Recent decades have experienced an increasing frequency of smaller fires (Moritz 1997, Keeley et al. 1999). Throughout the century, there has been a growth in fire frequency that parallels human population growth (Keeley and Fotheringham 2003). Much of the population growth has been in coastal valleys and foothills, where natural fire frequencies were lowest. In the latter half of the twentieth century, fire rotation intervals shortened and average fire size decreased in all southern California counties (Conard and Weise 1998, Keeley et al. 1999, Weise et al. 2002). Human impacts on montane environments have been slower to develop, although air pollution has caused substantial changes in forest structure (McBride and Laven 1999).

Major Ecological Zones

Burning patterns in the lower-elevation coastal valley and foothill zone show that, despite vigorous fire-suppression efforts throughout the twentieth century, over half of the landscape has burned within the past several decades (Fig. 15.6A, B, C). This in fact is an underestimate of the extent of twentieth century burning because these data are for just national forest lands (Stephenson and Calcarone 1999), and much of the foothill landscape outside the forests have experienced higher rates of burning (Keeley 1982).

Widespread burning should not be interpreted to suggest that fire-suppression activities have had no impact. Considering the fact that humans account for more than 95% of all fires (Keeley 1982), it seems reasonable that the primary impact of suppression has been to maintain these landscapes closer to their natural fire regime than if fires were not suppressed (Keeley et al. 1999). Within this zone it appears that roughly 10% to 25% of the landscape has never had a recorded fire (Table 15.1). Based on estimates of burning made by Leiberg, and discussed in the historical section, it would appear that this proportion of unburned landscape is not likely to be far outside the natural range of variability for the region.

Burning patterns for the montane zone (Fig. 15.6D, E, F) suggest that vigorous fire-suppression efforts throughout the twentieth century have had a substantial impact in excluding fires from this landscape (Stephenson and Calcarone 1999). Roughly 50% to 75% of these forests have never had a recorded fire (Table 15.1), which is likely outside the natural range of variability for these conifer forests. Effective fire exclusion in this zone contrasts markedly with the foothill zone where suppression has not been effective at excluding fire (Fig. 15.6A, B, C).

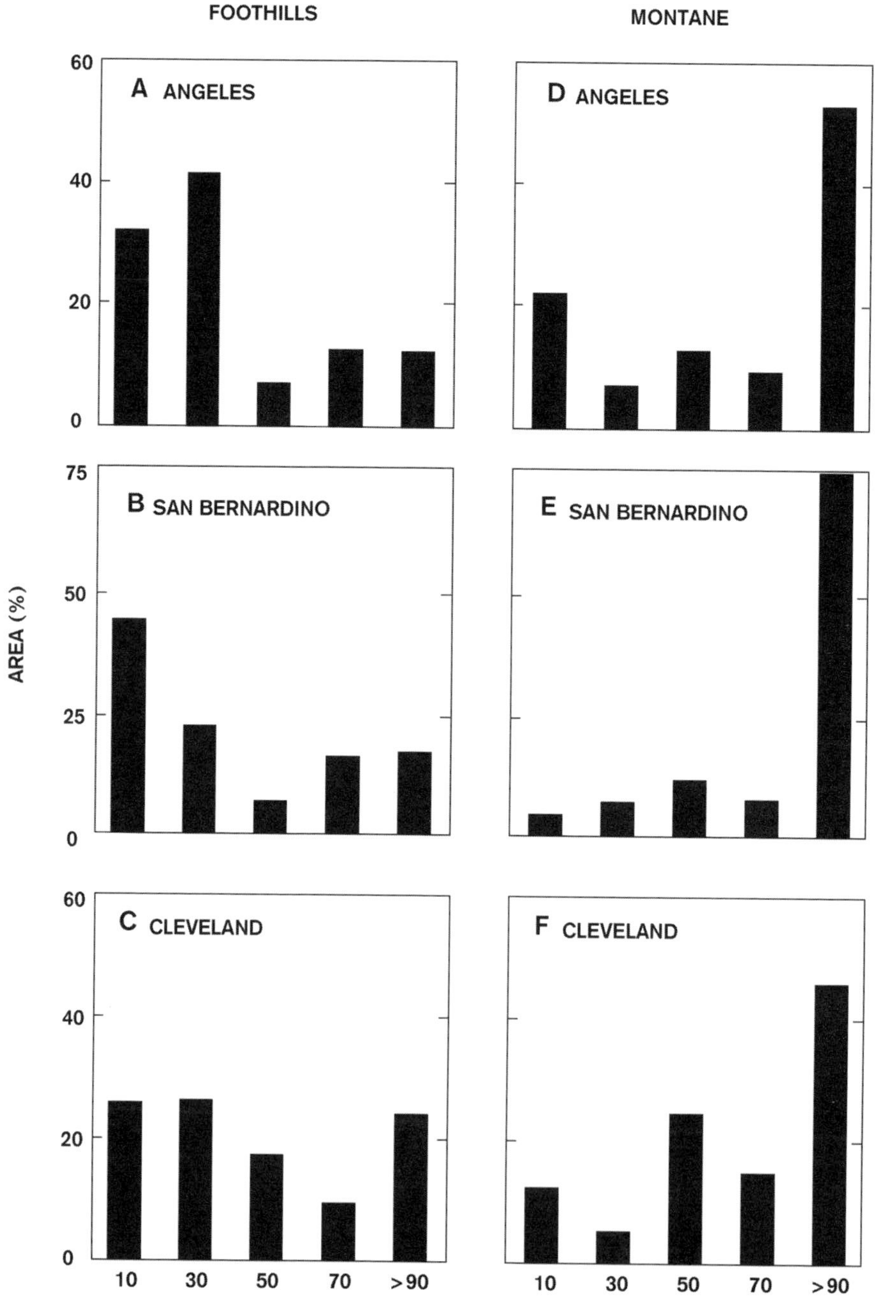

FIGURE 15.6. Time since last fire for foothill (A, B, C) and montane (D, E, F) environments in the Angeles, San Bernardino, and Cleveland USFS national forests. The Angeles includes most of the San Gabriel Mountains and surrounding foothills, the San Bernardino includes the San Bernardino and San Jacinto mountains and the Cleveland includes largely the Santa Ana and Laguna mountains. (Data from Stephenson and Calcarone 1999.)

Grasslands

A substantial proportion of native bunchgrass rootstocks survive grassland fires and resprout as moisture becomes available in autumn (Table 15.2). These grasses flower and disperse seeds in the first post-fire spring, and seedling recruitment is commonly very abundant in the second and the next few post-fire years (Keeley 1990b), although recruitment may only be successful in years of high precipitation (Hamilton et al. 1999). These patterns are the same for a rich diversity of native herbaceous perennial forbs as well, including species of *Calochortus, Dichelostemma, Sanicula,* and *Lomatium* among others. Although annual species (both native and non-

native) lack much long-term seed storage, annual recruitment and seed production ensure a ready seed bank at the time of fire, and low-intensity fires generated by herbaceous fuels enhance seed survival.

Grasslands are resilient to a wide range of fire frequencies. Although annual fires are not part of the natural fire regime, they present little threat to either herbaceous perennial or annual species. This is because both life history types are adapted to persisting through the dry season with dormant rhizomes, bulbs, or seeds. Surviving fire apparently presents no greater challenge than the long summer drought. In the absence of fire for extended periods of time, natural grassland patches persist because of the greater competitive ability of

Dodge (1975) postulated that burning patterns were likely to be different between chaparral and coniferous forests on the two sides of the U.S. border because, unlike the United States, south of the border fire suppression was not practiced outside of towns and there was a common practice of setting fire to the brush as soon as sufficient dead material had accumulated to carry a fire. He found that the most significant difference between the vegetation of these two regions was the near total absence of grass and other herbaceous plants by the end of summer due to intense grazing by cows and horses. With the lack of fire suppression, frequent burning of the shrublands, and over-grazing in Baja California, he suggested land use patterns were at the same stage as was the case north of the border in the late nineteenth century.

Minnich (1983) used Landsat remote imagery to compare patterns of burning in sage scrub and chaparral shrublands between 1972 and 1980 on both sides of the border. He concluded that during this nine-year period, fires were larger north of the border. However, fire size was not compared statistically, and critics have suggested there is no difference evident in these data (Strauss et al. 1989, Keeley and Fotheringham 2001a). The primary motivation for concluding fires were larger north of the border was based on the inclusion of two fires reported in written historical records north of the border (Minnich 1983). Because written records were not available south of the border, it has been argued that this is a biased comparison (Keeley and Fotheringham 2001a). To compensate for the lack of written records south of the border, Minnich (1989, 1995, 1998; Minnich and Dezzani 1991; Minnich and Chou 1997) estimated fire size for an 80-year period south of the border using historical aerial photographs, and concluded that during this period, large fires were absent from the northern Baja California landscape. The conclusion from these studies is that the smaller fires south of the border are reflective of the natural southern California fire regime and larger fires north of the border are a modern artifact of fire suppression and illustrate the need for doing landscape-scale prescription burning in southern California.

This conclusion has been criticized because historical records show that prior to fire suppression in southern California, large fires were always part of this landscape (Barrett 1935), and through the twentieth century there has been no increase in frequency of large fires (Keeley et al. 1999, Mensing et al. 1999, Weise et al. 2002). Additionally, it has been proposed that the present fire regime in Baja California is not likely representative of the natural regime, and that it is largely the result of contemporary land use practices (Keeley and Fotheringham 2001a, 2001b). These latter authors contended that the patterns observed north and south of the border should not be the basis for southern California fire management policy.

More recent studies have focused on north-south comparisons of mixed conifer forest structure in the San Bernardino and San Jacinto Mountains in southern California with the San Pedro Martir Mountains of Baja California (Savage 1997; Minnich et al. 2000, 2001; Stephens and Gill 2005). These studies have attributed differences in forest structure to differences in fire suppression policy. Although the general conclusions are consistent with accepted dogma, there are reasons to question whether the more open forests, with minimal in-growth of white fir, reported for Baja California are primarily a result of different fire management practices.

Climate could play a bigger role than fire management practices. For example, north of the border yellow pine forests on the more arid end of the precipitation gradient commonly exhibit characteristics of Baja forests—for example, lack of white fir in-growth (Laven 1978, Dolph et al. 1995). Because the San Pedro Martir Mountain Range is approximately 3° latitude further south, there is little justification for ruling out climatic factors as explanations for differences in forest structure. There are clear north-south gradients in distribution of both winter (Keeley and Fotheringham 2001a, 2001b) and summer storms (Douglas et al. 1983). Indeed, the precipitation reported for 2,000 m in the San Pedro Martir (Minnich 1987b, Minnich et al. 2000) is comparable to what would be received at 500 to 1,000 m lower elevation north of the U.S.-Mexican border (NOAA Climatogical Summary).

Climatic differences are also suggested by differences in fire seasons north and south of the border (Stephens et al. 2003), and by patterns of tree distribution (Minnich 1987b). For example, ponderosa pine and big-cone Douglas-fir reach their southernmost distribution more than 200 km north of the Baja mountain range San Pedro Martir, and this is very likely climatically controlled (Thorne 1977, Stephenson 1990). Even trees that co-occur in both regions exhibit different patterns of distribution. Minnich (1987b) lists several examples, but the point is well illustrated by incense cedar. This conifer is widespread in forests of southern California (Thorne 1977, Minnich et al. 1995), yet in the San Pedro Martir it is concentrated along stream courses.

Also limiting the usefulness of these regions for understanding fire management north of the border is the fact that Jeffrey pine and mixed conifer forests of Baja California have experienced twentieth century reductions in the mean fire return interval over what was observed in pre-settlement times (Stephens et a. 2003). Some of this may be the result of a fire suppression policy that has been in effect for several decades in the national parks of Baja California. However, fire exclusion is not solely dependent on fire suppression activities, but rather may result from consumption of herbaceous fuels by livestock grazing (Savage and Swetnam 1990)—and Baja California forests have had a long history of livestock grazing (Henderson 1964, Stephens et al. 2003).

Until we have a clearer understanding of the extent to which climate and grazing determine forest structure in the mountain ranges south of the border, it would be prudent to rely on more direct measures of fire suppression impacts on forests of southern California for directing fire management.

TABLE 15.1

Fire frequency in foothills (below 900 m) and montane (above 1500 m)
portions of the three southern California USFS national forests

	Percentage of Area Burned							
	Foothills				Montane			
	NUMBER OF RECORDED FIRES				NUMBER OF RECORDED FIRES			
	0	1	2	≥3	0	1	2	≥3
Angeles	11	34	33	22	52	31	14	3
San Bernardino	16	38	25	21	73	22	4	1
Cleveland	24	37	24	16	45	47	8	0

NOTE: From Stephenson and Calcarone 1999.

TABLE 15.2

Fire-response types for important species in grasslands in the South Coast bioregion

	Type of Fire Response			
Lifeform	Sprouting	Seeding	Individual	Species
Herbaceous perennial	Yes, as a normal phenological response, not fire stimulated	No, dormant seed bank; seeds are produced by first year resprouts and generate seedlings in subsequent post-fire years	Aboveground portions of plants usually dead at time of fire	Mariposa lilies (Calochortus spp.), blue dicks (Dichelostemma capitatum), Lomatium (Lomatium spp.), needlegrass (Nassella spp.), sanicle (Sanicula spp.)
Herbaceous perennial	None	Yes, largely from current year seed bank	Plants dead at time of fire	Oats (Avena spp.), bromegrasses (Bromus spp.)

TABLE 15.3

Natural fire regime characteristics for grasslands
in the South Coast bioregion

Temporal	
Seasonality	Summer–fall
Fire-return interval	Moderate–long
Spatial	
Size	Moderate–large
Complexity	Low
Magnitude	
Intensity	Low
Severity	Low
Fire type	Crown

grasses over shrubs on fine-grained soils. These substrates retain moisture in the upper-soil profiles and reduce percolation to deeper soil layers, which is lethal for shrub taproots that depend on it for surviving summer drought. Annual grassland persistence in the absence of fire is more complicated and a function of plant community interactions as discussed below.

FIRE REGIME–PLANT COMMUNITY INTERACTIONS

Historically, fire-return intervals were likely heavily influenced by proximity to Native American settlements (Keeley 2002a), being frequent in those areas, but on remote sites, where lightning was the primary ignition source, more on the order of one to several times a century (Table 15.3). Today, grassland fires are almost entirely ignited by humans, and fire frequency is very high, particularly at the interface of urban areas. Historically, it is to be expected that most fires burned in summer and fall, but wherever human ignitions have been or are a factor, the fire season is extended to include late spring and early winter, and year round during droughts.

Anthropogenic burning beginning with Native Americans and continued by Euro-American settlers has greatly expanded grassland distribution at the expense of sage scrub, chaparral, and woodland (Wells 1962; Keeley 1990b, 2002a; Hamilton 1997). Initially these "grasslands" were likely dominated by native forbs, as the state lacks aggressive colonizing native annual grasses. It is to be expected that where these type conversions occurred adjacent to native grasslands that bunchgrasses such as purple (*Nassella pulchra*) and nodding needlegrass (*Nassella cernua*) would have invaded, although the long and extreme summer drought in this region might have made persistence on well-drained course substrates precarious. One native bunchgrass, foothill needlegrass (*Nassella lepida*), which is a common component of coastal sage scrub (Keeley and Keeley 1984), likely persisted in these disturbance-maintained grasslands. However, prior to European entry into California, these "grasslands" probably were dominated by annual forbs, many of which were important food resources for Native Americans (Timbrook et al. 1982, Keeley 2002a).

During the first half of the nineteenth century, California grasslands, both bunchgrass-dominated and annual forb-dominated grasslands, were rapidly and thoroughly invaded by non-native grasses and forbs brought by the European colonizers (Mack 1989). Overgrazing and drought during the mid- to late nineteenth century are commonly given as causal factors behind our present non-native–dominated grasslands. However, some species, such as wild oats (*Avena fatua*) and black mustard (*Brassica nigra*), appear to have dominated rapidly in the absence of overgrazing (Heady 1977). The primary factors driving the rapid non-native invasion of grasslands over much of the landscape were: (1) Holocene climate warming, which favored annuals over perennials; (2) long co-evolution of European annuals with human disturbance, which selected for aggressive colonizing ability; and (3) the disequilibrium in native ecosystems created by high frequency of burning by Native Americans (Keeley 2002a), which favored rapid invasion.

Annual grasslands thrive on frequent fires due to copious seed production and high seed survival under low-intensity fires. These non-native–dominated grasslands originated from disturbance and are not restricted by substrate, being found on soils that support most other vegetation types (Wells 1962). In the absence of fire or other disturbances, their persistence is a function of recolonization ability of woody associations (Wells 1962; DeSimone and Zedler 1999, 2001). Chaparral species colonize open grassland sites poorly, because species most tolerant of open xeric sites have weak dispersal and species with high dispersal establish poorly on open sites (Keeley 1998b). In the absence of disturbance, sage scrub species recolonize much more readily than chap-

arral (McBride 1974, Freudenberger et al. 1987, Callaway and Davis 1993).

Sage Scrub

In coastal communities the most common subshrubs are obligate resprouters after fire (Table 15.4), including California brittlebush (*Encelia californica*), saw-toothed goldenbush (*Hazardia squarrosa*), and coastal buckwheat (*Eriogonum cinereum*); although in the long absence of fire these species are capable of continued basal sprouting and canopy regeneration (Malanson and Westman 1985). Many subshrubs are facultative seeders and regenerate after fire from resprouts and dormant seed banks, although on many sites resprouting is the dominant means for recapturing post-fire sites (Malanson and O'Leary 1982). The most common facultative seeders include bush monkeyflower (*Mimulus* spp), California sagebrush (*Artemisia californica*), purple sage (*Salvia leucophylla*), and black sage (*Salvia mellifera*). Seeds produced by the first-year resprouts are largely non-dormant and produce a massive flush of seedlings in the second post-fire year (Keeley and Keeley 1984, Keeley et al. 2006b). Several of these species are known to produce polymorphic seed banks with a portion of the seeds having deep dormancy broken by smoke or other combustion products (Keeley and Fotheringham 2000). Deerweed (*Lotus scoparius*) is the only obligate-seeding woody species typical of coastal sage scrub, and it exhibits massive seedling recruitment in the first post-fire year from dormant seed banks. In this, and all other legumes, chemical cues such as smoke play no role in stimulating germination; rather, heat shock triggers germination in the first post-fire year. As a consequence, germination may be triggered in the absence of fire on open substrates due to solar heating of the soil. For example, deerweed continues to recruit at low levels in subsequent years, particularly following high rainfall (Keeley et al. 2005b). This species is not long lived, perhaps a decade or two, and occasionally is subject to mass die off as was observed on many 5-year post-fire sites in spring following the extremely wet El Niño winter of 1997–1998 (J. Keeley personal observations).

Two larger-stature evergreen shrubs, laurel sumac (*Malosma laurina*) and lemonadeberry (*Rhus integrifolia*), are widely dispersed throughout coastal sage scrub. They are both vigorous resprouters but have very different seedling recruitment dynamics. The former species often has substantial seedling recruitment following fire (Keeley et al. 2006b), whereas the latter species typically recruits under fire-free conditions (Lloret and Zedler 1991).

Much of the post-fire woody flora in southern California is rather promiscuously distributed in both chaparral and coastal sage scrub (Keeley et al. 2005b). Some species such as deerweed, golden yarrow (*Eriophyllum confertiflorum*), California buckwheat (*Eriogonum fasciculatum*), chaparral mallow (*Malacothamnus fasciculatus*), laurel sumac, and black sage are equally common in both vegetation types. Coastal sage communities also have a very rich annual and herbaceous perennial flora, many of which are ephemeral post-fire

TABLE 15.4
Fire-response types for important species in sage scrub in the South Coast bioregion

		Type of Fire Response		
Lifeform	Sprouting	Seeding	Individual	*Species*
Shrub	Fire stimulated	Fire stimulated	Top-killed	Laurel sumac *(Malosma laurina)*
Shrub	Fire stimulated	None	Top-killed	Lemonadeberry *(Rhus integrifolia)*
Subshrub	Fire stimulated	Polymorphic seed bank, a portion is dormant and fire stimulated	Top-killed or killed	California sagebrush *(Artemisia californica)*, coastal buckwheat, *(Eriogonum cinereum)*, California buckwheat, *(Eriogonum fasciculatum)*, bush monkeyflower *(Mimulus aurantiacus)*, purple sage *(Salvia leucophylla)*, black sage *(Salvia mellifera)*
Subshrub	Fire stimulated	No, dormant seed bank; seeds are produced by first year; resprouts generate seedlings in subsequent post-fire years	Top-killed	California brittlebush *(Encelia californica)*, saw-toothed goldenbush *(Hazardia squarrosa)*
Suffrutescent	None	Fire stimulated	Killed or present only as dormant seeds	Deerweed *(Lotus scoparius)*

followers. The floristic overlap between chaparral and sage scrub in both the annual and the herbaceous floras is even more pronounced than with woody species; thus, they are discussed in the chaparral section. On the more mesic slopes, rhizomatous grasses, including giant wildrye *(Leymus condensatus)* and species of bent grass *(Agrostis spp.)*, often dominate, particularly under high fire frequencies.

INTERIOR SAGE SCRUB

This more arid interior version of sage scrub lacks some of the most vigorous resprouting species, and the facultative seeders on these sites tend to behave more like obligate seeders, as fire-caused mortality often can be 100% on interior sites. Resprouting success appears to be more closely tied to plant age than to fire severity. In a study of several thousand burned shrubs it was found that for both California buckwheat and California sagebrush, mortality was not related to height of the burned skeleton, suggesting fire severity was not a factor determining resprouting (Keeley 1998a, Keeley in press). Rather, stem diameter (an indicator of plant age) was the primary determinant of resprouting success: as stems increased in diameter their probability of resprouting declined, a phenomenon shared by the northern California coastal scrub dominant coyote brush

(Hobbs and Mooney 1985). Less resprouting in older plants appears to derive from the loss of functional adventitious buds due to wood production, and may be the result of the evolution of secondary wood in taxa derived from herbaceous perennial ancestors (Keeley in press). Other interior shrubs regenerating heavily from seed are black sage, white sage *(Salvia apiana)*, deerweed, and chaparral mallow, and all except brittlebush are shared with coastal sage scrub associations. Most of these species have light wind-dispersed seed, so if populations are extirpated from a site they readily disperse in from nearby source populations (Wells 1962; DeSimone and Zedler 1999, 2001).

Interior sage scrub communities have a similar ephemeral post-fire flora of annual and herbaceous perennial species that overlap greatly with coastal sage scrub and chaparral associations (Keeley et al. 2005a, b).

FIRE REGIME–PLANT COMMUNITY INTERACTIONS

Historically, fires burned primarily summer to winter but today the bulk of this landscape burns in the fall (Table 15.5). As with grasslands, human ignitions have increased both the frequency of fires (Wells et al. 2004) and length of the fire season, and during severe droughts, fires can burn year round. Size of fires is extremely variable and can be very large,

TABLE 15.5
Natural fire regime characteristics for sage scrub in the South Coast bioregion

Temporal
  Seasonality   Late summer–fall
  Fire-return interval   Moderate–long

Spatial
  Size   Moderate–large
  Complexity   Low

Magnitude
  Intensity   Moderate
  Severity   Low–high
  Fire type   Passive-active crown

on the order of thousands of hectares, but modal fire size has decreased (Keeley et al. 1999), due to increased human ignitions coupled with increasingly effective fire suppression, as well as habitat fragmentation.

Natural lightning-ignited fires are rare in the low-elevation coastal sites; however, under autumn Santa Ana wind conditions fires would have readily burned in from adjoining chaparral and woodlands. Contemporary burning patterns in the western end of the Transverse Ranges result in much of this vegetation burning at roughly five-year intervals, and nearly all of this type burns before 20 years of age (McBride and Jacobs 1980, Keeley and Fotheringham 2003). It is unlikely that natural lightning-ignited fires ever burned at such a short fire-return interval. Although this vegetation is reasonably resilient to high fire frequencies, the current levels are near the lower threshold of tolerance, and many such sites are experiencing accelerated non-native invasion (Keeley 2001, 2004c).

Vogl (1977) hypothesized that sage scrub was an artifact of fire suppression and livestock grazing, and that its current distribution was greatly expanded due to human disturbance. This model would appear to be based on the well-known mesquite invasion of Texas grasslands, which has been clearly linked to overgrazing (Archer 1994). However, coastal sage species share little in common with mesquite, and empirical studies demonstrate sage scrub species colonize grassland sites when grazing pressure is relieved (Hobbs 1983, Freudenberger et al. 1987, Callaway and Davis 1993, McBride 1974). These patterns are more consistent with the model that sage scrub loses ground to annual grassland under frequent disturbance, although it is capable of recolonizing when disturbance frequency declines. Sage scrub also expands into chaparral sites when fire frequencies exceed the disturbance tolerance of chaparral (Cooper 1922, Wells 1962, Freudenberger et al. 1987, Callaway and Davis 1993).

Increased burning in the interior valleys, as illustrated for Riverside County (Fig. 15.3) is certainly a major stress for these shrubs, most of which must regenerate from seed. Historical studies show that there has been a substantial type conversion of sage scrub to non-native grasslands during the twentieth century (Minnich and Dezzani 1998). It has been hypothesized that in addition to increased fire frequency, nitrogen deposition in this region of high air pollution has contributed to this shift from sage scrub to non-native grasslands (Allen et al. 2000). It is unclear to what extent this affects post-fire invasion, because soil nitrate levels normally increase by an order of magnitude in the first spring after fire (Christensen 1973). Consistent with the role of air pollution driving the invasion process is the much greater presence of non-natives during the first five post-fire years in interior sage scrub than in coastal sage scrub (Keeley et al. 2005c). However, there is also a very strong negative relationship between shrub cover and non-native presence in both the coastal and the interior sage scrub associations. Certainly a contributing factor to the greater inviability of interior sage scrub is the much slower shrub canopy recovery rate resulting from more limited resprouting and greater reliance on seedling recruitment (Fig. 15.7).

Chaparral

The primary differences in chaparral fire response are best understood by comparing responses on arid, usually south-facing slopes and ridges, with mesic, north-facing exposures. As a general rule, species that recruit seedlings after fire (Table 15.6) tend to occupy the more xeric sites, that is, low elevations and south-facing exposures (Keeley 1986, Meentemeyer and Moody 2002). Resprouting species that do not recruit after fire—for example, obligate resprouters—are usually on the more mesic slopes (Keeley 1998b). These are extremes of a gradient, and each comprises a collection of floristically different associations, not readily distinguished from one another by fire ecology or fire regime. Distribution of arid and mesic chaparral types is commonly determined by slope aspect; thus, landscapes usually comprise a mixture of different fuels and post-fire ecologies. This fine-grained distribution of different associations results in a great deal of diversity of fire behaviors and post-fire responses arising out of large fires that cover extensive portions of the landscape.

ARID SITES

Chamise is the nearly ubiquitous dominant on most arid chaparral sites. With respect to fire response, this needle-leaved shrub is a facultative seeder and often exhibits massive seedling recruitment in the first post-fire year from a dormant seed bank (Keeley 2000). There is substantial site-to-site variation in the ratio of seedlings to resprouts; on some sites regenerating almost entirely from seedling recruitment and other sites from resprouts (Keeley et al. 2005b). Fire intensity, season of burn, and level of precipitation in the first post-fire winter appear to be the primary factors determining these patterns (Moreno and Oechel 1994, Keeley and Fotheringham

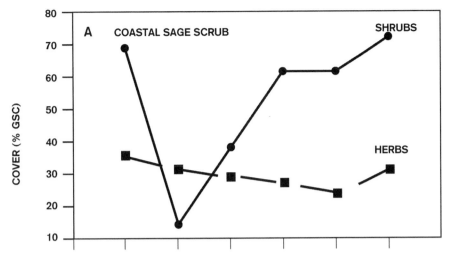

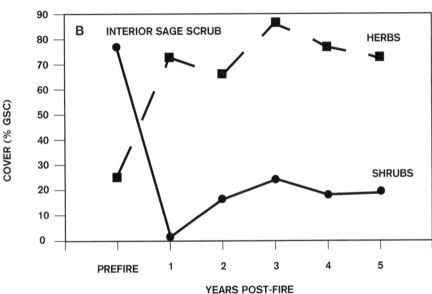

FIGURE 15.7. Foliar cover before and after fire at coastal (A) and interior (B) sage scrub sites. (Redrawn from O'Leary and Westman 1988.)

2003, Keeley et al. 2005b). Other facultative seeders include Eastwood's manzanita *(Arctostaphylos glandulosa),* chaparral whitethorn *(Ceanothus leucodermis),* yerba santa *(Eriodictyon* spp.*),* and flannelbush *(Fremontodendron californicum),* although these latter broad-leaved species often occupy less-arid sites.

Also at the arid end of the gradient are species that lack any ability to resprout vegetatively after fire, and their persistence is entirely a function of successful seedling recruitment from a dormant seed bank. These shrubs are termed *obligate-seeding* (Wells 1969) species, or *obligate seeders* (Keeley 1977). Chaparral, along with three of the other mediterranean-climate shrublands, is unique among woody shrublands of the world in having a large proportion of species that lack the ability to resprout following fire or other disturbance (Keeley 1986). These obligate-seeding species of manzanita and California-lilac *(Ceanothus* spp.*)* recruit heavily in the first post-fire year from dormant seed banks, and recruitment is typically nil until the next fire on the site (Keeley et al. 2005b). The bulk of the seed bank is dispersed

locally (Zedler 1995b) and with deep dormancy; thus, these species disperse more in time than in space. They are very sensitive to repeat fires and may be extirpated from a site if fires occur too frequently (Keeley 2000). Some coastal species appear to require more than 40 years without fire to establish seed banks sufficient to maintain populations (Odion and Tyler 2002).

Demography of obligate seeders is quite variable. Bush poppy *(Dendromecon rigida)* is a short-lived shrub that has massive recruitment in the first post-fire year (Bullock 1989). Shrubs die within a decade after fire and seed banks remain dormant until the next fire. On many sites, it is known that this dormant seed bank remained viable and produced a dense vigorous population after more than 125 years in the soil (Keeley et al. 2003, Keeley et al. 2005d).

Obligate-seeding California-lilac varies markedly in longevity (Zedler 1995b). Some species (e.g., woolyleaf ceanothus *[Ceanothus tomentosus]*) appear to be relatively short lived, on the order of three to five decades, whereas

TABLE 15.6
Fire-response types for important species in chaparral in the South Coast bioregion

Lifeform	Type of Fire Response			Species
	Sprouting	Seeding	Individual	
Tree	None	Serotinous cones	Killed	Tecate cypress (Cupressus forbesii), Cuyamaca cypress (Cupressus arizonica), knobcone pine (Pinus attenuata)
Tree	None	Variable, low level serotiny; often dependent on parent tree survival	Killed or survive	Coulter pine (Pinus coulteri), Torrey pine (Pinus torreyana)
Subshrub or suffrutescent	None	Fire stimulated	Largely present only as dormant seed banks	California buckwheat (Eriogonum fasciculatum), deerweed (Lotus scoparius), black sage (Salvia mellifera)
Shrub	None	Fire stimulated	Killed	Woolyleaf ceanothus (Ceanothus tomentosus), desert ceanothus (Ceanothus greggii), bigberry manzanita (Arctostaphylos glauca)
Shrub	Fire stimulated	Fire stimulated	Top-killed or killed	Chamise (Adenostoma fasciculatum), Eastwood's manzanita (Arctostaphylos glandulosa), chaparral whitethorn (Ceanothus leucodermis), greenbark ceanothus (Ceanothus spinosus), yerba santa (Eriodictyon spp.), flannelbush (Fremontodendrun californicum)
Shrub	Fire stimulated	None	Top-killed or killed	Birch-leaf mountain-mahogany (Cercocarpus betuloides), silk tassel bush (Garrya spp.), chaparral holly (Heteromeles arbutifolia), chaparral cherry (Prunus ilicifolia), scrub oak (Quercus berberidifolia), California coffeeberry (Rhamnus californica), spiny redberry (Rhamnus crocea)
Herbaceous perennials	Fire stimulated in some, in others sprouting is normal phenological stage	None	Aboveground portions of plants dead at time of fire	Sacapellote (Acourtia microcephala), mariposa lily (Calochortus spp.), soap plant (Chlorogalum pomeridianum), larkspur (Delphinium spp.), blue dicks (Dichelostemma capitatum), Lomatium (Lomatium spp.), Cucamonga man-root (Marah macrocarpus), smallflower melicgrass (Melica imperfecta), death camas (Zigadenus spp.)

TABLE 15.6 (continued)

| | Type of Fire Response | | | |
Lifeform	Sprouting	Seeding	Individual	Species
Annuals	None	None	Present only as a dormant seed bank	Snapdragon *(Antirrhinum* spp.)*, red maids *(Calandrinia breweri, C.)*, common pussypaws *(Calyptridium monandrum)*, sun cup *(Camissonia* spp.)* white pincushion *(Chaenactis artemisiifolia)*, cryptantha *(Cryptantha* spp.)*, spotted hideseed *(Eucrypta chrysanthemifolia)*, whispering bells *(Emmenanthe penduliflora)*, gilia *(Gilia* spp.)*, lotus *(Lotus* spp.)*, lupine *(Lupinus* spp.)*, San Luis blazingstar *(Mentzelia micrantha)*, fire poppy *(Papaver californicum)*, phacelia *(Phacelia* spp.)*, manynerve catchfly *(Silene multinervia)*, chia *(Salvia columbariae)*

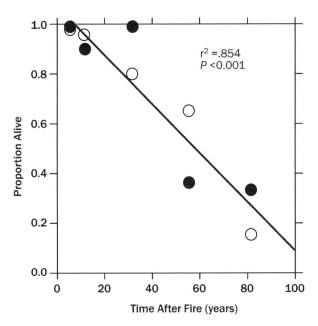

FIGURE 15.8. Mortality patterns of the obligate-seeding desert ceanothus *(Caeanothus greggii)* in different-aged chaparral stands in eastern San Diego County (from Zedler 1995). Closed circles are for north-facing exposures, and open circles are for south-facing exposures.

others persist far longer (e.g., desert ceanothus *[Ceanothus greggii]*) (Fig. 15.8). Mortality appears to be driven by competition and increases on more mesic slopes (Keeley 1992a). As stands age, there is a shifting balance in the competitive

relationships resulting in a successional replacement of obligate seeders by species more competitive under long fire-free conditions. Even where populations experience complete mortality, they are highly resilient to long fire-free periods as soil-stored seed banks survive hundreds of years (Zavitokovski and Newton 1968, Franklin et al. 2001, Keeley et al. 2005b). Obligate-seeding manzanita generally have smaller seed banks, take longer to establish seed banks, recruit fewer seedlings, exhibit greater early seedling survivorship and perhaps greater longevity than California-lilac (Keeley 1977, Odion and Tyler 2002). All post-fire–seeding species exhibit structural and physiological characteristics selected to tolerate the severe conditions on open sites during the long summer-autumn drought (Davis et al. 1998, Keeley 1998b).

This community comprises a rich diversity of herbaceous species, the bulk of which form an ephemeral post-fire successional flora. Most of this flora is composed of annuals that arise from dormant seed banks, and are endemic to burned sites, and do not persist more than one or two years (Keeley et al. 2005a, b). Herbaceous perennials are almost all obligate resprouters, arising from dormant bulbs, corms, or rhizomes (Keeley 2000), although a few are short lived and are present in post-fire environments only as seedlings. Post-fire resprouts flower and disperse non-dormant seeds that readily recruit in the subsequent post-fire years. Once the canopy closes, these species may remain entirely dormant for many years (Epling and Lewis 1952) or continue to produce foliage but not flower (Tyler and Borchert 2002).

Dormant seed banks are triggered to germinate by either heat shock or chemicals from smoke or charred wood (Keeley and Fotheringham 2000). In general, species are stimulated by one or the other of these cues; however, there are a few species where both appear to play a role—for example, the nearly ubiquitous chamise is equally stimulated by either smoke or heat (Keeley, Bolton, and McGinnis unpublished data). There is a very strong phylogenetic component to germination response, with certain families responding only to heat and others only to chemicals. For example, all California-lilac species are stimulated by heat, and smoke plays no role in their germination. This pattern is typical for other fire-stimulated buckthorns, for example, *Phylica* spp. in South African fynbos (Keeley and Bond 1997). Other common families in chaparral and sage scrub with heat-stimulated germination include the legumes (Fabaceae), morning-glories (Convolvulaceae), mallows (Malvaceae), and bladdernuts (Sterculeaceae). However, the majority of species with seedling recruitment in the post-fire flora of both chaparral and sage scrub are not stimulated by heat, but rather by smoke or other chemicals produced during combustion (Keeley and Fotheringham 2000). This behavior is common in woody and herbaceous species in the sunflower (Asteraceae), borage (Boraginaceae), mustard (Brassicaceae), pink (Caryophyllaceae), waterleaf (Hydrophyllaceae), mint (Lamiaceae), evening primrose (Onagraceae), poppy (Papaveraceae), phlox (Polemoniaceae), figwort (Scrophulariaceae), and nightshade (Solanaceae) families (Keeley 1991, Keeley and Fotheringham 2000).

One factor that plays an important role in determining post-fire patterns is fire intensity. Davis et al. (1989) demonstrated that microscale patterns in post-fire regeneration resulted from spatial variation in seed banks and apparent fire intensities. Fire-intensity impacts are complex because seedling recruitment of some species is greatly inhibited by high fire intensity, whereas for others it is enhanced (Keeley et al. 2005a, b).

MESIC SITES

Broadleaved evergreen shrubs dominate these sites and include scrub oak, California coffeeberry, spiny redberry, silk tassel bush, chaparral cherry, and Christmas berry. Throughout much of the region the dominant oak is scrub oak, but in the interior ranges interior live oak dominates (Scott and Sawyer 1994). The proportion of shrubs that are killed and fail to resprout is generally very low in most of these species, and they seldom recruit seedlings except in the long absence of fire (Keeley 1992a,b). These obligate-resprouting species avoid the stressful summer drought by deep roots that gain access to water in deep rock and soil layers; however, this option is unavailable to seedlings and thus recruitment success is dependent on establishment in favorable mesic microsites (Keeley 1998b). All of these shrubs have animal-dispersed fruits and successful establishment is dependent on finding safe sites with shade and highly organic soils, usually in the understory of chaparral or woodlands. Seedlings that recruit in the understory often remain suppressed for decades; however,

they do resprout after fire, and it may be that fires are required for successful emergence into the canopy (Keeley 1992a).

There are a number of facultative seeders such as greenbark ceanothus, chaparral whitethorn, and Eastwood's manzanita that often form mixed chaparral on either arid or mesic sites and their response to fire is similar to chamise, often recruiting seedlings and resprouting. Another species that seems to have a wide range of tolerances, occurring on both xeric and mesic sites, is birch-leaf mountain-mahogany, a post-fire obligate resprouter. However, unlike other obligate resprouters, it does not recruit in the understory of mature chaparral; rather, it appears to be dependent on openings created by other types of disturbance (Keeley 1992a).

Mesic sites contribute to higher fuel moisture conditions that may reduce fire intensity and fire severity; however, these mesic sites lead to higher primary production and under severe fire weather they may experience much higher fire intensity (Keeley and Fotheringham 2003). When these productive sites burn in low-intensity fires, much of the larger woody fuels are not consumed, thus putting the community on a trajectory for potentially more intense fires during the next fire.

FIRE REGIME–PLANT COMMUNITY INTERACTIONS

With rare exceptions, chaparral always burns as active crown fires. Fire-return intervals are on the order of one to several times a century, and are heavily influenced by human ignitions (Table 15.7). Complexity is commonly low to moderate, and is a function of topography, vegetation mosaic, antecedent climate, and weather. Fire intensity is generally high, but variable depending on fuels and weather.

Today, fire frequency is highest in the summer, but the bulk of the landscape burns in the fall (Keeley and Fotheringham 2003). Historically, fire frequency also would have peaked in the summer due to the timing of lightning ignitions. These summer fires spread slowly and often reached sizes of only 100 to 1,000 ha after months of burning (Minnich 1987). Fire size would have increased markedly when lightning-ignited fires persisted until the autumn Santa Ana wind season, where, within a day, these fires would have expanded to 100,000 ha and, with typical Santa Ana wind episodes lasting several days to a week, may have generated fires on the order of a million ha (Keeley et al. 2004). Today, modal fire size has greatly decreased due to habitat fragmentation and high human ignitions coupled with effective fire suppression; however, the bulk of the landscape still burns in large fires (Strauss et al. 1989) at rotation intervals of 30 to 40 years (Keeley et al. 1999). One exception to this rule is the chaparral on the Channel Islands (see Sidebar 15.2).

An alternative opinion has been expressed that large fires are a modern artifact of twentieth-century fire-suppression policy (Philpot 1974; Minnich 1995, 1998; Chou and Minnich 1997). These authors contend that fire exclusion has resulted in an unnatural fuel build-up on the southern California landscape, which is directly responsible for increasing

TABLE 15.7

Natural fire regime characteristics for chaparral in the
South Coast bioregion

Temporal	
Seasonality	Summer–fall
Fire-return interval	Moderate–long
Spatial	
Size	Moderate–large
Complexity	Low
Magnitude	
Intensity	High
Severity	Low–high
Fire type	Active crown

fire size. The hypothesis that fire suppression has excluded fire has been tested and shown to be unsupported (Moritz 1997, Conard and Weise 1998, Keeley et al. 1999, Weise et al. 2002). Indeed, during the twentieth century much of this landscape received a higher frequency of burning (30–40-year rotation intervals) than would be expected under natural conditions (Keeley and Fotheringham 2003). The role of fuel age in controlling fires is further developed in the chaparral fuels and fire sidebar (Sidebar 15.3).

Extensive chaparral dieback has the potential to cause a rapid change in fire hazard (Riggan et al. 1994). It commonly hits large patches of a single species, typically species of ceanothus in the subgenus Cerastes. This was once thought to be driven by fungal pathogens, but experimental studies demonstrate conclusively that it is a result of drought (Davis et al. 2002). These are obligate-seeding shrubs whose shallow root systems subject these plants to excessive water stress during extended droughts.

Non-native annuals frequently invade post-fire chaparral sites and may persist for several years until shrub canopies return (Keeley et al. 2005c). Invasion is largely a function of proximity of post-fire seed sources, and this is largely determined by pre-fire stand age. Mature chaparral stands generate sufficient fuels to produce fire intensities that kill seed banks of non-native grasses. However, when fires occur too frequently, shrub canopies fail to close and a substantial non-native grass flora persists (Zedler et al. 1983). These surface fuels increase the chances of another fire, and because the fuels are a mixture of shrubs and grasses, they generate lower fire intensities (Odion and Davis 2000) and greater non-native seed bank survival (Keeley 2001, 2004c).

Closed-Cone Cypress

Fire regime characteristics match that of chaparral (Table 15.7). Both Tecate *(Cupressus forbesii)* and Cuyamaca cypress *(Cupressus arizonica)* have characteristics shared by closed-cone pines—specifically, high stand density, lack of self-pruning and thin bark, and relatively long fire-return intervals—characteristics typical of stand-replacing crown fire regimes (Keeley and Zedler 1998). These obligate-seeding trees disperse seeds shortly after fire from aerial seed banks and recruit heavily in the first post-fire spring (Table 15.6). They form monotypic even-aged stands that may require many decades of fire-free conditions in order to develop a seed bank sufficient to withstand a repeat fire (Zedler 1977). Studies of seed production show that populations younger than 30 years of age are extremely vulnerable to extinction, and seed production continues up to a century and perhaps beyond (Zedler 1995b). Canopy fuels typically produce extremely high fire intensities and sterilize the soil seed bank of competing plants. Cypress seeds are protected by cones, and following dispersal beneath the parent skeleton, seedlings are released from competition compared with microsites just outside the canopy shadow (Ne'eman et al. 1999).

Historical fire-return intervals were undoubtedly very long, perhaps once a century. Contemporary fire frequencies are much higher (Zedler 1995a), and when stands are hit with high fire frequencies they may be extirpated, though recolonization from metapopulations that survive in ravines or other fire-free refugia are likely an important means of long-term persistence (Zedler 1980). Fire frequencies greater than once or twice a century appear to be the primary threat to the persistence of these cypress populations (Zedler 1977, Reveal 1978)

Low-Elevation Pines

These pines are typically distributed in patches within a mosaic of chaparral, and thus their fire regime characteristics match that of chaparral (Table 15.7). Knobcone pine *(Pinus attenuata)* is similar to the closed-cone cypress species in its deeply serotinous cones that initiate dense monotypic stands following crown fires (Keeley and Zedler 1998, Stuart and Stephens this volume).

Coulter pine *(Pinus coulteri)* spans a range of habitats from chaparral to forests. Fire regimes vary from stand-replacing to stand-thinning fire regimes, largely dependent on associated vegetation (Dodge 1975, Minnich 1977). When associated with chaparral, cones are serotinous and recruitment is synchronized to the immediate post-fire environment, whereas on forested sites cones are not serotinous and recruitment may occur between fires (Table 15.6), and consequently stands are uneven aged (Vale 1979, Borchert 1985, Borchert et al. 2002). Torrey pine is associated with chaparral and thus naturally exposed to stand-replacing fires. Although most recruitment is tied to fire, stands comprise different age cohorts that recruit after different fire events (Wells and Getis 1999).

Both of these latter two pines share characteristics that are tied to the stand-replacing fire regime characteristic of chaparral shrublands. They typically do not self-prune lower branches, something that enhances their flammability and increases the probability of them as well as their neighbors

Eight islands ranging in size from approximately 3 to 250 km^2 lie within 100 km of the South Coast bioregion mainland (Schoenherr et al. 1999). The highest peak is 750 m and is on Santa Cruz Island. During Pleistocene glacial episodes (last one ending about 12,000 years ago), the size of islands and distance from the coast varied. At this time the four northernmost islands were connected as one island, but were still separated from the mainland by more than 4 km of ocean. Some of the earliest Native American populations were established on these islands and at the time of contact with Europeans there were sizable settlements on the larger islands (Jones 1992). Over the past 200 years, livestock, primarily goats and sheep, have expanded populations to the point of denuding vegetation from large portions of most of the islands (Schoenherr et al. 1999).

The ecosystems on these islands are broadly similar to and share a substantial number of plant species with those on the mainland. Plant communities include grassland, coastal sage scrub, chaparral, and oak woodland. The presence of fire-dependent shrubs chamise and species of ceanothus and manzanita (Minnich 1980b), fire-following annuals whispering bells and spotted hideseed (Carroll et al. 1993), and closed-cone pines (Linhart et al. 1967) are evidence that fires have historically been a predictable feature of this landscape. However, since settlement by Euro-Americans in the nineteenth century, fires have been relatively rare. During the period 1830 to 1986, only 73 fires were recorded in written records, 65% less than 10 ha and only 7% greater than 1,000 ha (Carroll et al. 1993). These numbers provide crude estimates of fire rotation intervals on the order of hundreds of years. Also, during this period only three lightning-ignited fires were recorded; however, this is likely below the historical range of variability because of greatly reduced fuels due to intense grazing pressure during the period of record.

Prior to the exploitation of these islands with over-grazing, there is evidence that communities such as chaparral and coastal sage scrub formed more contiguous vegetation capable of carrying fire (Minnich 1982). The presence of Native American settlements for the last 10,000 years, coupled with their use of fire as a land management tool (Keeley 2002a), makes it seem likely that fires were a regular feature of some of these islands. Prior to Indian occupation, lightning was an occasional source of ignition and it need not have been frequent to maintain fire-type species on the islands. The high frequency of winds on the islands (Yoho et al. 1999) would have contributed to the drying of fine fuels, as well as ensuring fire spread. Fire spread would also have been enhanced during Pleistocene glacial episodes when some of the islands were connected.

In chaparral, the limited fire activity over the historical period since Euro-American settlement appears to have reduced the extent of fire-dependent shrubs such as chamise and species of ceanothus and manzanita, and favored species capable of regenerating in fire-free periods such as species of cherry, Christmas berry, oak, coffeeberry and redberry, and lauril sumac (Minnich 1980b, Landis 2000). Although some of the fire-dependent species still retain fire-stimulated germination, some produce a smaller proportion of dormant seeds than mainland taxa (Carroll et al. 1993). In the absence of fire, closed-cone pines exhibit a low level of seed release and seedling recruitment and an uneven age structure (Linhart et al. 1967, Walter and Taha 1999).

Several lines of evidence cast doubt on the strict control of fires by fuel age in these crown fire regimes. For example, large fires (>5,000 ha) in the westernmost portion of the Transverse Range are fueled primarily by shrublands that are less than 20 years of age (Keeley et al. 1999). In addition, across all of Los Angeles County there is no statistically significant change in probability of burning after approximately 20 to 25 years (Schoenberg et al. 2003). A thorough analysis of the role of fuel age by Moritz et al. (2004) included ten chaparral landscapes from Baja California to Monterey, a span of 500 km, with each data set representing tens of thousands of hectares and hundreds of fires over an 85-year period (in most cases). For nine of the ten landscapes they observed a near constant probability of burning with age. Hazard functions calculated with the Weibull function indicated that the rate of fire hazard did not change over time, ranging from 2%–4% in year 20 and 4%–7% in year 60. Collectively, these data refute the hypothesis that large fires are determined by a build-up of dead fuels. Indeed, several lines of evidence suggest the primary determinant of fire size is the coincidence of ignitions and Santa Ana winds (Davis and Michaelsen 1995; Conard and Weise 1998; Keeley and Fotheringham 2001a, 2001b; Moritz 2003).

This does not mean that fuel age has no effect on chaparral fires. In general it appears that fuel age is primarily a controlling factor under moderate weather conditions, and relatively unimportant under severe weather conditions accompanying Santa Ana winds (Keeley et al. 2004). However, Zedler and Seiger (2000) contend that it is unlikely that fuel age alone has ever maintained a landscape pattern of small fires. Their modeling studies demonstrate that it would take only a single large Santa Ana fire to set the landscape to the same age class, and thus, if subsequent fires were controlled by fuel age, the landscape would be forever doomed to burn in large fires.

not surviving fires (Keeley and Zedler 1998, Schwilk and Ackerly 1999, Schwilk and Kerr 2002, Schwilk 2003). Chaparral populations of Coulter pine are strongly serotinous (Borchert 1985), but Torrey pine (Pinus torreyana) is not, although some seeds persist in the cones for years after seed maturity (McMaster and Zedler 1981). This delayed seed dispersal is thought by McMaster and Zedler (1981) to result from selection in an environment where large crown fires occur at long and unpredictable intervals, often longer than one generation. Such relaxed serotiny is also found in other closed-cone pines when distributed in coastal environments where natural lightning-ignited fires are rare (e.g., Millar 1986). These coastal pines also have a very subtle form of serotiny in that seeds dispersed in the year of maturity typically disperse months later than most pine species, thus dispersing seeds in winter, following the autumn fire season (Keeley and Zedler 1998).

Both of these pines have large seeds and exhibit far less capacity for wind dispersal than montane pines such as ponderosa pine (Johnson et al. 2002). Localized dispersal in these chaparral-associated pines has likely been selected for because large stand-replacing fires generate suitable habitat close to the now-dead parent tree. In contrast, low-severity surface fire or mixed-severity fire regimes typical of ponderosa pine forests present fewer safe sites for recruitment, thus selection for the ability to disperse into gaps produced by the patchiness of mixed-severity fires (see yellow pine forest section).

Big-Cone Douglas-Fir

Big-cone Douglas-fir (Pseudotsuga macrocarpa) is one of only three conifers in California capable of resprouting after fire (Pacific yew [Taxus brevifolia] and coast redwood [Sequoia sempervirens] also resprout), but unlike the other two, big-cone Douglas-fir typically does not resprout from the base, rather from epicormic buds present throughout the length of the bole and branches (Fig. 15.9). Trees less than 10 cm dbh fail to resprout (Bolton and Vogl 1966); however, Minnich (1980a) reported that sprouting success appeared to be dependent primarily on fire severity rather than on tree size (Table 15.8).

FIGURE 15.9. Big-cone Douglas-fir *(Pseudotsuga macrocarpa)* tree in the early stages of resprouting from epicormic buds following wildfire in the San Gabriel Mountains. (Photo by J. Keeley.)

Minnich (1974) hypothesized that resprouting ability was not an adaptation to fire; rather, it evolved in response to mechanical damage from strong winds and excess snow. This seems improbable since most other Northern Hemisphere conifers are exposed to wind and snow, yet very few resprout. Also, big-cone Douglas-fir has one of the highest wood densities of any conifer (McDonald 1990), which should reduce mechanical damage relative to many other conifers. In this regard, pines provides a useful study in that in this large genus, the few species that resprout exist in stand-replacing fire regimes conducive to vegetative regeneration (Keeley and Zedler 1998), as is the case with big-cone Douglas-fir.

Seedling recruitment occurs sporadically during fire-free periods often under chaparral or oak woodland (Bolton and Vogl 1969, McDonald and Litterell 1976). Seedlings and saplings are very sensitive to burning, and thus successful establishment requires extended fire-free periods of at least two decades (Minnich 1980a). Unless recruitment occurs in a very sheltered environment, a further hiatus in burning for many more decades is apparently required for successful establishment of mature trees (Bolton and Vogl 1969). Seedling recruitment is uncommon on south-facing exposures, and it seems likely that the more mesic conditions on north-facing slopes, coupled with longer fire-free intervals

TABLE 15.8

Fire-response types for important species in big-cone Douglas-fir forests in the South Coast bioregion

	Type of Fire Response			
Lifeform	Sprouting	Seeding	Individual	Species
Tree	Fire stimulated, only epicormic	None	Top-killed or survive	Big-cone Douglas-fir (Pseudotsuga macrocarpa)
Tree	Fire stimulated basal or epicormic	None	Top-killed or survive	Canyon live oak (Quercus chrysolepis)

due to higher fuel moisture, are factors contributing to greater seedling recruitment on those slopes.

Aspects of this species' life history seem anomalous. Adult trees survive and resprout after fires only if fires are of low to moderate intensity. The habitat of this tree includes chaparral and oak woodlands, and low-intensity fires in these fuels are most likely if they occur frequently. However, seedling and sapling recruitment is eliminated under frequent fires of any intensity, and successful emergence into a canopy-level tree may require 50 to 100 years of fire-free conditions. In short, frequent fires favor adult persistence and infrequent fires favor population expansion.

FIRE REGIME–PLANT COMMUNITY INTERACTIONS

Fire regimes in big-cone Douglas-fir forests vary spatially and temporally (Table 15.9). Historically, higher-elevation groves associated with conifer forests likely experienced fires on decadal time scales, but lower elevations more on the scale of once or twice a century. Fires can burn as surface fires, but burn mostly as crown fires; thus complexity is high, being heavily influenced by topography and associated vegetation.

Big-cone Douglas-fir forests are typically restricted to ravines and steep slopes, comprising groves of a few trees to thousands of trees. There is the widespread belief that this species has become more restricted with Euro-American and Mexican settlement due to increased fire frequency or more severe fires due to ignition during severe fire weather (Leiberg 1900b, Horton 1960, Gause 1966). Groves that occur amidst chaparral are particularly vulnerable to high-severity fire that results in substantial mortality, whereas forests in more sheltered ravines and steep slopes are often immune to destruction (Minnich 1988). In the San Bernardino Mountains between 1938 and 1975, Minnich (1980a) reported 25% mortality of this species and that survivorship increased with increasing slope inclination, from 37% on slopes less than 20° to greater than 90% on slopes exceeding 40°. In a study of big-cone Douglas-fir mortality on two different aspects following a lightning-ignited wildfire in the San Gabriel Mountains (Keeley et al. unpublished data), it was found that pop-

TABLE 15.9

Natural fire regime characteristics for big-cone Douglas-fir in the South Coast bioregion

Temporal	
Seasonality	Late summer–fall
Fire-return interval	Moderate–long
Spatial	
Size	Small–moderate
Complexity	High
Magnitude	
Intensity	Mix of low and high
Severity	Low–high
Fire type	Surface, active or passive crown

ulations on relatively level terrain suffered 100% mortality, whereas a population on a steep north-facing slope had substantial survivorship, but only of large trees (Fig. 15.10A, B).

Bolton and Vogl (1969) observed that big-cone Douglas-fir could invade chaparral on gentler slopes only in the absence of fire, usually during a series of wet years following a severe fire that had destroyed the existing vegetation. These invasions were most often terminated with fire, unless the trees had grown large enough in the fire-free period to become fire resistant. Dense chaparral on shallow slopes is generally free of big-cone Douglas-fir because of frequent high-severity fires (e.g., Fig. 15.10B).

Minnich (1988) suggested that infrequent high-severity fires in these forests are an artifact of fire suppression, and under natural conditions, low-intensity fires would burn at frequent intervals under more moderate summer weather conditions. As a consequence, fire intensity would be less and tree mortality would be limited. While this model would ensure survival of existing big-cone Douglas-fir, frequent fires greatly restrict population expansion since recruitment of seedlings and saplings is dependent on long fire-free periods.

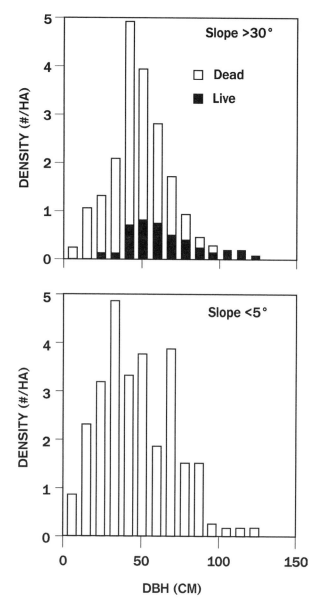

FIGURE 15.10. Live and dead big-cone Douglas-fir trees 13 years after a wildfire in the San Gabriel Mountains on sites of different incline. Approximate elevations were: site A, 1,700 m, and site B, 1,500 m. Sites burned in the Sage Fire of 1979 and were sampled in autumn of 1992. (Data from Keeley, Crandell, and Calderon, unpublished data.)

Long-term dynamics of this chaparral conifer are best explained by a metapopulation model involving fire-free refugia. This "fire refugia model" is based on the premise that frequent fires will be conducive to maintaining static adult populations, but a dynamic population capable of expansion would require extended fire-free conditions. During extreme fire events, such as illustrated in Figure 15.10B, populations would retreat to steep fire-resistant slopes that act as refugia (Fig. 15.10A). From these refugia, the species disperses back into more hazardous habitats during extended fire-free conditions. Subsequent fires on these sites will eliminate all of the younger trees and the extent to which mature trees survive will be dependent on fuels and severity of the fire weather. Thus,

understanding the dynamics of big-cone Douglas-fir requires an understanding of the long-term role of metapopulations and not the short-term effects of fires on individual populations. This model is based on a similar idea proposed by Zedler (1981) who highlighted the importance of refugia to the long-term persistence of closed-cone cypress, particularly in the face of increased anthropogenic fires. The general dynamic of population contraction and expansion under altering fire regimes possibly applies to other chaparral conifers such as Coulter pine and the more northerly gray pine.

Riparian Woodland and Shrublands

Response to fire is uniform, as nearly all are vigorous resprouters, either from rootcrowns or rhizomes (Davis et al. 1989). None of the riparian species are post-fire seeders, because all have transient seed banks; indeed, most have extraordinarily short-lived seeds measured on the order of days or weeks (Table 15.10). A number of factors account for the lack of selection for post-fire seedling recruitment: (1) the unpredictability of fire penetrating riparian woodlands, (2) the ready water source favors rapid and dense vegetative regrowth that results in intense competition for seedings, and (3) the severe surface scour resulting from annual winter flooding, which carries away any soil stored seed banks. Differences in species response to fire are largely unexplored, although these differences are to be expected based on species differences in distribution along disturbance gradients (Harris 1987, Bendix 1994).

FIRE REGIME–PLANT COMMUNITY INTERACTIONS

Riparian zones maintain communities that, relative to upland species, have higher fuel moistures during severe fire weather. As a consequence, they potentially pose an important barrier to fire spread, and thus play a role in determining landscape patterns of burning (Dwire and Kauffman 2003). The deciduous habit of dominant species, coupled with increased water availability during winter to summer, greatly limits the fire season, except during severe droughts (Table 15.11). Although most fires burn as crown fires with high intensity, fire severity is generally low due to the predominance of vigorous sprouting species.

Riparian areas are of particular ecological concern because of their disproportionate share of biodiversity and propensity to non-native invasion (Rundel and Sturmer 1998). A major threat to southern California riparian communities is the highly aggressive non-native grass known as giant reed (*Arundo donax*) or bamboo, which has displaced substantial portions of the native vegetation in southern California riparian ecosystems (Rieger and Kreager 1989). It has invaded thousands of hectares of riparian habitat, including all major drainages from Ventura to San Diego counties (Bell 1997). It is extremely flammable and can change green riparian corridors that are barriers to fire spread into highly combustible fire conduits. Giant reed is a very vigorous resprouter capable of dominating riparian sites far more quickly than the native species.

TABLE 15.10

Fire-response types for important species in riparian woodland-shrubland in the South Coast bioregion

| | Type of Fire Response | | | |
Lifeform	Sprouting	Seeding	Individual	Species
Tree	Fire stimulated	None	Top-killed or survive	White alder (Alnus rhombifolia), western sycamore (Platanus racemosa), Fremont cottonwood (Populus fremontii), willow (Salix spp.)
Shrub	Fire stimulated	None	Top-killed or survive	Mule fat (Baccharis salicifolia), black-berry (Rubus spp.), poison oak (Toxicodendron diversilobum)

TABLE 15.11

Natural fire regime characteristics for riparian woodland and shrublands in the South Coast bioregion

Temporal
    Seasonality   Fall
    Fire-return interval   Moderate–long

Spatial
    Size   Moderate
    Complexity   Low

Magnitude
    Intensity   Moderate–high
    Severity   Low
    Fire type   Active crown

Oak and Walnut Woodlands

The dominant oaks in this association have thick bark and are quite resistant to frequent fires. Based on bark thickness and mortality following fires (Table 15.12), it appears that Engelmann oak (Quercus engelmannii) is more fire resistant than coast live oak (Quercus agrifolia) (Lawson 1993). Where understory fuels have accumulated, fires may carry into the canopy, producing lethal crown fires, since these older trees seldom resprout from the base when top-killed. They have long juvenile periods and thus frequent fires may inhibit successful establishment (Plumb 1980, Lawson 1993). Seedlings and saplings often resprout from the base after fire, but if fires are frequent enough they remain suppressed for many decades. They apparently require an extended fire-free period to emerge to a size capable of withstanding fires, a pattern typical of recruitment in many savanna trees (e.g., Bond et al. 2001). For these southern California oaks, Lawson (1993) reported a negative relationship between fire frequency and density of both saplings and mature trees.

In walnut (Juglans californica) woodlands, all of the dominant species are vigorous basal resprouters after fire. There is no information on how burning during the growing versus dormant season affects resprouting of this winter-deciduous tree. Seedling recruitment is limited following fires, but in the long absence of fire, walnut seedling recruitment is abundant, and successful establishment generates an uneven age structure that appears to form a stable age distribution (Keeley 1990a). Also in the absence of fire, mesic-type chaparral shrubs persist as "gap-phase" species capable of seedling recruitment into openings in the walnut canopy, as well as gaps in other woodland associations (Campbell 1980).

FIRE REGIME–PLANT COMMUNITY INTERACTIONS

Fire regimes in oak and walnut woodlands are variable depending on moisture status, woodland density, and location in the landscape (Table 15.13). Fire-return intervals occur on the order of one to several times a century. On mesic sites, the higher fuel moisture, coupled with the closed canopy, which reduces drying of surface fuels, act in concert to reduce fire frequency. On these sites, fire complexity can be high with patches of crown fire and surface fire interspersed with unburned patches. At the xeric end of the gradient, more-open woodlands today support surface fuels of annual grasses, which increase fire frequency, but reduce fire intensity and complexity. The rapid growth rates of understory subshrubs and herbs make it likely that historically the primary limitation to fires was ignitions. Thus, it is to be expected that fire-return intervals varied along a gradient from the coast to the interior in conjunction with the distribution of summer lightning storms. Due to the mosaic distribution of woodlands, fires typically burn into them from adjacent shrublands.

With the mid-Holocene shift of Native American diets to emphasize acorns and other seeds (Erlandson and Glassow 1997), settlements centered around oak woodlands increased fire frequency, both to maintain herbaceous understories and reduce pathogens (Anderson 1993). Wells (1962) hypothesized

TABLE 15.12
Fire-response types for important species in oak and walnut woodlands in the South Coast bioregion

| | Type of Fire Response | | | |
Lifeform	Sprouting	Seeding	Individual	Species
Tree	Fire stimulated, basal when young, epicormic in mature trees	None	Top-killed or survive	Coast live oak *(Quercus agrifolia)*, Engelmann oak *(Quercus engelmannii)*
Tree	Fire stimulated	None	Top-killed	California black walnut *(Quercus kelloggii)*

TABLE 15.13
Natural fire regime characteristics for southern oak woodland in the South Coast bioregion

Temporal
  Seasonality   Summer–fall
  Fire-return interval Moderate–long

Spatial
  Size   Moderate–large
  Complexity   Low–high

Magnitude
  Intensity   Low–moderate
  Severity   Low–high
  Fire type   Surface–passive crown

that prior to extensive Native American burning, oak woodlands in coastal California supported subshrub understories, which would have contributed to a greater incidence of high-severity fire. He contended that throughout the region, Native American burning converted oak woodland sage scrub associations to oak savannas (Cooper 1922, Wells 1962), although remnants of this woodland sage scrub association are still evident in the central coast. Historical studies of oak woodlands indicate that twentieth-century fire regimes have had no discernable impact on woodland cover in San Diego County (Scheidlinger and Zedler 1980).

Black Oak Woodlands

At higher elevations, black oak *(Quercus kelloggii)* woodland often interfaces between the crown-fire chaparral ecosystem below and the surface-fire yellow pine forests above. Although little specific information is available, this community likely had a mixed fire regime such that surface fires burning downslope from pine forests were low-intensity surface fires and those burning upslope from chaparral were high-intensity crown fires. Considering the elevational distribution of lightning fires it seems likely that fires more

often burned in from higher-elevation conifer forests. Thick bark would have contributed to surviving surface fires, although these trees would succumb to high-intensity crown fires. Fire-free conditions in adjacent yellow pine forests are said to promote invasion by black oak (Laven 1978).

Yellow Pine Forests

The dominant pines are adapted to a mix of low-severity surface fires and high-intensity crown fires. Thick bark and self-pruning of dead branches ensure survival of the larger trees under low-intensity surface fires (Keeley and Zedler 1998), but a mix of high and low fire severity patches is requisite for reproduction (Table 15.14). Seedling recruitment requires gaps produced by localized high-severity fire, which exposes mineral soil by removing surface duff, and opens the canopy to sunlight. Critically important is the size of these gaps, because recruitment is dependent on survival of parent seed trees in adjacent patches of forest that are either unburned or burned by low-severity surface fire. The high-severity crown fires are also critical because by opening the canopy these microhabitats accumulate fuels at a slower rate and inhibit subsequent fires from burning in and destroying recruitment cohorts (Keeley and Stephenson 2000).

Understory species have received limited attention in these forests, although many of the patterns observed in Sierra Nevada forests following fires of different severities (Keeley et al. 2003) likely hold here as well. The dominant species are typically greenleaf manzanita *(Arctostaphylos patula)* and deer brush *(Ceanothus intergerrimus)* that often germinate *en masse* after fire from soil seed banks. Recruitment, however, is not restricted to burned sites, and these species often recruit into gaps caused by other disturbances. Herbaceous species are mostly perennials that resprout after fire, and it is to be expected that seedling recruitment would follow in subsequent years.

FIRE REGIME–PLANT COMMUNITY INTERACTIONS

Fire history studies in the San Bernardino Mountains show that the pre-settlement fire return intervals were slightly longer than for Sierra Nevada forests, with estimates of 10 to 14 years

TABLE 15.14

Fire-response types for important species in montane coniferous forests in the South Coast bioregion and includes yellow pine forests on drier sites and white fir–dominated mixed conifer forests on more mesic sites

Lifeform	Type of Fire Response			Species
	Sprouting	Seeding	Individual	
Tree	None	Recruitment from seeds dispersed by parent trees that survive fire, in first year or later	Survive or killed	White fir (Abies concolor), incense-cedar (Calocedrus decurrens), Jeffrey pine (Pinus jeffreyi), sugar pine (Pinus lanbertiana), ponderosa pine (Pinus ponderosa)
Shrub	None	Fire stimulated	Killed	Greenleaf manzanita (Arctostaphylos patula)
Shrub	Fire stimulated	Fire stimulated	Top-killed	Mountain whitethorn (Ceanothus cordulatus), deer brush (Ceanothus intergerrimus)
Shrub	Fire stimulated	None	Top-killed	Bush chinquapin (Chrysolepsis sempervirens), bitter cherry (Prunus emarginata), currant (Ribes spp.), snowberry (Symphoricarpos spp.)
Herbaceous perennial	Yes, as a normal phenological response, not fire stimulated	None	Top-killed	Rock cress (Arabis spp.), Indian paintbrush (Castilleja spp.), squirreltail (Elymus elymoides), imbricate phacelia (Phacelia imbricata), Lemmon's catchfly (Silene lemmonii), violet (Viola spp.)
Annual	None	A few fire stimulated, mostly transient seed banks that escape high-intensity fire	Killed or dead at time of fire	Groundsmoke (Gayophytum spp.), lotus (Lotus spp.), blazing star (Mentzelia spp.), monkeyflower (Mimulus spp.).

for ponderosa pine forests (Table 15.15) and longer intervals for the drier Jeffrey pine forests (McBride and Laven 1976, McBride and Jacobs 1980). Historically, fires were primarily from summer lightning storms and were predominately surface fires with patches of passive crown fire (Minnich 1974). Due to the short fire season and low-intensity surface fires, humans have been very effective at suppressing fires, and as a consequence the contemporary fire-return interval is much longer and far outside the historical range of variability (Table 15.1; Figure 15.6). As with other parts of the western United States, during the twentieth century much of this landscape has escaped fire entirely (Stephenson and Calcarone 1999).

Evidence of the impacts of management practices on forest structure in the eastern Transverse Ranges is presented by Minnich et al. (1995). They utilized VTM (Vegetation Type Map) plot data from 1932 as a baseline for measuring historical changes in these forests by comparing with contem-

porary samples. Their study showed increased in-growth of white fir and incense cedar into yellow pine forests over the 60 years of study, reflecting the impact of fire suppression. This generalization primarily applies to ponderosa forests as Jeffrey pine forests have had far less white fir in-growth under long fire-free periods (Laven 1978, Minnich et al. 1995). These ponderosa pine forests present a greater fire hazard for crown fires than would be expected under natural fire regimes, though it is worth noting that stand densities of 200 to 300 per hectare (Minnich et al. 1995) are substantially lower than those commonly observed in contemporary Sierra Nevada forests (Rundel et al. 1977).

Other historical changes in mixed conifer forest structure reported by Minnich et al. (1995) include 79% mortality of all ponderosa pine greater than 30 cm dbh during the 60 years between the 1930s VTM plots and their samples, attributed to ozone pollution. However, other studies have not reported

TABLE 15.15
Natural fire regime characteristics for the montane coniferous forests in the South Coast bioregion.

Temporal
Seasonality	Summer–fall
Fire-return interval	Short–moderate

Spatial
Size	Small–moderate
Complexity	Moderate–high

Magnitude
Intensity	Mix of low to high
Severity	Low–high
Fire type	Surface and passive crown, rarely active crown

twentieth-century mortality levels anywhere near these values (McBride and Laven 1999), and some of this estimated mortality may be tied to errors associated with use of VTM plots (Bouldin 1999, Keeley 2004b). However, this level of ponderosa pine mortality has been observed in the early years of the twenty-first century, and is attributed to severe drought and associated beetle damage (USDA Forest Service 2004).

Although the success of fire-suppression activities is certainly a factor in driving these structural changes, past logging practices have perhaps created a bigger problem. Data from Minnich et al. (1995) show that stand density was 51% higher on logged, as opposed to unlogged sites. This is important in light of the fact that over a 30-year period beginning in 1950, roughly 350 million board feet were removed from the rather limited conifer forests of the Transverse Ranges (McKelvey and Johnston 1992). In-growth from this cutting has greatly added to the contemporary fire hazard in these forests.

The high fire hazard in these forests has contributed to some significant crown fire damage. For example, crown fires with tree mortality of 90% or more in ponderosa and Jeffrey pine forests have been reported for several twentieth- and twenty-first-century fires in the Peninsular Ranges (Dodge 1975, Halsey 2004), and similar fires have occurred in the eastern Transverse Ranges (Minnich 1988). However, it is unclear how far outside the natural range of variation such fires are because historical records show large high-intensity fires did occur in these forests during the nineteenth century (Minnich 1978, p. 134). Also, evidence of former conifer forests now occupied by chaparral indicates high-intensity crown fires prior to the twentieth century (Minnich 1999).

Mixed Conifer Forests

These are white fir–dominated forests with incense-cedar (*Calocedrus decurrens*), sugar pine (*Pinus lambertiana*), and Jeffrey pine (*Pinus jeffreyi*) as co-dominants. They are more mesic than yellow pine forests and occur either at higher elevations

or lower on north-facing slopes. Productivity, and thus fuel loads, are typically higher and largely comprise needles and branches, with relatively little of the fuel load from herbaceous fuels as in the drier ponderosa type.

Both white fir and incense cedar can persist and recruit seedlings and saplings in the absence of fire. This characteristic allows them to expand into drier yellow pine forests when fires are excluded. Under a mixed fire regime, both white fir and incense cedar are also capable of taking advantage of fire-induced gaps and recruiting into them. These species have thick fire-resistant bark and are tolerant of surface fires, although less tolerant than associated yellow pines. Although both white fir and incense cedar can recruit after fire, unlike the yellow pines, recruitment is not fire dependent. Sugar pine is very long lived, capable of surviving low-intensity surface fires, and recruiting both after and between fires.

Associated shrubs that are typically restricted to permanent or temporary gaps in the forest canopy include bush chinquapin (*Chrysolepis sempervirens*), huckleberry oak (*Quercus vaccinifolia*), bitter cherry (*Prunus emarginata*), and mountain whitethorn (*Ceanothus cordulatus*). All of these are vigorous resprouters after fires or other disturbances, and the last species recruits seedlings after fire.

FIRE REGIME–PLANT COMMUNITY INTERACTIONS

Fire return intervals historically were frequent—10 to 30 years—but since the turn of the century fires have been excluded from much of the higher-elevation mixed conifer landscape (McBride and Laven 1976, Everett 2003). It has been suggested that north-facing slopes in these forests have historically had a higher fire frequency (Minnich et al. 1995). This is based on the higher productivity of these slopes and more rapid fuel production. However, that model assumes fuel load is the only determinant of fire return interval. Historical studies of fire return intervals in mixed conifer forests of the Sierra Nevada show that north-facing slopes have had longer fire return intervals, presumably because high fuel moisture levels inhibit ignition more often than on south-facing slopes (Tony Caprio, Sequoia National Park, unpublished data; Fites-Kaufman 1997). The importance of fuel moisture is suggested by the observation that in the eastern Transverse Ranges, severe fires consistently burn a greater percentage of the landscape on south-facing than on north-facing slopes (Minnich 1999).

Savage (1994) examined patterns of mortality in forest dieback in the San Jacinto Mountains and recorded that the bulk of the mortality occurred in the older age classes of ponderosa and Jeffrey pines, with relatively few trees older than 60 years surviving. Roughly half of the white fir older than 40 years died, whereas sugar pine and incense cedar suffered little or no mortality. Of particular interest to understanding fire-suppression impacts is the fact that stand density did not differ between high-mortality and low-mortality plots; thus, in-growth from fire suppression does not appear to have been a major contributing factor to dieback. Periodic severe drought followed by bark beetle attack seems to be the primary factors affecting pine survival. These mortality events may be a natural part of this system and would contribute sufficient fuels to produce high-intensity crown fires resulting in a burning mosaic of gaps, suggesting that mixed fire regimes of low and high severity are likely within the range of natural variation.

In summary, a fire suppression appears to have excluded natural fires over much of the mixed conifer landscape (Fig. 15.6D, E, F), it is not clear how much structural change in these forests can be specifically attributed to fire management policy. The natural fire regime included substantial surface fire burning, but the natural range of variation in high-severity crown fires, their frequency and size, are unknown.

Lodgepole Pine Forests

In this bioregion, lodgepole pine *(Pinus contorta* var. *murrayana)* forests are at the highest end of the elevational gradient for forests exposed to fire on any regular basis. Lodgepole pine has thin bark and is not highly tolerant of even moderately intense surface fires. Recruitment is not tied to fire and stands tend to be uneven aged (Keeley and Zedler 1998).

FIRE REGIME–PLANT COMMUNITY INTERACTIONS

These forests are characterized by a shorter growing season, lower fuel accumulation, more infrequent droughts, and lower lightning fire incidence than characterize lower-elevation forest types (Sheppard and Lassoie 1998). As is common in other high-elevation pines, lodgepole pine is quite long lived (more than 600 yrs, Fowells 1965). Periodic seedling recruitment is restricted to gaps created by wind-thrown trees or to meadows experiencing a drop in water table, or seedlings may initiate primary succession on granitic outcrops (Rundel 1975). Lodgepole pine forests are not replaced by more shade-tolerant species, perhaps due to the shallow granitic soils (Rundel et al. 1977). Where this species comes together with more stress-tolerant taxa (e.g., Jeffrey pine), forests appear to result from a lottery-type coexistence, which derives from infrequent, species-specific pulses of seedling recruitment in response to differing sets of environmental conditions.

These high-elevation forests receive a frequent bombardment of lightning strikes but ignitions are limited by fuels and fuel moisture. The porous soils in combination with the mediterranean-climate summer drought are not conducive to herbaceous growth sufficient to form a cover that will carry fire. Fuels are primarily short needles and woody litter, and in forests that have experienced a century of fire suppression, fuel loads are 15 to 19 Mg/ha (Hanawalt and Whittaker 1976, Sheppard and Lassoie 1998). Low productivity in these high-elevation forests and the lack of continuity of fuels are important limitations to fire spread. Fires in this type generally are low-severity surface fires that usually are rather localized and spread slowly, often being contained by lack of fuel continuity to areas on the scale of hectares or less. Minnich (1988) reviewed a number of historical accounts that reported crown fires on the scale of hundreds to thousands of hectares. It appears that on a frequency of perhaps once a century, the surface fire regime may be punctuated by larger high-intensity fires that cover thousands of hectares (Sheppard and Lassoie 1998). The impact of these high-intensity fire events on forest structure is apparently highly variable. Sheppard and Lassoie (1998) report that such fire events reduce the smaller size classes but have little impact on the larger trees.

Management Issues

Fire regimes vary markedly between the crown fire regimes of the foothill zone and the mixed surface and crown fire regimes of the montane zone, and fire suppression policy has played a very different role in each.

Montane environments have experienced an unnaturally low level of fires this past century, and there is reason to believe fire exclusion has resulted from both fire-suppression policy and the loss of herbaceous surface fuels due to livestock grazing (Minnich et al. 1995). Fire hazard is currently higher than was likely the case historically and is largely the result of increased surface fuels and increased in-growth of saplings (Everett 2003, USDA Forest Service 2004). Although higher fuel loads are often blamed on fire exclusion, an equally important factor is past logging practices that promoted recruitment of young trees induced by the removal of over-story canopy trees (Minnich 1980a, Everett 2003). Severe drought during the years 2002 to 2003 has resulted in substantial pine mortality in southern California forests, potentially exacerbating the fire hazard situation (USDA Forest Service 2004). The bulk of mortality occurred in ponderosa pine, which is at the southernmost limits of its distribution on the West Coast, and it is unclear how much of this is natural mortality to be expected at the limits of a species' range or is the result of increased competition for water due to increased forest density during the twentieth century (Keeley et al. 2004).

These forests require some form of fuel manipulation to reduce the fire hazard for human safety and diminish negative ecosystem impacts. Prescription burning is a viable option in parts of these ranges but not widely applicable in areas highly fragmented by private in-holdings. In addition, atmospheric circulation in most of these ranges is closely linked with foothills and valleys, and as a consequence, air quality constraints greatly limit the window of opportunity for prescription burning. Mechanical thinning is perhaps the only viable option in many of these forests; however, it is costly, particularly if the prescriptions focus just on removing those size cohorts most responsible for fire hazard. Thinning projects can pay for themselves, but usually only if larger trees are taken. This creates a dilemma because removing large trees promotes further in-growth and exacerbates the fire hazard problem, requiring future mechanical thinning at shorter intervals. It is unknown if this required reentry interval is long enough to allow sufficient growth to regenerate larger, commercially acceptable trees needed to fund these operations.

In the lower coastal valley and foothill zone, fire suppression has not reduced the natural fire frequency (Table 15.1). Currently there are many more fires than historically, but fire-suppression policy has kept many of these in check so that, although fire rotation intervals are shorter, most stands burn within the range of natural variability, albeit at the lower end of the range. However, landscapes surrounding urban areas fires have been of sufficient frequency to affect widespread type conversion to non-native grasslands (Keeley and Fotheringham 2003). During severe fire weather, a small percentage of fires escape containment and account for the bulk of the landscape that burns in this region (Minnich and Chou 1997, Moritz 1997). The limited number of lightning ignitions in this zone, coupled with historical accounts of relatively little area burned by these summer fires (Minnich 1987), suggests they were not responsible for most of the area burned. However, the infrequent occurrence of lightning-ignited fires persisting until the Santa Ana wind season (Fig. 15.1) would readily account for massive fires capable of burning huge fragments of the landscape in a matter of days (Keeley and Fotheringham 2003).

Maintaining this historical fire regime creates a major management dilemma because chaparral and sage scrub share this landscape with people in an ever-expanding urban sprawl. On these landscapes, fire is as much a social and political problem as it is a fire management problem (Rodrigue 1993). The primary driver of large fires that are often catastrophic to humans is the coincidence of fire ignitions and Santa Ana winds (Davis and Michaelsen 1995; Moritz 1997, 2003; Moritz et al. 2004; Conard and Weise 1998). Under these severe fire weather conditions, fuel age is ineffective as a barrier to fire spread, which limits the value of pre-fire fuel manipulations (Keeley and Fotheringham 2001b, 2003; Keeley et al. 2004).

The important management implication of these conclusions is that landscape scale prescription burning on a rotational basis is a questionable management strategy in this bioregion. The notion that a mosaic of age classes will act as a barrier to the spread of Santa Ana wind–driven fires is not supported (Dunn 1989, Keeley 2002b, Keeley and Fotheringham 2003). Illustrative of this are the massive wildfires that burned more than 300,000 ha in the last week of October 2003 (Halsey 2004). Within the perimeters of these large fires were substantial areas that had burned by either prescription burns or wildfires within the previous 10 years (Keeley et al. 2004). Fires either burned through or skipped over or around these younger age classes. The San Diego County Cedar fire, which was larger than any other fire recorded for the twentieth century in California, burned through extensive areas of young fuels that spanned nearly the entire width of the fire in two separate areas. On its southern boundary the Cedar fire burned through three-year-old chaparral (with fuel loads of 10 to 20 metric tons/ha; Keeley and Halsey, unpublished data) and then proceeded to skip over a six-lane freeway. North of this fire was the Piru fire that burned substantial areas of sage scrub that had previously burned in 1997. At the southern end of the bioregion,

the Otay fire burned through thousands of hectares of chaparral that previously had burned in 1996, and then continued to burn across the Mexican border until halted by the Tijuana River and a change in weather that brought rain.

This does not suggest that prescription burning has no place in the chaparral management arsenal, only that it needs to be used strategically with a clear understanding of its limitations. Even during severe fire weather, young fuels do reduce fire intensity and thus provide defensible space for fighting fires. This argues for the use of prescription burning and other fuel manipulations in strategic sites that could be utilized during extreme fire events. Fuel treatments in the backcountry, far removed from the urban interface, have limited value because of the extreme danger of frontal attacks on Santa Ana wind-driven fires when firefighters are completely surrounded by shrubland fuels. In addition, these fires move at such a rapid pace that by the time firefighting resources can be mobilized, the fires are already threatening homes and lives at the wildland-urban interface (Rohde 2002). As this interface zone expands and increases in complexity, an increasingly greater proportion of firefighter resources will be diverted to protecting homes, and fewer resources will be available for directly attacking these potentially catastrophic fires. These considerations argue for greater diversion of pre-fire fuel manipulations from the backcountry to the wildland-urban interface (Keeley et al. 2004).

Broader application of fuel manipulations may be warranted for managing fires that occur under mild weather conditions and are not wind-driven events. These so-called plume-dominated fires differ because the flame is nearly vertical and fuels ahead of the fire front are not preheated by hot gases (Morvan and Dupuy 2004). Under these conditions, age mosaics of young chaparral fuels can provide barriers to fire spread as suggested by anecdotal observations (Philpot 1974). Age mosaics also may control burning patterns south of the U.S.-Mexico border where wildfires are generally fanned by mild on-shore breezes, and are seldom under Santa Ana conditions (Minnich 1989, 1998; Minnich and Everett 2002). In southern California, fires that ignite under mild weather are seldom responsible for major property damage or loss of lives (Halsey 2004). Thus, the critical question about the widespread use of prescription burning to inhibit the spread of these fires is whether or not it is cost effective; further research on this question is needed. This is particularly important when considering the high cost of burning in crown fire ecosystems, which is often increased in southern California due to temporal restrictions imposed by air quality constraints (Conard and Weise 1998).

Costs of prescription burning also need to be evaluated in terms of impacts on resources. The lower-elevation chaparral and sage scrub in this region are already stressed with unnaturally high fire frequencies that threaten to replace much of this landscape with non-native annual plants (Keeley 2001, 2004c; USDA Forest Service 2004b). The primary concern with prescription burning is that it makes these stands vulnerable to type conversion by reburning due to the high frequency of anthropogenic fires. Other suggested benefits of prescription burning include the effects of mosaic age classes on reducing post-fire flooding and mudflows (Loomis et al. 2003); however, winter precipitation is a far greater factor, and high-frequency fires increase the chances of fire being followed by a winter of high rainfall (Keeley et al. 2004).

This analysis suggests that the appropriate currency for successful prescription burning is not "total acres burned," as is commonly employed, but rather strategic placement of fuel manipulation projects. For much of southern California, this represents a major paradigm shift from the widely accepted model of landscape scale rotational burning. Some agencies appear to be making this paradigm shift. For example, the recent fire management plan for the Santa Monica Mountains has proposed a major switch from the former rotational burning model to one that uses more limited and strategic application of fuel management practices (USDI National Park Service 2004). Similar ideas have been included as alternatives in southern California forest plans (USDA Forest Service 2004a).

It is important to recognize that there is much intra-regional variation in fire regimes, evident in different levels of fire hazard (Moritz 2003, Moritz et al. 2004) and different fire seasons (Keeley and Fotheringham 2003) throughout central and southern California chaparral. The lack of fire-suppression impacts on chaparral in this region is not necessarily shared throughout the state. For example, marked fire exclusion is documented for chaparral in the southern Sierra Nevada (Keeley et al. 2005d), which suggests a need for different approaches to fire management in different regions.

A problem that is likely to capture more and more attention in the future is the impact of fire management practices on invasive species problems. One illustration is the widespread use of black mustard (Brassica nigra) and shortpod mustard (Hirschfeldia incana) for post-fire rehabilitation projects in the 1940s and 1950s. These seed sources were abandoned long ago because of their aggressive invasive tendencies, particularly into economically important citrus orchards. However, we still see the ghost of past seedings because these species produce dormant seed banks that are fire stimulated; thus, after fire many shrublands are rapidly invaded from within. Most of the data to date do not support use of these or any other non-native species for post-fire management, both because they are not particularly effective and because they have serious negative ecosystem impacts (Conard et al. 1995).

Another area in serious need of consideration is the impact of fuel breaks on invasive species (Keeley 2004a). By removing the native shrub and tree cover these sites act as sources for non-native species to further spread into wildlands. The fact that fuel breaks typically form long corridors makes them ideal mechanisms for transporting non-native species into remote wildlands. When sites are burned, the non-native seed banks in shrubland vegetation are generally killed by the high fire intensities, but are not killed by lower fire intensities in the fuel breaks, and thus provide a ready seed source for invasion of burns. Co-locating fuelbreaks with roadways may be one way to minimize the non-native invasion of wildland areas.

What about planning for the future? Anticipated climate changes include an approximately 25% greater winter rainfall, coupled with a 1°C–3°C increase in temperature, and these have been used to predict higher primary productivity, higher fuel loads, and thus a worsening of the current fire hazard problems (Davis and Michaelsen 1995, Field et al. 1999). That scenario is not likely to be borne out in chaparral shrublands since contemporary fire problems are not closely linked to fuel level, and antecedent climate seems to have minimal impact on large fires (Keeley 2004a). These predicted climate changes, however, might increase the fire hazard in montane forests where fuel load does appear to be an important determinant of fire hazard. However, predictions are complicated, and the present modeling effort falls short of including all of the important ecosystem processes. For example, because the primary fuels in conifer forests are dead material on the surface, increased decomposition due to the expected higher temperatures and moisture could act to reduce fuels. On the other hand, the greater mineralization and release of nutrients could, through increased productivity, have the opposite impact. Regardless of how climate affects fuels, based on current patterns of burning it appears that throughout this region the primary threat to future fire regimes is more tied to future patterns of human demography than to climate.

References

Alexander, E. B. 1993. Gabbro and its soils. Fremontia 21:8–10.

Allen, E. B., S. A. Eliason, V. J. Marquez, G. P. Schultz, N. K. Storms, C. D. Stylinski, T. A. Zink, and M. F. Allen. 2000. What are the limits to restoration of coastal sage scrub in southern California? Pages 253–262 in J. E. Keeley, M. B. Keeley, and C. J. Fotheringham, editors. 2nd interface between ecology and land development in California. U.S. Geological Survey, Sacramento, CA.

Anderson, K. 1993. Native Californians as ancient and contemporary cultivators. Pages 151–174 in B.T.C. and K. Anderson, editors. Before the wilderness: environmental management by native Californians. Ballena Press, Menlo Park, CA.

Anderson, M. K., M. G. Barbour, and V. Whitworth. 1998. A world of balance and plenty. Pages 12–47 in R. A. Gutierrez and R. J. Orsi, editors. Contested Eden. California before the gold rush. University of California Press, Los Angeles.

Anderson, R. S., and B. F. Byrd. 1998. Late-Holocene vegetation changes from the Las Flores Creek coastal lowlands, San Diego County, California. Madroño 45:171–182.

Anderson, R. S., M. J. Power, S. J. Smith, K. Springer, and E. Scott. 2002. Paleoecology of a middle Wisconsin deposit from southern California. Quaternary Research 58:310–317.

Archer, S. 1994. Woodland plant encroachment into southwestern grasslands and savannas: rates, patterns and proximate causes. Pages 13–68 in M. Vavra, W. A. Laycock, and R. D. Pieper, editors. Ecological implications of livestock herbivory in the west. Society for Range Management, Denver, CO.

Armstrong, W. P. 1966. Ecological and taxonomic relationships of Cupressus in southern California. M.A. thesis. California State University, Los Angeles.

Axelrod, D. I. 1938. A Pliocene flora from the Mount Eden Beds, southern California. Pages 125–183 in Miocene and Pliocene floras of western North America. Carnegie Institution of Washington, Washington, DC.

Axelrod, D.I. 1939. A Miocene flora from the western border of the Mohave Desert. 516:125–183.

Axelrod, D.I. 1950a. Further studies of the Mount Eden flora, southern California. Pages 73–117 + plates in D.I. Axelrod, editor. Studies in late Teritiary paleobotany. Carnegie Institution of Washington, Washington, DC.

Axelrod, D.I. 1950b. The Anaverde flora of southern Califonria. Pages 119–157 + plates in D.I. Axelrod, editor. Studies in late Teritiary paleobotany. Carnegie Institution of Washington, Washington, DC.

Axelrod, D.I. 1950c. The Piru Gorce flora of southern California. Pages 159–213 + plates in D.I. Axelrod, editor. Studies in late Teritiary paleobotany. Carnegie Institution of Washington, Washington, DC.

Axelrod, D.I. 1978. The origin of coastal sage vegetation, Alta and Baja California. American Journal of Botany 65:1117–1131.

Axelrod, D.I., and F. Govean. 1996. An early Pleistocene closed-cone pine forest at Costa Mesa, Southern California. International Journal of Plant Science 157:323–329.

Barrett, L.A. 1935. A record of forest and field fires in California from the days of the early explorers to the creation of the forest reserves. USDA Forest Service, San Francisco.

Bell, G.P. 1997. Ecology and management of *Arundo donax*, and approaches to riparian habitat restoration in southern California. Pages 103–133 in J.H. Brock, M. Wade, P. Pysek, and D. Green, editors. Plant invasions: studies from North America and Europe. Backhuys Publishers, Leiden, The Netherlands.

Bendix, J. 1994. Among-site variation in riparian vegetation of the southern California transverse ranges. American Midland Naturalist 132:136–151.

Bolton, R.B., Jr. 1966. Ecological requirements of big-cone spruce (*Pseudotsuga macrocarpa*) in the Santa Ana Mountains. M.A. thesis. California State University, Los Angeles.

Bolton, R.B., and R.J. Vogl. 1969. Ecological requirements of *Pseudotsuga macrocarpa* (Vasey) Mayr. in the Santa Ana Mountains. Journal of Forestry 69:112–119.

Bond, W.J., K.-A. Smythe, and D.A. Balfour. 2001. *Acacia* species turnover in space and time in an African savanna. Journal of Biogeography 28:117–128.

Borchert, M. 1985. Serotiny and cone-habit variation in populations of *Pinus coulteri* (Pinaceae) in the southern Coast Ranges of California. Madroño 32:29–48.

Borchert, M., D. Schreiner, T. Knowd, and T. Plumb. 2002. Predicting postfire survival in Coulter Pine (*Pinus coulteri*) and Gray pine (*Pinus sabiniana*) after wildfire in Central California. Western Journal of Applied Forestry 17:134–138.

Bouldin, J.R. 1999. Twentieth-century changes in forests of the Sierra Nevada, California. Ph.D. dissertation. University of California, Davis, CA.

Bradbury, D.E. 1978. The evolution and persistence of a local sage/chamise community pattern in southern California. Yearbook of the Association of Pacific Coast Geographers 40:39–56.

Byrne, R., E. Edlund, and S. Mensing. 1991. Holocene changes in the distribution and abundance of oaks in California. Pages 182–188 in R.B. Standiford, editor. Proceedings of the symposium on oak woodlands and hardwood rangeland management. USDA Forest Service, Pacific Southwest Research Station.

Bullock, S.H. 1989. Life history and seed dispersal of the short-lived chaparral shrub *Dendromecon rigida* (Papaveraceae). American Journal of Botany 76:1506–1517.

Callaway, R.M., and F.W. Davis. 1993. Vegetation dynamics, fire, and the physical environment in coastal central California. Ecology 74:1567–1578.

Carroll, M.C., L.L. Laughrin, and A.C. Bromfield. 1993. Fire on the California Islands: does it play a role in chaparral and closed-cone pine forest habitats? Pages 73–88 in F.G. Hochberg, editor. Third California Islands Symposium: Recent Advances in Research on the California Islands. Santa Barbara Museum of Natural History, Santa Barbara, CA.

Campbell, B.M. 1980. Some mixed hardwood forest communities of the coastal range of southern California. Phytocoenologia 8:297–320.

Christensen, N.L. 1973. Fire and the nitrogen cycle in California chaparral. Science 181:66–68.

Christenson, L.E. 1990. The late prehistoric Yuman people of San Diego county, California: Their settlement and subsistence system. Ph.D. dissertation. Arizona State University.

Coffin, H. 1959. Effect of marine air on the fire climate in the mountains of southern California. USDA Forest Service, Pacific Southwest Forest and Range Experiment Station, Technical Paper 39.

Cole, K.L., and E. Wahl. 2000. A late Holocene paleoecological record from Torrey Pines State Reserve, California. Quaternary Research 53:341–351.

Collett, R. 1992. Frost report: towns and temperatures. Pacific Horticulture 53:7–9.

Conard, S.G., J.L. Beyers, and P.M. Wohlgemuth. 1995. Impacts of postfire grass seeding on chaparral systems—what do we know and where do we go from here? Pages 149–161 in J.E. Keeley and T. Scott, editors. Wildfires in California brushlands: ecology and resource management. International Association of Wildland Fire, Fairfield, WA.

Conard, S.G., and D.R. Weise. 1998. Management of fire regime, fuels, and fire effects in southern California chaparral: lessons from the past and thoughts for the future. Tall Timbers Ecology Conference Proceedings 20:342–350.

Conroy, C.C. 1928. Thunderstorms in the Los Angeles district. Monthly Weather Review 56:310.

Cooper, W.S. 1922. The broad-sclerophyll vegetation of California. An ecological study of the chaparral and its related communities. Publication No. 319, Carnegie Institution of Washington.

Davis, F.W., M.I. Borchert, and D.C. Odion. 1989. Establishment of microscale vegetation pattern in maritime chaparral after fire. Vegetatio 84:53–67.

Davis, F.W., E.A. Keller, A. Parikh, and J. Florsheim. 1989. Recovery of the chaparral riparian zone after wildfire. Pages 194–203 in D.L. Abell, editor. Proceedings of the California riparian systems conference: protection, management, and restoration for the 1990s. USDA Forest Service, Pacific Southwest Forest and Range Experiment Station, Berkeley, CA.

Davis, F.W., and J. Michaelson. 1995. Sensitivity of fire regime in chaparral ecosystems to climate change. Pages 435–456 in J.M. Moreno and W.C. Oechel, editors. Global change and mediterranean-type ecosystems. Springer-Verlag, New York.

Davis, F.W., P.A. Stine, and D.M. Stoms. 1994. Distribution and conservation status of coastal sage scrub in southwestern California. Journal of Vegetation Science 5:743–756.

Davis, F. W., P. A. Stine, D. M. Stoms, M. I. Borchert, and A. D. Hollander. 1995. Gap analysis of the actual vegetation of California 1. The southwestern region. Madroño 42:40–78.

Davis, O. K. 1992. Rapid climatic change in coastal southern California inferred from pollen analysis of San Joaquin Marsh. Quaternary Research 37:89–100.

Davis, S. D., F. W. Ewers, J. S. Sperry, K. A. Portwood, M. C. Crocker, and G. C. Adams. 2002. Shoot dieback during prolonged drought in Ceanothus (Rhamnaceae) chaparral of California: a possible case of hydraulic failure. American Journal of Botany 89:820–828.

Davis, S. D., K. J. Kolb, and K. P. Barton. 1998. Ecophysiological processes and demographic patterns in the structuring of California chaparral. Pages 297–310 in P. W. Rundel, G. Montenegro, and F. M. Jaksic, editors. Landscape disturbance and biodiversity in Mediterranean-type ecosystems. Springer-Verlag, New York.

DeSimone, S. A., and P. H. Zedler. 1999. Shrub seedling recruitment in unburned Californian coastal sage scrub and adjacent grassland. Ecology 80:2018–2032.

DeSimone, S. A., and P. H. Zedler. 2001. Do shrub colonizers of southern Californian grassland fit generalities for other woody colonizers? Ecological Applications 11:1101–1111.

Dodge, J. M. 1975. Vegetational changes associated with land use and fire history in San Diego County. Ph.D. dissertation. University of California, Riverside.

Dolph, K. L., S. R. Mori, and W. W. Oliver. 1995. Long-term response of old-growth stands to varying levels of partial cutting in the Eastside pine type. Western Journal of Applied Forestry 10:101–108.

Douglas, M. W., R. A. Maddox, and K. Howard. 1993. The Mexican monsoon. Journal of Climate 6:1665–1677.

Dunn, A. T. 1989. The effects of prescribed burning on fire hazard in the chaparral: toward a new conceptual synthesis. Pages 23–29 in N. H. Berg, editor. Proceedings of the symposium on fire and watershed management. USDA Forest Service, Pacific Southwest Forest and Range Experiment Station.

Dwire, K. A., and J. B. Kauffman. 2003. Fire and riparian ecosystems in landscapes of the western USA. Forest Ecology and Management 178:61–74.

Epling, C., and H. Lewis. 1952. Increase of the adaptive range of the genus Delphinium. Evolution 6:253–267.

Erlandson, J. M., and M. A. Glassow (eds.). 1997. Archaeology of the California coast during the middle Holocene. Perspectives in California Archaeology, Volume 4. Institute of Arcahaeology, University of California, Los Angeles.

Everett, R. G. 2003. Grid-based fire-scar dendrochronology and vegetation sampling in the mixed-confer forests of the San Bernardino and San Jacinto Mountains of southern California. Ph.D. dissertation, University of California, Riverside.

Faber, P. M., E. Keller, A. Sands, and B. M. Massey. 1989. The ecology of riparian habitats of the southern California coastal region: a community profile. Biological Report 85(7.27), U.S. Fish and Wildlife Service.

Field, C. B., G. C. Daily, F. W. Davis, S. Gaines, P. A. Matson, J. Melack, and N. L. Miller. 1999. Confronting climate change in California. Ecological impacts on the Golden State. Union of Concerned Scientists and Ecological Society of America., Cambridge, MA, and Washington, DC.

Franklin, J., A. D. Syphard, D. J. Mladenoff, H. S. He, D. K. Simons, R. P. Martin, D. Deutschman, and J. F. O'Leary. 2001. Simulating the effects of different fire regimes on plant functional groups in southern California. Ecological Modelling 142:261–283.

Freudenberger, D. O., B. E. Fish, and J. E. Keeley. 1987. Distribution and stability of grasslands in the Los Angeles Basin. Bulletin of the Southern California Academy of Sciences 86:13–26.

Gause, G. W. 1966. Silvical characteristics of bigcone Douglas-fir. Research Paper PSW-39, USDA Forest Service.

Griffin, J. R., and W. B. Critchfield. 1972. The distribution of forest trees in California. Research Paper PSW-82, USDA Forest Service, Pacific Southwest Forest and Range Experiment Station.

Gumprecht, B. 1999. The Los Angeles River. Johns Hopkins University Press, Baltimore, MD.

Halsey, R. W. 2004. Fire, chaparral and survival in southern California. Sunbelt Publications, El Cajon, California.

Hamilton, J. G. 1997. Changing perceptions of pre-European grasslands in California. Madroño 44:311–333.

Hamilton, J. G., C. Holzapfel, and B. E. Mahall. 1999. Coexistence and interference between a native perennial grass and non-native annual grasses in California. Oecologia 121: 518–526.

Hanawalt, R. B., and R. H. Whittaker. 1976. Altitudinally coordinated patterns of soils and vegetation in the San Jacinto Mountains, California. Soil Science 121:114–124.

Harris, R. R. 1987. Occurrence of vegetation on geomorphic surfaces in the active floodplain of a California alluvial stream. American Midland Naturalist 118:393–405.

Henderson, D. A. 1964. Agriculture and livestock raising in the evolution of the economy and culture of the state of Baja California, Mexico. Ph.D. dissertation. University of California, Los Angeles.

Hickman, J. C. (ed.). 1993. The Jepson manual. University of California Press, Los Angeles.

Hinds, N. E. A. 1952. Evolution of the California landscape. Department of Natural Resources/Division of Mines, San Francisco.

Hobbs, E. R. 1983. Factors controlling the form and location of the boundary between coastal sage scrub and grassland in southern California. Ph.D. dissertation. University of California, Los Angeles.

Hobbs, R. J., and H. A. Mooney. 1985. Vegetative regrowth following cutting in the shrub Baccharis pilularis ssp. consanguinea (DC) C. B. Wolf. American Journal of Botany 72:514–519.

Holstein, G. 1984. California riparian forests: deciduous islands in an evergreen sea. Pages 2–22 in R. E. Warner and K. M. Hendrix, editors. California riparian systems. Ecology, conservation, and productive management. University of California Press, Berkeley.

Horton, J. S. 1960. Vegetation types of the San Bernardino Mountains. Technical Paper No. 44, USDA Forest Service, Pacific Southwest Forest and Range Experiment Station.

Huenneke, L. F. 1989. Distribution and regional patterns of Californian grasslands. Pages 1–12 in L. F. Huenneke and H. A. Mooney, editors. Grassland structure and function. California annual grasslands. Kluwer Academic Publishers, Dordrecht, The Netherlands.

Johnson, D. L. 1977. The California ice-age refugium and the Rancholabrean extinction problem. Quaternary Research 8:149–153.

Johnson, M., S. B. V. Wall, and M. Borchert. 2002. A comparative analysis of seed and cone characteristics and seed-dispersal strategies of three pines in the subsection Sabinianae. Plant Ecology 168:69–84.

Jones, T. L. 1992. Settlement trends along the California coast. Pages 1–37 in T. L. Jones, editor. Essays on the prehistory of maritime California. Center for Archaeological Research, Davis, CA.

Keeley, J. E. 1977. Seed production, seed populations in soil, and seedling production after fire for two congeneric pairs of sprouting and non-sprouting chaparral shrubs. Ecology 58:820–829.

Keeley, J. E. 1982. Distribution of lightning and man-caused wildfires in California. Pages 431–437 in C. E. Conrad and W. C. Oechel, editors. Proceedings of the symposium on dynamics and management of Mediterranean-type ecosystems. USDA Forest Service, Pacific Southwest Forest and Range Experiment Station, General Technical Report PSW-58.

Keeley, J. E. 1986. Resilience of Mediterranean shrub communities to fire. Pages 95–112 in B. Dell, A.J.M. Hopkins, and B. B. Lamont, editors. Resilience in Mediterranean-type ecosystems. Dr. W. Junk, Dordrecht, The Netherlands.

Keeley, J. E. 1990a. Demographic structure of California black walnut (*Juglans californica;* Juglandaceae) woodlands in southern California. Madroño 37:237–248.

Keeley, J. E. 1990b. The California valley grassland. Pages 2–23 in A. A. Schoenherr, editor. Endangered plant communities of southern California. Southern California Botanists, Fullerton.

Keeley, J. E. 1991. Seed germination and life history syndromes in the California chaparral. Botanical Review 57:81–116.

Keeley, J. E. 1992a. Demographic structure of California chaparral in the long-term absence of fire. Journal of Vegetation Science 3:79–90.

Keeley, J. E. 1992b. Recruitment of seedlings and vegetative sprouts in unburned chaparral. Ecology 73:1194–1208.

Keeley, J. E. 1993. Native grassland restoration: the initial stage—assessing suitable sites. Pages 277–281 in J. E. Keeley, editor. Interface between ecology and land development in California. Southern California Academy of Sciences, Los Angeles.

Keeley, J. E. 1998a. Postfire ecosystem recovery and management: the October 1993 large fire episode in California. Pages 69–90 in J. M. Moreno, editor. Large forest fires. Backhuys Publishers, Leiden, The Netherlands.

Keeley, J. E. 1998b. Coupling demography, physiology and evolution in chaparral shrubs. Pages 257–264 in P. W. Rundel, G. Montenegro, and F. M. Jaksic, editors. Landscape diversity and biodiversity in mediterranean-type ecosystems. Springer-Verlag, New York.

Keeley, J. E. 2000. Chaparral. Pages 203–253 in M. G. Barbour and W. D. Billings, editors. North American terrestrial vegetation. Cambridge University Press, Cambridge, England.

Keeley, J. E. 2001. Fire and invasive species in Mediterranean-climate ecosystems of California. Pages 81–94 in K.E.M. Galley and T. P. Wilson, editors. Proceedings of the invasive species workshop: the role of fire in the control and spread of invasive species. Miscellaneous Publication No. 11. Tall Timbers Research Station, Tallahassee, FL.

Keeley, J. E. 2002a. Native American impacts on fire regimes of the California coastal ranges. Journal of Biogeography 29:303–320.

Keeley, J. E. 2002b. Fire management of California shrubland landscapes. Environmental Management 29:395–408.

Keeley, J. E. 2004a. Impact of antecedent climate on fire regimes in southern California. International Journal of Wildland Fire 13:173–182.

Keeley, J. E. 2004b VTM plots as evidence of historical change: Goldmine or landmine? Madroño 51:372–378.

Keeley, J. E. 2004c. Invasive plants and fire management in California Mediterranean-climate ecosystems. No pagination in

M. Arianoutsou and V. P. Panastasis, editors. Ecology, conservation and management of mediterranean climate ecosystems. Millpress, Rotterdam, Netherlands.

Keeley, J. E. Fire severity and plant age in postfire resprouting of woody plants in sage scrub and chaparral. Madroño. In press.

Keeley, J. E., and W. J. Bond. 1997. Convergent seed germination in South African fynbos and Californian chaparral. Plant Ecology 133:153–167.

Keeley, J. E., and C.J. Fotheringham. 2000. Role of fire in regeneration from seed. Pages 311–330 in M. Fenner, editor. Seeds: the ecology of regeneration in plant communities, 2nd edition. CAB International, Oxon, UK.

Keeley, J. E., and C.J. Fotheringham. 2001a. Historic fire regime in Southern California shrublands. Conservation Biology 15:1536–1548.

Keeley, J. E., and C.J. Fotheringham. 2001b. History and management of crown-fire ecosystems: a summary and response. Conservation Biology 15:1561–1567.

Keeley, J. E., and C. J. Fotheringham. 2003. Impact of past, present, and future fire regimes on North American mediterranean shrublands. Pages 218–262 in T. T. Veblen, W. L. Baker, G. Montenegro, and T. W. Swetnam, editors. Fire and climatic change in temperate ecosystems of the Western Americas. Springer, New York.

Keeley, J. E., C.J. Fotheringham, and M. B. Keeley. 2005a. Determinants of postfire recovery and succession in mediterranean-climate shrublands of California. Ecological Applications 15:1515–1524.

Keeley, J. E., C.J. Fotheringham, and M. B. Keeley. 2006b. Demographic patterns of postfire regeneration in Mediterranean-climate shrublands of California. Ecological Monographs 76:235–255.

Keeley, J. E., C.J. Fotheringham, and M. Morais. 1999. Reexamining fire suppression impacts on brushland fire regimes. Science 284:1829–1832.

Keeley, J. E., C.J. Fotheringham, and M. A. Moritz. 2004. Lessons from the October 2003 wildfires in southern California. Journal of Forestry 102(7):26–31.

Keeley, J. E., M. B. Keeley, and C. J. Fotheringham. 2005c. Alien plant dynamics following fire in mediterranean-climate California shrublands. Ecological Applications 15:2109–2125.

Keeley, J. E., and S. C. Keeley. 1984. Postfire recovery of California coastal sage scrub. American Midland Naturalist 111: 105–117.

Keeley, J. E., D. Lubin, and C.J. Fotheringham. 2003. Fire and grazing impacts on plant diversity and alien plant invasions in the southern Sierra Nevada. Ecological Applications 13:1355–1374.

Keeley, J. E., A. H. Pfaff, and H. D. Safford. 2005d. Fire suppression impacts on postfire recovery of Sierra Nevada chaparral shrublands. Intermountain Journal of Wildland Fire 14:225–265.

Keeley, J. E., and N. L. Stephenson. 2000. Restoring natural fire regimes in the Sierra Nevada in an era of global change. Pages 255–265 in D. N. Cole, S. F. McCool, and J. O'Loughlin, editors. Wilderness science in a time of change conference. RMRS-P-15, Vol. 5. USDA Forest Service, Rocky Mountain Research Station, Missoula, MT.

Keeley, J. E., and P. H. Zedler. 1998. Evolution of life histories in Pinus. Pages 219–250 in D. M. Richardson, editor. Ecology and biogeography of *Pinus*. Cambridge University Press, Cambridge, England.

Kellogg, E.M., and J.L. Kellogg. 1990. A study of the distribution and pattern of perennial grassland on the Camp Pendleton Marine Corps Base. Contract No. M00681-88-P03161. U.S. Marine Corps, Camp Pendleton, CA.

Kinney, A. 1887. Report on the forests of the counties of Los Angeles, San Bernardino, and San Diego, California. First biennial report, California State Board of Forestry, Sacramento, CA.

Kinney, A. 1900. Forest and water. Post Publishing Company, Los Angeles, CA.

Kirkpatrick, J. B., and C.F. Hutchinson. 1977. The community composition of California coastal sage scrub. Vegetatio 35:21–33.

Landis, F.C. 2000. Unburned and grazed chaparral: a case study. Pages 60–69 in J.E. Keeley, M. Baer-Keeley, and C.J. Fotheringham, editors. 2nd interface between ecology and land development in California. U.S. Geological Survey, Sacramento, CA.

Lawson, D.M. 1993. The effect of fire on stand structure of mixed *Quercus agrifolia* and *Quercus engelmannii* woodlands. M.S. thesis. San Diego State University, San Diego, CA.

Ledig, F.T. 1999. Genic diversity, genetic structure, and biogeography of *Pinus sabiniana* Dougl. Diversity and Distributions 5:77–90.

Ledig, F.T. 2000. Founder effects and the genetic structure of Coulter pine. Journal of Heredity 91:307–315.

Lee, R.G., and T.M. Bonnicksen. 1978. Brushland watershed fire management policy in southern California: biosocial considerations. Contribution No. 172, California Water Resources Center, University of California, Davis.

Leiberg, J. B. 1899a. San Jacinto Forest Reserve. U.S. Geological Survey, Annual Report 19:351–357.

Leiberg, J.B. 1899b. San Bernardino Forest Reserve. U.S. Geological Survey, Annual Report 19:359–365.

Leiberg, J.B. 1899c. San Gabriel Forest Reserve. U.S. Geological Survey, Annual Report 19:367–371.

Leiberg, J.B. 1900a. San Gabriel Forest Reserve. U.S. Geological Survey, Annual Report 20:411–428.

Leiberg, J.B. 1900b. San Bernardino Forest Reserve. U.S. Geological Survey, Annual Report 20:429–454.

Leiberg, J.B. 1900c. San Jacinto Forest Reserve. U.S. Geological Survey, Annual Report 20:455–478.

Linhart, Y. B., B. Burr, et al. 1967. The closed-cone pines of the northern Channel Islands. Pages 151–177 in R.N. Philbrick, editor. Proceedings of the symposium on the biology of the California Islands. Santa Barbara, CA, Santa Barbara Botanic Garden, Santa Barbara.

Lloret, F., and P.H. Zedler. 1991. Recruitment of *Rhus integrifolia* in chaparral. Journal of Vegetation Science 2:217–230.

Loomis, J. , P. Wohlgemuth, A. Gonzale-Caban, and D. English. 2003. Economic benefits of reducing fire-related sediment in southwestern fire-prone ecosystems. Water Resources Research 39(No 9, WES 3):1–8.

Mack, R.N. 1989. Temperate grasslands vulnerable to plant invasions: characteristics and consequences. Pages 155–179 in J. A. Drake, H. A. Mooney, F. d. Castri, R.H. Groves, F.J. Kruger, M. Rejmanek, and M. Williamson, editors. Biological invasions: a global perspective. John Wiley & Sons, New York.

Major, J. 1977. California climate in relation to vegetation. Pages 11–74 in M.G. Barbour and J. Major, editors. Terrestrial vegetation of California. John Wiley & Sons, New York.

Malanson, G.P. 1984. Fire history and patterns of Venturan subassociations of Californian coastal scrub. Vegetatio 57:121–128.

Malanson, G.P., and J.F. O'Leary. 1982. Post-fire regeneration strategies of California coastal sage shrubs. Oecologia 53:355–358.

Malanson, G.P., and W.E. Westman. 1985. Postfire succession in Californian coastal sage scrub: the role of continual basal sprouting. American Midland Naturalist 113:309–318.

McBride, J.R. 1974. Plant succession in the Berkeley Hills, California. Madroño 22:317–380.

McBride, J.R., and D.F. Jacobs. 1980. Land use and fire history in the mountains of southern California. Pages 85–88 in M.A. Stokes and J.H. Dieterich, editors. Proceedings of the fire history workshop. USDA Forest Service, Rocky Mountain Forest and Range Experiment Station, General Technical Report RM-81.

McBride, J.R., and R.D. Laven. 1976. Scars as an indicator of fire frequency in the San Bernardino Mountains, California. Journal of Forestry 74:439–442.

McBride, J.R., and R.D. Laven. 1999. Impact of oxidant air pollutants on forest succession in the mixed conifer forests of the San Bernardino Mountains. Pages 338–352 in P. R. Miller and J.R. McBride, editors. Oxidant air pollution impacts in the montane forests of southern California. A case study of the San Bernardino Mountains. Springer, New York.

McDonald, P.M. 1990. *Pseudotsuga macrocarpa* (Vasey) Mayr bigcone Douglas-fir. Pages 520–525 in R.M. Burns and B.H. Honkala, editors. Silvics of North America. Volume 1, Conifers. Agriculture Handbook 654. USDA Forest Service, Washington, DC.

McDonald, P.M., and E.E. Litterell. 1976. The bigcone Douglas-fir—canyon live oak community in southern California. Madroño 23:310–320.

McKelvey, K.S., and J.D. Johnston. 1992. Historical perspectives on forests of the Sierra Nevada and the Transverse Ranges of Southern California: forest conditions at the turn of the century. Pages 225–246 in J. Verner, K. S. McKelvey, B.R. Noon, R.J. Gutierrez, G.I. Gould, and T.W. Beck, editors. The California spotted owl: a technical assessment of its current status. USDA Forest Service, General Technical Report PSW-GTR-133.

McMaster, G.S., and P.H. Zedler. 1981. Delayed seed dispersal in *Pinus torreyana* (Torrey pine). Oecologia 51:62–66.

McMillan, C. 1956. Edaphic restriction of *Cupressus* and *Pinus* in the coast ranges of central California. Ecological Monographs 26:177–212.

Meentemeyer, R.K., and A. Moody. 2002. Distribution of plant history types in California chaparral: the role of topographically-determined drought severity. Journal of Vegetation Science 13:67–78.

Mensing, S.A., J. Michaelsen, and R. Byrne. 1999. A 560-year record of Santa Ana fires reconstructed from charcoal deposited in the Santa Barbara Basin, California. Quaternary Research 51:295–305.

Miles, S.R., and C.B. Goudey. 1997. Ecological subregions of California. R5-EM-TP-005. USDA Forest Service, Pacific Southwest Region, San Francisco.

Millar, C.I. 1986. Bishop pine (*Pinus muricata*) of inland Marin County, California. Madroño 33:123–129.

Minnich, R.A. 1974. The impact of fire suppression on southern California conifer forests: a case study of the Big Bear fire, November 13 to 16, 1970. Pages 45–57 in M. Rosenthal, editor. Symposium on living with the chaparral, proceedings. Sierra Club, San Francisco.

Minnich, R.A. 1977. The geography of fire and big cone Douglas-fir, Coulter pine and western conifer forest in the east Transverse Ranges, southern California. Pages 343–350 in H.A. Mooney and C.E. Conrad, editors. Proceedings of the symposium on environmental consequences of fire and fuel management in Mediterranean ecosystems. USDA Forest Service.

Minnich, R.A. 1980a. Wildfire and the geographic relationships between canyon live oak, Coulter pine, and bigcone Douglas-fir forests. Pages 55–61 in T.R. Plumb, editor. Proceedings of the symposium on ecology, management and utilization of California oaks. USDA Forest Service, Pacific Southwest Forest and Range Experiment Station.

Minnich, R.A. 1980b. Vegetation of Santa Cruz and Santa Catalina Islands. Pages 123–139 in D.M. Power, editor. The California islands: proceedings of a multidisciplinary symposium. Santa Barbara Museum of Natural History, Santa Barbara, CA.

Minnich, R.A. 1982. Grazing, fire, and the management of vegetation on Santa Catalina Island, CA. Pages 444–449 in C.E. Conrad and W.C. Oechel, editors. Proceedings of the symposium on dynamics and management of mediterranean-type ecosystems. USDA Forest Service, Pacific Southwest Forest and Range Experiment Station, General Technical Report PSW-58.

Minnich, R.A. 1983. Fire mosaics in southern California and northern Baja California. Science 219:1287–1294.

Minnich, R.A. 1987a. Fire behavior in southern California chaparral before fire control: the Mount Wilson burns at the turn of the century. Annals of the Association of American Geographers 77:599–618.

Minnich, R.A. 1987b. The distribution of forest trees in northern Baja California, Mexico. Madroño 34:98–127.

Minnich, R.A. 1988. The biogeography of fire in the San Bernardino Mountains of California. A historical study. University of California Publications in Botany 28:1–120.

Minnich, R.A. 1989. Chaparral fire history in San Diego County and adjacent northern Baja California: an evaluation of natural fire regimes and the effects of suppression management. Pages 37–47 in S.C. Keeley, editor. The California chaparral: paradigms reexamined. Natural History Museum of Los Angeles County, Los Angeles.

Minnich, R.A. 1998. Landscapes, land-use and fire policy: where do large fires come from? Pages 133–158 in J.M. Moreno, editor. Large forest fires. Backhuys Publishers, Leiden, The Netherlands.

Minnich, R.A. 1999. Vegetation, fire regimes, and forest dynamics. Pages 44–83 in P.R. Miller and J.R. McBride, editors. Oxidant air pollution impacts in the montane forests of southern California. A case study of the San Bernardino Mountains. Springer, New York.

Minnich, R.A. 2001. Fire and elevational zonation of chaparral and conifer forests in the peninsular ranges of La Frontera. Pages 120–142 in G.L. Webster and C.J. Bahre, editors. Changing plant life of La Frontera, observations on vegetation in the United States/Mexico borderlands. University of Mexico Press, Albuquerque, NM.

Minnich, R.A., M.G. Barbour, J.H. Burk, and R.F. Fernau. 1995. Sixty years of change in Californian conifer forests of the San Bernardino Mountains. Conservation Biology 9:902–914.

Minnich, R.A., M.G. Barbour, J.H. Burk, and J. Sosa-Ramirez. 2000. Californian conifer forests under unmanaged fire regimes in the Sierra San Pedro Martir, Baja California, Mexico. Journal of Biogeography 27:105–129.

Minnich, R.A., and Y.H. Chou. 1997. Wildland fire patch dynamics in the chaparral of southern California and northern Baja California. International Journal of Wildland Fire 7:221.

Minnich, R.A., and R.J. Dezzani. 1991. Suppression, fire behavior, and fire magnitudes in Californian chaparral at the urban/wildland interface. Pages 67–83 in J.J. DeVries, editor. California watersheds at the urban interface, proceedings of the third biennial watershed conference. University of California, Davis.

Minnich, R.A., and R.J. Dezzani. 1998. Historical decline of coastal sage scrub in the Riverside-Perris Plain, CA. Western Birds 29:366–391.

Minnich, R.A., and R.G. Everett. 2002. What unmanaged fire regimes in Baja California tell us about presuppression fire in California mediterranean ecosystems. Pages 325–338 in N.G. Sugihara, M.E. Morales, and T.J. Morales, editors. Proceedings of the symposium: fire in California ecosystems: integrating ecology, prevention and management. Miscellaneous Publication No. 1, Association for Fire Ecology, Sacramento.

Minnich, R.A., E.F. Vizcaino, and R.J. Dezzani. 2000. The El Niño/Southern Oscillation and precipitation variability in Baja California, Mexico. Atm_sfera 13:1–20.

Mooney, H.A., and C. Chu. 1974. Seasonal carbon allocation in *Heteromeles arbutifolia,* a California evergreen shrub. Oecologia 14:295–306.

Morvan, D., and J.L. Dupuy. 2004. Modeling the propagation of a wildfire through a Mediterranean shrub using a multiphase formulation. Combustion and Flame 138:199–210.

Moreno, J.M., and W.C. Oechel. 1994. Fire intensity as a determinant factor of postfire plant recovery in southern California chaparral. Pages 26–45 in J.M. Moreno and W.C. Oechel, editors. The role of fire in Mediterranean-type ecosystems. Springer-Verlag, New York.

Moritz, M.A. 1997. Analyzing extreme disturbance events: fire in the Los Padres National Forest. Ecological Applications 7:1252–1262.

Moritz, M.A. 2003. Spatiotemporal analysis of controls on shrubland fire regimes: age dependency an fire hazard. Ecology 84:351–361.

Moritz, M.A., J.E. Keeley, E.A. Johnson, and A.A. Schaffner. 2004. Testing a basic assumption of shrubland fire management: How important is fuel age? Frontiers in Ecology and the Environment 2:67–70.

Ne'eman, G., C.J. Fotheringham, and J.E. Keeley. 1999. Patch to landscape patterns in post fire recruitment of a serotinous conifer. Plant Ecology 145:235–242.

Norris, R.M., and R.W. Webb. 1976. Geology of California. John Wiley & Sons, New York.

Oberbauer, A.T. 1978. Distribution dynamics of San Diego County grasslands. M.S. thesis. San Diego State University, San Diego, CA.

Odion, D.C., and F.W. Davis. 2000. Fire, soil heating, and the formation of vegetation patterns in chaparral. Ecological Monographs 70:149–169.

Odion, D., and C. Tyler. 2002. Are long fire-free periods needed to maintain the endangered, fire-recruiting shrub *Arctostaphylos morroensis* (Ericaceae)? Conservation Ecology 6:4 [http://www.consecol.org/Journal].

Owen, L.A., R.C. Finkel, R.A. Minnich, and A.E. Perez. 2003. Extreme southwestern margin of late Quaternary glaciation in North America: Timing and controls. Geology 31:729–732.

Parish, S.B. 1903. A sketch of the flora of southern California. Botanical Gazette 36:203–222, 259–279.

Pequegnat, W.E. 1951. The biota of the Santa Ana Mountains. Journal of Entomology and Zoology 42:1–84.

Phillips, C.B. 1971. California aflame! September 22–October 4, 1970. State of California, Department of Conservation, Division of Forestry.

Philpot, C.W. 1974. The changing role of fire on chaparral lands. Pages 131–150 in M. Rosenthal, editor. Symposium on living with the chaparral, proceedings. Sierra Club, San Francisco.

Plumb, T.R. 1980. Response of oaks to fire. Pages 202–215 in T.R. Plumb, editor. Proceedings of the symposium on ecology, management and utilization of California oaks. USDA Forest Service, Pacific Southwest Forest and Range Experiment Station.

Plummer, F.G. 1911. Chaparral—studies in the dwarf forests, of elfin-wood, of southern California. Bulletin No. 85, USDA Forest Service.

Quinn, R.D. 1990. The status of walnut forests and woodlands (*Juglans californica*) in southern California. Pages 42–54 in A.A. Schoenherr, editor. Endangered plant communities of southern California. Southern California Botanists, Fullerton.

Radtke, K. W-H., A.M. Arndt, and R.H. Wakimoto. 1982. Fire history of the Santa Monica Mountains. Pages 438–443 in C.E. Conrad and W.C. Oechel, editors. Proceedings of the symposium on dynamics and management of Mediterranean-type ecosystems. USDA Forest Service, Pacific Southwest Forest and Range Experiment Station, General Technical Report PSW-58.

Reveal, J.L. 1978. A report on the autecology and status of Cuyamaca cypress (*Cupressus arizonica* var. *stephensonii*), Cleveland National Forest California. USDA Forest Service, Cleveland National Forest, unpublished report, Order No. 1191-PSW-77.

Rhode, D. 2002. Early Holocene juniper woodland and chaparral taxa in the central Baja California Peninsula, Mexico. Quaternary Research 57:102–108.

Rieger, J.P., and D.A. Kreager. 1989. Giant reed (*Arundo donax*): a climax community of the riparian zone. Pages 222–225 in D.L. Abell, editor. Proceedings of the California riparian systems conference: protection, management, and restoration for the 1990s. USDA Forest Service, Pacific Southwest Forest and Range Experiment Station, Berkeley, CA.

Riggan, P.J., S.E. Franklin, J.A. Brass, and F.E. Brooks. 1994. Perspectives on fire management in mediterranean ecosystems of southern California. Pages 140–162 in J.M. Moreno and W.C. Oechel, editors. The role of fire in Mediterranean-type ecosystems. Springer-Verlag, New York.

Robert, C. 2004. Late Quaternary variability of precipitation in southern California and climatic implications: clay mineral evidence from the Santa Barbara Basin, ODP Site 893. Quaternary Science Reviews 23:1029–1040.

Rodrigue, C.M. 1993. Home with a view: chaparral fire hazard and the social geographies of risk and vulnerability. California Geographer 33:29–42.

Rohde, M.S. 2002. Command decisions during catastrophic urban-interface wildfire: a case study of the 1993 Orange County Laguna Fire. M.S. thesis, California State University, Long Beach.

Rundel, P.W. 1975. Primary succession on granite outcrops in the montane southern Sierra Nevada. Madroño 23:209–219.

Rundel, P.W., D.J. Parsons, and D.T. Gordon. 1977. Montane and subalpine vegetation of the Sierra Nevada and Cascade Ranges. Pages 559–599 in M.G. Barbour and J. Major, editors. Terrestrial vegetation of California. John Wiley & Sons, New York.

Rundel, P.W., and S.B. Sturmer. 1998. Native plant diversity in riparian communities of the Santa Monica Mountains, California. Madroño 45:93–100.

Sargent, C.S. 1884. Report on the forests of North America (exclusive of Mexico). Report on the productions of agriculture as returned at the tenth census, Volume 9. U.S. Government Printing Office, Washington, DC.

Savage, M. 1994. Anthropogenic and natural disturbance and patterns of mortality in a mixed conifer forest in California. Canadian Journal of Forest Research 24:1149–1159.

Savage, M. 1997. The role of anthropogenic influences in a mixed-conifer forest mortality episode. Journal of Vegetation Science 8:95–104.

Savage, M., and T.W. Swetnam. 1990. Early 19th century fires decline following sheep pasturing in a Navajo ponderosa pine forest. Ecology 71:2374–2378.

Sawyer, J.O., and T. Keeler-Wolf. 1995. A manual of California vegetation. California Native Plant Society, Sacramento, California.

Scheidlinger, C.R., and P.H. Zedler. 1980. Change in vegetation cover of oak stands in southern San Diego County: 1928–1970. Pages 81–85 in T.R. Plumb, editor. Proceedings of the symposium on the ecology, management, and utilization of California oaks. USDA Forest Service, Pacific Southwest Forest and Range Experiment Station.

Schoenberg, F.P., R. Peng, Z. Huang, and P. Rundel. 2001. Detection of non-linearities in the dependence of burn area on fuel age and climatic variables. International Journal of Wildland Fire 12:1–6.

Schoenherr, A.A. 1992. A natural history of California. University of California Press, Los Angeles.

Schoenherr, A.A., C.R. Feldmeth, and M.J. Emerson. 1999. Natural history of the islands of California. University of California Press, Los Angeles.

Schroeder, M.J., et al. 1964. Synoptic weather types associated with critical fire weather. U.S. Department of Commerce, National Bureau of Standards, Institute for Applied Technology, AD 449-630. 372 p.

Schwilk, D.W. 2003. Flammability is a niche construction trait: canopy architecture affects fire intensity. American Naturalist 162:725–733.

Schwilk, D.W., and D.D. Ackerly. 2001. Flammability and serotiny as strategies: correlated evolution in pines. Oikos 94:326–336.

Schwilk, D.W. and B. Kerr. 2002. Genetic niche-hiking: an alternative explanation for the evolution of flammability. Oikos 99:431–442.

Sharp, R.P., C.R. Allen, and M.F. Meier. 1959. Pleistocene glaciers on southern California mountains. American Journal of Science 257:81–94.

Sheppard, P.R., and J.P. Lassoie. 1998. Fire regime of the lodgepole pine forest of Mt. San Jacinto, California. Madroño 45:47–56.

Simpson, L.B. 1938. California in 1792. The expedition of Jose Longinos Martinez, San Marino, CA.

Stephens, S.L. and S.J. Gill. 2005. Forest structure and mortality in an old-growth Jeffrey pine–mixed conifer forest in northwest Mexico. Forest Ecology and Management 205:15–28.

Stephens, S.L., C.N. Skinner, and S.J. Gill. 2003. Dendrochonology-based fire history of Jeffrey pine–mixed conifer forests in the Sierra San Pedro Martir, Mexico. Canadian Journal of Forest Research 33:1090–1101.

Stephenson, J.R., and G.M. Calcarone. 1999. Southern California mountains and foothills assessment. USDA Forest Service,

Pacific Southwest Research Station, General Technical Report GTR-PSW-172, Albany, CA.

Stephenson, N.L. 1990. Climatic control of vegetation distribution: the role of the water balance. American Naturalist 135:649–670.

Strauss, D., L. Dednar, and R. Mees. 1989. Do one percent of forest fires cause ninety-nine percent of the damage? Forest Science 35:319–328.

Stromberg, M.R., and J.R. Griffin. 1996. Long-term patterns in coastal California grasslands in relation to cultivation, gophers, and grazing. Ecological Applications 6:1189–1211.

Thorne, R.F. 1977. Montane and subalpine forests of the Transverse and Peninsular Ranges. Pages 537–557 in M.G. Barbour and J. Major, editors. Terrestrial vegetation of California. John Wiley & Sons, New York.

Timbrook, J., J.R. Johnson, and D.D. Earle. 1982. Vegetation burning by the Chumash. Journal of California and Great Basin Anthropology 4:163–186.

Tyler, C., and M. Borchert. 2002. Reproduction and growth of the chaparral geophyte, *Zigadenus fremontii* (Liliaceae), in relation to fire. Plant Ecology 165:11–20.

USDA Forest Service. 2004a. Draft environmental impact statement for revised land management plans. Angeles National Forest, Cleveland National Forest, Los Padres National Forest, San Bernardino National Forest. USDA Forest Service, Pacific Southwest Region, R5-MB-05.

USDA Forest Service. 2004b. Draft land management plan. Part 2: Cleveland National Forest Strategy. USDA Forest Service, Pacific Southwest Region, R5-MB-042.

USDOI National Park Service. 2004. Draft environmental impact statement. Fire management plan, Santa Monica Mountains National Recreation Area, CA. USDOI National Park Service.

Vale, T.R. 1979. *Pinus coulteri* and wildfire on Mount Diablo, California. Madroño 26:135–140.

van Wagtendonk, J.W., and D.R. Cayan. 2007. Temporal and spatial distribution of lightning strikes in California in relationship to large-scale weather patterns. Fire Ecology. (in press).

Vogl, R.J. 1973. Ecology of knobcone pine in the Santa Ana Mountains, California. Ecological Monographs 43:125–143.

Vogl, R.J. 1977. Fire frequency and site degradation. Pages 151–162 in H.A. Mooney and C.E. Conrad, editors. Proceedings of the symposium on environmental consequences of fire and fuel management in Mediterranean ecosystems. USDA Forest Service.

Walter, H.S. and L.A. Taha. 1999. The Regeneration of bishop pine (*Pinus muricata*) in the absence and presence of fire: a case study from Santa Cruz Island, California. Pages 172–181 in Proceedings of the fifth California Islands symposium, March 29–April 1, 1999. U.S. Department of the Interior, Minerals Management Service, Pacific OCS Region, Ventura, CA.

Ward, J.K., J.M. Harris, T.E. Cerling, A. Wiedenhoeft, M.J. Lott, M-D. Dearing, J.B. Coltrain, and J.R. Ehleringer. 2005. Carbon starvation in glacial trees recovered from the La Brea tar pits, southern California. Proceedings of the National Academy of Sciences 102:690–694.

Weide, D.L. 1968. The geography of fire in the Santa Monica Mountains. M.S. thesis. California State University, Los Angeles.

Wells, M.L., and A. Getis. 1999. The spatial characteristics of stand structure in *Pinus torreyana*. Plant Ecology 143: 153–170.

Wells, M.L., J.F. O'Leary, J. Franklin, J. Michaelsen, and D.E. McKinsey. 2004. Variations in a regional fire regime related to

vegetation type in San Diego County, California (USA). Landscape Ecology 19:139–152.

Wells, P.V. 1962. Vegetation in relation to geological substratum and fire in the San Luis Obispo quadrangle, California. Ecological Monographs 32:79–103.

Wells, P.V. 1969. The relation between mode of reproduction and extent of speciation in woody genera of the California chaparral. Evolution 23:264–267.

Wells, P.V. 2000. Pleistocene macrofossil records of four-needled pinyon or juniper encinal in the northern Vizcaino Desert, Baja California del Norte. Madroño 47:189–194.

Weise, D.R., J.C. Regelbrugge, T.E. Paysen, and S.G. Conard. 2002. Fire occurrence on southern California national forests— has it changed recently? Pages 389–391 in N.G. Sugihara, M.E. Morales, and T.J. Morales, editors. Proceedings of the symposium: fire in California ecosystems: integrating ecology, prevention and management. Miscellaneous Publication No. 1, Association for Fire Ecology, Sacramento, CA.

Westerling, A.L., A. Gershunov, D.R. Cayan, and T.P. Barnett. 2002. Long lead statistical forecasts of area burned in western U.S. wildfires by ecosystem province. International Journal of Wildland Fire 11:257–266.

White, S.D., and J.J.O. Sawyer. 1994. Dynamics of *Quercus wislizenii* forest and shrubland in the San Bernardino Mountains, California. Madroño 41:302–315.

Yoho, D., T. Boyle, and E. McIntire. 1999. The climate of the Channel Islands, California. Pages 81–99 in Proceedings of the fifth California Islands symposium, March 29–April 1, 1999. U.S. Department of the Interior, Minerals Management Service, Pacific OCS Region, Ventura, CA.

Zavitokovski, J., and M. Newton. 1968. Ecological importance of snowbrush, *Ceanothus velutinus*, in the Oregon Cascades. Ecology 49:1134–1145.

Zedler, P.H. 1977. Life history attributes of plants and the fire cycle: a case study in chaparral dominated by *Cupressus forbesii*. Pages 451–458 in H.A. Mooney and C.E. Conrad, editors. Proceedings of the symposium on environmental consequences of fire and fuel management in Mediterranean ecosystems. USDA Forest Service.

Zedler, P.H. 1981. Vegetation change in chaparral and desert communities in San Diego County, CA. Pages 406–430 in D. C. West, H.H. Shugart, and D. Botkin, editors. Forest succession. Concepts and applications. Springer-Verlag, New York.

Zedler, P.H. 1995a. Fire frequency in southern California shrublands: biological effects and management options. Pages 101–112 in J.E. Keeley and T. Scott, editors. Wildfires in California brushlands: ecology and resource management. International Association of Wildland Fire, Fairfield, WA.

Zedler, P.H. 1995b. Plant life history and dynamic specialization in the chaparral/coastal sage shrub flora in southern California. Pages 89–115 in M.T.K. Arroyo, P.H. Zedler, and M.D. Fox, editors. Ecology and biogeography of Mediterranean ecosystems in Chile, California and Australia. Springer-Verlag, New York.

Zedler, P.H., C.R. Gautier, and G.S. McMaster. 1983. Vegetation change in response to extreme events: the effect of a short interval between fires in California chaparral and coastal scrub. Ecology 64:809–818.

Zedler, P.H., and L.A. Seiger. 2000. Age mosaics and fire size in chaparral: a simulation study. Pages 9–18 in J.E. Keeley, M. Baer-Keeley, and C.J. Fotheringham, editors. 2nd interface between ecology and land development in California. U.S. Geological Survey, Sacramento, CA.

CHAPTER 16

Southeastern Deserts Bioregion

MATTHEW L. BROOKS AND RICHARD A. MINNICH

> Because of the inescapably close correlation between prevalence
> of fire and amount of fuel, deserts are characteristically less
> affected by fire than are most ecosystems ... however, even
> though fire frequency and severity may be relatively low in any
> rating scale, their effect on the ecosystem may be extreme.
>
> HUMPHREY 1974

Description of Bioregion

Physical Geography

The southeastern deserts bioregion (desert bioregion) occupies the southeastern 27% of California (110,283 km² or 27,251,610 ac) (Miles and Goudy 1997) (Map 16.1). The desert bioregion is within the basin and range geomorphic province of western North America, and includes two ecoregional provinces comprised of five ecological sections. The American Semi-Desert and Desert Province (hot-desert province) includes the Mojave Desert, Sonoran Desert, and Colorado Desert sections in the southern 83% of the desert bioregion (Table 16.1). The Intermountain Semi-Desert Province (cold-desert province) includes the Southeastern Great Basin and Mono sections in the northern 17% of the desert bioregion.

The geomorphology of the desert bioregion is characterized by isolated mountain ranges with steep slopes separated by broad basins containing alluvial fans, lava flows, dunes, and playas. Elevations range from −85 m (−280 ft) below sea level in Death Valley, to 4,328 m (14,200 ft) above sea level in the White Mountains. Soil taxa range widely from hyperthermic or thermic, aridic Aridisols and Entisols in the Colorado, Sonoran, and Mojave Desert sections, to thermic, mesic, frigid, or cryic, aridic, xeric, or aquic Alfisols, Aridisols, Entisols, Inceptisols, Mollisols, and Vertisols in the Mono and Southeastern Great Basin sections (Miles and Goudy 1997). This wide range in geomorphology and soil conditions translates into a wide range of vegetation and fuel types, which include arid shrublands and semi-arid shrublands, grasslands, woodlands, and forests.

Climatic Patterns

Although frontal cyclones of the jet stream pass through the region during winter (November through April), virtually the entire desert bioregion is arid due to rain shadows of the Sierra Nevada, Transverse, and Peninsular ranges (Chapter 2, this volume). Precipitation increases locally with orographic lift in desert ranges, particularly those that rise above 2,000 m (6,096 ft). From July to early September, the region experiences 10 to 25 days of afternoon thunderstorms from the North American monsoon originating in the Gulf of California and Mexico. Thunderstorm cells tend to concentrate over high terrain, especially the eastern escarpments of the Sierra Nevada, Transverse, and Peninsular ranges, in the mountains of the eastern Mojave Desert, and in the high basin and range terrain between the White Mountains and Death Valley. The average annual precipitation on valley floors ranges from 10 to 20 cm (3.9–7.9 in) in the Mojave Desert and Southeastern Great Basin, to 7 to 10 cm (2.8–3.9 in) in the Colorado and Sonoran deserts. The average annual rainfall total at Death Valley (5.8 cm, 2.3 in) is the lowest in North America. Precipitation ranges from 20 to 30 cm (7.9–11.8 in) in the mountains above 2,000 m (6,562 ft), 40 cm (15.8 in) in the White Mountains, and 60 cm (23.6 in) in the upper leeward catchments of the Sierra Nevada, Transverse, and Peninsular ranges. The percentage of annual precipitation falling during summer (May through October) ranges from approximately 20% in the southeastern Great Basin to 40% at the Colorado River in the Sonoran Desert.

Interannual variation in rainfall is relatively high compared to other California bioregions, resulting in highly variable frequency and extent of fires among years. High rainfall produces fine fuels that promote fire spread, especially in the hot desert sections where fuels are otherwise sparse. Low rainfall causes shrub mortality, which reduces woody fuel moisture and may promote fire spread in the cold desert sections where woody fuel cover is relatively high, although low fine fuel loads caused by low rainfall is probably more limiting to fire spread. Multi-decadal variation in rainfall has also been significant, with periods of relatively high rainfall

391

TABLE 16.1
General descriptions and lightning frequencies (1985–2001) in the ecological sections of the Southeastern
Deserts bioregion

Ecological Section[a]	Percentage of Bioregion	Constituent Ecological Zones[b]	Predominant Küchler Vegetation Types[c]	Lightning Strikes/ 100 km²/yr[d]
Mojave	61	Low, mid, high, montane, riparian	Desert shrub 58% barren 37%	30
Sonoran	12	Low, riparian	Barren 82% desert shrub 18%	25
Colorado	10	Low, mid, riparian	Desert shrub 57% barren 38%	12
SE Great Basin	10	High montane, riparian	Desert shrub 74% juniper-pinyon 18%	29
Mono	7	High, montane, riparian	Sagebrush 46% juniper-finyon 15%	32

[a] Miles and Goudy (1997).

[b] Low-elevation desert shrubland, middle-elevation desert shrubland and grassland, high-elevation desert shrubland and woodland, desert montane woodland and forest, desert riparian woodland and oasis (see detailed descriptions in the text).

[c] Potential natural vegetation types (Küchler 1964) that constitute 15% or more of the ecological section.

[d] Bureau of Land Management lightning detection data (van Wagtendonk and Cayan, 2007).

from the turn of the century until 1946, a mid-century drought from 1947 to 1976, and a period of high rainfall 1977 to 1998 (Hereford et al. in press). This approximately 30-year cycle, coupled with below-average rainfall from 1999 to 2004, suggests that another 30-year drought period may be establishing, which could lead to reduced frequency and size of fires in most of the desert bioregion entering the twenty-first century.

The entire desert bioregion has a large annual range of temperature due to its isolation from the stabilizing influences of the Pacific Ocean. There is also large local variability due to variable elevational relief. Average January temperatures on valley floors range from −3°C–0°C (27°F–32°F) in the northeastern Great Basin to 7°C–10°C (45°F–50°F) in the Mojave Desert, and 11°C–13°C (52°F–55°F) in the Sonoran and Colorado deserts. Temperatures decrease with altitude to about 0°C (32°F) at 2,000 m (6,562 ft) and −8°C (18°F) at 3,000 m (9,842 ft.). During summer, average temperatures vary near the dry adiabatic lapse rate due to intense atmospheric heating in the absence of evapotranspiration under high rates of insolation. July average temperatures on valley floors range from 18°C–20°C (64°F–68°F) in the northeastern Great Basin to 25°C–30°C (77°C–86°F) in the Mojave Desert and 30°C–35°C (86°F–95°F) in the Sonoran and Colorado deserts. Maximum temperatures average higher than 40°C (104°F) below 1,000 m (3,281 ft) elevation and occasionally reach 50°C (122°F) in Death Valley, the Colorado River Valley, and

the Salton Sea trough. In the desert mountains, average temperatures decrease to 20°C (68°F) at 2,000 m (6,562 ft) and 10°C (50°F) at 3,000 m (9,842 ft). The decrease in temperature with altitude results in a rapid decrease in evapotranspiration, which in phase with increasing precipitation results in a corresponding increase in woody biomass of ecosystems. Light snowpacks 10 to 15 cm (3.9–5.9 in) deep can develop in winter but typically disappear by spring above 2,000 m (6,562 ft), although deeper snow of 100 cm (39.4 in) can persist into the spring in subalpine forests higher than 3,000 m (9,842 ft).

Relative humidity during the afternoon in the summer fire season, when fires are most likely to spread, is very low throughout the desert bioregion. Average relative humidity in July ranges from 20% to 30% in the northeastern Mojave Deserts to 10% to 20% in the Mojave, Sonoran, and Colorado deserts. Values are low because moisture of the Pacific Coast marine layer is mixed aloft with dry subsiding air masses upon dissipation of the marine inversion, as well as from high temperatures produced by convective heating of surface air layers. The lowest humidity of the year (frequently less than 10%) typically occurs in late June, just before the arrival of the North American monsoon.

Lightning frequency is higher in the desert than in any other California bioregion (van Wagtendonk and Cayan 2007). Lightning strikes/100 km²/year averaged 27 (SD = 16) from 1985 through 2000, ranging from 32 in the Mono to 12 in the Colorado Desert sections (Table 16.1). The bioregions

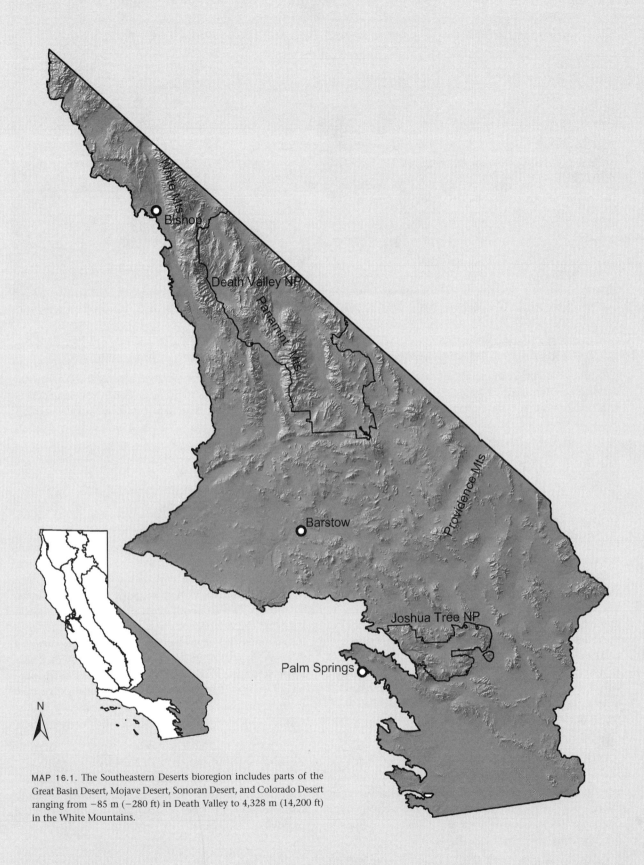

MAP 16.1. The Southeastern Deserts bioregion includes parts of the
Great Basin Desert, Mojave Desert, Sonoran Desert, and Colorado Desert
ranging from −85 m (−280 ft) in Death Valley to 4,328 m (14,200 ft)
in the White Mountains.

FIGURE16.1. The low-elevation desert shrubland ecological zone. This photo shows a creosote bush scrub vegetation typical of the Sonoran Desert, and lower elevations of the Mojave Desert.

with the next most-frequent lightning strikes were the Northeastern Plateaus (22 strikes/100 km²/year) and Sierra Nevada (20 strikes/100 km²/year) bioregions. Most lightning in the desert bioregion occurred from July to September (78%), resulting from summer monsoons that developed in the Colorado, Sonoran, and eastern Mojave deserts, and from summer storms that developed in the Sierra Nevada mountains and drifted into the southeastern Great Basin and Mono sections. Lightning also occurred primarily during daylight hours, with 81% between 0600 and 1800.

Ecological Zones

From a fire ecology perspective, much of the variation in the desert bioregion relates to patterns of fuel characteristics and fire regimes. Vegetation (fuels), topography, and lightning strikes per unit area vary locally with elevation, and elevational vegetation gradients are correlated positively with latitudinal gradients and ecotones with more mesic regions in the immediate rain shadow of the Sierra Nevada, Transverse, and Peninsular ranges. Accordingly, we consider elevation to be the primary determinant of fire ecology zones in the desert bioregion. The ecological zones described below are listed in order of increasing elevation, except for the riparian zone, which transcends many of the other zones.

Low-Elevation Desert Shrubland Zone   This is the predominant ecological zone in the Sonoran Desert section and in the lower elevations of the Mojave Desert section. Major vegetation types include alkali sink vegetation and the lower elevations of creosote bush scrub (Munz and Keck 1959) and succulent scrub (Rowlands 1980). Surface fuel loads and continuity are typically low, hindering the spread of fire (Fig 16.1).

Middle-Elevation Desert Shrubland and Grassland Zone   This is the predominant ecological zone in the Mojave Desert, Col-

orado Desert, and Southeastern Great Basin sections, where it typically occurs as an elevational band above the low-elevation zone and below the high-elevation zone. It also occurs at the regional ecotone between the Mojave and Great Basin deserts. Major vegetation types include Joshua tree woodland, shadscale scrub, the upper elevations of creosote bush scrub (Munz and Keck 1959), blackbrush scrub, and desert scrub-steppe (Rowlands 1980). Surface fuel characteristics are variable, but loads and continuity can be relatively high compared with the low-elevation zone, facilitating the spread of fire (Fig. 16.2).

High-Elevation Desert Shrubland and Woodland Zone   This is the predominant ecological zone in the Mono section. It also occurs at the tops of most Mojave Desert Mountains or just below desert montane forests, and along the margins of the Sierra Nevada, Transverse, and Peninsular mountain ranges where they intergrade with yellow pine forests. Major vegetation types include sagebrush scrub, pinyon-juniper woodland, and desert chaparral (Munz and Keck 1959). Surface fuel loads and continuity are high where sagebrush scrub and chaparral dominate, facilitating the spread of fire. However, surface fuels are replaced by very high loads of crown fuels in closed pinyon-juniper woodlands, where fires only occur under extreme fire weather conditions and are typically very intense (Fig. 16.3).

Desert Montane Woodland and Forest Zone   This zone is very limited in total area, and occurs almost exclusively in the Mono and Southeastern Great Basin sections. Major vegetation types include bristlecone pine forest and alpine fellfields (Munz and Keck 1959). Surface fuels are typically sparse, separating patches of crown fuels and hindering the spread of fire (Fig. 16.4).

Desert Riparian Woodland and Oasis Zone   This zone includes a diverse set of vegetation types that do not fit into any single elevational range. Vegetation types include oases

FIGURE 16.2. The middle-elevation desert shrubland and grassland ecological zone. This photo shows a blackbrush scrubland, which typically includes blackbrush, Mojave yucca, and Joshua tree.

FIGURE 16.3. The high-elevation desert shrubland and woodland ecological zone. This photo shows a pinyon-juniper woodland.

and riparian woodlands, shrublands, grasslands, and marshes. Surface fuels loads and continuity can be very high, facilitating fire spread, although vertical continuity of ladder fuels and horizontal continuity of crown fuels are often insufficient to carry crown fires (Fig. 16.5).

Overview of Historic Fire Occurrence

The primary factor controlling fire occurrence in the desert bioregion is fuel condition, specifically fuel continuity and fuel type. Where fuel continuity is low, as in most of the low-elevation and desert montane ecological zones, fires will not typically spread beyond ignition points. Even where continuity is relatively high, fuelbeds may be comprised primarily of fuel types that do not readily burn except under the most extreme fire weather conditions. The coarse, woody fuels of pinyon-juniper woodlands in the high-elevation ecological zone are a good example. Thus, variations in fuel condition are central to any attempts to evaluate past or current patterns of fire occurrence.

FIGURE 16.4. The desert montane woodland and forest ecological zone. This photo shows a bristlecone pine forest.

FIGURE 16.5. The desert riparian woodland and oasis ecological zone. This photo shows a riparian shrubland and woodland.

Prehistoric Period

Prehistoric fire regimes have not been quantitatively described for most of the desert regions of southwestern North America, largely because the usual tools for reconstructing fire histories, such as analyzing trees for fire scars or coring sediments in swamps or lakes for charcoal deposits, cannot be used where the requisite trees or lakes are not present. As a result, past fire regimes must be inferred indirectly from prehistoric vegetation studies or current observations and data.

Fossil packrat midden data suggest that most of the desert bioregion has been under arid to semi-arid conditions since the beginning of the Holocene (~10,000 years B.P.), with pinyon and juniper woodlands on upper slopes and at higher elevations, and low scrub and perennial grasslands in valleys and at lower elevations (Van Devender and Spaulding 1979, Koehler et al. 2005). Most interior basins in the desert bioregion did not support permanent lakes except those receiving runoff from the Sierra Nevada, Transverse, or Peninsular ranges. Thus, the major vegetation types that presently occur in the desert bioregion and the ecological zones described in this chapter were likely present in the desert bioregion throughout the Holocene, expanding and contracting relative to each other as they shifted up and down elevational gradients with periods of low and high rainfall.

The low-elevation ecological zone probably contained low and discontinuous fuels, hindering fire spread and resulting in low-intensity, patchy burns and long fire-return intervals. Consecutive years of high rainfall would have increased fine fuel loads and continuity, and may have allowed fire to spread periodically in this ecological zone, especially were rainfall was highest along the western margins of the Mojave and Colorado deserts close to the Transverse and Peninsular mountain ranges.

The middle-elevation, high-elevation, and riparian zones likely had sufficient perennial plant cover to periodically carry fire in the prehistoric past without significant amounts of fine fuels. Because these fires would have been carried by relatively high cover of perennial shrubs and grasses, they were likely moderate-severity, stand-replacing fires, as they typically are today.

Fuels in the desert montane zone were probably discontinuous, resulting in small, patchy, and very infrequent surface or passive crown fires. Evidence of this is the presence of the long-lived (older than 3,000 years), but fire-sensitive, western bristlecone pines *(Pinus longaeva)*.

It seems highly probable that fuel conditions and fire regimes have remained relatively constant across the desert bioregion during the Holocene, although their spatial distributions likely varied as the ecotones between vegetation formations shifted with alternating periods of low and high rainfall. Current climate conditions have generally persisted since ~1,440 years B.P. in the Mojave Desert (Koehler et al. 2005), supporting the supposition that relative distributions of fuel conditions and ecological zones have remained relatively constant during at least the latter part of the Holocene. It is also likely that fuel conditions and fire regimes have changed significantly since the late 1880s due to land-use activities and invasions by non-native annual grasses. We discuss these changes in more detail below.

Historic Period

Livestock grazing can reduce perennial plant cover, especially cover of perennial grasses (Brooks et al. in press), which may have led to reduced flammability to native fuels since grazing began in the desert bioregion during the late 1880s. However, at the same time that fuels were reduced due to grazing, ignitions probably increased as fire came into use by livestock operators to convert shrublands into grasslands and increase forage production, especially in the Mono and middle to high elevations of the Southeastern Great Basin and Mojave Desert sections. For example, rangelands in southern Nevada, southwestern Utah, and northwestern Arizona were extensively burned during the early 1900s to reduce shrub cover and promote the growth of perennial grasses (Brooks et al. 2003). Similar rangeland burns may have also been implemented in the southern and eastern Mojave Desert and the far western Colorado Desert, where summer rainfall occurs in sufficient amounts to support large stands of perennial grasses. However, most of the southern hot desert regions are too dry to support sufficient native fuels to carry

fire, so even if ranchers tried to burn, they may have often been unsuccessful.

Analyses of historic aerial photos from 1942, 1953, 1954, 1968, 1971 to 1974, 1998, and 1999 at Joshua Tree National Park indicate that there were periodic fires prior to 1942 (Minnich 2003), during a 30-year period of relatively high rainfall that lasted until 1946 (Hereford et al. in press). However, most fires were less than 121 ha (300 ac) with the largest encompassing 607 ha (1,500 ac), and all occurred in the middle- and high-elevation ecological zones (Minnich 2003). The spatial clustering of burns in some areas suggests that deliberate burning by humans was practiced, possibly to improve range production for livestock. During the mid-century drought, only three small fires occurred, all during the 1960s and in Joshua tree woodlands of the middle-elevation ecological zone. Soon after the drought ended in 1977, fires again became more prevalent, but their size and numbers eclipsed what was observed prior to the mid-century drought. The first was a 2,428-ha (6,000-ac) fire in 1978, and the most recent large fire was a 6,070-ha (15,000-ac) complex of fires that burned over a period of five days in 1999, in both the middle- and the high-elevation ecological zones. These recent fires at Joshua Tree National Park were fueled largely by old stands of native trees, shrubs, and perennial grasses, but fire spread was additionally facilitated by stands of the non-native annual grasses red brome *(Bromus madritensis* ssp. *rubens)* and cheat grass *(Bromus tectorum)*, especially where fire passed through previously burned areas where cover of these grasses was especially high (National Park Service, DI-1202 fire reports).

Current Period

Records from land management agencies provide information on recent fires that can be used to reconstruct current fire regimes across the desert bioregion. We extracted data from fire occurrence records (DI-1202 fire reports) archived by the United States Department of the Interior and Department of Agriculture between 1980 and 2001 to create basic summaries for each of the five ecological sections in the California desert (Map 16.2, Table 16.2). This 21-year database is too short to capture the full range of potential burning conditions, because it was coincident with a period of above-average rainfall from 1977 to 1998 (Hereford et al. in press). However, it represents the best data available to approximate fire regimes since 1980 in the desert bioregion of California.

The primary message from these fire records is that the proportion of total area that burned per year from 1980 to 2001 is very small, peaking in the Mono section at 0.3%/yr (292 ha/1,000 km^2/yr, Table 16.2), resulting in a fire cycle of 342 years in that ecological section. The annual fire frequency and area burned were highest in the Mono section, and lowest in the Southeastern Great Basin section (Map 16.2, Table 16.2), peaking from May through September. Among the hot desert regions, fire frequency was highest in the Mojave and Colorado deserts, and the annual area burned

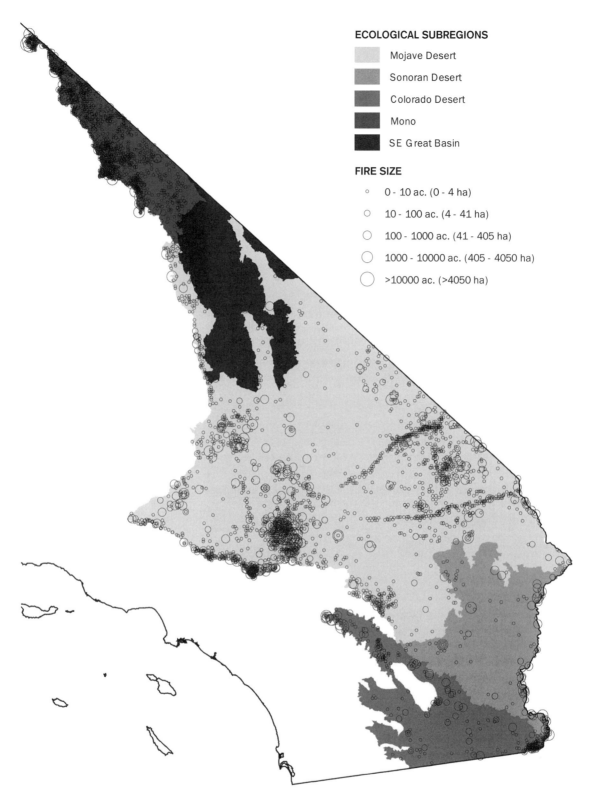

MAP 16.2. Recent fire occurrences (1980–2001) in the five ecological sections of the Southeastern Deserts bioregion.

TABLE 16.2
Recent fire history (1980–2001) in the ecological sections of the Southeastern Deserts bioregion

Ecological Section[a]	Total Fires	Total Area Burned (ha)	Fire Frequency (Fires/1000 km²/yr)	Annual Area Burned (ha/1000 km²/yr)	Fire Size (ha/Fire)	Human: Lightning Fires	Percentage of Lightning Strikes That Resulted in Fires[b]
Mojave Desert	3,158	69,110	2.1	47	22	3.6	0.6
Sonoran Desert	175	13,217	0.6	47	76	7.5	0.2
Colorado Desert	525	21,340	2.2	88	41	44.2	1.8
Mono	1,630	49,292	9.6	292	30	0.5	2.0
SE Great Basin	90	5,460	0.4	23	61	1.0	0.1
TOTAL	5,578	158,419	2.3	66	28	2.0	

[a] Miles and Goudy (1997).

[b] Lightning frequency (van Wagtendonk and Cayan, 2007) per lightning fires.

NOTE: From fire records (DI-1202 reports) of the Department of the Interior and Department of Agriculture, screened for errors as recommended by Brown et al. (2002).

was highest in the Colorado Desert. The percentage of lightning strikes that resulted in fire was highest in the Mono and Colorado Desert sections, probably due to high fuel continuity caused by the prevalence of sagebrush steppe in the Mono section, and red brome-dominated creosote bush scrub in the western Colorado section. The Colorado Desert section had the highest ratio of human-caused to lightning-caused fires. This is probably due to both the high human population density and agricultural activity in the Coachella and Imperial valleys, and the low frequency of lightning in the Colorado Desert (Table 16.1). The northern cold desert regions had the lowest frequency of fires caused by humans, probably due to its remoteness from major human population centers.

In a separate analysis of agency fire data from 1980 to 1995 in the Mojave, Colorado, and Sonoran desert sections, fires were found to be clustered in regional hotspots (Brooks and Esque 2002), where they were much more frequent and burned more proportional area than the desert-wide averages indicated in Table 16.2. Annual fire frequency increased significantly from 1980 through 1995 ($r^2 = 0.27$) (Brooks and Esque, 2002), but the increase was only significant in the low- and middle-elevation zones below 1,280 m (4,200 ft) ($r^2 = 0.32$, 1980 to 2001) (M. Brooks unpublished data). A few areas burned three separate times during this 15-year interval. The increase in fire frequency was due to increased number of fires caused by humans, since the number of lightning-caused fires remained constant (Brooks and Esque 2002). Another major contributor to increased fire frequency was a general increase in fine fuel loads caused by heightened dominance of non-native annual grasses beginning in the late 1970s (e.g., Hunter 1991) and continuing on through the 1990s (M. Brooks personal observation), probably the result of above-average rainfall from 1976 to 1998 (Hereford et al. in press). Although most fires were small and started along roadsides, most of the large fires occurred in remote areas far from major roads, and were typically started by lightning (Brooks and Esque 2002).

During the summer of 2005, approximately 400,000 ha (988,440 acres) burned in the Mojave Desert (DI-1202 fire reports). This single year of burning covered one and a half times more area than burned during the previous 25 years in the Mojave Desert (1980-2004). Eight percent of the area burned during 2005 was in California, with the remainder in Nevada, Arizona, and Utah. Details of these fires will be presented in a future publication (M. Brooks, in prep).

Major Ecological Zones

In this section we describe the basic fire ecology of the predominant plant species in each ecological zone. We also discuss patterns of post-fire succession, and interactions among plant communities, fire behavior, and fire regimes. More details on the fire ecology of a wider range of desert species can be found in other recent publications (Brown and Smith 2000, Esque and Schwalbe 2002) and on the Fire Effects Information System Web site (www.fs.fed.us/database/feis).

Low-Elevation Desert Shrubland Zone

This zone includes two primary vegetation types. Alkali sink vegetation occurs on poorly drained saline and/or alkaline playas, flats, and fans approximately –80 to 1,200 m (–63–3,937 ft) throughout all the ecological sections. Plant communities include iodine bush-alkali scrub, allscale-alkali scrub, Mojave saltbush-allscale scrub, and saltgrass meadow (Rowlands 1980). Creosote bush scrub vegetation occurs 0 to 1,200 m (0-3,937 ft) on well-drained flats, fans, and upland slopes of the Mojave, Colorado, and Sonoran Desert ecological sections. However, only the lower elevations below about 900 m (2,953 ft), where perennial plant cover is relatively low, are typical of the low-elevation desert shrubland zone. Plant communities include creosote bush scrub, cheesebush (*Hymenoclea salsola*), and succulent scrub (Rowlands 1980).

TABLE 16.3
Fire responses of some dominant plant species in the Southeastern Deserts bioregion

| | Predominant Type of Fire Response[a] | | |
Lifeform	Sprouting	Individual	Species
Conifer pinyon	None	Killed	Western bristlecone pine, limber pine, pine, Utah juniper
Hardwood	Fire stimulated	Top-killed	Scrub live oak, saltcedar,[b] honey mesquite, willows
	Fire stimulated	Underburned	Fremont cottonwood
Shrub	Fire stimulated	Top-killed	Catclaw acacia, smoke tree, desert willow, fourwing saltbush, white bursage, rubber rabbitbrush, spiny hopsage, antelope bitterbrush
	None	Killed	Shadscale, blackbrush, creosote bush, brittlebrush, snakeweed, cliffrose
Stem and Leaf Succulents	None	Killed	Cacti
	Fire stimulated	Top-killed	Mojave yucca, banana yucca, Joshua tree[c]
Herb	Fire stimulated	Top-killed	Bulbs
	None	Killed	Annual forbs
Grass	Fire stimulated	Top-killed	Perennial grasses (e.g., galleta grass, Indian ricegrass, desert needlegrass, fountaingrass[b])
	None	Killed	Annual grasses (e.g. red brome[b] Mediterranean grass[b], cheat grass[b], sixweeks fescue)

[a] Varies depending on fire intensity and percentage of plants consumed.

[b] Non-native species.

[c] After initially resprouting, Joshua trees often die within 5 years if most or all of their foliage was scorched or consumed.

FIRE RESPONSES OF IMPORTANT SPECIES

Most shrubs in the low-elevation zone do not survive after being completely consumed by fire (Humphrey 1974, Wright and Bailey 1982) (Table 16.3), but because many fires in this zone are patchy and of low intensity, plants frequently survive in unburned islands. Low fire temperatures in interspaces, and high temperatures beneath woody shrubs, likely result in relatively higher seedbank mortality for annual plants that frequent beneath-shrub than interspace microhabitats (Brooks 2002). A few perennial species that evolved to resprout after floods often resprout after burning, such as desert-willow (Chilopsis linearis), catclaw acacia (Acacia greggi),

smoke tree (Psorothammus spinosus), and white bursage, (Ambrosia dumosa) (Table 16.3). Cheesebush can have almost 100% survival rates even after being totally consumed by fire (Table 16.4). Cacti are usually only scorched during fires, as flames propagate through their spines, but the stems do not ignite due to their high moisture content. Individuals with high levels of scorching typically die from uncontrolled desiccation that occurs post-fire. Cactus regeneration can occur from resprouting of partially scorched plants, or rooting of fallen unburned stem fragments, and less frequently from establishment of new seedlings.

The most frequently encountered and dominant shrub in this zone, creosote bush (Larrea tridentata), can have 25% to

TABLE 16.4
Survival rates of perennial shrubs after fires in August 1995 at three low-elevation shrubland sites

Species[a]	Sample Size	Percentage Survival[b]			Notes on Fire Behavior[c]
		Year 1	Year 4	Year 8	
Central Mojave Site					Fire did not spread from ignition
White bursage					points. Therefore, the litter beneath
Unburned	n=20	100	100	85	each shrub, but not the shrub itself,
Consumed	n=20	20	20	10	was ignited. Most creosote bushes
Creosote bush					were consumed, because accumu-
Unburned	n=25	100	100	100	lated dead branches beneath them
Scorched	n=4	25	25	25	provided supplemental surface fuels
Consumed	n=21	0	0	0	that increased flame residency time
					beneath them, and ladder fuels that
					helped carry fire up into the creosote
					bush canopies.
Southern Mojave Site					Fire spread rapidly from a few igni-
Creosote bush					tion points and burned 50% of the
Unburned	n=25	100	100	100	site. Few shrubs were consumed due
Scorched	n=13	77	70	62	to low fuel loads beneath creosote
Consumed	n=12	8	8	8	bushes, and low cover of finely tex-
					tured subshrubs.
Western Mojave Site					Fire spread slowly from multiple
White bursage					ignition points and burned 50%
Unburned	n=10	100	100	90	of the site. Most shrubs were con-
Consumed	n=10	20	20	20	sumed due to high fuel loads
Cheesebush					beneath creosote bushes and the
Unburned	n=10	100	100	60	presence of many finely textured
Consumed	n=10	100	100	80	subshrubs.
Creosote bush					
Unburned	n=25	100	100	100	
Scorched	n=8	88	75	75	
Consumed	n=17	12	12	12	
Wolfberry					
Unburned	n=20	100	100	90	
Scorched	n=5	100	100	80	
Consumed	n=20	75	75	50	

[a] Dominant perennial plant species at each site. Not all were represented by both scorched and consumed plants. White bursage = *Ambrosia dumosa*, creosote bush = *Larrea tridentata*, cheesebush = *Hymenoclea salsola*, wolfberry = *Lycium andersonii*.

[b] Shrub survival was defined as possessing live leaf tissue, either on unburned or resprouted stems, when sampled during May of 1996, 1999, and 2003.

[c] Additional descriptions of the fires and study sites are reported in Brooks 1999.

NOTE: Data from M. Brooks, unpublished. All three fires were 2.25 ha (5.6 acre) in size. "Unburned" is defined as 0% of living biomass burned, "scorched" as 1 to 10%, and "consumed" as 11% to 100%.

80% survival rates eight years post-fire when it is only scorched (1% to 10% biomass loss), and 0% to 12% survival rates by year eight when it is consumed by fire (11% to 100% biomass loss) (Table 16.4). Individuals with slight to moderate scorching displayed 30% to 40% survival in the Sonoran Desert in Arizona (Dalton 1962), and in general, fire intensity and duration is inversely correlated with resprouting potential (White 1968).

The wide range in survival rates among creosote bushes appears to be associated with their variable physiognomy and variable fuel loads beneath their canopies and across the landscape, which translate into variable fire intensity and vertical continuity from surface to canopy fuels. Individuals with canopies in the shape of inverted cones tend to occur in water-limited environments (De Soyza et al. 1997), resulting in relatively low fuel loads beneath their canopies and across the

TABLE 16.5
Fire regime classification for desert shrubland zones

Vegetation type	Low-elevation shrubland	Middle-elevation shrubland and grassland	High-elevation shrubland and woodland
Temporal			
Seasonality	Spring–summer–fall	Spring–summer–fall	Summer–early fall
Fire-return interval	Truncated long	Long	Long
Spatial			
Size	Small	Moderate–large	Moderate–large
Complexity	High	Multiple	Low–moderate
Magnitude			
Intensity	Low	Moderate	Moderate–high
Severity	Moderate	Moderate–high	High
Fire type	Surface	Passive crown–active crown	Active crown

landscape and a relatively low probability of being completely consumed by fire. In contrast, individuals with hemispherical canopies that extend to the ground tend to occur in less water-limited environments (De Soyza et al. 1997), resulting in higher fuel loads beneath their canopies and across the landscape and a higher probability of being completely consumed by fire. Resprouting in creosote bushes also probably varies throughout the extensive range of this species, especially at ecotones with vegetation types that support more frequent burning. For example, moderate (O'Leary and Minnich 1981, Brown 1984) to high (Brown 1984) rates of post-fire resprouting were reported at the ecotone of the western Colorado Desert with shrubland vegetation in the Peninsular Ranges.

FIRE REGIME–PLANT COMMUNITY INTERACTIONS

This is the zone that Humphrey (1974) was primarily referring to when he stated that in desert shrublands "... fires are a rarity, and the few fires that do occur cause little apparent damage to the various aspects of the ecosystem..." (337). This is largely because fuels are discontinuous and characterized by a sparse 8% to 15% cover of woody shrubs, and the large interspaces between shrubs are mostly devoid of vegetation, inhibiting fire spread (Fig. 16.1). A recent summary of fire regimes of the United States (Schmidt et al. 2002) assumed that Küchler's "barren vegetation type" (Küchler 1964), which covers most of the low-elevation desert shrubland zone, is mostly devoid of vegetation and therefore fireproof. However, 9% of fires and 7% of the total area burned between 1980 and 2001 occurred within the barren vegetation type in the California desert bioregion. Thus, fires do occur in the low-elevation desert shrubland zone, although not as frequently as, and over less area than, in the other zones of the desert bioregion.

Fire behavior and fire regimes in this zone are affected primarily by the ephemeral production of fine fuels from annual plants. Years of high winter and spring rainfall can increase continuity of fine fuels by stimulating the growth of annual plants that fill interspaces and allow fire to spread (Brown and Minnich 1986, Rogers and Vint 1987, Schmid and Rogers 1988, Brooks 1999). Native annuals that produce some of the most persistent fuelbeds include the annual grasses sixweeks fescue (*Vulpia octoflora*) and small fescue (*Vulpia microstachys*), and the large forbs fiddleneck (*Amsinkia tessellata*), tansy mustard (*Descurainia pinnata*), and lacy phacelia (*Phacelia tanacetifolia*), compared with a whole suite of smaller native forbs (119 species, Brooks 1999). Infrequently, successive years of high rainfall may have allowed these native annuals to build up fine fuel loads sufficient to carry fire across the interspaces between larger perennial plants. Low-elevation fires carried by high loads of native annuals typically only burn dead annual plants and finely textured sub-shrubs, leaving many of the larger woody shrubs such as creosote bush unburned. Thus, the historic fire regime was likely characterized by relatively small, patchy, low-severity surface fires, and a truncated long fire-return interval (Table 16.5).

The invasion of non-native annual grasses into the desert bioregion introduced new fuel conditions. Species such as red brome and Mediterranean grass (*Schismus arabicus* and *Schismus barbatus*) provide more persistent and less patchy fine fuelbeds than do native annual plants, breaking down more slowly and persisting longer into the summer and subsequent years (Brooks 1999). These new fuel conditions have the potential to increase the size, decrease the complexity, and shorten the time interval between desert fires, although fire intensity will likely decrease because fine herbaceous non-native fuels are replacing coarse woody native fuels. These fire regime changes have occurred over a small fraction of the low-elevation ecological zone, and fire regimes over the vast majority of this zone are still within the historic range of variation.

Mediterranean grass is the most widespread and abundant non-native annual grass in the low-elevation shrubland zone, although red brome may predominate under large shrubs or in the less arid parts of this ecological zone. Mediterranean grass has fueled fires as large as 41 ha (100 ac) (Bureau of Land Management DI-1202 records), and interspace fuel loads of as little as 112 kg/ha (100 lb/ac) are sufficient to carry fire (Brooks 1999). Because these fires burn with low intensity, soil heating is negligible and most woody shrubs are left unburned.

The recent spread of Sahara mustard (*Brassica tournefortii*) throughout the low-elevation shrublands has caused concern that this invasive mustard may introduce a significant new fuel type to the desert bioregion. During years of high rainfall this invasive annual can exceed 1 m (3.3 ft) in height with a rosette of basal leaves 1 m (3.3 ft) across, and even moderately sized plants can produce as many as 16,000 seeds (M. Brooks unpublished data). Plants can remain rooted and upright through the summer fire season, and when they finally do break off they blow like a tumbleweed and lodge in shrubs or fencerows, accumulating piles of fuels similar to Russian thistle (*Salsola tragus*). The combination of Sahara mustard with red brome in the understory helped fuel a 20.2-ha (50-ac) fire in creosote bush scrub in northwest Arizona (M. Brooks, personal observation). During the five years after this fire, Sahara mustard and red brome have come to dominate this site while the native creosote bush has yet to show signs of recovery.

Non-native annual plants that evolved in other desert regions will likely be most successful at persisting in the California desert bioregion. For example, Mediterranean grass and Sahara mustard, respectively, evolved in the arid Middle East and Northern Africa, and they have also successfully established in the desert bioregion (Brooks 2000, Minnich and Sanders 2000). At three sites in the western Colorado Desert, these non-native species successfully persisted through two major droughts, which occurred during the end of the 1980s and 1990s (R. Minnich unpublished data). Their cover values in 1983, 1988, and 1990 through 2001 were comparable or higher than those of the non-native forb red-stemmed filaree (*Erodium cicutarium*), which is a poorer fuel source for fires (Brooks 1999), and compared with all native forbs combined.

Middle-Elevation Desert Shrubland and Grassland Zone

This zone includes five primary vegetation types. The upper elevations of creosote bush scrub generally occur at 900 to 1,200 m (2,953–3,937 ft) and contain higher perennial plant cover than do the lower elevations of this vegetation type. Joshua tree woodland occurs on well-drained loamy, sandy, or fine gravelly soils of mesas and gentle slopes from 760 to 1,300 m (2,493–4,265 ft) in the Mojave Desert and Southeastern Great Basin sections. Shadscale scrub occurs on heavy, rocky, often calcareous soils with underlying hardpan from 1,000 to 1,800 m (3,281–5,906 ft) in the Mono, Southeastern Great Basin, and Mojave Desert sections. Blackbrush (*Coleogyne ramo-*

sissima) occurs on well-drained, sandy to gravelly, often calcareous soils from 1,000 to 2,000 m (3,281–6,562 ft) in the southern Mono, Southeastern Great Basin, and Mojave Desert sections. Desert scrub-steppe vegetation types are intermixed with a wide range of other plant communities from the low- to high-elevation ecological zones, but they are most common in the middle-elevation zone. Indian ricegrass scrub-steppe and desert needlegrass scrub-steppe typically occur where winter rainfall predominates within creosote bush scrub (Rowlands 1980). Big galleta scrub-steppe typically occurs in creosote bush scrub below 1,000 m (3,281 ft), and in Joshua tree woodland and blackbrush scrub above 1,000 m (3,281 ft).

FIRE RESPONSES OF IMPORTANT SPECIES

Higher fuel loads and more continuous fuelbeds in the middle-elevation ecological zone result in higher-intensity fires and higher frequency of top-killing in plants than in the low-elevation zone. However, more species in this zone are likely to resprout after being top-killed. Perennial grasses such as desert needlegrass (*Achnatherum speciosum*), galleta grass (*Pleuraphis jamesii*), and Indian ricegrass (*Achnatherum hymenoides*) readily resprout after burning (Table 16.3). Spiny menodora (*Menodora spinescens*) and Mormon tea (*Ehedra* spp.) often survive fire because their foliage does not readily burn. In contrast, some shrub species such as blackbrush and winterfat (*Kraschennikovia lantata*) rarely survive burning.

Blackbrush is one of the more flammable native shrubs in the desert bioregion, due to its high proportion of fine fuels and optimal packing ratio. In the rare case that only a portion of a shrub is consumed, it may survive and resprout from the root crown. This resprouting was observed within the first few post-fire years (Bates 1984), and these resprouts were still evident 20 years later (M. Brooks personal observation) at a site in the Mono section near Bishop, California. It seems probable that the ability of blackbrush to resprout after burning varies across its wide geographic range, which extends from the Colorado Plateau and southern Great Basin on through the Mojave Desert.

It is commonly thought that blackbrush stands take centuries to recover (Bowns 1973, Webb et al. 1988). However, analyses of historic photographs from Joshua Tree National Park and southern Nevada indicate that blackbrush stands can recover within 50 to 75 years (Minnich 2003, M. Brooks unpublished data), although other historic photographs from other locations do not indicate recovery within this time interval (M. Brooks, unpublished data).

Yucca species such as Joshua tree (*Yucca brevifolia*), Mojave yucca (*Yucca schidigera*), banana yucca (*Yucca baccata*), and Our Lord's candle (*Yucca whipplei*) are typically scorched as flames propagate through the shag of dead leaves that line their trunks. The relatively small size and more optimal packing ratio of dead Joshua tree leaves compared with dead Mojave or banana yucca leaves increase the frequency at which they are completely burned. This may partly explain why Joshua trees are more frequently killed by fire. All four yucca species readily resprout after fire, but Joshua tree resprouts are often eaten by herbivores or otherwise die soon after burning. Post-fire recruitment of new Joshua trees is infrequent, and likely occurs during years of high rainfall. No seedlings or saplings were observed in burns less than 10 years old, and only fewer than 10 individuals/ha were present on burns more than 40 years old in Joshua Tree National Park (Minnich 2003). Joshua tree populations along the extreme western edge of the desert bioregion often resprout and survive more readily after fire than those further east (M. Brooks personal observation). A cycle of relatively frequent fire and resprouting can result in short, dense clusters of Joshua tree clones, such as those found near Walker Pass, in the western end of the Antelope Valley, and in pinyon-juniper woodlands at ecotones with the Transverse Ranges. High resprouting rates of Joshua trees in these areas may have evolved in local ecotypes that became adapted to relatively high fire frequencies at the ecotone between the desert bioregion and more mesic ecosystems to the west.

FIRE REGIME–PLANT COMMUNITY INTERACTIONS

Some of the most continuous native upland fuels in the desert bioregion occur at the upper elevations of this zone, especially in areas dominated by blackbrush (Fig. 16.2). Invasive annual grasses have contributed to increased fire frequencies since the 1970s (Brooks and Esque, 2002), although the native perennial vegetation in this zone can at times be sufficient alone to carry fire during extreme fire weather conditions (Humphrey 1974). Between 1980 and 2001, 49% of all fires and 45% of total area burned occurred in Küchler's desert shrubland vegetation type, which is roughly analogous to the middle-elevation ecological zone.

At the lower elevations within this zone, where creosote bush is co-dominant with a wide range of other shrubs and perennial grasses, fire spread is largely dependent on high production of fine fuels filling interspaces during years of high rainfall (Brown and Minnich 1986, Rogers and Vint 1987, Schmid and Rogers 1988, Brooks 1999). At higher elevations within this zone, where blackbrush is often the primary dominant plant, fire spread is not so dependent on the infilling of shrub interspaces during years of high rainfall and fire occurrence does not vary as much interannually compared with lower elevations (M. Brooks unpublished data). Thus, the historic fire regime was likely characterized by relatively moderate- to large-sized, patchy to complete, moderate-severity, surface-to-crown fires, and a long fire return interval (Table 16.5).

The post-fire response of plant communities in blackbrush scrub is illustrative of the general responses of other desert scrub communities in the middle- and high-elevation ecological zones. Blackbrush fires remove cover of woody shrubs, which is soon replaced by equivalent cover of herbaceous perennials and annual plants (Brooks and Matchett 2003). Non-native species such as red brome, cheat grass, and red-stemmed filaree typically increase in cover after fire, but only if rainfall is sufficient to support their growth and reproduc-

tion. Recovery of blackbrush stands may occur within 50 years (Minnich 2003, M. Brooks unpublished data), but perhaps more typically takes more than 100 years (Webb et. 1988, Bowns 1973).

Red brome is the dominant invasive grass at middle elevations in the California desert bioregion. This invasive grass produces higher fuel loads and fuel depths than Mediterranean grass does, and accordingly produces longer flame lengths that carry fire into the crowns of large woody shrubs more readily, producing more-intense fires (Brooks 1999). Cover of red brome can become greater and more continuous after fire, promoting recurrent fire (Sidebar 16.1). This positive-invasive plant/fire regime cycle (*sensu* Brooks et al. 2004) has shifted fire regimes outside of their historic range of variation in some regional hotspots (Brooks and Esque 2002), although current fire regimes in most of the middle-elevation zone are probably similar to historic conditions.

The recent invasion of the non-native annual grass African needlegrass (*Achnatherum capense*) into the ecotone between the Colorado Desert and the Peninsular Ranges in the 1990s has helped fuel at least one 243-ha (600-ac) fire (R. Minnich personal observation). There are early indications that this species can survive relatively dry years, suggesting that it may spread and become another source of fine fuels that may further alter fire regimes in the desert bioregion.

High-Elevation Desert Shrubland and Woodland Zone

This zone includes three primary vegetation types. Sagebrush scrub occurs at 1,100 to 2,800 m (3,600–9,186), although it can extend to 3,800 m (12,467 ft) in the White Mountains. Pinyon-juniper woodland occurs at 1,300 to 2,400 m (4,265–7,874 ft), and can reach 2,700 m (8,858 ft) in the White Mountains. Both vegetation types occur in the Mono, Southeastern Great Basin, and Mojave sections. Among the pinyon-juniper vegetation types, the Utah juniper (*Juniperus osteosperma*)–singleleaf pinyon (*Pinus monophylla*) association is the most widespread, occurring in the Mono, Southeastern Great Basin, and eastern Mojave Desert ecological sections of California (Minnich and Everett 2001). The California juniper (*Juniperus californica*)–singleleaf pinyon association occurs along the desert slopes of the Transverse Ranges at the edge of the Mojave Desert section, with California juniper dominating below 1,700 m and singleleaf pinyon dominating above. Desert chaparral is the least prevalent of the major vegetation types in this ecological zone. It occurs on the middle slopes of the Transverse Ranges adjacent to the Mojave Desert, and the Peninsular Ranges adjacent to the Colorado Desert, below the mixed conifer forests, and in the same general elevation range as sagebrush scrub and pinyon-juniper woodland.

FIRE RESPONSES OF IMPORTANT SPECIES

Relatively high fuel loads result in high fire intensity, but plant mortality rates can vary widely among species. Wyoming sage-

Non-native annual grasses in the genera *Bromus*, *Avena*, and others have become dominant components of many grasslands, shrublands, woodlands, and forests in western North America during the twentieth century. These invasions have negatively affected native plant species by directly competing with them for limited soil nutrients and water, and by altering ecosystem properties such as fuel characteristics and fire regimes. The positive feedback between non-native grass dominance and increased fire frequency, or the "grass/fire cycle" (D'Antonio and Vitousek 1992), is the most clearly understood and well-documented example of the more general "invasive plant/fire regime cycle" (Brooks et al. 2004).

Fire frequencies increased beyond their historical range and variation can have dramatic and far-reaching ecological effects. For example, invasion of the non-native cheat grass has altered fuelbed characteristics and shortened fire return intervals from 30 to 100 years to 5 years in areas of the Great Basin (Whisenant 1990). This new fire regime promotes the dominance of cheat grass over native species, resulting in large-scale conversions of high-diversity, native sagebrush steppe to low-diversity, non-native annual grassland. This vegetation change has negatively affected animals that require sagebrush steppe for forage and cover such as the sage grouse *(Centrocercus urophasianus)* (Sidebar 11.2, this volume), and prey species such as black-tailed jackrabbits *(Lepus* spp.*)* and the Paiute ground squirrel *(Spermophilus mollis)*, which are important for golden eagles *(Aquila chrysaetus)* and prairie falcons *(Falco mexicanus)* (Knick and Rotenbery 1995, Knick et al. 2003). Although similar large-scale higher-order effects have not been documented in the Mojave, Colorado, or Sonoran deserts, non-native grass/fire cycles have degraded habitat for the desert tortoise *(Gopherus agassizii)* in localized hotspots within these desert regions (Brooks and Esque 2002; Sidebar 16.3, this volume).

Invasive plant/fire regime cycles represent ecosystem shifts to alternative stable states that will likely persist unless fuels, climate, or ignition patterns significantly change (Brooks et al. 2004). For example, non-native annual grasses such as cheat grass and medusahead *(Taeniatherum caput-medusae)* persist in cold desert regions like the Great Basin because rainfall is typically sufficient to support reproduction during any given year. Although the fuelbeds they create may only significantly affect fire behavior following years of high rainfall, their populations will likely persist even during years of low rainfall. As a result, non-native grasses and the altered fire regimes they cause are now relatively permanent features in many parts of the cold desert region.

In contrast, the hot desert regions of the Mojave, Colorado, and Sonoran deserts receive less annual rainfall than the cold desert regions, increasing the chances of population crashes of non-native annual grasses such as cheat grass and red brome. Rainfall events as small as 5 mm (2 in) can stimulate their germination, and when there is little subsequent rainfall, the plants often die before reproducing (M. Brooks and R. Minnich personal observations), potentially depleting the soil seedbank. This is probably why red brome became locally extinct at two low-elevation sites after the late 1980s drought and at one low-elevation site after the late 1990s drought (R. Minnich unpublished data). However, extirpation of red brome did not occur at many higher-elevation sites following these same drought periods (M. Brooks personal observation). Broad-scale responses by non-native grasses to droughts indicate that they are typically not regionally extirpated and can recover to ecologically significant numbers relatively quickly in hot desert regions. For example, after the end of the approximately 30-year mid-century drought (Hereford et al. in press) red brome density and biomass jumped 700% and 150%, respectively, between the last year of the drought (1975) and the first year of higher rainfall (1976), and by 1988 the increase above 1975 levels reached 15,646% for density and 1,596% for biomass at a Mojave Desert/Great Basin ecotone in southern Nevada (Hunter 1991). During this time interval, density and biomass of native annuals decreased (Hunter 1991), whereas the frequency and size of fires across the Mojave Desert steadily increased (Brooks and Esque 2002). In addition, the shorter 1987–1991 drought was followed in 1993 by one of the biggest fire years in the 1980–2001 agency fire record for the hot desert regions, and the spread of many of these fires was facilitated by substantial fine fuebeds of red brome and cheat grass.

Thus, non-native annual grasses will not likely ever become extirpated from the hot desert regions under the current climate regime, although their landscape dominance and effects on fire frequency and behavior will undoubtedly continue to be highly episodic in response to rainfall. Non-native grass/fire cycles have already become established in some localized hotspots within the hot desert region (Brooks and Esque 2002). The extent of area affected by these vegetation and fire regime type-conversions may expand during periods of high rainfall in the future, although most of this expansion will probably be confined to the middle-elevation desert shrubland and grassland ecological zone. Below the middle-elevation zone, extreme drought conditions will cause more frequent population crashes of red brome and cheat grass and thus limit their influence on fire regimes, and above the middle-elevation zone, native woody plants and perennial grasses are the primary factors affecting fire regimes.

brush (*Artemisia tridentata,* ssp. *Wyomingenesis*) is typically killed by fire, but it often re-establishes readily from wind-dispersed seeds. Cliffrose (*Purshia mexicana* var. *stansburyana*) is typically killed by fire, whereas its close relative, antelope bitterbrush (*Purshia tridentata*), exhibits highly variable responses to fire, sometimes resprouting (Table 16.3). Interior chaparral species, such as Muller's oak (*Quercus cornelius-mulleri*), scrub live oak (*Quercus turbinella*), birch-leaf mountain-mahogany (*Cercocarpus betuloides* var. *betuloides*), bigberry manzanita (*Arctostaphylos glauca*), Eastwood's manzanita (*Arctostaphylos glandulosa*), and beargrass (*Nolina* spp.), either resprout or reseed soon after fire, but lower rainfall and sparser vegetation cover result in less frequent fire and slower recovery rates than is typical of coastal chaparral.

Singleleaf pinyon pine, Colorado pinyon pine (*Pinus edulis*), Utah juniper, and California juniper are typically killed by fire, but these woodlands can re-establish after 100 or more years of fire exclusion. Juniper typically re-establishes from seed sooner than pinyon pine. Initial establishment of singleleaf pinyon pine appears to be delayed 20 to 30 years by sun scald and/or freeze-thaw soil heaving until the establishment of the shrub layer and young juniper trees, which act as nurse plants (Wangler and Minnich 1996). The first pinyon recruits establish within the canopies of nurse plants, often near root axes. The establishment of a pinyon pine canopy after about 75 years eventually reduces freeze-thaw processes, setting off a chain reaction of spatially random recruitment throughout old burns. Pinyons develop complete canopy closure after 100 to 150

years, which is accompanied by a decline in the surface vegetation, due apparently to shrub senescence and shade stress.

FIRE REGIME–PLANT COMMUNITY INTERACTIONS

Fuel continuity is similar to that of the middle-elevation zone, but the fuels are generally more woody and difficult to ignite. In addition to high plant cover, the prevalence of steep slopes in this ecological zone facilitates the spread of fire. Due to the high biomass of woody fuels created by juniper and pinyon pine, and to a lesser extent, sagebrush, bitterbrush, cliffrose, and scrub live oak, the fires that do start are among the most intense encountered in the desert bioregion. Between 1980 and 2001, 33% of fires and 45% of the total area burned occurred in Küchler's sagebrush, juniper-pinyon, and chaparral vegetation types that are characteristic of the high-elevation ecological zone.

Fire spread can occur most any year in sagebrush steppe, although it is more likely when fine fuel loads (especially cheat grass and red brome) are high following years of high rainfall, or during periods of high winds and low relative humidity. Fires are patchy to complete, moderate-severity passive crown-to-crown fires, depending on the continuity of the woody shrub fuels. Fire spread in pinyon-juniper woodlands is most probable when live fuel moisture and relative humidity are low and winds are high. When fires did historically occur, they were mostly large, intense crown fires, burning through woodland crown fuels. At the interface between sagebrush steppe and pinyon-juniper woodland, a surface-to-passive-crown fire regime is the norm, as fire spreads through woody and herbaceous surface fuels and occasionally torches woodland fuels, especially younger trees. The historic fire regime was likely characterized by relatively large, patchy to complete, moderate-severity surface-to-crown fires, and a long fire return interval (Table 16.5).

Sagebrush stands generally require 30 to 100 years to recover following fire (Whisenant 1990). Where cheat grass has dramatically shortened fire-return intervals, especially in the lower-elevation Wyoming big sagebrush communities, sagebrush steppe has been converted to non-native annual grassland (Sidebar 16.1). In the higher-elevation mountain sagebrush communities, this type conversion is much less common, because the native shrubs and perennial grasses recover much more rapidly after fire.

Fire suppression coupled with removal of fine fuels by live-stock grazing has allowed pinyon-juniper woodlands to encroach on sagebrush steppe across much of the western United States (Miller and Tausch 2001), including the Mono section of the desert bioregion. However, it is less likely that woodland encroachment has occurred in the more arid hot desert regions, due to low primary productivity rates. Recent resampling of 1929 to 1934 California Vegetation Type Map (VTM) survey plots reveal no significant changes in wood-land densities at the western edge of the hot desert regions (Wangler and Minnich 1996). Pinyon-juniper woodlands adjacent to the Transverse Ranges have experienced long periods between stand-replacement fires both before and after fire suppression began (fire rotation periods, ~450 years; Wangler and Minnich 1996).

Fires in pinyon-juniper woodlands are least frequent in open stands at lower elevations and more frequent in dense forests at higher elevations, in response to changing productivity and fuel accumulation gradients with increasing elevation and rainfall. The upper-elevation ecotones between pinyon-juniper wood-lands and mixed conifer forest are typically very narrow, due to truncated gradients related to fire behavior and stem mortality (Minnich 1988). The thin bark of pinyon pine prevents their survival in the frequent surface fire regime typical of mixed conifer forests. Alternatively, post-fire surface fuels appear to lack sufficient biomass to support short-period burns, and as canopy closure occurs in pinyon and juniper woodlands, surface fuel loads and continuity are further reduced. Thus, a historic dis-continuity in fire return intervals probably existed along the ecotones between mixed conifer forests and pinyon woodlands in which more frequent understory surface fires at high eleva-tions shift to less frequent stand-replacement crown fires at lower elevations in response to differences in stand structure, fire behavior, and tree survivorship (Minnich 1988).

Desert Montane Woodland and Forest Zone

There are two primary vegetation types in this ecological zone. Bristlecone-limber pine forests occur on well-drained, shallow, dolomitic soils from 2,600 to 3,800 m (8,530–12,467 ft) in the Inyo, White, Panamint, Funeral, and Grapevine mountains. Alpine fell-fields occur above timberline, primarily in the White Mountains. Small white fir (Abies concolor) forest enclaves also occur on north-facing slopes from 1,900 to 2,400 m (6,234–7,874 ft) in the New York, Clark, and Kingston mountains of the Mojave Desert section (Rowlands 1980).

FIRE RESPONSES OF IMPORTANT SPECIES

The flagship tree species of this ecological zone—bristlecone pine and limber pine—have thin bark that makes them sus-ceptible to mortality during fires (Table 16.3). Although most individuals are struck by lightning by the time they are 1,000 years old, strikes may not result in the entire tree burning, since many old individuals have scars resulting from multi-ple lighting strikes. The presence of ancient bristlecone pine individuals is testimony to the historic infrequency of fire. As a result, most plant species in this zone are not adapted to recovery from fire, although species associated with other periodic natural events such as from colluvial erosion may be able to resprout after burning.

FIRE REGIME–PLANT COMMUNITY CNTERACTIONS

Fuels are very discontinuous, but in contrast to the low-elevation zone, ephemeral production by annuals during years of high rainfall adds very little to the fuel bed, due to shallow soils, low temperatures, and a short growing season. As a result, surface fires are extremely rare, and most fires that do occur spread through the crowns of pines only during extreme fire weather conditions, but even these fires are very small (less than 1ha [2.5 ac]). Between 1980 and 2001, less than 1% of all fires and total area burned occurred in Küch-ler's great basin pine, alpine meadows-barren, and mixed conifer vegetation types characteristic of the desert montane ecological zone.

Low productivity results in very low fuel loads and conti-nuity in desert montane forests. Except on steep, north-facing canyons, heavy fuels are widely spaced and fine fuels are low and relatively unflammable, making it difficult to carry fire in this landscape. Thus, the historic fire regime is characterized by truncated small, patchy, variable severity, passive crown fires, and a truncated long fire return interval (Table 16.6).

Desert Riparian Woodland and Oasis Zone

Riparian woodlands occur primarily along the Colorado and Mojave river corridors adjacent to low-elevation shrublands in the southern desert region. Other examples can be found in the Amargosa Gorge, Whitewater River, Andreas Canyon, and Palm Canyon. In the northern desert region, riparian woodlands occur along the Owens and Walker rivers and the many creeks along the east slope of the Sierra Nevada Moun-tains. Oasis woodlands occur in isolated stands such as the Palm Canyon, Thousand Palms, and Twentynine-palms oases in the Colorado Desert section.

TABLE 16.6

Fire regime classification for the desert montane woodland and riparian woodland/oasis zones

Vegetation type		
	Desert montane woodland	Riparian woodland/ oasis zone
Temporal		
Seasonality	Summer–early fall	Spring–summer–fall
Fire-return interval	Truncated long	Short–moderate
Spatial		
Size	Truncated small	Small–moderate
Complexity	Moderate	Low
Magnitude		
Intensity	Multiple	High
Severity	Multiple	Multiple
Fire type	Passive Crown	Passive–active crown

FIRE RESPONSES OF IMPORTANT SPECIES

Woodland dominants such as Fremont cottonwood *(Populus fremontii)*, honey mesquite *(Prosopis glandulosa* var. *torreyana)*, and willows *(Salia* spp.) typically resprout after being top-killed (Table 16.3). However, resprouting individuals and seedlings are susceptible to mortality during recurrent fires. Oasis species such as California fan palm *(Washingtonia filifera)* benefit from frequent, low-severity fire, which reduces competition for water from other plants growing at the surface, and allows new seedlings to become established.

FIRE REGIME–PLANT COMMUNITY INTERACTIONS

Fuel characteristics and fire behavior are extremely variable, due to the wide range of vegetation types that characterize the riparian zone. In general, fuels are typically continuous and fuel loads high, but fuel moisture content is also often high. Fires may not carry except under extreme fire weather conditions. Thus, the historic fire regime is characterized by small- to moderate-sized, complete, high-severity passive-to-active crown fires, and a short-to-moderate fire return interval (Table 16.6).

In riparian woodlands, the invasives tamarisk *(Tamarix* spp.) and less frequently giant reed *(Arundo donax)* create ladder fuels that allow fire to spread from surface fuels of willow, saltbush *(Atriplex* spp.), sedge *(Carex* spp.), bulrush *(Scirpus* spp.), and arrow weed *(Pluchea sericea)* into the crowns of overstory Fremont cottonwood trees, top-killing them. After an initial fire, these invasives quickly recover and surpass their pre-fire dominance, promoting increasingly more frequent and intense fires that can eventually displace many native plants (Sidebar 16.2).

In palm oases, Washington fan palms depend on surface fire to clear understory species and facilitate recruitment. However, these sites can be preempted by tamarisk as it rapidly recovers after fire. The ladder fuels tamarisk creates can also carry fire into the tops of Washington fan palms, increasing the incidence of crown fires (Sidebar 16.2)

Management Issues

Fuels Management

The deserts of southwestern North America are one of the fastest-growing regions in terms of human populations in the United States. As human populations increase, so too do the number of people living at the wildland-urban interface, which complicates fire management in many ways (Chapter 19, this volume). Increasing human populations can also potentially change fuel characteristics, through increased air pollution, which can increase deposition rates of atmospheric nitrogen, and potentially increase fine fuel loads (Brooks 2003). Burgeoning human populations can also increase the introduction rates of new plant species that could add new fuel components and fire hazards to the region (Chapter 22, this volume). Because fire spread is mostly limited by the availability of contiguous fuels, fuel management can be a very important tool for fire managers in the California desert bioregion, even though the areas in which it is used may be a small percentage of the total region.

HERBACEOUS FUEL MANAGEMENT

The fuel component of greatest concern in the desert bioregion is the continuous cover of the non-native annual grasses red brome, cheat grass, and Mediterranean grass that appear during years of high rainfall. Although populations of these non-native annual plants and their resultant fine fuel loadings wax and wane with annual and multi-decadal fluctuations in rainfall (Sidebar 16.1), they have changed fire behavior and fire regimes in many parts of the desert bioregion, especially in the low-elevation ecological zone where their presence is almost a prerequisite for large fires.

Despite all the concern surrounding the non-native species already dominating the desert bioregion, new grass invaders

Saltcedar was brought to North America in the early 1800s by European colonists as a horticultural plant, and by the early 1900s it became widely used to provide windbreaks and erosion control along railways and other erosion-prone sites. Its ability to tolerate periodic drought and harsh soil conditions helped ensure its establishment persistence where other species failed. It was recognized as an invader of desert watercourses around the 1920s, and, with the advent of water control and diversion projects, took advantage of the altered conditions to expand its range during the middle and latter part of the century (Robinson 1965).

Saltcedar is deciduous and produces a fine-structured, water-repellent litter layer that is highly flammable in late summer and fall. Because stand densities can be very high, and litter is slow to decompose, a nearly continuous layer of surface fuels can develop that carries fire throughout the stand (Busch and Smith 1992). The standing trees are also flammable, and can carry fire from surface fuels up into the canopies of native riparian trees. These fuel characteristics can create a frequent, high-intensity, crown fire regime where an infrequent, low- to moderate-intensity, surface fire regime previously existed. After burning, saltcedar stump-sprouts readily and benefits from nutrients released by fire, whereas native riparian plants such as cottonwood and willow do not resprout as vigorously (Ellis 2001). Recurrent high-intensity fire may lead to monoculture stands of saltcedar. Thus, saltcedar has turned many watercourses from barriers of fire movement to pathways for fire spread.

As stands of saltcedar increase in density and cover, native cottonwood and willow trees decrease. In some cases, this is coincident with changing environmental conditions that do not favor the native species (e.g., decreased water tables caused by water diversion projects; Everitt 1998), but in other cases, it is clear that saltcedar is responsible for the decline in native trees, directly through competition and indirectly through altered fire regimes (Busch and Smith 1995). Because it provides lower quantity and quality of shade, forage, and insect prey species, wildlife generally avoid large stands of saltcedar in preference for native stands (Shafroth et al. in press). This includes numerous threatened and declining riparian birds which find better nesting and feeding resources on native trees. In addition, saltcedar can have higher evapotranspiration rates than native trees, potentially reducing water tables (Sala et al. 1996). All of these symptoms of saltcedar invasion have caused major management problems in southwestern riparian ecosystems.

Mechanical and chemical methods are typically used to manage saltcedar, however they can be very expensive ($300–$6,000/ha; Shafroth et al. in press), their effectiveness is often limited and temporary, and they can have other undesirable ecosystem effects. After more than a decade of pre-release testing, a leaf-feeding beetle from Eurasia, *Diorhabda elongata*, has been experimentally released in several western states as a biological control agent against saltcedar (Dudley et al. 2000). At one site in northern Nevada this beetle defoliated approximately 2 ha in 2002, and spread to defoliate more than 400 ha in 2003. The physiological stress experienced by defoliated plants may lead to lowered live fuel moisture, and definitely increases the amount of dead wood and foliage. In the short term, this biocontrol may increase the chance of high-intensity fire, but in the long run the conversion of saltcedar stands back to native riparian woodlands will likely reduce fire hazards. —*Tom Dudley, MB* such as crimson fountaingrass (*Pennisetum setaceum*), buffel grass (*Cenchus ciliaris*), and African needlegrass, and invasive mustards such as Sahara mustard may pose additional fire hazards in the future. For example, in the Sonoran Desert, buffel grass invasion coupled with frequent fire has converted desertscrub to non-native grassland in Mexico (Búrquez et al. 1996), created fuels sufficient to carry fire in Arizona, and recently appeared in southeastern California (M. Brooks personal observation). Land managers who once lamented the damage caused by fires fueled by red brome in southern Arizona are even more concerned now about the potential effects of buffel grass (S. Rutman, Organ Pipe Cactus National Monument, personal communication). Buffel grass is currently being considered for addition to the Arizona Department of Agriculture Noxious Weed List, due primarily to its ability to alter fire regimes (E. Northam personal communication). Thus, fine fuels management should be closely tied to invasive plant management, because the predominant plant invaders in the southern part of the desert bioregion are relatively flammable herbaceous species (Brooks and Esque, 2002). This is important from the perspective of both managing invasive plant fuels that are currently present and preventing the establishment of new invasive plants that may change fuel structure and potentially cause even greater fire management problems in the future.

Livestock grazing has been mentioned as a possible tool for managing fine fuels in the desert bioregion (Brooks et al. 2003, Minnich 2003). It may temporarily reduce fine fuel loads and be effective for managing fuels in specific areas such as within the wildland-urban interface. However, grazing may also reduce cover of late seral native plants and replace them with non-native annual and other early seral plant species that can be more flammable (Brooks et. al 2003). Grazing treatments must be applied with attention to the potential responses of all dominant plant species, both in the short term, based on the phenologic stage during which they are grazed, and in the long term, based on their life history characteristics and interrelationships among species.

WOODY FUEL MANAGEMENT

Where native plant cover is sufficient to carry fire without the addition of fine fuels from non-native plants, coarse woody fuels are the major concern of fire managers. In the central and southern parts of the desert bioregion, blackbrush intermixed with perennial grasses, Joshua trees, and juniper produce the right mix of high fuel continuity, fuel loads, and fuel packing ratio that can cause large, intense fires with frequent spotting ahead of the flaming front. Although infrequent, intense, stand-replacing fires are a natural part of blackbrush shrubland ecology, these types of fires are not desirable when they occur near human habitations, or where they may damage cultural resources such as historic buildings or prehistoric sites. Once these fires start, they often require indirect firefighting tactics to suppress, which complicates efforts to pro-

tect specific areas from burning. As a result, land managers and scientists are testing ways to reduce the chances of extreme fire behavior in this vegetation type (M. Brooks et al. unpublished data). They are comparing the effects of fire and mechanical blackbrush thinning on subsequent fuel conditions, fire behavior, and plant community structure. The goal is to find tools that will allow managers to manipulate fuel characteristics to reduce fire hazards near areas identified for protection from fire, while having minimal negative ecological effects, such as increased dominance of invasive non-native plants.

Sagebrush and pinyon-juniper fuels are the primary focus of fuel management in the northern parts of the desert bioregion, especially in the Mono section. Sagebrush intermixed with perennial grasses is generally considered to be a greater fire hazard than the blackbrush communities described above. A century or more of fire exclusion, livestock grazing, and climate change can also result in encroachment by pinyon-juniper woodlands into sagebrush steppe (Miller and Tausch 2001). This has been documented in the northeast bioregion of California (Schaefer et al. 2003) and has also occurred where rainfall is relatively high in the desert bioregion at the ecotone of the Great Basin desert with the Sierra Nevada Mountains (Anne Halford, botanist, BLM-Bishop Field Office). Dense stands of mature trees in that area increase the chance of intense, stand-replacing, crown fire. Unfortunately, these same mature woodlands are desirable for use as homesites, especially in the Mono section, complicating the implementation of fuels management treatments and the protection of homes during fires.

Millions of hectares are planned for fuels reduction in the western United States (http://www.fireplan.gov), and much will involve thinning of smaller size classes of pinyon and juniper trees to allow surface fuels to increase and moderate-severity surface fires to return to the ecotone between pinyon-juniper woodlands and sagebrush steppe. Because very little is known about the effectiveness of these treatments in changing fire behavior or the potential ecological effects of these treatments, a research project was recently begun to quantify the effects of pinyon and juniper thinning on subsequent fuel condition, fire behavior, and ecosystem variables (M. Brooks et al. unpublished data).

Where sagebrush and pinyon-juniper vegetation interface in the southern desert sections, they are either at high elevations far from major roads and human habitations, or they contain surface fuels of insufficient amount and continuity to carry fire. These stands only burn under extreme fire weather conditions. Analyses of aerial photographs and VTM survey data from the 1930s show no evidence of pinyon-juniper expansion in the southern parts of the California desert region (R. Minnich unpublished data). Accordingly, management of pinyon-juniper fuels is not advisable in this region, except where needed for specific cultural resource or safety reasons.

SIDEBAR 16.3. FIRE EFFECTS ON THE DESERT TORTOISE

Changing fire regimes threaten 12 of the 40 major tortoise species worldwide (Swingland and Klemens 1989). Only general habitat destruction is listed as a threat for more species (23 of 40 species). In general, tortoises are poorly adapted to fire because they evolved in arid or semi-arid habitats where fire was historically rare. The desert tortoise, Mojave population, is a Federally Threatened species listed partly because of threats posed by fire.

Fires can kill desert tortoises, especially fires that occur in the spring and early summer when they are most active aboveground throughout their range (Esque et al. 2002). Years of high rainfall produce the profuse annual plant growth that is required for desert tortoise reproduction, but it also contributes to fire occurrence, especially at the low- and middle-elevation zones within the desert tortoise range. Thus, years when growth and reproduction are expected to be greatest can be coincident with years of increased fire occurrence. Although mortality from individual fires is generally considered insignificant for wildlife populations compared with the habitat changes that can follow, loss of a few individuals may be catastrophic for local populations of species that are already in decline (Esque et al. 2003).

Fires can also affect desert tortoises indirectly, by changing habitat structure and plant species composition. Loss of cover sites that provide protection from the sun and predators, and loss of native forage plants are specific examples of the potential negative effects of fire (Brooks and Esque 2002, Esque et al. 2002). Individual fires may have relatively small indirect effects within desert tortoise habitat, since they are often patchy, leaving unburned islands of native vegetation. In contrast, recurrent fires pose a much greater threat, as they often burn through previously unburned islands of vegetation, and can produce broad landscapes devoid of shrub cover and dominated by non-native annual grasses. These conditions are currently focused within a number of regional hotspots in the desert bioregion (Brooks and Esque 2002).

When fighting fires that occur within desert tortoise habitat in the low- and middle-elevation zones, land managers follow guidelines developed to reduce the chance of killing desert tortoises such as not burning out unburned habitat islands when feasible, checking under tires before moving vehicles, and walking ahead of vehicles when they are required to travel off-road (Duck et al. 1997). Results of firefighting activities in desert tortoise habitats have proven that the benefit of fighting fires in desert tortoise habitat far outweighs the potential danger of damage to habitats and tortoise populations when appropriate guidelines are followed (Duck et al. 1997).—*MB, Todd Esque*

Fire Suppression

There is specific concern about the effect of fire suppression activities on the federally threatened desert tortoise where it occurs in low- and middle-elevation zones (Sidebar 16.3). More generally, fire suppression in desert wilderness areas became a significant issue after the California Desert Protection Act (1994) applied this designation to many new areas. Wilderness areas often encompass mountain ranges in the desert bioregion, where locally high fuel loads from both native and non-native plants, and steep slopes, facilitate the spread of fire. Fire suppression options are generally more limited in these areas by the constraints outlined in wilderness management plans, and often the primary tactic is to wait for fire to spread downslope and attempt to stop it along preexisting roads. This can result in large portions of desert mountain ranges burning during a single event. The question is, which causes greater ecological damage, activities associated with aggressive firefighting (e.g., construction of hand or bulldozer control lines, fire retardant drops) or large-scale, sometimes recurrent, fire occurring where fires were historically small and infrequent? We recommend that suppression be a high priority where fire frequency has been recently high in regional hotspots and non-native grass/fire cycles have become locally established, where local populations of non-native plants may be poised to expand their range and landscape dominance following fire (mostly in the middle-elevation ecological zone), or where there are other management reasons to exclude fire. Otherwise, a let burn policy for natural fires may be appropriate.

Post-Fire Restoration

Burn Area Emergency Rehabilitation (BAER) teams have developed post-fire restoration/rehabilitation plans after the large fires that have recently occurred in the Mono section (e.g., Cannon and Slinkard fires), and further south in the desert bioregion at its ecotone with the Transverse and Peninsular ranges (e.g., the Juniper Complex and Willow fires). Much of this effort is focused on protecting watersheds from soil erosion, and one of the common tools is the seeding of rapidly growing plants (Sidebar 20.1, this volume). In general, seeding treatments establish more readily in the cold deserts than in the hot deserts, although relative establishment rates and the ecological effects of seeding in these two regions have not been experimentally compared.

Post-fire seeding may also be used to compete with and reduce the cover of invasive grasses associated with the grass/fire cycle (Sidebar 16.1). The idea is to replace highly flammable species such as cheat grass with less flammable seeded species. Non-native perennial grasses such as desert crested wheatgrass (*Agropyron desertorum*) have been used to compete with and reduce cover of cheat grass in Great Basin sagebrush steppe. However, there has been a recent move toward using native species in post-fire seeding, which may not have the same effect as non-native perennial grasses in suppressing the growth of non-native annual grasses such as cheat grass. A current study is evaluating the relative effectiveness of non-native versus native perennial grasses to compete with and reduce cover of cheat grass after fires in sagebrush steppe in the Mono section, and at sites in the Great Basin and Colorado Plateau (M. Brooks unpublished data).

Fire Management Planning

One of the biggest challenges in fire management planning is determining desired future conditions to use as management goals. In cases where historic fire regimes can be reconstructed (e.g., ponderosa pine forest), the natural range and variation of historic fire regime characteristics may be a realistic and appropriate target. However, management goals may be elusive where historic fire regimes cannot be easily reconstructed, such as in the desert bioregion where one must rely on indirect inferences.

Fire histories alone may not be enough to establish management goals when protection of specific natural or cultural resources are priorities, or where plant invasions have changed the rules of the game. For example, if plant invasions have shifted fuel characteristics outside of their natural range of historic variation, then restoration of historic fire regimes may be impossible without first dealing with the invasive plants that are at the root of the problem (Brooks et al. 2004). Although it appears that fire regimes, and at least woody fuel conditions, across much of the desert bioregion may be within their historic range of variation, it is difficult to quantify the impact that non-native plant invasions have had, aside from recognizing that fire regimes have been altered dramatically in some regional hotspots (Brooks and Esque 2002). Further complicating this process are the effects of potential future changes in rainfall patterns (Hereford et al. in press), and levels of atmospheric CO_2 (Mayeaux et al. 1994) and nitrogen deposition (Brooks 2003), on fuel conditions and fire regimes. All of these potential variables need to be considered when determining fire management goals in the desert bioregion.

The recent mandate by federal land management agencies to create fire management plans for all management units has resulted in a flurry of activity as new plans are drafted and old plans are revised. In many cases, plans developed for desert management units are supported by relatively few scientific studies, due to the paucity of fire research that has been conducted in the desert regions of North America. Decisions on when and where fuels should be managed, fires should be suppressed or allowed to burn, or post-fire restoration projects should be implemented, are difficult to make given the limited data available. Recent reviews have attempted to provide land managers and others with current information on desert fire ecology and management (Brooks and Pyke 2001, Brooks and Esque 2002, Esque and Schwalbe

2002, Esque et al. 2002, Brooks et al. 2003). Along these same lines, a primary purpose of this desert bioregion chapter is to provide additional information that can be used in the development of fire management plans in the deserts of southwestern North America.

References

Bates, P. A. 1984. The role and use of fire in blackbrush (*Coleogyne ramosissima* Torr.) communities in California. Doctoral dissertation, University of California, Davis. 56 p.

Bowns, J. E. 1973. An autecological study of blackbrush (*Coleogyne ramosissima* Torr.) in southwestern Utah. Doctoral dissertation, Utah State University, Logan. 115 p.

Brooks, M. L 1999. Alien annual grasses and fire in the Mojave Desert. Madroño 46:13–19.

Brooks, M. L. 2000. *Schismus arabicus* Nees, *Schismus barbatus* (L.) Thell. Pages 287–291 in C. Bossard, M. Hoshovsky, and J. Randall (eds.), Invasive plants of California's wildlands. University of California Press, Berkeley.

Brooks, M. L. 2002. Peak fire temperatures and effects on annual plants in the Mojave Desert. Ecological Applications 12:1088–1102.

Brooks, M. L. 2003. Effects of increased soil nitrogen on the dominance of alien annual plants in the Mojave Desert. Journal of Applied Ecology 40:344–353.

Brooks, M. L. C. M. D'Antonio, D. M. Richardson, J. Grace, J. E. Keeley, DiTomaso, R. Hobbs, M. Pellant, D. Pyke. 2004. Effects of invasive alien plants on fire regimes. BioScience 54:677–688.

Brooks, M. L., and T. C. Esque. 2002. Alien annual plants and wildfire in desert tortoise habitat: status, ecological effects, and management. Chelonian Conservation and Biology 4:330–340.

Brooks, M. L., T. C. Esque, and T. Duck. 2003. Fuels and fire regimes in creosotebush, blackbrush, and interior chaparral shrublands. Report for the Southern Utah Demonstration Fuels Project, USDA, Forest Service, Rocky Mountain Research Station, Fire Science Lab, Missoula, MT. 17 p.

Brooks, M. L., and J. R. Matchett. 2003. Plant community patterns in unburned and burned blackbrush (*Coleogyne ramosissima*) shrublands in the Mojave Desert. Western North American Naturalist 63:283–298.

Brooks, M. L., J. R. Matchett, and K. Berry. In press. Alien and native plant cover and diversity near livestock watering sites in a desert ecosystem. Journal of Arid Environments.

Brooks, M. L., and D. Pyke. 2001. Invasive plants and fire in the deserts of North America. Pages 1–14 in K. Galley and T. Wilson (eds.), Proceedings of the invasive species workshop: the role of fire in the control and spread of invasive species. Fire Conference 2000: The First National Congress on Fire, Ecology, Prevention and Management. Miscellaneous Publications No. 11, Tall Timbers Research Station, Tallahassee, FL.

Brown, D. E. 1984. Fire and changes in creosote bush scrub on the western Colorado Desert, California. M.S. thesis, University of California, Riverside.

Brown, D. E., and R. A. Minnich. 1986. Fire and creosote bush scrub of the western Sonoran Desert, California. American Midland Naturalist 116:411–422.

Brown, J. K., and J. K. Smith (eds.). 2000. Wildland fire in ecosystems: effects of fire on flora. Gen. Tech. Rep. RMRS-GTR-42-vol.

2. Ogden, UT: U.S. Department of Agriculture, Forest Service, Rocky Mountain Research Station. 257 p.

Brown, T. J., B. L. Hall, C. R. Mohrle, and H. J. Reinbold. 2002. Coarse assessment of federal wildland fire occurrence data. CEFA Report 02-04. Desert Research Institute, Division of Atmospheric Sciences, Reno, NV.

Búrquez, A. M., A. Y. Martinez, M. Miller, K. Rojas, M. A. Quintana, and D. Yetman. 1996. Mexican grasslands and the changing arid lands of Mexico: an overview and a case study in northwestern Mexico. Pages 21–32 in B. Tellman, D. M. Finch, E. Edminster, and R. Hamre (eds.), The future of arid grasslands: identifying issues, seeking solutions. Proceedings RMRS-P-3. U.S. Forest Service, Rocky Mountain Station, Fort Collins, CO.

Busch, D. E., and S. D. Smith. 1992. Fire in a riparian shrub community: postburn water relations in the *Tamarix-Salix* association along the lower Colorado River. Pages 52–55 in W. P. Clary, M. E. Durant, D. Bedunah, and C. L. Wambolt (comp.), Proc. ecology and management of riparian shrub communities. USDA-FS GTR-INT-289.

Busch, D. E., and S. D. Smith. 1995. Mechanisms associated with decline of woody species in riparian ecosystems of the southwestern U.S. Ecol. Monogr. 65:347–370.

Dalton, P. D. 1962. Ecology of the creosotebush *Larrea tridentata* (D.C.) Cov. Doctoral Dissertation, University of Arizona.

D'Antonio, C. M., and P. M. Vitousek. 1992. Biological invasions by exotic grasses, the grass/fire cycle, and global change. Annual Review of Ecology and Systematics 3:63–87.

De Soyza, A. G., W. G. Whitford, E. Martinez-Meza, and J. W. Van Zee. 1997. Variation in creosotebush (*Larrea tridentate*) canopy morphology in relation to habitat, soil fertility, and associated annual plant communities. American Midland Naturalist 137:13–26.

Duck, T. A., T. C. Esque, and T. J. Hughes. 1997. Fighting wildfires in desert tortoise habitat, considerations for land managers. Proceedings for symposium on fire effects on rare and endangered species habitats conference. November 13–16, 1995. International Wildland Fire Association, Coeur D'Alene, ID.

Dudley, T. L., C. J. DeLoach, J. E. Lovich, and R. I. Carruthers. 2000. Saltcedar invasion of western riparian areas: impacts and new prospects for control. Pages 345–381 in R. E. McCabe and S. E. Loos (eds.), Tran. 65th No. Amer. wildlife mgt. inst., Washington, DC.

Ellis, L. M. 2001. Short-term response of woody plants to fire in a Rio Grande riparian forest. Biol. Cons. 97:159–170.

Esque, T. C., A. M. Búrquez, C. R. Schwalbe, T. R. VanDevender, M.J.M. Nijhuis, and P. Anning. 2002. Fire ecology of the Sonoran desert tortoise. Pages 312–333 in The Sonoran desert tortoise: natural history, biology, and conservation. Arizona-Sonora Desert Museum and the University of Arizona Press, Tuscon, AZ.

Esque, T. C., and C. R. Schwalbe. 2002. Alien annual plants and their relationships to fire and biotic change in Sonoran desertscrub. Pages 165–194 in B. Tellman (ed.), Invasive exotic species in the Sonoran region. Arizona-Sonora Desert Museum and the University of Arizona Press, Tuscon, AZ.

Esque, T. C., C. R. Schwalbe, L. A. DeFalco, R. B. Duncan, and T. J. Hughes 2003. Effects of wildfire on desert tortoise (*Gopherus agassizii*) and other small vertebrates. The Southwestern Naturalist. 48:103–111.

Everitt, B. L. 1998. Chronology of the spread of tamarisk in the central Rio Grande. Wetlands 18:658–668.

Hereford, R., R. H. Webb, R.H., C. I. Longpr_. In press. Precipitation history and ecosystem response to multidecadal precipitation variability in the Mojave Desert region, 1893–2001. Journal of Arid Environments.

Humphrey, R.R. 1974. Fire in deserts and desert grassland of North America. Pages 365–401 in T.T. Kozlowski and C.E. Ahlgren (eds.), Fire and ecosystems. Academic Press, New York.

Hunter, R. 1991. *Bromus* invasions on the Nevada Test Site: present status of *B. rubens* and *B. tectorum* with notes on their relationship to disturbance and altitude. Great Basin Naturalist 51:176–182.

Koehler, P. A., R. S. Anderson, and W. G. Spaulding. 2005. Development of vegetation in the central Mojave Desert of California during the late Quaternary. Paleogeography, Paleoclimatology, Paleoecology 215:297–311.

Küchler, A. W. 1964. Potential natural vegetation of the conterminous United States. Special Publication 36, American Geographical Society, New York.

Knick, S.T., D. S. Dobkin, J.T. Rotenberry, M.A Schroeder, W.M. Vander Hagen, and C. Van Riper III. 2003. Teetering on the edge or too late? Conservation and research issues for avifauna of sagebrush habitats. The Condor 105:611–634.

Knick, S.T., and J.T. Rotenberry. 1995. Landscape characteristics of fragmented shrubsteppe habitats and breeding passerine birds. Conservation Biology 9:1059–1071.

Mayeaux, H.S., H.B. Johnson, and H.W. Polley. 1994. Potential interactions between global change and Intermountain annual grasslands. Pages 95–110 in S. B. Monsen and S.G. Kitchen (eds.), Proceedings of ecology and management of annual rangelands. Intermountain Research Station, Ogden, UT.

Miles, S.R., and C.B. Goudy. 1997. Ecological subregions of California: section and subsection descriptions. USDA Forest Service, R5-EM-TP-005.

Miller, R.F., and R.J. Tausch. 2001. The role of fire in juniper and pinyon woodlands: as descriptive analysis. Pages 15–30 in K. Galley and T. Wilson (eds.), Proceedings of the invasive species workshop: the role of fire in the control and spread of invasive species. Fire Conference 2000: The First National Congress on Fire, Ecology, Prevention and Management. Miscellaneous Publications No. 11, Tall Timbers Research Station, Tallahassee, FL.

Minnich, R.A. 1988. The biogeography of fire in the San Bernardino Mountains of California. University of California Publications in Geography 28:1–121.

Minnich, R.A. 2003. Fire and dynamics of temperate desert woodlands in Joshua Tree National Park. Report submitted to the National Park Service, Joshua Tree National Park. Contract number P8337000034/0001. 32 p.

Minnich, R.A., and R.G. Everett. 2001. Conifer tree distributions in southern California. Madrono 48:177–197.

Minnich, R.A., and A.C. Sanders. 2000. *Brassica tournefortii* (Gouan). Pages 68–71 in C. Bossard, M. Hoshovsky, and J. Randall (eds.), Invasive plants of California's wildlands. University of California Press, Berkeley.

Munz, P.A, and D.D. Keck, 1959. A California flora. University of California Press, Berkeley. 1681 p.

O'Leary, J.F., and R.A. Minnich. 1981. Postfire recovery of creosote bush scrub vegetation in the Western Colorado Desert. Madroño 28:61–66.

Robinson, T.W. 1965. Introduction , spread and areal extent of saltcedar *(Tamarix)* in the western states. USGS Prof. Paper 491-A.

Rogers, G. F., and M.K. Vint. 1987. Winter precipitation and fire in the Sonoran Desert. Journal of Arid Environments 13:47–52.

Rowlands, P.G. 1980. The vegetational attributes of the California Desert Conservation Area. Pages 135–183 in J. Latting (ed.), The California desert: an introduction to its resources and man's impact. California Native Plant Society Special Publication 5.

Sala, A., S. D. Smith, and D. A. Devitt. 1996. Water use by *Tamarix ramosissima* and associated phreatophytes in a Mojave Desert floodplain. Ecol. Applic. 6:888–898.

Schaefer, R. J., D. J. Thayer, and T. S. Burton. 2003. Forty-one years of vegetation change on permanent transects in northeastern California: implications for wildlife. California Fish and Game 89:55–71.

Schmid, M.K., and G.F. Rogers. 1988. Trends in fire occurrence in the Arizona upland subdivision of the Sonoran Desert, 1955 to 1983. The Southwestern Naturalist 33:437–444.

Schmidt, K.M., J. P. Menakis, C.C. Hardy, W.J. Hann, and D.L. Bunell. 2002. Development of coarse-scale spatial data for wildand fire and fuel management. United States Department of Agriculture, Forest Service, General Technical Report, GTR-RMRS-87.

Shafroth, P. B., J. R. Cleverly, T. L. Dudley, J. N. Stuart, J. P. Taylor, C. van Riper, and E. P. Weeks. Saltcedar removal, water salvage, and wildlife habitat restoration along rivers in the southwestern U.S. Frontiers in Ecology. (In press.)

Swingland, I.R., and M.W. Klemens. 1989. The conservation biology of tortoises. Occasional Papers of the IUCN Species Survival Commission (SSC), No. 5. Gland, Switzerland: International Union for Conservation of Nature and Natural Resources. 204 p.

Van Devender, T.R., and W.G. Spaulding. 1979. Development of vegetation and climate in the southwestern United States. Science 204:701–710.

van Wagtendonk, J.W., and D. Cayan. 2007. Temporal and spatial distribution of lightning strikes in California in relationship to large-scale weather patterns. Fire Ecology. (In press.)

Wangler, M, and R.A. Minnich. 1996. Fire and succession in pinyon-juniper woodlands of the San Bernardino Mountains. Madroño 43:493–514.

Webb, R.H., J. W. Steiger, and E. B. Newman. 1988. The response of vegetation to disturbance in Death Valley National Monument, California. U.S. Geological Survey Bulletin 1793.

Whisenant, S.G. 1990. Changing fire frequencies on Idaho's snake river plains: ecological and management implications. Pages 4–7 in E. D. McArthur, E.D. Romney, E.M. Smith, and S.D. Tueller (eds.), Proceedings—symposium on cheatgrass invasion, shrub die-off, and other aspects of shrub biology and management, 5–7 April 1989, Las Vegas, NV. General Technical Report INT-276, Department of Agriculture, Forest Service, Intermountain Research Station.

White, L.D. 1968. Factors affecting the susceptibility of creosotebush (*Larrea tridentata* [D.C.] Cov.) to burning. Doctoral dissertation, University of Arizona.

Wright, H.E., and A.W. Bailey. 1982. Fire ecology, United States and Canada. Wiley, New York.

PART III

FIRE MANAGEMENT ISSUES IN CALIFORNIA'S ECOSYSTEMS

In the first two parts of the book, we have presented details about fire as an ecological process and the role fire plays in the nine bioregions of California. It should be obvious that fire has been a dynamic force in these ecosystems and will continue to be so in the future. How then, must we reconcile this ecological fact with the need for human society to coexist with fire? There are several issues Californians must face if they are to continue to live in a fire-prone landscape. In Part III, we address these issues.

Chapter 17 takes a look at Native American use of fire and discusses how this important cultural activity has influenced ecosystems and how it can continue in light of conflicting land management objectives. Since European settlement, our population has expanded, and fire policies have evolved as our understanding of fire has become more sophisticated. Chapter 18 chronicles this evolution and asks how policies must change in the future. One of the greatest challenges faced by Californians is the accumulation of fuels in areas within and surrounding communities. Dealing with this challenge is the subject of Chapter 19. If fire is to be reintroduced as an ecological process and a management tool, conflicting societal goals must be reconciled. Chapter 20 discusses the impacts of fire on watersheds and aquatic resources, Chapter 21 addresses smoke and air quality concerns, Chapter 22 deals with the problem of invasive plants, and Chapter 23 deals with the conflict between fire and at-risk species. In Chapter 24, we summarize the concepts developed in the book and challenge Californians to accept the fact that they live in fire-prone ecosystems.

CHAPTER 17

The Use of Fire by Native Americans in California

M. KAT ANDERSON

Speech, tools, and fire are the tripod of culture and have been so,
we think, from the beginning.

SAUER, 1981

The use of fire as a land management tool in human history has been universal. Setting fires to influence vegetation patterns was one of the most potent achievements of the human species; it literally shifted our status from that of foragers to true cultivators of nature (Lewis and Anderson 2002). The use of fire by *Homo erectus* may be more than 400,000 years old (Weiner et al. 1998). Indigenous use of fire is an important dimension of human evolution, enabling our species to move around the world and occupy higher latitudes and elevations, thriving in extremely cold environments. From about 400,000 years ago, proper hearths consisting of rings of stones, burned bones, and other clear evidence of fire become common throughout Europe (McCrone 2000). There is archaeological evidence that fire was used to drive and hunt wildlife at this time also (Boyd 1999). Thus, its application to California landscapes for hunting is most likely as ancient as the first human occupation some 11,000 years ago (Moratto 1984).

When Spanish explorer Juan Rodríguez Cabrillo anchored in San Pedro Bay in October of 1542, it was the chaparral fires that gave him the signal that the coast was occupied by humans (Kelsey 1986:143) (Map 17.1). A succession of explorers, missionaries, and settlers thereafter would continually note the "smoky air" from these fires in their journals in every corner of the state—in the coastal redwood forests, the tule marshes of the Delta, the southern oak woodlands, the mixed conifer forests, and the northern hazelnut flats (Sutter 1939, Thompson 1991, Timbrook et al. 1993).

Former indigenous burning patterns are a significant part of the historical ecology of many environments—a fact that makes this topic relevant to ecologists, conservation biologists, and land managers interested in restoring various areas to their pre-European settlement condition. Alfred Kroeber, the father of California anthropology, wrote of the benefits of Indian-set fires: "Travel was better, views farther, ambuscades more difficult, certain kinds of hunting more remunerative,

and a crop of grasses and herbs was of more food value than most brush" (Kroeber 1976). With California population densities some of the highest in North America, and their population level about 310,000 (Cook 1971), the acreage that was burned by California's earliest humans may have been significant; Martin and Sapsis (1992) estimate that between 5.6 and 13 million acres of California burned annually under both lightning and indigenous peoples' fire regimes.

The success of indigenous economies depended on setting fires. In many areas of California, setting fires was integral to the maintenance of food, cordage, and basketry production systems—three essential cultural use categories that required enormous quantities of high-quality plant material to satisfy human needs. Furthermore, Native Americans thoroughly understood the necessity of "fighting fire with fire." Their deliberately set fires were often designed to preclude the kinds of catastrophic fires that regularly devastate large areas today.

Native Americans from various tribes continue to gather, prepare, use, and manage plants within their surroundings, reenacting age-old traditions (Ortiz and Staff 1991, Anderson 2005). National park and forest managers and private landowners have begun to take a more active role by becoming advocates of maintaining, tending, and encouraging growth of plants important to California Indians. This involves surveying the resources, recording their conditions and numbers, matching these with indigenous needs, and reintroducing Native American fire as a horticultural technique to enhance cultural resources.

The major technologies of California Indians such as digging sticks, seed beaters, knocking sticks, knives, stone axes, deer antlers, and fire-making kits may appear "primitive" and unable to affect vast areas. Yet it was the invention and the modification of the fire-making kit that revolutionized human ability to alter landscapes. Tribes in California made fire either by drilling or percussion. *Drilling* refers to the rotating of a slender wooden shaft in a hole in a stationary

MAP 17.1. The territories associated with California Indian language groups. Names in bold represent a language family of two or more languages and multiple dialects.

board called the *hearth* to create intense heat by friction; *percussion* refers to striking two objects together, such as two stones to create sparks (Driver and Massey 1957). Most tribes utilized a slow match or torch, which consisted of a tightly packed flammable material that would smolder at one end for a considerable period of time. The torch provided continuous light for nighttime activities and enabled travelers to start fires without the aid of a fire drill (Barrett 1907, Dixon 1905).

Native American Uses of Fire

Native Americans' uses of fire pervaded their everyday lives. These uses included applying fire in fields and forests, keeping the country open, managing wildlife, manufacturing cultural items, and enhancing the growth of basketry material.

Fire in the Fields and Forests

Fire was the most significant, effective, efficient, and widely employed vegetation management tool utilized by California Indian tribes. Native Americans conducted purposeful burning to meet specific cultural objectives, strongly suggesting that they understood fire effects such as the reproductive response of vegetation at different levels of biological organization (e.g., organism, population, community, and landscape scales) (Blackburn and Anderson 1993, Anderson 2005). Fire as a habitat management tool was so commonly used by Native Americans that it threatened the agricultural, ranching, lumbering, and gold mining plans of the new settlers; thus, edicts, agreements, and proclamations were drawn up to prohibit burning by American Indians. The first regulation prohibiting burning in California was proclaimed by Spanish Governor José Joaquín de Arrillaga in 1793, who was in Santa Barbara at the time (see Timbrook et al. 1993:129–132).

The slow match or torch gave Native Americans the technological capability to burn both small patches and extensive tracts of vegetation in a systematic fashion. Vegetation types that occur as continuous fuelbeds—such as grasslands—meant that fires could conceivably burn uninterrupted for miles. Additionally, most tribes had the ability to fell trees with fire for meeting cultural needs. These tools were used for type conversions of areas for villages and conversions of riparian habitat and floodplains for farming in southeastern California. A combination of burning and hand weeding of young conifers or hardwoods were two methods used in tandem to keep trees from encroaching on meadows or prairies. Galen Clark, guardian of the Yosemite grant for many years, observed burning and weeding among the Southern Sierra Miwok/Mono Lake Paiute in Yosemite Valley (Clark 1894).

Although many reasons for indigenous burning are unrelated to ecological effects (e.g., communication, animal drives, ease of travel, increased visibility, clearing underbrush that could hide enemies), setting fires to produce specific ecological consequences probably was the most significant motivation for Native Americans. Many of these ecological purposes are under-recorded in the earlier historical and ethnographic literature because ethnographers talked only to the men. These practices often benefited plants gathered by women. Some of these purposes include: increasing abundance and densities of edible tubers, greens, and mushrooms; enhancing feed for wildlife; decreasing insects and diseases of wild foods and basketry material; increasing quantity and quality of material for basketry and cordage; decreasing detritus; increasing sprouts for household items, granaries, fish weirs, clothing, games, hunting and fishing traps, and weapons; removing dead material and promoting growth through the recycling of nutrients; decreasing plant competition; and maintaining specific plant community types (Lewis 1993, Stewart 2002). For example, black oak–ponderosa pine forests in the Sierra Nevada of California were managed by the Western Mono, Sierra Miwok/Mono Lake Paiute, and Foothill Yokuts tribes for at least seven purposes: increasing mushroom (*Peziza* spp. and *Morchella elata)* production; facilitating acorn collection, increasing rapid elongation of epicormic branches on oaks for the manufacture of items, reducing the incidence of insect pests that inhabit acorns (*Curculio* and *Cydia* spp.) (Fig. 17.1), promoting useful understory grasses and forbs, promoting a vegetative structure that increases acorn production; and eliminating brush to inhibit catastrophic fires (Anderson 1993).

Fire to Keep the Country Open

Burning areas to "decrease the brush" was a nearly ubiquitous practice in California. Not only did it facilitate hunting and provide greater ease of travel and increased visibility, but thick underbrush could hide enemies and harbor dangerous animals such as rattlesnakes.

De Massey (1926:154) reported of the Indians of northern California: "The Indians, particularly in the spring and autumn, set the stubble in the pastures on fire to destroy the insects and reptiles, and to make hunting easier." According to Jack Voitich (pers. comm. 1990), Jess Duncan and Steve Shelton (both Sierra Miwok) said that the land used to be clear because the Miwok burned in the fall. They started fires above the pine forests in white fir and incense cedar forests. Voitich said, "When they built the road around the Big Trees Park you didn't have all those young pines, you had only the big trees. Even in my time, when I'd go hunting quail and deer all around this country it was easy to get through." The former openness of the country was substantiated by the fact that numerous tribes ran down deer. A fast Sierra Miwok runner could tire a deer in a day (Barrett and Gifford 1933).

Kroeber (1976) noted that: "It appears that forest fires have been far more destructive since American occupancy, owing to the accumulated underbrush igniting the large trees." A severe fire in a tribal territory, would not only have meant immediate loss of life, but would have spelled disaster for the long-term well-being of a village. If, for example, the kind of stand-replacing fire that we have often witnessed in our forests during the last decade had occurred, it would have destroyed thousands of acres of important tree food resources. And if many of the foothill pines and blue oaks had been destroyed in blue oak woodland, and California black oaks and sugar pines had been destroyed in mixed conifer forests—all at important tribal gathering sites—this would have automatically cut 30% to 40% of the food supply and cost villages part of their livelihood for many years to come. Although these trees would eventually have been replaced through seed or vegetative means, it would not have been within the lifetime of the inhabitants or their children (Anderson 1993). Thus, it was not in their best interest to allow catastrophic fires to occur.

During a study conducted on indigenous burning in the Yosemite and Sequoia-Kings Canyon regions, Native American elders commonly stressed that Indian-set fires "did not hurt the big trees" (Anderson 1993). Burning to keep the brush down provided the environmental context within which more localized burning could then be conducted for specific cultural purposes. With the possibility of a catastrophic fire very remote with frequent burning, the long-term welfare of humans, other animals, and plant gathering sites was assured. Frequent burning was the insurance policy against annihilation of important gathering and village sites.

Fire to Manage Wildlife

An extremely important reason for setting fires was to increase forage for wildlife. Anthropologist Harold Driver

FIGURE 17.1. Acorn of California blue oak (*Quercus douglasii*) with insect damage of filbert weevil (*Curculio pardus*) in the larval stage. Different tribes burned under black, blue, and tan oak trees to help rid areas of this pest. (Courtesy of and photographed by Tedmund Swiecki.)

(1939) recorded that the Wiyot burned every two or three years to increase feed for deer. José Joaquin Moraga, a chronicler of the second Anza expedition jotted down in 1776 that, "The heathen [probably the Ohlone] had burned many patches [southeast of the Mission of San Francisco], which doubtless would produce an abundance of pasturage."

Today, Native American elders from different tribes substantiate the importance of burning for wildlife. Sierra Miwok elder Bill Franklin learned about burning from his father and grandfather: "They said the Indians used to burn in the fall—October and November. They set the fires from the bottom of the slope to decrease the snowpack, get rid of the debris so there's no fire danger and they burned in the hunting areas so there was more food for the deer. They burned every year and in the same areas."

Ingenious methods using fire to lure, capture, or drive wildlife were abundant. The Tubatulabal waved torches under trees where quail were roosting at night; as the birds flew down they were easily clubbed (Voegelin 1938). Ishi (Yahi) told of hunters using fire to kill bears. A number of men would surround an animal, building a circle of fire about him. They then would discharge arrows at him, attempting to shoot him in the mouth. If the bear charged an Indian, he defended himself with a fire brand (Heizer and Kroeber 1979). The golden beaver was hunted by the Sierra Miwok by first burning off the tule around its pond, thus exposing the entrances to the animal's house, and creating bare ground in which to dig out the beaver (Barrett and Gifford 1933). Many tribes drove deer using fire, including the Pit River and the Owens Valley Paiute (Steward 1935, Olmstead and Stewart

1978). According to the Wobonuch Mono, "When game was needed in a hurry, as for a ceremony or special feast, an encircling fire would be set at the base of one of the many small conical hills of the Wobonuch region. Several hunters were posted about to shoot the animals as they broke through the ring of flames" (Elsasser [1962] 1972).

The use of fire to capture grasshoppers was a widespread phenomenon in California. It was a tool of the Yuki, Pomo, Pit River and many other tribes (Foster 1944, Merriam 1955, Olmstead and Stewart 1978). Anthropologist Cora Du Bois described this drive among the Wintu: "Grasshoppers were obtained by burning off large grass patches. Two or three villages might participate in a drive. The grass was set with torches three to five feet long made of dry wormwood or of devils' stems tied into bundles" (Du Bois 1935:14). Both grasslands and meadows were burned, including the grassland understory within mixed conifer forests.

Fire for Manufacturing Cultural Items

Over half of the plant material culture of California Indian tribes was made with young shrub or tree growth that comes up after fires. These cultural items include weapons, cordage, tools, structures, baskets, traps and snares, fishing gear, musical instruments, clothing, ceremonial regalia, games, and boats. On the other hand, older growth that was hard and inelastic also was required to accommodate some of the plant material culture, but these uses were minuscule compared to those for young growth. Most of these items required small quantities of older wood to satisfy the demand, and did not require the use of fire for their manufacture. However, firewood and larger support wood for structures did require significant amounts of older wood.

The young shoots of shrubs and trees used to make various cultural items are termed "sprouts" or "suckers" by horticulturists and "epicormic" or "adventitious" shoots by plant morphologists. The plants selected for these products have adaptive traits that enhance their survival and regeneration (Keeley and Zedler 1978, Philpot 1980, Kauffman and Martin 1990). These shoots have vigorous growth that is characterized by both an upsurge of vertical development and retardation of lateral branching. These specialized growth forms do not occur readily in nature in the absence of perturbations (e.g., flooding, fire, herbivory). These shoots also tend to exhibit juvenile characteristics and flowering is generally absent until the shoots have reached a certain stage of maturity.

Some examples of items that are made with fire-managed growth include rod armor, which was worn in battle by some of the Northwest Coast tribes; fire drills, which were long, straight shafts of wood with no lateral branches averaging more than two feet in length; looped stirring sticks used for cooking; and fish weirs (Anderson 1993).

Fire as a Tool for Enhancing Basketry Materials

One of the most significant reasons for the indigenous fire management of wildlands in California was for the production of weaving material for a myriad of baskets. The technology of basketry was central to daily living in each household in every traditional society. These containers were the single most ubiquitous and essential possessions in every family (Anderson 2005). Each woman utilized workbaskets several times every day. The shrubs, trees, perennial bunchgrasses, herbaceous plants, sedges, rushes, and ferns selected for use were harvested for raw materials through repeated visits over many years. Many of these plants were managed with fire to enhance their quality and quantity.

BURNING TO ENHANCE SHRUBS AND TREES

Plant characteristics that are of critical importance for making well-crafted baskets include: flexibility, straightness, no lateral branching, bark color, no bark blemishes, even diameter, and long length. These characteristics were (and continue to be) important for both twined and coiled basketry, and were key when considering the quality of both whole shoots used in the foundations (*warp*) and split shoots used for sewing strands (*weft*) of different types of baskets (Bates 1984; Anderson 1993, 1999; Mathewson 1998). Basketmakers adhered to the strict practice of using only young (first-, second-, or third-year) growth for making baskets. However, in many instances, the wild plants gathered by indigenous cultures for basketry do not exhibit the proper qualities or age to make excellent weaving material, and thus, must be managed *in situ*. Indigenous people in California utilized burning and pruning, and in more recent times, *coppicing* (a severe form of pruning) as vegetation management tools to promote long, straight branches for basketry material. In the absence of management, these plants are largely composed of old, brittle, and crooked branch growth—sometimes harboring insects and diseases—that is useless for basketry materials (Anderson 1999). Thus, patches in coastal sage scrub, streamsides, chaparral, oak woodlands, hazelnut flats, mixed conifer forests, and other vegetation types that had not recently been burned or pruned, yielded few "usable" shoots for this indigenous industry (Figs. 17.2 and 17.3).

Some of the major plant genera that had widespread use and were managed with burning include: *Cercis* (redbud), *Ceanothus* (wild lilac), *Corylus* (hazelnut), *Rhus* (sumac or sourberry), and *Salix* (willow) (Merrill 1923, Potts 1977, Farmer 1993, Anderson 1999). These genera have widespread distributions, exhibit suitable characteristics for basketry, and readily regenerate after repeated burning and pruning. Other less widely used genera include *Cornus* (dogwood), *Acer* (maple), *Quercus* (oak), and *Prunus* (western choke-cherry). Large quantities of these young shoots were needed for basketry, such as 500 to 675 sourberry sticks from six separate patches that had been burned or pruned prior to being harvested for the making of one cradleboard (Fig. 17.4).

BURNING TO ENHANCE DEERGRASS AND BEAR-GRASS

Deergrass (*Muhlenbergia rigens*) is a large native perennial bunchgrass occurring below 2,150 m along streams and in

FIGURE 17.2. Eliza Coon, a Pomo woman, weaving a basket. Note the long straight branches protruding from the basket, signifying that the shrub from which the branches were obtained was pruned or burned prior to harvest. (Photo courtesy of the Smithsonian Institute #47,749-D. Photo taken by H.W. Henshaw, circa 1892–1893.)

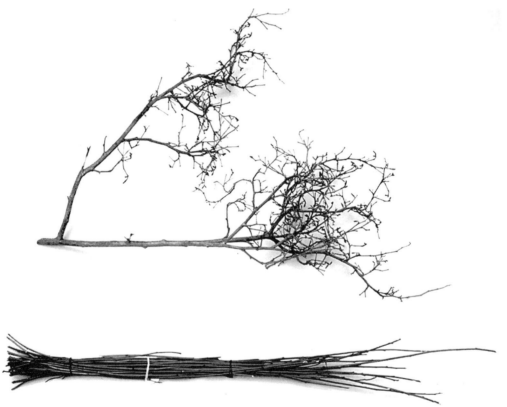

FIGURE 17.3. Contrasting plant architectures of managed versus wild sourberry (*Rhus trilobata*) (read from bottom to top). Weavers select branches with strict parameters: they must be flexible, straight, long, and with no lateral branching. Weavers burn or prune shrubs to create this young growth. Wild growth, which is several to many years old, on the other hand, exhibits many short lateral branches that are crooked and unsuitable for weaving.

chaparral, oak woodland, and other plant community types (Peterson 1993). It was used as basketry material by tribes whose territories covered more than half of California. Valuable parts of the plant were the flower stalks used in the foundation of coiled baskets (Merrill 1923). Deergrass is still gathered today and is highly valued by contemporary weavers.

The stalks are gathered in the late spring, while still green, or in summer or fall when golden brown (Anderson 1996).

A Western Mono cooking basket would take 3,750 flower stalks to complete, requiring at least three dozen large bunchgrass plants. A small Western Mono gift basket would require over 1,000 stalks (Anderson 1993). Yet, when surveying

FIGURE 17.4. Wahnomkot
(Wukchumni Yokuts) displaying coils
of split basketry materials that come
from hundreds of branches of young
shrubs and rhizomes from sedges.
(Courtesy of the Yosemite Museum,
Yosemite National Park. Photograph
by Frank F. Latta.)

wildlands in many areas, deergrass is difficult to find in large colonies, although formerly it must have existed in great abundance (Beetle 1947). Today, plants are usually found in small scattered populations of less than a dozen plants along roads, streams, and in meadows. And frequently the grasses contain very few stalks.

Traditionally areas were burned by different tribes to decrease detritus, increase flower stalk production, reduce competition, and recycle nutrients (Shipek 1989, Anderson 1996). Another very important reason to burn was to create and maintain openings conducive to the sunlight requirements of deergrass (Lathrop and Martin 1982). Thus, deergrass not only occurred along streams and in mountain meadows, but also large patches were maintained and encouraged within lower mixed conifer forests and chaparral.

Without indigenous fires, many colonies are being out-competed by surrounding vegetation types (Anderson 1996).

Another plant that is used for basketry that requires periodic burning is bear-grass. The young leaves of this plant were gathered by the Wailaki, Karuk, Tolowa, Yurok and other tribes in northern California for the making of baskets (Clarke Memorial Museum 1985, Turnbaugh and Turnbaugh 1986) and are still highly valued today by contemporary basketweavers (Heffner 1984). Bear-grass grows on dry open slopes, ridges, and montane coniferous forests below 2,300 m (7,546 ft) (McNeal 1993). Burning of areas for bear-grass has been recorded among the Karuk, Yurok, and Chilula in northwestern California (Gibbs 1851:29, Gifford 1939, Kroeber 1939, Clarke Memorial Museum 1985:51). The best bear-grass leaves are the new green leaves after a burn, which are

FIGURE 17.5. Mrs. Freddie, a Hupa woman, pouring water from a basket cup into acorn meal being leached in a hollow in the sand. To her right is an acorn-collecting basket. Setting fires under various kinds of oaks ensured a continual supply of non-wormy, disease-free acorns. (Photograph by Pliny E. Goddard, 1902. Photo courtesy of the Phoebe Hearst Museum, #15-3329.)

more easily picked and worked in this state, being more pliable, stronger, and thinner.

Fire as an Agricultural Tool

Many food plants that contain edible plant parts—bulbs, leaves, fruits, and seeds—occurred in open woods, meadows, prairies, or grasslands in California and required systematic burning to keep plant populations healthy and abundant, and to keep surrounding vegetation from encroaching. Large, venerable oak trees of various species produced acorns that were the staff of life to Native American cultures for millennia. Many tribes in California used fire as a vegetation management tool to ensure continual yields of high-quality acorns (Schenck and Gifford 1952, McCarthy 1993) (Fig. 17.5). In addition to acorns, the grains of many native grasses and seeds of diverse wildflowers were eaten and relished by all tribal cultures. Grains and seeds were eaten raw, parched, or made into cakes, bread, or soup by many tribes.

To facilitate harvesting, stimulate seed production, protect the perennial stock, replenish the annual stock, recycle nutrients, and remove detritus to allow for new growth and easy access, areas were burned by indigenous groups in many parts of California (Driver and Massey 1957, Anderson 2005). The Paiute burned the brush in the hills near their winter villages and then broadcast seeds of *Mentzelia* and *Chenopodium* (Steward 1938). Shipek (1977) recorded burning by the Luiseño in southern California to eliminate insect pests and parasites that damaged seed crops.

The underground swollen stems of many other species were relished by California tribes and were second in impor-

tance in the vegetal diet, next to grains and seeds. Eaten raw, boiled, or baked in an earth oven, these plant parts were referred to as "Indian potatoes" and are also called bulbs, corms, or tubers. Some of these also formed important medicines. They were harvested with a digging stick before, during, or after flowering—depending on the plant species, tribe, and individual family. Habitats, as well as specific plant populations, were manipulated with deliberately set fires. Areas were burned to reduce plant competition, facilitate gathering, recycle nutrients, and increase the size and number of bulbs and tubers (Baxley 1865, Peri and Patterson 1979, Shepherd 1989, Anderson 1993) (Fig. 17.6).

Greens, although ranking third in importance in the indigenous diet after bulbs and seeds, were nonetheless attractive for their storage value and vitamins and minerals. Greens are defined as the leaves and stems of various herbaceous plants. These were eaten raw, boiled, or steamed. Plant species that harbored edible greens weren't "naturally" productive continuously, over many years, but required fire to maintain their quality and quantity. Clover patches were burned by the Wukchumni Yokuts, North Fork Mono, and Pomo (Peri et al. 1982, Anderson 1993. Aginsky (1943) records the "burning of herbage for better wild crops" among the Valley Yokuts, Chukchansi Yokuts, Western Mono, and Southern, Central, and Northern Miwok. The Maidu burned areas to encourage the growth of bulbs and greens (Duncan 1964).

Fruits were gathered in substantial quantities and often dried and stored for winter use. Fire was used as a management tool to maintain or increase fruit production of native shrubs such as manzanita (*Arctostaphylos* spp.), elderberry (*Sambucus* spp.), choke-cherry (*Prunus virginiana* var.

FIGURE 17.6. Alferetta and Grapevine Tom (both Pit River) digging *bulidum'* (*Lomatium californicum*) near Black Tom Bar. The tubers were probably used medicinally and ceremonially. (Courtesy of the Santa Barbara Museum of Natural History.) The digging of many different kinds of bulbs and tubers with a hardwood digging stick; replanting propagules; and burning over areas to increase numbers, densities, and size of subterranean organs of wild plants for food was a common practice in many parts of California.

demissa), wild strawberry *(Fragaria vesca)*, blackberry, wild grape *(Vitis californica)*, and gooseberry *(Ribes* spp.). The Pit River, for example, burned fields and forests to stimulate growth of seed and berry plants (Garth 1953). Peri et al. (1982) reported that the Pomo people burned manzanita shrubs and that berries provided foods, leaves provided medicines, and branches were used for clubs. The Karuk burned huckleberry areas to enhance shrub growth and productivity (Harrington 1932). The Maidu, Foothill Yokuts, Western Mono, and Miwok tribes burned shrubs in order to thin dense shrub canopies and reduce insect activity by eliminating old wood, thus increasing fruit production (Jewell 1971 as quoted in Roper-Wickstrom 1987, Anderson 1993).

Possible Ecological Impacts of Indigenous Burning

Indigenous burning was conducted at different levels of biological organization. Thus, the ecological consequences of these practices would register at the organism, population, community, and landscape scales.

Organism Level

Individual favored shrubs and trees were manipulated through spot burning, weeding, pruning, and knocking to enhance production and quality of a desired plant part and change the plant architecture (Fig. 17.7). California tribes knocked the branches of oak trees and pinyon pines with poles, causing the edible acorns and pine nuts to fall to the ground. Knocking acted as a pruning process because, "some branch tips and leaves and brittle and dead twigs were also removed in the process, while dead or diseased limbs were intentionally broken off. This autumnal 'pruning' increased the surface area of the canopy and fruit production by stimulating the growth of new branchlets and foliage the following year" (Peri and Patterson 1979:39). Many indigenous cultures, such as the Miwok, climbed into trees or used

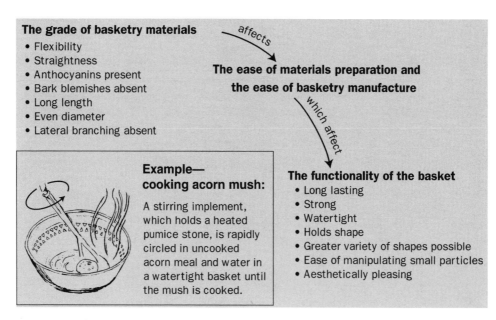

The grade of basketry materials
- Flexibility
- Straightness
- Anthocyanins present
- Bark blemishes absent
- Long length
- Even diameter
- Lateral branching absent

affects

The ease of materials preparation and the ease of basketry manufacture

which affect

Example— cooking acorn mush:

A stirring implement, which holds a heated pumice stone, is rapidly circled in uncooked acorn meal and water in a watertight basket until the mush is cooked.

The functionality of the basket
- Long lasting
- Strong
- Watertight
- Holds shape
- Greater variety of shapes possible
- Ease of manipulating small particles
- Aesthetically pleasing

FIGURE 17.7. There are strong links between quality and quantity of plant material, ease of manufacture, and functionality of finished product. Frequently, native plants were not abundant enough or of the proper grade in their wild state, necessitating fire management.

hooked sticks and broke off dead or dying branches for firewood, removing diseased and dying wood that could harbor disease and insects (Barrett and Gifford 1933). Tribes in different parts of California purposefully pruned individual shrubs and trees repeatedly or piled brush onto individual shrubs and set them on fire to induce their rapid elongation of young shoots for arrows, looped stirring sticks, musical instruments, traps, baskets, regalia, cages, and many other items. By keeping plants in a physiologically young state, it may have prolonged their life spans.

Population Level

Encouragement of plant populations by burning, sowing, tilling, weeding, and other techniques changed their arrangement in space, affecting species' densities and abundances. Burning and sowing seeds of wildflowers such as *Wyethia helenoides, Clarkia* sp., and *Mentzelia* sp. (Hudson 1901, Steward 1938) probably promoted high concentrations of one favored species in an area encouraging them to grow in a clumped or aggregated pattern. Over time, Native Americans assert, these techniques expanded certain gathering tracts for populations of that species. Selection for these desirable species probably led to the reduction of other less desirable species that grew in association with these favored species.

The visual effect of encouraging populations of plant species at particular gathering sites was a high degree of "patchiness" with some areas devoted to one species. Many journals of early settlers describe these wildflower patches of one color (Purdy 1976, Mayfield 1993). Patches of basketry grasses also were encouraged, such as deergrass colonies in ponderosa pine forests, chaparral, and blue oak woodlands.

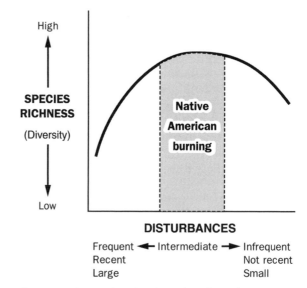

FIGURE 17.8. Intermediate disturbance hypothesis after Connell 1978. It can be postulated that the temporal and spatial scales of Native American burning and other indigenous disturbances most closely fit the "intermediate" zone (*gray region*).

These patches were burned to increase flower stalk production for basketry, decrease dead material, and expand the tract.

Plant Community Level

Indigenous burning practices probably changed the physiognomy of many communities, such as woodlands, shrublands, and forests, and encouraged a variety of plant species in the understory. Techniques, especially burning, changed

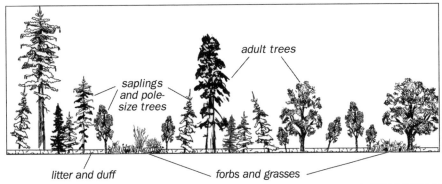

FIGURE 17.9. Mixed conifer forest types created by three local fire regimes. At *top,* medium-density forest with fires due to lightning only (every 15 years); medium biodiversity, with medium rate of nutrient cycling and medium depth of litter and duff. In the *middle,* park-like, pine-dominated forest with fires due to Native American burning (every 2 to 5 years) and lightning (every 15 years); greatest biodiversity, with highest rate of nutrient cycling and thinnest layer of litter and duff. At *bottom,* dense, fir-dominated forest due to fire suppression management or rocky area not susceptible to burning by lightning or Native Americans; least biodiversity, with lowest rate of nutrient cycling and thickest layer of litter and duff. (Adapted from article "Simulated indigenous management: a new model for ecological restoration in national parks" published in Ecological Restoration, 2003, 21:269–277.)

the species richness, evenness, and diversity. Under indigenous burning regimes, hardwood and softwood forests were comprised of widely spaced trees. Increased insolation on the forest floor and exposed bare mineral soil, heightened seed germination rates of herbaceous plants, and probably led to an increase in plant species diversity on an area basis (Figs. 17.8 and 17.9).

Landscape Level

Landscapes can be viewed as mosaics of ecosystems, generated by physical and ecological processes (Pickett 1976). In addition to natural processes, Indians introduced systematic changes that probably maximized landscape heterogeneity (Figs. 17.9 and 17.10). It was recognized by many Native American groups that some plant community types, while covering small land surface areas, harbored extremely useful and varied plant life. Hand clearing and burning were used to maintain ponds, marshes, meadows, and prairies. Burning probably expanded special plant community subtypes such as black oak–ponderosa pine, prolonged the life of dry meadows by destroying trees, and recycled the nutrients of dead

tules and cattails in marshlands (Anderson 1993, Anderson and Moratto 1996). Fire mosaics promoted an abundance of water in numerous springs and creeks (Duncan 1964; James Rust, Southern Sierra Miwok, pers. comm. 1989). Fire was used in many ways, some revealing a highly sophisticated understanding of natural processes. For example, in California, burning at mid-elevations was for the express purpose of removing shrub and duff layers, promoting a more tightly assembled snowpack, reducing transpiration, and reducing foliage interception of snow. This dense snowpack melted off more slowly in the spring, reducing flooding and causing ephemeral creeks and streams to run longer in the summer (Jewell 1971).

Extent of Human Influence with Fire

Given the diverse habitat types in California, the uneven indigenous occupation in some types, and the flammability of some kinds of vegetation, indigenous influence with fire was neither uniform nor equally effective across landscapes. The upper montane and subalpine forests, the drier desert regions of southern California, the lower salt marsh areas, the

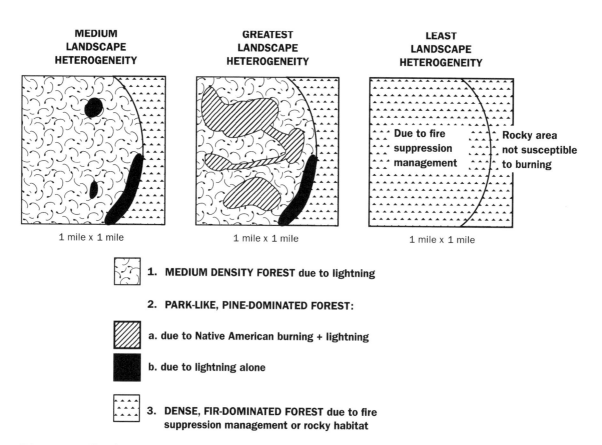

MEDIUM
LANDSCAPE
HETEROGENEITY

GREATEST
LANDSCAPE
HETEROGENEITY

LEAST
LANDSCAPE
HETEROGENEITY

Due to fire
suppression
management

Rocky area
not susceptible
to burning

1 mile x 1 mile   1 mile x 1 mile   1 mile x 1 mile

1. **MEDIUM DENSITY FOREST** due to lightning

2. **PARK-LIKE, PINE-DOMINATED FOREST:**

a. due to Native American burning + lightning

b. due to lightning alone

3. **DENSE, FIR-DOMINATED FOREST** due to fire
suppression management or rocky habitat

FIGURE 17.10. Hypothetical mosaic as seen from above of mixed conifer forest types created by three different regional fire regimes. Types 1, 2, and 3 are those shown in Figure 17.9. It can be postulated that lightning and Native American burning resulted in the greatest landscape heterogeneity.

beach and dune communities, and the alkali flats and serpentine balds with widely spaced plants do not burn readily. Remote areas in the back country that were not visited by Native Americans may have been shaped very little, if at all by Indian burning. Furthermore, there were also areas that were off limits to burning by Indians.

Perhaps a more reasonable and accurate way of viewing Indian interventions in California landscapes is as part of a continuum that would encompass a full range of human modifications from very little or no Native American influence to fully human-created ecosystems. The serpentine barrens and subalpine flora of various parts of California would qualify as uninfluenced wilderness at one endpoint, whereas the agricultural fields of the Mojave, the coastal prairies of the northwest coastal tribes of California and the desert fan palm oases of the Cahuilla in southern California are heavily influenced at the other endpoint. Other landscapes fall somewhere in the middle of the continuum, reflecting some degree of indigenous influence. The most heavily influenced landscapes make up about 20 percent of California.

Vale (2002) also suggests that Native American influences varied along gradients from a humanized to a pristine landscape. He defined three gradients at different scales. The *intensity* scale varies with different levels of occupation and activities from village sites to remote hunting areas. The *spatial* scale encompasses variation in the degree to which the effect

of local humans extends spatially. The *temporal* scale indicates the degree to which areas once occupied by humans continue to be in evidence on the landscape. While the degree of human influence might be arguable, it is irrefutable that Native Americans influenced California landscapes.

Management of the landscape for cultural purposes remains an important activity for Native Americans today. A major issue for land management agencies is to provide opportunities for these practices to continue. As their cultures evolve, their practices will also evolve, but it is important that their heritage be preserved. Without opportunities for continuing Native American cultural practices, California is in danger of not only losing that heritage, but also the ecosystem patterns and elements that were maintained by anthropogenic fire and its effects on biodiversity and ecosystem function.

References

Aginsky, B. W. 1943. Culture element distributions, XXIV, Central Sierra. University of California Anthropological Records 8(4).

Anderson, M. K. 1993. Indian fire-based management in the sequoia-mixed conifer forests of the central and southern Sierra Nevada. Final Report to the Yosemite Research Center, Yosemite National Park. United States Department of Interior. National Park Service. Western Region. Cooperative Agreement Order Number 8027–002.

Anderson, M. K. 1996. The ethnobotany of deergrass, *Muhlenbergia rigens* (Poaceae): Its uses and management by California Indian tribes. Economic Botany 50(4):409–422.

Anderson, M. K. 1999. The fire, pruning, and coppice management of temperate ecosystems for basketry material by California Indian tribes. Human Ecology 27(1):79–113.

Anderson, M. K. 2005. Tending the wild: Native American knowledge and the management of California's natural resources. University of California Press, Berkeley.

Anderson, M. K., and M. J. Moratto. 1996. Native American land-use practices and ecological impacts. Sierra Nevada Ecosystem Project: Final report to Congress, vol. II. Assessments and Scientific Basis for Management Options. University of California-Davis, Centers for Water and Wildland Resources.

Barrett, S. A. 1907. The material culture of the Klamath Lake and Modoc Indians of northeastern California and southern Oregon. Univ. of California Publications in American Archaeology and Ethnology 6(4):239–260.

Barrett, S. A., and Gifford, E. W. 1933. Miwok material culture: Indian life of the Yosemite region. Yosemite Association, Yosemite National Park, CA.

Bates, C. D. 1984. Traditional Miwok basketry. American Indian Basketry and Other Native Arts 4(13):3–18.

Baxley, W. H. 1865. What I saw on the west coast of South and North America and at the Hawaiian Islands. D. Appleton & Company, New York.

Beetle, A. A. 1947. Distribution of the native grasses of California. Hilgardia 17(9):309–357.

Blackburn, T. C., and K. Anderson. 1993. Introduction: managing the domesticated environment. Pages 15–25 in T. C. Blackburn and K. Anderson (eds.), Before the wilderness: native Californians as environmental managers. Ballena Press, Menlo Park, CA.

Boyd, R. T. (ed.). 1999. Indians, fire, and the land. Oregon State University Press, Corvallis, OR.

Clark, G. 1894. Letter to the board of commissioners of the Yosemite Valley and Mariposa Big Tree Grove. August 30. Contained in the Yosemite Research Library. Yosemite National Park, CA.

Clarke Memorial Museum. 1985. The Hover Collection of Karuk baskets. Clarke Memorial Museum, Eureka, CA.

Connell, J. H. 1978. Diversity in tropical rainforests and coral reefs. Science 199:1302–1310.

Cook, S. F. 1971. The aboriginal population of Upper California. Pages 66–72 in R. F. Heizer and M. A. Whipple (eds.), The California Indians: a source book. University of California Press, Berkeley, CA.

de Massey, E. 1926. A Frenchman in the goldrush, Part V. Translated by M. E. Wilbur. California Historical Society Quarterly 5(2):149.

Dixon, R. B. 1905. The Northern Maidu. The Huntington California Expedition. Bulletin of the American Museum of Natural History 17(3):119–346.

Driver, H. E. 1939. Culture element distributions X: northwest California. University of California Anthropological Records 1(6):297–433.

Driver, H. E., and W. C. Massey. 1957. Comparative studies of North American Indians. Transactions of the American Philosophical Society 47(2):1–456.

Du Bois, C. A. 1935. Wintu ethnography. University of California Publications in American Archaeology and Ethnology 36(1): 1–148.

Duncan III, J. W. 1964. Maidu Ethnobotany. Unpublished master's thesis. Sacramento State University, Sacramento.

Elsasser, A. B. [1962] 1972. Indians of Sequoia and Kings Canyon National Parks. Sequoia Natural History Association, Three Rivers.

Farmer, J. F. 1993. Preserving Diegueno basket weaving. Pages 141–147 in Christopher L. Moser (ed.), Native American basketry of Southern California. Riverside Museum Press. Riverside, CA.

Foster, G. M. 1944. A summary of Yuki culture. University of California Anthropological Records 5(3):155–244.

Garth, T. R. 1953. Atsugewi ethnography. UCPAR 14(2):129–212.

Gibbs, G. 1851. Journal of the expedition of Colonel Redick through northwestern California, 1851. In Archives of aboriginal knowledge collected by H. R. Schoolcraft, 1860. 3:115–134.

Gifford, E. W. 1939. Karok field notes, Part 1. Ethnological Document No. 174 in Dept. and Museum of Anthropology, University of California; Manuscript in University Archives, Bancroft Library, Berkeley.

Harrington, J. P. 1932. Tobacco among the Karuk Indians of California. Bureau of American Ethnology Bulletin 94. Washington, DC.

Heffner, K. 1984. Following the smoke: contemporary plant procurement by the Indians of northwest California. Unpublished document. Six Rivers National Forest. Eureka. 94 pp.

Heizer, R. F., and T. Kroeber. 1979. Ishi the last Yahi. University of Californi Press, Berkeley.

Hudson, J. W. 1901. Field notebook. G. H. M. Acc. No. 20,004. Collection of Grace Hudson Museum and Sun House, Ukiah, CA.

Jewell, D. 1971. Letter to R. Riegelhuth, Sequoia and Kings Canyon National Parks. On file, Research Office, Sequoia and Kings Canyon National Parks, Three Rivers, CA.

Kauffman, J. B., and R. E. Martin. 1990. Sprouting shrub response to different seasons and fuel consumption levels of prescribed fire in Sierra Nevada mixed conifer ecosystems. Forest Science 36(3):748–764.

Keeley, J. E., and P. H. Zedler. 1978. Reproduction of chaparral shrubs after fire: a comparison of the sprouting and seeding strategies. American Midland Naturalist 99:142–161.

Kelsey, H. 1986. Juan Rodríguez Cabrillo. Huntington Library, San Marino, CA

Kroeber, A. L. 1939. Unpublished field notes on the Yurok. University Archives, Bancroft Library (quoted from Stewart 2002).

Kroeber, A. L. 1976. Handbook of the Indians of California. Bureau of American Ethnology Bulltetin 78. Washington D.C. Reprinted in 1976 by Dover Publications, New York.

Lathrop, E., and B. Martin. Fire ecology of deergrass *(Muhlenbergia rigens)* in Cuyamaca Rancho State Park, California. Crossosoma 8(5):1–4, 9–10.

Lewis, H. T. 1993. Patterns of Indian burning in California: ecology and ethnohistory. Pages 55–116 in Before the wilderness: environmental management by native Californians. Ballena Press, Menlo Park, CA.

Lewis, H. T., and M. K. Anderson. 2002. Introduction. Pages 3–16 in O. C. Stewart, H. T. Lewis, and M. K. Anderson, (eds.), Forgotten fires: Native Americans and the transient wilderness. University of Oklahoma Press, Norman.

Martin, R. E., and D. B. Sapsis. 1992. Fires as agents of biodiversity–pyrodiversity promotes biodiversity. Proc. of the Symp. on Biodiversity of Northwestern California. October, 1991. R. R. Harris and D. C. Erman (eds.), Div. of Agric. and Nat'l. Res., University of California.

Mathewson, M. 1998. The living web: contemporary expressions of Californian Indian basketry. Ph.D. thesis, unpublished. University of California, Berkeley.

Mayfield, T.J. 1993. Indian summer: traditional life among the Choinumne Indians of California's San Joaquin Valley. Heyday Books, Berkeley, CA.

McCarthy, H. 1993. Managing oaks and the acorn crop. In T.C. Blackburn and M.K. Anderson (eds.), Before the wilderness: Native Californians as environmental managers. Ballena Press, Menlo Park, CA.

McCrone, J. 2000. Fired up. New Scientist 166(2239):30–34.

McNeal, D.W. 1993. *Xerophyllum*: bear-grass, Indian basket-grass. Pages 1208–1210 in J.C. Hickman (ed.), The Jepson manual: higher plants of California. University of California Press, Berkeley.

Merriam, C.H. 1955. Studies of California Indians. University of California Press, Berkeley.

Merrill, R.E. 1923. Plants used in basketry by the California Indians. University of California Publications in American Archaeology and Ethnology, Berkeley 20(13):215–242.

Moratto, M.J. 1984. California Archaeology. Academic Press, Orlando, FL.

Olmstead, D.L., and O.C. Stewart. 1978. Achumawi. Pages 225–235 in R.F. Heizer (ed.), Handbook of North American Indians, Vol. 8. California. Smithsonian Institution, Washington, DC.

Ortiz, B., and staff (eds.). 1991. California Indian basketweavers gathering June 28–30, 1991: a special report. News from Native California: An Inside View of the California Indian World 6(1): 13–36.

Peri, D.W., and S.M. Patterson. 1979. Ethnobotanical resources of the Warm Springs Dam–Lake Sonoma Project Area, Sonoma County, California. Final Report (unpublished) for the U.S. Army Corps of Engineers Contract No. DACW07–78–C–0043. Elgar Hill Environmental Planning and Analysis and Sonoma State University.

Peri, D.W., S.M. Patterson, and J.L. Goodrich. 1982. Ethnobotanical mitigation Warm Springs Dam—Lake Sonoma California. In Elgar Hill and Richard N. Lerner (eds.), Report of Elgar Hill, environmental analysis and planning, Penngrove, CA.

Peterson, P.M. 1993. *Muhlenbergia: muhly*. Pages 1272–1274 in J.C. Hickman (ed.), The Jepson manual: higher plants of California. University of California Press, Berkeley.

Philpot, C.W. 1980. Vegetative features as determinants of fire frequency and intensity. Pages 202–215 in H.A. Mooney and C.E. Conrad (eds.), Proceedings of the symposium on the environmental consequences of fire and fuel management in mediterranean ecosystems, August 1–5, 1977. Palo Alto, CA. Gen. Tech. Rep. WO–3. Washington, DC.

Pickett, S.T.A. 1976. Succession: an evolutionary interpretation. The American Naturalist 110:(971):107–119.

Potts, M. 1977. The Northern Maidu. Naturegraph, Happy Camp, CA.

Purdy, C. 1976. My life and my times. Privately published by E. E. Humphrey and M.E. Humphrey. (No location listed).

Roper Wickstrom, C.K. 1987. Issues concerning Native American use of fire: a literature review. Yosemite Research Center Yosemite National Park, National Park Service, U.S. Department of Interior. Publications in Anthropology No. 6.

Sauer, C.O. 1981. The agency of man on the earth. Pages 330–363 in Selected Essays 1963–1975. University of California Press, Berkeley.

Schenck, S.M., and E.W. Gifford. 1952. Karok ethnobotany. Anthropological Records 13(6):377–392.

Shepard, A. 1989. Wintu Texts. University of California Press, Berkeley.

Shipek, F.C. 1977. A strategy for change: the Luiseño of southern California. Ph.D. Dissertation in Anthropology at the University of Hawaii.

Shipek, F.C. 1989. An example of intensive plant husbandry: the Kumeyaay of southern California. Pages 159–170 in D.R. Harris and G.C. Hillman (eds.), Foraging and farming: the evolution of plant exploitation. Unwin-Hyman Publishers, London.

Steward, J.H. 1935. Indian tribes of Sequoia National Park region. U.S. Department of Interior, National Park Service, Berkeley, CA.

Steward, J.H. 1938. Basin-Plateau aboriginal sociopolitical groups. Smithsonian Institution Bureau of American Ethnology Bulletin 120. United States Government Printing Office Washington, DC.

Stewart, O.C. 2002. Forgotten fires: Native Americans and the transient wilderness. H.T. Lewis and M.K. Anderson (eds.). University of Oklahoma Press, Norman.

Sutter, J.A. 1939. New Helvetia diary: a record of events kept by John A. Sutter and his clerks at New Helvetia, California, from September 9, 1845, to May 25, 1848. Grabhorn Press, in arrangement with the Society of California Pioneers, San Francisco.

Thompson, L. [1916] 1991. To the American Indian: reminiscences of a Yurok woman. Heyday Press, Berkeley, CA.

Timbrook, J., J.R. Johnson, and D.D. Earle. 1993. Vegetation burning by the Chumash. Pages 117–149 in Before the wilderness: environmental management by Native Californians. Ballena Press, Menlo Park, CA.

Turnbaugh, S.P., and W.A. Turnbaugh. 1986. Indian baskets. Schiffer Publishing, Ltd., West Chester, PA.

Vale, T.R. 2002. Pre-European landscape of the United States: pristine or humanized? Pages 1–40 in T.R. Vale (ed.), Fire, native peoples, and the natural landscape. Island Press, Washington, DC. 315 p.

Voegelin, E.W. 1938. Tubatulabal ethnography. University of California Anthropological Records 2(1):1–84.

Weiner, S., Q. Xu, P. Goldberg, J. Liu, and O. Bar-Yosef. 1998. Evidence for the use of fire at Zhoukoudian, China. Science 281(5374):251–253.

CHAPTER 18

Fire Management and Policy Since European Settlement

SCOTT L. STEPHENS AND NEIL G. SUGIHARA

Everywhere, and from the earliest times, humans have altered
the natural fire regimes they have encountered.

PYNE *et al.* 1996

Since European explorers first touched the shores of California, their activities, shaped by their needs and values, have changed the state's fire regimes. Fire regime changes have resulted, directly and indirectly, from a variety of human activities. At times, these influences have been unintentional consequences of other land management activities; in other instances, they have been well planned and even codified. All of the activities that have affected fire regimes are considered here as fire *management,* but only those that have been intentionally and formally adopted by society are considered fire *policies*.

Formal fire policy since European settlement is a response to society's and institutions' views of fire. These change as human relationships with the land, natural resources, and fire change. Our understanding of the historical relationships between fire and society is greatly enhanced if we review the setting in which that society existed. It is common for us to blame our current fire situation on the shortcomings and lack of perspective of past land managers. But this is rarely the case. The needs and values of society were the driving force of past policies, and those needs and values have changed and will continue to change. In this chapter, we discuss the activities and events that have had the greatest effect on fire in California, why they occurred, and how they influenced fire regimes.

European Exploration Era

The earliest European explorers to visit California came by ship. The "discovery" of Alta (upper) California by European explorers is generally credited to Juan Rodriguez Cabrillo, who sailed up the coast from Baja (lower) California in 1542. Following his death at San Miguel Island in January of 1543, his crew continued to explore northward reaching what is now southern Oregon. They could make no landings north of Point Conception and eventually returned to Mexico. No other European explorers visited the coast of Upper California until Francis Drake and his party landed at Drakes Bay near what is now called Point Reyes in 1579. The first overland journey that extended far into the state was not made until 1769 when Gaspar de Portola's expedition "discovered" San Francisco Bay.

These early explorers were motivated by discovery, conquest, and the pursuit of riches. The voyages were challenging, and landings were difficult and very few. Most of this early discovery was merely a view from off shore. These explorers were not settlers and had little long-term contact with the land, people, or ecosystems that they discovered. So why, as fire ecologists, do we care about their exploits? Because their visits had unintended, long-lasting, and important influences on California fire regimes.

The first significant impacts on fire regimes that the European civilization brought to California actually predate the arrival of large-scale permanent settlers by over a century. The impacts were the introduction of the human diseases that decimated the populations of indigenous peoples and the introduction of plants from other parts of the world. Although both of these impacts involved the expansion of the historic ranges of biological organisms, they had very different mechanisms for influencing fire regimes. Both of these actions were inadvertent but were to have enormous impacts on California ecosystems that continue to the present.

Removal of Native American Fire Use

Manipulation of fire by Native Americans had many important impacts on the character and geographic distribution of California's fire regimes, and greatly modified fire as an ecological process (Anderson 2005). The removal of the Native Americans and their fire use had variable effects on California's ecosystems. Although there was little or no change to ecosystems where fire was very rare, or where fire regimes were not altered by the activities of the Native Americans, there was often a profound change on ecosystems in the areas where they actively managed with fire, including many oak woodlands, montane meadows, coastal grasslands, and coniferous forests. These ecosystems now supported a different burning pattern, replacing the specific pattern of Native American ignitions and lightning with a new combination of settler burning and lightning. Coastal areas experience little lightning, and fire regimes in these areas were dominated by anthropogenic ignitions (Keeley 2005, Stephens and Fry 2005, Stephens and Libby 2006). Removal of anthropogenic fire from these ecosystems has brought about wholesale changes in species composition, by encroachment of invasive species, conversion to other vegetation types, and increased fire hazards (van Wagtendonk 1996; Stephens 1998, 2004, Stephens and Fule 2005, Stephens and Moghaddas 2005).

Introduction of Invasive Non-Native Plant Species

The introduction of non-native invasive plant species began when the explorers visited the California coast during the 1500s and 1600s. The establishment of the Jesuit Missions in the late 1700s with their livestock and horticultural activities greatly accelerated the establishment and expanded the ranges of non-native grasses and forbs in California (Menke et al. 1996).

Cattle ranching in California began on the coast in 1769 when the Spanish brought about 200 head of cattle to San Diego. By 1823, livestock grazing was an established activity, to various degrees, at all 21 missions. At its peak, the missions may have had more than 400,000 cattle grazing one sixth of California's land area. In the Central Valley, grazing by domestic livestock was light until after the gold rush. In 1860, the U.S. Census reported nearly a million beef cattle (not including open range cattle), just over a million sheep, and 170,000 horses in California. As range quality declined, sheep ranching gained in favor with a peak of 5.7 million animals in 1880 (Barbour et al. 1993).

Among the newly introduced plants were several species that were adapted to the rangelands in the mediterranean climates of southern Europe. They had invasive habits and rapidly out-competed the native species in many of the plant communities, especially those dominated by herbaceous plants. Changes in climate over the last centuries could also have influenced plant community responses and composition (Millar and Woolfenden 1999).

Many of California's grasslands and woodlands are currently dominated by invasive species (Menke et al. 1996), and changes in species composition have influenced fire regimes. For example, fuel from introduced annual grasslands cures earlier, recovers faster, and has greater continuity than the native vegetation that previously occupied the sites. This allows the fire season to begin in the late spring, shortens fire-return intervals, and increases fire size. In general, invasive plant species have a greater impact in mesic conditions and at lower elevations than harsher alpine or subalpine ecosystems. Non-native species also aggressively colonize many ecosystems when openings are created by mechanical methods or high-severity fire. Chapter 22 includes an in-depth treatment of invasive species and fire in California ecosystems.

Early Settlement

California Mission Era—Alta California

During the time period from 1769 to 1823, a string of Spanish missions were established as the first permanent outposts of European settlements. These were expansions of the established footholds in Mexico and grew from San Diego northward to as far as Sonoma in northern California (Bean 1973, Watkins, 1983).

Private Spanish land grants to establish pueblos or towns were introduced in California starting in 1775 and used extensively beginning in 1784. These grants provided colonists with livestock to establish herds to be grazed on common lands. Each grantee was required to build a storehouse and to stock his holdings with at least 2,000 head of cattle. By 1790, there were 19 private rancheros in California. During the Spanish and Mexican periods, more than 800 large grants of land were given to Hispanics and some European immigrants who settled in California. The effect of these grants was to expand the area of California being utilized by domestic livestock.

The Treaty of Guadalupe Hidalgo explicitly guaranteed that these land grants would be honored by the United States. Several of the land grants were larger than 40,468 ha (100,000 acres). With the beginning of the Gold Rush and the influx of new settlers, Americans complained about the size of such land claims. The U.S. Senate sympathized with the new immigrants, not the rancheros, most of whom were Hispanic, and passed legislation that allowed multiple appeals on land claim decisions. Thus, most claims remained unresolved for years. The Californios had to prove ownership, a difficult task because few accurate surveys had ever been made. The cost of court proceedings often consumed more than the property was worth.

Although fur trappers worked the rivers and streams throughout the state in the 1830s, they did not establish permanent settlements. The missions and small communities such as Monterey and Sutter's Fort near present-day Sacramento were the major European outposts in California until the arrival of settlers from the east in the early 1840s.

Although the missions were small outposts, their establishment represents an important historic and ecological milestone for two main reasons. First, they continued the decline in Native American population and ecological influences, replacing them with influences of European ancestry, who had a different land ethic. Second, they expanded the introduction of domestic livestock and also introduced herbaceous plants from other parts of the world. The domestic livestock served to extend the ranges of the non-native plants in California. Both of these milestones initiated major alterations to California flora and fire regimes that are still important today.

Although no large-scale direct manipulations of the fire regimes were made during this time period, it still resulted in drastic alterations in the role of fire in California's ecosystems. The removal of widespread and often-focused Native American burning was accomplished indirectly by relocating the people and decimating the population by introducing diseases. This was an especially important change to fire regimes where focused, long-term, Native American burning maintained vegetation under conditions that would not persist without them. As detailed in Chapter 17, these ecosystems were often manipulated using fire to increase the reliability of food crops and cordage materials (Anderson 2005). This abrupt halt in the use of fire initiated ecosystem change in many areas of California.

The Gold Rush and Early Statehood

Growth of the non-indigenous population was slow during the years following the establishment of the missions. This changed in a single year with the discovery of gold in January 1848 at Sutter's Mill east of Sacramento in the foothills of the Sierra Nevada. The California Gold Rush of 1849 saw the population explode from about 2,000 non-indigenous people at the time of the discovery to more than 53,000 by the close of 1849 (Shinn 1885, Farquhar 1966). The flood of settlers following the discovery of gold created a need for effective civil government in California. In September 1849, a convention met at Monterey and adopted a state constitution. The constitution was approved by popular vote on November 13, and on December 15 the first legislature met at San Jose to create an official state government. On September 9, 1850, California officially became the 31st state in the Union. The population growth during this time period was not just a growth in numbers, but was a sudden expansion of the population into many remote areas of the state.

The miners and early settlers had several direct and indirect impacts on the fire regimes during this era. Early settlers used fire to clear land for improved grazing and to facilitate the search for gold. Sheepherders often set fires on the way out of the mountains in the fall to improve forage for the next year. The developing railroad system served as a new source of ignitions. Widespread logging occurred in many areas near major mining centers to support both the mines and the population needed to work them (Stephens and Elliott-Fisk 1998, Stephens 2000). Much of the Lake Tahoe basin and areas of the eastern Sierra Nevada were logged to support the mines (Elliott-Fisk et al. 1997). Meanwhile, fire suppression efforts were confined to the immediate protection of structures.

Fire Control Era

Yellowstone and Yosemite were designated as national parks in 1872 and 1890, respectively, but at first no agency was assigned responsibility for their administration (van Wagtendonk 1991). When the United States Army was given the responsibility for managing Yellowstone in 1886, and

Yosemite and Sequoia in 1891, the policy of suppressing all fires began (Agee 1974, van Wagtendonk 1991). The National Park Service was established in 1916 and its administration passed into civilian hands.

Federal fire policy was formally started with establishment of large-scale forest reserves during the late 1800s and early 1900s. In 1891, congress authorized President Harrison to establish forest reserves, later to be known as National Forests (Pinchot 1907, Ruth 2000, Stephens and Ruth 2005). The U.S. Forest Service was established as a separate agency in 1905 with Gifford Pinchot as its first chief. Under his direction, a national forest fire policy was initiated and the agency began systematic fire suppression including the development of an infrastructure of fire control facilities, equipment, fire stations, lookouts, and trails. The forest reserves were created partly because Congress believed the nation's forests were being destroyed by fire and reckless cutting (Pinchot 1907). Pinchot declared that one of the objectives of the National Forests was to make sure that "timber was not burnt up."

A policy of fire suppression was not universally supported during this period. One of the most vocal groups that argued for the use of fire in forest management was a group of private foresters from the northern Sierra Nevada and southern Cascades (Clar 1959, Pyne 1982). In the late 1880s, they promoted the concept of "light burning" modeled after earlier Native American uses of fire. The main objective of this burning was to reduce fuel loads and associated damage when the inevitable wildfire occurred. Federal managers disagreed with this policy because of the damage to small trees and problems with fire escapes. Most foresters at this time believed that western forests were understocked and elimination of fire would ultimately produce higher yields of timber (Show and Kotok 1924).

There were many large forest fires in the late 1880s and early 1900s that influenced early federal forest fire policy (Pyne 1982, 1997, 2001). These fires included the Peshtigo (Wisconsin and Michigan, 1871), Michigan (Michigan 1881), Hinckley (Minnesota 1894), Wisconsin (Wisconsin 1894), Yacoult (Washington and Oregon, 1902), and Great Idaho (Idaho and Montana, 1910). Together these fires burned more than 4 million ha and killed approximately 2,500 people (Guthrie 1936). There was some awareness that forest harvesting practices may have contributed to some of these fires in some forest types (Perkins 1900, Stephens 2000), but this was not recognized by many early forest managers.

The Great Idaho fire of 1910 was pivotal in the development of early fire policy (Pyne 2001). In this wildfire, 78 firefighters were killed and over a million hectares of national forest lands were burned. It was time to "do something" about the wildfire threat and the 1910 fires instigated the creation of a national system of wildland fire protection.

Henry Graves, the second chief of the Forest Service was against the "light burning" policy, declaring "the first measure necessary for the successful practice of forestry is protection from fire" (Graves 1910). The earliest comprehensive federal fire control policy was written shortly after Graves was appointed (DuBois 1914). William Greeley, the third Forest Service chief, took over the agency in 1920 and continued the strong endorsement of fire suppression stating, "The conviction burned into me that fire prevention is the number one job of American foresters." (Greeley 1951). During Greeley's nine-year tenure, fire suppression was paramount in federal and private forest management.

A scientific study was initiated in California on the merits of fire suppression versus light underburning, and its conclusions supported a strong fire suppression policy (Show and Kotok 1924). The philosophy that nature could be dominated and controlled contributed to these early policies. Passage of the federal Clarke-McNary Act in 1924 tied federal appropriations to the state first adopting fire suppression and this law effectively created a national fire suppression policy.

The Berkeley fire of September 17, 1923 is a story of wildland fire on the interface with a new and rapidly growing urban area that has become all too familiar to Californians in recent decades. Biswell (1989) describes the progression of the 1923 fire:

> A strong hot, dry northeast wind quickly drove a fire through the grasslands and eucalyptus groves along the crest of the ridge above Berkeley. Firebrands from the eucalyptus allowed the fire to spread out of the wildlands onto the shingle rooftop of the first house at 2:20 pm. Within 40 minutes the fire spread throughout a one-half square mile area. Over a period of just two hours, 625 houses and other buildings were destroyed. At about 4:30 pm the cool moist coastal breeze took over and the firefighters extinguished the blaze.

Perhaps the most effective change that occurred with the industrialization of America and the subsequent scientific revolution was making the philosophy of "taming the wilderness" a possibility. Society was now developing effective tools and strategies for the protection of its valuable timber supply. Fire was seen as a potential threat to that timber supply, and large amounts of resources were committed to the removal of fire from America's forests.

In 1935, federal forest fire policy was updated to incorporate the "10 AM" policy, aimed at increasing suppression efficiency. This policy directed that all fires should be controlled in the first burning period or by 10 AM the following morning. To accomplish this objective, a large labor force and improved access to wildlands were necessary. The newly created Civilian Conservation Corps (CCC) provided thousands of workers to assist in this effort (Anderson et al. 1941, Pyne 1982). Efforts were made to increase the effectiveness of fire suppression by developing better access to further reduce response times, mapping vegetation and fuel hazards, and keeping detailed records of any large fires that occurred (van Wagtendonk 1991).

The first national education campaign designed to influence public behavior regarding forest fire began when the Forest Service created the Cooperative Forest Fire Prevention Program in 1942 (USDA 1995a). This program encouraged citizens nationwide to make a personal effort to prevent forest fires. The campaign was modified three years later to produce the national "Smokey Bear" campaign that is still in existence. Smokey Bear has been one of the most successful public education campaigns in the United States.

World War II had a lasting influence on fire suppression. During the war, fire suppression efforts were modest, due to the war effort. However, after the war there was a new, much more intensive fire suppression effort that included the widespread use of the tools that were developed and refined in the war (Stephens 2005). Aerial retardant drops, helitack crews, bulldozers, and smokejumpers became the new tools of choice and this new firefighting force was very effective in continuing the policy of full fire suppression (USDA 1960, van Wagtendonk 1991).

The public was now well shielded from the history of human–wildland fire relationships and fighting fires had become "The moral equivalent of war" (Pyne 1997). After World War II, firefighting efforts were further intensified. Science and technology were applied to the firefighting efforts and important strides were made toward understanding wildfire and its control. The study of fire concentrated on fire physics, fire behavior, and the relationships between meteorology and fire.

Beginning of Fire Use

The use of fire in the management of California private rangelands was common in the early 1900s to the 1960s (Biswell 1989, McClaran and Bartolome 1989, Stephens 1997). Private ranchers would pool resources and burn rangelands to increase forage for livestock. Fire use was tolerated by the state agencies that had oversight authority on private lands, but the burning was done by private citizens (Biswell 1989).

The effectiveness of fire protection was partly responsible for the beginnings of a shift in policy from fire control to fire management (van Wagtendonk 1991). Research was indicating that exclusion of fire caused shifts in species composition and forest structure, and increased fuel accumulations. Harold Biswell advocated the use of prescribed fire to reduce fuel accumulations in Sierra Nevada ponderosa pine forests (Biswell 1959). Hartesvelt and Harvey (1967) considered the greatest threat to giant sequoia (*Sequoiadendron giganteum* [*Lindley*] *Buchholz*) groves was not trampling by humans, but catastrophic fire burning through understory thickets and unnaturally high fuel accumulations.

In 1951, the first use of fire by the National Park Service occurred in Everglades National Park in Florida (Kilgore 1974). Several vegetation types in the park were fire adapted, including pine and mixed hardwood forests. The initial burns were designed to reduce understory vegetation and to promote pine regeneration (Robertson 1962).

In 1962, the Secretary of the Interior requested a wildlife management report, and it identified fire suppression as a policy that was adversely impacting wildlife habitats (Leopold et al. 1963). In 1968, the Leopold Committee report was incorporated into National Park Service policy, and for the first time since 1916, the National Park Service viewed fire as a natural process rather than a menace (van Wagtendonk 1991). Shortly after the report was commissioned, the first western federal prescribed fire occurred in California at Sequoia-Kings Canyon National Parks (1968) and two years later in Yosemite National Park (USDI 1968, van Wagtendonk 1991). This was the beginning of the use of fire on federal forested lands in the western United States. Creation of the national Wilderness System in 1964 also advanced the idea of wildland fire use in remote forested areas (Pyne 1982).

In 1968, the first experimental prescribed natural fire program (managed lightning fires to meet resource objectives) in Sequoia-Kings Canyon National Parks was created (USDI 1968, Kilgore 1974, Parsons et al. 1986). This program became possible because of earlier research on the fire ecology of mixed-conifer forest in the Sierra Nevada (Biswell 1961, Hartesveldt and Harvey 1967, Kilgore and Briggs 1972) and because of the recent change in National Park Service fire policy. The era of wildland fire use in the National Park Service had begun; the long era of total suppression that began in the early 1900s had ended (Agee 1974, Kilgore 1974, van Wagtendonk 1978).

Prescribed fire in the California State Park system was initiated in 1972 at Montana de Oro State Park on the Central Coast and then Calaveras Big Trees State Park in the Sierra Nevada. The program was initially the target of high levels of political and academic criticism, but persistent efforts to evaluate the biological impacts of fire and fire exclusion have supported the need for prescribed fire to maintain ecosystems (Biswell 1989). The prescribed fire program expanded to treat more than 4,000 acres a year by 1996. Today the program is coordinated on a statewide basis and focuses on restoring the natural role of fire in California (Barry and Harrison 2002).

Forest fire policy in the Forest Service changed from fire *control* to fire *management* in 1974. Henry DeBruin, Director of Fire and Aviation Management for the Forest Service, stated: "we are determined to save the best of the past as we change a basic concept from fire is bad to fire is good and bad" (DeBruin 1974). This was a major policy shift for the Forest Service, but fire suppression was still to dominate for the coming decades. Some Forest Service Wilderness areas such as the Selway-Bitterroot Wilderness in Idaho and Montana, and the Gila Wilderness in New Mexico began a program of prescribed natural fire but areas with similar management philosophies were few in number (Stephens and Ruth 2005). During this change, some Forest Service managers believed suppression would have to be increased to meet the demand of the new fire management policy (Sanderson 1974). In 1978, the Forest Service abandoned the 10 AM policy in favor of a new one that encouraged the use of prescribed fire. No Forest Service Wilderness areas in California adopted a prescribed natural fire program until the mid 1990s and areas with this type of management are still rare today.

In 1978, the National Park Service further refined its fire management policy to describe the conditions under which fire could be used and specified that any management fire would be suppressed if it posed a threat to human life, cultural resources, physical facilities, threatened or endangered species or if it threatened to escape from predetermined zones (van Wagtendonk 1991). In 1986, the National Park Service issued Wildland Fire Management Guidelines that detailed procedures and standards for managing wildfires, prescribed natural fires, and prescribed burns. These guidelines required that condition limits under which naturally ignited fires could be allowed to burn, the maximum size and boundaries, and daily monitoring and evaluation must be pre-planned (USDI National Park Service 1986). In 1988, a series of very large fires in the Greater Yellowstone Area again brought federal fire policy under review. Whereas fire policy was generally reaffirmed, greater emphasis was placed on the development of fire management plans (van Wagtendonk 1991).

Although management of fire on many jurisdictions is changing, protection of people and property is still the top priority. The State Board of Forestry and the California Department of Forestry (CDF) drafted a comprehensive update of the fire plan for wildland fire protection in California entitled "California Fire Plan—A Framework for Minimizing the Costs and Losses from Wildland Fires" (CDF 1996). This approach to management of wildland fire is focused on the reduction of the damage caused by wildfire and does not generally emphasize the role of fire in wildland natural resource management. This difference in perspective is explained by the fact that CDF is primarily a firefighting organization tasked with fire prevention and suppression on private and state lands. In contrast, the Forest Service, Bureau of Land Management, and National Park Service are primarily land management agencies tasked with land management as their primary mission.

In the last decade, CDF has increased the size and scope of their Vegetation Management Program, which encourages partnerships between private land owners to reduce fire hazards, primarily in the urban-wildland interface. Although this program has been successful in a relatively small number of communities, CDF still emphasizes fire suppression. Without a well-funded program of fuels management to complement their already strong fire suppression capability, it will be difficult or impossible to reduce fire losses in lands overseen by CDF. Certainly the added complexity of CDF not owning the majority of the lands where it has fire responsibility makes it difficult to initiate fuels management programs, but they are as essential as strong suppression programs. Without investments in both suppression and prevention, large, expensive, and destructive wildfires will continue on CDF-administered lands.

One area in which the state and counties can significantly improve fire management is by passing and enforcing laws that mandate the use of combustion-resistant construction materials and defensible space for every structure in the urban–wildland interface. Presently, counties have the majority of the jurisdiction in this area, but in most cases, they have been unwilling or incapable of providing this essential oversight. Losses of life and property in the urban–wildland interface will only be reduced when both private homeowners and adjacent wildland managers take steps to reduce fire hazards and risks. If only one side of the interface (private homeowners or adjacent wildland managers) takes steps to reduce its vulnerability to wildfire, the result will be continued large losses in this expanding area of California.

Fire science and management continue to change. Starting in the late 1960s and continuing today, the emphasis of fire research has become more focused on natural resource values and the influence of fire as an ecosystem process. There has been widespread acceptance of the idea that fire is an important part of many ecosystems, and that changes in the patterns of occurrence of fire have had many large-scale ecosystem impacts. Today, fire management has become the central issue in land management throughout the state.

In 1989, Harold Biswell asked, "Is fire management on a collision course with disaster?" and answered, "Perhaps, because wildfires continue to become more intense and destructive of resources, and expenses in fire control are increasing at an astronomical rate" (Biswell 1989). Today, the practice of managing wildland fuel to modify future fire behavior has become an important land management activity (Stephens and Moghaddas 2005). The wildland–urban interface has become one of the focal points for the application of fuel management in California. Although society as a whole continues to value the suppression of wildfire, and we continue to negatively affect ecosystems by reducing fire's impact as an important ecosystem process, there is an increasing recognition among land managers that the long-term exclusion of fire has changed fuel dynamics and is changing the patterns of uncontrollable wildfires.

Overview of Some Key Historic Fires, 1923–2005

Human interaction with fire during the period since European settlers first set foot in California is defined by the struggle to reduce the negative impacts of wildfire on society. Throughout this period, there have been efforts to remove fire from California's ecosystems. Even to this day, in which fire is widely recognized as an important ecosystem process, the efforts to restore and manage fire in the state's wildlands are dwarfed by the efforts to suppress unwanted fire. As technology develops and resources become available, they are continuously used to *control* wildfire. Despite our intensive efforts over several decades to remove fire as a threat to society and natural resources, large-scale fires continue to occur at an alarming rate. Although we have often altered its pattern, we have not eliminated fire from California ecosystems, nor have we eliminated fire as a threat to human life and property.

Although fire suppression is very effective over most of California, there are a few situations in which very large fires still occur despite the intensive effort and resources applied to suppressing them. These are settings and conditions in which fire intensity is extremely high over large areas. It is a relatively rare, but predictable, set of circumstances that leads to conditions that can produce the largest and most destructive fires in California.

Tables 18.1 and 18.2 list the 20 largest fires, in terms of area burned and structure loss, that occurred in California between 1923 and 2005. The fires are located on Maps 18.1 and 18.2. The entire 2002 Biscuit fire is included in this table although only a portion of it burned within California. Several important patterns are evident in these tables. The largest and most destructive fires have occurred in relatively few settings under a small number of weather conditions and continue to occur during those conditions in the same ecosystems.

Chaparral and Woodland Fires in the Central and South Coastal Mountains

The current pattern is for large chaparral fires to occur in the south and central California Coastal Mountains, or the Sierra Nevada foothills in two distinct scenarios. During the extended periods of hot dry summer conditions that are common in these ecosystems, fires occur that can burn for several weeks or even months in very steep inaccessible terrain. The 1999 Kirk and 1977 Marble Cone fires in the Central Coast and portions of the McNally fire in the Southern Sierra Nevada are examples. The second type of very large chaparral fire occurs in the fall and early winter during short periods of extreme fire weather characterized by foehn winds, locally known as Santa Ana, Sundowner, or North Winds (Keeley et al. 2004, Moritz et al. 2004). These winds are characteristically gusty, strong, dry, and warm and drive the fires rapidly over very large areas in periods of time lasting from a few hours to a few days. The intensity of the winds coincides with the period of time when the live fuel moistures are the lowest, thereby producing explosive fire conditions. Because there is virtually no lightning activity during this part of the year, these fires historically may have started with holdover fires burning in from higher-altitude vegetation types, but are now almost universally human caused. The 2003 Cedar and 1970 Laguna fires are examples of this type of fire. These fires are responsible for most of the highest structure loss fires since 1923, including the 2003 Cedar fire (2820 structures lost), 1991 Tunnel fire (2843 structures lost), Old (1,003) fires, 1990 Paint fire (641) and 1923 Berkeley fire (584). Both the 1991 Tunnel fire and the 1923 Berkeley fire burned through urban forest landscapes occupied by Eucalyptus and other urban trees, and were driven by foehn winds.

Forest and Chaparral Fires in the Sierra Nevada and Klamath Mountains

A second type of very large fire occurs in the Klamath Mountains and Sierra Nevada foothills and mountains. These fires can be human caused, or started by numerous lighting strikes over a large area, overwhelming fire suppression forces. The fires burn over a relatively long period of time with fire

TABLE 18.1
The 20 largest fires (by area burned) in California from 1923 to 2005

		Bioregion(s)	Hectares	(Acres)
Biscuit	July 2002	Klamath Mountains	202,328	(499,965)
Cedar	October 2003	South Coast	110,579	(273,246)
Matilija	September 1932	South Coast	89,031	(220,000)
Marble Cone	July 1977	Central Coast	71,980	(177,866)
Laguna	September 1970	South Coast	70,992	(175,425)
McNally	July 2002	Sierra Nevada	60,985	(150,696)
Stanislaus Complex	August 1987	Sierra Nevada	59,076	(145,980)
Big Bar Complex	August 1999	Klamath Mountains	57,040	(140,948)
Campbell Complex	August 1990	North Coast	50,947	(125,892)
Wheeler	July 1985	South Coast	47,753	(118,000)
Simi	October 2003	South Coast	43,789	(108,204)
Highway 58	August 1996	Central Coast	43,167	(106,668)
Clampitt	September 1970	South Coast	42,578	(105,212)
Wellman	June 1966	South Coast	37,879	(93,600)
Old	October 2003	South Coast	36,940	(91,281)
Kirk	September 1999	Central Coast	35,086	(86,700)
Refugio	September 1955	South Coast	34,305	(84,770)
Fork	August 1996	North Coast	33,581	(82,980)
Scarface	August 1977	Northeastern Plateaus	32,336	(79,904)
Las Pilitas	July 1985	Central Coast	30,206	(74,640)

NOTE: Data from California Department of Forestry and Fire Protection. Area for the Biscuit fire includes California and Oregon.

TABLE 18.2
The 20 most destructive wildland fires (by number of structures lost) in California from 1923–2005

		Bioregion	Structures Lost	Hectares	(Acres)
Tunnel	October 1991	Central Coast	2843	647	(1,600)
Cedar	October 2003	South Coast	2820	202,328	(273,246)
Old	October 2003	South Coast	1,003	36,940	(91,281)
Jones	October 1999	Central Valley	954	10,603	(26,200)
Paint	June 1990	South Coast	641	1,983	(4,900)
Fountain	August 1992	Southern Cascades	636	25,884	(63,960)
Berkeley	September 1923	Central Coast	584	53	(130)
Bel Air	November 1961	South Coast	484	2,465	(6,090)
Laguna	October 1993	South Coast	441	5,842	(14,437)
Laguna	September 1970	South Coast	382	70,992	(175,425)
Panorama	November 1980	South Coast	325	9,551	(23,600)
Topanga	November 1993	South Coast	323	7,284	(18,000)
49er	September 1988	Sierra Nevada	312	13,638	(33,700)
Simi	October 2003	South Coast	300	43,789	(108,204)
Sycamore	July 1977	South Coast	234	326	(805)
Canyon	September 1999	Central Valley	230	1,044	(2,580)
Kannan	October 1978	South Coast	224	10,273	(25,385)
Paradise	October 2003	South Coast	223	22,946	(56,700)
Kinneloa	October 1993	South Coast	196	2,220	(5,485)
Old Gulch	August 1992	Sierra Nevada	170	7,036	(17,386)

NOTE: Data from California Department of Forestry and Fire Protection.

MAP 18.1 Location of the 20 fires burning the largest area between 1923 and 2005.

behavior highest in areas where the fire can make long uphill runs, through many vegetation zones, and over steep terrain and canyons. The 1987 Stanislaus Complex, 2002 Biscuit, and 1999 Big Bar Complex fires are examples of these lightning-ignited fires. The 2002 McNally fire is similar but was human caused. Although most of these fires burn in uninhabited landscapes, they can cause a great deal of structure loss when they occur in landscapes with numerous developments mixed into the wildlands. The 1988 49er (312) and 1992 Old Gulch (170) fires are examples of fires that burned numerous structures.

Patterns of Large Fires

The 20 fires burning the largest area in California from 1923 to 2005 (Table 18.1) are illustrated by decade in Figure 18.1 and by month in Figure 18.2. In the 81 years of record, 90% of the largest fires have occurred in the last 39 years after 1966. The 1990s and 2000s were the decades with the most large fires (with five). The first six years of the 2000s have produced more of the largest fires than there were in the first half of the recorded period. Nine of the 12

largest fires have occurred since 1985. All of these largest fires occurred in steep inaccessible terrain. The fires were well distributed during the four-month period from July to October with one occurring in June. Increasing fuel continuity and fuel loads from successful fire suppression have probably contributed to the increase in large fires since 1970.

The 20 fires burning the most structures in California since 1923 (Table 18.2) are illustrated by decade in Figure 18.1 and by month in Figure 18.2. Although there were a variety of specific causes, all of the ignitions were human caused. Thirteen of the 20 fires occurred since 1990, including those causing the six highest structure losses. Eighteen of the 20 fires occurred since 1970. Nearly half of the fires occurred in October, including the top four that combined to burn more than 7,600 structures. Nineteen of the 20 largest structure-loss fires occurred between July and November. There is an increasing rate of occurrence of the state's largest and most destructive fires. This is despite increasing efforts, effectiveness, and expenditures for fire suppression. All of the fires occurred during extreme fire weather conditions, and all were actively suppressed.

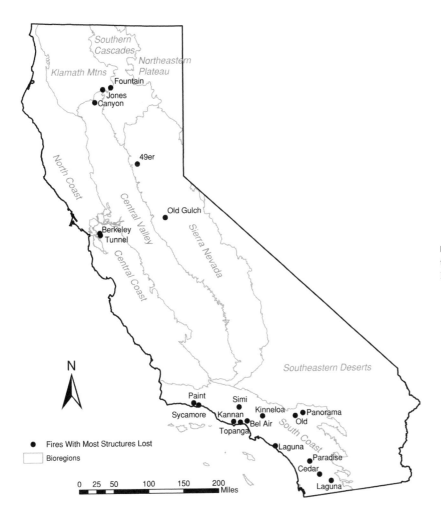

MAP 18.2. Location of the 20 fires burning the most structures between 1923 and 2005. Berkeley and Tunnel are two separate fires.

Current Fire Policies, Initiatives, and Direction

In recent years, societal concerns for managing natural resources have shifted to include the role of fire as a dynamic and predictable part of wildland ecosystems. This has served to thrust fire management into the forefront of wildland management. It is now widely recognized that fire plays an important role in the functioning of natural ecosystems. It is also recognized that if we value ecosystem components such as plant and animal species and their habitats, water, and air, then fire must be managed rather than eliminated from ecosystems. The focus of fire policy and management has shifted away from the overall goal of removing fire toward the much more complex goal of managing fire.

In response to 14 firefighter fatalities at the South Canyon fire in Colorado in 1994, and the growing recognition that fire problems are caused by fuel accumulation, the Bureau of Land Management, Forest Service, National Park Service, Fish and Wildlife Service, Bureau of Indian Affairs, and the National Biological Service released a joint Federal Wildland Fire Management Policy and Program Review in 1995 (USDI-USDA 1995, USDA 1995b). The key findings of this policy and program review are as follows:

1) The protection of human life is reaffirmed as the first priority in wildland fire management.

2) The second priority is the joint protection of property and natural and cultural resources.

3) "Wildland fire, as a critical natural process, must be reintroduced into the ecosystem. This will be accomplished across agency boundaries and will be based upon the best available science."

4) Treatment of hazardous fuel buildups, particularly in the wildland-urban interface, and approved fire management plans are needed.

It concluded, "Agencies and the public must change their expectations that all wildfires can be controlled or suppressed." For the first time, the federal land management agencies jointly took responsibility for managing fire as a natural process in America's wildlands.

The 1995 fire policy was reviewed and updated in the aftermath of the Cerro Grande fire. This incident started with an escaped prescribed fire that eventually burned 235 structures in and around Los Alamos, New Mexico, and threatened the Los Alamos National Laboratory in May of

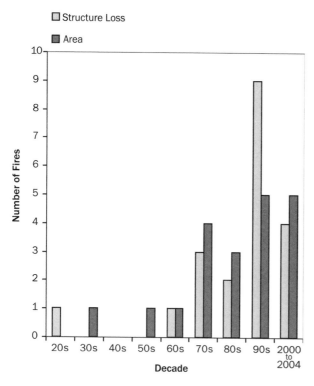

FIGURE 18.1. Distribution of the 20 fires burning the most structures and largest areas between 1923 and 2003, by decade.

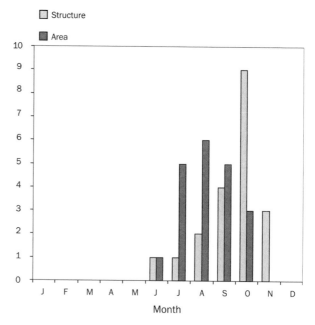

FIGURE 18.2. Seasonal distribution of the 20 fires burning the most structures and largest area between 1923 and 2005.

2000 (USDI 2001). The review supported the 1995 fire policy and fine tuned its implementation. The key findings of the review are as follows:

1) The 1995 policy is generally sound and continues to provide a solid foundation for wildland fire management activities and for natural resources management activities of the federal government.

2) As a result of fire exclusion, the condition of fire-adapted ecosystems continues to deteriorate; the fire hazard situation in these areas is worse than previously understood.

3) The fire hazard situation in the wildland-urban interface is more complex and extensive than understood in 1995.

One of the main objectives of the 1995 policy was to reduce fire hazards annually on 1,200,000 ha (3,000,000 acres) of forests using mechanical and prescribed fire treatments by 2005. Re-introducing fire and restoring large areas of forests is a formidable management challenge for both political and ecological reasons (Cole and Landres 1996, Ruth 2000, Stephens and Ruth 2005). Progress has been slower than forecasted (GAO 2003), because of constraints on smoke production, difficulties in plan preparation, possible effects on rare and endangered species, and budgetary procedures that have delayed the implementation of fuel management projects.

The National Fire Plan, established in "A Report to the President in Response to the Wildfires of 2000" (USDA-USDI 2000), is now being implemented using the "Collaborative Approach for Reducing Wildfire Risks to Communities and the Environment: Ten-Year Comprehensive Strategy" (WGA 2001). The Plan and the Strategy state: "Unless hazardous fuel is reduced, the number of severe wildland fires and the costs associated with suppressing them will continue to increase." Implementation of the National Fire Plan is designed to be a long-term, multibillion-dollar effort (GAO 2003). The Ten-Year Comprehensive Strategy recognizes that key decisions in setting priorities for restoration, fire, and fuel management should be made collaboratively at local levels. As such, the Strategy requires an ongoing process whereby the local, tribal, state, and federal land management, scientific, and regulatory agencies exchange the required technical information to facilitate the decision-making process.

Today's complex land management objectives will be achieved by the long-term incorporation of fire as an ecosystem process as a part of a broadly based wildland management program. Fire management includes a combination of methods that are used individually or in combination to meet different objectives (Stephens 1998, Stephens and Moghaddas 2005). Methods include the general categories of fuel management, using naturally occurring fire to achieve natural resource objectives (wildland fire use), modifying future fire behavior and home construction in the wildland–urban interface, and restoration of historic fire regimes.

Fire management has developed from a relatively simple straightforward suppression program, tasked with protecting lives, property, and natural resources, into an immensely complex program of land management, tasked with the additional needs to maintain plant and animal species and their habitats, air, soil and water quality, and visual, recreational, and residential landscapes. Fuels management must be applied in appropriate ecosystems (Stephens and Ruth 2005) at necessary spatial scales and arrangements (Finney 2001) before it will have the ability to reduce losses from large high-severity wildfires.

In October of 2003, a group of 10 fires burned more than 303,514 ha (750,000 ac) of chaparral, woodlands, and forest in and around the cities of the greater San Diego and Los Angeles areas. More than 4,000 structures were burned and 22 lives were lost over a one-week period. This was a dramatic demonstration of several points that define our current place in the history of fire ecology, management, and policy:

1) High-intensity wildland fires continue to operate on large landscapes. Removal of smaller and low-to moderate-intensity fires in forests by effective fire suppression serves to greatly increase the proportion of the burned area that experiences extreme fire behavior.

2) Fire management can be effective in modifying fire behavior in certain ecosystems. However, in ecosystems characterized by very high-intensity fire, such as chaparral and some forest types, management of wildlands as natural ecosystems is not likely to reduce the threat to adjacent urban areas. In such cases, it is likely that we must rely on the design of structures and the development of buffers between the wildlands and urban areas. These buffers may consist of unnatural vegetation that can reduce fire intensity and result from the modification of urban area designs.

3) Fire policy must continue to focus on three primary areas: promoting the restoration of the role of fire in natural ecosystems, moderating the impacts of wildland fire on society, and producing better building codes and wildland management in and adjacent to the urban–wildland interface.

4) Fire management is a very important part of wildland management. Despite great effort over several decades, we have not managed to remove fire from ecosystems, even in wildlands adjacent to the nation's largest population centers. In fact we have had little impact on the frequency or intensity of fire in these ecosystems. Fire is a very basic part of these ecosystems and will not likely be removed in the near future. We must continue to improve our understanding of the natural role of fire in ecosystems, how fire can be a threat to society and how to co-exist with fire in California's wildlands.

Fires in a Changing Climate

Despite the complexity inherent in local fire regimes, regional fire activity often oscillates in phase with year-to-year climatic variability (Clark 1988, Swetnam 1993, Stephens and Ruth 2005). For example, the area burned annually across the southwestern United States tends to decrease in El Niño years and increase during La Niña years (Swetnam and Betancourt 1990). In northern California, the impact of climatic change on wildland fire and suppression effectiveness is projected to change in the inland regions of the state (Fried et al. 2004). Despite enhancement of fire suppression efforts, the number of escaped fires (those exceeding initial containment limits) is projected to increase by 51% in the south San Francisco Bay area and 125% in the Sierra Nevada; no increase in the number of escaped fires is projected in the wet coastal forests of northwestern California. In addition to the increased suppression costs and economic damages, changes in fire severity of this magnitude would have widespread impacts on vegetation distribution, forest condition, and carbon storage, and greatly increase the risk to property, natural resources, and human life.

Conclusion

Industrialization and urbanization of America from the late 1800s to the mid 1900s generated an increasing need to manage wildlands for commodity production to supply an increasingly urban population. Protection of forests and rangelands from wildland fire was a central part of this evolution in management philosophy. The application of a fire-protection philosophy that was developed to protect European forests was applied to every plant community in North America during this period (Wright and Bailey 1982).

The challenge today is to develop fire policies, management actions, and budgets that recognize the need for both fire suppression and the management of fire as an ecosystem process and hazard reduction tool. Fire will continue as an important agent of change in many western ecosystems but we must strive to produce conditions where fire can become a positive force in most of California. This is a challenge of magnitude and complexity that is unprecedented in the history of wildland resource management. The stakes are extremely high and the future of both the relationship of wildlands to society and the integrity of natural ecosystems are at risk.

Global climate change may further complicate fire management in California (Torn and Fried 1992, Karl 1998, Fried et al. 2004). Climate change may lead to differences in plant distributions (Bachelet et al. 2001), lightning frequency (Price and Rind 1994), and the length of fire season, which could increase ignitions and further exacerbate wildfire effects. Changing climates may necessitate creation of fire policies that are easily adaptable because of large uncertainties (Stephens and Ruth 2005).

References

Agee, J. K. 1974. Fire management in the national parks. Western Wildlands 1:27–33.

Anderson, R. E., B. L. Rasmussen, and V. V. Church. 1941. Adapting advanced principles of organization and fire-line construction to CCC suppression crews. Fire control notes 5(3): 123–128.

Anderson, M. K. 2005. Tending the wild: Native American knowledge and the management of California's natural resources. University of California Press. Berkeley, 526 p.

Bachelet, D., R. P. Neilson, J. M. Lenihan, and R. J. Drapek. 2001. Climate change effects on vegetation distribution and carbon budget in the United States. Ecosystems 4:164–185.

Barbour, M., B. Pavlik, F. Drysdale, and S. Lindstrom. 1993. California's changing landscapes. California Native Plant Society. Sacramento, CA. 244 p.

Barry, W. J., and R. W. Harrison. 2002. Prescribed burning in the California State Park system. P. 203–212 in Proceedings of the symposium: fire in California ecosystems: integrating ecology, prevention and management. Miscellaneous Publication No. 1, Association for Fire Ecology.

Bean, W. 1973. California: an interpretive history McGraw-Hill, New York. 622 p.

Biswell, H. H., 1959. Man and fire in ponderosa pine in the Sierra Nevada of California. Sierra Club Bulletin 44:44–53.

Biswell, H. H. 1961. The big trees and fire. National Parks and Conservation Magazine 35:11–14.

Biswell, H. H., 1989. Prescribed burning in California wildland vegetation management. University of California Press, Berkeley. 255 p.

CDF. 1996. California fire plan—a framework for minimizing costs and losses from wildland fires. California State Board of Forestry. State of California, Sacramento. 104 p.

Clar, C. R. 1959. California government and forestry. Division of Forestry. State of California, Sacramento.

Clark, J. S. 1988. Effects of climate change on fire regimes in Northwestern Minnesota. Nature 334:233–235.

Cole, D. N., and P. B. Landres. 1996. Threats to wilderness ecosystems: impacts and research needs. Ecological Applications 6(1): 168–184.

DeBruin, H. W. 1974. From fire control to fire management: a major policy change in the Forest Service. P. 11–17 in Proceedings of the 14th Tall Timbers fire ecology conference. Missoula, MT. Tall Timbers Research Station, Tallahassee FL.

DuBois, C. 1914. Systematic fire protection in the California forests. USDA Forest Service. Washington DC. 99 p.

Elliott-Fisk, D. L., T. C. Cahill, O. K. Davis, L. Duan, C. R. Goldman, G. E. Gruell, R. Harris, S. L. Stephens, et al. 1997. Lake Tahoe Case Study. Sierra Navada Ecosystem project. Addendum (Davis: University of California, Centers for Water and Wildland Resources). pp. 217–276.

Farquhar, F. P. 1966. History of the Sierra Nevada. University of California Press, Berkeley. 262 p.

Finney, M. A. 2001. Design of regular landscape fuel treatment patterns for modifying fire growth and behavior. Forest Science 47:219–228.

Fried, J. S., M. S. Torn, and E. Mills. 2004. The impact of climate change on wildfire severity: a regional forecast for Northern California. Climate Change 64:169–191.

GAO. 2003. Forest service fuels reduction. U.S. General Accounting Office Report GAO-03-689R. Washington, DC. 43 p.

Graves, H. S. 1910. Protection of forests from fire. U.S. Forest Service Bulletin 82. Washington DC. 48 p.

Greeley, W. B. 1951. Forests and men. Doubleday Publishing, Garden City, NY.

Guthrie, J. D. 1936. Great forest fires of America. USDA Forest Service, Washington, DC. 10 p.

Hartesveldt, R. J., and Harvey, H. T., 1967. The fire ecology of sequoia regeneration. P. 65–77 in Proceedings of the 6th Tall Timbers fire ecology conference, Tallahassee, FL.

Karl, T. R. 1998. Regional trends and variations of temperature and precipitation. P. 412–425 in R. T. Watson, M. C. Zinyowera, R. H. Moss, and D. J. Dokken (eds.), The regional impacts of climate change: an assessment of vulnerability. Cambridge University Press, Cambridge, MA.

Keeley, J. E. 2002. Native American impacts on fire regimes of the California coastal ranges. Journal of Biogeography 29:303–320.

Keeley, J. E., C. J. Fotheringham, and M. A. Moritz, 2004. Lessons from the 2003 wildfires in southern California. Journal of Forestry 102:26–31.

Kilgore, B. M. 1974. Fire management in national parks: an overview. P. 45–57 in Proceedings of the 14th Tall Timbers fire ecology conference, Missoula, MT. Tall Timbers Research Station, Tallahassee, FL.

Kilgore, B. M., and G. S. Briggs. 1972. Restoring fire to high elevation forests in California. Journal of Forestry 70(5):266–271.

Leopold, S. A., S. A. Cain, C. A. Cottam, I. N. Gabrielson, and T. L. Kimball. 1963. Wildlife management in the national parks. American Forestry 69:32–35, 61–63.

McClaran, M. P., and J. W. Bartolome. 1989. Fire-related recruitment in stagnant Quercus douglasii populations. Canadian Journal of Forest Research 19:580–585.

Menke, J. W., C. Davis, and P. Beesley. 1996. Rangeland assessment. in Sierra Nevada Ecosystem Project, final report to congress, Vol. III: assessments, commissioned reports, and background information. Wildland Research Center, University of California, Davis.

Millar, C. I., and W. B. Woolfenden. 1999. The role of climate change in interpreting historical variability. Ecological Applications 9:1207–1216.

Moritz, M. A., J. E. Keeley, E. A. Johnson, and A. A. Schaffner. 2004. Testing a basic assumption of shrubland fire management: does the hazard of burning increase with the age of fuels? Frontiers in Ecology and the Environment 2:67–72.

Parsons, D. J., D. M. Graber, J. K Agee, and J. W. van Wagtendonk. 1986. Natural fire management in national parks. Environmental Management. 10(1):21–24.

Perkins. 1900. Report on the big trees of California. USDA Division of Forestry. 56th Congress, 1st Session. Senate Document No. 393. Government Printing Office, Washington, DC.

Pinchot, G. 1907. The use of the national forests. USDA Forest Service. 42p.

Price, C., and D. Rind. 1994. The impact of a 2 x CO2 climate on lightning caused fires. Journal of Climate 7:1484–1494.

Pyne, S. J. 1982. Fire in America: a cultural history of wildland and rural fire. Princeton University Press, Princeton, NJ. 654 p.

Pyne, S. J. 1997. America's fires: management on wildlands and forests. Forest History Society, Durham, NC. 54 p.

Pyne, S.J. 2001. Year of the fires: the story of the great fires of 1910. Viking Publishing, New York. 322 p.

Robertson, W.B. 1962. Fire and vegetation in the Everglades. P. 67–80 in Proceedings of the 1st Tall Timbers fire ecology conference, March 1–2, Tallahassee, FL.

Ruth, L. 2000. Conservation on the cusp: the reformation of national forest policy in the Sierra Nevada. UCLA Journal of Environmental Law and Policy 18:1–97.

Sanderson, J.E. 1974. The role of fire suppression in fire management. P. 19–31 in Proceedings of the 14th Tall Timbers fire ecology conferenc, Missoula, MT. Tall Timbers Research Station, Tallahassee, FL.

Shinn, C.H. 1885. Mining camps: a study in American frontier government. New York (new edition 1948).

Show, S.B., and E. I. Kotok. 1924. The role of fire in the California pine forests. USDA Bulletin No. 1294. Washington, DC. 80 p.

Stephens, S.L. 1997. Fire history of a mixed oak-pine forest in the foothills of the Sierra Nevada, El Dorado County, California. P. 191–198 in Symposium on oak woodlands: ecology, management, and urban interface issues. USDA Forest Service General Technical Report PSW GTR-160.

Stephens, S.L. 1998. Evaluation of the effects of silvicultural and fuels treatments on potential fire behavior in Sierra Nevada mixed conifer forests. Forest Ecology and Management 105:21–34.

Stephens, S.L. 2000. Mixed conifer and uper montane forest structure and uses in 1899 from the central and northern Sierra Nevada, CA. Madrono 47:43–52.

Stephens, S.L., 2004. Fuel loads, snag abundance, and snag recruitment in an unmanaged Jeffrey pine-mixed conifer forest in northwestern Mexico. Forest Ecology and Management 199:103–113.

Stephens, S.L. 2005. Forest fire causes and extent on United States Forest Service lands. International Journal of Wildland Fire 14:213–222.

Stephens, S.L., and D.L. Elliott-Fisk. 1998. *Sequoiadendron giganteum*-mixed conifer forest structure in 1900-1901 from the Southern Sierra Nevada, CA. Madroño 45:221–230.

Stephens, S.L. and D.L. Fry. 2005. Fire history in coast redwood stands in the Northeastern Santa Cruz Mountains, California. Fire Ecology 1:2–19.

Stephens S.L., and P.Z. Fule. 2005. Western pine forests with continuing frequent fire regimes: Possible reference sites for management. Journal of Forestry 103:357–362.

Stephens, S.L., and J.J. Moghaddas. 2005. Experimental fuel treatment impacts on forest structure, potential fire behavior, and predicted tree mortality in a mixed conifer forest. Forest Ecology and Management 215:21–36.

Stephens, S.L., and W.J. Libby. 2006. Anthropogenic fire and bark thickness in coastal and island pine populations from Alta and Baja California. Journal of Biogeography 33:648–652.

Stephens, S.L., and L.W. Ruth. 2005. Federal forest fire policy in the United States. Ecological Applications 15:532–542.

Swetnam, T. W. 1993. Fire history and climate change in sequoia groves. Science 262:885–889.

Swetnam, T.W., and J.I. Betancourt. 1990. Fire—southern oscillation relations in the southwestern United States. Science 249:1017–1020.

Torn, M.S., and J.S. Fried. 1992. Predicting the impact of global warming on wildfire. Climatic Change 21:257–274.

USDA. 1960. Air attack on forest fires. U.S. Forest Service Agricultural Information Bulletin 229. Washington, DC. 32 p.

USDA. 1995a. Smokey Bear, the first fifty years. USDA Forest Service Publication FS-551.

USDA. 1995b. Course to the future: positioning fire and aviation management. Department of Fire and Aviation Management. Washington, DC. 19 p.

USDA–USDI. 2000. A report to the President in response to the wildfires of 2000. Available at www.fireplan.gov\president.cfm [accessed 22 May 2003].

USDI. 1968. Compilation of the fire administrative policies for the national parks and monuments of scientific significance. U.S. National Park Service. Washington, DC. 138 p.

USDI. 2001. Review and update of the 1995 federal wildland fire management policy. Report to the Secretaries of the Interior, Agriculture, Energy, Defense, and Commerce; the Administrator, Environmental Protection Agency; the Director, Federal Emergency Management Agency; and the National Association of State Foresters, by an Interagency Federal Wildland Fire Policy Review Working Group. National Interagency Fire Center, Boise, ID.

USDI-NPS. 1986. Wildland fire management guideline: NPS-18. Washington, D.C: U.S. Department of the Interior, National Park Service. 22 chapters, 8 appendixes.

USDI–USDA. 1995. Federal wildland fire management: policy and program review. Final Report, December 18, 1995. 45 p.

van Wagtendonk, J. W. 1978. Wilderness fire management in Yosemite National Park. P. 324–335 in E. A. Schofield (ed.), Proceedings of the 14th biennial wilderness conference, June 5–8, 1975, New York. Westview Press, Boulder, CO.

van Wagtendonk, J.W. 1991. The evolution of national park fire policy. Fire Management Notes 52:10–15.

van Wagtendonk, J.W. 1996. Use of a deterministic fire growth model to test fuel treatments. P. 1155–1165 in Sierra Nevada Ecosystem Project, final report to congress, Vol. II: assessments and scientific basis for management options. Wildland Research Center, University of California, Davis.

Watkins, T.H. 1983. California: an illustrated history. American Legacy Press, New York. 543 p.

WGA. 2001. A collaborative approach for reducing wildland fire risk to communities and the environment: 10-year comprehensive strategy. Western Governors' Association. Available at www.westgov.org/wga/initiatives/fire/final_fire_rpt.pdf [accessed 25 May 2003].

Wright, H.A., and A.W. Bailey. 1982. Fire ecology: United States and southern Canada. John Wiley and Sons, Inc. New York. 501 p.

CHAPTER 19

Fire and Fuel Management

SUE HUSARI, H. THOMAS NICHOLS, NEIL G. SUGIHARA,
AND SCOTT L. STEPHENS

The only alternative to planned and managed vegetation
patterns in Southern California appears to be the acceptance
of great economic damage, threat to human life, and the
unpleasant aesthetic and environmental effects of
unmanageable wildfire.

CLIVE COUNTRYMAN, 1974

Even though fire is itself an inexorable force of nature, we need
not view its worst effects as inevitable.

STEPHEN F. ARNO AND STEVEN ALLISON-BUNNELL, 2002

The complex set of tasks we now characterize as *fire management* evolved from the single-minded pursuit of fire control. The management of wildland fuel has become one of the more important aspects of fire management (Biswell 1989, Carle 2002). In the last 20 years, fuel management has come to play a leading role in managing ecosystems and natural resources. Scientists and managers have improved their shared understanding of the importance of natural processes in ecosystem function. Attempts to exclude fire events merely delay, alter, and intensify subsequent fires. The build-up of fuel in some California ecosystems has contributed to the destructive power of recent fires. To be effective at protecting social values and natural resources, California land managers have focused attention on the manipulation of wildland fuel. Toward this end, fuel management is the most significant land management activity in many parts of California.

As a society, we recognize the necessity of managing the effects of wildland fire on both humans and natural resources. We have learned from experience that we cannot simply eliminate fire from fire-adapted ecosystems, nor can we ignore it. We have the responsibility to manage the range of fire patterns and fire effects that occur on wildlands. Although fuel management is not limited to the reintroduction of fire as an ecosystem process, prescribed fire remains a critical component of responsible management.

Fuel management is important simply because it gives us the opportunity to modify the pattern of future fire by modification of today's fuel. Climate and topography cannot be changed although fuel management can effect some local weather characteristics (van Wagtendonk 1996). This leaves fuel and ignitions as the two main means by which wildfires can be affected (Martin et al. 1989). Hence, fuel management

and fire prevention have joined fire suppression as key components of fire management programs.

This chapter builds on the concepts and processes developed in Part I and described for the bioregions in Part II of this book. The historical, social, and political considerations in the other chapters in Part III define the management setting in which fuel management operates. This chapter first provides an overview of basic fuel management concepts. We then describe the setting in which fuel management programs operate within the various land management agencies and fire departments in California's diverse wildfire environment.

Fuel Management Objectives

The direct goal of any fuel treatment is the modification of potential fire behavior or fire effects to achieve a defined condition. Federal and state fuel management programs have the purpose of reducing risks to human communities and improving ecosystem health. To ensure these programs are coordinated, common priorities for fuel treatments have been established that follow the guidelines and policies under the National Fire Plan (USDA and USDI 2004).

Common goals are reducing potential fire intensity and rate of spread, reducing the severity of fire effects, and restoring historic fuel quantity and structure. Achieving these goals creates the potential for reestablishing presettlement fire regimes. Manipulation of fuel is the most common and effective way to influence future wildland fires.

The land management objectives requiring management of fuel are diverse and often complex. Reestablishing or restoring historic fire regimes can be, but are not always, the objective of fuel management. Modified or redefined fire regimes that accept currently occurring fire regimes or a fire regime distribution that differs from the historic pattern are often the objective of wildland management. These goals may be driven by the need to manage for habitat for individual species (see Chapter 23), or as part of an effort to exclude wildland fire from an ecosystem for public safety purposes.

Fuel Management Basics

Fuel is accumulated live and dead plant biomass. Chapter 3 discusses in detail how the characteristics of fuel influence its potential to burn. Fuel moisture, chemical composition, surface area to volume ratio, size, and structural arrangement of the fuel in the stand and on the landscape influence the conditions under which fuel will burn, as well as help characterize the resulting fires.

Fuel management is the planned manipulation of the amount, composition, and structure of the biomass within wildland ecosystems for the purpose of modifying potential fire behavior and effects (NPS 2004). Fuel has several characteristics that can be manipulated to influence its potential to burn, and the characteristics of the potential wildland fire. Fuel management includes the manipulation of a number of different fuel characteristics to achieve a defined modification of future fire behavior (Pyne et al. 1996, Stephens and Ruth 2005). Table 19.1 explains how different fuel characteristics are modified by fuel treatment. Fuel characteristics that are typically manipulated are as follows:

Fuel Quantity The overall amount of fuel in the ecosystem is an important factor determining the character and impact of fires. The metric used to describe the quantity of fuel is oven dry weight per unit area (tons per acre). This dry weight is often subdivided into size classes. The size classes are based on the time the fuel takes to reach equilibrium with moisture in the air. Small fuels, such as pine needles, respond to changes in relative humidity more rapidly than do large, dense fuels, such as logs. Fuel can be removed from a site by a variety of means, thereby reducing fuel quantity.

Fuel Size The sizes of fuel particles are very important in determining fire behavior and effect. Fine fuels—less than a quarter inch in diameter—have the greatest influence on the ignition and spread of fires. Removal of fine fuel is a primary focus of many fuel management projects.

Packing Ratio Packing ratio is a measure of how densely packed the fuel particles are. Fuel may be compacted through a variety of mechanical treatments including mastication, chipping, and shredding. Compact fuel burns more slowly because the oxygen required for combustion is not available to the fuel away from the surface.

Surface Fuel Surface fuel is composed of small shrubs, grasses, and plant debris lying on the surface of the ground.

Surface fuel is necessary for fire to spread continuously across landscapes. Surface fuel continuity can be interrupted to achieve fuel management goals.

Crown Fuel The branches and foliage of the trees and large shrubs (over 6 feet in height) make up crown fuel. Continuous crown fuel is required for fire to spread through the crowns of trees. Crown fires may also occur in discontinuous stands of trees if supported by surface fire. Wind speed and, to a lesser extent, foliar moisture are important to propagation of crown fires. Crown fire risk reduction may be accomplished through removing trees and ladder fuel, treating surface fuel, or a combination of the above. Such treatments reduce the continuity and bulk density of crown fuel and increase the separation between crown fuel and surface fuel.

Horizontal Fuel Continuity Within any ecosystem, horizontal fuel continuity is necessary to allow fire to spread laterally across a surface or through crowns. Surface fuel discontinuities act as barriers to fire spread under most conditions. Fires can spot across bare areas, especially under dry, hot, windy conditions. Fuel treatments designed to interrupt fuel continuity include fuel breaks and strategically placed area treatments.

Vertical Fuel Continuity Vertical fuel continuity is necessary for surface fire to spread into the crowns of trees within forested ecosystems. Vertical fuel continuity can be reduced to increase the separation between the surface fuel and the crown fuel. Fuel treatments are often designed to separate surface fuel and crown fuel to reduce the probability of crown involvement.

Ladder Fuel Intermediate-sized trees or shrubs provide a fuel conduit that can allow a surface fire to "climb" into the crown fuel. Fuel treatments can remove shrubs and small trees or the lower branches of trees to reduce ladder fuel.

Types of Fuel Treatments

The term *fuel management* is a new term, not found even as recently as the second edition of the classic text by Brown and Davis (1973), *Forest Fire Control and Use*. Fuel management as a concept first appeared about the same time fire *control* became fire *management*—1977—and is now ubiquitous in discussions of fire management.

Fuel treatments take on a wide assortment of forms but can generally be divided into two categories—fire treatments and mechanical treatments. Fire treatments are the application, use, or management of wildland fire to modify fuel. Mechanical treatments rely on a variety of methods to manually modify or remove fuel. Fuel treatment programs often include the use of mechanical treatments to restore the fuel to a condition where fire can be used to maintain the desired range of conditions over a longer period of time.

TABLE 19.1

Fire and non-fire treatment effects on fuel and potential fire

	Non-fire Treatments			Fire Treatments		
	Thinning	Grazing	Mastication	Surface Fire	Mixed Severity Fire	Crown Fire
Total fuel quantity	Reduced	Reduced	No effect	Reduced	Removes fuel, may create new dead fuel	Removes fuel, may create new dead fuel
Fuel size	Reduces aerial (crown) fuel of all sizes	Reduces fine fuel Browsing may remove twigs and branches	Increases the percentage of small-sized fuel particles	Reduces fuel of all sizes depending on moisture content of fuel and duration of burning	Reduces fuel of all sizes depending on moisture content of fuel and duration of burning	Reduces fuel of all sizes depending on moisture content of fuel and duration of burning
Packing ratio of surface fuel	Not directly influenced	Increases packing ratio because fine fuels are decreased	Increases packing ratio because of compaction	Variable effect	Variable effect	Variable effect
Surface fuel continuity	Can be used to decrease surface fuel continuity	Can be used to decrease surface fuel continuity	Can be used to decrease surface fuel continuity	Reduces surface fuel continuity	Reduces surface fuel continuity	Reduces surface fuel continuity
Crown fuel continuity	Can be used to reduce crown fuel continuity	No effect	No effect on mature canopy	Can reduce crown fuel continuity	Reduces crown fuel continuity	Reduces crown fuel continuity
Surface fuel	Increases surface fuel if branches or debris are left on site after thinning	Reduces total surface fuel	Compacts surface fuel, can increase total surface fuel if brush or small trees are converted to surface fuel	Reduces total surface fuel	Reduces total surface fuel	Reduces total surface fuel

Fuel characteristic						
Crown fuel	Reduces crown fuel	Minimal impact from browsing	No effect on mature canopy	Minimal effect from scorching or tree mortality in sensitive species	Reduces crown fuel through mortality and scorching	Reduces crown fuel through consumption of leaves and small twigs
Horizontal fuel continuity	Can be used to reduce horizontal fuel continuity, primarily in aerial fuels	Can be used to reduce horizontal fuel continuity	Can be used to reduce horizontal fuel continuity through rearrangement	Reduces horizontal fuel continuity	Reduces horizontal fuel continuity	Reduces horizontal fuel continuity
Vertical fuel continuity	Can be reduced by removal of ladder fuel, increasing the separation of surface and crown fuel	Browsing can reduce ladder fuel	Can be reduced by removal of ladder fuel, increasing the separation of surface and crown fuel	Can be reduced by removal of ladder fuel, increasing the separation of surface and crown fuel	Can be reduced by removal of ladder fuel, increasing the separation of surface and crown fuel	Can be reduced by removal of ladder fuel, increasing the separation of surface and crown fuel
Ladder fuel	Can be used to reduce ladder fuel	Browsing can reduce ladder fuel	Can be used to reduce ladder fuel	Reduces ladder fuel	Reduces ladder fuel	Reduces ladder fuel
Potential for surface fire	Not directly influenced	Reduces potential for surface fire	Can reduce potential for surface fire	Reduces potential for surface fire	Reduces potential for surface fire	Reduces potential for surface fire
Potential for crown fire	Reduces potential for crown fire	Reduces potential for crown fire by decreasing surface fire potential	Can reduce potential for crown fire by decreasing surface fire potential and increasing height to live crown base	Reduces potential for crown fire by decreasing surface fire potential	Reduces potential for crown fire by decreasing surface fire potential and crown fuel continuity	Reduces potential for crown fire by decreasing surface fire potential and crown fuel continuity

FIGURE 19.1. Prescribed burning in Yosemite Valley is used to reduce fire hazard, maintain meadows, and to open vistas. (National Park Service photo.)

Fire Treatments

Fire treatments may include prescribed fires purposely ignited to achieve established objectives, or naturally caused fires allowed to burn in designated locations under specific conditions. Both types of fire treatments maintain the presence of fire as an ecological process, but prescriptions may or may not be designed to mimic the historic influences of fire.

PRESCRIBED FIRE

Civilizations around the world have used prescribed fire for millennia to accomplish a wide array of objectives. Pyne (1982) notes, "To discriminate between influences of climatic change, biotic migrations, natural fire, and aboriginal firing of the landscape is all but impossible." Prescribed fire has often been a supplement to natural sources of ignition or, in some areas, a replacement for such ignitions.

The uses and purposes of prescribed fire in California are widely varied. A general differentiation can be made between *restoration* burns, in which the current ecological condition is modified, and *maintenance* burns, in which existing conditions are maintained within a specified range. Modifications may include the reduction of hazardous amounts of dead and down fuel, the stimulation of fire-dependent species, the control or removal of non-native species, improvement of range condition, or the creation of wildlife habitat.

Prescriptions for burning consider the variables that influence fire behavior, the ecological role of fire, and the ability to control the fire and minimize the potential for escapes. Site considerations include slope, aspect, topographic position, and role of fire in the project area. Prescribed conditions at the time of burning include the season, weather, fuel conditions, and the availability of qualified personnel.

Methods for ignition can greatly influence the intensity and severity of prescribed fires. Ignition patterns are used to modify and control fireline intensity and fire severity patterns. A wide variety of hand-held, mechanized, and aerial ignition methods are used to accomplish the desired fire patterns. The most effective method for a given project will depend on the terrain, fuel type, prescribed conditions, type and pattern of fire, and the scale of the project.

Whether for restoration or maintenance purposes, the establishment of measurable objectives, and monitoring methods to measure them, are critical. The value of prescribed fire to land managers decreases with the inability to quantify the purpose of the fire and its accomplishments (or lack of them). Prescribed burning within an adaptive management context is critical to each agency (Fig. 19.1).

WILDLAND FIRE USED FOR RESOURCE BENEFITS

The concept of allowing lightning fires to burn originated in 1968 in Sequoia and Kings Canyon National Parks, followed by other agencies and other units (Kilgore 1974). Much like maintenance prescribed fires, areas in which wildland fires are allowed to burn are generally considered to be within historic or natural ranges of variability. The original justification for such areas is that they were sufficiently remote to have been unaffected by fire suppression activities.

Following the 1988 Yellowstone Area fires, additional requirements for planning, approving, and implementing the wildland fire use program were established. With greater emphasis in federal fire policy on the restoration of fire to its more natural role and the revision of fire management plans that this entailed, the program in California has grown (Fig.19.2). Smoke from these fires is a concern to air quality

FIGURE 19.2. The Bluff wildland fire use project was successfully managed in Lassen Volcanic National Park in the summer of 2004. (Photo by Mike Lewelling, Lassen Volcanic National Park.)

regulators, and land managers will continue to balance the importance of clean air with the reality that wildland fires will occur. Representatives from the National Parks, National Forests, state air regulators, and local air districts developed protocols in 2004 for implementation of the wildland fire use program. All recognize that smoke from these fires is transported throughout the state and across jurisdictions from areas with relatively clean air to other areas where visibility and human health are already at risk from elevated levels of particulate matter and other pollutants.

Mechanical Treatments

Many kinds of vegetation management remove, rearrange, or modify biomass. Mechanical fuel treatments must also include the objective of modifying potential fire behavior. Many vegetation management strategies have multiple objectives. The question of which mechanical vegetation management treatments reduce hazardous fuel and which do not is a contentious issue in California and throughout the West (Agee and Skinner 2005, Stephens and Moghaddas 2005a). This has been the subject of much debate, intellectual discourse, and some legal action focused on timber salvage and forest management. Land management agencies, the fire service, large landowners, elected representatives, and the public need improved fire behavior models, analysis, research, and, especially, monitoring, to resolve this issue. A long-term study is underway to compare the efficacy, the economics, and the effects of prescribed fire, mechanical thinning, and a combination of the two on a series of linked study sites in fire-adapted ecosystems throughout the country (Knapp et al. 2004).

Removal of both live and dead woody fuel can utilize equipment such as feller bunchers, skidders, and grapplers. Trees may also be thinned to a variety of densities. Crushing,

chipping, shredding, chopping, and other mechanical methods of changing the fuel characteristics are commonly used. Woody material can be chipped or burned in piles. Mechanical treatments can be more precise than prescribed fire. Smoke impacts and damage from scorching are avoided when mechanical methods are used instead of fire. In some cases, the fuel can be removed from the area and used to produce wood products or to generate electricity, as described in Sidebar 19.1. However, removal of organic material reduces the amount of carbon and nutrients on the site. The application of mechanical methods on a scale matching the fuel problem in California is dependent on continued partnerships with research and industry to find uses of the material and cost-effective methods of removing it. Work remains to be done on use of these methods in remote or steep locations.

Other mechanical methods may include grazing to remove fine fuel and type conversions such as brush to grass. In many cases, however, the need for prescribed fire to maintain the conditions once established mechanically still remains. Although the risk of wildland fire may be reduced through mechanical means, these treatments rarely prove a perfect surrogate for fire (Stephens and Moghaddas 2005b,c). The presence of heat and smoke, as well as the recycling of specific nutrients are fire-specific cues that cannot be simulated by mechanical treatments.

FOREST THINNING

Thinning is used as a treatment to modify the fuel structure in forests that have become denser due to fire exclusion. Thinning projects that reduce ladder fuel or crown fuel continuity can be effective at moderating crown fire behavior. Thinning is often proposed as a fuel management treatment because it can provide economic returns and produce some commercial timber products. In most cases, thinning projects

SIDEBAR 19.1. BIOMASS REMOVAL

FIGURE 19.1.1. Mechanized harvest of sawtimber and biomass from the Wrights Creek burn plantation. (Photo by Dave Horak, Stanislaus National Forest.)

In forest management, biomass removal commonly refers to the mechanical removal of small trees, branches and tops of larger trees, and portions of down woody material from the forest floor. It can provide for substantial reductions of hazardous fuel. Forest thinning may remove a wide range of tree sizes, with trees smaller than 25 cm in diameter at breast height and 1.5 m above the uphill ground line providing the majority of biomass yield. This practice is regarded as a valuable component of the forest management toolkit, especially where fuel hazard reduction is a major management objective.

Like other ground-based mechanical operations, biomass removal is generally limited to slopes less than 40%; however, recently designed equipment now provides for access to steeper slopes (Fig. 19.1.1). In some cases, a skyline-yarder aerial harvesting system is used to collect woody material from steep slopes. Numerous strategies exist for cutting, collecting, and transporting biomass from the stump to a roadside landing. Equipment type, size, and capability vary widely. One common strategy uses a rubber-tired feller-buncher, to cut and concentrate the biomass, and a grapple skidder, to transport the concentrated material to the landing. At the landing site, the biomass is fed into a chipper and blown into a van for transport to a local power generation facility.

Economic considerations play a substantial role in biomass removal projects. The material is commonly chipped at roadside landings and hauled to wood-fired electrical generation plants. Harvesting and transportation costs are substantial and are not always offset by the value of the delivered chips. When forest thinning includes valuable saw timber products, the connected costs of biomass harvest and transportation may be absorbed more easily. In some cases, Forest Service fuel reduction projects often provide additional funding to cover expenditures beyond those covered by the value of the chips. In other cases, subsidies from governmental agencies can play an important role in providing for cost-effective projects. There are several other promising end uses of biomass material; however the use as fuel is the most common at this time. —*Joseph W. Sherlock* are only effective as a fuel management technique when fine surface fuel is also reduced (Agee and Skinner 2005).

Thinning can remove trees to create specified stand densities, patterns, distributions, and species compositions. Thinning is an effective fuel management method if it reduces the likelihood that a surface fire will transition into a crown fire by breaking up vertical and horizontal fuel continuity. The thinning specifications, by density and by diameter classes of trees, are important characteristics of thinning prescriptions. Considerable progress has been made in developing guidelines to implement fuel reduction goals through thinning projects as summarized by Peterson et al. (2004).

MASTICATION

Mastication is the mechanical grinding, crushing, shredding, chipping, and chopping of fuel that can reduce fireline intensity and the rate of fire spread. Mastication and some other mechanical modifications of the fuel are used to reduce potential fire behavior by reducing fuelbed depth and thereby increasing packing ratio. An ever-increasing selection of mechanical equipment is available to accomplish these tasks.

Mastication can effectively accomplish the modification of potential fire behavior with a great deal of precision. It can be applied to specific areas and fuel and can be effective without the need to remove fuel or soil cover from the site. Ladder fuel, specific fuel sizes, or shrub layers can be the specific target for projects. These mechanical treatments differ greatly from historical fire in ecological effects. They do not replace the biological role of fire and can create a significant impact on the site by the presence of equipment. Mastication, like other mechanical treatments is most commonly applied in the restoration rather than in maintenance of wildland ecosystems.

GRAZING

Prior to the arrival of domestic livestock, native grazers undoubtedly had a great influence on herbaceous fuel. Domestic livestock have been effective at modifying fuel in California since the establishment of the missions as described in Chapter 18. Concentrated livestock grazing is still used to reduce surface fuel loads and the rate of fire spread. Grazing or browsing for the specific purpose of reducing fuel is applied on a limited scale, mostly on the wildland-urban interface in shrublands or grasslands. Its use is growing as a maintenance tool on fuel breaks and other linear fuel reduction projects. Nonetheless, the impact of grazing on vegetation and fire regimes in present-day California should not be discounted. Grazing of cattle influences fire regimes on the Northeastern Plateaus and Southwestern Desert bioregions, especially on lands administered by the Bureau of Land Management. The removal of fine fuel by domestic animals shortens the fire season and reduces fire potential.

Owners of large tracts of private land have used fire to improve forage and grazing throughout the twentieth century (Biswell 1989). The Vegetation Management Program (VMP), administered by the California Department of Forestry and Fire Protection (CDF), was established in 1983 to provide a means to share the cost of mechanical treatment and prescribed burning on private land in California. VMP has enabled CDF and landowners to conduct safe and effective prescribed burns on ranchlands throughout the state. A second objective was wildlife habitat improvement in cooperation with the California Department of Fish and Game. The number of acres burned under the VMP program has declined somewhat in recent years, but at its peak, more than 24,000 ha (60,000 ac) were burned each year.

Fuel Management Phases: Restoration and Maintenance

The restoration and long-term maintenance of ecosystems for a defined set of desired conditions including the range of variability for wildland fuel requires knowledge about fire regimes. These fire regimes may or may not have persisted on the same landscapes in the past, or even exist there currently. The desired condition is typically a manifestation of society's needs from that wildland landscape. Establishment or restoration of a changed fire regime will often require both an initial restoration phase and a long-term maintenance phase. The importance of analyzing the costs and the frequency of restoration and maintenance has been highlighted by federal agencies' current efforts to define condition class and fire regime on a spatial basis. These concepts are designed to assist fire managers and the public in setting priorities for fuel management based on the frequency and severity of fire under pre- European conditions (fire regime) and departure from these regimes that has occurred during the fire suppression era (condition class) (Schmidt et al. 2002). The growing availability of spatial data describing fuel characteristics allows managers to use these data to set priorities for fuel treatments and to quantify the extent of the fire hazard problem at a variety of scales.

The *restoration phase* is designed to re-establish the fuel structure and composition before prescribed fires can be introduced or reintroduced. During this phase, the techniques that are used are not necessarily the ones that occurred historically or the ones that will be prescribed for a long-term program. Mechanical treatments such as thinning of overly dense forest stands are important tools. These treatments must maintain the desired focal characteristics of the landscape while accelerating the progress toward desired fuel conditions. Duration of the restoration phase can range from a single treatment to several decades of treatments. The restoration will effectively and efficiently set up the landscape for fire to operate as an ecosystem process, enabling continuance during the maintenance phase. In some cases, prescribed fire alone can be used in the restoration and maintenance phases (Stephens and Moghaddas 2005b).

The *maintenance phase* is the long-term application of prescribed fire or other fuel management techniques to the landscape. The maintenance phase can be accomplished once the restoration phase is completed. If the landscape is already in a condition that can support the desired prescribed fire regime, restoration is not necessary. Maintenance phase treatments are characterized by greater variability and "more random" fire applications within normal ranges of fire regime attributes for given ecosystems. In many cases, application of herbicides, scraping, chopping, or other methods are used to maintain mechanical fuel treatments. There are many challenges to completing maintenance treatments on thinned areas and fuel breaks. The costs of developing the initial treatments can sometimes be defrayed by the economic value of the trees that are removed. As more areas are restored, the cost of completing maintenance on previously treated areas multiplies. Fire managers must choose between doing restoration work on new areas and maintaining areas that have received initial restoration treatments. The challenge of following through on maintenance has come up repeatedly in California (Cermak 1988). Perhaps the most striking example of this is the Ponderosa Way and Truck Trail, a 1,047-km (650-mi) long fuel break completed in the 1930s to stop the spread of fire from the foothills into forested areas. It stretched from the Pit River to the southern end of the Sierra Nevada near Kernville (Green 1977). The Truck Trail persists as a street name in many foothill communities, but the fuel break is gone, due to lack of maintenance.

Choosing Management Methods on Complex Landscapes

The primary objective of fuel management is the reduction of potential fire behavior and effects. We know how to monitor and evaluate the effects of individual fuel treatments (Brown et al. 1982, Miller 1996, Lutes et al. 2006, NPS 2003, Agee and Skinner 2005, Stephens and Moghaddas 2005b). It is far more challenging to design and monitor treatments on a landscape scale. This requires the application of large numbers of treatments over entire watersheds and the development of measures to evaluate the interaction of wildfires with these treatments over long periods of time. Such data are essential in making the most efficient use of scarce funds and setting priorities and schedules for treatment. Essential questions, including how to arrange fuel treatments, how often to maintain them, how much of the landscape must be treated, and how these treatments interact with critical wildlife habitat and riparian areas, require both complex tools and difficult trade-offs.

Reducing surface fuel will limit the potential intensity of fires, provide a higher probability of controlling wildfires, and allow more of the forest to survive when it does burn (Agee 2003). Thinning treatments can be directed to effectively reduce ladder and crown fuel. Prior to 1990, the majority of fuel management treatments on forested areas in California were aimed at removing debris generated by forestry activities. These treatments were funded by the Forest Service

under the Brush Disposal program. The Brush Disposal (BD) Fund was created in 1916 to burn the excess brush and slash resulting from logging operations. The BD Fund requires timber purchasers to pay a brush disposal fee in addition to the timber sale price. Fuel treatments funded by these fees consisted primarily of piling and burning residue left after timber harvest or fire salvage. These deposits were also used to conduct broadcast burning of large areas that had been thinned as well as to burn clear-cut blocks. The BD program is still an important part of the Forest Service fuel management program, but its use has declined from its peak in the 1980s. The gradual decline of the BD program can be attributed to two things: first, the decline of timber program sales on national forests in California, and second, the loss of revenues on individual timber sales as the cost of harvest increased and the size, and therefore value, of the material being harvested declined. Little usable data exist on the extent and distribution of treatments conducted historically under the program in California, although we do know that thousands of acres were treated and millions of dollars spent. The distribution of these treatments in the landscape was not designed to influence wildfires.

Today, the focus of fuel treatments in many public and private forests is the removal of dense trees and modification of surface fuel. The purpose of these treatments is to reduce the risk of crown mortality during wildfires, to increase the probability of successful fire suppression, and to improve forest health. The Healthy Forest Restoration Act of 2003 establishes these as high priorities for federal agencies and gives stewardship authority to the Forest Service and the Bureau of Land Management.

It is important to note that logging residues (activity fuels) that are left on site can result in potential fire behavior that is more extreme or similar to an untreated forest (van Wagtendonk 1996, Stephens 1998). Fuel treatments in forests that once experienced frequent, low- to moderate-intensity fire regimes should focus on surface first and then ladder and crown fuel (Stephens 1998, Agee 2003, Stephens and Ruth 2005).

One method of establishing priorities and arrangements of fuel treatments on a landscape scale is to link them to past fire causes. Strategically placed area treatments may be an effective strategy to reduce landscape fire behavior in large, heterogeneous areas (Finney 2001). These treatments are a system of overlapping-area fuel treatments designed to minimize the area burned by high-intensity head fires in diverse terrain.

Human-caused fires commonly occur near highways, roads, trails, campgrounds, and urban areas, making it possible for fire managers to forecast areas of higher ignition potential. Defensible fuel profile zones placed near areas of high human-caused ignitions can be used to decrease the probability of large, high-severity fires by improving suppression efficiency (Agee et al. 2000, Stephens and Ruth 2005). The defensible fuel profile zone idea originated on the Lassen National Forest (Olson et al. 1995). The proposal was further developed by Weatherspoon and Skinner (1996) as a fuel management strategy. The concept was popularized by the Quincy Library Group, a grassroots community group centered in Quincy, California. This group sought to influence the Forest Service to reduce the risk of large damaging wildfires and improve the local economy by putting local people to work and revitalizing the declining forest products industry. The Quincy Library Group succeeded in convincing the federal government to plan and finance fuel management efforts on three national forests in northern California. Their original proposal was funded by Congress in 1999 to plan and construct a network of wide, shaded, fuel breaks on the Lassen, Plumas, and Tahoe National Forests. These networks differ from traditional fuel breaks by being wider and emphasizing retention of overstory trees. The purpose of these networks was to provide an area with road access where firefighters could take action safely on wildfires. One of the primary goals of the program was to implement the network of fuel breaks and monitor the effect that they had on this fire-prone ecosystem over the long term (Quincy Library Group 1994).

Fuel breaks have a long history California. The chaparral management program in Southern California reached its peak in the 1970s, and was supported by extensive research conducted at the Forest Service Riverside Fire Lab (Green and Shmimke 1971, Green 1977). According to Green (1977), there were 2,977 km (1,850 mi) of fuel break wider than 30 m (100 ft) in California in 1972. The original management plans for the Angeles, Cleveland, San Bernardino, and Los Padres National Forests proposed ambitious programs to maintain a complex network of fuel breaks extending from national forests into the adjoining cities and suburbs. These plans also proposed management of age classes in chaparral through a mosaic of prescribed burning. Countryman (1974) discussed the short intervals needed for effective rotational burning, as well as the high costs, and risks of escaped prescribed burns. Debate continues today on whether such strategies are effective under the worst-case weather conditions that typify Southern California wildfires (Keeley et al. 2004, Moritz et al. 2004). Concerns have been raised over the effects of out-of-season burning and increased fire frequency on biodiversity (see Chapters 15 and 22).

In forested areas, installation and maintenance of fuel breaks, strategically placed fuel treatments, and defensible fuel profile zones at appropriate spatial scales (Finney 2001) should reduce wildfire area and severity. Defensible fuel profile zones and fuel breaks will only be effective in reducing losses in the urban–wildland intermix if they are used in combination with combustion-resistant homes that are surrounded by a defensible space free of flammable vegetation and fuel.

Several California forest types are currently experiencing elevated levels of high-intensity, high-severity wildfire, and active management is necessary to slow or reverse this trend. Prescribed fire can be used to reduce fuel hazards but

constraints can severely limit operation periods. It is common for many fire managers to have a single week or less when constraints (e.g., air quality, wildlife, weather, crew availability) actually allow burning. It is not possible to restore and maintain hundreds of thousands of hectares of forests with high fire hazards within these constraints (Stephens and Ruth 2005).

The social and political aspects of fuel management, although always factors in land management, are of even greater consequence today. It is of increasing importance for land managers to articulate and quantify the nature of the fuel hazard issue and the rationale behind the selection of tools and programs to mitigate it.

Within the context of fuel management, several social and political issues predominate. One set of issues revolves around the changing ecological role of fire. In some areas, the use of fire may make a situation worse ecologically, while in others, fire may be a useful tool to restore and maintain ecosystems in a desired state. In still other areas, the volume of fuel is so great that some fuel should be removed mechanically before fire can be safely restored.

Fire managers determine which situations exist on the land in question. Each situation will be affected by many ecological effects, such as the vulnerability of soil to erosion caused by prescribed versus wildland fire, and therefore the likelihood of erosion impacting watersheds. Air quality regulators want land managers to consider the use of mechanical fuel reduction methods before the use of prescribed fire. The use of mechanical methods to reduce fuel, and the threat of wildland fire, will cause controversy over which fuel should be removed; if live trees, then how many? Of what diameter? To what density? And mechanical treatment methods will have their own ecological impacts. Although the issues can be displayed fairly easily, the acquisition and analysis of data to arrive at the best combination of fuel techniques is not such an easy process. The Forest Service has recently completed work on analytical tools to assist fire and land managers in laying out fuel treatments in watersheds and across multiple jurisdictions. This tool, known as FIRESHED analysis (Bahro and Barber 2004), makes use of spatial data layers to allow the design of treatments and the testing of these tools using fire modeling methods (Sidebar 19.2).

The fuel manager must make candid evaluation of the wildland fire and fuel situation, including an assessment of the ecological impact of various fuel-reduction techniques and their influence on wildland fire behavior. This evaluation is the fundamental explanation to the public and to those who appropriate funds so that the program will be both effective and efficient. The amount of controversy that arises in fuel programs is proportional to the degree to which evaluation is not done, or explained, well. Clear description of the consequences of fuel management action—or inaction—will also help managers comply with air quality, cultural resource, threatened and endangered species, and other laws and regulations.

Fireshed assessment is an interdisciplinary and collaborative process for designing and scheduling fuels and vegetation management treatments across broad landscapes to meet goals for changing outcomes associated with large, severe wildland fires (Fig. 19.2.1). The fireshed assessment process is based on the premise that management actions (in the form of fuels treatments located to modify fire behavior) can affect the outcome of a wildland fire (how large it gets, where it burns, and how severely it affects communities, habitats, and watersheds).

FIGURE 19.2.1. Fire behavior at the landscape scale.

The approach for modifying landscape-scale fire behavior is anchored in the concept that, by using a carefully designed pattern of treatment areas, managers can treat a fraction of the landscape to achieve intended modifications in wildland fire behavior. The design of treatment area patterns is based on the premise that disconnected fuels treatment areas overlapping across the general direction of fire spread are theoretically effective in changing fire spread. Research conducted by Dr. Mark Finney (2001) suggests that fire spread rates can be reduced, even outside of treated areas, if a fire is forced to flank areas where fuels have been reduced or otherwise modified. Hence, treated areas function as "speed bumps," slowing the spread and reducing the intensity of oncoming fires, thereby reducing damage to both treated and untreated areas, and ultimately reducing the size and severity of wildland fires. Two criteria must be met for this strategy to be effective: (1) the pattern of area treatments across the landscape must interrupt fire spread, and (2) treatment prescriptions must be designed to significantly modify fire behavior within the treated areas. As landscape-scale wildfire behavior is modified over time, fire suppression opportunities are enhanced, leading to smaller fires that are less damaging and less costly. Treatments for modifying wildfire behavior can also be designed to meet multiple resource objectives, such as improving forest health and providing habitats for at-risk species over the long-term.

During fireshed assessment, interdisciplinary natural resource teams, working with partners from government agencies, stakeholders, and other collaborators, use the following process to design fuels treatments and assess their performance in changing outcomes of potential large "problem" fires.

Step 1: Determine Wildfire Threats by Identifying "Problem" Fires. "Problem" fires are the potential wildfires of greatest concern based on impacts to lives, property, forests, and watersheds. Such fires occur when suppression resources are unable to contain them under initial attack. Problem fires are the 2% of wildfires that escape initial attack, and are the most costly and damaging fires. Problem fires (along with data from historical large fires) are used to identify and delineate firesheds during Step 2.

Step 2: Frame the Analysis Area (Fireshed) for Assessment. Firesheds are large (thousands of acres) landscapes that share similar historical large wildland fire characteristics as well as potential fire behavior

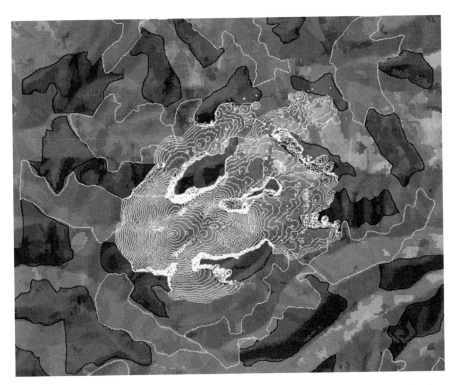

FIGURE 19.2.2. A modeled example of wildland fire moving across a treated landscape *(white lines).* Note the reduced rate of fire spread in treatment areas *(dark-shaded areas in the fire perimeter).*

characteristics. The purpose of delineating firesheds is to identify areas that are sufficiently large to assess the effectiveness of fuels treatment at changing the outcome of a large wildland fire.

Step 3: Characterize the Likely Behavior of the Problem Fire(s) Within the Fireshed. The problem fire defines the weather conditions of concern (wind directions, wind speeds, fuel moistures, and expected fire behavior) under which fuels treatments in the fireshed must perform. The location, size, and severity of the problem fire provide the baseline for assessing the extent to which various treatment scenarios change potential large wildfire outcomes. Spatial modeling tools, such as FARSITE and FLAMMAP, are used to analyze, display, and game multiple iterations of the problem fire's behavior.

Step 4: Develop a Treatment Pattern and Prescriptions Aimed at Changing the Outcome of the Problem Fire. First, a pattern of treatment areas is laid out across the fireshed to interrupt potential fire spread. Each treatment area is then assigned a prescription or prescriptions. Treatment prescriptions must be designed to significantly modify fire behavior within each treated area by removing sufficient material to cause a fire to burn at lower intensities and slower rates of spread. Prescriptions focus on removing fuels in a sequential manner, starting with surface, then ladder, and finally crown fuels to achieve desired effects on fire behavior. Prescriptions also consider existing vegetation and fuels conditions; for example, in previously treated areas, a maintenance treatment may be prescribed. Treatment methods can include prescribed burning, hand treatments, and/or mechanical treatments.

This step also involves demonstrating how the combination of treatment area patterns and prescriptions (referred to collectively as *the treatment scenario*) modifies wildland fire spread, resulting in a smaller potential fire with less severe effects (Fig. 19.2.2). The performance of Step 4's treatment scenario in changing the outcome of the problem fire is assessed by comparing the potential fire in the treated landscape with the problem fire in the untreated landscape based on fire location, size (acres), and type (acreages experiencing surface fire, passive crowning, and active crowning). As in Step 3 above, FLAMMAP and FARSITE are useful tools for displaying these outcomes.

Step 5: Adjust Treatments from Step 4 to Incorporate Landscape-Scale Desired Outcomes for Other Resources Where Possible While Still Meeting the Intended Effect of Changing the Outcome of the Problem Fire. Treatment patterns and prescriptions from Step 4 are adjusted and refined to incorporate multiple resource objectives, such as reducing stand densities, maintaining habitats, making treatments cost effective, and mitigating potential impacts to watershed conditions and landscape visual character. The primary goal, however, is to continue to maintain a treatment scenario that meets the primary objective of changing the outcome of the problem fire. As in Step 4, performance in changing wildfire outcomes is assessed.

Step 6: Adjust and Refine the Treatment Scenario Developed in Step 4 Based on Information from the Field and Other Relevant Sources. During this step, some potential treatment areas as well as past treatments are reviewed in the field, especially those that have been affected by wildland fire. Information from past treatments and fire impacts inform the current fireshed assessment process in making coarse-scale refinements or adjustments to treatment designs, analysis assumptions, or both. —*Bernhard Bahro, Laurie Perrot*

Focusing fuel management funds on the wildland–urban interface may preclude or hinder the use of prescribed fire because of safety or air quality concerns. Fuel buildup near communities may require mechanical fuel reduction before prescribed fire can be safely used, if it can be used at all. Although prescribed fire managers have effectively worked for years with impacts on air quality (see Chapter 21), sensitive species (see Chapter 23), cultural resources, and other environmental issues, many of these projects were in remote areas away from the public. With the current emphasis on fuel reduction projects in the wildland-urban interface, there is greater likelihood of public interest, concern, and involvement. Controversy can arise when smoke blows into neighborhoods or concerns arise about mechanical treatments, particularly with regard to thinning being a pretext to allow logging.

Choosing the methods to be used for fuel management is becoming a more complex process with more choices available and more considerations necessary. As fire and fuel management become a greater focus of the land managers and the public, more information and scientific understanding are needed to answer the public's questions. Public acknowledgment of the scope and scale of the fire and fuel issues in California wildlands brings with it increased levels of scrutiny and accountability.

History of Fuel Management: The Evolution of a Fuel Emergency

As detailed in Chapter 17, Native Americans used fire to modify fuel for several thousand years prior to the arrival of European settlers. Some Native American fire practices were continued in modified forms by the early European settlers. Ironically, one of the first widespread modifications of Native American fuel patterns came with the introduction of large numbers of domestic livestock, which eliminated most of the surface fuel over large areas during the late 1800s. This was unintentional fuel management, but did result in widespread modification of fire patterns. The effort to exclude fire from ecosystems during the 1900s has resulted in additional fire pattern changes (see Chapter 18). We now know that the effect of these management efforts was to maximize fuel loads by allowing the uninterrupted accumulation of fuel.

A fuel condition emergency has been developing over the past 200 years and is now manifesting. From 2002 to 2004, four states—California, Arizona, Oregon, and Colorado—have experienced their largest wildland fires ever recorded. Additionally, Montana had thousands of acres burn during the 2003 fire season. The annual cost of suppression and rehabilitation are exceeding a billion dollars.

These catastrophic situations were foreseen decades ago by the pioneers in prescribed fire use in California. As noted by Carle (2002), government advocates of fire protection overrode ranchers, loggers, and other practitioners of "light burning." Interestingly, many of the arguments used against the practice of light burning are as valid today as they were in 1924: Fire damages young trees, is expensive, and is difficult to adapt to variations in fuel and topography. Fire suppression was viewed as more straightforward and practical. The difference today is the understanding we now have about the effects on both ecosystems and fire behavior that result from the accumulation of understory vegetation and fuel in the absence of fire.

The research and teaching of Dr. Biswell remains the cornerstone of the use of fire in California. His work and the work of his students, such as Bruce Kilgore, James Agee, Jan van Wagtendonk, Tom Nichols, and Ron Wakimoto, were instrumental in the establishment of prescribed fire and wildland fire use programs at Sequoia and Kings Canyon and Yosemite National Parks. Similar programs were established in national forests, refuges, and parks throughout California.

Therefore, it is useful to examine in some detail the techniques that Dr. Biswell and others used to support the transition of policy. The translation of Dr. Biswell's techniques from small demonstration burns to large prescribed burn units to landscape or drainage-sized prescribed fire projects has continued to be a challenge. The teachings of Dr. Biswell, however, contain the solution to this transition: patience and public education.

Dr. Biswell's lesson of patience has two elements. One is the more obvious technique of conducting prescribed burns slowly and carefully, not exceeding the holding capacity of the personnel present, as well as not exceeding the capacity of the ecosystem to absorb heat with undesirable amounts of damage or mortality. The other is bringing along the public, agency administrators, and cooperators slowly enough that their comfort level with the use of prescribed fire is not exceeded. It is often said that it has taken a century of fire suppression to cause the fuel condition of ecosystems we see today, and it might take a century of prescribed fire to restore these ecosystems.

The difficult task of the modern fire manager is to increase the size and magnitude of fuel management programs so that the fuel can be reduced and ecosystems can be restored at a significant rate while also building public support. Many land management agencies conduct prescribed fires, but at a rate and size trivial when compared to the size of the unit and scale of the wildland fire risk. It is the advancement of the size of prescribed fire programs from small research burns to ecologically significant landscape burns that requires skill and patience. This also requires a concomitant public education effort, which was the critical element of Dr. Biswell's methods, as well as those of the other early researchers in the successful use of prescribed fire.

Fire policy itself has become more complex, and in particular the measurement and mitigation of risk associated with prescribed fire operations. Although very few prescribed fires escape and cause damage to structures or property, the few that do cause such damage receive much media attention and result in even more risk mitigation policies to be written and managers to become more risk adverse and cautious. Escaped prescribed fires in California have had a profound impact on interagency cooperation in the implementation of prescribed programs. In 1957, the 202-ha (500-ac) Bogus Burn on the Klamath National Forest escaped and was controlled at 5,192 ha (12,831 ac) (Cermak 1988). After the Bogus Burn escape, prescribed burning on National Forests in California was severely reduced until the 1970s. The 1990 Bedford Canyon fire, an escaped prescribed burn on the Cleveland National Forest, burned onto private land into a subdivision and destroyed a dozen homes. This fire prompted state legislation that led to the development of the Cooperative Prescribed Fire Agreement between California and the federal agencies. The agreement formalized the multi-agency coordination to implement prescribed burns on multiple jurisdictions.

In 1999, the Lowden Ranch Fire escaped and burned through part of the town of Lewiston, destroying 23 homes. This escape served to increase public anxiety about the use of prescribed fire adjacent to towns and homes and increased northern California communities' interest in finding mechanical alternatives to prescribed fire in the urban-wildland interface. The Lowden Ranch escape also had significant impacts on fire management professionals. In the years following this fire, managers and prescribed burn bosses have become much more risk averse and concerned about both personal liability and the risk associated with performance of their jobs.

Air quality and smoke management policies frequently limit agencies' abilities to conduct fire management programs—ironically so because one of the purposes of prescribed burning is to *reduce* wildfires, which emit much more smoke than do prescribed fires (Agee 1989). The 1997 Beaver Creek prescribed fire on the Stanislaus National Forest was a turning point regarding prescribed fire and smoke management. Prior to this time, many county burn rules exempted all prescribed burns above 1,500 meters (6,000 feet) elevation in the Sierra Nevada. Counties frequently approved these exemptions to allow fire managers to burn on "no burn" days. The Beaver Creek burn and a number of other burns on adjacent parklands, CDF management units, and forests were approved simultaneously. An unforecasted weather pattern caused the smoke from these fires to impact most of the Sierra Nevada, the Central Valley, and the Reno and Lake Tahoe areas. This event precipitated the revision of the state burning regulations and heralded a new era in regulation of smoke from prescribed burns. Public concerns about smoke put air quality regulators in the difficult position of trying to both protect the public from unhealthful air and support fire managers in their use of fire.

The issues of invasive plants, which may take advantage of prescribed fire or mechanical fuel treatment to become established, is a growing concern (see Chapter 22). This problem is particularly severe in the deserts and chaparral of California and is thoroughly discussed in Chapter 16. The effects of prescribed fire on sensitive species are often poorly understood; managers are often reluctant to allow prescribed fires that may have deleterious effects on sensitive species or their habitats (Knapp et al. 2005, Stephens and Moghaddas 2005c) (see Chapter 23). Because of these and many other issues, the responsibilities of state and federal fuel managers have become increasingly more rigorous. Considerable time and effort are spent addressing technical issues such as burn plan development and approval, acquisition of permits, budget formulation and tracking, and the mobilization of sufficient fire resources to conduct burns or implement treatments.

Too often lost in the effort to conduct fuel management has been the more qualitative issue of public education, the same issue that was so important in the original public promotion of the need for prescribed fire to the public. One of the most encouraging developments of the last few years is the cooperative education and planning efforts of fire managers and the public. The California Department of Forestry and Fire Protection, in trying to develop community involvement at the local level through the state's California Fire Plan, encouraged the development of fire-safe councils throughout the state. These councils have sprung up in both rural and suburban communities. The primary objective of the councils is involving citizens in creating defensible space around their homes and in working together to design protection strategies for their communities. These groups are increasingly interested, as they should be, in influencing fuel management priorities on areas adjacent to their communities and are influencing the design of projects and the expenditures of funds by federal, state, and local government fuel managers.

Another interagency group, the California Fire Alliance, created a one-stop grants application web site for National Fire Plan grants in California. The purpose of this clearinghouse is to provide a California-wide view of community-based fuel treatment projects to estimate funding needs and to evaluate the capacity of communities and organizations to conduct fuel treatment, education, and fire hazard reduction planning.

These are encouraging trends in a state that clearly needs a force to galvanize interagency cooperation and cohesion in development of fuel management strategies. The continued implementation of fuel management in California absolutely requires the involvement of the public in issues such as smoke management that require cooperation between a variety of agencies and regulators. The ability of land managers to educate the public and gain their support for prescribed fire programs is directly linked to the survival of these programs.

Managing Fuel in Twenty-First–Century California

Recent fire history in California is characterized by what have been come to be called "fire sieges" (CDF and USDA Forest Service 2004). These are periods when multiple, large fires briefly overwhelm the considerable fire-suppression capability of federal, state, and local government fire departments. These events are costly and large enough to capture the attention of media, government, and the people of California. Such fires directly impact the cities and towns in the paths of the fires. Homes, businesses, and lives are lost. Closed highways, electrical power disruptions, and large-scale evacuations impact the economies of large areas of the state. During a 13-day period in 1970, wildfires in Southern California burned 230,000 hectares (580,000 acres), destroyed 772 homes, and killed 16 people. The most recent of these sieges occurred in Southern California in late October of 2003 when wildfires burned 303,514 hectares (750,000 acres), destroyed 3,652 residences, and killed 22 people.

California's forested mountain ranges have also been affected by fire sieges. These sieges are characterized by multiple, large, lightning fires burning under very dry conditions (Weatherspoon et al. 1992). Numerous fires start in remote or rural areas and burn large areas in the national forests, parks, and rangelands of the Klamath Mountains, Coastal Ranges, Cascades, and Sierra Nevada. The most notable recent sieges were in 1977 and 1987. Throughout the course of the twentieth century, such events in the Sierra Nevada have shown an increased *percentage* of the area burned being impacted by crown fire and exhibiting tree mortality, even though the *number* of hectares burned in the Sierra Nevada range and California has not increased significantly (McKelvey and Busse 1996, Stephens 2005).

Each of these fire sieges has had a profound impact on the fuel management program in the state, stimulating fact-finding reviews and investigations. Reports, commissions, and local government bodies uniformly recommend that fuel management be expanded to protect communities, improve the efficiency of fire suppression, and lessen impacts on natural resources. There is a surge of public and government support for fuel management programs in the wake of these events. This support translates into increases in funding for all types of fuel treatment. A task force on California's wildland fire problem was convened after the severe fires of 1970 and made a number of recommendations that still ring true today: require hazardous fuel abatement adjacent to structures, strengthen research efforts, improve fuel management planning efforts, expand the prescribed burning program in chaparral, and create a network of fuel breaks and greenbelts (Anonymous 1972). The requirement for defensible space subsequently became part of the state code. And the other recommendations were implemented, but only for a time. Funding gradually decreased, treated acres declined, and fuel breaks were left unmaintained. More importantly, the initial efforts failed because the treatments were not monitored, and we learned little about the effects of those treatments on fire hazard and fire regimes. In every case, there has been a marked increase in treated acres subsequent to these sieges, but a failure to carry through on the recommendations over the longer term and gather vital landscape-level data to adapt and improve programs in the future.

It has been said that the wildland–urban interface is a defining fire management issue of the twenty-first century. Pyne (1982) noted, however, that these interface issues have been a part of fire management as long as fires have burned from wildlands into communities. The 1991 Oakland Hills fire, for example, had a precedent in the 1923 Berkeley fire. What was new was the number of homes and communities that have been, and continue to be, constructed in the interface, greatly increasing the number of people and amount of property at risk. Many of these homes are at risk not so much because of the build-up of fuel, but because homes and towns are constructed in vegetation types that naturally burn with high intensity and rapid spread. Comparisons of structure density in the footprint of the Laguna fire of 1970—an area burned again in the Cedar fire of 2003—showed that the number of structures has increased fivefold (Husari et al. 2004). Fire management in the interface is clearly one of the major natural resource issues for California as the twenty-first century begins.

Continuing development in the interface area is reorienting fire resources and funding for fuel management programs. Allocating firefighting resources to protect homes and communities, rather than to suppress the fire itself, is one reason for increasing costs and size of wildfires. Simultaneously, the increased threat of wildland fire to the public has also influenced the magnitude and pattern of allocation of fuel management funding appropriations at the national level.

Increasing loss of homes in the interface has spurred Congress to allocate more fuel management funds to treat more acres at risk. Congress has accepted the argument made by land managers that expanding fuel treatment to work in concert with suppression resources is an important part of the solution to the escalating costs of wildland fires.

The Risk of Fuel Management Projects

It is important to recognize that fuel management, particularly prescribed fire, involves inherent risk to both natural resources and communities. Changes in the federal policy emphasizing the importance of the restoration of the natural role of fire have led to a greater use of prescribed fire. This, in turn, has led to an increased potential for escaped prescribed fires or for smoke episodes from larger or multiple burns.

The 2000 Cerro Grande prescribed fire, which escaped from Bandelier National Monument and burned into the community of Los Alamos, New Mexico, led to a number of refinements to increase control of prescribed fire by federal agencies, including an emphasis on the availability of fire suppression resources should weather conditions deteriorate. Prescribed fire does carry inherent risk with it, but the risk can be analyzed, mitigated, and reduced with better identification of the nature of the risk.

Similarly, health impacts from smoke continue to be a source of liability. Planning, modeling, and mitigation of the volume and extent of smoke impacts are needed to anticipate and avoid those impacts. As with other aspects of prescribed fire, the use of monitoring equipment to show what health standards have, or have not, been violated is a basic part of the program.

Even without the risk of escaped fire, fuel management brings additional risks. Fuel management in forested ecosystems commonly seeks to reduce the potential for catastrophic, high-intensity crown fires. This is accomplished by reducing the overall fuel loads and reducing the continuity of crown fuel. Over time, this is a transition from a high-severity crown

fire regime to a low-severity surface fire regime. It is important to understand that this does not usually mean less fire, but rather more frequent fire. Although surface fires are certainly more easily controlled by suppression efforts, the amount of fire over time often increases.

The Cost of Not Implementing Fuel Treatments

Since the 1940s, many wildfire experts have warned of the effects of allowing fuel to accumulate far beyond natural levels. Harold Weaver, Harold Biswell, Roy Komarek, Ed Komarek, and Bruce Kilgore all stressed the need for the restoration of fire to the ecosystem and for the need to manage fuel loads to mitigate the occurrence of high-intensity, destructive wildland fires. Their predictions have proven all too accurate. The cost of *not* doing fuel management projects, therefore, is increasing damage to cultural and natural resources, higher suppression costs, degraded air quality, loss of revenue to communities, and, of paramount importance, increased risk to firefighter and public safety.

The cost of not doing fuel treatments is larger and more damaging fires, because incident commanders and fire chiefs will not put firefighters in harm's way to bring more-intense fires under control under worst-case fire conditions. Changing climates may further escalate the fire management problem (Fried et al. 2004).

The Future of Fuel Management in California

The future of fuel management in California, and its implementation at a level of activity that significantly reduces hazardous amounts of wildland fuel and restores and maintains healthy ecosystems, will require state, local, and federal fire managers to work more closely with the citizens of California. This will require the ability to make the highly technical field of fuel management intelligible to the citizens of California and greater efforts by fire managers to understand the public's point of view. It requires a balance of treatment types and careful decisions concerning priorities for use of mechanical fuel reduction methods, prescribed fire, and wildland fire use based on monitoring treatments and adapting programs (Sidebar 19.3).

Communities and fire management agencies must cooperate in the development of risk reduction fire and fuel management programs. It is this cooperation between the public and the government agencies in the reduction of wildfire damage, and the restoration of fire to a more beneficial ecological influence, that is the cornerstone of the new fire policies.

Beyond these efforts to inform and communicate, there is an even greater need to educate, which brings us back full circle to the lessons taught by Dr. Biswell and others. Support for and understanding of fuel management programs should be a year-round activity—and not limited to fire season. The future of fuel management, which must include the increased use of mechanical treatment and prescribed fire, depends on not only the acquisition of funding, personnel,

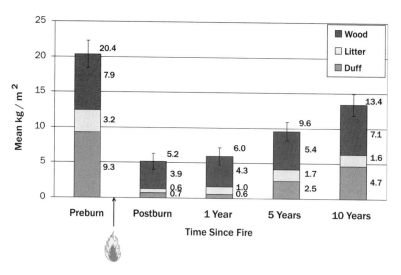

FIGURE 19.3.1. Fuel accumulation in the Giant sequoia-mixed conifer forest type (n = 26 plots). Error bars indicate 80% confidence interval.

Early studies in the giant sequoia forests of the Sierra Nevada demonstrated that a long period of fire exclusion had created heavy accumulations of fuels and an increased density of young trees. Scientists recognized that these conditions, if left unchecked, might promote uncharacteristically intense and/or extensive fires with potentially undesirable effects. In response, National Park Service managers at Sequoia and Kings Canyon National Parks began a prescribed fire program in 1969 (Fig. 19.3.1). Although early observations and limited short-term data indicated that these prescribed fires seemed to be effective, consistent, reliable data to demonstrate program success and long-term trends were lacking (Keifer et al. 2006).

How to Burn

The Sequoia-Kings Canyon National Park fire effects monitoring program was started in 1982 to provide feedback to help guide the prescribed fire management program (National Park Service 2003). Monitoring efforts are designed to determine if fuel reduction and other objectives are being met, to help detect unexpected consequences of prescribed burning, and to provide this information to fire managers, other park staff, and the public.

To most efficiently monitor fire effects, the mixed-conifer forest is stratified into three different types based on species composition and physiographic characteristics: the giant sequoia–mixed conifer, white fir–mixed conifer, and low-elevation–mixed conifer forest types. The fuels portion of the monitoring program measures dead and down organic matter on the forest floor (surface fuels) including litter, duff, and woody fuel using a planar intercept method (Brown 1974, Brown et al 1982). Surface fuels are measured in plots before and after the area is burned under a specified range of environmental conditions (temperature, relative humidity, wind, and fuel moisture).

The objective for fuel reduction in all forest types is a 60%–95% removal of total surface fuel load. Postburn monitoring results have revealed that the fuel reduction objective is met or exceeded in all

TABLE 19.3.1
Reduction in total surface fuels immediately after prescribed fire by forest type

Forest Type	Fuel Reduction: 80% Confidence Interval (Mean)
Giant sequoia-mixed conifer (n = 28 plots, 18 fires)	71%–81% (76%)
White fir-mixed conifer (n = 10 plots, 6 fires)	62%–85% (73%)
Low-elevation mixed conifer (n = 5 plots, 3 fires)	75%–93% (84%)

FIGURE 19.3.2. The prescribed fire program at Sequoia and Kings Canyon National Parks treats undesirable fuel conditions. (Photo by MaryBeth Keifer, National Park Service.)

three mixed-conifer forest types (Table 19.3.1), indicating that the range of burning conditions are appropriate for the desired fuel reduction.

When to Burn

Tens of thousands of acres of mixed-conifer forest in the parks were in need of prescribed fire treatment to reduce fuels and restore fire. It has taken decades to attempt to apply fire over such a large area, and returning to areas for repeat prescribed burns was not a priority early in the management program. More recently, managers have begun to apply repeat treatments; therefore, making decisions about the timing of second (and subsequent) prescribed burns is necessary to prioritize areas for treatment.

Results from long-term monitoring provide managers with critical data that track the accumulation of fuels over time in areas burned and thus can provide insight into when future fuels treatments are needed. In the giant sequoia-mixed conifer forest, fuel load had reached 66% of pre-burn levels by 10 years post-burn (Fig. 19.3.2). This result means that reburns for fuel reduction should be considered after 10 years following the initial burns if managers want to avoid a return to heavy pre-burn fuel load conditions in this forest type. By 10 years post-burn in the white fir–mixed conifer forest type, mean total fuel load was 83% of pre-burn levels, indicating that reburns for fuel reduction should be more strongly considered after 10 years in this forest type.

In the low-elevation–mixed conifer forest, total fuel load accumulated to 58% of pre-burn levels by five years post-burn, faster than in other forest types. Much of this accumulation is woody fuel due to the high amount of post-burn tree mortality that occurred in this forest type. While the sample size is limited (five plots), data from these five-year post-burn plots indicate that reburning may be warranted sooner than in other forest types to prevent fuels from accumulating to pre-burn levels.

The timing of reburns based on fuel accumulation also corresponds to historic fire return intervals (time between fires) and the differences in return intervals by elevation. Historic fire return intervals in the giant sequoia–mixed conifer and white fir–mixed conifer forests ranged from 2 to 30 years, with a mean of 10 years (Kilgore and Taylor 1979, Swetnam 1993, Stephens and Collins 2004, Moody et al. 2006). Fire return intervals decrease with decreasing elevation (Caprio and Swetnam 1995), therefore, the more xeric low-elevation–mixed conifer forests are likely to have had more frequent fires than the other mixed conifer types. The correspondence of fuel accumulation patterns with historic fire return intervals demonstrates that park managers may be able to achieve the simultaneous goals of reducing fuel hazard and restoring natural fire regimes.

Long-term fuel monitoring may also have important implications for smoke management and emissions modeling. For example, the dominant component of the pre-burn fuel complex is duff, while woody fuel, which produces less smoke than smoldering duff, tends to make up a greater proportion of the post-burn fuelbed (Fig. 19.3.2). Monitoring results from seven giant sequoia–mixed conifer plots show lower total fuel reductions for second treatments (48%) than in the initial burns (76%). In addition, a smaller proportion of duff was consumed in the reburns (47%) than in the initial prescribed fires (89%). It seems likely that the amount of smoke produced by individual burn units will be reduced after multiple treatments are implemented.

Integrating Results into Management Actions

Fuel and fire effects monitoring has become a critical component of Sequoia and Kings Canyon National Parks' fire management program and results from the monitoring program demonstrate the usefulness of long-term information. The ecology of fire and fuels management is often not simple. The issues are made even more complex by agency missions and political mandates that may present managers with multiple goals such as reducing fuel hazards while at the same time restoring and maintaining natural processes. Understanding fuel dynamics through long-term monitoring in these systems is an important part of helping managers to answer critical questions that will better address complex goals and continually improve the way that public lands are managed. —*MaryBeth Keifer* and technology, but also the construction of a base of public support for the program. This base of support will help cushion the program from incidents that may occur, such as smoke episodes, changes in scenic resources, and even escapes. The building of support is a year-round process, and its success or lack of success will directly affect the activity and acceptance of the fuel management program. This is the lesson we can learn from Dr. Biswell and the other prescribed fire pioneers, and was the key to their success in convincing agencies to change from fire control to fire management.

Conclusion

Fuel management programs in California do not suffer from a lack of public interest. However, they consistently have lacked a clear focus that could carry across the multiple jurisdictions, varied fire regimes, and political and demographic landscapes of California in a way that could truly influence large fires and sustain biodiversity and ecosystem health. Every fire siege, expensive fire season, and escaped prescribed fire generates new fuel management policies and initiatives before previous decisions have been tested or evaluated. There is an increasing call for fire management strategies and programs that are developed and monitored in a consistent and cohesive manner (USDI 2001). The National Fire Plan of 2001 kicked off efforts to establish a single federal fire policy rather than a set of loosely coordinated agency approaches to fire management. The National Fire Plan has been expanded to do a better job of considering the needs of state and local fire departments, as reflected in the Western Governors' Association's 10-Year Strategy (www. westgov.org/wga/initiatives/fire/final_fire_rpt.pdf). The California Fire Plan, released by the CDF in 1999, takes a collaborative and iterative approach to involving citizens in designing fuel management strategies and aggregating these up into a statewide approach to fuel management and fire protection.

Priority setting for fuel management will always be a difficult task in California. The sheer number of vegetation types and fire regimes described in the preceding chapters illustrates the difficulty of sorting out fuel management techniques appropriate to each of these assemblages of fire-adapted plants and animals. The selection of fuel management techniques is further complicated by how the land is used and how many people live nearby. Is it wilderness or is it private land? Is it allowable or practical to use mechanical treatment methods to reduce accumulated fuel? These factors also influence how fuel treatments are distributed in the landscape. With all the barriers to implementation, it is clear that we should use every tool available to us, including—and especially—decision support tools, which help us in distributing fuel treatments in the most efficient way, and monitoring, which helps us understand what works and what does not. There may come a time when mechanical treatments are the dominant fuel treatment available to managers for reducing fuel. Prescribed fire and wildland fire use may only be possible in a few areas that we designate, where fire is absolutely essential to preserve a few of the best examples of fire-adapted ecosystems. That time has not

arrived—yet. We must work together to make sure that we delay, rather than hurry, that day into existence. The alternative is that we lose much of what we have worked so hard to describe in this book, in all its beauty, variety, and complexity.

References

Agee, J.K. 1989. Wildfire in the Pacific west: a brief history and implications for the future. P. 11–16 in Proceedings of the symposium on fire and watershed management, October 26–28, 1988, Sacramento, CA. Gen. Tech. Rep. PSW-109.

Agee, J.K. 2003. The fallacy of passive management. Conservation Biology in Practice 1:18–25.

Agee, J.K., B. Bahro, M.A. Finney, P.N. Omi, D.B. Sapsis, C.N. Skinner, J.W. Wagtendonk, and C.P. Weatherspoon. 2000. The use of shaded fuelbreaks in landscape fire management. Forest Ecology and Management 127:55–66.

Agee, J.K., and Skinner, C.N. 2005. Basic principles of fuel reduction treatments. Forest Ecology and Management 211:83–96.

Anonymous. 1972. Recommendations to solve California's wildland fire problem. Report to Resources Agency Secretary Norman B. Livermore, Jr., by the Task Force on California's Wildland Fire Problem, June 1972. 62 p.

Arno, S.F., and S. Allison-Bunnell. 2002. Flames in our forest—Disaster or renewal? Island Press, Washington, DC. 227 p.

Bahro, B., and K. Barber. 2004. Fireshed assessment. An integrated approach to landscape planning. USDA Forest Service. R5-TP-017. 2 p.

Biswell, H.H. 1989. Prescribed burning in California wildland vegetation management. University of California Press, Berkeley. 255 p.

Brown, A.A., and K.P. Davis. 1973. Forest fire: control and use. McGraw-Hill, New York. 686 p.

Brown, J.K. 1974. Handbook for inventorying downed woody material. U.S. Forest Service, General Technical Report INT-16. 24p.

Brown, J.K., R.D. Oberheu, and C.M. Johnson. 1982. Handbook for inventorying surface fuels and biomass in the Interior West. U.S. Forest Service, General Technical Report INT-129. 48p.

California Department of Forestry and Fire Protection and USDA Forest Service. 2004. The story. California fire siege 2003. 98 p.

Caprio, A.C., and T.W. Swetnam. 1995. Historic fire regimes along an elevational gradient along the west slope of the Sierra Nevada, California. P. 173–179 in J.K. Brown, R.W. Mutch, C.W. Weatherpoon, and R. H. Wakimoto (tech. coord.), Proceedings: symposium on fire in wilderness and park management. U.S. Forest Service, Intermountain Research Station, Ogden, UT. General Technical Report, INT-320.

Carle, D. 2002. Burning questions—America's fight with nature's fire. Praeger Publishers, Westport, CT. 298 p.

Cermak, R.W. 1988. Fire control in the California National Forests: 1898–1955. Unpublished report. 669 p.

Countryman, C.M. 1974. Can Southern California wildland conflagrations be stopped? Pacific Southwest Forest and Range Exp. Stn. Gen. Tech. Rep PSW-7, Berkeley, CA. 11 p.

Finney, M.A. 2001. Design of regular landscape fuel treatment patterns for modifying fire growth and behavior. Forest Science 47:219–228.

Fried, J.S., M.S. Torn, and E. Mills. 2004. The impact of climate change on wildfire severity: a regional forecast for Northern California. Climatic Change 64:169–191.

Green L., 1977. Fuelbreaks and other fuel modification for wildland fire control, USDA Forest Service Agriculture Handbook No 499. 79 p.

Green, L. R., and H. E. Schmimke. 1971. Guides fuel-breaks in the Sierra Nevada mixed-conifer type. USDA For. Serv. Pac. Southwest For. and Range Exp. Stn., Berkeley, CA. 14 p.

Husari, S. H., D. Brown, N. Cleaver, G. Glotfelty, D. Golder, R. Green , T. Hatcher, K. Hawk, N. Hustedt, P. Kidder, J. Millar, M. Sandeman, and T. Walsh. 2004. The 2003 San Diego County fire siege fire safety review. Unpublished report on file at the Cleveland National Forest.

Keeley, J. E., C. J. Fotheringham, and M. A. Moritz. 2004. Lessons from the 2003 wildfires in southern California. Journal of Forestry 102:26–31.

Keifer, M., J. W. van Wagtendonk, and M. Buhler. 2006. Long-term surface fuel accumulation in burned and unburned mixed-conifer forests of the central and southern Sierra Nevada, CA. Fire Ecology 2:53–72.

Kilgore, B. M. 1974. Fire management in national parks: an overview. P. 45–57 in Proceedings of the 14th Tall Timbers fire ecology conference, Missoula, MT. Tall Timbers Research Station, Tallahassee, FL.

Kilgore, B. M., and D. Taylor. 1979. Fire history of a sequoia-mixed conifer forest. Ecology 60(1):129–142.

Knapp, E. E., Keeley, J. E., Ballenger, E. A., Brennan, T. J., 2005. Fuel reduction and coarse woody debris dynamics with early season and late season prescribed fire in a Sierra Nevada mixed conifer forest. Forest Ecology and Management. 208:383–397.

Knapp, E., S. L. Stephens, J. D. McIver, J. J. Moghaddas, and J. E. Keeley. 2004. The fire and fire surrogate study in the Sierra Nevada: evaluating restoration treatments at Blodgett Experimental Forest and Sequoia National Park. October 7–10. The Sierra Science Symposium, Lake Tahoe, CA. P. 79–86. USDA RSW-GTR-193.

Lutes, D. C., R. E. Keane, J. F. Caratti, C. H. Key, N. C. Benson, S. Sutherland, and L. J. Gangi, 2006. FIREMON: The fire effects monitoring and inventory system. Gen. Tech. Rep. RMRS-GTR-164-CD. Fort Collins, CO. U.S. Department of Agriculture, Forest Service, Rocky Mountain Research Station.

Martin, R. E, J. B. Kauffman, and J. D. Landsberg. 1989. Use of prescribed fire to reduce wildfire potential. P. 11–16 in Proceedings of the symposium on fire and watershed management, October 26–28, 1988, Sacramento, CA. Gen. Tech. Report PSW-109.

McKelvey K. S.,and K. K. Busse. 1996. Twentieth-century fire patterns on Forest Service lands. P. 1119–1138 in Sierra Nevada Ecosystem Project, final report to Congress, Vol. II: assessments and scientific basis for management options. University of California, Centers for Water and Wildland Resources, Davis.

Miller, M. (ed.). 1996. Fire effects guide. NWCG PMS #2394. National Interagency Fire Center, Boise, ID.

Moody, T. J., J. Fites-Kaufman, and S. L. Stephens. 2006. Fire history and climate influences from forests in the Northern Sierra Nevada, USA Fire Ecology 2:115–141.

Moritz, M. A., J. E. Keeley, E. A. Johnson, and A. A. Schaffner. 2004. Testing a basic assumption of shrubland fire management: does the hazard of burning increase with the age of fuels? Frontiers in Ecology and the Environment. 2:67–72.

National Park Service. 2003. Fire monitoring handbook. Boise (ID) Fire Management Program Center, National Interagency Fire Center, Boise, ID. 274 pages.

National Park Service, 2004. Fire management plan for Yosemite National Park, Yosemite National Park.

Olson, R., R. Heinbockel, and S. Abrams. 1995. Technical fuels report. Unpublished report. Lassen, Plumas, and Tahoe National Forests. U.S. Forest Service.

Peterson, D. L., M. C. Johnson, J. K.Agee T. B. Jain, D. McKenzie, and E. D. Reinhardt. 2004. Fuel planning: science synthesis and integration-forest structure and fire hazard. Gen Tech Rep. PNW-GTR, Portland, OR; USDA Forest Service Northwest Research Station.

Pyne, S. J. 1982. Fire in America: a cultural history of wildland and rural fire. Princeton University Press, Princeton, NJ. 654 p.

Pyne, S. F., P. L. Andrews, and R. D. Laven. 1996. Introduction to wildland fire. John Wiley and Sons, Inc. New York. 769 p.

Quincy Library Group. 1994. Fuels management for fire protection. Unpublished report. Quincy Library Group position paper. Quincy, CA.

Schmidt, K. M., J. P. Menakis, and C. C. Hardy. 2002. Development of coarse scale spatial data for wildland fire and fuel management. Gen Tech Rep. RMRS-GTR-87. Fort Collins, CO. USDA Forest Service, Rocky Mountain Research Station. 41 p.

Stephens, S. L. 1998. Effects of fuels and silvicultural treatments on potential fire behavior in mixed conifer forests of the Sierra Nevada, CA. Forest Ecology and Management 105: 21–34.

Stephens, S. L. 2005. Forest fire causes and extent on United States Forest Service Lands. International Journal of Wildland Fire 14:213–222.

Stephens, S. L. and Collins, B. M. 2004. Fire regimes of mixed conifer forests in the north-central Sierra Nevada at multiple spatial scales. Northwest Science 78:12–23.

Stephens, S. L. and J. J. Moghaddas. 2005a. Silvicultural and reserve impacts on potential fire behavior and forest conservation: 25 years of experience from Sierra Nevada mixed conifer forests. Biological Conservation 25:369–379.

Stephens, S. L., and J. J. Moghaddas. 2005b. Experimental fuel treatment impacts on forest structure, potential fire behavior, and predicted tree mortality in a mixed conifer forest. Forest Ecology and Management 215:21–36.

Stephens, S. L. and J. J. Moghaddas. 2005c. Fuel treatment effects on snags and coarse woody debris in a Sierra Nevada mixed conifer forest. Forest Ecology and Management 214:53–64.

Stephens, S. L., and L. W. Ruth. 2005. Federal forest fire policy in the United States. Ecological Applications 15:532–542.

Swetnam, T. W. 1993. Fire history and climate change in giant sequoia groves. Science 262:885–889.

USDA and USDI. 2004. Interagency standards for fire and fire aviation operations 2004. NFES 2724.

USDI. 2001. Review and update of the 1995 federal wildland fire management policy. Report to the Secretaries of the Interior, Agriculture, Energy, Defense, and Commerce; the Administrator, Environmental Protection Agency; the Director, Federal Emergency Management Agency; and the National Association of State Foresters, by an Interagency Federal Wildland Fire Policy Review Working Group. National Interagency Fire Center, Boise, ID.

van Wagtendonk, J. W. 1996. Use of a deterministic fire growth model to test fuel treatments. P. 1155–1166 in Sierra Nevada

Ecosystem Project, final report to Congress, Vol. II: assessments and scientific basis for management options. University of California, Centers for Water and Wildland Resources, Davis.

Weatherspoon, C.P., S.J. Husari, and J.W. van Wagtendonk. 1992. Fire and fuel management in relation to owl habitat in forests of the Sierra Nevada and Southern California. P. 247–260 in The California spotted owl: a technical assessment of its current status. Gen. Tech. Rep. PSW-GTR-133.

Albany, CA; Pacific Southwest Research Station, Forest Service, U.S. Department of Agriculture.

Weatherspoon, C.P., and C.N. Skinner. 1996. Landscape-level strategies for forest fuel management. P. 1471–1492 in Sierra Nevada Ecosystem Project, final report to Congress, Vol. II: assessments and scientific basis for management options. University of California, Centers for Water and Wildland Resources, Davis.

CHAPTER 20

Fire, Watershed Resources, and Aquatic Ecosystems

ANDREA E. THODE, JEFFREY L. KERSHNER, KEN ROBY,
LYNN M. DECKER, AND JAN L. BEYERS

> When we study the individual parts or try to understand the
> system through discrete quantities, we get lost. Deep inside the
> details, we cannot see the whole. Yet to understand and work
> with the system, we need to be able to observe it as a system, in
> its wholeness.
>
> MARGARET WHEATLEY IN LEADERSHIP AND THE NEW SCIENCE, 1999

Fire is a major process within many California watersheds causing natural fluctuations of water, nutrients, and sediment that are transmitted through aquatic ecosystems. Historic fire regimes and other watershed processes have shifted and changed with anthropogenic disturbances. In addition, more homes and communities are being located along streams and in floodplains. These changes cause social and ecological issues to arise concerning fire as a process within watersheds. This chapter first examines the current perspective of fires in watersheds and the social and ecological reactions to changes in the historic fire regimes. It then discusses issues surrounding the restoration of fire regimes within watersheds, and ends with the concept of integrated watershed restoration.

The Effects of Fire on Watershed Processes and Functions

The effects of fire on watershed processes in California are as diverse as the landscape itself and involve a variety of ecosystems and physical processes. These watersheds include a diverse mosaic of intermittent, ephemeral, and perennial streams of various sizes. All are shaped by the dynamics of water and sediment, which ultimately determine the size and function of streams and rivers. This balance of water and sediment is influenced by physical and biological perturbations, including fire, at a variety of scales.

The relationship of water and sediment in watersheds is shaped by a number of factors including climate, topography, geology, vegetation, and the frequency and magnitude of disturbances. Ecological processes such as fire play an important role in determining the timing and magnitude of sediment, nutrient, and water delivery to streams. Timing and magnitude are influenced by aspects of the fire regime including fire size, seasonality, fire-return interval, intensity, severity, spatial complexity, and fire type. Keep in mind that fire regimes

have often played an important role in shaping the watershed conditions we see today.

The influence of fire on hillslope erosion is manifested in many different ways. Surface erosion occurs where surface litter and duff are removed by wildfire, allowing direct raindrop impact and overland flow with the subsequent displacement of soil. Large erosional events such as landslides and debris torrents may be initiated where slopes are steep and root-strength of vegetation has been reduced by fire. The eroded products of this sediment mobilization are transported downslope into streams.

Once sediment reaches the channels, it moves downstream, alternately transported and deposited through the stream network. This sequence of transport and deposition is influenced by the timing and amount of runoff and sediment, local stream gradient, and the hydraulic complexity of the channels. This sediment is delivered to channels in pulses for the first few years post-fire and is reworked and resorted for a number of years until eventually sediment loads return to pre-fire levels (Fig. 20.1) (Minshall et al. 1989). Responses of other components of stream ecosystems to fire generally follow a similar trajectory. The direction, duration, and magnitude of stream ecosystem response are governed by the intensity, severity, and spatial complexity of the fire event. Uniform high-intensity wildfires, resulting in severe effects that cover large landscapes, will generate a more dramatic response than low-intensity fires that remove little ground cover and are patchy in their effects.

Aquatic Habitats

The impacts of wildfires on streams are generally viewed as "pulses" (Detenbeck et al. 1992) that may be initially severe, but are generally short lived. In some cases, these pulses may actually renew and rejuvenate stream habitats (Benda et al. 2003). Post-fire recovery of watersheds and aquatic ecosystems

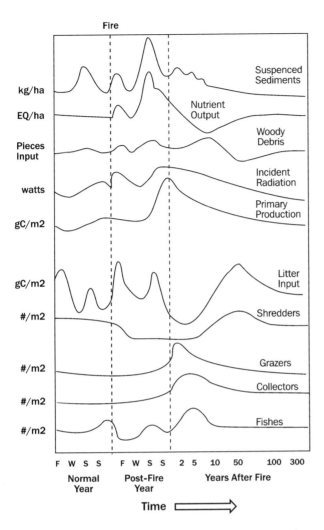

kg/ha   Suspenced Sediments

EQ/ha   Nutrient Output

Pieces Input   Woody Debris

watts   Incident Radiation

gC/m2   Primary Production

gC/m2   Litter Input

#/m2   Shredders

#/m2   Grazers

#/m2   Collectors

#/m2   Fishes

F W S S   F W S S   2   5   10   50   100 300

Normal Year   Post-Fire Year   Years After Fire

Time ⟹

FIGURE 20.1. A conceptual, temporal sequence of the recovery of components of stream ecosystems in response to fire. (Redrawn from Minshall et al. 1989). Short-term inputs of sediment and nutrients may occur in the first few years after a fire. Most other fire-related disturbances to streams, such as debris flows or flooding typically occur within the first few years after a fire.

is influenced by the integrity of the surrounding landscape and the proximity of high-quality habitats as a source of new colonists for stream organisms that have been locally extirpated. Recovery of the stream-riparian interface generally parallels the surrounding vegetation recovery (Minshall et al. 1989).

Chronic or "press" events may truncate or retard the recovery of watershed processes and aquatic systems. The current situation in many parts of California represents a highly altered landscape where historic fire regimes have been modified and watersheds are influenced by land management practices including water development, mining, road building, urbanization, fire suppression, timber harvest, and recreation. The full expression of aquatic ecosystems has been significantly altered from the conditions that existed prior to European settlement. In many cases, stream and watershed recovery may be inhibited or truncated by these additional disturbances by humans (Dunham et al. 2003). For example,

the amount of sediment delivered post-fire will eventually decline as vegetation creates ground cover and promotes root building and soil cohesion. Subsequent vegetative removal or road building may promote continued inputs of fine and coarse sediment into streams. These additional amounts of sediment may delay or interrupt the recovery of sediment-delivery mechanisms and ultimately delay the recovery of aquatic organisms.

Major ecological effects occur when local extirpations of fish and other organisms are caused by fire effects, such as stream heating, temporary changes in stream chemistry, or post-fire debris torrents (Spencer et al. 2003). In well-connected stream networks, individuals from surrounding areas can re-colonize recovering streams once living conditions are again favorable. Migration barriers from poorly placed road culverts, irrigation diversions, and dams may limit the movement of organisms through stream networks. This impact can be particularly severe where small population fragments exist in headwaters susceptible to wildfire.

There is a range of responses of the post-fire aquatic ecosystem that will vary with the intensity, severity, and temporal length of the fire event (Bisson et al. 2003). In some cases, wildfire in watersheds may benefit aquatic ecosystems by restoring ecological processes that were altered by past management practices. In others, the combination of wildfire and anthropogenic influences may compound effects to severely alter aquatic ecosystems for much longer time periods. After the Hayman fire in Colorado, upslope and riparian areas that experienced high fire severity contributed large amounts of sediment to streams immediately after the burn. The fire-related sediment contribution from these areas will eventually decline as they revegetate, but sediment input to streams is unlikely to be eliminated because roads located within the riparian areas will continue to contribute large sediment pulses to streams after most storm events (Kershner et al. 2003). Ultimately, the speed and trajectory of post-fire recovery will be influenced by the amount and location of anthropogenic disturbances.

Although aquatic ecosystem recovery after fire is a long-term process, there are often immediate public concerns over the short-term effects of fire on water quality, particularly where the water is used for human consumption. A variety of laws and policies are in place that guide the management of water quality within California (see Sidebar 20.1). Where there are concerns for downstream water quality or potential threats to life or property, federal agencies have undertaken post-fire rehabilitation to accelerate the recovery process.

Watershed Rehabilitation and Restoration

Land management agencies have a long history of undertaking post-fire rehabilitation activities in watersheds. The Forest Service has implemented procedures since the 1930s that are still practiced today, and the Bureau of Land Management has had programs in place at least since the 1960s. The intention of these procedures is to minimize risks to life

When discussing prescribed fire and mechanical fuel treatments, there are several water quality laws and policies that can come into play. The main water quality issue that stems from fuels treatments is generally sedimentation, which is addressed through non–point-source pollution laws. However, herbicide use to eliminate or suppress understory growth also presents water quality issues and could entail regulation as point-source pollution. It is critical to understand the general structure and relationships between federal and state laws to understand how these laws and policies can affect fuels treatments. The following is a summary of the main points of water quality law and policy in California.

Three principal laws govern water quality in California: the Federal Clean Water Act of 1972 (33 USC 1251-1387); the state's Porter-Cologne Water Quality Control Act (California Water Code 13000-14958); and the Federal Coastal Zone Management Act (16 USC 1451 et seq.).

Water quality protection is the responsibility of the State Water Resources Control Board (State Board) and the regional water quality control boards. The state is split into nine regions based on watersheds. Within each region, the regional boards establish regional water quality plans and work on water quality under the policies of the State Board (Ruffolo 1999). Under the Clean Water Act and the Coastal Zone Management Act, California is required to adopt water quality standards and to submit those standards for approval to the U.S. Environmental Protection Agency (EPA) and to the National Oceanic and Atmospheric Administration (NOAA).

The Clean Water Act

The Clean Water Act establishes nationwide minimum standards for water quality control in waters subject to federal jurisdiction (i.e., "navigable" waters and tributaries to navigable waters); it addresses water quality pollution from two distinct sources—point sources and non–point sources. *Point sources* include direct discharge from factories, sewers, and other sources that have direct contact with surface waters. Section 402 of the Clean Water Act and regulations set by the EPA (33 USC 1342, 40 CFR 122, *et seq.*) require that these point sources are regulated by permits or requirements that implement the National Pollutant Discharge Elimination System (NPDES). *Non–point sources* are those associated with activities such as agriculture and forestry practices, where many activities are spread across large areas and water quality is affected by runoff from the activity areas, rather than from a discrete location. Specific sections of the Clean Water Act provide guidance on the assessment and treatment of non–point-source pollution and these are applicable to wildfire and fuel treatment activities. However, the Clean Water Act does not require non-point sources to be regulated under the NPDES; instead, non–point sources are regulated more indirectly through section 303d.

Section 303d of the Clean Water Act provides a structure for states to assess water quality (Houck 2002). States must evaluate all water bodies and identify those that fail to meet water quality standards despite the application of effluent limits for point sources. Total maximum daily loads (TMDLs) of pollutants must be established for these waters (Ruffolo 1999, Houck 2002). TMDLs are defined as the maximum amount of a pollutant that can occur daily in a water body to meet water quality standards. However, in practice, the term "daily" has been expanded to include various times such as weekly, monthly, or annually. This part of the act was dormant until the 1990s when environmental and citizen groups began to utilize its power in court (Houck, 2002), and refinement of the total daily load process is ongoing. Current interpretation of this section and the implications of TMDLs to non–point-source polluters and regulators are in flux.

Section 319, added to the Clean Water Act in 1987, established the non–point-source grant program that requires states to develop non–point-source management plans (CWA section 319, 33 USC 1329). These plans generally depend on nonregulatory approaches to control non–point-source pollution and include voluntary efforts, incentives, education, and training to help implement "Best Management Practices" (BMPs) (Ruffolo 1999). BMPs are guidelines designed to offset or mitigate land use practices with potential to affect water quality from non–point sources. These practices have been developed by state and federal agencies for a variety of land use activities including timber harvest, road construction and maintenance, fire suppression, fuel management, and many others.

The Porter-Cologne Water Quality Control Act

Section 303d requires states to set TMDLs and section 319 requires states to develop management plans that depend on nonregulatory actions. However, the actual regulatory authority over non–point-source pollution is not contained within the federal policy but rather lies within California's Porter-Cologne Act (Ruffolo 1999). This act does not distinguish between point and non–point sources, but instead focuses on "discharges" of waste to water bodies and regulates the quality of those discharges. Regulatory power over non–point sources comes through the state's "waste discharge requirement" permitting program. Waste discharge requirements permits must be obtained by any person or entity that intends to discharge waste into California's waters.

The Coastal Zone Management Act

The 1972 federal Coastal Zone Management Act set a framework for management, protection, development, and beneficial use of the coastal zone (SWRCB and CCC 2000). However, this act did not specifically deal with water quality until the 1990 Coastal Zone Act Reauthorization Amendments. The reauthorization required that California's Water Resources Control Board and the California Coastal Commission jointly develop a coastal non–point-source pollution control program (SWRCB and CCC 2000). This was done with the realization that non–point-source pollution was a major polluter of coastal resources as well as of the state's fresh water resources.

California's Non–Point-Source Programs: The 1998 and 2000 Plans

In response to section 319, California developed the 1988 Plan for California's Non–Point Source Pollution Control Program (1988 Plan), which applies three tiers, or levels, of regulatory involvement (Ruffolo 1999). The first tier relies on voluntary implementation of BMPs, and for the most part California has used this level of regulation. The second tier is regulatory-based encouragement of BMPs where the regional water quality control boards have discretion over the waver of waste discharge requirements. Regional boards may enter into management agency agreements with other agencies capable of enforcing BMPs. These agreements have been initiated with the Forest Service, the California Board of Forestry, and the California Department of Forestry and Fire Protection to control discharges of waste and pollutants associated with silvicultural activities (SWRCB and CCC 2000). The third tier contemplates the issuance and enforcement of waste discharge requirements prescribing BMPs and effluent limits for proposed or existing non–point-source discharges (SWRCB 1988, Ruffolo 1999).

The first significant revision of the 1988 Plan occurred in 1998 with the Plan for California's Non–Point-Source Pollution Control Program (SWRCB and CCC 2000). Because of the 1990 changes in the Coastal Zone Management Act, the 1998 Plan was written in conjunction with the California Coastal Commission. This revision adds 61 management measures as goals for six non–point-source pollution categories. Two pollution categories—forestry and urban areas—include management measures that relate to fire suppression, prescribed fire, and fuel treatments. —*AET* and property related to flood runoff, erosion, off-site sedimentation, and hydrologic damage (Robichaud et al. 2000). In addition, other non-emergency post-wildfire activities may be planned and implemented. These often include plans to capture economic value from burned trees (often termed *salvage logging*) and actions intended to promote longer-term restoration of ecosystem products and services. The definitions of mitigation, emergency rehabilitation, post-fire activities (including timber salvage), and restoration are often confused. However, each has different goals, implementation methods, and consequences to long-term ecosystem recovery, and, in many cases, the goals and methods conflict. Rehabilitation and restoration are not mutually exclusive, and most of the tools and practices used in rehabilitation are often used for restoration. Grass seeding with fast-growing, non-native species may be done to increase plant cover for erosion control—a form of rehabilitation. Alternatively, an integrated watershed approach might use seeding of native species to out-compete invasive species and re-establish a historic native plant community, along with the natural processes that accompany that plant community (e.g., fire, flooding).

Post-Fire Rehabilitation

From the perspective of ecosystems, fires are not an emergency. However, there is a social desire to respond to large wildfires, particularly when they are in proximity to communities and municipal water resources. The common context for rehabilitation typically occurs where wildfires exhibit low spatial complexity, high intensity, and high severity. These fires often result in increased erosion and overland flow of water from burned watersheds. The effects are initially expressed during the first rainy seasons after fire, resulting in flooding, debris flows, and sedimentation. Life and property may be at risk when developments are located downstream. Given these concerns, federal land management agencies, such as the Forest Service, National Park Service, and Bureau of Land Management, are required to assess burned areas and determine whether emergency resource or human health and safety conditions exist. Assessment teams—called Burned Area Emergency Response (BAER) teams by the Forest Service and National Park Service and Emergency Rehabilitation and Stabilization teams by the Bureau of Land Management—are convened to evaluate: (1) threats to life and property, (2) potential for loss of control of water, (3) likely reduction in water quality, and (4) potential for loss of soil productivity in the burned area (U.S. GAO 2003). If an emergency is found to exist, assessment teams prescribe short-term stabilization treatments designed to alleviate the immediate threats. Treatments are undertaken when analyses show that the planned actions are likely to significantly reduce risk of adverse impacts in a cost-effective manner. A report (Robichaud et al. 2000) and a U.S. General Accounting Office Audit (U.S. GAO 2003) questioned the efficacy and cost of many of these treatments. Costs for post-fire rehabilitation have escalated over the past decade, and in fiscal years 2001 and 2002 combined, the Department of Agriculture and Department of the Interior spent $205 million and $125 million, respectively, to treat burned lands. As costs have increased, however, more questions have been raised about the effectiveness and ecological impacts of various rehabilitation methods (Table 20.1). In response to the GAO report, efforts to consistently monitor the effectiveness of Forest Service and Department of the Interior burned area treatments have increased.

Post-Fire Restoration

Treatments included in Table 20.1 indicate that most rehabilitation has focused on controlling sediment and runoff and restoring vegetative cover. Although effects of fires vary, many vegetation communities recover quite well from fire without human intervention. This is often the case when the fire falls within the historic fire regime for a vegetation community. Chaparral, many types of grasslands, and low-severity fires in ponderosa pine forests are good examples. However, there are cases where restoration actions are implemented to accelerate recovery. These include landscapes where fire effects have been severe, large, and homogenous; where fire occurred soon after a previous fire and an adequate seed bank has not formed; or where undesirable non-native species grow back more quickly than native flora.

Restoration of a vegetative community is generally a longer-term process than rehabilitation, and restoration activities can occur concurrently with or after rehabilitation and stabilization projects. Most restoration treatments, such as tree or shrub planting, are not carried out until after emergency rehabilitation treatments have been implemented. Restoration treatments that control competing vegetation around planted tree seedlings, such as grazing, chemical applications, or prescribed fire, may continue for many years. Native plant seeding to increase forage for wildlife may be done concurrently with erosion-control rehabilitation grass seeding. Native perennial grasses often do not grow quickly enough from seed to provide effective erosion control immediately after fire, but their introduction can help return a forest type to its historic condition. In sagebrush rangelands, native or well-adapted non-native bunch grasses and forbs are often seeded after fire in an attempt to reduce successful invasion by cheatgrass (*Bromus tectorum*) or noxious weeds. These invasives tend to cover burn sites if they occur near the burn or were present before the fire. This kind of seeding, as well as direct control of noxious weeds using hand or chemical methods, can meet both vegetation restoration and long-term rehabilitation goals. For a more detailed look at post-fire seeding refer to Sidebar 20.2.

Restoring long-term ecological processes and functions of watersheds may require other types of rehabilitation and restoration. The post-fire timeframe provides a window of opportunity to assess the impacts of roads on a watershed's hydrology and to implement actions to reduce these effects. Actions include removing roads or moving roads out of

TABLE 20.1
Post-fire rehabilitation treatments

	Purpose	Benefits	Concerns	Literature
Hillslope Treatments Non-native grass seeding	Rapidly increase vegetation cover, reduce hillslope erosion, or prevent undesirable non-native species establishment	Can accelerate development of cover from vegetation; application is relatively inexpensive if non-native species are used, so can be applied to large areas	May take several growing seasons for effective cover to become established; abundant grass can create early reborn hazard; seeded species may compete with native vegetation (may not increase total cover); grazing too early can affect the plant community that will develop	Noble 1965, Orr 1970, Dyrness 1976, Tiedemann and Klock 1976, Ratliff and McDonald 1987, Robichaud et al. 2000
Native grass seeding	Same as above	Accelerate development of vegetation cover. May be less aggressive competitor with natural regeneration than non-native species. Natural part of ecosystem.	Same as above; generally more expensive than non-native seed. May not be available in large quantities when needed; concerns about genetic contamination if non-local genotypes are used—often unknown is "how local is 'local'?"	Griffith 1998, Richards et al. 1998
Mulch	Provide ground cover, protect the soil surface, and promote water infiltration	Effective cover can be provided in short term, prior to precipitation.	Application expensive, especially away from roads; mulch may contain seed of non-native species; unknown effects on vegetation recovery.	Bautista et al. 1996, Edwards et al. 1995
Contour-felled logs and straw wattles	Provide breaks in slope, slowing runoff and promoting infiltration; also act to trap sediment	Utilizes materials available on site, provides some cover. Rilling and gullying are reduced if successfully applied.	Difficult to achieve contact between ground surface and logs	McCammon and Hughes 1980, Miles et al. 1989
Contour trenching or raking	Breaks through the soil, water-repellent soil layer, and promotes infiltration	Reduced soil erosion and runoff	Difficult to economically treat enough area to achieve watershed scale benefits	DeByle 1970a, b, Costales and Costales 1984
Channel Treatments Straw bale check dams and gabions	Replace channel structure removed by fire. Check store sediment and slow water.	Sediment storage, improved channel stability, reduced channel erosion	Very hard to provide design that mimics natural system; straw bales may fail in high flows	Collins and Johnston 1995, Goldman et al. 1986

TABLE 20.1 (continued)

	Purpose	Benefits	Concerns	Literature
Channel hardening	Uses logs or rocks to keep channels from eroding during high flow	Improved channel stability, reduced channel erosion	Expensive for broad-scale application. May not mimic natural structure or morphology and may conflict with long-term recovery	Miles et al. 1989
Debris basins	Store large amounts of sediment	Catch sediment and wood that would otherwise damage downstream improvements	Unnatural intrusion into channel system; difficult to size adequately to protect from largest (most damaging) events	Robichaud et al. 2000
Removal of large woody debris	Prevents damage to downstream culverts or structures during peak post-fire flows	Provides protection to in-channel and flood plain improvements	Large wood provides in-channel structure and habitat post-fire	Robichaud et al. 2000
Roads and Trails Treatments				
Water bars on trails	Divert water from trail, preventing it from eroding into a channel	Prevents concentrated flow (rills and gullies); cheap and effective	Site disturbance to soil if improperly constructed	Furniss et al. 1998
Rolling dips on roads	Reduce connection of road surfaces with channel system	Avoids concentrated surface flow; reduces road ditch and surface erosion	None if properly designed and maintained, though dips may not be compatible with large vehicle traffic	Furniss et al. 1998
Culvert upgrades	Improve passage of water, wood, and sediment	Reduces risk of crossing failure, improves connectivity	Short-term impacts during construction; may be expensive	Furniss et al. 1998

riparian areas to prevent degradation of riparian condition and chronic sediment delivery, and reconstructing roads and road crossings to reduce their hydrologic impacts. In addition to efforts of reducing sediment delivery to streams, there is also an opportunity for reconnecting fragmented aquatic habitats and re-establishing both terrestrial and aquatic native species. This would move efforts past post-fire rehabilitation to include longer-term restoration of watersheds beyond immediate fire effects.

Many burned areas do not need emergency rehabilitation or restoration treatments. If the characteristics of the fire are within the historic range of variation, and human or natural resource values are not at risk, a burned area can be left to recover on its own. This is consistent with a view of fire as one of the functions and processes that form and support watershed and aquatic processes.

Ecological and Social Values

When discussing rehabilitation and restoration it becomes clear that ecological and social values often result in conflicting actions. In general, post-fire rehabilitation and other post-fire

The most common practice for post-fire emergency watershed rehabilitation is broadcast grass seeding, usually from aircraft (Robichaud et al. 2000). Hillslope erosion is inversely related to vegetative cover, and rapid vegetation establishment is regarded as the most cost-efficient way to keep soil on hillslopes and out of channels and downstream areas (Noble 1965, Rice et al. 1965, Miles et al. 1989). Grasses are particularly desirable for this purpose because their quick growth along with extensive, fibrous root systems increase water infiltration and hold soil in place. Grass seeding after fire for range improvement began decades ago, with the intent to gain useful outputs (e.g., livestock production) from land that would not yield harvestable timber for decades (Christ 1934, McClure 1956). Seed mixes were developed regionally based on germination and establishment success. Most mixes contain annual grasses to provide quick cover and short-lived perennials to establish longer-term protection, with legumes sometimes included for their ability to add nitrogen to the soil (Klock et al. 1975, Ratliff and McDonald 1987). Fast-growing non-native species have typically been used. They are inexpensive and readily available in large quantities when an emergency arises (Barro and Conard 1987, Agee 1993).

Post-fire grass seeding has generated considerable controversy (Conrad 1979, Barro and Conard 1987, Robichaud et al. 2000, Beyers 2004, Keeley et al. 2006). Critics point to evidence that seeded grasses suppress native herbaceous plant establishment, out-compete tree and shrub seedlings, create flashy fuel conditions conducive to an early reburn of the site, and do not demonstratively reduce erosion in many cases (e.g., Schultz et al. 1955, Keeley et al. 1981, Griffin 1982, Gautier 1983, Zedler et al. 1983, Nadkarni and Odion 1986, Taskey et al. 1989, Conard et al. 1991, Conard et al. 1995, Beyers et al. 1998, Wohlgemuth et al. 1998). Persistent seeded species may delay recovery of native flora and potentially alter local plant diversity. Defenders argue that even small reductions in hillslope erosion due to grass seeding are justified by the method's relatively low cost and wide applicability (Rice et al. 1965, Miles et al. 1989); no other rehabilitation treatment can be applied relatively cheaply to thousands of acres after a large fire (Robichaud et al. 2000). The dilemma between short-term suppression of forest regeneration and long-term soil productivity maintenance is well recognized (Ruby 1989, Van de Water 1998).

In California, much of the concern over the impacts of grass seeding focused on the use of annual ryegrass (*Lolium multiflorum*) in chaparral ecosystems (Barro and Conard 1987). This fast-growing non-native species typically persists for less than five years on chaparral sites. However, a specialized native annual flora exists that takes advantage of the light, space, and soil nutrients available immediately after fire in chaparral ("fire followers") (Sweeney 1956, Keeley et al. 1981). In addition, some dominant shrub species, particularly in the genera *Arctostaphylos* and *Ceanothus*, regenerate after fire only from seed that germinates during the first growing season after the fire (Sampson 1944, Keeley 1991). Both groups of plants can be negatively affected by competition from seeded grass. Many studies have shown reduced cover of native chaparral species on ryegrass-seeded plots, but most found no increase in total vegetation cover due to seeding (reviewed in Beyers et al. 1998, Beyers 2004). Very few studies (published or unpublished) have demonstrated that seeding reduced erosion on chaparral sites in the first or second year after a fire (see Robichaud et al. 2000). Instead, Wohlgemuth et al. (1998) found erosion reduction attributable to seeded ryegrass occurred only after sediment movement had dropped to pre-fire rates or lower. As a result of these studies, the use of broadcast grass seeding after fire in California chaparral has declined considerably (Robichaud et al. 2000).

High-intensity fires that consume all aboveground vegetation, with the consequent soil effects, are well within the range of natural variation for chaparral ecosystems and thus not of particular concern from the standpoint of soil productivity. This is not true in most conifer forest types, where low-severity fires that seldom killed mature trees are thought to have been typical of pre-European fire regimes. Especially on sites with good soils and high tree-growing capability, seeding is often prescribed after crown fires to help hold soil in place and maintain site productivity. As in chaparral, however, seeded grasses can compete with tree seedlings and native shrubs. Several species commonly used for post-fire seeding, because of their rapid growth and wide adaptability (Klock et al. 1975), have been found to be strongly competitive with conifer seedlings. For example, the non-natives orchardgrass *(Dactylis glomerata)*, perennial ryegrass *(Lolium perenne)*, and timothy *(Phleum pratense)* reduced growth of ponderosa pine *(Pinus ponderosa)* seedlings in experimental plots (Baron 1962). Low pine seedling densities were found on aerially seeded sites with annual ryegrass cover greater than 40% (Griffin 1982, Conard et al. 1991). These species can persist for several years after fire, affording extended soil protection but also increasing the competitive impact on tree regeneration. Grasses can provide some benefit to tree seedlings if they displace shrubs that would otherwise compete with the trees for soil moisture and nutrients (McDonald 1986, Amaranthus et al. 1993). In general, however, burned area rehabilitation assessment teams must take into consideration the cost of suppressing seeded grasses during reforestation efforts as part of their cost-benefit analysis when developing watershed treatment prescriptions (Griffith 1998). As with chaparral, there has been a decrease in the amount of seeding performed on forested areas in recent years as the impacts and effectiveness have been debated (Robichaud et al. 2000).

Most land management agencies now have direction to use native species wherever possible for revegetation projects, including emergency watershed rehabilitation. However, seed of locally adapted native grasses is seldom available in sufficient quantity to use after large fires, and costs are high compared to non-natives such as annual ryegrass (Robichaud et al. 2000). Many rehabilitation assessment teams now prescribe nonreproducing annuals, such as cereal grains or sterile hybrids, which could provide quick cover and then die out to let native vegetation reoccupy the site. Few studies have been conducted on the effectiveness or ecosystem impacts of these grasses; preliminary information suggests that cereals largely die out after one year unless disturbed by grazers or salvage logging operations (Robichaud et al. 2000). If establishment success of cereals is high, first-year cover of native herbaceous species and tree seedling density can be reduced (Keeley 2004), just as with annual ryegrass. The cost of sterile hybrids, such as proprietary Regreen (a wheat-wheatgrass hybrid), can be very high compared to ordinary cereals, and they are generally prescribed only for highly sensitive areas such as wilderness (Beyers *in press*).

Burned-area assessment teams must weigh the likelihood of successful establishment and erosion reduction by seeded grasses against the economic and potential ecological costs of treatment when making the decision to seed or not after fire. Public pressure to do *something* to burned slopes, especially in the wildland–urban interface, can be intense. Seeding is probably most appropriate in high-value timberlands where fire intensity has been outside the range of natural variation, increasing the probability that soil seed banks have been damaged and excessive erosion will occur, and where tree seedlings can be planted if natural regeneration fails due to grass competition (Beyers 2004). Where protection of private property and public infrastructure from sediment movement after fire is essential, more reliable and immediately effective treatments such as straw mulch are more appropriate. —*JLB* activities treat fire as an emergency, not as an expression of the ecosystem process. Social values drive the view of fire as being external to the ecosystem. As discussed in the first part of the chapter, fire plays a role in creating watersheds and is an integral part of ecosystem processes, influencing fluctuations in water and sediment yield. However, there are now homes and entire communities along streams, in floodplains, and adjacent to fire-prone ecosystems in much of California. The propensity for burned watersheds to move large amounts of water and sediment into people's yards, houses, and businesses creates social demand for post-fire rehabilitation. Post-fire restoration such as tree, shrub, and native species plantings are used to bring burned landscapes back to pre-fire conditions faster than would occur naturally. Although this can be considered restoration, the goals and objectives are not necessarily ecologically based as much as socially based. Goals focus on a "quick recovery," which is a human concept rather than an ecological one. Although becoming more understanding in recent years, many in society do not want to live with the impacts of fire, natural or not. As a result, societal demands and expectations play a large role in post-fire rehabilitation and restoration.

Ideally, restoring fire regimes and reintroducing fire as an essential ecological process would be an integral part of watershed restoration. Socially, this would mean less expenditure on fire suppression and rehabilitation, and less loss of property and lives. Ecologically it would mean the restoration of sediment and runoff regimes that more closely resembled those that occurred prior to European settlement. This is the future of watershed management for certain vegetation types; however, it will be difficult for a number of reasons as discussed in the next section.

What Are the Issues in Restoring Fire as a Process in Watersheds?

As discussed previously, watersheds are dynamic and fire is part of that dynamism, playing an important role in shaping watersheds and the aquatic systems they support. The return of historic fire regimes in areas where fire regimes have changed would likely be beneficial to watersheds and aquatic systems, because a key formative process would be restored. Numerous obstacles to restoring historic fire regimes exist and include administrative, legal, cultural, and technical aspects of resource management. In many cases, recent proposals to implement fuel and fire projects have not been embraced by agency watershed and aquatic specialists, or some publics, despite the fact that such projects are often designed to reduce fire severity and would, if successfully implemented, reduce the adverse impacts of wildfire on watersheds. The most important issues that form obstacles to restoring fire regimes, and a possible approach to overcome them, are discussed below.

Existing Watershed and Habitat Condition

Aquatic and riparian conditions in many California watersheds are in an altered or degraded state due to past activities

(Kattleman 1996). In headwater streams, disturbances include road construction and logging. These activities are also present in larger stream systems, along with impacts from historic and current mining activities, historic and current grazing, recreation use, and urban development. Farther downstream, dams, diversions, and flood control structures have radically altered river flow regimes and channel conditions. In many locations in California, the combination of dams and road channel crossings has disrupted the longitudinal connection of channel systems (Moyle et al. 1996). Aquatic communities in all systems have been further stressed by the widespread introduction of non-native species (Moyle et al. 1996). In this context of anthropogenic change, proposals for fuel management and fire treatments are often viewed as just adding to existing disturbance (Reiman and Clayton 1997).

Scale: Site versus Landscape Level

Unless fuel treatments are frequently applied at a broad scale, they have low potential of influencing fire behavior at a landscape scale. Site treatments have a high probability of altering fire severity at the site scale, and they are likely to reduce impacts to soils as described in Chapter 5. However, the utility of the treatments in affecting high-severity fire across a watershed and at a landscape scale is unclear.

A major long-term goal of managers may be to return fire regimes to those that more closely resemble their historic frequency and intensity distributions. Unfortunately, existing fuel conditions and air quality concerns seriously constrain the use of prescribed fire, often necessitating a prescription of mechanical fuel manipulation. The amount of landscape protection gained from individual, site-level fire and fuel treatments is difficult to measure, and the effectiveness of mechanical fuel treatments in emulating fire is uncertain. In contrast, the incremental risk associated with site-level ground-disturbing activities, particularly mechanical treatments, is known. This makes it difficult for managers to justify large-scale treatment plans designed to change fire behavior and fire effects at a landscape level.

It has been difficult to approach resource management from greater than a site or project scale. For example, watershed restoration projects have typically selected "problem" sites (e.g., a channel headcut) for treatment, in absence of a broader-scale assessment of condition or cause. Although such an approach may be warranted in some cases to prevent degradation of water quality, it essentially treats symptoms and falls short of the goal of restoring hydrologic system process or function. Fairly recently, watershed restoration and aquatic conservation needs have pushed forward watershed analyses (Regional Ecosystem Office 1995). Results have been mixed. Some efforts have been successful in providing context and a strategic approach to watershed improvement efforts. However, further integration of fuel treatments and fire are needed in multi-resource–based restoration plans.

A Lack of Monitoring Data

It is important to recognize that current decisions involving fire management are constrained by a lack of information due in large part to a lack of monitoring. Scant information was collected on past management practices, and this trend continues with current activities. Had effective monitoring programs been in place, uncertainty about fire management projects discussed in this section would have been reduced.

Treatment in Riparian Areas: A Case in Point

The important influences of riparian areas on the condition and function of stream and other aquatic systems are well documented (Swanson et al. 1982). Due to the importance of these areas, many management activities, including mechanical fuel treatments and prescribed fire, have been excluded from riparian areas. This "exclusion approach" to management certainly meets some objectives for management of these areas, such as recent protection of riparian corridors from timber harvest and vegetation trampling by livestock. However, this approach may not meet other objectives, such as restoring historic fire regimes. This is particularly true where past activities, prior to exclusion (fire suppression, timber harvest, grazing, mining, etc.), have changed vegetation composition and structure of the riparian area. There is considerable debate regarding the efficacy of fuel treatments, and this debate is intensified with the application of treatments in riparian zones. Proponents of fuel treatments argue riparian areas must be treated to protect them from the consequences of wildfire. Opponents question the value of the treatments, and believe they are either unnecessary or will produce damage that outweighs benefits. Debate over management of riparian areas is a microcosm of the broader debate regarding fuel management.

In many areas of California, riparian systems have been impacted by multiple disturbances. Historic mining, grazing, and roads are often concentrated in or near streams. Disturbances in areas close to channels are more readily transferred to aquatic systems. Fire impacts vary in riparian zones and range from positive (thinning and restoring historic fire frequency) to negative (mortality of organisms, increased erosion, removal of shade, large wood, recruitable wood, etc.) (see Chapter 7).

Very little research or monitoring has been performed to evaluate either the effects of fire management activities in riparian zones or the natural role of fire in riparian system function. Beche et al. (2005) looked at the effects of a low to moderate prescribed fire on a riparian zone and stream in the Sierra Nevada. The authors found that the small prescribed fire resulted in few short-term effects and reduced fuel loads in the riparian zone up to 80%. The fire burned a small portion of the watershed (14%) and was low to moderate-severity. Skinner (2002) evaluated fire return intervals in several riparian zones in the Klamath Mountains. He found return intervals varied with stream type and topographic location. Stream sides higher in the watershed, with steeper channels, and vegetation more like the surrounding slopes (versus low-gradient channels with riparian vegetation) had the shortest return intervals. Such distinctions do not usually find their way into discussion of fuel treatments in riparian areas. Often the discussion is simplified to a "do" or "don't" argument, in which the natural variation of fire effects, riparian community types, and the role of fire in the landscape are overlooked.

Lack of experience in managing riparian systems is a major factor in the inability of resource specialists to develop integrated objectives for riparian zones. Training and experience of many aquatic specialists has been to protect streamside areas from human activities, rather than determining and using land management practices to enhance or conserve riparian systems. Combined with a lack of relevant monitoring or research, the result is a reluctance to plan treatments where the potential for negative impacts (for instance, ground disturbance from fuel treatments) is easier to envision than benefits of restoring fire to the system in ways that mimic the historic regime.

The reluctance to accept the risk of negative short-term effects is magnified by several factors. First, proposals are often small in scale, and second, their objective is treating fuel rather than restoring the fire regime. Last, in almost all cases, treatment proposals are aimed only at fuel or fire. They are not integrated to include treatments to improve system function (erosion, barriers, etc.) when other actions are needed in the riparian system where fire proposals are under consideration. As with the broader question of landscape level treatments, land management actions in critical parts of watersheds and riparian zones would be more effectively approached in a collaborative and integrated manner based on sound monitoring and research.

An Integrated Landscape Approach

A revised approach to restoring fire regimes and watersheds is needed. The ideal approach to restoration is preemptive, restoring process and function in watersheds, including fire regimes, rather than reactive application of emergency measures to burned watersheds. Re-establishment of fire as a watershed process requires an integrated landscape approach at large (river basin) scales, with fire, wildlife, terrestrial, and aquatic specialists working together to develop priorities for treatment. However, there are places where restored fire regimes will not be possible or desired, such as some wildland-urban interfaces. Developments in fire-prone areas will complicate the restoration of historic fire regimes but do not negate the need for an integrated landscape approach. Though there has been much discussion about landscape or ecological approaches to management, there are few, if any, examples to emulate. If fuel treatments are going to benefit watershed resources, watershed managers and aquatic specialists need to involve themselves in the development of prescriptions for the use of fire and fuel treatments in watersheds.

A Broad-Scale Context for Analysis: Planning and Priority Setting

As fire and other important ecosystem processes function across and at scales larger than watersheds, planning and priority setting would best be done at multiple scales. The need for improvement in watershed and fire conditions is widespread, so prioritizing the treatments is key for several reasons. If an integrated approach is planned, decades will be needed for implementation, due to likely limited levels of funding, infrastructure, and personnel. Therefore, identifying those areas in greatest need of treatment and where success is most likely is critical. Linked to this practical consideration is the recognition that not all areas (or watersheds) are equal. Some watersheds contain the best habitat, or last refugia for aquatic species, making them high priority for restoration from an aquatic species perspective. Other watersheds might rate as high priority because they supply water for domestic uses, or are the site of heavy fuel loading near substantial property improvements and urban interfaces (see Chapters 18 and 19). Due to the uncertainty of treatment effectiveness discussed earlier, it is likely that watersheds that lack critical resources might be a priority for initial treatment. Identifying priorities, considering risk to resources, importance of the watershed to those resources, and other criteria for a range of resource areas (fire, recreation, wildlife, etc.) is a complex task.

Monitoring

Monitoring and evaluation of integrated, landscape-level projects is critical. Given the long time frames necessary to assess effectiveness of treatments, land managers generally find it necessary to supplement useful, short-term monitoring (e.g., implementation, evaluation of effects on soils, riparian vegetation) with modeling of long-term processes (e.g., fire behavior, sediment yield). Correct interpretation of monitoring findings and modeling outputs allows more information from which to base decisions and increases the probability of applying treatments in the most sensitive areas.

Monitoring to assess project implementation and effectiveness would take commitment from land managers and resources. Fortunately, some recent schemes for effectiveness monitoring at both the site (USDA Forest Service 1992) and landscape scale (Kershner et al. 2004) have been implemented and might serve as models for other monitoring efforts.

Integrated Treatments

An integrated approach to restoration assesses and addresses multiple restoration needs on a given watershed at the same time. Watersheds form natural boundaries across the landscape; they are the units that support aquatic systems and beneficial uses of water, thus providing logical management units. Treatments within selected watersheds would naturally vary, dependent both on local existing conditions and the ability to move them toward a state where natural processes function more closely to historic or desired conditions. This means fire management activities are integrated with watershed, wildlife, and other resource-improvement activities. Sediment and flow regimes are improved by decommissioning or improving roads, and road crossings can be improved to enhance connectivity and flow of watershed products (e.g., bedload, wood). Riparian function in meadows can be improved by revising range management activities. In the same implementation cycle, fire management treatments should be undertaken. Fuel treatments should include the use of prescribed fire and mechanical manipulation of fuel, and a schedule to return fire to key areas in the future. This combination of actions can improve conditions of several ecosystem processes: aquatic and hydrologic connectivity, sediment, water flow, and fire regimes. Short-term impacts from fire management activities are balanced and surpassed by short-term improvement in sediment regime, and long-term improvements to all these processes.

Collaboration

As noted earlier, many fuel treatment proposals meet with opposition from the public, who are concerned about the risks of escaped prescribed fire, aesthetics, smoke from planned ignitions, or removal of timber from public lands. Additionally, projects are often delayed, and sometimes deferred, when regulatory processes are not fully anticipated by project planners. These delays are often related to listed or focus wildlife species (see Chapter 23) or air quality (see Chapter 21) or water quality concerns. An integrated approach emphasizes the importance of interdisciplinary planning. Land managers, the public, and regulatory agencies need to work together in planning fuel treatment and watershed restoration projects.

Summary and Next Steps

Application of an integrated approach has positive consequences to an overall goal of ecosystem restoration in the long term. As the condition of watersheds is slowly improved, improvements to conditions at larger scales should be evident. Linking areas where physical and biological processes function closer to their natural states would contribute to the ability to use self-sustaining treatments (e.g., "let burn," see Chapters 18 and 19). It is also likely that incentive for implementing treatments would be increased, if they were demonstrated to be effective and conditions improved at broad scales.

Moving from situations where restoration projects are applied after ecosystem damage has occurred, or at small scales based on the objectives of a single resource, to an integrated, landscape approach is a difficult journey. The obstacles, including fiscal and administrative barriers barely discussed in this chapter, may seem overwhelming.

Our suggestion for implementing the latter approach is to try to improve our performance where and when we can. At smaller scales, managers and specialists can implement some elements of the integrated landscape approach. Integration can be improved at all scales. Useful monitoring can be conducted on all projects. Managers can improve the degree and quality of public and agency communication. Successes at small scales will translate to application to larger landscapes. Meanwhile, those with policy and funding authority should look for opportunities to implement an integrated landscape approach.

The reality is that funding will come for both watershed restoration and fire management. Projects will be planned and implemented; financial, ecological, administrative, and personnel resources will be invested. An integrative approach would help realize a maximum return on those investments.

Conclusion

Fire is a natural process within most California watersheds and must be considered when managing for riparian, aquatic, and water resources. Sedimentation, mass-wasting, and flooding are also natural processes that work within watersheds. Issues concerning fire and watershed resources are difficult, because they mix social and ecological values. Communities, homes, and municipal water supplies sit at the base of large watersheds, and increased water and sediment flows from large wildfires may threaten these investments. In addition, many aquatic species are endangered or extremely limited in their habitat and populations due to a variety of anthropogenic activities. Fires out of their natural regime can and do cause serious damage to these limited ecological assets. These concerns have resulted in a post-fire rehabilitation approach to watershed management. The idea of preemptive work that restores historic fire regimes has not been widely discussed, considered, or used to address both the ecological and social issues surrounding fires and watershed resources. Until society understands that fires are not something that happens to a watershed but something that is part of what creates and maintains watersheds, the social issues will be difficult to integrate into a more comprehensive management strategy. Finally, until watershed managers and aquatic ecologists actively prescribe the restoration of fire regimes, fire regimes that benefit watersheds likely will not be realized.

References

Agee, J.K. 1993. Fire ecology of Pacific Northwest forests. Island Press, Washington, DC., 493 p.

Amaranthus, M.P., J.M. Trappe, and D.A. Perry. 1993. Soil moisture, native revegetation, and *Pinus lambertiana* seedling survival, growth, and mycorrhiza formation following wildfire and grass seeding. Restoration Ecology 1:188–195.

Baron, F.J. 1962. Effects of different grasses on ponderosa pine seedling establishment. Res. Note PSW-199. Berkeley, CA, USDA Forest Service, Pacific Southwest Forest and Range Experiment Station. 8 p.

Barro, S.C., and S.G. Conard. 1987. Use of ryegrass seeding as an emergency revegetation measure in chaparral ecosystems. Gen. Tech. Rep. PSW-102. Berkeley, CA, USDA Forest Service, Pacific Southwest Forest and Range Experiment Station. 12 p.

Bautista, S., J. Bellot, and V.R. Vallejo. 1996. Mulching treatment for post-fire soil conservation in a semiarid ecosystem. Arid Soil Research and Rehabilitation 10:235–242.

Beche, L.A., S.L. Stephens, and V.H. Resh. 2005. Effects of a prescribed fire on a Sierra Nevada (California, USA) steam and its riparian zone. Forest Ecology and Management 218:37–59.

Benda, L., D. Miller, P. Bigelow, and K. Andras. 2003. Effects of post-wildfire erosion on channel environments, Boise River, Idaho. Forest Ecology and Management 178:105–119.

Beyers, J.L. 2004. Postfire seeding for erosion control: Effectiveness and impacts on native plant communities. Conservation Biology 18:947–956

Beyers, J.L. *In press*. Growth of Regreen, seeded for erosion control, in the Manter fire area, southern Sierra Nevada. In M G. Narog (tech. coord.) Proceedings of the 2002 fire conference on managing fire and fuels in the remaining wildlands and open spaces of the southwestern United States. December 2–5, 2002, San Diego, CA. Gen. Tech. Rep. PSW-189. USDA Forest Service, Pacific Southwest Research Station, Albany, CA.

Beyers, J.L., C.D. Wakeman, P.M. Wohlgemuth, and S.G. Conard,. 1998. Effects of postfire grass seeding on native vegetation in southern California chaparral. P. 52–64 in Proceedings, nineteenth annual forest vegetation management conference: wildfire rehabilitation, January 20–22, 1998. Forest Vegetation Management Conference, Redding, CA.

Bisson, P.A., B.R. Rieman, C. Luce, P.F. Hessburg, D.C. Lee, J.L. Kershner, G.H. Reeves, and R.E. Gresswell. 2003. Fire and aquatic ecosystems: current knowledge and key questions. Forest Ecology and Management 178:213–229.

Christ, J.H. 1934. Reseeding burned-over lands in northern Idaho. University of Idaho Agricultural Experiment Station Bulletin 201. University of Idaho, Moscow. 27 p.

Collins, L.M., and C.E. Johnston. 1995. Effectiveness of straw bale dams for erosion control in the Oakland Hills following the fire of 1991. P. 171–183 in J.E. Keeley and T. Scott (eds.), Brushfires in California wildlands: ecology and resource management. International Association of Wildland Fire, Fairfield, WA.

Conard, S.G., J.L. Beyers, and P.M. Wohlgemuth. 1995. Impacts of postfire grass seeding on chaparral systems—what do we know and where do we go from here? P. 149–161 in J.E. Keeley and T. Scott (eds.), Brushfires in California wildlands: ecology and resource management. International Association of Wildland Fire, Fairfield, WA.

Conard, S.G., J.C. Regelbrugge, and R.D. Wills. 1991. Preliminary effects of ryegrass seeding on postfire establishment of natural vegetation in two California ecosystems. P. 314–321 in P.L. Andrews and D.F. Potts (eds.), Proceedings of the 11th conference on fire and forest meteorology, April 16–19, 1991, Missoula, MT. Society of American Foresters, Bethesda, MD.

Conrad, C.E. 1979. Emergency postfire seeding using annual grass. CHAPS Newsletter, March 1979 p 5–8. Chaparral Research and Development Program, Riverside, CA.

Costales, E.F., Jr., and A.B. Costales. 1984. Determination and evaluation of some emergency measures for the quick rehabilitation of newly burned watershed areas in the pine forest. Sylvtrop Philippine Forestry Research 9:33–53.

DeByle, N. V. 1970a. Do contour trenches reduce wet-mantle flood peaks? Res. Note INT-108. USDA Forest Service, Intermountain Forest and Range Experiment Station, Ogden, UT. 8 p.

DeByle, N. V. 1970b. Infiltration in contour trenches in the Sierra Nevada. Res. Note INT-115. USDA Forest Service, Intermountain Forest and Range Experiment Station, Ogden, UT. 5 p.

Detenbeck, N. E., P. W. DeVore, G. J. Niemi, and A. Lima. 1992. Recovery of temperate-stream fish communities from disturbance: a review of case studies and synthesis of theory. Environmental Management 16:33–53.

Dunham, J. B., M. K. Young, R. E. Gresswell, and B. E. Rieman. 2003. Effects of fire on fish populations: landscape perspectives on persistence of native fishes and nonnative fish invasions. Forest Ecology and Management 178:183–196.

Dyrness, C. T. 1976. Effect of wildfire on soil wetability in the High Cascades of Oregon. Res. Pap. PNW-202. USDA Forest Service, Pacific Northwest Forest and Range Experiment Station, Portland, OR. 18 p.

Edwards, L., J. Burney, and R. DeHaan. 1995. Researching the effects of mulching on cool-period soil erosion in Prince Edward Island, Canada. Journal of Soil and Water Conservation 50:184–187.

Furniss, M. J., T. S. Ledwith, M. A. Love, B. C. McFadin, S. A. Flanagan. 1998. Response of road-stream crossings to large flood events in Washington, Oregon, and northern California. USDA Forest Service, Technology and Development Program, 9877 1806-San Dimas Technology Development Center, San Dimas, CA. 14 p.

Gautier, C. R. 1983. Sedimentation in burned chaparral watersheds: is emergency revegetation justified? Water Resources Bulletin 19:793–802.

Goldman, S. J., K. Jackson, and T. A. Bursztynsky. 1986. Erosion and sediment control handbook. McGraw-Hill, San Francisco 360 p.

Griffin, J. R. 1982. Pine seedlings, native ground cover, and Lolium multiflorum on the Marble-Cone burn, Santa Lucia Range, California. Madroño 29:177–188.

Griffith, R. W. 1998. Burned area emergency rehabilitation. P. 4–7 in Proceedings, nineteenth annual forest vegetation management conference: wildfire rehabilitation, January 20–22, 1998. Forest Vegetation Management Conference, Redding, CA.

Houck, O. A. 2002. Clean Water Act TMDL Program: law, policy, and implementation. Environmental Law Institute, Washington, DC. 362p.

Kattleman. R. 1996. Hydrology and water resources. P. 855–920 in Sierra Nevada Ecosystem Project: final report to Congress, Vol. II: assessments and scientific basis for management options. University of California, Centers for Water and Wildland Resources, Davis.

Keeley, J. E. 2004. Ecological impacts of wheat seeding after a Sierra Nevada wildfire. International Journal of Wildland Fire 13:73–78.

Keeley, J. E. 1991. Seed germination and life history syndromes in the California chaparral. The Botanical Review 57:81–116.

Keeley, J. E., C. D. Allen, J. Betancourt, G. W. Chong, C. J. Fotheringham, and H. D. Safford. 2006. A 21st Century Perspective on Postfire Seeding. Journal of Forestry 104:1–2.

Keeley, S. C., J. E. Keeley, S. M. Hutchinson, and A. W. Johnson. 1981. Postfire succession of herbaceous flora in southern California chaparral. Ecology 62:1608–1621.

Kershner, J. L., M. Coles-Ritchie, E. Cowley, R. C. Henderson, K. Kratz, C. Quimby, D. M. Turner, L. C. Ulmer, and M. R. Vinson. 2004. Guide to effective monitoring of aquatic and riparian resources. General Technical Report, RMRS-GTR-121. USDA Forest Service, Rocky Mountain Research Station, Fort Collins, CO.

Kershner, J. L., L. MacDonald, Z. Libohova, L. M. Decker, and D. Winters. 2003. Where are aquatic ecosystems likely to be changed by the Hayman fire and how will the changes be manifested on the landscape/watershed? In R. Graham (ed.), A case study analysis of the Hayman fire. General Technical Report RMRS-GTR 114, Rocky Mountain Research Station, Fort Collins, CO.

Klock, G. O., A. R. Tiedemann, and W. Lopushinsky. 1975. Seeding recommendations for disturbed mountain slopes in north central Washington. Res. Note PNW-244. USDA Forest Service, Pacific Northwest Forest and Range Experiment Station, Portland, OR. 8 p.

McCammon, B. P., and D. Hughes. 1980. Fire rehab in the Bend municipal watershed. P. 252–259 in Proceedings of the 1980 watershed management symposium, July 21–23, 1980, Boise, ID. American Society of Civil Engineers, New York.

McClure, N. R. 1956. Grass and legume seedings on burned-over forest lands in northern Idaho and adjacent Washington. Master's Thesis, University of Idaho. 125 p.

McDonald, P. M. 1986. Grasses in young conifer plantations—hindrance and help. Northwest Science 60(4):271–278.

Miles, S. R., D. M. Haskins, and D. W. Ranken. 1989. Emergency burn rehabilitation: cost, risk, and effectiveness. P. 97–102 in N. H. Berg (tech. coord.), Proceedings of the symposium on fire and watershed management, October 26–28, 1988, Sacramento, CA. Gen. Tech. Rep. PSW-109. USDA Forest Service, Pacific Southwest Forest and Range Experiment Station, Berkeley, CA.

Minshall, G. W., J. T. Brock, and J. D. Varley. 1989. Wildfires and Yellowstone's stream ecosystems. BioScience 39:707–715.

Moyle, P. B., R. M. Yoshiyama, and R. A. Knapp. 1996. Status of fish and fisheries. P. 953–973 in Sierra Nevada Ecosystem Project: final report to Congress, Vol. II: assessments and scientific basis for management options. University of California, Centers for Water and Wildland Resources, Davis.

Nadkarni, N. M., and D. C. Odion. 1986. Effects of seeding an exotic grass Lolium multiflorum on native seedling regeneration following fire in a chaparral community. P. 115–121 in J. J. DeVries (ed.), Proceeding of the chaparral ecosystems research conference, May 16–17, 1985, Santa Barbara, CA. Report No. 62, California Water Resources Center, University of California, Davis.

Noble, E. L. 1965. Sediment reduction through watershed rehabilitation. P. 114–123 in Proceedings of the federal interagency sedimentation conference 1963. Miscellaneous Publication 970. U.S. Department of Agriculture, Washington, DC.

Orr, H. K. 1970. Runoff and erosion control by seeded and native vegetation on a forest burn: Black Hills, South Dakota. Res. Pap. RM-60. USDA Forest Service, Rocky Mountain Forest and Range Experiment Station, Fort Collins, CO. 12 p.

Ratliff, R. D., and P. M. McDonald. 1987. Postfire grass and legume seeding: what to seed and potential impacts on reforestation. P. 111–123 in Proceedings, ninth annual forest vegetation management conference, November 3–5, 1987. Forest Vegetation Management Conference, Redding, CA.

Regional Ecosystem Office. 1995. Ecosystem analysis at the watershed scale. Federal Guide for Watershed Analysis, Version 2.2. Portland, OR. 27 pp.

Reiman, B., and J. Clayton. 1997. Wildfire and native fish: issues of forest health and conservation of sensitive species. Fisheries 22(11):6–15.

Rice, R.M., R.P. Crouse, and E.S. Corbett. 1965. Emergency measures to control erosion after a fire on the San Dimas Experimental Forest. P. 123–130 in Proceedings of the federal inter-agency sedimentation conference, 1963. Miscellaneous Publication 970. U.S. Department of Agriculture, Washington, DC.

Richards, R.T., J.C. Chambers, and C. Ross. 1998. Use of native plants on federal lands: policy and practice. Journal of Range Management 51:625–632.

Robichaud, P.R., J.L. Beyers, and D.G. Neary. 2000. Evaluating the effectiveness of postfire rehabilitation treatments. General Technical Report RMRS-GTR-63. USDA Forest Service, Rocky Mountain Research Station, Fort Collins, CO. 85 p

Ruby, E.C. 1989. Rationale for seeding grass on the Stanislaus Complex burn. P. 125–130 in N. H. Berg (tech. coord.), Proceedings of the symposium on fire and watershed management, October 26–28, 1988, Sacramento, CA. Gen. Tech. Rep. PSW-109. U. S. Department of Agriculture, Forest Service, Pacific Southwest Forest and Range Experiment Station, Berkeley, CA.

Ruffolo, J. 1999. TMDLs: The revolution in water quality regulation. California Research Bureau. CRB-99-005, Sacramento.

Sampson, A.W. 1944. Plant succession on burned chaparral lands in northern California. California Agricultural Experiment Station Bulletin 685. 144 p.

Schultz, A.M., J.L. Launchbaugh, and H.H. Biswell. 1955. Relationship between grass density and brush seedling survival. Ecology 36:226–238.

Skinner, C.N. 2002. Fire history in riparian reserves of the Klamath Mountains. P. 164–169 in Association for fire ecology miscellaneous publication No. 1: fire in California ecosystems: integrating ecology, prevention and management.

Spencer, C.N., F.R. Hauer, K.O. Gabel. 2003. Wildfire effects on stream food webs and nutrient dynamics in Glacier National Park, USA. Forest Ecology and Management 178:141–153.

Swanson, F.J., S.V. Gregory, J.R. Sedell, and A.G. Campbell. 1982. Land-water interactions: the riparian zone. P. 267–291 in R.L. Edmonds (ed.), Analysis of coniferous forest ecosystems in the western United States. Hutchinson Ross, Stroudsburg, PA.

Sweeney, J.R. 1956. Responses of vegetation to fire: a study of the herbaceous vegetation following chaparral fires. University of California Publications in Botany 28:143–249.

SWRCB, 1988. Nonpoint Source Management Plan. State Water Resources Control Board, Division of Water Quality, Sacramento, CA. November 1988.

SWRCB and CCC. 2000. Volume I: Nonpoint Source Program Strategy and Implementation Plan, 1998-2013 (PROSIP). In Plan for California's nonpoint source pollution control program. State Water Resources Control Board and the California Coastal Commission. Sacramento, CA. January 1999.

Taskey, R.D., C.L. Curtis, and J. Stone. 1989. Wildfire, ryegrass seeding, and watershed rehabilitation. P. 149–161 in N.H. Berg (tech. coord.), Proceedings of the symposium on fire and watershed management, October 26–28, 1988, Sacramento, CA. Gen. Tech. Rep. PSW-109. USDA Forest Service, Pacific Southwest Forest and Range Experiment Station, Berkeley, CA.

Tiedemann, A.R., and G.O. Klock. 1976. Development of vegetation after fire, seeding, and fertilization on the Entiat Experimental Forest. P. 171–191 in Proceedings, annual Tall Timbers fire ecology conference, number 15: Pacific Northwest. Tall Timbers Research Station, Tallahassee, FL.

USDA Forest Service. 1992. Investigating water quality in the Pacific southwest region. Best management practices evaluation program: A user's guide. Forest Service, Pacific Southwest Region, San Francisco.

U.S. GAO. 2003. Wildland fires: better information needed on effectiveness of emergency stabilization and rehabilitation treatments. GAO-03-430. U.S General Accounting Office, Washington, DC.

Van de Water, R. 1998. Post-fire riparian zone management: the Salmon River experience. P. 25–40 in Proceedings, nineteenth annual forest vegetation management conference: wildfire rehabilitation, January 20–22, 1998. Forest Vegetation Management Conference, Redding, CA.

Wheatley, M.J. 1999. Leadership and the new science: discovering order in a chaotic world (2nd ed.). Berrett-Koehler Publishers, San Francisco. 197 p.

Wohlgemuth, P.M., J.L. Beyers, C.D. Wakeman, and S.G. Conard. 1998. Effects of fire and grass seeding on soil erosion in southern California chaparral. P. 41–51 in Proceedings, nineteenth annual forest vegetation management conference: wildfire rehabilitation, January 20–22, 1998. Forest Vegetation Management Conference, Redding, CA.

Zedler, P.H., C.R. Gautier, G.S. McMaster. 1983. Vegetation change in response to extreme events: the effect of a short interval between fires in California chaparral and coastal scrub. Ecology 64:809–818.

CHAPTER 21

Fire and Air Resources

SURAJ AHUJA

There is no fire without some smoke.

HEYWOOD, *Proverbs*, 1546

Fire is an important part of California ecosystems, but it also produces combustion byproducts that are potentially harmful to human health and welfare. A challenge of managing wildland fire is balancing public interest objectives while still sustaining ecological integrity. Minimizing adverse effects of smoke on human health and welfare, while maximizing the effectiveness of using wildland fire, will need to become an integrated and collaborative activity. Awareness of air quality regulations, smoke production, transport, and effects from prescribed and wildland fires will enable land managers to refine existing smoke management strategies and develop better smoke management plans and programs in the future. Land managers need to ensure that using wildland fire is the most effective alternative for achieving their land management objectives. At the same time, federal, state, local, and tribal air resource regulators must ensure that air quality rules and regulations are equitable (Hardy and Leenhouts 2001). Additionally, public support plays an important role in achieving these objectives. California is such a large and diverse state that one simple formula cannot work for all types of landscapes, vegetation types, community locations, and receptor sites.

Composition of Smoke

Carbon dioxide and water are the two products of complete combustion and generally make up over 90% of the total emissions from wildland fire. In the incomplete combustion that occurs under wildland conditions, smoke is composed of carbon dioxide, water vapor, carbon monoxide, particulate matter, hydrocarbons and other organic compounds, nitrogen oxides, trace minerals, and several thousand other compounds (Ryan and McMahon 1976, Peterson and Ward 1992).

Particulate matter is the principal pollutant of concern to human health from wildfire smoke for the short-term exposures typically experienced by firefighters and the public.

Studies indicate that 90% of smoke particles emitted during wildland burning are particles less than ten microns in size (PM_{10}), and about 90% of these are less than 2.5 microns ($PM_{2.5}$) (Ward and Hardy 1991).

Other pollutants of concern include carbon monoxide, nitrogen oxides, and hydrocarbons. Carbon monoxide is a colorless, odorless gas, produced by incomplete combustion of wood or other organic materials. Carbon monoxide levels are highest during the smoldering stages of a fire.

Nitrogen oxides are produced primarily from oxidation of the nitrogen contained in the fuel. Most fuel contains less than 1% nitrogen, of which about 20% is converted to nitrogen oxides when burned (Hardy et al. 2001). Hydrocarbons and nitrogen oxides from large wildland fires contribute to increased ozone formation (which causes injury to plants) under certain conditions.

Other air toxics, such as acrolein, benzene, and formaldehyde, are present in smoke, but in much lower concentrations than particulate matter and carbon monoxide. These air toxics have been known to be carcinogenic (Kane and Alarie 1977, U.S. Dept. Labor 1987).

Emission factors (pounds of emissions per ton of fuel consumed) for more than 25 compounds have been identified and described by Ward (1990) and Ward and Hardy (1991). Table 21.1 shows pounds of emissions produced from one ton of fuel consumed, by vegetation type and combustion phase (Hardy et al. 1996). Fuel loading estimation is one of the parameters that can introduce a major error in estimation of the emissions. Table 21.2 summarizes the fuel loading by vegetative grouping.

Health and Environmental Effects of Smoke

The level and duration of exposure, age and susceptibility of the individual, and other factors play significant roles in determining whether someone will experience smoke-related

TABLE 21.1
Pounds of emissions per ton of fuel consumed by combustion phase

Fuel/Fire Configuration	Combustion Phase	Emission Factors						
		PM	PM_{10}	$PM_{2.5}$	CO	CO_2	CH_4	NMHC
Broadcast burned slash								
Douglas fir/hemlock	Flaming	24.7	16.6	14.9	143	3,385	4.6	4.2
	Smoldering	35	27.6	26.1	463	2,804	15.2	8.4
	Average	29.6	23.1	21.83	312	3,082	11	7.2
Hardwoods	Flaming	23	14	12.2	92	3,389	4.4	5.2
	Smoldering	38	25.9	23.4	366	2,851	19.6	14
	Average	37.4	25	22.4	256	3,072	13.2	10.8
Ponderosa pine/lodgepole pine	Flaming	18.8	11.5	10	89	3,401	3	3.6
	Smoldering	48.6	36.7	34.2	285	2,971	14.6	9.6
	Average	39.6	25	22	178	3,202	8.2	6.4
Mixed conifer	Flaming	22	11.7	9.6	53	3,458	3	3.2
	Smoldering	33.6	25.3	23.6	273	3,023	17.6	13.2
	Average	29	20.5	18.8	201	3,165	12.8	9.8
Juniper	Flaming	29.1	15.3	13.9	82	3,401	3.9	5.5
	Smoldering	35.1	25.8	23.8	250	3,050	20.5	15.5
	Average	28.3	20.4	18.7	163	3,231	12	10.4
Pile-and burn slash								
Tractor-piled	Flaming	11.4	7.4	6.6	44	3,492	2.4	2.2
	Smoldering	25	15.9	14	232	3,124	17.8	12.2
	Average	20.4	12.4	10.8	153	3,271	11.4	8
Crane piled	Flaming	22.6	13.6	11.8	101	3,349	9.4	8.2
	Smoldering	44.2	33.2	31	232	3,022	30	20.2
	Average	36.4	25.6	23.4	185	3,143	21.7	15.2
Average piles	Average	28.4	19	17.1	169	3,207	16.6	11.6
Broadcast-burned brush								
Sagebrush	Flaming	45	31.8	29.1	155	3,197	7.4	6.8
	Smoldering	45.3	29.6	26.4	212	3,118	12.4	14.5
	Average	45.3	29.9	26.7	206	3,126	11.9	13.7
Chaparral	Flaming	31.6	16.5	13.5	119	3,326	3.4	17.2
	Smoldering	40	24.7	21.6	197	3,144	9	30.6
	Average	34.1	20.1	17.3	154	3,257	5.7	19.6
Wildfires fires (in forests)								
	Average		30	27				

NOTE: Adapted from Hardy et al. 2001. Fire averages are weighted averages based on measured carbon flux. PM_{10} values are derived from known size class distribution of particulates using PM and $PM_{2.5}$.

TABLE 21.2
Summary of fuel load and consumption by National Fire Danger Rating System (NFDRS) model for wildfires

Model	Description	Fuel Load (Tons/Acre)
A	Western grasses (annual)	0.5
B	California chaparral	19.5
C	Pine-grass savanna	4.7
E	Hardwood litter (winter)	3.8
F	Intermediate brush	15
G	Short needle (heavy dead)	43.5
H	Short needle (normal dead)	27.5
I	Heavy slash	55.1
J	Intermediate slash	34
K	Light slash	14.4
L	Western grasses (perennial)	0.75
R	Hardwood litter (summer)	3.1
T	Sagebrush-grass	4.5
U	Western pines	19.1

NOTE: Use the fuel load numbers given in the table only when field-verified numbers are not available.

problems. The effects of smoke range from eye and respiratory tract irritation to more serious disorders, including reduced lung function, bronchitis, exacerbation of asthma, and premature death. Studies have found that fine particles are linked (alone or with other pollutants) with increased mortality and aggravation of preexisting respiratory and cardiovascular disease. In addition, particles are respiratory irritants, and laboratory studies show that high concentrations of particulate matter can cause persistent cough, phlegm, wheezing, and difficulty breathing. Particles can also affect healthy people, causing respiratory symptoms, transient reductions in lung function, and pulmonary inflammation. Particulate matter can alter the body's immune system and make it more difficult to remove inhaled foreign materials such as pollen and bacteria from the lung. Table 21.3 shows the PM_{10} health-protective and visibility-range values for different concentrations of PM_{10} (Sharkey 1997).

Carbon monoxide enters the bloodstream through the lungs, reducing oxygen delivery to the body's organs and tissues. Individuals experiencing health effects (e.g., chest pain and cardiac arrhythmias) from lower levels of carbon monoxide include those with cardiovascular disease. At higher levels, carbon monoxide exposure causes headaches, dizziness, visual impairment, reduced work capacity, and reduced manual dexterity, even in otherwise healthy individuals. At even higher concentrations (seldom associated solely with a wildfire), carbon monoxide can be deadly.

Wildfire smoke contains significant quantities of respiratory irritants. Formaldehyde and acrolein are two of the principal irritant chemicals that add to the cumulative irritant properties of smoke, even though the concentrations of these chemicals individually may be below levels of public health concern. People exposed to toxic air pollutants at sufficient concentrations and durations may have slightly increased risks of cancer or other serious health problems. However, in general, the long-term risk from short-term smoke exposure is quite low (Reinhardt 2000, Reinhardt et al. 2000).

Besides its impacts on human health, air pollution has long been recognized as having adverse effects on the environment. In addition to damaging agricultural and timber yields, air pollution can affect global climate, alter wildland and aquatic ecosystems, and have detrimental impacts on visibility. Particulate matter from wood smoke has a size range near the wavelength of visible light (0.4–0.7 micrometers) and efficiently scatters light and reduces visibility (see Table 21.3).

Current Emission Patterns

For California, the estimated daily emissions (by major source category) for total organic gases, reactive organic gases, carbon monoxide, nitrogen oxides, sulfur oxides, and particulate matter less than 10 microns (PM_{10}) are summarized in Table 21.4 (CARB 2002). The contributing sources are categorized as *stationary, area-wide, mobile,* and *natural.* Natural sources include wildfires; area-wide sources include prescribed and agricultural burning. The numbers are daily average based on annual estimates (annual emissions are divided by 365 to get the daily average). The California Air Resources Board Statewide Emissions Inventory (Table 21.4) shows that wildland fires contribute a significant portion of total emissions (CARB 2002). Because wildfires are event based and are not emitted every day, wildfire emissions are high during the actual event day.

It is important to know background-level emissions by county and air basin for management purposes. Inyo County has the highest PM_{10} emission levels, due mainly to wind-blown dust-exposed lakebeds from the Owens and Mono lakes. Los Angeles and south San Diego lead in nitrogen oxide emissions that result from onsite and mobile sources. Table 21.5 shows the comparative emission values for different factors for wildfire and prescribed fires in the 13 western states including California.

California's Environment

Managing smoke from fires in California requires knowledge of airflow and pollution sources and patterns and an understanding of the state's regulatory framework, population patterns, meteorology, and physical features for fire emissions production and transport prediction.

For example, in the Central Valley, horizontal air movement is restricted by mountain ranges: the coastal mountains to the west, the Tehachapi Mountains to the south, and the Sierra to the east. In the spring and summer when the marine layer is shallow, westerly winds enter through low coastal gaps, primarily the Carquinez Straits, and flow down the valley toward the southeast. Daytime wind speeds increase as the valley heats up and are strongest in the afternoon. During storm-free periods in the fall and winter, flow is more variable with light

TABLE 21.3

The health-protective and visibility range values for different concentrations of PM_{10}

Concentration of PM_{10} ($\mu g/m^3$)	Health-Protective Value	Visibility Range (miles)
0–40	Good	10 and up
41–80	Moderate	7 to 9
81–175	Unhealthy for sensitive groups	2.5 to 3 (mild smoke conditions)
176–300	Unhealthy	1.24 to 2 (moderate smoke conditions)
301–500	Very unhealthy	1 (heavy smoke conditions)
>500	Hazardous	0.75 or less (extremely heavy smoke conditions)

NOTE: $\mu g/m^3$ = microgram per cubic meter.

TABLE 21.4

Statewide Emission Inventory 2002

	Emissions (tons/day, annual average)					
	TOG	ROG	CO	NOx	SOx	PM_{10}
Stationary Sources	2,568	588	362	587	137	139
Fuel Combustion	203	43	304	478	53	42
Waste Disposal	1,422	22	3	3	0	1
Cleaning and Surface Coatings	401	285	0	0	0	0
Petroleum Production and Marketing	458	168	9	14	55	3
Industrial Processes	85	69	45	92	28	94
Area-Wide Sources	2,032	749	2,309	96	5	2,076
Solvent Evaporation	561	504	0	0	0	0
Miscellaneous Processes	1,471	244	2,309	96	5	2,076
Residential Fuel Combustion	152	66	1,009	81	5	143
Wood Combustion	145	64	985	12	2	139
Agricultural Burning	38	22	251	5	0	30
Non-Agricultural Burning	100	55	1,038	9	0	99
Mobile Sources	1,816	1,672	14,394	2,741	161	123
On Road Motor Vehicles	1,296	1,197	11,636	1,767	12	53
Other Mobile Sources	519	474	2,759	974	149	70
Natural Sources						
Wildfires	106	38	409	18	0	80
Total	6,522	3,046	17,474	3,441	302	2,418

NOTE: Does not include biogenic sources. These summaries do not include emissions from wind blown dust-exposed lake beds from Owens and Mono Lakes. TOG = total organic gases, ROG = reactive organic gases, CO = carbon monoxide, NOx = nitrogen oxides, SOx = sulfur oxides, PM_{10} = particles less than 10 microns in size.

TABLE 21.5
Summary of fire activity and emissions from wildfires
and prescribed fires in 1996

	Wildfire	Prescribed Fire	Total
No. of individual fires	1,348	14,696	16,044
Mean fire duration (days)	3.6(1–117)	Set at 1 day	n/a
No. of fire days (original)	4,902 (24%)	14,696 (75%)	19,598
No. of fire days (+ smoldering)	5,311	16,603	21,914
Area burned (acres × 10³)	5,030 (88%)	555 (10%)	5,585
Area burned per fire day, mean (acres, smoldering excluded)	1,026	38	n/a
Fuel consumed (tons × 10³)	48,085 (90%)	5,243 (10%)	5,3328
Fuel consumed per fire day, mean (tons, smoldering excluded)	9,809	357	n/a
Total emissions (tons × 10³)			
TSP	917 (93%)	64 (7%)	981
PM$_{10}$	756 (94%)	50 (6%)	806
PM$_{2.5}$	648 (93%)	44 (6%)	694
Elemental Carbon	40 (93%)	3 (7%)	43
Organic Carbon	312 (93%)	22(7%)	334
VOC	366 (93%)	27 (7%)	396
CH$_4$	366 (85%)	30 (7%)	396
NH$_3$	35 (92%)	2 (5%)	37
NO$_x$	167 (91%)	17 (9%)	184
CO	7,770 (94%)	505 (6%)	8,275
SO$_2$	46 (90%)	5 (10%)	51
PM-Coarse	108 (95%)	6 (5%)	114

NOTE: TSP = total solid particles, PM$_{10}$ = particles less than 10 microns, PM$_{2.5}$ = particles less than 2.5 microns, VOC = volatile organic carbon, CH$_4$ = methane, NH$_3$ = ammonia, NOx = nitrogen oxide, CO = carbon monoxide, SO$_2$ = sulfur dioxide
(Source: Adapted from WRAP–Air Sciences Inc 2003.)

wind speeds resulting in less air movement (Map. 21.1). Computer modeling during a summer pollution episode showed that the Bay Area and Sacramento Area contributed 27%, 10%, and 7% to the ozone exceedences in the northern, central, and southern valleys, respectively (San Joaquin Valley Unified Air Pollution Control District 1994c).

Since 1975, California's population has increased by approximately 56% from 22.1 million to nearly 34.5 million in the year 2000. The increase in the average number of vehicle miles traveled each day has increased from 359 million miles per day in 1975 to 797 million miles per day in 2000 (CARB 2002). These increases in population and

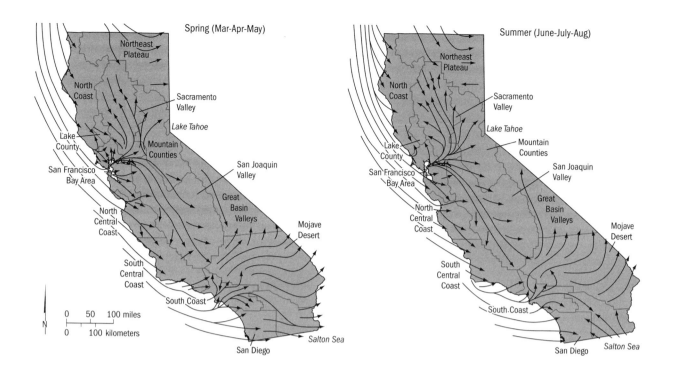

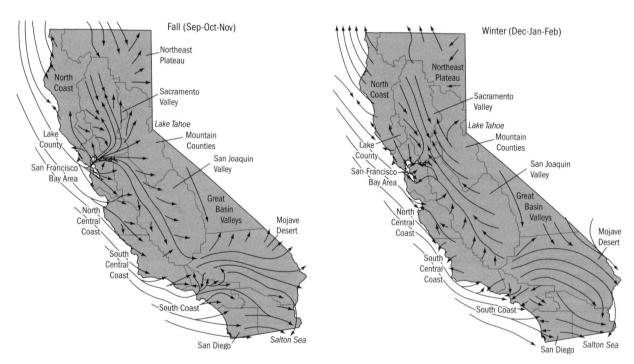

MAP 21.1. General statewide seasonal airflow patterns. (Source: California Air Resources Board Aerometric Data Division, April 1984.)

vehicle miles traveled have created challenges for controlling emissions to improve air quality. Thus, mobile sources are one of the biggest contributors to the ozone problem. Further improvement in auto exhaust emissions and people's driving habits are needed to bring reduction in ozone concentrations.

Air Regulatory Framework

Air quality is managed through federal, state, and local laws and regulations. The national Environmental Protection Agency (EPA) has the primary federal role of ensuring compliance with the requirements of the Clean Air Act. The EPA issues national air quality regulations, approves and oversees State Implementation Plans, and conducts major enforcement actions. If a proposed or active State Implementation Plan (or Tribe Implementation Plan) is deemed inadequate or unacceptable, the EPA can take over enforcing all or parts of the Clean Air Act requirements for that state or tribe through implementation of a Federal Implementation Plan.

The Clean Air Act recognizes that states should take the lead in carrying out its provisions, since appropriate and effective design of pollution control programs requires an understanding of local industries, geography, transportation, meteorology, urban and industrial development patterns, and priorities. The California Air Resource Board and local Air Pollution Control Districts/Air Quality Management Districts have the primary responsibility of carrying out the development and execution of State Implementation Plans, which must provide for the attainment and maintenance of air quality standards.

The original Clean Air Act was passed in 1963. This act was followed by the Clean Air Act Amendments in 1970, 1977, and 1990 (Public Law 1963, 1967, 1970, 1977, and 1990). The amendments of 1970, Section 109, required the EPA to develop primary National Ambient Air Quality Standards to protect human health and secondary standards to protect welfare.

National Ambient Air Quality Standards

To protect human health, the EPA established National Ambient Air Quality Standards for six pollutants: PM_{10}, sulfur dioxide, nitrogen dioxide, ozone, carbon monoxide, and lead. These standards are shown along with California Standards in Table 21.6. If the federal standards are violated in an area, that area is designated as "non-attainment" for that pollutant, and the state must develop a State Implementation Plan for bringing that area back into "attainment." All management activities must conform to State Implementation Plans.

The EPA published Conformity Regulations for non-attainment areas (Map. 21.2 A, B, C) in the Federal Register on November 30, 1993. The conformity provisions of the Clean Air Act, Section 176(c), prohibit federal agencies from taking any action that causes or contributes to any new violation of the National Ambient Air Quality Standards, increases the frequency or severity of an existing violation, or delays timely attainment of a standard in these areas.

Conformity rules apply to the activities on federal lands in non-attainment areas that have total direct and indirect emissions equal to or exceeding the *de minimis* levels for criteria pollutants (see Table 21.7). Conformity determination is also required if the project emissions are at a significant level—that is, constitute 10% of emissions in the non-attainment area. In addition to total emission analyses, area-wide or local air quality modeling analyses must be performed. The modeling analysis must show that the action does not cause or contribute to a new violation of standard or increase the severity or frequency of existing violations. Any action subject to this rule can be determined to conform

TABLE 21.6
National and California Ambient Air Quality Standards

| Pollutant | Averaging Time | Primary Standards ($\mu g/m^3$) | |
		Federal	State
PM_{10}	Annual	50	30
	24 hours	150	50
$PM_{2.5}$	Annual	15	None
	1 hour	65	None
NO_2	Annual	100(0.053)	None
	1 hour	None	470 (0.25)
CO	8 hours	10,000(g)	10,000
	1 hour	40,000(35)	20,000
SO_2	Annual	80(0.03)	None
	24 hours	365(0.14)	105 (0.04)
	3 hours	None	None
	1 hour	None	655 (025)
O_3	1 hour	235(0.12)	180 (0.09)
	8 hour	(0.08)	(0.07)
Pb	Calendar average	1.5	None
	30-day average	None	1.5

NOTE: Annual standards are never to be exceeded. Other standards are not to be exceeded more than once a year. The numbers in the bracket are ppm.

if the total emissions are specifically identified and accounted for in the State Implementation Plan. No conformity rules have been proposed by the state, so conformity applies to federal standards only.

State Implementation Plans

Section 110 of the Clean Air Act requires states to develop State Implementation Plans that identify how the state will attain and maintain National Ambient Air Quality Standards. For all federal non-attainment areas, the state must demonstrate when and how these areas will be able to maintain National Ambient Air Quality Standards.

Controls can include more stringent pollution control requirements for industry, tighter requirements on wood-burning stoves or prescribed burning, or more stringent controls on mobile sources of emissions. States also have the authority to include air quality standards and regulations more stringent than federal standards and regulations. The air pollution districts will have to demonstrate that the control measures in the State Implementation Plans provide for attainment of the National Ambient Air Quality Standards. The emissions will have to be tracked to ensure progress. The attainment plans must encompass an air quality monitoring

MAP 21.2A. Attainment and nonattainment areas for PM$_{10}$ 24-hour state standard. (Source: CARB (2004). http://www.arb.ca.gov/desig.htm)

network, an emission inventory and tracking program, a modeling/control strategy demonstration, legal authority for rules and regulations, emission-limiting regulations, enforcement procedures and policies, and resources for program implementation.

Prevention of Significant Deterioration Program

The Prevention of Significant Deterioration program was established in 1978 as a result of a lawsuit alleging that the Clean Air Act Amendments of 1977 required that a program

be established to prevent degradation of air quality in regions in attainment. The program requires permits for new air pollution sources above a certain size. The emission from new sources cannot cause deterioration of ambient air quality beyond certain increments (referred to as Prevention *of Significant Deterioration increments*). The Prevention of Significant Deterioration increments for nitrogen dioxide, sulfur dioxide, and PM$_{10}$ and total particulates were established for three classes of attainment areas. Prevention of Significant Deterioration increments for Class I, Class II, and Class III areas are shown in Table 21.8.

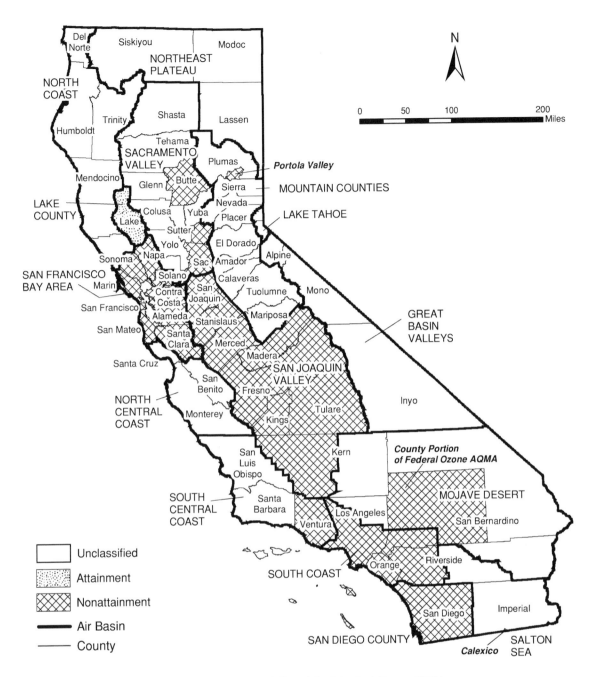

MAP 21.2B. Attainment and nonattainment areas for $PM_{2.5}$ 24 hour-federal standard. (Source: CARB.)

Class I areas include international parks, national parks larger than 6,000 acres, national wilderness areas greater than 5,000 acres, and national wildlife refuges in existence as of August 17, 1977, when the amendments were signed into law. There are 29 Class I Areas located in California (including nine national parks). According to the act, federal land managers have "An affirmative responsibility to protect the Air Quality Related Values within a Class I area." Air Quality Related Values include visibility, flora, fauna, bodies of water, and other resources that may be potentially damaged by air pollution. Table 21.9 gives examples of Air Quality Related Values, sensitive receptors of pollution, and factors potentially changed

by air pollutants (NPS 1997). Areas that are not Class I are classified as Class II. No Class III areas have been established.

Regional Haze Regulations for Protection of Visibility

The EPA issued final regional haze regulations on July 1, 1999 (40 CFR 1999), to improve visibility, or visual air quality, in 156 important Class I areas across the country.

Visibility impairment occurs as a result of the scattering and absorption of light by particles and gases in the atmosphere. Without the effects of pollution, a natural visual range is approximately 140 miles in the western United States and

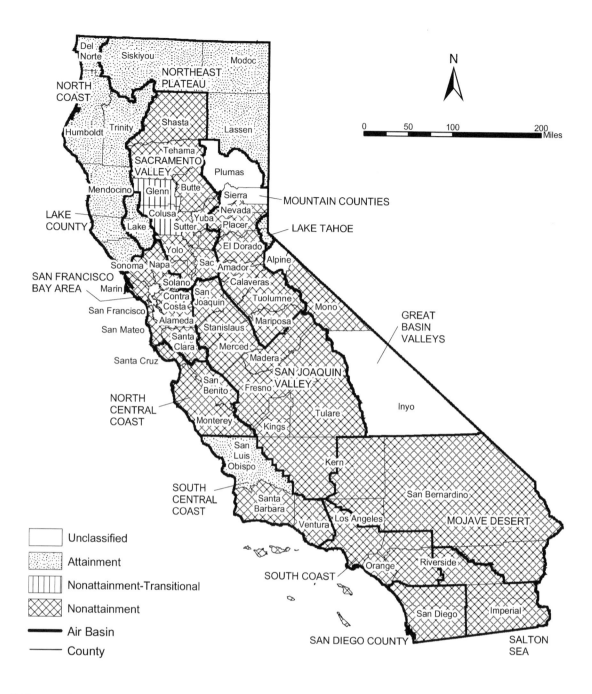

MAP 21.2C. Attainment and nonattainment areas for ozone 8-hour federal standard. (Source: CARB.)

90 miles in the east. However, over the years and in many parts of the United States, fine particles have significantly reduced the range that people can see. In the west, the current range is 60 to 90 miles; in the east, the current range is only 15 to 30 miles (NPS 1997).

IMPROVE Network

Because most visibility degradation is from fine particulate matter, the EPA initiated continuous size-selective monitoring and elemental analysis of particles in 1977. This was replaced by the Interagency Monitoring of Protected Visual Environments (IMPROVE) program. The National Park Service started the IMPROVE program as a cooperative effort with three other federal land management agencies (Forest Service, U.S. Fish and Wildlife Service, and Bureau of Land Management) and the EPA to monitor visibility at selected Class I areas. IMPROVE is now a cooperative monitoring effort between the EPA, federal land management agencies, and state air agencies. The objectives of IMPROVE are to: (1) establish current background visibility in Class I areas, (2) identify chemical species and emission sources responsible

TABLE 21.7
De minimus levels for conformity

Pollutant 1	Type of Area	Tons/Year
Nonattainment Areas (NAA)		
Ozone (VOC or NOx)	Serious	50
	Severe	25
	Extreme	10
Other ozone NAA outside an ozone transport region		100
CO	All	100
SO_2 or NOx	All	100
PM_{10}	Moderate	100
	Serious	70
Lead	All	25
Maintainence Areas		
Ozone (NOx, NO_2)		100
Ozone (VOC's)	Inside transport region	50
	Outside transport region	100
PM_{10}		100
Lead		25
CO		100

TABLE 21.8
Prevention of significant deterioration increments ($\mu g/m^3$)

Pollutant	Measure Interval	Class I	Class II	Class III
PM_{10}	Annual	4	17	34
	24-Hour	8	30	60
Total Particulates	Annual	5	19	38
	24-Hour	10	37	74
SO_2	Annual	2	20	40
	24-Hour	5	91	182
	3-Hour	25	512	700
NO_2	Annual	2.5	N/A	50

NOTE: $\mu g/m^3$ = micrograms per cubic meter.

for existing manmade visibility impairment, and (3) document long-term trends (IMPROVE 1994, NPS 1997, Malm 1999).

The standard protocol is to collect 24-hour samples, every third day. The samples are analyzed for nitrate (NO_3), sulfate (SO_4), elemental and organic carbon, dust, soot, and $PM_{2.5}$ and PM_{10} mass.

The haze rule regulations, when implemented, are designed to improve visibility on the most-impaired days and prevent further degradation on the least-impaired days.

Both the proposed regional haze program and the Clean Air Act require consultation between the state and the federal land managers responsible for managing Class I areas. Such collaboration will help in developing state implementation and monitoring plans, and in predicting the visibility impacts of potential new sources. The haze regulations respond to *Recommendations for Improving Western Vistas*, the

TABLE 21.9
Examples of Air Quality Related Values (AQRVs), sensitive receptors, and factors potentially
changed by air pollution

AQRVs	Sensitive Receptors	Factors Changed by Air Pollution
Flora	Ponderosa pine, lichens	Growth, death, reproduction visible injury
Water	Alpine lakes	Total alkalinity, pH, metal concentration, dissolved oxygen
Soil	Alpine soils	pH, cation exchange capacity, base saturation
Visibility	High-usage vista	Contrast, visual range, coloration
Cultural/Archaeological Values	Pictographs	Decomposition rate
Odor	Popular hiking trails	Ozone odor

report provided to the EPA by the Grand Canyon Visibility Transport Commission (GCVTC 1996a, 1996b, 1996c).

Grand Canyon Visibility Transport Commission: Recommendations

As a part of the Clean Air Act Amendments of 1990, congress established the Grand Canyon Visibility Transport Commission in 1991 to advise the EPA on strategies for protecting visual air quality at national parks and wilderness areas on the Colorado Plateau. On June 10, 1996, the Commission submitted recommendations that were aimed at protecting clear days and reducing dirty days at national parks and wilderness areas on the Colorado Plateau (GCVTC 1996a, 1996b, 1996c). Some of the Commission's recommendations that are important to wildland fire management include the following:

Clean Air Corridors   The Commission recommends careful tracking of emissions growth that may affect air quality in these corridors.

Areas In and Near Class I Areas   The Commission recommends that local, state, tribal, federal, and private parties cooperatively develop strategies, expand data collection, and improve modeling for reducing or preventing visibility impairment in areas within and adjacent to parks and wilderness areas.

Fire   The Commission recognizes that fire plays a significant role in visibility on the Plateau. In fact, land managers propose aggressive prescribed fire programs aimed at correcting the build-up of biomass due to decades of fire suppression. Therefore, prescribed fire and wildfire levels are projected to increase significantly during the coming years. The Commission recommends the implementation of pro-

grams to minimize emissions and visibility impacts from prescribed fire, as well as to educate the public.

Future Regional Coordinating Entity   Finally, the Commission believes there is a need for an entity like the Commission to oversee, promote, and support many of the recommendations in this report.

Since the Commission recognized the impact of wildland fires on visibility, the EPA prepared the Interim Air Quality Policy on Wildland and Prescribed Fire. This policy had been prepared in response to plans by some federal, tribal, and state wildland owners/managers to significantly increase the use of wildland and prescribed fires to achieve resource benefits in the wildlands. The policy statement integrates two public policy goals: (1) to allow fire to function, as nearly as possible, in its natural role in maintaining healthy wildland ecosystems; and (2) to protect public health and welfare by mitigating the impacts of air pollutant emissions on air quality and visibility.

This policy document provides guidance on mitigating air pollution impacts caused by fires in the wildlands and the wildland–urban interface. The EPA does not directly regulate the use of fire within a state or on Indian lands. Rather, the EPA's authority is to enforce the provisions of the Clean Air Act, which requires states and tribes to attain and maintain the National Ambient Air Quality Standards adopted to protect public health and welfare. This policy recommends that states/tribes implement Smoke Management Programs to mitigate the public health and welfare impacts of fires managed for resource benefits.

Federal land management agencies sometimes manage naturally ignited fires to achieve resource benefits. Planning for naturally ignited fires is obviously limited, but the agencies require fire management plans to be included in land use plans for an area before a naturally ignited fire can be managed for resource benefits. Fires ignited in areas without fire management plans are unwanted or wildfires.

This policy does not apply to open burning of agricultural waste, crop residue, or land in the United States Department of Agriculture, Conservation Reserve Program. The EPA worked with the United States Department of Agriculture, Agriculture Air Quality Task Force to develop equitable policies for emissions from activities that could be classified as agricultural burning.

The Western Regional Air Partnership Policy on Categorizing Fire Emissions

The Western Regional Air Partnership, as the successor to the Grand Canyon Visibility Transport Commission, is charged with implementing the commission recommendations as well as addressing broader air quality issues, such as the Regional Haze Rule. The EPA recognizes the Western Regional Air Partnership as the regional planning organization that is developing the guidance and means to implement the Rule in the Western Regional Air Partnership region.

There are a number of sources that the EPA has identified as potential contributors to natural background conditions, one of which is fire. The Regional Haze Rule Preamble stipulates that fire of all kinds contributes to regional haze and that fire can have both natural and human-caused sources. The Preamble further states that some fire that is human ignited may be included in a state's or tribe's determination of natural background conditions.

Under the Policy, most fire emissions sources are classified "anthropogenic," which is in keeping with the Rule's primary objective of the development of long-term strategies for reducing emissions of visibility-impairing pollutants. However, some fire emissions sources are classified as "natural" in recognition of fire's inherent occurrence as part of the landscape.

The Western Regional Air Partnership approved a guidance document that states:

- All fires must be managed to minimize visibility impacts.
- All emissions from fires classified as an "anthropogenic" source will be controlled to the maximum extent feasible, subject to economic, safety, technical, and environmental considerations.
- Emissions from all fires will be tracked.
- Prescribed fire is an "anthropogenic" source, except where it is utilized to maintain an ecosystem that is currently in an ecologically functional and fire-resilient condition, which is classified as a "natural" source.
- Wildfire that is suppressed by management action is a "natural" source. Wildfire, when suppression is limited for safety, economic, or resource limitations, remains a "natural" source. Wildfires managed for resource objectives are classified the same as prescribed.
- Native American cultural burning for traditional, religious, and ceremonial purposes is a "natural" source.

This will provide states and tribes an equitable and practical method for determining which fire emissions will be considered part of the natural background conditions in federal Class I areas. In so doing, the Policy will enable states and tribes to address natural reductions of visibility from fire as well as identify those fire emissions that need to be controlled to achieve progress toward the 2064 natural conditions goal. The Fire Emission Joint Forum, working under the Western Regional Air Partnership, has also developed policy and technical tools that will support this Policy and its implementation, such as: guidance on Enhanced Smoke Management Program elements, recommendations for creation of an annual emissions goal, availability and feasibility of alternatives to burning, recommendations for managing fire emissions sources, guidance for feasibility determinations, a methodology for tracking fire emissions, and a stepwise progression for the Program Management elements of the Policy (Fire Emission Joint Forum 2002).

The Enhanced Smoke Management Program elements are: authorization to burn, minimizing air pollution emissions, smoke management components of burn plans, public education and awareness, surveillance and enforcement, program evaluation and reporting, air quality monitoring, evaluation of smoke dispersion, and regional coordination.

California Clean Air Act

The California Air Resources Board (CARB) administers the California Clean Air Act of 1988. CARB added several requirements concerning plans and control measures to attain and maintain the state ambient air quality standards. One such requirement is for the board to establish designation criteria and to designate areas of the state as *attainment, non-attainment,* or *unclassified* for any state standards. Table 21.6 shows the state and national standards for six criteria pollutants. California has also established ambient air quality standards for sulfate, hydrogen sulfide, vinyl chloride, and visibility-reducing particles.

The states have direct responsibility for meeting requirements of the Federal Clean Air Act and corresponding federal regulations. As authorized by Division 26 of the California Health and Safety Code, CARB is directly responsible for regulating emissions from mobile sources. However, authority to regulate stationary sources has been delegated to Air Pollution Control and Air Quality Management Districts at the county and regional levels. The state still has an oversight authority to monitor the performance of district programs and can even assume authority to monitor the performance of district programs. It can even assume authority to conduct district functions if the district fails to meet certain responsibilities.

California Air Basin and Air Pollution Control Districts

California contains a wide variety of climates, physical features, and emission sources adding complexity to tasks leading to improvement in air quality. To better manage the air quality

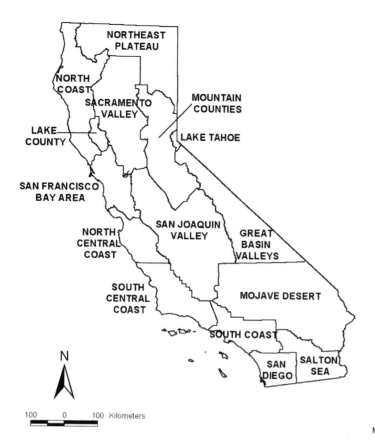

MAP 21.3. California air basins.

problems, California is divided into 15 air basins as shown in Map 21.3. An air basin has similar meteorological and geographical conditions and thus is supposed to be similar in air quality. Most of the boundary lines follow along political county lines though air moves freely from basin to basin. As a result, pollutants such as ozone and PM_{10} can be transported across air basin boundaries. Thus, interbasin/interregional transport needs to be addressed by the state.

California is divided into 35 Air Pollution Control Districts or Air Quality Management Districts. California is a diverse state with many sources of air pollution. To estimate the sources and quantities of pollution, CARB, in cooperation with Air Pollution Control Districts/Air Quality Management Districts and industry, maintains an inventory of emission sources. These sources are divided into four categories. *Stationary* source emissions are based on estimates made by the Air Pollution Control Districts. *Area-wide* emissions are estimated by CARB and staff. Prescribed fire and wildfire use come under this category. *Mobile* source emissions are regulated and estimated by CARB. *Natural* sources are estimated by CARB staff and air districts. Wildfires are classified under this category.

Title 17 Revision

California's agricultural burning guidelines were established in 1971 in response to statewide legislation that recognized the need to reduce the harmful health effects

caused by smoke from unrestrained open burning of vegetative material on public and private lands. CARB amended the guidelines in 2000 to elevate the importance of smoke management planning, collaboration, and consultation between burners, including federal and state land management agencies, and air agencies. CARB and the state's 35 Air Pollution Control Districts/Air Quality Management Districts are responsible for administering the guidelines. CARB has oversight authority and assists Air Pollution Control Districts through daily forecasts to make daily burn/no-burn decisions.

CARB issued Title 17 guidelines for updating California's prescribed burning regulations in March, 2000, with the following two objectives: (1) to accommodate large increases in prescribed burning without unacceptable decreases in air quality, and (2) to define a workable management plan for California's smoke management by working with all affected parties, local air districts, land management agencies, private industry, and the public. The revised guidelines also respond to the requirements of the EPA's Interim Air Quality Policy on Wildland and Prescribed Fires (CARB 2003).

California Nuisance Rule

The nuisance rule states, "No person shall discharge from any source whatsoever such quantities of air contaminants or other material which cause injury, detriment, nuisance, or annoyance to any considerable number of persons or to the public or which endanger the comfort, repose, health or safety of any such persons or the public or which cause, or which have a natural tendency to cause, injure or damage to business or property." The rule can lead to the shutting down of wildland burns if smoke becomes a nuisance, even if emissions concentrations are within the standards.

Nuisance smoke is defined by the EPA as the amount of smoke in the ambient air that interferes with a right or privilege common to members of the public, including the use or enjoyment of public or private resources (US EPA 1990).

Air Quality Trends

Ozone levels have improved in California over the last two decades. However, despite aggressive state emission controls, maximum measured ozone concentrations are still above the state standards in 11 air basins and federal standards in 9. Highest ozone concentrations occur in the anterior portion of the South Coast air basin where peak 1-hour indicator is more than twice the state standard indicating mobile and industrial sources being the biggest contributor to the problem. Ozone concentrations are lower near the coast and in rural areas. This can be explained in part by the characteristics of ozone, including pollutant reactivity, transport, and deposition. Based on the current ozone concentrations, substantial additional emission control measures will be needed (including on wildland fires that have potential to substantially contribute ozone precursors, nitrogen oxides, and hydrocarbons) to attain the standard (CARB 2002). Rise in ozone concentrations increases the potential for alterations to the structure and function of ecosystems (Miller et al. 1989, Plymale et al. 2003, Procter et al. 2003).

CARB (2002) projected baseline emissions for agricultural and prescribed burning emissions to reach maximum by 2010 and then level off at 81, 14, 1,394, and 136 tons per day of Reactive Organic Gases (ROG), nitrogen oxides, PM_{10}, and carbon monoxide respectively.

Smoke management requires collaborative efforts between land managers and air regulators. They are the key operators that can develop strategies leading to a reduction of smoke emissions. Smoke management strategies are described as follows from both air regulator and land manager points of view, CARB (2002) and Hardy et al. (2001).

Air Regulator Strategies

To reduce the impacts of smoke emissions from wood burning, CARB (2002) has proposed two strategies—targeting residential wood combustion and smoke management. This section focuses on the second strategy that considers changes to the meteorological criteria used to declare burn days in order to reduce health- and visibility-related impacts of smoke while minimizing the potential for catastrophic wildfires in forests.

Agricultural burning refers to the intentional use of fire for removal of vegetation waste, disease and pest prevention, forest operations, and range improvement in areas such as agricultural fields, orchards, and wildlands. *Prescribed burning* is a subset of agricultural burning and consists of fires intentionally ignited to meet specific land management objectives.

In 1998, approximately 1.6 million acres of agricultural burning occurred in California, of which 208,000 acres were treated using prescribed burning by federal and state land management agencies, the U.S. military, the California Department of Forestry and Fire Protection, and timber companies. CARB staff estimates that while agricultural burning acreage is expected to remain the same, or decrease slightly, federal land management agencies predict a substantial increase in prescribed burning in order to prevent catastrophic wildfires (National Interagency Fire Center 2001, 2002).

California's agricultural burning guidelines were established in 1971. They were adopted in response to statewide legislation that recognized the need to reduce the harmful health effects caused by smoke from unrestrained open burning of vegetative material on public and private lands (Subchapter 2, Chapter 1, Division 3, Title 17, California Code of Regulations). In March 2000, CARB amended the guidelines. These amendments place primary emphasis on smoke management through improved planning, collaboration, and consultation between burners, including federal and state land management agencies, and air agencies. The amendments contain new basic provisions like: requirements for a "burn authorization system," requirements for a "smoke management plan," requirements for "post-burn evaluations and monitoring" for large burns, and provisions for the use of a "marginal" burn day. CARB is planning to develop a Prescribed Fire Incident Reporting System (PFIRS) that will allow burners and regulators to plan burns that will help prevent violations of standards and reduce nuisance calls. Monitoring of burns (Ahuja 2002) will help strategize future planning.

The objective of the proposed strategy is to ensure that agricultural and prescribed burning shall not take place on days forecasted to exceed either the state or federal standards.

This proposed strategy would not reduce emissions from agricultural and prescribed burning but would ensure that burning does not inadvertently exceed either the state or federal standards.

Land Management Strategies

Effective strategies must include techniques that reduce emissions. Emission reduction techniques vary widely in their applicability and effectiveness by vegetation type, objective, county or region, and whether fuel is natural or activity generated (Ottmar et al. 2001). Emission reduction techniques can cause negative effects on other resources such as through soil compaction, loss of nutrients, impaired water quality, and increased tree mortality.

According to Hardy et al. (2002) there are two general strategies to managing wildland fire smoke: (1) emission reduction and (2) emission redistribution. Twenty-nine emission reduction and emission redistribution methods within seven major classifications were identified by Hardy et al. (2002).

Emission Reduction Strategies

All pollutants except nitrous oxide are negatively correlated with combustion efficiency, so actions that reduce one pollutant result in the reduction of all (except nitrogen oxides). Nitrous oxide and carbon monoxide can increase if the emission reduction technique increases combustion efficiency. Optimal use of reduction techniques can reduce emissions by approximately 20%–25%, assuming all other factors (vegetation types, acres, etc.) were held constant and land management goals were still met. Hardy et al. (2001) describe the following strategies to effectively reduce emissions:

Reducing the Area Burned   Area burned can be reduced by not burning or by burning a subset of the area within the project boundary. Specific techniques include burn concentrations, fuel isolation, and mosaic burning within the treatment area. The area reduction does not mean deferral of emissions to some future date. This technique has limited application to restoring ecosystem function in fire-adapted vegetation types and is least applicable when fire is needed for ecosystem or habitat management, or forest health enhancement (Hardy et al. 2001).

Reducing Fuel Loading   Methods like mechanical removal, mechanical processing, firewood sales, biomass removal for electrical power generation, grazing, site conversion, and land use change can be used to reduce the fuel.

Reducing Fuel Production   Chemical treatment can shift species composition to vegetation types that produce less biomass per acre per year, or produce biomass that is less likely to burn or that burns more efficiently with less smoke.

Reducing Fuel Consumption   Burning during high moisture in large woody fuel, or moist duff layer, and before large fuel cure can lead to less fuel consumption. Real emission reductions are achieved only if the fuel left behind will biologically decompose or be otherwise sequestered at a time of subsequent burning.

Schedule Burning before New Fuel Appears   Burning before litter fall and green-up can result in less fuel consumption and less emissions being produced.

Increasing Combustion Efficiency   Burning in piles, using backing fires, burning under dry conditions, rapidly mopping-up, aerial ignition, and burning fuel in a large metal container or pit with a fan-like device can lead to increased flaming phase and reduced smoldering phase. This shift can result in less emissions being produced.

Emission Redistribution Strategy

Title 17 requires the burning to be conducted on a burn day designated by the local Air Pollution Control Districts. Regulators generally authorize a burn based on redistribution strategy on a day forecast to be a *burn day*. This is often the most effective way to prevent direct smoke impacts to the public or sensitive areas. Emissions can be spatially and temporally redistributed by burning during periods of good atmospheric dispersion (*dilution*) and when prevailing winds will transport smoke away from sensitive areas (*avoidance*) so that air quality standards are not violated. Using this strategy, total emissions are not necessarily reduced though impact to the receptor site is.

Strategies that are commonly applied to achieve the redistribution/avoidance of emissions are: burning when dispersion is good, sharing the air basins, burning more frequently, burning in smaller units, especially in non-attainment areas, and avoiding sensitive areas.

Summary

California is a highly diverse state with more than one third of its area in non-attainment for PM_{10} and ozone national ambient air quality standards. Air regulators are concerned about allowing burning without application of alternatives to burning in those areas. Land managers are concerned about the use of other treatments that do not replicate the ecological role that fire plays in the environment. Land managers are also concerned that any constraints placed by regulators like California and Nevada Air Consortium (CANSAC) on fuel reduction projects will reduce their ability to achieve reduction in large, more intense wildfires There is a need to develop coordination among land managers and regulators. Air quality regulators and land managers must work together to better understand the effectiveness, options, difficulties, applicability, and trade-offs of emission reduction techniques. CARB, with the cooperation of other agencies, is developing a centralized reporting system (Prescribed Fire Incident Reporting System). This system will help burners, local regulators, and the public in air quality smoke management planning and decision making.

Land managers and regulators have developed strategies to reduce the impacts on air quality that result from fire. Current knowledge of air quality impacts from fire has increased, though current models and tools like Blue Sky (www.airfare.org/bluesky/) to estimate emissions lack precision (Fox and Riebau 2000). Additionally, the linkage of Geographic Information Systems to emission production, meteorology, and dispersion models needs further development. Fire emissions lead to ozone formation and nitrogen deposition. Fire contribution to ozone and nitrogen deposition needs more research. Models predicting these and their quantitative impacts to biological processes need refinement for the proper utilization of fire in ecological management. The Fire Emission Trade-off Model can predict reduction in emissions achieved when prescribed fires are applied to landscape to prevent large-intensity wildfires. This model is new and needs more field validation.

References

40 CFR Part 51. Vol. 64 No. 126. Regional Haze Regulations—Final Rule. July 1, 1999.

Ahuja, S. 2002. Monitoring fire emissions to notify the public—mobile monitoring. Association for Fire Ecology Miscellaneous Publication No. 1:45–49.

Air Sciences Inc. 2002. Draft final report—1996 Fire Emission Inventory. WGA/WRAP.

CARB 2002. Air Resources Board's Clean Air Plan: Strategies for a Healthy Future. Volume I. Basic and Impacts. 2002.

CARB 2002. Air Resources Board's Clean Air Plan: Strategies for a Healthy Future 2002–2020. Volume II. (Marvin, Cynthia). 2002.

CARB 2002. Emissions Inventory Data. http://www.arb.ca.gov/ei/emissiondata.htm.

CARB 2006. Non-Attainment Area Maps for $PM_{2.5}$ and Ozone. http://www.arb.ca.gov/smp/progdev/alm/alm.htm.

Ferguson, S. A., J. Peterson, and A. Acheson. 2001. Automated, real-time predictions of cumulative smoke impacts from prescribed forest and agricultural fires. P. 168–175 in Fourth symposium on fire and forest meteorology. American Meteorological Society, Boston, MA.

Fire Emissions Joint Forum. 2002. WRAP policy: enhanced smoke management programs for visibility, http://www.wrapair.org/forums/FEJF/esmptt/policv/WRAP ESMP Policy O90202.pdf. [September 2002].

Fox, D. G., and A. R. Riebau. 2000. Technically advanced smoke estimation tools (TASET). Final report. Colorado State University, Cooperative Institute for Research in the Atmosphere, Fort Collins, CO. 99 p.

Grand Canyon Visibility Transport Commission. 1996a. Alternative assessment committee report. Western Governors' Association, Denver, CO.

Grand Canyon Visibility Transport Commission. 1996b. Recommendations for improving western vistas. Western Governors' Association, Denver, CO.

Grand Canyon Visibility Transport Commission. 1996c. Report of the Grand Canyon Visibility Transport Commission to the United States Environmental Protection Agency (1996). Western Governors' Association, Denver, CO. 85 p.

Hardy, C. C., S. G. Conard, J. C. Regelbrugge, and D. T. Teesdale. 1996. Smoke emissions from prescribed burning of southern California chaparral. Res. Pap. PNW-RP-486. USDA Forest Service, Pacific Northwest Research Station, Portland, OR. 37 p.

Hardy, C. C., and B. Leenhouts. 2001. Why do we need a Smoke Management Guide, in Hardy et al. (eds.). Smoke Management Guide for Prescribed and Wildland Fire; 2001 edition. PMS 420-2. National Wildfire Coordinating group, Boise, ID. 226 p.

Hardy, C. C., R. D. Ottmar, J. L. Peterson, J. E. Core, and P. Seamon (comps., eds.). 2001. Smoke management guide for prescribed and wildland fire: 2001 edition. PMS 420-2. National Wildfire Coordinating Group, Boise, ID. 226 p.

IMPROVE. 1994. Visibility protection. Interagency monitoring of protected visual environments brochure. Ft. Collins, CO. August 1994. Available at: ww2.nature.nps.gov/ard/impr/index.htm.

Kane, L. E., and Y. Alarie. 1977. Sensory irritation to formaldehyde and acrolein during single and repeated exposures in mice. American Industrial Hygiene Association Journal 38(10): 509–522.

Malm, W. C. 1999. Introduction to visibility. Cooperative Institute for Research in the Atmosphere. NPS Visibility Program, Colorado State University, Fort Collins, CO. 79 p.

Miller, P., J. McBride, S. Schilling, and A. Gomez. 1989. Trends of ozone damage to conifer forests between 1974 and 1988 in the San Bernardino Mountains of southern California. P. 309–323 in Pro. air pollution effects on western forests. 32nd Ann. Mtg. Air Waste Manag. Assoc.

National Interagency Fire Center. 2001. Prescribed fire statistics. http://www.nifc.gov/stats/prescribedfirestats.htnil. [August 8, 2002]

National Interagency Fire Center. 2002. Wildland fires statistics. http://www.nifc.gov/stats/wildlandfirestats.html. [October 5, 2002]

National Park Service. 1997. Visibility protection. National Park Service Air Resources Division Web Page. Available at www.nature.nps.gov/ard/vis/visprot.html.

National Wildfire Coordinating Group. 1985. Smoke management guide. PNW 420-2. NFES 1279. National Interagency Fire Center, National Interagency Coordinating Group, Prescribed Fire and Fire Effects Working Team, Boise, ID. 28 p.

Ottmar, R. D., et al. 2001 Smoke management techniques to reduce or redistribute emissions, in Hardy et al. (eds.). Smoke Management Guide for Prescribed and Wildland Fire; 2001 edition. PMS 420-2. National Wildfire Coordinating group, Boise, ID. 226 p.

Peterson, J. L., and D. Ward. 1992. An inventory of particulate matter and air toxic emissions from prescribed fires in the United States for 1989. Final report. U.S. EPA Office of Air Quality Programs and Standards.

Plymale, E., M. Arbaugh, T. Procter, S. Ahuja, G. Smith, and P. Temple. 2003. Towards an air pollution effects monitoring system for the Sierra Nevada. Development in Env. Sci. 2:285–298.

Procter, T., S. Ahuja, and M. McCorison. 2003. Managing air pollution effected forests in the Sierra Nevada. Development in Env. Sci. 2:359–370.

Public Law 88-206. Clean Air Act of 1963. Act of December 17, 1963, 77 Stat. 392.

Public Law 90-148. Air Quality Act of 1967. Act of November 1, 1967. 42 U.S.C. 7401. 81 Stat. 485, 501.

Public Law 91-604. Clean Air Act Amendments of 1970. Act of December 31, 1970. 42 USC 1857h-7 et seq.

Public Law 95-95. Clean Air Act as Amended August 1977. 42 U.S.C. s/s 1857 et seq.

Public Law 101-549. Clean Air Act as amended. November 15, 1990. 104 Stat. 2399.

Reinhardt, E. D., R. E. Keane, and J. K. Brown. 1997. First order fire effects model: FOFEM 4.0, users guide. Gen. Tech. Rep. INT-GTR-344. USDA Forest Service, Intermountain Research Station, Ogden, UT. 65 p.

Reinhardt, T. E. 2000. Effects of smoke on wildland firefighters. URS/Radian International, Seattle, WA.

Reinhardt, T. E. R. D. Ottmar, and A. J. S. Hanneman. 2000. Smoke exposure among firefighters at prescribed burns in the Pacific Northwest. Res. Pap. PNW-RP-526. USDA Forest Service, Pacific Northwest Research Station, Portland, OR. 45 p.

Ryan, P. W., and C. K. McMahon. 1976. Some chemical characteristics of emissions from forest fires. In Proceedings of the 69th annual meeting of the air pollution control association, Portland, OR. Air Pollution Control Association, Pittsburgh, PA. Paper No. 76-2.3.

Sandberg, D. V., J. M. Bierovich, D. G. Fox, and E. W. Ross. 1979. Effects of fire on air: a state-of-knowledge review. Gen. Tech. Rep. WO-9. USDA Forest Service. 40 p.

Sharkey, B. (ed.). 1997. Health hazards of smoke: recommendations of the April 1997 consensus conference. Tech. Rep. 9751-2836-MTDC. USDA Forest Service, Missoula Technology and Development Center, Missoula, MT. 84 p.

U.S. Department of Agriculture and U.S. Department of the Interior. 2000. A report to the President in response to the wildfires of 2000. http://www.fireplan.gov/president.cfm. [September 2002]

U.S. Department of Labor, Occupational Safety and Health Administration. 1987. Occupational exposure to formaldehyde, final rule. Federal Register 52(233): 46312, Washington DC. 1987.

U.S. Environmental Protection Agency. 1990. Air quality criteria for particulate matter, vol. II of III (p. 8-82–8-89). Office of Research and Development. EPA/600/P-95/OOibF.

U.S. Environmental Protection Agency. 1999. Guideline for reporting of daily air quality—air quality index (AQI). EPA-454/R-99-010. Office of Air Quality Planning and Standards, Research Triangle Park, NC. 25 p.

U.S. Environmental Protection Agency. 2000a. Compilation of air pollutant emission factors AP-42, fifth edition, volume I: stationary point and area sources. U.S. Environmental Protection Agency, Research Triangle Park, NC. January 1995–September 2000. AP-42 reference.

U.S. Environmental Protection Agency. 2000b. National ambient air quality standards (NAAQS). http://www.epa.gov/airs/ criteria.html. [5 December 2000]

Ward, D. E. 1990. Airborne monitoring and smoke characterization of prescribed fires on forest lands in western Washington and Oregon. Gen. Tech. Rep. PNW-GTR-251. Portland, OR.

Ward, D.E., and C.C. Hardy. 1991. Smoke emissions from wildland fires. Environmental International. 17:117–134.

Model: FOFEM 4.0, users guide. Gen. Tech. Rep. INT-GTR-344. Ogden, UT: USDA Forest Service, Intermountain Research Station. 65 p.

Western Governors' Association. 2001. A collaborative approach for reducing wildland fire risks to communities and the environment: 10-year comprehensive strategy, http://www.westgov.org/ wga/imtiatives/fire/final fire rpt.pdf. [August 2001]

CHAPTER 22

Fire and Invasive Plant Species

ROBERT C. KLINGER, MATTHEW L. BROOKS,
AND JOHN M. RANDALL

Just as there is honor among thieves, so there is solidarity and
co-operation among plant and animal pests. Where one pest is
stopped by natural barriers, another arrives to breach the same
wall by a new approach. In the end every region and every
resource get their quota of uninvited ecological guests.

ALDO LEOPOLD, 1949

One of the most significant issues in conservation is the effect
of invasive species on natural communities and ecosystems.
Conservation scientists generally agree that only habitat
destruction poses a greater threat to native biological diversity
and the integrity of ecosystems (Wilcove et al. 1998, Mack
et al. 2000). Invasive species can have impacts on populations
of individual species as well as entire communities (Vitousek
et al. 1996, Lonsadale 1999). In recent years, their impact on
ecosystem processes, including fire regimes, has been increasingly well documented (Mack and D'Antonio 1998, Mack
et al. 2001). Although these impacts are varied and sometimes
poorly understood (Parker et al. 1999), there is no argument
that invasive species have long-term implications for management of many (or even most) natural areas. In a world
where biological diversity is considered imperiled, the transformation of ecological interactions and ecosystem properties
by invasive species poses both an immediate and a chronic
threat to preservation, management, and restoration of parks,
refuges, and reserves (Harty 1986, Gordon 1998).

Interest regarding the interrelationship between invasive
species and fire is not a recent phenomenon. A small number
of papers appeared sporadically from the 1930s to the 1970s
(Pickford 1932, Hervey 1949, Furbush 1953, Sharp et al. 1957,
Daubenmire 1968, Young and Evans 1971, Heady 1972, Vogl
1974). These papers were mainly reviews or short observa-
tional studies (≤1 year), and focused primarily on range
degradation in grasslands and prairies of the central and western United States. Since the early 1990s, the publication rate
of studies on fire and invasive species has increased exponentially (Fig. 22.1), as has the geographic scope, method of
study, and emphasis of research (see Table 1 in D'Antonio
2000 for an overview). Most reviews on invasive species and
fire have been written in the last 12 years. D'Antonio and
Vitousek (1992), Mack and D'Antonio (1998), D'Antonio
(2000), D'Antonio et al. (2000), and Brooks et al. (2004) focus
primarily on general patterns of how invasive species have

altered fire regimes and other ecosystem processes throughout
the world. Regional patterns from North America were
reviewed in a series of papers from a 2000 workshop on the
relationship between fire and invasive species (Galley and
Wilson 2001). Keeley (2006) discussed fire management and
invasive plant issues in conifer forests and shrublands in the
western United States. Although our understanding of the
interaction between fire and invasive species has rapidly
increased in the last decade, it is important to note that it is
one of the "youngest" areas of study on fire and ecology. Consequently, many variations to some of the seemingly general
patterns that have emerged in the last decade will likely be
found.

The management of fire and invasive plants creates unique
challenges. Fire occurs (or occurred) naturally in many
ecosystems, and there have been extensive changes in many
communities as a result of fire exclusion. Consequently, the
restoration of fire is often seen as a critical component for
managing natural communities where fire was a naturally
occurring process (Parsons and Debenedetti 1989, Pyne 1984,
Parsons and Swetnam 1989, Minnich et al. 1995, Biswell
1999). However, many invasive species are known to exploit
areas burned by fires (Bossard 1991, Hobbs and Huenneke
1992, Vitousek et al. 1996). By creating seedbeds and reducing competition, fire opens the way for invasion or expansion of new species. In North America, invasive non-native
species have been reported to invade burn sites and/or alter
fire regimes in most regions of the continent (Brooks and
Pyke 2001, Grace et al. 2001, Harrod and Reichard 2001,
Keeley 2001, Mueller-Dombois 2001, Richburg et al. 2001).

Plant invasions have especially affected fire regimes in
regions with mediterranean climates, such as South Africa,
Australia, Chile, southern Europe, and California. This is
especially problematic in terms of conservation because areas
with mediterranean climates contain some of the highest
recorded levels of biodiversity outside of the tropics (Wilson

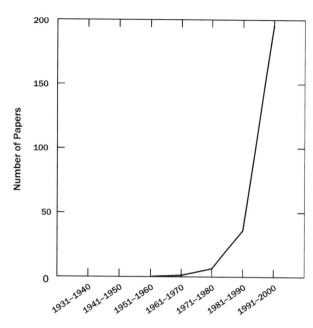

FIGURE 22.1. The number of studies published on fire and invasive species.

and Peter 1988). These regions also tend to have relatively high human population densities, and human activities both transport non-native species and disturb vegetation and soils, making systems more vulnerable to invasion. Other North American ecosystems where alteration of fire regimes by invasive species has been particularly severe include Great Basin woodlands and shrublands (Whisenant 1990), Mojave Desert scrub (Hunter 1991, Brooks 1999, Brooks and Pyke 2001), and Midwest grasslands (Grace et al. 2001).

Fire can also be an effective tool for managing some species of invasive plants (Nuzzo 1991, Lonsdale and Miller 1993, Gann and Gordon 1998, DiTomaso et al. 1999, Myers et al. 2001). Compared to other cultural and mechanical types of management (e.g., herbicides, grazing, plowing, and cutting), fire is a relatively inexpensive method that can be applied in a short period of time. The timing, frequency, and extent of burning can be managed to a certain extent. Fire is effective at killing individual plants and/or reducing aboveground biomass. But responses of plants to fire are complex, species-specific, and can vary both within a site and between sites. This complexity and variability are reflected in the outcomes of many efforts to control invasive species with fire.

In this chapter, we examine the relationship between fire and invasive species in California from three different perspectives: (1) the general interrelationships between fire and invasive plants, (2) specific examples from within or near California, and (3) the use of fire as a management tool to control non-native species. We will conclude by synthesizing these three perspectives into a more general conservation and social context. But first, we begin by discussing just what an invasive species is and identifying the species that are thought or known to present the greatest threats to conservation in California.

Invasive Species Definitions

Different authors have used different definitions for the terms *native, non-native,* and *invasive,* and some authors have not been clear about which definition they were following (Richardson et al. 2000). To avoid that problem we use the following definitions in this chapter:

Native Plant Species Those present in an area without direct or indirect human intervention, growing within their native range and natural dispersal potential. Other terms for native species include indigenous and aboriginal.

Non-native Plant Species Those whose introduction to the area under consideration was a direct or indirect result of human activity. Other terms that are often used as synonyms for non-native include *alien, exotic, introduced, adventive, non-indigenous,* and *non-aboriginal.* Many non-native plants were deliberately introduced for use in agriculture, horticulture, or forestry. Others, including some of the most common weeds of croplands and pastures, were unintentionally introduced as contaminants in seed or soil, or in the hair of domesticated animals. The distinction between locally native and non-native plants can be important in conservation. With few exceptions, conservation programs are dedicated to the preservation of native species and communities. However, in rare cases, non-native species may be deliberately introduced or maintained in a conservation area when their presence is important to management objectives, for example, in the use of non-native grazers or the introduction of selected biological control agents.

Native ranges generally do not conform to political or administrative boundaries. For example, bush lupine (*Lupinus arboreus*) is native to the state of California, but its native range is more specifically only the central and southern coasts of the state. It is a non-native plant along California's north coast, where it persists and spreads from intentional plantings outside its native range (Miller 1988, Hickman 1993, Pickart 2000).

Invasive Species Those that spread into areas where they are not native (Rejmánek 1995). Some authors, such as Cronk and Fuller (1995) and White et al. (1993), define invasive species as only those that cause significant negative ecological effects such as displacing natives or bringing about changes in species composition, community structure, or ecosystem function, but we include all non-native species that escape cultivation whether they have known harmful effects or not. However, it is important to note that not all non-native plants are invasive. In fact, only a small minority of the thousands of species introduced to California have escaped cultivation, and a minority of those that have escaped are invasive in wildlands.

Invasive Non-native Plants That Threaten Biodiversity Plants in a specified region that: (1) are present but not native there, (2) maintain themselves in conservation areas or other native species habitats, and (3) negatively affect the native species

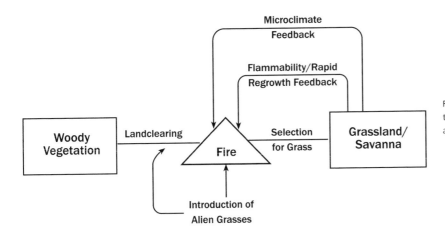

FIGURE 22.2. Schematic representation of the grass-fire cycle. (Redrawn from D'Antonio and Vitousek 1992.)

and other natural biodiversity within the region, generally by displacing or hybridizing with native species, or altering ecological communities or ecosystem processes. Similar terms include *harmful invasive* plants and *environmental weeds*.

Plants that are harmful invaders in some wildlands may not be troublesome elsewhere. For example, the empress tree *(Paulownia tomentosa)* is a pest in deciduous forests of the eastern United States, particularly in the southern Appalachians, but it is not known to escape from cultivation in California, although it is used as an ornamental landscape tree there. Some species that are troublesome in agricultural or urban areas rarely, if ever, become wildland weeds. The term *environmental weeds* is used by many Australians (Groves 1991, Humphries et al. 1991) to refer to wildland weeds, but few North America land managers or researchers use this term.

Interrelationships between Fire and Invasive Plants

General Patterns

Much of the research on fire and invasive species has focused on how fire facilitates plant invasions, and how invasive species in turn may alter fire regimes (Billings 1990, Whisenant 1990, D'Antonio and Vitousek 1992, D'Antonio 2000, D'Antonio et al. 2000, Brooks et al. 2004). Many invasive species readily exploit areas of disturbance (Hobbs and Huenneke 1992), and fire can promote invasion of non-native species into burned areas (D'Antonio 2000). As invasive species increase in abundance, plant species composition and ecosystem processes change, which in turn alters fuel characteristics and, ultimately, fire regimes (Holmes and Cowling 1997, Brooks et al. 2004).

Probably the most widespread mechanism of alteration of fire regimes by invasive species is through the "grass-fire cycle" (D'Antonio and Vitousek 1992). Invasive grass species become established in an area dominated by woody vegetation, either as a result of disturbance or, in some instances, where there has been a long history of fire suppression (Grace et al. 2001). As the invasive grasses increase in abundance, a

continuous layer of highly combustible fine fuel develops. The fine fuel has higher probability of ignition than the woody vegetation, resulting in increased fire starts, rates of fire spread, and increased fire frequency. Then, as a result of shortened fire-return intervals, areas that once were shrublands or forest dominated by native species are converted to grasslands dominated by non-natives (Fig. 22.2).

The grass-fire cycle has been reported in many parts of the world, including Hawaii, South Africa, Australia, and the western United States (D'Antonio 2000, Brooks et al. 2004, Keeley 2005). In the western United States, the most notable examples are invasion of cheat grass *(Bromus tectorum)* in the Great Basin (Mack 1981), red brome *(Bromus madritensis* ssp. *rubens)* and Mediterranean split grass *(Schismus* spp.) in the Mojave desert (Brooks 1999), and Italian ryegrass *(Lolium multiflorum)* in chaparral and coastal scrub areas of southern California (Zedler et al. 1983, Haidinger and Keeley 1993).

Examples of invasive species altering fire regimes by reducing fire frequency are far less common than examples of those that increase fire frequencies, but alteration of ecosystem properties can be as severe. In the southeastern United States, Chinese tallow *(Triadica sebifera;* synonym *Sapium sebiferum)* has invaded extensive areas of coastal prairie, marsh, and swamp along the Gulf coastal plain, forming dense thickets that suppress herbaceous species growth that would otherwise produce continuous surface fuel (Grace et al. 2001). The lowered levels of surface fuel results in reduced fire frequency, which promotes Chinese tallow dominance and leads to the establishment of nearly monotypic stands (Bruce et al. 1995).

The Fire and Invasive Plant Situation in California

During the past two decades, scientists and land managers have become increasingly aware of the magnitude of the problem biotic invasions pose to California's wildlands (Jackson 1985, Baker 1986, Rejmanek et al 1991, Randall 1996, Randall et al. 1998). Although the spread of species into new areas is a common and natural occurrence, the rate of introduction, escape from cultivation, and subsequent spread of non-native plants in California increased tremendously with the

$$Y = a/1 + (b-1)e^{-cX})$$

Hickman et al, 1993

Munz 1968

Munz & Keck 1959

Estimates by
Frenkel (1970)

Jepson 1925

Brewer et al. 1876 & Watson 1880

$$Y = ae^{bX}$$

1600
1400
1200
100
800
600
400
200

Alien Species Number

35
30
25
20
15
10
5
0

**Human Population
(in Millions)**

1700   1750   1800   1850   1900   1950   2000   2050
Year

FIGURE 22.3. The increase in invasive plant species recorded in California. (Redrawn from Randall et al. 1998.) The dashed line is from data analyzed by Randall et al. (1998) and the solid line from an earlier analysis by Frenkel (1970). Note the higher number of species considered invasive in 1998 relative to the prediction of the 1970 analysis.

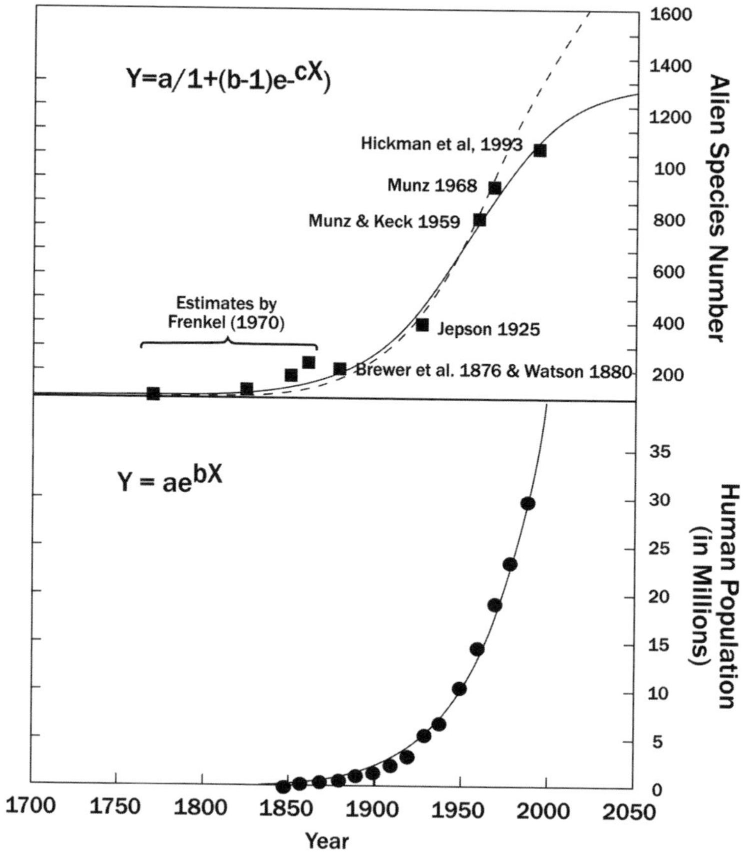

influx of European and American settlers since the late 1700s (Fig. 22.3). In just over 200 years, 1,045 intentionally and unintentionally introduced plant species have established populations outside cultivation in the state (Rejmanek and Randall 1994). The ranges of many of these species did not increase substantially beyond their points of introduction, or if their ranges did increase they never reached levels of abundance to have significant, detectable effects on natural systems. But other species did flourish, and as early as the late 1800s, major alterations to some plant communities were being noted (Mooney et al. 1989). It was not uncommon to consider some of these community-level changes to be beneficial, especially in terms of improved range forage for livestock and of erosion control. However, it was also clear that non-native species could have undesirable effects on communities.

GRASSLANDS

California's grasslands have been particularly susceptible to invasions by non-native species (Bossard et al. 2000). The native California prairie has been converted to grasslands dominated by non-native annual grasses and forbs, but it is important to note that this was not due solely to fire. Most likely it was a result of a number of interacting factors, including climate change, human disturbance, the introduction of large numbers of non-native grazing mammals by

Euro-American settlers, seed transport on the hides and in the feed of the grazers, and fire (Jackson 1985, Mack 1989, Mooney et al. 1989, Hamilton 1997). Fire alone can, but does not necessarily, promote invasion or dominance of non-native species in grassland ecosystems. The key consideration is that the overwhelming majority of grasslands in California are now dominated by non-native species (Heady 1988). Seasonality and frequency of fire play a role in the relative abundance of particular non-native species in grasslands (Foin and Hektner 1986, Meyer and Schiffman 1999), but fire alone typically does not change dominance of these systems by non-natives (Parsons and Stohlgren 1989, Klinger and Messer 2001).

Precisely how the shift in grasslands to dominance by non-native species has affected fire regimes is unknown (Heady 1988, Sims and Risser 2000; see also Chapters 8, 9, 14, 15). The size of fires in these grasslands has likely decreased as a result of fire suppression and reduced fuel continuity caused by anthropogenic features arising from agriculture and urban developments. However, it is unknown if the frequency, intensity, or seasonality of fire has changed since the region was settled in the 1700s and 1800s (see Chapter 9).

Although many of the non-native species in California grasslands are highly invasive (Heady 1988), this has not resulted in any single non-native species having a particularly strong individual effect on fire behavior. For example, yellow star-thistle (*Centaurea solstitialis*) is one of the most invasive species in California grasslands, but it has had relatively little effect on fire regimes. Fire behavior in California's grasslands is generally determined by the assemblage of herbaceous species, and there is little dispute that non-native annual grasses comprise the most important fuel type in the system.

MEDITERRANEAN SHRUBLANDS

In contrast with California's grasslands, fire has certainly played a central role in the conversion of native-dominated shrublands into grasslands dominated by non-native species (Keeley 2001). Type conversion of shrublands to grasslands is a major concern in southern California, especially in chaparral and coastal scrub ecosystems (Keeley 2006). These ecosystems are relatively intact shrub communities (i.e., where the horizontal and vertical arrangement of vegetation is relatively continuous) and have relatively few non-native species. Two interrelated mechanisms have led to widespread conversion of chaparral and coastal scrub communities to grasslands in southern California: (1) greater fragmentation of shrub patches as a result of urbanization, and (2) an increase in fire frequency, especially fires started by humans after long periods of fire suppression and the subsequent buildup of fuel.

Many shrub communities in California are fire adapted, with a fire-return interval of 20 to 50 years (Wright and Bailey 1982, Biswell 1999, Caprio and Lineback 2002). If fire-return intervals remain within this range, invasive non-native plants can become *established* in the burned area, but it is difficult for them to *persist*. This is because most non-native species that invade burned areas are herbaceous and not shade tolerant. As the canopy closes in, the non-native species that have become established are shaded out.

However, when fire-return intervals decrease to just 1 to 15 years, the more-frequent fires kill many shrub seedlings and saplings and may stunt or even kill resprouting adults. The end result is that the shrub canopy cannot re-establish, and invasive non-native herbaceous species (mainly annual grasses and forbs) become the community dominants. Once dense stands of grass develop, it becomes extremely difficult for woody and herbaceous native species to become established and regenerate (Schultz et al. 1955, Eliason and Allen 1997). When a stand of chaparral or coastal scrub is converted to grassland, not only is the woody community lost but also the community that replaces it is comprised primarily of non-native species.

This situation has been exacerbated by management programs in which non-native herbaceous species swamp out native species that would normally regenerate in the burned areas. The most common way for this to occur is when seeds of non-native grasses and forbs are spread across burned sites to prevent erosion in the first months and years following a fire (Beyers et al. 1998). This practice has been shown to be of little benefit (Conrad et al. 1995), and it is uncommon for it to now occur. Unfortunately, previously seeded areas continue to be dominated by non-natives. These areas act as propagule sources for non-native species, particularly where chaparral and coastal scrub vegetation is already highly fragmented (Zedler 1995, Allen 1998).

There appears to be a negative relationship between the distance of a burned area from areas infested with non-native species and rates of invasion into the burn (Giessow and Zedler 1996, Merriam et al. 2006). This is important in areas fragmented by urban development, especially for smaller burns with a high edge/area ratio. Fragmented stands are often in close proximity to degraded plant communities with a high proportion of invasive species. When these fragments burn, invasion rates into them from surrounding degraded vegetation can be very high (Allen 1998, Minnich and Dezzani 1998).

In addition, fire suppression activities (e.g., fuel break construction, heavy equipment and vehicle use) can create corridors or act as vectors of transport that invasive species can exploit (Giessow and Zedler 1996). There is increasing evidence this situation is widespread and severe (Stylinski and Allen 1999, Backer et al. 2004, Merriam et al. 2006).

DESERT SHRUBLANDS AND WOODLANDS

The invasion of cheat grass into the Great Basin Desert of eastern Oregon, Idaho, and Nevada and its effect on fire regimes has been well studied (see Chapter 16, Sidebar 16.1). Although relatively few of those studies have been conducted in the Great Basin regions of eastern California, there is little doubt that similar alteration in vegetation structure and fire regimes has resulted there.

In contrast to the changes in fire regimes in the Great Basin resulting predominantly from cheat grass, changes in the Mojave Desert have resulted from invasion by red brome, cheat grass, and to a lesser extent, Mediterranean split grass (Chapter 16, Sidebar 16.1). These species were introduced into the Mojave Desert through livestock grazing, military activities, or off-road vehicle use (Brooks and Pyke 2001), and have spread throughout the region. These invasive annual grasses produce fuel that is more persistent and continuous than fuel produced by native annuals (Brooks 1999), facilitating the spread of fire where fire was previously infrequent (Brooks and Pyke 2001; Fig. 22.4).

In shrub-steppe communities of the Great Basin there is an example of a *native* species invading areas and altering fire regimes. Juniper trees *(Juniperus occidentalis)* and pinyon pine *(Pinus monophylla, P. quadrifolia)* have increased in distribution in western North America (Miller and Tausch 2001). The expansion of juniper and pinyon woodland may have been initially due to fire suppression programs and livestock grazing, which reduced fire frequency. As the forest canopy closed, cover of herbaceous species and small shrubs was reduced as trees overtopped them. With the increase in coarse woody fuel, fire intensity has also increased. This can result in stand-replacement fires, which may be followed by invasions by non-native annual grass species (such as cheat grass) into the burned areas. It is unclear whether this dynamic is as prevalent

FIGURE 22.4. Burned/invaded creosotebush scrub (A) compared with unburned/uninvaded creosostebush scrub (B) in the Opal Mountain region of the central Mojave Desert in California. Non-native annual grasses have rapidly invaded and now dominate the burned area.

in California as it is elsewhere in western North America. However, it seems much more plausible to occur in the Great Basin regions of California than in the more southerly Mojave and Colorado desert regions, where low rainfall rather than lengthened fire-return intervals is more likely the limiting factor to the downslope spread of pinyon-juniper woodlands.

CONIFEROUS FORESTS

Fire regimes in montane conifer forest ecosystems have been drastically altered by fire exclusion practices, but invasive species have not invaded these ecosystems in great numbers and have had relatively little effect on their fire regimes (Keeley 2001, Klinger et al. 2006). Most invasive species in montane conifer forests are herbaceous, although there are concerns that some woody non-native species present potentially severe threats as well. These include scotch broom (*Cytisus scoparius*), salt cedar (*Tamarix* spp.), Russian olive (*Elaeagnus angustifolia*), and tree-of-heaven (*Ailanthus altissima*) (Schwartz et al. 1996).

An important aspect of the relatively low rates of invasion into montane conifer forests is that there is a negative relationship between elevation and non-native species richness (Schwartz et al. 1996, Randall et al. 1998, Keeley 2001, Klinger et al. 2006). Factors that may reduce the likelihood of establishment by invasive species in higher-elevation plant communities include less activity by humans, relatively intact shrub and tree canopies, and relatively harsh climates and other physical conditions. Presumably, reduced human activity would result in reduced propagule pressure (Schwartz et al. 1996, Randall et al. 1998). It is telling that sites in montane conifer forests where invasive species have become established and are relatively abundant are usually those that had previously been disturbed by human activities (Harrod and Reichard 2001).

Preliminary data suggest that invasive species are more abundant in conifer forests where the canopy is broken (Crawford et al. 2001, Keeley 2001). Because most of the non-native species that do invade conifer forests are herbaceous (Klinger et al. 2006), reduced light availability under intact canopies may generally prevent or minimize their establishment. Elevation per se

probably has little to do with the decreasing incidence of invasive species at higher elevations, but instead is correlated with physical factors that do affect establishment and growth of plants (e.g., reduced moisture, low temperatures, short growing seasons, etc.). Rejmanek (1989) pointed out that as a general rule, more extreme environments may be less susceptible to invasion.

There is concern that alteration of fire regimes in montane conifer forests *could* occur, primarily because of increasing invasion by annual species such as cheat grass and disturbance resulting from land use and fire suppression activities (Harrod and Reichard 2001). Despite this concern over *potential* effects, there is relatively little published data on the relationship between fire and invasive species in montane conifer ecosystems (Randall and Rejmanek 1993, Bossard and Rejmanek 1994, Schoennagel and Waller 1999, Crawford et al. 2001, Keeley 2001). There is evidence from Ponderosa pine forests in Arizona that non-native invasive species are altering post-burn succession patterns (Crawford et al. 2001), but the limited data available from California are inconclusive (Keeley 2001, Keeley et al. 2003, Klinger et al. 2006). In Sequoia and Kings Canyon National Parks, Keeley et al. (2003) found that frequency and cover values of invasive non-native species were low in virtually all burned conifer sites, but that invasion was greater in areas with higher-severity fires. Based on an analysis of two different data sets from Yosemite National Park, Klinger et al. (2006) found that species richness and cover of non-native species were relatively low in conifer forests and did not differ significantly between burned and unburned sites (Fig. 22.5). Of perhaps greater significance, Klinger et al. (2006) found that there was a negative relationship between richness and cover of non-native species and time since burn (Fig. 22.6), suggesting that even though non-native plants can invade burned conifer forests they are shaded out as the canopy closes (Keeley et al. 2003).

RIPARIAN ECOSYSTEMS

California's riparian systems have been heavily invaded by non-native species. In terms of extent of distribution and

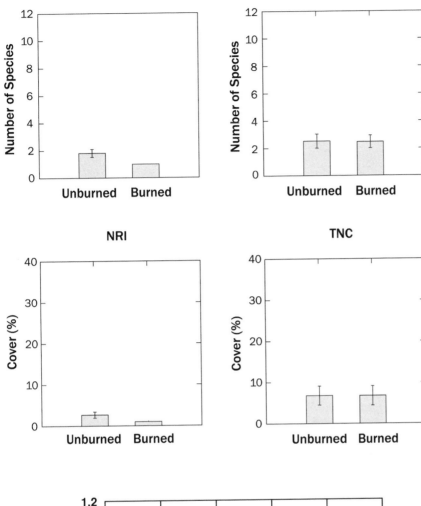

FIGURE 22.5. Mean species richness and absolute cover of invasive alien species in burned and unburned plots in Yosemite National Park. The data are from 356 0.1-ha plots sampled by the National Park Service from 1991 to 1993 (NRI) and 236 plots ranging in size from 0.05 ha to 0.1 ha sampled by The Nature Conservancy from 1998 to 1999 (TNC).

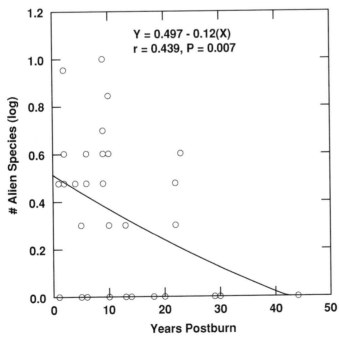

FIGURE 22.6. The relationship between species richness of non-native plants and the number of years since burning in Yosemite National Park, California.

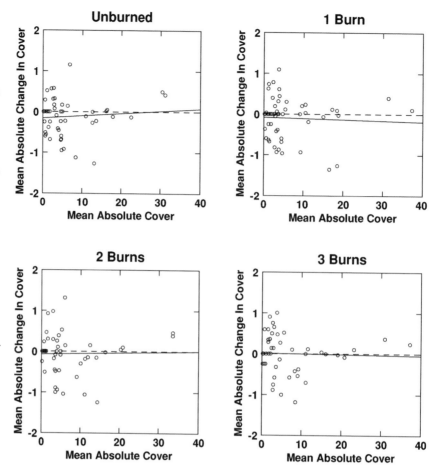

FIGURE 22.7. The relative change in abundance of alien herbaceous species (individual points) in control (unburned) and treatment (burn frequency) conditions in grasslands on Santa Cruz Island, California, 1996–2000. Each point represents the mean annual change in cover over a five-year period for a given species. Note the flat regression lines, indicating that regardless of how frequently an area was burned, the number of species that increased was about the same as the number of those that decreased. These results indicate the highly individualistic response of species, and that management prescriptions for collectively trying to control guilds of species (e.g., nonnative annual grasses) have a low likelihood of succeeding. (R. Klinger, unpublished, data.)

impacts to native species and ecosystem properties, the two taxa of greatest concern are giant reed *(Arundo donax)* and saltcedar. Both have invaded riparian areas throughout much of the state, although giant reed tends to be more common and have greater impacts in coastal parts of the state (Bell 1997), whereas saltcedar has had greater impacts in the southeastern desert region. Both are also present in the Central Valley and inner Coast Ranges. Both taxa are known to have altered species composition in riparian areas, as well as flooding regimes and other aspects of riparian hydrology. However, both have also had some effect on fire regimes. Bell (1997) reported that fires occurred more frequently and were more intense in areas where giant reed dominates riparian communities. Busch and Smith (1993) and Busch (1995) concluded that riparian forests along the Colorado River in Arizona have been drastically changed because saltcedar resprouts vigorously after a burn whereas most native trees (e.g., cottonwood, *[Populus fremontii]*) do not.

Fire and the Management of Invasive Species

Fire is often recommended as a way of managing invasive species (Randall et al. 1998, Bossard et al. 2000), and there are a number of examples where it has been used success-fully for this purpose (Nuzzo 1991, DiTomaso et al. 1999, Myers et al. 2001). But there are also examples where fire alone is not effective at decreasing the abundance of target species or guilds, or where there is an increase in the abundance of other invasive species (see Sidebar 22.1). In Arizona, fire enhanced germination of Lehman lovegrass *(Eragrostis lehmanniniana)* (Ruyle et al. 1988), and in Montana, fire increased biomass and seed production of dalmation toadflax *(Linaria genistifolia* spp. *dalmatica)* after a single spring burn (Jacobs and Sheley 2003). In the prairies of the mid-western United States, the abundance of native herbaceous species often increases following fires, but so does the abundance of non-native grasses and forbs (Howe 1995).

These inconsistent patterns underscore the importance of the interactions between the fire regimes and the natural history of different species. Invasive species show the same range of adaptations and responses to fire as native species do (Rowe 1981). The details of the fire regime in the system they invade may differ from those in their natural range, but the species life history characteristics may still allow them to persist or even thrive. Consequently, it is reasonable to expect there to be a tremendous range of responses by individual species to burning (Fig. 22.7), which makes broad management prescriptions for multiple species difficult to devise.

There are few ecosystems in California that have been impacted by just a single non-native species. Most ecosystems have been invaded by multiple species, which presents many challenges for developing, implementing, and evaluating control programs. Organizations in charge of managing parks, forests, refuges, and preserves have to carefully evaluate which invasive species pose the greatest threats, what the biological traits of the species are that make them both invasive and pose a threat, and how the species can potentially be controlled or, in some instances, eradicated. But perhaps the most critical aspect of controlling invasive species is what the outcomes of a control or eradication program are. Control and eradication programs are usually very expensive and long-term projects, and expectations about their outcomes can be quite high. But while expectations of success for these programs can be high, a number of different factors can affect their outcomes. Evaluating the success of a control program requires not just focusing on the target species, but analyzing how other species are affected as well. Some of the complexities involved in conducting and evaluating alien species control programs using fire can be illustrated from several studies conducted on Santa Cruz Island in the 1990s.

Like many islands throughout the world, the California Channel Islands off the coast of southern California have been subject to myriad impacts from accidentally and intentionally introduced non-native plant and animal species. These impacts have been well described in a series of symposiums dealing with the biology and management of the islands, and include outright destruction of vegetation communities, dominance of some vegetation communities by non-native species (e.g., grasslands, the understory of oak woodlands), species extinctions, altered hydrology, and extreme erosion. In addition to the impacts from non-native species, other human activities have played a major role in the transformation of the islands' ecosystems. One of these activities has been fire suppression. None of the islands have had any extensive burns from the 1850s up through the 1990s. Although the historic fire regimes on the islands are not well understood, many of the species on the islands show the same range of adaptations to fire that their counterparts on the mainland do (Carroll et al. 1993, Ostoja and Klinger 2000). So, presumably, fire once played an important role on the islands.

Santa Cruz Island is the largest and most diverse of the Channel Islands, and is held in joint ownership and managed as an ecological preserve by The Nature Conservancy and the National Park Service. There are 42 plants on Santa Cruz that are endemic to the Channel Islands, eight of which occur only on Santa Cruz itself (Junak et al. 1995) However, 25% of the flora on the island is non-native (Junak et al. 1995). Grasslands are the most extensive vegetation community on the island, but this is likely a result of type-conversion from coastal scrub and chaparral communities from overgrazing by feral sheep. Alien grasses and forbs now comprise more than 90% of the cover of grasslands and the understory of oak woodlands. The existing stands of chaparral, Bishop pine forest, and coastal scrub communities are comprised predominantly of native species, but they have been severely fragmented from overgrazing and are surrounded by grasslands. Recruitment of some shrub and tree species was extremely low as a result of either pathogens or high seed and seedling mortality from feral pig rooting.

Because conditions on the island had been so drastically altered, an evaluation of the contemporary role of fire needed to be done as the first step in a more comprehensive fire management plan. A central question in this evaluation was how fire affected the abundance of non-native species. Fire could potentially decrease abundance of some non-native species, but it might also lead to an increase in others. A series of exploratory experiments was undertaken by The Nature Conservancy to try to answer two questions: (1) Could prescribed burns be used to control the spread of fennel (*Foeniculum vulgare)* on the island? and (2) Would prescribed burns in grassland reduce the species richness and cover of non-native species and increase that of native species?

Fennel is considered one of the most invasive plants in California (Cal IPC 2006). Following the removal of cattle in 1988 and the end of a drought in 1991, the distribution and density of fennel on Santa Cruz increased dramatically. A series of three experiments from 1991 to 2001 was conducted to determine an effective method for controlling fennel, and to evaluate the effects on groups of species other than fennel as a result of the control methods (Brenton and Klinger 1994, 2002). One of these experiments tested whether fire alone or in combination with an herbicide (Triclopyr®) reduced fennel cover. Fire alone was ineffective at reducing fennel cover and was no more effective at reducing fennel cover when combined with herbicide spraying than spraying alone was. In areas where fennel cover was reduced, alien grasses and forbs dominated the community. Native species richness and cover increased in the burned and sprayed plots, but they comprised less than 10% of the mean cover and less than 15% of the species.

Two experiments that differed greatly in scale were conducted in grasslands on the island from 1993 to 2000. Although the experiments each had their own specific objectives, a common objective was to determine whether fire alone was effective at reducing abundance of non-native species and increasing that of natives (Klinger and Messer 2001). A large-scale experiment (1993–1998) involved burning three different areas (270–490 ha) once in the fall in separate years (1993–1995) and then monitoring vegetation response in each area for three years post-burn. The response of alien species to the burns was generally consistent; there was an initial decrease in cover of annual grasses but an increase in that of annual forbs. However, the response of native species in each area varied. In one area there was an initial increase in native forbs, in another area there was no change, and in the third area they decreased. Of most interest was that the response of both alien and native species varied by topography (primarily aspect) as well as rainfall patterns (Klinger and Messer 2001). Burning had a greater effect on species composition than topography in the first year post-burn, but it declined in importance each year after.

The second grassland burning experiment (1996–2000) was much smaller in scale (burn plots were 50 m^2), but rather than using just a single fall burn, both season (spring and fall) and frequency (0–3 burns in consecutive years) of burning were manipulated. The experimental plots were arranged along an aspect gradient, so that the interaction between burn season, frequency, and topography could be analyzed. There was strong variation in species composition from year to year, but this was due mainly to variation in interannual rainfall patterns. There were some differences in species composition as a result of the fire treatments within any given year, but aspect explained much more of this variation than did burning. As in the larger-scale grassland burn study, non-native grasses and forbs dominated both species composition and cover in all years.

These three studies underscore the challenges of using fire to try to control non-native species in heavily invaded systems. Fire alone was not effective at controlling fennel, and did not substantially reduce fennel cover more when used in conjunction with spraying than did spraying alone. The best justification for using fire with herbicide spraying was that this was the only treatment where native species showed a significant increase in species richness and cover. Nevertheless, reduction in fennel cover was compensated for primarily by non-native annual grasses and forbs. In both grassland studies, factors other than burning had a more pronounced effect on variation in species composition than burning did, fire effects were transient and varied from year to year or site to site, and non-native species continued to dominate the communities. In all three studies, responses to fire were species specific, so that reduction in cover of one species was compensated for by an increase in cover by another.

Are the outcomes from these studies unique to Santa Cruz Island? It appears that they are not, and may actually be quite representative of broader patterns throughout the state. Sue Bainbridge from the Jepson Herbarium at UC Berkeley, along with several other collaborators, collected all known studies (published and unpublished) on fire and grasslands in California. Synthesizing the results from 36 studies with a statistical technique known as *meta-analysis,* Bainbridge et al. (unpubl. data) concluded that fire generally has no effect on or even increases cover of non-native species. Annual grasses are often reduced the first year after burning, but by the second or third year after a burn, their cover has returned to pre-burn levels. The reduction in cover of annual grasses is compensated by an increase in non-native forbs, although this may vary depending on whether a site is burned repeatedly and/or grazed. Native species, especially forbs, increase in the first year after burning in ungrazed sites and in the second year after burning in grazed sites. Season of burning had no significant effect on post-fire response for native or non-native taxa. Precipitation did influence response of different taxa, although the magnitude of this effect and how different guilds responded to precipitation were highly variable.

Although these outcomes do not necessarily argue against using fire as a management tool for non-native species, they do highlight the need to set appropriate management expectations and goals and to recognize the complexity inherent in the systems being managed. They also show that development of control methods that are part of a more comprehensive restoration program will require a long-term investment in research before full-scale implementation is initiated over large areas. Even then, results are likely to vary from year to year at any given site because of factors that are beyond the control of the managing organization.

Fire and the Control of Invasive Herbaceous Species

Fire has been used in attempts to control or manage invasive species in California for more than 50 years, with the most extensive use being in grasslands (Table 22.1). Non-native annual grasses and forbs have flourished in California for at least 150 years (Mack 1989). These non-natives suppress regeneration by native species through competitive interactions (Dyer and Rice 1997, Eliason and Allen 1997, Brooks 2000), primarily by development of a dense layer of "thatch" that reduces light and increases moisture (Heady 1988). Direct and indirect evidence indicates that many non-native annual grass and forb species exploit moisture and do better under conditions of reduced light than do native species (Evans and Young 1970, Dyer and Rice 1997, 1999). Therefore, prescribed burning has been recommended as a way of reducing competition intensity in grasslands by increasing the amount of light available to native species for germination and development of seeds and seedlings, and also as a way of directly reducing the abundance of non-native grasses and forbs (Dix 1960, Heady 1972, Menke 1992, Gillespie and Allen 2004).

Studies on managing grasslands in California with fire have varied broadly in their objectives. Some have focused on range improvement (Hervey 1949), others on increasing diversity of particular native herbaceous species (Dyer and Rice 1997, 1999, Gillespie and Allen 2004, Hatch et al. 1999),

some on reducing populations of particular non-native species and increasing diversity of natives (Pollak and Kan 1998, DiTomaso et al. 1999, Hopkinson et al. 1999, DiTomaso et al. 2001), and others on a community-level decrease in abundance of non-native species and increased abundance of natives (Parsons and Stohlgren 1989, Meyer and Schiffman 1999, Klinger and Messer 2001, Wills 2000, Marty 2002).

Despite the variation in objectives of these studies some limited generalities can be drawn from them. The timing and frequency of burning are critical factors for reducing the abundance of individual non-native species. DiTomaso et al. (2001) concluded that barbed goatgrass (*Aegilops triuncialis*) could be controlled with two late spring or early summer burns in consecutive years, whereas Hopkinson et al. (1999) reported that single summer burns were effective at reducing the cover but not the spread of goat grass. Hopkinson et al. (1999) also suggested that repeated burning in different seasons would be the best strategy for reducing cover and spread of barbed goatgrass, but this has yet to be tested. Although some range ecologists previously believed efforts to control medusahead *(Taenitherium caput-medusae)* with fire would be ineffective (Heady 1972), Pollak and Kan (1998) reported that medusahead was virtually eliminated the first growing season after a spring burn in a vernal pool/grassland system. DiTomaso et al. (1999) reported a 91% reduction in cover of yellow star-thistle following three consecutive summer burns. However, Kyser and DiTomaso

TABLE 22.1
Examples of studies on the use of fire to control invasive species and increase abundance or diversity of native species in grasslands in California

Reference	Target	Native Species Response	Alien Species Response
Hervey 1949	Community	None reported	Decrease in annual grass and increase in annual forbs
Furbush 1953	T. capat-medusae	None reported	T. capat-medusae nearly eliminated, but other annual herbaceous species dominated post-fire
Parsons and Stohlgren 1989	Community	Short-term increase in forbs; no change in grass biomass	Short-term decrease in grass; increase in forb biomass
Ahmed 1983	N. pulchra	Results varied among response variables, but generally positive response	Burning reduced cover and biomass of alien grass, primarily Bromus hordeaceous
Dyer et al. 1996	N. pulchra		Not measured
Dyer and Rice 1997	N. pulchra	Short-term increase in size; depended on reduced competition	Not measured
Pollak and Kan 1998	T. capat-medusae Community	"Early" annual forbs increased	T. capat-medusae reduced; annual forbs increased and dominated cover
DiTomaso et al. 1999	Centaurea solstitialis	Short-term increase in forbs and grass in some areas	No change in cover of grasses and forbs
Hatch et al. 1999	Danthonia californica Nasella lepida N. pulchra	No change in Danthonia or N. lepida. N. pulchra response varied unpredictably with topographic position	Not measured
Hopkinson et al. 1999	A. triuncialis	No response by N. pulchra	Cover reduced but no effect on spread
Meyer and Schiffman 1999	Community	Short-term increase in forb and grass cover	Short-term decrease in grass cover; Alien grasses and forbs dominate cover
DiTomaso et al. 2001	A. triuncialis	Species-specific changes. No overall changes in cover but an increase in frequency	Reduction in cover site-specific; depended on "completeness" of burn
Klinger and Messer 2001	Community	Short-term increase in cover of annual forbs; no change in grass	Short-term decrease in cover of annual grass; increase in annual forbs
Kyser and DiTomaso 2002 (post-burn monitoring only)	C. solstitialis	Decrease in forbs and perennial grasses	Increase in cover, seedling density, and seed bank of C. solstitialis

TABLE 22.1 (continued)

Reference	Target	Native Species Response	Alien Species Response
Marty 2002	Community	Increase in species richness and cover of annual and perennial forbs	Increase in species richness and cover of forbs; increase in species richness of grass but no change in cover
Alexander and D' Antonio 2003	*Genista monspessulana*	Greater density of native forbs in seedbank for stands that had burned 3–4 times	Reduction in seedbank of *G. monspessulana* following burning. Multiple burns did not further deplete seedbank.

NOTE: Target is whether the goal of burning was to alter abundance of a particular species or produce community-level changes in species composition.

(2002) found that within four years of the cessation of burning, the seedbank, seedling density, and cover of yellow starthistle rose rapidly.

In studies focused on community-level changes, a short-term decrease (≤2 years) in cover (or biomass) of annual grasses and short-term increase (1–2 years) in annual forbs usually occurs beginning in the first, and sometimes the second, growing season after the fire (but see Marty 2002). However, non-native species still dominate the burned sites and within two to three years, burn effects are largely gone (Parsons and Stohlgren 1989, Klinger and Messer 2001), a pattern that has been recognized for many decades (Hervey 1949, Heady 1972).

These results are not surprising, because most invasive non-native species in California grasslands: (1) evolved in a fire-prone environment with a mediterranean climate; (2) are annuals and can respond rapidly to fire; and (3) what is likely the most important factor, non-native herbaceous species dominate the aboveground cover of most grasslands in California, and it is likely they dominate the seed bank as well (Major and Pyott 1966, Maranon and Bartolome 1989).

A particularly important aspect in using fire to manage invasive species is that environmental variability and factors interacting with fire can have more important effects on both non-native and native species than does fire alone. For example, Harrison et al. (2003) reported species richness of non-native plants in a burned grassland community in the Central Coast Range to be greater on more productive soils. Klinger and Messer (2001) found that species composition in burned grasslands on Santa Cruz Island was determined largely by an interaction between rainfall, topography (aspect and elevation), and fire, and that native species were suppressed during years of high rainfall, apparently because of increased cover of non-native grasses and forbs in wetter years. Hatch et al. (1999) also found that fire effects were modified by topography, and that some native species showed a positive response to burning, whereas others did not. Pollak and Kan (1998) reported different responses by both native and non-native species in a vernal pool/grassland complex depending on small-scale variation in topography between "uplands" (raised mounds) and "swales" (low-lying areas between mounds).

The only study in which burning led to an unequivocal and relatively long-term positive response by native species has been on the Santa Rosa Plateau in eastern Riverside County (Wills 1999). Following a long-term program of spring burning, the percent cover of native species (bunchgrasses and forbs) is now roughly equal or greater than that of non-native species. What is significant about this study is that the initial (pre-treatment) cover of native species on the Santa Rosa Plateau was far greater than in the other studies. Similarly, Harrison and Safford (2003) concluded that post-fire herbaceous species composition in chaparral and grassland communities was related to the relative abundance of species prior to burning. The dominant groups of species prior to burning were the ones that tended to be most abundant after a burn, a phenomena they called the ". . . rich getting richer and the poor getting poorer" (Harrison et al. 2003).

These results have very important implications for grassland restoration and management programs throughout the state; fire will likely be most effective as a means of maintaining areas that already have a significant component of native species. In other areas where native species are not particularly abundant, fire will probably have to be integrated with other techniques (e.g., seeding, planting) if the goal is enhancement of native species diversity. Aside from Wills' (1999) study, there is little evidence at this time that grasslands in California can be restored to significant levels of native species cover simply by burning.

Attempting to generalize any further from studies of fire and invasive species control in California is somewhat tenuous because coordinated, systematic studies of fire regimes and control of non-native species are lacking (Table 22.2). The ad hoc nature of the studies conducted to date makes direct comparisons difficult because of variation in site characteristics, site history (e.g., land use patterns), and weather. Variation in the spatial and temporal scales of the studies likely has a strong influence on how post-fire

TABLE 22.2
Location, duration, and components of fire regimes in selected studies on the use of fire to control invasive species and
increase abundance or diversity of native species in grasslands in California

Reference	Location	Duration	Season	Frequency
Hervey 1949	Berkeley foothills (Alameda County)	1 year	Summer	1
Furbush 1953	Coast Range (Mendocino County)	2 years	Summer	1
Parsons and Stohlgren 1989	Sierra foothills (Sequoia National Park)	4 years	Spring and fall	1–3 with 1-year interval
Dyer et al. 1996	Central Valley grassland (Solano County)	2 years	Late spring	1
Dyer and Rice 1997	Central Valley grassland (Solano County)	4 years	Late spring	1
Pollak and Kan 1998	Central Valley grassland (Solano County)	1 year	Late spring	1
DiTomaso et al. 1999	Coast Range (Sonoma County)	3 years	Late spring	3 with 1-year interval
Hatch et al. 1999	Coastal grassland (San Mateo County)	1 year	Fall	1
Hopkinson et al. 1999	Coast Range (Contra Costa County)	3 years (effectivel y2)	Summer	2 with 3-year interval
Meyer and Schiffman 1999	Carrizo Plain (San Luis Obispo County)	1 year	Late spring, fall, winter	1
DiTomaso et al. 2001	Coast Range (Mendocino County)	2 years	Late spring	1
Klinger and Messer 2001	Santa Cruz Island (Santa Barbara County)	5 years	Fall	1
Marty 2002	Sierra foothills (Yuba County)	2 years	Summer	1
Alexander and D'Antonio 2003	Coastal grassland (Marin County)	1 year	Not specified	1–3 (interval not specified)

NOTE: *Duration* is the length of the study; *season* is the season that burns were conducted; and *frequency* is how often plots were burned, with *interval* being the amount of time between repeated burns.

responses are interpreted as well. The size of both the burn area and the sampling units used to collect data may introduce a spatial bias. Many of the studies on fire management of invasive species in California have used very small burn plots (<0.1 ha) and/or sampling plots (e.g., quadrats 0.25–1.0 m^2). Edge effects in these studies are probably substantial, and there is the potential for different interpretations of post-fire responses at different scales (Klinger and Messer 2001, Marty 2002).

Study duration introduces temporal bias in interpreting post-burn outcomes. The mean duration of studies on fire as means of controlling invasive species in California has been approximately two years (Table 22.2). Because of the pronounced post-fire response of annual species to fire, conclusions based on just a single year or even two of post-burn monitoring are likely misleading (Parsons and Stohlgren 1989, Klinger and Messer 2001, Kyser and DiTomaso 2002, Marty 2002).

The most commonly manipulated component of fire regimes has been burn season (Table 22.2). Very few studies have manipulated both season and frequency of burn (e.g., Parsons and Stohlgren 1989), and none have manipulated fire-return intervals. Other aspects of fire regimes that are difficult or virtually impossible to manipulate but can be measured, such as fire intensity and rate of spread, have rarely been quantified. Systematic, coordinated studies of fire effects on non-native and native species conducted at multiple grassland sites would be extremely important.

It is generally assumed that spring is probably the most effective season to conduct prescribed burns in grasslands because there would be much higher mortality of seed crops. There is evidence that spring burns can lead to greater reduction of non-native species and greater increases of native species than fall burns (DiTomaso et al. 1999, Meyer and Schiffman 1999, Wills 2000). However, other studies using fall burns have also documented significant decreases in cover of non-native species and significant increases in species richness and cover of native species, at least over short-term periods (Parsons and Stohlgren 1989, Klinger and Messer 2001).

The spring burning paradigm largely reflects the strong emphasis originally given to native perennial bunchgrass restoration (Menke 1992, Dyer 2002). It was thought that perennial bunchgrasses would have superior resprouting ability than invasive non-native species, and that this would enable them to regenerate at higher rates following a spring burn where seeds of annual species would presumably be destroyed before they became buried in the litter layer. However, bunchgrasses have high seedling mortality and do not have particularly good dispersal characteristics (Dyer and Rice 1997). The spring burning paradigm also ignores the likelihood that native annual forb species were a significant component of California's native grasslands (Hamilton 1997). In addition, natural fires in California occurred throughout the summer and fall. This implies that there was probably a mosaic of patches differing in species composition that reflected differential temporal responses to burning as a result of different species life history characteristics.

Fire and the Control of Invasive Woody Species

Management of woody invasive species in California with fire has been used less frequently than with herbaceous species, primarily because most invasive plants in California are herbaceous (Randall et al 1998). The effect of fire on most woody invasive species in the state is largely unstudied. Burning does not seem to be effective at controlling tamarisk (*Tamarix* ssp.) (Busch 1995), but some studies indicate burning can reduce density and/or the seedbank of Scotch brooms (*Cytisus scoparius* and *Genista monspessulana*) (Boyd 1995, Roja and Poepnoe 1998, Odion and Hausenback 2002, Alexander and D'Antonio 2003). Using fire to control brooms is complicated by non-native annual grasses rapidly becoming established in the burned areas (Swezey and Odion 1997).

As with herbaceous species, the timing and frequency of burning are important factors for controlling woody invasive species as well as enhancing habitat for native species. However, one particular type of prescribed burn that is effective at controlling spread or abundance of woody invasive species may not increase richness or abundance of native species. Alexander and D'Antonio (2003) reported that multiple burns done in consecutive years did not contribute to further reduction of the seedbank of French broom than a single burn. However, the seedbank of native forbs increased and that of non-native grasses decreased when burns were done in three consecutive years (Alexander and D'Antonio 2003).

Many woody invasive species either have biological traits or occur in areas that make them inappropriate candidates for burning programs. A particularly good example of this is Tasmanian blue gum (*Eucalyptus globulus*), which is rated as one of the most invasive species in the state (CALEPPC 1999). In localized areas it can form dense stands that are more than 40 m tall. Bark from the trunk exfoliates and leaves are shed prolifically, so a dense mat of organic litter can build up rapidly in the stands. This results in an understory virtually devoid of native species.

Although there is good conservation justification for controlling Tasmanian blue gum, the species has certain biological traits that complicate management options (Boyd 1997). Tasmanian blue gum evolved in fire-prone environments in Australia, and the bark on adult trees is extremely thick and resists burning in all but the hottest fires. The leaves have a high content of volatile oils, and fire intensity in the stands is extremely intense (Sapsis et al. 1995, Cole 2002). Seeds of Tasmanian blue gum have a tough coat that resists burning, and annual seed production is prolific. Although Tasmanian blue gum seeds don't require fire to germinate, germination rates after even intense burns are very high (R. Klinger pers. obs.). In addition, Tasmanian blue gum frequently occurs near urban areas. If fire were intense enough to ignite adults in mature stands, the extreme fire behavior would make control tenuous and present a severe hazard to human life and property.

Summary: Fire and the Control of Invasive Species

The complex and often unpredictable outcomes of trying to control invasive species with fire do not imply that using fire for this purpose is inappropriate. On the contrary, it is a reasonable justification for initiating management actions when they are most likely to be effective, which is before an invasive species begins to spread and/or dominate and alter ecological systems. However, in most instances, resource managers are faced with managing sites that have already been invaded. In some cases, carefully timed fires will be effective at reducing abundance of certain non-native species. But the outcomes from burning will become less predictable in sites that have been invaded by a number of different non-native species (see Sidebar 22.1), especially when the goal is to produce wholesale shifts in species composition throughout an entire community. A number of factors will modify burn effects, and variation in outcomes among sites and years.

Selecting where, when, and how fire is used is critical to the success of an invasive species management program. This will likely involve a number of years of research and monitoring before a large-scale control program can be developed and effectively implemented, which presents a dilemma because populations of one or more invasive species could increase during this time. In the long run though, an investment in a focused and comprehensive research and monitoring program will more times than not save investment in an expensive but ultimately ineffective management program.

Synthesis and Conclusions: The Ecological, Conservation, and Social Context of Fire and Invasive Species

The invasion and establishment of non-native species into natural communities raise two major questions relating to fire: (1) what has been the range of effects on fire regimes and fire behavior as a result of invasive species?, and (2) when should fire be used as a tool to control the spread or reduce the impacts of non-native species on natural communities? These questions are related of course, but it is important to keep in mind that they must be evaluated by different criteria.

The first question is an ecological one, and it must be addressed within an ecological context. It implies that effects need to be studied on a broad enough spatial scale and over a long enough period of time so that patterns can be understood and properly interpreted at multiple scales. More importantly, it is critical that the mechanisms producing the patterns be identified, because this will increase the ability to predict effects in areas where new invasions occur. The second question is management related, and it is at this point that value judgments must be made. What species or areas will be prioritized for management action? What level of invasion will be the threshold for initiating management actions? What measures will be used to determine success of management programs? And what period of time will be considered adequate to evaluate management actions? These are just some of the questions that must be considered before undertaking a fire management program targeted at a non-native species.

How ecologists and management agencies react to biological invasions is conditioned to a great extent on our values and perceptions. Biological invasions have effects on ecosystem properties, of which altered fire regimes are only one. Fire regimes and invasive species interact with other processes: fire with physical aspects of the ecosystem such as rainfall, temperature, soil properties, and fuel type; invasive species with herbivores (e.g., grazing regimes), predators, and pathogens. Whether a non-native species can displace a native species, exploit burn areas, alter fire regimes, or be controlled with fire will depend on inherent aspects of its biology,

its interactions with other species in the system, and how and when fire is applied. However, the underlying philosophy of conservation is based on value judgments; although, in its best application conservation is informed by ecological knowledge. In this context it is appropriate to attempt to determine what the harmful impacts of invasive species are and try to mitigate them. It is difficult to predict what our attitudes toward invasive species will be in the coming century. But they are likely to be modified as we learn more about how they interact within natural systems, the role human activities play in their spread and establishment, and their economic and social impacts (Pimentel et al. 2000; Zavaleta 2000a, 2000b).

Ultimately, the reason to prevent and control biological invasions is to maintain ecosystem properties that humans find desirable. Because invasive species can rapidly alter these properties, control (or eradication) is really only a step in a longer-term management process that focuses on maintaining or restoring conditions beneficial to native species (Randall et al. 1997). This means that controlling invasive species is not an end in itself, but must be evaluated relative to its contribution to maintaining or helping to restore desired ecosystem properties.

As we have seen throughout this text, fire can be used as a management tool for many different reasons. It is not necessarily applied to solely achieve ecological or conservation goals, and the potential proliferation of invasive species may be a secondary concern in some, or even many, fire management programs. Even in fire management programs where controlling invasive species is a priority, conflicts with other management programs may exist. Examples of such conflicts include management of threatened or endangered species (Germano et al. 2001) or bio-control programs (Briese 1996, Fellows and Newton 1999).

Because natural systems are being destroyed or altered at such a rapid pace, conservation actions have been largely driven by perceptions of how the world "should be," without an adequate understanding of how most ecological systems actually function or vary over time. But our time frames often are short, our perspectives limited, and we use simplistic (and possibly fallacious) targets for restoration and management programs such as "returning a system to a state similar to that prior to European settlement." We forget that just as human value systems change, so do ecosystems change. Our blurry image of what we want to restore and how we manage ecosystems must be re-focused on the fact that ecological conditions now are different from what they were 200 or 2,000 years ago. Most important, even without humans, they still would be different now from what they were in the past.

Management of natural areas must be based on current conditions. Historical information is useful, but primarily as a measure of what the range of variability in an ecosystem was, not as a target for management programs. Trying to manage ecosystems at some perceived historical state is likely a recipe for failure, especially since conditions are different now from the arbitrary periods we have chosen to use as our baselines. Management programs and ecological studies must recognize the irreversible nature of the transformation that these systems have undergone. It must be accepted that those invasive species now established as a dominant component of an ecosystem will be difficult to control, or even less likely, to eradicate.

Most research on fire and invasive species in the last decade has focused on the direct effect of invasive species on fire regimes and the direct effect of fire on invasive species. But we know very little about how large-scale changes in geophysical processes interact with invasive species to alter fire regimes (e.g., Fenn et al. 2003), or how management programs that use fire to try to control invasive species affect trophic structure, predator-prey relationships, and numerous other ecological relationships. For example, there have been very few studies on animal responses to fire and invasive plants, either as a result of altered fire regimes or where fire is being used as a management or restoration tool. Animals play critical roles as herbivores, seed predators and dispersers, pollinators, and disturbance agents, and we are almost completely ignorant about their interactions with fire and invasive species (for an exception, see D'Antonio et al. 1993). Just what are the effects of *our* management actions on these ecological interactions when we "restore" a fire regime to an ecological system, or use fire to try to control invasive species? These interactions and relationships are just starting to be studied (e.g., Bock and Bock 1992, Howe 1995, Howe and Brown 2001, Collins 2002, D'Antonio et al. 2003, Espeland et al. 2005), but ultimately they will drive our perceptions and use of fire to manage invasive species.

References

Allen, E.B. 1998. Restoring habitats to prevent exotics. Pages 41–44 in M. Kelly, E. Wagner, and P. Warner, editors. Proceedings California Exotic Pest Plant Council Symposium Volume 4. CALEPPC, Ontario, CA.

Alexander, J.M., and C.M. D'Antonio. 2003. Seed bank dynamics of French Broom in Coastal California grasslands: effects of stand age and prescribed burning on control and restoration. Restoration Ecology 11:185–197.

Baker, H.G. 1986. Patterns of plant invasions in North America. Pages 44–57 in H.A. Mooney and J.A. Drake (eds.), Ecology of Biological Invasions of North America and Hawaii. Springer-Verlag, New York.

Baker, W.L. 1994. Restoration of landscape structure altered by fire suppression. Conservation Biology 8:763–769.

Backer, D.M., S.E. Jensen, and G.R. McPherson. 2004. Impacts of fire-suppression activities on natural communities. Conservation Biology 18:937–946.

Bell, G.P. 1997. Ecology and management of *Arundo donax* and approaches to riparian habitat restoration in southern California. Pages 103–113 in J. H. Brock (ed.), Plant Invasions: Studies from North America and Europe. Backhuys Leiden, The Netherlands.

Beyers, J.L., C.D. Wakeman, P.M. Wohlgemuth, and S.G. Conard. 1998. Effects of postfire grass seeding on native vegetation in southern California chaparral. Proceedings of the Annual Forest Vegetation Management Conference 19:52–64.

Billings, W.D. 1990. *Bromus tectorum*, a biotic cause of ecosystem impoverishment in the Great Basin. Pages 301–322 in G.M. Woodwell (ed.), The Earth in Transition: Patterns and Processes of Biotic Impoverishment. Cambridge University Press, Cambridge.

Biswell, H. 1999. Prescribed Burning in California Wildlands Vegetation Management, Second edition. University of California Press, Berkeley.

Bock, C.E., and J.H. Bock. 1992. Response of birds to wildfire in native versus exotic Arizona grassland. Southwestern Naturalist 37:73–81.

Bossard, C., J.M. Randall, and M.C. Hoshovsky. 2000. Invasive Plants of California's Wildlands. University of California Press, Berkeley.

Bossard, C., and M. Rejmanek. 1994. Herbivory, growth, seed production, and resprouting of an exotic invasive shrub *Cytisus scoparius*. Biological Conservation 67:193–200.

Bossard, C.C. 1991. The role of habitat disturbance, seed predation, and ant dispersal on the establishment of the exotic shrub *Cytisus scoparius* (Scotch Broom) in California. Madroño 40:47–61.

Boyd, D. 1995. Use of fire to control French broom. Pages 9–12 in J. Lovich, J. Randall, and M. Kelly (ed.), Proceedings California Exotic Pest Plant Council Symposium, Pacific Grove, CA.

Boyd, D. 1997. Eucalyptus removal on Angel Island. Pages 73–75 in M. Kelly, E. Wagner, and P. Warner (eds.), Proceedings California Exotic Pest Plant Council Symposium Volume 3, Concord, California.

Brenton, B., and R.C. Klinger. 1994. Modeling the expansion and control of fennel *Foeniculum vulgare* on the Channel Islands. Pages 497–504 in W.L. Halvorson and G.J. Maender (eds.), The Fourth California Islands Symposium: Update on the Status of Resources. Santa Barbara Museum of Natural History, Santa Barbara, CA.

Brenton, B., and R.C. Klinger. 2002. Factors influencing the control of fennel *Foeniculum vulgare* using Triclopyr on Santa Cruz Island. Natural Areas Journal 22:135–147.

Briese, D.T. 1996. Biological control of weeds and fire management in protected natural areas: are they compatible strategies? Biological Conservation 77:135–141.

Brooks, M.L. 1999. Alien annual grasses and fire in the Mojave Desert. Madroño 46:13–19.

Brooks, M.L. 2000. Competition between alien annual grasses and native annual plants in the Mojave Desert. American Midland Naturalist 144:92–108.

Brooks, M.L., C.M. D'Antonio, D.M. Richardson, J.B. Grace, J.E. Keeley, J.M. DiTomaso, R.J. Hobbs, M. Pellant, and D.A. Pyke. 2004. Effects of invasive alien plants on fire regimes. BioScience 54:677–688.

Brooks, M.L., and D.A. Pyke. 2001. Invasive plants and fire in the deserts of North America. Pages 1–14 in K.E.M. Galley and T.P. Wilson (eds.), Proceedings of the Invasive Species Workshop: The Role of Fire in the Control and Spread of Invasive Species. Fire Conference 2000: The First National Congress on Fire Ecology, Prevention, and Management. Tall Timbers Research Station, Tallahassee, Florida.

Brown, D.E., and R.A. Minnich. 1986. Fire and changes in creosote bush scrub of the western Sonoran Desert, California [USA]. American Midland Naturalist 116:411–422.

Bruce, K. A., G. N. Cameron, and P. A. Harcombe. 1995. Initiation of a new woodland type on the Texas Coastal Prairie by the Chinese tallow tree (*Sapium sebiferum* (L.) Roxb.). Bulletin of the Torrey Botanical Club 122:215–225.

Busch, D. E., 1995. Effects of fire on southwestern riparian plant community structure. Southwestern Naturalist 40:259–267.

Busch, D. E., and S. D. Smith. 1993. Effects of fire on water and salinity relationships of riparian woody taxa. Oecologia 94:186–194.

Cal-IPC. 2006. California Invasive Plant Inventory, February 2006. Cal-IPC Publication 2006–02. California Invasive Plant Council, Berkeley.

Caprio, A. C., and P. Lineback. 2002. Pre-twentieth century fire history of Sequoia and Kings Canyon National Parks: a review and evaluation of our knowledge. Pages 180-199 in N. G. Sugihara, M. Morales, and T. Morales (eds.), Proceedings of the Symposium: Fire in California Ecosystems: Integrating Ecology, Prevention, and Management. Miscellaneous Publication No. 1, Association for Fire Ecology.

Carroll, M. C., L. L. Laughrin, and A. Bromfield. 1993. Fire on the California islands: does it play a role in chaparral and closed cone pine forest habitats. Pages 73–88 in F. G. Hochberg (ed.), The Third California Islands Symposium: Recent Advances in Research on the California Islands. Santa Barbara Museum of Natural History, Santa Barbara, CA.

Cole, D. 2002. California's urbanizing wildlands and the "Fire of the Future." Pages 231–238 in N. G. Sugihara, M. Morales, and T. Morales (eds.), Proceedings of the Symposium: Fire in California Ecosystems: Integrating Ecology, Prevention, and Management. Miscellaneous Publication No. 1, Association for Fire Ecology.

Collins, S. L. 2000. Disturbance frequency and community stability in native tallgrass prairie. American Naturalist 155:311–325.

Conard, S. G., J. L. Beyers, and P. M. Wohlgemuth. 1995. Impacts of postfire grass seeding on chaparral systems—what do we know and where do we go from here? Pages 149–161 in J. E. Keeley and T. Scott (eds.), Wildfires in California Brushlands: Ecology and Resource Management. International Association of Wildland Fire, Fairfield, WA.

Crawford, J. A., C. H. A. Wahren, S. Kyle, and W. H. Moir. 2001. Responses of exotic plant species to fires in *Pinus ponderosa* forests in northern Arizona. Journal of Vegetation Science 12:261–268.

Cronk, C. B., and J. L. Fuller. 1995. Plant Invaders: The Threat to Natural Ecosystems. Chapman & Hall, New York.

Crooks, J., and M. E. Soule. 1996. Lag times in population explosions of invasive species: causes and implications. Pages 39–46 in O. T. Sandlund, P. J. Schei, and A. Viken (eds.), Proceedings Norway/UN Conference on Alien Species. Directorate for Nature Management and Norwegian Institute for Nature Research, Trondheim, Norway.

D'Antonio, C. M. 2000. Fire, plant invasions, and global changes. Pages 65–93 in H. A. Mooney and R. J. Hobbs (eds.), Invasive Species in a Changing World. Island Press, Washington, D.C.

D'Antonio C. M., D. C. Odion, and C. M. Tyler. 1993. Invasion of Maritime Chaparral by the Introduced Succulent Carpobrotus-Edulis. Oecologia 95(1):14–21.

D'Antonio, C. M., J. T. Tunison, and R. K. Loh. 2000. Variation in the impact of exotic grasses on native plant composition in relation to fire across an elevation gradient in Hawaii. Austral Ecology 25:507–522.

D'Antonio, C. M., and P. M. Vitousek. 1992. Biological invasions by exotic grasses, the grass/fire cycle and global change. Annual Review of Ecology and Systematics 23:63–87.

Daubenmire, R. 1968. Ecology of grasslands. Advances in Ecological Research 5:209–266.

DiCastri, F. 1989. History of biological invasions with emphasis on the Old World. Pages 1–30 in J. A. Drake, H. A. Mooney, F. DiCastri, R. H. Groves, F. J. Kruger, M. Rejmanek, and M. Williamson (eds.) Biological Invasions: A Global Perspective. Wiley, New York.

DiTomaso, J. M., K. L. Hiese, G. B. Kyser, A. M. Merenlender, and R. J. Keiffer. 2001. Carefully timed burning can control barb goatgrass. California Agriculture (November–December 2001) 55(6):47–53.

DiTomaso, J. M., G. B. Kyser, and M. S. Hastings. 1999. Prescribed burning for control of yellow starthistle *(Centaurea soltitialis)* and enhanced native plant diversity. Weed Science 47:233–242.

Dix, R. L. 1960. The effects of burning on the mulch structure and species composition of grasslands in western North Dakota. Ecology 41:49–56.

Dyer, A. R. 2002. Burning and grazing management in a California grassland: effect on bunchgrass seed viability. Restoration Ecology 10:107–111.

Dyer, A. R., H. C. Fossum, and J. W. Menke. 1996. Emergence and survival of *Nassella pulchra* in a California grassland. Madroño 43:316–333.

Dyer, A. R., and K. J. Rice. 1997. Intraspecific and diffuse competition: the response of *Nassella pulchra* in a California grassland. Ecological Applications 7:484–492.

Dyer, A. R., and K. J. Rice. 1999. Effects of competition on resource availability and growth of a California bunchgrass. Ecology (Washington, DC) 80:2697–2710.

Eliason, S. A., and E. B. Allen. 1997. Exotic grass competition in suppressing native shrubland reestablishment. Restoration Ecology 5:245–255.

Espeland, E. K., T. M. Carlsen, and D. Macqueen. 2005. Fire and dynamics of granivory on a California grassland forb. Biodiversity and Conservation 14:267–280.

Evans, R. A., and J. A. Young. 1970. Plant litter and establishment of alien annual weed species in rangeland communities. Weed Science 18:697–703.

Fellows, D. P., and W. E. Newton. 1999. Prescribed fire effects on biological control of leafy spurge. Journal of Range Management 52:489–493.

Fenn, M. E., R. Haeuber, G. S. Tonnesen, J. S. Baron, S. Grossman-Clarke, D. Hope, D. A. Jaffe, S. Copeland, L. Geiser, H. M. Rueth, and J. O. Sickman. 2003. Nitrogen emissions, deposition, and monitoring in the western United States. BioScience 53:391–403.

Fischer, R. A., K. P. Reese, and J. W. Connelly. 1996. An investigation of fire effects within xeric sage grouse brood habitat. Journal of Range Management 49:194–198.

Foin, T. C., and M. M. Hektner. 1986. Secondary succession and the fate of native species in a California coastal prairies. Madroño 33:189–206.

Furbush, P. 1953. Control of medusa-head on California ranges. Journal of Forestry 51:118–121.

Galley, K. E. M., and T. P. Wilson (eds.). 2001. Proceedings of the Invasive Species Workshop: The Role of Fire in the Control and Spread of Invasive Species. Tall Timbers Research Station Miscellaneous Publications No. 11, Tallahassee, FL.

Gann, G., and D.R. Gordon. 1998. *Paederia foetida* (skunk vine) and *P. cruddasiana* (sewer vine): threats and management strategies. Natural Areas Journal 18:169–174.

Germano, D.J., G.B. Rathbun, and L.R. Saslaw. 2001. Managing exotic grasses and conserving declining species. Wildlife Society Bulletin 29:551–559.

Giessow, J., and P. Zedler. 1996. The effects of fire frequency and firebreaks on the abundance and species richness of exotic plant species in coastal sage scrub. Pages 86–94 in J. Lovich, J. Randall, and M. Kelly (eds.), Proceedings California Exotic Pest Plant Council Symposium Volume 2, San Diego, CA.

Gillespie, I.G., and E.B. Allen. 2004. Fire and competition in a southern California grassland: impacts on the rare forb *Erodium macrophyllum*. Journal of Applied Ecology 41:643–652.

Gordon, D.R. 1998. Effects of invasive, nonindigenous plant species on ecosystem processes: lessons from Florida. Ecological Applications 8:975–989.

Grace, J.B., M.D. Smith, S.L. Grace, S.L. Collins, and T.J. Stohlgren. 2001. Interactions between fire and invasive plants in temperate grasslands of North America. Pages 40–65 in K.E.M. Galley and T.P. Wilson (eds.), Proceedings of the Invasive Species Workshop: The Role of Fire in the Control and Spread of Invasive Species. Fire Conference 2000: The First National Congress on Fire Ecology, Prevention, and Management. Tall Timbers Research Station, Tallahassee, FL.

Haidinger, T.L., and J.E. Keeley. 1993. Role of high fire frequency in destruction of mixed chaparral. Madroño 40:141–147.

Hamilton, J.G. 1997. Changing perceptions of pre-European grasslands in California. Madroño 44:311–333.

Harrison, S., B.D. Inouye, and H.D. Safford. 2003. Ecological heterogeneity in the effects of grazing and fire on grassland diversity. Conservation Biology 17:837–845.

Harrod, R.J., and S. Reichard. 2001. Fire and invasive species within the temperate and boreal coniferous forests of North America. Pages 95–101 in K.E.M. Galley and T.P. Wilson (eds.), Proceedings of the Invasive Species Workshop: The Role of Fire in the Control and Spread of Invasive Species. Fire Conference 2000: The First National Congress on Fire Ecology, Prevention, and Management. Tall Timbers Research Station, Tallahassee, FL.

Harty, F.M. 1986. Exotics and their ecological ramifications. Natural Areas Journal 6:20–26.

Hatch, D.A., J.W. Bartolome, J.S. Fehmi, and D.S. Hillyard. 1999. Effects of burning and grazing on a coastal California grassland. Restoration Ecology 7:376–381.

Heady, H.F. 1972. Burning and the grasslands in California. Pages 97–107 in Proceedings 12th Annual Tall Timbers Fire Ecology Conference. Tall Timbers Research Station, Tallahassee, FL.

Heady, H.F. 1988. Valley grassland. Pages 491–514 in M.G. Barbour and J. Major (eds.), Terrestrial Vegetation of California. Wiley Interscience, New York.

Hervey, D.F. 1949. Reaction of a California annual-plant community to fire. Journal of Range Management 2:116–121.

Hickman, J.C. 1993. The Jepson Manual: Higher Plants of California. University of California Press, Berkeley.

Hobbs, R.J., and L.F. Huenneke. 1992. Disturbance, diversity, and invasion: implications for conservation. Conservation Biology 6:324–337.

Holmes, P.M., and R.M. Cowling. 1997. The effects on invasion by *Acacia saligna* on the guild structure and regeneration capabilities of South African fynbos shrublands. Journal of Applied Ecology 34:317–332.

Hopkinson, P., J.S. Fehmi, and J.W. Bartolome. 1999. Summer burns reduce cover, but not spread, of barbed goatgrass in California grassland. Ecological Restoration 17:168–169.

Howe, H.F. 1995. Succession and fire season in experimental prairie plantings. Ecology 76:1917–1925.

Howe, H.F., and J.S. Brown. 2001. The ghost of granivory past. Ecology Letters 4:371–378.

Humphries, S.E., R.H. Groves, and D.S. Mitchell (eds.). 1991. Plant Invasions: The Incidence of Environmental Weeds in Australia. Kowari 2. Aust. Nat. Parks Wildlife Service, Canberra.

Hunter, R. 1991. Bromus invasions on the Nevada test site: present status of *B. rubens* and *B. tectorum* with notes on their relationship to disturbance and altitude. Great Basin Naturalist 51(2):176–182.

Jackson, L.E. 1985. Ecological origins of California's mediterranean grasses. Journal of Biogeography 12:349–361.

Jacobs, J.S., and R.L. Shelley. 2003. Prescribed fire effects on dalmation toadflax. Journal of Range Management 56:193–197.

Junak, S., T. Ayers, R. Scott, D. Wilken, and D. Young. 1995. A Flora of Santa Cruz Island. Santa Barbara Botanic Garden, Santa Barbara, CA. 397 p.

Keeley, J.E. 2001. Fire and invasive species in mediterranean-climate ecosystems of California. Pages 81–94 in K.E.M. Galley and T.P. Wilson (eds.), Proceedings of the Invasive Species Workshop: The Role of Fire in the Control and Spread of Invasive Species. Fire Conference 2000: The First National Congress on Fire Ecology, Prevention, and Management. Tall Timbers Research Station, Tallahassee, FL.

Keeley, J.E. 2006. Fire management impacts on invasive plants in the western United States. Conservation Biology 20:375–384.

Klinger, R.C., E.C. Underwood, and P.E. Moore. 2006. The role of environmental gradients in non-native plant invasions into burnt areas of Yosemite National Park, California. Diversity and Distributions 12:139–156.

Kyser, G.B., and J.M. DiTomaso. 2002. Instability in a grassland community after the control of yellow starthistle *(Centaurea solstitialis)* with prescribed burning. Weed Science 50:648–657.

Lonsdale, W.M. 1999. Global patterns of plant invasions and the concept of invasibility. Ecology 80:1522–1536.

Lonsdale, W.M., and I.L. Miller. 1993. Fire as a management tool for a tropical woody weed: *Mimosa pigra* in North Australia. Journal of Environmental Management 33:7–87.

Mack, M.C., and C.M. D'Antonio. 1998. Impacts of biological invasions on disturbance regimes. Trends in Ecology and Evolution 13:195–198.

Mack, M.C., C.M. D'Antonio, and R.E. Ley. 2001. Alteration of ecosystem nitrogen dynamics by exotic plants: a case study of C4 grasses in Hawaii. Ecological Applications 11:1323–1335.

Mack, R.N. 1981. Invasion of *Bromus tectorum* L. into western North America: an ecological chronicle. Agro-Ecosystems 7:145–165.

Mack, R.N. 1989. Temperate grasslands vulnerable to invasions: characteristics and consequences. Pages 155–179 in J.A. Drake, H.A. Mooney, F. DiCastri, R.H. Groves, F.J. Kruger, M. Rejmanek, and M. Williamson (eds.), Biological Invasions: A Global Perspective. Wiley and Sons, New York.

Mack, R.N., D. Simberloff, W.M. Lonsdale, H. Evans, M. Clout, and F.A. Bazzaz. 2000. Biotic invasions: causes, epidemiology, global consequences, and control. Ecological Applications 10:689–710.

Major, J., and W.T. Pyott. 1966. Buried, viable seeds in two California bunchgrass sites and their bearing on the definition of a flora. Vegetatio 13:253–282.

Maranon, T., and J.W. Bartolome. 1989. Seed and seedling populations in two contrasted communities: open grassland and oak understory in California. Acta Oecologia, Oecologia Plantarum 10:147–158.

Marty, J.T. 2002. Spatially-dependent effects of fire and grazing in a California annual grassland plant community. Ph.D. thesis (Chapter 3). University of California, Davis.

Menke, J.W. 1992. Grazing and fire management for native perennial grass restoration in California grasslands. Fremontia 20:22–25.

Merriam, K.E., J.E. Keeley, and J.L. Beyers. 2006. Fuel breaks affect nonnative species abundance in California plant communities. Ecological Applications 16:515–527.

Meyer, M.D., and P.M. Schiffman. 1999. Fire season and mulch reduction in a California grassland: a comparison of restoration strategies. Madroño 46:25–37.

Miller, L.M. 1988. How yellow bush lupine came to Humboldt Bay. Fremontia 16:6–7.

Miller, R.F., and R.J. Tausch. 2001. The role of fire in juniper and pinyon woodlands: a descriptive analysis. Pages 15–30 in K.E.M. Galley and T.P. Wilson (eds.), Proceedings of the Invasive Species Workshop: The Role of Fire in the Control and Spread of Invasive Species. Fire Conference 2000: The First National Congress on Fire Ecology, Prevention, and Management. Tall Timbers Research Station, Tallahassee, FL.

Minnich, R.A., M.G. Barbour, J.H. Burk, and R.A. Fernau. 1995. Sixty years of change in Californian conifer forests of the San Bernardino Mountains. Conservation Biology 9:902–914.

Minnich, R.A., and R.J. Dezzani. 1998. Historical decline of coastal sage scrub in the Riverside-Perris Plain, California. Western Birds 29:366–391.

Mooney, H.A., S.P. Hamburg, and J.A. Drake. 1989. The invasions of plants and animals into California. Pages 250–272 in J.A. Drake, H.A. Mooney, F. DiCastri, R.H. Groves, F.J. Kruger, M. Rejmanek, and M. Williamson (eds.), Biological Invasions: A Global Perspective. Wiley, New York.

Mueller-Dombois, D. 2001. Biological invasion and fire in tropical biomes. Pages 112– in K.E.M. Galley and T.P. Wilson (eds.), Proceedings of the Invasive Species Workshop: the Role of Fire in the Control and Spread of Invasive Species. Fire Conference 2000: The First National Congress on Fire Ecology, Prevention, and Management. Tall Timbers Research Station, Tallahassee, FL.

Myers, R.L., H.A. Belles, and J.R. Snyder. 2001. Prescribed fire in the management of Melaleuca quinquenervia in subtropical Florida. Pages 132–140 in K.E.M. Galley and T.P. Wilson (eds.), Proceedings of the Invasive Species Workshop: The Role of Fire in the Control and Spread of Invasive Species. Fire Conference 2000: The First National Congress on Fire Ecology, Prevention, and Management. Tall Timbers Research Station, Tallahassee, FL.

Nuzzo, V.A. 1991. Experimental control of garlic mustard (Alliaria petiolata [Bieb.] Cavara & Grande) in northern Illinois using fire, herbicide, and cutting. Natural Areas Journal 11:158–167.

Odion, D.C., and K. Hausenback. 2002. Response of French Broom to fire. Pages 296–307 in N.G. Sugihara, M. Morales, and T. Morales (eds.), Proceedings of the Symposium: Fire in California Ecosystems: Integrating Ecology, Prevention, and Management. Miscellaneaous Publication No. 1, Association for Fire Ecology.

Ostoja, S.M., and R.C. Klinger. 2000. The relationship of Bishop pine Pinus muricata morphology to serotiny on Santa Cruz Island, California. Pages 167–171 in D.R. Browne, K.L. Mitchell, and H.W. Chaney (eds.), Proceedings of the Fifth California Islands Symposium, Santa Barbara Museum of Natural History, Santa Barbara, CA.

Parker, I.M., D. Simberloff, W.M. Lonsdale, K. Goodell, M. Wonham, P.M. Kareiva, M.H. Williamson, B. Bon Holle, P.B. Moyle, J.E. Byers, and L. Goldwasser. 1999. Impact: toward a framework for understanding the ecological effects of invaders. Biological Invasions 1:3–19.

Parsons, D.J., and S. DeBenedetti. 1979. Impact of fire suppression on a mixed-conifer forest. Forest Ecology and Management 2:21–33.

Parsons, D.J., and T.J. Stohlgren. 1989. Effects of varying fire regimes on annual grasslands in the southern Sierra Nevada of California. Madroño 36:154–168.

Parsons, D.J., and T.W. Swetnam. 1989. Restoring natural fire to the sequoia-mixed conifer forest: should intense fire play a role? Tall Timbers Fire Ecology Conference 20:20–30.

Pickart, A.J. 2000. Lupinus arboreus Sims. Pages 231–235 in C.C. Bossard, J.M. Randall, and M.C. Hoshovsky (eds.), Invasive Plants of California's Wildlands. University of California Press, Berkeley.

Pickford, G.D. 1932. The influence of continued heavy grazing and promiscuous burning on spring-fall ranges in Utah. Ecology 13:159–171.

Pimentel, D., L. Lach, R. Zuniga, and D. Morrison. 2000. Environmental and economic costs on nonindigenous species in the United States. BioScience 50:53–65.

Pollak, O., and T. Kan. 1998. The use of prescribed fire to control invasive exotic weeds at Jepson Prairie Preserve. Pages 241–249 in C.W. Witham, E.T. Bauder, D. Belk, W.R. Ferren Jr., and R. Onduff (eds.), Ecology, Conservation, and Management of Vernal Pool Ecosystems. California Native Plant Society, Sacramento.

Pyne, S.J. 1984. Introduction to Wildland Fire: Fire Management in the United States. Wiley, New York.

Randall, J.M. 1996. Weed control for the preservation of biological diversity. Weed Technology 10:370–383.

Randall, J.M., R.R. Lewis, and D.B. Jensen. 1997. Ecological restoration. Pages 205–219 in D. Simberloff, D.C. Schmitz, and T.C. Brown (eds.), Strangers in Paradise. Island Press, Washington, DC.

Randall, J.M., and M. Rejmanek. 1993. Interference of bull thistle (Cirsium vulgare) with growth of ponderosa pine (Pinus ponderosa) seedlings in a forest plantation. Canadian Journal of Forest Research 23:1507–1513.

Randall, J.M., M. Rejmanek, and J.C. Hunter. 1998. Characteristics of the exotic flora of California. Fremontia 26:3–12.

Rejmanek, M. 1989. Invasibility of plant communities. Pages 369–388 in J.A. Drake, H.A. Mooney, F. DiCastri, R.H. Groves, F.J. Kruger, M. Rejmanek, and M. Williamson (eds.), Biological Invasions: A Global Perspective. Wiley, New York.

Rejmanek, M. 1995. What makes a species invasive? Pages 3–13 in P. Pysek, K. Prach, M. Rejmanek, and P.M. Wade (eds.), Plant Invasions. SPB Academic Publishing, The Hague, The Netherlands.

Rejmanek, M., and J.M. Randall. 1994. Invasive alien plants in California: 1993 summary and comparisons with other areas in North America. Madroño 41:161–177.

Rejmanek, M., C.D. Thomsen, and I.D. Peters. 1991. Invasive vascular plants of California. Pages 81–101 in R.H. Groves and D. DiCastri (eds.), Biogeography of Mediterranean Invasions. Cambridge University Press, Cambridge.

Richardson, D.M., P. Pysek, M. Rejmanek, M.G. Barbour, F.D. Pannetta, and C.J. West. 2000. Naturalization and invasion of alien plants: concepts and definitions. Diversity and Distributions 6:93–107.

Richburg, J.A., A.C. Dibble, and W.A.I. Patterson. 2001. Woody invasive species and their role in altering fire regimes of the Northeast and Mid-Atlantic states. Pages 104–111 in K.E.M. Galley and T.P. Wilson (eds.), Proceedings of the Invasive Species Workshop: the Role of Fire in the Control and Spread of Invasive Species. Fire Conference 2000: The First National Congress on Fire Ecology, Prevention, and Management. Tall Timbers Research Station, Tallahassee, FL.

Roja, D., and J. Popenoe. 1998. Fire effects on first-year scotch broom in Redwood National and State Parks. Pages 59–60 in M. Kelly, E. Wagner, and P. Warner (eds.), Proceedings California Exotic Pest Plant Council Symposium, Vol. 4, Ontario, CA.

Rowe, J.S. 1981. Concepts of fire effects on plant individuals and species. Pages 135–154 in R.W. Wein and D.A. Maclean (eds.), The Role of Fire in Northern Circumpolar Ecosystems. Wiley, New York.

Ruyle, G.B., B.A. Roundy, and J.R. Cox. 1988. Effects of burning on germinability of Lehmann lovegrass. Journal of Range Management 41:404–406.

Sapsis, D.B., D.V. Pearman, and R.E. Martin. 1995. Progression of the Oakland/Berkeley Hills "Tunnel Fire." Pages 187–189 in D.R. Weise and R.E. Martin (eds.), The Biswell Symposium: Fire Issues and Solutions in Urban Interface and Wildland Ecosystems. USDA Forest Service General Technical Report PSW-GTR-158. Albany, CA.

Schoennagel, T.L., and D.M. Waller. 1999. Understory responses to fire and artificial seeding in an eastern Cascades Abies grandis forest, U.S.A. Canadian Journal of Forest Research 29:1393–1401.

Schultz, A.M., J.L. Launchbaugh, and H. Biswell. 1955. Relationship between grass density and brush seedling survival. Ecology 36:226–238.

Schwartz, M.W., D.J. Porter, J.M. Randall, and K.E. Lyons. 1996. Impact of nonindigenous plants. Pages 1203–1217 in Sierra Nevada Ecosystem Project: Final Report to Congress II: Assessments and Scientific Basis for Management Options.

Sharp, L.A., M. Hironaka, and E.W. Tisdale. 1957. Viability of medusa-head (Elymus caput-medusae L.) seed collected in Idaho. Journal of Range Management 10:123–126.

Simms, P.L., and P.G. Risser. 2000. Grasslands. Pages 323–356 in M.G. Barbour and W.D. Billings (eds.), North American Terrestrial Vegetation, 2nd edition. Cambridge University Press, New York.

Stylinski, C.D., and E.B. Allen. 1999. Lack of native species recovery following severe exotic disturbance in southern Californian shrublands. Journal of Applied Ecology 36:544–554.

Swezey, M., and D.C. Odion. 1997. Fire on the mountain: a land manager's manifesto for broom control. Pages 76–81 in M. Kelly, E. Wagner, and P. Warner (eds.), Proceedings California Exotic Pest Plant Council Symposium, Vol. 3, Concord, CA.

Vitousek, P.M., C.M. D'Antonio, L.L. Loope, and R. Westbrooks. 1996. Biological invasions as global environmental change. American Scientist 84:468–478.

Vogl, R.J. 1974. Effects of fire on grasslands. Pages 139–194 in C.E. Ahlgren (ed.), Fire and Ecosystems. Academic Press, New York.

Whisenant, S.G. 1990. Changing fire frequencies on Idaho's Snake River Plains: ecological and management implications. Pages 4–10 in Symposium on Cheatgrass Invasion, Shrub Die-Off and Other Aspects of Shrub Biology and Management. USDA Forest Service, Las Vegas, NV.

White, D.J., E. Haber, and C. Keddy. 1993. Invasive Plants of Natural Habitats in Canada: An Integrated Review of Wetland and Upland Species and Legislation Governing Their Control. Canadian Wildlife Service, Environment Canada, and Canadian Museum of Nature, Ottawa, Canada.

Wilcove, D.S., D. Rothstein, J. Dubow, A. Phillips, and E. Losos. 1998. Quantifying threats to imperiled species in the United States. BioScience 48:607–615.

Wills, R.D. 1999. Effective fire planning for California native grasslands. Pages 75–78 in J.E. Keeley, M. Baer-Keeley, and C.J. Fotheringham (eds.), 2nd Interface Between Ecology and Land Development in California. U.S. Geological Survey, Sacramento, CA.

Wills, R.D. 2001. Effects of varying fire regimes in a California native grasslands. Ecological Restoration 19:109.

Wilson, E.O., and F.M. Peter (eds.). 1988. Biodiversity. National Academy Press, Washington, DC.

Wright, H.A., and A.W. Bailey. 1982. Fire Ecology: United States and Canada. Wiley, New York.

Young, J.A., and R.R. Blank. 1995. Cheatgrass and wildfires in the intermountain west. Pages 6–8 in J. Lovich, J. Randall, and M. Kelly (eds.), Proceedings California Exotic Pest Plant Council Symposium, Pacific Grove, CA.

Young, J.A., and R.A. Evans. 1971. Invasion of medusahead into the Great Basin. Weed Science 18:89–97.

Zavaleta, E. 2000a. The economic value of controlling an invasive shrub. Ambio 29:462–467.

Zavaleta, E. 2000b. Valuing ecosystem services lost to Tamarix invasion in the United States. Pages 261–299 in H.A. Mooney and R.J. Hobbs (eds.), Invasive Species in a Changing World. Island Press, Washington, DC.

Zedler, P. 1995. Fire frequency in southern California shrublands: biological effects and management options. Pages 101–112 in J.E. Keeley and T. Scott (eds.), Brushfires in California: Ecology and Resource Management. International Association of Wildfire.

Zedler, P.H., C.R. Gautier, and G.S. McMaster. 1983. Vegetation change in response to extreme events: the effect of a short interval between fires in California chaparral and coastal scrub. Ecology 64:809–818.

CHAPTER 23

Fire and At-Risk Species

KEVIN E. SHAFFER

Nothing is more priceless and more worthy of preservation than the rich array of animal life with which our country has been blessed.

PRESIDENT RICHARD NIXON, *signing the federal Endangered Species Act, December 28, 1973*

Is fire management on a collision course with disaster? Perhaps, because wildfires continue to become more intense and destructive of resources, and expenses in fire control are increasing at an astronomical rate.

HAROLD H. BISWELL, 1989

A Summary of the Conflict

Previous chapters have described the essential ecological function of fire and society's struggle to control and manage it. As described in Chapter 18, modern-era management of fire commenced at the turn of the nineteenth century, and even the issue of wildland fire burning at the urban interface has been part of the California landscape since the 1920s. The middle of the twentieth century not only represented a growing attention to fire management and the use of fire, but also society's growing attention to the welfare of animals and plants. In the 1960s, federal protection was afforded to laboratory animals, and over the next 20 years several important laws and conventions to protect native plant and animals were enacted (Table 23.1).

Perhaps the most significant statute was the federal Endangered Species Act of 1972 (ESA). ESA was the first law of its kind, specifically affording native plants and animals threatened or endangered with extinction federal attention and protection. And in 1986, the State of California passed its own law to protect its native plants and animals, the California Endangered Species Act (CESA).

As California's human population has increased and urban development has pushed into the state's wildlands, homeowners' and entire communities' experience and familiarity with wildfire has become more frequent and more disconcerting. California Department of Forestry and Fire Protection (CDF) statistics reveal the trend in large wildland fire conflagrations. Including the devastating fires that burned in southern California in the autumn of 2003, 15 of the 20 largest fires have taken place since the inception of ESA (CDF 2003a); 17 of the top 20 fires as measured by structures lost also occurred during this same period (CDF 2003b). And

perhaps even more important to the general public, of the 62 fatalities that occurred during the 20 fires referenced in the second statistic, 57 perished in fires since 1980. Growing human population and expanding urban areas not only have brought more people into conflict with wildfires but also affect how wildlands are managed. For example, as described in Chapter 19, the ability to use prescribed fire or allow wildfires to burn has become exceedingly difficult. Population growth into wildlands has made management of vegetation more complex. Agencies responsible for conserving wilderness and natural resources (e.g., California Department of Fish and Game [CDFG], U.S. Fish and Wildlife Service, California Department of Parks and Recreation, National Park Service, Forest Service, Bureau of Land Management) and agencies responsible for addressing vegetation fuel on public lands (e.g., National Park Service, Forest Service, Bureau of Land Management, California Department of Forestry and Fire Protection, U.S. Fish and Wildlife Service, Bureau of Indian Affairs, local fire districts) increasingly spend more time and money addressing fuel management, and agency policies come into conflict when trying to manage fire and fuel while protecting ecological values and at-risk species. California citizens, though wanting to protect the state's native biota, have become increasingly concerned with the impacts of large fires to lives, property, and finances.

Laws protecting at-risk species were enacted when both the California and federal governments recognized the ever-increasing threat to many species. Rectifying the causes of endangerment or the threat of future endangerment of extinction are the essential goals of both ESA and CESA. The primary intents of the other laws and policies are conservation and protection of at-risk species *before* they become threatened or endangered. Fire and fuel management regulations,

TABLE 23.1

Laws and conventions applicable to California to protect animals and plants, year enacted, and regional scope of authority

Law or Convention	Year Enacted (Last Amended)	Governing Authority and Responsibility
Migratory Bird Treaty Act	1918 (1998)	Canada, USA, Mexico, Japan, and Russia
Bald Eagle Act	1940 (1978)	National
Airborne Hunting Act	1956	National
Animal Welfare Act	1966 (1984)	National
Wildlife Protection Practices (Article 9 of Forest Practices Regulations of the California [Z'Berg-Nejedly] Forest Practice Act [CFPA]	1973 (2003)	State
Convention on International Trade in Endangered Species of Wild Fauna and Flora (CITES)	1973 (2003)	International
Federal Endangered Species Act (ESA)	1973 (2003)	National
Native Plant Protection Act (NPPA)	1977	State
California Endangered Species Act (CESA)	1986 (2003)	State
Neotropical Migratory Bird Conservation Act (NMBCA)	2000	Western hemisphere

policies, and activities sometimes conflict with protecting at-risk species because loss and alteration of habitat and human activities often create need for increased protection (Box 23.1). Fire suppression, prescribed burning, vegetation reduction, post-fire restoration, air quality control, and protection of homes and lives rarely fully consider or integrate conservation or protection of at-risk species. The reality that each of these two sets of laws and activities do not consider adequately the other may seem understandable, but this lack of integration, or perhaps adjustment, may be the basic reason for the conflicts that have occurred over the last two decades in California. To date, this conflict seemingly has pitted species protection against protection of humans, homes, and other natural resource values.

With late summer and early autumn come news reports of wildfires raging somewhere in California. Over the last 12 years, a tangent issue, the conflicts between species protection and fire management, often shares headlines and occupies the time and energy of those tasked with responsibilities of the two goals. Though the contention between these protections is not unique to California, it may be more pronounced because of many complicated and integrated issues and values: hundreds of thousands of acres that burn (annual average from 1972 to 2002: 249,173 acres [CDF 2003c]); private property lost due to wildfire (annual average from 1972 to 2002: $97,266,559.00 [CDF 2003c]); the approximately 34,336,000 people that inhabit California (as of January 1, 2000, California Department of Finance); the many ecosystems that are fire adapted or dependent; the thousands of species that live in those systems; and the hundreds of species that are either state or federally listed (as of January 2004, 282 plant and 148 animal species are listed under CESA and/or ESA [CDFG 2003, 2004]). Nowhere else in the continental United States are fire regimes more complex, bioregions so variable, and so many species listed—all of this ecological diversity coinciding with the nation's largest economy and population.

Air quality management	Restricted season for prescribed burning
Invasive plant species control	Timing of prescribed burning
	Mechanical treatment
Vegetation management to lower risk of fire:	Chemical application to vegetation
	Mechanical removal or crushing of vegetation
	Road construction
	Prescribed burning
	Use of grazing herds to lower vegetation load
Fire suppression:	Mechanical removal or clearance
	Use of heavy machinery (i.e., compaction of soil)
	Road construction
	Back-burning and burning out of vegetation
	Water drafting
	Application of fire-surfacant
	Establishing incident command camps and additional
	locales for firefighting equipment and staff
Post-wildfire rehabilitation and watershed restoration:	Application of seed
	Additional removal or clearance of vegetation
	Fire incident mop-up
	Road construction
	Engineering technologies for erosion control

The struggle begins well before fire season. Activities to reduce the dry and dead vegetation that feeds wildfires are scrutinized, in part because of their possible or actual effects to native plants and animals and habitat. Residents and communities clear, chip, or crush brush, burn-off grass, or thin trees. Agencies and land conservancies apply broader mechanical treatment or conduct prescribed burns. And agencies develop long-term land management plans, which include fire and fuel management. In many circumstances, at-risk species potentially are affected. Addressing species and habitat needs takes planning and time and more resources. Simply put, to-date in California, fire and fuel management and at-risk species conservation and protection have often been more in conflict than in accord with one another because of the lack of planning, time, and resources dedicated to the conflicts. Ironically, the enforce-

ment of ESA and CESA has neither interfered with fire management activities nor affected any parties participating in fuel or fire management activities. It has been the real or perceived constraints that ESA and CESA place on fire and fuel management activities that form the basis for the conflict in California. Nonetheless, the conflict is real and increasingly has set various organizations and agencies at odds with one another.

What Is an At-Risk Species?

At risk refers to legal or land management status; it is not a biological trait. Several terms the reader may be familiar with (e.g., *candidate, rare, threatened, endangered, sensitive, special concern*) are included in the *at-risk* designation. The phrase refers to native plants and animals identified through a variety

TABLE 23.2
Legal protection and special consideration afforded California native plants and animals
under various federal and state laws

Federal Protection Opportunities	California Protection Opportunities
Species listing, ESA	Species listing, CESA
Incidental take permits, ESA	Incidental take permits, CESA
Government agency consultation, ESA	Recovery planning, CESA
Critical habitat designation, ESA	Natural community conservation planning, NCCP
Habitat conservation planning, ESA	Special sensitive species listing and protection, CFPR
Recovery planning, ESA	
Evaluating and mitigating significant impacts to species, NEPA	Evaluating and mitigating significant impacts to species, CEQA
Evaluation, planning, and avoidance, NMBCA	

of formal means, by one or more organizations or agencies, to be deserving of special protection and/or land management attention, and includes those: (1) formally identified and protected by law, (2) given special management protection by agency policy, and (3) specially monitored because of vulnerable status or circumstances. At-risk species include those with legal protection, usually referring to CESA or ESA. Legal protection also is afforded to some animals under California's Forest Practice Rules. Also, the California Environmental Quality Act (CEQA) defines *sensitive* to include species determined to meet the criteria for listing under CESA and needing investigation and consideration for impacts that may be significant during the development of environmental impact reports. Results of such investigations must be made available to the public. Last, some agencies give special attention to species identified as sensitive (e.g., U.S. Forest Service and Bureau of Land Management) or of special concern (e.g., CDFG) because of their rarity or susceptibility. These designations do not usually include regulatory or legal protection but do allow agencies to develop policies and programs for conserving species before listing becomes necessary (Table 23.2).

Chapters 18 and 19 discuss how land management agencies and the California public have been keenly interested and involved in managing fire for decades. This chapter focuses on the fundamental issues that surround efforts to protect and conserve at-risk species while managing fire and vegetation. The chapter briefly highlights the essential aspects of species protection laws and policies that have been points of relevance or contention with fire and fuel management. It describes how fuel treatment can impact at-risk species and how protection of at-risk species can influence fuel reduction. Finally, the chapter puts forth ideas and perspectives on how protecting native species and their habitat and managing wildfire could and should be better integrated.

Protecting At-Risk Species

Agency and public attention has focused on threatened and endangered species. These are the most visible at-risk species. Protection under ESA and CESA is not identical in all aspects, but both have specific elements that are relevant in fire and fuel management (Table 23.2). The most obvious element is the listing of species as threatened or endangered. Such a designation means that many fuel management activities must take into consideration the potential harmful or deathly impacts to listed species. Such consideration has been seen as restricting or preventing fuel management activities. Under ESA, critical habitat is also identified, and these areas require special considerations regarding any land practices. Agencies and parties may pursue permits to allow for incidental take[1] to their otherwise lawful fuel management activities and, if dealing with federally listed species, may also pursue a Habitat Conservation Plan, where all land management activities are evaluated and planned for in relation to species needs. Both ESA and CESA allow recovery planning for listed species, and this planning and implementation process allows the consideration of: (1) the impacts that might occur from fuel and fire management activities and (2) what benefit such activities would actually provide for species and habitat.

---

1. In California, take is defined as "hunt, pursue, catch, capture, or kill, or attempt to hunt, pursue, catch, capture, or kill" [Section 86, California Fish and Game Code]. For the federal Endangered Species Act, take is defined as harass, harm, pursue, hunt, shoot, wound, kill, trap, capture, or collect any threatened or endangered species. Take, under the California and federal endangered species acts, is prohibited.

Incidental take is the unexpected, but not necessarily unforeseen, take of protected species. Under California and federal law, incidental take may be permitted if activities (i.e., causes) are otherwise legal, minimize impact, and are not foreseen to impact the species in total [see CFGC, §2080–2085; sections 7 and 10, ESA].

Several other conventions and laws addressing protection of plants and animals (Table 23.1) afford less direct protection or address a much smaller group of at-risk animals and plants. Nine species of birds are listed as sensitive under Forest Practice Rules of the California Forest Practices Act and are given special rules for forestry practices, including vegetation management and broadcast burning. Native birds migrating through or to the state are protected by the Neotropical Migratory Bird Treaty Act, but ironically, the federal courts have found that federal agencies are exempt to protections provided by the act when conducting fuel and fire management activities. Hence, protection only applies to private, local, and state agencies and private, regional, and state property. Two additional laws, the National Environmental Protection Act (NEPA) and CEQA, afford species listed under ESA and CESA, respectively, consideration in fuel and fire management projects. CEQA also affords consideration to species that meet the criteria of CESA. But for both environmental acts, the consideration is relative, and often fuel and fire management activities are deemed less than significant or even exempt from consideration.

The Interface between At-Risk Species and Fire and Fuel Management

Many questions arise when addressing the interface between managing fuel and fire and protecting at-risk species. What means of reducing fuel are available that do not impact species or at least minimize the effects? How does controlling invasive species affect native species? How can fires best be fought, burned areas restored, and species be either minimally affected or actually benefited by such actions? How can land management actions regarding fire be undertaken without contributing to the future California or federal listing? And possibly most important of all, what is the role of fire in restoring, enhancing, or simply maintaining the ecological integrity of a landscape so that the native animals and plants dependent on that landscape may be viable into the future? These are but a few of the questions that local, state, and federal agencies, land owners and conservancies, fire departments and districts, and conservation and environmental groups are asking and trying to answer.

As with the immediate and longer-term effects that wildfire has on plants and animals (Chapters 6 and 7), management actions also can have immediate and longer-term effects on at-risk species. Fuel reduction activities, prescribed fire, and post-fire seeding historically have been the primary issues of concern, but other issues, such as some firefighting tactics, use of chemicals and grazing to reduce fuel, and use of heavy machinery after fires are either potential issues or have some example where they have posed a threat to at-risk species.

Much already has been discussed in this section with regard to managing fire in California. All of these management issues (i.e., fuel reduction, air quality, watershed health, invasive species control) are even more complicated when protecting at-risk species is added to the equation. With more than 400 listed species in California, it is nearly impossible not to have at least one species potentially affected by such activities. Often, the goals of managing fire or fuel have conflicted with protection of species. In general, the integration of fire management with protection of at-risk species historically has been inconsistent. This has not always been the situation, but unfortunately, it has been the norm.

There is a range of issues related to fuel and fire management and species protection, from conducting prescribed burns (e.g., as a tool for recovering at-risk species versus reducing fuel load) to addressing potential effects from firefighting tactics (e.g., blading a given area) and post-fire restoration (i.e., impacts to native flora from grasses seeded to reduce erosion). Table 23.3 lists many of the general conflicts that have arisen between fuel and fire management and species protection. These activities span the entire range of fire and fuel management—fuel reduction and prescribed burning, fire suppression, and post-fire rehabilitation. Planning and implementation of activities can be altered to protect species and habitat, but the necessary changes are often not seen as being conducive to the primary goals of the fire or fuel management objectives. In essence, protection of at-risk species and their habitats is often identified as a hindrance, even a barrier, to planning and implementing fuel and fire management activities.

Road construction is one activity that is universally utilized in fuels and fire management, and just as universally affects at-risk species. Roads are constructed to both access more-isolated areas and break up such areas in pre-fire treatments. Roads are built and widened during fire suppression activities, and road construction can also be part of post-fire rehabilitation efforts. Roads split and alter habitat, are sites of erosion and sediment delivery to watercourses (see Chapter 20), and facilitate the spread of invasive species (see Chapter 22).

The conflicts have risen steadily during the last 25 years. Fire scientists and ecologists have become more involved in fire and fuel management, providing technical advice and recommendations on fire incidents and post-fire restoration and rehabilitation teams, aiding in the development of fuel reduction and prescribed fire plans, studying the effects of fire and fire surrogates on biotic communities and species, and describing historical and current fire regimes in various ecosystems. In fact, the first conference dedicated to fire effects and rare and endangered species and habitats took place in Coeur d' Arlene, Idaho (Greenlee 1997) because of the growing knowledge about the fire ecology of species and the more frequent, more contentious fire issues, and the ecological functioning of fire.

There are many considerations for protecting at-risk species and their habitat when planning and implementing fire and fuel management activities (Box 23.2), and such considerations do place restrictions and conditions on land management activities. Prescribed burning in the spring may be desirable because of safety and air quality issues, but may pose a threat to migratory bird nesting, ground-nesting birds, sprouting or flowering plants, or even nursing mammals. Using

TABLE 23.3
Potential conflicts between mechanical fuel reduction and protection of at-risk species

Consideration or Technique	Potential Conflicts
Timing (seasonal)	Feasibility to do project and attaining desired results versus impacting crucial aspect of species life cycle
Level of complexity and detail	Affordability, time required to conduct treatment, level of personnel needed versus planning for the special needs and variety of species involved
Scope (spatial)	Attaining a lower fire risk versus accomplishing what is feasible versus treating an area too small to reduce future threat to biota or to allow fire to play a future ecological role
Re-entry for further treatment	The need for additional or continual treatment versus repeated stress on species or fire not being used in the future
Techniques:	
Fuel buffer	The height needed for effect versus impacts to plants and animal habitat
Fuel break	Exposure of soil and elimination of plants and animal habitat; potential disturbance to animal home range or migration; stimulation of invasive plant species
Shaded fuel break	Removal of habitat elements; fundamental alteration of vegetation community; disturbance of migration corridors, cover, or shelter

particular types of machinery or treating particular stands or quantities of vegetation might be advantageous for reducing fuel before fire season, during a wildfire, or even as post-fire treatment, but may threaten unique or rare at-risk plant populations and animal habitat, or disturb critical animal behavior (this relates to pre-season treatment specifically).

Vegetation Management to Lower Risk of Fire

There are four general categories of techniques available to reduce vegetation: chemical, biological, mechanical, and prescribed burning. Each category has various applications and each application has various degrees of effectiveness and potential impact to biota. Chemical and biological treatments are not known to have caused great harm to at-risk species, though this conclusion would be expected because these two strategies are rarely used. For all intents and purposes, chemical treatments are not used by public agencies and are rarely used by private landowners to control or reduce fuel load and do not represent a threat currently to at-risk species. If chemical treatments were to be used by agencies in the future, there clearly would be a need to evaluate the impacts to at-risk species, especially plants and amphibi-

ous and aquatic animals. Biological treatment is also a rarely used strategy. Biological treatment is the use of grazing animals to keep down fuel by strategically or broadly allowing herds to graze and browse grasses and shrubs. There is the potential that the use of grazing herds (e.g., cattle, sheep, goats) would impact plants (e.g., by trampling, through consumption), animals (e.g., through disturbance of animal behavior, short-term displacement, trampling of nests), and habitat (e.g., through encroachment of invasive plant species, destruction of native seed banks, alteration in solar radiation penetration). Perhaps the best-known example of the interaction between a biological treatment and an at-risk species is Laguna Beach. Goats have been used in the Laguna Beach area since the Laguna fire of 1993. There has been the concern that the goats' consumption of surrounding vegetation, disturbance of the soil, and increased solar radiation penetration has impacted the health of some populations of Laguna Beach dudleya (*Dudleya stolonifera*), listed as threatened under both ESA and CESA. However, it is still unclear what effect the goats have had both on Laguna Beach dudleya and reducing the risk or impact of future fires.

Whereas chemical and biological treatments are relatively minor or non-existent issues currently, mechanical treatment

Air quality management	What is the effect of limiting the burn window for prescribed fire?
Invasive plant species control	What are the immediate and longer-term effects to native species and habitat from
	Prescribed burning?
	Herbicide application?
	Mechanical treatment?
Fuel reduction and prescribed burning	Will species or habitat be directly impacted? Will species habitat be impacted longer term? Are incidental take permits required? What is the pretreatment condition?
Fire suppression	Are there tactical options that would avoid or minimize impact to species or habitat? Can unburned areas be left as biological refugia?
Post-fire rehabilitation	What are the effects of post-fire clean-up? What are the effects of seeding on native plant communities and herbivorous animals? What are the effects of check dams, silt fences, and other technologies on riparian and aquatic ecosystems? Will monitoring occur to verify and validate both effectiveness of efforts and effects to species and habitat?

Protection of life and property has been universally accepted as paramount, so planning and implementation of tactics is always done within the context of judgment and decisions of the agency or agencies responsible for suppressing the wildfire.

and prescribed fire are major issues. Both types of treatments have the potential to both reduce the risk and impact of wildfire and contribute to the conservation of at-risk species. But often, consideration of at-risk species is secondary or even interpreted as an obstacle to specific, preferred activities or to entire plans.

MECHANICAL TREATMENTS

Mechanical treatments represent some of the most common and desired treatments currently used to reduce vegetation fuel. There are many reasons for this, including the lower cost, ready availability and variety of techniques, the social acceptance, and relative low risk to field personnel and local residents. But the immediate physical changes to the vegetation community and soil and longer-term ecological changes affect at-risk species and their habitats. Alteration and removal of vegetation equates to alteration of plant and animal habitat. Mechanical treatment upturns and compacts

soil, affecting plants and surface and subterranean animals. Removing overstory trees and shrubs alters arboreal animal habitat, allowing increased solar radiation to reach understory and herbaceous plants, and exposing understory and surface animal cover and shelter. The use of mechanical equipment and presence of field personnel can disturb animal behavior, and many techniques disturb soil and vegetation in such a way as to promote invasive plant species to expand or colonize an area (also see Chapter 20). In many regions of California, especially in the urban intermix, managing vegetation for the purposes of protecting human life and property has immediate and longer-term ecological consequences for native species (see Sidebar 23.1).

Regardless of the complications and complexities of integrating species needs, these issues do not dictate that mechanical treatment has to be contrary to protection of at-risk species. In fact, many scientists and conservationists believe that the application of fire is inevitably necessary to recovery or stabilization of many at-risk species and that

FIGURE 23.1.1 Fuel modifications around structures on the urban-wildland interface often influence habitat over a much wider area.

To reduce the risk to life and property from structures burning in wildfires, reduction of combustible fuel around structures is mandated by law and insurers. These actions include removal of native vegetation, often accompanied by installation of landscaping species and irrigation. This practice of "fuel modification" or "vegetation management" contributes, along with structural design (i.e., roofing, chimneys, siding) and local infrastructure (access routes, water supply), to reducing fire danger for homes (Vicars 1999).

The fuel modification requirements prescribed by local fire officials are reinforced by insurance carriers. For properties with high fire hazard, the insurer of last resort in California is the California Fair Access to Insurance Requirements (FAIR) Plan. For properties within designated "brush areas" (so designated by the Insurance Services Office), the FAIR Plan assesses a surcharge based on the amount of clearance surrounding a property. Since the most recent revision of these charges in 1999, all structures with less than 200 feet of brush clearance are assessed surcharges, ranging from $0.13 to $2.52 per hundred dollars of insurance, based on clearance distance and other hazard factors, including distance to fire station, roof type, and type of coverage. For a new structure not adjacent to existing structures, a 200-foot fuel modification zone results in the destruction of a minimum of three acres of natural vegetation through direct removal or manipulation. However, the effects of fuel modification activities extend well beyond the 200-foot radius, and these activities degrade habitats over a much greater area (Fig. 23.1.1).

Birds, mammals, and other vertebrates are affected by fuel modification practices. By increasing the amount of edge habitats, fire clearance will greatly exacerbate the effects of urbanization. Urbanization, and fire clearance with it, increases the abundance of urban-tolerant bird species and reduces populations of interior habitat specialists (Bolger et al. 1997, Stralberg 2000). By transforming bird communities, fuel modification often increases abundance of nest predators (e.g., Western scrub-jay *[Aphelocoma coerlescens]*, American crow *[Corvus brachyrhynchos]*). An increase in edges and abundance of these species will increase nest predation on habitat specialists in, for example, chaparral (Langen et al. 1991).

Fuel modification often results in the introduction of invasive exotic plant species to wildland areas. For example, Capeweed (*Arctotheca calendula*) and Chinese tallow tree (*Sapium sebiferum*) are recommended by the County of Los Angeles in fuel modification zones, but are listed as "Red Alert" species with the potential to spread explosively by the California Exotic Pest Plant Council (1999). Other weedy plant species recommended by the County include *Acacia* spp., *Gazania rigens, Lonicera japonica, Echium fatuosum, Cotoneaster* spp., *Eucalyptus* spp., and *Verbena* spp. In addition to the purposeful introduction of invasive species, the disturbance associated with fire clearance promotes the invasion of plant species already associated with residential development (Rundel 2000). Disturbance promotes invasion of alien plants throughout California and in other mediterranean regions (Kotanen 1997, Rundel 1998). The understories of areas subject to fuel modification are rapidly dominated by invasive exotic grasses and forbs, which increases the movements of aliens into wildlands, and produces seeds that may invade wildlands after fire (Keeley 2002). Invasive plant species can profoundly affect ecosystem structure and function by modifying fire regimes, nutrient cycling, and erosion patterns (Mooney et al. 1986, Minnich and Dezzani 1998, Rundel 1998).

Fuel modification activities also disrupt native arthropod communities, including relations such as seed dispersal mutualisms. Fuel modification usually requires the introduction of a permanent water source in the form of an "irrigated zone" surrounding structures. This irrigated zone, along with disturbance of clearance, promotes the invasion of alien insect species, such as the Argentine ant (*Linepithema humile*), into native habitats. The deleterious effect of Argentine ants on native arthropods is well documented, with numerous studies reporting a decrease in arthropod diversity as Argentine ant abundance increases (Erickson 1971, Human and Gordon 1997, Kennedy 1998). Fuel modification increases the abundance of Argentine ants by providing two conditions that increase invasion: a water source (Holway 1998) and increased disturbance (Human et al. 1998). Argentine ants invade far beyond the water sources and into surrounding undisturbed habitats, with increased abundance documented to a distance of up to 650 feet (Suarez et al. 1998).

Community-level analysis indicates that arthropod species composition changes and overall diversity decreases when habitats are subjected to fuel modification. For example, disturbed coastal sage scrub sites have fewer arthropod predator species, such as scorpions and trap-door spiders, and are dominated by exotic arthropods, such as Argentine ants, European earwigs (*Forficula auricularia*), and pillbugs and sowbugs (*Armadillidium vulgare* and *Porcellio* spp.) (Longcore 2003b). These changes in arthropod species diversity will have resonating impacts on vertebrates that use arthropods as prey species. Suarez et al. (2000) show that coast horned lizards (*Phrynosoma coronatum*) prefer native ants (*Pogonomyrmex* and *Messor* spp.) as their food source and suffer when invading Argentine ants eliminate these species.

The cumulative ecological effects of fuel modification have not been adequately incorporated into environmental review for development proposals. The effects of fuel modification on landscape and local habitat has not been the topic of significant research, perhaps because it is considered as another edge effect of development. But as residential development is pushed deeper into wildlands for first and second homes, the cumulative impacts of these practices can no longer be ignored. The opportunity exists for changed fuel modification policies. Research has shown that 200 feet of fire clearance is not necessary for structure protection in most circumstances, especially if the structure itself is built in a firewise manner (see review in Longcore 2003a). The type of materials used in construction is ultimately more important than vegetation management in determining whether structures survive a wildland fire. Natural resource managers and firefighters should work together to develop comprehensive fire risk management that reduces fire clearance zones in a sensible way while strengthening controls on other more important site conditions such as roof type. —*Travis Longcore*

1994   BOF and California Fish and Game Commission adopts a joint policy of
         wildland fire in an attempt to coordinate fire and fuels management and
         wildlife protection and conservation between CDF and CDFG.

1995   CDFG adopts policy and procedures to address activities regarding pre-, dur-
         ing-, and post-fire, especially in conjunction with CDF. This includes a
         CDFG policy of post-fire seeding.

1995   CDF convenes two multi-agency working groups to review and make recom-
         mendations for revision of its Vegetation Management Program and Emer-
         gency Watershed Protection Program. One result of this effort was the revi-
         sion of CDF's VMP programmatic environmental impact report.

1995   CDFG signs a Memorandum of Understanding (MOU) exempting land own-
         ers and agencies conducting activities to increase fire safety around homes
         and structures from prosecution for incidental take of listed species under
         CESA if those activities were conducted under the conditions of fire safety
         regulations (California Code, §4260-4263). The MOU was valid through Sep-
         tember 1999.

1996   CDF, CDFG, and USFWS enter into MOUs in Riverside and San Diego coun-
         ties to address the incidental take of species under both ESA and CESA and
         fuels management for the purposes of protecting life and property.

current fuel loads either would disallow for the application of fire because of the risk or would result in undesired fire behavior. Therefore, mechanical treatment would be a prerequisite in many places in California so that fire could eventually fulfill its ecological role again.

Mechanical treatments can create conditions where fire would be both safe for humans and within an appropriate fire regime to benefit biota and natural communities. However, there are many aspects of mechanical treatments that might be in conflict with at-species protection. Often, the conflicts relate to timing of treatment, specific effects from the techniques chosen, or the degree of alteration of vegetation desired. Planning and implementing mechanical treatment that also addresses at-risk species requires additional planning time, knowledge, and detail, and the involvement of more agencies and experts and more resources, time, and, often, staffing in the field. Windows of operation are shorter so as to avoid crucial biological phenomena (e.g., flowering, seeding seed, migration, nesting, rearing). Types of appropriate activities might therefore be fewer. For example, larger machinery might not be used where there are plant populations that would be impacted by compaction or disturbance of soil or where the use of machinery would disturb critical animal behavior or activities. In addition, sometimes special treatments, such as marking off of crucial plots, even individual plants or stands of shrubs and trees, might need to occur prior to the primary activities commencing.

Thus, there may be many disincentives to integrating at-risk species protection with mechanical treatments. Interestingly, implementation of ESA and CESA has been indicted as both halting fuel treatment projects and even contributing to wildfires by disallowing for fuel reduction.

This allegation was a prominent issue following the 1993 wildland fire storms that saw 21 fires burn approximately 197,000 acres in six Southern California counties and, up until 2003, represented the largest fires to impact any region of California. Though no example of such conflicts between fire and fuel management and species protection was ever confirmed, various agencies decided to pursue conspicuous agreements to: (1) establish cooperative efforts to integrate species needs with fire and fuel management, (2) demonstrate that ESA and CESA protection would be secondary to fire safety regulations, and (3) provide fire management agencies and organizations the flexibility necessary to treat fuel loading without the concern of being in conflict with either law (Box 23.3). Since 1993 and even with these agreements in place, there still exists tension and a lack of clarity related to developing mutual benefits between fuel reduction and species protection.

PRESCRIBED BURNING

Many of the concerns related to mechanical fuel treatment are also pertinent to prescribed fire—the narrow window for

TABLE 23.4
Bioregion examples of at-risk species affected by the exclusion of fire

Sierra Nevada	California spotted owl *(Strix occidentalis)*
Central Valley	Colusa grass *(Neostapfia colusana)*
Central Coast	Monterey pine *(Pinus radiata)*
South Coast	California gnatcatcher *(Poliocalifornica)*
Southeast Deserts	Bighorn sheep *(Ovis canadensis)*

operations, the seasonal timing and spatial scope to achieve prescribed fire goals, the necessity of more personnel, funding, and knowledge. But the use of fire also presents unique problems and offers unique opportunities different from all other fuel or fire management techniques. Fundamentally, use of fire restores fire back to natural communities; at-risk species have existed in fire-adapted ecosystems, and the long-term viability of these species is tied to ecological processes such as the fire cycle. Wildfire's ability to perform its ecological functions has become rare, and as wildfires become more of a threat to human populations, prescribed fire becomes the only feasible alternative to fill the vital role of wildfire. On the other hand, the threat of prescribed burning to human life and property, the cost for staffing and equipment to control burns, and the public's opposition to prescribed fire's smoke and resulting poorer air quality (see Chapter 21) have prevented the broad application of prescribed fire for any purposes, let alone conservation of at-risk species.

Many studies have demonstrated the benefits of prescribed fire to native animals and plants. For most of the twentieth century, the focus was on the benefits to wildlife game species and the vegetation communities they inhabit (Biswell 1957, 1969). There has, however, been an increasing appreciation of the potential recovery role of prescribed fire for California's native, at-risk biota. Since the middle of the 1980s, prescribed fire has been proposed or actually used to manage and benefit at-risk species, such as the California spotted owl (Weatherspoon et al. 1992), Stephen's kangaroo rat (Price and Tayler 1993), butterfly diversity (Huntzinger 2000), at-risk native plants (USFWS 2002a), and Alameda whipsnake (*Masticophis lateralis euryxanthus*) and pallid manzanita (*Arctostaphylos pallida*) (2002b). But logistical, safety, and health conflicts have prevented prescribed fire from becoming a major tool for conservation. The needs and priorities for both the public and agencies conducting burns have prevented the majority of prescribed fires from being carried out during periods of greatest ecologic value (e.g., late summer and autumn) and allowed prescribed fire during times when fire is of either less ecological value or ecological impact (e.g., spring burning). It has been postulated that in a state with so many fire-adapted or fire-dependent natural communities and species, prescribed fire may be a mandatory tool for the conservation and recovery of at-risk species (Biswell 1989). It also is likely that in a state with so many people and so much urban intermix, either prescribed fire will have a selective minor role, or Californians will have to make a wholesale re-examination of prescribed burning in the future.

Fire Suppression

Fire suppression activities represent an interesting issue and threat to at-risk species and habitat. On the one hand, there is the cumulative effect of fire suppression activities over approximately the last 80 years across much of California, and on the other hand, there are the specific effects of fire suppression activities for an individual fire. Interestingly, the success of fire suppression in excluding fire from many vegetation communities is now considered to have been one of the major causes of critical deleterious shifts in those vegetation communities. The loss of the normal range of fire regime attributes and the subsequent loss of more natural fire behavior and substitution of altered fire behavior can only be seen as being negative to biotic communities. In fact, recent endeavors to alter how wildfire is managed have cited the impacts of successful fire suppression to ecological health, wildlife, at-risk species, and habitat as being a reason for changing how fire and fuel is managed (CBOF 1999, USFS/ USDI 2001, USA 2002).

Absence of fire or major shifts in fire regime have had a critical effect on fire-adapted or fire-dependent at-risk plant species, and there are examples of these changes being identified as a cause of decline (e.g., Baker's manzanita [*Arctostaphylos bakeri* spp. *bakeri*], USFWS 1998a). Plant survival and population viability are linked both to seed bank viability during the time between fires and the effects that subsequent fires have both on plants and on seed (see Chapter 6). The absence of fire also has had profound effects on vegetation structure and composition and has thereby affected at-risk animal species. In many California bioregions, the changes to vegetation communities and their consequences have been the topic of conservationists, land managers, and the general public with regard to many at-risk species (Table 23.4).

Unlike other fuel and fire management, fighting a wildfire is immediate and urgent in nature. Hence, the ability to alter suppression activities in lieu of at-risk species is less, and the actual impacts to at-risk species are more acceptable and understandable because human life and property are also at risk. In recent years, agencies responsible for suppressing fire have appreciated the needs of at-risk species and habitats to

TABLE 23.5

Potential issues and solutions for fire-suppression impacts to at-risk species

Fire-suppression Activity	Potential Impact	Potential Solution
Use of heavy machinery	Soil: impacting future vegetation and increasing sedimentation; Vegetation: destruction of subterranean, surface, and arboreal species habitat	Evaluate the options for: other locations; amount of area that needs to be cleared (e.g., the blade width of a fuel break); fuel buffers vs. fuel breaks; use of existing or natural fuel breaks
Burning out	Critical post-fire, biologic refugia for wildlife	Set aside unburned refugia
Water drafting	Aquatic species and habitat	Alternate drafting sites
Application of fire surfactant	Native plants	Avoid application to at-risk plant populations
Incident command camps and other fire-fighting bases	Disturbance to biotic community in and around base	Evaluate options for; locations of camps; marking off sensitive areas within or adjacent to camps

the point of having biologists and ecologists as part of the fire incident infrastructure to act as technical advisors, giving fire-fighters and fire incident commanders options for addressing the fire and minimizing or avoiding impacts to biotic resources. Some of the more important suppression activities that have been examined include the use of heavy machinery to clear away vegetation, burning out unburned areas after a fire front passes, drafting water for fighting fire, applying fire surfactant to vegetation, and setting up the incident base camp and other firefighting bases. Table 23.5 lists some of the potential impacts and solutions of fire suppression activities on at-risk species. In some cases, fire suppression activities have contributed to the declined status of an at-risk species (e.g., western lily *[Lilium occidentale]*) (USFWS 1998b), whereas in other cases, guidelines and recommendations have been developed specifically for fire activities in an attempt to promote conservation of an at-risk species (e.g., California red-legged frog *[Rana aurora draytonii]*) (USFWS 2002a).

Post-Wildfire Rehabilitation and Restoration

Post-wildfire rehabilitation and restoration (post-fire rehabilitation) have similarities to both vegetation management and fire suppression, with some activities being more considered while others are more emergency in nature. Several activities conducted during post-fire rehabilitation can impact at-risk species, including fire mop-up, removal of additional vegetation, compaction of soil (i.e., when using heavy machinery), use of engineered structures (e.g., check dams), and application of seed to burned areas. The potential for immediate impacts to at-risk species may be relatively low, and there are few cases where there has been concern of

such impacts. One exception is Laguna Beach. As with the use of sheep for vegetation control (see above), Laguna Beach dudleya was impacted by post-fire seeding (hydro- and not aerial) following the Laguna fire in 1993. There may be many reasons for the lack of documented impacts, including that (1) rehabilitated areas are areas that have already been burned or affected by suppression activities, and thus species were already affected or had left the area, or (2) there usually is sufficient time for planning and technical input from scientists to avoid or minimize effects to habitat and species. Some post-fire rehabilitation activities have been seen as posing a real longer-term threat to vegetation communities, species, and habitat. Such activities all fall within actions taken to minimize or control delivery of sediment off and downstream of burned slopes. Hay bales, log dams, check dams, mulch, netting, and seeding all are methods undertaken to trap or hold sediment back (e.g., dams) or stabilize the slopes themselves (e.g., netting, aerial seeding). Most of these activities are localized in both their application and effect, though a check dam does affect all downstream aquatic and riparian habitats as long as the dam is kept in place. The major exception is aerial seeding, and it is this post-fire rehabilitation practice that has been considered the greatest impact historically and threat in the future.

For most of the twentieth century, aerial seeding using non-native annual grasses was seen as the most viable and cost-efficient means of stabilizing large areas after fires. Research and post-fire monitoring in the 1980s, and especially in the 1990s, not only questioned the effectiveness of seeding but also recognized the threats to biodiversity and native vegetation communities (Conard et al. 1995, Keeler-Wolf 1995, O'Leary 1995). Impacts to native biota from early twentieth-century seeding or from post-fire rehabilitation since enactment of ESA and CESA are difficult to identify due to lack of recognition of the issue and not enough time having elapsed, respectively. To date, attention has been focused on the effects to the native plant species that define the local plant community and not to at-risk plant or animal species. Nevertheless, in the mid-1990s, CDFG and the California Native Plant Society adopted a policy and statement, respectively, highly critical of the use of non-native grasses and encouraging the use of native grasses or natural reseeding wherever possible. It is yet to be seen if and how fire management agencies will alter the nearly century-long practice of the use of non-native grass seed for emergency rehabilitation when downstream values are considered at risk. And it is yet to be seen what research and monitoring might tell of effects to at-risk species on the slopes or downstream of seeding activities.

Potential Solutions and the Future

At the end of 2003, significant changes occurred to federal law that at least complicate, if not detract from, opportunities to integrate the needs of protecting human life and property and at-risk species. In the fall of 2003, ESA was amended significantly twice. The passage of the 2003 Defense Bill generally affected ESA and the Neotropical Migratory Bird Treaty Act, and specifically in regard to ESA, by prohibiting setting aside any further critical habitat on military lands that already have a plan for managing natural resources. In addition, the federal Healthy Forest Initiative (USA 2002) and passage of the Healthy Forests Restoration Act (2003 Act; HR 2003) allowed for federal land management agencies special, focused consideration and autonomy from many important elements of federal laws related to natural resources and at-risk species, including safe harbor provision under ESA, discretionary limitations and categorical exemptions for analysis under NEPA, formal integration with the Western Governors' Association 10-year strategy for fuel management, and limiting injunctions against activities under the 2003 Act. Focus on protecting human society appears to have created an even greater disparity between mutuality in managing fuel and fire and protecting at-risk species. Many fire regimes in California have already been greatly altered and there are already hundreds of listed species and hundreds more considered at risk. Reducing the consideration, and likely the protection, for at-risk species, rather than giving more consideration to them and their fire ecology, does not bode well for the near-term future for at-risk species or for finding solutions to both protect species and human values concurrently.

Notwithstanding these most recent events at the national level, one of the most interesting trends in recent years has been a seemingly ubiquitous government agency policy perspective that reducing vegetation fuel loading is necessary and beneficial to protecting, enhancing, or restoring ecosystem health and at-risk species. In California, this viewpoint, and subsequent collaboration, funding, and land management planning, can be tied to the development of both the

California Fire Plan (CBOF 1999) and the National Fire Plan (USDA/USDI 2001). Several critical documents affecting significant wildland regions, if not the entire state, have been developed (e.g., Sierra Nevada Forest Plan, USDAFS 2003), regionally (e.g., Western Governors' Association 10-Year Comprehensive Strategy, WGA 2001), or nationally (National Fire Plan). All of these efforts to plan and implement substantial fuel reduction in shrub, woodland, and forest communities are early in their development or implementation. Each endeavor has the potential to improve or degrade the natural environment, or do both. It is yet to be seen whether such comprehensive plans and activities will alter fire regimes to benefit natural communities, and whether at-risk species will benefit from these alterations. It is also unknown what impacts will occur to at-risk species during activities to alter fuel load, and ultimately, fire behavior, and if any at-risk species might not endure to ever benefit from longer-term changes. And lastly, it is unknown if there will be the longer-term commitment by agencies and the public essential to achieving changes to the landscape that benefit natural communities, let alone the commitment necessary to conserve at-risk species. Notwithstanding these uncertainties, at-risk species protection will depend, at least in part, on the success of these comprehensive plans to manage both wildlands and fire.

Success in achieving both the goals of fuel and fire management and conservation of species and habitat already has a history in California. And with a growing knowledge of the fire ecology of California's bioregions and many of its native flora, and the ever-increasing capabilities and variety of fire and fuel management techniques, the potential to meet both goals should be greater than ever before. Combined with the many land management plans and collaborations mentioned above, protecting California's at-risk species, even with an ever-growing urban intermix, may be more of a possibility in the future than at any time in the state's past.

Achieving Both Goals

Fuel management can be done in a way that minimizes impacts, is neutral, or is beneficial to local biotic communities. Often this requires a combination of mechanical treatment and prescribed fire and the longer-term planning and management of the area in question. Since the 1980s, such planning and implementation has been undertaken in several regions in California (Table 23.6). The efforts have protected life and property, maintained ecological function, and promoted the recovery of at-risk species. In places like the Santa Rosa Plateau, the Channel Islands, and the Jepson Prairie, successful conservation of at-risk species had to be integrated with the management of fire, fuel, and invasive plant species.

As mentioned above, comprehensive planning and implementation of land management activities represent a practical solution to accomplishing protection and conservation of at-risk species while allowing for effective fuel and fire management. Many plans cover large acreages with multiple at-risk species, and involve many agencies and landowners. To

TABLE 23.6
Examples in California of integrating fire and fuels management and conservation and
protection of at-risk species and habitat

Location	Management Activities
Santa Rosa Plateau Ecological Reserve, southern Riverside County	Mechanical treatment of vegetation, prescribed burning
Western Riverside County Multiple Species Habitat Conservation Plan	Mechanical treatment of vegetation
Channel Island National Park System	Mechanical treatment of vegetation, prescribed burning, control of invasive plant species
U.C. Davis Jepson Prairie Reserve, Solano County	Mechanical treatment of vegetation, prescribed burning, control of invasive plant species
Pine Hills Preserve, El Dorado County	Mechanical treatment of vegetation, prescribed burning

protect at-risk species and habitats, management plans must address the temporal and spatial characteristics of vegetation communities and fire regimes in regard to the fire ecology of at-risk species and the short-term and longer-term consequences that any activity might have on the at-risk populations and habitats. Though this may seem to be a difficult mission to accomplish, the several examples in California that have already occurred demonstrate that such planning and implementation is possible.

Other land management options can initially come from either the perspective of species protection or fire and fuel management and then integrate the needs of the other. From the perspective of fuel and fire management, the California Fire and National Fire plans provide for integrating vegetation communities, species, and habitat needs into fuel and fire management. From the perspective of at-risk species, California's Natural Community Conservation Planning program, recovery plans under CESA and ESA, and Habitat Conservation Plans under ESA allow for reciprocal planning. Under the California Fire Plan, CDF has successfully conducted fuel treatment and prescribed burning projects that have addressed the conservation needs of at-risk species in southern California (e.g., rodents, birds, butterflies, and plants), the western foothills of the Sierra Nevada (e.g., plants), and several regions' grassland and vernal pool ecosystems (e.g., crustaceans and plants). Yosemite National Park and Calaveras Big Trees State Park have managed vegetation and conducted prescribed burning for several years benefiting the forest ecosystem and their native species while addressing fire and fuel management goals. Such management does the most to prevent native species from becoming at risk. Even such ecosystem-based management should investigate and address specific fire ecology needs of already at-risk species; conditions

BOX 23.4. EXAMPLES OF SMALL-SCALE
RECOVERY EFFORTS FOR AT-RISK SPECIES
THAT HAVE UTILIZED VEGETATION AND FIRE
MANAGEMENT ACTIVITIES

Large-flowered fiddleneck, *Amsinkia grandiflora*
Morro manzanita, *Arctostaphylos morroensis*
Ione manzanita, *Arctostaphylos myrtifolia*
Santa Cruz tarplant, *Holocarpha macrodenia*

and activities that benefit the majority of native species might not benefit particular at-risk species.

Not all efforts to integrate species protection and fuel management need be large scale. Many smaller, local efforts have been attempted across the state. Often, these activities focus on a single at-risk species, and to-date, often address an at-risk plant (Box 23.4, USFWS 1997b). It is not explicitly known why this is the case. There is both an agency and public sensitivity to incidental take of animal species and a more obvious ecological relationship between fire and plant population viability. These factors may be the foundation for a relative lack of application of fire and fuel management to animal recovery. The programs that have addressed rodent and bird species in the South Coast bioregion and the potential extensive fire and fuel program in the East San Francisco Bay region may signal the acknowledgment that at-risk animal recovery can benefit from fuel and fire management activities (see Sidebar 23.2).

There are many threatened and endangered species that call fire-prone communities home. One such species, the Alameda whipsnake *(Masticophis lateralis euyxanthus)*, is associated with the chaparral/scrub communities east of the San Francisco Bay. Measuring 30–60 inches, the Alameda whipsnake is a dark brown to black snake with a conspicuous cream-colored to orange strip down each side of its body. It primarily inhabits chaparral and shrubland communities of Contra Costa and Alameda counties, often landscapes of gullies and canyons with scattered grass and chaparral and rocky outcrops but also ranging into the mixed conifers of the foothills. It preys upon other snakes, lizards, frogs, and insects, and may seek shelter in among rocks or in burrows.

The tragic Tunnel fire of 1991, one that claimed 25 lives, understandably was a foundation for the attention and emotional reaction to the U.S. Fish and Wildlife Service's (USFWS) actions to protect the snake—the listing of the whipsnake as threatened under the Endangered Species Act (USFWS 1997a), the designation of critical habitat (USFWS 2000), and the draft recovery plan (2002b), which also covered pallid manzanita *(Arctostaphylos pallida)*, also federally listed, and other chaparral/scrub community species.

Many of the landscape changes that put homes and people at risk of a repeat firestorm—houses built on steep slopes and ridge lines, planting of volatile non-native vegetation such as eucalyptus, and 50 years of fire suppression—are the same changes that led to the listing of the whipsnake. However, remedies for protecting the "community" of one have not necessarily been seen as protecting the "community" of the other.

To determine what was fiction and what was fact in relation to threats to the communities on both sides of the urban intermix, a cooperative effort, which integrated research on the whipsnake species with actual fuel reduction and wildfire suppression techniques, was launched in 1999. This effort is scheduled to last several years and to include prescribed burning to promote the recovery of the whipsnake and reduce fuel load, development of comprehensive fire and fuel management planning and the potential development of an Habitat Conservation Plan (HCP), and research on the response of the whipsnake and chaparral plant species to prescribed fire and other fuel-reduction activities. This effort coincided with the drafting of the recovery plan and provided an opportunity for interested cooperators to present to USFWS their techniques and their concerns, and, most importantly, their expertise. These cooperators included water districts, park districts, federal and state agencies, non-governmental organizations, fire-safe councils, and fire districts.

Some of the questions that will hopefully be answered are:

Does the size of the fuels treatment area affect re-colonization of an area by the whipsnake listed species or its prey?

Does the timing of the fuels treatment affect the amount of harm or mortality to listed species?

Will winter controlled burns, which are safer for the public, inhibit rather than promote reproduction of chaparral plants?

Does the frequency of the fuels treatment play a role in shaping the future of the chaparral community in such as way as to cause long-term declines in listed species?

Pursuing preliminary answers through this multiple-year planning and research effort may mean weighing short-term and long-term gains and losses, a delicate line when you are working with a species that is already threatened! Because this effort is unprecedented, there is no clear solution or strategy to recovering the whipsnake and preventing another Tunnel fire. The collaboration likely will include an HCP for Mt. Diablo State Park and the implementation of recommendations in USFWS's draft recovery plan. Even though the most visible species in this effort is the Alameda whipsnake, this partnership between the many affected parties bodes well not only for the whipsnake and other at-risk species of the east San Francisco Bay region but also for other at-risk species and biotic communities inhabiting the ever-growing urban intermix areas all across California.

One thing is known—the design and implementation of any fire and fuel management program in the East Bay urban intermix community will play a pivotal role in the recovery of the chaparral/scrub community's threatened and endangered species. —*Heather Bell, KES*

TABLE 23.7

Examples of at-risk species recovery where prescribed fire has been recommended, researched, or used as a recovery action

Region to Be Treated with Prescribed Fire	Targeted At-Risk Species
San Francisco Bay	More than 12 serpentine-soil plants and dependent insects; East Bay chaparral species, including Alameda whipsnake
Central Sierra Nevada foothills	6 rare plants
Channel Islands	More than 12 rare plants
Vernal pools (from Butte to San Diego County)	More than 30 plants and crustaceans, including several grass species and fairy shrimp (*Branchinecta* ssp.)
Southern California shrub and chaparral	Species of coastal and interior chaparral and coastal sage brush communities, including California gnatcatcher and cactus wren

As mentioned above, the use of prescribed fire may provide the last best opportunity for at-risk species and habitat where fire has been absent or where, because of human development, it is not likely to be allowed to return naturally. Prescribed burning has been identified as being a tool for recovery for a variety of at-risk species across many regions of California, including the San Francisco Bay area, Central Valley grasslands, the central Sierra Nevada foothills, southern California chaparral and shrublands, and the Channel Islands (Table 23.7). One effort that may provide a model for

the future has been evolving in the foothills east of the San Francisco Bay region. Agencies (i.e., USFWS, CDFG, CDPR), water districts, and land owners in counties east of San Francisco Bay have been working to develop a broad, large-scale management plan that would include fuel load reduction and prescribed burning to protect suburban communities and watersheds; recover two federally listed species, the Alameda whipsnake and pallid manzanita; and protect four additional sensitive species (see Sidebar 23.2). If this planning effort comes to fruition, it will represent a remarkable accomplishment in integrating complex land management needs across a vast area of multiple land ownerships.

There are numerous examples across California's nine bioregions demonstrating that fire and fuel management activities, whether vegetation or invasive species control and reduction, prescribed burning, fire suppression, or post-fire rehabilitation and restoration, can be integrated with conserving and protecting at-risk species and their habitats and ecological processes needed to promote species recovery. Such integration has been done on small and large scales, has addressed single- and multiple-species conservation, and has occurred in isolated wild areas as well as the urban intermix. And possibly as important, has not resulted in loss of property or life and has not caused insurmountable or excessive financial burden to either the private or public sectors of California. Human communities cannot afford the risk that large intense fire presents. At-risk species, and the ecological systems they depend on, cannot be sustained or recovered without the immediate and longer-term ecological functioning provided by fire. Clearly, the viability of both human communities and at-risk species depends on integrating fire and fuel management with at-risk species conservation and protection wherever both activities overlap.

References

Biswell, H.H. 1957. The use of fire in California chaparral for game habitat improvement. From Proceedings, Society of American Foresters, Syracuse, New York. 5 p.

Biswell, H.H. 1969. Prescribed burning for wildlife in California brushlands. Transactions of the 34th North American Wildlife and Natural Resources Conference, March 2–5. Wildlife Management Institute. 9 p.

Biswell, H.H. 1989. Prescribed Fire in California Wildlands Vegetation Management. University of California Press, Berkeley. 255 p.

Bolger, D.T., T.A. Scott, and J.T. Rotenberry 1997. Breeding bird abundance in an urbanizing landscape in coastal Southern California. Conservation Biology 11:406–421.

California Board of Forestry and Fire Protection. 1999. California Fire Plan. California Department of Forestry and Fire Protection. 126 p.

California Department Fish and Game. 2003. State and federally listed endangered and threatened animals of California. 10 p.

California Department Fish and Game. 2004. State and federally listed endangered, threatened, and rare plants of California. 14 p.

California Department of Forestry and Fire Protection. 2003a. 20 largest California wildland fires (by acreage burned). 1 p.

California Department of Forestry and Fire Protection. 2003b. 20 largest California wildland fires (by structures destroyed). 1 p.

California Department of Forestry and Fire Protection. 2003c. CDF jurisdiction fires, acres, and dollar damage: 1943–2002. 2 p.

California Exotic Pest Plant Council. 1999. The CalEPPC list: exotic pest plants of greatest ecological concern in California. California Exotic Pest Plant Council, San Juan Capistrano, CA.

Conard, S.G., J.L. Beyers, and P.M. Wohlgemuth. 1995. Impacts of postfire grass seeding on chaparral systems—what do we know and where do we go from here? In J.E. Keeley and T. Scott, editors. Brushfires in California Wildlands: Ecology and Resource Management. International Association for Wildland Fire, Fairfield, WA. Pages 149–161.

Erickson, J.M. 1971. The displacement of native ant species by the introduced Argentine ant *Iridomyrmex humilis* (Mayr). Psyche 78:257–266.

Greenlee, J.M., (ed.) 1997. Proceedings: First Conference on Fire Effects on Rare Endangered Species and Habitats, November 13–16, 1995, Coeur d'Arlene, Idaho. International Association for Wildland Fire, Fairfield, WA.

Holway, D.A. 1998. Factors governing rate of invasion: a natural experiment using Argentine ants. Oecologia 115:206–212.

House of Representatives. [1904] 2003. Healthy Forests Restoration Act of 2003. 7 p.

Human, K.G., and D.M. Gordon. 1997. Effects of Argentine ants on invertebrate biodiversity in Northern California. Conservation Biology 11:1242–1248.

Human, K.G., S. Weiss, A. Weiss, B. Sandler, and D.M. Gordon. 1998. Effects of abiotic factors on the distribution and activity of the invasive Argentine ant (Hymenoptera: Formicidae). Environmental Entomology 27:822–833.

Huntzinger, P.M. 2000. Effects of fire management practices on butterfly diversity in the forested western United States. Master of Science thesis, University of California–Davis. 52 p.

Keeler-Wolf, T. 1995. Post-fire emergency seeding and conservation in southern California shrublands. In J.E. Keeley and T. Scott, editors. Brushfires in California Wildlands: Ecology and Resource Management. International Association for Wildland Fire, Fairfield, WA. Pages 127–140.

Keeley, J.E. 2002. Fire and invasive species in mediterranean-climate ecosystems of California. Pages 81–94 in K.E.M. Galley and T.P. Wilson, editors. Proceedings of the invasive species workshop: the role of fire in the control and spread of invasive species. Fire conference 2000: the first national congress on fire ecology, prevention and management. Tall Timbers Research Station, Tallahassee, FL.

Kennedy, T.A. 1998. Patterns of an invasion by Argentine ants (*Linepithema humile*) in a riparian corridor and its effects on ant diversity. American Midland Naturalist 140:343–350.

Kotanen, P.M. 1997. Effects of experimental soil disturbance on revegetation by natives and exotics in coastal Californian meadows. Journal of Applied Ecology 34:631–644.

Langen, T.A., D.T. Bolger, and T.J. Case. 1991. Predation on artificial bird nests in chaparral fragments. Oecologia 86:395–401.

Longcore, T. 2003a. Ecological effects of fuel modification on arthropods and other wildlife in an urbanizing wildland. P. 111–117 in K.E.M. Galley, R.C. Klinger, and N.G. Sugihara, editors. Proceedings of Fire Conference 2000: The First National Congress on Fire Ecology, Prevention and Management. Miscellaneous Publication No. 13, Tall Timbers Research Station, Tallahassee, FL.

Longcore, T. 2003b. Terrestrial arthropods as indicators of ecological restoration success in coastal sage scrub (California, U.S.A.). Restoration Ecology 11:397–409.

Minnich, R.A., and R.J. Dezzani. 1998. Historical decline of coastal sage scrub in the Riverside-Perris Plain, California. Western Birds 29:366–391.

Mooney, H.A., S.P. Hamburg, and J.A. Drake. 1986. The invasions of plants and animals into California. P. 250–272 in H.A. Mooney and J.A. Drake, editors. Ecology of Biological Invasions of North America and Hawaii. Springer Verlag, New York.

O'Leary, J.F. 1995. Potential impacts of emergency seeding on cover and diversity pattern of California's shrubland communities. P. 141–148 in J.E. Keeley and T. Scott, (eds.). Brushfires in California Wildlands: Ecology and Resource Management. International Association for Wildland Fire, Fairfield, WA.

Price, M.V., and K.E. Tayler. 1993. The potential value of fire for managing Stephens' kangaroo rate habitat at Lake Perris State Recreational Area. Final Report. Lake Perris Recreational Area Stephens' Kangaroo Rat Habitat Restoration. California Department of Parks and Recreation. 25 p.

Rundel, P.W. 1998. Landscape disturbance in mediterranean-type ecosystems; an over view. P. 3–22 in P.W. Rundel, G. Montenegro and F. Jaksic (eds.). Landscape disturbance and biodiversity in mediterranean-type ecosystems. Springer-Verlag, Berlin.

Rundel, P.W. 2000. Alien species in the flora and vegetation of the Santa Monica Mountains, California: patterns, processes, and management implications. P. 145–152 in J.E. Keeley, M. Baer-Keeley, and C.J. Fotheringham (eds.). 2nd Interface between Ecology and Land Development in California. U.S. Geological Survey, Sacramento, CA.

Stralberg, D. 2000. Landscape-level urbanization effects on chaparral birds: a Santa Monica Mountains case study. P. 125–136 in J.E. Keeley, M. Baer-Keeley, and C.J. Fotheringham (eds.). 2nd Interface between Ecology and Land Development in California. U.S. Geological Survey, Sacramento, CA.

Suarez, A.V., D.T. Bolger, and T.J. Case. 1998. Effects of fragmentation and invasion on native ant communities on coastal southern California. Ecology 79:2041–2056.

Suarez, A.V., J.Q. Richmond, and T.J. Case. 2000. Prey selection in horned lizards following the invasion of Argentine ants in southern California. Ecological Applications 10:711–725.

United States Department of Agriculture Forest Service. 2003. Draft Supplemental Environmental Impact Statement. USDA Forest Service, Pacific Southwest Region, R5-MB-019. 382 p.

United States Departments of Agriculture and Interior. 2001. The National Fire Plan: A Report to the President in Response to the Wildfires of 2000 (September 8, 2000). Managing the Impact of Wildfires on Communities and the Environment. 19 p.

United States Fish and Wildlife Service. 1997a. Final Rule: Endangered and Threatened Wildlife and Plants; Determination of Endangered Status for the Callippe Silverspot Butterfly and the Behren's Silverspot Butterfly and Threatened Status for the Alameda Whipsnake. Federal Register 62 (234): 64306–64320.

United States Fish and Wildlife Service. 1997b. Recovery plan for large-flowered fiddleneck, Amsinckia grandiflora. Region 1, U.S. Fish and Wildlife Service, Portland, OR. 50 p.

United States Fish and Wildlife Service. 1998a. Recovery plan for serpentine soil species of the San Francisco Bay area. Region 1, U.S. Fish and Wildlife Service, Portland, OR. 449 p.

United States Fish and Wildlife Service. 1998b. Final recovery plan for the endangered western lily (Lilium occidentale). Region 1, U.S. Fish and Wildlife Service, Portland, OR. 82 p.

United States Fish and Wildlife Service. 2000. Endangered and Threatened Wildlife and Plants; Final Determination of Critical Habitat for the Alameda Whipsnake (Masticophis lateralis euryxanthus). Federal Register 65 (192):58933–58962.

United States Fish and Wildlife Service. 2002a. Recovery plan for the California red-legged frog (Rana aurora draytonii). Region 1, U.S. Fish and Wildlife Service, Portland, OR. 173 p.

United States Fish and Wildlife Service. 2002b. Draft recovery plan for chaparral and scrub community species east of San Francisco Bay, California. Region 1, U.S. Fish and Wildlife Service, Portland, OR. 332 p.

United States of America, Office of the President. 2002. Healthy Forests: An Initiative for Wildfire Prevention and Stronger Communities. 22 p.

Vicars, M. 1999. FireSmart: protecting your community from wildfire. Partners in Protection, Edmonton, Alberta.

Weatherspoon, C.P., S.J. Husari, and J.W. van Wagtendonk. 1992. Fire and fuels management in relation to owl habitat in forests of the Sierra Nevada and southern California. In The California spotted owl: a technical assessment of its current status. U.S.D.A. Forest Service, Pacific Southwest Region, General Technical Report PSW-GTR-133. 14 p.

Western Governors' Association. 2001. A Collaborative Approach for Reducing Wildland Fire Risks to Communities and the Environment 10-Year Comprehensive Strategy. 24 p.

CHAPTER 24

The Future of Fire in California's Ecosystems

NEIL G. SUGIHARA, JAN W. VAN WAGTENDONK, JOANN FITES-
KAUFMAN, KEVIN E. SHAFFER, AND ANDREA E. THODE

> A thing is right when it tends to preserve the integrity, stability,
> and beauty of the biotic community. It is wrong when it tends
> otherwise.
>
> ALDO LEOPOLD, 1952

> It's not a matter of if fire will occur but when it will occur.
>
> MARK FINNEY, *Research Forester, Forest Service*
> *Fire Science Lab, Missoula, Montana*

This book has covered a wide array of topics that are unified by wildland fire. In this concluding chapter, we take the opportunity to summarize the three parts of the book, focussing on some of the most important overarching concepts. We then address where the future is likely to lead us and end with a challenge for managing and living with fire in California.

Concepts of Fire Ecology

The vegetation in California is a product of its evolutionary past, current and past climates, topography, and fire. From the dense, moist forests of the North Coast to the grasslands of the Central Valley to the dry southeast deserts and Northeastern Plateaus, fire has played a varying but important role. Similarly, the forests of the Klamath Mountains, the Southern Cascades, and the Sierra Nevada have evolved with periodic fire. Nowhere in California, however, is fire more dramatic than in the chaparral-covered mountains of the South and Central Coasts. California's variety of fire regimes are products of its wide diversity of vegetation, climate, topography, and ignitions.

Although much of California's climate is mediterranean in nature, the state's climate in fact is as variable as its vegetation. Rainfall ranges from an annual average of 204 cm (80 in) along the north coast to 5 cm (2 in) in the desert. Normal temperatures vary from −4°C (24°F) in January in the Sierra Nevada to 39°C (102°F) in July in Death Valley. Winds are also variable, but the Santa Ana winds are the ones that have the greatest effect on fires, particularly in the mountains of the South Coast. Lightning strikes occur throughout California at all times of the year but are most prevalent in the Southeastern Deserts, the Northeastern Plateaus, and the Sierra Nevada, primarily in July and August. All of these variations create a diverse fire landscape with a wide variety of fire regimes.

Fire also interacts with the physical components of the ecosystem. The process of combustion is dependent on the presence of sufficient heat, oxygen, and fuel to sustain ignition and spread. Fire behavior characteristics such as rate of spread and intensity are influenced by the amount of available fuel, weather conditions, and topography. Fires with different behavior characteristics produce different fire types and effects. Fire also interacts with soil, water, and air ranging from minute changes in soil structure, to alterations in stream water quantity and quality, to changes in air quality across broad regions. However, these are not isolated effects, as fire interactions in one part of the ecosystem can influence outcomes in other areas. High-intensity fire can cause hydrophobic layers in the soil and result in elevated erosion when the rains come in the fall. Eroding soil affects water quality and chemistry and influences downstream stream channel morphology with pulses of sediment that both impact aquatic habitat and form the substrate for many riparian and wetland ecosystems.

Fire interactions with living components of the ecosystem are equally diverse. Effects to plants include the direct effects of heat and smoke and the indirect effects of changes in nutrient and light availability. Plant responses to fire can be categorized as fire dependent, fire enhanced, fire neutral, or fire inhibited. Many species have physical characteristics, such as thick bark, that enable them to survive fires. Other species are adversely affected by fire and proliferate during long fire-free periods. Fire regime attributes affect plant survival and reproduction and, consequently, plant community structure and composition. The plant community, in turn, affects fire regimes through feedback mechanisms. Fires affect animals through direct mortality and through indirect effects on habitats. Although individual animals may die and populations may be impacted, animal community health is maintained by fire fulfilling its ecological role. Fire maintains habitat complexity, recycles and makes available nutrients and water, and changes the trophic relationships between the various animal species in a given community. Since many animal species evolved with fire, it is essential for their continued existence that fire be retained as an important ecological process.

Our Changing Perceptions

Throughout this book, we have shown that fire is an integral part of California ecosystems, and that from an ecological perspective, it is rarely useful to view it as an exogenous disturbance. The state's diverse climate and topographic patterns have facilitated the development of a rich array of vegetation and habitats. Ecological processes including fire, flood, and erosion have sculpted the landscapes and plant communities into complex, continuously changing ecosystems. Therefore, fire should not be characterized as a disturbance or retrogressive event that delays progress toward some hypothetical, static, climatic climax, but as a vital, incorporated ecosystem process that has a major role in defining California's dynamic ecosystems.

The role fire plays in an ecosystem is characterized by the fire regime attributes that describe the pattern of fire occurrence, behavior, and effects. Temporal attributes include seasonality and fire return interval. Spatial attributes are fire size and spatial complexity of the burns. Magnitude attributes are fire intensity, fire severity, and fire type. Distributions of these seven attributes form the fire regimes. Fire regimes and vegetation are intricately linked, one perpetuated by the other as interdependent components within an ecosystem.

Fire regimes vary both within and between the bioregions. Variation is often pronounced along a gradient inland from the coast due to differential marine influence on fire weather and climate. Fire tends to be less frequent in the cool, moist conditions found on the immediate coast than in the more interior locations where it is typically hot and dry during the summer. Elevation gradients also produce variations in fire regimes that are moderated near the coast but become more pronounced in the Sierra Nevada, Southern Cascades, and Klamath Mountains. Within these three mountain bioregions, there is often a change in fire regimes due to the higher precipitation on western slopes and rain shadows on eastern slopes. In the Central Valley, variation in the fire regimes is more subtle and related to north-south gradients in climate and hydrology.

Additional sources of variation in fire regimes and responses to fire within and among bioregions include the duration of the fire season and the productivity of the sites. Wetter bioregions and wetter portions of drier bioregions produce abundant fuel, but there are fewer years and shorter seasons when fuel is dry enough to burn. Consequently, fire regimes in these areas are characterized by longer fire return intervals and a tendency toward higher fire severities. In drier bioregions and drier portions of other bioregions that produce less fuel, there are more years and extended periods of the year

when the fuel will burn. These areas are characterized by shorter fire-return intervals and a tendency toward lower fire severities. In the harshest alpine climates of California, plant establishment and growth are restricted to the point where fires are limited by the lack of fuel and extremely limited fire season. Similarly, plants in hot, dry deserts produce little fuel and burn infrequently.

Fire regime descriptions are useful in determining and describing which attributes have changed and how these attributes differ from historic patterns. Comparison of the changed fire regime with the regimes of adjacent plant communities allows us to predict the trajectory of vegetation change and, potentially, the direction that plant communities will expand or contract. Land managers are now able to focus on the fire regime attributes that are biologically significant in their ecological restoration efforts.

Fire Is an Integral Part of California Ecosystems but Variability Occurs across Them

Martin and Sapsis (1992) introduce the notion that *pyrodiversity*—the variability within fire regimes over long periods of time—promotes biological diversity. This concept is needed to understand fire as an ecological process and its value in restoring and maintaining ecosystems. Pyrodiversity is particularly important in ecosystems where variation of fire severity provides much of the fine-scale habitat variability. Pyrodiversity promotes biodiversity in many fire regimes, especially those that are characterized by short fire return interval, low-intensity, and low-severity surface fires. Severity variation is also important in vegetation that depends on fire for providing age-class mosaics such as many riparian woodlands and red and white fir forests.

Although it is clear that the levels of pyrodiversity that historically occurred maintained the biodiversity, it is important to note that further increases in pyrodiversity beyond historic ranges may not always promote elevated levels of native biodiversity. Within the wide variety of fire-vegetation relationships, there are two general classes of settings in which pyrodiversity may not promote biodiversity:

1. The first is the group of ecosystems characterized by truncated fire return interval distributions. Only limited amounts of pyrodiversity can be tolerated because they are subject to type conversion when intervals between fires are too long or too short. For example, if closed-cone pine or cypress stands burn even a single time before seeds are produced, or remain unburned long enough to exhaust the seed source, these specialized conifers are lost. Effective fire suppression can exclude fire long enough for this to happen. This is an expansion of the variability in fire regimes that decreases biodiversity.

2. The second class of settings involves the fire-limited or fire-induced spread of native or non-native

invasive species. Annual grasses can temporarily expand the range of pyrodiversity in some deserts, but once they become dominant enough to provide a continuous fuel bed they reduce both pyrodiversity and biodiversity. Douglas-fir encroachment into Oregon white oak woodlands on the north coast increases pyrodiversity while reducing biodiversity by replacing the more species-rich woodlands.

Although pyrodiversity certainly does promote biodiversity in most California ecosystems, restoring and maintaining historic levels of pyrodiversity is the wise approach to take if natural levels of biodiversity are the goal.

Enough individual organisms of a given species must have the ability to survive fire, or to recolonize after fire, to remain a part of an ecosystem. They must be able to persist in order to reproduce and become a viable component of the biotic community. Even rare fires that occur in the wrong season, or that are too large, intense, severe, or uniform, can greatly reduce, displace, or even extirpate a species from an area. Enough individuals of a species need to persist throughout the range of variability that is characteristic of the fire regimes for that species to remain viable in fire-affected ecosystems.

California has a diverse flora comprised of plants that have evolved under a variety of climates and evolutionary pressures. Some species of chaparral are unequivocally dependent on fire and require smoke or chemicals from charcoal to germinate. Other species, primarily from moist regions, have low to no resistance to fire. But across all bioregions, many species have some characteristics that allow them to persist, and often thrive, with fire. Exclusion of fire has contributed to the demise of some endemic and rare species throughout the state.

Most of the state's dominant native vegetation depends on fire to maintain its structure, composition, and function, and the relationship of fire and California vegetation can be traced back for thousands of years. Giant sequoia, mixed conifer, ponderosa pine, and Douglas-fir forests are greatly influenced by fire. When fire is excluded for even a few decades, these forests take on an entirely different structure and provide a greatly different habitat. Coast redwood forests in the fog belt of the North Coast, blue oak woodlands on the hot, dry Central Valley foothills, and the rich array of shrub communities in the South Coast coexisted with recurring fire. The closed-cone pine and cypress communities, Oregon white oak woodlands of the North Coast, and quaking aspen stands in the high Sierra Nevada would likely be extirpated or drastically reduced without recurring fire. A significant portion of California's biological heritage is directly dependent on the recurrence of fire.

It is a mistake to assume that a given plant community always has the same fire regime. Several plant communities are characterized by more than one fire regime both within and between bioregions. Trees in open stands on sites that are unproductive, open, rocky, or ultramafic have very discontinuous fuels, and fires are typically limited to single trees that are struck by lightning. Where the same trees grow on more productive sites that produce more fuel, fires are larger and become a more important ecological process. Coast redwood, Douglas-fir, mixed evergreen, and a number of other communities occur over a wide range of environments and are thus characterized by more than one fire regime.

Over millennia, climate changes have occurred and vegetation has responded by changing geographic distribution and range. Bioregional climates have varied, as have the flora and fire regimes. Human-induced fire regime changes can also be the driver of vegetation change. Modification of fire regimes during post-European settlement has changed some of the boundaries between ecological zones. Fire exclusion has allowed the white fir zone in the Sierra Nevada to expand down to lower elevations. Removal of fire from sage communities on the east side of the Cascades and Sierra Nevada has allowed the expansion of juniper and pinion woodlands. Fire scar records in giant sequoia show evidence of decadal, centennial, and millennial variation. Exclusion of fire from these giant sequoia stands limits their regeneration and allows encroachment by other conifers. Separating the influences of climate change from the influences of fire exclusion on post-European fire biota is often a difficult, but important, consideration in understanding the current ecological role of fire in California.

Fire ecology is an emerging and rapidly expanding field of science—but there are many gaps in our knowledge. Until recently, research concentrated on chaparral in the South Coast and the mixed conifer forests of the Sierra Nevada. Information on the role of fire in the Central Coast, North Coast, Southeastern Deserts, and other bioregions has developed more recently. Research is beginning to be conducted on fire effects in the other bioregions of the state. Given the diversity of flora and fire regimes across California, we are far from having a comprehensive body of research on fire ecology. A targeted, strategic approach aimed at answers to key ecological questions that can be extrapolated across the broadest array of species and bioregions is needed.

There are also gaps in our knowledge about fire and management issues. The most common management issues transcend multiple bioregions and include invasive species impacts, urban development, habitat fragmentation, fuel hazard reduction, fire suppression impacts, at-risk species, and air quality.

Management of Fire in California Ecosystems Must Be Based in Ecology

California is the most populous state in the United States, and the challenge of living with fire is ever present in most parts of the state. As long as we choose to inhabit fire-prone ecosystems, our choices are to allow fire to occur on its own terms, to adjust our communities to fire, or to continue to interfere with the natural range of fire regimes and essential ecological function of fire itself. How we as a society decide to accommodate—or interfere with—fire will say a great deal about our social ecological sophistication and how much we value our native biota and natural environment.

It is impossible to separate the actions of people from ecosystems because we influence and are part of fire regimes and ecosystems. Humans have been using fire for hundreds of thousands of years to manipulate their environment. The use of fire shifted our status from foragers to cultivators and contributed to enabling our species to expand around the world. Fire application to California landscapes is as ancient as the first human occupation about 11,000 years ago. Fire was the most significant, effective, efficient, and widely employed vegetation management tool utilized by California Indian tribes, and they conducted purposeful burning to meet specific cultural objectives and maintained specific plant communities. The influence of Native Americans on California ecosystems has varied across a spectrum from little to none in remote areas to considerable in human-maintained ecosystems.

Since European explorers arrived in 1542, they have directly or indirectly influenced the state's fire regimes. Removal of anthropogenic fire from these ecosystems has allowed widespread changes to species composition, encroachment of invasive species, conversion to other vegetation types, and increased fire hazards. The California gold rush permanently established the European-American population in 1848. Formal fire policy arrived with establishment of large-scale forest reserves during the late 1800s and early 1900s. A series of devastating fires resulted in a policy of full fire suppression following the fires of 1910. Starting during the 1970s, federal fire policy changed to incorporate a combination of fire suppression and fire management. During the late 1990s and early 2000s, fire and land management have focused on managing the fuel that accumulates in ecosystems as a pre-suppression and ecosystem management treatment. Fire increasingly has become recognized as an important ecological process, and fire management is increasingly addressing ecosystem values by focusing on the restoration of natural fire regimes. It is important that we remember that humans have influenced fire regimes since our arrival and that we must take responsibility for knowing what effects our actions will have.

It seems that no matter how hard we try, total fire control still eludes us. Since the Berkeley fire in 1923, the issue of fire in the wildland-urban interface has become one of the most important land management issues facing Californians. Despite intensive efforts and the application of great amounts of technology and money to the effort to exclude wildfires, they continue to have great effects on society and ecosystems. The largest and most destructive fires are occurring at an increasing rate and the expansion and intermixing of urban and wildland areas make the impacts of the largest fires even greater. There is increasing recognition that if we are to moderate the impact of fires burning out of the wildlands into the urban landscapes, we must understand and manage both the fire regimes that are inherently associated with the ecosystems in the wildlands and the fuel characteristics of the urban areas.

Even though there are a greater number of large fires in California today, there is probably less fire overall in most of the state's landscape than in any point in time since the arrival of humans, yet we consider the occurrence of fire to be an environmental emergency. This is particularly true with fire effects on watersheds and air. Maybe we are the victims of our own success. We like our health, clean air, and clean water, and we would like to protect all of our native species and ecosystems. Historically, there was a lot of fire, a lot of smoke, and a lot of fire-accelerated erosion in California. But wildland fire produces smoke and other combustion byproducts that can be harmful to human health and particulate matter that reduces visibility. Fire increases erosion, reduces water quality, and kills vegetation. Although society might not like these changes because they can have detrimental effects on human health and quality of life, they are, to a large extent, natural. Today, we have excluded fire to the point where we have experienced, and are expecting far less fire impacts to air and water quality than existed before Euro-American settlement of California.

We clearly need to protect the quality of our air and water. The question is, how do we do this in fire-prone ecosystems? Uncontrolled wildfires are responsible for the most widespread, prolonged, and severe periods of air quality degradation, but local, state, and federal regulatory agencies focus on the activities that are considered discretionary, including managed fire. The challenge in managing wildland fire is to understand the tradeoffs of balancing public interest objectives while sustaining ecological integrity. Minimizing the adverse effects of smoke on human health and welfare, while maximizing the effectiveness of using wildland fire, is an integrated and collaborative activity.

Today, watersheds and fire regimes are highly altered by human activities. Past and current management practices including water development, mining, road building, urbanization, fire suppression, timber harvesting, and recreation are impacting watersheds. The largest erosion events typically follow very large, uniformly high-severity wildfires in steep, erosive landscapes. Fire and its associated pulses of sedimentation, mass wasting, and flooding are natural processes that work within ecosystems and are part of the process that creates and maintains watersheds. However, like air quality management, the focus of watershed management is often to minimize the impacts of prescribed fire because it is considered discretionary. Unless watershed managers, local communities, aquatic ecologists, and other resource mangers actively support the restoration of historic fire regimes for the management of their resources, it is likely that the exclusion of fire will continue. In some ecosystems, this means that fire will be less frequent, but the fires that do occur will be more uniformly high in severity and sometimes cause an elevated level of watershed instability.

One of the most significant ecosystem changes has been the arrival of non-native, invasive species, starting with the earliest European contact in the 1500s. Fire management in ecosystems with non-native, invasive plants creates unique challenges. In some ecosystems, fire facilitates the expansion of non-native, invasive species, and in other cases, fire can be used to control or eradicate them. In the dynamic cycle between grasses and fire, invasive grass species become established in an area dominated by woody vegetation. As the invasive grasses increase in abundance, a continuous layer of highly combustible fine fuel develops, resulting in increased rates of fire spread and fire frequency. Shrublands and forests composed of native species are converted to grasslands comprised mainly of non-native species. Although fire maintained native plant communities, invasive species are responsible for altering fire regimes in large areas in southern California chaparral, the Great Basin, the Central Valley, and the Mojave Desert. Managing fire and invasive species is an important area of future work.

When Aldo Leopold (1952) stated, "To keep every cog and wheel is the first precaution of intelligent tinkering," he spoke of species. The Federal Endangered Species Act and the California Endangered Species Act were specifically enacted to protect native plants and animals that are threatened or endangered with extinction. In California, fire and fuel management and at-risk species conservation and protection have more often been in conflict than in accord. Species protection often has meant fire exclusion. Although there are difficulties, there are also potential opportunities for fire management to aid in the protection of at-risk species. The use of prescribed fire may provide the best opportunity for these species where the absence of fire has degraded habitat or where fire is not likely to be allowed to return naturally. There are numerous examples across California where fire and fuel management activities, prescribed burning, fire suppression, or post-fire rehabilitation and restoration have been integrated while conserving and protecting at-risk species, their habitats, and ecological processes. Many at-risk species, and the ecological systems they depend on, cannot be sustained or recovered without the immediate and longer-term ecological functioning provided by fire. Fire as an ecological process is a necessary part of California's ecosystems, and if we really intend to keep all of the parts, fire should be returned to the extensive inventory of California's diverse "cogs" and "wheels."

Where Do We Go from Here?

As humans, we feel the need to control fire in our environment, and as we develop the ability to control fire, the role that fire plays in California ecosystems has become both more controlled and more unpredictable. However, controlling fires and extensively manipulating vegetation have not always benefited California's ecosystems or provided the control and assurance that society has desired. The fires of 1993 and 2003 exemplify how little control we really have and that other options must be considered. Although this book synthesizes and consolidates our understanding of fire, it does not answer the question of what we want our relationship with wildland fire to be. This is not an ecological ques-

tion; rather it is a social one; and societal wants and needs are as dynamic as fire regimes and ecosystems. What is clear is that if fire is to continue to play out its role in ecosystems, we need to better understand that role and incorporate it into our land stewardship.

An assessment of the largest fires in California's recorded history will quickly give the impression that fires are getting larger and more destructive. It is true that the largest fires and the most destructive fires are occurring at an increasing rate. There are a number of explanations for this trend, but the answer lies in the nature of fire-ecosystem interactions and the history of our management practices.

It seems illogical that the more effective our firefighting forces become, the worse the fire events become. But it makes ecological sense. Ecosystems that are biologically productive but relatively non-flammable will tend to burn in fires that are infrequent and very high in intensity and severity. For example, southern California chaparral burns less frequently than most of the surrounding vegetation types, but because it burns in less frequent and more extreme weather conditions, the fires are often uniformly high in intensity and severity. Suppressing fires tends to eliminate the smaller and less intense fires burning in lighter fuel accumulations during less severe weather conditions. These fires are easily suppressed, resulting in atypical, uniform, high fuel loads and fires that spread only under severe weather conditions. This amplifies the naturally occurring high-intensity fire regime. Unless we can develop the technology to completely exclude fire from chaparral ecosystems, the more effective our fire suppression becomes, the larger and more severe the fires that do occur can become.

In terms of human loss, the most destructive fires burn out of the wildlands and into the rapidly expanding urban development. These are fires that are burning through landscapes much as they have for thousands of years. They are not necessarily more intense or more frequent or faster moving than they were before humans were present. The difference is that subdivisions or small communities lie in their path, and the only fires that we allow to reach the urban interface are those that are too intense to stop. As long as we continue to suppress all of the other fires and expand urban development into high-intensity fire regime wildlands, we will continue to see more and more destructive fires. Although the destructive fires cannot be eliminated, the design of the urban side, fuel management of the wildland side, and creation of buffers and barriers in the interface can moderate the level of damage.

The Future of Fire and Land Management

With the exception of aquatic ecosystems, sand dunes, extremely arid deserts with very sparse fuel, and alpine ecosystems, fire plays an essential ecological role throughout the state. The habitats and species on all of these landscapes have evolved with fire. Perhaps the most universal changes to California's ecosystems during the historic period have been the alteration of past fire regimes and changes in the pattern of fire on the landscape. Nearly all native biota and communities have been and are affected by these alterations.

However, no matter how important fire is to ecosystems, we will not universally restore fire to its historical role in California ecosystems. There are several reasons for this, including the fact that many of those ecosystems simply no longer exist and others are impacted by human actions beyond the point where restoration is feasible. Biologically, California ecosystems have been altered and are mostly composed of an unprecedented mix of native and non-native species from many continents. Discontinuities exist throughout the natural landscape, preventing fires from achieving their historic patterns. The only way that fire regimes will be fully restored to California is if humans were to value the restoration of historic ecosystems and processes to the exclusion of all other land uses—and that is against human nature.

In the wildlands where managing for natural ecosystems and processes are the priority, it is important that fire be incorporated into long-term management plans. Although land management planning needs to recognize the numerous constraints of society, prescriptions must incorporate the variability of fire regimes. Narrowly focused prescriptions that apply only parts of the historic fire regime or use mean values for the fire regime attributes do not restore historic fire patterns and need to be applied in very special cases or not at all. Without the dynamic nature of natural fire regimes, restored ecosystems are not likely to maintain historic levels and patterns of species distribution and diversity.

A few details are clear when looking into the future of fire and land management. The population of California will continue to grow, the wildland-urban interface will continue to expand, wildlands will be valued as both habitat and open space, and the regulation of fire and other land management activities will continue to increase. The understanding of fire and its role in ecosystems is vital to making land management decisions.

The restoration of fire as an ecosystem process is a complex undertaking. Substituting mechanical treatments that can only mimic some aspects of fire will accomplish only portions of fire's role. There is one simple rule that applies to the restoration of fire into ecosystems: To completely restore fire as an ecological process, there is no substitute for fire. In the words of Sue Husari, fire management officer for the Pacific West Region of the National Park Service and one of the true pioneers in fire management: *"You can't restore fire without fire."*

Ecosystems change, and it is a mistake to manage any complex, dynamic ecosystem for a single, static state or condition. It is contrary to the basic nature of ecosystems, because all ecosystems continuously change, develop, and cycle over time and space. It is that long-term pattern of change and subsequent species responses that allow those species to persist, adapt, and interact with the other biotic and physical attributes of the natural environment.

Intentionally or unintentionally, we are affecting fire regimes on all wildlands in which we manage or suppress fire. The management of fire regimes is among the most important land management activities on most wildlands. Fire exclusion has resulted in alteration of ecosystems on a massive scale, and this has influenced the habitats for thousands of species in hundreds of ecosystems. The decision to impose a fire regime on an ecosystem should be taken seriously. Whether we intentionally prescribe a detailed fire regime or simply decide to suppress all fires, we are making a decision about what our desired fire regime will be; there is no real "no action alternative."

Managing fuel should be an extension of managing fire regimes. Because both surface and crown fires rely on surface fuel to generate fire spread, treating surface fuel is an essential step in effective fuel management programs. Fuel treatments can make fire exclusion more effective by facilitating fire suppression. In other cases, fuel management is the first step in restoring historic fuel conditions for the purposes of restoring historic fire regimes. The intentional manipulation of fuel to achieve desired fire conditions should be the focus of a variety of fire and land management activities.

We will never know everything that we would like to know about fire in California ecosystems, but we do need to use what we do know. We have been influencing ecosystems by manipulating fire regimes for more than a hundred years. Most fires have been successfully suppressed because we were able to control and manage them. We currently have the ability to apply prescribed fire and manage wildfires, and in the future, we may be able to totally exclude wildfire. Clearly, California ecosystems will not be the same without fire playing its ecological role. If we are to maintain California ecosystems for future generations, it is time to start deciding if, where, and how we will move forward with restoration of fire. And this time, humans will be almost solely responsible for determining future fire regimes.

References

Leopold, A. 1952. A sand county almanac, and sketches here and there. Oxford University Press, New York. 226 p.

Martin, R. E., and D. B. Sapsis. 1992. Fires as agents of biodiversity: pyrodiversity promotes biodiversity. P. 150–157 in R. R. Harris and D. C. Erman (eds). Proceedings of the symposium on biodiversity of northwestern California. Report 29, Wildland Resources Center, University of California, Berkeley.

Plant Common and Scientific Names

This appendix contains two lists. The first alphabetizes plants by common name, the second by Latin name.

Taxonomy follows these sources: J.C. Hickman, editor. 1993. The Jepson Manual: higher plants of California. University of California Press: Berkeley and Los Angeles; J.O. Sawyer and T. Keeler-Wolf. 1995. A manual of California vegetation. California Native Plant Society; The PLANTS Database, U.S. Department of Agriculture, Natural Resources Conservation Service, http://plants.usda.gov

Common Name	**Latin Name**
acorn	*Curculio* and *Cydia* spp.
African needlegrass	*Achnatherum capense*
agave	*Agave* spp.
agoseris	*Agoseris* spp.
Ahart's dwarf rush	*Juncus leiospermus* var. *ahartii*
alder	*Alnus* spp.
alkali sacaton	*Sporobolus airoides*
alkali sacaton	*Sporobolus airoides*
annosus root rot	*Heterobasidion annosum*
antelope bitterbrush	*Purshia tridentata*
annual ryegrass	*Lolium multiflorum*
Arabian schismus	*Schismus arabicus*
arrow weed	*Pluchea sericea*
Aspen ash	*Populus* spp.
aster	*Aster* spp.
avens	*Geum* spp.
Baker's manzanita	*Arctostaphylos bakeri* spp. *bakeri*
balsam-root	*Balsamorhiza* spp.
baltic rush	*Juncus balticus*
banana yucca	*Yucca baccata*
barbed goatgrass	*Aegilops triuncialis*
basin big sagebrush	*Artemisia tridentata* ssp. *tridentata*
basin wildrye	*Leymus cinereus*
beach pine	*Pinus contorta* ssp. *contorta*
bearbrush	*Garrya fremontii*
beargrass	*Nolina* spp.
bear-grass	*Xerophyllum tenax*
bent grass	*Agrostis* spp.
big galleta grass	*Pleuraphis rigida*
big sagebrush	*Artemisia tridentata*
bigberry manzanita	*Arctostaphylos glauca*
bigcone Douglas-fir	*Pseudotsuga macrocarpa*
bigleaf maple	*Acer macrophyllum*
bigpod ceanothus	*Ceanothus megacarpus* var. *megacarpus*
birch-leaf mountain-mahogany	*Cercocarpus betuloides* var. *betuloides*
Bishop pine	*Pinus muricata*
bitter brush	*Purshia tridentata*
bitter cherry	*Prunus emarginata*
black brush	*Coloegyne ramossisima*

black cottonwood	*Populus balsamifera* ssp. *trichocarpa*
black morel	*Morchella elata*
black mustard	*Brassica nigra*
black sage	*Salvia mellifera*
black sagebrush	*Artemisia nova*
Blackberry	*Rubus* spp.
Blackbrush	*Coloegyne ramosissima*
blazing star	*Mentzelia* spp.
blister sedge	*Carex vesicaria*
blue blossom	*Ceanothus thyrsiflorus*
blue dicks	*Dichelostemma capitatum*
blue larkspur	*Delphinium parryi*
blue oak	*Quercus douglasii*
blue wildrye	*Elymus glaucus*
bluebells, lungwort	*Mertensia* spp.
bluebunch wheatgrass	*Pseudoroegneria spicata*
bluejoint reedgrass	*Calamagrostis canadensis*
Bolander pine	*Pinus contorta* ssp. *bolanderi*
Bolander's bedstraw	*Galium bolanderi*
Booth's willow	*Salix boothii*
box elder	*Acer negundo* var. *californicum*
Brainerd's sedge	*Carex brainerdii*
Brewer oak	*Quercus garryana* var. *breweri*
Brewer spruce	*Picea breweriana*
Brewer's redmaids	*Calandrinia breweri*
Brewer's reedgrass	*Calamagrostis breweri*
brittlebrush	*Encelia farinosa*
broadleaf lupine	*Lupinus latifolius*
broadleafed cattail	*Typha latifolia*
brodiaea	*Brodiaea* spp.
Brown's peony	*Paeonia brownii*
buck brush	*Ceanothus cuneatus* var. *cuneatus*
buffel grass	*Cenchrus ciliaris*
bulrush	*Scirpus lacustris*
burrobrush	*Hymenoclea salsola*
bush chinquapin	*Chrysolepis sempervirens*
bush lupine	*Lupinus arboreus*
bush monkeyflower	*Mimulus aurantiacus*
bush poppy	*Dendromecon rigida*
butter-and-eggs	*Triphysaria eriantha*
cactus	*Cactaceae* spp.
California bay	*Umbellularia californica*
California black oak	*Quercus kelloggii*
California black walnut	*Juglans californica*
California blackberry	*Rubus ursinus*
California blue oak	*Quercus douglasii*
California brittlebush	*Encelia californica*
California buckeye	*Aesculus californica*
California buckwheat	*Eriogonum fasciculatum*
California bulrush	*Scirpus californicus*
California coffeeberry	*Rhamnus californica*
California fan palm	*Washingtonia filifera*
California gnatcatcher	*Polio californica*
California goldfields	*Lasthenia californica*
California juniper	*Juniperus californica*
California lilac	*Ceanothus* spp.

California melic	*Melica californica*
California nutmeg	*Torreya californica*
California oatgrass	*Danthonia californica*
California pitcher plant	*Darlingtonia californica*
California red fir	*Abies magnifica* var. *magnifica*
California sagebrush	*Artemisia californica*
California wild grape	*Vitus californica*
camphorweed	*Pluchea* spp.
canby bluegrass	*Poa secunda* ssp. *secunda*
canyon live oak	*Quercus chrysolepis*
capeweed	*Arctotheca calendula*
catclaw acacia	*Acacia greggi*
cattail	*Typha* spp.
chamise	*Adenostoma fasciculatum*
chaparral cherry	*Prunus ilicifolia*
chaparral mallow	*Malacothamnus fasciculatus*
chaparral whitethorn	*Ceanothus leucodermis*
cheat grass	*Bromus tectorum*
cheesebrush	*Hymenoclea salsola*
chia	*Salvia columbariae*
Chilean bird's-foot trefoil	*Lotus subpinnatus*
Chilean bird's-foot trefoil	*Lotus wrangelianus*
Chinese tallow	*Sapium sebiferum*
Christmas berry	*Heteromeles arbutifolia*
cinquefoil	*Potentilla* spp.
clarkia	*Clarkia* spp.
cliffrose	*Purshia mexicana* var. *stansburyana*
club-hair mariposa lily	*Calochortus clavatus*
coast buckwheat	*Eriogonum latifolium*
coast live oak	*Quercus agrifolia*
coastal redwood	*Sequoia sempervirens*
Colorado pinyon pine	*Pinus edulis*
Columbia needlegrass	*Achnatherum lemmonii*
Colusa grass	*Neostapfia colusana*
common Mediterranean grass	*Schismus barbatus*
common pussypaws	*Calyptridium monandrum*
common rice	*Oryza sativa*
common stickyseed	*Blennosperma nanum*
common velvetgrass	*Holcus lanatus*
cord grass	*Spartina* spp.
corn lily	*Veratrum californicum*
cosmopolitan bulrush	*Scirpus maritimus*
cotton-thorn, horsebrush	*Tertradymia canescens*
Coulter pine	*Pinus coulteri*
coyotebrush	*Baccharis pilularis*
creeping barberry	*Berberis repens*
creeping snowberry	*Symphoricarpos mollis*
creeping wildrye	*Leymus triticoides*
creosote bush	*Larrea tridentata*
crimson fountaingrass	*Pennisetum setaceum*
cryptantha	*Cryptantha* spp.
Cucamonga man-root	*Marah macrocarpus*
cup fungus	*Peziza* spp.
curl-leaf mountain-mahogany	*Cercocarpus ledifolius*
currant	*Ribes* spp.
Cuyamaca cypress	*Cupressus arizonica* ssp. *stephensonii*

cypress	*Cupressus* spp.
dalmation toadflax	*Linaria genistifolia* ssp. *dalmatica*
dandelion	*Taraxacum* spp.
Davidson's penstemon	*Penstemon davidsonii*
death camas	*Zigadenus* spp.
deer brush	*Ceanothus intergerrimus*
deergrass	*Muhlenbergia rigens*
deerweed	*Lotus scoparius*
desert ceanothus	*Ceanothus greggii*
desert crested wheatgrass	*Agropyron desertorum*
desert gooseberry	*Ribes velutinum*
desert needlegrass	*Achnatherum speciosum*
desert-willow	*Chilopsis linearis*
devil's lettuce	*Amsinckia tessellata*
dichlostemma	*Dichelostemma*
dogwood	*Cornus* spp.
dotseed plantain	*Plantago erecta*
Douglas' buckwheat	*Eriogonum douglasii*
Douglas-fir	*Pseudotsuga menziesii* var. *menziesii*
dwarf birch	*Betula nana*
dwarf brodiaea	*Brodiaea terrestris*
Eastwood manzanita	*Arctostaphylos glandulosa*
elderberry	*Sambucus* spp.
empress tree	*Paulownia tomentosa*
Engelmann oak	*Quercus engelmannii*
Engleman spruce	*Picea engelmannii*
Ephedra, Mormon tea	*Ephedra* spp.
Eucalyptus	*Eucalyptus* spp.
evergreen huckleberry	*Vaccinium ovatum*
fennel	*Foeniculum vulgare*
fiddleneck	*Amsinckia tessellata*
fig-marigold	*Carpobrotus edulis*
fire poppy	*Papaver californicum*
fireweed	*Epilobium angustifolium*
flannelbush	*Fremontodendron californicum*
fleabane daisy	*Erigeron* spp.
foothill ash	*Fraxinus dipetala*
Foothill death camas	*Zigadenus paniculatus*
foothill needlegrass	*Nassella lepida*
foothill pine	*Pinus sabiniana*
fourwing saltbush	*Atriplex canescens*
foxtail pine	*Pinus balfouriana* spp. *balfouriana*
Fremont cottonwood	*Populus fremontii*
Fremont's death camas	*Zigadenus fremontii*
French broom	*Genista monspessulana*
galleta grass	*Pleuraphis jamesii*
geranium	*Geranium* spp.
Geyer's willow	*Salix geyeriana*
golden chinquapin	*Chrysolepis chrysophylla*
giant reed	*Arundo donax*
giant sequoia	*Sequoiadendron giganteum*
giant wildrye	*Leymus condensatus*
gilia	*Gilia* spp.
goat's beard	*Tragopogon dubius*
goldenbush	*Ericameria ericoides*
golden chinquapin	*Chrysolepis chrysophylla*

golden-eye	*Heliomeris* spp.
goldenrod	*Solidago* spp.
golden-yarrow	*Eriophyllum confertiflorum*
Goodding's black willow	*Salix gooddingii*
gooseberry	*Ribes* spp.
goosefoot violet	*Viola purpurea*
grand fir	*Abies grandis*
gray alder	*Alnus incana*
greasewood	*Sarcobatus vermiculatus*
greasewood	*Sarcobatus* spp.
green rabbitbrush	*Chrysothamnus teretifolius*
greenbark ceanothus	*Ceanothus spinosus*
greenleaf manzanita	*Arctostaphylos patula*
groundsmoke	*Gayophytum* spp.
hairy brackenfern	*Pteridium aquilinum* var. *pubescens*
hairy wallabygrass	*Danthonia pilosa*
hawksbeard	*Crepis* spp.
hawkweed	*Hieracium* spp.
hayfield tarweed	*Hemizonia congesta*
hazelnut	*Corylus cornuta*
heartleaf arnica	*Arnica cordifolia*
hoaryleaf ceanothus	*Ceanothus crassifolius*
holly-leaf redberry	*Rhamnus ilicifolia*
honey mesquite	*Prosopis glandulosa* var. *torreyana*
Hooker's manzanita	*Arctostaphylos hookeri* ssp. *hookeri*
horsebrush	*Tetradymia* spp.
huckleberry oak	*Quercus vaccinifolia*
Idahoe fescue	*Festuca idahoensis*
imbricate phacelia	*Phacelia imbricata*
incense-cedar	*Calocedrus decurrens*
Indian paintbrush	*Orthocarpus attenuatus*
Indian paintbrush, owl's -clover	*Castilleja* spp.
Indian ricegrass	*Achnatherum hymenoides*
interior live oak	*Quercus wislizenii*
interior rose	*Rosa woodsii* ssp. *ultramontana*
iodine brush	*Allenrolfea* spp.
ione manzanita	*Arctostaphylos myrtifolia*
iris	*Iris* spp.
Italian ryegrass	*Lolium multiflorum*
jack pine	*Pinus banksiana*
Jeffrey pine	*Pinus jeffreyi*
Johnny-jump-up	*Viola pendunculata*
Joshua tree	*Yucca brevifolia*
Junegrass	*Koeleria macrantha*
juniper	*Juniperus* spp.
Kentucky bluegrass	*Poa pratensis* ssp. *Pratensis*
knobcone pine	*Pinus attenuata*
La Purisima manzanita	*Arctostaphylos purissima*
lacy phacelia	*Phacelia tanacetifolia*
Laguna beach dudleya	*Dudleya stolonifera*
lambstongue ragwort	*Senecio intergerrimus*
large-flowered flddleneck	*Amsinckia grandiflora*
largehead clover	*Trifolium macrocephalum*
larkspur	*Delphinium* spp.
laurel sumac	*Malosma laurina*
Lehman lovegrass	*Eragrostis lehmanniana*

Lemmon's catchfly	*Silene lemmonii*
Lemmon's ceanothus	*Ceanothus lemmonii*
Lemmon's willow	*Salix lemmonii*
lemonadeberry	*Rhus integrifolia*
lewisia	*Lewisia* spp.
lily	*Lilium* spp.
limber pine	*Pinus flexilis*
lodgepole pine	*Pinus contorta* var. *murrayana*
lomatium	*Lomatium* spp.
longleaf phlox	*Phlox stansburyi*
lotus	*Lotus* spp.
low sagebrush	*Artemisia arbuscula*
lupine	*Lupinus* spp.
MacNab cypress	*Cupressus macnabiana*
mahala mat	*Ceanothus prostratus*
manynerve catchfly	*Silene multinervia*
many-stemmed sedge	*Carex multicaulis*
manzanita	*Arctostaphylos* spp.
marigold navarretia	*Navarretia tagetina*
mariposa lily	*Calochortus* spp. *clavatus*
Mariposa manzanita	*Arctostaphylos viscida,* ssp. *mariposa*
matted buckwheat	*Eriogonum caespitosum*
meadow barley	*Hordeum brachyantherum*
Mediterranean split grass	*Schismus* spp.
medusahead	*Taeniatherum caput-medusae*
mesquite	*Prosopis* spp.
Mexican elderberry	*Sambucus mexicana*
milkvetch	*Astragalus* spp.
mission manzanita	*Xylococcus bicolor*
Modoc cypress	*Cupressus bakeri*
Modoc plum	*Prunus subcordata*
Mojave yucca	*Yucca schidigera*
monkeyflower	*Mimulus* spp.
Monterey cypress	*Cupressus macrocarpus*
Monterey pine	*Pinus radiata*
Morro manzanita	*Arctostaphylos morroensis*
mountain alder	*Alnus incana* ssp. *tenuifolia*
mountain big sagebrush	*Artemisia tridentata* ssp. *vaseyana*
mountain dogwood	*Cornus nuttallii*
mountain gooseberry	*Ribes montigenum*
mountain hemlock	*Tsuga mertensiana*
mountain lady's slipper	*Cypropedium montanum*
mountain-mahogany	*Cercocarpus* spp.
mountain maple	*Acer glabrum*
mountain misery	*Chamaebatia foliolosa*
mountain sedge	*Carex scopulorum*
mountain snowberry	*Symphoricarpos oreophilus*
mountain whitethorn	*Ceanothus cordulatus*
Mt. Hood pussypaws	*Cistanthe umbellata* var. *umbellata*
mule fat	*Baccharis salicifolia*
mule's ears	*Wyethia* spp.
Muller's oak	*Quercus cornelius-mulleri*
mustard	*Brassica* spp.
narrow-leaved willow	*Salix exigua*
Nebraska sedge	*Carex nebrascensis*
needlegrass	*Achnatherum* spp.

Nevada pea	*Lathyrus lanszwertii*
nineleaf biscuitroot	*Lomatium triternatum*
nodding needlegrass	*Nassella cernua*
northern bishop pine	*Pinus muricata* var. *borealis*
Northwest territory sedge	*Carex urticulata*
oak	*Quercus* spp.
oats	*Avena* spp.
One-sided bluegrass	*Poa secunda* ssp. *secunda*
onion/garlic	*Allium* spp.
oniongrass	*Melica bulbosa*
orchard grass	*Dactylis glomerata*
orcutt brome	*Bromus orcuttianus*
Oregon ash	*Fraxinus latifolia*
Oregon grape	*Berberis* spp.
Oregon white oak	*Quercus garryana*
Our Lord's candle	*Yucca whipplei*
Pacific madrone	*Arbutus menziesii*
Pacific starflower	*Trientalis latifolia*
Pacific yew	*Taxus brevifolia*
Pajaro manzanita	*Arctostaphylos pajaroensis*
pallid manzanita	*Arctostaphylos pallida*
pampas grass	*Cortaderia jubata*
papershell pinyon	*Pinus remota*
Parish's snowberry	*Symphoriocarpus rotundifolius* var. *parishii*
Parry pinyon pine	*Pinus quadrifolia*
Parry's larkspur	*Delphinium parryi*
Parry's rabbitbrush	*Chrysothamnus parryi*
parsnipflower buckwheat	*Eriogonum heracleoides*
penstemon	*Penstemon* spp.
perennial ryegrass	*Lolium perenne*
perennial veldtgrass	*Erharta calycina*
phacelia	*Phacelia* spp.
pigweed, goosefoot	*Chenopodium*
pine bluegrass	*Poa secunda*
pinemat manzanita	*Arctostaphylos nevadensis*
poison oak	*Toxicodendron diversilobum*
ponderosa pine	*Pinus ponderosa*
popcornflower	*Plagiobothrys nothofulvus*
Port Orford-cedar	*Chamaecyparis lawsoniana*
prairie cordgrass	*Spartina pectinata*
prickly lettuce	*Lactuca serriola*
prickly sandwort	*Arenaria aculeata*
princess tree	*Paulownia tomentosa*
purple needlegrass	*Nassella pulchra*
purple sage	*Salvia leucophylla*
pussy-toes	*Antennaria* spp.
pygmy cypress	*Cupressus goveniana* ssp. *pigmaea*
pygmyweed	*Crassula connata*
quackgrass	*Elytrigia repens*
quaking aspen	*Populus tremuloides*
rabbitbush	*Ericameria bloomeri*
red alder	*Alnus rubra*
red brome	*Bromus madritensis* ssp. *rubens*
redbud	*Cercis occidentalis*
red fescue	*Festuca rubra*
red maids	*Calandrinia ciliata*

red pine	*Pinus resinosa*
red shank	*Adenostoma sparsifolium*
redstem-filaree	*Erodium cicutarium*
red willow	*Salix laevigata*
reed canary grass	*Phalaris arundinacea*
rock cress	*Arabis* spp.
Ross' sedge	*Carex rossii*
roundfruited carex	*Carex globosa*
roundleaf snowberry	*Symphoriocarpus rotundifolius*
rubber rabbitbrush	*Chrysothamnus nauseosus*
rush	*Juncus* spp.
Russian olive	*Elaegnus angustifolius*
Russian thistle	*Salsola tragus*
sacapellote	*Acourtia microcephala*
sagebrush	*Artemisia* spp.
Sahara mustard	*Brassica tournefortii*
salal	*Gaultheria shallon*
salmonberry	*Rubus spectabilis*
saltbush	*Atriplex* spp.
saltcedar	*Tamarix ramosissima*
saltgrass	*Distichlis spicata*
San Luis blazingstar	*Mentzelia micrantha*
sand buck brush	*Ceanothus cuneatus* var. *fasciculatus*
sand mesa manzanita	*Arctostaphylos rudis*
Sandberg bluegrass	*Poa secunda* ssp. *sanbergii*
sandmat manzanita	*Arctostaphylos pumila*
sandscrub ceanothus	*Ceanothus dentatus*
sandwort	*Arenaria* spp.
sanicles	*Sanicula* spp.
Santa Barbara ceanothus	*Ceanothus impressus*
Santa Cruz tarplant	*Holocarpha macrodenia*
Santa Lucia fir	*Abies bracteata*
Sargent cypress	*Cupressus sargentii*
Saw-toothed goldenbush	*Hazardia squarrosa*
Scotch broom	*Cytisus scoparius*
Scouler's willow	*Salix scouleriana*
scrub live oak	*Quercus turbinella*
scrub oak	*Quercus berberidifolia*
seaside woolly sunflower	*Eriophyllum staechadifolium*
sedges	*Carex* spp.
seep monkeyflower	*Mumulus guttatus*
shadscale	*Atriplex confertifolia*
Shasta red fir	*Abies magnifica* var. *shastensis*
shining willow	*Salix lucida* ssp. *lasiandra*
short-beaked sedge	*Carex simulata*
shorthair sedge	*Carex filifolia* var. *erostrata*
shortpod mustard	*Hirschfeldia incana*
shrub tan oak	*Lithocarpus densiflorus* var. *echinoides*
Sierra gooseberry	*Ribes roezlii*
Sierra juniper	*Juniperus occidentalis* ssp. *australis*
silk tassel bush	*Garrya* spp.
silver sagebrush	*Artemisia cana* ssp. *bolanderi*
singleleaf pinyon pine	*Pinus monophylla*
Sitka spruce	*Picea sitchensis*
sixweeks fescue	*Vulpia octoflora*
skunkbrush	*Rhus trilobata*

slender buckwheat	*Eriogonum microthecum*
slender penstemon	*Penstemon gracilentus*
slender phlox	*Phlox gracilis*
slenderbeak sedge	*Carex athrostachya*
small fescue	*Vulpia microstachys*
smallflower melicgrass	*Melica imperfecta*
smallhead clover	*Trifolium microcephalum*
smoke tree	*Psorothamnus spinosus*
snapdragon	*Antirrhinum* spp.
snowberry	*Symphoricarpos* spp.
snowdrop bush	*Styrax officinalis*
snowfield sagebrush	*Artemisia spiciformis*
soap plant	*Chlorogalum pomeridianum*
soft chess	*Bromus hordeaceus*
softstem bulrush	*Scirpus tabernaemontani*
southern bishop pine	*Pinus muricata* var. *muricata*
spiny hopsage	*Grayia spinosa*
spiny menodora	*Menodora spinescens*
spiny phlox	*Phlox hoodii*
spiny redberry	*Rhamnus crocea*
spirea	*Spiraea* spp.
spotted hideseed	*Eucrypta chrysanthemifolia*
squirreltail	*Elymus elymoides*
sticky cinquefoil	*Potentilla glandulosa*
sticky currant	*Ribes viscosissimum*
sticky snakeweed	*Gutierrezia microcephala*
strawberry	*Fragaria* spp.
subalpine fir	*Abies lasiocarpa*
sugar pine	*Pinus lambertiana*
sulfur flower	*Eriogonum umbellatum*
sumac or sugarbrush	*Rhus* spp.
sun cup	*Camissonia* spp.
sweet cicely	*Osmorhiza* spp.
sweet vernalgrass	*Anthoxanthum odoratum*
tailcup lupine	*Lupinus caudatus*
tallow tree	*Triadica sebifera*
tamarisk	*Tamarix* spp.
tanoak	*Lithocarpus densiflorus*
tarweed	*Hemizonia* spp.
Tasmanian blue gum	*Eucalyptus globulus*
Tecate cypress	*Cupressus forbesii*
thimbleberry	*Rubus parviflorus*
thinleaf alder	*Alnus viridis* ssp. *sinuata*
thistle	*Cirsium* spp.
Thurber needlegrass	*Achnatherum thurberianum*
timothy	*Phleum pratense*
tobacco brush	*Ceanothus velutinus* var. *velutinus*
Torrey pine	*Pinus torreyana*
toyon	*Heteromeles arbutifolia*
trail plant	*Adenocaulon bicolor*
tree-of-heaven	*Ailanthus altissima*
tufted hairgrass	*Deschampsia cespitosa* ssp. *holciformis*
tumble mustard	*Sisymbrium altissimum*
Utah juniper	*Juniperus osteosperma*
Utah service-berry	*Amelanchier utahensis*
Utah snowberry	*Symphoricarpos oreophilus* var. *utahensis*

valley oak	*Quercus lobata*
variable linanthus	*Linanthus parviflorus*
vine maple	*Acer circinatum*
violet	*Viola* spp.
walnut	*Juglans* spp.
Washoe pine	*Pinus washoensis*
water birch	*Betula occidentalis*
water chickweed	*Montia fontana*
water jacket and wolfberry	*Lycium andersonii*
wax currant	*Ribes cereum*
western blue flag	*Iris missouriensis*
western bristlecone pine	*Pinus longaeva*
western choke-cherry	*Prunus virginiana* var. *demissa*
western hemlock	*Tsuga heterophylla*
western juniper	*Juniperus occidentalis* ssp. *occidentalis*
western larch	*Larix occidentalis*
western lily	*Lilium occidentale*
western needlegrass	*Achnatherum occidentalis*
western redcedar	*Thuja plicata*
western sycamore	*Platanus racemosa*
western tansy mustard	*Descurainia pinnata*
western white pine	*Pinus monticola*
Wheeler's bluegrass	*Poa wheeleri*
whispering bells	*Emmenanthe penduliflora*
white alder	*Alnus rhombifolia*
whitebark pine	*Pinus albicaulis*
white bursage	*Ambrosia dumosa*
white fir	*Abies concolor*
white pincushion	*Chaenactis artemisiifolia*
white sage	*Salvia apiana*
whitebark pine	*Pinus albicaulis*
whitehead mule's ears	*Wyethia helenioides*
whiteleaf manzanita	*Arctostaphylos viscida*
whiteveined wintergreen	*Pyrola picta*
Wild buckwheat	*Eriogonum* spp.
wild mock orange	*Philadelphus lewisii*
wild oat	*Avena fatua*
wild pea	*Lathryus lanszwertii*
willow	*Salix* spp.
winterfat	*Kraschennikovia lanata*
woodrose	*Rosa gymnocarpa*
woolly mule's ears	*Wyethia mollis*
woollypod milkvetch	*Astragalus purshii*
woolyleaf ceanothus	*Ceanothus tomentosus*
Wyoming big sagebrush	*Artemisia tridentata* ssp. *wyomingenesis*
yampah	*Perideridia* spp.
yarrow	*Achillea millifolium*
yellow bush lupine	*Lupinus arboreus*
yellow rabbitbrush	*Chysothamnus viscidiflorus*
yellow star-thistle	*Centaurea solstitialis*
yellowflower tarweed	*Holocarpha virgata*
yerba santa	*Eriodictyon californicum*
zigzag groundsmoke	*Gayophytum heterozygum*

Latin Name	Common Name
Abies bracteata	Santa Lucia fir
Abies concolor	white fir
Abies grandis	grand fir
Abies lasiocarpa	subalpine fir
Abies magnifica var. *magnifica*	California red fir
Abies magnifica var. *shastensis*	Shasta red fir
Acacia greggi	catclaw acacia
Acer circinatum	vine maple
Acer glabrum	mountain maple
Acer macrophyllum	bigleaf maple
Acer negundo var. *califonricum*	box elder
Achillea millifolium	yarrow
Achnatherum capense	African needlegrass
Achnatherum hymenoides	Indian ricegrass
Achnatherum lemmonii	Columbia needlegrass
Achnatherum occidentalis	western needlegrass
Achnatherum spp.	needlegrass
Achnatherum speciosum	desert needlegrass
Achnatherum thurberianum	Thurber needlegrass
Acourtia microcephala	sacapellote
Adenocaulon bicolor	trail plant
Adenostoma fasciculatum	chamise
Adenostoma sparsifolium	redshank
Aegilops triuncialis	barbed goatgrass
Aesculus californica	California buckeye
Agave spp.	agave
Agoseris spp.	agoseris
Agropyron desertorum	desert crested wheatgrass
Agrostis spp.	bent grass
Ailanthus altissima	tree-of-heaven
Allenrolfea spp.	iodine brush
Allium spp.	onion/garlic
Alnus incana	gray alder
Alnus incana ssp. *tenuifolia*	mountain alder
Alnus rhombifolia	white alder
Alnus rubra	red alder
Alnus spp.	alder
Alnus viridis ssp. *sinuata*	thinleaf alder
Ambrosia dumosa	white bursage
Amelanchier utahensis	Utah service-berry
Amsinckia grandiflora	large-flowered fiddleneck
Amsinckia tessellata	devil's lettuce
Antennaria spp.	pussy-toes
Anthoxanthum odoratum	sweet vernalgrass
Antirrhinum spp.	snapdragon
Arabis spp.	rock cress
Arbutus menziesii	Pacific madrone
Arctostaphylos bakeri spp. *bakeri*	Baker's manzanita
Arctostaphylos glandulosa	Eastwood manzanita
Arctostaphylos glauca	bigberry manzanita
Arctostaphylos hookeri ssp. *hookeri*	Hooker's manzanita
Arctostaphylos morroensis	Morro manzanita
Arctostaphylos myrtifolia	ione manzanita
Arctostaphylos nevadensis	pinemat manzanita

Arctostaphylos pajaroensis	Pajaro manzanita
Arctostaphylos pallida	pallid manzanita
Arctostaphylos patula	greenleaf manzanita
Arctostaphylos pumila	sandmat manzanita
Arctostaphylos purissima	La Purisima manzanita
Arctostaphylos rudis	sand mesa manzanita
Arctostaphylos spp.	manzanita
Arctostaphylos viscida	whiteleaf manzanita
Arctostaphylos viscida, ssp. *mariposa*	Mariposa manzanita
Arctotheca calendula	capeweed
Arenaria aculeata	prickly sandwort
Arenaria spp.	sandwort
Arnica cordifolia	heartleaf arnica
Artemisia arbuscula	low sagebrush
Artemisia californica	California sagebrush
Artemisia cana ssp. *bolanderi*	silver sagebrush
Artemisia nova	black sagebrush
Artemisia spp.	sagebrush
Artemisia spiciformis	snowfield sagebrush
Artemisia tridentata	big sagebrush
Artemisia tridentata ssp. *tridentata*	basin big sagebrush
Artemisia tridentata ssp. *vaseyana*	mountain big sagebrush
Artemisia tridentata ssp. *wyomingenesis*	Wyoming big sagebrush
Artostaphylos viscida ssp. *mariposa*	Mariposa manzanita
Arundo donax	giant reed
Aster spp.	aster
Astragalus purshii	woollypod milkvetch
Astragalus spp.	milkvetch
Atriplex canescens	fourwing saltbush
Atriplex confertifolia	shadscale
Atriplex spp.	saltbush
Avena fatua	wild oat
Avena spp.	oats
Baccharis pilularis	coyotebrush
Baccharis salicifolia	mule fat
Balsamorhiza spp.	balsam-root
Berberis repens	creeping barberry
Berberis spp.	Oregon grape
Betula nana	dwarf birch
Betula occidentalis	water birch
Blennosperma nanum	common stickyseed
Brassica nigra	black mustard
Brassica spp.	mustard
Brassica tournefortii	Sahara mustard
Brodiaea spp.	brodiaea
Brodiaea terrestris	dwarf brodiaea
Bromus hordeaceus	soft chess
Bromus madritensis ssp. *rubens*	red brome
Bromus orcuttianus	orcutt brome
Bromus tectorum	cheat grass
Cactaceae spp.	cactus
Calamagrostis breweri	Brewer's reedgrass
Calamagrostis canadensis	bluejoint reedgrass
Calandrinia breweri	Brewer's redmaids
Calandrinia ciliata	red maids
Calocedrus decurrens	incense-cedar

Calochortus clavatus	clubhair mariposa lily
Calochortus spp. *clavatus*	mariposa lily
Calyptridium monandrum	common pussypaws
Camissonia spp.	sun cup
Carex athrostachya	slenderbeak sedge
Carex brainerdi	Brainerd's sedge
Carex filifolia var. *erostrata*	shorthair sedge
Carex globosa	round-fruited carix
Carex multicaulis	many-stemmed sedge
Carex nebrascensis	Nebraska sedge
Carex rossii	Ross' sedge
Carex scopulorum	mountain sedge
Carex simulata	short-beaked sedge
Carex spp.	sedges
Carex urticulata	northwest territory sedge
Carex vesicaria	blister sedge
Carpobrotus edulis	fig-marigold
Castilleja spp.	Indian paintbrush, owl's -clover
Ceanothus cordulatus	mountain whitethorn
Ceanothus crassifolius	hoaryleaf ceanothus
Ceanothus cuneatus var. *cuneatus*	buck brush
Ceanothus cuneatus var. *fasciculatus*	sand buck brush
Ceanothus dentatus	sandscrub ceanothus
Ceanothus greggii	desert ceanothus
Ceanothus impressus	Santa Barbara ceanothus
Ceanothus intergerrimus	deer brush
Ceanothus lemmonii	Lemmon's ceanothus
Ceanothus leucodermis	chaparral whitethorn
Ceanothus megacarpus var. *megacarpus*	bigpod ceanothus
Ceanothus prostratus	mahala mat
Ceanothus spp.	California lilac
Ceanothus spinosus	greenbark ceanothus
Ceanothus thyrsiflorus	blue blossom
Ceanothus tomentosus	woolyleaf ceanothus
Ceanothus velutinus var. *velutinus*	tobacco brush
Cenchrus ciliaris	buffel grass
Centaurea solstitialis	yellow star-thistle
Cercis occidentalis	redbud
Cercocarpus betuloides var. *betuloides*	birch-leaf mountain-mahogany
Cercocarpus ledifolius	curl-leaf mountain-mahogany
Cercocarpus spp.	mountain-mahogany
Chaenactis artemisiifolia	white pincushion
Chamaebatia foliolosa	mountain misery
Chamaecyparis lawsoniana	Port Orford-cedar
Chenopodium	pigweed, goosefoot
Chilopsis linearis	desert-willow
Chlorogalum pomeridianum	soap plant
Chrysolepis chrysophylla	golden chinquapin
Chrysolepis sempervirens	bush chinquapin
Chrysothamnus nauseosus	rubber rabbitbrush
Chrysothamnus parryi	Parry's rabbitbrush
Chrysothamnus teretifolius	green rabbitbrush
Chysothamnus viscidiflorus	yellow rabbitbrush
Cirsium spp.	thistle
Cistanthe umbellata var. *umbellata*	Mt. Hood pussypaws
Clarkia spp.	clarkia

Coloegyne ramosissima	blackbrush
Cornus nuttallii	mountain dogwood
Cornus spp.	dogwood
Cortaderia jubata	pampas grass
Corylus cornuta	hazelnut
Crassula connata	pygmyweed
Crepis spp.	hawksbeard
Cryptantha spp.	cryptantha
Cupressus arizonica spp. *stephensonii*	Cuyamaca cypress
Cupressus bakeri	Modoc cypress
Cupressus forbesii	Tecate cypress
Cupressus goveniana ssp. *pigmaea*	pygmy cypress
Cupressus macnabiana	MacNab cypress
Cupressus macrocarpus	Monterey cypress
Cupressus sargentii	Sargent cypress
Cupressus spp.	cypress
Curculio and *Cydia* spp.	acorn
Cypropedium montanum	mountain lady's slipper
Cytisus scoparius	Scotch broom
Dactylis glomerata	orchard grass
Danthonia californica	California oatgrass
Danthonia pilosa	hairy wallaby grass
Darlingtonia californica	California pitcher plant
Delphinium parryi	blue larkspur
Delphinium parryi	Parry's larkspur
Delphinium spp.	larkspur
Dendromecon rigida	bush poppy
Deschampsia cespitosa ssp. *holciformis*	tufted hairgrass
Descurainia pinnata	western tansy mustard
Dichelostemma capitatum	blue dicks
Distichlis spicata	saltgrass
Dudleya stolonifera	Laguna beach dudleya
Elaeagnus angustifolius	Russian olive
Elymus elymoides	squirreltail
Elymus glaucus	blue wildrye
Elytrigia repens	quackgrass
Emmenanthe penduliflora	whispering bells
Encelia californica	California brittlebush
Encelia farinosa	brittle brush
Ephedra spp.	Ephedra, Mormon tea
Epilobium angustifolium	fireweed
Eragrostis lehmanniana	Lehman lovegrass
Erharta calycina	perennial veldtgrass
Ericameria bloomeri	rabbitbush
Ericameria ericoides	goldenbush
Erigeron spp.	fleabane daisy
Eriodictyon californicum	yerba santa
Eriogonum caespitosum	matted buckwheat
Eriogonum douglasii	Douglas' buckwheat
Eriogonum fasciculatum	California buckwheat
Eriogonum heracleoides	parsnipflower buckwheat
Eriogonum latifolium	coast buckwheat
Eriogonum microthecum	slender buckwheat
Eriogonum spp.	wild buckwheat
Eriogonum umbellatum	sulfur flower
Eriophyllum confertiflorum	golden-yarrow

Eriophyllum staechadifolium	seaside woolly sunflower
Erodium cicutarium	redstem filaree
Eucalyptus globulus	blue gum
Eucalyptus spp.	Eucalyptus
Eucrypta chrysanthemifolia	spotted hideseed
Festuca idahoensis	Idaho fescue
Festuca rubra	red fescue
Foeniculum vulgare	fennel
Fragaria spp.	strawberry
Fraxinus dipetala	foothill ash
Fraxinus latifolia	Oregon ash
Fremontodendron californicum	flannelbush
Galium bolanderi	Bolander's bedstraw
Garrya fremontii	bearbrush
Garrya spp.	silk tassel bush
Gaultheria shallon	salal
Gayophytum heterozygum	zigzag groundsmoke
Gayophytum spp.	groundsmoke
Genista monspessulana	French broom
Geranium spp.	cranesbill, geranium
Geum spp.	avens
Gilia spp.	gilia
Grayia spinosa	spiny hopsage
Gutierrezia microcephala	snakeweed
Hazardia squarrosa	saw-toothed goldenbush
Heliomiris spp.	golden eye
Hemizonia congesta	hayfield tarweed
Hemizonia spp.	tarweed
Heterobasidion annosum	annosus root rot
Heteromeles arbutifolia	Christmas berry
Heteromeles arbutifolia	toyon
Hieracium spp.	hawkweed
Hirschfeldia incana	shortpod mustard
Holcus lanatus	common velvetgrass
Holocarpha macrodenia	Santa Cruz tarplant
Holocarpha virgata	yellowflower tarweed
Hordeum brachyantherum	meadow barley
Hymenoclea salsola	cheesebrush
Hymenoclea salsola	burrobrush
Iris missouriensis	western blue flag
Iris spp.	iris
Juglans californica	California black walnut
Juglans spp.	walnut
Juncus balticus	baltic rush
Juncus leiospermus var. *ahartii*	Ahart's dwarf rush
Juncus spp.	rush
Juniperus californica	California juniper
Juniperus occidentalis ssp. *australis*	Sierra juniper
Juniperus occidentalis ssp. *occidentalis*	western juniper
Juniperus osteosperma	Utah juniper
Juniperus spp.	juniper
Koeleria macrantha	junegrass
Kraschennikovia lanata	winterfat
Lactuca serriola	prickly lettuce
Larix occidentalis	western larch
Larrea tridentata	creosote bush

Lasthenia californica	California goldfields
Lathyrus lanszwertii	Nevada pea
Lathryus lanszwertii	wild pea
Lewisia spp.	lewisia
Leymus cinereus	Basin wildrye
Leymus condensatus	giant wildrye
Leymus triticoides	creeping wildrye
Lilium occidentale	western lily
Lilium spp.	lily
Linanthus parviflorus	variable linanthus
Linaria genistifolia ssp. *dalmatica*	dalmation toadflax
Lithocarpus densiflorus	tanoak
Lithocarpus densiflorus var. *echinoides*	shrub tanoak
Lolium multiflorum	annual ryegrass
Lolium multiflorum	Italian ryegrass
Lolium perenne	perennial ryegrass
Lomatium spp.	Lomatium
Lomatium triternatum	nineleaf biscuitroot
Lotus subpinnatus	Chilean bird's-foot trefoil
Lotus spp.	lotus
Lotus wrangelianus	Chilean bird's-foot trefoil
Lupinus arboreus	bush lupine
Lupinus arboreus	yellow bush lupine
Lupinus caudatus	tailcup lupine
Lupinus latifolius	broadleaf lupine
Lupinus spp.	lupine
Lycium andersonii	water jacket and wolfberry
Malacothamnus fasciculatus	chaparral mallow
Malosma laurina	laurel sumac
Marah macrocarpus	Cucamonga manroot
Melica bulbosa	oniongrass
Melica californica	California melic
Melica imperfecta	smallflower melicgrass
Menodora spinescens	spiny menodora
Mentzelia micrantha	San Luis blazingstar
Mentzelia spp.	blazing star
Mertensia spp.	bluebells, lungwort
Mimulus aurantiacus	bush monkeyflower
Mimulus spp.	monkeyflower
Mimulus guttatus	seep monkeyflower
Montia fontana	water chickweed
Morchella elata	black morel
Muhlenbergia rigens	deergrass
Nassella cernua	nodding needlegrass
Nassella lepida	foothill needlegrass
Nassella pulchra	purple needlegrass
Navarretia tagetina	marigold navarretia
Neostapfia colusana	Colusa grass
Nolina spp.	beargrass
Orthocarpus attenuatus	Indian paintbrush
Oryza sativa	common rice
Osmorhiza spp.	sweet cicely
Paeonia brownii	Brown's peony
Papaver californicum	fire poppy
Paulownia tomentosa	empress tree
Paulownia tomentosa	princess tree

Pennisetum setaceum	crimson fountaingrass
Penstemon davidsonii	Davidson's penstemon
Penstemon gracilentus	slender penstemon
Penstemon spp.	Penstemon
Perideridia spp.	yampah
Peziza spp.	cup fungus
Phacelia imbricata	imbricate phacelia
Phacelia spp.	phacelia
Phacelia tanacetifolia	lacy phacelia
Phalaris arundinacea	reed canary grass
Philadelphus lewisii	wild mock orange
Phleum pretense	timothy
Phlox gracilis	slender phlox
Phlox hoodii	spiny phlox
Phlox stansburyi	longleaf phlox
Picea breweriana	Brewer spruce
Picea engelmannii	Engleman spruce
Picea sitchensis	Sitka spruce
Pinus albicaulis	whitebark pine
Pinus attenuata	knobcone pine
Pinus balfouriana spp. *balfouriana*	foxtail pine
Pinus banksiana	jack pine
Pinus contorta ssp. *bolanderi*	Bolander pine
Pinus contorta ssp. *contorta*	beach pine
Pinus contorta var. *murrayana*	lodgepole pine
Pinus coulteri	Coulter pine
Pinus edulis	Colorado pinyon pine
Pinus flexilis	limber pine
Pinus jeffreyi	Jeffrey pine
Pinus lambertiana	sugar pine
Pinus longaeva	western bristlecone pine
Pinus monophylla	singleleaf pinyon pine
Pinus monticola	western white pine
Pinus muricata	Bishop pine
Pinus muricata var. *borealis*	northern bishop pine
Pinus muricata var. *muricata*	southern bishop pine
Pinus ponderosa	ponderosa pine
Pinus quadrifolia	Parry pinyon pine
Pinus radiata	Monterey pine
Pinus remota	papershell pinyon
Pinus resinosa	red pine
Pinus sabiniana	foothill pine
Pinus torreyana	Torrey pine
Pinus washoensis	Washoe pine
Plagiobothrys nothofulvus	popcornflower
Plantago erecta	dotseed plantain
Platanus racemosa	western sycamore
Pleuraphis jamesii	galleta grass
Pleuraphis rigida	big galleta grass
Pluchea sericea	arrow weed
Pluchea spp.	camphorweed
Poa pratensis ssp. *pratensis*	Kentucky bluegrass
Poa secunda	pine bluegrass
Poa secunda ssp. *secunda*	canby bluegrass
Poa secunda ssp. *secunda*	one-sided bluegrass
Poa secunda, ssp. *sanbergii*	Sandberg bluegrass

Poa wheeleri	Wheeler's bluegrass
Polio californica	California gnatcatcher
Populus balsamifera ssp. *trichocarpa*	black cottonwood
Populus fremontii	Fremont cottonwood
Populus spp.	Aspen ash
Populus tremuloides	quaking aspen
Potentilla glandulosa	sticky cinquefoil
Potentilla spp.	cinquefoil
Prosopis glandulosa var. *torreyana*	honey mesquite
Prosopis spp.	mesquite
Prunus emarginata	bitter cherry
Prunus ilicifolia	chaparral cherry
Prunus subcordata	Modoc plum
Prunus virginiana var. *demissa*	western choke-cherry
Pseudoroegneria spicata	bluebunch wheatgrass
Pseudotsuga macrocarpa	bigcone Douglas-fir
Pseudotsuga menziesii var. *menziesii*	Douglas-fir
Psorothamnus spinosus	smoke tree
Pteridium aquilinum var. *pubescens*	hairy brackenfern
Purshia mexicana var. *stansburyana*	cliffrose
Purshia tridentata	antelope bitterbrush
Purshia tridentata	bitter brush
Pyrola picta	whiteveined wintergreen
Quercus agrifolia	coast live oak
Quercus berberidifolia	scrub oak
Quercus chrysolepis	canyon live oak
Quercus cornelius-mulleri	Muller's oak
Quercus douglasii	blue oak
Quercus douglasii	California blue oak
Quercus engelmannii	Engelmann oak
Quercus garryana	Oregon white oak
Quercus garryana var. *breweri*	Brewer oak
Quercus kelloggii	California black oak
Quercus lobata	valley oak
Quercus spp.	oak
Quercus turbinella	scrub live oak
Quercus vaccinifolia	huckleberry oak
Quercus wislizenii	interior live oak
Rhamnus californica	California coffeeberry
Rhamnus crocea	spiny redberry
Rhamnus ilicifolia	holly-leaf redberry
Rhus integrifolia	lemonadeberry
Rhus spp.	sumac or sugarbrush
Rhus trilobata	skunkbrush
Ribes cereum	wax currant
Ribes montigenum	mountain gooseberry
Ribes roezlii	Sierra gooseberry
Ribes spp.	gooseberry
Ribes velutinum	desert gooseberry
Ribes viscosissimum	sticky currant
Rosa gymnocarpa	wood rose
Rosa woodsii ssp. *ultramontana*	interior rose
Rubus parviflorus	thimbleberry
Rubus spectabilis	salmonberry
Rubus spp.	blackberry
Rubus ursinus	California blackberry

Salix boothii	booth's willow
Salix exigua	narrow-leaved willow
Salix geyeriana	Geyer's willow
Salix gooddingii	Goodding's black willow
Salix laevigata	red willow
Salix lemmonii	lemmon's willow
Salix lucida ssp. *lasiandra*	shining willow
Salix scouleriana	Scouler's willow
Salix spp.	willow
Salsola tragus	Russian thistle
Salvia apiana	white sage
Salvia columbariae	chia
Salvia leucophylla	purple sage
Salvia mellifera	black sage
Sambucus mexicana	Mexican elderberry
Sambucus spp.	elderberry
Sanicula spp.	sanicles
Sapium sebiferum	Chinese tallow
Sarcobatus spp.	greasewood
Sarcobatus vermiculatus	greasewood
Schismus arabicus	Arabian schismus
Schismus barbatus	common Mediterranean grass
Schismus spp.	Mediterranean split grass
Scirpus californicus	California bulrush
Scirpus lacustris	bulrush
Scirpus maritimus	cosmopolitan bulrush
Scirpus tabernaemontani	softstem bulrush
Senecio intergerrimus	lambstongue ragwort
Sequoia sempervirens	coastal redwood
Sequoiadendron giganteum	giant sequoia
Silene lemmonii	Lemmon's catchfly
Silene multinervia	manynerve catchfly
Sisymbrium altissimum	tumble mustard
Solidago spp.	goldenrod
Spartina pectinata	prairie cordgrass
Spartina spp.	cord grass
Spiraea spp.	spirea
Sporobolus airoides	alkali sacaton
Styrax officinalis	snowdrop bush
Symphoricarpos mollis	creeping snowberry
Symphoricarpos oreophilus	mountain snowberry
Symphoricarpos oreophilus var. *utahensis*	Utah snowberry
Symphoriocarpus rotundifolius	roundleaf snowberry
Symphoriocarpus rotundifolius var. *parishii*	Parish's snowberry
Taeniatherum caput-medusae	medusahead
Tamarix ramosissima	saltcedar
Tamarix spp.	tamarisk
Taraxacum spp.	dandelion
Taxus brevifolia	Pacific yew
Tertradymia canescens	cotton-thorn, horsebrush
Tetradymia spp.	horsebrush
Thuja plicata	western redcedar
Torreya californica	California nutmeg
Toxicodendron diversilobum	poison oak
Tragopogon dubius	goat's beard
Triadica sebifera	tallow tree

Trientalis latifolia	Pacific starflower
Trifolium macrocephalum	largehead clover
Trifolium microcephalum	smallhead clover
Triphysaria eriantha	butter-and-eggs
Tsuga heterophylla	western hemlock
Tsuga mertensiana	mountain hemlock
Typha latifolia	broadleafed cattail
Typha spp.	cattail
Umbellularia californica	California bay
Vaccinium ovatum	California huckleberry
Veratrum californicum	corn lily
Viola pendunculata	Johnny-jump-up
Viola purpurea	goosefoot violet
Viola spp.	violet
Vitaceae californica	California wild grape
Vulpia microstachys	small fescue
Vulpia octoflora	sixweeks fescue
Washingtonia filifera	California fan palm
Wyethia helenioides	whitehead mule's ears
Wyethia mollis	woolly mule's ears
Wyethia spp.	mule's ears
Xerophyllum tenax	bear-grass
Xylococcus bicolor	mission manzanita
Yucca baccata	banana yucca
Yucca brevifolia	Joshua tree
Yucca schidigera	Mojave yucca
Yucca whipplei	our Lord's candle
Zigadenus fremontii	Fremont's death camas
Zigadenus paniculatus	Foothill death camas
Zigadenus spp.	death camas

APPENDIX 2

Animal Common and Scientific Names

This appendix contains two lists. The first alphabetizes animals by common name, the second by Latin name.

Taxonomy follows these sources.

INSECTS: Jerry A. Powell and Charles L. Hogue. 1979. California insects. University of California Press, Berkeley and Los Angeles; H.E. Jaques. 1951. How to know the beetles. Wm. C. Brown Company Publishers, Dubuque, Iowa.

AMPHIBIANS AND REPTILES: M.R. Jennings. 2004. An annotated check list of the amphibians and reptiles of California and adjacent waters. California Department of Fish and Game Journal, 90(4):161–228.

FISHES: Nelson, J.S., E.J. Crossman, H. Esponosa~Perez, L.T. Findley, C.R. Gilbert, R.N. Lea, and J.D. Williams. 2004. Common and scientific names of fishes from United States, Mexico, and Canada, sixth edition. American Fisheries Society Special Publication 29, American Fisheries Society.

BIRDS: American Ornithologists' Union. 1998. The Check-list of North American Birds: The species of birds of North America from the Arctic through Panama, including the West Indies and the Hawaiian Islands, seventh edition. Buteo Books: Shipman, Virginia; Joseph Grinnell and Alden H. Miller. 1944. The distribution of the birds of California, Pacific Coast Avifauna No. 27.

MAMMALS: D.E. Wilson and D.M. Reeder. 2005. Mammal species of the world, third edition, revised. John Hopkins University Press, Baltimore, MD.

Common name	Latin name
Alameda whipsnake	*Masticophis lateralis euryxanthus*
American crow	*Corvus brachyrhynchos*
American pine marten	*Martes americana*
Argentine ant	*Linepithema humile*
bark beetle	*Scolytidae* spp. *scolytus*
bark beetle	*Dendroctonus* spp.
beetle	*Diorhabda elongata*
bighorn sheep	*Ovis canadensis*
black bear	*Ursus americanus*
brook trout	*Salvelinus fontinalis*
brown trout	*Salmo trutta*
cactus mouse	*Peromyscus eremicus*
California gnatcatcher	*Polioptila californica*
California red-legged frog	*Rana aurora draytonii*
chipmunk	*Tamius* spp.
Clark's nutcracker	*Nucifraga columbiana*
coast horned lizard	*Phrynosoma coronatum*
coho salmon	*Oncorhynchus kisutch*
deer mouse	*Peromyscus maniculatus*
desert tortoise	*Gopherus agassizii*
Douglas' squirrel	*Tamiasciurus douglasii*
Douglas-fir tussock moth	*Orgyia psedotsugata*
dusky-footed wood rat	*Neotoma fuscipes*
European earwig	*Forficula auricularia*
fairy shrimp	*Branchinecta* ssp.
filbert weevil	*Curculio pardus*
filbertworm	*Melissopus latferreanus*
gelechiid moth	*Gelechia* spp.
Gila trout	*Oncorhynchus gilae*
beaver	*Castor canadensis*
golden eagles	*Aquila chrysaetus*
grizzly bear	*Ursus arctos*

ground squirrel	*Spermophilus* and *Ammospermophilus* spp.
jackrabbit	*Lepus* spp.
kangaroo rats	*Dipodomys* spp.
long horn beetle	*Phymatodes nitidus*
long horn beetle	*Cerambycidae*
flat-headed boring beetle	*Buprestidae*
Modoc budworm	*Choristoneura viridis*
mountain lion	*Felis concolor*
mule deer	*Odocoileus hemionus*
native ant genera	*Pogonomyrmex* and *Messor* spp.
northern flying squirrel	*Glaucomys sabrinus*
northern goshawk	*Accipiter gentilis*
northern sage grouse	*Centrocercus urophasianus*
northern spotted owl	*Strix occidentalis caurina*
Pacific fisher	*Martes pennanti pacifica*
Pacific kangaroo rat	*Dipodomys agilis*
Paiute ground squirrel	*Spermophilus mollis*
peregrine falcon	*Falco peregrinus*
pillbug	*Armadillidium vulgare*
porcupine	*Erethizon dorsatum*
prairie falcon	*Falco mexicanus*
pronghorn	*Antilocapra americana*
rainbow trout	*Oncorhynchus mykiss*
riparian brush rabbit	*Sylvilagus bachmani riparius*
sage grouse	*Centrocercus urophasianus*
sowbug	*Porcellio* spp.
spotted owl	*Strix occidentalis*
Stephens' kangaroo rat	*Dipodomys stephensi*
Townsend's chipmunk	*Tamias townsendii*
tree frog	*Hyla* spp.
tree squirrels	*Sciurus and Tamiasciurus*
voles, rodents	*Microtus* spp.
water mold (fungus)	*Phytophthora ramorum*
weevils	*Curculio*
western gray squirrel	*Sciurus griseus*
western screech owl	*Megascops kennicottii*
western scrub-jay	*Aphelocoma coerlescens*
western toad	*Bufo boreas*
white-headed woodpecker	*Picoides albolarvatus*
woodpecker	*Sphyrapicus, Melanerpes, Picoides, Dryocopus*
woodrat	*Neotoma* spp.

Latin name	Common name
Accipiter gentilis	northern goshawk
Antilocapra americana	pronghorn
Aphelocoma coerlescens	western scrub-jay
Aquila chrysaetus	golden eagles
Armodillidium vulgare	pillbug
Branchinecta ssp.	fairy shrimp
Buprestidae	metallic wood-boring beetle
Castor canadensis	beaver
Centrocercus urophasianus	sage grouse
Cerambycidae	long-horned beetle
Choristoneura viridis	Modoc bugworm
Corvus brachyrhynchos	American crow
Curculio	weevils
Curculio pardus	filbert weevil

Dendroctonus spp.	bark beetle
Diorhabda elongata	beetle
Dipodomys agilis	Pacific kangaroo rat
Dipodomys spp.	kangaroo rats
Dipodomys stephensi	Stephens' kangaroo rat
Erethizon dorsatum	porcupine
Falco mexicanus	prairie falcon
Falco peregrinus	peregrine falcon
Felis concolor	mountain lion
Forficula auricularia	European earwig
Ghelechia spp.	gelechiid moth
Glaucomys sabrinus	northern flying squirrel
Gopherus agassizii	desert tortoise
Hyla spp.	tree frog
Lepus spp.	jackrabbit
Linepithema humile	Argentine ant
Martes americana	American marten
Martes pennanti pacifica	Pacific fisher
Masticophis lateralis euryxanthus	Alameda whipsnake
Megascops kennicottii	western screech owl
Melissopus latferreanus	filbertworm
Messor spp.	native art genera
Microtus spp.	voles, rodents
Neotoma fuscipes	dusky footed wood rat
Neotoma spp.	woodrat
Nucifraga columbiana	Clark's nutcracker
Odocoileus hemionus	mule deer
Oncorhynchus gilae	Gila trout
Oncorhynchus kisutch	coho salmon
Oncorhynchus mykiss	rainbow trout
Orgyia psedotsugata	Douglas-fir tussock moth
Ovis canadensis	bighorn sheep
Peromyscus eremicus	cactus mouse
Peromyscus maniculatus	deer mouse
Phrynosoma coronatum	coast horned lizard
Phymatodes nitidus	long-horned beetle
Phytophthora ramorum	water mold (fungus)
Picoides albolarvatus	white-headed woodpecker
Pogonomyrmex spp.	native art genera
Polioptila californica	California gnatcatcher
Porcellio spp.	sowbugs
Rana aurora draytonii	California red-legged frog
Salmo trutta	brown trout
Salvelinus fontinalis	brook trout
Sciurus and Tamiasciurus	tree squirrels
Sciurus griseus	western gray squirrel
Scolytidae	bark and ambrosia beetle
Spermophilus mollis	Paiute ground squirrel
Spermophilus and Ammospermophilus spp.	ground squirrel
Sphyrapicus, Melanerpes, Picoides, and Dryocopus	woodpeckers
Strix occidentalis caurina	northern spotted owl
Strix occidentalis occidentalis	spotted owl
Sylvilagus bachmani riparius	riparian brush rabbit
Tamias townsendii	Townsend's chipmunk
Tamiasciurus douglasi	Douglas squirrel
Tamius spp.	chipmunk
Ursus americanus	black bear
Ursus arctos	grizzly bear

Bioregions, Ecological Zones, and Plant Alliances of California That Occur in This Text

BIOREGION Ecological Zone	Plant Alliance[1] Scientific Nomenclature	Common Nomenclature
NORTH COAST		
North Coastal Scrub and Prairie	*Baccharis pilularis*	Coyote Brush Scrub and Dwarf Scrub
	Danthonia californica	California Oatgrass Bunchgrass Grassland
	Deschampsia caespitosa	Tufted Hairgrass
	Festuca idahoensis	Idaho Fescue
	Festuca rubra	Red Fescue
	Gaultheria shallon-Vaccinium ovatum	Salal–Black Huckleberry Scrub and Dwarf Scrub
	Lupinus arboreus	Yellow Bush Lupine Scrub
	Salix hookeriana	Hooker Willow Riparian Forests
Sitka Spruce Forest	*Abies grandis*	Grand Fir Forest
	Alnus rubra	Red Alder
	Chamaecyparis lawsoniana	Port Orford Cedar Forest
	Gaultheria shallon-Vaccinium ovatum	Salal–Black Huckleberry Scrub and Dwarf Scrub
	Picea sitchensis	Sitka Spruce Forest
	Pseudotsuga menziesii	Douglas-fir Forest
	Tsuga heterophylla	Western Hemlock Forest
Redwood Forest	*Ceanothus thyrsiflorus*	Blue Blossom Chaparral
	Gaultheria shallon-Vaccinium ovatum	Salal–Black Huckleberry Scrub and Dwarf Scrub
	Sequoia sempervirens	Redwood Forest
	Umbellularia californica	California Bay Forest and Woodland
Douglas-fir and Tan-Oak Forest	*Pseudotsuga menziesii*	Douglas-fir Forest
	Pseudotsuga menziesii-Lithocarpus densiflora	Douglas-fir–Tanoak Forest
	Lithocarpus densiflora	Tanoak Forest and Woodland
	Pseudotsuga menziesii-Pinus ponderosa	Douglas-fir–Ponderosa Pine Forest
	Quercus chrysolepis	Canyon Live Oak Forest and Woodland
	Umbellularia californica	California Bay Forest and Woodland
Oregon Oak Woodland	*Danthonia californica*	California Oatgrass Bunchgrass Grassland
	Festuca idahoensis	Idaho Fescue
	Pseudotsuga menziesii	Douglas-fir Forest
	Pseudotsuga menziesii-Lithocarpus densiflora	Douglas-fir–Tanoak Forest
	Quercus garryana var. *garryana*	Oregon White Oak Woodland
	Quercus kelloggii	Black Oak Forests and Woodland
	Umbellularia californica	California Bay Forest and Woodland
North Coast Pine Forest	*Cupressus goveniana* ssp. *goveniana*	Pygmy Cypress Dwarf Woodland
	Pinus contorta ssp. *contorta*	Beach Pine Forest
	Pinus muricata	Bishop Pine Forests

[1]Plant alliances based on Manual for California Vegetation, Second Edition (in draft).

BIOREGION Ecological Zone	Plant Alliance Scientific Nomenclature	Common Nomenclature
KLAMATH MOUNTAINS		
Lower Montane	*Adenostoma fasciculatum*	Chamise Chaparral
	Aesculus californica	California Buckeye Woodland
	Arctostaphylos patula	Greenleaf Manzanita Chaparral
	Arctostaphylos viscida	Whiteleaf Manzanita Chaparral
	Ceanothus integerrimus	Deerbrush Montane Chaparral
	Cercocarpus betuloides var. *betuloides*	Birchleaf Mountain-mahogany Woodland
	Pinus jeffreyi	Jeffrey Pine Forest and Woodland
	Pinus ponderosa	Ponderosa Pine Forest and Woodland
	Pinus sabiniana	Foothill Pine Woodland
	Pseudotsuga menziesii	Douglas-fir Forest
	Pseudotsuga menziesii-Lithocarpus densiflora	Douglas-fir–Tanoak Forest
	Pseudotsuga menziesii-Pinus ponderosa	Douglas-fir–Ponderosa Pine Forest
	Pseudotsuga menziesii-Quercus chrysolepis	Douglas-fir–Canyon Live Oak Forest
	Quercus chrysolepis	Canyon Live Oak Forest and Woodland
	Quercus chrysolepis	Canyon Live Oak Chaparral
	Quercus garryana var. *breweri*	Brewer Oak Chaparral
	Quercus kelloggii	Black Oak Forests and Woodland
	Toxicodendron diversilobum	Poison Oak Scrub
	Umbellularia californica	California Bay Forest and Woodland
Mid to Upper Montane	*Abies concolor*	White Fir Forest
	Abies magnifica	Red Fir Forest
	Arbutus menziesii	Pacific Madrone
	Betula occidentalis	Water Birch Scrub
	Ceanothus velutinus	Tobacco Brush Montane Chaparral
	Cercocarpus ledifolius	Curlleaf Mountain-mahogany Woodland and Scrub
	Chamaecyparis lawsoniana	Port Orford-Cedar Forest
	Chrysolepis chrysophylla	Giant Chinquapin Scrub
	Chrysolepis sempervirens	Bush Chinquapin Montane Chaparral
	Quercus chrysolepis	Canyon Live Oak Forest and Woodland
	Quercus chrysolepis	Canyon Live Oak Chaparral
	Quercus kelloggii	Black Oak Forests and Woodland
	Juniperus occidentalis ssp. *occidentalis*	Western Juniper Woodland
	Lithocarpus densiflora	Tanoak Forest and Woodland
	Picea breweriana	Brewer Spruce Forest
	Pinus attenuata	Knobcone Pine Forest and Woodland
	Pinus jeffreyi-Abies concolor	Jeffrey Pine–White Fir Forest
	Pinus monticola	Western White Pine Woodland
	Pinus ponderosa	Ponderosa Pine Forest and Woodland
	Pseudotsuga menziesii–Calocedrus decurrens	Douglas-fir–Incense-cedar Forest
	Quercus douglasii	Blue Oak Woodland
	Quercus garryana var. *garryana*	Oregon White Oak Woodland
	Quercus vaccinifolia	Huckleberry Oak Chaparral
	Tsuga mertensiana	Mountain Hemlock Forest
Subalpine	*Abies magnifica*	Red Fir Forest
	Cercocarpus ledifolius	Curlleaf Mountain-mahogany Woodland and Scrub
	Pinus albicaulis	Whitebark Pine Woodland
	Pinus balfouriana	Foxtail Pine Woodland
	Pinus jeffreyi	Jeffrey Pine Forest and Woodland
	Pinus monticola	Western White Pine Woodland
	Tsuga mertensiana	Mountain Hemlock Forest

(continued)

BIOREGION Ecological Zone	Plant Alliance Scientific Nomenclature	Common Nomenclature
SOUTHERN CASCADES		
Southwestern Foothills	*Aesculus californica*	California Buckeye Woodland
	Arctostaphylos manzanita	Common Manzanita
	Arctostaphylos viscida	Whiteleaf Manzanita Chaparral
	Ceanothus cuneatus	Wedgeleaf Ceanothus Chaparral
	Cercocarpus betuloides var. *betuloides*	Birchleaf Mountain-mahogany Woodland
	Juniperus californica	California Juniper Woodland and Scrub
	Pinus ponderosa	Ponderosa Pine Forest and Woodland
	Pinus ponderosa-Calocedrus decurrens	Ponderosa Pine–Incense-cedar Forest
	Pinus sabiniana	Foothill Pine Woodland
	Quercus douglasii	Blue Oak Woodland
	Quercus kelloggii	Black Oak Forests and Woodland
	Quercus lobata	Valley Oak Forests and Woodlands
	Quercus wislizeni	Interior Live Oak Woodland
	Quercus wislizeni	Interior Live Oak Chaparral
	Quercus wislizeni-Quercus chrysolepis	Interior Live Oak–Canyon Live Oak Chaparral
	Umbellularia californica	California Bay Forest and Woodland
Northwestern Foothills	*Arctostaphylos patula*	Greenleaf Manzanita Chaparral
	Artemisia tridentata	Big Sagebrush Scrub
	Bromus tectorum	Cheatgrass
	Carex spp.	Sedge
	Ceanothus velutinus	Tobacco Brush Montane Chaparral
	Cercocarpus ledifolius	Curlleaf Mountain-mahogany Woodland and Scrub
	Chrysothamnus nauseosus	Rubber Rabbitbrush Scrub
	Chrysothamnus parryi	Parry Rabbitbrush Dwarf Scrub
	Juniperus occidentalis ssp. *occidentalis*	Western Juniper Woodland
	Quercus chrysolepis	Canyon Live Oak Forest and Woodland
	Quercus kelloggii	Black Oak Forests and Woodland
Low Elevation Eastside	*Arctostaphylos patula*	Greenleaf Manzanita Chaparral
	Bromus tectorum	Cheatgrass
	Cercocarpus ledifolius	Curlleaf Mountain-mahogany Woodland and Scrub
	Chrysothamnus nauseosus	Rubber Rabbitbrush Scrub
	Juniperus occidentalis ssp. *occidentalis*	Western Juniper Woodland
	Pinus attenuata	Knobcone Pine Forest and Woodland
	Pinus ponderosa	Ponderosa Pine Forest and Woodland
	Pinus ponderosa-Calocedrus decurrens	Ponderosa Pine–Incense-cedar Forest
	Pinus sabiniana	Foothill Pine Woodland
	Pseudotsuga menziesii–Calocedrus decurrens	Douglas-fir–Incense-cedar Forest
	Pseudotsuga menziesii-Pinus ponderosa	Douglas-fir–Ponderosa Pine Forest
	Purshia tridentata	Antelope Bitterbrush Scrub
	Quercus garryana var. *garryana*	Oregon White Oak Woodland
	Quercus kelloggii	Black Oak Forests and Woodland
Mid-Montane Westside/Eastside	*Abies concolor*	White Fir Forest
	Abies concolor-Pinus lambertiana	White Fir–Sugar Pine Forest
	Abies magnifica var. *magnifica-Abies concolor*	Red Fir–White Fir Forest
	Arctostaphylos patula	Greenleaf Manzanita Chaparral
	Artemisia tridentata	Big Sagebrush Scrub
	Bromus tectorum	Cheatgrass
	Carex spp.	Sedge
	Ceanothus integerrimus	Deerbrush Montane Chaparral

BIOREGION Ecological Zone	Plant Alliance Scientific Nomenclature	Common Nomenclature
Mid-Montane Westside/Eastside	*Ceanothus velutinus*	Tobacco Brush Montane Chaparral
	Cercocarpus ledifolius	Curlleaf Mountain-mahogany Woodland and Scrub
	Chrysolepis sempervirens	Bush Chinquapin Montane Chaparral
	Chrysothamnus nauseosus	Rubber Rabbitbrush Scrub
	Juniperus occidentalis ssp. *occidentalis*	Western Juniper Woodland
	Pinus attenuata	Knobcone Pine Forest and Woodland
	Pinus contorta ssp. *Murrayana*	Lodgepole Pine Forest and Woodland
	Pinus jeffreyi	Jeffrey Pine Forest and Woodland
	Pinus jeffreyi-Abies concolor	Jeffrey Pine–White Fir Forest
	Pinus jeffreyi-Pinus ponderosa	Jeffrey Pine–Ponderosa Pine Forest and Woodland
	Pinus lambertiana	Sugar Pine Forest and Woodland
	Pinus ponderosa	Ponderosa Pine Forest and Woodland
	Pinus ponderosa-Calocedrus decurrens	Ponderosa Pine–Incense-dedar Forest
	Populus tremuloides	Aspen Upland and Riparian Forests and Woodlands
	Pseudotsuga menziesii–Calocedrus decurrens	Douglas-fir–Incense-cedar Forest
	Pseudotsuga menziesii-Pinus ponderosa	Douglas-fir–Ponderosa Pine Forest
	Purshia tridentata	Antelope Bitterbrush Scrub
	Quercus chrysolepis	Canyon Live Oak Forest and Woodland
Upper Montane	*Abies concolor*	White Fir Forest
	Abies magnifica	Red Fir Forest
	Abies magnifica var. *magnifica-Abies concolor*	Red Fir–White Fir Forest
	Arctostaphylos patula	Greenleaf Manzanita Chaparral
	Artemisia tridentata	Big Sagebrush Scrub
	Carex spp.	Sedge
	Ceanothus cordulatus	Mountain Whitethorn Montane Chaparral
	Ceanothus velutinus	Tobacco Brush Montane Chaparral
	Chrysothamnus nauseosus	Rubber Rabbitbrush Scrub
	Chrysothamnus parryi	Parry Rabbitbrush Dwarf Scrub
	Chrysolepis sempervirens	Bush Chinquapin Montane Chaparral
	Pinus contorta ssp. *murrayana*	Lodgepole Pine Forest and Woodland
	Pinus jeffreyi	Jeffrey Pine Forest and Woodland
	Pinus jeffreyi-Abies concolor	Jeffrey Pine–White Fir Forest
	Pinus jeffreyi-Pinus ponderosa	Jeffrey Pine–Ponderosa Pine Forest and Woodland
	Pinus monticola	Western White Pine Woodland
	Pinus ponderosa	Ponderosa Pine Forest and Woodland
	Quercus kelloggii	Black Oak Forests and Woodland
	Quercus vaccinifolia	Huckleberry Oak Chaparral
Subalpine	*Abies magnifica*	Red Fir Forest
	Pinus albicaulis	Whitebark Pine Woodland
	Tsuga mertensiana	Mountain Hemlock Forest

NORTHEASTERN PLATEAUS

Sagebrush Steppe	*Artemisia cana*	Silver Sagebrush Scrub
	Atriplex confertifolia	Shadscale Scrub
	Atriplex spp.	Mixed Saltbush
	Bromus tectorum	Cheatgrass
	Cercocarpus ledifolius	Curlleaf Mountain-mahogany Woodland and Scrub
	Chrysothamnus nauseosus	Rubber Rabbitbrush Scrub
	Chrysothamnus teretifolius	Needle-leaved Rabbitbrush
	Elymus elymoides	Squirreltail
	Festuca idahoensis	Idaho Fescue

(continued)

BIOREGION Ecological Zone	Plant Alliance Scientific Nomenclature	Common Nomenclature
	Grayia spinosa	Hop-sage Scrub
	Juniperus occidentalis ssp. *occidentalis*	Western Juniper Woodland
	Krascheninnikovia lanata	Winter Fat Dwarf Scrub
	Phlox covillei-Elymus elymoides	Coville Phlox–Squirreltail
	Pseudoroegneria spicata spp. *spicata*	Bluebunch Wheatgrass Bunchgrass Grassland
	Purshia tridentata	Antelope Bitterbrush Scrub
	Sarcobatus vermiculatus	Greasewood Scrub
Lower Montane	*Arctostaphylos patula*	Greenleaf Manzanita Chaparral
	Artemisia nova	Black Sagebrush Dwarf Scrub
	Artemisia tridentata	Big Sagebrush Scrub
	Carex spp.	Sedge
	Cercocarpus ledifolius	Curlleaf Mountain-mahogany Woodland and Scrub
	Festuca idahoensis	Idaho Fescue
	Juniperus occidentalis ssp. *occidentalis*	Western Juniper Woodland
	Pinus attenuata	Knobcone Pine Forest and Woodland
	Pinus jeffreyi	Jeffrey Pine Forest and Woodland
	Pinus jeffreyi-Pinus ponderosa	Jeffrey Pine–Ponderosa Pine Forest and Woodland
	Pinus ponderosa	Ponderosa Pine Forest and Woodland
	Pinus ponderosa-Calocedrus decurrens	Ponderosa Pine–Incense-cedar Forest
	Populus tremuloides	Aspen Upland and Riparian Forests and Woodlands
	Purshia tridentata	Antelope Bitterbrush Scrub
	Quercus kelloggii	Black Oak Forests and Woodland
Mid-Montane	*Abies concolor*	White Fir Forest
	Arctostaphylos patula	Greenleaf Manzanita Chaparral
	Artemisia tridentata	Big Sagebrush Scrub
	Ceanothus velutinus	Tobacco Brush Montane Chaparral
	Cercocarpus ledifolius	Curlleaf Mountain-mahogany Woodland and Scrub
	Juniperus occidentalis ssp. *occidentalis*	Western Juniper Woodland
	Purshia tridentata	Antelope Bitterbrush Scrub
	Pinus jeffreyi	Jeffrey Pine Forest and Woodland
	Pinus jeffreyi-Abies concolor	Jeffrey Pine–White Fir Forest
	Pinus jeffreyi-Pinus ponderosa	Jeffrey Pine–Ponderosa Pine Forest and Woodland
	Pinus ponderosa	Ponderosa Pine Forest and Woodland
	Populus tremuloides	Aspen Upland and Riparian Forests and Woodlands
	Quercus kelloggii	Black Oak Forests and Woodland
Upper Montane	*Abies concolor*	White Fir Forest
	Artemisia tridentata	Big Sagebrush Scrub
	Ceanothus velutinus	Tobacco Brush Montane Chaparral
	Cercocarpus ledifolius	Curlleaf Mountain-mahogany Woodland and Scrub
	Juniperus occidentalis ssp. *occidentalis*	Western Juniper Woodland
	Pinus albicaulis	Whitebark Pine Woodland
	Pinus contorta ssp. *murrayana*	Lodgepole Pine Forest and Woodland
	Pinus jeffreyi	Jeffrey Pine Forest and Woodland
	Pinus jeffreyi-Pinus ponderosa	Jeffrey Pine–Ponderosa Pine Forest and Woodland
	Pinus jeffreyi-Abies concolor	Jeffrey Pine–White Fir Forest
	Pinus monticola	Western White Pine Woodland
	Pinus washoensis	Washoe Pine Woodland
	Populus tremuloides	Aspen Upland and Riparian Forests and Woodlands

BIOREGION Ecological Zone	Plant Alliance Scientific Nomenclature	Common Nomenclature
Subalpine	*Abies concolor*	White Fir Forest
	Pinus albicaulis	Whitebark Pine Woodland
	Pinus contorta ssp. *murrayana*	Lodgepole Pine Forest and Woodland
	Pinus monticola	Western White Pine Woodland
Non Zonal	*Populus balsamifera*	Black Cottonwood Riparian Forests and Woodlands

SIERRA NEVADA

Foothill Shrub and Woodlands	*Adenostoma fasciculatum*	Chamise Chaparral
	Adenostoma fasciculatum-Ceanothus cuneatus	Chamise–Wedgeleaf Ceanothus Chaparral
	Aesculus californica	California Buckeye Woodland
	Alnus incana	Mountain Alder Scrub
	Arctostaphylos viscida	Whiteleaf Manzanita Chaparral
	Baccharis pilularis	Coyote Brush Scrub and Dwarf Scrub
	Ceanothus cuneatus	Wedgeleaf Ceanothus Chaparral
	Ceanothus leucodermis	Chaparral Whitethorn Chaparral
	Cercocarpus betuloides	Birchleaf Mountain-mahogany Scrub
	Pinus attenuata	Knobcone Pine Forest and Woodland
	Pinus sabiniana	Foothill Pine Woodland
	Quercus chrysolepis	Canyon Live Oak Forest and Woodland
	Quercus douglasii	Blue Oak Woodland
	Quercus durata	Leather Oak Chaparral
	Quercus wislizeni	Interior Live Oak Chaparral
	Quercus wislizeni	Interior Live Oak Woodland
	Quercus wislizeni-Ceanothus leucodermis	Interior Live Oak–Chaparral Whitethorn Chaparral
	Umbellularia californica	California Bay Forest and Woodland
Lower Montane	*Abies concolor*	White Fir Forest
	Abies concolor-Pinus lambertiana	White Fir–Sugar Pine Forest
	Arctostaphylos patula	Greenleaf Manzanita Chaparral
	Calocedrus decurrens	Incense-cedar Forest
	Ceanothus integerrimus	Deerbrush Montane Chaparral
	Lithocarpus densiflora	Tanoak Forest and Woodland
	Pinus lambertiana	Sugar Pine Forest and Woodland
	Pinus ponderosa	Ponderosa Pine Forest and Woodland
	Pinus ponderosa-Calocedrus decurrens	Ponderosa Pine–Incense-cedar Forest
	Populus balsamifera	Black Cottonwood Riparian Forest and Woodland
	Pseudotsuga menziesii	Douglas-fir Forest
	Pseudotsuga menziesii–Calocedrus decurrens	Douglas-fir–Incense-cedar Forest
	Pseudotsuga menziesii-Pinus ponderosa	Douglas-fir–Ponderosa Pine Forest
	Quercus kelloggii	Black Oak Forests and Woodland
	Sequoiadendron giganteum	Giant Sequoia Forest
Upper Montane Forest	*Abies magnifica*	Red Fir Forest
	Abies magnifica var. *magnifica-Abies concolor*	Red Fir–White Fir Forest
	Ceanothus cordulatus	Mountain Whitethorn Montane Chaparral
	Deschampsia caespitosa	Tufted Hairgrass
	Juniperus occidentalis ssp. *australis*	Mountain Juniper Woodland
	Pinus jeffreyi	Jeffrey Pine Forest and Woodland
	Pinus jeffreyi-Abies concolor	Jeffrey Pine–White Fir Forest
	Pinus jeffreyi-Pinus ponderosa	Jeffrey Pine–Ponderosa Pine Forest and Woodland
	Pinus monticola	Western White Pine Woodland
	Populus tremuloides	Aspen Upland and Riparian Forest and Woodland
	Quercus vaccinifolia	Huckleberry Oak Chaparral

(continued)

BIOREGION Ecological Zone	Plant Alliance Scientific Nomenclature	Common Nomenclature
Subalpine Forest	*Calamagrostis breweri*	Shorthair Reedgrass
	Carex filifolia	Shorthair Sedge
	Carex nebrascensis	Nebraska Sedge
	Pinus albicaulis	Whitebark Pine Woodland
	Pinus balfouriana	Foxtail Pine Woodland
	Pinus contorta ssp. *murrayana*	Lodgepole Pine Forest and Woodland
	Pinus flexilis	Limber Pine Forest and Woodland
	Tsuga mertensiana	Mountain Hemlock Forest
Alpine Meadows and Shrublands	*Salix eastwoodiae*	Sierra Willow Riparian Scrub
	none	Alpine Fell-field
Eastside Forest and Woodland	*Abies concolor*	White Fir Forest
	Abies magnifica	Red Fir Forest
	Arctostaphylos patula	Greenleaf Manzanita Chaparral
	Artemisia tridentata	Big Sagebrush Scrub
	Ceanothus cordulatus	Mountain Whitethorn Montane Chaparral
	Ceanothus velutinus	Tobacco Brush Montane Chaparral
	Cercocarpus ledifolius	Curlleaf Mountain-mahogany Woodland and Scrub
	Pinus contorta ssp. *murrayana*	Lodgepole Pine Forest and Woodland
	Pinus jeffreyi	Jeffrey Pine Forest and Woodland
	Pinus jeffreyi-Pinus ponderosa	Jeffrey Pine–Ponderosa Pine Forest and Woodland
	Pinus monophylla	Singleleaf Pinyon Woodland
	Pinus ponderosa	Ponderosa Pine Forest and Woodland
	Pinus washoensis	Washoe Pine Woodland
	Populus balsamifera	Black Cottonwood Riparian Forests and Woodlands
	Populus tremuloides	Aspen Upland and Riparian Forest and Woodland
	Pseudotsuga menziesii-Pinus ponderosa	Douglas-fir–Ponderosa Pine Forest

CENTRAL VALLEY

Foothill Woodland	*Elymus elymoides*	Squirreltail
	Elymus glaucus	Blue Wildrye
	Nassella pulchra	Purple Needlegrass
	Pinus sabiniana	Foothill Pine Woodland
	Quercus douglasii	Blue Oak Woodland
	Quercus garryana var. *garryana*	Oregon White Oak Woodland
	Quercus lobata	Valley Oak Forest and Woodland
	Quercus wislizeni	Interior Live Oak Chaparral
Valley Grassland	*Achnatherum* spp.	Valley Needlegrass Grassland
	Bromus diandrus–Bromus hordeaceus	Annual Brome
	Distichlis spicata	Saltgrass
	Elymus elymoides	Squirreltail
	Elymus glaucus	Blue Wildrye Grassland
	Nassella pulchra	Purple Needlegrass
	Populus fremontii	Fremont Cottonwood Riparian Forests and Woodlands
	Sporobolus airoides	Alkali Sacaton Bunchgrass Grassland
	Trifoloium–Lotus–Lessengia-Holocarpha	California Annual Herbland
Riparian Forest	*Platanus racemosa*	California Sycamore
	Populus fremontii	Fremont Cottonwood Riparian Forests and Woodlands
	Quercus lobata	Valley Oak Forests and Woodlands
	Salix gooddingii	Black Willow Riparian Forests and Woodlands

BIOREGION Ecological Zone	Plant Alliance Scientific Nomenclature	Common Nomenclature
Freshwater Marsh	*Typha* spp.	Cattail Wetland
	Scirpus spp.-*Typha* spp.	Bulrush–Cattail Wetland
	Scirpus spp.	Bulrush
	Salix gooddingii	Goodding's Black Willow
	Salix laevigata	Red Willow Riparian Forests
	Salix spp.	Mixed Willow Riparian Forests and Woodlands
	Baccharis salicifolia	Mulefat Scrub

CENTRAL COAST

BIOREGION Ecological Zone	Plant Alliance Scientific Nomenclature	Common Nomenclature
Coastal Prairie and Coastal Sage Scrub	*Artemisia californica*	California Sagebrush Scrub
	Artemisia californica-Eriogonum fasciculatum	California Sagebrush–California Buckwheat Scrub
	Artemisia californica–Salvia mellifera	California Sagebrush–Black Sage Scrub
	Baccharis pilularis	Coyote Brush Scrub and Dwarf Scrub
	Danthonia californica	California Oatgrass Bunchgrass Grassland
	Deschampsia caespitosa	Tufted Hairgrass
	Nassella pulchra	Purple Needlegrass
	Quercus agrifolia	Coast Live Oak Forest and Woodland
Coast Redwood~ Douglar-fir and Mixed Evergreen Forest	*Arbutus menziesii*	Pacific Madrone
	Lithocarpus densiflora	Tanoak Forest and Woodland
	Pseudotsuga menziesii	Douglas-fir Forest
	Pseudotsuga mensiesii-Lithocarpus densiflora	Douglas-fir–Tanoak forest
	Quercus agrifolia	Coast Live Oak Forest and Woodland
	Sequoia sempervirens	Redwood Forest
	Umbellularia californica	California Bay Forest and Woodland
Chaparral and Oak Woodland	*Adenostoma fasciculatum*	Chamise Chaparral
	Quercus agrifolia	Coast Live Oak Forest and Woodland
	Quercus lobata	Valley Oak Forests and Woodlands
Coastal Plain and Foothills	*Adenostoma fasciculatum*	Chamise Chaparral
	Adenostoma fasciculatum– Arctostaphylos glandulosa	Chamise–Eastwood Manzanita Chaparral
	Adenostoma fasciculatum– Arctostaphylos glauca	Chamise–Bigberry Manzanita Chaparral
	Adenostoma fasciculatum-Ceanothus greggii	Chamise–Cupleaf Ceanothus Chaparral
	Artemisia californica	California Sagebrush Scrub
	Baccharis pilularis	Coyote Brush Scrub and Dwarf Scrub
	Pinus attenuata	Knobcone Pine Forest and Woodland
	Pinus muricata	Bishop Pine Forests
	Pinus radiata	Monterey Pine Forest
	Quercus agrifolia	Coast Live Oak Forest and Woodland
Lower Montane	*Adenostoma fasciculatum*	Chamise Chaparral
	Adenostoma fasciculatum-Ceanothus cuneatus	Chamise–Wedgeleaf Ceanothus Chaparral
	Adenostoma fasciculatum-Salvia mellifera	Chamise–Black Sage Chaparral
	Artemisia californica	California Sagebrush Scrub
	Artemisia californica-Eriogonum fasciculatum	California Sagebrush–California Buckwheat Scrub
	Artemisia californica–Salvia mellifera	California Sagebrush–Black Sage Scrub
	Cupressus sargentii	Sargent Cypress Woodland
	Eriogonum fasciculatum	California Buckwheat Scrub
	Quercus agrifolia	Coast Live Oak Forest and Woodland
	Quercus berberidifolia	Scrub Oak Chaparral
	Salvia mellifera	Black Sage Scrub
	Salvia leucophylla	Purple Sage Scrub

(continued)

BIOREGION Ecological Zone	Plant Alliance Scientific Nomenclature	Common Nomenclature
Upper Montane	*Abies bracteata*	Santa Lucia Fir Woodland
	Arbutus menziesii	Pacific Madrone
	Lithocarpus densiflora	Tanoak Forest and Woodland
	Pinus ponderosa	Ponderosa Pine Forest and Woodland
	Pinus coulteri	Coulter Pine Woodland
	Pinus coulteri/Arctostaphylos glandulosa	Coulter Pine/Eastwood Manzanita Woodland
	Pinus coulteri-Quercus chrysolepis	Coulter Pine–Canyon Live Oak Woodland
	Quercus chrysolepis	Canyon Live Oak Forest and Woodland
	Umbellularia californica	California Bay Forest and Woodland
Interior Foothill	*Adenostoma fasciculatum*	Chamise Chaparral
	Artemisia californica-Eriogonum fasciculatum	California Sagebrush–California Buckwheat Scrub
	Quercus douglasii	Blue Oak Woodland
	Quercus lobata	Valley Oak Forests and Woodlands

SOUTH COAST

Ecological Zone	Scientific Nomenclature	Common Nomenclature
Coastal Valley and Foothill–Grassland	*Bromus* spp.	Annual Brome
	Nassella cernua	Nodding Needlegrass
	Nassella lepida	Foothill Needlegrass
	Nassella pulchra	Purple Needlegrass
Coastal Valley and Foothill–Coastal Sage Scrub	*Artemisia californica*	California Sagebrush Scrub
	Artemisia californica-Eriogonum fasciculatum	California Sagebrush–California Buckwheat Scrub
	Baccharis salicifolia	Mulefat Scrub
	Encelia farinosa	Brittlebush Drought Deciduous Scrub
	Eriogonum fasciculatum	California Buckwheat Scrub
	Eriogonium fasciculatum-Salvia apiana	California Buckwheat–White Sage Scrub
	Rhamnus californica	Coffeeberry Scrub
	Rhus sp., *Malosma laurinab*	Sumac Scrub
	Salvia apiana	White Sage Scrub
	Saliva mellifera	Black Sage Scrub
	Salvia leucophyll	Purple Sage Scrub
	Salvia spp.	Mixed Sage Scrub
Coastal Valley and Foothill–Chaparral	*Adenostoma fasciculatum*	Chamise Chaparral
	Adenostoma fasciculatum-Salvia mellifera	California Sagebrush–Black Sage Scrub
	Arctostaphylos glandulosa	Eastwood Manzanita Chaparral
	Arctostaphylos glauca	Bigberry Manzanita Chaparral
	Artemisia californica–Salvia mellifera	Chamise–Black Sage Chaparral
	Ceanothus leucodermis	Chaparral Whitethorn Chaparral
	Ceanothus megacarpus-Rhamnus ilicifolia	Bigpod Ceanothus–Hollyleaf Redberry Chaparral
	Ceanothus spinosus	Greenbark Ceanothus Scrub
	Cercocarpus betuloides	Birch-Leaf Mountain-mahogany Scrub
	Cercocarpus betuloides-Eriogonum fasciculatum	Birchleaf Mountain-mahogany–California Buckwheat Chaparral
	Quercus berberidifolia	Scrub Oak Chaparral
	Quercus berberidifolia-Adenostoma fasciculatum	Scrub Oak–Chamise Chaparral
	Quercus berberidifolia-Ceanothus leucodermis	Scrub Oak–Chaparral Whitethorn Chaparral
	Quercus berberidifolia-Cercocarpus betuloides	Scrub Oak–Birchleaf Mountain-mahogany Chaparral
	Quercus wislizeni	Interior Live Oak Chaparral
	Quercus wislizeni-Quercus berberidifolia	Interior Live Oak–Scrub Oak Chaparral
	Rhamnus californica	Coffeeberry Scrub

BIOREGION Ecological Zone	Plant Alliance Scientific Nomenclature	Common Nomenclature
Coastal Valley and Foothill–Woodlands	*Alnus rhombifolia*	White Alder Forest and Woodland
	Platanus racemosa	California Sycamore
	Populus fremontii	Fremont Cottonwood Riparian Forests and Woodlands
	Quercus wislizeni	Interior Live Oak Woodland
	Quercus lobata	Valley Oak Forests and Woodlands
	Quercus engelmannii	Engelmann Oak Woodland
	Quercus kelloggii	Black Oak Forests and Woodland
	Salix spp.	Mixed Willow Riparian Forests and Woodlands
Montane	*Abies concolor*	White Fir Forest
	Arctostaphylos patula	Greenleaf Manzanita Chaparral
	Ceanothus cordulatus	Mountain Whitethorn Montane Chaparral
	Ceanothus integerrimus	Deerbrush Montane Chaparral
	Chrysolepis sempervirens	Bush Chinquapin Montane Chaparral
	Juglans californica var. *californica*	California Walnut Woodland and Forest
	Pinus attenuata	Knobcone Pine Forest and Woodland
	Pinus contorta spp. *murrayana*	Lodgepole Pine Forest and Woodland
	Pinus couleri	Coulter Pine Woodland
	Pinus jeffeyi	Jeffrey Pine Forest and Woodland
	Pinus ponderosa	Ponderosa Pine Forest and Woodland
	Pinus ponderosa-Calocedrus decurrens	Ponderosa Pine–Incense-cedar Forest
	Pseudotsuga macrocarpa	Bigcone Douglas-fir forest
	Quercus agrifolia	Coast Live Oak Forest and Woodland
	Quercus engelmannii	Englemann Oak Woodland
	Quercus kelloggii	Black Oak Forests and Woodland

SOUTHEASTERN DESERTS

Low Elevation Desert Scrubland	*Acacia greggii*	Catclaw Acacia Thorn Scrub
	Agave deserti	Desert Agave Succulent-leaved Scrub
	Allenrolfea occidentalis	Desert Iodine Bush Scrub
	Atriplex polycarpa	Allscale Scrub
	Atriplex spp.	Mixed Saltbush
	Bromus madritensis ssp. *Rubens*	Red Brome
	Bromus tectorum	Cheatgrass
	Cercidium floridum-Olneya tesota– *Psorothamnus spinosus*	Blue Palo Verde–Ironwood–Smoke Tree Woodland
	Distichlis spicata	Saltgrass
	Hymenoclea salsola	Cheesebush Scrub
	Larrea tridentata	Creosote Bush Scrub
	Opuntia bigelovii	Teddy-bear Cholla Succulent Scrub
	Psorothamnus spinosus	Smoke Tree Woodland and Scrub
Middle Elevation Desert Scrubland and grassland	*Achnatherum hymenoides*	Indian Ricegrass
	Achnatherum speciosum	Desert Needlegrass Grassland
	Atriplex confertifolia	Shadscale Scrub
	Bromus madritensis ssp. *Rubens*	Red Brome
	Bromus tectorum	Cheatgrass
	Coleogyne ramosissima	Blackbush High Desert Scrub
	Ephedra californica	California Ephedra
	Ephedra nevadensis	Nevada Ephedra Scrub

	Isomeris arborea-Ephedra californica-
	   Ericameria linearifolia
		Bladderpod–California Ephedra–Narrowleaf
		   Goldenbush Scrub

	Larrea tridentata	Creosote Bush Scrub

(continued)

BIOREGION Ecological Zone	Plant Alliance Scientific Nomenclature	Common Nomenclature
	Menodora spinescens	Spiny Menodora Scrub
	Pleuraphis jamesii	Little Galleta Grassland
	Pleuraphis rigida	Big Galleta Bunchgrass Grassland
	Yucca brevifolia	Joshua Tree Tall Scrub and Open Woodland
	Yucca schidigera	Mojave Yucca Scrub
High Elevation Desert Scrubland and Woodland	*Arctostaphylos glauca*	Bigberry Manzanita Chaparral
	Arctostaphylos glandulosa	Eastwood Manzanita Chaparral
	Artemisia tridentata	Big Sagebrush Scrub
	Cercocarpus betuloides	Birchleaf Mountain-mahogany Scrub
	Chrysothamnus nauseosus	Rubber Rabbitbrush Scrub
	Juniperus californica	California Juniper Woodland and Scrub
	Juniperus monosperma	Utah Juniper Woodland
	Nolina spp.	Nolina Scrub
	Pinus monophylla	Singleleaf Pinyon Woodland
	Pinus monophylla~Juniperus spp.	Singleleaf Pinyon–Utah Juniper Woodland
	Pinus ponderosa	Ponderosa Pine Forest and Woodland
	Pinus quadrifolia	Parry Pinyon Woodland
	Purshia mexicana	Stanbury's Antelope Brush Scrub
	Purshia tridentata	Antelope Bitterbrush Scrub
	Quercus cornelius-mulleri	Muller Oak
	Quercus turbinella	Shrub Live Oak Scrub
Desert Montane Woodland and Forest	*Pinus longaeva* *none*	Bristlecone Pine Woodland Alpine Fell-field
Desert Riparian Woodland and Oasis	*Arundo donax*	Giant Reed
	Pluchea sericea	Arrow Weed Scrub
	Populus fremontii	Fremont Cottonwood Riparian Forest and Woodland
	Prosopis glandulosa	Honey Mesquite Scrub
	Salix spp.	Mixed Willow Riparian Forests and Woodlands
	Tamarix spp.	Tamarisk Scrubs and Woodlands
	Washingtonia filifera	Fan Palm Woodland

GLOSSARY

ACTIVE CROWN FIRE A crown fire that is dependent on and synchronous with a supporting surface fire.

ADIABATIC HEATING Heating of air parcels due to volumetric changes caused by subsidence without the addition or subtraction of heat.

ANABATIC FLOW Airflow moving up sloping terrain in response to heating of the upper slopes

ANABATIC WINDS Winds caused by the upward movement of heated air.

ANNUAL PLANTS Plant species with life histories with a yearly periodicity, living for one year.

ARBOREAL SPECIES Species living in trees or adapted for life in trees.

ASPECT The direction a slope faces.

AVOIDER A life-history strategy of plants that have little adaptation to fire.

BIENNIAL PLANTS Plants lasting two years, requiring two years to complete their life cycle.

BIOMASS The total mass of the organisms comprising all or part of a population or ecosystem.

BIOREGION A bio-geographical region or formation, a major regional ecological community characterized by distinctive life forms and principal plant and animal species. In this text, nine bioregions are defined for California.

BIOTIC COMMUNITIES All the species that occur together and interact on a particular site. Three major aspects of plant communities include: (1) species composition, (2) community structure, and (3) interactions among plants and between plants and their environment.

BURL A swollen growth including many dormant buds from which primary sprouts may arise. Often occurring at the junction of roots and stems, but sometimes occurring on other stem tissues.

CAMBIUM A thin layer of tissue between the bark and wood of woody plants. A plant's cambium tissues are responsible for stem diameter growth in trees and shrubs.

CANOPY FUELS Fuels located within the overstory tree canopy that feed and sustain crown fires.

CANOPY STORED SEED Seeds that are retained in serotinous or non-serotinous cones within the live tree canopy for multiple years. These seeds serve as a reserve that is released en mass for recolonization following fire.

CAT FACE An open fire scar located at the base of a tree.

CLIMATE The average condition of weather at a place over time.

COMBUSTION One of many types of oxidation processes combining materials that contain hydrocarbons with oxygen to produce carbon dioxide, water, and energy.

COMBUSTION PHASE In wildland fuels, burning occurs in three combustion phases: preheating, gaseous, and smoldering.

PREHEATING Fuel ahead of the flaming front of the fire is heated, water is driven out of the fuel, and gases are partially distilled.

GASEOUS Ignition occurs and gases continue to be distilled as active burning begins. Oxidation is initiated and an active flaming front develops.

SMOLDERING Charcoal and other unburned material remaining after the flaming phase continue to burn leaving a small amount of residual ash. The fuel burns as a solid and oxidation occurs on the surface of the charcoal.

CONDUCTION The transfer of heat from molecule to molecule; the only mechanism that can transfer heat through an opaque solid.

CONVECTION, AIR Small-scale vertical movement of air parcels and heat transport, driven mostly by buoyancy (thermal convection), and to a limited extent by wind shear (mechanical convection).

CONVECTION, THERMAL The transfer of heat through movement of a gas or a liquid.

CROWN FIRE A fire burning in the crowns of forest vegetation; can be passive, active, or independent.

CROWN SPROUTING The re-growth of foliage and branches from dormant buds in scorched crowns.

DORMANCY (1) A state of relative metabolic quiescence, or (2) A state in which viable seeds, spores, or buds fail to germinate under conditions favorable for germination and vegetative growth.

DUFF A product of litter decomposition. Incompletely decomposed organic matter in which the original structure is no longer discernible.

ECOLOGICAL SUCCESSION The gradual and predictable process of progressive community change and replacement; the process of continuous colonization and extinction of species populations at a particular site.

ECOSYSTEM A community of organisms and their physical environment interacting as an ecological unit

ECOTONE The boundary or transition zone between adjacent communities or biomes.

ENDEMIC A population with an endemic distribution is one in which the distribution of the species is limited geographically to a small area.

FIRE-ADAPTED ECOSYSTEMS Ecosystems that incorporate the repeated occurrence of fire as an integral ecological process.

FIRE BEHAVIOR The manner in which a fire reacts to the influences of fuel, weather and topography.

FIRE CYCLE A fire return interval calculated using current age-class structure on the landscape.

FIRE ECOLOGY The study of the interrelationships between living organisms, their environments, and fire.

FIRE EXCLUSION The intentional or unintentional removal of fire as a process from ecosystems.

FIRE FREQUENCY Temporal fire occurrence described as a number of fires occurring within a defined area within a given time period.

FIRE REGIME The long-term fire pattern characteristic of an ecosystem described as a combination of seasonality, fire return interval, size, spatial complexity, intensity, severity, and fire type.

FIRE RESISTANT A characteristic of plant species that allows individuals to resist damage or mortality during fires.

FIRE RETURN INTERVAL The length of time between fires on a particular area of land.

FIRE ROTATION The length of time necessary to burn an area equal to the area or landscape of interest.

FIRE SCAR A healing or healed-over injury on a woody plant that was caused or aggravated by a fire.

FIRE SEVERITY The magnitude of fire effect on organisms, species, and the environment. Commonly applied to a number of ecosystem components including but not restricted to soils, vegetation, trees, animals, and watersheds.

FIRE SIZE A measure of the amount of area inside the perimeter of the fire, including both burned and unburned areas.

FIRE-STIMULATED GERMINATION The requirement of the seeds of some species for heating, smoke, or charrate as cues to stimulate germination.

FIRE TYPE Flaming front patterns that are characteristic of a fire. Ground, surface, passive crown, active crown, and independent crown fires are fire types.

FIRE WEATHER The weather conditions that influence fire behavior. Fire weather is concerned with weather variations within the first 8 km to 16 km (5 mi to 10 mi) above the earth's surface that influence wildland fire behavior. Fire weather includes air temperature, atmospheric moisture, atmospheric stability, and clouds and precipitation.

FIRELINE INTENSITY The rate of energy release per unit length of flaming front. The amount of heat you would be exposed to per second while standing immediately in front of a fire.

FLAME LENGTH The average distance from the base of the flame to its highest point. Flame length is the only measurement that can be taken easily in the field that is related to fireline intensity.

FLAMING FRONT The primary area of active burning on the leading edge of a wildland fire.

FLAMING ZONE DEPTH The flaming zone depth is the distance from the front to the back of the active flaming front and is calculated by multiplying the rate of spread by the residence time.

FOEHN WIND A dry wind associated with wind flow down the lee side of a plateau or mountain range and with adiabatic warming. Santa Ana and Mono winds are examples.

FUEL The source of heat that sustains the combustion process. In wildland fire, fuel is combustible plant biomass including the grass, leaves, ground litter, plants, shrubs, and trees.

FUEL LOAD The amount of fuel that is potentially available for combustion.

FUEL MOISTURE The moisture content expressed as a percentage of the dry weight of the fuel.

GEOPHYTE A perennial plant with regenerating organs with buds, such as corms or rhizomes, buried well below the soil surface. Geophytes are insulated from heating during fire by the soil.

GROUND FIRE A fire that burns in the ground. Typically this is a fire in thick organic soil layers, peat, or very thick duff.

HEAT-STIMULATED GERMINATION Stimulation of the germination of seeds by heat.

HEAT TRANSFER The means by which heat is transferred including conduction, convection, and radiation.

HYDROPHOBICITY A physical property of the soil that limits soil water infiltration rate due to the coating of soil particles with organic compounds. In a hydrophobic soil, water will not readily penetrate and infiltrate into the soil, but will "ball up" and remain on the surface.

IGNITION POINT The location of the ignition.

IGNITION SOURCE The origin or source of the fire. Types of ignition sources include lightning, volcanoes, and humans.

IMMATURITY RISK When the fire return intervals are shorter than the time required for individual plants to grow to a fire-resistant reproductive state.

INDEPENDENT CROWN FIRE A crown fire that burns independently of a surface fire. The crown fire advances over a given area ahead of the occurrence of the surface fire.

INFILTRATION The process by which water seeps into a soil, influenced by soil texture, soil structure, and vegetative cover.

INTERCEPTION That part of the total precipitation retained on the surface of vegetation before reaching the ground and returned to the atmosphere by evaporation.

INVASIVE PLANT Plants that aggressively expand their ranges over the landscape. Many invasive species are widely recognized as major threats to biological diversity.

INVERSION A layer of increasing atmospheric temperature with height.

JET STREAM A relatively narrow stream of fast-moving air in the middle and upper troposphere (the Polar Front). Surface cyclones develop and move eastward along the jet stream.

LADDER FUELS Fuels that provide vertical continuity between strata that allows fire to carry from surface fuels into the crowns of trees or shrubs with relative ease.

LAPSE RATE The rate of the fall of temperature with increasing height.

LATENT HEAT The heat that is given out (absorbed) when gases and liquids condense (evaporate) or freeze (melt).

LIFE CYCLE Those stages through which an organism passes between the production of gametes by one generation and the production of gametes by the next. (LBC)

LIFE HISTORY The significant features of the life cycle through which an organism passes, with particular reference to strategies influencing survival and reproduction.

LIFEFORM The characteristic structural features of plants. The basic forms of vascular plants include trees, shrubs, grasses, and herbs.

LITTER Recently fallen plant material that is only partially decomposed and in which the organs of the plant are still discernible, forming a surface layer on some soils.

MAGNITUDE Refers to both a fire's intensity and its severity.

MEDITERRANEAN CLIMATE The climate characteristic of the mediterranean region and much of California. Typically hot, dry summers and cool, wet winters.

MICROCLIMATE The climate of the immediate surroundings or habitat as a result of the influences of local topography, vegetation, and soil.

MINERAL SOIL Soil consisting predominantly of, and having its properties determined by mineral matter. Usually contains less than 20% organic matter.

NON-VASCULAR PLANT Plants without specialized tissues to conduct water and sap.

PACKING RATIO Fuel bed compactness, called the *packing ratio*, is measured by dividing the bulk density of the fuel bed, including fuel and air, by the fuel particle density.

PASSIVE CROWN FIRE (TORCHING) Burning of individual trees or groups of trees limited to vertical torching. The fire does not perpetuate itself horizontally. (NS)

PERENNIAL A plant life history in which the plant continues to live more than one year.

PHENOLOGY The temporal development of plants and animals, birth, growth and development, and death.

RADIATION Heat transfer occurring through transparent solids, liquids, and gases.

RAIN SHADOW A reduction in precipitation in an area on the leeward side of a mountain or range of mountains caused by release of moisture on the windward side and subsidence.

RATE OF SPREAD The speed at which the flaming front advances.

REACTION INTENSITY The rate of energy release per unit of area; the source of heat that keeps the chain reaction of combustion in motion.

RECRUITMENT RISK Occurs in species that rely on recruitment by seed when the fire return interval is shorter than the time required for individuals to mature and set seed.

RELATIVE HUMIDITY The amount of moisture in a parcel of air divided by the maximum amount of moisture that parcel could contain.

RESIDENCE TIME The amount of time that it takes for the flaming front to pass over a point.

RHIZOMES Underground root-like stems sending leafy stems upward and roots down.

SCARIFICATION The scratching of hard seed coats to facilitate germination.

SCORCH Tissue death that occurs when the internal temperature of the leaves or needles of a plant are raised to lethal levels but there is not enough heating to ignite the plant. Both the temperature and its duration are important in determining the severity of scorch.

SEASONALITY The timing of a fire during the year.

SEDIMENT Organic and inorganic matter that has been transported by wind, water, or ice and subsequently deposited.

SEDIMENT YIELD The amount of sediment that is produced from a watershed during a defined period of time.

SEED DISPERSAL The movement of seeds into or out of an area or population. (TX, NS)

SEEDBANK A reserve of seeds stored in the soil or in the canopy that becomes available to germinate following the fire.

SENESCENCE RISK The risk associated with time intervals between fires exceeding survival time, thereby reducing reproductive abilities of populations during the fire-free period

SEROTINY A condition where seeds are retained within cones that only open and release seeds en mass following fire. The mechanism varies, with some cones sealed by resin and waxes that melt during the fire, allowing the cones to open afterwards, releasing the seeds.

SMOKE-STIMULATED GERMINATION Germination of seeds that require stimulation by smoke.

SOIL STORED SEED Seed that is stored and acts as a reserve for recolonization following fire. Includes long-lived seeds that have thick, hard seed coats that require scarification or heating to stimulate germination.

SPATIAL COMPLEXITY The pattern of patchiness and spatial variability of burned areas and fire severity occurring within the fire perimeter.

SPECIES COMPOSITION The array of species that comprises a community or ecosystem.

SPOT FIRES Ignitions resulting from embers from the fireline becoming transported aerially in front of the fireline and often increasing fire spread.

SPROUTING A general term used to describe a number of plant responses involving the stimulation of dormant bud growth. Post-fire sprouting is typically from root crowns, lignotubers, basal burls, rootstocks, tubers, or from aboveground stems.

STAND-REPLACING FIRE A level of fire severity in which all of the aboveground plant parts are killed.

STOLON A modified aboveground horizontal stem that may root at the nodes developing new plantlets, as in a strawberry.

SURFACE AREA-TO-VOLUME RATIO The ratio of the surface area of a fuel particle to its volume. A measure of fuel particle coarseness or fineness.

SURFACE EROSION Removal of the soil surface by the action of water runoff and raindrop splash.

SURFACE FIRE A fire burning along the surface without significant movement into the understory or overstory, with flame length usually below 1 m.

UNDERSTORY FIRE A fire burning in the understory, more intense than a surface fire

VAPOR PRESSURE The partial pressure of water vapor.

VASCULAR PLANTS Plants with specialized tissues to conduct water and sap within roots, stems, and leaves.

WATER REPELLENCY See hydrophobicity.

WATER YIELD The amount of water produced by a watershed over a defined period of time.

WATERSHED The area contributing to the water supply of a river or lake; drainage basin.

WEATHER The short-term state of the air or atmosphere with respect to heat or cold, wetness or dryness, calm or storm, clearness or cloudiness, or any other meteorologic phenomena.

INDEX

restoring historic, 444, 475–76; during settlement, 431, 433; Sierra Nevada bioregion, 270, 272–73, 274*t*, 279*t*, 282–83*t*, 285*t*, 288–89; South Coast bioregion, 352, 354, 355, 359, 363–66, 370–71*t*, 373–75, 377*t*–383*t*; Southeastern Deserts bioregion, 396, 397, 402*t*, 404, 406–9, 412; Southern Cascades bioregion, 201, 203, 205–6*t*, 209*t*–212, 214–18, 214*t*–215; surface, 112

fire resistance, 94–99, 202, 278–80, 281, 287, 336

fire response, 103–4; Central Coast bioregion, 334*t*, 338*t*; Central Valley bioregion, 306*t*, 309*t*, 312*t*; Klamath bioregion, 181, 184–85, 186*t*, 189*t*; Northeastern Plateaus bioregion, 230, 233–37, 243–44*t*, 247*t*, 251–53*t*; Sierra Nevada bioregion, 270–72, 271–72, 273*t*, 274–75, 276*t*, 281–82, 284–85*t*; South Coast bioregion, 363*t*, 365*t*, 366, 368*t*, 375*t*, 377*t*–379*t*, 378*t*–379*t*; Southeastern Deserts bioregion, 399–402, 400*t*, 403, 407–8; Southern Cascades bioregion, 205, 206*t*, 210*t*, 212*t*, 213–14, 213*t*. *See also* fire ecology

fire return interval. *See* return interval, fire

fires: by decade, 438–39*f*; 1932-2003 historic fires, 436–38, 439*f*, 440*f*

fires, named: Barkley, 203, 207; Beaver Creek, 457; Bedford Canyon, 457; Berkeley, 434, 459; Biscuit, 173, 179; Blue, 249, 252; Bogus Burn, 457; Boise River basin, 137; Bolam, 198; Calaveras Big Trees State Park, 435, 533; Campbell, 202, 207; Cedar, 459; Cerro Grand, 439–40, 459; Cleveland National Forest, Eldorado County, 107; Cone, 198; Crank, 249; Everglades National Park, 434; Fountain, 198, 202, 218; Greater Yellowstone Area, 435; Great Idaho, 433; Gunn, 202, 203; Hayfork, 173; Jones, 172, 190; Kirk Complex, 333; Laguna, 459, 525; Lexington, 333; Lincoln Hill, 333; Lost, 198, 202; Lowden Ranch, 457; Marble Cone, 316, 333, 437*t*; Megram, 172, 179; Michigan, 433; Montana de Oro State Park, 435; Oakland Hills, 459; Oregon, 173; Peshtigo, 433; San Diego County Cedar, 382; San Diego/Los Angeles, 441; Scarface, 249, 437*t*; Sequoia-Kings Canyon National Parks, 435; South Canyon, 439; Southern California, 529; Sugar Hill, 230; Tunnel, 340, 534; Wisconsin, 433; Yacoult, 433; Yellowstone, 127, 129; Yosemite National Park, 435

fire scar, 35, 130, 160, 540; Central Coast bioregion, 330, 342; Central Valley bioregion, 307; Klamath bioregion, 182, 185, 186; Sierra Nevada bioregion, 270, 275, 277, 282; Southeastern Deserts bioregion, 396; Southern Cascades bioregion, 203, 204*f*, 208, 209, 216, 218

fire-sensitive species, 212

fire severity, 53, 68–69, 106, 119, 158; Klamath bioregion, 179–81*f*; Northeastern Plateaus bioregion, 229*t*, 250; Southern Cascades bioregion, 203, 205, 205*f*, 211, 218*f*

fire-tolerant species, 186. *See also* fire resistance

Fischer, R., 252

fish, 137–38, 203

Fish and Wildlife Service, U.S. (USFWS), 439, 534–35

Fites-Kaufman, Joann, 58, 94, 265, 538

flaming front equation, 46–47

flammability, 13, 23, 99, 112–13

FLAMMAP spatial modeling tool, 455, 456

flannelbush (*Fremontodendron californicum*), 206*t*, 273

flooding, 295

Florida, fire in, 434

floristic provinces, 5

foehn winds, 296, 322, 358, 436. *See also* Santa Ana winds

foliage, 95–97

Fons, W., 48

foothill pine (*Pinus sabinana*), 271, 272*f*, 273*t*. *See also* gray pine (*Pinus sabinana*)

foothills: Central Coast bioregion, 332–33; Central Valley bioregion, 304–7; Sierra Nevada bioregion, 267–68, 271–74, 535*t*; South Coast bioregion, 360*f*; Southern Cascades bioregion, 198, 199*f*, 205–6*t*, 210

forbs: Central Valley bioregion, 303, 305, 308, 311, 312; Northeastern Plateaus bioregion, 235*t*, 237, 244*t*, 247*t*, 251*t*, 253*t*, 255; Sierra Nevada bioregion, 273*t*, 276*t*, 282*t*; South Coast bioregion, 355, 358, 360, 364

Ford, L., 339

Forest Fire Control and Use (Brown and Davis), 445

Forest Practice Rules, 523

Forest Service, U.S., 335, 433, 435, 439, 452–53, 467, 469–70

forest/woodland, 148, 149, 237, 433–34; age of, 162; areas dominated by, 139; Central Coast bioregion, 341; Central Valley bioregion, 304–7, 311*f*; density of, 211; fire in, 436; fuel reduction in, 460; industrial, 165; Klamath bioregion, 174, 175; management of, 190; montane, 322, 335, 357, 396*f*; Native American use of, 418–19; Northeastern Plateaus bioregion, 256; shifts in, 135; South Coast bioregion, 354, 370; Southeastern Deserts bioregion, 395*f*; Southern Cascades bioregion, 198, 199–201; structural diversity of, 211, 217; systems dominated by, 139; thinning of, 449–51. *See also* canopy; crown; and *individual species*

foxtail chess (*Bromus madritensis ssp. rubens*), 397, 403, 404, 405–6

foxtail pine (*Pinus balfouriana*), 281*t*, 285*t*

Frandsen, W. H., 48

French, M. G., 129

French, S. P., 129

French broom (*Genista monspessulana*), 511*t*, 513

Frenkel, R. E., 308

frequency of fire, 111, 119, 405, 501; Central Coast bioregion, 329; North Coast bioregion, 152–53; Northeastern Plateaus bioregion, 229; South Coast bioregion, 359, 363*t*, 365, 370, 377, 381; Southeastern Deserts bioregion, 397, 398*m*, 399, 404; Southern Cascades bioregion, 202

fresh water marsh, 295, 313–15. *See also* wetlands

Frost, C. C., 237

fruits, 418–19

fuel, 240, 274; age of, 328, 373; category of, 46–47; Central Coast bioregion, 322, 324*f*, 333, 337, 344, 345; Central Valley bioregion, 300, 302*f*, 303–4, 313; combustible fine, 501; continuity of, 6, 445, 446*t*, 447*t*; and fuel load, 42, 162, 460–62, 481–83, 496; Klamath bioregion, 181, 186, 189–90; ladder, 445, 447*f*; mastication of, 451; modifications to protect structure, 527–28; moisture of, 41–42; Northeastern Plateaus bioregion, 229–30, 238, 245, 246, 252, 254; packing ratio of fuelbed, 41–42, 445, 446*t*; profile zone for, 452–53; reduction of, 529, 539; Sierra Nevada bioregion, 270, 271, 273–74, 278, 280, 282, 285–86, 289; South Coast bioregion, 326, 352, 370–71, 377, 378, 381–82; Southeastern Deserts bioregion, 391, 394–95, 397, 399, 401–2, 404, 406–8; Southern Cascades bioregion, 198, 202, 203, 205, 211, 213–15; surface, 445, 446*t*, 447*t*, 452; threshold of, 23. *See also* management, fire and fuel

Fuller, J. L., 500

fungi activity, 105–6, 139

fur-bearers, 217

Furbush, P., 510*t*, 512*t*

Furniss, M. J., 472

Gannett, H., 194

gases, 13–14, 40. *See also* nitrogen; carbon monoxide, 481, 482*t*, 483; ozone, 89, 90, 491*t*, 495–96

gelechiid moth (*Ghelechia sp.*), 277

Geographic Information Systems, 496

geography: human, 319, 321, 322

geography, physical: Central Coast bioregion, 321; Central Valley bioregion, 295, 296; Klamath bioregion, 170–71*m*; North Coast bioregion, 147, 149*m*; Northeastern Plateaus bioregion, 225–26; Sierra Nevada bioregion, 264, 266; South Coast bioregion, 350–51; Southeastern Deserts bioregion, 391–92*m*; Southern Cascades bioregion, 195, 197*m*

geology, 260, 281, 391

Sussott, R. A., 48
Swain Mountain Experimental Forest, 214
Sweeney, J. R., 78
Sweiecki, T., 307
Swetnam, T. W., 52, 114, 270

Tahoe National Forest, 453
tamarisk *(Tamarix ssp.)*, 513
tan oak *(Lithocarpus densiflorus)*, 150–52f, 161–64, 184, 271, 275t, 331
Tansley, A. G., 60
Tasmanian blue gum *(Eucalyptus globules)*, 513
Taylor, A. H., 170, 195, 203–4, 212, 215, 271, 287
Taylor, D., 270
temperature, 16, 17, 18m, 44; in aquatic ecosystems, 136; Central Coast bioregion, 322, 327m; Central Valley bioregion, 296, 298t; fire, 119; Klamath bioregion, 172, 172t; Sierra Nevada bioregion, 266, 266t; soil, 75–78; South Coast bioregion, 352; Southeastern Deserts bioregion, 393; water, 124, 138. *See also* climate
temporal attributes: of fire-animal interactions, 118–19; of fire regime, 64–67; of forest continuity, 134–35; of fuel, 41; of landscape, 428; of management, 514–15. *See also* fire return intervals
Thode, A. E., 466
Thode, Andrea E., 538
Thompson Ridge study area, 178f, 182f
thunderstorms, 20–21, 226, 228, 267, 296, 391. *See also* lightning
Thurber needlegrass *(Achnatherum thurberianum)*, 237, 241
Tiedermann, A. R., 86
Tietje, W., 307
timber harvesting. *See* logging (timber harvest)
Timbrook, J., 333
timothy *(Phleum pratense)*, 474
toads, 123
tobacco brush *(Ceanothus velutinus var. velutinus)*, 249, 286, 287, 289
topography: Central Coast bioregion, 321, 324; Central Valley bioregion, 296, 308; Klamath bioregion, 173, 179, 180f, 182f, 185; North Coast bioregion, 147; Sierra Nevada bioregion, 266; South Coast bioregion, 355, 370; Southern Cascades bioregion, 195, 198, 211, 215, 218
Torrey pine *(Pinus torreyana)*, 356, 373
total maximum daily loads (TMDLs), 468–69
treatment: for at-risk species, 522b, 524–26, 529–32; cost of, 470; fuel, 445–52; scale of, 475–78; scenario of, 455; seeding as, 470–71, 473–74; for watersheds, 467–72, 475. *See also* management; fire and fuel
tree frogs *(Hyla spp.)*, 123
trees: bark of, 112, 160, 162–63, 275, 281; canopy of, 43, 130; crown of, 53;

fire-resistant, 202; mortality of, 124, 132; Native American use of, 419; in North Coast bioregion, 148, 157t; removal of, 453; seedlings of, 474; stand of, 201, 207f, 214, 216, 220, 374. *See also specific species*
tree squirrels *(Sciurus and Tamiasciurus)*, 123
truffles, 215
tubers, 419f
tufted hairgrass *(Deschampsia cespitosa ssp. holciformis)*, 155, 282, 283, 283t
Tunnel fire, 340, 437t, 534
Turner, M. G., 61, 103
Tussock moth, 248
Tyler, C., 338

underbrush, 164, 419
ungulates, 119, 127, 128; elk, 135; mule deer, 123, 135, 230, 231, 232; pronghorn, 123, 127, 135
U.S. Army, 267, 433
U.S. Bureau of Indian Affairs, 439
U.S. Bureau of Land Management, 21, 435, 439, 452, 467, 470
U.S. Census (1860), 432
U.S. Coastal Zone Management Act (1972,1990), 468, 469
U.S. Congress, 432, 459
U.S. Department of Agriculture, 397, 470, 493
U.S. Department of Interior, 397, 434, 470
U.S. Environmental Protection Agency (EPA): and Clean Air Act (1963), 88, 486–88, 491–94; and National Environmental Protection Act (NEPA), 524; on nuisance smoke, 495; on visibility, 489–90
U.S. Fish and Wildlife Service (USFWS), 439, 534–35
U.S. Forest Service, 433, 435, 439, 452–53, 467, 469–70
U.S. General Accounting Office Audit, 470
U.S. military, 267, 433, 495
United States government: on California land grants, 432; laws on water quality, 468; regulation of air quality, 486–87. *See also under* National
University of California Davis Jepson Prairie Reserve, 533t
upper montane: Central Coast bioregion, 332, 334; Klamath bioregion, 174–76, 184–86, 184t, 186t; Northeastern Plateaus bioregion, 225, 228, 249–52; Sierra Nevada bioregion, 268, 281–83; Southern Cascades bioregion, 201, 213
urban-wildland interface, 382, 439–40, 458–59, 469, 541; Central Coast bioregion, 345; fuel in, 456, 527; grazing in, 451; Klamath bioregion, 190; property/structures in, 434–41, 459, 521, 527–28; Sierra Nevada bioregion, 289; Southern Cascades bioregion, 218
Utah, 123

Utah service-berry *(Amelanchier utahensis)*, 244

Vale, T. R., 6, 248, 428
valley oak *(Quercus lobata)*, 335
values, ecological and social, 453, 472, 475, 478, 514. *See also* public interest
Van Wagner, C. E., 51, 53, 54
van Wagtendonk, Jan W., 38, 54, 58, 457, 538; on Sierra Nevada bioregion, 264, 282, 286
vaporization, 38
Vasquez, F. J., 105
vegetation assemblages, 1–5, 113, 148, 538; as animal food source, 130; Central Coast bioregion; Central Valley bioregion, 295, 299, 300f, 306, 308; coastal, 324, 325m; erosion of, 473; fire weather window in, 27–28; as fuel, 13, 22–23, 43, 520; Klamath bioregion, 174, 178, 183, 191; management of, 338, 418, 470, 525–26, 529–30; Northeastern Plateaus bioregion, 225, 228, 229, 243f, 245, 246, 256; Sierra Nevada bioregion, 267, 270, 271, 274; South Coast bioregion, 358, 364; Southeastern Deserts bioregion, 394, 402; Southern Cascades bioregion, 198, 199, 201, 211; structures or, 96t; in watershed, 467. *See also* plant
Vegetation Management Program (VMP), 451
Veirs, S. D., 159
vernal pools, 124, 301f–303, 535t
Vesk, P. A., 101
visibility impairment, 484, 489, 492. *See also* air quality; smoke
Vitousek, P.M., 499
Vogl, R. J., 366, 375
Voitich, Jack, 419
volcanism, 225, 264

Wagener, W. W., 271
Wakimoto, Ron, 457
Walker, L. R., 61
walnut woodlands *(Juglans spp.)*, 357, 377–78
Ward, D. E., 481
Washoe pine *(Pinus washoensis)*, 245, 248, 251–52
water: for aquatic animals, 136–38; interactions with fire, 75; quality of, 8, 85–88, 468–71, 473–74, 541; repellency of soil to, 79; runoff from soil, 23; for sprouting, 101; temperature of, 124, 138. *See also* precipitation
watershed, 466–78; hydrology of, 87–88, 137; in integrated landscape approach, 476–78; management of, 541; processes of, 466–67; rehabilitation and restoration of, 467–72, 475–76; and seeding, 470–71t, 473–74; Southern Cascades bioregion, 218; water quality in, 468–69. *See also* riparian areas

Interior Design: Victoria Kuskowski

Composition: Techbooks, Inc.

Text: 9/13.5 Scala, Scala Caps

Display: Scala Sans, Scala Sans Caps

Printer and Binder: Sheridan Books, Inc.